Giant philodendron leaves in the rain forest of St. Kitts. See chapter 22. © Catherine Karnow Photography.

The idyllic cove of Anse Chastanet on the lush, mountainous island of St. Lucia. See chapter 23. © Susan Pierres Photography.

Beach on the laid-back island of Cayman Brac. See chapter 9. © Stephen Frink/Waterhouse.

Aerial view of Little Bay on the small, secluded island of Anguilla. See chapter 3. © Susan Pierres Photography.

The sheltered harbor of Gustavia, the capital of St. Barthélemy. See chapter 20. © Susan Pierres Photography.

Rafting on the Great River, near Montego Bay, Jamaica. See chapter 15. © M. Timothy O'Keefe Photography.

The top places to snorkel in the Caribbean include Bonaire (see chapter 7), Grand Cayman (chapter 9), Curaçao (chapter 10), Tobago (chapter 26), and the U.S. Virgin Islands (chapter 27). © M. Timothy O'Keefe Photography.

The Anse Chastanet reef off St. Lucia (see chapter 23). Other great dive sites are Bonaire (chapter 7), Virgin Gorda (chapter 8), Grand Cayman (chapter 9), Saba (chapter 19), and St. Croix (chapter 27). © *M. Timothy O'Keefe Photography.*

La Fortaleza, Old San Juan, Puerto Rico, is a national historic site, with medieval towers dating back more than four centuries. See chapter 18. © Andrea Pistolesi Photography.

Vibrant shops and restaurants, along with colorful local architecture, mark the town of Philipsburg, the Dutch capital of St. Maarten. See chapter 24. © Andrea Pistolesi Photography.

The little fishing port of Soufrière on St. Lucia. See chapter 23. © Susan Pierres Photography.

Pink Gin Beach, on Grenada, offers clear waters perfect for swimming, reef snorkeling, or kayaking. See chapter 13. © M. Timothy O'Keefe Photography.

For a different side of Grenada, visit the market in St. George, especially lively on Saturday mornings, with everything from spices to sandals for sale. See chapter 13. © Susan Pierres Photography.

Carnival transforms Port-of-Spain, Trinidad, into one big, colorful party, complete with dazzling costumes, calypso, and dancing. See chapter 26. © Robert Holmes Photography.

The Rawlins Plantation, a hotel set among the remains of an old sugar mill on St. Kitts. See chapter 22. © Catherine Karnow Photography.

The beach at Maracas Bay, Trinidad, with a protected cove. See chapter 26. © Robert Holmes Photography.

Codrington Theological College, one of the many historic sites on Barbados. The Anglican seminary was constructed of coral in 1745. See chapter 6. © *Robert Holmes Photography.*

The lush rain forest in Morne Trois Pitons National Park, Dominica, is dotted with hot springs and waterfalls. See chapter 11. © Markham Johnson/Robert Holmes Photography.

A view of Antigua's historic English Harbour from Shirley Heights. The harbor is known for its sailing facilities. See chapter 4. © Susan Pierres Photography.

Nevis's reef-protected Pinney's Beach, a 3-mile strip of golden sand that culminates in a sleepy lagoon. See chapter 17. © Susan Pierres Photography.

The Baths, Virgin Gorda, where giant boulders form a series of pools and caves. A great spot for swimming and snorkeling. See chapter 8. © M. Timothy O'Keefe Photography.

Frommer's® 2000

Caribbean

by Darwin Porter & Danforth Prince

with Online Directory by Michael Shapiro

MACMILLAN • USA

ABOUT THE AUTHORS

A native of North Carolina, **Darwin Porter** was a bureau chief for the *Miami Herald* when he was 21, and later worked in television advertising. A veteran travel writer, he is the author of numerous best-selling Frommer's guides, notably to England, France, Italy, and Spain. He is assisted by **Danforth Prince,** formerly of the Paris Bureau of the *New York Times.* They have been frequent travelers to the Caribbean for years, and are intimately familiar with what's good there and what isn't. They have also written Frommer's *Caribbean from $70 a Day,* the most candid and up-to-date guide to budget vacations on the market. In this guide, they share their secrets and discoveries with you.

MACMILLAN TRAVEL

Macmillan General Reference USA, Inc.
1633 Broadway
New York, NY 10019

Find us online at **www.frommers.com**

ISBN 0-02-862993-0
ISSN 1044-2375

Editor: Leslie Shen
With thanks to Lisa Renaud and Maureen Clarke
Production Editor: Donna Wright
Photo Editor: Richard Fox
Design by Michele Laseau
Staff Cartographers: John Decamillis, Roberta Stockwell
Page Creation by Toi Davis, Natalie Evans, Angel Perez

SPECIAL SALES

Bulk purchases (10+ copies) of Frommer's and selected Macmillan travel guides are available to corporations, organizations, mail-order catalogs, institutions, and charities at special discounts, and can be customized to suit individual needs. For more information write to Special Sales, Macmillan General Reference, 1633 Broadway, New York, NY 10019.

Manufactured in the United States of America

5 4 3 2 1

Contents

List of Maps

AN INVITATION TO THE READER

In researching this book, we discovered many wonderful places—hotels, restaurants, shops, and more. We're sure you'll find others. Please tell us about them, so we can share the information with your fellow travelers in upcoming editions. If you were disappointed with a recommendation, we need to know that, too. Please write to:

Frommer's Caribbean 2000
Macmillan Travel
1633 Broadway
New York, NY 10019

AN ADDITIONAL NOTE

Please be advised that travel information is subject to change at any time—and this is especially true of prices. We therefore suggest that you write or call ahead for confirmation when making your travel plans. Entry requirements for each island are also subject to change, so we suggest confirming the latest word on what documents you need before you travel. The authors, editors, and publisher cannot be held responsible for the experiences of readers while traveling. Your safety is important to us, however, so we encourage you to stay alert and be aware of your surroundings. Keep a close eye on cameras, purses, and wallets, all favorite targets of thieves and pickpockets.

WHAT THE SYMBOLS MEAN

✪ Frommer's Favorites

Our favorite places and experiences—outstanding for quality, value, or both.

The following abbreviations are used for credit cards:

AE	American Express	MC	MasterCard
DC	Diners Club	V	Visa
DISC	Discover		

The following abbreviations are used in hotel listings:

MAP (Modified American Plan): usually means room, breakfast, and dinner, unless the room rate has been quoted separately, and then it means only breakfast and dinner.
AP (American Plan): includes your room plus three meals.
CP (Continental Plan): includes room and a light breakfast.
EP (European Plan): means room only.

FIND FROMMER'S ONLINE

Arthur Frommer's Budget Travel Online (**www.frommers.com**) offers more than 6,000 pages of up-to-the-minute travel information—including the latest bargains and candid, personal articles updated daily by Arthur Frommer himself. No other Web site offers such comprehensive and timely coverage of the world of travel.

Choosing the Perfect Island: The Best of the Caribbean

In the Caribbean, you can hike through national parks and scuba dive along underwater mountains. But perhaps your idea of the perfect island vacation is to plunk yourself down on the sands with a frosted drink in hand. Whether you want a veranda with a view of the sea or a plantation house set in a field of sugarcane, this chapter will help you choose the lodgings that best suit your needs. Whether you're looking for a rum-and-reggae cruise or an utterly quiet evening, read on.

For a thumbnail portrait of each island, see "The Islands in Brief," in chapter 2.

1 The Best Beaches

Good beaches with soul-warming sun, crystal-clear waters, and fragrant sea air can be found on virtually every island of the Caribbean, with the possible exceptions of Saba (which has rocky shores) and Dominica (where the few beaches have dramatically black sands that reflect the hot sun).

- **Shoal Bay** (Anguilla): Often so empty you can pretend it's Eden, this silvery beach helped put Anguilla on the world tourism map. Divers are drawn to the schools of iridescent fish that dart among the coral gardens offshore. You can also take the trail walk from Old Ta to little-known Katouche Beach, which offers perfect snorkeling and is also a prime site for a beach picnic under shade trees. See chapter 3.
- **Cane Garden Bay** (Tortola): One of the Caribbean's more spectacular stretches of beach, Cane Garden Bay has 1½ miles of white sand and is a jogger's favorite. It's a much better choice than the more obvious (and crowded) Magens Bay beach on neighboring St. Thomas. See chapter 8.
- **Seven Mile Beach** (Grand Cayman): It's really about 5½ miles long, but who's counting? Lined with condos and plush resorts, this beach is known for its array of water sports and its translucent aquamarine waters. Australian pines dot the background, and the average winter temperature of the water is a perfect 80°F. See chapter 9.
- **Grand Anse Beach** (Grenada): This 2-mile beach is reason enough to go to Grenada. Although the island has some 45 beaches, most with white sand, this is the fabled one, and rightly

The Caribbean Islands

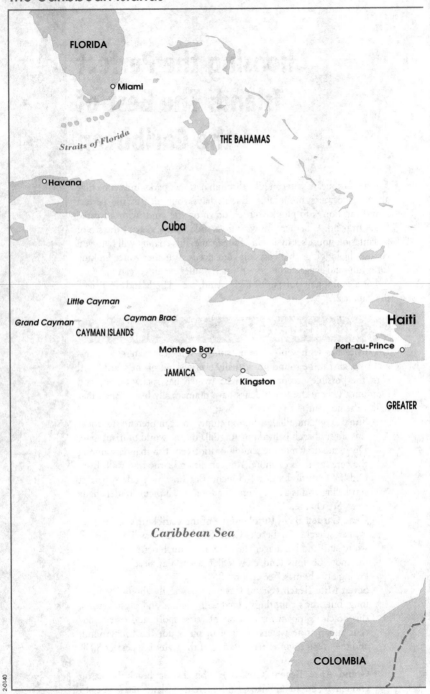

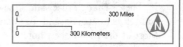

0   300 Miles

0   300 Kilometers

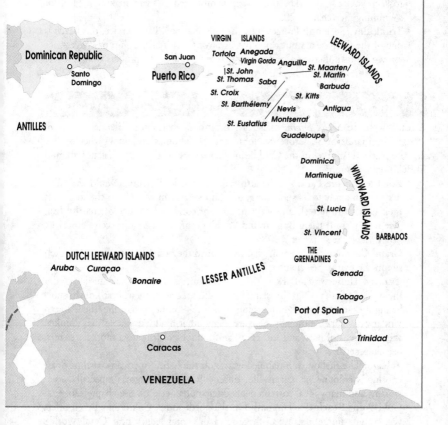

Atlantic Ocean

TURKS AND CAICOS ISLANDS

Dominican Republic
○ Santo Domingo

San Juan
○
Puerto Rico

VIRGIN ISLANDS
Tortola Anegada
Virgin Gorda Anguilla
|St. John
St. Thomas Saba
St. Croix
St. Barthélemy
St. Eustatius

LEEWARD ISLANDS

St. Maarten/
St. Martin
Barbuda
St. Kitts
Nevis Antigua
Montserrat
Guadeloupe

ANTILLES

Dominica
Martinique

St. Lucia

St. Vincent

WINDWARD ISLANDS

BARBADOS

DUTCH LEEWARD ISLANDS
Aruba Curaçao
Bonaire

LESSER ANTILLES

THE GRENADINES

Grenada

Tobago

Port of Spain
○
Trinidad

○
Caracas

VENEZUELA

3

so. There's enough space and so few visitors that you'll likely find a spot just for yourself. The sugary sands of Grand Anse extend into deep waters far offshore. Most of the island's best hotels are within walking distance of this beach strip. See chapter 13.

- **Negril Beach** (Jamaica): In the northwestern section of the island, this beach stretches for seven miles along the sea, and in the backdrop lie some of the most hedonistic resorts in the Caribbean. Not for the conservative, the beach also contains some nudist patches along with bare-all Booby Cay offshore. See chapter 15.

- **Le Diamant** (Martinique): This bright, white sandy beach stretches for about 6½ miles, much of it undeveloped. It faces a rocky offshore island, Diamond Rock, which has uninhabited shores. See chapter 16.

- **Luquillo Beach** (Puerto Rico): This crescent-shaped public beach, 30 miles east of San Juan, is the local favorite. Much photographed because of its white sands and coconut palms, it also has tent sites and picnic facilities. The often-fierce waters of the Atlantic are subdued by the coral reefs protecting the crystal-clear lagoon. See chapter 18.

- **St. Jean** (St. Barthélemy): A somewhat narrow, golden sandy beach, St. Jean is the gem of the island, reminiscent of the French Riviera (though you're supposed to keep your top on). The beach strip is protected by reefs, making it ideal for swimming. See chapter 20.

- **Trunk Bay** (St. John): Protected by the U.S. National Park Service, this beach is one of the Caribbean's most popular. A favorite with cruise-ship passengers, it's known for its underwater trail, where markers guide beachcombers along the reef just off the white-sand beach. See chapter 27.

2 The Best Snorkeling

A reader's poll in *Scuba Diving* magazine confirmed what Virgin Islanders knew all along: The islands of St. Croix, St. John, and St. Thomas are among the top-five favorite places to snorkel in the Caribbean. The waters off the Virgin Islands abound in rich flora and fauna.

- **Bonaire Marine Park:** All the attributes that make Bonaire a world-class dive destination apply to its snorkeling, too. Snorkelers can wade from the shores off their hotels to the reefs and view an array of coral and a range of colorful fish. The reefs just off Klein Bonaire and Washington/Slagbaai Park receive especially rave reviews. See chapter 7.

- **Grand Cayman:** Stingray City has been called the best 12-foot dive (or snorkel) site in the world. See chapter 9.

- **Curaçao Underwater Park** (Curaçao): In contrast to Curaçao's sterile terrain, the marine life that rings the island is rich and spectacular. The best-known snorkeling sites stretch for 12½ miles along Curaçao's southern coastline (the Curaçao Underwater Park), although there are many other highly desirable sites. Sunken ships, gardens of hard and soft coral, and millions of fish are a snorkeler's treat. See chapter 10.

- **Tobago:** The shallow, sun-dappled waters off the Latin American coastline boast enormous colonies of marine life. Buccoo Reef on Tobago is especially noteworthy, and many local entrepreneurs offer snorkel cruises. See chapter 26.

- **Coki Point Beach** (St. Thomas): On the north shore, Coki Point Beach offers year-round snorkeling, especially around the coral ledges near Coral World's underwater tower, a favorite with cruise-ship passengers. See chapter 27.

- **Trunk Bay** (St. John): Trunk Bay's self-guided 225-yard-long trail has large underwater signs that identify species of coral and other items of interest. The beach offers showers, changing rooms, equipment rentals, and a lifeguard. See chapter 27.
- **Leinster Bay** (St. John): With easy access from land and sea, Leinster Bay is filled with calm, clear, and uncrowded waters, with an abundance of sea life. See chapter 27.
- **Haulover Bay** (St. John): A favorite with locals, this small bay is rougher than Leinster and often deserted. The snorkeling is dramatic, with ledges, walls, nooks, and sandy areas set close together. At this spot, only about 200 yards separate the Atlantic Ocean from the Caribbean Sea. See chapter 27.
- **Buck Island** (St. Croix): More than 250 species of fish, as well as a variety of sponges, corals, and crustaceans, have been found at this 850-acre island and reef system, 2 miles off St. Croix's north shore. The reef is strictly protected by the National Park Service. See chapter 27.
- **Cane Bay** (St. Croix): One of the island's best diving and snorkeling sites is off this breezy north-shore beach. On a clear day, you can swim out 150 yards and see the Cane Bay Wall that drops off dramatically to deep waters below. Multicolored fish and elkhorn and brain coral are in abundance here. See chapter 27.

3 The Best Dive Sites

All the major islands offer diving trips, lessons, and equipment, but here are the top picks:

- **Bonaire:** The highly accessible reefs that surround Bonaire have never suffered from poaching or pollution, and the island's environmentally conscious dive industry will ensure that they never do. Created from volcanic eruptions, the island is an underwater mountain, with fringe reefs right off the beach of every hotel on any part of the island. See chapter 7.
- **Virgin Gorda:** Many divers plan their entire vacations around exploring the famed wreck of the HMS *Rhone*, off Salt Island. This royal mail steamer, which went down in 1867, is the most celebrated dive site in the Caribbean. See chapter 8.
- **Grand Cayman:** A world-class diving destination. There are 34 dive operators on Grand Cayman (with five more on Little Cayman, plus three on Cayman Brac). A full range of professional dive services is available, including equipment sales, rentals, and repairs; instruction at all levels; underwater photography; and video schools. See chapter 9.
- **Saba:** Islanders can't brag about its beaches, but Saba is blessed with some of the Caribbean's richest marine life. It's one of the premier diving locations in the Caribbean, with 38 official dive sites. The unusual setting includes underwater lava flows, black sand, large strands of black coral, millions of fish, and underwater mountaintops submerged under 90 feet of water. See chapter 19.
- **St. Croix:** Increasingly known as a top diving destination, St. Croix hasn't overtaken Grand Cayman yet, but it has a lot going for it. Beach dives, reef dives, wreck dives, nighttime dives, wall dives—they're all here. But the highlight is the underwater trails of the national park at Buck Island, off St. Croix's mainland. Other desirable sites include the drop-offs and coral canyons at Cane Bay and Salt River. Davis Bay is the location of the 12,000-foot-deep Puerto Rico Trench, the fifth-deepest body of water on earth. See chapter 27.

4 The Best Sailing

Virtually any large-scale hotel in the Caribbean will provide small sailboats (especially Sunfish, Sailfish, and small, one-masted catamarans) for its guests. For larger craft, the Virgin Islands and the Grenadines come instantly to mind for their almost-ideal sailing conditions. These two regions offer many options for dropping anchor at secluded coves surrounded by relatively calm waters. Both areas are spectacular, but while the Virgin Islands offer more dramatic, mountainous terrain, the Grenadines offer insights into island cultures little touched by the modern world.

Other places to sail in the Caribbean include Antigua, Barbados, St. Martin, and the French-speaking islands. But if you plan on doing a lot of sailing, know in advance that the strongest currents and biggest waves usually occur on the northern and eastern sides of most islands—the Atlantic (as opposed to the Caribbean) side.

- **The Virgin Islands:** Perhaps because of their well-developed marina facilities (and those of the nearby United States), the Virgin Islands receive the lion's share of really devoted yachties. The reigning capital for sailing is Tortola, the largest island of the British Virgins. On site are about 300 well-maintained sailing craft available for bareboat rentals, and perhaps 100 charter yachts.

  The largest of the Caribbean's yacht chartering services is **The Moorings** (☎ 284/494-2332). Run by Ginny and Charlie Cary, this yachting charter center is described more fully in chapter 8, "The British Virgin Islands," as are the other outfits in this paragraph. If you'd like sailing lessons, consider **Steve Colgate's Offshore Sailing School** (☎ 284/494-5119) or Tortola's **Treasure Isle Hotel** (☎ 284/494-2501), which offers courses in seamanship year-round. (One of their programs is exclusively on how to sail catamarans.) On the island of Virgin Gorda, in the British Virgin Islands, the best bet for both boat rentals and accommodations, as well as for a range of instruction, is the **Bitter End Yacht Club** (☎ 800/872-2392 in the U.S., or 284/494-2746).

  Some of the biggest charter business in the Caribbean is conducted on St. Thomas, especially at **American Yacht Harbor,** Red Hook (☎ 800/736-7294 in the U.S., or 340/775-6454), which offers bareboat and fully crewed charters. Other reliable rental agents include **Charteryacht League,** at Flagship (☎ 800/524-2061 or 340/774-3944). The U.S. Virgin Islands are covered in chapter 27; look there for more information.

  On St. Croix, boating is less a factor in the local economy than it is on St. Thomas or in the British Virgins.

- **The Grenadines:** Boating is a way of life in the Grenadines, partly because access to many of the remote islands is difficult or impossible by airplane. One of the most prominent local charter agents is **Nicholson Yacht Charters** (☎ 800/662-6066 in the U.S.), headquartered in nearby St. Vincent. On Bequia, Mustique, Petit St. Vincent, and Union Island, all the hotels can put you in touch with local entrepreneurs who rent sailing craft. See chapters 2 and 25 for more details.

5 The Best Golf Courses

Some of the world's most famous golf architects, including Robert Trent Jones (both junior and senior), Pete Dye, Gary Player, and others, have designed challenging courses in the Caribbean.

- **Teeth of the Dog and The Links,** both at Casa de Campo (Dominican Republic; ☎ 800/877-3643 in the U.S. and Canada, or 809/523-3333):

Hispaniola's most challenging golf course, Teeth of the Dog, is one of designer Pete Dye's masterpieces. Seven holes are set adjacent to the sea, whereas the other 11 are confoundedly labyrinthine. The resort also has a second golf course, The Links, which some claim is even more difficult. See chapter 12.

- **Golf de St-François** (Guadeloupe; ☎ **0590/88-41-87**): Six of its 18 holes are ringed with water traps, the winds are devilishly unpredictable, and the par is a sweat-inducing 71. This fearsome course displays the wit and skill of its designer, Robert Trent Jones, Sr. Most of the staff is multilingual, and because it's owned by the local municipality, it's a lot less snobby than you might expect. See chapter 14.

- **Tryall** (Montego Bay, Jamaica; ☎ **800/238-5290** in the U.S., or 876/ 956-5660): This is the finest golf course on an island known for its tricky breezes. The site, now occupied by the Tryall Golf, Tennis, and Beach Club, was once the home of one of Jamaica's best-known sugar plantations; the only remnant is a ruined waterwheel. The promoters of Johnnie Walker Scotch, who know a lot about golfing, selected this place for their most prestigious competition. In winter, the course is usually open only to guests of the Tryall Beach Club. See chapter 15.

- **Wyndham Rose Hall Resort** (Rose Hill, Jamaica; ☎ **800/624-7326** in the U.S., or 876/953-2650): This is one of the top five courses in the world, even though it faces other tough competition in Montego Bay. The signature hole is number 8, which doglegs onto a promontory and a green that thrusts about 200 yards into the sea. The back nine, however, is the most scenic and most challenging, rising into steep slopes and deep ravines on Mount Zion. See chapter 15.

- **The Four Seasons** (Nevis; ☎ **800/332-3442** in the U.S., 800/268-6282 in Canada, or 869/469-1111): We consider this our personal favorite in all of the Caribbean, and so do readers of *Caribbean Travel & Life*. It was carved out of a coconut plantation and tropical rain forest in the 1980s, and its undulating beauty is virtually unequaled. Designed by Robert Trent Jones, Jr., the course begins at sea level, rises to a point midway up the slopes of Mount Nevis, then slants gracefully back down near the beachfront clubhouse. Electric carts carry golfers through a labyrinth of well-groomed paths, some of which skirt steep ravines. See chapter 17.

- **El Conquistador Resort & Country Club** (Puerto Rico; ☎ **800/468-8365** in the U.S., or 787/863-1000): Its fairways meander over the rolling hills that surround one of Puerto Rico's most fabled resorts. The par-72 layout was designed by Robert Von Hagge in 1967, and redesigned by Arthur Hills & Associates (who flattened some of the more daunting slopes). Golfers, who must be guests of the El Conquistador Resort, enjoy sweeping views of the sea. The winds are tricky and change frequently, adding to the challenge. See chapter 18.

- **Hyatt Dorado Beach Resort** (Puerto Rico; ☎ **800/233-1234** in the U.S., or 787/796-1234): This resort maintains two golf courses, both set on what were originally citrus and coconut plantations. Both courses were designed by Robert Trent Jones, Sr. No one can agree on which of the two courses is the more interesting, but the elegance of both is breathtaking. If you're an absolute golf glutton, the Hyatt's companion resort, the Cerromar, a short drive down the coastal road, offers an additional pair of golf courses. See chapter 18.

- **Palmas del Mar** (Puerto Rico; ☎ **800/725-6273** in the U.S., or 787/ 852-6000): Designed by Gary Player, this par-72 golf course near Humacao is one of the most noteworthy anywhere. Its botanical highlights include thousands of mature palm trees and carefully maintained sections of tropical rain forest. The course is so good that many golf-playing retirees have bought homes adjacent to the fairways. The most challenging holes? Numbers 11 through 16, although many beginners have lost their tempers over number 18 as well. Lessons are offered to players of all different levels. See chapter 18.

6 The Best Tennis Facilities

- **Curtain Bluff** (Antigua; ☎ **888/289-9898** in the U.S., or 268/462-8400): It's small, select, and carefully run by people who love tennis, and it's also the annual site of a well-known spring tournament. The courts are set in a low-lying valley. See chapter 4.
- **Casa de Campo** (Dominican Republic; ☎ **800/877-3643** in the U.S., Canada, Puerto Rico, and the Virgin Islands, or 809/523-3333): The facilities here include 13 clay courts (half are lighted, and two are ringed with stadium seating), four all-weather Laykold courts, a resident pro, ball machines, and tennis pros who are usually available to play with guests. During midwinter, residents and clients of Casa de Campo have first crack at court times. See chapter 12.
- **Half Moon Golf, Tennis, and Beach Club** (Montego Bay, Jamaica; ☎ **800/ 626-0592** in the U.S., or 876/953-2211): This resort sprawls over hundreds of acres, with about a dozen tennis courts and at least four squash and/or racquet-ball courts. Jamaica has a strong, British-based affinity for tennis, and Half Moon keeps the tradition alive. See chapter 15.
- **El Conquistador** (Puerto Rico; ☎ **800/468-8365** in the U.S., or 787/ 863-1000): Facilities at this megaresort include seven Har-Tru tennis courts, a resident pro, and a clubhouse with its own bar. If you're looking for a partner, the hotel will find one for you. Only guests of the hotel can use the courts, some of which are illuminated for night play. See chapter 18.
- **Hyatt Regency Cerromar Beach/Hyatt Dorado Beach** (Puerto Rico; ☎ **800/ 233-1234** in the U.S., or 787/796-1234): These twin beachfront resorts are within a 15-minute walk of each other. There are 15 Laykold tennis courts, some lit, some ringed with stadium seats; all are administered by a tennis pro who gives lessons. If you want pointers on improving your serve or strokes, someone will be on hand to videotape you. These facilities are open only to resort guests. See chapter 18.
- **Wyndham Sugar Bay Resort** (St. Thomas; ☎ **800/WYNDHAM** in the U.S., or 340/777-7100): The resort offers the U.S. Virgin Islands' first stadium tennis court, with a capacity of 220 spectators. In addition, it has about half a dozen Laykold courts, each of which is lit for night play. There's an on-site pro shop and lessons are available. See chapter 27.
- **The Buccaneer** (St. Croix; ☎ **800/255-3881** in the U.S., or 340/773-2100): Hailed as having the best tennis facilities in the Virgin Islands, this resort hosts several tournaments every year. There are eight all-weather Laykold courts, two of which are illuminated at night; there's also a pro shop. Nonguests can play here for a fee. See chapter 27.

7 The Best Honeymoon Resorts

More and more couples are exchanging their vows in the Caribbean. Many resorts will arrange everything from the preacher to the flowers, so we've included in the following list some outfits that provide wedding services. For more information about the various options and the legal requirements for marriages on some of the more popular Caribbean islands, see chapter 2, "Planning a Trip to the Caribbean."

- **St. James's Club** (Antigua; ☎ **800/345-0271** or 561/994-5640 in the U.S.): There are enough diversions available at this very posh, British-style resort to keep a honeymoon couple up and about for weeks. Breakfast, lunch, and dinner are included along with unlimited drinks. Among the perks is a private, candlelit dinner for two in a romantic setting. See chapter 4.
- **Biras Creek Estate** (Virgin Gorda, B.V.I.; ☎ **800/608-9661** in the U.S., or 284/494-3555): If you're eager to escape your in-laws and bridesmaids after a wedding ceremony, this is the place. It's a quintessential mariner's hideaway, reached only by a boat ride of several miles across the open sea. Perched on a narrow promontory jutting into the Caribbean, it's an intensely private retreat set on 150 acres with a crisscrossing network of signposted nature trails. Honeymooners can get better acquainted in the spacious, open-air walled showers in each bathroom. See chapter 8.
- **Hyatt Regency Grand Cayman** (Grand Cayman; ☎ **800/233-1234** or 345/949-1234): Hands down, this is the most glamorous and best-landscaped resort in the Cayman Islands. Honeymooners can buy a package that includes champagne and wine, a room with an oversize bed, a 1-day jeep rental, a romantic sundowner sail on a 65-foot catamaran, and discounts at clothing stores, the resort's restaurants, and a golf course. They'll even present you with a honeymoon memento for your home. See chapter 9.
- **Sandals** (Jamaica; ☎ **800/SANDALS**): There are half a dozen members of this resort chain in Jamaica alone (plus two others on St. Lucia). Each one prides itself on providing an all-inclusive (cash-free) environment where meals are provided in abundance to any couple. Enthusiastic members of the staff bring heroic amounts of community spirit to ceremonies celebrated on site. Sandals will provide everything from a preacher to petunias (as well as champagne, a cake, and all the legalities) for you to get hitched here. Any of these resorts can provide a suitable setting, but one of the most appealing is Sandals Royal Jamaican, outside Montego Bay, Jamaica. See chapter 15.
- **The SuperClubs of Jamaica** (☎ **800/859-SUPER [7873]**): These all-inclusive properties are for upscale honeymooners who can afford a little more elegance and luxury. They operate somewhat like Sandals, but have far more style and a higher price tag. Prices are high in winter, but when mid-April arrives, rates plummet. SuperClubs, such as Grand Lido and Grand Lido Sans Souci, are scattered between Ocho Rios and Negril. If you pay for the food and room packages, the hotel chain will throw in the wedding for free—they'll provide the license, the witnesses, the minister, and even a two-tier wedding cake. They'll see that you're married in the garden or on a white sandy beach. See chapter 15.
- **Four Seasons** (Nevis; ☎ **800/332-3442** in the U.S., 800/268-6282 in Canada, or 869/469-1111): Though not as historic as some of the island's plantation-style inns, the Four Seasons rules without peer as the most deluxe hotel on the island, with the most extensive facilities. Set in a palm grove adjacent to the island's finest beach, it has the atmosphere of a supremely indulgent country club. The Four Seasons offers a 4-day wedding package with a choice of ceremony styles (in a church or on a beach, with a judge or with a civil magistrate). Your wedding cake will be individually designed by the resort's pastry chef, and music, photographs, flowers, legalities, and virtually anything else you want can be arranged by the staff. See chapter 17.

- **El Conquistador** (Puerto Rico; ☎ **800/468-5228** in the U.S., or 787/ 863-1000): A complex of hotels set on a forested bluff overlooking the sea, this is one of the most lavish resorts ever built in the Caribbean. The architecture incorporates Moorish gardens and Andalusian fortresses. You'll find hammocks for two on the resort's offshore private island, as well as about a dozen private Jacuzzis artfully concealed by vegetation throughout the grounds. See chapter 18.
- **Petit St. Vincent Resort** (The Grenadines; ☎ **800/654-9326** in the U.S., or 784/458-8801): If your idea of a honeymoon is to run away from everybody except your new spouse, this is the place. It takes about three planes and a boat to reach it, but the effort to get here is worth it—that is, if you want total isolation and privacy. Even the staff doesn't bother you unless you raise a flag for room service. If the honeymoon's going well, you may never have to leave your stone cottage by the beach. See chapter 25.
- **The Buccaneer** (St. Croix; ☎ **800/255-3881** in the U.S., or 340/773-2100): Posh and discreet, this resort boasts some of the most extensive vacation facilities on St. Croix—three beaches, eight tennis courts, a spa and fitness center, an 18-hole golf course, and 2 miles of carefully maintained jogging trails. The accommodations include beachside rooms with fieldstone terraces leading toward the sea. The resort's stone sugar mill (originally built in 1658) is one of the most popular sites for weddings and visiting honeymooners on the island. See chapter 27.

8 The Best Romantic Hideaways

- **Cap Juluca** (Anguilla; ☎ **888/858-5822** in the U.S., or 264/497-6666): A unique resort in the Caribbean, it utilized the skills of top postmodern architects, a couple of million dollars, and a thrillingly beautiful beach to create just the right atmosphere. The result: something like a Saharan Casbah whose domed villas seem to float against the scrubland and azure sky. You'll always have the feeling that someone very famous is enjoying a romantic off-the-record tryst behind the sheltering walls of this extremely stylish resort. See chapter 3.
- **Peter Island Resort** (B.V.I.; ☎ **800/346-4451** or 284/495-2000): Romantics appreciate its isolation on a 1,800-acre private island south of Tortola and east of St. John. Reaching it requires a 30-minute waterborne transfer, which many urban refugees consider part of the fun. It's very laid-back—bring a companion and/or a good book, and enjoy the comings and goings of yachts at the island's private marina. See chapter 8.
- **Trident Villas and Hotel** (Port Antonio, Jamaica; ☎ **876/993-2602**): This is a retreat straight out of *Lifestyles of the Rich and Famous*. Perhaps you'll opt for a studio cottage or tower, or a room within the hotel's antique-filled main building. Imperial suites are the ultimate in luxury. The white-gloved waiters with their silver service and crystal evoke the heyday of the British Empire. See chapter 15.
- **Horned Dorset Primavera Hotel** (Puerto Rico; ☎ **800/633-1857** in the U.S., or 787/823-4030): This resort, on the western side of Puerto Rico, has a main clubhouse that's reminiscent of an Iberian villa. Great care is lavished on the sophisticated continental/California cuisine, and drinks are served in a well-stocked library. The comfortable, dignified accommodations contain oversize mahogany beds and large private verandas, with views of lushly planted hillsides sloping down to a narrow sandy beach. See chapter 18.
- **Rawlins Plantation** (St. Kitts; ☎ **800/346-5358** in the U.S., or 869/ 465-6221): Surrounded by 25 acres of carefully clipped lawns and tropical

shrubbery, and set on a panoramic hillock about 350 feet above sea level, this hotel evokes a 19th-century plantation with its rugs of locally woven rushes and carved four-poster beds. You'll be separated from the rest of the island by hundreds of acres of sugarcane, and there are few phones and no televisions. See chapter 22.

- **The Golden Lemon** (St. Kitts; ☎ **869/465-7260**): It started its life as a French manor house during the 17th century, but by the time its present owners began restoring it, it was decidedly less glamorous. It required the refined tastes of Arthur Leaman, a former editor at *House & Garden,* to bring it to its full potential. Today the Golden Lemon is an authentic Antillean retreat—luxurious, laid-back, and romantic—set in an isolated fishing village loaded with charm. See chapter 22.
- **Anse Chastanet Beach Hotel** (St. Lucia; ☎ **800/223-1108** in the U.S., or 758/459-7000): Offering panoramic views of mountains and jungle, this hotel is a winner with romantics. With its small size, it offers a lot of privacy and rustic charm. See chapter 23.
- **Petit St. Vincent (PSV) Resort** (The Grenadines; ☎ **800/654-9326** in the U.S., or 784/458-8801): The sheer distance of PSV from the United States makes it the most secluded of the Caribbean's luxury hideaways. Located on a privately owned island, the artfully built clubhouses and bungalows were crafted from tropical woods and local stone. The results are simultaneously rustic and lavish. Your bungalow is designed in such a way that if you don't put on any clothes until dinnertime, no one will see you au naturel except your companion. See chapter 25.
- **The Cotton House** (The Grenadines; ☎ **800/826-2809** in the U.S., or 784/456-4777): Cosmopolitan and evoking fashionable London, this hotel was built as a cotton warehouse on the tiny island of Mustique during the 18th century. Richly overhauled in the 1970s by one of Britain's most tasteful designers, it now houses 20 airy accommodations. Although the glamour that was associated with the Cotton House in the 1970s has dimmed, recent renovations have brought back its undeniable charm and romance. See chapter 25.

9 The Best Places to Get Away from It All

- **Biras Creek Estate** (Virgin Gorda, B.V.I.; ☎ **800/608-9661** in the U.S., or 284/494-3555): The only access to this resort is by private launch. The sea air and the views over islets, cays, and deep blue waters will relax you in your charming guest room. The nautical atmosphere will quickly remove all thoughts of the 9-to-5 job you left behind. See chapter 8.
- **Guana Island Club** (B.V.I.; ☎ **914/967-6050** in the U.S., or 284/494-2354): One of the most secluded hideaways in the entire Caribbean, this resort occupies a privately owned 850-acre bird sanctuary with nature trails. Head here for views of rare plant and animal life, and for several excellent uncrowded beaches, but remember that there's no nightlife. See chapter 8.
- **Little Cayman Beach Resort** (Cayman Islands; ☎ **800/327-3835** in the U.S. and Canada, or 345/948-1033): The only practical way to reach the 10-square-mile island where this resort is located is by airplane. Snorkelers will marvel at some of the most spectacular and colorful marine life in the Caribbean. The resort has the most complete water-sports facilities on the island, and bikes are available for exploring. See chapter 9.

- **Ottley's Plantation Inn** (St. Kitts; ☎ **800/772-3039** in the U.S., or 869/465-7234): As you approach, its dignified verandas appear majestically at the crest of 35 acres of impeccably maintained lawns and gardens. It's one of the most charming plantation-house inns anywhere in the world, maintained with style and humor by its expatriate American owners. The food is the best on the island, and the setting will soothe your tired nerves within a few hours after your arrival. See chapter 22.

10 The Best Family Resorts

- **Hyatt Regency Aruba** (Aruba; ☎ **800/233-1234** in the U.S. and Canada, or 297/8-61234): Designed like a luxurious hacienda, with award-winning gardens, this resort is the most upscale on Aruba. There are supervised activities for children 3 to 12 that include games and contests such as crab races and hula-hoop competitions. See chapter 5.
- **Sandy Beach Hotel** (Barbados; ☎ **246/435-8000**): Set amid lots of fast-food and family-style restaurants on the southwest coast, this family-oriented hotel offers one- and two-bedroom suites. Each unit has a kitchen, so you can cook for yourself and save money. The beach is a few steps away, and the ambience is informal. If you bring the kids, they'll have plenty of playmates. See chapter 6.
- **Hyatt Regency Grand Cayman** (☎ **800/233-1234** or 345/949-1234): Safe and serene, Grand Cayman Island with its 7-mile sandy beach seems designed for families with children. No one coddles children as much as the Hyatt people, who offer not only baby-sitting but also a Camp Hyatt, with an activity-filled agenda, for children ages 3 to 12. See chapter 9.
- **FDR** (Runaway Bay, Jamaica; ☎ **800/654-1FDR** in the U.S., or 876/973-4591): FDR gives you a suite with its own kitchen, and a so-called "Vacation Nanny" whose duties include baby-sitting. Neither its beach nor its pool is the most appealing on Jamaica, but the price is right, and the baby-sitting is part of the all-inclusive price. Programs for children include dress-up parties, donkey rides, basketball, tennis, and snorkeling. See chapter 15.
- **Four Seasons** (Nevis; ☎ **800/332-3442** in the U.S., 800/268-6282 in Canada, or 869/469-1111): The staff of the Kids for All Seasons day camp are kindly, matronly souls who work well with children. During the adult cocktail hour, when parents might opt for a romantic sundowner, kids attend a supervised children's hour that resembles a really good birthday bash. Other activities include tennis lessons, water sports, and storytelling. See chapter 17.
- **Hyatt Regency Cerromar Beach Hotel** (Puerto Rico; ☎ **800/233-1234** or 787/796-1234): This is the best place for kids on the whole island. The big attraction is a water playground that contains the world's longest freshwater swimming pool: a 1,776-foot fantasy pool with five different depths, five interconnected free-form pools, and 14 waterfalls with tropical landscaping. As if that weren't enough, Hyatt also offers Camp Hyatt, a day camp for kids 3 to 12. See chapter 18.
- **El Conquistador** (Puerto Rico; ☎ **800/468-5228** in the U.S., or 787/863-1000): Children aren't forgotten amid the glamour and hoopla of this fabulous resort. Camp Coquí provides day care daily from 9am to 3pm for children 3 to 12, at a price of $38 per child per day. Activities include fishing, sailing, arts and crafts, and nature treks. Baby-sitting services are available, and children 15 and under stay free in a room with their parents. See chapter 18.

- **Doubletree Sapphire Beach Resort and Marina** (St. Thomas; ☎ **800/ 524-2090** in the U.S., or 340/775-6100): More than any other hotel on St. Thomas, this well-designed resort caters to both adults and children. There's supervised activities for preteens at the Little Gems Kids Klub, and a baby-sitting service for children under 4. Other activities can include the entire family. The white sandy beaches are among the safest and most desirable on the island. See chapter 27.
- **The Buccaneer** (St. Croix; ☎ **800/255-3881** in the U.S., or 340/773-2100): Posh, upscale, and offering extremely good service, this hotel is a longtime favorite that occupies a 240-acre former sugar estate. Its kids' programs (for ages 2 to 12) include a half-day sailing excursion to Buck Island Reef and guided nature walks that let kids touch, smell, and taste tropical fruit. See chapter 27.

11 The Best Inns

- **The Admiral's Inn** (Antigua; ☎ **800/223-5695** in the U.S., or 268/460-1027): The most historically evocative corner of Antigua is Nelson's Dockyard, which was originally built in the 1700s to repair His Majesty's ships. The brick-and-stone inn that flourishes here today was once a warehouse for turpentine and pitch. In the late 1960s it was transformed into a well-designed and very charming hotel. If you're trying to escape from urban pressures, you might be bothered by the sometimes raucous scene in the hotel's bar and restaurant. See chapter 4.
- **Drake's Anchorage Resort Inn** (Mosquito Island, B.V.I.; ☎ **617/969-9913** in Massachusetts, or 284/494-7045): Set off the northeastern coast of Virgin Gorda, this simple, austere, 12-room inn is the only establishment of any kind on Mosquito Island. Guests can enjoy the island's 125 acres of forest and scrubland, and snorkeling opportunities abound offshore. The island has a restaurant, a bar frequented by yachters, and a kind of roguish charm. Don't expect luxurious amenities—everything is almost studiously simple here. But if you want an insight into the way the Caribbean used to be, this is the place. See chapter 8.
- **Avila Beach Hotel** (Curaçao; ☎ **599/9-4614377**): This hotel's historic core, built in 1780 as the "country house" of the island's governor, retains its dignity and lack of excess ornamentation. Although it has functioned as a hotel since the end of World War II, a new owner added 40 bedrooms in motel-like outbuildings and upgraded the sports and dining facilities in the early 1990s. Today the Avila provides a sandy beach and easy access to the shops and distractions of nearby Willemstad. See chapter 10.
- **Spice Island Inn** (Grenada; ☎ **800/742-4276** in the U.S., or 473/444-4258): Each of this hotel's 56 accommodations is a suite (with Jacuzzi) either beside the beach (one of Grenada's best) or near a swimming pool. Friday nights feature live music from the island's most popular bands. See chapter 13.
- **Montpelier Plantation Inn and Beach Club** (Nevis; ☎ **800/223-9832** or 869/469-3462): Style and grace are the hallmarks of this former 18th-century plantation, now converted to an inn and set on a 100-acre estate. Guests have included the late Princess of Wales. Cottage rooms are spread across 10 acres of ornamental gardens. Swimming, horseback riding, windsurfing, a private beach, and "ecorambles" fill the agenda. See chapter 17.
- **Hermitage Plantation** (Nevis; ☎ **800/682-4025** in the U.S., or 869/ 469-3477): Guests stay in clapboard-sided cottages separated by carefully maintained bougainvillea and grasslands. The beach is a short drive away, but this slice

of 19th-century plantation life (complete candlelit dinners amid the antiques and polished silver of the main house) is decidedly romantic. See chapter 17.

- **François Plantation** (St. Barthélemy; ☎ **0590/29-80-22**): At this inn, about a dozen pastel-colored bungalows are scattered among the lushest gardens on St. Barts. The mood is discreet, permissive, and fun (as long as you don't bother any of the other guests). The food is French-inspired and served on a wide veranda decorated in a whimsical colonial style. See chapter 20.

- **Frangipani Hotel** (Bequia, the Grenadines; ☎ **784/458-3255**): This is the century-old homestead of the Mitchell family, whose most famous scion later became prime minister of St. Vincent. Today it's a small, very relaxed inn. It's fun to watch the yachts making their seaward forays from the nearby marina. See chapter 25.

- **Villa Madeleine** (St. Croix; ☎ **800/496-7379** or 340/778-8782): This recently built, almost perfect re-creation of a 19th-century great house occupies the summit of a scrub-covered ridge. The food is among the best on St. Croix. Accommodations include richly furnished hideaway suites with sweeping views over the coastline. See chapter 27.

12 The Best Destinations for Serious Shoppers

Since the American government allows U.S. citizens to take (or send) home more duty-free goods from the U.S. Virgins than from other ports of call, the U.S. Virgin Islands remain the shopping bazaar of the Caribbean. U.S. citizens may carry home $1,200 worth of goods untaxed, as opposed to only $400 worth of goods from most islands in the Caribbean. (The only exception to this rule is Puerto Rico, where any purchase, regardless of the amount, can be carried tax free back to the U.S. mainland.)

- **Aruba:** The wisest shoppers on Aruba are cost-conscious souls who have carefully checked the prices of comparable goods before leaving home. Duty is relatively low (only 3.3%). Much of the European china, jewelry, perfumes, watches, and crystal have a disconcerting habit of reappearing in every shopping mall and hotel boutique on the island, so after you determine exactly which brand of watch or china you want, you can comparison-shop. See chapter 5.

- **Barbados:** Local shops seem to specialize in all things English. Merchandise includes bone china from British and Irish manufacturers, watches, jewelry, and perfumes. Bridgetown's Broad Street is the shopping headquarters of the island, although some of the stores here maintain boutiques (with similar prices but a less extensive range of merchandise) at many of the island's hotels and in malls along the congested southwestern coast. Except for cigarettes and tobacco, duty-free items can be hauled off by any buyer as soon as they're paid for. Duty-free status is extended to anyone showing a passport or ID and an airline ticket with a date of departure from Barbados. See chapter 6.

- **Cayman Islands:** Goods are sold tax free from a daunting collection of malls and minimalls throughout Grand Cayman. Most of these are along the highway that parallels Seven Mile Beach; you'll need a car to shop around. There are also lots of stores in George Town, which you can explore on foot, poking in and out of some large emporiums in your search for bargains. See chapter 9.

- **Curaçao:** Curaçao has been a mercantile center since the 1700s. In the island's capital, tidy and prosperous Willemstad, hundreds of merchants will be only too happy to cater to your needs. A handful of malls lie on Willemstad's outskirts, but most shops are clustered within a few blocks of the center of town. During seasonal sales, goods might be up to 50% less than comparable prices in the States; most of the year, you'll find luxury items (porcelain, crystal, watches, and gemstones) priced at about 25% less than back home. Technically, you'll pay import duties on virtually everything you buy, but rates are so low you may not even notice. See chapter 10.

- **Dominican Republic:** The island's best buys include handcrafts, amber from Dominican mines, and the distinctive pale-blue semiprecious gemstone known as *larimar*. The amber sold by street vendors may be nothing more than orange-colored, transparent plastic; buy only from well-established shops if your investment is a large one. Other charming souvenirs might include a Dominican rocking chair (remember the one JFK used to sit in?), which is sold boxed, in ready-to-assemble pieces. Malls and souvenir stands abound in Santo Domingo, in Puerto Plata, and along the country's northern coast. See chapter 12.

- **Jamaica:** The shopping was better in the good old days, before new taxes added a 10% surcharge. Despite that, Jamaica offers a wealth of desirable goods, including flavored rums, Jamaican coffees, handcrafts (such as wood carvings, woven baskets, and sandals), original paintings and sculpture, and cameras, watches, and VCRs. Unless you're a glutton for handmade souvenirs (which are available on virtually every beach and street corner), you'd be wise to limit most of your purchases to bona fide merchants and stores. See chapter 15.

- **Puerto Rico:** For U.S. citizens, there's no duty on anything (yes, anything) you buy in Puerto Rico. That doesn't guarantee that prices will be particularly low, however. Jewelry and watches abound, often at competitive prices, especially in the island's best-stocked area, Old San Juan. Also of great interest are such Puerto Rican handcrafts as charming folkloric papier-mâché carnival masks and *santos*, carved wooden figures depicting saints. See chapter 18.

- **St. Maarten/St. Martin:** Although there's no duty on any purchases you make on either side of the island's Dutch/French border, goods are not especially cheap. Merchants have been suspected of fixing prices on both sides of the border, and after a few days, you may grow exceedingly tired of displays of electronic gadgets. It's best to arrive on the island as a well-educated consumer, with a firm grip on what is and what isn't a favorable price for whatever you really need. Philipsburg, capital of the island's Dutch side, is the best place to shop. See chapter 24.

- **St. Thomas:** Many of its busiest shops are in restored warehouses that were originally built in the 1700s. Charlotte Amalie, the capital, is a shopper's town, with a staggering number of stores stocked with more merchandise than anywhere else in the entire Caribbean. However, despite all the fanfare, real bargains are hard to come by. Regardless, the island attracts hordes of cruise-ship passengers on a sometimes frantic hunt for bargains, real or imagined. Look for two local publications, *This Week* and *Best Buys*; either might steer you to the type of merchandise you're seeking. If at all possible, try to avoid shopping when more than one cruise ship is in port—the shopping district is a madhouse on those days. See chapter 27.

- **St. Croix:** This island is a poor stepchild of St. Thomas, but there's still much to interest the "born-to-shop" visitor here, and merchandise has never been more wide-ranging than it is today. Even though most cruise ships call at Frederiksted, a colorful but isolated town near the island's western tip, most of the shops are in Christiansted, the capital. You'll see many of the same shops and chains on St. Croix that you find on St. Thomas, including such omnipresent names as Little Switzerland. Prices are about the same as on St. Thomas. See chapter 27.

13 The Best Nightlife

It's sleepy time on the following islands: The British Virgins, Montserrat, Nevis, Anguilla, St. Eustatius, Saba, St. Barthélemy, Dominica, Bonaire, St. Vincent, and all of the Grenadines. The serious partyer will probably want to choose the following destinations:

- **Aruba:** This island has 10 casinos, each with its own unique decor and each with a following of devoted gamblers. Some offer their own cabaret or comedy shows, dance floors with live or recorded music, restaurants of all degrees of formality, and bars. See chapter 5.

- **Barbados:** Bridgetown is home to at least two boats (the *Bajan Queen* and the *Jolly Roger*) that embark at sundown for rum-and-reggae cruises, as well as over-size music bars like Harbour Lights. Otherwise, a host of bars, British-style pubs, dozens of restaurants, and discos (both within and outside of large hotels) beckon from St. Lawrence Gap or the crowded southwest coast. See chapter 6.

- **Dominican Republic:** Large resort hotels in the Dominican Republic evoke a Latino version of Las Vegas. If cabaret shows aren't your thing, there are casinos and enough discos to keep a *soca* or hip-hop fan busy for weeks. However, Santo Domingo is not the safest place to be out at night, so take a cab back to your hotel. See chapter 12.

- **Jamaica:** Many visitors are drawn here by a love for the island's distinct musical forms. Foremost among these are reggae and *soca*, both of which are performed at hotels, resorts, and raffish dives throughout the island. Hotels often stage folkloric shows that include entertainers who sing, dance, swallow torches, and walk on broken glass. There are also plenty of indoor/outdoor bars where you might actually be able to talk to people. Local tourist boards in Negril and Montego Bay sometimes organize weekly beach parties called "Boonoonoonoos." See chapter 15.

- **Puerto Rico:** Puerto Rico contains all the raw ingredients for great nightlife, including casinos, endless rows of bars and bodegas, cabaret shows with girls and glitter, and discos that feature everything from New York imports to some of the best salsa and merengue anywhere. If you're a really serious partyer, you'll have lots of company in Puerto Rico. Be prepared to stay out very late; you can recover from your Bacardi hangover on a palm-fringed beach the next day. See chapter 18.

- **St. Maarten/St. Martin:** This island has a rather cosmopolitan nightlife and contains the densest concentration of restaurants in the Caribbean, each with its own bar. Discos are often indoor/outdoor affairs. Hotel casinos abound, and if you're addicted to the jingle of slot machines and roulette wheels, you won't lack for company. See chapter 24.

- **St. Thomas:** The Virgin Islands' most active nightlife is found here. Don't expect glitzy shows like those in San Juan's Condado area, or any kind of casino. Nearby, the Greenhouse Restaurant features recorded music, live concerts, and golden-oldies nights. See chapter 27.

- **St. Croix:** It's very similar to St. Thomas, but with fewer options. A consistently good choice is the Buccaneer Hotel, which stages limbo/folkloric shows, reggae players, and concerts by local stars. Otherwise, the funky clubs and hole-in-the-wall bars of Christiansted dominate the nightscape. See chapter 27.

14 The Best Gambling

- **Aruba:** After dark, visitors throng to the island's 10 casinos. The casinos are big, splashy, colorful, and, yes, people even occasionally win. Drinks are usually free while you play. Conveniently, the legal tender in most of Aruba's casinos is the U.S. dollar. See chapter 5.
- **Curaçao:** The canny merchants of Curaçao have known how to make a guilder since the early colonial days. There are at least a dozen casinos beckoning from strategic points throughout the island. See chapter 10.
- **Dominican Republic:** The tourist areas of Puerto Plata and Santo Domingo are sprinkled with casinos, and the island's ever developing north shore contains its share of jingle-jangle, too. Our favorite is the casino in the Renaissance Jaragua Hotel & Casino in Santo Domingo, which offers floor shows, live merengue concerts, a wraparound bar, and at least five different restaurants. See chapter 12.
- **Puerto Rico:** The country's gaming headquarters lies along the Condado in San Juan, although there are also casinos in megaresorts scattered throughout the island. The casinos here are the most fun in the Caribbean, and also some of the most spectacular. Each contains lots of sideshows (restaurants, merengue bars, art galleries, piano bars, shops) that can distract you from the roulette and slots. Puerto Ricans take pride in dressing well at their local casinos, which enhances an evening's glamour. No drinking is permitted at the tables, and tight controls are exerted by U.S. gaming authorities. See chapter 18.
- **St. Maarten:** Gambling is illegal on the island's French side (St. Martin), so the casinos are the exclusive domain of the Dutch. The gaming halls have an atmosphere of nonchalance, which might appeal to you if you dislike gaming halls with high stakes and lots of intensity. There are about seven casinos on St. Maarten, usually in large resort hotels. Hotels on the French side sometimes arrange gambling junkets to the Dutch side. See chapter 24.

2

Planning a Trip to the Caribbean

Golden beaches shaded by palm trees and crystalline waters teeming with colorful sea creatures—it's all just a few hours' flight from the east coast of the United States. Dubbed the "Eighth Continent of the World," the Caribbean islands have an amazing variety of terrain that ranges from thick rain forests to haunting volcanoes, from white- to black-sand beaches. Spicy food, spicier music, and the gentle, leisurely lifestyle of the islands draw millions of visitors each year, all hoping to find the perfect place in the sun.

1 The Islands in Brief

ANGUILLA (British Leewards)   Although it's developing rapidly as sunseekers discover its 12 miles of arid but spectacular beaches, Anguilla is still quiet, sleepy, and relatively free of racial tensions. A flat, coral-based island, it maintains a maritime tradition of proud fisherfolk, many of whom still make a living from the sea, mainly catching lobsters and selling them at high prices to expensive resorts and restaurants. Although a handful of moderately priced accommodations is available, Anguilla is a very expensive destination.

ANTIGUA (British Leewards)   Antigua is famous for having a different beach for each day of the year. Some British traditions (including a passion for cricket) linger on even though the nation became independent in 1981. The island has a population of 80,000, mostly descended from the African slaves of plantation owners. Antigua's resorts are isolated and conservative but very glamorous, its highways are horribly maintained, and its historic naval sites are some of the most interesting in the British maritime world. Antigua is politically linked to the sparsely inhabited and largely undeveloped island of Barbuda, about 30 miles north. In spite of its small size, Barbuda has two resorts that are pockets of posh, with lethal prices to match.

ARUBA (Dutch Leewards)   Until its beaches were "discovered" in the late 1970s, Aruba was an almost forgotten outpost of Holland, valued mostly for its oil refineries and salt factories. Today it's favored for the lunar landscapes of its desertlike terrain, spectacular beaches, constant sunshine, and an almost total lack of racial tensions. Its population of 70,000 is culturally diverse, with roots in Holland, Portugal, Spain, Venezuela, India/Pakistan, and Africa. A building boom in the 1980s transformed this island into a pale version of Las Vegas—come here if you're interested in gambling and splashy resorts.

BARBADOS   Originally founded on a plantation economy that made its aristocracy rich (on the backs of slave laborers), this Atlantic outpost was a staunchly loyal member of the British Commonwealth for generations. Barbados is the Caribbean's easternmost island, floating in the mid-Atlantic like a great coral reef and ringed with beige-sand beaches. Cosmopolitan Barbados has the densest population of any island in the Caribbean, a sports tradition avidly devoted to cricket, and a loyal group of return visitors who appreciate its many stylish, medium-size hotels (many of which carry a hefty price tag). Service is usually extremely good, a by-product of its British mores, which have flourished since the turn of the century. Topography varies from rolling hills and savage waves on the eastern (Atlantic) coast to densely populated flatlands, rows of hotels and apartments, and sheltered beaches in the southwest.

BONAIRE   Its strongest historical and cultural links are to Holland, and although it has always been a poor relation of nearby Curaçao, Bonaire boasts better scuba diving and better bird life than any of its larger and richer neighbors. The terrain is as dry and inhospitable as anything you'll find in the Caribbean, a sparse desert landscape offset by a wealth of marine life that thrives along miles of offshore reefs.

THE BRITISH VIRGIN ISLANDS (B.V.I.)   Still a British Crown Colony, this lushly forested chain contains about 50 mountainous islands (depending on how many rocks, cays, and uninhabited islets you want to include). Superb for sailors, the B.V.I. are less densely populated, less developed, and have fewer social problems than the U.S. Virgin Islands. **Tortola** is the main island, followed by **Virgin Gorda,** which boasts some of the poshest hotels in the West Indies. **Anegada,** a coral atoll geologically different from the other members of the B.V.I., mainly attracts the yachting set.

THE CAYMAN ISLANDS   This is a trio of islands set near the southern coast of Cuba. Flat and prosperous, this tiny nation depends on Britain for its economic survival and attracts millionaire expatriates from all over because of its lenient tax and banking laws. Relatively unattractive, these islands are covered with scrubland and swamp, but boast more than their share of expensive private homes and condominiums. Until recently, **Grand Cayman** enjoyed one of the most closely knit societies in the Caribbean, although with recent prosperity, some of it is beginning to unravel. Because of the marine life above the offshore reefs, scuba divers seek out the Caymans almost as avidly as tax exiles. Many hotels have begun to line the sands of the nation's most famous sunspot, Seven Mile Beach.

CURAÇAO (Dutch Leewards)   Since much of the island's surface is an arid desert that grows only cactus, its canny Dutch settlers ruled out farming and developed Curaçao into one of the Dutch Empire's busiest trading posts. Until the post–World War II collapse of the oil refineries, Curaçao was a thriving mercantile society with a capital (Willemstad) that somewhat resembled Amsterdam and a population with a curious mixture of bloodlines, including African, Dutch, Venezuelan, and Pakistani. The lingua franca here is Papiamentu, a mixture of African and European dialects. Dutch, Spanish, and English are spoken here as well. Tourism began to develop during the 1980s, and many new hotels have been built since then. Overall, Curaçao is more than just a hotel industry: It's a well-defined society in its own right.

DOMINICA (British Windwards)   An English-speaking island set midway between Guadeloupe and Martinique, Dominica (*doh-mi-NEE-kah*), the largest and most mountainous island of the Windwards, is not to be confused with the Dominican Republic (see below). A mysterious, little-visited land of waterfalls, rushing streams, and rain forests, it has only a few beaches, which are mainly lined with black volcanic sand. But if you like the offbeat and unusual, you may find this the lushest and most fascinating island in the Caribbean. Some 82,000 people live here, including 2,000 descendants of the once-fierce Carib Indians. The capital is Roseau. Dominica is one of the poorest islands in the Caribbean, and has the misfortune of lying directly in the hurricane belt.

THE DOMINICAN REPUBLIC   Occupying the eastern two-thirds of Hispaniola, the island it shares with Haiti, the mountainous Dominican Republic is the second-largest country of the Caribbean. Longtime victim of an endless series of military dictatorships, it now has a more favorable political climate and offers some of the least expensive vacation options in the entire Caribbean. Its crowded capital is Santo Domingo, with a population of 2 million. The island offers lots of Latin color, zesty merengue music, and many opportunities to dance, drink, and party. The contrast between the wealth of foreign tourists and the poverty of locals is especially obvious here, and it's not the safest of the islands. Unfortunately, the Dominican Republic was hard-hit by Hurricane Georges in 1998.

GRENADA (British Windwards)   The southernmost nation of the Windward Islands, Grenada (*gre-NAY-dah*) is one of the lushest in the Caribbean. With its gentle climate, extravagantly fertile volcanic soil, and denizens who cultivate nutmeg and cloves for a living, it's one of the largest producers of spices in the western hemisphere. There's a lot of very appealing local color on Grenada, particularly since the political troubles of the 1980s seem, at least for the moment, to have ended. The beaches are white and sandy, and the populace (a mixture of English expatriates and islanders of African descent) is friendly. Once a British Crown Colony but now independent, the island nation also incorporates two smaller islands: Carriacou and Petit Martinique, neither of which has many tourist facilities. Grenada's capital, St. George's, is one of the most raffishly charming towns in the Caribbean.

GUADELOUPE (French West Indies)   It isn't as sophisticated or cosmopolitan as the two outlying islands over which it holds administrative authority, St. Barthélemy and the French section of St. Martin. Despite that, there's a lot of natural beauty in this département of mainland France. With a relatively low population density (only 340,000 people live here, mostly along the coast), butterfly-shaped Guadeloupe is actually two distinctly different volcanic islands separated by a narrow saltwater strait, the Rivière Salée. It's ideal for scenic drives and Creole color, offering an unusual insight into the French colonial world.

JAMAICA   A favorite of North American honeymooners, Jamaica is a mountainous island that rises abruptly from the sea 90 miles south of Cuba and about 100 miles west of Haiti. One of the most densely populated nations in the Caribbean, with a vivid sense of its own identity, Jamaica has a history rooted in the plantation economy and some of the most turbulent and impassioned politics in the western hemisphere. In spite of its economic and social problems, Jamaica is one of the most successful black democracies in the world. The island is large enough to allow the more or less peaceful coexistence of all kinds of people within its beach-lined borders, including everyone from expatriate English aristocrats to dyed-in-the-wool Rastafarians. Its tourist industry has been plagued by the island's reputation for aggressive vendors and racial tension, but is taking steps to improve the situation. Overall, and despite its long history of social unrest, increasing crime, and poverty, Jamaica is a fascinating island. It offers excellent beaches, golf, ecotourism adventures, and fine hotels in all price brackets, making it one of the most popular destinations in the Caribbean, especially since you can often find package deals galore.

MARTINIQUE (French West Indies)   One of the most exotic French-speaking destinations in the Caribbean, Martinique was the site of a settlement demolished by volcanic activity (St. Pierre, now only a pale shadow of a once-thriving city). Like Guadeloupe and St. Barts, Martinique is legally and culturally French (certainly many islanders drive with a Gallic panache—read: very badly), although many Creole customs and traditions continue to flourish. The beaches are beautiful, the Creole cuisine is full of flavor and flair, and the island has lots of tropical charm.

NEVIS   Now forging its own road to independence from St. Kitts, from which it is separated by two miles of water, this island was spotted by Columbus in 1493 on his second voyage to the New World. He called it Nieves—Spanish for snows—when he saw the cloud-crowned volcanic isle that evoked for him the snow-capped peaks of the Pyrenees. Known for its long beaches of both black and white sand, Nevis, more than any other island in the Caribbean, has turned its former great houses, built during the plantation era, into some of the most charming and atmospheric inns in the West Indies. It also boasts the Four Seasons Resort for those who want world-class elegance and service. The capital city of Charlestown looks like a real Caribbean backwater, though it is home to hundreds of world-wide businesses, drawn to Nevis for its tax laws and bank secrecy.

PUERTO RICO   Home to 3.3 million people whose primary language is Spanish, the Commonwealth of Puerto Rico is under the jurisdiction of the United States. It's the most urban island of the Caribbean, with lots of traffic, glittering casinos, relatively high crime, and a more-or-less comfortable mix of Latin culture with imports from the U.S. mainland. The island's interior is filled with ancient volcanic mountains; the coastline is ringed with sandy beaches. The commonwealth also includes a trio of small offshore islands: Culebra, Mona, and Vieques (the last has the most tourist facilities). San Juan, the island's 16th-century capital, has some of the most extensive and best-preserved Spanish colonial neighborhoods in the New World, lots of things to see and do, and a steady flow of cruise-ship passengers who keep the stores and casinos filled throughout much of the year. You can usually find great package deals offered by Puerto Rico's hotels and resorts.

SABA (Dutch Windwards in the Leewards)   Saba is a cone-shaped extinct volcano that rises abruptly and steeply from the watery depths of the Caribbean. There are no beaches to speak of, but the local Dutch- and English-speaking populace has traditionally made a living from fishing, trade, and needlework rather than tourism. Hotel choices are limited and are often designed in the traditional Saban style with white walls, red roofs, and stone foundations terraced into sloping hillsides. Saba's thrifty, seafaring folk can offer insights into the old-fashioned lifestyle of the Antilles. There's only one road on the island, and unless you opt to hike away from its edges, you'll have to follow the traffic along its narrow, winding route.

ST. BARTHÉLEMY (also called St. Barts or St. Barths; French West Indies)   Part of the French département of Guadeloupe, lying 15 miles from St. Martin, St. Barts is a small, hilly island with a population of 3,500 people who live on 13 square miles of verdant terrain ringed by pleasant white-sand beaches. A small number of African descendants live harmoniously on this chic Caribbean island with descendants of Norman and Breton mariners and a colony of more recent expatriates from Europe's mainland. An expensive and exclusive stamping ground of the rich and famous, with a distinctive seafaring tradition and a decidedly French flavor, St. Barts has a "storybook" capital in Gustavia.

ST. EUSTATIUS (known as Statia; Dutch Windwards in the Leewards)   During the 1700s, this Dutch-controlled island ("The Golden Rock") was one of the most important trading posts in the Caribbean. During the U.S. War of Independence, a brisk arms trade helped to bolster the local economy, but the glamour ended in 1781, when British Admiral Romney sacked the port, hauled off most of the island's wealth, and propelled St. Eustatius onto a path of obscurity—where it remained for almost 200 years, until the advent of tourism. Today the island is among the poorest in the Caribbean, with 8 square miles of arid landscape, beaches with strong and sometimes dangerous undertows, a population of around 1,700 people, and a sleepy capital named Oranjestad. Out of desperation, the island is very committed to maintaining its political and fiscal links to the Netherlands.

ST. KITTS (British Leewards)   The first English settlement in the Leeward Islands, St. Kitts has a rich sense of British maritime history. With 68 square miles of land, St. Kitts (also known as St. Christopher) enjoyed one of the richest sugarcane economies of the plantation age. This island lies somewhat off the beaten tourist track and has a very appealing small-scale charm. A lush, fertile mountain island with a rain forest and waterfalls, it is crowned by the 3,792-foot Mount Liamuiga—a crater that thankfully has remained dormant (unlike the one at Montserrat). St. Kitts is home to some 35,000 people and Brimstone Hill, the Caribbean's most impressive fortress.

ST. LUCIA (British Windwards)   St. Lucia (*LOO-sha*), 24 miles south of Martinique, is the second largest of the Windward Islands, with a population of around 150,000. Although in 1803 Britain eventually won control of the island, French influence is still evident in the Creole dialect spoken here. A volcanic island with lots of rainfall and great natural beauty, it has both white- and black-sand beaches, bubbling sulfur springs, and beautiful mountain scenery. Most tourism is concentrated on the island's northwestern tip, near the capital (Castries), but the arrival of up to 200,000 visitors a year has definitely altered the old agrarian lifestyle throughout the island.

ST. MAARTEN/ST. MARTIN (Dutch Windwards in the Leewards/French West Indies)   Lying 144 miles east of Puerto Rico, this scrub-covered island has been divided between the Dutch (Sint Maarten) and the French (Saint Martin) since 1648. Regardless of how you spell its name, it's the same island on both sides of the unguarded border—though the two halves are quite different. The Dutch side contains the island's more important airport, more shops, and more tourist facilities, while the French side has some of the poshest hotels and superior food. Both sides are modern, urbanized, and cosmopolitan. And both suffer from traffic jams, a lack of parking space in the capitals, tourist-industry burnout (especially on the Dutch side), and a disturbing increase in crime. There's a lot to do on this island, with many dining and drinking options, as the recent tourist boom proves.

ST. VINCENT & THE GRENADINES (British Windwards)   Despite its natural beauty and its population of 105,000 people (of mostly African descent), tourists have only recently discovered this miniarchipelago, though it has always been known to divers and the yachting set, who consider its north-to-south string of cays and coral islets one of the most beautiful sailing regions in the world. St. Vincent, 18 miles long and 11 miles wide, is by far the largest and most fertile island in the country. Its capital is the sleepy, somewhat dilapidated town of Kingstown (not to be confused with Kingston, Jamaica). The Grenadines, some 32 neighboring islands, stretch like a pearl necklace to the south of St. Vincent. These include the charming boatbuilding communities of Bequia and Mustique, where Princess Margaret has a home. Less densely populated islands in the chain include the tiny outposts of Mayreau, Canouan, Palm Island, and Petit St. Vincent, which was mostly covered with scrub until hotel owners planted much-needed groves of palm and hardwood trees.

TRINIDAD & TOBAGO   The southernmost of the West Indies, this two-island nation lies just 7 miles off the coast of Venezuela. Both islands once had sugar-plantation economies and enjoyed fantastic wealth during the 18th century. Trinidad is the most industrialized island in the Caribbean, with oil deposits and a polyglot population derived from India, Pakistan, Venezuela, Africa, and Europe. Known for its calypso music and carnival, Trinidad is one of the most culturally distinctive nations in the Caribbean, with a landmass of more than 1,800 square miles, a rich artistic tradition, a bustling capital (Port-of-Spain), and an impressive variety of exotic flora and fauna.

About 20 miles northeast of Trinidad, tiny Tobago (9 miles wide and 26 miles long) is calmer and less heavily forested, with a rather dull capital (Scarborough) and an impressive array of white-sand beaches. While Trinidad seems to consider tourism only one of many viable industries, Tobago is absolutely dependent on it.

THE U.S. VIRGIN ISLANDS   Formerly Danish possessions, these islands became part of the United States in 1917. Originally based on a plantation economy, St. Croix is the largest and flattest of the U.S. Virgins, whereas St. Thomas and St. John are more mountainous. St. Thomas and, to a lesser degree, St. Croix possess all the diversions, facilities, and amusements you'd find on the U.S. mainland, including bars, restaurants, and lots of modern resort hotels. St. Thomas, which is way overbuilt, is sometimes referred to as the shopping mall of the Caribbean, and cruise-ship passengers constantly pass through. Much of the surface of St. John is devoted to a national park, a gift from Laurance Rockefeller to the national park system. All three islands offer sailing, snorkeling, and unspoiled vistas. Crime is on the increase, however—an unfortunate fly in the ointment of this otherwise soothing U.S.-owned corner of paradise.

2 Visitor Information

All the major islands have tourist representatives who will supply information before you go; we list each one in the "Fast Facts" section of the individual island chapters.

The **Caribbean Tourism Organization**, 80 Broad St., 32nd Floor, New York, NY 10004 (☎ 212/635-9530), can also provide general information.

INFO ON THE WEB   The Internet is a great source of travel information. **Yahoo** (www.yahoo.com), **Excite** (www.excite.com), **Lycos** (www.lycos.com), **Infoseek** (www.infoseek.com), and the other major Internet indexing sites all have subcategories for travel, country/regional information, and culture—click on all three for links to travel-related Web sites.

Other good clearinghouse sites for information are **Microsoft's Expedia** (www.expedia.msn.com), **Travelocity** (www.travelocity.com), the **Internet Travel Network** (www.itn.com), and **TravelWeb** (www.travelweb.com). Another good site is **www.city.net/regions/caribbean**, which will point you toward a wealth of Caribbean travel information on the Web.

Of the many, many online travel magazines, two of the best are **Arthur Frommer's Budget Travel Online** (www.frommers.com), written and updated by the guru of budget travel himself, and **Condé Nast's Epicurious** (www.epicurious.com), based on articles from the company's glossy magazines *Traveler* and *Bon Appetit*.

That covers some of the top general Web sites. As often as possible throughout this chapter, we've included specific Web sites along with phone numbers and addresses. We've also given each resort's Web site if it has one, so you can see pictures of a property before you make your reservation. See also the *Online Directory* at the back of this book.

TRAVEL AGENTS   Travel agents can save you plenty of time and money by steering you toward the best package deals, hunting down the best airfare for your

---

Web Sites for Divers

For useful information on scuba diving in the Caribbean, check out the Web site of the Professional Association of Diving Instructors (PADI) at **www.padi.com.** This site provides descriptions of dive destinations throughout the Caribbean and a directory of PADI-certified dive operators. *Rodale's Scuba Diving Magazine* also has a helpful Web site at **www.scubadiving.com.** Both sites list dive package specials and display gorgeous color photos of some of the most beautiful dive spots in the world.

---

route, and arranging for cruise and rental cars. For the time being, most travel agents still charge nothing for their services—they're paid through commissions from the airlines and other agencies they book for you. A number of airlines, however, have begun to cut commissions, and increasingly agents are finding they have to charge a fee to hold the bottom line. In the worst instances, unscrupulous agents will only offer you travel options that bag them the juiciest commissions. Shop around and ask hard questions—use this book to become an informed consumer.

If you decide to use a travel agent, make sure the agent is a member of the **American Society of Travel Agents** (ASTA), 1101 King St., Alexandria, VA 22314 (☎ 703/739-8739; www.astanet.com). If you send a self-addressed stamped envelope, ASTA will mail you the free booklet *Avoiding Travel Problems.*

3 Entry Requirements & Customs

ENTRY REQUIREMENTS

Even though most of the Caribbean islands are independent nations and, thereby, classified as international destinations, passports may not be strictly required of Americans. We recommend carrying them nevertheless. You'll certainly need identification, and a passport is the best form of ID for speeding through Customs and Immigration. Other acceptable documents include an ongoing or return ticket, plus a birth certificate (the original or a copy that has been certified by the U.S. Department of Health). You will also need some photo ID, such as a driver's license or an expired passport; however, driver's licenses are not acceptable as a sole form of ID. Visas are usually not required, but some countries may require you to fill out a tourist card (see the individual island chapters for details).

Before leaving home, make two copies of your documents, including your passport and your driver's license, your airline ticket, and any hotel vouchers. If you're on medication, you should also make copies of prescriptions.

CUSTOMS

Each island has specific requirements that will be detailed in the destination chapters that follow. Generally, you're permitted to bring in items intended for your personal use, including tobacco, cameras, film, and a limited supply of liquor—usually 40 ounces. Here's what you can bring home from the islands:

U.S. CUSTOMS The U.S. government generously allows $1,200 worth of duty-free imports every 30 days from the U.S. Virgin Islands; those who go over their exemption are taxed at 5% rather than the usual 10%. The limit is $400 for such international destinations as the French islands of Guadeloupe and Martinique, and $600 for many other islands. If you visit only Puerto Rico, you don't have to go through Customs at all, since the island is a U.S. commonwealth.

Joint Customs declarations are possible for members of a family traveling together. For instance, if you are a husband and wife with two children, your purchases in the U.S. Virgin Islands become duty free up to $4,800! Unsolicited gifts can be sent to friends and relatives at the rate of $100 per day from the U.S. Virgin Islands (or $50 a day from the other islands). U.S. citizens, or returning residents at least 21 years of age, traveling directly or indirectly from the U.S. Virgin Islands, are allowed to bring in free of duty 1,000 cigarettes, 5 liters of alcohol, and 100 cigars (but not Cuban cigars). Duty-free limitations on articles from other countries are generally 1 liter of alcohol, 200 cigarettes, and 200 cigars.

Collect receipts for all purchases made abroad. You must also declare on your Customs form the nature and value of all gifts received during your stay abroad. It's prudent to carry proof that you purchased expensive cameras or jewelry on the U.S. mainland. If you purchased such an item during an earlier trip abroad, you should carry proof that you have previously paid Customs duty on the item.

Sometimes merchants suggest a false receipt to undervalue your purchase. *Warning:* You could be involved in a sting operation—the merchant might be an informer to U.S. Customs.

If you use any medication that contains controlled substances or requires injection, carry an original prescription or note from your doctor.

For more specifics, write to the **U.S. Customs Service,** 1301 Constitution Ave., P.O. Box 7407, Washington, DC 20044 (☎ **202/927-6724**), and request the free pamphlet *Know Before You Go.*

U.K. CUSTOMS   U.K. citizens returning from a non-EC country such as one of the Caribbean nations have a customs allowance of 200 cigarettes; 50 cigars; 250g of smoking tobacco; 2 liters of still table wine; 1 liter of spirits or strong liqueurs (over 22% volume); 2 liters of fortified wine, sparkling wine or other liqueurs; 60cc (ml) perfume; 250cc (ml) of toilet water; and £145 worth of all other goods, including gifts and souvenirs. People under 17 cannot have the tobacco or alcohol allowance. For more information, contact **HM Customs & Excise,** Passenger Enquiry Point, 2nd Floor Wayfarer House, Great South West Road, Feltham, Middlesex, TW14 8NP (☎ **0181/910-3744,** or 44/181-910-3744 from outside the U.K.; www.open. gov.uk).

CANADIAN CUSTOMS   For a clear summary of Canadian rules, write for the booklet *I Declare,* issued by **Revenue Canada,** 2265 St. Laurent Blvd., Ottawa K1G 4KE (☎ **613/993-0534**). Canada allows its citizens a $500 exemption, and you're allowed to bring back duty free 200 cigarettes, 2.2 pounds of tobacco, 40 imperial ounces of liquor, and 50 cigars. In addition, you're allowed to mail gifts to Canada from abroad at the rate of Can$60 a day, provided they're unsolicited and don't contain alcohol or tobacco (write on the package "Unsolicited gift, under $60 value"). All valuables should be declared on the Y-38 form before departure from Canada, including serial numbers of valuables you already own, such as expensive foreign cameras. *Note:* The $500 exemption can only be used once a year and only after an absence of 7 days.

4 Money

CASH/CURRENCY   Widely accepted on many of the islands, the U.S. dollar is the legal currency of the U.S. Virgin Islands, the British Virgin Islands, and Puerto Rico. Many islands use the Eastern Caribbean dollar, even though your hotel bill will most likely be presented in U.S. dollars. French islands use the French franc, although

Dollars & Pounds

The U.S. dollar is widely accepted throughout the Caribbean, even on islands that print their own currency. At press time, the Canadian dollar trades at an average of around $1.50 CAN = $1 U.S. The British pound trades at an average of around 61p = $1 U.S. The chart below gives a rough approximation of conversion rates you're likely to find at the time of your trip, but confirm before you make transactions.

U.S.$	Can$	U.K.£	U.S.$	Can$	U.K.£
0.25	0.38	0.15	15.00	22.50	9.15
0.50	0.75	0.31	20.00	30.00	12.20
0.75	1.13	0.46	25.00	37.50	15.25
1.00	1.50	0.61	50.00	75.00	30.50
2.00	3.00	1.22	75.00	112.50	45.75
3.00	4.50	1.83	100.00	150.00	61.00
4.00	6.00	2.44	150.00	225.00	91.50
5.00	7.50	3.05	200.00	300.00	122.00
6.00	9.00	3.66	250.00	375.00	152.50
7.00	10.50	4.27	300.00	450.00	183.00
8.00	12.00	4.88	350.00	525.00	213.50
9.00	13.50	5.49	400.00	600.00	244.00
10.00	15.00	6.10	500.00	750.00	305.00

many hotels often quote their prices in U.S. dollars. For details, see "Fast Facts" in the individual island chapters.

TRAVELER'S CHECKS   Traveler's checks are something of an anachronism from the days before the ATM made cash accessible at any time. These days, traveler's checks seem less necessary, as most islands have 24-hour ATMs that allow you to withdraw small amounts of cash as needed. However, if you want to avoid ATM service charges, or if you just want the security of knowing you can get a refund in the event that your wallet is stolen, you may want to purchase traveler's checks, which you can do at almost any bank. American Express offers denominations of $10, $20, $50, $100, $500, and $1,000. You'll pay a service charge ranging from 1% to 4%. You can also get **American Express** traveler's checks over the phone by calling ☎ **800/ 221-7282;** by using this number, Amex gold and platinum cardholders are exempt from the 1% fee. AAA members can obtain checks without a fee at most AAA offices.

Visa offers traveler's checks at **Citibank** locations nationwide and several other participating banks. The service charge ranges from 1½% to 2%; checks come in denominations of $20, $50, $100, $500, and $1,000. **MasterCard** also offers traveler's checks. Call ☎ **800/223-9920** for a location near you.

If you opt to carry traveler's checks, be sure to keep a record of their serial numbers separate from the checks, so you're ensured a refund in case of lost or theft.

ATMs   ATMs are linked to a national network that most likely includes your bank at home. **Cirrus** (☎ **800/424-7787;** www.mastercard.com/atm) and **Plus** (☎ **800/843-7587;** www.visa.com/atms) are the two most popular networks; check the back of your ATM card to see which network your bank belongs to. Use the toll-free numbers to locate ATMs in your destination.

If you're traveling abroad, ask your bank for a list of overseas ATMs. Be sure to check the daily withdrawal limit before you depart, and ask whether you need a new personal ID number.

CREDIT CARDS   Credit cards are invaluable when traveling. They are a safe way to carry money and provide a convenient record of all your expenses. You can also withdraw cash advances from your credit cards at any bank (though you'll start paying hefty interest on the advance the moment you receive the cash, and you won't receive frequent-flyer miles on an airline credit card). At most banks, you don't even need to go to a teller; you can get a cash advance at the ATM if you know your PIN number. (If you've forgotten your PIN or didn't even know you had one, call the phone number on the back of your credit card and ask the bank to send it to you. It usually takes 5 to 7 business days, though some banks will provide the number over the phone if you tell them your mother's maiden name or pass some other security clearance.)

THEFT   Almost every credit-card company has an emergency toll-free number that you can call if your wallet or purse is stolen. They may be able to wire you a cash advance off your credit card immediately, and in many places, they can deliver an emergency credit card in a day or two. The issuing bank's toll-free number is usually on the back of the credit card—though of course that doesn't help you much if the card was stolen. In that case, call the toll-free information directory at ☎ **800/555-1212. Citicorp Visa's** U.S. emergency number is ☎ **800/336-8472. American Express** cardholders and traveler's check holders should call ☎ **800/221-7282** for all money emergencies. **MasterCard** holders should call ☎ **800/307-7309.**

Odds are that if your wallet is gone, the police won't be able to recover it for you. However, after you realize that it's gone and you cancel your credit cards, it is still worth informing them. Your credit-card company or insurer may require a police report number.

5 When to Go

CLIMATE

The temperature variations in the Caribbean are surprisingly slight, averaging between 75° and 85° Fahrenheit in both winter and summer. It can get really chilly, however, especially in the early morning and at night. The Caribbean winter is usually like a perpetual May. Overall, the mid-80s prevail throughout most of the region, and trade winds make for comfortable days and nights, even without air-conditioning.

The humidity and bugs can be a problem here year-round. However, more mosquitoes come out during the rainy season, which traditionally occurs in the autumn. If you come in the summer, be prepared for really broiling sun in the mid-afternoon.

HURRICANES   The curse of Caribbean weather, the hurricane season lasts—officially, at least—from June 1 to November 30. But there's no cause for panic: Satellite forecasts give adequate warnings so that precautions can be taken.

To get a weather report before you go, call the nearest branch of the **National Weather Service,** listed in your phone directory under the "U.S. Department of Commerce." You can also call **Weather Trak.** For the telephone number for your particular area, call ☎ **900/370-8725.** A taped message gives you the three-digit access code for the place you're interested in; the call costs 95¢ per inquiry. On the Web, check **www.weather.com.**

THE HIGH SEASON & THE OFF-SEASON

The Caribbean has become a year-round destination. The "season" runs roughly from mid-December to mid-April. Hotels charge their highest prices during the peak winter period, which is generally the driest season. Even the winter can be wet, however, in mountainous areas, and you can expect showers, especially in December and January, on Martinique, Guadeloupe, Dominica, St. Lucia, on the north coast of the Dominican Republic, and in northeast Jamaica.

For a winter vacation, make reservations 2 to 3 months in advance—or earlier for trips at Christmas and in February.

The off-season in the Caribbean—roughly from mid-April to mid-December (although this varies from hotel to hotel)—is one big summer sale. In most cases, hotels, inns, and condos slash 20% to 60% off their winter tariffs.

Dollar for dollar, you'll spend less money by renting a summer house or self-sufficient unit in the Caribbean than you would on Cape Cod, Fire Island, Laguna Beach, or the coast of Maine. Sailing and water sports are better, too, because the West Indies are protected from the Atlantic on their western shores, which border the calm Caribbean Sea. You just have to be able to tolerate strong sun if you're considering coming in the summer.

Because there's such a drastic difference in high-season and low-season rates at most hotels, we've included both on every property we review. You'll see the incredible savings you can enjoy if your schedule allows you to wait a couple of months for your fun in the sun!

6 Organized Adventure Tours

You might also inquire about the offerings from **Ecosummer Expeditions,** 5640 Hollybridge Way, Richmond, B.C., Canada V76 4N3 (☎ **800/465-8884** or 604/214-7484).

BIRD WATCHING   Victor Emanuel Nature Tours (☎ **800/328-8368**) offers weeklong bird-watching trips led by a biologist in Trinidad and Tobago, costing approximately $2,000 per person. The trip is based at the **Asa Wright Nature Center,** which has 150 of the more than 400 species of birds found in Trinidad. Discussion sessions on the symbiosis between plant and bird life are offered, along with field trips.

The company also operates weeklong birding trips to Jamaica (home to some 30 species of birds found nowhere else in the world), also costing from $2,000 per person. A Jamaican ornithologist conducts the trips.

CRUISES FOR NATURALISTS & DIVERS   Some of the best wildlife cruises are packaged by **Oceanic Society Expeditions,** Fort Mason Center, Building E, San Francisco, CA 94123 (☎ **800/326-7491** in the U.S., or 415/441-1106). Whale-watching jaunts and some research-oriented trips are also featured. You can swim with humpback whales in the Dominican Republic, or be part of the research swim with dolphins in the Bahamas. Another specialist in this field is **Tropical Adventures,** 111 Second Ave. N., Seattle, WA 98109 (☎ **800/247-3483** in the U.S., or 206/441-3483), which offers adventurous scuba packages to Saba.

ECOTOURS TO PUERTO RICO   Puerto Rico's varied and often hard-to-reach natural treasures have been conveniently packaged into a series of economical ecotours, operated by **Tropix Wellness Tours** (☎ **787/268-2173;** fax 787/268-1722). Five major tours are offered, including the exploration of sea turtles' nesting sites in Culebra, the phosphorescent bay in Vieques, the Rio Camuy cave system in Camuy,

In Search of the Big Wahoo

Some of the world's premier fishing grounds are found in the Caribbean—the waters are teeming with a spectacular variety of deep-sea game fish, including wahoo, sailfish, tuna, marlin, and dolphin (the fish, not the mammal). Among the shallow-water fish are tarpon, bonefish, pompano, and barracuda.

Spring through autumn is the best time to fish, although the sport is still practiced during the winter.

Puerto Rico is the fishing capital of the Caribbean—some 30 world records have been set here. Charters are plentiful in San Juan and Palmas del Mar.

Some of the other excellent fishing grounds are in the Cayman Islands, where waters offshore are filled with tuna, yellowtail, and other catches; and the Dominican Republic, which attracts anglers in pursuit of sailfish and bonito.

Those in search of marlin head for the north coast of Jamaica from September to April and favor the south coast in winter. Port Antonio is Jamaica's major fishing center.

The U.S. Virgin Islands are popular with vacationers pursuing Allison tuna, bonito, marlin, and wahoo. Red Hook on St. Thomas is the major charter center, although St. John and St. Croix lure anglers as well.

the dry, desertlike forest in Guanica, and the mountains in Maricao. All tours include equipment, and most include accommodations and at least some meals.

Prices range from $473 per person for the 4-day, 3-night turtle expedition on Cuelbra (including inter-island air transportation), to $243 per person for the 3-day, 2-night cave tour in Camuy.

Tropix Wellness Tours will customize an itinerary for those traveling to Puerto Rico alone, or for groups of six or more. Add-ons to the fixed tours, such as body-rafting expeditions through underground cave rivers and hiking excursions, can also be arranged.

HIKING   Unlike many of its neighboring islands, Jamaica offers mountain peaks of up to 7,400 feet. The flora, fauna, waterfalls, and panoramas of those peaks have attracted increasing numbers of hikers and hill climbers, each determined to experience the natural beauty of the island firsthand. Because of possible dangers involved, it's always best to go on an organized tour, the best of which are offered by **Sunventure Tours,** 30 Balmoral Ave., Kingston 10, Jamaica W.I. (☎ **876/960-6685**). For more data, refer to "Climbing Blue Mountain," in chapter 15.

Nature Expeditions (☎ **800/869-0639**) runs the best 9-day excursions to Trinidad and Tobago, going for $1,990 per person, not including airfare. Trip participants are based at the Asa Wright Nature Center, a bucolic 200-acre reserve on a former coffee plantation. Guests stay in individual cabins or in the center's guest house.

SAILING (FOR WOMEN)   A program for women of all ages and levels of nautical expertise is offered by **Womanship,** The Boat House, 410 Severn Ave., Annapolis, MD 21403 (☎ **800/342-9295** in the U.S., or 410/267-6661). It offers expert sailing instruction by women for a maximum of six students with one or two instructors. Tortola is the primary port of departure for the Caribbean trips, and sailing instruction takes place in the British Virgin Islands. Courses, which last 7 days, are offered year-round. Trips can be arranged for couples and families as well.

SEA KAYAKING Arawak Expeditions, P.O. Box 853, Cruz Bay, St. John (☎ **800/238-8687** in the U.S., or 340/693-8312), is the only outfitter in the Virgin Islands that offers overnight sea-kayaking/island-camping excursions. Full- and half-day trips are also available. You cruise through the island somewhat as the Arawaks did, except that they used dugout canoes. Today's vessels are two-person fiberglass kayaks complete with a foot-controlled rudder. The outfit provides kayaking gear, healthy meals, camping equipment, and two experienced guides. The cost of a full-day trip is $75, a half-day trip is $45, and multiday excursions range in price from $750 to $1,150.

7 Getting Married in the Caribbean

See also "The Best Honeymoon Resorts," in chapter 1, for specific resorts that offer wedding and honeymoon packages. **Club Med** (☎ **800/CLUB-MED**) and **Sandals** (☎ **800/SANDALS**) are two chains that have helped many couples tie the knot.

If you yearn to take the plunge on a sun-dappled island, here are some wedding basics on the islands:

ANGUILLA Couples need to file a license application on Anguilla, which takes approximately 48 hours to process. You'll need to present a passport or a birth certificate and photo ID, and, if applicable, you'll have to show proof of divorce or the death certificate of a deceased spouse. The fee for the license and stamp duty is $284. For further information, contact Ms. Carmencita Davis, **Registrar of Births, Deaths, and Marriages,** Judicial Department, The Valley, Anguilla, B.W.I. (☎ **264/ 497-2377**). A local wedding service, **Sunshine Lady Productions,** Box 85, The Valley, Anguilla, Leeward Islands, B.W.I. (☎ **264/497-2911;** fax 264/497-3884), will make the arrangements.

ANTIGUA There's a 24-hour waiting period for marriages on Antigua. A couple appears at the Ministry of Justice in the capital of St. John to complete and sign a declaration before a marriage coordinator and pays a $150 license fee. The coordinator will arrange for a marriage officer to perform a civil ceremony at any of Antigua's hotels or another place the couple selects. The fee for the marriage officer is $50. Several hotels and resorts offer wedding/honeymoon packages. For more information on civil or religious wedding ceremonies, contact the **Antigua Department of Tourism,** 610 Fifth Ave., Suite 311, New York, NY 10020 (☎ **212/541-4117**).

ARUBA Civil weddings are possible on Aruba only if one of the partners is an Aruban resident. Couples who qualify can arrange Roman Catholic, Protestant, and Jewish weddings on the island. Of course, because of restrictions, the average couple marries elsewhere, then visits Aruba for a honeymoon. For more information about planning a wedding on Aruba, contact the **Aruba Tourism Authority,** 1000 Harbor Blvd., Weehawken, NJ 08707 (☎ **800/TO-ARUBA** or 201/330-0800).

BARBADOS Couples can now marry the same day they arrive on Barbados, but they must first obtain a marriage license from the **Ministry of Home Affairs** (☎ **246/228-8950**). Bring either a passport or a birth certificate and photo ID, $50 (U.S.) in fees, $12.50 for the revenue stamp which you can obtain at the local post office, a letter from the authorized officiant who will perform the service, plus proof, if applicable, of pertinent deaths or divorces from any former spouse(s). A Roman Catholic wedding on Barbados carries additional requirements. For more information, contact the **Barbados Tourism Authority,** 800 Second Ave., New York, NY 10017 (☎ **800/221-9831** or 212/986-6516).

BONAIRE   The bride and/or groom must have a temporary residency permit, obtained by writing a letter to the governor of the **Island Territory of Bonaire,** Wilhelminaplein 1, Kralendijk, Bonaire, N.A. (☎ **599/7-5350**). The letter, submitted within 2 months of departure for Bonaire, should request permission to marry on Bonaire and to apply for temporary residency. You'll also need to inform the governor of your arrival and departure dates and the date you wish to marry. The partner who applies for residency must be on the island for 7 days prior to the wedding. A special dispensation must be issued by the governor if there is less than a 10-day time period between the announcement of the marriage and the ceremony. In addition, send three passport photos, copies of the bride's and groom's passports, birth certificates, and proof of divorce or, in the case of widows and widowers, the death certificate of the deceased spouse.

If you desire, you can arrange your wedding on Bonaire through **Multro Travel and Tours,** Attn: Mrs. Marvel Tromp, Kaya Amazon 27B (P.O. Box 237), Bonaire, N.A. (☎ **599/7-8334;** fax 599/7-8416), or check with the hotel where you're planning to stay. Some hotels arrange weddings on special request. For further information, contact the **Bonaire Tourist Office** (☎ **800/826-6247** or 212/956-5911).

THE BRITISH VIRGIN ISLANDS   Island residency is not required, but a couple must apply for a marriage license at the attorney general's office and must stay in the B.V.I. for 3 days while the application is processed. Present a passport or original birth certificate and photo identification, plus certified proof of your marital status and any divorce or death certificates that apply to any former spouse(s). Two witnesses must be present. The fee is $110. Marriages can be performed by the local registrar or by the officiant of your choice. Contact the **Registrar's Office,** P.O. Box 418, Road Town, Tortola, B.V.I. (☎ **284/494-3134** or 284/494-3701).

THE CAYMAN ISLANDS   Visitors have to call ahead and arrange for an authorized person to marry them. The name of the "marriage officer," as it is called, has to appear on the application for a marriage license. The application for a special marriage license costs $200 and can be obtained from the Deputy Secretary's Office, 3rd Floor, **Government Administration Building,** George Town (☎ **345/949-7900**). There is no waiting period. Present a birth certificate, the embarkation/disembarkation cards issued by the island's immigration authorities, and, if applicable, divorce decrees or proof of a spouse's death. Complete wedding services and packages are offered by **Cayman Weddings of Grand Cayman,** which is owned and operated by Caymanian marriage officers Vernon and Francine Jackson. For more information, contact them at P.O. Box 678, Grand Cayman (☎ **345/949-8677;** fax 345/949-8237). A brochure, *Getting Married in the Cayman Islands,* is available from **Government Information Services,** Broadcasting House, Grand Cayman (☎ **345/949-8092;** fax 345/949-5936).

CURAÇAO   Couples must be on-island 2 days before applying for a marriage license, for which there is a 14-day waiting period. Passport, birth certificate, return ticket, and divorce papers (if applicable) are required. The fee is subject to change, so check in advance. For further information, call the **Curaçao Tourist Board,** 475 Park Ave. S., Suite 2000, New York, NY 10016 (☎ **212/683-7660;** fax 212/683-9337).

JAMAICA   In high season, some Jamaican resorts witness several weddings a day. Many of the larger resorts can arrange for an officiant, a photographer, and even the wedding cake and champagne. Some resorts, however, will even throw in your wedding with the cost of your honeymoon at the hotel. Both the Jamaican Tourist Board and your hotel will assist you with the paperwork. Participants must reside on Jamaica for 24 hours before the ceremony. Bring birth certificates and affidavits saying you've never been married before. If you've been divorced or widowed, bring copies of your divorce papers or a copy of the deceased spouse's death certificate. The license and stamp duty costs $200. The cost of the ceremony can range from $50 to $200, depending on how much legwork you want to do yourself. You may apply in person at the **Ministry of National Security and Justice,** 12 Ocean Blvd., Kingston, Jamaica (☎ 876/922-9500).

PUERTO RICO   There are no residency requirements. You'll need parental consent if either party is under 18. Blood tests are required, although a test conducted within 10 days of the ceremony on the U.S. mainland will suffice. A doctor in Puerto Rico must sign the license after conducting an examination of the bride and groom. For complete details, contact the **Commonwealth of Puerto Rico Health Department,** Demographic Register, 171 Quisaueya St., Hato Rey, PR 00917 (☎ 787/767-9120).

ST. LUCIA   Both parties must have remained on the island for 48 hours prior to the ceremony. Present your passport or birth certificate, plus (if either participant has been widowed or divorced) proof of death or divorce from the former spouse(s). It usually takes about 2 days before the ceremony to process all the paperwork. Fees run around $150 for a lawyer (one is usually needed for the application to the governor-general), $25 for the registrar to perform the ceremony, and $37.75 for the stamp duty and the license. Some resorts and vacation properties also offer wedding packages that include all the necessary arrangements for a single fee. For more information, contact the **St. Lucia Tourist Board,** 800 Second Ave., Suite 400J, New York, NY 10017 (☎ 212/867-2950; fax 212/370-7867).

THE U.S. VIRGIN ISLANDS   No blood tests or physical examinations are necessary, but there is a $25 license fee, a $25 notarized application, and an 8-day waiting period, which is sometimes waived depending on circumstances. Civil ceremonies before a judge of the territorial court cost $200 each; religious ceremonies performed by clergy are equally valid. Fees and schedules for church weddings must be negotiated directly with the officiant. More information is available from the **U.S. Virgin Islands Division of Tourism,** 1270 Ave. of the Americas, New York, NY 10020 (☎ 212/332-2222).

The U.S.V.I. tourism offices distribute the guide *Getting Married in the U.S. Virgin Islands,* which gives information on all three islands, including wedding planners, places of worship, florists, and limousine services. The guide also provides a listing of island accommodations that offer in-house wedding services.

Couples can apply for a marriage license for **St. Thomas** or **St. John** by contacting the **Territorial Court of the Virgin Islands,** P.O. Box 70, St. Thomas, U.S.V.I. 00804 (☎ 340/774-6680). You can apply for weddings on **St. Croix** by contacting the **Territorial Court of the Virgin Islands,** Family Division, P.O. Box 929, Christiansted, St. Croix, U.S.V.I. 00821 (☎ 340/778-9750).

8 Health & Insurance

STAYING HEALTHY

Try to take proper precautions the week before you depart to avoid falling ill while you're away from home. Make an extra effort to eat and sleep well the week before you go—especially if you feel an illness coming on. Keep the following suggestions in mind.

- It's best to drink bottled mineral water during your trip.
- If you experience diarrhea, moderate your eating habits and drink only mineral water until you recover. If symptoms persist, consult a doctor.

- The Caribbean sun can be brutal. Wear sunglasses and a hat and use sunscreen liberally. Limit your time on the beach the first day. If you do overexpose yourself, stay out of the sun until you recover. If your exposure is followed by fever or chills, a headache, or a feeling of nausea or dizziness, see a doctor.
- One of the biggest menaces are the "no-see-ums," which appear mainly in the early evening. You can't see these gnats, but you sure can "feel-um." Screens can't keep these critters out, so carry your favorite bug repellent.
- Mosquitoes are a nuisance. Malaria-carrying mosquitoes in the Caribbean are confined largely to Haiti and the Dominican Republic. If you're visiting either, consult your doctor for preventive medicine at least 8 weeks before you leave. Dengue fever is prevalent in the islands, most prominently on Antigua, St. Kitts, Dominica, and the Dominican Republic. Once thought to have been nearly eliminated, it has made a comeback. To date, no satisfactory treatment has been developed; visitors are advised to avoid mosquito bites—as if that were possible.
- Vaccinations are not required for entering the Caribbean if you're coming from the United States, Britain, or Canada.
- Infectious hepatitis has been reported on islands such as Dominica and Haiti. Unless you have been immunized for both hepatitis A and B, consult your doctor about the advisability of getting a gamma-globulin shot before you leave.

WHAT TO DO IF YOU GET SICK AWAY FROM HOME

Finding a good doctor in the Caribbean is not a problem, and most speak English. See the "Fast Facts" section in each chapter for specific names and addresses on each individual island.

If you worry about getting sick away from home, you may want to consider medical travel insurance (see the section on travel insurance later in this chapter). In most cases, however, your existing health plan will provide all the coverage you need. Be sure to carry your identification card in your wallet.

If you suffer from a chronic illness, consult your doctor before your departure. For conditions like epilepsy, diabetes, or heart problems, wear a **Medic Alert Identification Tag** (☎ **800/825-3785;** www.medicalert.org), which will immediately alert doctors to your condition and give them access to your records through Medic Alert's 24-hour hot line. Membership is $35, plus a $15 annual fee.

Pack prescription medications in your carry-on luggage. Bring written prescriptions in generic, not brand-name form, and dispense all prescription medications from their original labeled vials. Also bring along copies of your prescriptions in case you lose your pills or run out.

If you wear contact lenses, pack an extra pair in case you lose or tear one.

Contact the **International Association for Medical Assistance to Travelers** (IAMAT) (☎ **716/754-4883** or 416/652-0137; www.sentex.net/~iamat) for tips on travel and health concerns in the countries you'll be visiting, plus lists of local English-speaking doctors. The **United States Centers for Disease Control and Prevention** (☎ **404/332-4559;** www.cdc.gov) provides up-to-date information on necessary vaccines and health hazards by region or country (by mail, their booklet is $20; on the Internet, it's free).

Once you're abroad, any local consulate can provide a list of area doctors who speak English. If you do get sick, you may want to ask the concierge at your hotel to recommend a local doctor—even his or her own. This will probably yield a better recommendation than any toll-free number would. If you can't find a doctor who can help you right away, try the emergency room at the local hospital. Many emergency rooms have walk-in-clinics for emergency cases that are not life-threatening.

INSURANCE

There are three kinds of travel insurance: trip-cancellation, medical, and lost-luggage coverage.

Trip-cancellation insurance is a good idea if you have paid a large portion of your vacation expenses up front, say, by purchasing a package or a cruise. Trip-cancellation insurance should cost approximately 6% to 8% of the total value of your vacation. (Don't buy it from the same company from which you've purchased your vacation—talk about putting all your eggs in one basket!)

The other two types of insurance, however, don't make sense for most travelers. Rule number one: Check your existing policies before you buy any additional coverage.

Your existing health insurance should cover you if you get sick on vacation (though if you belong to an HMO, you should check to see whether you are fully covered while you're away from home). If you need hospital treatment, most health insurance plans and HMOs will cover out-of-country hospital visits and procedures, at least to some extent. Most make you pay the bills up front at the time of care, however, and you'll get a refund only after you've returned and filed all the paperwork. Members of **Blue Cross/Blue Shield** can now use their cards at select hospitals in most major cities worldwide (☎ **800/810-BLUE** or www.bluecares.com/blue/bluecard/wwn for a list of hospitals).

Note that **Medicare** only covers U.S. citizens traveling in Mexico and Canada.

Your homeowner's insurance should cover stolen luggage. The airlines are responsible for $1,250 if they lose your luggage on domestic flights; if you plan to carry anything more valuable than that, keep it in your carry-on bag.

If you do require additional insurance, try one of the following companies: **Access America,** 6600 W. Broad St., Richmond, VA 23230 (☎ 800/284-8300); **Travel Guard International,** 1145 Clark St., Stevens Point, WI 54481 (☎ 800/826-1300); **Travel Insured International, Inc.,** P.O. Box 280568, East Hartford, CT 06128 (☎ 800/243-3174); **Columbus Travel Insurance,** 279 High St., Croydon CR0 1QH (☎ 0171/375-0011 in London; www2.columbusdirect.com/columbusdirect). For medical coverage, try **MEDEX International,** P.O. Box 5375, Timonium, MD 21094-5375 (☎ 888/MEDEX-00 or 410/453-6300; fax 410/453-6301; www.medexassist.com); or **Travel Assistance International** (Worldwide Assistance Services, Inc.), 1133 15th St. NW, Suite 400, Washington, DC 20005 (☎ 800/ 821-2828 or 202/828-5894; fax 202/828-5896). The **Divers Alert Network** (DAN) (☎ 800/446-2671 or 919/684-2948) insures scuba divers.

9 Tips for Travelers with Special Needs

FOR TRAVELERS WITH DISABILITIES

A disability shouldn't stop anyone from traveling. There are more resources out there than ever before. *A World of Options,* a 658-page book of resources for disabled travelers, covers everything from biking trips to scuba outfitters. It costs $35 ($30 for members) and is available from **Mobility International USA,** P.O. Box 10767, Eugene, OR, 97440 (☎ **541/343-1284,** voice and TDD; www.miusa.org). Annual membership for Mobility International is $35, which includes their quarterly newsletter, *Over the Rainbow.*

The **Moss Rehab Hospital** (☎ 215/456-9600) has been providing friendly and helpful phone advice and referrals to disabled travelers for years through its **Travel Information Service** (☎ 215/456-9603; www.mossresourcenet.org).

You can join the **Society for the Advancement of Travel for the Handicapped** (SATH), 347 Fifth Ave. Suite 610, New York, NY 10016 (☎ 212/447-7284 fax 212-725-8253; www.sath.org), for $45 annually, $30 for seniors and students, to gain access to a vast network of connections in the travel industry. SATH provides information sheets on travel destinations and referrals to tour operators that specialize in traveling with disabilities; its quarterly magazine, *Open World for Disability and Mature Travel,* is full of good information and resources. A year's subscription is $13 ($21 outside the U.S.).

Travelers with disabilities may also want to consider joining a tour that caters specifically to them. One of the best operators is **Flying Wheels Travel,** 143 West Bridge (P.O. Box 382), Owatonna, MN 55060 (☎ 800/535-6790). It offers various escorted tours and cruises, with an emphasis on sports, as well as private tours in minivans with lifts. Other reputable specialized tour operators include **Access Adventures** (☎ 716/889-9096), which offers sports-related vacations; **Accessible Journeys** (☎ 800/TINGLES or 610/521-0339), for slow walkers and wheelchair travelers; **The Guided Tour, Inc.** (☎ 215/782-1370); **Wilderness Inquiry** (☎ 800/728-0719 or 612/379-3858); and **Directions Unlimited** (☎ 800/533-5343).

Vision-impaired travelers should contact the **American Foundation for the Blind,** 11 Penn Plaza, Suite 300, New York, NY 10001 (☎ 800/232-5463), for information on traveling with seeing-eye dogs.

FOR GAY & LESBIAN TRAVELERS

Some of the islands are more gay friendly than others. These would include all the U.S. possessions—notably Puerto Rico, which is hailed as the "gay capital of the Caribbean" and offers gay guest houses, nightclubs, bars, and discos. To a lesser extent, much of St. Thomas, St. John, and St. Croix are welcoming, though they have nowhere near the number of gay-oriented establishments as Puerto Rico.

The French islands—St. Barts, St. Martin, Guadeloupe, and Martinique—are technically an extension of mainland France, and the French have always regarded homosexuality with a certain blasé tolerance.

The Dutch islands of Aruba, Bonaire, and Curaçao are quite conservative, so discretion is suggested.

Gay life is fairly secretive in many of the sleepy islands of the Caribbean. Some islands even have repressive antihomosexual laws. Homosexuality is actively discouraged in places like the Cayman Islands. Gay travelers might also note that the Cayman Islands recently refused to allow an all-gay cruise ship to dock on Grand Cayman, and several gay advocacy groups have even called for a boycott on travel to the Caymans in response. In Barbados, it is illegal, and there is often a lack of tolerance in spite of the large number of gay residents and visitors on the island. Jamaica is the most homophobic island in the Caribbean, with harsh antigay laws, even though there is a large local gay population. One local advised that it's not smart for a white gay man to wander the streets of Jamaica at night.

Many all-inclusive resorts, notably the famous Sandals of Jamaica, have discriminatory policies, allowing only male-female couples; gay men and lesbians are definitely excluded from their love nests. However, not all the all-inclusives practice such blatant discrimination. **Hedonism II,** a rival of Sandals in Negril, is not a "couples-only" resort, though they will help you find a roommate so that you can travel on the lower double-occupancy rate. The **Grand Lido,** a more upscale all-inclusive in Negril, will welcome whatever combinations show up (even singles, for that matter). For more information on all these resorts, see chapter 15.

The **International Gay & Lesbian Travel Association** (IGLTA) (☎ 800/ 448-8550 or 954/776-2626; fax 954/776-3303; www.iglta.org) links travelers with the appropriate gay-friendly service organization or tour specialist. With around 1,200 members, it offers quarterly newsletters, marketing mailings, and a membership directory that's updated quarterly. Membership often includes gay or lesbian businesses but is open to individuals for $150 per year, plus a $100 administration fee for new members. Members are kept informed of gay and gay-friendly hoteliers, tour operators, and airline and cruise-line representatives. Contact the IGLTA for a list of its member agencies, who will be tied into IGLTA's information resources.

General gay and lesbian travel agencies include **Family Abroad** (☎ 800/999-5500 or 212/459-1800; gay and lesbian); **Above and Beyond Tours** (☎ 800/397-2681; mainly gay men); and **Yellowbrick Road** (☎ 800/642-2488; gay and lesbian).

There are also two good, biannual English-language gay guidebooks, both focused on gay men but including information for lesbians as well. You can get the *Spartacus International Gay Guide* or *Odysseus* from most gay and lesbian book stores, or order them from **Giovanni's Room** (☎ 215/923-2960) or **A Different Light Bookstore** (☎ 800/343-4002 or 212/989-4850). Both lesbians and gays might want to pick up a copy of *Gay Travel A to Z* ($16). **The Ferrari Guides** (www.q-net.com) is yet another very good series of gay and lesbian guidebooks.

Out and About, 8 W. 19th St. #401, New York, NY 10011 (☎ 800/929-2268 or 212/645-6922), offers guidebooks and a monthly newsletter packed with good information on the global gay and lesbian scene. A year's subscription to the newsletter costs $49. *Our World,* 1104 North Nova Rd., Suite 251, Daytona Beach, FL 32117 (☎ 904/441-5367), is a slicker monthly magazine that promotes and highlights travel bargains and opportunities. Annual subscription rates are $35, $45 outside the U.S.

Several companies now assemble gay travel packages. **RSVP Vacations** (☎ 800/ 328-RSVP or 619/379-4697; www.rsvp.net), based in Minneapolis, offers gay cruises on ships both large and small in the Caribbean. **Atlantis Events** (☎ 800/628-5268 or 310/281-5450; www.atlantisevents.com), based in West Hollywood, books Club Med resorts for all-gay, all-inclusive vacations; they also do all-gay cruises, often in the Caribbean.

Many travel agencies are affiliated with the **International Gay Travel Association,** based in Key West. Any of these agencies can work with you to choose gay-friendly destinations and accommodations. (You'll find a list of gay-friendly travel agencies across the U.S. on the RSVP Vacations and Out & About Web sites mentioned above.) Two gay-friendly agencies are **Now Voyager Travel,** in San Francisco (☎ 800/255-6951 or 415/626-1169), and **Islanders' Kennedy Travel** (☎ 800/ 988-1181 or 516/352-4888). There are many others, all over the United States.

FOR SENIORS

Don't be shy about asking for discounts, but always carry some kind of identification, such as a driver's license, that shows your date of birth. Also, mention the fact that you're a senior citizen when you first make your travel reservations; many hotels offer senior discounts.

Members of the **American Association of Retired Persons** (AARP), 601 E St. NW, Washington, DC 20049 (☎ 800/424-3410 or 202/434-2277), get discounts not only on hotels but also on airfares and car rentals. AARP offers members a wide range of special benefits, including *Modern Maturity* magazine and a monthly newsletter.

The **National Council of Senior Citizens,** 8403 Colesville Rd., Suite 1200, Silver Spring, MD 20910 (☎ **301/578-8800**), a nonprofit organization, offers a newsletter six times a year (partly devoted to travel tips) and discounts on hotels and auto rentals. Annual dues are $13 per person or couple.

Mature Outlook, P.O. Box 9390, Des Moines, IA 50306 (☎ **800/336-6330**), began as a travel organization for people over 50, though it now caters to people of all ages. Members receive a bimonthly magazine and discounts on hotels. Annual membership is $19.95, which entitles members to discounts and, often, free coupons for discounted merchandise from Sears.

Golden Companions, P.O. Box 5249, Reno, NV 89513 (☎ **702/324-2227**), helps travelers over 45 to find compatible companions through a personal voice-mail service. Contact them for more information.

The Mature Traveler, a monthly 12-page newsletter on senior travel, is a valuable resource. It's available by subscription ($30 a year) from GEM Publishing Group, Box 50400, Reno, NV 89513-0400 (☎ **800/460-6676**). Another helpful publication is *101 Tips for the Mature Traveler,* available from Grand Circle Travel, 347 Congress St., Suite 3A, Boston, MA 02210 (☎ **800/221-2610** or 617/350-7500; fax 617/346-6700).

Grand Circle Travel is also one of the hundreds of travel agencies that specialize in vacations for seniors. Many of these packages, however, are of the tour-bus variety, with free trips thrown in for those who organize groups of 10 or more. Seniors seeking more independent travel should probably consult a regular travel agent. **SAGA International Holidays,** 222 Berkeley St., Boston, MA 02116 (☎ **800/343-0273**), offers inclusive tours and cruises for those 50 and older. SAGA also sponsors the more substantial **Road Scholar Tours** (☎ **800/621-2151**), which are fun-loving but with an educational bent.

10 Package Deals

For popular destinations like the Caribbean, packages are really the smart way to go, because they can save you a ton of money. Especially in the Caribbean, package tours are *not* the same thing as escorted tours. You'll be on your own, but in most cases, a package to the Caribbean will include airfare, hotel, and transportation to and from the airport—and it'll cost you less than just the hotel alone if you booked it yourself. This is really the way to save hundreds and hundreds of dollars! It may not be for you if you want to stay in a more intimate inn or guest house, but if you like resorts, read on.

You'll find an amazing array of packages to popular Caribbean destinations. Some packages offer a better class of hotels than others. Some offer the same hotels for lower prices. Some offer flights on scheduled airlines, while others book charters. In some packages, your choices of accommodations and travel days may be limited. Remember to comparison shop among at least three different operators, and always compare apples to apples.

One of the reasons visitors flock to the Caribbean is not just for the beaches, but also to visit various restaurants. Since many land-and-sea packages include meals, you may find yourself locked into your hotel dining room every night since your meals are already pre-paid. If you're seeking a more varied dining experience, avoid **AP (American Plan),** which means full-board, and opt for **MAP (Modified American Plan),** meaning breakfast and either lunch or dinner). That way, you'll at least be free for one main meal of the day and can sample a variety of an island's regional fare. Another way you can avoid being hotel-bound for meals is to book into an apartment or condo. Then you can either cook in, if there's a kitchenette, or take all your meals outside.

The best place to start your search is the travel section of your local Sunday newspaper. Also check the ads in the back of national travel magazines like *Travel & Leisure, National Geographic Traveler,* and *Condé Nast Traveler.* **Liberty Travel** (☎ 888/271-1584 to be connected with the agent closest to you; www.libertytravel.com), is one of the biggest packagers in the Northeast, and usually boasts a full-page ad in Sunday papers. You won't get much in the way of service, but you will get a good deal. **American Express Vacations** (☎ 800/241-1700; www.leisureweb.com) is another option. Check out its **Last Minute Travel Bargains** site, offered in conjunction with Continental Airlines (www6.americanexpress.com/travel/lastminutetravel/default. asp), with deeply discounted vacation packages and reduced airline fares that differ from the E-savers bargains that Continental e-mails weekly to subscribers. **Northwest Airlines** offers a similar service. Posted on Northwest's Web site every Wednesday, its **Cyber Saver Bargain Alerts** offer special hotel rates, package deals, and discounted airline fares.

Another good resource is the airlines themselves, which often package their flights together with accommodations. Fly-by-night packagers are uncommon, but they do exist; when you buy your package through an airline, however, you can be pretty sure that the company will still be in business when your departure date arrives. Among the airline packagers, your options include **American Airlines FlyAway Vacations** (☎ 800/321-2121), **Delta Dream Vacations** (☎ 800/872-7786), and **US Airways Vacations** (☎ 800/455-0123). Pick the airline that services your hometown most frequently.

The biggest hotel chains, casinos, and resorts also offer package deals. If you already know where you want to stay, call the resort itself and ask if they offer land/air packages.

To save time comparing the prices and value of all the package tours out there, consider calling **TourScan, Inc.,** P.O. Box 2367, Darien, CT 06820 (☎ 800/962-2080 or 203/655-8091). Every season, the company computerizes the contents of travel brochures that contain about 10,000 different vacations at 1,600 hotels in the Caribbean, the Bahamas, and Bermuda. TourScan selects the best-value vacation at each hotel and condo. Two catalogs are printed each year, which list a choice of hotels on most of the Caribbean islands in all price ranges. Write to TourScan for their catalogs, the price of which ($4) is credited to any TourScan vacation.

Other tour operators include the following:

Caribbean Concepts Corp., 99 Jericho Turnpike, Jericho, NY 11793 (☎ 800/423-4433 or 516/867-0700), offers low-cost air-and-land packages to the islands, including apartments, hotels, villas, and condo rentals, plus local sightseeing (which can be arranged separately).

Horizon Tours, 1010 Vermont Ave. NW, Suite 202, Washington, DC 20005 (☎ 888/SUN-N-SAND or 202/393-8390), specializes in good deals for all-inclusive resorts in the Bahamas, Jamaica, Aruba, Puerto Rico, Antigua, and St. Lucia.

Club Med, Club Med Sales, P.O. Box 4460, Scottsdale, AZ 85261-4460 (☎ 800/258-2633), has various all-inclusive options throughout the Caribbean and the Bahamas.

Globus, 5301 S. Federal Circle, Littleton, CO 80123 (☎ 800/851-0728, ext. 7518), gives escorted island-hopping expeditions to three or four islands, focusing on the history and culture of the West Indies.

11 Finding the Best Airfare

You shouldn't have to pay a regular fare to the Caribbean. Why? There are so many deals out there—in both summer and winter—that you can certainly find a discount fare. That's especially true if you're willing to plan on the spur of the moment: If a flight is not fully booked, an airline will discount tickets to try to fill it up.

Before you do anything else, read the section above on "Package Deals." But if you decide a package isn't for you, and you need to book your airfare on your own, read on, and we'll give you lots of money-saving tips.

If you fly in summer, spring, and fall, you're guaranteed substantial reductions on airfares to the Caribbean. You can also ask if it's cheaper to fly Monday through Thursday. And don't forget to consider air-and-land packages, which offer considerably reduced rates.

Most airlines charge different fares according to the season. Peak season, which is winter in the Caribbean, is most expensive; basic season, in the summer, offers the lowest fares. Shoulder season refers to the spring and fall months in between.

- **Keep an eye out for sales.** Check your newspaper for advertised discounts or call the airlines directly and ask if any promotional rates or special fares are available. You'll almost never see a sale during the peak winter vacation months of February and March, or during the Thanksgiving or Christmas seasons; but in periods of low-volume travel, you should find a discounted fare. If your schedule is flexible, ask if you can get a cheaper fare by staying an extra day or by flying midweek. (Many airlines won't volunteer this information.) If you already hold a ticket when a sale breaks, it may even pay to exchange your ticket, which usually incurs a $50 to $75 charge.

  Note, however, that the lowest-priced fares are often nonrefundable, require advance purchase of 1 to 3 weeks and a certain length of stay, and carry penalties for changing dates of travel.

- **Consolidators, also known as bucket shops, are a good place to find low fares.** Consolidators buy seats in bulk from the airlines and then sell them back to the public at prices below even the airlines' discounted rates. Their small boxed ads usually run in the Sunday travel section at the bottom of the page. Before you pay a consolidator, however, ask for a record locator number and confirm your seat with the airline itself. Be prepared to book your ticket with a different consolidator—there are many to choose from—if the airline can't confirm your reservation. Also be aware that bucket-shop tickets are usually non-refundable or rigged with stiff cancellation penalties, often as high as 50% to 75% of the ticket price.

- **Council Travel** (☎ 800/226-8624; www.counciltravel.com) and **STA Travel** (☎ 800/781-4040; www.sta.travel.com) cater especially to young travelers, but their bargain basement prices are available to people of all ages. **Travel Bargains** (☎ 800/AIR-FARE; www.1800airfare.com) was formerly owned by TWA but now offers the deepest discounts on many other airlines, with a 4-day advance purchase. Other reliable consolidators include **1-800-FLY-CHEAP** (www.1800flycheap.com); **TFI Tours International** (☎ 800-745-8000 or 212/736-1140), which serves as a clearinghouse for unused seats; or "rebators" such as **Travel Avenue** (☎ 800/333-3335 or 312/876-1116) and the **Smart Traveller** (☎ 800/448-3338 in the U.S., or 305/448-3338; www.smarttraveller@juno.com), which rebate part of their commissions to you.

- **Consider a charter flight.** Discounted fares have pared the number available, but they can still be found. Most charter operators advertise and sell their seats through travel agents, thus making these local professionals your best source of information for available flights. Before deciding to take a charter flight, however, check the restrictions on the ticket: You may be asked to purchase a tour package, to pay in advance, to be flexible if the day of departure is changed, to pay a service charge, to fly on an airline you're not familiar with (this usually is not the case), and to pay harsh penalties if you cancel—but be understanding if the charter doesn't fill up and is canceled up to 10 days before departure. Summer charters fill up more quickly than others and are almost sure to fly, but if you decide on a charter flight, seriously consider cancellation and baggage insurance.

- **Join a travel club** such as **Moment's Notice** (☎ **718/234-6295**) or **Sears Discount Travel Club** (☎ **800/433-9383,** or 800/255-1487 to join), which supply unsold tickets at discounted prices. You pay an annual membership fee to get the club's hot-line number. Of course, you're limited to what's available, so you have to be flexible.

- **Search for the best deal on the Web.** The Web sites highlighted below are worth checking out, especially since all services are free. Always check the lowest published fare, however, before you shop for flights on line.

- **Arthur Frommer's Budget Travel** (www.frommers.com) offers detailed information on destinations around the world and up-to-the-minute ways to save dramatically on flights, hotels, car rentals, and cruises. Book an entire vacation on line and research your destination before you leave. Consult the message board to set up "hospitality exchanges" in other countries, to talk with other travelers who have visited a hotel you're considering, or to direct travel questions to Arthur Frommer himself. The newsletter is updated daily to keep you abreast of the latest breaking ways to save, to publicize new hot spots and best buys, and to present veteran readers with fresh, ever-changing approaches to travel.

- **Microsoft Expedia** (www.expedia.com) offers a Fare Tracker that e-mails you weekly with the best airfare deals from your hometown on up to three destinations. The site's Travel Agent will steer you to bargains on hotels and car rentals, and with the help of hotel and airline seat pinpointers, you can book everything right on line. Before you depart, log on for maps and up-to-date travel information, including weather reports and foreign exchange rates.

- **Travelocity** (www.travelocity.com) is one of the best travel sites out there, especially for finding cheap airfares. In addition to its Personal Fare Watcher, which notifies you via e-mail of the lowest airfares for up to five different destinations, Travelocity will track the three lowest fares for any routes on any dates in minutes. You can book a flight, then find the best hotel or car-rental deals via the SABRE computer reservations system. Click on "Last Minute Deals" for the latest travel bargains.

- **The Trip** (www.thetrip.com) is really geared toward the business traveler, but vacationers-to-be can also use its exceptionally powerful fare-finding engine, which will e-mail you weekly with the best city-to-city airfare deals for as many as 10 routes. The Trip uses the Internet Travel Network, another reputable travel-agent database, to book hotels and restaurants.

Here's a partial list of airlines and their Web sites, where you can not only get on the e-mailing lists, but also book flights directly: **Air Jamaica** (www.airjamica.com); **American Airlines** (www.aa.com); **British Airways** (www.british-airways.com)**; BWIA** (www.bwee.com); **Canadian Airlines International** (www.cdnair.ca); **Continental Airlines** (www.flycontinental.com); **Delta** (www.delta-air.com); and **US Airways** (www.usairways.com).

12 Cruises

Here's a brief rundown of some of the major cruise lines that serve the Caribbean. For more detailed information, pick up a copy of *Frommer's Caribbean Cruises & Ports of Call 2000*.

BOOKING YOUR CRUISE

How should you book your cruise and get to the port of embarkation before the good times roll? If you've developed a relationship over the years with a favorite travel agency, then by all means, leave the details to the tried and true specialists. Many agents will propose a package deal from the principal airport closest to your residence to the airport nearest to the cruise-departure point. It's possible to purchase your air ticket on your own and book your cruise ticket separately, but in most cases, you'll save big bucks by combining the fares into a package deal.

You're also likely to save money—sometimes *lots* of money—by contacting a specialist who focuses on cruise bookings. He or she will be likely to match you with a cruise line whose style suits you, and can also steer you toward any of the special promotions that come and go as frequently as Caribbean rainstorms.

Here are some travel agencies to consider: **Cruises, Inc.,** 5000 Campuswood Dr. E., Syracuse, NY 13057 (☎ 800/854-0500 or 315/463-9695); **Cruise Fairs of America,** Century Plaza Towers, 2029 Century Park E., Suite 950, Los Angeles, CA 90067 (☎ 800/456-4FUN or 310/556-2925); **The Cruise Company,** 10760 Q St., Omaha, NE 68127 (☎ 800/289-5505 or 402/339-6800); **Kelly Cruises,** 1315 W. 22nd St., Suite 105, Oak Brook, IL 60523 (☎ 800/837-7447 or 630/990-1111); **Hartford Holidays Travel,** 129 Hillside Ave., Williston Park, NY 11596 (☎ 800/828-4813 or 516/746-6670); and **Mann Travel** and **Cruises American Express,** 6010 Fairview Rd., Suite 104, Charlotte, NC 28210 (☎ 800/849-2301 or 704/556-8311). These companies stay tuned to last-minute price wars; cruise lines don't profit if these megaships don't fill up near peak capacity, so sales pop up all the time.

You're likely to sail from Miami, which has become the cruise capital of the world. Other departure ports include San Juan, Port Everglades, New Orleans, Tampa, and (via the Panama Canal) Los Angeles.

CRUISE LINES

- **American Canadian Caribbean** (☎ 800/556-7450) These tiny, 80- to 100-passenger coastal cruisers make 7- to 12-day excursions through the Caribbean, visiting smaller, more out-of-the-way ports than the big cruise ships and offering an experience that's quiet and completely unpretentious. The line operates three almost identical ships, at least one of which spends part of the winter cruising around the Bahamas, Puerto Rico, the Virgin Islands, the Panama Canal, and the coasts of Central America.
- **Carnival Cruise Lines** (☎ 800/438-6744) Offering affordable vacations on some of the biggest and most brightly decorated ships afloat, Carnival is the boldest, brashest, and most successful mass-market cruise line in the world. Twelve of its vessels depart for the Caribbean from Miami, Tampa, New Orleans, Port Canaveral, and San Juan, and eight of them specialize in 7-day or longer tours that feature stopovers at selected ports throughout the eastern, western, and southern Caribbean, including St. Lucia, San Juan, Guadeloupe, Grenada, Grand Cayman, and Jamaica; four others offer 3- to 5-day itineraries visiting such ports as Nassau, Key West, Grand Cayman, and Playa del Carmen/ Cozumel. Its fleet has many ships, including the megaship *Paradise*. Launched in

1998 and weighing in at 70,367 tons, it's noteworthy as the only completely smoke-free cruise ship in the Caribbean. Most of the company's Caribbean cruises offer good value and feature nonstop activities. Food and party-colored drinks are plentiful, and the overall atmosphere is comparable to a floating theme park. Lots of single passengers opt for this line, as do families attracted by the line's well-run children's program. The average onboard age is a relatively youthful 42, although ages range from 3 to 95.

- **Celebrity Cruises** (☎ 800/437-3111)   Celebrity maintains five newly built, stylish, medium to large ships with cruises that last between 7 and 15 nights to ports such as Key West, San Juan, Grand Cayman, St. Thomas, Ocho Rios, Antigua, and Cozumel, Mexico, to name a few. It's classy but not stuffy, several notches above mass-market, and provides an experience that's both elegant and fun—and all for a competitive price. Accommodations are roomy and well-equipped, cuisine is the most refined of any of its competitors, and its service is impeccable.

- **Clipper Cruise Line** (☎ 800/325-0010). Clipper, a line whose small ships visit ports around the world, has two ships on Caribbean itineraries every winter. Like the vessels of American Canadian Caribbean line, the Clipper ships are small, conservative, and lacking the flashy amenities of the megaships (though between the two lines, Clipper's ships are much more comfortable—and their prices commensurately higher). Each weighs under 100 tons and has a shallow draft that allows it access to small, out-of-the-way ports in the Virgin Islands, plus such southern Caribbean ports as Dominica and the Grenadine islands of Bequia, Union Island, Mayreau, Mustique, and Petit St. Vincent. Other stops include Bonaire, Isla Margarita, Tobago and Trinidad, and destinations along the banks of Venezuela's Orinoco River. Vessels also make transits of the Panama Canal (many of which are sold out months in advance) and stop in more frequently visited ports of call like St. Thomas, St. Kitts and/or Nevis, and St. Lucia.

- **Club Med Cruises** (☎ 800/4-LESHIP)   Club Med Cruises is basically Club-Med-at-sea, but with a more upscale, couples-oriented feel and with fewer children. The line's one ship, the *Club Med II*, sails the Caribbean during the winter months and is the largest cruise ship afloat that purports to be sail-powered—though frankly, it used engines much more than sails to get between its home port of Martinique and its out-of-the-way ports of call, which include isolated beaches in the Grenadines and the Virgin Islands; an almost uninhabited bird refuge (La Blanquilla) and a small island (La Roque), both off the coast of Venezuela; such French-speaking ports of call as St. Barts and St. Martin; and other ports that include St. Kitts, Grenada, Bonaire, and San Juan. The food aboard is quite satisfactory and is served in ample portions, and the onboard atmosphere is, per the Club Med formula, French as all get out.

- **Commodore Cruise Line** (☎ 800/237-5361)   Commodore's two ships are both small, solid, not particularly glamorous, but highly seaworthy vessels, and are based year-round in New Orleans. The *Enchanted Isle* sails through the western Caribbean and usually spends 3 full days of its 7 cruise days at sea, occupying the remaining 4 days at ports in Montego Bay, Jamaica; the Cayman Islands; and at either Mexico or Honduras. The *Enchanted Capri* sails 2- and 5-night cruises: The former sails the Gulf of Mexico, visiting no ports, while the latter visits Progreso (a beach resort on the tip of Mexico's Yucatán peninsula) and Cozumel, where passengers can opt for a day excursion to Cancún. Both ships lack state-of-the-art facilities, but their low rates make a Caribbean cruise a reality for many first-time cruisers without a lot of cash. Theme cruises are especially pronounced aboard the *Enchanted Isle,* while the *Enchanted Capri* in very gambling-oriented, particularly on its 2-night sailings. Both ships attract goodly numbers of unattached singles.

- **Costa Cruise Lines** (☎ 800/462-6782)   Costa, the U.S.-based branch of a cruise line that has thrived in Italy for about a century, maintains hefty to mega-size vessels, two of which offer virtually identical jaunts through the western and eastern Caribbean on alternate weeks, each of them departing from Fort Lauderdale. Ports of call during the eastern Caribbean itineraries of both vessels include stopovers in San Juan, St. Thomas, Serena Cay (a private island off the coast of the Dominican Republic known for its beaches), and Nassau. Itineraries through the western Caribbean include stopovers at Grand Cayman; either Ocho Rios or Montego Bay, Jamaica; Key West; and Cozumel. There's an Italian flavor and lots of Italian design on board here, and an atmosphere of relaxed indulgence.

- **Disney Cruise Line** (☎ 800/951-3532)   The *Disney Magic* and its sister ship, the *Disney Wonder* (set to debut in August of 1999) are the famous company's first foray into cruising, and boast a handful of truly innovative, Disney-style features including a rotating series of restaurants on every cruise, cabins designed for families, monumental Disney entertainment, and the biggest kids' facilities at sea. In many ways, the experience is more Disney than it is cruise—there's no casino or library, for instance, and fewer adult activities in general. On the other hand, the ships are beautifully designed. In the spirit of Disney's penchant for organization, its 3- and 4-day cruises from Port Canaveral to Nassau and Disney's private island, Castaway Cay, are designed to be combined with a visit to Disney World to create a weeklong all-Disney vacation. They even whisk you from Disney World to the ship in a fleet of custom Disney buses. The upside: The ships have the best kids' facilities at sea, and practically the only cabins designed with families in mind. The downside: They're more expensive than their competition (and much more expensive than the other primarily family-oriented ship, Premier's *Big Red Boat*).

- **Holland America Line–Westours** (☎ 800/426-0327)   Holland America is the most high-toned of the mass-market cruise lines, with nine respectably hefty and good-looking ships, seven of which spend substantial time cruising the Caribbean. They offer solid value, with very few jolts or surprises, and attract a solid, well-grounded clientele of primarily older travelers (so late-night revelers and serious partyers might want to book cruises on other lines, such as Carnival). Cruises stop at deep-water mainstream ports throughout the Caribbean and last for an average of 7 days, but in some cases for 10 days, visiting such ports as Key West, Grand Cayman, St. Maarten, St. Lucia, Curaçao, Barbados, and St. Thomas.

- **Norwegian Cruise Line** (☎ 800/327-7030)   Norwegian operates a diverse fleet ranging from the classic though now massively renovated *Norway* (formerly the *France*) to the medium-sized *Norwegian Majesty, Norwegian Wind, Norwegian Dream,* and *Norwegian Sea.* The first three are based throughout the winter in Miami and embark on 7-day jaunts through the eastern and/or western Caribbean. Ships on either itinerary usually spend a day allowing passengers to sun, swim, and surf at the company's private island, Great Stirrup Cay. *Norwegian Dream* follows a year-round 7-day itinerary departing from San Juan, Puerto Rico, to such ports as Aruba, Curaçao, Tortola, Virgin Gorda, St. Thomas, St. Lucia, Antigua, St. Kitts, and St. Croix. The *Norwegian Sea* sails year-round from Houston, making continuous circuits across the Gulf of Mexico to such Yucatán ports as Cancún and Cozumel, and Honduras's Roatan Bay. On board ship, NCL administers a snappy, high-energy array of activities and, in many cases, a revolving array of international sports figures for game tips and lectures. Look for yet another NCL ship, the 80,000-ton, 2,000-passenger *Norwegian Sky,* to be added to the company armada in August 1999, likely sailing year-round from Miami on eastern and western Caribbean itineraries.

- **Premier Cruises** (☎ 800/990-7770)   Premier is a budget-minded line operating ships that are oldies and, in most cases, goodies. They offer good value, though they don't boast the state-of-the-art facilities of newer, custom-designed cruise ships at better-financed lines. One of the line's ships, the *Big Red Boat,* is marketed primarily to families and offers an extensive kids' program. It sails year-round from Port Canaveral on alternating 3- and 4-day cruises visiting Nassau and Port Lucaya. The line's best ship, the *Rembrandt,* is a classic ocean liner built in 1959 and until recently sailed as Holland America's *Rotterdam V.* Still boasting its original beautiful decor, the ships sails 10- and 11-night round-trip itineraries from Ft. Lauderdale December though late March, visiting ports that, depending on the exact itinerary, include Tortola, St. John, Dominica, St. Croix, San Juan, Grand Cayman, Curaçao, Aruba, and Jamaica. The 842-passenger, 21,010-ton *SeaBreeze* was built in 1958 as Costa's luxury flagship, *Frederico C.,* and today sails 7-night western Caribbean itineraries round-trip from Ft. Lauderdale October through June, visiting Cozumel, Belize, Roatan, and Key West.

  Premier offers cost-effective—and sometimes free—hotel packages that allow participants to extend their holiday in either Jamaica or Aruba before or after their cruise experience.

- **Princess Cruises** (☎ 800/421-0522)   Currently operating 10 megavessels, four of which cruise through Caribbean and Bahamian waters, Princess offers a cruise experience that's one part Carnival- or Royal Caribbean–style party-time fun and one part Celebrity-style classy enjoyment. The *Ocean Princess, Dawn Princess,* and *Sea Princess,* almost identical vessels all built in the late 90s, offer the bulk of Princess's Caribbean itineraries, with the *Dawn* and *Ocean* running two alternating 7-night southern Caribbean itineraries round-trip from San Juan, while the *Sea* sails 7-night western Caribbean runs round-trip from Fort Lauderdale. Depending on the exact itinerary, ports on the southern Caribbean runs include Curaçao, Isla Magarita (Venezuela), La Guaira/Caracas (Venezuela), Grenada, Dominica, St. Vincent, St. Kitts, St. Thomas, Trinidad, Barbados, Antigua, Martinique, St. Lucia, and St. Maarten. Western Caribbean itineraries visit Ocho Rios (Jamaica), Grand Cayman, Cozumel, and Princess Cays, the line's private island. The *Grand Princess,* at press time the largest cruise ship in the world, sails 7-night eastern Caribbean itineraries round-trip from Fort Lauderdale, visiting St. Thomas, St. Maarten, and Princess Cays. All of the line's ships are stylish and comfortable, though the *Grand* ups it a notch in the style department, offering amazing open deck areas and some really beautiful indoor public areas.

- **Royal Caribbean International (RCI)** (☎ 800/327-6700 or 305/539-6000)   RCI leads the industry in the development of megaships. Most of this company's dozen or so vessels weigh in at around 73,000 tons, though at press time its scheduled to up the ante on the whole industry by launching the just plain unbelievably enormous *Voyager of the Seas,* weighing in at 142,000 tons, carrying 3,114 passengers, and offering such cruise ships firsts as an ice-skating rink and a rock-climbing wall. A mass-market company that has everything down to a science, RCI encourages a house-party theme that's just a little less frenetic than the mood aboard Carnival. There are enough onboard activities to suit virtually any taste and age level. Though accommodations are more than adequate, they are not upscale, and tend to be a bit more cramped than the industry norm. Using either Miami, Fort Lauderdale, or San Juan as their home port, Royal Caribbean ships call regularly at St. Thomas, San Juan, Ocho Rios, St. Maarten, Grand Cayman, St. Croix, Curaçao, and one or the other of the line's private beaches—one in the Bahamas, the other along an isolated peninsula in northern Haiti. Most of the company's cruises last 7 days, although some weekend jaunts from San Juan to St. Thomas are available for 3 nights, and some Panama Canal crossings last for 11 and 12 nights.

- **Seabourn Cruise Line** (☎ **800/929-9595**)   Seabourn is deservedly legendary for the unabashed luxury aboard its elegant, small-scale ships. The *Seabourn Pride* conducts 10-day November-and-December cruises in the Caribbean as part of a year-long itinerary devoted mostly to Europe and Asia. Its identical twin, the *Seabourn Legend,* spends the entire winter from home ports of San Juan and Fort Lauderdale. Ports of call for both ships include Jamaica, St. Barts, St. Martin, St. Lucia, Bequia, Tobago, Barbados, St. Croix, and Virgin Gorda, some of which are visited before or after transits of the Panama Canal. There are more activities than you'd expect aboard such a relatively small ship (10,000 tons), and an absolutely amazing amount of onboard space per passenger. Cuisine is superb, served in a dining room that's unapologetically formal. Throughout every venue, the emphasis is on top-notch service, luxury, discretion, and impeccably good taste. All in all, you get what you pay for—and you pay *a lot.*

- **Star Clippers** (☎ **800/442-0553**)   Star Clippers two replica 19th-century clipper ships were built as the hobby of a Swedish industrialist, and are the fastest sailing vessels ever constructed. Though based on the best shipbuilding principles of the 19th century, the ships are thoroughly modern, utilizing space-age materials and all the latest computerized equipment—for instance, aboard each ship, just 10 deckhands are needed to hoist sails that would have required four dozen hands on the original clippers. In winter, one of the line's two vessels, *Star Clipper,* operates from a base in Antigua and includes weeklong jaunts that stop in obscure, rarely visited cays in the Grenadines, St. Lucia, Tortola, St. Kitts, St. Martin, and St. Barts.

- **Tall Ship Adventures** (☎ **800/662-0090**)   Tall Ship Adventures has only one ship—a tall-masted 1917 schooner that was built to carry copper ore from the coast of Chile to the Baltic ports of Germany. Today, after extensive refittings, the *Sir Francis Drake* carries sailing-ship aficionados on meandering, down-to-earth trips through the Caribbean. In winter, it focuses on the British Virgin Islands, exploring such relatively remote outposts as Peter Island, Norman Island, Cooper Island, Jost Van Dyke, Marina Cay, Long Bay, and sites on or slightly offshore from Virgin Gorda and Tortola. In summer, the ship moves south to a home port in St. Lucia, embarking on alternate weeks for 7-day explorations of the Grenadines.

- **Windjammer Barefoot Cruises** (☎ **800/327-2601**)   Windjammer is similar in ambience to Tall Ship Adventures and operates six sailing ships, most of which are faithful renovations of antique schooners or sail-driven private yachts. The company offers a real "yo ho ho and a bottle of rum" kind of cruise, and true to the line's name, few passengers ever bring more than shorts and T-shirts for their time aboard. From bases as divergent as San Juan, St. Martin, Grenada, Tortola, Antigua, and Grenada, the ships travel to rarely visited outposts, with special emphasis on the scattered reefs and cays of the Virgin Islands and the

Grenadines. Port calls often mean just anchoring off a small beach and shuttling passengers ashore, and the ships often stay in port late into the evening, giving passengers an opportunity to enjoy nightlife ashore. A feature on the line's Web site, www.windjammer.com, offers e-mail updates of last-minute bargains. If you're able to travel at short notice, you can often get a weeklong cruise for under $500.

13　Chartering Your Own Boat

Experienced sailors and navigators can charter "bareboat," a fully equipped rental boat with no captain or crew. You're on your own on such a craft, and you'll have to prove your qualifications before you're allowed to rent one. Even an experienced skipper may want to take along someone familiar with local waters, which may in some places be tricky.

You can also charter a boat with a skipper and crew. Charter yachts, ranging from 50 to more than 100 feet, can accommodate 4 to 12 people.

Most yachts are rented on a weekly basis, with a fully stocked bar and equipment for fishing and water sports. The average charter carries four to six passengers, and usually is reserved for 1 week.

✪ **The Moorings,** 19345 U.S. 19 North, 4th Floor, Clearwater, FL 33764 (☎ **800/535-7289** in the U.S. and Canada, or 888/952-8402 in Clearwater; fax 813/530-9747), operates the largest charter yacht fleet in the Caribbean. Its main branch is located in the British Virgin Islands, but it has Caribbean and Bahamian outposts in St. Martin, Guadeloupe, Martinique, St. Lucia, and Grenada, to name a few. Each has a regatta of yachts available for chartering. Depending on their size, yachts are rented to as many as four couples at a time. You can arrange to rent bareboat (for qualified sailors only) or rent yachts with a full crew and cook. Depending on circumstances, the vessels come equipped with a barbecue, snorkeling gear, a dinghy, and linens. The boats are serviced by an experienced staff of mechanics, electricians, riggers, and cleaners. If you're going out on your own, you'll get a thorough briefing on Caribbean waters, reefs, and anchorages. Seven-night combined hotel-and-crewed-yacht packages can run $835 to $1,218 per person in Tortola, $800 to $1,195 in St. Lucia, and $870 to $1,320 in Grenada.

✪ **Nicholson Yacht Charters,** 29 Sherman St., Cambridge, MA 02138 (☎ **800/662-6066** in the U.S., or 617/661-0555; fax 617/661-0554), or P.O. Box 103, St. John's, Antigua, W.I., is one of the best in the business, handling charter yachts for use throughout the Caribbean basin, particularly the route between Dutch-held St. Maarten and Grenada and the routes around the U.S. Virgin Islands and British Virgin Islands and Puerto Rico. Featuring boats of all sizes, the company can arrange rentals of motorized vessels or sailing yachts up to 298 feet long. According to one popular arrangement, two or more yachts (each sleeping eight guests in four double cabins) race each other from island to island during the day and anchor near each other in secluded coves or at berths in Caribbean capitals at night. The price for renting a yacht depends on the number in your party, the size of the vessel, and the time of the year. Weekly rates range from $3,500 up to $85,000 or so. You can get a nice, comfortable vessel for $6,000 to $12,000 weekly. At that price, why not?

Sunsail, 980 Awald Rd., Suite 302, Annapolis Landing Marina, Annapolis, MD 21403 (☎ **800/327-2276** in the U.S., or 410/280-2553; fax 410280-2406), specializes in yacht chartering from its bases in the British Virgin Islands, Antigua, St. Vincent, and the French West Indies. More than 60 bareboat and crewed yachts, between 30 and 52 feet, are available for cruising these waters. Programs include Caribbean racing and regattas, flotilla sailing, skippered sailing, and one-way or stay-and-sail bareboat cruises. The company usually requires a deposit of 25% of the total rental fee; arrangements should be made 4 to 6 months in advance. Clients with flexible schedules need only reserve a month in advance. Sunsail also offers charter flights from the United States to the Virgin Islands.

14 Tips on Accommodations

WATCH OUT FOR THOSE EXTRAS!   Nearly all islands charge a government tax on hotel rooms, usually 7½%, but that rate varies from island to island. This tax mounts quickly, so ask if the rate you're quoted includes this room tax. Sometimes the room tax depends on the quality of the hotel, relatively low for a guest house but steeper for a first-class resort. Determine the tax before you accept the rate.

Furthermore, most hotels routinely add 10% to 12% for "service," even if you didn't like the service or didn't see much evidence of it. That means that with tax and service, some bills are 17% or even 25% higher than originally quoted to you! Naturally, you need to determine just how much the hotel, guest house, or inn plans to add to your bill at the end of your stay.

That's not all. Some hotels slip in little hidden extras that mount quickly. For example, it's common for many places to quote rates that include a continental breakfast. Should you prefer ham and eggs, you will pay extra charges. If you request special privileges, like extra towels for the beach or laundry done in a hurry, surcharges may mount. It pays to watch those extras, and ask questions before you commit.

WHAT THE ABBREVIATIONS MEAN   Rate sheets often have these classifications:

MAP (Modified American Plan) usually means room, breakfast, and dinner, unless the room rate has been quoted separately, and then it means only breakfast and dinner.

CP (Continental Plan) includes room and a light breakfast.

EP (European Plan) means room only.

AP (American Plan) includes your room plus three meals a day.

HOTELS & RESORTS   Many budget travelers assume they can't afford the big hotels and resorts. But there are so many packages out there (see section 10 of this chapter) and so many frequent sales, even in winter, that you might be pleasantly surprised.

The rates given in this book are only "rack rates"—that is, the officially posted rate that you'd be given if you just walked in off the street. Almost no one actually pays them! Always ask about packages and discounts. Think of the rates in this book as guidelines to help you comparison shop.

A savvy travel agent can help save you serious money. Some hotels are often quite flexible about their rates, and many offer discounts and upgrades whenever they have a big block of rooms to fill and few reservations. The smaller hotels and inns are not as likely to be generous with discounts, much less upgrades. Even if you book into one of these bigger hotels, ask for the cheaper rooms—that is, those that don't open directly onto the ocean. Caribbean hoteliers charge dearly for the view alone.

ALL-INCLUSIVE RESORTS   The promises are persuasive: "Forget your cash, put your plastic away." Presumably, everything's all paid for in advance at an "all-inclusive" resort. But is it?

The all-inclusives have a reputation for being expensive, and many of them are, especially the giant SuperClubs of Jamaica or even the Sandals properties (unless you book in a slow period or off-season).

In the 1990s, so many competitors entered the all-inclusive game that the term now means different things to the various resorts that use this marketing strategy. The ideal all-inclusive is just that—a place where everything, even drinks and water sports, is included. But in the most narrow sense, it means a room and three meals a day, with extra charges for drinks, sports, cigarettes, whatever. When you book, it's important to ask and to understand exactly what's included in your so-called all-inclusive. Watersports programs and offerings vary greatly at the various resorts. Extras might include options for horseback riding or sightseeing on the island.

The all-inclusive market is geared to the active traveler who likes to participate in organized entertainment, a lot of sports, and workouts at fitness centers, and who also likes a lot of food and drink.

If you're single or gay, avoid Sandals. If you have young children, stay away from Hedonism II in Negril, Jamaica, which lives up to its name. Even some Club Meds are targeted more for singles and couples, although many now aggressively pursue the family market. Some Club Meds have Mini Clubs, Baby Clubs, and Teen Clubs at some of its properties, at least during holiday and summer seasons.

The trick is to look for that special deal and to travel in off-peak periods, which doesn't always mean just from mid-April to mid-December. Discounts are often granted for hotels during certain slow periods, called "windows," most often after the New Year's holiday. If you want a winter vacation at an all-inclusive, choose the month of January—not February or the Christmas holidays, when prices are at their all-year high.

One good deal might be **Club Med's "Wild Card,"** geared to singles and couples. You must be 18 or over. Reservations must be made two or more weeks before departure. One week prior to departure, Club Med tells you which "village" on which island you're going to visit. If this uncertainty doesn't bother you, you can save $150 to $300 per weekly package. The complete per-person Wild Card cost for a week's package is a flat $999 per person. Each package includes round-trip air transportation from New York, double-occupancy accommodations, all meals with complimentary wine and beer (other alcoholic drinks are extra), use of all sports facilities except scuba gear (extra charges), nightly entertainment, and other recreational activities such as boat rides, snorkeling expeditions, and picnics. For more information, call ☎ **800/ CLUB-MED.**

Consult a good travel agent for other good deals that might be available.

GUEST HOUSES   An entirely different type of accommodation is the guest house, where most of the Antilleans themselves stay when they travel. In the Caribbean, the term guest house can mean anything. Sometimes so-called guest houses are really like simple motels built around swimming pools. Others are small individual cottages, with their own kitchenettes, constructed around a main building in which you'll often find a bar and a restaurant that serves local food. Some are surprisingly comfortable, often with private baths and swimming pools. You may or may not have air-conditioning.

For value, the guest house can't be topped. You can always journey over to a big beach resort and use its seaside facilities for only a small charge, perhaps no more than $5. Although bereft of frills, the guest houses we've recommended are clean and safe for families or single women. The cheapest ones are not places where you'd want to spend time, because of their simple, modest furnishings.

DOING YOUR OWN COOKING   Particularly if you're a family or a group of friends, a "housekeeping holiday" can be one of the least expensive ways to vacation in the Caribbean. Accommodations with kitchens are now available on nearly all the islands. Some are individual cottages, others are housed in one building, and some are private homes that owners rent out while they're away. Many self-catering places include maid service in the rental, and you're given fresh linen as well.

In the simpler rentals, doing your own cooking and laundry or even your own maid service may not be your idea of a good time in the sun, but it saves money—a lot of money.

The disadvantage of many of these self-catering cottages is their remote locations, which may mean you'll need a car. Public transportation on any island in the Caribbean is simply inadequate, if it exists at all.

You'll have to approach these rental properties with a certain sense of adventure and a do-it-yourself independence. These rentals are not for everybody, but they can make a Caribbean vacation possible for families or other groups on a tight budget.

For a list of agencies that arrange rentals, refer to the hotel sections of the individual island chapters.

PRIVATE APARTMENTS, EFFICIENCIES & COTTAGES   There are lots of private apartments for rent, either with or without maid service. This is more of a no-frills option than a villa or condo. The apartments may not be in buildings with swimming pools, and they may not have a front desk to help you.

Cottages are the most freewheeling way to stay. Most are fairly simple. Many open onto a beach, while others may be clustered around a communal pool. Many contain no more than a simple bedroom with a small kitchen and bathroom. For the peak winter season, reservations should be made at least 5 or 6 months in advance.

Dozens of agents throughout the United States and Canada offer these types of rentals; we've noted some in the destination chapters that follow. You can also ask each island's tourist office for good suggestions.

The savings, especially for a family of three to six people, or two or three couples, can range from 50% to 60% of what a hotel would cost. If there are only two members in your party, these savings don't apply. However, groceries are sometimes priced 35% to 60% higher than the average on the U.S. mainland, as nearly all foodstuffs have to be imported. Even so, preparing your own food will be a lot cheaper than dining at restaurants.

RENTING YOUR OWN VILLA OR CONDO   Even Princess Margaret rents out her private villa on Mustique in the Grenadines, with proper references. Throughout the Caribbean, you can find good deals by renting privately owned villas and condos, and not all of them charge royal rates.

Many villas have a staff, or at least a maid who comes in a few days a week, and they also provide the essentials for home life, including linens and housewares. Condos usually come with a reception desk and are often comparable to a suite in a big resort hotel. Nearly all condo complexes have pools (some more than one). Like condos, villas range widely in price and may begin at $500 per week for a modest one and go up to $35,000 a week for a luxurious one. More likely, the prices will be somewhere in between.

Villas of Distinction, P.O. Box 55, Armonk, NY 10504 (☎ **800/289-0900** in the U.S., or 914/273-3331; fax 914/273-3387; www.villasofdistinction.com), offers private villas with one to six bedrooms and a pool. Domestic help is often included. They have offerings on St. Martin, Anguilla, Mustique, Barbados, the U.S. and British Virgins, the Cayman Islands, St. Lucia, St. Barts, and Jamaica. Descriptions, rates, and photos are available on line.

At Home Abroad, 405 E. 56th St., Suite 6-H, New York, NY 10022-2466 (☎ **212/421-9165;** fax 212/752-1591), has a roster of private upscale homes for rent on Barbados, Jamaica, Mustique, St. John, St. Lucia, St. Martin, St. Thomas, Tortola, and Virgin Gorda, most with maid service included.

Caribbean Connection Plus Ltd., P.O. Box 261, Trumbull, CT 06611 (☎ **800/ 893-1100** or 203/261-8603; fax 203/261-8295), offers many apartments, cottages, and villas in the Caribbean, especially on St. Kitts, Nevis, and Montserrat, but also on some of the more obscure islands such as St. Eustatius, Tobago, St. Vincent, Dominica, and Nevis. Caribbean Connection specializes in island-hopping with Inter-Island Air, and offers especially attractive deals for U.S. West Coast travelers. This is one of the few reservations services staffed by people who have actually been on the islands, so members can talk to people who really know the Caribbean.

VHR, Worldwide, 235 Kensington Ave., Norwood, NJ 07648 (☎ **800/633-3284** in the U.S. and Canada, or 201/767-9393; fax 201/767-5510), offers the most comprehensive portfolio of luxury villas, condominiums, resort suites, and apartments for rent in not only the Caribbean, but the Bahamas, Mexico, and the United States as well. The company can also arrange for airfare and car rental. Its more than 4,000 homes and suite resorts are handpicked by the staff, and these accommodations are generally less expensive than comparable hotel rooms.

Hideaways International, 767 Islington St., Portsmouth, NH 03801 (☎ **800/ 843-4433** in the U.S., or 603/430-4433; fax 603/430-4444; www.hideaways.com), publishes *Hideaways Guide,* a pictorial directory of home rentals throughout the world, including the Caribbean, especially the British Virgin Islands, the Cayman Islands, Jamaica, and St. Lucia, with full descriptions so you know what you're renting. Rentals range from cottages to staffed villas to whole islands! On most rentals you deal directly with owners. At condos and small resorts, Hideaways offers member discounts. Other services include yacht charters, cruises, airline ticketing, car rentals, and hotel reservations. Annual membership is $99; a 4-month trial membership is $39. Membership information, listings, and photos are available on line.

Heart of the Caribbean Ltd., 17485 Penbrook Dr., Brookfield, WI 53045 (☎ **800/231-5303** or 414/783-5303; fax 414/781-4026; www.hotcarib.com), is a villa wholesale company offering travelers a wide range of private villas and condos on several islands, including St. Maarten/St. Martin, Barbados, and St. Lucia. Accommodations range from one to six bedrooms, and from modest villas and condos to palatial estates. Homes have complete kitchens and maid service. Catering and car rentals can also be provided. Rates, listings, and photos are available on line.

Rent-a-Home International, 7200 34th Ave. NW, Seattle, WA 98117 (☎ **800/ 488-RENT** or 206/789-9377; fax 206/789-9379; www.rentavilla.com), maintains an inventory of several thousand properties, specializing in condos and villas with weekly rates ranging from $700 to $25,000. It arranges bookings for weeklong stays or longer. For a color catalog including prices, descriptions, and pictures, send $15, which will be applied to your next rental. Prices, descriptions, and pictures are also available on line.

Sometimes local tourist offices will also advise you on vacation-home rentals if you write or call them directly.

If you want a small, serene, secluded island, this place is for you—especially if you look like Tom Cruise or Demi Moore and have millions in the bank. The northernmost of the British Leeward Islands in the eastern Caribbean, 5 miles north of St. Maarten, Anguilla (rhymes with *vanilla*) is only 16 miles long, with 35 square miles in land area. Scant rainfall makes for unproductive soil, with mainly low foliage and sparse scrub vegetation. Anguilla's white coral sand beaches, however, are reason enough to visit. More than 30 of them, shaded by sea-grape trees, dot the coast here.

The little island has a population of approximately 9,000 people. Most are of African descent, though many are European, predominantly Irish. The locals work primarily in the tourist industry or fish for lobster.

Once part of the federation with St. Kitts and Nevis, Anguilla gained its independence in 1980 and has since been a self-governing British possession. In 1996, however, London issued a policy statement that locals have viewed as a move to shove them toward independence. Many Anguillians believe that Britain has now reduced its global ambitions and wants to relinquish colonies that have become too expensive to maintain. Many islanders fear going it alone as a nation just yet. They know, however, that to retain Britain's protection, they would also have to abide by British laws—including its liberal position on gay rights. For the most part, islanders remain archly conservative and often homophobic.

Anguilla used to be a destination for the adventurous. With the opening of some superdeluxe (and superexpensive) hotels in the 1980s and 1990s, however, it has become one of the Caribbean's most chic destinations, rivaling even St. Barts. Recently more moderately priced hotels have opened, too. Operations tend to be small and informal, though, as Anguilla has tried to control development and conserve natural beauty and resources.

1 Essentials

VISITOR INFORMATION

The **Anguilla Department of Tourism,** P.O. Box 1388, The Valley, Anguilla, B.W.I. (☎ **264/497-2759**), is open Monday to Saturday from 8am to 5pm. They're on the Web at **www.candw.com.ai/~atbtour**.

In the United Kingdom, contact the **Anguilla Tourism Office,** 3 Epirus Rd., London SW6 7UI (☎ **0171/937-7725**).

GETTING THERE

BY PLANE More than 50 flights into Anguilla are scheduled each week, not counting various charter flights. There are no nonstop flights from mainland North America, however, so visitors usually transfer through San Juan, Puerto Rico, or nearby St. Maarten. Some visitors also come in from St. Kitts, Antigua, and St. Thomas.

Anguilla's most reliable carrier, **American Eagle** (☎ 800/433-7300 in the U.S.), the commuter partner of American Airlines, has two nonstops daily to Anguilla from its hub in San Juan. Flights leave at different times based on the seasons and carry 44 to 46 passengers. Schedules are subject to change, so check with the airline or your travel agent.

From Dutch St. Maarten, **Winair** (Windward Islands Airways International; ☎ 800/634-4907) schedules three daily flights to Anguilla, usually on Twin Otters.

LIAT (☎ 800/468-0482 in the U.S. and Canada, or 869/465-2286), flies to Anguilla daily from Antigua and St. Kitts. On some days it might operate two or three flights to Anguilla from either Antigua or St. Kitts, but it's not the promptest airline.

Air Anguilla (☎ 264/497-2643) schedules one flight daily from St. Thomas to Anguilla. It also operates charter flights from St. Maarten, Tortola (British Virgin Islands), and San Juan.

Tyden Air (☎ 264/497-2719) offers daily flights between St. Maarten and Anguilla, and a charter service between San Juan and Anguilla. It maintains a kiosk at the St. Maarten airport.

Flights from St. Maarten to Anguilla take 7 minutes; from San Juan and Antigua, 50 minutes; and from St. Thomas and St. Kitts, 30 minutes.

BY FERRY Ferries run between the ports of Marigot Bay, French St. Martin, and Blowing Point, Anguilla, at approximately 45- to 60-minute intervals daily. The first ferry leaves St. Martin at 8am and the last at 7pm; from Blowing Point, the first ferry leaves at 7:30am and the last at 6:15pm. The one-way fare is $10, which rises to $12 in the early evening. There's a $2 departure tax for those leaving by boat. No reservations are necessary; schedules and fares, of course, are always subject to change. Ferries are small, and none take vehicles.

GETTING AROUND

BY RENTAL CAR To explore the island in any detail, it's best to rent a car. Several rental agencies on the island can issue the mandatory Anguillian driver's license, which is valid for 3 months. You can also get a license at police headquarters in the Valley and at ports of entry. You'll need to present a valid driver's license from your home country and pay a one-time fee of $6. Remember to *drive on the left!*

Most experienced visitors take a taxi from the airport to their hotel and arrange, at no extra charge, for a rental agency to deliver a car there the following day. All the rental companies offer slight discounts for rentals of 7 days or more.

Budget (☎ 800/527-0700 or 264/497-2217) and **Hertz** (☎ 800/654-3001 or 264/497-2934) operate on Anguilla. Local firms, which offer jeeps and cars, include

A Special Celebration

Anguilla's most colorful annual festival is **Carnival,** held jointly under the auspices of the Ministries of Culture and Tourism. Boat races are Anguilla's national sport, and they form 60% of the Carnival celebration. The festival begins on Friday before the first Monday in August and lasts a week. Carnival harks back to Emancipation Day, or "August Monday," in 1834, when all enslaved Africans were freed.

Anguilla

Atlantic Ocean

Scrub Island

Seal Island

Prickly Pear Cays

Shoal Bay **5**

Captain's Bay
Island Harbour
Junk's Hole Bay

Savannah Bay

Little Bay
Crocus Bay

The Valley

East End

Sandy Isle

Road Bay
Sandy Ground **3** **4**

The Quarter

Sandy Hill Bay

Meads Bay **2**

South Hill **7**

Little Harbour **6**

Forest Bay

Barnes Bay

West End

Blowing Point

Blowing Point Harbour

10 **9** Rendezvous Bay

Shoal Bay West   Maunday's Bay

Caribbean Sea

Anguilla Great House & Beach Resort **8**
Cap Juluca **9**
Cinnamon Reef Resort **6**
CoveCastles **10**
Easy Corner Villas **4**
Fountain Beach Hotel **5**
La Sirena **1**
Malliouhana **2**
Mariners Cliffside Beach Resort **3**
Sonesta Beach Resort & Villas Anguilla **7**

0   3 Miles
0   3 Kilometers

Airport ✈ Beach

2-0188

Bennie & Sons, Blowing Point (☎ 264/497-2788), and **Connor's Car Rental,** c/o Maurice Connor, South Hill (☎ 264/497-6433).

BY TAXI   Typical taxi fares are $20 from the airport to Cap Juluca; $14 to the Fountain Beach Hotel; and $16 to the Malliouhana Hotel.

Fast Facts: Anguilla

Banking Hours   Banks are open Monday to Thursday from 8am to 3pm, Friday from 8am to 5pm.

Currency   The Eastern Caribbean dollar (EC$) is the official currency of Anguilla, although U.S. dollars are the actual "coin of the realm." The official exchange rate is about EC$2.70 to each U.S.$1 (EC$1 = 37¢ U.S.).

Customs   Even for tourists, duties are levied on imported goods at varying rates: from 5% on foodstuffs to 30% on luxury goods, wines, and liquors.

Documents   All visitors must have an onward or return ticket. For U.S. and Canadian citizens, the preferred form of ID is a passport, even if it has expired within the last 5 years. In place of a passport, photo ID with an original birth certificate or a driver's license is required (we suggest you bring a passport anyway). Citizens from the United Kingdom must have a valid passport.

Drugstores   See "Pharmacies," below.

Electricity　The electricity is 110 volts AC (60 cycles), so no transformers or adapters are necessary for U.S. appliances.

Hospitals　For medical services, consult the **Princess Alexandra Hospital,** Stoney Ground (☎ **264/497-2551**), or one of several district clinics.

Language　English is spoken here, often with a West Indian accent.

Pharmacies　Go to the **Government Pharmacy** at the Princess Alexandra Hospital, Stoney Ground (☎ **264/497-2551**), open Monday to Friday from 8am to noon and 1 to 4pm; on Saturday from 10am to noon. In addition, **Paramount Pharmacy,** Water Swamp (☎ **264/497-2366**), has a 24-hour emergency service.

Police　You can reach the police at their headquarters in the Valley (☎ **264/497-2333**) or the substation at Sandy Ground (☎ **264/497-2354**). In an emergency, dial ☎ **911.**

Post Office　The main post office is in the Valley (☎ **264/497-2528**). Collectors consider Anguilla's stamps valuable, and the post office also operates a philatelic bureau, open Monday to Friday from 8am to 3:30pm.

Safety　Although crime is rare here, secure your valuables; never leave them in a parked car or unguarded on the beach. Anguilla is one of the safest destinations in the Caribbean, but you should still take standard precautions.

Taxes　The government collects an 8% tax on rooms and a departure tax of $10 U.S. if you leave the island by air, $2 if you leave by boat.

Telephone　Telephone, cable, and Telex services are offered by **Cable & Wireless Ltd.,** Wallblake Road, The Valley (☎ **264/497-3100**), open Monday to Friday from 8am to 5pm and on Saturday from 9am to 1pm.

Time　Anguilla is on Atlantic standard time year-round, which means it's usually 1 hour ahead of the U.S. East Coast—except during daylight saving time, when the clocks are the same.

Weather　The hottest months in Anguilla are July to October; the coolest, December to February. The mean monthly temperature is about 80°F.

2　Where to Stay

Besides the properties listed below, two popular restaurants also rent out rooms. See the listings for the **Ferryboat Inn** and for **Roy's Place** under "Where to Dine," below.

You may also want to consider renting a villa from an absentee owner, an increasingly popular option on the island. Several rental agencies list villas in a vast range of prices. One of the best is **Anguilla Connection** (☎ **800/916-3336** in the U.S., or 264/497-4403; fax 264/497-4402). Choices range from luxurious, secluded hideaways to condo-style quarters.

Don't forget that the government adds an 8% tax to your hotel bill, and you'll pay 10% for service. Be sure to read the section on package tours in chapter 2 before you book your hotel on your own!

VERY EXPENSIVE

✪ **Cap Juluca.** Maunday's Bay (P.O. Box 240), Anguilla, B.W.I. ☎ **888/858-5822** in the U.S., 264/497-6666, or 305/932-3460 in Miami. Fax 264/497-6617. www.capjuluca.com. E-mail: capjuluca@anguilla.net.com. 98 units. A/C TEL. Winter/Spring $380–$770 double; from $830 suite. Off-season $290–$560 double; from $565 suite. MAP $85 per person extra. AE, MC, V.

This is one of the most boldly conceived, luxurious oases in the Caribbean. On a rolling 179-acre site, Cap Juluca caters to Hollywood stars and financial barons and offers some serious pampering on one of the island's best beaches.

The villa-style accommodations evoke Marrakesh, Morocco. Most have soaring domes, walled courtyards, labyrinthine staircases, and concealed swimming pools ringed with thick walls. Inside, a mixture of elegantly comfortable wicker furniture is offset with Moroccan accessories. Each unit faces one of the world's perfect beaches. Rooms are spacious, with luxurious beds and mattresses, and floors are made from Italian tile. Ceiling fans evoke *Casablanca*, and lights are wired to rheostats so you can dim them if you're feeling romantic. Amenities include private safes. The large marble and mirrored baths are luxuriously appointed and equipped with hair dryers and a rack of fluffy towels in various sizes.

Dining: Pimms (see "Where to Dine," below), is one of the island's finest restaurants. George's is a more casual alternative.

Amenities: Water sports and instruction (including waterskiing, fishing, windsurfing, Sunfish sailing, scuba, and snorkeling), championship tennis court, large pool, fitness center, business center, laundry, massage, concierge, baby-sitting, children's programs, golf carts from the guest rooms to the hotel's restaurants and bars.

Cinnamon Reef Resort. Little Harbour, Anguilla, B.W.I. ☎ **800/222-2530** in the U.S., or 264/497-2727. Fax 264/497-3727. www.cinnamon-reef.com. E-mail: cinnamon-reef@cinnamon-reef.com. 22 units. MINIBAR TEL. Winter $300–$350 suite; $400 villa suite. Off-season $175–$225 suite; $250 villa suite. Rates include continental breakfast. MAP (breakfast and dinner) $50 per person extra. Extra person $60. All-inclusive packages available. AE, MC, V. Closed Sept–Oct.

Five miles west of the airport on the southern coast, this intimate hotel sits astride a circular cove with calm waters that make for the best windsurfing on the island. The resort's Mediterranean-inspired, 12-acre core is surrounded by 18 acres of rolling scrubland. The limited size of the resort makes it feel like a pleasantly informal private estate. Accommodations are in individual white stucco villas and garden suites; each unit contains well-appointed bedrooms and dressing areas, plus ceiling fans. Each of the spacious units has oversized beds with firm mattresses, a sunken living room, and a private patio. Each suite also has a private dressing room and an opulent bathroom with a step-down shower. Along with fluffy bathroom towels, the hotel also provides fresh beach towels three times a day.

Dining/Diversions: The Palm Court Restaurant and the bar area are the focal points. The veranda offers views of the reef-sheltered harbor. Some entertainment and occasional dancing are offered at night.

Amenities: Freshwater pool, hot tub and Jacuzzi, two championship tennis courts, beach sheltered by a reef, free sailboats, paddleboats, Windsurfers, kayaks, and snorkeling and fishing equipment; scuba diving can be arranged. Room service, laundry.

CoveCastles. Shoal Bay West (P.O. Box 248), Anguilla, B.W.I. ☎ **800/223-1108** in the U.S., or 264/497-6801. Fax 264/497-6051. E-mail: covecastles@Anguillianet.com. 14 units. TV TEL. Winter $695–$895 beach house; $995–$1,195 villa. Off-season $425–$525 beach house; $525–$725 villa. AE. Closed Sept.

A cross between a collection of private homes and a luxury hotel on a lovely beach, this is a wonderful (if shockingly expensive) small resort, with an attentive staff. Designed by award-winning architect Myron Goldfinger in 1985, the structure combines elements from North Africa, the Caribbean, and the futuristic theories of Le Corbusier. The units include an interconnected row of town house–style beach structures that accommodate two to four persons, and a handful of larger, fully detached villas that house up to six. Large bedrooms have twin- or king-size beds with hand-embroidered linens and deluxe mattresses. Stylish large bathrooms have luxurious toiletries and fluffy towels.

Each building has optimal views of the sea, amid the dunes and scrublands of the southwestern coast. Each contains louvered doors and windows crafted from Brazilian walnut, terra-cotta tiles, comfortably oversized rattan furniture, a fully equipped kitchen, and a hammock. The most spectacular place to stay is its four-bedroom grand villa that opens directly on the beach; this is one of the most fabulous accommodations in the Caribbean.

Dining: The resort's French chef serves candlelit dinners in an intimate private dining room that overlooks the beach, or en suite. Breakfast and lunch are delivered upon request to your villa.

Amenities: Sunfish sailboats, kayaks, free bicycles, lit tennis court, snorkeling, deep-sea fishing, scuba, windsurfing, glass-bottom boat excursions, aerobics, concierge, massage, car rental, baby-sitting, room service, laundry, personal housekeeper, secretarial service.

✪ **Malliouhana.** Meads Bay (P.O. Box 173), Anguilla, B.W.I. ☎ **800/835-0796** in the U.S., or 264/497-6111. Fax 264/497-6011. www.malliouhana.com. 55 units. MINIBAR TEL. Winter $505–$650 double; from $800 suite. Off-season $240–$430 double; from $410 suite. No credit cards.

One of the most elegants hotel in the Caribbean, this cliff-side retreat conjures up images of Positano in the tropics. It looks even more spectacular than Cap Juluca—opulent and lavishly decorated with a splashy 1980s overkill. Established in 1984 by the Anglo-French Roydon family, it occupies a rocky bluff between miles of white-sand beaches in the southwest, 8 miles west of the airport. The complex occupies 25 acres of sloping scrubland with landscaped terraces, banks of flowers, pools, and fountains. Thick walls and shrubbery provide seclusion.

The famed "Boston Brahmin" decorator, Lawrence Carleton Peabody II, assembled the resort's Haitian art and decorations. Spacious bedrooms and suites are distributed among the main buildings and outlying villas. Each room has tropical furnishings and wide, private verandas; the villas can be rented as a single unit or subdivided into three. Most of the rooms are air-conditioned. With a 224-member staff attending to 55 units, the motto here is "Your wish is my command." Three of the suites have a private Jacuzzi, and one unit comes with a private pool. Some accommodations open onto garden views, while others front Mead's Bay Beach or Turtle Cove. Many rooms have luxurious four-poster beds with plush mattresses, plus spacious Italian marble baths with tubs and shower stalls, an array of fluffy towels, a hair dryer, and deluxe toiletries.

Dining: The resort's French restaurant is one of the most prestigious in the Caribbean (see "Where to Dine," below), if you can get a table in winter. Scattered over the premises are a handful of bars for drinking and snacking throughout the day.

Amenities: Beauty salon, boutiques, TV room, library, water-sports center with instruction in practically everything, four tennis courts (three lit for night play), gym with resident instructor, swimming pools, state-of-the-art children's playground on Meads Bay Beach, room service (7am to 10pm), concierge, laundry, massage.

Sonesta Beach Resort & Villas Anguilla. Rendezvous Bay West, Anguilla, B.W.I. ☎ **800/ SONESTA** or 264/497-6999. Fax 264/497-6899. www.sonesta.com. E-mail: sonesta@ Anguillianet.com. 92 units. A/C MINIBAR TV TEL. Winter $350–$450 double; $580–$725 suite. Off-season $200–$280 double; $385–$550 suite. MAP (breakfast and dinner) $65 per person extra. AE, MC, V.

On the edge of a 3-mile strip of beachfront, this hotel offers views of St. Martin's nearby mountains. In the 1980s, Arab investors commissioned architects to emulate a Moroccan palace beside an oasis. Moroccan artisans spent months on marble floors, intricate geometric mosaics, and imperial green tile roofs that glisten against the surrounding scrub-covered landscape.

Designed to compete with some of the hyper-expensive hotels nearby (especially Cap Juluca and the Malliouhana), the hotel never really attained the glamour or cachet of its neighbors. After back-to-back hurricanes damaged the property in 1995, it was sold to Sonesta, which poured money into its refurbishment and softened (some say weakened) aspects of the original Moorish design. Accommodations are scattered among a complex of buildings set either beside the beach or in a garden. Each room features Italian marble, a private patio, and high ceilings with fans. Beds are plush, with excellent mattresses and fine linens. Baths have large circular tubs, stall showers, marble counters, hair dryers, and plenty of fluffy towels.

Dining/Diversions: Continental cuisine is served in the Casablanca Restaurant and Bar. A grill also serves food in an indoor/outdoor setting overlooking the pool and the sea, and complimentary tea is served daily from 3 to 5pm.

Amenities: One of the most exotic-looking swimming pools on Anguilla, health club with exercise machines overlooking the sea, two lit tennis courts, games room, wide array of land and water sports (some of them complimentary). Massage, room service (7am to midnight), baby-sitting, concierge, valet, twice-daily maid service, hair salon, shops.

EXPENSIVE

Anguilla Great House & Beach Resort. Rendezvous Bay (P.O. Box 157), Anguilla, B.W.I. ☎ **800/583-9247** in the U.S. outside Florida, 407/994-5640 in Florida, or 264/497-6061. Fax 264/497-6019. www.erols.com/gafaxa/aghbr.html. E-mail: flemingw@zemn. candw.com.al. 27 units. Winter $230–$260 double. Off-season $130–$175 double. AE, DISC, MC, V.

On the white sands of Rendezvous Bay near Anguilla's southernmost tip, this property is designed around a central garden/courtyard with a view of the beach. Colonial-inspired, single-story units have front verandas that are connected like the wings of an old-fashioned plantation house. Some rooms have air-conditioning, but most just have ceiling fans. Beds are queen- or king-size, with good mattresses. Baths have only showers (no tubs), medium-size towels, and adequate plumbing.

Dining/Diversion: Most of the resort's social life revolves around an open-sided bar and restaurant, which serves good Caribbean and continental cuisine.

Amenities: Freshwater pool; a water-sports program that includes windsurfing, reef fishing, kayaking, snorkeling, and sailing.

Fountain Beach Hotel. Shoal Bay Beach, Anguilla, B.W.I. ☎ **264/497-3491.** Fax 264/497-3493. www.fountainbeach.com/aboutourplace.htm. 12 units, 2 cottages. Winter $215–$280 double, $315–$365 two-bedroom unit. Off-season $100–$125 double, $175–$200 two-bedroom unit. AE, DISC, MC, V.

Built right on the beach in 1989, this coral-colored resort was inspired by Mediterranean architecture, and it's more like a Caribbean B&B or a small inn than a hotel. Surrounded by 5 acres of sloping and forested land on the island's underpopulated north coast, it's simple, with few amenities, but conducive to reading, sunbathing, or doing nothing. The bedrooms are large and airy, with ceramic-tile floors, sliding glass windows, and pastel color schemes. Each unit has an unstocked refrigerator, and some have kitchenettes. Accommodations range from a junior suite (the smallest) to a roomy two-bedroom cottage with full kitchen and two bathrooms. Each has a marble bath, fluffy towels, and first-class mattresses. You won't find TVs, VCRs, or many people. Each unit has a sitting area, and some also offer private balconies.

La Sirena. Meads Bay (P.O. Box 200), Anguilla, B.W.I. ☎ **800/331-9358** in the U.S., 800/223-9815 in Canada, or 264/497-6827. Fax 264/497-6829. www.la-sirena.com/Default.htm. E-mail: masshardtr@Anguillianet.com. 25 units. A/C MINIBAR TEL. Winter $245–$315 double; $330–$530 villa. Off-season $145–$190 double; $230–$360 villa. MAP $48 per person extra. AE, MC, V.

Built in 1989 on 3 acres of sandy soil, a 4-minute walk from the beach, this Swiss-owned resort is pleasant, intimate, and small—more understated than the ultra-sophisticated and chic ambience of Cap Juluca and Malliouhana. At least 80% of its clientele comes from Switzerland or Germany. Accommodations, arranged in two-story bougainvillea-draped wings, are large and airy, with fine rattan and wicker furnishings. Some have air-conditioning; all have ceiling fans. Rooms have large double-, queen-, or king-size beds with fine linens and good mattresses. Bathrooms are spacious, with shower stalls, medium-size towels, and a hair dryer. To reach the beach, guests walk down through the garden and a sandy footpath. Beach hats, umbrellas, and lounge chairs await you on the sand.

   Dining: The Top of the Palms restaurant, open only for dinner, is recommended separately (see "Where to Dine," below). For breakfast and lunch, the Coconuts Café is less formal and specializes in pastas, sandwiches, and ice cream.

   Amenities: Two freshwater pools, baby-sitting, laundry.

The Mariners Cliffside Beach Resort. (P.O. Box 241) Road Bay, Sandy Ground, Anguilla, B.W.I. ☎ **264/497-2671.** Fax 264/497-2901. www.Anguillianet.com/ai/mariners. E-mail: mariners@Anguillianet.com. 61 units, 20 cottages. TV TEL. Winter $250–$275 double; from $450 cottage. Off-season $150–$175 double; from $280 cottage. Rates are all-inclusive. AE, DISC, MC, V.

This rare all-inclusive resort sits on 8½ acres beside an isolated beach with an access road that winds between flowering shrubs and hillocks. Accommodations are housed in three two-story buildings and cottages delightfully embellished with West Indian gingerbread. All rooms have ceiling fans (some are air-conditioned), and resemble New England summer cottages in the 1930s. Accommodations vary from small rooms with twin beds and shower baths to spacious two-bedroom, two-bath cottages close to the water's edge. Baths are adequate, with hair dryers and medium-size towels. All the mattresses are good. The staff is very laid back.

   Dining: The food is zesty but rather standard.

   Amenities: Pool, tennis court lit at night, two Jacuzzis, water sports. Room service, laundry, baby-sitting, boat charters.

INEXPENSIVE

Easy Corner Villas. South Hill (P.O. Box 65), Anguilla, B.W.I. ☎264/497-6433. Fax 264/497-6410. 12 units. A/C TV. Winter $110–$240 apt; off-season $90–$195 apt. AE, MC, V. No children under 2.

On the main road west of the airport, Easy Corner Villas is owned by Maurice E. Connor, the same entrepreneur who rents many of the cars on the island. The one-, two-, and three-bedroom apartment units are simply furnished and set on landscaped grounds with views of a good beach from their private porches. Each comes equipped with a kitchen, combination living and dining room, a decent mattress, and large, airy living areas, plus small baths with medium-size towels. All have ceiling fans and air-conditioning. Daily maid service is available for an extra charge.

3 Where to Dine

VERY EXPENSIVE

✪ **Blanchards.** Meads Bay. ☎ **264/497-6100.** Reservations recommended. Main courses $26–$36. AE, MC, V. Mon–Sat 6:30–9pm. INTERNATIONAL.

Bob and Melinda Blanchard, also the founders of a salad dressing and condiment business in Vermont, have celebrated a love affair with Anguilla and the restaurant trade for about a decade. They have masterminded this elegantly casual, intensely fashionable restaurant on a garden-swathed pavilion beside the sea, next to the Hotel Malliouhana's beach. The cuisine is among the most creative and interesting on the island, and they've attracted a sprinkling of celebs (say hi to Robert de Niro or Janet Jackson if you see them).

Behind very tall teal shutters (which can be opened to the sea breezes), you're likely to find upscale, sophisticated food with a Caribbean flair enhanced with spices from Spain, Asia, California, and the American Southwest. Dishes change according to the inspiration of chef Melinda but are likely to include Cajun grouper on a bed of onion marmalade; swordfish stuffed with toasted corn dressing; and jerk Jamaica-style chicken with bananas grilled and glazed with molasses and rum. It's unlikely that you'll ever order a bad dish here.

KoalKeel Restaurant. The Valley. ☎ **264/497-2930.** Reservations recommended for dinner. Main courses $22–$45. AE, MC, V. Tues–Sun 7am–11pm. Closed Sept to mid-Oct. CONTINENTAL/CARIBBEAN.

Housed in a dignified coral stone and clapboard manor built in 1790, this restaurant is set on a hillside that overlooks the island's administrative center, The Valley. The two-story dining area has an airy decor and sea views from its outdoor patio and second story.

Some of the menu items (slow-cooked lamb and rock-oven chicken with locally grown herbs) are cooked in the stone-sided, wood- and charcoal-burning oven (the KoalKeel) that was part of the original building. Grilled snapper with Creole sauce, lobster crêpes, lobster-studded pasta, and smoked grouper on a bed of leeks are deservedly popular.

On the premises, **Le Dôme** (a wine cellar and retail wine shop) stocks thousands of bottles of the most desirable wines on Anguilla, and the **Old Rum Shop** is an antique-studded outlet for "designer" rums (some of them vintage and very old). A tearoom upstairs (**Le Petit Pâtissier**) serves steaming pots of tea and deliciously fattening, freshly made Viennese and French pastries. All three shops maintain the same hours as the restaurant.

✪ **Malliouhana Restaurant.** Meads Bay (8 miles west of the airport). ☎ **264/497-6111.** Reservations required. Main courses $28–$39. AE, MC, V. Daily 12:30–3:30pm and 7:30–10:30pm. FRENCH/CARIBBEAN.

This restaurant, with the Caribbean's most ambitious French menu, offers fluidly choreographed service, fine food, a 25,000-bottle wine cellar, and a glamorous clientele. Michel Rostang, the successful son of the legendary Jo Rostang, one of the most acclaimed chefs of southern France, is often in charge. You'll dine in an open-sided pavilion on a rocky promontory over the sea. At night your candlelit table will be set with French crystal, Limoges china, and Christofle silver. There are well-spaced tables, an ocean view, and a splashing fountain.

The hors d'oeuvres selection is the finest on the island, including warm lobster medallions with celery pancake and curry sauce; seasoned diced fresh tuna with onion cream; a fabulous smoked-salmon purse filled with yogurt, cucumber, and mint; and a delectable beef carpaccio with fresh tomato and basil. Main courses are likely to range from a perfectly prepared braised fillet of mahimahi served with a sweet potato purée, to roasted whole lobster with a basil butter sauce. They also feature local specialties, such as grilled Anguillian crayfish with a lemon butter sauce, or fillet of salmon grilled with watercress and parsnips.

Pimms. In the Cap Juluca, Maunday's Bay. ☎ **264/497-6666.** Reservations required. Main courses $25–$36. AE, MC, V. Daily 7–9:30pm. CONTINENTAL/CARIBBEAN.

This pocket of posh is one of the most elegant restaurants on Anguilla. Set among the archways and domes of Anguilla's most spectacular resort, Cap Juluca, it blends the finest culinary standards of the Old and New Worlds with fresh and exotic ingredients flown in regularly. Lit with flickering candlelight, tables overlook the island's best beach.

The executive chef, George Reid, is Anguillian, and he has earned praise for his Euro-Caribe style of cooking. The menu changes every night, but count on an imaginative seafood-based selection of dishes that often show Asian influences. Pimm's also features a selection of freshly made salads, pizzas, pastas, and other specialties.

You can dine less expensively and more informally at **George's,** the chef's namesake restaurant. Dining terraces open onto the beach and pool, and on Monday night George's offers a lavish West Indian buffet accompanied by a festive "scratch" band. Try the Anguilla conch chowder, the curried sweet potato, the breadfruit salad, the grilled local lobster, and the roast red snapper. A big beach barbecue also takes place every week under the stars. You can visit George's during the day to sample a vast array of salads, burgers, chicken, or fish prepared on the grill. The chef makes the island's best bouillabaisse. Wait until you sample his chicken pie with curry and his simple but delectable sautéed fillet of sole with lemon butter.

MODERATE/EXPENSIVE

✪ **Arlo's.** South Hill. ☎ **264/497-6810.** Reservations recommended. Main courses $6–$25 lunch, $15–$35 dinner. AE, DC, MC, V. Mon–Sat noon–2:30pm (mid-Dec to Apr only); Mon–Sat 6:30–9:30pm. Closed mid-Aug to mid-Oct. ITALIAN/FRENCH.

On a cliff about 50 feet above the sea, this restaurant brings a Mediterranean flair to the Caribbean, thanks to French and Italian dishes that meld island ingredients with European preparations. French-born Philippe Kim, the owner, gathers a stylish crowd from a wide cross-section of the island's hotels in his mostly white dining room with a wide terrace and sea view. Mr. Kim is a master at flavoring, zest, and spice, and he imports only the finest ingredients when he's not making use of fresh local goods. Menu items include bow-tie pasta with salmon in dill sauce, chicken stuffed with mushrooms and spinach in lobster sauce, tartare of tuna, platters of marinated fish, spaghetti carbonara, and penne with shrimp and clam sauce. Lobster risotto is an ongoing favorite. His pizzas are the best on the islands, and you can choose your own toppings.

Barrel Stay Beach Bar & Restaurant. Sandy Ground. ☎ **264/497-2831.** Reservations recommended. Main courses $20–$40. AE, MC, V. Daily 11am–3pm and 6:30–9:30pm. FRENCH/CREOLE.

Set beside the beach, this restaurant has an outdoor drinks terrace and a smaller bar inside. Though pricey, it has many fans. The fish soup served here in the French fashion is as good as any you'll find in Martinique. Conch Creole is a delight, and the fresh catch of the day prepared with a garlic sauce is a sure bet. You're likely to find barbecued lobster on the menu or else a Black Angus steak. The well-heeled diners also go for the stuffed crab. A selection of expensive French wines is also available.

Leduc's. West End Bay. ☎ **264/497-6393.** Reservations required. Main courses $18.50–$27. AE, MC, V. Daily 6:30–9:30pm.

Chef Maurice Leduc has opened one of the island's leading gourmet French restaurants on the main West End road, between CoveCastles and Cap Juluca. Veronica and Maurice will welcome you into this cozy enclave decorated with folk-art murals. Select a table on their terrace and peruse the delectable menu that might begin with *escargot en croûte* or a blue cheese salad. You can sample main courses such as grilled whole snapper baked with spices and garlic, French country style *coq au vin* (chicken with wine), or even frog's legs Provençal. This chef's grilled Black Angus steak topped with diced plum tomatoes, fresh garlic, and parsley, laced with an herb-infused virgin olive oil, is magical.

✪ **Mango's.** Seaside Grill. Barnes Bay. ☎ **264/497-6479.** Reservations required for dinner as far in advance as possible. Main courses $20–$33. AE, MC, V. Wed–Mon 6:30–9pm. Closed Aug–Oct. AMERICAN/CARIBBEAN.

In a pavilion a few steps from the edge of the sea, on the northwestern part of the island, is a great choice with healthier cuisine than any of the island's top restaurants. Mango's serves the freshest obtainable fish, meat, and produce, cooked on the grill with an absolute minimum of added fats or calories. All the breads and desserts, including the ice cream and sorbet, are made fresh daily on the premises. You might start with delectable lobster cakes and homemade tartar sauce or creamy conch chowder. Grilled local lobster and spicy whole snapper are featured main courses, but the best entree is simply grilled fish with lemon-and-herb butter.

✪ **Ripples.** Sandy Ground. ☎ **264/497-3380.** Reservations recommended. Main courses $5–$20 lunch, $16–$28 dinner. AE, DISC, MC, V. Daily noon–midnight. INTERNATIONAL.

This restaurant is earthier and more British than most of the other restaurants in Sandy Ground, the densest concentration of bars and restaurants on Anguilla. With a cheerful staff, and a long, busy bar, it has been compared to the set of *Cheers.* Set in a restored clapboard house, it has a raised deck, a casual West Indian decor, and a crowd of regulars. Local fish is served here—mahimahi, snapper, tuna, and grouper, prepared any way you'd like but always zesty. The coconut shrimp, puffy Brie in beer batter, and Creole-style conch are superb.

Top of the Palms. In La Sirena Hotel, Meads Bay. ☎ **264/497-6827.** Reservations recommended. Main courses $17.50–$29.50. AE, MC, V. Daily 7–9pm. INTERNATIONAL.

This restaurant is open to cool ocean breezes and offers views over Meads Bay and the surrounding treetops. A well-trained local chef, Sherman Niles, prepares specialties like conch fritters or quesadillas, perhaps followed by fillet of beef grilled the way you like it. Top of the Palms features a different specialty menu nightly, which offers everything from beef carpaccio to fish caught in local waters. The local lobster is grilled every night, and pan-fried grouper and baked, thyme-crusted snapper also make regular appearances. Fondues are served on Saturday nights. You can cook your own lobster, fish, beef, or chicken in a West Indian fondue broth flavored with tomatoes, peppers, and rum, or else stick to the classic cheese fondue of the Alps. Homemade tropical fruit sorbets provide a smooth finish to a meal.

INEXPENSIVE

In addition to the following budget restaurants, look into **Roy's Place,** Crocus Bay (☎ 264/497-2470), which serves savory, inexpensive meals and rents out affordable guest rooms on the premises.

Cora's Pepperpot. The Valley. ☎ **264/497-2328.** Reservations recommended for dinner, not necessary at lunch. Main courses $4–$12 lunch, $16–$18 dinner. MC, V. WEST INDIAN.

This is one of the most charming and authentic restaurants in Anguilla, run by Ms. Cora Richardson, a former local police officer. Find the blue-gray, concrete-sided building adjacent to the island's secondary school, and prepare to sample Cora's Pepperpot rotis. Inspired by the roti of Trinidad, but justifiably praised as all-new food items invented by Cora herself, they come in five different varieties, including versions with minced stuffings made with conch, meat, duck, vegetables, and potato. Other featured dishes include Anguilla pea soup, grilled lobster or snapper, and steamed and curried goat meat.

✪ **Ferryboat Inn**. Cul de Sac Rd., Blowing Point, Anguilla, B.W.I. ☎ **264/497-6613.** www. ai/ferryboatinn. Reservations recommended. Main courses $8.50–$37. AE, MC, V. Mon–Sat noon–3pm and daily 7:30–10pm. Closed Tues Apr to mid-Dec. Turn right just before the Blowing Point Ferry Terminal and travel 150 yards before making a left turn. CARIBBEAN/ FRENCH.

Established by English-born John McClean and his Anguillian wife, Marjorie, this place is one of the best values on the island. On the beach, a short walk from the Blowing Point ferry pier, it features French onion soup, black bean soup, some of the best lobster Thermidor on the island, and scallop of veal Savoyard.

The McCleans also rent six one-bedroom apartments and one two-bedroom beach house. In winter, apartments cost $150 to $175, and the beach house is $275. Offseason, an apartment is $80 to $90, and the beach house is $175.

4 Beaches

Superb beaches put Anguilla on the tourist map. There are no fewer than 39 of them, plus another half dozen or so on the outer cays. Inland, the island appears barren, but there's no denying the beauty of its shores. Miles and miles of pristine, powdery soft sands open onto crystal-clear waters. Many of them are reached via a bone-jarring dirt path that ultimately gives way to sand and sea. All the beaches are open to the public, though you may have to walk through the lobby of a deluxe hotel to reach them.

The best beaches are on the west end of the island, site of the most expensive hotels. **Rendezvous Bay** is the island's most famous, and it was also the point where French soldiers invaded from St. Martin, before the two islands began coexisting peacefully 150 years ago. Today it's invaded by the bikini-clad set. Located in the southwest part of the island, it's a long curving ribbon of pale gold sand that stretches along the bay for 2½ miles. It's calmer, warmer, and shallower than Shoal Bay, which is on the Atlantic side and draws the widest cross-section of people, including day-trippers from French St. Martin. With an alfresco beach bar, it attracts all kinds, from families to romantic couples.

Other good beaches include ✪ **Shoal Bay** in the southeast. With white-silver, powder-soft sands, it also boasts some of Anguilla's best coral gardens, the habitat of hundreds of tiny iridescent fish. This 2-mile beach is one of the best in the entire Caribbean Basin. Umbrellas, beach chairs, and other equipment are available here so you can enjoy the backdrop of coconut palms and seagrape trees. This beach is often called "Shoal Bay East" to distinguish it from "Shoal Bay West" (see below). The waters are usually luminous, transparent, and brilliant blue. At noon the sands are so white they almost blind you, but at sunrise or sunset, they turn so pink they could rival any beach in Bermuda.

Music graces the shores from the terraces of the Hard Broke Café or Uncle Ernie's. The Upper Shoal Bar serves first-rate tropical drinks. On the beach, souvenir shops hawk T-shirts and suntan lotion. In the offshore coral reefs, snorkeling is good, and you can arrange dives, sailing, and fishing trips.

Grilled Lobster on a Remote Cay

At Island Harbor, just wave your arms and a boatman will hasten to pick you up and transport you across the water to **Scilly Cay,** pronounced "silly key." You wouldn't really call this place an island. It's more like a spit of sand 170 yards off the coast of the main island's northeastern shoreline. At a little cafe and bar here, you can select a lobster that is, in our view, the finest in the Caribbean. Grilled while you wait, the lobster is marinated in a sauce of honey-laced orange juice, orange marmalade, roasted peanuts, virgin olive oil, curry, and tarragon. Chicken is prepared here the same way. Lunch is daily Tuesday to Sunday from noon to 3pm.

Shoal Bay West, next to Maunday's Bay, has pristine white sands opening onto the southwest coast. You'll find some deluxe accommodations rising from these shores, including CoveCastles (see "Where to Stay," above, for a review).

Adjoining Shoal Bay West is **Maunday's Bay Beach,** justifiably one of the island's most popular shorelines. This mile-long beach of white sands is known for its good snorkeling and swimming. The most famous resort here is Cap Juluca (see above). Though the waters are luminescent and usually calm, sometimes the wind blows enough to attract windsurfers and sailboats. On a clear day you can see the French island of St. Martin across the way.

Sandy Isle, on the northwest coast, is a tiny islet with a few palms surrounded by a coral reef. It lies offshore from Road Bay. Once here, you'll find a beach bar and restaurant, plus free use of snorkeling gear and underwater cameras. **Sandy Island Enterprises** (☎ 264/497-5643) has daily trips from the pier by Johnno's Beach Bar at Sandy Ground. The cost of a round-trip ticket is $8, and the first boat leaves at 10am. The last boat back usually departs at 4pm. You can also go farther out to Prickly Pear Cay, which stretches like a sweeping arc all the way to a sand spit populated by sea birds and pelicans.

The northwest coast has a number of other beaches worth seeking out, notably **Barnes Bay Beach,** filled with powdery white sand and opening onto clear blue waters. You can relax in the shade of the chalky hillside or a beach umbrella, or join the windsurfers and snorkelers who come here. It's usually less crowded after lunch.

Almost never crowded, **Little Bay Beach** is also one of the most dramatic in Anguilla, set against steep cliffs. Here the sands are grayish, but snorkelers and scuba divers don't seem to mind. The beach also attracts bird-watchers and picnickers. Local weddings are sometimes performed here.

Road Bay Beach, also on the northwest coast, is known for spectacular sunsets and clear blue waters filled with yachties, many of whom sail over from French St. Martin. A watersports center here on the beach will equip you for sports like waterskiing and windsurfing. You can also watch fishermen set out in their boats to pursue the elusive, valuable Anguillian lobster.

The beaches along the northeast coast are a beach buff's fantasy—especially if you've got a four-wheel drive. Calm and tranquil, the incredibly blue waters of **Island Harbour Beach** attract both locals and the odd visitor or two. For centuries Anguillians have set out from these shores to haul in Anguillian lobster. There are a few beach bars and alfresco dining rooms here, so you can make a day of it—or take a 3-minute boat ride over to Scilly Cay.

Chances are you'll have **Captain Bay's Beach** all to yourself. Near Junk's Hole, it's better for enjoying the sun and sand than it is for swimming. The undertow is dangerous, though the setting is dramatic and appealing.

5 Sports & Outdoor Pursuits

FISHING   Your hotel can arrange for you to cast your line with local fishers, but you should bring your own tackle. Agree on the cost before setting out, however, to avoid "misunderstandings," which have been reported.

Malliouhana, Meads Bay (☎ 264/497-6111), has a 34-foot fishing cruiser, Kyra, that holds up to eight passengers at a time. You can charter it for fishing parties for $400 for up to 4 hours, with a $100 surcharge for each additional hour. All fishing gear is included, and they can pack you a box lunch for an additional charge.

SCUBA DIVING & SNORKELING   Most of the coastline of Anguilla is fringed by coral reefs, and the island's waters are rich in marine life, with sunken coral gardens and brilliantly colored fish offshore. Conditions for scuba diving and snorkeling on the island are ideal. In addition, the government of Anguilla has artificially enlarged the existing reef system, a first for the Caribbean. Battered and outmoded ships, deliberately sunk in carefully designated places, act as nurseries for fish and lobster populations and provide new dive sites.

The Dive Shop, Sandy Ground (☎ **264/497-2020**), is a five-star PADI international training center and offers a complete line of PADI certification courses. They carry several lines of scuba equipment for sale or rental. A two-tank dive costs $80, and night dives go for $60.

TENNIS   Most of the resorts have their own tennis courts (see "Where to Stay," above). **Malliouhana,** Meads Bay (☎ **264/497-6111**), has a pro-shop and four championship Laykold tennis courts with a year-round professional coach, Peter Burwash. Three courts are lit for night games. There are also two courts at **Cinnamon Reef Resort,** Little Harbour (☎ **264/497-2727**).

WINDSURFING   Many hotels and villa properties offer windsurfing to guests: Cap Juluca, the Cinnamon Reef Beach Club, Fountain Beach, La Sirena, Malliouhana, the Mariners Cliffside Beach Resort, Shoal Bay Villas, and Rendezvous Bay. Water-sports facilities also offer windsurfing. The Mariners has windsurfing or Sunfish sailboats for $15 per half hour for rental or lessons, and $25 per hour for rental or lessons.

6 Exploring the Island

The best way to get an overview of the island is on a **taxi tour.** In about 2½ hours, a local driver (all of them are guides) will show you everything for $45. They will also arrange to let you off at your favorite beach after a look around, and then pick you up and return you to your hotel or the airport.

You can arrange a boat trip to **Sombrero Island,** 38 miles northwest of Anguilla. With its lone lighthouse, this mysterious island is 400 yards wide at its broadest point and three-quarters of a mile in length. Abandoned by phosphate miners in 1890, the treeless, waterless terrain evokes a moonscape, ringed by eroded limestone cliffs. Adventure seekers can sometimes arrange to visit on the supply boat that serves the island on the first and sixteenth of each month. A boat leaves Anguilla between 6 and 7am and returns at noon. Call **Ed Carty** (☎ **264/497-2337**) if you'd like to arrange such a free trip.

If you'd like to while away the afternoon in a beach bar, see section 8 of this chapter, "Anguilla After Dark."

7 Shopping

Anguillian handcrafts are simple. The handcrafted mats are quite beautiful, made from stripped corn husks and sisal rope. Tablecloths and bedspreads are woven into spidery lace designs. Many of these are grabbed up by shops on neighboring islands, however, and sold there at high prices. You'll also find model schooners and small pond boats for sale, along with wooden dolls and gifts made of shells.

Anguilla Arts & Crafts, The Valley (☎ **264/497-2200**), next door to the library, is one of the best outlets for island handcrafts and art: painted wood carvings, pottery, ceramics, textiles, and primitive art.

The Boutique at Malliouhana, in the Malliouhana Hotel, Meads Bay (☎ **264/ 497-6111**), is the most interesting and upscale boutique on Anguilla, with jewelry, sportswear and casual beachwear for men and women, evening dresses, gifts, designer bathing suits, and Kaminsky Rafia hats.

Cheddie's Carving Shop, The Cove (☎ **264/497-6027**), near the Sonesta Beach Resort, showcases the work of Anguilla-born Cheddie Richardson, a self-taught carver whose unique pieces have attracted the notice of collectors of Caribbean art.

Devonish Art Gallery, George Hill Landing Mall (☎ **264/497-2949**), offers paintings by Anguillian, Caribbean, and international artists and also features the work of well-known proprietor-artist Courtney Devonish. Visitors might get to watch handmade pottery production on Saturdays.

New World Gallery, Old Factory Plaza, the Valley (☎ **264/497-5950**), features exquisite fine-art pastels, paintings, and prints. New World also stocks a range of international artifacts, textiles, and jewelry.

Stamp collectors should head to the **Valley Post Office** (☎ **264/497-2528**).

8 Anguilla After Dark

Nightlife on Anguilla centers mainly on the various hotels, especially in winter when they offer barbecues, West Indian parties, or singers and musicians. The hotels hire calypso combo groups and other bands, both local and imported.

The **Mayoumba Folkloric Theater** (☎ **264/497-6827**), plays Thursday night at La Sirena on Meads Bay. Call for details before you go. African drums and a string band will give you an insight into Antillean culture.

Johnno's Beach Bar, Sandy Ground (☎ **264/497-2728**), is a favorite of Michael J. Fox and other Hollywood types when they visit Anguilla. Open-air, with sunlight and sea winds wafting into its unpretentious premises, the club offers Beck's beer on the beach, barbecued spareribs, grilled chicken, and fresh fish. Live entertainment takes place Wednesday, Friday, Saturday, and Sunday from 8pm to 1am. A weekly Sunday barbecue begins at 11am.

Other hot spots (make sure they're open before you head there) include **Rafe's,** on South Hill (☎ **264/497-3914**), with late-night dancing, music, and a simple menu: barbecue ribs, chicken, garlic bread, and the like. The decor is mainly driftwood, with cast-off chairs and furnishings under a galvanized roof. The location is on a backroad cliff that overlooks Sandy Ground and Road Bay. You can hear the music from Johnno's a mile away.

At **Dune Preserve,** Rendezvous Bay (☎ **264/497-7910**), check out **Bankie BanX,** the best-known recording star on Anguilla. As Bankie picks up his guitar and begins to sing, he weaves magic—a cross between Bob Dylan, Bob Marley, Richie Havens, and Ray Charles. His son tends bar, and they work the tiny space in casual harmony. The best times to show up are on Wednesday and Friday nights after 10pm. Saturday it's sunset-to-sunrise reggae, which picks up again on Sunday afternoon.

A restaurant-cum-beach bar, **Palm Grove Bar & Grill,** Junk's Hole Bay (☎ 264/497-4224), offers a long stretch of uncrowded curving white sand and off-shore reefs full of eels, squid, and manta ray. Nat Richardson, the owner, is waiting to boil or grill for you fresh-caught lobster, crayfish, or shrimp. *Bon Appétit* liked his johnnycakes so much they stole the recipe and published it. On Friday nights, party-goers rock the sands to live music.

✪ **The Pumphouse,** Sandy Ground (☎ 284/497-5154) is the island's latest hotspot, called "The People's Place." Of all the dives in Anguilla, this one has the best-stocked bar—a total of 30 different rums. The food is delicious too. Go any time from 7pm to 2am, except Sunday and Monday when it's closed. Reggae lovers show up on Wednesday and Saturday nights, and Thursday nights are often devoted to merengue.

Uncle Ernie's, Shoal Bay (no phone), is perhaps the most casual place on island. Yell out your order—maybe the barbecued spare ribs, which connoisseurs claim are the island's best—and wash it down with cold local beer or fruit punch. Directly on Shoal Bay Beach, the bar lures locals and visitors with finger food, good times, gossip, and those ribs.

Antigua 4

Antiguans boast that they have a different beach for every day of the year. This is an exaggeration, but the beaches here are certainly spectacular: Most are protected by coral reefs, and the sand is often sugar white. Antigua is also known for its sailing facilities in English Harbour. Most hotels, restaurants, beach bars, and water-sports facilities lie north of the capital of St. John's in the northwest.

Antigua, Barbuda, and Redonda form the independent nation of Antigua and Barbuda, within the Commonwealth of Nations. Redonda is an uninhabited rocky islet of less than a square mile located 20 miles southwest of Antigua. Barbuda is covered at the end of this chapter.

Independence has come, but Antigua is still British in many of its traditions. Economically, it has transformed itself from a poverty-stricken island of sugar plantations to a 20th-century vacation haven. American millionaires seeking British serenity under a tropical sun turned Antigua into an elegant destination around the exclusive Mill Reef Club (where you'll only be accepted if you're recommended by a member). The island has now developed a broader base of tourism and now attracts middle- and lower-income travelers in addition to the jet-setters.

The landscape of rolling, rustic Antigua (*an-TEE-gah*) is dotted with stone towers that were once sugar mills. The inland scenery isn't as dramatic as what you'll find on St. Kitts, but, oh, those beaches!

The capital is **St. John's,** a large, neatly laid-out town 6 miles from the airport and less than a mile from Deep Water Harbour Terminal. The port is the focal point of commerce and industry and the seat of government and shopping. Protected within a narrow bay, St. John's is charming, with cobblestone sidewalks and weather-beaten wooden houses with corrugated iron roofs and louvered Caribbean verandas. Trade winds keep the wide streets cool.

1 Essentials

VISITOR INFORMATION

Before you leave, you can contact the **Antigua and Barbuda Department of Tourism,** 610 Fifth Ave., Suite 311, New York, NY 10020 (☎ **212/541-4117**); or 25 SE Second Ave., Suite 300, Miami, FL 33131 (☎ **305/381-6762**). A new toll-free number also provides information: ☎ **888/268-4227.** Live operators are available Monday to Friday 9am to 5pm—that's Eastern Standard Time.

In Canada, contact the **Antigua and Barbuda Department of Tourism & Trade,** 60 St. Clair Ave. E., Suite 304, Toronto, ON, M4T 1N5 (☎ **416/961-3085**).

In the United Kingdom, information is available at **Antigua House,** 15 Thayer St., London, England W1M 5LD (☎ **0171/486-7073**).

The official Web site is **www.antigua-barbuda.org**.

On the island, the **Antigua and Barbuda Department of Tourism,** at Thames and Long streets in St. John's (☎ **268/462-0480**), is open Monday to Thursday from 8am to 4:30pm and on Friday from 8am to 3pm.

GETTING THERE

Before you book your airline ticket on your own, refer to the section on "Package Deals," in chapter 2. Buying an air/land package can save you a ton of money! If you don't buy a package, still read over our tips on how to get the best airfare in chapter 2.

BY PLANE The major airline that flies to Antigua's V. C. Bird Airport is **American Airlines** (☎ **800/433-7300** in the U.S.; www.aa.com), which offers three daily (morning, afternoon, and evening) nonstop flights to Antigua from its Caribbean hub in San Juan, Puerto Rico; flights take about 1½ hours. Each of these departs late enough in the day to allow easy transfers from other flights.

Continental (☎ **800/231-0856** or 268/462-5355; www.flycontinental.com) has daily flights out of Newark, New Jersey.

British Airways (☎ **800/247-9297** in the U.S.; www.british-airways.com) offers flights four times a week from London's Gatwick Airport.

Air Canada (☎**800/776-3000** in the U.S., 800/268-7240 in Canada; www.aircanada.ca) has regularly scheduled flights from Toronto to Antigua on Saturday only.

BWIA (☎ **800/292-1183** in the U.S.; www.bwee.com) is increasingly popular. Each week, four flights depart for Antigua from Miami; two from Toronto; five from Kingston, Jamaica; two from London; and two from Frankfurt.

GETTING AROUND

BY TAXI Taxis meet every airplane, and drivers wait outside the major hotels. If you're going to spend a few days here, a particular driver may try to "adopt" you. The typical one-way fare from the airport to St. John's is $12, but to English Harbour it's $25 and up. The government of Antigua fixes rates, and taxis are meterless.

Private taxis are costly, but they are the best way to see Antigua, as the drivers also act as guides. Most taxi tours go from the St. John's area to English Harbour. Drivers will generally charge $40 for three or four passengers and will often wait 30 minutes or more while you sightsee around English Harbour. If you split the cost with another couple, these tours become reasonably affordable.

To call a taxi in St. John's, dial ☎ **268/462-0711;** after 6pm, ☎ **268/462-5190**.

BY RENTAL CAR Renting a car on Antigua is not advisable. Newly arrived drivers quickly learn that the island's roads are terribly potholed and poorly signposted.

If you still want to drive despite these caveats, you must obtain an Antiguan license, which costs $20 and requires a valid driver's license from home. Most car-rental firms

Special Events

The week before the first Tuesday in August, summer **Carnival** envelops the streets in exotic costumes that recall Antiguan's African heritage. Festivities include a beauty competition and calypso and steel-band competitions. The big event in spring is Antigua's annual **Sailing Week** in late April or early May.

Atlantic Ocean

Hodges Bay

Dutchman's Bay

Dickenson Bay
Cedar Grove
Runaway Beach **3**
Deep Water Harbour Fort James V. C. Bird Airport
Long Island **4**

Hawksbill Beaches **1** Five Islands
St. John's
Guiana Island

Parham
Pineapple Beach **5** Long Bay
Indian Town Point

Darkwood Beach Jennings All Saints
Willikies
Devil's Bridge

Jolly Harbour Bolans
Megaliths Potworks Dam
Freetown

Driftwood Beach Boggy Peak
Half Moon Bay

Johnson's Point **6** Urlings
Falmouth **9** **10**
Willoughby Bay

Morris Bay Old Road *Falmouth Bay* **8** English Harbour **11** **13** *Mamora Bay*

Turner's Beach **7** Pigeon Point
Carlisle Bay Nelson's Dockyard National Park **12** Shirley Heights

Caribbean Sea

0 ——— 5 Miles
0 ——— 5 Kilometers

Airport ✈ Beach ☂ Mountain ▲

2-0189

Admiral's Inn **12**
Antigua Village **3**
Catamaran Hotel & Marina **8**
Copper and Lumber Store Hotel **9**
Curtain Bluff **7**
Falmouth Harbour Beach Apartments **10**

Hawksbill Beach Resort **1**
Inn at English Harbour **11**
Jumby Bay **4**
Long Bay Hotel **5**
Rex Blue Heron **6**
St. James's Club **13**
Yepton Beach Resort **2**

can issue you an Antiguan license, which they usually do without a surcharge. Note that *motorists drive on the left.*

The best rental agencies are major American affiliates. **Avis** (☎ **800/331-1212** in the U.S., or 268/462-2840 in Antigua) and **Hertz** (☎ **800/654-3131** in the U.S., or 268/462-6450 in Antigua) offer pickup service at the airport. Antigua has several car-rental agencies, but some are financially precarious and their vehicles can be somewhat battered. They do offer one advantage: They may make a cheaper deal. Try **Anjam Rent-a-car,** Sunset Cove, Dickenson Bay (☎ **268/462-0959**), or **J&L Rent-a-Car,** Crosbies (☎ **268/461-7496**). The average rental costs about $50 a day. If you're arriving off-season, insist on a "summer discount"—they will often grant one.

BY MOTORCYCLE & SCOOTER For the cheapest wheels on the island, rent a motorcycle or scooter from **Shipwreck,** English Harbour (☎ **262/460-2711**). Yamaha or Honda motorcycles rent for about $35 per day or $150 per week; scooters cost $25 per day or $85 per week. You'll save so much that you may not even mind the bumpy ride.

BY BUS   We don't recommend buses for the average visitor, though they are an inexpensive option. Service is erratic and undependable, and roads are impossibly bumpy. Buses are supposed to operate between St. John's and the villages daily from 5:30am to 6pm, but don't count on it. In St. John's, buses leave from two different "stations"— near the Central Market and near the Botanical Gardens. Most fares cost $1.

Fast Facts: Antigua

Banking Hours   Banks are usually open Monday to Thursday from 8am to 1pm and on Friday from 8am to 1pm and 3 to 5pm.

Currency   These islands use the Eastern Caribbean dollar (EC$). Nearly all hotels bill in U.S. dollars, however, and only certain tiny restaurants present their prices in EC$. When you inquire about a price, make sure you know the type of dollars quoted. The EC dollar is worth about 37¢ in U.S. currency (EC$2.70 = U.S.$1). Unless otherwise specified, *rates in this chapter are quoted in U.S. dollars.*

Customs   Arriving visitors are allowed to bring in 200 cigarettes, one quart of liquor, and six ounces of perfume.

Documents   A valid passport is preferred from U.S., British, and Canadian nationals. An original birth certificate accompanied by a photo ID is also acceptable, but we recommend that you carry a passport when visiting a foreign country. All arriving visitors must have a departing ticket.

Electricity   Most of the island's electricity is 220 volts AC (60 cycles), which means that American appliances require transformers. The Hodges Bay area and some hotels, however, are supplied with 110 volts AC (60 cycles).

Emergencies   In an emergency, contact the police (☎ 268/462-0125), the fire department (☎ 268/462-0044), or an ambulance (☎ 268/462-0251). You can also call ☎ 911 or ☎ 999 for any type of emergency.

Hospital   The principal medical facility on Antigua is **Holberton Hospital,** on Hospital Road (☎ 268/462-0251).

Language   The official language is English.

Safety   Antigua is generally safe, but that doesn't mean you should wander alone at night on St. John's near-deserted streets. Don't leave valuables unguarded on the beach either.

Taxes & Service Charges   Visitors must pay a departure tax of U.S.$20 and an 8.5% government tax on hotel bills. Most hotels also add a 10% service charge.

Telephone   Telephone calls can be made from hotels or the office of **Cable & Wireless,** 42–44 St. Mary's St., in St. John's (☎ 268/462-0840). You can also send faxes and telegrams from here.

Time   Antigua is on Atlantic standard time year-round, so it's 1 hour ahead of U.S. eastern standard time. When daylight saving time takes over in the States, then Antigua's time is the same as in the eastern United States.

Water   Tap water is generally safe to drink here, but many visitors prefer to only drink bottled water.

Weather   The average year-round temperature ranges from 75° to 85°F.

2 Where to Stay

Antigua's hotels are excellent, plentiful, and generally small—a 100-room hotel is rare on the island. (Check summer closings. Owners may decide to shut down early if business isn't good.) Air-conditioning is uncommon, except in first-class hotels.

An 8.5% government tax and 10% service charge are added to your hotel bill, which makes quite a difference in your final tab.

Antigua has lots of shockingly expensive hotels and resorts, but there are ways you can bring down the prices. Consider booking a package if you're interested in one of those pricey places! Refer back to the section on "Package Deals," in chapter 2.

VERY EXPENSIVE

✪ **Curtain Bluff.** Old Rd. (P.O. Box 288, St. John's), Antigua, W.I. ☎ **888/289-9898** in the U.S., or 268/462-8400. Fax 268/462-8409. www.curtainbluff.com. 63 units. Dec 19–Apr 14 $695–$895 double; from $965 suite. Apr 15–May 14 and Oct 12–Dec 18 $545–$750 double; from $795 suite. Rates are all-inclusive. AE. Closed May 15 to mid-Oct.

This serene, comfortable oasis is the island's premier resort, with price tags to match. Fifteen miles from the airport on the southwest shore, the hotel occupies the most lushly tropical section of the island, in the village of Old Road, and sits on two beautiful beaches (one turbulent, the other calm as can be). Once a pilot for Texaco, founder Howard W. Hulford discovered his Shangri-la back in the 1950s while flying over it, and established the hotel in 1961. Now it hosts Sailing Week each year and has good sports facilities.

The setting resembles a subtropical forest, with beautifully furnished accommodations, including deluxe units with king-size beds; a terrace room with a king-size, four-poster bed; and suites. The luxurious mattresses are the island's best. The roomy bathrooms have beautiful tiles, deluxe toiletries, dual vanities, and bidets. Fluffy towels are supplied twice daily. Ceiling fans and trade winds keep the rooms cool, and individual terraces open onto the water.

Dining/Diversions: Some guests come primarily for the superb food. Swiss-born Ruedi Portmann keeps his continental menu limited, so he can freshly prepare and artistically arrange everything. The Curtain Bluff restaurant boasts the Caribbean's most extensive wine selection. Guests can dance to live music under the stars, and once a week a steel band entertains guests. Jackets are required for men at dinner in winter.

Amenities: Sailing, waterskiing, skin diving, deep-sea fishing, scuba diving (for certified divers only), four championship tennis courts (plus a pro shop and a full-time pro), squash, exercise room, aerobics classes—all at no extra charge. Large free-form swimming pool with two lanes, room service (from 8am to 9pm), baby-sitting.

Hawksbill Beach Resort. Five Islands Village (P.O. Box 108, St. John's), Antigua, W.I. ☎ **800/223-6510** in the U.S., or 268/462-0301. Fax 268/462-1515. www.hawksbill.com. E-mail: hawksbill@candw.ag. 111 units. TEL. Winter $300–$380 double; $1,800 great house. Off-season $210–$250 double; $1,330 great house. AE, MC, V.

Named after an offshore rock that resembles a hawksbill turtle, this 37-acre resort is 10 miles west of the airport and 4 miles southwest of St. John's. Set on four brown-sand beaches (one reserved for those who want to go home sans tan lines), it caters to active types and is popular for weddings and honeymoons. The hotel revolves around an open-air, breezy central core. A former sugar mill on the premises now functions as a boutique. Bedrooms are small and comfortably furnished, with ceiling fans and showers. The least expensive accommodations open onto a garden. Note that rooms have neither TVs nor air-conditioning. The great house has three bedrooms for three to six occupants.

Dining/Diversions: There are two restaurants (one on the beach) and two bars. It's usually lively here, with limbo dancers and calypso singers four nights a week in season.

Amenities: Pool, tennis court, Sunfish sailing, windsurfing, snorkeling, waterskiing (for a nominal charge), laundry, baby-sitting.

The Inn at English Harbour. English Harbour (P.O. Box 187, St. John's), Antigua, W.I. ☎ **268/460-1014.** Fax 268/460-1603. www.theinn.ag. E-mail: info@theinn.ag. 28 units. Winter $290–$410 double. Off-season $140–$210 double. MAP $60 per person extra. AE, MC, V. Closed Aug 5–Oct 3. From St. John's, head south, through All Saints and Liberta, until you reach the south coast.

This small inn occupies one of the finest sites on Antigua, with terrace views over Nelson's Dockyard and English Harbour. The late actor Richard Burton liked it so well he spent two of his honeymoons here. Amenities include hair dryers, wall safes, balconies, ceiling fans, and small fridges. White-tile floors, screened plantation shutters, and excellent beds invite you to linger. The least expensive units are farthest from the beach, on a hillside.

Dining/Diversions: The inn is known for high-quality cooking. Lunch is served both at the beach house and in the main dining room. Have a drink before dinner in the old-style English Bar with stone walls and low overhead beams. Live entertainment is provided in winter.

Amenities: Complimentary water sports (including Sunfish sailing, windsurfing, snorkeling, and rowing), daytime water taxi to Nelson's Dockyard, lit tennis courts nearby, room service, laundry, baby-sitting. Waterskiing and day sailing available at an extra cost. Deep-sea fishing, scuba diving, golf, and horseback riding can be arranged.

✪ **Jumby Bay.** Long Island, (P.O. Box 243, St. Johns) Antigua, W.I. ☎ **800/223-7636,** or 268/462-6000. Fax 268/462-6020. 51 units. TEL. Winter $650 double; $750 junior suite; $1,500 two-bedroom villa; $2,150 three-bedroom villa. Off-season $350–$450 double; $450–$550 junior suite; $800–$1,200 two-bedroom villa; $1,250–$1,750 three-bedroom villa. Extra person $100. Lunch and dinner $95 extra. Children 12 and under stay free in parents' room in summer only. AE, DC, MC, V.

After years of legal wrangling, this retreat of the rich and famous has reopened. Managed by Rockresorts International, it occupies a 300-acre offshore island 2 miles away. Management has already poured some $3 million into refurbishments, and it's likely they will have spent an additional $12 million before you check in. Boats depart from the Antiguan "mainland" every hour from 10am to 10pm daily. You can preregister on the Antiguan side. With white sandy beaches along a coastline protected by coral reefs, the grounds have been handsomely planted with loblolly and white cedar.

Guests are coddled and pampered in luxury, as they should be at these prices. Only Curtain Bluff matches this place. A haven for naturalists, the resort features Pasture Bay Beach on the island's windward side, home to endangered species of turtles, rare birds, and sheep. All the accommodations are newly refurbished, including a 12-unit Mediterranean-style complex, two- and three-bedroom luxury villas, and several spacious private manor houses. Beds are luxurious, as are the spacious bathrooms with deluxe toiletries, bidets, hair dryers, and lots of fluffy towels. All rooms have twice-daily maid service, monogrammed terry robes, and a personal safe, along with umbrellas and bikes for every guest. Note that rooms have neither air-conditioning nor TVs.

Dining/Diversions: For breakfast and lunch, it's casual fare at the open-air Beach Pavilion. Dinner six nights a week is at the historic Estate House, the signature restaurant in the 230-year-old English plantation manor. Imaginative dishes reflect the popular cuisines of Europe, America, and the Caribbean. Two bars are ideal for evening drinks. A new bistro restaurant offers good food in a less formal setting.

Amenities: Room service for continental breakfast (from 7 to 10am), water sports, three tennis courts, 4½ miles of hiking trails, a croquet court, a putting green, golf arranged at an 18-hole course, freshwater pool, spa and wellness Center.

Long Bay Hotel. Long Bay (P.O. Box 442, St. John's), Antigua, W.I. ☎ **800/291-2005** in the U.S., or 268/463-2005. Fax 268/463-2439. E-mail: hotel@longbay-antigua.com. 24 units. Winter $375–$405 double; $375–$435 cottage for two. Off-season $265–$295 double; $265–$350 cottage for two. Rates include MAP (breakfast and dinner). Extra person $110. AE, MC, V.

On a remote spit of land between the open sea and a sheltered lagoon, Long Bay is on the eastern shore, a mile beyond the hamlet of Willikie's. It was hit hard by Hurricane Luis in 1995, but it's since bounced back. It faces one of the island's best beaches and a lagoon that is safe for water sports. Owned and operated by the Lafaurie family since 1966, it's more of an inn than a resort, with breezy rooms and six furnished cottages for more privacy. The spacious rooms, in motel-like wings along the lagoon, have ceiling fans and firm mattresses. The bathrooms have fluffy towels, excellent plumbing, and half-size tubs with showers. Instead of TV, you get the sound of waves crashing on the beach.

Dining/Diversions: The resort centers on a clubhouse within the stone-walled Turtle Restaurant. The bar provides a relaxing environment. There's also the Beach House Restaurant and Bar.

Amenities: Championship tennis court, complete scuba facilities, sailboats, Windsurfers, snorkeling, golf nearby. Fishing, waterskiing, and boat trips can be arranged. Room service, laundry, baby-sitting, special dinner seating for children, library, games room.

✪ St. James's Club. Mamora Bay (P.O. Box 63, St. John's), Antigua, W.I. ☎ **800/345-0271** or 561/994-5640 in the U.S. Fax 561/994-6344. 105 units, 73 villas. A/C TV TEL. Winter $295–$335 double; $410 suite; from $595 villa for two. Off-season $235–$280 double; $325 suite; from $475 villa for two. Children 5 and under stay free in parents' room. AE, DC, MC, V.

This luxurious, remote, 100-acre resort on Mamora Bay closed after Hurricane Luis hit, in 1995. Though it sustained much damage, the club bounced back in the autumn of 1998 with more lush, tropical landscaping. Some of the great rooms are standard and medium in size, but others are spacious. All have excellent beds, combination baths (tub and shower), commodious vanities, dual basins, fluffy towels, private safes, hair dryers, and sliding-glass doors that open onto private balconies or patios. Pricey two-bedroom villas and hillside homes are also available. The sports facilities are among the Caribbean's best, and guests can choose between two lovely beaches.

Dining/Diversions: You can relax amid elegance in the Rainbow Garden Restaurant or dine alfresco by candlelight at the Docksider Café overlooking Mamora Bay. Guests can top off the evening at the Jacaranda nightclub. Many enjoy gambling in the high-ceilinged but small European-style casino. Children will love the playhouse, playground, and activity programs, which include donkey rides.

Amenities: 18-slip, full-service marina; water sports, including sailboats (Sunfish and Hobie cats), sailboards, aqua bikes, deep-sea fishing, waterskiing, snorkeling, scuba diving (with a scuba school offering American and European certification); seven hard tennis courts (two lit for night play), with a center court for tournaments; complete Universal-equipped gym; Jacuzzi; massage facility; beauty salon; croquet court; three pools; a playground and playhouse for children; room service; laundry; baby-sitting.

EXPENSIVE

Antigua Village. Dickenson Bay (P.O. Box 649, St. John's), Antigua, W.I. ☎ **268/462-2930.** Fax 268/462-0375. 65 units. A/C TV TEL. Winter $190–$215 studio for two; $230–$270 one-bedroom apt for two; $420–$485 two-bedroom apt for four. Off-season $110–$130 studio for two; $130–$155 one-bedroom apt for two; $240–$285 two-bedroom apt for four. AE, DISC, V.

On a peninsula that stretches into turquoise waters 2 miles from St. John's, Antigua Village is like a self-contained condo community—with a freshwater pool and mini-market on the premises. Guests can use the neighboring tennis court, a nearby course, and comprehensive water-sports facilities. The studio apartments and villas all have kitchenettes, patios and balconies, twin beds with firm mattresses, and sofa beds in the living room. The units are generally spacious, and a tropical decor brightens things considerably; expect standard motel-style bathrooms. Most accommodations open onto views of the water.

The Copper and Lumber Store Hotel. Nelson's Dockyard, English Harbour (P.O. Box 184, St. John's), Antigua, W.I. ☎ **268/460-1058.** Fax 268/460-1529. 14 units. Winter $195–$275 double; $215–$325 suite. Off-season $85–$145 double; $95–$175 suite. MC, V. From St. John's, follow the signs southeast to English Harbour.

As its name suggests, this charming, 18th-century building was originally a store that sold wood and copper for repairing British sailing ships. The store and its adjacent harbor structures are built of brick that once was used as ships' ballast. Each of the period units is brick-lined, uniquely designed, and filled with fine Chippendale and Queen Anne reproductions, antiques, brass chandeliers, hardwood paneling, and hand-stenciled floors. The showers look as if they belong in a sailing vessel, with thick mahogany panels and polished brass fittings. All suites have kitchens, private bathrooms (with showers only), and ceiling fans. Request a room with a half-tester bed and mosquito netting. All the mattresses are first rate. Towels are fluffy, and even the toilet seat is mahogany.

Dining: A traditional English pub serves food daily from 10:30am to midnight. The Wardroom serves dinner nightly.

Amenities: Room service, laundry, baby-sitting. There is no pool or beach, but the hotel provides a ferry service to Galleon Beach.

Rex Blue Heron. Johnson's Point Beach (P.O. Box 1715, St. John's), Antigua, W.I. ☎ **800/255-5859** or 305/471-6170 in the U.S., or 268/462-8564. Fax 305/471-9547 in the U.S., or 268/462-8005. www.rexcaribbean.com. E-mail: rbheron@candw.ag. 64 units. Year-round $268–$348 double. Rates are all-inclusive. AE, DC, DISC, MC, V.

On the most beautiful beach on Antigua, about 15 miles from either St. John's or the airport, this hotel offers peace and quiet, and tends to appeal to couples and honey-mooners. Casually comfortable, it crowns Johnson's Point with two-story white-stone buildings with rooms that overlook either well-kept gardens, the pool, or the beach. The beachfront units have air-conditioning, ceiling fans, and TVs; the standard rooms offer only ceiling fans. Each room has a patio or balcony. Standard rooms have only one double bed, while most of the others contain twins.

Dining/Diversions: An intimate on-site restaurant serves West Indian meals at affordable prices. You can choose between two bars. Most evenings feature live enter-tainment.

Amenities: A full range of water sports is available, including complimentary wind-surfing, snorkeling equipment, and Sunfish sailing. Deep-sea and offshore scuba diving is also offered.

Yepton Beach Resort. Hog John Beach, P.O. Box 1427, St. John's, Antigua, W.I. ☎ **800/361-4621** in the U.S., or 268/462-2520. Fax 268/462-3240. www.yepton.com. Winter $190–$280 double; $245 suite with kitchen for up to three; $575 suite with kitchen for up to six. Mid-Apr to mid-Dec $125–$190 double; $170 suite with kitchen for up to three; $380 suite with kitchen for up to six. MC, V.

At one edge of Hog John Beach, this small but choice 37-acre beachfront resort was built in the late 1980s. The neo-Hispanic, three-story white-walled building has a red terra-cotta roof and a verdant lawn that extends to the sandy beach on the Five Islands Peninsula. Don't expect glitz or razzle-dazzle or a sense of chic. What you get here is laid-back, unpretentious charm and intimacy that some visitors compare to a private house party among friends. Bedrooms have beige-tile floors and streamlined modern furniture, including firm mattresses; bathrooms are rather routine, motel-style affairs. Ground-floor bedrooms have direct beach access.

Dining/Diversions: There's a restaurant and bar on the premises, with live reggae or calypso music three nights a week.

Amenities: Two tennis courts, a kidney-shaped swimming pool.

MODERATE

✪ **The Admiral's Inn.** English Harbour (P.O. Box 713, St. John's), Antigua, W.I. ☎ **800/223-5695** in the U.S., or 268/460-1027. Fax 268/460-1534. E-mail: admirals@candw.ag. 15 units. Winter $120–$150 double; $154–$166 triple; $250 suite for two. Off-season $84–$100 double; $114–$122 triple; $150 suite. AE, MC, V. Closed Sept to mid-Oct. Take the road southeast from St. John's, following the signs to English Harbour.

Designed in 1785, the year Nelson sailed into the harbor as captain of the HMS *Boreas,* and completed in 1788, the building here once used to house dockyard services. Loaded with West Indian charm, this place in the heart of Nelson's Dockyard is constructed of weathered brick that was brought from England to be used as ships' ballast. The terrace opens onto a centuries-old garden. The ground floor—with brick walls, giant ship beams, and island-made furniture—has a tavernlike atmosphere, with decorative copper, boat lanterns, old oil paintings, and wrought-iron chandeliers.

There are three types of character-filled accommodations. The most expensive are the ground-floor rooms of a tiny brick building across the courtyard from the main structure. Each of these spacious units has a little patio, a garden entry, and optional air-conditioning. The front rooms on the first floor of the main building, with views of the lawn and harbor, are also more expensive. The back rooms on this floor are less pricey, and all have air-conditioning. With dormer-window views over the yacht-filled harbor, the least expensive chambers on the top floor are smaller and quiet, but they may get warm on summer afternoons. All units have twin beds, ceiling fans, and good mattresses. The Joiner's Loft, an upstairs suite, has a large living room overlooking the water, two bedrooms, two baths, and a full kitchen.

For the inn's restaurant, see "Where to Dine," below. On Saturday night a steel band plays. Amenities include room service, laundry, baby-sitting, free transportation to two nearby beaches, snorkeling equipment, and Sunfish craft.

Falmouth Harbour Beach Apartments. English Harbour Village, Yacht Club Rd. (P.O. Box 713, St. John's), Antigua, W.I. ☎ **268/460-1094.** Fax 268/460-1534. E-mail: admirals@candw.ag. 20 units. Winter $135–$150 double, $160–$175 triple. Off-season $90–$98 double, $114–$122 triple. Children 15 and under stay for $15 when sharing their parents' studio. AE, MC, V. Free parking. Take the road southeast from St. John's and follow the signs to English Harbour.

If you'd like to be near historic English Harbour, this relatively simple place may be for you. It offers an informal Antiguan atmosphere on a small sandy beach and rents twin-bedded studio apartments. Each studio has a ceiling fan, electric stove, fridge, oven, and terrace overlooking the water. They don't, however, have air-conditioning, phones, or TVs. A dozen studios sit on the beach; the others occupy a hillside just behind. Nearby you'll find restaurants, a supermarket, a bank, a post office, boutiques, and galleries. Next door, Temo Sports offers tennis and squash facilities. A dive operation in the dockyard arranges sailing and fishing boat charters. Bus service runs daily to and from St. John's, so you don't need a car.

INEXPENSIVE

✪ **The Catamaran Hotel & Marina.** Falmouth Harbour (P.O. Box 958, St. John's), Antigua, W.I. ☎ **800/223-6510** in the U.S., 800/424-5500 in Canada, or 268/460-1339. 16 units. Winter $65–$150 double; off-season $55–$115 double. Extra person $25; children under 10 pay $15. AE, MC, V. Closed Sept.

A longtime favorite on Antigua, the Catamaran opens onto a palm-lined beach at Falmouth Harbour, a 2-mile drive from English Harbour. When we first discovered the property years ago, a film crew had taken it over to make a movie about pirates of the West Indies. The management had to post a sign: TODAY'S "PIRATES" MUST WEAR BATHING SUITS ON THE BEACH. It's not as wild around here anymore, and peace and tranquillity prevail.

On the second floor, each of eight self-contained rooms has a four-poster bed, a queen-size mattress, and a balcony over the water. The Captain's Cabin is the most luxurious rental. The standard rooms are small, well maintained, and comfortable. The efficiencies at water's edge can be rented by one person or two. Each efficiency has a balcony and an equipped kitchen, plus a small bathroom with somewhat thin towels. Boaters will like the hotel's location at the 30-slip Catamaran Marina. You can purchase supplies at a nearby grocery store or enjoy the reasonably priced meals at the hotel restaurant and bar. Sportfishing and diving can be arranged, and the hotel offers Sunfish dinghies and rowboats.

3 Where to Dine

Although the Eastern Caribbean dollar (EC$) is used on these islands, only certain tiny restaurants present their prices in the local currency. When you inquire about a price, make sure you know which type of dollars is being quoted. Unless otherwise specified, rates quoted in this section are given in U.S. dollars.

IN ST. JOHN'S

✪ **Big Banana Holding Company.** Redcliffe Quay, St. John's. ☎ **268/462-2621.** Main courses $8–$32. AE, DC, MC, V. Mon–Sat 8:30am–midnight. PIZZA.

In former slave quarters, some of the best pizza in the eastern Caribbean is served amid the most stylish shopping and dining emporiums in town, a few steps from the Heritage Quay Jetty. Its ceiling fans and laid-back atmosphere will almost make you expect Sydney Greenstreet to stop in for a drink. The frothy libations, coconut or banana crush, are practically desserts. You can also order overstuffed baked potatoes, fresh-fruit salad, or conch salad. On Thursday a reggae band entertains from 10pm to 1am.

✪ **Julians.** Church Lane and Corn Alley. ☎ **268/461-3868.** Reservations recommended. Main courses EC$52–EC$78 (U.S.$19.25–$28.85). AE, DISC, MC, V. Tues–Sun 7–10pm. Closed mid-July to Aug. CONTINENTAL.

In an antique, white-and-green-shuttered wooden house, this restaurant is the island's best. There's no air-conditioning, but ceiling fans twirl above a black-and-white decor with lots of green plants. You can also opt to eat in the English-style garden in back. The inspired cuisine of Julian Waterer, the English owner and chef, has earned many fans. Presenting the most sophisticated food on the island, the menu changes frequently according to season and the owner's whim. A different homemade soup—perhaps a red bean or a cold fruit variety—is prepared daily. The kitchen knows how to rustle up some delectable main courses: pork chops with mustard sauce, wonderfully seasoned jerk chicken, or roast rack of lamb. Savvy local foodies swear by the Cajun rib eye.

Russell's. Fort James. ☎ **268/462-5479.** Reservations recommended. Main courses $4–$22 lunch, $12–$22 dinner. MC, V. Daily noon–3pm and 6–11pm. Hours vary according to owners' whims during low season. INTERNATIONAL.

In a dark-stained wooden house on a hillside about 20 feet above sea level, this restaurant is best known for its bar, live music, and potent drinks—which sometimes elevate the West Indian setting into a raucous party. Visit during the cocktail hour, especially when live music is playing (usually Wednesday to Saturday from 7 to 10pm). Rum-based drinks are popular—especially the pink sort flavored with guava, paw-paw, and cinnamon. Menu items range from simple burgers, salads, and hot dogs to more ambitious fare like grilled wahoo, grouper with hollandaise sauce, or Creole-style snapper.

Redcliffe Tavern. Redcliffe Quay. ☎ **268/461-4557.** Reservations recommended. Main courses $10–$22; lunch from $6.90. AE, DISC, MC, V. Mon–Sat 8am–11pm. CARIBBEAN/INTERNATIONAL.

This waterside restaurant is owned by Ian Fraser. Originally a warehouse constructed by the British in the 18th century, the place displays plantation-era water pumps and other Antiguan artifacts from that time. Don't expect a quiet and romantic evening here, however; the place is usually crowded. The menu includes plantain-stuffed chicken breasts in tomato or basil sauce, Brie wrapped in phyllo with a tomato-raspberry vinaigrette, and steaks with mushrooms or peppercorn sauce. The Normandy-style apple tart is superb.

ELSEWHERE AROUND THE ISLAND

✪ **The Admiral's Inn.** In Nelson's Dockyard, English Harbour. ☎ **268/460-1027.** Reservations recommended, especially for dinner in high season. Main courses $20–$27. AE, MC, V. Daily 7:30–10am, noon–2:30pm, and 7–9:30pm. Closed Sept to mid-Oct. AMERICAN/CREOLE.

Partake of lobster, seafood, and steaks in this 17th-century hotel (see "Where to Stay," above). Our favorite appetizer is pumpkin soup. Four or five main courses are served daily, such as local red snapper, grilled steak, or lobster. The service is agreeable, and sometimes the atmosphere is more exciting than the cuisine, which is good but rather standard. Before dinner, drink up in the bar and read where sailors carved their names in wood 100 years ago.

Alberto's. Willoughby Bay. ☎ **268/460-3007.** Reservations recommended. Main courses $22–35. AE, DC, MC, V. Tues–Sun 7–10pm. Closed May–Nov. INTERNATIONAL.

One of the most stylish and cosmopolitan restaurants on Antigua is Alberto's, the creative statement of Venice-born Alberto Ravanello and his English wife, Vanessa, who prepares much of the food herself. You'll find it close to the edge of the sea, near the St. James Club, in an open-sided pavilion lavishly draped with bougainvillea. The owners' frequent travels inspired the menu's satisfying medley of Italian, French, and continental dishes. Examples include ravioli stuffed with pulverized asparagus and smoked salmon; roasted rabbit with polenta; pasta with clams; stuffed crabs; and snapper in a caper, olive, and tomato sauce. Lobster, a favorite here, is boiled in sea-water, then grilled and served simply, usually with garlic-flavored butter.

✪ **Chez Pascal.** Galley Bay Hill, Five Islands. ☎ **268/462-3232.** Reservations recom-mended. Main courses $22–$40. AE, DC, MC, V. Daily 11:30–3:30pm and 6–10pm. Closed Sept. FRENCH.

This small but well-groomed corner of France blooms with tropical vegetation and well-prepared cuisine on the west coast. On a plateau near the Royal Antiguan Hotel, it centers on a terrace with an illuminated swimming pool. French colonial trappings include copper pots, rough-textured ceramics, dark-stained wicker and rattan, and tropically inspired fabric designs. The chef, Pascal Milliat (former saucier at La Samanna, a hyper-upscale hotel in St. Martin), inherited generations of cooking skills in his former home, Lyon. Assisted by his Brittany-born wife, Florence, he prepares and serves dishes with sublime sauces and seasonings. Examples include chicken liver mousse with basil-flavored butter sauce, lobster bisque en croute, sea scallops on a bed of leeks, roasted rack of lamb with herbes de Provence (prepared only for two diners at a time), and grouper with beurre blanc sauce.

On the premises are four very large bedrooms, none with TV, phone, or air-conditioning. (Friends and fans of the Milliats have urged them never to add these modern "inconveniences.") Each unit has a whirlpool tub, fridge, rattan furniture, sea views, and color schemes influenced by the sand and sky. With breakfast included, singles or doubles range from $85 to $100 in low season, from $120 to $170 in winter.

Coconut Grove. In the Siboney Beach Club, Dickenson Bay. ☎ **268/462-1538.** Reserva-tions required for dinner. Main courses $11–$30. AE, DC, MC, V. Daily 7–11pm. INTERNATIONAL/SEAFOOD.

North of St. John's in a coconut grove right on the beach, simple tables on a flagstone floor beneath a thatch roof are cooled by sea breezes. A food critic for the *Times* of London said that this is "every visitor's dream of what a Caribbean restaurant should be." We agree—this restaurant is one of the island's best. Soup is prepared fresh daily from local ingredients like ginger, carrot, or pumpkin. Appetizers include a seafood delight—scallops, shrimp, crab, lobster, and local fish with a mango-and-lime dressing. Lobster and shrimp dishes figure prominently, along with a catch of the day and a daily vegetarian special. Lunch fare is lighter. During happy hour at the bar (from 3:30 to 7pm), all drinks are half price.

Colombo's Restaurant. In the Galleon Beach Club, English Harbour. ☎ **268/460-1452.** Reservations required. Main courses $15–$27. AE, DC, DISC, MC, V. Daily 12:30–2:30pm and 7–10pm. Closed Sept–Oct 5. ITALIAN.

Colombo's serves the island's best Italian food on a Polynesian-style, open-air terrace sheltered by a woven palm-frond ceiling. It's only a few steps across the flat sands to the water. Lunches might include spaghetti marinara, lobster salad, and sandwiches. Dinners are more elaborate, with daily specials from a classic Italian inventory of veal scaloppine, veal pizzaiola, and lobster Mornay. Some dishes lack polish, but most selections are brimming with flavor. You can choose from a wide assortment of French or Italian wines. Live reggae, rock, jazz, and calypso music is offered on Wednesday or Friday night. (There's no cover, but there is a two-drink minimum.)

✪ **Le Bistro.** Hodges Bay. ☎ **268/462-3881.** Reservations recommended. Main courses EC$55–EC$85 (U.S.$20.35–$31.45). AE, MC, V. Tues–Sun 6:30–10:30pm. Closed July. FRENCH.

Antigua's Best Beach Bar

As you whiz along the winding road, you spot the initials of ✪ **O.J.,** Crab Hill (☎ **268/460-0184**), and you wonder for a moment if the Juice is hiding out in Antigua. Not so. O.J. stands for Oliver Joseph, who returned to his childhood home after being what he calls a "Toronto suit." His bar overlooks the sea on a half acre between Curtain Bluff and Jolly Harbour, both south of St. John's along the coastal road. This is the classic cliché of a Caribbean beach bar, with sea shells, tablecloths in flamboyant prints, and coral from the reefs. In a relaxed atmosphere, you can sample local Wadadli beer or one of the dark Cavalier rums so beloved by Antiguans. The piña coladas, made from home-grown plantains, guava, coconuts, and mangos, are the island's best. O.J. even grows his own herbs for chicken, fresh fish, and lobster dishes. If you want to stay for a big lunch, it'll cost around $12—rarely more than $20 for dinner. The big resort hotels just don't have this kind of atmosphere.

A half mile inland from the coast of Hodges Bay, this restaurant occupies a stone-sided structure that was built as a clubhouse for a golf course, now defunct. Sporting low-key European pizzazz, it's the oldest continuously operated restaurant in Antigua (since 1981). The owners are English-born Philippa Esposito and her husband, Raffaele, from Capri. Together, they concoct a mostly French menu that includes succulent lobster with creamy basil sauce, roasted snapper in a pumpkin-thyme sauce, snails in a creamy garlic sauce in puff pastry, duck with mango sauce, and medallions of veal with passion fruit and pink peppercorns. One of the rare Italian dishes here is ziti Raffaele, made from cream, fresh tomatoes, fresh basil, and Parmesan cheese. A favorite dessert is apple crêpes in a spiced honey sauce.

Shirley Heights Lookout. Shirley Heights. ☎ **268/460-1785.** Reservations recommended. Main courses EC$45–EC$65 (U.S.$16.65–$24.05). AE, DC, MC, V. Daily 9am–10pm. AMERICAN/SEAFOOD.

In the 1790s, this was a lookout station for unfriendly ships heading toward English Harbour, site of a powder magazine constructed to strengthen Britain's position in this strategic location. Today this panoramic spot, directly east of English Harbour, is one of Antigua's most romantic places. Specialties include pumpkin soup, grilled lobster in lime butter, garlic-flavored shrimp, and good desserts, such as pecan pie flambée. It's not the world's grandest cuisine—overcooking is the most frequent flaw—but it's a fun crowd-pleaser, and who can argue with that view? Less expensive hamburgers and sandwiches are available in the bar downstairs. It's best at lunch.

4 Beaches

There's a lovely white-sand beach on **Pigeon Point** at Falmouth Harbour, about a 4-minute drive from Admiral's Inn (see above). With calm waters and pristine sands, this is the best beach near English Harbour, but it's likely to be crowded, especially when a cruise ship is in port. It's ideal for snorkelers and swimmers of most ages and abilities.

✪ **Dickenson Bay** in the northwest, directly north of St. John's, has long been one of the island's finest, with its wide strip of powder-soft sand and blissfully calm waters. This safe beach often attracts families with small children in tow. The center point here is the **Halcyon Cove Hotel,** where you can rent water-sports equipment. You can visit the hotel for refreshments, or mosey over to the casual bars and restaurants nearby. Shimmering turquoise waters make this beach especially alluring. On the north side of Dickenson Bay, you'll find more secluded beaches and some ideal snorkeling areas along this fan-shaped northern crown of Antigua. For a fee, locals will sometimes take beachcombers to one of the uninhabited offshore islets, such as **Prickly Pear Island,** enveloped by beautiful coral gardens. Glass-bottom excursions often visit one of the island's best snorkeling spots— **Paradise Reef,** a mile-long coral garden of stunning beauty north of Dickenson Bay.

If you want to escape from everybody, flee to **Johnson's Point.** Between the hamlets of Johnson's Point and Urlings at Antigua's southwestern tip below Jolly Harbour, it opens onto the tranquil Caribbean Sea. There are no facilities, but the sand is a dazzling white, and the clear, calm waters are populated with schools of rainbow-hued tropical fish.

Near Johnson's Point on the southwest coast, **Turner's Beach** is idyllic. This is one of the best places to lie out in the tropical sun, cooled by trade winds. The beach has fine white sand and gin-clear waters. If the day is clear (as it usually is), you can see the volcanic island of Montserrat.

If you head east of Urlings, toward the hamlet of "Old Road," you'll reach **Carlisle Bay,** site of one of the island's most celebrated shores. One beach buff said, "Snow White must have designed these sands." Against a backdrop of coconut groves, two long beaches extend from the spot where **Curtain Bluff,** the island's most deluxe hotel, sits atop a bluff. The waters are impossibly blue here, where the calm Caribbean Sea meets the more turbulent Atlantic.

South of Jolly Harbour, **Driftwood Beach** is directly north of Johnson's Point, in the southwest. The white sands and calm, clear waters are delightful. It is close to all the villas at Jolly Harbour Beach Resort Marina, however, and may be overcrowded.

In the same vicinity is **Darkwood Beach,** a 5-minute drive south of Jolly Harbour Marina and the Jolly Harbour Golf Club. Here the shimmering waters are almost crystal blue. The snorkeling is great, and you can bet that gentle trade winds will keep you cool. Located in a crowded tourist zone, it is likely to be crowded—almost impossibly so when cruise ships are in port.

If you continue north toward St. John's and cut west at the turnoff for Five Islands, you'll reach the four secluded **Hawksbill Beaches** on the Five Islands peninsula. The beaches here have white sands, dazzling blue and green waters, and coral reefs ideal for snorkeling. On one of them, you can sunbathe and swim in the buff. The Five Islands Peninsula is the site of major hotel developments. Though it's secluded, the beaches might be crowded.

Perhaps Antigua's most beautiful beach, ✪ **Half Moon Bay** stretches along nearly a mile of white sand on the eastern coast. The Atlantic surf is liable to be rough—which doesn't stop a never-ending stream of snorkelers and windsurfers. Half Moon is now a public park and is an ideal choice for a family outing, as it is completely protected by a reef. The location is a 5-minute drive from Freetown village on the southeast coast. With its fine pink sand, trade winds, and active surf, it has long been one of our favorites. The Half Moon Bay lies east of English Harbour in the vicinity of Mill Reef.

Directly north of Half Moon Bay, east of Willikies, **Long Bay** fronts the Atlantic on the far eastern coast of Antigua. Guests of the Long Bay Hotel and the Pineapple Beach Club are likely to populate this sandy strip. The shallow waters here are home to stunning coral reefs. Great snorkeling.

In the same vicinity, **Pineapple Beach** is a 5-minute drive from the village of Willikies heading east. It opens onto Long Bay and the west coast (Atlantic side) of Antigua. Crystal blue waters make it ideal for snorkeling. Most beach buffs come here just to sun on nearly perfect white sands.

5 Sports & Outdoor Pursuits

A SAILING CRUISE   All the major hotel desks can book a day cruise on the 108-foot "pirate ship," the *Jolly Roger,* Redcliffe Quay (☎ 268/462-2064), which is the largest sailing ship in Antiguan waters. For $55 to $60 for adults and $30 for children, you get a fun-filled day of sightseeing, with drinks and barbecued steak, chicken, or lobster. Lunch is combined with a snorkeling trip. On the poop deck, members of the crew teach passengers how to dance calypso. Daily cruises last 5½ hours, from 9:30am to 3pm. A Saturday-night dinner cruise is $40, leaving Heritage Quay in St. John's at 7pm and returning at 11pm.

FISHING   Many anglers visit Antigua just for the big-game fishing offshore, where wahoo, tuna, and marlin abound. The *Obsession* (☎ 268/462-2824) is a 50-foot Hatteras Sportfisherman with excellent equipment. You can battle the big ones in a featured "fighting chair." For the day, the *Obsession* charges $1,300, a fee that is shared by all the passengers. A competitor of similar size, the *Nimrod* (☎ 268/463-8744), is captained by Terry Bowen, who knows where the best catches are. You can arrange for the *Nimrod* to circle the island or go on sunset cruises. The full day costs $780; a half day is $440.

GOLF   Antigua's facilities are not on par with some of the other islands', but its premier course is good. The 18-hole, par-69 **Cedar Valley Golf Club,** Friar's Hill Road (☎ 268/462-0161), is 3 miles east of St. John's, near the airport. With panoramic views of Antigua's northern coast, the island's largest course was designed by the late Richard Aldridge to fit the contours of the area. Daily greens fees are $35 for 18 holes. Cart fees are $30 for 18 holes, and club rentals are $10.

PARASAILING   This sport is gaining popularity on Antigua. Facilities are available during the day, Monday to Saturday on the beach at Dickenson Bay.

✪ SCUBA DIVING, SNORKELING & OTHER WATER SPORTS   The reefs that fringe Antigua are home to beautiful, brilliantly colored fish. Many of the island's beaches (see above) have clear, pure, calm waters that make for great snorkeling.

Scuba diving is best arranged through **Dive Antigua,** at the Rex Halcyon Cove, Dickenson Bay (☎ 268/462-3483), Antigua's most experienced dive operation. A resort course is $88, and a two-tank dive costs $73. A five-dive package goes for $295, and open-water certification costs $492. Prices include equipment.

On the northeastern coast of the island, **Long Bay Hotel** (☎ 268/463-2005) is a good location for swimming, sailing, waterskiing, and windsurfing. The hotel also has complete scuba facilities. Beginning snorkelers and divers alike are welcome. A boat will take groups of four or more to Green Island and Great Bird Island. The shallow side of the double reef across Long Bay is ideal for the novice, and the northeastern tip has many reefs of varying depths. A one-afternoon resort course costs $85.

TENNIS   True tennis buffs—well-heeled ones, that is—check into **Curtain Bluff** (see "Where to Stay," above). Its courts are the finest on island. Most of the major hotels have courts as well, and some are lit for night games. (We don't recommend playing tennis at noon—it's just too hot!) Guests of a hotel usually play free; if you're not a guest, you'll have to book a court and pay charges that vary from place to place. If your hotel doesn't have a court, try the **Royal Antiguan Resort,** Deep Bay (☎ 268/462-3733). You might also try the **Temo Sports Complex** at Falmouth Bay (☎ 268/463-1781), which offers two floodlit tennis courts.

WINDSURFING   Located at the Lord Nelson Beach Hotel, on Dutchman's Bay, **Windsurfing Antigua** (☎ 268/462-9463) offers windsurfing for the absolute beginner, the intermediate sailor, and the hard-core windsurfer. The outfit guarantees beginners will enjoy the sport after a 2-hour introductory lesson for $60. A 1-hour rental costs $20; a half day, $50.

6　Exploring the Island

IN ST. JOHN'S

In the southern part of St. John's, the **market** is colorful and interesting, especially on Saturday morning from 8am to noon. Fruit and vegetable vendors bargain and gossip. The semi-open-air market takes place at the lower end of Market Street.

St. John's Cathedral, the Anglican church between Long Street and Newgate Street at Church Lane (☎ 268/461-0082), has resurrected itself time and again—destroyed by earthquakes and rebuilt on the same site at least three times since the original structure was constructed in 1683.

Exhibits at the **Museum of Antigua & Barbuda,** at Market and Church streets (☎ 268/462-1469), cover the island-nation's prehistoric days up to its independence from Britain in 1981. The full-size replica of a house built by Arawaks, the earliest settlers, is most intriguing. You can also see models of sugar plantations, paintings, and historical prints. It's open Monday through Friday from 8:30am to 4pm and on Saturday from 10am to 1pm; admission is free.

AROUND THE ISLAND

After leaving St. John's, most visitors head southeast for 11 miles to ✪ **Nelson's Dockyard National Park** (☎ 268/460-1379), one of the eastern Caribbean's biggest attractions. English ships took refuge from the hurricanes in this harbour as early as 1671. The park's centerpiece is the restored Georgian naval dockyard, which was used by Admirals Nelson, Rodney, and Hood, and was the home of the British fleet during the Napoleonic Wars. From 1784 to 1787, Nelson commanded the British navy in the Leeward Islands and made his headquarters at English Harbour.

The dockyard museum recaptures the 18th-century era of privateers, pirates, and battles at sea. A sort of Caribbean Williamsburg, its colonial naval buildings stand as they did when Nelson was here. Although Nelson never lived at **Admiral House** (☎ 268/463-1379)—it was built in 1855—his telescope and tea caddy are displayed here, along with other nautical memorabilia. Hours are daily from 8am to 6pm; admission is $2.

The park itself has sandy beaches and tropical vegetation, with various species of cactus and mangroves. A migrating colony of African cattle egrets shelters in the mangroves. Archaeological sites here predate Christ. Nature trails, with coastal views, lead you through the flora. Tours of the dockyard last 15 to 20 minutes; nature walks along the trails can last anywhere from 30 minutes to 5 hours. The entrance fee is $5 for a tour of the dockyard; the nature trail costs an additional $2.50. Children 12 and under are admitted free. The dockyard and its museum are open daily from 9am to 5pm.

Another major attraction is the **Dow's Hill Interpretation Center** (☎ 268/460-2777), just 2½ miles from the dockyard. The only one of its kind in the Caribbean, it offers multimedia presentations that cover six periods of the island's history, including the era of Amerindian hunters, the era of the British military, and the struggles connected with slavery. A belvedere opens onto a panoramic view of the park. Admission to the center, including the multimedia show, is EC$15 ($5.55). Hours are daily from 9am to 5pm.

On a low hill overlooking Nelson's Dockyard, **Clarence House** (☎ 268/463-1026) was built by English stonemasons to accommodate Prince William Henry, later known as the Duke of Clarence—and even later known as William IV. The future king stayed here when he was in command of the *Pegasus* in 1787. At present it's the country home of the governor of Antigua and Barbuda and is open to visitors

---

Photo Ops

Once, in the 1700s, the coastline of the island was ringed with British forts, though they're all in ruins today. Even if there isn't much left to see, the views from these former military strongholds are among the most panoramic in the Caribbean—and you can visit them for free. You can begin at St. John's harbor (the capital), which was once guarded by **Fort Barrington** on the south and **Fort James** on the north. Later you can head down to **Fort James Bay** where you'll find a couple of bars right on the sand, including **Russell's Beach Bar,** which is most active on Sunday afternoon. It's an ideal place to unwind with a beer. In the south, near English Harbour, check out the view from Shirley Heights.

---

when His Excellency is not in residence. A caretaker will show you through (it's customary to tip), and you'll see many pieces of furniture on loan from the National Trust. Princess Margaret and Lord Snowdon stayed here on their honeymoon.

On the way back, take ✪ **Fig Tree Drive,** a 20-some-mile circular drive across the main mountain range. It passes through lush tropical hills and fishing villages along the southern coast. You can pick up the road just outside Liberta, north of Falmouth. Winding through a rain forest, it passes thatched villages, every one with a church and lots of goats and children running about. But don't expect fig trees—*fig* is an Antiguan name for bananas.

The Potworks Dam, holding back the largest artificial lake on Antigua, is surrounded by an area of great natural beauty. The dam holds a billion gallons of water and provides protection for Antigua in case of a drought.

Betty's Hope (☎ 268/462-1469), just outside the village of Pares on the eastbound route to Long Bay, is Antigua's first sugar plantation (from 1650). You can tour it for free, Tuesday to Saturday from 10am to 4pm. Exhibits in the visitor's center trace the sugar era, and you can also see two windmills. Plans are underway to excavate the adjacent slave village—the first dig of a slave village in the Caribbean.

Indian Town is one of Antigua's national parks, on the island's northeastern point. Over the centuries, Atlantic breakers have lashed the rocks and carved a natural bridge known as Devil's Bridge. It's surrounded by numerous blowholes spouting surf, a dramatic sight. An environmentally protected area, Indian Town Point lies at the tip of a deep cove, Indian Town Creek. The park fronts the Atlantic at Long Bay, just west of Indian Town Creek at the eastern side of Antigua. Birders flock here to see some 36 different species. The park is blanketed mainly by the acacia tree—a dry shrub locally known as "cassie." A large, meadowy headland around Devil's Bridge makes a great spot for a picnic. Arm yourself with directions and a good map before you start out. The main highway ends at Long Bay, but several hiking trails lead to the coastline. Long Bay is also great for snorkeling, if you bring along your gear.

A long climb brings you to the **Megaliths,** at Greencastle Hill. Their origins are disputed: Some say humans built them to worship a sun god and moon goddess. Geologists believe the arrangement is natural—an unusual geological formation known as a volcanic rockfall.

Antigua Rum Distillery, at Rat Island (☎ 268/462-1072), turns out fine Cavalier rum. Check at the tourist office about arranging a tour.

7 Shopping

Most of the shops are clustered on **St. Mary's Street** or **High Street** in St. John's. Some stores are open Monday to Saturday from 8:30am to noon and 1 to 4pm, but this rule varies greatly from place to place—Antiguan shopkeepers are an independent lot. Many of them close at noon on Thursday.

Duty-free items include English woolens and linens. You can also purchase Antiguan goods: local pottery, straw work, rum, mammy bags, floppy foldable hats, shell curios, and hand-printed fabrics.

If you want an island-made bead necklace, just lie on the beach, anywhere, and a "bead lady" will find you.

If you're in St. John's on a Saturday morning, visit the **fruit and vegetable market.** The juicy Antiguan black pineapple alone is worth the trip.

Bargain hunt in St. John's at the **Redcliffe Quay** waterfront on the southern edge of town. Set around tree-shaded, landscaped courtyards, nearly three dozen boutiques set in former warehouses offer specialty items sold nowhere else. Our favorite is **A Thousand Flowers** (☎ 268/462-4264), which sells Indonesian batiks crafted on Antigua into sundresses, knock-'em-dead shirts, sarongs, and rompers. Many of the garments are one-size-fits-all. You can also purchase jewelry here.

The Pottery Shop, also at Redcliffe Quay (☎ 268/462-5503), is the best place for locally made vases, mugs, plates, and more. **The Toy Shop** (☎ 268/462-0141) is a big hit with kids, offering British toys, beach games, island crafts, and more. Additional Redcliffe Quay shops include **Isis** (☎ 268/461-2066) for unique Egyptian jewelry, leather, finely woven cotton, and handcrafts; **The Rum Shoppe** (☎ 268/460-6355) for a full range of the local brew; and **The Goldsmitty** (☎ 268/462-4601) for precious stones and gold designed by Hans Smit and made on the premises. Black opal, imperial topaz, and other exotic gemstones are set in unique, exquisite creations of 14- and 18-karat gold.

Noreen Phillips, Redcliffe Quay (☎ 268/462-3127), is one of the island's major fashion outlets. Cruise-ship passengers beeline here for both casual wear and beaded glitzy dress clothes. **Island Hopper,** Jardine Court, St. Mary's Street (☎ 268/462-2972), specializes in Caribbean-made gifts and clothing, including T-shirts and casual wear, spices, coffees, and handcrafts.

The Scent Shop, Lower High Street (☎ 268/462-0303), is the oldest and best perfume shop on the island, and also stocks an array of crystal. **Shoul's Chief Store,** St. Mary's Street at Market Street (☎ 268/462-1140), is an all-purpose department store selling fabric, appliances, souvenirs (more than 300 kinds), and general merchandise.

Heritage Quay, Antigua's first shopping-and-entertainment complex, features some 40 duty-free shops and an arcade for local artists and craftspeople. Its restaurants and food court offer a range of cuisines and views of St. John's Harbour. Many shops are open all day, Monday through Saturday.

At the foot of St. Mary's Street, stop in at **Benjies Photo Centre** (☎ 268/462-3619), a Kodak distributor and photofinisher, selling film and brand-name cameras. **Fashiondock** (☎ 268/462-9672) is known for its duty-free Gianni Versace jeans and accessories, plus other Italian styles. **Sunseakers** (☎ 268/462-4523) carries the largest collection of duty-free swimwear in the Caribbean. **Colombian Emeralds** (☎ 268/462-3462) is the world's largest retailer of these gemstones. **Little Switzerland** (☎ 268/462-3108) sells the best selection of Swiss watches on Antigua, plus china and crystal. Little Switzerland has opened a perfume shop in Heritage Quay called **La Perfumery by Little Switzerland** (☎ 268/462-2601).

Island Arts, upstairs at Heritage Quay (☎ 268/462-2787), was founded by Nick Maley, a makeup artist who worked on *Star Wars* and *The Empire Strikes Back.* You can purchase his own fine-art reproductions or browse through everything from low-cost prints to works by artists exhibited at the Museum of Modern Art in New York. You can also visit Nick's home and studio at Aiton Place, on Sandy Lane directly behind the Hodges Bay Club, 4 miles from St. John's. The residence is open Monday through Saturday from 10am to 4pm, but it's wise to call first (☎ 268/461-6324).

Other worthwhile specialty stores include **Caribelle Batik,** St. Mary's Street (☎ 268/462-2972), a reasonably priced outlet for the Romney Manor workshop on St. Kitts. The Caribelle label consists of batik and tie-dye items such as beach wraps, scarves, and casual wear for women and men. On the same street, **Specialty Shoppe** (☎ 268/462-1198) sells various gift items, including cosmetics, local hand carvings, and imported china.

Rain Boutique, Lower St. Mary's (☎ 268/462-0118), sells casual clothes, formal wear, and a well-chosen collection of hats, scarves, shoes, jewelry, and handbags.

At Falmouth Harbour, **Seahorse Studios, Art Gallery & Gift Shop** (☎ 268/460-1417) specializes in original art and limited-edition prints, with lots of seascapes, plus the pottery of Nancy Nicholson, considered the island's best craftsperson. Batiks, T-shirts, and much more are also sold.

The best for last: Head for ✪ **Harmony Hall,** in Brown's Bay Mill, near Freetown (☎ 268/460-4120), following the signs along the road to Freetown and Half Moon Bay. This restored 1843 plantation house and sugar mill overlooking Nonsuch Bay is ideal for a luncheon stopover or a shopping expedition. It displays an excellent selection of Caribbean arts and crafts. Lunch is served daily from noon to 4pm, featuring Green Island lobster, flying fish, and other specialties. Sunday is barbecue day.

8 Antigua After Dark

Antigua has some of the best steel bands in the Caribbean. Most nightlife revolves around the hotels. If you want to roam Antigua at night looking for that hot local club, arrange to have a taxi pick you up, so you're not stranded in the wilds somewhere.

The **Royal Casino,** in the Royal Antiguan Hotel, Deep Bay (☎ **268/462-3733**), has American games, including blackjack, baccarat, roulette, craps, and slot machines. It's open daily from 6pm until around 2 or 3am, and there's no cover. Other casino action can be found at the **St. James's Club** at Mamora Bay (☎ **561/994-5640**), which has the island's most flamboyant gambling palace, and at **King's Casino** on Heritage Quay (☎ **268/463-1727**), the only casino in St. John's proper.

Steel bands, limbo dancers, calypso singers, folkloric groups—there's always something happening by night on Antigua. Your hotel can probably tell you where to go on any given night. The following clubs are reliable hot spots:

Ribbit Night Club, in Donovans, Green Bay (☎ **268/462-7996**), is the nicest club on Antigua and attracts mostly locals, ranging from the prime minister to young people who come here to dance. Overlooking Deep Water Harbour and St. John's, it's known for hot music and dancing that lasts 'til all hours. You can hear reggae, some of the best Caribbean steel bands, and international music. There's a cover of EC$10 (U.S.$3.70) on Friday, EC$20 (U.S.$7.40) on Saturday.

Stop in at the **Bay House,** Tradewinds Hotel, Marble Hill (☎ **268/462-1223**), for the island's best mix of singles (both straight and gay). Live reggae is often performed on Wednesday night at **Colombo's** at the Galleon Beach Club in English Harbour (☎ **268/460-1452**).

Live nightly entertainment takes place right on the beach at **Millers by the Sea,** at Runaway Beach (☎ **268/462-9414**). Spilling over onto the sands, its happy hour is the best in town. The **Crazy Horse Saloon,** Redcliffe Quay (☎ **268/462-7936**), is a genuine country-western hangout. Burgers, jerk pork, lobster (prepared 15 different ways), and Caribbean smoked fish round out the menu, along with seafood and grilled steaks. Friday is party night, with a live dance band, and Sunday is devoted to a jazz brunch and karaoke.

At English Harbour, action centers around the **Admiral's Inn** (☎ 268/460-1027), a barefoot-friendly kind of place. In the British style, you can always play a game of darts. Thursday and Saturday nights feature live music, most often a local 14-piece steel band or a 5-piece string and flute combo. Try one of Norman's daiquiris—the island's best—and ask the bartender about the famous guests he's served, from Richard Burton to Prince Charles.

9 Barbuda

Barbuda is part of the independent nation of Antigua and Barbuda. It's the Caribbean's last frontier, even though it is home to two of the region's most expensive and exclusive resorts (see below). Charted by Columbus in 1493, the island is 26 miles north of Antigua. Fifteen miles long by 5 miles wide, it has a population of only 1,200 hardy souls, most of whom live around the unattractive village of Codrington.

Don't come here seeking lush, tropical scenery, as Barbuda is flat, consisting of coral rock. There are no paved roads, few hotels, and only a handful of restaurants.

So what's the attraction? The pink- and white-sand beaches—almost like those of Bermuda. The most famous one stretches for over 17 miles. (We prefer the sands north of Palmetto Point.) Barrier reefs protect the island and keep most of the waters tranquil. Beaches on the southwestern shore stretch uninterrupted for 10 miles; these are the best for swimming. Fronting the Atlantic, the beaches on the island's eastern shore are somewhat rougher, but suitable for beachcombing and shell-collecting. The temperature seldom falls below an average of 75°F.

ESSENTIALS

GETTING THERE   The island is a 15-minute flight from Antigua's V. C. Bird Airport. Barbuda has two airfields: one at Codrington, the other a private facility, the Coco Point Airstrip, which lies some 8 miles from Codrington at the Coco Point Lodge.

To reach Barbuda from Antigua, you can contact **Carib Aviation** (☎ 268/ 462-0701), which operates two daily flights from Antigua to Barbuda's Codrington Airport. One to three persons rent the plane for $265; three to eight persons fly for $330, dividing the cost among them.

GETTING AROUND   Many locals rent small four-wheel-drive Suzukis, which are the best way to get around the island. They meet incoming flights at Codrington Airport, and prices are negotiable. You'll need an Antiguan driver's license (see "Getting Around," in the Antigua section of this chapter) if you plan to drive.

WHERE TO STAY & DINE

✪ **K-Club.** Barbuda, Antigua, W.I. ☎ **268/460-0304.** Fax 268/460-0305. 47 units. A/C MINIBAR TEL. Winter $700–$1,200 cottage for two; $1,700 suite; from $2,800 villa. Off-season $750–$900 cottage for two; $1,300 suite; from $2,100 villa. Rates include all meals. AE, DC, MC, V. Closed Sept–Nov 15. No children under 12.

The most interesting, and superexpensive, hotel to open in the Caribbean in recent years, the beachfront K-Club brings a chic Italian panache to one of the most far-flung backwaters of the Antilles. The resort opened in 1990 when a planeload of glitterati, spearheaded by Giorgio Armani, headed for Barbuda en masse. A 15-minute taxi ride from the airport, the K-Club is the creative statement of Italy's Krizia Mariuccia

Airport ✈ Beach ☚ Reef ||||

Goat Point

Atlantic Ocean

Cobb Cove

Cedar Tree
Point

Hog Point

**Wa' Omoni
Beach Park**

Two Foot Bay

Codrington Lagoon

Low Bay

○ Codrington
✈

■ **Martello Tower**

*Pelican
Bay*

Palmetto
Point

■ **K-Club**

Coco Point ☚

Caribbean Sea

*Gravener
Bay*

*Spanish
Point*

0   3 Miles
0   3 Kilometers

2-0191

Mandelli, whose sports and evening-wear empire has grossed a spectacular fortune. It's set on more than 200 acres, adjacent to the island's only other major hotel. Conceived by Italian architect Gianni Gamondi, the roof of the cottages and main clubhouse are supported by a forest of white columns. Accommodations come in a huge range of styles and shapes; a stylish insouciance predominates throughout. The furnishings include Hamptons-style wicker and sumptuous beds. Bathrooms have two sinks, a bidet and adjacent shower, a hair dryer, a basket of deluxe toiletries, and a set of fluffy towels. Rooms also have a private wall safe and plenty of space for luggage.

Dining: The all-inclusive rates provide for all meals (but no drinks or wine). The cuisine is Mediterranean, with an emphasis on Italian specialties and fresh pasta. Chef Jeremy O'Connor passionately believes in fresh ingredients, and his food not only is the finest on Barbuda but also tops anything on Antigua. Try his sliced crayfish tails or his grilled spiny lobster and you'll know why he pleases the palates of the most demanding Italians who check into this pocket of posh.

Amenities: Two tennis courts, seawater swimming pool, waterskiing, snorkeling, Sunfish sailing, windsurfing, deep-sea fishing. Transportation from Codrington Airport.

EXPLORING THE ISLAND

Hunters, anglers, and beachcombers gravitate here to see fallow deer, guinea fowl, pigeons, and wild pigs. You can also negotiate with small-boat owners to fish for bonefish and tarpon.

Day visitors usually head for **Wa'Omoni Beach Park,** to visit the frigate bird sanctuary, snorkel for lobster, and eat barbecue. A most impressive sight, the frigate bird sanctuary is one of the world's largest. Visitors can see the birds, *Fregata magnificens,* sitting on their eggs in the mangrove bushes, which stretch for miles in a long lagoon accessible only by small motorboat. At various hotels and resorts on Antigua, you can arrange tours to the sanctuary. The island attracts about 150 other species of birds, including pelicans, herons, and tropical mockingbirds.

While you're here, look into the **"Dividing Wall,"** which once separated the imperial Codrington family from the African islanders. Also visit the **Martello Tower,** which predates the known history of the island. Purportedly the Spanish erected it before the British occupied the island. Several tours explore interesting **underground caves** on the Barbuda. Stamp collectors might want to stop in at the **Philatelic Bureau** in Codrington.

Aruba 5

Aruba has a growing number of fans, from honeymooners and sun worshippers to snorkelers, sailors, and weekend gamblers. When you lie back along the 7-mile stretch of white-sand beach, you'll enjoy an average 82°F daytime temperature, trade winds, and very low humidity. Moreover, you won't be harassed by peddlers on the beach, you'll find it relatively safe, and you won't feel racial tensions.

Aruba stands outside the hurricane path. Its coastline on the leeward side is smooth and serene, with white-sand beaches; but on the eastern coast, the windward Atlantic side, it looks rugged and wild. Dry and sunny almost year-round, Aruba has clean, exhilarating air, like in the desert of Palm Springs, California. Forget lush vegetation here, as Aruba receives only 17 inches of rainfall annually.

Its own Palm Beach, one of the best in the world, draws droves of tourists, as do its glittering casinos. Aruba is for vacationers who think that sun-drenched flesh is best complemented by an elegant evening gown.

Though it is still a Dutch protectorate, Aruba became a nation unto itself in 1986. With more than a dozen resort hotels populating its once-uninhabited beaches, it is now one of the Caribbean's most popular destinations. A recent moratorium on hotel construction, however, has halted the building of newer resorts—so for now, Aruba remains safe from rampant overdevelopment.

1 Essentials

VISITOR INFORMATION

Before you leave home, contact the **Aruba Tourism Authority** at the following locations: 1000 Harbor Blvd., **Weehawken, NJ** (☎ 201/330-0800; fax 201/330-8757; E-mail: newjersey@toaruba.com); One Financial Plaza, Suite 136, **Fort Lauderdale, FL** 33394 (☎ 954/767-6477; fax 954/767-0432; E-mail: ata.florida@toaruba.com); 199 14th St., N.E., Suite 2008, **Atlanta, GA** 39309 (☎ 404/892-7822; fax 404/873-2193; E-mail: ata.atlanta@toaruba.com); 401 Wilmette Ave., **Westmont, IL** 60559 (☎ 603/663-1363; fax 630/663-1362; E-mail: ata.chicago@toaruba.com); 1207 North Freeway, Suite 138, **Houston, TX** 77060 (☎ 281/872-7822; fax 281/872-7872; E-mail: ata.houston@toaruba.com); 86 Bloor St. W., Suite 204, **Toronto, Canada** M5S 1M5 (☎ 416/975-1950; fax 416/975-1947; E-mail: ata.canada@toaruba.com).

Information is on the Web at **www.aruba.com**.

Once on the island, for information go to the **Aruba Tourism Authority** at L. G. Smith Blvd. 172, Oranjestad (☎ **297/8-23777**).

GETTING THERE

Before you book your airline tickets, read the section on "Package Deals" in chapter 2—it could save you a bundle! Even if you don't book a package, see that chapter's tips on finding the best airfare.

On **American Airlines** (☎ **800/433-7300**; www.aa.com), Aruba–bound passengers can catch a daily nonstop 4½-hour flight from New York's JFK airport. American also offers daily nonstop flights from Miami and San Juan, Puerto Rico. American offers lots of great-value packages to Aruba, including a selection of several resorts. Ask for their tour department, or talk to your travel agent.

ALM (☎ **800/327-7230**; www.alm-airlines.com) has good connections into Aruba from certain parts of the United States. Direct flights depart from Atlanta on Thursday and Sunday. Daily flights from Miami stop first in Curacao.

Tiny **Air Aruba** (☎ **800/88-ARUBA**; www.interknowledge.com/air-aruba), the country's national carrier, boasts several flights weekly. Daily flights depart from both Newark and Miami: one flight per day from Monday to Friday, two flights per day on weekends. From Tampa, one flight per day departs from Thursday to Sunday; and from Baltimore, one flight departs per day from Friday to Monday.

Continental Airlines (☎ **800/231-0856**; www.flycontinental.com) also flies to Aruba from Houston, with nonstop service on Saturday and Wednesday.

Air Canada (☎ **800/268-7240** in Canada, or 800/776-3000 in the U.S.; www.aircanada.ca) has good connections from Toronto and Québec to Miami. Once in Miami, Canadians and other passengers can fly Air Aruba to the island.

GETTING AROUND

BY RENTAL CAR   It's easy to rent a car in Aruba. Excellent roads connect major tourist attractions, and all the major rental companies accept valid U.S. or Canadian driver's licenses. The three major U.S. car-rental companies maintain offices on Aruba at the airport and at major hotels. No taxes are imposed on car rentals on Aruba, but insurance can be tricky. Even when you purchase a collision-damage waiver, you are still responsible for the first $300 to $500 worth of damage. (Avis doesn't even offer this waiver. In the event of an accident, you would be liable for up to the full value of damage to your car unless you have private insurance.) Rental rates range between $50 and $70 per day.

Try **Budget Rent-a-Car,** at Divi Aruba Beach Resort, L. G. Smith Blvd. 93 (☎ **800/472-3325** in the U.S., or 297/8-24185); **Hertz,** L. G. Smith Blvd. 142 (☎ **800/654-3001** in the U.S., or 297/8-24545), and **Avis,** Kolibristraat 14 (☎ **800/331-1212** in the U.S., or 297/8-25496). Budget requires that renters be at least 25; Avis, 23; and Hertz, 21.

For a better deal, consider **Hedwina Car Rental,** Bubali 93A (☎ **297/8-76442,** or 297/8-30880 at the airport). If you rent for a week, you sometimes pay for only 5 days. Also consider **Thrifty Car Rental,** Balashi 65 (☎ **297/8-55300,** or 297/

Carnival

Many visitors come here for the annual pre-Lenten Carnival, a monthlong festival with events day and night. With music, dancing, parades, costumes, and "jump-ups" (Caribbean hoedowns), Carnival is the highlight of Aruba's winter season.

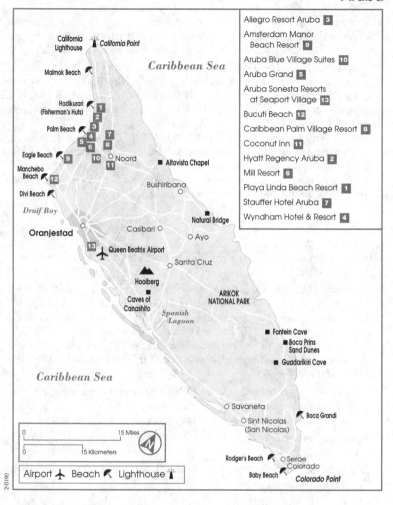

Allegro Resort Aruba **3**
Amsterdam Manor Beach Resort **9**
Aruba Blue Village Suites **10**
Aruba Grand **5**
Aruba Sonesta Resorts at Seaport Village **13**
Bucuti Beach **12**
Caribbean Palm Village Resort **8**
Coconut Inn **11**
Hyatt Regency Aruba **2**
Mill Resort **6**
Playa Linda Beach Resort **1**
Stauffer Hotel Aruba **7**
Wyndham Hotel & Resort **4**

California Lighthouse · California Point
Malmok Beach
Caribbean Sea
Hadikurari (Fisherman's Huts) **1**
Palm Beach **3** **4** **7** **8**
5 **6**
Eagle Beach **9** **10** ○ Noord **11**
Manchebo Beach **12**
Divi Beach
Druif Bay
Oranjestad
13 · Queen Beatrix Airport
■ Altovista Chapel
Bushiribana ○
Natural Bridge ■
Casibari ○
○ Ayo
○ Santa Cruz
▲▲ Hooiberg
■ Caves of Canashito
Spanish Lagoon
ARIKOK NATIONAL PARK
■ Fontein Cave
■ Boca Prins Sand Dunes
■ Guadarikiri Cave
Caribbean Sea
○ Savaneta
○ Sint Nicolas (San Nicolas)
Boca Grandi
Rodger's Beach ○ Seroe Colorado
Baby Beach · *Colorado Point*

0 ————— 15 Miles
0 ————— 15 Kilometers
Airport ✈ Beach ◤ Lighthouse 🌟

8-35335 at the airport), which offers rentals starting from $42 per day. You can also rent jeeps starting from $65 per day.

BY BUS Aruba has excellent bus service, with regular daily service from 6am to midnight. Round-trip fare between the beach hotels and Oranjestad is $2. Bus schedules are available at the Arubus Office at the central bus station on Zoutmanstraat. Your hotel reception desk will know when the buses pass by. Try to have the exact change. For bus schedules and information, call the **Arubus Co.** (☎ **297/8-27089**).

BY TAXI Taxis are unmetered but rates are fixed, so tell the driver your destination and ask the fare before you get in. The main office is on Sands Street between the bowling center and Taco Bell. A dispatch office is located at the Bosabao (☎ **297/ 8-22116**). A ride from the airport to most of the hotels, including those at Palm Beach, costs about $16 to $18 per car, with a four-passenger maximum. Some locals don't tip, but we suggest you do, especially if the driver has helped you with luggage. On some parts of the island, it's next to impossible to locate a taxi. If you're going to a remote location, it's a good idea to ask the driver to return for you at a certain time.

The English-speaking drivers are usually willing tour guides. Most seem well informed and eager to share their knowledge with you. A 1-hour tour (you don't need much more than that) costs from $30 for a maximum of four passengers.

BY MOTORCYCLE & MOPED   Since Aruba's roads are good, and the terrain is flat, many visitors like to rent mopeds and motorcycles. They're available at **George's Scooter Rental,** L. G. Smith Blvd. 136 (☎ **297/8-25975**), and **Nelson Motorcycle Rental,** Gasparito 10A, Noord (☎ **297/8-66801**). Scooters rent for $25 per day and motorcycles for $49 to $84.

Melcor Cycle Rental, Bubali 106B (☎ **297/8-75203**), in front of the Adventure Golf Club, rents scooters for $32 per day. You can also rent dirt bikes and street bikes, beginning at $45 per day. These are cash prices; a 4% handling charge is assessed if you use a credit or charge card. You can also find rentals at **Semver Cycle Rental,** Noord 22 (☎ **297/8-66851**), where bikes begin at $25 per day.

Fast Facts: Aruba

Banking Hours   Banks are open Monday to Friday from 8am to noon and 1:30 to 3:45pm.

Currency   The currency is the Aruba florin (AFl), which is divided into 100 cents. Silver coins are in denominations of 5¢, 10¢, 25¢, and 50¢ and 1 and 2½ florins. The 50-cent piece, the square *yotin,* is Aruba's best-known coin. The current exchange rate is 1.77 AFl to $1 U.S. (1 AFl is worth about 56¢). U.S. dollars, traveler's checks, and major credit and charge cards are widely accepted throughout the island. *Unless otherwise stated, prices are quoted in U.S. dollars in this chapter.*

Documents   To enter Aruba, U.S. and Canadian citizens and British subjects may submit a valid passport or a birth certificate along with photo ID. We always recommend carrying your passport whenever you visit a foreign country.

Electricity   The electricity is 110 volts AC, 60 cycles, the same as in the United States.

Emergencies   For the police, dial ☎ **11100.** For a medical emergency, dial ☎ **74300.** For the fire department, call ☎ **115.**

Hospital   To receive medical care, go to the **Horacio Oduber Hospital** on L. G. Smith Boulevard (☎ **297/8-74300;** also the number to call in case of a medical emergency). This modern building near Eagle Beach has excellent medical facilities. Hotels also have medical doctors on call, and there are good dental facilities as well (appointments can be made through your hotel).

Language   The official language is Dutch, but nearly everybody speaks English. Spanish is also widely spoken.

Safety   Aruba is one of the Caribbean's safer destinations, in spite of its numerous hotels and casinos. Pickpockets and purse-snatchers are around, of course, but they're rare. Still, it's wise to guard your valuables. Never leave them unattended on the beach or even in a locked car.

Taxes & Service Charges   The government of Aruba imposes a 6% room tax and a $20 airport departure tax. Your hotel will add a 15% to 20% service charge for room, food, and beverages.

Telephone   To call Aruba from the United States, dial **011** (the international access code), then **297** (the country code for Aruba), then **8** (the area code) and the five-digit local number. Once you're in Aruba, dial only the five-digit local number for locations on the island.

Time   Aruba is on Atlantic standard time year-round, so most of the year Aruba is one hour ahead of eastern standard time (when it's 10am on Aruba, it's 9am in New York). When daylight saving time is in effect in the United States, clocks in New York and Aruba show the same time.

Water   The water, which comes from the world's second-largest desalination plant, is pure.

2 Where to Stay

Most of Aruba's hotels are bustling, self-contained resorts. There's a tremendous dearth of family or budget hotels. Guest houses are also few and tend to fill up early in winter with faithful return visitors.

In season, it's imperative to make reservations well in advance; don't ever arrive expecting to find a room on the spot. You must give Immigration the address where you'll be staying when you arrive.

Don't forget to ask if the 6.66% room tax and service charge are included in the rates quoted when you make your reservation.

Before you try to book your hotel on your own, read the section on "Package Deals" in chapter 2. Lots of the big resorts here are frequently featured in packages, which can bring their rates down dramatically.

VERY EXPENSIVE

Allegro Resort Aruba. L. G. Smith Blvd., Oranjestad, Aruba. ☎ **800/858-2258** in the U.S., or 297/8-64500. Fax 297/8-63191. www.arubatourism.com/stay/h-allegro.html. E-mail: allegro@setarnet.aw. 419 units. A/C MINIBAR TV TEL. Winter $480–$530 double; $610–$690 suite. Off-season $390–$440 double; $520–$600 suite. Rates are all-inclusive and based on double occupancy. AE, DC, MC, V.

Rising high above Palm Beach, this hotel was originally built in the 1970s by American Airlines as the Americana. In 1998, after a $25-million renovation, it was reconfigured as the Aruba branch of a 30-member chain of resorts based in the Dominican Republic. Today, the ambience is that of an ongoing, all-inclusive house party. Drinks flow liberally from half a dozen bars, and guests have direct access to one of the island's prime beachfronts. This hotel is not quite as luxurious as some of its competitors in this price range, but the service is exceptionally good.

The hotel was designed as a pair of nine-story interconnected towers in a landscaped garden with a lagoon-shaped swimming pool in the center. Bedrooms have carpeting, rattan furniture, comfortable beds, hair dryers, and small balconies overlooking the beach. Well-managed, the resort attracts families, repeat guests, and international tour groups.

Dining/Diversions: The Caruso is the establishment's most upscale and formal restaurant, and requires advance reservations. More casual choices include The Trade Winds, and the Brazilian Garden Restaurant, which is set on a verdant second-floor veranda that overlooks the pool's splashing fountains. A casino and a half-dozen bars are scattered strategically around the property.

Amenities: Lagoon-shaped pool, two tennis courts, exercise room, beauty salon, massage, laundry, baby-sitting, drugstore, jeweler, deli. Room service is available only for continental breakfast. Beach chairs and snorkeling equipment are provided free. A PADI-registered dive facility and a sailboat provider operate from a cabin on the beach, though these activities are not part of the all-inclusive price.

Aruba Grand. J. E. Irausquin Blvd. 79, Oranjestad, Aruba. ☎ **800/345-2782** in the U.S. and Canada, or 297/8-63900. Fax 297/8-61-941. www.arubagrand.com. E-mail: resv@aruba-grand.com. 170 units. A/C MINIBAR TV TEL. Winter $445 double; $640–$1,400 suite. Off-season $125–$205 double; $450–$850 suite. AE, DC, DISC, MC, V.

This eight-story, pale-yellow concrete tower lies in a palm grove 5 miles south of the commercial center of Oranjestad. It recently underwent an $11-million renovation and reopened with many new amenities and special features. The medium-sized, summery accommodations have white walls, tropical-print fabrics, refrigerators, and comfortable beds. Bathrooms are medium-sized, with good towels and hair dryers. Full-time gardeners tend the beautiful grounds, which include a bougainvillea-draped garden near the beach.

Dining/Diversions: You can choose among four restaurants. A poolside grill and deli are the least formal option. The Fantail Bistro offers light, savory cuisine in the style of a Caribbean bistro. The Sea Watch restaurant is the most formal and expensive, with Caribbean and international food. A lobby lounge has an ornate carved wood bar and a baby grand piano.

Amenities: Olympic-sized lap pool set into landscaped gardens; a small-scale casino; and an activities director who arranges water sports and excursions.

Aruba Sonesta Resorts at Seaport Village. L. G. Smith Blvd. 9, Oranjestad, Aruba. ☎ **800/SONESTA** in the U.S. and Canada, or 297/8-36000. Fax 297/8-25317. www.arubasonesta.com. 550 units in 2 resorts. A/C MINIBAR TV TEL. Winter $300–$400 double; $400–$480 suite; $300–$400 one-bedroom suite. Off-season $205–$305 double; $305–$385 suite; $205–$305 one-bedroom suite. Extra person $30. Children 11 and under stay free in parents' room. AE, DC, DISC, MC, V.

This place is two resorts in one, located in the Seaport Village Complex (the island's largest shopping and entertainment facility). Next to two marinas and a recreational park, it's the only major resort at Oranjestad Harbor and the only one on Aruba that boasts a private island and six beaches. The first resort, Aruba Sonesta Resort & Casino (with 300 units), is adjacent to the Seaport Mall with an outdoor pool and terrace. The Aruba Sonesta Suites & Casino (with 250 one-bedroom suites) is a time-share resort that caters to yachties; rooms are rented out when time-share owners are not present. Each of the one-bedroom suites opens onto a beach. Units have kitchenettes, blond rattan furniture with floral pastel prints, and small balconies, plush carpeting, private safes, and either a king- or two queen-size beds with firm mattresses. Bathrooms have deluxe toiletries, a hair dryer, fluffy towels, and a combination tub and shower.

Dining/Diversions: The top restaurant, L'Escale, is reviewed below (see "Where to Dine"). The restaurant is connected to Aruba's only 24-hour casino. The Crystal Lounge presents local entertainment.

Amenities: Each resort has a pool, a casino, tennis courts, a gym on a 40-acre off-shore island, water sports, room service, laundry, baby-sitting, and a year-round program of counselor-supervised activities for children 5 to 12.

✪ **Hyatt Regency Aruba.** J. E. Irausquin Blvd. 85, Palm Beach, Aruba. ☎ **800/233-1234** in the U.S. and Canada, or 297/8-61234. Fax 297/8-61682. E-mail: Sd.hyattaruba@setarnet.av. 354 units. A/C MINIBAR TV TEL. Winter $390–$495 double; from $650 suite. Off-season $205–$335 double; from $495 suite. MAP (breakfast and dinner) $65 per person extra. AE, CB, DC, DISC, MC, V.

The most glamorous resort on Aruba lies on 12 landscaped beachfront acres about 2 miles north of Oranjestad. Built in the early 1990s for over $57 million, it offers a series of public rooms reminiscent of a large-scale Latin American hacienda, with soaring ceilings and an art deco–inspired facade. Its gardens, Aruba's finest, are dotted with waterfalls, reflecting pools, exotic birds, and stonework. The bedrooms are luxurious, with many amenities, including original artworks commissioned from around the Americas. Rooms are generous, with sitting areas; many guests prefer the overhead fans to air-conditioning. Extras include private safes, desk space, king or two double beds (with luxury mattresses), and big bathrooms with combination tubs and showers, tile floors, fluffy towels, and hair dryers. Guests in the hotel's 29 Regency Club rooms enjoy a private concierge, upgraded linens, and other amenities.

Dining/Diversions: Choose among several restaurants and lounges, including the indoor/outdoor Ruinas del Mar restaurant. Fashioned out of native island stone, it's positioned on the edge of the lagoon and offers scenic ocean views; the cuisine is Mediterranean. For more casual dining, the beachfront Palms Restaurant presents an open-air Caribbean-style seafood grill. Other dining choices include the Olé Restaurant, serving Spanish tapas with singing waiters and other live entertainment, and Café Piccolo, an Italian-style cafe and bistro. The Casino Copacabana with its entertainment and gaming tables evokes the Côte d'Azur.

Amenities: A $2.5-million multilevel pool complex and lagoon (with waterfalls, tropical gardens, and slides), health and fitness facilities (including exercise room, saunas, massage, steam rooms, outdoor whirlpool, and aerobics sundeck), two tennis courts (lit at night), 24-hour room service, laundry, massages, baby-sitting. Scuba diving can be arranged. Supervised activities and special programs for children 3 to 12 on weekends and holidays in summer.

Wyndham Hotel & Resort. J. E. Irausquin Blvd. 77, Palm Beach, Aruba. ☎ **800/ WYNDHAM** or 297/8-64466. Fax 297/8-863403. www.arubatourism.com/stay/ h-wyndham.html. 24 units. A/C MINIBAR TV TEL. Winter $315–$375 double; from $405 suite. Off-season $185–$265 double; from $310 suite. AE, DC, MC, V.

This 14-story "skyscraper" rises beside a white-sand beach in a cluster of other high-rise hotels north of Oranjestad. It recently underwent a renovation worth millions, and the lobby is now sheathed in layers of stucco tinted in desert-inspired colors of terra-cotta and cerulean blue. Each of the bedrooms has a balcony, an ocean view, comfortable furniture, fresh draperies, first-rate mattresses, a coffeemaker, and a private safe. Accommodations are available for people with disabilities. Bathrooms are small but well organized, with adequate shelf space, fluffy towels, hair dryers, and combination tubs and showers.

Dining/Diversions: The Casablanca Casino occupies a large room near the lobby. Rick's Cabaret Lounge and the Baci Café serve Italian cuisine. The Pago Pago serves touristy Polynesian cuisine. The Café Royale hosts dinner shows.

Amenities: State-of-the-art health club, water-sports facilities, one tennis court, free-form Olympic-size swimming pool (on three different levels, with waters rippled by waterspouts and fountains), room service (from 7am to 11pm), laundry, baby-sitting, concierge.

EXPENSIVE

Bucuti Beach. Eagle Beach, Aruba. ☎ **800/223-1108,** or 297/8-31100. Fax 297/8-25272. www.bucuti.com. E-mail: bucuti@setaxnet.aw. 63 units. A/C MINIBAR TV TEL. Winter $200– $260 double. Off-season $120–$160 double. Tax and 11% service extra. AE, DC, DISC, MC, V.

At the Bucuti, you get personal service and European charm on one of the Caribbean's best beaches. Each spacious, well-furnished bedroom is on the beach and has two queen-size beds or one king-size bed with good mattresses and a sleeper sofa. The most expensive units have two queen-size beds and an oceanfront balcony or terrace.

Room amenities include coffeemakers, safety-deposit boxes, microwaves, refrigerators, ceiling fans, designer toiletries, fluffy towels, and hair dryers in the roomy bathrooms.

Dining/Diversions: Across from the Alhambra Bazaar and Casino, the hotel operates the Pirates' Nest Restaurant, a replica of a 17th-century Dutch galleon that specializes in good steaks, fresh seafood, and theme nights.

Amenities: Bike rental, pool, health club, business center, self-service Laundromat, car-rental desk, tour desk.

MODERATE

Amsterdam Manor Beach Resort. J. E. Irausquin Blvd., 252 (P.O. Box 1302), Oranjestad, Aruba. ☎ **800/932-6509** in the U.S., or 297/8-71492. Fax 297/8-71463. E-mail: impress525@aol.com. 73 units. A/C TV TEL. Winter $165–$195 double; $235–$255 one-bedroom suite for two; $290–$295 two-bedroom suite for four. Off-season $115–$125 double; $155 one-bedroom suite for two; $260 two-bedroom suite for four. Extra person $20. AE, DC, MC, V.

Inspired by the canal-front row houses in Amsterdam, this hotel sports one of the most interesting facades on the island. In an arid landscape across the street from Eagle Beach, it has a series of inner courtyards, a swimming pool fed by a pair of splashing waterfalls, and a simple bar and restaurant.

Even the accommodations draw from 19th-century Dutch models, with pine furniture, country-rustic blues, dull reds, and greens. In some cases, high ceilings lead to gable-capped peaks. Both studios and one- or two-bedroom apartments have fully equipped kitchens. This is an especially good choice for families, with baby-sitting, use of washer/dryers, and a children's playground. Units are small but well maintained and inviting, with ceiling fans, balconies or terraces (often with a sea view), white tile floors, and textured walls. Mattresses are frequently replaced as needed. Some of the rather tiny bathrooms lack tubs but have showers.

Caribbean Palm Village Resort. Noord 43-E, Aruba. ☎ **800/992-2015** in the U.S., or 297/8-62700. Fax 297/8-62380. 228 units. A/C TV TEL. Winter $160–$170 double; $215–$225 one-bedroom suite; $280–$305 two-bedroom suite. Off-season $90–$100 double; $115–$125 one-bedroom suite; $155–$165 two-bedroom suite. Service and tax extra. AE, DC, DISC, MC, V.

The place doesn't have a beachfront, one of its major drawbacks. It has pools for all ages, however, and public beaches are within a minute's drive. It's located in the village of Noord in the Palm Beach district, half a mile from the beach and 7 miles from the airport. It's the site of Aruba's only five-star Italian restaurant, Valentino's (see "Where to Dine," below). In the Spanish style, the resort offers handsomely decorated and streamlined bedrooms, plus one- and two-bedroom suites in a tropical garden setting. Suites come with full kitchen facilities. Every room has air-conditioning and ceiling fans, queen- or king-size beds with good mattresses, a pull-out sofa, and a private safe. Roomy bathrooms have combination tubs and showers and adequate shelf space.

The Mill Resort. L. G. Smith Blvd. 330, Palm Beach, Aruba. ☎ **297/8-67700.** Fax 297/8-67271. 200 units. A/C TV TEL. Winter $160–$170 double with fridge; $195–$205 minisuite with kitchenette for two. Off-season $90–$100 double with fridge; $107–$117 studio or minisuite with kitchenette for two. AE, DC, MC, V.

This complex of two-story concrete buildings with red roofs is set in an arid, rather dusty location inland from the beach. It's adjacent to a large, modern re-creation of a Dutch windmill, a kitschy Aruban landmark. Units ring a large swimming pool, and Eagle Beach (which is used by such megahotels as the Hilton) lies across the highway, a 7-minute trek away. The room decor is tropical, with white rattan furniture and carpeting or white floor tiles; many units have king-size beds and Jacuzzi-style tubs.

This hotel is best for self-motivated visitors who don't mind venturing out to find their own dining and fun. You'll find very limited bar and restaurant service here, but since most units have kitchenettes (or at least a refrigerator), many guests cook in. There's a launderette, a sauna, a fitness center, an exercise room, a beauty salon, and massage services.

Playa Linda Beach Resort. J. E. Irausquin Blvd. 87, Palm Beach (P.O. Box 1010, Oranjestad), Aruba. ☎ **297/8-61000.** Fax 297/8-63479. E-mail: plbr@setarnet.aw. 194 units. A/C TV TEL. Winter $250 studio for 1–4; $350 one-bedroom suite; $700 two-bedroom suite. Off-season $170 studio for 1–4; $220 one-bedroom suite; $420 two-bedroom suite. Rates include continental breakfast. Extra person $30. AE, DC, V.

Designed in an M-shape of receding balconies, this salmon-colored time-share complex sits amid tropical foliage on a desirable stretch of white-sand beachfront, 6 miles northwest of the airport. The units offer private verandas and foldaway sofa beds suitable for children. Accommodations are generally roomy, with attractive tropical decor, rattan furniture, ceiling fans, and fully equipped kitchens. The mattresses are firm and replaced as often as needed. Baths have toiletries, fluffy towels, and adequate shelf space.

Amenities and facilities at Playa Linda include a large, lagoon-shaped pool, a separate children's pool, outdoor whirlpool baths, tennis courts, access to an 18-hole professional golf course, and a shopping arcade featuring a beauty parlor, perfumery, and souvenir and gift shop. The Linda Vista Restaurant serves Italian food. Laundry and baby-sitting are available.

INEXPENSIVE

Aruba Blue Village Suites. Cunucu Abao 37, Aruba. ☎ **297/8-78618.** Fax 297/8-70081. 56 units. Winter $100 junior suite; $111 one-bedroom suite; $140 two-bedroom suite. Off-season, $70 junior suite; $88 one-bedroom suite; $105 two-bedroom suite. AE, MC, V.

If you can forgo a beachfront location, you'll find one of Aruba's best deals at this single-story complex in a residential area removed from the hotel strip. Off-season, it's a sweet bargain—from $16 per person a night if four people share a junior suite or six people share a two-bedroom suite. The typical resort-style accommodations are plain but comfortable. Features include cable TV, a safety-deposit box, a separate bath with shower, and a fully equipped kitchenette. Twenty-six suites come with pull-out sofas. You're 5 minutes from the beach (free bus service will haul you there) and close to casinos and nightlife. Guests who stay on the property can enjoy two spacious pools, two large sun terraces, table tennis and other indoor and outdoor games, a children's playground, and poolside bar and barbecue facilities.

Coconut Inn. Noord 31, Aruba. ☎ **297/8-66288.** Fax 297/8-65433. 40 units. A/C TV TEL. Winter $75 studio for 2; $90 double or one-bedroom suite for 2. Off-season $55 studio for two; $70 double or one-bedroom suite for two. Rates include breakfast. Extra person $20 in winter, $15 in off-season. MC, V.

Set inland from the sea, within a 7-minute walk from the village of Noord, this affordable hotel was built in five yellow-and-white sections between 1975 and 1996. Its rates are a steal. Though you won't be near the beach, the location is convenient to supermarkets and a public bus stop. The conventional rooms and one-bedroom suites contain almost the same amount of floor space; the studios are relatively cramped. All motel-style accommodations have a balcony or patio and either a kitchenette or a microwave and refrigerator. There's no maid service on Sunday. A swimming pool, restaurant, and bar are on the premises.

⊙ **Stauffer Hotel Aruba.** J. E. Irausquin Blvd. 370, Aruba. ☎ **297/8-60855.** Fax 297/8-60856. 101 rms. A/C TV. Winter $120 double; off-season $100 double. Extra person $10. Children 11 and under stay free in parents' room. AE, DC, DISC, MC, V.

Although the accommodations are rather standard, the Stauffer (not to be confused with Stouffer) is a very good buy on high-priced Aruba. This plain, square, three-story building is surrounded by high-rise hotels and a variety of restaurants. A bus stops in front, and the beach is across the street (the hotel provides free chairs and beach towels). The bedrooms are large, with two double beds, tables, and phones, but no balconies. Although the hotel opened only in the mid-1990s, it has become well known and is already drawing many repeat visitors (book early!). Services and facilities, however, are very limited; there's no restaurant, bar, or pool.

3 Where to Dine

Sometimes—at least on off-season package deals—visitors on the MAP plan (breakfast and dinner) are allowed to dine around on an exchange plan with other hotels.

IN ORANJESTAD
EXPENSIVE

Boonoonoonoos. Wilhelminastraat 18. ☎ **297/8-31888.** Reservations recommended for dinner in winter. Main courses $15.75–$33.75. AE, DC, MC, V. Mon–Sat 11:30am–10:30pm, Sun 4–10:30pm. CARIBBEAN/INTERNATIONAL.

Named after the legendary Jamaican beach parties, this restaurant in an old-fashioned Aruban house on the capital's main shopping street celebrates the widely divergent traditions of Caribbean cuisine. The decor is a confectionary mix of blues, greens, and pinks, rows of hard-bottomed benches line the bar, and waiters wear carnival-colored shirts.

You can go on a culinary tour of the Caribbean by wandering across the menu. Try an appetizer known as *ajaka*, an Aruban chicken dish wrapped in banana leaves. The local callaloo soup and homemade fish soup are also a good way to start. The most popular main dish is Aruban: *keshi yena*, Aruban chicken casserole. You can also order Jamaican jerk ribs, based on a 300-year-old recipe. A small section of the menu is devoted to French cuisine, including filet mignon and Dover sole meunière. This place continues to draw mixed reactions from readers, everything from raves to attacks. Slow service is one of the major complaints. Let us know what you think.

⊙ **Chez Mathilde.** Havenstraat 23. ☎ **297/8-34968.** Reservations recommended. Main courses $22–$36. AE, DC, MC, V. Mon–Sat 11:30am–2:30pm; daily 6–11pm. FRENCH.

Oranjestad's restaurant français is expensive, but most satisfied customers agree that it's worth the price. The chef's bouillabaisse contains over a dozen different sea creatures. We also recommend rack of lamb chops with fine French herbs, juicy veal sirloin cooked in a raspberry liqueur and lime sauce and topped with melted Brie, and fillet of red snapper prepared with a lightly peppered crust and lemon dressing. You get not only distinguished food and service but an elegant setting as well. In this carefully preserved 19th-century building, dining rooms are intimate, tables are beautifully set, and the decor is restrained but romantic. Live piano music enhances the total experience. The restaurant is near the Sonesta hotel complex, a 5-minute drive north of the airport.

Gasparito. Gasparito 3. ☎ **297/8-67144.** Reservations recommended. Main courses $18.50–$37.50. AE, DISC, MC, V. Mon–Sat 5–11pm. ARUBAN/INTERNATIONAL.

This bright, upbeat restaurant is set in a traditional Aruban-style house, with yellow walls and local artwork. The atmosphere is lively, and the food varied. With zest, flair, and consummate skill, the chef uses only top-quality ingredients. Diners can enjoy baked chicken stuffed with a peach, filet mignon served with either sautéed mushroom or black-pepper sauce, or a variety of *keshi yena* (Dutch cheese stuffed with a choice of beef, chicken, or seafood). The menu also features an array of fresh seafood, including lobster served with a garlic-butter sauce or sautéed with onions, green peppers, tomatoes, and a multitude of spices.

La Trattoria "El Faro Blanco." At the California Lighthouse, North Aruba. ☎ **297/8-60787.** Reservations required. Main courses $16–$35. AE, DISC, MC, V. Mon–Sat 11am–3pm and 6–11pm. ITALIAN.

Charming and authentically Italian, this ochre, tile-roofed restaurant, built in 1914, was originally the local lighthouse keeper's home. It's now managed by the same people who maintain the nearby golf course. The staff is mostly European, and the head chef studied in Italy. Views sweep out over the sea, the island's northern coastline, and the island's largest golf course. The menu covers a full range of Italian cuisine, with a heavy dose of pungent Neapolitan specialties. Examples include heaping platters of fish and vegetable antipasti; linguine with shrimp, octopus, scallops, clams, and tomatoes; red snapper cooked in a potato crust with olive oil and rosemary; and veal shank (osso buco) served with parmesan-laced risotto Milanese. The desserts are excellent; we recommend tiramisu or pears poached in red wine served with ice cream. The bar, a favorite stopover for golfers, is open Monday to Saturday from 11am to 11pm.

✪ **L'Escale.** In the Aruba Sonesta Resort & Casino at Seaport Village, L. G. Smith Blvd. 82. ☎ **297/8-36000.** Reservations recommended in winter. Main courses $22–$49. AE, DC, DISC, MC, V. Daily 6:30–11pm; Sat–Sun brunch 10am–2pm. CARIBBEAN/INTERNATIONAL.

Some savvy locals prefer this to Chez Mathilde (see above) and claim that l'Escale is Aruba's best restaurant. We think it's a toss-up between the two. It offers direct access to Oranjestad's bustling Crystal Casino, but remains calm, elegant, and peaceful, thanks to a raised bar area that separates it from the action nearby. Designed in a French Empire style, it offers panoramic views of the harbor, formal service, and well-prepared cuisine. The service here is formal, although formal attire is not required. The Hungarian string quartet plays every night except Monday.

The meals rely on imported foodstuffs, but they are perfectly cooked. The chefs skillfully handle only the best ingredients. Try *vol-au-vent* chicken with island spices served in puff pastry or an award-winning lobster bisque. A 5-ounce portion of tenderloin steak transforms the seafood pasta into the Caribbean's most elegant surf-and-turf ("seafood mignon").

MODERATE

Frankie's Prime Grill. In the Royal Plaza Mall, L. G. Smith Blvd. ☎ **297/8-38471.** Reservations recommended. Main courses $14.50–$28.50. AE, DC, DISC, MC, V. Mon–Sat noon–4:30pm; daily 6–10:30pm. STEAKS/SEAFOOD.

Come here for two-fisted portions of steak and seafood—some of it grilled in the churrasco style you might expect on the Argentinian pampas. You can dine either inside, where it's air-conditioned, or on an outdoor terrace with views of potted palms, busy downtown streets, and boats bobbing at anchor in the harbor. A wide selection of pastas includes penne with vodka sauce or a spicy l'arrabiata sauce; there's also filet mignon, barbecued ribs, and a mixed grill with various sausages and cuts of meat. Seafood crêpes, shrimp in garlic sauce, and various preparations of grouper and snapper will please most fish lovers.

Kowloon. Emmastraat 11, Oranjestad. ☎ **297/8-24950.** Reservations recommended. Main courses $17–$20. Set-price rijstaffel (rice table), $35 for 2 diners. AE, DISC, MC, V. Daily 11am–10pm. CHINESE/INDONESIAN.

This elegant Asian restaurant has two red-and-black dining rooms, accented with varnished hardwoods and Chinese lamps, that overlook one of the capital's thoroughfares. Skilled at preparing Hunan, Szechuan, and Shanghai cuisine, chefs here also offer Indonesian staples such as *nasi goreng* and *bami goreng,* made with rice or noodles and tidbits of pork, vegetables, and shrimp. The elaborate *rijstaffel* combines dozens of small curried vegetables in one impressive display, and the house special seafood combines fish, scallops, lobster, shrimp, and Szechuan-style black-bean sauce.

La Dolce Vita. Palm Beach 29. ☎ **297/8-65241.** Reservations recommended, especially in winter. Main courses $11.95–$30.95. AE, DISC, MC, V. Daily 6–11pm. ITALIAN.

La Dolce Vita has long been among the most acclaimed Italian restaurants on Aruba, recognized by the food and wine critics at *Gourmet* magazine. In an arid neighborhood inland from the sea, this rustic restaurant is ringed with a cactus garden. The creative Italian menu includes most of the usual favorites and a scattering of unusual dishes. A meal might include slices of veal served either Parmesan style, cordon bleu style, with marsala sauce, la Florio (with artichokes), or la Bartolucci (with ricotta, spinach, and mozzarella). Snapper comes four ways: simmered with clams and mussels, broiled with lemon or with wine, or stuffed with pulverized shrimp. A stewpot of fish comes with linguine in either red or white clam sauce.

The Waterfront Crabhouse. In the Seaport Market, L. G. Smith Blvd., Oranjestad. ☎ **297/8-35858.** Reservations recommended. Main courses $13.95–$39.95; lunch from $7. AE, MC, V. Daily 11am–11pm. SEAFOOD/STEAK.

This restaurant overlooks a manicured lawn at the most desirable end of a shopping mall in downtown Oranjestad. With painted murals of underwater life, rattan furniture, and dining indoors and outdoors on a garden terrace, it evokes a restaurant on the California coast. Menu items include stuffed clams and fried squid with a marinara sauce and linguine with white or red clam sauce. The chef lists "crabs, crabs, crabs" as his specialty, including garlic crabs, Alaska crab legs, and (in season) soft-shell crabs. Over an open fire, he grills a wide range of fish, including yellowfin tuna and swordfish. He also serves stuffed Maine lobster and Cajun grilled shrimp. All fish are caught by hook-and-line, never from drift nets. The restaurant's steak menu includes a 10-ounce Black Angus filet mignon, as well as a less expensive chopped sirloin smothered in onions.

INEXPENSIVE

Mama's & Papa's. Noord 41C. ☎ **297/8-67913.** Main courses $11–$25. AE, DC, MC, V. Mon–Sat 6–11pm. ARUBAN/SPANISH.

North of Oranjestad, this small place serves Aruban and Spanish specialties and some West Indian dishes. Local favorites include *keshi yena,* a casserole of chicken and cheese, and *kreeft di cay reef,* broiled lobster. Fish comes in a variety of dressings, including Creole sauce and garlic butter. If you're in the mood for West Indian food, try the curried chicken, stewed goat, or conch stew. The cooks here serve the island's best paella. Most nights a guitar player entertains with music from the 1960s.

The Paddock. 13 L. G. Smith Blvd. Oranjestad. ☎ **297/8-32334.** Sandwiches, snacks, and salads $3.70–$5.50; main courses $8.50–$14.50. MC, V. Mon–Thurs 10am–2am, Fri–Sun 10am–3am. INTERNATIONAL.

In the heart of Oranjestad, this cafe and bistro overlooks the harbor, a short walk from virtually every shop in town. Much of the staff is blonde, hip, and European. No one will seem to mind whether you opt for a drink, a cup of tea or coffee, a snack of sliced sausage and Gouda cheese, or a full-fledged meal. The menu offers crab, salmon, shrimp, and tuna sandwiches; salads; pita-bread sandwiches stuffed with sliced beef and an herb sauce with plenty of tang; fresh poached or sautéed fish; and a glazed tenderloin of pork. Happy hours change frequently, but whenever they're offered, drink prices drop and the place is as crowded and animated as anything else on the island.

NEAR PALM BEACH
EXPENSIVE

De Olde Molen (The Old Mill). L. G. Smith Blvd. 330, Palm Beach. ☎ **297/8-62060.** Reservations recommended. Main courses $20–$35. AE, DC, DISC, MC, V. Mon–Sat 6–11pm. INTERNATIONAL.

This landmark structure is just across the street from the Wyndham and within walking distance of a number of other Palm Beach hotels. A gift from the queen of Holland, the windmill housing the restaurant was built in the Netherlands in 1804 and was torn down, shipped to Aruba, and reconstructed piece by piece. Since 1960, it has been a restaurant, albeit mostly for tourists. International and regional cuisine are served, including thick Dutch split-pea soup, Châteaubriand for two, veal cordon bleu, shrimp Provençal, and red snapper arubiano (with a Creole sauce). Although the windmill setting may seem gimmicky, the cuisine is basically noteworthy—although we've found some dishes too heavy for a hot night. Don't come here expecting anything adventurous; everything's tried and true.

The Old Cunucu House. Palm Beach 150. ☎ **297/8-61666.** Reservations recommended. Main courses $16.95–$31.95. AE, DC, MC, V. Mon–Sat 6–10pm. ARUBAN/INTERNATIONAL.

When it was originally constructed as a private house in the 1920s, this was the only building in the neighborhood. Today it retains its original decor of very thick, plaster-coated walls, ultra-simple furniture, and tile floors. Many visitors appreciate a before-dinner drink under a shed-style roof in front, where chairs and tables overlook a well-kept garden studded with desert plants. The restaurant maintains a warm, traditional feeling, and focuses on local and international recipes including fish soup, fried squid, coconut fried shrimp, and broiled swordfish. Several dishes are served with *funchi* (made of cornmeal) and *pan bati* (a local pancake). The skilled chef knows how to embroider a traditional repertoire with first-class ingredients. Mariachi bands provide entertainment every Saturday night.

MODERATE

Chalet Suisse. J. E. Irausquin Blvd. 246. ☎ **297/8-75054.** Reservations recommended. Main courses $14–$25. AE, DC, MC, V. Mon–Sat 6–10pm. SWISS/INTERNATIONAL.

Set beside the highway close to La Cabana Hotel, this alpine-chalet restaurant is the closest replica of an old-fashioned Swiss dining room in the entire Caribbean. In deliberate contrast to the arid scrublands that surround it, the restaurant is an air-conditioned refuge of thick plaster walls, pinewood panels, and a sense of *gemütlichkeit* (well-being). Menu items include a lobster bisque, Dutch pea soup, beef Stroganoff, a pasta of the day, Wiener schnitzel, roast duckling with orange sauce, red snapper with Creole sauce, and an array of high-calorie desserts. The food is what you'd find in a quality roadside inn along a ski trail in Switzerland—not bad, but a bit heavy for the tropics.

Mi Cushina. In the La Quinta Beach Resort, J. E. Irausquin Blvd. 228. ☎ **297/8-72222.** Reservations recommended. Main courses $14–$30. AE, DC, MC, V. Tues–Sun noon–2pm and 6–10pm. ARUBAN/INTERNATIONAL.

For years, this recently relocated restaurant was known for some of the most authentic Aruban dishes on the island, when nearly everyone else had gone international. The world used to come to its door, even in its former location, which was difficult to reach. Now, Mi Cushina has moved into the heart of the hotel belt. The decor isn't as quaint as it used to be, and the prices are a lot higher, but they still serve the old recipes. Yes, you'll find conch stir-fry, stewed goat, and slices of fish cooked Aruban style, but the new menu is more international, with lobster Thermidor and filet mignon. International dishes are better elsewhere, but here you can still order excellent local fare like *funchi* (cornmeal), a fried concoction that accompanies many dishes, and *pan bati* (a pancake).

IN OR NEAR NOORD
EXPENSIVE

✪ **Valentino's.** In the Caribbean Palm Village, Noord 43–E. ☎ **297/8-62700.** Reservations recommended. Main courses $18.95–$49.95. AE, DC, MC, V. Mon–Sat 6–11pm. ITALIAN.

This is the most elegant Italian restaurant on Aruba. In the central courtyard of an upscale condominium complex, it offers guests cocktails near the entrance, then invites them to climb a flight of stairs to the peak-ceilinged dining room. Here you can check out the glassed-in, well-designed kitchen, and enjoy views over the palms and pools of the condominium complex and the attentions of the young but well-trained international staff. The prices are a bit high, but forgivable once you taste the food. It's a cozy, comfortable place. Menu items might include chicken Parmesan, veal scaloppine, tenderloin pepper steak, rack of lamb in rosemary sauce with mint jelly, and a selection of fish dishes.

MODERATE

The Buccaneer. Gasparito 11–C. ☎ **297/8-66172.** Reservations not accepted. Main courses $12–$19. AE, MC, V. Mon–Sat 5:30–10pm. SEAFOOD/INTERNATIONAL.

In a rustic-looking building near the hamlet of Noord, close to many of the island's biggest high-rise hotels, this is one of Aruba's most reasonably priced, popular seafood restaurants. Inside, you'll find a decor of varnished pine, nautical accessories, and bubbling aquariums. Menu items include crabmeat cocktail, escargots, shrimp in Pernod sauce, lobster Thermidor, and a land-and-sea platter with fish, shrimp, and tenderloin. The food is hearty and delicious. A spacious bar area is a good place to linger over drinks.

La Paloma. Noord 39. ☎ **297/8-62770.** Reservations recommended. Main courses $12–$29. AE, MC, V. Wed–Mon 6–11pm. ITALIAN/INTERNATIONAL.

A 10-minute drive north of Oranjestad, La Paloma contains a semi-circular bar area and a crowded, convivial dining area filled with bamboo and rattan furniture. The place is often packed with both visitors and locals seeking a fun-loving, casual atmosphere. The chefs have made each dish thousands of times, but they're still good, decent, and uncomplicated. Choices include linguine scampi marinara, lobster Provençal, red snapper *en papillotte,* a seafood platter, a 12-ounce filet mignon, and a 14-ounce strip loin steak.

AT TIERRA DEL SOL

Ventanas del Mar. In the Clubhouse of the Tierra del Sol Golf Course, Malmokweg. ☎ **297/8-67800.** Reservations recommended for dinner. Main courses $7.50–$12.95 lunch, $21.50–$37 dinner. AE, MC, V. Tues–Sun 6am–10am, 11am–3pm, and 6–10:30pm. SEAFOOD.

Surrounded by an emerald golf green, this restaurant offers views that sweep out over the coastline and a comfortably contemporary decor. Lunches are less formal than dinners and feature sandwiches and salads in addition to the steaks and grilled fish offered at dinner. Evening meals focus instead on Caribbean lobster, seafood pasta, conch ceviche, grilled garlic shrimp, and sautéed grouper. One of the best dishes is fried whole red snapper served in a ginger-soy sauce. A bar on the premises, decorated with golf memorabilia, remains open throughout the afternoon.

EAST OF ORANJESTAD

Brisas del Mar. Savaneta 222A. ☎ **297/8-47718.** Reservations required. Main courses $12–$32. AE, MC, V. Tues–Sun noon–2:30pm; daily 6:30–9:30pm. SEAFOOD.

A 15-minute drive east of Oranjestad, near the police station, Brisas del Mar, in very simple surroundings right at the water's edge, is a little hut with an air-conditioned bar where locals gather to drink the day away. The place is often jammed on weekends with many of the same locals who come here to drink and dance. In back the tables are open to sea breezes, and nearby you can see the catch of the day, perhaps wahoo, being sliced and sold to local buyers. Specialties include a mixed seafood platter, baby shark, and broiled lobster; you can order meat and poultry dishes as well, including tenderloin steak and broiled chicken. Don't expect subtle cuisine. This is the type of food Arubans enjoyed back in the 1950s, and nothing much has changed since then.

Charlie's Bar and Restaurant. B. v/d Veen Zeppenveldstraat 56 (Main St.), San Nicolas. ☎ **297/8-45086.** Daily soup $4.75; main courses $15–$20. AE, MC, V. Mon–Sat noon–9:30pm. (Bar, Mon–Sat noon–10pm.) SEAFOOD/INTERNATIONAL.

Charlie's is the best reason to visit San Nicolas. The bar dates from 1941 and is the most overly decorated joint in the West Indies, sporting an array of memorabilia and local souvenirs. Where roustabouts and roughnecks once brawled, you'll now find tables filled with contented tourists admiring thousands of pennants, banners, and trophies dangling from the high ceiling. Two-fisted drinks are still served, but the menu has improved since the good old days, when San Nicolas was one of the toughest towns in the Caribbean. You can now enjoy freshly made soup, grilled scampi, Creole-style squid, and churrasco. Sirloin steak and red snapper are usually featured. Come here for the good times and the brew—not necessarily for the food, although it isn't bad. Charlie's is a 25-minute drive east of Oranjestad.

4 Beaches

The western and southern shore, called the Turquoise Coast, attracts sun seekers to Aruba. Palm Beach and Eagle Beach (the latter closer to Oranjestad) are the best. No hotel along the strip owns the beaches, all of which are open to the public (if you use any of the hotel's facilities, however, you'll be charged).

The major resort hotels are built on the southwestern and more tranquil strip of Aruba. These beaches open onto calm waters, ideal for swimming. The beaches on the northern side of Aruba, although quite beautiful, face choppy waters and are good for only skilled swimmers. On this, the Atlantic side, you'll see white waves crash against a jagged rock coast.

✪ **Palm Beach** is a superb stretch of wide white sand that fronts hotels such as the previously recommended Allegro Resort. All sorts of activities take place here—not just swimming and sunbathing but sailing and fishing as well. Unfortunately, it's crowded in the winter. The waters off this beach are incredibly blue and teeming with neon-yellow fish and flame-bright coral reefs. Billowing rainbow-colored sails complete the picture.

Quite similar to Palm Beach, ✪ **Eagle Beach** is next door on the southern coast, fronting a number of time-share units. With gentle surf along miles of white-powder sand, swimming conditions here are excellent. Hotels along the strip organize water sports and beach activities.

The white-powder sands of **Punta Brabo**, also called **Manchebo Beach**, are a favorite among topless sunbathers. Actually Manchebo is part of the greater Eagle Beach (see above), and the hotel is a good refueling stop, as it offers a dive shop and will rent snorkeling gear. It's also set amid 100 acres of gardens, filled with everything from cacti to bougainvillea.

Eagle Beach and Palm Beach are known to nearly all visitors. If you'd like something more private, head for ✪ **Baby Beach** on the eastern end of Aruba. The beach has white-powder sand and tranquil, shallow waters, making this an ideal place for swimming and snorkeling. There are no facilities other than a refreshment stand and shaded areas. (Our local friends love this beach, and may be furious at us for telling you about it!) You'll spot the Arubans themselves here on weekends. Baby Beach opens onto a vast lagoon shielded by coral rocks that rise from the water. Bring your own towels, lotion, and snorkeling gear.

Also worth seeking out is **Hadikurari** (Fisherman's Huts), where swimming conditions, in very shallow water, are excellent. The only drawback to this white powder-sand beach is some pebbles and stones at water's edge. This beach is known for some of the finest wind-surfing on island. It is, in fact, the site of the annual **Hi-Winds Pro-Am Windsurfing Competition.** Facilities include picnic tables.

Next to Baby Beach on the eastern tip of the island, **Rodger's Beach** also has white powder sand and excellent swimming conditions. The backdrop, however, is an oil refinery at the far side of the bay. But the waters remain unpolluted, and you can admire large and small multicolored fish here and strange coral formations. The trade winds will keep you cool.

5 Sports & Outdoor Pursuits

CRUISES For a boat ride and a few hours of snorkeling, contact **De Palm Tours,** with offices in eight of the island's hotels. Its main office is at L. G. Smith Blvd. 142, in Oranjestad (☎ **800/766-6016** or 297/8-24400). De Palm Tours offers a 1½-hour glass-bottom-boat cruise that visits two coral reefs and the German shipwreck *Antilla* on Thursday and Friday. The cost is $19.50 per person.

DEEP-SEA FISHING In the deep waters off the coast of Aruba you can test your skill and wits against the big ones—wahoo, marlin, tuna, bonito, and sailfish. **De Palm Tours,** L. G. Smith Blvd. 142, in Oranjestad (☎ **297/8-24400**), takes a max-imum of six people (four can fish at the same time) on one of its four boats, which range in length from 27 to 41 feet. Half-day tours, with all equipment included, begin at $250 for up to four people and $30 per person for five or six. The prices double for full-day trips. Boats leave from the docks in Oranjestad. De Palm maintains 11 branches, most of which are in Aruba's major hotels.

GOLF Aruba's **Tierra del Sol Golf Course** (☎ **297/8-67800**), designed by Robert Trent Jones, Jr., is on the northwest coast near the California Lighthouse. The 18-hole, par-71, 6,811-yard course was designed to combine lush greens with the beauty of the island's indigenous flora, such as the swaying divi-divi tree. Facilities include a restaurant and lounge in the clubhouse, plus a swimming pool. Golf Hyatt manages the course. In winter, greens fees are a whopping $130, including golf cart, or $95 after 3pm. Off-season, greens fees are $75, or $55 after 3pm. The course is open daily from 6am to 7pm.

A less pricey alternative is the **Aruba Golf Club,** Golfweg 82 (☎ **297/8-42006**), near San Nicolas on the southeastern end of the island. Although it has only 10 greens, you play them from different tees to simulate 18-hole play. Twenty-five different sand traps add an extra challenge. Greens fees are $18 for 18 holes and $10 for 9 holes. The course is open daily from 7:30am to 5pm, although anyone who wishes to play 18 holes must begin the rounds before 1pm. You can rent golf carts and clubs in the on-site pro shop. On the premises, you'll find an air-conditioned restaurant and changing rooms with showers.

HORSEBACK RIDING   De Palm Tours, L. G. Smith Blvd. 142 (☎ **297/ 8-24400**), will make arrangements for you to ride at **Rancho Del Campo** (☎ **297/ 8-50290**). Two daily rides last 3 hours and cut through a park to a natural pool where you can dismount and cool off with a swim. The price is $45 per person, and the minimum age is 10 years.

TENNIS   Most of the island's beachfront hotels have tennis courts, often swept by trade winds, and some have top pros on hand to give instruction. Many of the courts can also be lit for night games. We don't advise playing in Aruba's hot noonday sun. Some hotels allow only guests on their courts.

The best tennis is at the **Aruba Racket Club** (☎ **297/8-60215**), the island's first world-class tennis facility, with eight courts, an exhibition center court, a swimming pool, a bar, a small restaurant, an aerobics center, and a fitness center. The club is open Monday through Saturday from 8am to 11pm and on Sunday from 3 to 8pm. Rates are $10 per hour per court, and lessons are $20 for a half hour or $35 per hour. The location is part of the Tierra del Sol complex on Aruba's northwest coast, near the California Lighthouse.

WATER SPORTS   You can snorkel in shallow waters, and scuba divers find stunning marine life with endless varieties of coral and tropical fish in myriad hues; at some points visibility extends up to 90 feet. Most divers set out for the German freighter *Antilla,* which was scuttled in the early years of World War II off the northwestern tip of Aruba, not too far from Palm Beach.

Red Sails Sports, Palm Beach (☎ **297/8-61603**), is the island's best water-sports center. The extensive range of activities here includes sailing, waterskiing, and scuba diving. Red Sail dive packages include shipwreck dives and marine-reef explorations. Guests first receive a poolside dive-safety course from Red Sail's certified instructors. Those who wish to become certified can achieve full PADI certification in 4 days for $350. One-tank dives cost $40, and two-tank dives are $65.

Divi Winds Center, J. E. Irausquin Blvd. 41 (☎ **297/8-37841**), near the Tamarind Aruba Beach Resort, is the island's windsurfing headquarters. Equipment, made by Fanatic, rents for $15 per hour, $30 per half day, and $45 all day. The resort is on the tranquil (Caribbean) side of the island, safe from fierce Atlantic waves. A private Sunfish lesson is $45; group instruction is $30. You can also rent snorkeling gear.

6 Seeing the Sights

De Palm Tours, L. G. Smith Blvd. 142, Oranjestad (☎ **297/8-24400**), has desks at all the major hotels. Its latest attraction is De Palm Island, a complete entertainment facility on a private island 5 minutes by ferry from Aruba. Their tours include snorkeling, beach barbecues, and folklore shows. Its office is open Monday to Saturday from 8:30am to noon and 1 to 5pm. The organized jaunts start at $19.

IN ORANJESTAD

Aruba's capital, Oranjestad, attracts more shoppers than sightseers. The bustling city has a very Caribbean flavor, with part-Spanish, part-Dutch architecture. The main thoroughfare, Lloyd G. Smith Boulevard, cuts in from the airport along the waterfront and on to Palm Beach, changing its name along the way to J. E. Irausquin Boulevard. Most visitors cross it to head for **Caya G. F. Betico Croes** and the best duty-free shopping.

After a shopping trip, you might return to the harbor where fishing boats and schooners, many from Venezuela, are moored. Nearly all newcomers to Aruba like to photograph the **Schooner Harbor.** Colorful boats dock along the quay, and boat people display their wares in open stalls. The local patois predominates. A little farther along, at the **fish market,** fresh fish is sold directly from the boats. **Wilhelmina Park,** named after Queen Wilhelmina of the Netherlands, is also on the sea side of Oranjestad. The park features a tropical garden along the water and a sculpture of the Queen Mother.

AN UNDERWATER JOURNEY

One of the island's most fun activities is an underwater journey on one of the world's few passenger submarines, operated by ✪ **Atlantis Submarines,** Seaport Village Marina (opposite the Sonesta), Oranjestad (☎ **800/253-0493** or 297/8-36090). Even nondivers can witness a coral reef firsthand without risking the obstacles and dangers of a scuba expedition. Carrying 46 passengers to a depth of up to 150 feet, the ride provides all the thrills of an underwater dive—but keeps you dry. In 1995 an old Danish fishing vessel was sunk to create a fascinating view for divers and submariners.

The submarine organizes four departures from the Oranjestad harbor front every hour on the hour, Tuesday to Sunday from 10am to 2pm. Each tour includes a 30-minute catamaran ride to Barcadera Reef, 2 miles southeast of Aruba—a site chosen for the huge variety of its underwater flora and fauna. At the reef, participants are transferred to the submarine for a 1-hour underwater lecture and tour.

Allow 2 hours for the complete experience. The cost is $69 for adults and $32 for children 4 to 16 (children under 4 are not admitted). Advance reservations are essential. A staff member will ask for a credit-card number (and give you a confirmation number) to hold the booking for you.

IN THE COUNTRYSIDE

If you can lift yourself from the sands for one afternoon, you might like to drive into the *cunucu,* which in Papiamento means "the countryside." Here Arubans live in modest, colorful, pastel-washed houses, decorated with tropical plants that require expensive desalinated water. Visitors who venture into the center of Aruba will want to see the strange **divi-divi tree,** with its trade-wind-blown coiffure.

Aruba is studded with rocks. You'll find the most impressive ones at **Ayo** and **Casibari,** northeast of Hooiberg. Diorite boulders stack up as high as urban buildings. The rocks weigh several thousand tons and puzzle geologists. Ancient Amerindian drawings appear on the rocks at Ayo. At Casibari, you can climb to the top for a panoramic view of the island or a close look at rocks that nature has carved into seats or prehistoric birds and animals. Pay special attention to the island's unusual species of lizards and cacti. Casibari is open daily from 9am to 5pm, with no admission charge. There's a lodge at Casibari where you can buy souvenirs, snacks, soft drinks, and beer.

Guides can also point out drawings on the walls and ceiling of the **Caves of Canashito,** south of Hooiberg. You may get to see some giant green parakeets here as well.

Special Moments

- **Wandering the Beach Gardens.** Along Palm Beach, all the resorts are set in flowering gardens. Of course, a river of water keeps these gardens blooming in this otherwise arid landscape, but the gardens take on a special beauty precisely because the island is so dry. As you walk along the beach, you can wander through garden after garden, watching the native birdlife. The tropical mockingbird feeds on juicy local fruits, and the black-faced grass quit or the green-throated carib hover around the flowers and flowering shrubs. If you stop to have a drink at one of the hotels' open-air bars, chances are you'll be joined by a bananaquit hoping to steal some sugar from you.

- **Sunset at Bubali Pond.** This bird sanctuary lies on the north side of Eagle Beach (see above) at Post Chikito. It is south of De Olde Molen—a 19th-century windmill-turned-restaurant, Aruba's most famous landmark. Once this pond was used to extract salt from seawater. Flocks of birds cluster at salt-free water, particularly at sunset, which makes for a memorable sight. You can see pelicans galore, black olivaceous cormorants, the black-crowned night herons, great egrets with long, black legs and yellow bills, and spotted sandpipers. Even the large wood stork and the glossy scarlet ibis sometimes fly in from Venezuela.

- **A Desert in the Caribbean.** On the northeastern coast, Arikok National Park is a desert-like ecological preserve. The island's rich crust makes it one of the rare places in the world with geological origins you can trace with a naked eye. Hiking trails make it easy to explore the preserve's unusual terrain and diverse flora and fauna. Iguanas and many species of migratory birds nest in the park, and goats and donkeys graze on nearby brush trees. Some of the island's best examples of early Indian art and artifacts are preserved within its boundaries. If you're up for something new, try dune sliding with the locals at the nearby Boca Prins dunes. At dusk, parakeets and other birds bid a cacophonous farewell in Jaburibari.

Hooiberg is affectionately known as "The Haystack," Aruba's most outstanding landmark. Anybody with the stamina can climb steps to the top of this 541-foot-high hill. One Aruban jogs up here every morning. On a clear day, you can see Venezuela from here.

On the jagged, windswept northern coast, the unrelenting surf carved the **Natural Bridge** out of coral rock. You can order snacks in a little cafe overlooking the coast. You'll also find a souvenir shop with trinkets, T-shirts, and wall hangings for reasonable prices.

NEAR SAN NICOLAS

As you drive along the highway toward the island's southernmost section, you may want to stop at the **Spaans Lagoen** (Spanish Lagoon), where pirates hid and waited to plunder rich cargo ships in the Caribbean. Today it's an ideal place for snorkeling, and you can picnic at tables under the mangrove trees.

To the east, you'll pass an area called **Savaneta,** where some of the most ancient traces of human habitation have been unearthed. You'll see here the first oil tanks that marked the position of the **Lago Oil & Transport Company,** the Exxon subsidiary around which the town of San Nicolas developed. San Nicolas was a company town until 1985, when the refinery curtailed operations. Twelve miles from Oranjestad, it is now called the Aruba Sunrise Side, and tourism has become its main economic engine. In the area, you'll find caves with Arawak artwork on the walls and a PGA-approved golf course with sand "greens" and cactus traps.

Boca Grandi, on the windward side of the island, is a favorite windsurfing location; if you prefer quieter waters, you'll find them at Baby Beach and Rodgers Beach, on Aruba's leeward side. Baby Beach offers the island's best beach-based snorkeling. Seroe Colorado (Colorado Point) overlooks the two beaches. From here, you can see the Venezuelan coastline and the pounding surf on the windward side. If you climb down the cliffs, you're likely to spot an iguana; protected by law, the once-endangered saurians now proliferate in peace.

You can see cave wall drawings at the **Guadarikiri Cave** and **Fontein Cave**. At the **Huliba** and **Tunnel of Love** caves, guides and refreshment stands await visitors. In spite of its name, the Tunnel of Love cave requires some physical stamina to explore. It is filled with steep climbs, and its steps are illuminated only by hand-held lamps. Wear sturdy shoes and watch your step.

7 Shopping

Aruba manages to offer goods from six continents along the half-mile-long **Caya G. F. Betico Croes,** Oranjestad's main shopping street. Technically this is not a free port, but the duty is so low (3.3%) that prices are attractive—and Aruba has no sales tax. You'll find the usual array of Swiss watches; German and Japanese cameras; jewelry; liquor; English bone china and porcelain; Dutch, Swedish, and Danish silver and pewter; French perfume; British woolens; Indonesian specialties; and Madeira embroidery. Delft blue pottery is an especially good buy. Other good buys include Dutch cheese (Edam and Gouda), Dutch chocolate, and English cigarettes in the airport departure area.

Philatelists will love the wealth of colorful, artistic stamps issued in honor of Aruba's changed governmental status. You can purchase a complete assortment, and other special-issue stamps, at the post office in Oranjestad.

SHOPPING CENTERS

Try **Alhambra Moonlight Shopping Center,** adjacent to the Alhambra Casino, L. G. Smith Boulevard (☎ **297/8-35000**), with international shops, outdoor marketplaces, cafes, and restaurants.

Its major competitor is **Royal Plaza Mall,** L. G. Smith Blvd. 94, a bustling shopping center across from the cruise-ship terminal. It has a little bit of everything, including big-name Caribbean chains such as Gandelman's Jewelers and Little Switzerland. You'll also find outlets for American chains, including Tommy Hilfiger and Nautica. At the **Internet Café,** (☎ **297/8-24500**) you can send e-mail and order coffee.

Finally, check out **Seaport Mall/Seaport Market Place,** L. G. Smith Blvd. 82 (☎ **297/8-24622**). Aruba's densest concentration of shopping options is here in the heart of Oranjestad, in a pair of two-story malls. Overlooking the harbor, each mall contains its own casino. There's also a movie theater (☎ **297/8-30318**) with six screens and recently released films from Europe and the U.S. mainland, a convention center, several bars and cafes, and at least 200 stores. Most shops within the complex are open Monday to Saturday from 9am to 6pm, and the bars and cafes usually operate on Sunday as well.

SPECIALTY SHOPS

Notable specialty shops include **Agatha at Les Accessories,** in the Seaport Mall (☎ **297/8-37965**). Agatha Brown, an award-winning American designer, features her exclusive designs here, including stunning knitwear handbags.

Artistic Boutique, Caya G. F. Betico Croes 25 (☎ **297/8-23142**), carries 14- and 18-karat, fine-gold jewelry set with precious or semiprecious stones. It also sells porcelain figurines, Oriental antiques, handmade dhurries and rugs, fine linens, and organdy tablecloths. Its collections of Indonesian imports is the best on the island.

Aruba Trading Company, Caya G. F. Betico Croes 12 (☎ **297/8-22602**), has the island's best and most moderately priced selection of perfume, sold considerably cheaper than in the States because of the low duty. The company also offers a complete range of cosmetics, shoes, clothing for men and women, liquor, and cigarettes. Brand-name perfumes are often discounted here, but you'll have to search the store carefully to find the good buys.

Again, because of the low duty imposed on Aruba, even the budget traveler can sometimes find a good deal on jewelry. **Gandelman Jewelers,** Royal Plaza (☎ **297/8-34433**), offers an extensive collection of fine gold jewelry and famous-name timepieces at duty-free prices. Go here if you're in the market for a deluxe watch or some piece of jewelry you'll have for a lifetime. Prices are reasonable. There are branch stores in the Americana Aruba Hotel, Airport Departure Hall, Wyndham Hotel, Royal Plaza, and Hyatt Regency Aruba. **Jewelers Warehouse,** in the Seaport Mall (☎ **297/8-36045**), is a popular international jewelry store near the center of Oranjestad. It carries a complete line of rings, earrings, and bracelets, most of them inexpensively priced. **Little Switzerland Jewelers,** Caya G. F. Betico Croes 14 (☎ **297/8-21192**), is famous for its duty-free 14- and 18-karat-gold jewelry and watches.

New Amsterdam Store, Caya G. F. Betico Croes 50 (☎ **297/8-21152**), is the leading department store for linens, with napkins, place mats, and embroidered tablecloths from as far away as China.

Penha, Caya G. F. Betico Croes 11–13 (☎ **297/8-24161**), has offered large selections of top-name perfumes and cosmetics since 1865. A household name on Aruba, it's one of the most dependable stores around. A Tommy Hilfiger boutique has been added to the store, and the men's department on the second floor is Aruba's finest. Prices are usually lower than in the States, but shop carefully.

8 Aruba After Dark

THE CLUB & BAR SCENE

Nongamblers can usually drink in hotel cocktail lounges and supper clubs. You don't have to be a guest to see shows, but you should make a reservation. Tables at the big shows, especially in season, are likely to book up early in the day.

The Cellar, Kliebstraat 2, Oranjestad (☎ **297/8-28567**), scattered over two floors of a battered-looking building, boasts a fairly well-rounded clientele with an even mixture of tourists and locals. Upstairs, people dance to everything from disco to house to merengue. Downstairs, in the raucous cellar, people sit, talk, and people-watch. On weekends it can get pretty noisy and crowded, but it's a highly appealing, friendly place. The Cellar is open until 4am.

Cheers Bar, L. G. Smith Blvd. 17 (☎ **297/8-30838**), has four convivial, even raucous bars. The main one shows cable sports, especially European soccer. There's an enormous terrace with outside speakers and enough room for you to dance if you like.

Fans appreciate the resident DJ, who spins mostly house music during the week. Expect particularly animated mobs on Tuesday nights, when women drink for free. Sunday is Carnival night, with live salsa and merengue. A full menu of shrimp, fried fish, burgers, and sandwiches is available. The place is open from sundown until 2am weeknights and until 4am on Saturday and Sunday.

Mumbo Jumbo, in the Royal Plaza Mall, L. G. Smith Boulevard (☎ 297/8-33632), is sultry and relaxing. Expect a cosmopolitan blend of Dutch and Latino clients, and lots of Latin rhythms. The volume is kept at a tolerable level for wallflowers and conversationalists. There's an array of specialty drinks; imagine coconut shells, very colorful straws, and large fruit. Hours are from sunset until between 2 and 3am, depending on the night of the week.

Havana Beach Club, L. G. Smith Blvd. 4 (☎ 297/8-23380), is a seafront building that functions as a beach club during the day, with chair and parasol rentals and a swimming pool. After 8pm, however, it transforms into one of the island's busiest nightclubs, with recorded or live salsa music and lots of high-energy exhibitionism on the dance floor. It's open every night until 5am. The cover ranges from $6 to $8.

CASINOS: LET THE GOOD TIMES ROLL

The casinos of the big hotels along Palm Beach are the liveliest nighttime destinations. They stay open as long as business demands, often into the wee hours. In plush gaming parlors, guests try their luck at roulette, craps, blackjack, and, of course, the one-armed bandits.

Excelsior Casino, J. E. Irausquin Blvd. 230 (☎ 297/8-67777), wins the prize for all-around action. Its casino doors are open from 8am to 4am. The **Aruba Grand,** J. E. Irausquin Blvd. 79 (☎ 297/8-63900), opens its games at noon; it stays open until 2am. The **Casino Masquerade,** at the Radisson Aruba Caribbean Resort & Casino, J. E. Irausquin Blvd. 81, Palm Beach (☎ 297/8-66555), is one of the newest casinos on Aruba. On the lower-level lobby of the hotel, it's open from 10am to 4am daily. It offers blackjack, single deck, roulette, Caribbean stud, craps, and "Let It Ride."

One of the island's best casinos is the **Crystal Casino** at the Aruba Sonesta Resort & Casino at Seaport Village (☎ 297/8-36000), open daily 24 hours. The 14,000-square-foot casino offers 11 blackjack tables, 270 slot machines, four roulette tables, three Caribbean stud-poker tables, two craps tables, one minibaccarat table, and three baccarat tables. This place has luxurious furnishings, ornate moldings, marble, and crystal chandeliers.

Visitors have a tendency to flock to the newest casinos on the island, like the one at the **Wyndham Hotel and Resort,** J. E. Irausquin Blvd. 77 (☎ 297/8-64466), or the **Hyatt Regency Aruba,** J. E. Irausquin Blvd. 85 (☎ 297/8-61234). **Royal Cabana Casino,** at the **La Cabana All Suite Beach Resort & Casino,** J. E. Irausquin Blvd. 250 (☎ 297/8-79000), outdraws them all. It's known for its multitheme three-in-one restaurant and its showcase cabaret theater and nightclub, with Las Vegas–style revues, female impersonators, and comedy series on the weekend. The largest casino on Aruba, it offers 33 tables and games, plus 320 slot machines.

The **Alhambra,** J. E. Irausquin Blvd. 47 (☎ 297/8-35000), is a complex of buildings and courtyards designed like an 18th-century Dutch village. About a dozen shops here sell souvenirs, leather goods, jewelry, and beachwear. From the outside, the complex looks Moorish, with serpentine mahogany columns, arches, and domes. A busy casino operates on the premises (open from 10am 'til very early in the morning, usually 3am).

Barbados 6

Bajans like to think of their island as "England in the tropics," but endless pink- and white-sand beaches are what really put Barbados on the map. Rich in tradition, Barbados has a grand array of hotels (many of them super-expensive). Although it doesn't offer casinos, it has more than beach life for travelers interested in learning about the local culture, plus more sightseeing attractions than most islands of the West Indies.

Afternoon tea remains a tradition at many places, cricket is still the national sport, and many Bajans speak with a British accent. In spite of Barbados being called "Little England" in the Caribbean, many islanders are weighing the possibility of a divorce from the mother country. A government-appointed constitutional revision commission here is considering whether to discard Queen Elizabeth II as head of state. Such a divorce would make Barbados a republic, eliminating its formal ties to the British legal system.

There has been great dissatisfaction on the island about the Privy Council, the British high court whose members are appointed by the queen. This court is far too liberal for many local citizens, who want to break free of it. In general, Bajans favor capital punishment and find the court too lenient with criminals. Barbados has already restored the use of a whip with knotted cords to punish criminals and has widened grounds for corporal punishment in schools, all of which is against present British law.

Although crime has been on the rise in recent years, Barbados is still viewed as a safe destination. The difference between the haves and the have-nots doesn't cause the sometimes violent clash here that it does on other islands, such as Jamaica.

Don't rule out Barbados if you're seeking a peaceful island getaway. Although the south coast is known for its nightlife and the west-coast beach strip is completely built up, some of the island remains undeveloped. The east coast is fairly tranquil, and you can often be alone here (but since it faces the Atlantic, the waters aren't as calm as they are on the Caribbean side). Many escapists, especially Canadians seeking a low-cost place to stay in winter, don't seem to mind the Atlantic waters at all.

Because it's so developed with hotels and condos, Barbados offers more package deals than most islands. You can often get a steal in the off-season, which lasts from April until mid-December. And if you take the time to shop around, Barbados is filled with bargains,

Barbados

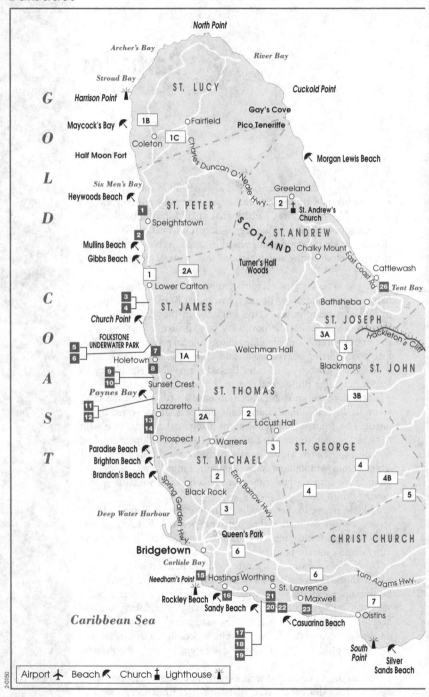

Airport ✈ Beach 🏄 Church † Lighthouse 🔆

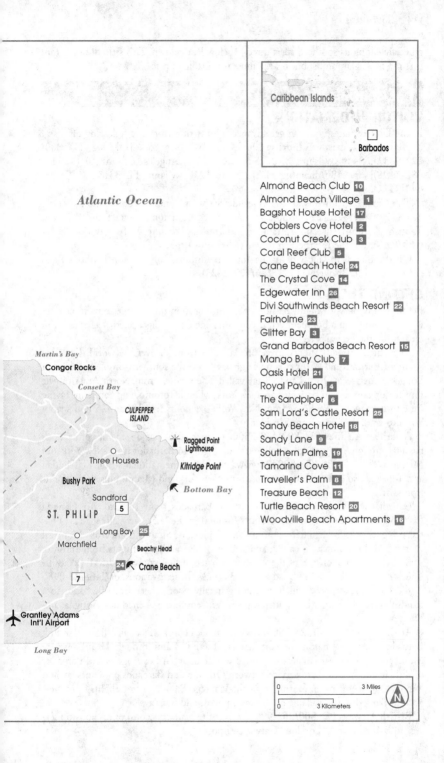

Atlantic Ocean

Caribbean Islands

Barbados

Almond Beach Club 10
Almond Beach Village 1
Bagshot House Hotel 17
Cobblers Cove Hotel 2
Coconut Creek Club 3
Coral Reef Club 5
Crane Beach Hotel 24
The Crystal Cove 14
Edgewater Inn 26
Divi Southwinds Beach Resort 22
Fairholme 23
Glitter Bay 3
Grand Barbados Beach Resort 15
Mango Bay Club 7
Oasis Hotel 21
Royal Pavillion 4
The Sandpiper 6
Sam Lord's Castle Resort 25
Sandy Beach Hotel 18
Sandy Lane 9
Southern Palms 19
Tamarind Cove 11
Traveller's Palm 8
Treasure Beach 12
Turtle Beach Resort 20
Woodville Beach Apartments 16

Martin's Bay
Congor Rocks

Consett Bay

CULPEPPER
ISLAND

Ragged Point
Lighthouse

Three Houses

Kitridge Point

Bushy Park

Bottom Bay

Sandford
ST. PHILIP
5

Long Bay 25
Marchfield

Beachy Head

24 Crane Beach

7

Grantley Adams
Int'l Airport

Long Bay

0   3 Miles
0   3 Kilometers

N

especially along its southern coast directly below Bridgetown. This strip of beachfront isn't the most glamorous, but it's the most reasonable in price.

1 Essentials

VISITOR INFORMATION

In the United States, you can get advance information from the following offices of the **Barbados Tourism Authority:** 800 Second Ave., New York, NY 10017 (☎ **800/ 221-9831**); 3440 Wilshire Blvd., Suite 1215, Los Angeles, CA 90010 (☎**213/ 380-2198**); or 158 Alhambra Circle, Suite 1270, Miami, FL 33134 (☎ **305/ 442-7471**).

The Canadian office is at 105 Adelaide St. West, Suite 1010, Toronto, Ontario M5H 1P9 (☎ **416/214-9880**). In the United Kingdom, contact the Barbados Tourism Authority at 263 Tottenham Court Rd., London W1P 0LA (☎ **0171/ 636-9448**). On the Internet, go to **www.barbados.org**.

On the island, the local Barbados Tourism Authority office is on Harbour Road (P.O. Box 242), Bridgetown (☎ **246/427-2623**).

GETTING THERE

Before you book your flight, be sure to read the section on package tours in chapter 2—it can save you a bundle! Even if you don't book a package, see that chapter's tips on finding the best airfare.

More than 20 daily flights arrive on Barbados from all over the world. **Grantley Adams International Airport** is on Highway 7, on the southern tip of the island at Long Bay, between Oistins and village called The Crane. From North America, the four major gateways to Barbados are New York, Miami, Toronto, and San Juan. Flying time to Barbados is 4½ hours from New York, 3½ hours from Miami, 5 hours from Toronto, and 1½ hours from San Juan.

American Airlines (☎ **800/433-7300;** www.aa.com) has dozens of connections passing through San Juan, plus daily nonstop flights to Barbados from New York and Miami. **BWIA** (☎ **800/538-2942;** www.bwee.com), the national airline of Trinidad and Tobago, also offers daily nonstops from New York and Miami, plus many flights from Trinidad.

Canadians may opt for nonstop flights to Barbados from Toronto. **Air Canada** (☎ **800/268-7240** in Canada, or 800/776-3000 in the U.S.; www.aircanada.ca) has seven flights per week from Toronto in winter, plus one Sunday flight from Montréal year-round. In summer, when demand slackens, there are fewer flights from Toronto.

Barbados is a major hub of the Caribbean-based airline known as **LIAT** (☎ **800/ 468-0482** in the U.S. and Canada, 246/434-5428 for reservations, or 246/428-0986 at the Barbados airport), which provides generally poor service from Barbados to a handful of neighboring islands, including St. Vincent in the Grenadines, Antigua, and Dominica.

Air Jamaica (☎ **800/523-5585;** www.airjamaica.com) offers daily flights that link Barbados to Atlanta, Baltimore, Fort Lauderdale, and Miami through the airline's new Montego Bay hub. Air Jamaica has added service between Los Angeles and Barbados on Friday and Sunday, and service between Orlando and Barbados on Thursday and Sunday (but requiring an overnight stay in Montego Bay). Nonstop flights from New York to Barbados are available on Tuesday, Friday, and Sunday.

British Airways (☎ **800/247-9297;** www.british-airways.com) offers nonstop service to Barbados from London's Gatwick Airport.

GETTING AROUND

BY RENTAL CAR   If you don't mind *driving on the left,* you may find a rental car ideal on Barbados. You'll need a temporary permit if you don't have an International Driver's License. The rental agencies listed below can all issue visitor's permits, or you can go to the police desk upon your arrival at the airport. You must have your own license and pay a registration fee of BD$10 ($5). The speed limit is 20mph inside city limits, 45mph elsewhere on the island. Due to frequent delays at airport counters, we suggest taking a taxi from the airport to your hotel, then calling for the delivery of your rental car. No taxes apply to car rentals on Barbados.

None of the major U.S.-based car-rental agencies maintain affiliates on Barbados, but a host of local companies rent vehicles. Except in the peak midwinter season, cars are usually readily available without prior reservations. Many local companies continue to draw serious complaints from readers, both for overcharging and for the poor conditions of their vehicles. Proceed very carefully with rentals on this island. Check the insurance and liability issues carefully when you rent.

The island's most frequently recommended agency is **National Car Rentals,** Bush Hall, Main Road, St. Michael (☎ **246/426-0603**), which offers a wide selection of Japanese cars (note that it's not affiliated with the U.S. chain of the same name). National is 3 miles northeast of Bridgetown, near the national stadium; it delivers cars to almost any location on the island upon request, and the driver who delivers it will carry the necessary forms for the Bajan driver's license, which may be purchased for $5.

Other comparable companies include **Sunny Isle Motors,** Dayton, Worthing Main Road, Christ Church (☎ **246/435-7979**), and **P&S Car Rentals,** Pleasant View, Cave Hill, St. Michael (☎ **246/424-2052**). One company conveniently close to hotels on the remote southeastern end of Barbados is **Stoutes Car Rentals,** Kirtons, St. Philip (☎ **246/435-4456**). Since it's closer to the airport than its competitors, it can theoretically deliver a car there within 10 minutes of a call placed when you arrive.

BY TAXI   Taxis aren't metered, but rates are fixed by the government; one cab can carry up to five passengers for the same fare. Taxis are plentiful and easily identifiable by the letter Z on their license plates. Drivers will produce a list of standard rates ($20 per hour, subject to change). To call a taxi, contact one of the following services: **Paramount Taxi Service** (☎ 246/429-3718), **Royal Pavilion Taxi Service** (☎ 246/422-5555), or **Lyndhurst Taxi Service** (☎ 246/436-2639).

BY BUS   Unlike most of the British Windwards, Barbados has a reliable bus system fanning out from Bridgetown to almost every part of the island. The nationally owned **buses** of Barbados are blue with yellow stripes. They're not numbered, but their destinations are marked on the front. On most major routes, buses run every 20 minutes or so. Wherever you go, the fare is BD$1.50 (75¢), exact change required. Departures are from Bridgetown, leaving from Fairchild Street for the south and east; from Lower Green and the Princess Alice Highway for the north going along the west coast. Call the **Barbados Tourist Board** (☎ 246/427-2623) for schedules and information.

Privately operated **minibuses** run shorter distances and travel more frequently. They are bright yellow, with their destinations displayed on the bottom-left corner of the windshield. Minibuses in Bridgetown are boarded at River Road, Temple Yard, and Probyn Street. The fare is BD$1.50 (75¢).

Fast Facts: Barbados

American Express The island's affiliate is **Barbados International Travel Services,** Horizon House, McGregor Street (☎ **246/431-2423**), in the heart of Bridgetown.

Business Hours Most banks are open Monday to Thursday from 9am to 3pm, Friday from 9am to 1pm and 3 to 5pm. Stores are open Monday to Friday from 8am to 4pm, Saturday from 8am to noon. Most government offices are open Monday to Friday from 8:30am to 4:30pm.

Consulates & High Commissions The **U.S. Consulate** is in the ALICO Building, Cheapside, Bridgetown (☎ 246/431-0225); the **Canadian High Commission** at Bishop Court Hill, Pine Road (☎ 246/429-3550); and the **British High Commission** at Lower Collymore Rock, St. Michael (☎ 246/436-6694).

Currency The Barbados dollar (BD$) is the official currency, available in $5, $10, $20, and $100 notes, as well as 10¢, 25¢, and $1 silver coins, plus 1¢ and 5¢ copper coins. The Bajan dollar is worth 50¢ in U.S. currency. *Currency quotations in this chapter are in U.S. dollars unless otherwise specified.* Most stores take traveler's checks or U.S. dollars. However, it's best to convert your money at banks and pay in Bajan dollars.

Dentists **Dr. Derek Golding,** with two other colleagues, maintains one of the busiest practices on Barbados, at the Beckwith Shopping Mall in Bridgetown (☎ **246/426-3001**). They will accept any emergency (they treat most of the cruise-ship passengers' emergencies) and often stay open late. Otherwise, hours are Monday to Saturday from 8am to 2:30pm. All members of this dental team received their training in the United States, Britain, Canada, or New Zealand.

Doctors Your hotel may have a list of doctors on call; some of the best recommended are **Dr. J. D. Gibling** (☎ **246/432-1772**) and **Dr. Adrian Lorde** or his colleague **Dr. Ahmed Mohamad** (☎ **246/424-8236**). All will pay house calls to patients unable or unwilling to leave their hotel rooms.

Documents U.S. or Canadian citizens coming directly from North America to Barbados for a period not exceeding 3 months must have proof of identity and national status, such as a passport, which is always preferred. However, a birth certificate (either an original or a certified copy) is also acceptable, provided it's backed up with photo ID. For stays longer than 3 months, a passport is required. An ongoing or return ticket is also necessary. British subjects need a valid passport.

Electricity The electricity is 110 volts AC (50 cycles), so at most places you can use your U.S.-made appliances.

Emergencies In an emergency, dial ☎ **119.** Other important numbers include the **police** at ☎ **112,** the **fire department** at ☎ **113,** and an **ambulance** at ☎ **115.**

Hospitals The **Queen Elizabeth Hospital** is on Martinsdale Road in St. Michael (☎ **246/436-6450**). Of the several private clinics, one of the most expensive and best recommended is the **Bayview Hospital,** St. Paul's Avenue, Bayville, St. Michael (☎ **246/436-5446**).

Language The Barbadians, or Bajans, as they're called, speak English, but with their own island lilt.

Safety Crimes against tourists used to be rare, but the U.S. State Department reports rising crime, such as purse snatching, pickpocketing, armed robbery, and even sexual assault. The department advises that you avoid leaving cash or valuables in your hotel room, beware of purse snatchers when walking, exercise caution on the beach or at tourist attractions, and be wary of driving in isolated areas.

Taxes A 7½% government sales tax is added to hotel bills. A new 15% VAT (value added tax) is levied on all meals. For example, if your hotel costs $200 per night, and you are charged $50 per person for a MAP, you'll have to pay a 7½% government tax plus the 10% additional service charge for the $200 room rate, then an additional 15% VAT on the MAP rate. Some visitors view these additional charges as "larcenous." They certainly won't make you happy when you go to pay your final bill. There's also a BD$25 ($12.50) departure tax.

Telephone To call Barbados from the United States, dial **1**, then **246** (the area code for Barbados) and the local number. Once on Barbados, to call another number on the island, only the local number is necessary.

Time Barbados is on Atlantic standard time year-round, placing it 1 hour ahead of New York. However, when the United States is on daylight saving time, Barbados matches the clocks of the U.S. East Coast.

Tipping Most hotels and restaurants add at least a 10% service charge to your bill.

Water Barbados has a pure water supply. It's pumped from underground sources in the coral rock that covers six-sevenths of the island, and it's safe to drink.

Weather Daytime temperatures are in the 75° to 85°F range throughout the year.

2 Where to Stay

Barbados has the best hotels in the Caribbean, many of which are small and personally run. Most of our recommendations are on fashionable St. James Beach. At press time, the biggest news on the hotel scene is the projected opening of one of Jamaican entrepreneur Butch Stewart's new Sandals resorts, on the west coast. This long-delayed project will be called—you guessed it—**Sandals Barbados.** For more information and details, call ☎ **800/SANDALS.**

Another bit of news is that **Sandy Lane,** St. James, Barbados (☎ **246/432-1310;** fax 246/432-2954), one of the most famous luxury resorts on the island, will be closed until the winter of 1999 or early 2000 for a $75-million renovation. The rooms will be completely refurbished; other plans include 45 new golf holes, seven new tennis courts, a spa, and a children's activity center. If you have to ask about the rates, you can't afford it; that part of the description is sure not to change. A complete review of the new Sandy Lane will be in *Frommer's Caribbean 2001.*

Now here's the bad news: Because Barbados is so popular with charter groups, hotels are often extremely expensive in high season. Many will also insist that you take their meal plans if you're there in the winter.

But Barbados does have some bargains, and we've surveyed the best of these as well. You'll have to head south from Bridgetown to such places as Hastings and Worthing for the best buys, which are often self-contained efficiencies or studio apartments where you can do your own cooking. See also the section on package tours in chapter 2.

Prices cited in this section, unless otherwise indicated, are in U.S. dollars. See "Taxes," above, for additional information.

ON THE WEST COAST
VERY EXPENSIVE

Almond Beach Club. Vauxhall, St. James, Barbados, W.I. ☎ **800/4-ALMOND** in the U.S., or 246/432-7840. Fax 246/432-2115. www.bajan.com/barbados/hotels/almondb/almondb/ htm. 161 units. A/C TV TEL. Winter $495–$660 double. Off-season $440–$595 double. Rates include all meals. AE, MC, V. Children under 16 not accepted.

Set on a flat and sandy beach about a 2-minute walk from its more famous neighbor, Sandy Lane, this hotel lies on the island's west coast, south of Holetown. The narrow beach here is less than ideal. This was the first of Barbados's all-inclusive resorts, established in 1991 as part of a $2-million refurbishment. The accommodations are spread among seven low-rise, three-story buildings (no elevators). Pool-view units open onto three freshwater pools and gardens planted with frangipani trees and palms; beach-front units open onto the Caribbean. Rooms are outfitted with island motifs, tropical fabrics, and tile floors. Each unit has a private safe, coffeemaker, walk-in closest, and bathroom with combination tub/shower, fluffy towels, and a hair dryer; most rooms have twin beds with good mattresses.

Dining/Diversions: The Almond Beach Restaurant serves decent continental fare. Enid's is our favorite, with its zesty Bajan cuisine. The Rum Shop Bar evokes 19th-century colonial days and offers virtually every kind of distilled rum on Barbados. There's lively nightly entertainment until 2am, including jazz and steel-drum bands, folk dancing, and contemporary music. The all-inclusive program offers a dine-around option, allowing guests to consume one lunch and one dinner per weeklong stay at one of three neighboring hotels.

Amenities: Three freshwater pools, a new spa, tennis and squash courts, fitness center with sauna, fishing, windsurfing, waterskiing, reef fishing, kayaking, and "banana boating." Laundry and baby-sitting; the guest services department will organize island tours.

Almond Beach Village. Speightstown (15 miles north of Bridgetown along Hwy. 2A), St. Peter, Barbados, W.I. ☎ **800/4-ALMOND** in the U.S., or 246/422-4900. Fax 246/422-1581. www.bajan.com/barbados/hotels/almondr/almondr.htm. E-mail: vacation@iag.net. 330 units. A/C TV TEL. Winter $520–$625 double; $635–$690 suite. Off-season $460–$545 double; $560–$615 suite. Rates are all-inclusive. AE, MC, V.

Set near a string of more expensive hotels (referred to as the island's Gold Coast), the Almond Beach Village occupies the site of a 19th-century sugarcane plantation. In 1994, it was acquired by Barbados Shipping and Trading and underwent a $13-million renovation. Today, it's the most desirable all-inclusive resort on the island (with all meals, drinks, and most sports included in one net price) and a good choice for families.

On 30 acres of tropically landscaped gardens and prime beachfront, its relatively isolated position makes leaving the premises awkward, although that doesn't seem to bother guests. Accommodations are clustered into seven different compounds to create something akin to a miniature, self-contained village. Rooms, though not large, are well appointed, with ceiling fans, private safes, well-upholstered chairs, good mattresses, and small bathrooms with combination tub/showers and hair dryers. Exchange privileges are available with the hotel's all-inclusive twin, the Almond Beach Club (see above).

Dining: La Smarita, the most formal of the restaurants, serves excellent seafood pastas. Horizons, the main dining room, offers standard fare. Least formal is Enid's, for spicy Bajan food. There's also a burger-and-hot-dog joint.

In case you want to be welcomed there.

We're here to see that you're always welcomed at establishments everywhere. That's why millions of people carry the American Express® Card – for peace of mind, confidence, and security, around the world or just around the corner.

do more AMERICAN EXPRESS

Cards

In case you're running low.

We're here to help with more than 190,000 Express Cash locations around the world. In order to enroll, just call American Express at 1 800 CASH-NOW before you start your vacation.

do more **AMERICAN EXPRESS**

Express Cash

And in case you'd rather be safe than sorry.

We're here with American Express® Travelers Cheques. They're the safe way to carry money on your vacation, because if they're ever lost or stolen you can get a refund, practically anywhere or anytime. To find the nearest place to buy Travelers Cheques, call 1 800 495-1153. Another way we help you do more.

do more

Travelers Cheques

Amenities: Five floodlit tennis courts, two air-conditioned squash courts, and a nine-hole, par-3 golf course (too easy for professionals but good for beginners). Laundry facilities, baby-sitting, room service. One of the best children's programs on the island, with videos, Nintendo, a computer lab, books, board games, two playgrounds, nine pools, an activity center, pool and beach games, nature walks, water sports, treasure hunts, storytelling, arts and crafts, and evening entertainment.

✪ **Cobblers Cove Hotel.** Road View, St. Peter, Barbados, W.I. ☎ **800/890-6060** in the U.S., 0181/367-5175 in London, or 246/422-2291. Fax 246/422-1460. www.barbados.org/hotels/ccove/index.htm. E-mail: cobblers@caribsurf.com. 40 units. A/C MINIBAR TEL. Winter $540–$880 double; $1,300–$1,500 suite. Off-season $356–$506 double; $796–$846 suite. Rates include MAP (breakfast and dinner). AE, MC, V. Closed late Sept to mid-Oct.

One of the small, exclusive hotels of Barbados, this former mansion was built in a mock-medieval style over the site of a former British fort. Now a member of Relais & Châteaux, the hotel is a favorite honeymoon retreat. First-class suites are housed in 10 Iberian-style villas, placed throughout the gardens of jasmine, bougainvillea, mango, red ginger lilies, and banana trees. Overlooking a white-sand beach, each unit has a spacious living room, a private balcony or patio, and a kitchenette. Each year nine bedrooms are completely redecorated, so the property is always in topnotch condition. The spacious bathrooms come with fluffy towels, combination shower/tubs, and hair dryers. Two of the most exclusive accommodations on the entire island are the Camelot and Colleton suites, on the rooftop of the original mansion; they're beautifully decorated and offer panoramic views of both the beach and the garden. The Colleton suite even has its own pool, and meals can be delivered so you can dine in privacy. The resort contains many acres of well-developed tropical gardens and lawns.

Dining/Diversions: The award-winning cuisine served at Cobblers Cove is generally lighter and more refined than the heavier French food offered at its competitor, Sandy Lane. The open-air dining room overlooks the sea. The emphasis is on Caribbean specialties from the sea—say, fish of the day grilled or poached with Bajan seasoning, or shrimp flavored with ginger. The Tuesday-night barbecue is an event. Nearby is the resort's social center, the bar. Tea is served poolside daily (and yes, there's even English-style cucumber sandwiches).

Amenities: Tennis courts (lit at night), pool, water sports (including waterskiing, Sunfish sailing, snorkeling, and windsurfing). Laundry, baby-sitting, arrangements for island tours, car rentals.

Coconut Creek Club. Derricks, St. James, Barbados, W.I. ☎ **800/223-6510** in the U.S., or 246/432-0803. Fax 246/432-0272. E-mail: aedghill@stjames.com. 53 units. A/C TEL. Winter $402–$532 double. Off-season $362–$486 double. Rates are all-inclusive. MC, V.

Small, intimate, and known as an escape for publicity-shy European celebrities, this is an elegantly informal and landscaped retreat, about a mile south of Holetown. Completely renovated in 1995, it resembles an exclusive country retreat in Devon, England. About half of the accommodations lie atop a low bluff overlooking what might be the two most secluded beaches on the island's west coast. Many of the rooms are built on the low cliff edge overlooking the ocean, while others open onto the pool or the garden. Each tropical-motif unit has white-washed wooden ceilings, a veranda or balcony (where breakfast can be served), a private safe, a small fridge, and rattan furnishings, including a king-size bed or twins with good mattresses. Bathrooms are well equipped with good-size towels and hair dryers.

Dining/Diversions: The restaurant, Cricketers, is modeled after an upscale English pub. Bajan buffets and barbecues are served on the vine-covered open pergola, overlooking the gardens and the sea. The inn's food has been praised by *Gourmet* magazine. There's dancing to West Indian calypso and steel bands almost every night. Clients on the MAP are encouraged to dine at the restaurants connected to this chain's three other properties—the Crystal Cove Hotel, the Tamarind Cove Hotel, and the Colony Club—for no additional charge.

Amenities: Freshwater pool, complimentary water sports (including waterskiing, windsurfing, snorkeling, and Hobie Cat sailing; scuba diving can be arranged for an extra charge), nearby tennis courts. Room service (from 7:30am to 10pm), baby-sitting, arrangements for island tours and rental cars.

Coral Reef Club. St. James Beach (a 5-minute drive north of Holetown), Barbados, W.I. ☎ **800/223-1108** or 246/422-2372. Fax 246/422-1776. www.barbados.org/hotels/coral.htm. E-mail: coral@caribsurf.com. 85 units. A/C TEL. Winter $680–$810 double; from $1,205 two-bedroom suite (sleeps up to 4). Off-season $400–$470 double; $830 suite. Rates include MAP (breakfast and dinner). AE, MC, V. Children under 12 not accepted in Feb.

This family-owned and -managed luxury hotel has set standards that are hard for competitors to match. It's one of the best and most respected establishments on the island, set on elegantly landscaped grounds beside a beach that's ideal for swimming. A collection of veranda-fronted private units is scattered about the main building and clubhouse on a dozen landscaped acres, fronting a long strip of white-sand beach. Rental units, housed in cottages, the main building, or in small, coral-stone wings in the gardens, can vary greatly, but each has a luxurious bed (a king, twins, or a four-poster) and a tiled bathroom with fluffy towels, combination shower/tub, and hair dryer. All have private patios, and some have separate dressing rooms. The reception staff is very helpful.

Dining/Diversions: You can lunch in an open-air area, then enjoy dinner in a room with three sides open to ocean views. A first-class chef runs the kitchen. There's a folklore show and barbecue every Thursday, plus a Monday Bajan buffet featuring an array of food (including whole baked fish) and local entertainment.

Amenities: Freshwater pool, tennis court (floodlit at night), water sports including windsurfing, snorkeling, scuba diving (which can be arranged), and use of a minifleet of small sailboats. Room service (during restaurant hours), laundry, massage, hair salon.

The Crystal Cove. Fitt's Village (4 miles north of Bridgetown), St. James, Barbados, W.I. ☎ **800/223-6510** in the U.S., 800/561-1366 in Canada, or 246/432-2683. Fax 246/432-8290. 88 units. A/C TEL. Winter $432–$584 double; $500–$610 suite. Off-season $312–$344 double; $352–$425 suite. Rates are all-inclusive. AE, MC, V.

Set on a 4-acre beachfront site at Fitt's Village, this hotel is a member of the Barbados-based St. James Beach Hotels, which owns some of the best properties on the island, including the Colony Club, Coconut Creek, and Tamarind Cove. Guests have access to the other hotels' combined facilities, and a water taxi provides transportation among the different properties. This, in fact, is one of the major reasons we recommend the Crystal Cove: If you want a change of scene, you can always visit the next member of the St. James group. There is a beach here, but be warned of the treacherous pilings and offshore rocks.

If you don't like the food here, you can prepare your own, since more than two dozen units have kitchenettes. Accommodations range from standard motel-like rooms to more upscale units, with separate living areas and bedrooms. Each opens onto the pool, garden, or ocean; most units have high ceilings. Decorated in soft tropical pastels, all rooms feature light-colored wood furniture, small fridges, private safes, private balconies or patios, small private bathrooms (with hair dryers), and good beds with comfortable mattresses.

Dining/Diversions: There are two restaurants here. You might not drive across the island to sample the food, but it's above average. Entertainment is provided most nights.

Amenities: Three pools and two tennis courts.

Glitter Bay. Porters (a mile north of Holetown), St. James, Barbados, W.I. ☎ **800/223-1818** in the U.S., 800/268-7176 in Canada, 0171/389-1126 in London, or 246/422-5555. Fax 246/422-3940. www.cphotels.ca. E-mail: gasher@cphotels.com. 83 units. A/C MINIBAR TEL. Winter $475–$600 double; $550–$750 one-bedroom suite for 2; from $1,060 two-bedroom suite for 4. Off-season $255–$330 double; $280–$365 one-bedroom suite; from $535 two-bedroom suite. MAP (breakfast and dinner) $65 per person extra. AE, DC, MC, V.

This carefully maintained resort, managed by Princess Hotels International, offers discreet charm and Mediterranean style, although it isn't as sophisticated or alluring as its next-door sibling, the Royal Pavilion (see below). But with its cottagelike suites with kitchenettes, plus a wide array of sports facilities, it's a favored choice for families (well-to-do families, that is). Built in 1981 by the Pemberton Group, a small Barbados-based hotel chain, it lies on a 10-acre plot of manicured lowlands near a sandy beachfront. The accommodations—in an Iberian-style minivillage with thick beams and terra-cotta tiles—surround a garden with a pool, an artificial waterfall, and a simulated lagoon. Most units contain art, built-in furniture, louvered doors, and spacious outdoor patios or balconies ringed with shrubbery. The larger units have small kitchenettes, and some of the most spacious suites can accommodate four to six people. Bedrooms have deluxe mattresses, plus small bathrooms that are well appointed with seersucker robes, hair dryers, fluffy towels, and bidets.

Dining/Diversions: The Piperade Restaurant serves American and international cuisine and has its own bar. The Sunset Beach Bar is a popular rendezvous spot. Guests can dance on an outdoor patio and enjoy local entertainment, such as a steel-drum band or calypso.

Amenities: 24-hour room service, concierge, laundry, baby-sitting, business services, limousine service, twice-daily maid service. Fitness and massage center, two tennis courts (lit at night), aerobics classes, complimentary water sports (including waterskiing, windsurfing, snorkeling, and catamaran sailing), two pools (one for kids), golf at nearby Royal Westmoreland (a Pemberton associated company). Horseback riding, scuba diving, and motorboating can be arranged.

Mango Bay Club. Holetown, Barbados, W.I. ☎ **877/MANGO-4-U**, or 246/432-1384. www.funbarbados.com/lodgings/mangobay/cfm. E-mail: mangob@caribsurf.com. 64 units. A/C TV TEL. Winter $381–$460 double. Off-season $291–$365 double. Extra person $105. Children 3 and under stay free in parents' room. Rates are all-inclusive. AE, DC, MC, V.

The island's newest all-inclusive resort offers barefoot elegance. The complex's several white-washed buildings are set in tropical gardens, opening onto a white-sand beach where most guests spend their lazy days. You get a lot for your money here: accommodations; three meals a day; afternoon tea; all drinks, including house wine with meals; water sports such as sunfish sailing, kayaking, snorkeling, and windsurfing; tennis; one catamaran cruise; one in-pool scuba lesson; glass-bottom boat rides; nightly entertainment; and walking tours.

Guest rooms range from standard to pool view to beachfront. Most units don't face the beach, but open onto the gardens instead. rooms are sold as standard, pool view, and beachfront. Decorated in tropical pastels, each accommodation has a double or king bed with a firm mattress, wicker furnishings, a private safe, and a private terrace or balcony. Bathrooms are a bit small, but do come with fluffy towels and a hair dryer.

Dining/Diversions: Tasty grilled steaks, fresh seafood (including flying fish), and island fruits are just some of the offerings in the resort's beachside restaurant. Nightly entertainment is offered in the piano lounge.

Amenities: Two freshwater pools, tennis courts, and water sports.

✪ **Royal Pavilion.** Porters (a mile north of Holetown), St. James, Barbados, W.I. ☎ **800/223-1818** in the U.S., 800/268-7176 in Canada, 0171/407-1010 in London, or 246/422-5555. Fax 246/422-3940. www.bajan.com/barbados/hotels/royalpav/royalpav.htm. 75 units. A/C MINIBAR TEL. Winter $895 suite for 2; $995–$1,180 villa for 4; $1,500–$1,770 villa for 6. Off-season $275–$365 suite for 2; $470–$750 villa for 4; $810–$1,070 villa for 6. MAP (breakfast and dinner) $65 per person extra. AE, DC, MC, V. Children 11 and under not accepted in winter.

British grace and Bajan hospitality meet at the Royal Pavilion, which became one of the finest resorts on Barbados the moment it opened. It sits next door to Glitter Bay (part of the same chain, whose gardens it shares) and was built on the site of the former Miramar Hotel, a pink-walled structure with lily ponds and splashing fountains. We find this lush resort far superior to the more famous Sandy Lane, which was closed at press time for a complete renovation.

The architects applied a California-hacienda style to the waterfront deluxe rooms and the villa, which houses three suites. Guest rooms are spacious and airy, with marble floors and beautiful rattan furnishings, including comfortable beds. The good-size bathrooms have hair dryers, deluxe toiletries, fluffy towels, and marble vanities. Guests staying here can visit the drinking, dining, and sports facilities at Glitter Bay (and vice versa).

Dining: Both the oceanfront Café Taboras and the more formal Palm Terrace, set below the seaside columns of an open-air loggia on the water, serve Caribbean and international fare. There's an international buffet on Wednesdays.

Amenities: 24-hour room service, concierge, laundry, baby-sitting, business services, limousine service. Freshwater pool overlooking the ocean, massage center, fitness center at Glitter Bay, two tennis courts (open day and night), water-sports program (including complimentary snorkeling, waterskiing, sailing, and windsurfing), duty-free shops, beauty shop with hairdresser. Guests also enjoy privileged tee times at the nearby Royal Westmoreland.

The Sandpiper. Holetown (a 3-minute walk north of town), St. James, Barbados, W.I. ☎ **800/223-1108** in the U.S., 800/567-5327 in Canada, or 246/422-2251. Fax 246/422-1776. E-mail: coral@caribsurf.com. 45 units. A/C TEL. Winter $545–$620 double; $730–$840 suite. Off-season $375–$410 double; $440–$485 suite. MAP (breakfast and dinner) $50 per person extra. AE, MC, V. Children not accepted in Feb.

The Sandpiper has more of a South Seas look than most of the hotels of Barbados. Affiliated with the Coral Reef Club (see above), it's a self-contained, intimate resort, set in a small grove of coconut palms and flowering trees right on the beach. A cluster of rustic-chic units surrounds the pool; some have fine sea views. The rooms open onto little terraces that stretch along the second story, where you can order drinks or have breakfast. Accommodations are generous in size, consisting of superior rooms and one- or two-bedroom suites which are beautifully furnished with tropical pieces. Each has a private terrace, luxurious bed, and small fridge. The medium-size bathrooms are equipped with fluffy towels, combination tub/showers, and hair dryers.

Dining: The cuisine is both continental and West Indian; weekly buffets are offered in winter. There are two bars, one of which sits a few paces from the surf.

Amenities: Pool, two lighted tennis courts. Room service (from 7am to 10:30pm), laundry, baby-sitting.

Tamarind Cove. Paynes Bay, St. James Beach (P.O. Box 429, Bridgetown), Barbados, W.I.
☎ **800/326-6898** in U.S., 800/561-1366 in Canada, or 246/432-1332. Fax 246/432-6317.
166 units. A/C TEL. Winter $406–$472 double; $486–$690 suite. Off-season $358–$372
double; $276–$381 suite. Half-board $75 per person extra. AE, DC, MC, V.

This is the flagship of a British-based hotel chain (St. James Beach Properties) and a
major challenger to the Coral Reef/Sandpiper properties, attracting somewhat the
same upmarket clientele. An $8-million restoration in 1990 made this one of the most
noteworthy hotels on Barbados. In 1995, a freshwater swimming pool with a beachfront terrace was added, as well as a new south wing with more than 40 luxurious
rooms and suites, some with private plunge pools.

Designed in an Iberian style, with pale-pink walls and red terra-cotta roofs, the
hotel occupies a desirable site immediately adjacent to white-sand St. James Beach, 1½
miles south of Holetown. The stylish and comfortable rooms are in a series of
hacienda-style buildings interspersed with vegetation. Each unit has a patio or balcony
overlooking the gardens or ocean. The well-appointed bathrooms boast dual basins,
spacious Roman tubs, stall showers, long marble counters, fluffy towels, and hair
dryers.

Dining/Diversions: The Tamarind Cove has an informal beachfront eatery, two
elegant restaurants (see "Where to Dine," below, for a review of Neptune's), and a
handful of bars. There's some kind of musical entertainment every night.

Amenities: Four freshwater pools, complimentary water sports (including waterskiing, windsurfing, catamaran sailing, and snorkeling). Golf, tennis courts, horseback
riding, and polo are available nearby. Room service, baby-sitting, laundry, massage,
concierge staff.

Treasure Beach. Paynes Bay (about half a mile south of Holetown), St. James, Barbados, W.I.
☎ **800/223-6510** in the U.S. and Canada, or 246/432-1346. Fax 246/432-1094. www.
barbados.org/hotels/h64.htm. E-mail: treasure@caribsurf.com. 29 units. A/C TEL. Winter
$482–$764 one-bedroom suite for 2; $1,704 superior luxury suite. Off-season $188–$318
one-bedroom suite for 2; $647 superior luxury suite. MAP (breakfast and dinner) $44
per person extra. AE, DC, DISC, MC, V. Children 11 and under accepted only by special
request.

Treasure Beach has a loyal following. It's small but choice, known for its well-prepared
food and the comfort and style of its amenities. The atmosphere is intimate and
relaxed, with personalized service a mark of the well-trained staff. Set on about an acre
of sandy beachfront land, this minivillage of two-story buildings is arranged in a
horseshoe pattern around a pool and garden. The accommodations, furnished in a
tropical motif, open onto private balconies or patios. Bedrooms have king-size beds or
twins, each with a first-class mattress, plus small, well-maintained bathrooms with
combination tub/showers and fluffy towels. The clientele is about evenly divided
between North American and British clients.

Dining: Even if you aren't staying here, try to sample some of the culinary specialties at the Treasure Beach Restaurant, including freshly caught seafood and favorites of
Bajan cuisine.

Amenities: Sailboat rentals, pool (which we find too small), access to nearby golf
and tennis courts. Room service (from 7:30am to 9:30pm), valet and laundry service,
safety-deposit boxes, and a receptionist available to arrange car rentals and island
tours.

INEXPENSIVE

Traveller's Palm. 265 Palm Ave., Sunset Crest, St. James, Barbados, W.I. ☎ **246/
432-7722.** 16 units. A/C. Winter $85 apt for 2. Off-season $60 apt for 2. MC, V.

Designed for independent travelers, this is a choice collection of simply furnished, one-bedroom apartments with fully equipped kitchens, a 5-minute drive south of Holetown. Stay here only for reasons of economy, and don't expect too much. The apartments have living and dining areas, as well as patios where you can have breakfast or a candlelit dinner you've prepared yourself (no meals are served here). The slightly worn apartments, filled with bright but fading colors, open onto a lawn with a pool. Maid service is available. A handful of beaches are within a 10-minute walk.

SOUTH OF BRIDGETOWN
EXPENSIVE

Grand Barbados Beach Resort. Aquatic Gap, Bay St. (P.O. Box 639),Bridgetown, St. Michael, Barbados, W.I. ☎ **800/814-2235** in the U.S., or 246/426-4000. Fax 246/429-2400. 133 units. A/C MINIBAR TV TEL. Winter $240–$270 double; from $300 suite. Off-season $130–$175 double; from $245 suite. MAP (breakfast and dinner) $50 per person extra. AE, DC, DISC, MC, V. The hotel is about a mile southeast of Bridgetown.

This well-designed eight-story resort is on scenic Carlisle Bay, opening onto a good white-sand beach, although it's close to an oil refinery whose smell sometimes drifts over. Set on 4 acres, it offers well-furnished (excellent beds) but often small bedrooms with many amenities, including mini-safes and eight-channel satellite TV; the storage space for luggage, however, is inadequate. Rooms open onto furnished balconies with views of the water and of Bridgetown. The spacious bathrooms have vanity areas, fluffy towels, dual basins, and hair dryers. The two top floors are devoted to executive rooms, including a lounge where a complimentary continental breakfast is served.

Dining/Diversions: The Schooner Restaurant, at the end of a 260-foot historic pier, specializes in seafood and buffet lunches. Pier One is an informal alfresco dining area, and it's also the hotel's entertainment center, where live shows are often presented.

Amenities: Water sports, tiny outdoor pool, Jacuzzi, sauna, Sunfish sailing, free use of the hotel's fitness center, complimentary tennis courts (lit at night) nearby, glass-bottom boat rides. Sports, such as golf, waterskiing, and horseback riding, can be arranged. Room service (from 7am to 11pm), exercise room, laundry, activity coordinator who can arrange tours and rentals.

ON THE SOUTH COAST
VERY EXPENSIVE

Turtle Beach Resort. Dover, near St. Lawrence Gap, Barbados, W.I. ☎ **246/438-4680.** Fax 246/428-6089. 167 units. A/C MINIBAR TV TEL. Winter $590–$700 double; $610–$736 suite for 2. Off-season $456–$490 double; $512 suite for 2. Rates are all-inclusive. AE, DC, MC, V.

Most deluxe hotels don't lie south of Bridgetown—this one breaks the rule. The newest member of the Elegant Hotels Group, a swank coterie of Bajan hotels, opened in 1998 on 1,500 feet of white-sand beach on the south coast. It's an all-inclusive property, a type of accommodation gaining in popularity on the island. Families, couples, and honeymooners are attracted to the resort, with its open-air lobby opening onto the beach. All rooms have ocean views, wicker furniture, ceiling fans, safes, and voice mail. Beds have luxury mattresses and fine linens, and the one-bedroom suites offer both a king-size bed and a sofa bed. If needed, free roll-away beds are provided. Bathrooms are luxurious.

Dining/Diversions: The open-air Chelonia serves fine creative cuisine. The casually elegant Waterfront offers informal food such as design-your-own pizzas. The even more casual Blue Turtle Sports Bar has four large TV screens. For diversity, Turtle Beach offers a dine-around program with its other tony properties, including Crystal

Cove and Coconut Creek. There's also nightly entertainment—calypso, jazz, and more.

Amenities: Three pools (one for children), water sports, two flood-lit tennis courts, fitness center, nearby golf, Kids' Club.

EXPENSIVE

Divi Southwinds Beach Resort. St. Lawrence Gap, Christ Church, Barbados, W.I. ☎ **800/367-3484** or 246/428-7181. Fax 246/428-4674. www.barbados.org/hotels/divi/index.htm. 166 units. A/C TV TEL. Winter $200–$245 studio double; $222–$260 suite. Off-season $120–$155 studio double; $150–$165 suite. MAP (breakfast and dinner) $45 per person extra. AE, MC, V.

Midway between Bridgetown and the hamlet of Oistins, this resort was created when two distinctly different complexes were combined. The present resort consists of buildings scattered over 20 or so acres of sandy flatlands. The showpiece is the newer (inland) complex, housing one- and two-bedroom suites with full kitchens. These units look like a connected series of town houses, with wooden balconies and views of a large L-shaped pool. From here, you need only cross through two groves of palm trees and a narrow lane to reach a white-sand beach. The older units, more modestly furnished but fully renovated, lie directly on the beachfront, ringed with palm trees, near an oval pool. The Aquarius Restaurant, which rises above the largest of the resort's pools, is the main dining and drinking venue, serving standard fare. A snack/drink bar is beside the beach, near the older units. Amenities include three pools (one for children), sailboat rentals, snorkeling equipment, a putting green, and a hair salon. Among the loyal clientele are many young families.

Oasis Hotel. Rockley Main Road, P.O. Box 39W, Worthing 14, Christ Church, Barbados, W.I. ☎ **246/435-7930.** Fax 246/435-8232. www.funbarbados.com/lodgings/oasis.cfm. E-mail: oasis@caribsurf.com. 23 units. A/C TV TEL. Winter $250–$280 double. Off-season $175–$200 double. Extra person $95; children 8–12 $50 year-round. Rates are all-inclusive. AE, DC, MC, V.

This is a well-designed, unpretentious, all-suite hotel that is marketed in the U.S. and Britain as one of the least expensive all-inclusive hotels on the island. It was built on sun-flooded flatlands in the heart of Barbados's densest concentration of hotels, restaurants, nightclubs, and pubs. Despite a name change and mid-1990s renovations, many residents still call it by its original name, the Sichris Hotel. Don't expect to be dazzled by a wide array of amenities, as the resort was originally intended as a small-scale compound of self-catering holiday apartments. Each unit, furnished like a standard hotel room, has ceiling fans, a good bed, a safe, and a limited collection of cooking utensils, though few guests opt to actually cook their own meals since the resort's rates are all-inclusive. Bathrooms are small but adequate. There's a modestly sized pool on the premises, tennis courts nearby, and—across the busy coastal highway—the sands of Rockley Beach. The dining room serves Caribbean and international cuisine.

MODERATE

Southern Palms. St. Lawrence, Christ Church, Barbados, W.I. ☎ **800/424-5500** in the U.S., or 246/428-7171. Fax 246/428-7175. www.southernpalms.net. E-mail: southernpalms@sunbeach.net. 118 units. A/C TV TEL. Winter $185–$220 double; $270 suite. Off-season $112–$140 double; $162 suite. MAP (breakfast and dinner) $40 per person extra. AE, DC, DISC, MC, V.

A seafront club with a distinct personality, Southern Palms lies on the Pink Beach of Barbados, midway between the airport and Bridgetown. The core of the resort is a pink-and-white manor house built in the Dutch style, with a garden-level colonnade of arches. Spread along the sands are arched two- and three-story buildings, with

Italian fountains and statues adding to the Mediterranean feel. In its more modern block, an eclectic mixture of rooms includes some with kitchenettes, some facing the ocean, others opening onto the garden, and some with penthouse luxury. The suites have small kitchenettes. A cluster of straw-roofed buildings, housing the drinking and dining facilities, link the accommodations together.

The Khus-Khus Bar and Restaurant serves both West Indian and continental cuisine. A local orchestra often entertains with merengue and steel-band music. Facilities include two beachside freshwater pools, sailboat rentals, and two tennis courts. Snorkeling and scuba diving are available.

INEXPENSIVE

✪ **Bagshot House Hotel**. St. Lawrence Coast Rd., St. Lawrence, Christ Church, Barbados, W.I. ☎ **246/435-6956.** Fax 246/435-9000. www.prideofbarbados.com/bagshot. E-mail: bagshot@caribsurf.com. 16 units. A/C TEL. Winter $120 double. Off-season $80 double. Rates include breakfast. AE, CB, DC, DISC, MC, V.

Completely renovated in 1996, this small, family-managed hotel, which has been painted pink since the 1940s, has flowering vines tumbling over the railing of the balconies and an old-fashioned, unhurried charm. The hotel was named after the early-19th-century manor house that once stood on this site. Some of the well-kept guest rooms boast views of the water and the white-sand beach stretching before you. A sunbathing deck, which doubles as a kind of living room for the resort, is perched at the edge of a lagoon. Also on site are the Sand Dollar restaurant (see "Where to Dine," below) and a deckside lounge, decorated with paintings by local artists.

Fairholme. Maxwell, Christ Church, Barbados, W.I. ☎ **246/428-9425.** Fax 246/420-2389. 31 units. Winter $30 double; $55 studio apt. Off-season $28 double; $35 studio apt. No credit cards.

This converted plantation house has been enlarged over the past 20 years with a handful of connected annexes. The main house and its original gardens are just off a major road, 6 miles southeast of Bridgetown and a 5-minute walk to the beach. The older section has 11 double rooms, each with a living-room area and a patio overlooking an orchard and pool. The 20 Spanish-style studio apartments, more recently added, have cathedral ceilings, dark beams, traditional furnishings, and balconies or patios. Air-conditioning is available only in the studios: The reception desk sells $3 brass tokens that you insert into your air-conditioning unit for around 8 hours of cooling-off time. The restaurant here has a reputation for home-cooking—wholesome, nothing fancy, but the ingredients are fresh. Guests may also use the waterfront cafe and bar at Fairholme's neighbor, the Sea Breeze.

✪ **Sandy Beach Hotel**. Worthing, Christ Church, Barbados, W.I. ☎ **246/435-8000.** Fax 246/435-8053. 89 units. A/C TV TEL. Winter $124 double; $220 one-bedroom suite; $328 two-bedroom suite. Off-season $88–$93 double; $134–$139 one-bedroom suite; $182–$268 two-bedroom suite. MAP (breakfast and dinner) $45 per adult extra. Extra person $25. Children 11 and under stay free in parents' room. AE, MC, V.

Definitely not to be confused with Sandy Lane, this hotel, originally established in 1980 and renovated in 1994, is an unexciting but thoroughly reliable choice. It rests on 2 acres of beachfront land, 4 miles southeast of Bridgetown. The Barbadian-owned property rises around its architectural centerpiece, a soaring, cone-shaped structure known as a *palapa*. Suitable for families, the resort contains standard motel-like double rooms, one- and two-bedroom suites, and 16 honeymoon suites. All of the simply decorated and spacious units have fully equipped kitchenettes, private balconies or patios, and locally made furniture. Facilities for disabled travelers are available in some of the ground-floor suites. Kolors, specializing in seafood and steaks, is under the palapa and opens onto a view of the sea and pool. Every Monday, when nonguests are welcome, the resort sponsors a rum-punch party and a Bajan buffet. Entertainment is offered 3 nights a week. Amenities include a pool with tropical waterfall, children's play area, and wading pool. Water sports, which cost extra, include 3-hour snorkeling trips, windsurfing, paddleboats, Sailfish, scuba lessons, and use of air mattresses, snorkels, fins, and masks. An activities desk can arrange island tours.

Woodville Beach Apartments. Hastings, Christ Church, Barbados, W.I. ☎ **246/435-6694.** Fax 246/435-9211. 36 units. TEL. Winter $110–$116 studio apt for 2; $145 one-bedroom apt for 2; $190 two-bedroom apt for up to 4. Off-season $85–$90 studio apt; $110 one-bedroom apt; $130 two-bedroom apt. AE, MC, V.

These apartments, last renovated in 1995, represent one of the best bargains on Barbados and are ideal for families. Directly on a rocky shoreline 2½ miles southeast of Bridgetown, the hotel is in the heart of the village of Hastings. The U-shaped complex is built around a pool terrace overlooking the sea. Functional and minimalist in decor, the apartments are clean and comfortable, with tiny but fully equipped kitchenettes. All have balconies or decks, and some units have air-conditioning. Although some athletic guests attempt to swim off the nearby rocks, most walk 5 minutes to the white sands of nearby Rockley (Accra) Beach. A small restaurant on the property serves American and Bajan fare. Supermarkets, stores, and banks are within easy walking distance.

ON THE EAST COAST
VERY EXPENSIVE

Sam Lord's Castle Resort. Long Bay, St. Philip, Barbados, W.I. ☎ **246/423-7350.** Fax 246/423-6361. www.barbados.org/hotels/samlords/index.htm. 248 units. A/C MINIBAR TV TEL. Winter $350–$375 double; $480–$510 triple. Off-season $250–$275 double; $360–$385 triple. Rates include all meals and afternoon tea. AE, DC, DISC, MC, V. The hotel is a 15-minute drive northeast of the airport.

In spite of its name, this is no castle but a great house built in 1820 by one of Barbados's most notorious scoundrels. According to legend, Samuel Hall Lord (the "Regency Rascal") constructed the estate with money acquired by luring ships to wreck on the jagged but hard-to-detect rocks of Cobbler's Reef. The house, near the easternmost end of the island, was built in the pirate's more mellow "golden years." Craftspeople were brought from England to reproduce sections of the queen's castle at Windsor. The decor includes the dubiously acquired but nonetheless beautiful art of Reynolds, Raeburn, and Chippendale.

Set on 72 landscaped acres, the estate has a wide, lengthy private beach edged by tall coconut trees. Guest rooms have private balconies or patios, and most come with king-size beds or twins, each with a good mattress. The main house contains only seven rooms, stylishly decorated with antique furnishings; three have canopied beds. The rest of the accommodations are in cottages and wings, either two or four floors high; there are some rather tacky motel rooms with a faux-castle theme. (Some of these units evoke southwest Miami in the 1950s—no great compliment.) For privacy's sake and to get more light, try to avoid the ground-floor units. The best (and most expensive) accommodations are in structures 7, 8, and 9.

The Wanderer Restaurant serves all three meals; you can order a hamburger at the Oceanus Café, right on the beach. There are many bars as well. Weekly events include a fiesta night in the hotel's Bajan Village, a shipwreck barbecue and beach party with a steel-drum band, a limbo show, and fire-eaters on South Beach. The concierge can arrange island tours and attend to your needs, but the staff often seems more concerned with the demands of the tour groups (the hotel is a favorite for conventions). Amenities include three pools, an exercise room, shuffleboard, table tennis, sailing, horseback riding, snorkeling, and fishing; other activities can be arranged.

MODERATE

Crane Beach Hotel. Crane Bay, St. Philip, Barbados, W.I. ☎ **800/223-6510** or 246/423-6220. Fax 246/423-5343. www.barbados.org/hotels/crane. E-mail: cranebeach@ sunbeach.net. 18 units. TEL. Winter $160 double; $250–$295 one-bedroom suite; $425 two-bedroom suite. Off-season $90 double; $150–$175 one-bedroom suite; $255 two-bedroom suite. MAP (breakfast and dinner) $50 per person extra. Honeymoon packages available. AE, MC, V. The hotel is about 14 miles from Bridgetown and a 15-minute drive from the airport.

Near the easternmost end of the island, this remote hilltop property stands on a cliff overlooking the Atlantic. The location may be beautiful, but the hotel leaves much to be desired. Time-share units are hawked in the lobby, housekeeping appears lax, and rubberneckers, who pay an entrance fee to enter the property and patronize the area around the pool and bar, often disturb the tranquillity. In other words, it's not for everybody—yet it's still one of the most famous hostelries in the southern Caribbean.

Located near Marriott's Sam Lord's Castle Resort, the hotel opens onto one of the most scenic beaches on Barbados, reached by walking down some 200 steps. At times, the water can be too rough for swimming. Many of the guest rooms boast panoramic views, canopied beds, and antique furnishings. Some units have kitchenettes, but only four have air-conditioning and are reserved for guests in dire need of it. Baths are small but tiled, with generous counter space.

Many nonguests head here just to have a drink on the panoramic terrace or to enjoy a meal. An international cuisine is served with West Indian flair; at night, you can dine by candlelight. The Sunday brunch is a well-attended event. The Roman-style swimming pool with columns, separating the main house from the dining room, has been used as a backdrop for more fashion layouts than any other place in the Caribbean. The resort also has tennis courts.

INEXPENSIVE

The Edgewater Inn. Bathsheba (13 miles northeast of Bridgetown on Hwy. 3), St. Joseph, Barbados, W.I. ☎ **246/433-9900.** Fax 246/433-9902. 20 units. Winter $115–$195 double; off-season $85–$145 double. AE, DISC, MC, V.

Built as a dramatically isolated private home on the site of a much older colonial building, and converted into a hotel in 1947, this inn is set directly on the Atlantic seacoast, a short drive southeast of the island's Scotland district. Located in a tropical rain forest atop a low cliff, the property opens onto ocean views, and a nearby wildlife sanctuary invites exploration. Cozy and intimate, the small inn is decorated with beveled leaded-glass windows from Asia; furnishings reflect an island motif, with mahogany pieces handcrafted by local artisans. The freshwater pool, shaped like the island of Barbados, is the focal point of the resort. Surfers and nonguests often drop by, either for a drink or a meal. The restaurant, serving West Indian cuisine, is open daily for lunch and dinner. A Bajan buffet is staged every Sunday from noon to 3:30pm, costing $22.50 per person.

3 Where to Dine

ON THE WEST COAST
EXPENSIVE

✪ **Bagatelle Restaurant.** Hwy. 2A, St. Thomas. ☎ **246/421-6767.** Reservations recommended. Lunch $14; dinner main courses $22.50–$45. MC, V. Daily 11am–2:30pm and

7–9:30pm. Cut inland near Paynes Bay north of Bridgetown, 3 miles from both Sunset Crest and the Sandy Lane Hotel. FRENCH/CARIBBEAN.

A 15-minute drive north of Bridgetown, Bagatelle is located in what was originally the residence of the island's first governor (Lord Willoughby), built in 1645. This sylvan retreat, one of the island's finest and most elegant choices for French cuisine with Caribbean flair, is in the cool uplands, just south of the island's center. Candles and lanterns illuminate the old archways and the ancient trees. The service is the best we've found on Barbados. Try the homemade duck-liver pâté, deviled Caribbean crab backs, or smoked flying-fish mousse with horseradish mayonnaise. The beef Wellington Bagatelle style with a chasseur sauce is a favorite, as is the crisp roast duckling with an orange-and-brandy sauce. The local catch of the day can be prepared grilled, barbecued, or in the style of Baxters Road (spicily seasoned and sautéed in deep oil). Different homemade desserts are featured nightly, and coffee can be served on the terrace. Cruise-ship passengers can take advantage of Bagatelle's light lunches before their ships sail at sunset.

✪ **Carambola.** Derricks (1½ miles south of Holetown), St. James. ☎ **246/432-0832.** Reservations recommended. Main courses $22–$50. AE, MC, V. Mon–Sat 6:30–9:30pm. Closed Aug. FRENCH/CARIBBEAN/ASIAN.

Built beside the road that runs along the island's western coastline, this restaurant sits atop a 20-foot seaside cliff and offers one of the most panoramic dining terraces in the Caribbean. However, you'll have to go early for dinner to see the view, since lunch isn't served. The prize-winning cuisine is creative, with modern, French-inspired touches. The dishes may sound continental, but they definitely have Caribbean flair and flavor, as exemplified by the fillet of swordfish or dolphin (mahimahi). A crowd-pleasing favorite is the chicken stuffed with crab, or look to the Far East and try the spicy Thai pork tenderloin. A selection of savory vegetarian dishes is offered as well. Do try to save room for one of the luscious desserts like lime mousse. The impressive wine list features mostly French vintages.

✪ **The Cliff.** Hwy. 1, Derrick, St. James. ☎ **246/432-1922.** Reservations required in winter. Main courses $28–$37.50. AE, DISC, MC, V. Mon–Sat 6:30–10pm. INTERNATIONAL/ CARIBBEAN.

Built atop a 10-foot coral cliff adjacent to the Coconut Creek Hotel, this open-air restaurant has a four-level dining room crafted with terra-cotta tiles and coral stone. Despite the fact that the owners don't consider it exclusive, posh, or even particularly formal, it has attracted Prince Andrew and other titled and bejeweled guests of the nearby upscale hotels. No one will mind, however, if you wear well-tailored shorts; the place really is surprisingly low-key. We agree with the praise of Frommer's reader and gourmet Dr. Stephen C. Bandy of Princeton, New Jersey, who writes: "The Cliff offers a menu of the highest quality: the best cuts of meat, the freshest and most interesting vegetables and greens I have ever eaten on the island, and dessert confections that would not be looked down on in New York restaurants like Bouley and Lespinasse." How right he is! Menu items include grilled snapper drizzled in three types of coriander sauce (cream-based, oil-based, and vinaigrette style), accompanied with garlic mashed potatoes and Thai-style curried shrimp. Sushi comes complete with wasabi and portions of fresh local tuna, scallops, and snapper. As you dine, watch for manta rays, which glide through the illuminated waters below; a sighting is considered a sign of good luck.

The Emerald Palm. Porters, St. James. ☎ **246/422-4116.** Reservations required. Main courses $20–$48. AE, MC, V. Tues–Sun 6:30–9:30pm (last seating). Closed Sept. INTERNATIONAL.

This stucco-and-tile house is 2 miles north of Holetown in a tropical garden dotted with a trio of gazebos. After passing under an arbor, you'll be invited to order a drink, served on one of the flowered banquettes that fill various parts of the restaurant. You can then enjoy a candlelit meal on the rear terrace, alfresco style. Come here for zesty dishes packed with international and island flavors. Begin, perhaps, with a spicy cucumber soup or a succulent version of Caribbean fish soup with fresh peppers. Move on to roast red snapper in coconut juice with local baby spinach (a specialty), or go for a simple dish like medallions of beef tenderloin in mustard sauce. For a real taste of Barbados, try the chargrilled scallops and baby squid seasoned with a chili-pepper dressing.

Ile de France. In the Settlers' Beach Hotel, Holetown, St. James. ☎ **246/422-3245.** Reservations recommended. Main courses $25–$40. MC, V. Daily 6:30–9:30pm (last order). CLASSIC FRENCH.

Located north of Holetown and 8 miles north of Bridgetown, this restaurant presents the finest and most authentic French cuisine on Barbados. Place yourself in the capable hands of Michel and Martine Gramaglia, two French-born expats who handle their kitchen and dining room with an enviable savoir-faire. Ingredients are obtained fresh on Barbados, or flown in from France or Martinique. Specialties might include escargots de Bourgogne, a flavorful version of fish soup with lobster, or a marinade of three fish based on the catch of the day. Other dishes include tournedos with a béarnaise sauce, rack of lamb, shrimp, and roast lobster. For dessert, try the tart tatin, crème brûlée, or banana terrine. The atmosphere here is both charming and traditional.

La Maison. Holetown, St. James. ☎ **246/432-1156.** Reservations required in winter. Main courses $24–$40. AE, MC, V. Tues–Sun 6:30–9:30pm. FRENCH/CARIBBEAN.

Located on the beach south of Holetown and open on two sides to the sea and to a flowering courtyard, La Maison has exposed coral walls and an intricate ceiling, crafted from a Guyanan hardwood called greenheart. The award-winning cuisine is served with quiet dignity. The intriguing appetizers are likely to include blackened flying-fish fillets set on a sweet-potato salad. Main courses feature such exotica as barracuda steamed with tomato fondue and vegetables, red snapper grilled and served with a seafood sauce, or, for something more familiar, grilled sirloin in a ragoût with sautéed fennel. For a delectable dessert, there's fresh fruit in a tulip basket with ice cream or sorbet.

✪ **Neptune's.** In the Tamarind Cove Beach Resort, Paynes Bay, St. James. ☎ **246/432-1332.** Reservations recommended. Main courses $30–$45. MC, V. Wed–Sun 6:30–10pm. Closed Tues in the off-season. SEAFOOD.

This is the best seafood place on Barbados and one of the island's most expensive restaurants, with management virtually insisting that every food and beverage tab exceed $60 per person. Located south of Holetown in one of Barbados's top resorts, it abandons the standard tropical Caribbean motif found in most of the island's other restaurants. Instead, you'll find a stylish octagonal room sheathed in faux malachite, whose emerald-green tones reflect the colors of an illuminated aquarium in the room's center. Service is impeccable.

Appetizers range from a smoked fish pâté with cucumber noodles and beetroot vinaigrette to seasoned crab claws with a salad of bean sprouts and bok choy. Neptune's catch is a selection of island fish, often served in a light orange sauce flavored with herbs. You can also order that island favorite, fillet of red snapper, or splurge on a cassoulet of lobster. The dessert menu is one of the most elaborate on Barbados,

ranging from a classic tiramisu to a coconut-and-mango parfait or a trio of rich chocolate mousses.

✪ **Olives Bar & Bistro.** Second St. at the corner of Hwy. 1, Holetown. ☎ **246/432-2112.**
Reservations required in winter. Main courses $14–$33. AE, MC, V. Daily 6:30–10:30pm.
MEDITERRANEAN/CARIBBEAN.

Established in 1994 by a couple from New Zealand, this restaurant is named for the
only oil used in preparing the cuisine. In addition, olives are the only snack served in
the bar, where there's a welcome rowdiness. The street-level, air-conditioned dining
room (where no smoking is permitted) spills out from its original coral-stone walls and
scrubbed-pine floorboards into a pleasant garden. The cuisine celebrates the warm climates of southern Europe and the Antilles, and does so exceedingly well. Even some
local chefs like to dine here on their nights off. The best items include yellowfin tuna,
marinated and seared rare and served on a bed of roast-garlic mashed potatoes with
grilled ratatouille. You can also order roast lamb flavored with honey, garlic, and fresh
herbs, or, for something more Caribbean, jerk tenderloin of pork. For dessert, try the
toffee-and-walnut tart or the Creole bread pudding. Next door is a sandwich bar
serving light luncheon fare, Monday through Friday from 8am to 4pm.

MODERATE

Angry Annie's Restaurant & Bar. First St., Holetown, St. James. ☎ **246/432-2119.** Main
courses $12.50–$27.50. MC, V. Daily 6–10pm (sometimes until midnight). INTERNATIONAL.

Don't ask Annie why she's angry—she might tell you! Annie and Paul Matthews, both
from the United Kingdom, run this friendly, cozy, 34-seat joint. It's decorated in tropical colors with a circular bar, and rock-and-roll classics play on the excellent sound
system. The dishes are tasty with lots of local flavor. The place is known for its ribs,
the most savory on the island. We like the garlic-cream potatoes and the use of local
vegetables whenever possible. Annie also turns out fresh fish and excellent pasta dishes.
There's take-out service if you'd like to dine back in your studio or apartment.

Bourbon Street Restaurant. Prospect, St. James. ☎ **246/424-4557.** Reservations recommended. Main courses $20–$28.50. MC, V. Daily 6:30–10pm. Closed Mon May–Nov.
NEW ORLEANS CREOLE/CAJUN.

The award-winning Bourbon Street adds a unique twist to a dining culture that is
dominated largely by Bajan menus. The main focus here is re-creating a New Orleans
atmosphere, with spicy Louisiana food and music. For appetizers, you'll find everything from oysters on the half shell to Bar-B-Que Shrimps à la Louisiana. Main
courses, which can be prepared as spicy as you like, range from "N'awlins" style jambalaya and crawfish to Cajun-style island cuisine like blackened red snapper. Bourbon
Street also boasts a view that overlooks the sea, and prides itself for being the "house
of blues and jazz" on Barbados, with live music every Wednesday, Friday, and Saturday
night.

✪ **The Fathoms.** Paynes Bay, St. James. ☎ **246/432-2568.** Reservations recommended
for dinner. Main courses $22–$29. AE, DISC, MC, V. Daily noon–3pm and 6:30–10pm (last
order); bar daily from 5pm. INTERNATIONAL.

Located in a red-roofed stucco house close to the surf of the island's western coastline,
this pleasant restaurant serves meals on an outdoor terrace, shaded by a mahogany
tree, and inside, in a room with terra-cotta, wood, and pottery accents. The fairly
ambitious menu does itself proud with appetizers like shrimp and crab étouffée,
herbed conch cakes, and blackened shrimp with mango. For a main dish, try the
caramelized barracuda, grilled pork medallions, or the zesty dorado fish Hunan.
Upstairs is a Santa Fe–style tapas bar, primarily for drinks, wines, and finger foods. A

pool table and board games will help you pass the evening away. This attractive watering hole is open daily from 5pm until the crowd finally departs.

Nico's Champagne Wine Bar & Restaurant. Derrick's, St. James. ☎ **246/432-6386.** Reservations recommended. Main courses $8.70–$13.50 lunch, $12–$36 dinner. AE, DISC, MC, V. Mon–Sat 11:30am–10:30pm. INTERNATIONAL.

Set on the landward side of a road that bisects some of the most expensive residential real estate on Barbados (the west coast), Nico's is a great value, an informal bistro inspired by the wine bars of London. In a 19th-century building originally constructed as the headquarters for a plantation, it does a thriving business from its air-conditioned bar area. Meals are served at tables under a shed-style roof in the back garden. About a dozen wines are sold by the glass; the flavorful food is designed to accompany the wine. Examples include deep-fried Camembert with passion-fruit sauce, chicken breasts stuffed with crab, and some of the best lobster (grilled simply and served with garlic butter) on Barbados.

✪ **Ragmuffins.** First St., Holetown, St. James. ☎ **246/432-1295.** Main courses $16–$25. AE, MC, V. Tues–Sun 6–10pm. CARIBBEAN.

The only restaurant on Barbados housed in the typical chattel house, this is a real discovery: an affordable, lively, and most inviting choice. Many hard-to-please locals recommend Ragmuffins when visitors ask where to go for authentic island cuisine. The broiled T-bones are juicy and perfectly flavored; there's always an offering of fresh fish; and vegetarians aren't ignored either, as the cooks are always willing to stir-fry some vegetables with noodles. Highlights on the menu include blackened fish, the local version of a spicy West Indian curry, and the jerk chicken salad.

SPEIGHTSTOWN

Mango's by the Sea. 2 West End, Queen St. ☎ **246/422-0704.** Reservations recommended. Main courses $13–$70. MC, V. Sun–Fri 6–9:30pm. INTERNATIONAL.

Speightstown was never noted for its dining choices until the opening of this restaurant and bar overlooking the water. It's best known for its seafood: The owners, Montréal natives Gail and Pierre Spenard, buy the catch of the day directly from the fishermen's boats. The food is exceedingly good and the seasonings aren't too overpowering, as they are at many Bajan restaurants. Market-fresh ingredients are used to good advantage. Appetizers might be anything from an intriguing green peppercorn pâté to pumpkin soup. If you don't want fish, opt for the 8-ounce U.S. tenderloin steak cooked to perfection or the fall-off-the-bone barbecued baby back ribs. Top your meal off with a passion-fruit cheesecake or a starfruit torte. There's live entertainment on some nights.

BRIDGETOWN

The Waterfront Cafe. The Careenage, Bridgetown. ☎ **246/427-0093.** Reservations required. Main courses $10–$20. AE, DC, MC, V. Mon–Sat 10am–midnight. INTERNATIONAL.

In a turn-of-the-century warehouse originally built to store bananas and freeze fish, this cafe serves international fare with a strong emphasis on Bajan specialties. Try the fresh catch of the day prepared Creole style, peppered steak, or the fish burger made with kingfish or dolphin. For vegetarians, the menu includes such dishes as pasta primavera, vegetable soup, and usually a featured special. Both diners and drinkers are welcome here for Creole food, beer, and pastel-colored drinks. Tuesday nights bring live steel-band music and a Bajan buffet ($20.50). To see the Thursday night Dixieland bands, reserve about a week in advance. There's jazz on Friday and Saturday.

Going Native at the Market

Every vendor at the major markets, in the centers of Bridgetown, Oistins, and Speightstown, seems to offer something delightful. Start off with a glass of *mauby*, a refreshing but slightly bitter iced tea made from a tree bark. Move on to pumpkin fritters, formed into a ball and fried in butter, or pepper pot, a meat stew preserved in cassava juice. On our recent rounds, we discovered a mango-based variation on gazpacho—it's addictive. For dessert, seek out a hawker pushing an oversize cart filled with coconuts; he'll take his machete to a green coconut, then offer you a cool drink followed by "the jelly," that soft essence that slithers sweetly down your throat.

SOUTH OF BRIDGETOWN

Brown Sugar. Aquatic Gap, St. Michael. ☎ **246/426-7684.** Reservations recommended. Main courses $14–$50; fixed-price buffet lunch $17.50. AE, DC, DISC, MC, V. Sun–Fri noon–2:30pm and 6–9:30pm (last order), Sat 6–9:30pm (last order). BAJAN.

Brown Sugar serves some of the tastiest Bajan specialties on the island. The alfresco restaurant is hidden behind lush foliage in a turn-of-the-century coral limestone bungalow. The ceiling is latticed, with slow-turning fans, and there's an open veranda for dining by candlelight beneath hanging plants. We suggest starting with hot gungo-peak soup (pigeon peas cooked in chicken broth and zested with fresh coconut milk, herbs, and a touch of white wine). Among the main dishes, Creole orange chicken is popular, or you might like stuffed crab backs. A selection of locally grown vegetables is also offered. Only the lobster is expensive; most of the other dishes are reasonably priced. For dessert, we recommend the walnut-rum pie with rum sauce. The restaurant is known for its buffet-style lunches—popular with local businesspeople for its good value.

ON THE SOUTH COAST
MODERATE

✪ **David's Place.** St. Lawrence Main Rd., Worthing, Christ Church. ☎ **246/435-9755.** Reservations recommended. Main courses $15–$40. AE, DISC, MC, V. Tues–Sun 6–10pm. BARBADIAN.

Owner/operators David and Darla Trotman promise you'll sample "Barbadian dining at its best"—and they deliver on that promise, at reasonable prices, too. The restaurant is south of Bridgetown between Rockley Beach and Worthing, in an old-fashioned seaside house on St. Lawrence Bay. The tables are positioned so that diners enjoy a view of the Caribbean. Everybody's favorites, pumpkin or cucumber soup, might get you going, or you can try the pickled chicken wings. If you're afraid to venture to Baxters Road at night, you can order Baxters road chicken here. It's seasoned the Bajan way—marinated in lime, salt, and herbs, then deep-fried. Pepper pot is a hot-and-spicy dish with beef, salt pork, chicken, and lamb. Fish steak, the best choice on the menu, might be dolphin (mahimahi), kingfish, barracuda, shark, or red snapper, served in a white-wine sauce or deep-fried Bajan style. Desserts are equally good: Here, at last, is a restaurant that offers that old drugstore favorite of the 1940s and 1950s, a banana split—or you might opt instead for the coconut cream pie or the carrot cake in rum sauce.

Luigi's Restaurant. Dover Woods, St. Lawrence Gap, Christ Church. ☎ **246/428-9218.** Reservations recommended. Main courses $13–$26. MC, V. Mon–Sat 6–10:30pm (last order). ITALIAN.

This open-air Italian trattoria has operated in a green-and-white private house since 1963. The atmosphere is contemporary, airy, and comfortable. Appetizers include pizzas, classic choices such as escargots or Caesar salad, and half orders of many pastas. The baked pastas, such as a creamy lasagna, are delectable, or you can go for the fresh fish or veal special of the day. For dessert, try the zabaglione and one of the wide selections of coffee, ranging from Italian to Russian or Turkish.

Pisces. St. Lawrence Gap, Christ Church. ☎ **246/435-6564.** Reservations recommended. Main courses $15–$38. AE, DC, MC, V. Daily 6–9:30pm (last order). From Bridgetown, take Hwy. 7 south about 4 miles; turn right at the sign toward St. Lawrence Gap. BAJAN/SEAFOOD.

This beautiful restaurant with a tropical decor offers alfresco dining at water's edge. Begin with one of the soups, perhaps split pea or pumpkin, or a savory appetizer like flying fish Florentine. Seafood lovers enjoy the Pisces platter—charcoal-broiled dolphin (mahimahi), fried flying fish, broiled kingfish, and butter-fried prawns. You might also be drawn to the seasonal Caribbean fish, which can be broiled, blackened, or pan-fried, then served with lime-herb butter. Another seasonal delight is snapper Caribe, which is stuffed with shrimp, tomato, and herbs, then baked and served with a white-wine sauce. A limited but good selection of poultry and meat is offered, including roast pork Barbados with a traditional Bajan stuffing. New restaurants come and go on Barbados, but this old favorite still hangs on.

Sand Dollar. In Bagshot House Hotel, St. Lawrence Coast Rd., Christ Church. ☎ **246/435-6956.** Reservations recommended. Main courses $10–$20 lunch, $15–$32 dinner. AE, DC, MC, V. Daily 7am–10pm. INTERNATIONAL.

The pink-walled hotel that houses the Sand Dollar has featured one kind of restaurant or another since it was originally established in the early 1940s, thus this location has become something of a staple in the minds of many longtime island residents. Opening onto a masonry terrace that extends almost to the edge of the water, the restaurant is less formal than in years past, with a modern outlook stemming from a complete renovation in 1996. Menu items include a well-seasoned pepper steak, Mount Gay ribs, brochettes of jerk shrimp, chicken with a honey-rum sauce, different preparations of steak and lobster, and a wide array of salads. Lunches feature a roster of sandwiches and salads. No one will object if you wear shorts, but bathing suits are not allowed.

Witch Doctor. St. Lawrence Gap, Christ Church. ☎ **246/435-6581.** Reservations recommended. Main courses $13–$30. MC, V. Daily 6:15–9:45pm. BAJAN/AFRICAN.

The Witch Doctor hides behind a screen of thick foliage in the heart of the southern coast. The decor, in honor of its name, features African and island wood carvings of witch doctors. The fascinating cuisine includes some unusual concoctions that are tasty and well prepared, a big change from bland hotel fare. For an appetizer, try the split-pea-and-pumpkin soup or the cold, lime-soused ceviche. Chef's specialties include various flambé dishes such as steak, shrimp Creole, fried flying fish, and chicken piri-piri (inspired by Mozambique).

INEXPENSIVE

The Ship Inn. St. Lawrence Gap, Christ Church. ☎ **246/435-6961.** Reservations recommended for the Captain's Carvery only. Main courses $8–$15; all-you-can-eat carvery meal $15 at lunch, $21 (plus $7.50 for appetizer and dessert) at dinner. MC, V. Sun–Fri noon–3pm and 6:30–10:30pm (last order), Sat 6:30–10:30pm. ENGLISH PUB/BAJAN.

South of Bridgetown between Rockley Beach and Worthing, the Ship Inn is a traditional English-style pub with an attractive, rustic decor of nautical memorabilia. As an alternative, you can also enjoy a drink in the garden bar's tropical atmosphere. On hand are beers from Jamaica, Trinidad, and Europe. Many guests come to play darts, to meet friends, and especially to listen to top local bands (see "Barbados After Dark," later in this chapter). The Ship Inn serves substantial bar food, such as homemade steak-and-kidney pie, shepherd's pie, and chicken, shrimp, and fish dishes. For more formal dining, visit the Captain's Carvery, where you can have your fill of succulent cuts from prime roasts from the buffet, plus an array of traditional Bajan food, like fillets of flying fish.

T.G.I. Boomers. St. Lawrence Gap, Christ Church. ☎ **246/428-8439.** American breakfast $6.50; lunch specials $3.50–$7; dinner main courses $9–$22.50; Sun buffet $12.50. AE, MC, V. Daily 7:30am–11:30pm. AMERICAN/BAJAN.

Four miles south of Bridgetown near Rockley Beach along Highway 7, T.G.I. Boomers offers some of the best bargain meals on the island. It has an active bar and a row of tables for diners, who usually order frothy pastel-colored drinks as well. The cook prepares a special catch of the day, which is served with soup or salad, rice or baked potato, and a vegetable. You can always count on seafood, steaks, and hamburgers. For lunch, there's the daily Bajan special and jumbo sandwiches. Be sure to try one of the 16-ounce daiquiris.

ON THE EAST COAST

✪ **Atlantis Hotel.** Bathsheba, St. Joseph. ☎ **246/433-9445.** Reservations required for Sun buffet and 7pm dinner, recommended at all other times. Two-course fixed-price lunch $12.50; fixed-price dinner $15.75; Sun buffet $18.75. AE. Daily 11:30am–3pm, dinner at 7pm (don't be late). BAJAN.

Harking back to the old-fashioned Barbados of many years ago, the slightly run-down Atlantis Hotel is often filled with both Bajans and visitors. It's located between Cattlewash-on-Sea and Tent Bay on the east (Atlantic) coast. From the sunny, breeze-filled restaurant, with a sweeping view of the turbulent ocean, Enid I. Maxwell has been welcoming visitors from all over the world ever since she opened the place in 1945. Her copious buffets are one of the best values on the island. From loaded tables, you can sample such Bajan foods as pumpkin fritters, peas and rice, macaroni and cheese, chow mein, souse (pig's feet marinated in lime juice), and a Bajan pepper pot. No one ever leaves here hungry.

4 Beaches

Bajans will tell you that their island has a beach for every day of the year. If you're only visiting for a short time, however, you'll probably be happy with the ones that are easy to find. They're all open to the public—even those in front of the big resort hotels and private homes—and the government requires that there be access to all beaches, via roads along the property line or through hotel entrances. The beaches on the west coast, the so-called **Gold Coast,** are the most popular.

WEST COAST   Waters are calm here. Major beaches include **Paynes Bay,** which is accessed from the Coach House, south of Holetown, and has a parking area. This is a good choice for water sports, especially snorkeling. The beach can get rather crowded, but the beautiful bay somehow makes it seem worth the effort to get here. Directly south of Payne's Bay, at Fresh Water Bay, are three of the best west-coast beaches: **Brighton Beach, Brandon's Beach,** and **Paradise Beach.**

Church Point lies north of St. James Church, opening onto **Heron Bay,** site of the Colony Club Hotel and one of the most scenic bays on Barbados. The swimming here is ideal, though the beach can get overcrowded. When you've had enough sun, you can seek cover under some shade trees or order drinks at the beach terrace operated by the Colony Club.

We also recommend **Mullins Beach,** where the glassy blue waters attract snorkelers. There's parking on the main road and some shady areas. At the Mullins Beach Bar, you can order that rum drink you've been craving.

SOUTH COAST   Beaches here include **Casuarina Beach,** with access from Maxwell Coast Road, going across the property of the Casuarina Beach Hotel. This is one of the wider beaches of Barbados, and we've noticed that it's swept by trade winds even on the hottest days of August. Windsurfers are especially fond of this one. Food and drinks can be ordered at the hotel.

Silver Sands Beach, to the east of Oistins, is near the southernmost point of Barbados, directly east of South Point Lighthouse and near the Silver Rock Hotel. This white-sand beach is a favorite with many Bajans (who probably want to keep it a secret from as many tourists as possible). Drinks are sold at the Silver Rock Bar.

Sandy Beach, reached from the parking lot on the Worthing main road, has tranquil waters opening onto a lagoon, the epitome of Caribbean charm. This is a family favorite, with lots of screaming and yelling on the weekends in particular. Food and drinks are sold here.

SOUTHEAST COAST   The southeast coast is the site of the big waves, especially at **Crane Beach,** the white-sand strip set against a backdrop of palms that you've probably seen in all the travel magazines. The beach is spectacular, as Prince Andrew, who has a house overlooking it, might agree. It offers excellent bodysurfing, but at times the waters may be too rough for all but the strongest swimmers. The beach is set against cliffs, with the Crane Beach Hotel towering above it. This is ocean swimming, not the calm Caribbean, so take precautions.

Bottom Bay, north of Sam Lord's Castle Resort, is one of our all-time Bajan favorites. Park on the top of a cliff, then walk down the steps to this much-photographed tropical beach with its grove of coconut palms; there's even a cave. The sand is brilliantly white against the aquamarine sea, a picture-postcard perfect beach paradise.

EAST (ATLANTIC) COAST   There are miles and miles of uncrowded beaches along the east coast, but this is the Atlantic side, thus swimming here is potentially dangerous. Many travelers like to visit the beaches here, especially those in the **Bathsheba/Cattlewash** areas, for their rugged grandeur. Waves are extremely high on these beaches, and the bottom tends to be rocky. The currents are also unpredictable. Otherwise, the beaches are ideal for strolling if you don't go into the water.

5 Sports & Outdoor Pursuits

If you've come to swim and sunbathe, head for the western coast's clear, buoyant Caribbean waters. You may also want to visit the surf-pounded Atlantic coast in the east, which is better for the views than for the swimming.

DEEP-SEA FISHING   The fishing is first-rate in the waters around Barbados, where fishers pursue dolphin (mahimahi), marlin, wahoo, barracuda, and sailfish, to name only the most popular catches. There's also an occasional cobia. The **Dive Shop,** Pebbles Beach, Aquatic Gap, St. Michael (☎ **800/693-3483** or 246/426-9947), can arrange half-day charters for one to six people, costing $350 per boat (including all equipment and drinks). A whole-day jaunt goes for $700.

Heading for the Hills

Be sure to check out the "Exploring the Green Hills" section under "Exploring the Island," later in this chapter, for details on hikes, hill climbs, and horseback rides through the lush interior of Barbados.

GOLF   Open to all is the 18-hole championship golf course of the **Sandy Lane Hotel,** St. James (☎ 246/432-1311), on the west coast. Greens fees are $135 in winter and $100 in summer for 18 holes, or $90 in winter and $60 in summer for 9 holes. Carts and caddies are available.

HIKING   **Barbados National Trust** (☎ 246/426-2421) offers Sunday morning hikes throughout the year, often attracting more than 300 participants. Led by young Bajans and members of the National Trust, the hikes cover a different area of the island each week, giving you an opportunity to learn about the natural beauty of Barbados. The guides give brief talks on subjects such as geography, history, geology, and agriculture. The hikes, free and open to participants of all ages, are divided into fast, medium, and slow categories. All hikes leave promptly at 6am, are about 5 miles long, and take about 3 hours to complete. There are also hikes at 3:30 and 5:30pm, the latter conducted only on moonlit nights. For more information, contact the Barbados National Trust.

In 1998, Barbados launched two nature trails that explore the natural history and heritage of Speightstown, once a major sugar port and even today a fishing town with old houses and a bustling waterfront. The **Arbib Nature & Heritage Trail** takes you through town, the mysterious gully known as "the Whim," and the surrounding districts. The first marked trail is a 4.7-mile trek which begins outside St. Peter's Church in Speightstown, traverses the Whim, crosses one of the last working plantations in Barbados (Warleight), and leads to the historic 18th-century Dover Fort, following along white-sand beaches at Heywoods before ending up back in town. Equally enchanting is the 3.4-mile trail for those looking for a more relaxing hike. Guided hikes are offered on Wednesday, Thursday, and Saturday. For information and reservations, call the Barbados National Trust.

The rugged, dramatic **east coast** stretches about 16 miles from the lighthouse at Ragged Point, the easternmost point of Barbados, north along the Atlantic coast to Bathsheba and Pico Tenerife. This is the island's most panoramic hiking area. Some adventurers do the entire coast; if your time is limited, hike the 4-mile stretch from Ragged Point to Consett Bay, along a rough, stony trail. Allow at least 2½ hours. A small picnic facility just north of Bathsheba is a popular spot for Bajan families, especially on Sundays.

HORSEBACK RIDING   A different view of Barbados is offered by the **Caribbean International Riding Centre,** Auburn, St. Joseph (☎ 246/433-1453). With nearly 40 horses, Mrs. Roachford and her daughters offer a variety of trail rides for all levels of experience, ranging from a 1-hour jaunt for $40 to a 2½-hour trek for $82.50. You'll ride through some of the most panoramic parts of Barbados, including the hilly terrain of the Scotland district. Along the way, you can see wild ducks and water lilies, with the rhythm of the Atlantic as background music.

PARASAILING   The best beaches for this sport are St. James and Christ Church. **Skyrider Parasail** (☎ 246/435-0570) is along Bay Street in Bridgetown, but its 32-foot speedboat will pick you up at any of several hotels along the west coast if arrangements are made in advance. Rates are $45 per session.

SCUBA DIVING & SNORKELING   The clear waters off Barbados have a visibility of more than 100 feet most of the year. More than 50 varieties of fish are found on the shallow inside reefs. On night dives, you can spot sleeping fish, night anemones, lobsters, moray eels, and octopuses. On a mile-long coral reef 2 minutes by boat from **Sandy Beach,** sea fans, corals, gorgonias, and reef fish are plentiful. J.R., a dredge barge sunk as an artificial reef in 1983, is popular with beginners for its coral, fish life, and 20-foot depth. The *Berwyn,* a coral-encrusted tugboat that sank in Carlisle Bay in 1916, attracts photographers for its variety of reef fish, shallow depth, good light, and visibility.

Asta Reef, with a drop of 80 feet, has coral, sea fans, and reef fish in abundance. It's the site of a Barbados wreck sunk in 1986 as an artificial reef. **Dottins,** the most beautiful reef on the west coast, stretches 5 miles from Holetown to Bridgetown and has numerous dive sites at an average depth of 40 feet and drop-offs of 100 feet. The SS *Stavronikita,* a Greek freighter, is a popular site for advanced divers. Crippled by fire in 1976, the 360-foot freighter was sunk a quarter of a mile off the west coast to become an artificial reef in **Folkestone Underwater Park.** The mast is at 40 feet, the deck at 80 feet, and the keel at 140 feet. It's encrusted with coral.

The **Dive Shop,** Pebbles Beach, Aquatic Gap, St. Michael (☎ **800/693-3483** or 246/426-9947), offers some of the best scuba diving on Barbados, charging $55 for a one-tank dive and $80 for a two-tank dive. Every day, three dive trips go out to the nearby reefs and wrecks; snorkeling trips and equipment rentals are also available. Visitors with reasonable swimming skills who have never dived before can sign up for a resort course. Priced at $70, it includes pool training, safety instructions, and a one-tank open-water dive. The establishment is NAUI- and PADI-certified, and is open daily from 9am to 5pm. Some other dive shops in Barbados that rent or sell snorkeling equipment include the following: **Carib Ocean Divers,** St. James (☎ **246/422-4414**); **Hazel's Water World,** Bridgetown, St. Michael (☎ **246/426-4043**); and **Explore Sub,** Christ Church, near Bridgetown (☎ **246/435-6542**).

Several companies also operate snorkeling cruises that take you to particularly picturesque areas; see "Tours & Cruises" under "Exploring the Island," below.

TENNIS   The big hotels have tennis courts that can be reserved even if you're not a guest. In Barbados, most tennis players still wear traditional whites. **Folkestone Park,** Holetown (☎ **246/422-2314**), is a public tennis court available for free. The **National Tennis Centre,** Sir Garfield Sobers Sports Complex, Wildey St., St. Michael (☎ **246/437-6010**), charges $12 per hour; you must reserve in advance. Courts at the **Barbados Squash Club,** Marine House, Christ Church (☎ **246/427-7913**), can be reserved for $9 for 45 minutes.

WINDSURFING   Experts say the windsurfing off Barbados is as good as any this side of Hawaii. Judging from the crowds who flock here, they're right. Windsurfing on Barbados has turned into a very big business between November and April, attracting thousands of windsurfers from as far away as Finland, Argentina, and Japan. The shifting of the trade winds between November and May and the shallow offshore reef of **Silver Sands** create unique conditions of wind and wave swells. This allows windsurfers to reach speeds of up to 50 knots and do complete loops off the waves. Silver Sands is rated the best spot in the Caribbean for advanced windsurfing (skill rating of five to six). In other words, one needs skills similar to those of a professional downhill skier to master these conditions.

An outfitter set up to handle the demand from the hordes of international windsurfers is **Barbados Windsurfing Club,** which maintains two branches on the island. Beginners and intermediates usually opt for the branch in Oistins

(☎ **246/428-7277**), where winds are constant but the sea is generally flat and calm. Advanced intermediates and experts usually go to the branch adjacent to the Silver Sands Hotel, in Christ Church (☎ **246/428-6001**), where stronger winds and higher waves allow surfers to combine aspects of windsurfing and conventional Hawaii-style surfing. Both branches use boards and equipment provided by the Germany-based Club Mistral. Lessons at either branch cost between $40 and $65 per hour, depending on how many people are in your class. Equipment rents for $25 per hour, or $55 to $65 per half day, depending on where and what you rent; rates are less expensive at the Oistins branch.

6   Exploring the Island

TOURS & CRUISES

Barbados is worth exploring, either in your own car or with a taxi-driver guide. Unlike so many islands of the Caribbean, Barbados has fair roads. They are, however, poorly signposted, and newcomers invariably get lost—not only once, but several times. If you lose your way, you'll find the people in the countryside generally helpful.

ORGANIZED TOURS   Bajan Tours, Glenayre, Locust Hall, St. George (☎ **246/ 437-9389**), is a locally owned and operated company. The best bet for the first-timer is the Exclusive Island Tour, departing daily between 8:30 and 9am and returning between 3:30 and 4pm. It covers all the highlights of the island, including the Barbados Wildlife Reserve, the Chalky Mount Potteries, and the rugged east coast. On Friday, the Heritage Tour takes in mainly the island's major plantations and museums. Monday through Friday, the Eco Tour explores the natural beauty of the island. All tours cost $56 per person and include a full buffet lunch.

CRUISES   **Largest of the coastal cruising vessels, the *Bajan Queen* is modeled after a Mississippi riverboat and is the only cruise ship offering table seating and dining on local fare produced fresh from the onboard galley. There's also cover available in case of rain or too much sun. The *Bajan Queen* becomes a showboat by night, with local bands providing music for dancing under the stars. You're treated to a dinner of roast chicken, barbecued steak, and seasoned flying fish, with a buffet of fresh side dishes and salads. Cruises are offered Wednesday from 6 to 10pm and Saturday from 5 to 9pm; they're usually sold out, so book early to avoid disappointment. Each cruise costs $44.50 and includes transportation to and from your hotel. For reservations, contact **Jolly Roger Cruises, Shallow Draft, Bridgetown Harbour (☎ **246/436-6424**).

The same company also owns two motorized replicas of pirate frigates, the *Jolly Roger I* and the *Jolly Roger II.* One or both of these, depending on demand, departs five mornings a week for daytime snorkeling cruises from 10am to 2pm. Included in the price of $61.50 is an all-you-can-eat buffet, drinks, and use of snorkel equipment, which requires a $20 refundable deposit. Each boat also has an onboard boutique. For information, call Jolly Roger Cruises or visit the berth at Bridgetown Harbour. A fourth boat, *Excellence,* is a catamaran that runs on Monday, Wednesday, and Friday from 9am to 2pm and on Sunday from 10am to 3pm. The price of $61.50 includes a continental breakfast, a lunch buffet, drinks, and snorkeling gear (no deposit required), plus inflatable water mattresses. Since it's a catamaran and holds fewer people, the ambience is more intimate.

Another touring option is **Limbo Lady Sailing Cruises,** Casamara, Inchmarlow (☎ **246/420-5418**). Patrick Gonsalves skippers the classic 44-foot CSY yacht *Limbo Lady,* while his wife, Yvonne, a singer and guitarist, serenades you on a sunset cruise.

Daily lunch cruises are also available, with a stop for swimming and snorkeling (equipment provided). Both lunch and sunset cruises offer a complimentary open bar and transportation to and from your hotel. Lunch cruises last 4½ hours and cost $63; 3-hour sunset cruises go for $52 and include a glass of champagne. Moonlight dinner cruises and private charters, both local and to neighboring islands, can also be arranged; call for details.

Part cruise ship, part nightclub, the **M/V Harbour Master** (☎ **246/430-0900**) is one of the island's newest attractions. A 100-foot, four-story coastal vessel, it contains theme decks, a modern gallery, and a trio of bars. It boasts a dance floor and a sit-down restaurant, also offering formal buffets on its Calypso Deck. On the Harbour Master Deck, there's a bank of TVs for sports buffs. The showpiece of the vessel is an onboard semi-submersible, which is lowered hydraulically to 6 feet beneath the ship. This is, in effect, a "boat in a boat," with 30 seats. Lunch and dinner cruises start at $25 per person; the semi-submersible experience costs another $10.

SUBMERGED SIGHTSEEING   You no longer have to be an experienced diver to see what lives 150 feet below the surface of the sea. Now all visitors can view the sea's wonders on sightseeing submarines. The air-conditioned submersibles seat 28 to 48 passengers and make several dives daily from 9am to 4pm. Passengers are transported aboard a ferryboat from the Careenage in downtown Bridgetown to the submarine site, about a mile from the west coast of Barbados. The ride offers a view of the west coast of the island.

The submarines, *Atlantic I* and *III,* have viewing ports that allow you to see a rainbow of colors, tropical fish, plants, and even a shipwreck that lies upright and intact below the surface. The cost is $80 to $87.50 for adults, $40 to $43.75 for children. For reservations, contact **Atlantis Submarines (Barbados),** Shallow Draught, Bridgetown (☎ **246/436-8929**).

It's also possible to go cruising over one of the shore reefs to observe marine life. You sit in air-conditioned comfort aboard the *Atlantis Seatrec,* a semi-submersible boat, which gives you a chance to get a snorkeler's view of the reef through large viewing windows. You can also relax on deck as you take in the scenic coastline. A second *Seatrec* tour explores wreckage sites. Divers go down with video cameras to three different wrecks on Carlisle Bay, and the video is transmitted to TV monitors aboard the vessel. Both tours cost $35 for adults, half for children 4 to 12 (not suitable for kids 3 and under). For reservations, call the number above.

EXPLORING BRIDGETOWN

Often hot and clogged with traffic, the capital, Bridgetown, merits no more than a morning's shopping jaunt (see "Shopping," below, for a rundown of the best stores).

Since some half million visitors arrive on Barbados by cruise ship each year, the government has opened a $6-million **cruise-ship terminal** with 20 duty-free shops, 13 local retail stores, and scads of vendors. Cruise passengers can choose from a range of products, including the arts and crafts of Barbados, jewelry, liquor, china, crystal, electronics, perfume, and leather goods. Some shops sell Barbadian wood carvings and art, as well as locally made fashions. The interior was designed to re-create an island street scene; some storefronts appear as traditional chattel houses in brilliant island colors, complete with streetlights, tropical landscaping, benches, and pushcarts.

Begin your tour at the waterfront, called **the Careenage** (the French word for turning vessels on their side for cleaning). This was a haven for clipper ships, and even though today it doesn't have the color of yesteryear, it's still worth exploring.

At **Trafalgar Square,** the long tradition of British colonization is immortalized. The monument here, honoring Lord Nelson, was executed by Sir Richard Westmacott and erected in 1813. The great gray Victorian/Gothic **Public Buildings** on the square look like those you might expect to find in London. The east wing contains the meeting halls of the Senate and the House of Assembly, with some stained-glass windows representing the sovereigns of England. Look for the "Great Protector" himself, Oliver Cromwell.

Behind the Financial Building, **St. Michael's Cathedral,** east of Trafalgar Square, is the symbol of the Church of England. This Anglican church was built in 1655 but was completely destroyed in a 1780 hurricane. Reconstructed in 1789, it was again damaged by a hurricane in 1831. George Washington supposedly worshipped here on his visit to Barbados.

The **Synagogue,** Synagogue Lane (☎ 246/426-5792), is one of the oldest in the western hemisphere and is surrounded by a burial ground of early Jewish settlers. The present building dates from 1833. It was constructed on the site of an even older synagogue, erected by Jews from Brazil in 1654. Sometime in the early–20th century, the synagogue was deconsecrated, and the structure has since served various roles. In 1983 the government of Barbados seized the deteriorating building, intending to raze it and build a courthouse on the site. An outcry went up from the small Jewish community on the island; money was raised for its restoration, and the building was saved and is now part of the National Trust of Barbados—and a synagogue once again. It's open Monday to Friday from 9am to 4pm; a donation is requested for admission.

First made popular in 1870, **cricket** is the national pastime on Barbados. Matches can last from 1 to 5 days. If you'd like to see a local match, watch for announcements in the newspapers or ask at the **Tourist Board,** on Harbour Road (☎ 246/427-2623). From Bridgetown, you can hail a taxi and visit **Garrison Savannah,** just south of the capital, a frequent venue for cricket matches and horse races.

The **Barbados Gallery of Art,** Bush Hill (☎ 246/228-0149), in a restored old building in the historic Garrison district, displays the very best Barbadian and Caribbean visual art. Changing exhibitions enliven the permanent collection, which consists of 160 drawings, paintings, and sculptures. The gallery also pays tribute to the memory of the late actress Claudette Colbert, longtime resident of Barbados. She is memorialized in a beautiful garden here, and the gallery even owns one of her own paintings. Hours are Tuesday through Saturday from 10am to 5pm. Admission is $5 for adults Tuesday through Friday, $2 on Saturday; for those under 18, $2 Tuesday through Friday, free on Saturday.

The **Barbados Museum,** St. Ann's Garrison, St. Michael (☎ 246/427-0201), is housed in a former military prison. Extensive collections show the island's development from prehistoric to modern times, as well as fascinating glimpses into the natural environment and fine examples of West Indian maps and decorative arts. The museum sells a variety of quality publications, reproductions, and handcrafts. Its cafe is a good place for a snack or light lunch. Hours are Monday to Saturday from 9am to 5pm, Sunday from 2 to 6pm. Admission is $5 for adults, $2.50 for children.

Nearby, the russet-red **St. Ann's Fort,** on the fringe of the savannah, garrisoned British soldiers in 1694. The fort wasn't completed until 1703. The Clock House survived the hurricane of 1831.

SEEING THE INLAND SIGHTS: TROPICAL GARDENS & A SPECTACULAR CAVE

Flower Forest. Richmond Plantation, St. Joseph. ☎ 246/433-8152. Admission $7 adults, $3.50 children 5 to 16, free for children 4 and under. Daily 9am–5pm.

This old sugar plantation stands 850 feet above sea level near the western edge of the Scotland district, a mile from Harrison's Cave. Set in one of the most scenic parts of

Barbados, it's more than just a botanical garden; it's where people and nature came together to create something beautiful. After viewing the grounds, visitors can purchase handcrafts at Best of Barbados (see "Shopping," below).

✪ **Harrison's Cave.** Welchman Hall, St. Thomas. ☎ 246/438-6640. Tour reservations recommended. Admission $8.75 adults, $4.35 children. Daily 8:45am–4pm. Closed Good Friday, Easter Sunday, and Christmas Day.

The beautiful underground world here, the number-one tourist attraction of Barbados, is viewed from aboard an electric tram and trailer. On the tour, you'll see bubbling streams, tumbling cascades, and subtly lit deep pools, while all around stalactites hang overhead like icicles, and stalagmites rise from the floor. Visitors may disembark and get a closer look at this natural phenomenon at the Rotunda Room and the Cascade Pool.

Welchman Hall Gully. Welchman Hall, St. Thomas. ☎ 246/438-6671. Admission $6 adults, $3 children 6 to 12, free for children 5 and under. Daily 9am–5pm. Take Hwy. 2 from Bridgetown.

This lush, tropical garden is owned by the Barbados National Trust. You'll see some specimens of plants that were here when the English settlers landed in 1627. Many of the plants are labeled—clove, nutmeg, tree fern, and cocoa, among others—and occasionally you'll spot a wild monkey. You can also see breadfruit trees that are supposedly descendants of the seedlings brought ashore by Captain Bligh, of *Bounty* fame.

OTHER HISTORIC SITES

Francia Plantation. St. George, Barbados. ☎ 246/429-0474. Admission $4.50. Mon–Fri 10am–4pm. On the ABC Hwy., turn east onto Hwy. 4 at the Norman Niles Roundabout (follow the signs to Gun Hill); after going half a mile, turn left onto Hwy. X (follow the signs to Gun Hill); after another mile, turn right at the Shell gas station and follow Hwy. X past St. George's Parish Church and up the hill for a mile, turning left at the sign to Francia.

A fine family home, the Francia Plantation stands on a wooded hillside overlooking the St. George Valley and is still owned and occupied by descendants of the original owner. Built in 1913, the house blends both West Indian and European architectural influences. You can explore several rooms, including the dining room with its family silver and an 18th-century James McCabe bracket clock. On the walls are antique maps and prints, including a map of the West Indies printed in 1522.

Gun Hill Signal Station. Hwy. 4. ☎ 246/429-1358. Admission $4.60 adults, $2.30 children 13 and under. Mon–Sat 9am–5pm. Take Hwy. 3 from Bridgetown, then go inland from Hwy. 4 toward St. George Church.

One of two such stations owned and operated by the Barbados National Trust, the Gun Hill Signal Station is strategically placed on the highland of St. George and commands a panoramic view from the east to the west. Built in 1818, it was the finest of a chain of signal stations and was also used as an outpost for the British army. The restored military cookhouse houses a snack bar and gift shop.

Heritage Park & Rum Factory. Foursquare Plantation, St. Philip. ☎ 246/423-6669. Admission $12. Sun–Thurs 9am–5pm, Fri–Sat 9am–9pm.

After driving through cane fields, you'll arrive at the first rum distillery to be launched on the island since the 19th century. Inaugurated in 1996, this factory is located on a former molasses and sugar plantation dating back some 350 years. Produced on site is ESA Field, a white rum praised by connoisseurs. Adjacent is an admission-free park where Barbadian handcrafts are displayed in the Art Foundry (see "Shopping," below). You'll also find an array of shops and carts selling local foods, handcrafts, and products.

The Great Tour

From mid-January through the first week of April, you can tour a different great house every Wednesday afternoon. Houses include those rarely seen by the public, as well as major attractions such as Francia. You'll see a great array of plantation antiques and get a feeling for the elegant colonial lifestyle once commonplace on Barbados. For more information, call ☎ **246/426-2421**.

Sunbury Plantation House. 6 Cross Rd., St. Philip. ☎ **246/423-6270**. Admission $6 adults, $3 children. Daily 10am–5pm.

This is the only great house on Barbados where all the rooms are open for viewing. The 300-year-old plantation house is steeped in history, featuring mahogany antiques, old prints, and a unique collection of horse-drawn carriages. Take the informative tour, then stop in the Courtyard Restaurant and Bar for a meal or drinks; there's also an on-site gift shop. A candlelight dinner is offered at least once a week; this five-course meal, served at a 200-year-old mahogany table, costs $75 per person. Call the number above for information and reservations.

Tyrol Cot Heritage Village. Codrington Hill, St. Michael. ☎ **246/424-2074**. Admission $5.75 adults, $2.85 children. Mon–Fri 9am–5pm.

If you arrived at the airport, you'll recognize the name of Sir Grantley Adams, the leader of the Bajan movement for independence from Britain. This was once his home, and his wife, Lady Adams, lived in the house until her death in 1990. Once you had to wrangle a highly prized invitation to visit, but it's now open to all who have the price of admission. It was built sometime in the mid-1850s from coral stone in a Palladian style. The grounds have been turned into a museum of Bajan life, including small chattel houses where potters and artists work.

SEEING THE SIGHTS AROUND THE ISLAND

In Bathsheba, visit the **Andromeda Botanic Gardens,** Bathsheba, St. Joseph (☎ 246/433-9384). On a cliff overlooking the town of Bathsheba on the rugged east coast, limestone boulders make for a natural 8-acre rock-garden setting. Thousands of orchids, hundreds of hibiscus and heliconia, and many varieties of ferns, begonias, palms, and other species grow here in splendid profusion. A simple guide helps visitors identify many of the plants. You'll occasionally see frogs, herons, lizards, hummingbirds, and sometimes a mongoose or a monkey. Admission is BD$12 ($6) for adults, BD$6 ($3) for children (free for kids 5 and under). Hours are daily from 9am to 5pm.

On Cherry Tree Hill, which is on Highway 1, signs point the way to **St. Nicholas Abbey** (☎ 246/422-8725), a Jacobean plantation great house and sugarcane fields that have been around since about 1650. It was never actually an abbey—around 1820 an ambitious owner simply christened it as such. More than 200 acres are still cultivated each year. The house, characterized by its curved gables, is believed to be one of three Jacobean houses in the western hemisphere. At least the ground floor of the structure is open to the public, Monday through Friday from 10am to 3:30pm. Admission is BD$10 ($5) for adults, free for children 12 and under. You can lunch or take afternoon tea at the cafe.

Across the road from Farley Hill National Park, in northern St. Peter Parish, the **Barbados Wildlife Reserve,** St. Peter (☎ 246/422-8826), is set in a mahogany forest that's run by the Barbados Primate Research Center. Visitors can stroll through what is primarily a monkey sanctuary and an arboretum. Aside from the uncaged monkeys, you can see wild hares, deer, tortoises, otters, wallabies (which were brought into Barbados), and a variety of tropical birds. Admission is BD$20 ($10) for adults, half price for children 12 and under. Hours are daily from 10am to 5pm.

EXPLORING THE GREEN HILLS

Unless you make a special effort to explore the lush interior of this former British colony, most of your time on Barbados might be confined to the island's densely populated coastal plain. But much of Barbados's true beauty can only be appreciated on a trek, tour, or hill climb through such rarely visited parishes as St. Thomas and St. George (both of which are landlocked) and the Atlantic coast parishes of St. Andrews and St. John (where the rough surf of the Atlantic usually discourages the embarkation of sailing vessels). Until recently, most visitors were asked to restrict their sightseeing in these relatively undeveloped parishes to the sides of the highways and roads. But the locally owned **Highland Outdoor Tours,** Canefield, St. Thomas (☎ 246/438-8069), conducts a series of tours across privately owned land. With its verdant, rolling hills and dramatic rock outcroppings, much of the terrain may remind you of a windswept—but balmy—version of Scotland.

You can tour on horseback, on foot, or as a passenger in a tractor-drawn jitney. Horseback rides and walking tours last anywhere from 2 to 5 hours. As you traverse what used to be some of the most productive sugar plantations in the British Empire, your guide will describe the geology, architecture, and historical references you'll see en route. All tours depart from the Highland Outdoor Tour Center, St. Thomas (in north-central Barbados). Transportation to and from your hotel is included in the price of 2-hour horseback tours (from $60), hiking tours (from $30 to $60), and tractor-drawn jitney tours (from $30).

7 Shopping

You may find duty-free merchandise here at prices 20% to 40% lower than in the United States and Canada—but you've got to be a smart shopper to spot bargains and also be familiar with prices back in your hometown. Duty-free shops have two prices listed on items of merchandise: the local retail price, and the local retail price less the government-imposed tax.

Some of the best duty-free buys include cameras (Leica, Fuji), watches (Rolex, Omega, Piaget, Seiko), crystal (Waterford and Lalique), gold jewelry, bone china (Wedgwood and Royal Doulton), cosmetics and perfumes, and liquor (including locally produced Barbados rum and liqueurs), along with tobacco products and cashmere sweaters, tweeds, and sportswear from Britain. If you purchase items made on Barbados, you don't have to pay duty.

Cruise passengers generally head for the **cruise-ship terminal** at Bridgetown Harbour, which has some 20 duty-free shops, 13 local shops, and many vendors (see "Exploring Bridgetown" under "Exploring the Island," above).

The outstanding item in Barbados handcrafts is black-coral jewelry. Another Bajan craft, clay pottery, originated at **Chalky Mount Potteries,** which is worth a visit. Potters turn out different products, some based on designs that are centuries old. The potteries (which are signposted) are north of Bathsheba on the east coast, in St. Joseph Parish near Barclay's Park. In shops across the island, you'll also find a selection of locally made vases, pots, pottery mugs, glazed plates, and ornaments.

Wall hangings are woven from local grasses and dried flowers, and island craftspeople also turn out straw mats, baskets, and bags with raffia embroidery. Still in its infant stage, leather work is also found on Barbados, particularly handbags, belts, and sandals.

The best shop on the island for local products is **Best of Barbados,** in the Southern Palms, St. Lawrence Gap, Christ Church (☎ 246/420-8040). Part of an islandwide chain of 12 stores, this tasteful shop sells only products designed and/or made on Barbados, such as prints, coasters, T-shirts, pottery, dolls, games, and cookbooks. Another location is at Mall 34, Broad Street, Bridgetown (☎ 246/436-1416).

At **Articrafts,** Broad Street, Bridgetown (☎ 246/427-5767), John and Rosyln Watson have assembled one of the most impressive displays of Bajan arts and crafts on the island. Roslyn's distinctive wall hangings are decorated with objects from the island, including sea fans and coral. The unique **Colours of De Caribbean,** the Waterfront Marina (next to the Waterfront Cafe, on the Careenage), Bridgetown (☎ 246/436-8522), carries original hand-painted and batik clothing, all made in the West Indies, plus jewelry and decorative objects.

Walker's Caribbean World, St. Lawrence Gap (☎ 246/428-1183), near the Southern Palms, offers many locally made items for sale, as well as handcrafts from the Caribbean Basin and the famous Jill Walker prints. **Pelican Village,** Harbour Road, Bridgetown (☎ 246/426-4391), offers bargains from Bajan artisans. In Bridgetown, go down Princess Alice Highway to the city's Deep Water Harbour, where you'll find this tiny colony of thatch-roofed shops. Some of the shops here are gimmicky, but interesting items can be found. Sometimes you can see craftspeople at work.

✪ **Earthworks Pottery/The Potter's House Gallery,** Edgehill Heights 2, St. Thomas (☎ 246/425-0223), is one of the artistic highlights of Barbados. Deep in the island's central highlands, Canadian-born Goldie Spieler and her son, David, create whimsical ceramics whose colors emulate the Bajan sea and sky; many objects are decorated with Antillean-inspired swirls and zigzags. On the premises are a studio and a showroom that sells the output of at least half a dozen other island potters. Purchases can be shipped virtually anywhere.

The **Art Foundry,** Heritage Park (☎ 246/418-0714), is a partnership between Bajan artist Joscelyn Gardner and R. L. Seale, the rum distiller. It displays some of the finest works of art on Barbados in its ground-floor gallery, with changing exhibitions upstairs. The **Great House Gallery,** at the Bagatelle Restaurant, Highway 2A, St. Thomas (☎ 246/421-6767), in one of the most historic great houses on Barbados, displays oils and watercolors by Caribbean, Latin American, and British artists.

The **Shell Gallery,** Carlton House, St. James (☎ 246/422-2593), has the best collection in the West Indies. Shells for sale come from all over the world. Featured is the shell art of Maureen Edghill, the finest artist in this field and the founder of this unique gallery. Also offered are hand-painted china, shell jewelry, local pottery and ceramics, and batik and papier-mâché artwork depicting shells and aquatic life.

Cave Shepherd, Broad Street, Bridgetown (☎ 246/431-2121), is the largest department store on the island and the best place for duty-free merchandise. There are branches at Sunset Crest in Holetown, Da Costas Mall, Grantley Adams Airport, and the Bridgetown cruise-ship terminal, but if your time is limited, try this outlet, as it has the widest selection. The store sells perfumes, cosmetics, fine crystal and bone china, cameras, jewelry, swimwear, leather goods, men's designer clothing, handcrafts, liquor, and souvenirs. You can take a break in the cool comfort of the Balcony, overlooking Broad Street, which serves vegetarian dishes and has a salad bar and beer garden.

Harrison's, 1 Broad Street, Bridgetown (☎ 246/431-5500), has 14 branch stores, all selling a wide variety of duty-free merchandise, including china, crystal, jewelry, leather goods, and perfumes—all at fair prices. Also for sale are some fine leather products handcrafted in Colombia. Harrison's is the major competitor to Cave Shepherd on the island, but we'd give the edge to Cave Shepherd.

Little Switzerland, in the Da Costas Mall, Broad Street, Bridgetown (☎ **246/ 431-0030**), offers a wide selection of fragrances and cosmetics from leading houses, fine European china and crystal, Mont Blanc pens, and an array of goodies from Waterford, Lalique, Swarovski, Baccarat, and others. Watches and jewelry include a variety of 14- and 18-karat-gold pieces and names such as Rolex, Swatch, Raymond Weil, Tag Heuer, and Ebel.

A competitor, **Luna Jewelers,** Bay Street at Bedford Avenue, a 10-minute drive south of Bridgetown, about four buildings from Barbados's Parliament (☎ **246/430-0355**), sells an appealing but predictable collection of diamonds and precious stones, watches and gift items. What makes Luna unusual is its emphasis on art-nouveau and art-deco designs set into gold and silver, crafted on Barbados in alluring designs. Of special note are the pieces that elevate fossilized Bajan coral into a high art form, thanks to careful polishing, gold or silver settings, and in some cases, intricate mosaic-style inlays.

Greenwich House Antiques, Greenwich Village, Trents Hill, St. James (☎ **246/ 432-1169**), a 25-minute drive from Bridgetown, feels like a genteel, appealingly cluttered private home where the objects for sale seem to have come from the attic of your favorite, and slightly dotty, great aunt. Dozens of objects fill every available inch of tabletop or display space.

8　Barbados After Dark

Most of the big resort hotels feature entertainment nightly, often steel-band dance music and occasional Bajan floor shows. Sometimes beach barbecues are staged.

For the most authentic Bajan evening possible, head for **Baxters Road** in Bridgetown, where there's always something cooking on Friday and Saturday after 11pm. In fact, if you stick around until dawn, the party's still going strong. The street is safer than it looks because Bajans come here to have fun, not to make trouble. The entertainment tends to be spontaneous. Some old-time visitors have compared Baxters Road to the backstreets of New Orleans in the 1930s. If you fall in love with the place, you can "caf crawl" up and down the street, where nearly every bar is run by a Bajan mama.

The most popular "caf" on Baxters Road is **Enid's** (she has a phone, "but it doesn't work"), a little ramshackle establishment where Bajans come to devour fried chicken at 3 in the morning. Her place is open daily from 8:30pm to 8:30am, when the last satisfied customer departs into the blazing morning sun and Enid heads home to get some sleep before the new night begins. Stop in for a Banks beer.

The bar and restaurant at **Baku Beach Club,** Sunset Crest, St. James (☎ **246/ 432-1309**), serve as a social focal point for Sunset Crest. Drinks are half price during happy hour, nightly from 5 to 6pm and 9 to 10pm. Fish fries, barbecues, or buffets are offered from 7 to 10pm nightly and cost $10 to $12.50. Most nights, there's live entertainment, including bands and amateur talent shows; the club recently added a dance floor. If you're not dining, the cover is $15.

Some say the green-and-white **Coach House,** Paynes Bay (on the main Bridgetown–Holetown road, just south of Sandy Lane, about 6 miles north of Bridgetown), St. James (☎ **246/432-1163**), is 200 years old. This is a Bajan version of an English pub, with an outdoor garden bar. From 6 to 10:30pm, you can order bar meals, including flying-fish burgers, priced at $8 and up. Most nights, there's live music—everything from steel bands to jazz, pop, and rock, attracting an attentive crowd from 9pm on. The lunchtime buffet, offered Monday through Friday ($14), is popular.

✪ **Harbour Lights,** Marine's Villa, Upper Bay Street, about a mile southeast of Bridgetown (☎ 246/436-7225), is the most popular weekend venue for dancing, drinking, and flirting on all of Barbados. In a modern seafront building with an oceanfront patio (which gives dancers a chance to cool off), the place plays reggae, soca, and whatever else is popular until the wee hours every night. The barbecue pit/kiosk serves up grilled meats and hamburgers. Monday is beach party night; the $44 charge includes transportation to and from your hotel, a barbecue buffet, drinks, and a live band. On Wednesday and Friday, there's a cover of $12 to $15. You must be 18 or older.

✪ **John Moore Bar,** on the waterfront, Weston, St. James (☎ 246/422-2258), is the most atmospheric and least pretentious bar on Barbados. Although its namesake died in 1987, the place is owned and managed by Lamont (Breedy) Addison, whose tenure here began as a teenager. If you think this bar functions only as a watering hole, think again: It's the nerve center of this waterfront town, filled throughout the day and night with a most congenial group of neighborhood residents. Most visitors opt for a rum punch or beer, but if you're hungry, platters of local fish can be prepared, after a moderate delay.

✪ **Plantation Restaurant and Garden Theatre,** Main Road (Hwy. 7), St. Lawrence, Christ Church (☎ 246/428-5048), is the island's most prominent showcase for evening dinner theater and Caribbean cabaret. Every Wednesday and Friday, dinner is served at 6:30pm, followed by a show, *Plantation Tropical Spectacular II,* at 8pm. The show involves plenty of elaborate costumes and lots of reggae, calypso, limbo, and Caribbean exoticism. For $61.50, you get dinner, the show, and transport to and from your hotel; the show alone costs $30. Reserve in advance.

1627 and All That, Barbados Museum, Highway 7, Garrison, St. Michael (☎ 246/428-1627), effectively combines music with entertainment and dancing. It's the most interesting place on Barbados on a Thursday night. A night out here involves a cocktail hour, a large buffet of Bajan food, and a historic and cultural presentation. The $57.50 charge includes transportation to and from your hotel. Dinner is served at 7pm; the show lasts from 6:30 to 10pm.

The Ship Inn, St. Lawrence Gap, Christ Church (☎ 246/435-6961), recommended earlier in this chapter as a restaurant, is now among the leading entertainment centers on the south coast. The pub is the hot spot: Top local bands perform nightly, offering reggae, calypso, and Top 40 music. The $5 entrance fee is redeemable for food or drink at any of the other bars or restaurants in the Ship Inn complex, so you're actually paying only $2 for the live entertainment.

The frugal traveler can spend an inexpensive Bajan night at one of the island's popular clubs and bars. **Bert's Bar,** at the Abbeville Hotel in Worthing, on the Main Road in Christ Church (☎ 246/435-7924), is known for the best daiquiris on the island. Sports fans head for **Bubba's Sports Bar,** Rockley Main Road, Christ Church (☎ 246/435-6217), which offers a couple of satellite dishes, a 10-foot video screen, and a dozen TVs. Wash a Bubba burger down with a Banks beer here. **The Boatyard,** Bay Street, Bridgetown (☎ 246/436-2622), has a pubby atmosphere, with a DJ and occasional live bands. The longest bar on the island is at **After Dark,** St. Lawrence Gap, Christ Church (☎ 246/435-6547), where you can often hear live reggae, soca, Bajan calypso, and jazz.

7

Bonaire

Untrampled by hordes of tourists, unspoiled Bonaire is only gently touched by development. Although your options here range from bird watching to doing nothing, Bonaire is foremost a scuba diver's delight. It also offers some of the Caribbean's best snorkeling. This sleepy island is devoid of the glitzy diversions of Aruba. Instead, powdery white sands and turquoise waters beckon.

Bonaire is a bird watcher's haven, where flamingos nearly outnumber the sparse human population. There are more than 190 different species—not only the flamingo, but also the big-billed pelican, as well as parrots, snipes, terns, parakeets, herons, and hummingbirds. A pair of binoculars is an absolute necessity.

Bonaireans zealously treasure their precious environment and will go to great lengths to protect it. Even though they eagerly seek tourism, they aren't interested in creating another Aruba, with its high-rise hotel blocks. Spearfishing isn't allowed in its waters, nor is the taking or destruction of any coral or other living animal from the sea. Unlike some islands, Bonaire isn't just surrounded by coral reefs— it *is* the reef, sitting on the dry, sunny top of an underwater mountain. Its shores are thick with rainbow-hued fish.

Bonaire is close to the coast of Latin America, known for many generations as the Spanish Main. It's just 50 miles north of Venezuela. Part of the Netherlands Antilles (an autonomous part of the Netherlands), Bonaire has a population of about 10,000. Its name is Amerindian for "low country." The capital is **Kralendijk.** It's most often reached from its neighbor island of Curaçao, 30 miles to the west; like Curaçao, it's desertlike, with a dry and brilliant atmosphere. Often it's visited by day-trippers, who rush through here in pursuit of the shy, elusive flamingo.

Boomerang-shaped Bonaire comprises about 112 square miles, making it the second largest of the ABC Dutch-affiliated grouping. Its northern sector is hilly, tapering up to Mount Brandaris, all of 788 feet. However, the southern half, flat as a pancake, is given over to bays, reefs, beaches, and a salt lake that attracts the flamingos.

1 Essentials

VISITOR INFORMATION

Before you go, you can contact the **Bonaire Government Tourist Office** at Adams Unlimited, 10 Rockefeller Plaza, Suite 900, New

Captain Don's Habitat **1**

Carib Inn **5**

Divi Flamingo Beach Resort & Casino **4**

Harbour Village Beach Resort **3**

Plaza Resort Bonaire **6**

Port Bonaire Resort **7**

Sand Dollar Condominium Resort **2**

Airport ✈ Beach ☚ Mountain ▲▲

York, NY 10020 (☎ **800/U-BONAIR** or 212/956-5911). There's also information on the Web at **www.bonaire.org**.

On the island, you can go to the **Bonaire Government Tourist Bureau,** Kaya Libertad Simón Bolívar 12, Kralendijk (☎ **599/7-8322**), open Monday to Friday from 7:30am to noon and 1:30 to 5pm.

GETTING THERE

ALM (☎ **800/327-7230;** www.alm-airlines.com) is one of your best bets for flying to Bonaire. It offers daily flights from both Miami and Atlanta. **Air Aruba** (☎ **800/882-7822;** www.interknowledge.com/air-aruba) offers direct flights from Newark to Bonaire on Thursday, Saturday, and Sunday. On Monday, Tuesday, Wednesday, and Friday, it has air links to Bonaire via Aruba.

American Airlines (☎ **800/433-7300;** www.aa.com) offers one daily nonstop flight to Curaçao from its hub in Miami. These depart late enough in the day (11am) to allow easy connections from cities all over the Northeast, and reach Curaçao early enough to allow immediate transfers to Bonaire. American will book (but not ticket) your connecting flight to Bonaire on Bonaire Airways.

Other routes to Bonaire are possible on any of American's daily nonstop flights to Aruba through American's hubs in New York, Miami, and San Juan, Puerto Rico. Once on Aruba, ALM will transfer passengers on to Bonaire, usually after a brief touchdown (or change of equipment) on Curaçao. Although these transfers are somewhat complicated, American will set up any of them, and will also offer reduced rates at some Bonairean hotels if you book your reservation simultaneously with your air passage.

GETTING AROUND

Even though the island is flat, renting a moped or motor scooter is not always a good idea. The roads are often unpaved, pitted, and peppered with rocks. Touring through Washington National Park is best done by van, jeep, or automobile.

BY RENTAL CAR   It pays to shop around: Sometimes—but not always—you can make a better deal with a local agency. Try **Avanti Rentals,** Kaya Herman Pop 2 (☎ 599/7-5661), which offers year-round rentals beginning at $46 per day, including tax and insurance. A Suzuki Samurai, for $61 a day, is ideal for touring this desertlike island. Reserve well in advance.

Flamingo Car Rental, Kaya Grandi 86, in Kralendijk (☎ 599/7-8888), also has a kiosk at the airport for your convenience. Its Japanese-made cars, mostly Nissans, cost $56 daily. **Avis** (☎ 800/331-1212) is at Flamingo Airport. Weekly arrangements are cheaper, but daily rates range from $43 to $68, with unlimited mileage.

Your valid U.S., British, or Canadian driver's license is acceptable for driving on Bonaire. *Driving on Bonaire is on the right.*

BY TAXI   Taxis are unmetered, but the government has established rates. All taxis carry a license plate with the letters *TX.* Each driver should have a price list to be produced upon request. As many as four passengers can go along for the ride, unless there's too much luggage. A trip from the airport to your hotel should cost about $10 to $12. From 8pm to midnight, fares are increased by 25%; from midnight to 6am, they go up by 50%.

Most taxi drivers can take you on a tour of the island, but you'll have to negotiate a price according to how long a trip you want and what you want to see. For more information, call **Taxi Central Dispatch** (☎ 599/7-8100).

BY BICYCLE   If you're in good shape, you might consider renting a bike, although you'll have to contend with the hot sun and powerful trade winds. Nevertheless, much of the island is flat, and if you follow the main road, you'll go along the water's edge. The best deals are at **Cycle Bonaire,** Kaya L. D. Gerjharts (☎ 599/7-7558), where you can rent a 21-speed or an 830 Trek for $15 to $20 per day. Rental includes a water bottle, lock, helmet, repair kit, and pump. A map is provided free for a 6-day rental; otherwise, it's $5.

Fast Facts: Bonaire

Banking Hours   Banks are usually open Monday to Friday from 8:30am to noon and 2 to 4pm.

Currency   Like the other islands of the Netherlands Antilles (Curaçao, St. Maarten, St. Eustatius, and Saba), Bonaire's coin of the realm is the Netherlands Antillean florin (NAf), sometimes called a guilder. The official rate is 1.77 NAf to the U.S. dollar. However, U.S. dollars are widely accepted.

It's a big world.

And we've got the network to cover it.

Global connection with the AT&T Network

AT&T direct service

Enjoy going to the corners of the earth? We're with you. With the world's most powerful network, **AT&T Direct** Service gives you fast, clear connections from more countries than anyone,* and the option of an English-speaking operator. All it takes is your AT&T Calling Card or credit card! And the planet is yours. FOR A LIST OF **AT&T ACCESS NUMBERS**, TAKE THE ATTACHED WALLET GUIDE.

AT&T

For Travelers
who want more than
the Official Line

Also Available:

- The Unofficial Guide to Branson
- The Unofficial Guide to California with Kids
- The Unofficial Guide to Chicago
- The Unofficial Guide to Cruises
- The Unofficial Disney Companion
- The Unofficial Guide to Disneyland
- The Unofficial Guide to the Great Smoky
  & Blue Ridge Region
- The Unofficial Guide to Miami & the Keys
- Mini-Mickey: The Pocket-Sized Unofficial
  Guide to Walt Disney World
- The Unofficial Guide to New Orleans
- The Unofficial Guide to New York City
- The Unofficial Guide to San Francisco
- The Unofficial Guide to Skiing in the West
- The Unofficial Guide to Washington, D.C.

Macmillan Publishing USA

Customs   There are no Customs requirements for Bonaire.

Documents   U.S. and Canadian citizens don't need a passport to enter Bonaire, although a birth or naturalization certificate or an alien registration card will be required, plus a return ticket and photo ID. British subjects may carry a British Visitor's Passport, obtainable at post offices on Bonaire, although a valid passport issued in the United Kingdom is preferred, especially if you plan to visit other countries in the area. We recommend that all travelers carry a valid passport.

Electricity   The electricity on Bonaire is slightly different from that used in North America (110–130 volts, 50 cycles, as opposed to U.S. and Canadian voltages of 110 volts, 60 cycles). Adapters and transformers are necessary for North American appliances, but because of the erratic current, you should still proceed with caution when using any appliance and try to avoid usage if at all possible. Be warned, further, that electrical current used to feed or recharge finely calibrated diving equipment should be stabilized with a specially engineered electrical stabilizer. Every dive operation on the island has one of these as part of its standard equipment for visiting divers.

Emergencies   In an emergency, call ☎ **110** for the police or ambulance service.

Hospital   The **St. Franciscus Hospital** is at Kaya Soeur Bartola 2 in Kralendijk (☎ **599/7-8900**). A plane on standby at the airport takes seriously ill patients to Curaçao for treatment.

Language   English is widely spoken, but you'll hear Dutch, Spanish, and Papiamento.

Safety   "Safe, safe Bonaire" might be the island's motto in this crime-infested world. But remember, any place that attracts tourists also attracts people who prey on them. Safeguard your valuables.

Taxes   The government requires a $5.50-per-person daily room tax on all hotel rooms. Upon leaving Bonaire, you'll be charged an airport departure tax of $10, so don't spend every penny. There's also an interisland departure tax of $5.75.

Telephone   To call Bonaire from the United States, dial **011** (the international access code), then **599** (the country code for Bonaire), and then **7** (the area code) and the four-digit local number. Once on Bonaire, to call another number on the island, only the four-digit local number is necessary.

Time   Bonaire is on Atlantic standard time year-round, 1 hour ahead of eastern standard time (when it's noon on Bonaire, it's 11am in Miami). When daylight saving time is in effect in the United States, clocks in Miami and Bonaire show the same time.

Tipping   Most hotels and guest houses add a 10% service charge in lieu of tipping. Restaurants generally add a service charge of 15% to the bill.

Water   Drinking water comes from distilled seawater and is pure and safe.

Weather   Bonaire is known for its climate, with temperatures hovering at 82°F. The water temperature averages 80°F. It's warmest in August and September, coolest in January and February. The average rainfall is 22 inches, and December to March are the rainiest months.

2 Where to Stay

Hotels, all facing the sea, are low-key, personally run operations where everybody gets to know everybody else in no time. *Reminder:* Taxes and service charges are seldom included in the prices you're quoted, so ask about them when making your reservations. Be sure to read the section on package tours in chapter 2 before you book your hotel on your own!

VERY EXPENSIVE

✪ **Harbour Village Beach Resort.** Kaya Gobernador N. Debrot, Playa Lechi (P.O. Box 312), Bonaire, N.A. ☎ **800/424-0004** in the U.S. and Canada, or 599/7-7500. Fax 599/7-7507. www.harbourvillage.com. 70 units. E-mail: reservations@harbourvillage.com. A/C TV TEL. Year-round $320–$490 double; $535–$1,030 suite. Rates include continental buffet. Dinner $43 per person extra. AE, DC, MC, V.

Conceived by one of the largest land developers in Venezuela, this complex, the most stylish on the island, is designed like an Iberian village, opening onto a sandy beach. One of the most upscale resorts in the Caribbean, it has brought a pocket of posh to Bonaire for those divers who don't want the more laid-back atmosphere of Captain Don's Habitat. Accommodations are in a cluster of Dutch Caribbean–style villas painted in pastels, with red-tile roofs and terraced balconies. Guest rooms have tropical decor, island-style ceiling fans as well as air-conditioning, and luxurious bathrooms, with deluxe toiletries, fluffy towels, hair dryers, and robes.

Dining/Diversions: Kasa Coral Dining Terrace serves an international menu and has live music on Friday evenings. Our favorite restaurant is La Balandra Bar and Grill, a gazebo-like structure set beside a massive pier; an octagonal bar area flanked by an open grill and salad bar is open to the sea view and breezes. Captain Wook's, a bar and grill, overlooks a 60-slip marina.

Amenities: Pool, scuba-diving shop (with state-of-the-art diving and underwater photographic equipment), four tennis courts, fitness center, bicycles. A full-service European spa offers a range of beauty treatments, fitness equipment, and massage. The only hotel on Bonaire to offer room service (from 7 to 10am), laundry and dry cleaning, baby-sitting, wake-up service, pickup at the airport (10 minutes from the resort).

EXPENSIVE

✪ **Captain Don's Habitat.** Kaya Gobernador N. Debrot 103, Pier 7, Bonaire, N.A. ☎ **599/7-8290.** Fax 599/7-8240. For all reservations and business arrangements, contact Captain Don's Habitat, 903 South America Way, Miami, FL 33132 (☎ **800/327-6709**; fax 305/371-2337). E-mail: nick@habitatdiveresorts.com. 62 units. A/C. Rates for 8-day/7-night stays: Winter $1,154–$1,239 per person. Off-season $798–$1,011 per person. Rates include breakfast, airport transfers, tax, service, equipment, 12 boat dives, and unlimited 24-hour shore dives. AE, MC, V.

Built on a coral bluff overlooking the sea about 5 minutes north of Kralendijk, this unique diving, snorkeling, and nature-oriented resort, with an air of congenial informality, has a philosophy and lifestyle for those whose souls belong to the sea. The resort and its staff are devoted to the many different possibilities for diving off the coast of Bonaire. Habitat and its accompanying dive shop are the creation of Captain Don Stewart, Caribbean pioneer and "caretaker of the reefs," a former Californian who sailed his schooner from San Francisco through the Panama Canal, arriving on a reef in Bonaire in 1962—and he's been here ever since. Called the "godfather of diving" on the island, Captain Don was instrumental in the formation of the Bonaire Marine Park, whereby the entire island became a protected reef.

More than 90% of the guests here opt for one of the packages, which incorporate a variable number of dives with accommodations in settings ranging from standard double rooms to oceanfront villas. The most popular arrangement is the 8-day/7-night package.

Dining/Diversions: This resort has an oceanfront restaurant and two seaside bars. A casual, laid-back crowd gathers for meals at Rum Runners, the social hub. Theme nights are staged weekly, which divert guests from the rather standard fare served here.

Amenities: Laundry, baby-sitting, boutique, pool, complete diving program.

✪ **Plaza Resort Bonaire.** J. A. Abraham Blvd. 80, Bonaire, N.A. ☎ **800/766-6016** or **599/7-2500.** Fax 599/7-7133. www.plazaresortbonaire.com. E-mail: info@plazaresort-bonaire.com. 174 units. Winter $180–$240 suite; $260–$300 one-bedroom apt; $305–$365 two-bedroom apt. Off-season $125–$185 suite; $200–$240 one-bedroom apt; $245–$305 two-bedroom apt. Extra person $30. AE, DC, MC, V.

One of Bonaire's two most consciously luxurious resorts, rivaled only by Harbour Village Beach Resort, lies a short drive from the airport, on a strip of land midway between a saltwater lagoon and a sandy stretch of Caribbean beachfront. Designed in 1995 by a team of Italian architects, it resembles a white-sided village along the arid seacoast of southern Portugal, thanks to terra-cotta roofs and a pair of bridges that traverse the lagoon for easy access to the far-flung 12-acre premises. Marketing some of the units to private investors—and charging relatively reasonable rates for the others—the operators have provided all the amenities of a much larger resort, and continue to stress the very large proportions of the standard accommodations. Be aware that what management here refers to as suites are actually very large bedrooms, without interior dividers. Each contains a kitchenette, ceiling fans, and the kind of airy but durable furnishings that might remind you of a private summer home. Most units are large and airy, with private safes and balconies, plus queen beds with deluxe mattresses. Bathrooms are roomy and luxurious, with hair dryers and fluffy towels. Views encompass either the sea, the lagoon, or, in a limited number of cases, the tarmac of the nearby airport.

Dining/Diversions: Four on-site restaurants include the Caribbean Point (see "Where to Dine," below); the Banana Tree, a Caribbean bistro beside the pool; the Tipsy Seagull, for burgers and salads beside the beach; and an eatery specializing in drinks, snacks, and Spanish-style tapas. The hotel's casino (see "Bonaire After Dark," below) is the larger of two on the island. Some evenings, there's live entertainment.

Amenities: Swimming pool, adjacent children's pool, four tennis courts, fully equipped dive center, water sports, marina with room for at least 50 boats, concierge.

Port Bonaire Resort. J. A. Abraham Blvd. 80, Bonaire, N.A. ☎ **800/766-6016** or 599/7-2500. Fax 599/7-7133. www.netcarib.com/bonaire/resort-bonaire.html. E-mail: plaza@bonairenet.com. 26 units. A/C TV TEL. Winter $210–$320 apt (sleeps up to 4). Off-season $180–$280 apt. AE, DC, MC, V.

Set within a short walk of the Plaza Resort Bonaire (see above), and operating under the same management, this is a small, very upscale complex of apartments that for the most part are owned by absentee investors who rent them out for at least part of the year. More luxurious—and more expensive—than their counterparts at their nearby sibling, units here have sweeping views over the sea and individualized decor influenced by the personal tastes of their owners. A small, low-rise resort of three floors, this complex is one of the eye-catchers of Bonaire. Each unit has a fully equipped kitchen and a private safe, plus an excellent bathroom with fluffy towels and a hair dryer. On-site facilities include a freshwater pool, a sundeck, a private dock, and parking. Guests of Port Bonaire Resort can use the more extended dining facilities and other amenities of the Plaza Resort Bonaire.

MODERATE

Divi Flamingo Beach Resort & Casino. J. A. Abraham Blvd., Bonaire, N.A. ☎ **800/367-3484** in the U.S., 919/419-3484 in Chapel Hill, N.C., or 599/7-8285. Fax 599/7-8238. 140

units. A/C. Winter $130–$190 double; from $210 studio. Off-season $100–$120 double; from $140 studio. Rates about 10% higher between Christmas and New Year's. MAP $42 per person extra. Several inclusive packages offered. AE, MC, V.

This beachfront resort, with its comfortable but rather worn bedrooms, was once a gone-to-seed hotel with a cluster of flimsy wooden bungalows used to intern German prisoners in World War II. With foresight and taste, the owners turned it into a resort, offering individual cottages and seafront rooms with private balconies resting on piers above the surf, so you can stand out and watch rainbow-hued tropical fish in the waters below.

The resort's original rooms were supplemented in 1986 with the addition of time-share units, forming Club Flamingo. These are the newest and best rooms, and each of the units is rentable by the day or the week. The accommodations in both sections are spacious and sunny, with ceiling fans and Mexican accents. The newer units are clustered into a green-and-white neo-Victorian pavilion facing its own curving pool. Each contains a kitchenette with carved cupboards and cabinets of pickled hardwoods. Many rooms are just basic sleeping quarters with tired mattresses, whereas some are better appointed and in less need of rejuvenation; it would be nice if you could take a look at your room before agreeing to take it, although with prebooking that isn't always possible. Regardless of which part of the resort you're in, you can take advantage of the water-sports facilities, the social hostesses, and the proximity of a good dive operation and a beautiful beach. A pair of restaurants, the Chibi-Chibi and the Calabase Terrace, provide satisfying but unspectacular meals.

Sand Dollar Condominium Resort. Kaya Gobernador N. Debrot 79, Bonaire, N.A. ☎ **800/288-4773** in the U.S., or 599/7-8738. Fax 599/7-8760. E-mail: sanddollar@bonairenet.com. 85 units. A/C TV. Winter $180 studio for 2; $230 one-bedroom apt; $270 two-bedroom apt; $370 three-bedroom apt. Off-season $165 studio; $195 one-bedroom apt; $220 two-bedroom apt; $310 three-bedroom apt. MAP $38.50 per person extra. AE, DISC, MC, V.

On the beachfront, just 1½ miles north of Kralendijk and 3 miles north of the airport, the Sand Dollar, with its fun-time, upbeat atmosphere, offers studios and apartments with all the style, comfort, and convenience of a full-service hotel. A kind of European design is blended with a Caribbean motif here. All accommodations are equipped with electric ranges, ovens, dishwashers, fridges, custom cabinets, and modern furnishings, including good beds, with decks or balconies facing the ocean. The resort mainly attracts serious divers. Bathrooms are routine but well maintained. The minuscule beach is engulfed at high tide. On the grounds is the Green Parrot Restaurant and Bar (see "Where to Dine," below), two lit tennis courts, a freshwater swimming pool with bar and cabana, and Sand Dollar Dive and Photo (see "Diving," below).

INEXPENSIVE

Carib Inn. J. A. Abraham Blvd. (P.O. Box 68), Kralendijk, Bonaire, N.A. ☎ **599/7-8819.** Fax 599/7-5295. E-mail: bruce@caribinn.com. 10 apts. A/C TV. Year-round $89 studio apt; $99 efficiency apt; $119 one-bedroom apt; $139 two-bedroom apt; $159 three-bedroom apt. AE, MC, V.

On the water, this hotel—owned and managed by the American diver Bruce Bowker—is occupied by dedicated scuba divers drawn to its five-star PADI dive facility. This is the most intimate little dive resort on Bonaire and remains one of the island's best values. Eight rooms have kitchens, all units are equipped with fridges, and maid service is provided daily. The accommodations are furnished with tropical rattan pieces, and the bathrooms have been enlarged and refurbished. There's no restaurant or bar. Repeat guests are likely to book this place far in advance in winter.

3 Where to Dine

EXPENSIVE

✪ **Capriccio.** Kaya Isla Riba 1. Kralendijk. ☎ **599/7-7230.** Reservations required. Pizzas and pastas $9–$21; main courses $16–$23; fixed-price menu $39.50. AE, MC, V. Mon and Wed–Sat noon–2pm; Wed–Mon 6:30–10:30pm. ITALIAN.

One of the most charming (and most consistently booked) restaurants on Bonaire is run by Andrea Scandeletti and his wife, Lola, experienced Italian restaurateurs whose efforts were well-received before their exodus from Italy to Bonaire. In a small, pink-and-green dining room that has room for 50 diners, they prepare skillful interpretations of modern Italian cuisine based largely on olive oil, and only rarely on cream and butter. Pizzas emerge from a brick oven in at least 10 different variations, and, if accompanied by a salad, can satisfy a light pair of appetites. More fulfilling is the set-price menu, which includes carpaccio, seafood pasta, filet mignon, and tiramisu. À la carte items include a platter of smoked fish, savory pastas, prosciutto with hearts-of-palm salad, and pumpkin ravioli with Parmesan cheese and sage. Mostly Italian and, to a lesser degree, French wines emerge from the establishment's air-conditioned wine cellar. Dining options include an alfresco area, set across the coastal road from the sea (it can get very hot in midsummer), and a more comfortable air-conditioned interior studded with flickering candles in the evening.

The Caribbean Point. Plaza Resort Bonaire, J. A. Abraham Blvd. 80. ☎ **599/7-2500.** Reservations recommended. Main courses $17.80–$25.70; five-course surprise menu $48. AE, DC, MC, V. Wed–Mon 6–11pm. INTERNATIONAL.

The island's swankiest restaurant offers its finest dining, a haute cuisine menu of fresh ingredients flown in from Europe. Diners are consistently satisfied at the array of dishes, including some very imaginative interpretations such as the rarely seen gorgonzola soup or the veal sweetbreads with raisins, both appetizers. A vegetarian main course is always offered, along with such main dishes as a perfectly delectable sea devil with champagne sauce or veal tournedos with lobster salad. Filet mignon appears with a perfectly made amaretto sauce, or you might opt for the salmon with crayfish in a saffron-flavored sauce. The forever changing dessert offerings are rich and refreshing. It's evident that great care has gone into all the dishes here. The most festive time to visit is on Monday, when a Caribbean folkloric night is presented.

✪ **Den Laman Restaurant.** Kaya Gobernador N. Debrot 77. ☎ **599/7-8955.** Main courses $16–$34. AE, MC, V. Wed–Mon 6–11pm. Closed Sept 1–22. SEAFOOD.

Located between the Sunset Beach Hotel and the Sand Dollar Condominium Resort, Den Laman serves the best seafood on Bonaire. An excellent beginning is the fish soup (the chef's special). You might move on to conch Flamingo, a local favorite, or lobster from the tank. Other dishes include grouper Creole and New York sirloin steak. When it's featured, we always go for the red snapper meuniére. It's easy to spend about $35 here, but it's also possible to dine for less. Meals are served on a breezy seaside terrace, and a 6,000-gallon aquarium complements the decor.

MODERATE

Beefeater Garden Restaurant. Kaya Grandi 12. ☎ **599/7-7776.** Reservations recommended. Main courses $10–$21. AE, DISC, MC, V. Mon–Sat 4–11pm. CARIBBEAN/SEAFOOD.

Don't interpret the name of this place as a sign that it's a steak-and-ale joint. It isn't. In fact, it offers more vegetarian platters (at least five) than any other restaurant on Bonaire. It was established in the mid-1970s by an English expatriate ("Beefeater"

Richard Dove) who was joined later by his German-born wife, Brigitte Kley, and their Dutch-born manager, Jeanette. Together, they maintain a trio of indoor dining rooms and an artfully lit garden. Outside, near a convivial bar area, you can enjoy such dishes as spinach or seafood crêpes; seafood pasta; Curaçaon goat-meat stew; the catch of the day garnished with crabmeat, mussels, and fruit sauce; and a well-seasoned array of curry dishes (pork, shrimp, fish, and lamb). What should you do if you accidentally stumble in thinking the place is just a steakhouse? Order the filet steak—it's very good.

Blue Moon. Kaya Hellmund 5. ☎ **599/7-8617.** Reservations recommended. Main courses $10–$18. AE, MC, V. Tues–Sun 6-10pm. INTERNATIONAL.

This sea-bordering bistro near the Divi Flamingo is in one of the island's oldest houses. Intimate tables and candlelight create a romantic ambience in the main restaurant, although you can dine less formally outside on the terrace overlooking the harbor. The menu always features the catch of the day as well as steak dishes. Sample a rather delectable stuffed chicken breast with mango, or jumbo shrimp hollandaise, followed by one of the homemade desserts. Finish off with one of their rich, Cuban-style coffees. Flavors are precisely defined, although nearly all ingredients have to be imported. Specials change daily.

Green Parrot Restaurant. In the Sand Dollar Condominium Resort, Kaya Gobernador N. Debrot 79. ☎ **599/7-8738.** Reservations recommended. Main courses $12.50–$20; lunch $6.85–$10. AE, MC, V. Daily 7:30am–10pm. CONTINENTAL.

On a breezy pier, this place is part of a resort complex that's a 15-minute drive from the airport. It serves burgers, pasta, sandwiches, and seafood dishes. You can gaze at the waves, enjoy a frozen tropical-fruit drink, and watch the sunset. The food consistently ranks as some of the island's best, especially the charcoal-grilled fish (based on the catch of the day). You might also try the barbecued chicken and ribs, various U.S. beef cuts (from T-bone to filet mignon), garlic shrimp, or the highly favored onion strings (like an onion loaf). Saturday nights bring a barbecue buffet with entertainment. Come here for fun and good times.

Mona Lisa. Kaya Grandi 15. ☎ **599/7-8718.** Reservations recommended. Main courses $14.50–$25; fixed-price menu $28. AE, MC, V. Mon–Sat 5:30–10pm. FRENCH/INTERNATIONAL.

A local favorite on the main street of town, this is one of the best places for food that tastes homemade. The prices are some of the best around, considering the quality of the food served and the generous portions. Although many regulars come just to patronize the Dutch bar and catch up on the latest gossip, the old-fashioned dining room deserves serious attention. Guests enjoy the fresh fish of the day (often wahoo) or such meat dishes as a leg of lamb fillet, tournedos, and sirloin steak. The most popular appetizers are onion soup, smoked fish, and shrimp cocktail. Mona Lisa is known for serving the freshest vegetables on an island where nearly everything is imported.

✪ Richard's Waterfront Dining. J. A. Abraham Blvd. 60. ☎ **599/7-5263.** Reservations recommended for groups of six or more. Main courses $14–$21. DC, MC, V. Tues–Sun 6:30–10:30pm. STEAK/SEAFOOD.

On a recent visit, we had our best meal on Bonaire here. On the airport side of Kralendijk, within walking distance of the Divi Flamingo Beach Resort, this restaurant, with its large covered terrace, was once a private home. Reasonable in price, it's the favorite of many locals who have sampled every restaurant on the island. Boston-born Richard Beady and his Aruban partner, Mario, operate a welcoming oasis with a happy hour at 5:30pm, an hour before dinner hours. Gathered around the coral bar, guests consider the chalkboard menu listing the offerings for the night: grilled wahoo or the fresh catch of the day, filet mignon béarnaise, U.S. sirloin with green-peppercorn sauce, shrimp scampi, or pasta. It's best to begin with the fish soup, if featured. The menu is wisely kept small so that each night's entrees can be given the attention they deserve. The kitchen focuses on bringing out the natural flavors of a dish without overwhelming it with sauces or too many seasonings. The fact that all diners are welcomed with such warm hospitality contributes to a thoroughly enjoyable evening.

Zeezicht Restaurant. Kaya Corsow 10. ☎ **599/7-8434.** Reservations not required. Main courses $8–$28. AE, MC, V. Daily 8am–11pm. INTERNATIONAL.

This is the best place in the capital to go for a sundowner. Join the old salts or the people who live on boats to watch the sun go down, and try to see the "green flash" that Hemingway wrote about. Zeezicht (pronounced *ZAY-zict* and meaning "sea view") has long been popular for its excellent local cookery. A two-story operation, it serves a small rijstaffel as well as fresh fish from the nearby fish market. Lobster is occasionally offered, and there's always steak.

4 Beaches

Sports lovers come to Bonaire for the diving (see below), not the beaches. For the most part, the beaches are full of coral and feel gritty to bare feet. Those on the leeward side (the more tranquil side of the island) are often narrow strips. To compensate, some hotels have shipped in extra sand for their guests.

Pink Beach, south of Kralendijk, out past Salt Pier, is the most desirable beach, despite its narrow strip of sand, shallow water, and lack of shade. It's aptly named: The beach really is a deep pink color, from the corals that have been pulverized into sand by the waves. Bring your own cooler and towels, as there are no refreshment stands or equipment rentals to mar the panoramic setting. It's also wise to bring along some sun protection, as the few palm trees bordering the dunes offer little shade. Enter the water at the southern end of this beach, as the northern tier has some exposed rock. Many Bonaireans flock here on weekends, but during the week you'll have the beach to yourself.

Playa Funchi, within Washington-Slagbaai National Park, is good for snorkeling. Regrettably, it has almost no sand, there are no facilities, and the area surrounding the beach is a bit smelly. On one side of the beach, there's a lagoon where flamingos nest; snorkelers find the water most desirable on the other side.

Also within the park, the more desirable **Boca Slagbaai** is a major target for snorkelers and picnickers. You can spot flamingos nearby. A 19th-century building houses decent toilets and showers; drinks and snacks are also available. Don't venture into the waters barefoot, as the coral beach can be quite rough.

A final beach at the national park is **Boca Cocolishi**, a black-sand strip on the northern coast. This is the windiest beach on Bonaire; you'll certainly stay cool as the trade winds whip the surf up. The waters are too rough for swimming, but it's a good picnic spot.

The best spot for windsurfers is **Lac Bay Beach,** on the southern shore of Lac Bay. There are mangroves at the north end of the bay. A couple of windsurfing concessions usually operate here, and food and drink are available.

Like the island's hotels, many of Bonaire's beaches are situated along the west coast. One of the more unusual is **Nukove Beach,** a minicave in a limestone cliff with a small white-sand channel, which cuts through the dense wall of elkhorn coral near the shore, giving divers and snorkelers easy access to the water. Further north is **1,000 Steps Beach,** where 67 steps (although it can feel like 1,000 on the way back up) carved out of the limestone cliff lead to the white-sand beach. This beach offers good snorkeling and diving, a unique location and view, and nearly perfect solitude.

Bonaire's offshore island, Klein Bonaire, just three-quarters of a mile offshore, has some of the most pristine beaches. Popular for snorkeling, scuba diving, and picnicking, **No Name Beach,** on the north side of Klein Bonaire, features a 300-yard white-sand beach and a rainbow of colorful fish. Accessible only by boat (see "Boating" under "Other Sports & Outdoor Pursuits," below), Klein Bonaire is an uninhabited island home to sea turtles and other indigenous wildlife.

5 Diving & Snorkeling

The true beauty on Bonaire is under the sea, where visibility is 100 feet, 365 days of the year, and the water temperatures range from 78° to 82°F. One of the richest reef communities in the entire West Indies, Bonaire has plunging walls that descend to a sand bottom at 130 or so feet. The reefs are home to various coral formations that grow at different depths, ranging from the knobby brain coral at 3 feet to staghorn and elkhorn up to about 10 feet deeper, and gorgonians, giant brain, and others all the way to 40 to 83 feet. Swarms of rainbow-hued tropical fish inhabit the reefs, and the deep reef slope is home to a range of basket sponges, groupers, and moray eels. Most of the diving is done on the leeward side, where the ocean is lake flat. There are more than 40 dive sites on sharply sloping reefs.

The waters off the coast of Bonaire received an additional attraction in 1984. A rust-bottomed general cargo ship, 80 feet long, was confiscated by the police along with its contraband cargo, about 25,000 pounds of marijuana. Known as the *Hilma Hooker* (familiarly dubbed "The Hooker" by everyone on the island), it sank unclaimed (obviously) and without fanfare one calm day in 90 feet of water. Lying just off the southern shore near the capital, its wreck is now a popular dive site.

The ✪ **Bonaire Marine Park** was created to protect the coral-reef ecosystem off Bonaire. The park incorporates the entire coastline of Bonaire and neighboring **Klein Bonaire.** Scuba diving and snorkeling are both popular here. The park is policed, and services and facilities include a Visitor Information Center at the **Karpata Ecological Center,** lectures, slide presentations, films, and permanent dive-site moorings.

Visitors are asked to respect the marine environment and to refrain from activities that may damage it, including sitting or walking on the coral. All marine life is completely protected. This means there's no fishing or collecting fish, shells, or corals— dead or alive. Spearfishing is forbidden, as is anchoring; all craft must use permanent moorings, except for emergency stops (boats shorter than 12 feet may use a stone anchor). Most recreational activity in the marine park takes place on the island's leeward side and among the reefs surrounding uninhabited Klein Bonaire.

Bonaire has a unique program for divers: The major hotels offer personalized, close-up encounters with the island's fish and other marine life under the expertise of Bonaire's dive guides.

Dive I and **Dive II,** at opposite ends of the beachfront of the Divi Flamingo Beach Resort & Casino, J. A. Abraham Boulevard (☎ **599/7-8285**), north of Kralendijk, are among the island's most complete scuba facilities. They're open daily from 8am to 12:30pm and 1:30 to 5pm. Both operate out of well-stocked beachfront buildings, renting diving equipment and offering expeditions (both branches charge the same rates). A resort course for first-time divers costs $88; for experienced divers, a one-tank dive goes for $55, a two-tank dive for $75.

Captain Don's Habitat Dive Shop, Kaya Gobernador N. Debrot 103 (☎ **599/ 7-8290**), is a PADI five-star training facility. The open-air, full-service dive shop includes a classroom, photo/video lab, camera-rental facility, equipment repair, and compressor rooms. Habitat's slogan is "Diving Freedom": Divers can take their tanks and dive anywhere, day or night. Most head for "The Pike," half a mile of protected reef right in front of the property. The highly qualified staff is here to assist and advise, but not to police or dictate dive plans. Diving packages include boat dives, unlimited offshore diving (24 hours a day), unlimited air, tanks, weights, and belt. Some dive packages also include accommodations and meals (see "Where to Stay," above). If you're not staying at the hotel as part of a dive package, you can visit for a beach dive, costing $21. If you want to rent snorkeling equipment, the charge is $7.45 a day. A half day of diving, with all equipment, goes for $37.

Sand Dollar Dive and Photo, at the Sand Dollar Condominium Resort, Kaya Gobernador N. Debrot (☎ 599/7-5252), is open daily from 8:30am to 5:30pm. It offers dive packages, PADI and NAUI instruction, and equipment rental and repairs; boat and shore trips with an instructor are available by appointment. The photo shop offers underwater photo and video shoots, PADI specialty courses by appointment, E-6 processing, print developing, and equipment rental and repair.

Bonaire's coral reefs are also an underwater paradise for snorkelers. They are unique in that they start in just inches of water and therefore have dense coral formations in very shallow surf. Most snorkeling on the island is conducted in 15 feet of water or less, and there's plenty to see even at this depth. As you travel around the island, particularly in the northern area, you'll see evidence of prehistoric reefs now 30 to 40 feet above sea level, having lived submerged for hundreds of thousands of years and then uplifted as the island slowly rose.

Snorkeling equipment can be rented at such previously recommended establishments as **Carib Inn,** J. A. Abraham Boulevard (☎ 599/7-8819); **Sand Dollar Dive and Photo,** Kaya Gobernador N. Debrot (☎ 599/7-5252); and **Captain Don's Habitat Dive Shop,** Kaya Governador N. Debrot (☎ 599/7-8290).

6 Other Sports & Outdoor Pursuits

The true beauty on Bonaire is under the sea (see "Diving & Snorkeling," above). Sailing is another favored pastime here, and the bird watching is among the best in the Caribbean. Beachcombers will find acres and acres of driftwood, along the shore from the salt flats to Lac.

BIRD WATCHING Bonaire is home to 190 species of birds, 80 of which are indigenous to the island. But most famous are its flamingos, which can number 15,000 during the mating season. For great places to bring your binoculars, see "Exploring the Island," below.

BOATING Most everyone will want to take a trip to tiny, uninhabited **Klein Bonaire.** This flat, rocky 1,500-acre island is known for its almost deserted white-sand beaches and its spectacular reefs, filled with stunning elkhorn coral. **Sunset Beach Hotel,** at Playa Lechi (☎ 599/7-5300), offers trips daily. You'll be left in the morning for a day of snorkeling, beachcombing, and picnicking, then be picked up later that afternoon. The cost is $35. Other hotels can also arrange trips to the islet.

FISHING The island's offshore fishing grounds offer some of the best fishing in the Caribbean. A good day's catch might include mackerel, tuna, wahoo, dolphin (mahimahi), blue marlin, Amber Jack, grouper, sailfish, or snapper. Bonaire is also one of the best-kept secrets of bonefishing enthusiasts.

Your best bet is Chris Morkos of **Piscatur Fishing Supplies,** Kaya Herman 4, Playa Pabao (☎ 599/7-8774). A native Bonairean, he has been fishing all his life. A maximum of six people are taken out on a 42-foot boat with a guide and captain, at a cost of $350 for a half day or $500 for a whole day, including all tackle and bait. Reef fishing is another popular sport, in boats averaging 15 and 19 feet. A maximum of two people can go out for a half day at $225 or a whole day at $400. For the same price, a maximum of two people can fish for bonefish and tarpon on the island's large salt flats.

HIKING **Washington-Slagbaai National Park** (see "Exploring the Island," below) has a varied terrain; those ambitious enough to climb some of its steep hills are rewarded with panoramic views. The hiking possibilities are seemingly endless. Small hidden beaches with crashing waters by the cliffs provide an ideal place for a picnic.

HORSEBACK RIDING Spend part of a day at one of Bonaire's fine horse ranches, where private lessons and trail rides are available. You can usually arrange a day in the saddle through your hotel. You can also call **Kunuku Warahama Ranch** (☎ **599/7-7324**), a 165-acre ranch that offers hour-long trail rides through fields studded with cactus, where you're likely to spot everything from an iguana to a colony of pink flamingos. The cost is $20.

MOUNTAIN BIKING Biking is an ideal way to see Bonaire's hidden beauty; you can explore more than 186 miles of trails and dirt roads, venturing off the beaten path to enjoy the scenery. Ask at the tourist office for a trail map that outlines the most scenic routes. You can check with your hotel about arranging a trip, or call **Cycle Bonaire,** Kaya L. D. Gerharts 11D (☎ **599/7-7558**), which rents 21-speed mountain bikes and arranges half- and full-day excursions. The cost is $40 and $65, respectively, in addition to the bike-rental charges.

SEA KAYAKING Paddle the protected waters of Lac Bay, or head for the miles of flats and mangroves in the south (the island's nursery), where you can see baby fish and wildlife. Kayak rentals are available at **Jive City,** Lac Bay (☎ **599/7-5233**), for $10 per hour or $20 per half day.

TENNIS The are two courts, lit for night play, at the **Sand Dollar Condominium Resort,** Kaya Governador N. Debrot 79, and **Divi Flamingo Beach Resort,** J. A. Abraham Boulevard.

WINDSURFING Consistent conditions, enjoyed by windsurfers with a wide range of skill levels, make the shallow, calm waters of Lac Bay the island's home to the sport. Call **Bonaire Windsurfing** (☎ **599/7-2288**) for details. A half day costs $40.

7 Exploring the Island

KRALENDIJK

The capital, Kralendijk, means "coral dike" and is pronounced *KROLL-en-dike,* although most denizens refer to it as *Playa,* Spanish for "beach." A dollhouse town of some 2,500 residents, Kralendijk is small, neat, pretty, Dutch-clean, and just a bit dull. Its stucco buildings are painted pink and orange, with an occasional lime green. The capital's jetty is lined with island sloops and fishing boats.

Kralendijk nestles in a bay on the west coast, opposite **Klein Bonaire,** or Little Bonaire, an uninhabited, low-lying islet that's a 10-minute boat ride away.

The main street of town leads along the beachfront on the harbor. A Protestant church was built in 1834, and **St. Bernard's Roman Catholic Church** has some interesting stained-glass windows.

At **Fort Oranje,** you'll see a lone cannon dating from the days of Napoleon. If possible, try to get up early to visit the **Fish Market** on the waterfront, where you'll see a variety of strange and brilliantly colored fish.

THE TOUR NORTH

The road north is one of the most beautiful stretches in the Antilles, with turquoise waters on your left and coral cliffs on your right. You can stop at several points along this road, where there are paved paths for strolling or bicycling.

After leaving Kralendijk and passing the Sunset Beach Hotel and the desalination plant, you'll come to **Radio Nederland Wereld Omroep (Dutch World Radio).** It's a 13-tower, 300,000-watter. Opposite the transmitting station is a lovers' promenade, built by nature; it's an ideal spot for a picnic.

Continuing, you'll pass the storage tanks of the Bonaire Petroleum Corporation, the road heading to **Goto Meer,** the island's inland sector, with a saltwater lake. Several flamingos prefer this spot to the salt flats in the south.

Down the hill, the road leads to a section called **Dos Pos** ("two wells"); the palm trees and vegetation here are a contrast to the rest of the island, where only the drought-resistant kibraacha and divi-divi trees, tilted before the constant wind, can grow, along with forests of cacti.

Bonaire's oldest village is **Rincón.** Slaves who used to work in the salt flats in the south once lived here. The Rincón Ice Cream Parlour makes homemade ice cream in a variety of interesting flavors; there's also a couple of bars here. Above the bright roofs of the village is the crest of a hill called Para Mira, or "stop and look."

A side path outside Rincón takes you to some **Arawak inscriptions** supposedly 500 years old. The petroglyph designs are in pink-red dye. At nearby **Boca Onima,** you'll find grotesque grottoes of coral.

Before going back to the capital, you might take a short bypass to **Seroe Largu,** which has a good view of Kralendijk and the sea. Lovers frequent the spot at night.

THE NATIONAL PARK

Washington-Slagbaai National Park (☎ 599/7-8444), created for the conservation of the island's fauna, flora, and landscape, has a varied terrain that includes desertlike areas, secluded beaches, caverns, and a bird sanctuary. Occupying 15,000 acres of Bonaire's northwesternmost territory, the park was once plantation land, producing divi-divi, aloe, and charcoal. It was purchased by the Netherlands Antilles government, and since 1967 part of the land, formerly the Washington plantation, has been a wildlife sanctuary. The southern part of the park, the Slagbaai plantation, was added in 1978.

You can see the park in a few hours, although it takes days to appreciate it fully. Touring the park by car or jeep is easy, with two routes: a 15-mile "short" route, marked by green arrows, and a 22-mile "long" route, marked by yellow arrows. The roads are well marked and safe, but somewhat rugged, although they're gradually being improved. For those wanting a closer look, the hiking possibilities are nearly endless. The entrance fee is $5 for adults and $1 for children 11 and under. The park is open daily except holidays from 8am to 5pm. You must enter before 3pm.

Whichever route you take, there are a few important stops you shouldn't miss. Just past the gate is **Salina Mathijs,** a salt flat that's home to flamingos during the rainy season. Beyond the salt flat on the road to the right is **Boca Chiquito,** a white-sand beach and bay. A few miles up the beach lies **Boca Cocolishi,** a two-part black-sand beach. Many a couple has raved about their romantic memories of this beach, perfect for a secluded picnic. Its deep, rough seaward side and calm, shallow basin are separated by a ridge of calcareous algae. The basin and the beach were formed by small pieces of coral and mollusk shells (*cocolishi* means "shells"), thus the black sand. The basin itself has no current, so it's perfect for snorkeling close to shore.

Flamingo Watching at the Salt Flats

During the 20th century, the number of nesting places for the Caribbean flamingo decreased from 30 to 4, and the birds quickly dwindled. To reverse this trend, Bonaire created a preserve for flamingos within its salt works. Today, Bonaire's flamingo population during the breeding season swells to almost 10,000, nearly outnumbering the island's human population. The best place to watch flamingos is at the salt ponds in the National Park, at Goto Meer, or at the southern end of the island at the solar salt works. While the solar sanctuary within the salt works requires a special permit for entry, the pink flamingos can be seen from the road. Every day at sunset, the entire flock flies the short 50-mile trip to Venezuela for feeding.

The main road leads to **Boca Bartol,** a bay full of living and dead elkhorn coral, sea fans, and reef fish. A popular watering hole good for bird watching is **Poosdi Mangel. Wajaca** is a remote reef, perfect for divers and home to the island's most exciting sea creatures, including turtles, octopuses, and triggerfish. Immediately inland towers 788-foot **Mount Brandaris,** Bonaire's highest peak, at whose foot is **Bronswinkel Well,** a watering spot for pigeons and parakeets. Some 130 species of birds live in the park, many with such exotic names as bananaquit and black-faced grassquit. Bonaire has few mammals, but you'll see goats and donkeys, perhaps even a wild bull.

HEADING SOUTH

Leaving the capital again, you pass the **Trans World Radio antennae,** towering 500 feet in the air, transmitting with 810,000 watts. This is one of the hemisphere's most powerful medium-wave radio stations, the loudest voice in Christendom, and the most powerful nongovernmental broadcast station in the world. It sends out interdenominational Gospel messages and hymns in 20 languages to places as far away as Eastern Europe and the Middle East.

You then come to the ✪ **salt flats,** where the brilliantly colored pink flamingos live. Bonaire shelters the largest accessible nesting and breeding grounds in the world. The flamingos build high mud mounds to hold their eggs. The best time to see the birds is in spring, when they're usually nesting and tending their young. The salt flats were once worked by slaves, and the government has rebuilt some primitive stone huts, bare shelters little more than waist high. The slaves slept in these huts, and returned to their homes in Rincón in the north on weekends. The centuries-old salt pans have been reactivated by the International Salt Company. Near the salt pans, you'll see some 30-foot obelisks in white, blue, and orange, built in 1838 to help mariners locate their proper anchorages.

Farther down the coast is the island's oldest lighthouse, **Willemstoren,** built in 1837. Still farther along, **Sorobon Beach, Lac Bay Beach,** and **Boca Cai** come into view. They're at landlocked Lac Bay, which is ideal for swimming and snorkeling. Conch shells are stacked up on the beach. The water here is so vivid and clear, you can see coral 65 to 120 feet down in the reef-protected waters.

A SIGHTSEEING TOUR

Bonaire Sightseeing Tours (☎ 599/7-8778) transports you on tours of the island, both north and south, taking in the flamingos, slave huts, conch shells, Goto Lake, the Amerindian inscriptions, and other sights. Each of these tours lasts 2 hours and costs $17 per person. You can also take a half-day "City and Country Tour," lasting 3 hours and costing from $22 per person, allowing you to see the entire northern section and the southern part as far as the slave huts.

8 Shopping

Walk along Kaya Grandi in Kralendijk to see an assortment of goods, including gem-stone jewelry, wood, leather, sterling, ceramics, liquors, and tobacco, priced 25% to 50% less than in the United States and Canada. Prices are often quoted in U.S. dollars, and major credit cards and traveler's checks are usually accepted.

Bonaire Art Gallery, Kaya L. D. Gerharts 10 (☎ 599/7-7120), is the island's only art gallery. It inventories an impressive collection of watercolors, oil paintings, acrylics, and photographs (many of underwater scenes) from artists who spend at least part of their year on Bonaire, returning afterward for sojourns in Holland, Venezuela, or the United States. Especially prominent is the work of Venezuelan-born Hugo Aguirre. Pieces range in price from $15 to $2,500.

Ki Bo Ke Pakus ("What Do You Want"), in the Divi Flamingo Beach Resort & Casino, J. A. Abraham Boulevard (☎ 599/7-8239), has some of the most popular merchandise on the island—T-shirts, handbags, and beach wear. **Things Bonaire,** Kaya Grandi 38C (☎ 599/7-8423), carries many gift items, including sunglasses, postcards, locally made shell and driftwood items, swimsuits, T-shirts, beach towels, guayaberas, hats, and visors.

Men might want to head for **Little Holland,** in the Harbourside Mall, Kralendijk (☎ 599/7-5670), which has silk neckties, Nautica clothing, and a sophisticated array of cigars. Crafted, usually by hand, in Cuba, the Dominican Republic, and to a lesser degree, Brazil, they include some of the most prestigious names in cigars. Be aware that at this writing, it's still illegal to bring Cuban cigars into the mainland U.S.

Littman Jewelers, Kaya Grandi 33 (☎ 599/7-8160), sells Tag Heuer dive watches and also carries Daum French crystal and Lladró Spanish porcelain. Steve and Esther Littman have restored this old house to its original state. Next door, the Littmans have a shop called **Littman's Gifts,** selling standard and hand-painted T-shirts, plus sandals, hats, Gottex swimsuits, gift items, costume jewelry, and toys.

9 Bonaire After Dark

Underwater **slide shows** provide entertainment for both divers and nondivers. The best shows are at **Captain Don's Habitat** (☎ 599/7-8290) (see "Diving & Snorkeling," above). Shows are presented in the hotel bar, Rum-Runner, Thursday night from 7 to 8:30pm.

The **Divi Flamingo Beach Resort & Casino,** J. A. Abraham Boulevard (☎ 599/7-8285), promoted as "The World's First Barefoot Casino," offers blackjack, roulette, poker, wheel of fortune, video games, and slot machines. Gambling on the island is regulated by the government. Entrance is free; hours are Monday to Saturday from 8pm to 2am.

The **Plaza Resort Bonaire Casino,** J. A. Abraham Blvd. 80 (☎ 599/7-2500), managed by the Dutch-based Van der Valk hotel chain, is the larger of Bonaire's two casinos—and usually the noisier and more animated. Don't expect vestiges of colonial Dutch charm; modeled directly on Las Vegas, it glitters, vibrates, and jangles with the sound of slot machines that cover entire walls, plus gaming tables that purvey all the games of chance you might want. It's open daily from 6pm to 4am. Jackets and ties aren't required, but shorts after dark are frowned upon.

✪ **Karel's Beach Bar**, on the waterfront (☎ 599/7-8434), is almost Tahitian in its high-ceilinged, open-walled design. This popular place is perched above the sea on stilts. You can sit at the long rectangular bar with many of the island's dive and boating professionals, or select a table near the balustrades overlooking the illuminated surf. Local bands entertain on weekends. Drink prices are reduced during happy hour, from 5:30 to 7pm.

Call **Klein Bonaire**, Kaya C. E. B. Hellmund 5 (☎ 599/7-8617), to see if they're offering live jazz on the weekends, as they often do. We nominate the **City Cafe,** Kaya Isla Riba 3 (no phone), as the island's funkiest bar. Painted in screaming Caribbean colors of electric blue, scarlet magenta, and banana, this bar is a popular local hangout, but "only for the crazy ones," in the words of one habitué.

Disco still lives at **Fantasy Disco,** Kaya L. D. Gerharts 11 (☎ 599/7-6345), the local dance spot on the island. Big-screen TVs and taped music, such as Jamaican reggae or merengue from the Dominican Republic, keep the crowd jumping. Live performances feature the island's best bands.

The British Virgin Islands

8

With their small bays and hidden coves, the British Virgin Islands are among the world's loveliest cruising grounds. Strung over the northeastern corner of the Caribbean, about 60 miles east of Puerto Rico, are some 40 islands, although that's including some small, uninhabited cays or spits of land. Only three of the British Virgins are of any significant size: Tortola ("Dove of Peace"), Virgin Gorda (the "Fat Virgin"), and Jost Van Dyke. Remote Norman Island is said to have been the inspiration for Robert Louis Stevenson's *Treasure Island.* On Deadman Bay, a rocky cay, Blackbeard marooned 15 pirates and a bottle of rum, which gave rise to the ditty.

Columbus came this way in 1493, but the British Virgins apparently made little impression on him. Although the Spanish and Dutch contested it, Tortola was officially annexed by the English in 1672. Today these islands are a British colony, with their own elected government and a population of about 17,000.

The vegetation is varied and depends on the rainfall. In some parts, palms and mangos grow in profusion, whereas other places are arid and studded with cactus.

There are predictions that mass tourism is on the way, but so far the British Virgins are still a paradise for escapists.

1 Essentials

VISITOR INFORMATION

Before you go, you can obtain information from the **British Virgin Islands Tourist Board,** 370 Lexington Ave., Suite 313, New York, NY 10017 (☎ **212/696-0400**). Other branches of the **British Virgin Islands Information Office** are at 1804 Union St., San Francisco, CA 94123 (☎ **415/775-0344**); 3450 Wilshire Blvd., Suite 108-17, Los Angeles, CA 90010 (☎ **310/287-2200**); and 3390 Peachtree Rd. NE, Suite 1000, Lenox Towers, Atlanta, GA 30326 (☎ **404/240-8018**).

In the United Kingdom, contact the **B.V.I. Information Office,** 110 St. Martin's Lane, London WC2N 4DY (☎ **0171/240-4259**).

Once on the islands, you'll find the **B.V.I. Tourist Board** in the center of Road Town (Tortola), close to the ferry dock, south of Wickhams Cay (☎ **284/494-3134**).

The tourist board's official Web site is **www.bviwelcome.com**.

GETTING THERE

BY PLANE   There are no direct flights from New York to the British Virgin Islands, but you can make connections from San Juan and St. Thomas to Beef Island/Tortola (see chapter 18, "Puerto Rico," and chapter 27, "The U.S. Virgin Islands," for information on flying to these islands).

Your best bet to reach Beef Island/Tortola is to take **American Eagle** (☎ **800/ 433-7300** in the U.S.), the most reliable airline in the Caribbean, with at least four daily trips from San Juan to Beef Island/Tortola.

Another choice, if you're on one of Tortola's neighboring islands, is the much less reliable **LIAT** (☎ **800/468-0482** in the U.S. and Canada, 284/495-2577, or 284/495-1187). This Caribbean carrier makes the short hops to Tortola from St. Kitts, Antigua, St. Maarten, St. Thomas, and San Juan in small planes not known for their frequency or careful scheduling. Reservations are made through travel agents or through the larger U.S.-based airlines that connect with LIAT hubs.

Beef Island, the site of the major airport serving the British Virgins, is connected to Tortola by the one-lane **Queen Elizabeth Bridge.**

BY FERRY   You can travel from Charlotte Amalie (St. Thomas) by public ferry to West End and Road Town on Tortola, a 45-minute voyage along Drake's Channel through the islands. Boats making this run include **Native Son** (☎ 284/495-4617), **Smith's Ferry Service** (☎ 284/495-4495), and **Inter-Island Boat Services** (☎ 284/ 495-4166). The latter specializes in a somewhat obscure routing—that is, from St. John to the West End on Tortola.

Fast Facts: The British Virgin Islands

American Express   Local representatives include **Travel Plan,** Waterfront Drive (☎ **284/494-2347**), in Tortola; and **Travel Plan,** Virgin Gorda Yacht Harbour (☎ **284/495-5586**), in Virgin Gorda.

Banking Hours   Banks are generally open Monday through Thursday from 9am to 3pm, Friday from 9am to 5pm. To cash traveler's checks, try **Bank of Nova Scotia,** Wickhams Cay (☎ **284/494-2526**), or **Barclays Bank,** Wickhams Cay (☎ **284/494-2171**), both near Road Town on Tortola.

Cameras & Film   The best place for supplies and developing on Tortola is **Bolo's Brothers,** Wickhams Cay (☎ **284/494-3641**).

Currency   The U.S. dollar is the legal currency, much to the surprise of British travelers.

Customs   You can bring items intended for your personal use into the British Virgin Islands. For U.S. residents, the duty-free allowance is only $400, providing you have been out of the country for 48 hours. You can bring unsolicited gifts home if they total less than $50 per day to any single address. You don't have to pay duty on items classified as handcrafts, art, or antiques.

Dentists   For dental emergencies, contact **Dental Surgery** (☎ 284/ 494-3274), which is in Road Town, Tortola, behind the Skeleton Building and next to the *BVI Beacon,* the local newspaper.

Doctors   Thirteen doctors practice on Tortola; see also "Hospital," below. One doctor practices on Virgin Gorda. If you need medical help, your hotel will put you in touch with the islands' medical staff.

The British Virgin Islands

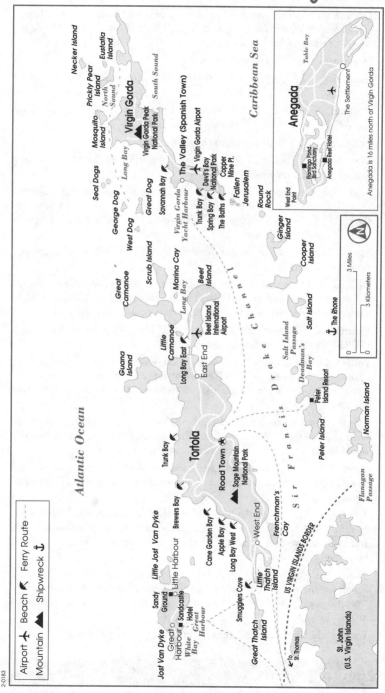

Airport ✈ Beach ⚓ Ferry Route ---
Mountain ▲ Shipwreck ⚓

2-0183

Atlantic Ocean

Jost Van Dyke
Sandy
Ground
Little Jost Van Dyke
Little Harbour
Sandcastle
Hotel
Great
Harbour
White
Bay
Smugglers Cove
Great Thatch
Island
Little
Thatch
Island
Brewers Bay
Cane Garden Bay
Apple Bay
Long Bay West
West End
Frenchman's
Cay
Trunk Bay
Tortola
Road Town
Sage Mountain
National Park

Guana
Island
Little
Camanoe
Long Bay East
East End
Great
Camanoe
Scrub Island
Marina Cay
Long Bay
Beef
Island
Beef Island
International
Airport

West Dog
George Dog
Seal Dogs
Great Dog
Savannah Bay
Trunk Bay
Spring Bay
The Baths
Virgin Gorda
Virgin Gorda Peak
National Park
The Valley (Spanish Town)
Virgin Gorda Airport
Devil's Bay
National Park
Copper
Mine Pt.
Fallen
Jerusalem
Virgin Gorda
Yacht Harbour

Mosquito
Island
Prickly Pear
Island
North
Sound
South Sound
Necker Island
Eustatia
Island
Long Bay

D r a k e   C h a n n e l

S i r   F r a n c i s

Salt Island
Passage
Deadman's
Bay
Peter
Island Resort
Peter Island
Salt Island
Round
Rock
Ginger
Island
Cooper
Island
⚓ The Rhone

Flanagan
Passage
Norman Island

US VIRGIN ISLANDS BORDER
To
St.Thomas
St.John
(U.S. Virgin Islands)

Caribbean Sea

Anegada
Table Bay
West End
Point
Flamingo Pond
Bird Sanctuary
Anegada Reef Hotel
The Settlement
✈
Anegada is 16 miles north of Virgin Gorda

N
3 Miles
3 Kilometers
0
0

167

Documents   U.S. citizens and Canadians need a valid passport or a birth certificate with a raised seal along with a government-issued photo ID. United Kingdom residents need a valid passport.

Drugstores   See "Pharmacies," below.

Electricity   The electrical current is 110 volts AC (60 cycles), as in the United States.

Hospital   On Tortola, **Peebles Hospital,** Porter Road, Road Town (☎ **284/494-3497**), has X-ray and laboratory facilities.

Language   The official language is English.

Liquor Laws   The legal minimum age for purchasing liquor or drinking alcohol in bars or restaurants is 21.

Mail   Postal rates in the British Virgin Islands are 30¢ for a postcard (airmail) to the U.S. or Canada, and 45¢ for a first-class airmail letter (half an ounce) to the United States or Canada, or 35¢ for a second-class letter (half an ounce) to the United States or Canada.

Maps   The best map of the British Virgin Islands is published by Vigilate and is sold at most bookstores in Road Town.

Newspapers & Magazines   The British Virgin Islands has no daily newspaper, but the *Island Sun,* published Wednesday and Friday, is a good source of information on local entertainment, as is the *Beacon,* published on Thursday.

Pharmacies   The best place to go is **J. R. O'Neal,** Main Street, Road Town (☎ **284/494-2292**), in Tortola; closed Sunday.

Police   The main police headquarters is on Waterfront Drive near the ferry docks on Sir Olva Georges Plaza (☎ **284/494-3822**), on Tortola. There are also police stations on Virgin Gorda (☎ **284/495-5222**) and on Jost Van Dyke (☎ **284/495-9828**).

Safety   Crime is rare here; in fact, the British Virgin Islands are among the safest places in the Caribbean. Still, you should take all the usual precautions you would anywhere, and don't leave items unattended on the beach.

Taxes   There is no sales tax. A government tax of 7% is imposed on all hotel rooms. A $10 departure tax is collected from everyone leaving by air, $5 for those departing by sea.

Telephone   You can call the British Virgins from the continental United States by dialing **011** (the international access code), area code **284,** followed by **49,** and then the five-digit number. Once here, omit both the 284 and the 49 to make local calls.

Time   The islands operate on Atlantic standard time year-round. In the peak winter season, when it's 6am in the British Virgins, it's 5am in Florida. However, when Florida and the rest of the East Coast go on daylight saving time, the clocks do not change here.

Water   The tap water in the British Virgin Islands is safe to drink.

2 Tortola

On the southern shore of this 24-square-mile island is **Road Town,** the capital of the British Virgin Islands. It's the seat of Government House and other administrative buildings, but it feels more like a small village than a town. The landfill at Wickhams Cay, a 70-acre town center development and marina in the harbor, has lured a massive yacht-chartering business here and has transformed the sleepy capital into more of a bustling center.

The entire southern coast, including Road Town, is characterized by rugged mountain peaks. On the northern coast are white sandy beaches, banana trees, mangos, and clusters of palms.

Close to Tortola's eastern end, **Beef Island** is the site of the main airport for passengers arriving in the British Virgins. The tiny island is connected to Tortola by the one-lane Queen Elizabeth Bridge, which the queen dedicated in 1966. On the north shore of Beef Island is Long Bay Beach.

ESSENTIALS

VISITOR INFORMATION   A **B.V.I. Tourist Board Office,** at the center of Road Town near the ferry dock (☎ **284/494-3134**), has information about hotels, restaurants, tours, and more. Pick up a copy of *The Welcome Tourist Guide,* which has a useful map of the island.

GETTING THERE   Because Tortola is the gateway to the British Virgin Islands, the information on how to get here is covered above.

GETTING AROUND   Taxis meet every arriving flight. Government regulations prohibit anyone from renting a car at the airport—visitors must take a taxi to their hotels. The fare from the Beef Island airport to Road Town is $15 for one to three passengers. A **taxi tour** lasting 2½ hours costs $45 for one to three people. To call a taxi in Road Town, dial ☎ **284/494-2322;** on Beef Island, ☎ **284/495-2378.**

A handful of local companies and U.S.-based chains rent cars. On Tortola, **Itgo** (☎ **284/494-2639**) is at 1 Wickhams Cay, Road Town; **Avis** (☎ **800/331-1212** or 284/494-3322) maintains offices opposite police headquarters in Road Town; and **Hertz** (☎ **800/654-3001** or 284/495-4405) has offices outside Road Town, on the island's West End, near the ferryboat landing dock. Rental companies will usually deliver your car to your hotel. All three companies require a valid driver's license and a temporary B.V.I. driver's license, which the car-rental agency can sell you for $10; it's valid for 3 months. Because of the volume of tourism to Tortola, you should reserve a car in advance, especially in winter.

Remember to *drive on the left.* Because island roads are narrow, poorly lit, and have few, if any, lines, driving at night can be tricky. It's a good idea to rent a taxi to take you to that difficult-to-find beach, restaurant, or bar.

Scato's Bus Service (☎ **284/494-2365**) operates from the north end of the island to the west end, picking up passengers who hail it down. Fares for a trek across the island are $1 to $3.

WHERE TO STAY

None of the island's hotels is as big, splashy, and all-inclusive as the hotels in the U.S. Virgin Islands, and that's just fine with most of the Tortola's repeat visitors. All rates are subject to a 10% service charge and a 7% government tax on the room. Be sure to read the section on package tours in chapter 2 before you book your hotel on your own!

VERY EXPENSIVE

✪ **Long Bay Beach Resort.** Tortola, B.V.I. ☎ **800/729-9599** in the U.S. and Canada, or 284/495-4252. Fax 914/833-3318 in Larchmont, N.Y. www.longbay.com. E-mail: reservations@longbay.com. 100 units. A/C. Winter $310–$360 double; $550–$650 two-bedroom villa; $775–$925 three-bedroom villa. Off-season $145–$195 double; $305–$350 two-bedroom villa; $420–$485 three-bedroom villa. MAP (breakfast and dinner) $45 per person extra. AE, MC, V.

A favorite of sophisticated travelers since the 1960s, this resort, the finest on Tortola, completed a recent upgrade by adding 18 new poolside overview studios. On the north shore, about 10 minutes from the West End, it's the only full-service resort on the island: a low-rise resort complex set in a 52-acre estate with a mile-long white-sand beach. The accommodations include hillside rooms and studios, the smallest and most basic with the simplest furnishings, and deluxe beachfront rooms and cabanas with either balconies or patios that overlook the ocean. The resort also offers two- and three-bedroom villas complete with a kitchen, a living area, and a large deck with a gas grill. Beachfront deluxe rooms and villas have cable TV. If you're not staying right on the beach, you'll still enjoy an ocean view from any of the other accommodations. All units have one four-poster king or two queen beds, each with a first-rate mattress, plus large bathrooms with fluffy towels and tiled showers.

Dining: The Beach Café offers breakfast, lunch, and informal à la carte suppers. In the ruins of an old sugar mill, the restaurant serves regular evening buffets with live entertainment. The Garden Restaurant offers dinner by reservation only and a tantalizing variety of local and international dishes in a more elegant, alfresco setting.

Amenities: Oceanside freshwater pool, two championship tennis courts and one regular court, beach bar, shops, summer children's activity program (ages 3 to 8). The hotel recently added a 130-foot pool, largest in the B.V.I., complete with a designated lap swimming area, a swim-up bar, and a water slide. Daily maid service, laundry, baby-sitting, car rental; chef available on request for villa renters.

The Sugar Mill. Apple Bay (P.O. Box 425, Road Town), Tortola, B.V.I. ☎ **800/462-8834** or 284/495-4355. Fax 284/495-4696. www.sugarmillhotel.com. E-mail: sugarmill@caribsurf. com. 21 units. A/C. Winter $295 double; $310 triple; $325 quad; $620 two-bedroom villa. Off-season $210–230 double; $225-245 triple; $240–$260 quad; $460–$500 two-bedroom villa. AE, MC, V. Closed Aug–Sept. Children 9 and under not accepted in winter.

Set in lush foliage on the site of a 300-year-old sugar mill on the north side of Tortola, this cottage colony sweeps down the hillside to its own little beach, with flowers and fruits brightening the grounds. Plain but comfortable apartments climb up the hillside. At the center is a circular swimming pool for those who don't want to go down to the beach. The accommodations are contemporary and well designed, ranging from suites and cottages to studio apartments, all self-contained with kitchenettes and private terraces with views. Rooms have twin or king beds, each with a good mattress, plus well-maintained private bathrooms with hair dryers and good towels. Four of the units are suitable for families of four.

Dining/Diversions: Lunch or dinner is served down by the beach at the Islands, which features Caribbean specialties along with burgers and salads. Dinner is also offered at the Sugar Mill Restaurant (see "Where to Dine," below). Breakfast is served on the terrace. The bars are open all day.

Amenities: Free snorkeling equipment.

EXPENSIVE

Frenchman's Cay Resort Hotel. West End (P.O. Box 1054), Tortola, B.V.I. ☎ **800/ 235-4077** in the U.S., 800/463-0199 in Canada, or 284/495-4844. Fax 284/495-4056. 9 units. Winter $235 one-bedroom villa; $350 two-bedroom villa. Off-season $140–$165 one-bedroom villa; $210–$245 two-bedroom villa. MAP (breakfast and dinner) $45 per person extra. AE, DISC, MC, V. From Tortola, cross the bridge to Frenchman's Cay, turn left, and follow the road to the eastern tip of the cay.

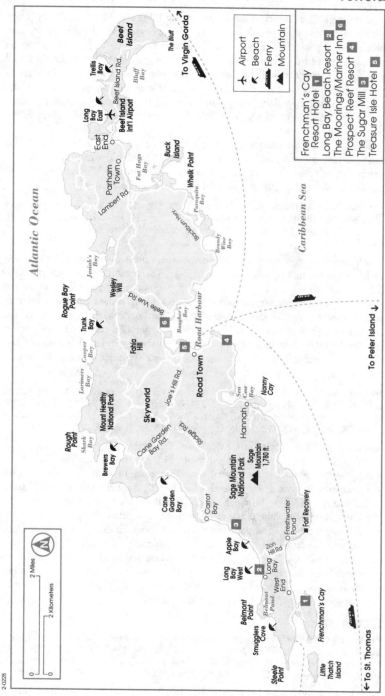

Tortola

Frenchman's Cay Resort Hotel 1
Long Bay Beach Resort 2
The Moorings/Mariner Inn 6
Prospect Reef Resort 4
The Sugar Mill 3
Treasure Isle Hotel 5

✈ Airport
🏖 Beach
⛴ Ferry
▲ Mountain

Atlantic Ocean

Caribbean Sea

Beef Island

The Bluff

To Virgin Gorda →

Trellis Bay
Beef Island Rd.
Bluff Bay

Long Bay East

Beef Island Int'l Airport

East End

Parham Town

Buck Island

Whelk Point

Fat Hogs Bay

Lambert Rd.

Blackburn Hwy.

Paraquita Bay

Brandy Wine Bay

Josiah's Bay

Wesley Will

Belle Vue Rd.

Rogue Bay Point

Trunk Bay

Fahia Hill

6

Beaugher's Bay

Road Harbour

Cooper Bay

Larimers Bay

Mount Healthy National Park

Skyworld ■

Joe's Hill Rd.

5

Road Town

4

Rough Point
Shark Bay

Brewers Bay

Cane Garden Bay Rd.

Ridge Rd.

Sea Cow Bay

Nanny Cay

To Peter Island →

Cane Garden Bay

Carrot Bay

Sage Mountain National Park

Sage Mountain 1,780 ft. ▲

Hannah ○

Apple Bay

3

Long Bay West

2

Long Bay

West End

Zion Hill Rd.

Freshwater Pond ○

Fort Recovery ■

Belmont Point

Smugglers Cove

1

Frenchman's Cay

Belmont Pond

← To St. Thomas

Steele Point

Little Thatch Island

N

2 Miles
2 Kilometers

0
0

2-0228

171

This intimate resort is tucked away at the windward side of Frenchman's Cay, a little island connected by bridge to Tortola. The 12-acre estate enjoys delightful year-round breezes and views of Sir Francis Drake Channel and the outer Virgins. The individual one- and two-bedroom villas—actually a cluster of condos—are well furnished, each with a shady terrace, full kitchen, dining room, and sitting room. The two-bedroom villas have two full bathrooms, a vacation in and of itself for families looking to escape the morning bathroom line. Pastel colors and tropical styling make for inviting accommodations, and each unit has quality mattresses, good linen, and fluffy towels. There's a beach with snorkeling.

The Clubhouse Restaurant and lounge bar is located in the main pavilion. The menu features a continental and Caribbean cuisine. Amenities include a freshwater swimming pool, tennis court, Sunfish sailboats, kayaks, and Windsurfers. Day-sail trips, horseback riding, island tours, and car rentals can be arranged.

The Moorings/Mariner Inn. Wickhams Cay (P.O. Box 139, Road Town), Tortola, B.V.I. ☎ **800/535-7289** in the U.S., or 284/494-2332. Fax 284/494-2226. 44 units. A/C TEL. Winter $170 double; $230 suite. Off-season $95 double; $125 suite. Extra person $15. AE, MC, V.

The Caribbean's most complete yachting resort is outfitted with at least 180 sailing yachts, some worth $2 million or more. On an 8-acre resort, the inn was obviously designed with the yachting crowd in mind, offering not only support facilities and services but also shoreside accommodations, a dockside restaurant and bar, swimming pool, tennis court, gift shop, and dive shop that rents underwater video cameras. The rooms are spacious; all suites have kitchenettes, and most of them open onto the water. The regular rooms contain refrigerators. Obviously the boaties get more attention here than do the landlubbers. The nearest beach is Cane Garden Bay, about 15 minutes away by car.

Treasure Isle Hotel. Pasea Estate, east end of Road Town (P.O. Box 68, Road Town), Tortola, B.V.I. ☎ **800/334-2435** in the U.S., or 284/494-2501. Fax 284/494-2507. E-mail: info@ treasureislehotelcom. 43 units. A/C TV TEL. Winter $187 double; $253 suite. Off-season $104–$143 double; $137–$209 suite. Extra person $15. AE, DISC, MC, V.

The most central resort on Tortola was built at the edge of the capital on 15 acres of hillside overlooking a marina (not on the beach). The core of the hotel is a rather splashy and colorful lounge and pool area. The motel-like rooms are on two levels along the hillside terraces; a third level is occupied by more elegantly decorated suites at the crest of a hill. Tropical touches such as local art, tile floors, white stucco walls, floral upholstery, and white rattan make for an inviting atmosphere.

Adjoining the lounge and pool area is a covered open-air dining room overlooking the harbor. The cuisine is respected here, with barbecue and full à la carte menus offered at dinner. On Wednesday, the hotel puts on a West Indian "grill out," complete with live entertainment and dancing. Amenities include complimentary transportation to the nearest beach and a fully equipped dive facility, which handles beginning instruction up to full certification courses.

MODERATE

Prospect Reef Resort. Drake's Hwy. (P.O. Box 104, Road Town), Tortola, B.V.I. ☎ **800/ 356-8937** in the U.S., 800/463-3608 in Canada, or 284/494-3311. Fax 284/494-5595. www.prospectreef.com. 131 units. TV TEL. Winter $147–$280 double; $420 two-bedroom villa for 4. Off-season $99–$242 double; $319 two-bedroom villa for 4. AE, DISC, MC, V.

Built by a consortium of British investors in 1979, this is the largest resort in the British Virgin Islands. It rises above a small, private harbor in a series of two-story concrete buildings scattered over 44 acres of steeply sloping, landscaped terrain. The panoramic view of Sir Francis Drake Channel from the bedrooms is one of the best anywhere, but there's no beach to speak of at this hotel.

Each of the resort's buildings contains up to 10 individual accommodations and is painted in hibiscus-inspired shades of pink, peach, purple, or aquamarine. Initially designed as condominiums, there are unique studios, town houses, and villas in addition to guest rooms. All include private balconies or patios; larger units have kitchenettes, living and dining areas, and separate bedrooms or sleeping lofts with firm mattresses. About a third of the rooms are air-conditioned; others are cooled by ceiling fans and the trade winds. Bathrooms are tiled and well maintained, and come with hair dryers.

The food at the hotel's Callaloo Restaurant (see "Where to Dine," below), offering a combination of continental specialties and island favorites, was praised by *Gourmet* magazine. Light meals are served on the terrace of the Scuttlebutt Bar and Grill.

On the property are four pools, including sand-terraced sea pools for snorkeling, plus a narrow, artificial beach by one of the pools. Six tennis courts are available, as well as a health and fitness center. Guest service staffers can fill you in on what's available from the harbor: day sailing, snorkeling, scuba diving, and sport fishing. The Offshore Sailing School is located on the resort's property.

WHERE TO DINE
EXPENSIVE

✪ **Brandywine Bay Restaurant.** Brandywine Estate, Sir Francis Drake Hwy. ☎ **284/ 495-2301.** Reservations required. Main courses $22–$30. AE, MC, V. Mon–Sat 6–9:30pm. Closed Aug–Oct. Drive 3 miles east of Road Town (toward the airport) on South Shore Rd. NORTHERN ITALIAN.

This restaurant is set on a cobblestone garden terrace along the south shore, overlooking Sir Francis Drake Channel. It's the most elegant choice for romantic dining. Davide Pugliese, the chef, and his wife, Cele, the hostess, have earned a reputation on Tortola for their outstanding Florentine fare. Davide changes his menu daily, based on the availability of fresh produce. Typical dishes include beef carpaccio, homemade pasta, his own special calf liver dish (the recipe is a secret), and homemade mozzarella with fresh basil and tomatoes. The skillful cookery ranges from the classic to the inspired. If you feel like indulging in game, you can order either pheasant or venison.

Callaloo. Prospect Reef Resort, Drake's Hwy. ☎ **284/494-3311.** Reservations recommended. Main courses $11–$31.50; fixed-price lunch $13. AE, MC, V. Daily 7am–11pm. INTERNATIONAL.

One of the better hotel restaurants on Tortola, this place is rather romantic at night, especially if it's a balmy evening and the tropical breezes are blowing. It's the kind of cliché Caribbean setting that is forever a turn-on, and the food is quite good, too. The menu is hardly imaginative, but the chefs do well with their limited repertoire. Begin with the conch fritters or shrimp cocktail, and don't pass on the house salad, which has a zesty papaya dressing. Main dishes include fresh lobster when available (not as good as the Maine variety, though), as well as fresh fish like tuna, swordfish, or mahimahi. For dessert, make it the orange bread pudding. If it's not available, then go for the key lime pie. Downstairs is the less expensive Scuttlebutt Pub.

Mrs. Scatliffe's Restaurant. Carrot Bay. ☎ **284/495-4556.** Reservations required by 5:30pm. Fixed-price meal $22–$29. No credit cards. Daily 7–8pm. WEST INDIAN.

Mrs. Scatliffe offers home-cooked meals on the deck of her island home, and some of the vegetables come right from her garden, although others might be from a can. You'll be served soup (perhaps spicy conch), followed by curried goat, "old wife" fish, or possibly chicken in a coconut shell. After dinner, your hostess and her family will entertain you with a fungi-band performance (except on Sunday) or gospel singing. *Be duly warned:* This entertainment isn't for everyone, including one reader who compared the hymns to a "screeching caterwaul." Service, usually from an inexperienced teenager, is not exactly efficient.

You may also be exposed to Mrs. Scatliffe's gentle and often humorous form of Christian fundamentalism. A Bible reading and a heartfelt rendition of a gospel song might be served up with a soft custard dessert. She often serves lunch in winter, but call ahead just to be sure.

✪ **Skyworld**, Ridge Rd., Road Town. ☎ **284/494-3567.** Reservations required. Main courses $18–$28. AE, MC, V. Daily 11am–3pm and 5:30–8:30pm. INTERNATIONAL.

Under new management, Skyworld continues to be all the rage, one of the worthiest dining excursions on the island. On one of Tortola's loftiest peaks, at a breezy 1,337 feet, it offers views of both the U.S. Virgin Islands and the British Virgin Islands. Completely renovated, the restaurant is now divided into two sections—a more upscale area, with a dress code for men (collared shirts and long trousers), and an enclosed garden area, where you can dine in shorts. Both sections offer the same menu.

The fresh pumpkin soup is an island favorite, but you can also begin with seafood chowder or—our favorite—mushrooms stuffed with conch. The fresh fish of the day is your best bet (we prefer to skip the steak with port and peaches). The best key lime pie on the island awaits you at the end of the meal, unless you succumb to chocolate-fudge ice-cream pie.

Sugar Mill Restaurant. Apple Bay. ☎ **284/495-4355.** Reservations required. Main courses $18–$28. AE, MC, V. Daily noon–2pm and 7–8:30pm. Closed Aug–Sept. From Road Town, drive west for about 7 miles, take a right turn over Zion Hill going north, and turn right at the T-junction opposite Sebastians; Sugar Mill is about half a mile down the road. CALIFORNIA/CARIBBEAN.

Here, you'll dine in an informal room that was transformed from a 3-century-old sugar mill (see "Where to Stay," above). Colorful works by Haitian painters hang on the old stone walls, and big copper basins once used in distilling rum have been planted with tropical flowers. Before going to the dining room, once part of the old boiling house, visit the open-air bar on a deck that overlooks the sea.

Your hosts, the Morgans, know a lot about food and wine. They have recently hired a new chef, Charles Delargy, who promises to keep the flair of the original menu intact, with additions of nightly specials. One of their most popular creations, published in *Bon Appétit,* is a curried-banana soup. You might also begin with smoked conch pâté. A good choice for dinner is Jamaican jerk pork roast with a green-peppercorn salsa, or perhaps ginger-lime scallops with pasta and toasted walnut sauce. Lunch can be ordered by the beach at the second restaurant, **Islands,** where dinner is also served Tuesday through Saturday from 6:30 to 9pm, from January to May. Try jerk ribs or stuffed crabs here.

MODERATE

✪ **Capriccio di Mare.** Waterfront Dr., Road Town. ☎ **284/494-5369.** Reservations not accepted. Main courses $6–$13. No credit cards. Daily 8–10:30am and 11am–9pm. ITALIAN.

Small, casual, and laid-back, this local favorite was created by the owners of the upmarket Brandywine Bay Restaurant in a moment of whimsy. It's the most authentic-looking Italian *caffè* in the Virgin Islands. At breakfast time, many locals stop in for a refreshing Italian pastry along with a cup of cappuccino. You can come back for lunch or dinner. If it's evening, you might also order the mango Bellini, a variation of the famous cocktail served at Harry's Bar in Venice (which is made with fresh peaches). Begin with such appetizers as *tiapina* (flour tortillas with various toppings), then move on to fresh pastas with succulent sauces, the best pizza on the island, or even well-stuffed sandwiches. We prefer the pizza topped with grilled eggplant. If you arrive on the right night, you might even be treated to lobster ravioli in a rosé sauce. Also try one of the freshly made salads: We like the *insalata mista* with large, leafy greens and slices of fresh parmesan.

Pusser's Landing. Frenchman's Cay, West End. ☎ **284/495-4554.** Reservations recommended. Main courses $13–$22. AE, DISC, MC, V. Daily 11am–10pm. CARIBBEAN/ENGLISH PUB/MEXICAN.

This second Pusser's (see below for the first) is even more desirably located in the West End, opening onto the water. In this nautical setting, you can enjoy fresh grilled fish or an English-inspired dish, like shepherd's pie. Begin with a hearty bowl of homemade soup and follow it with filet mignon, West Indian roast chicken, or a fillet of mahimahi. Mud pie is the classic dessert here, or else try key lime pie or, even better, the mango soufflé. Some dishes occasionally miss the mark, but on the whole this is a good choice. Happy hour is daily from 4 to 6pm.

✪ **Pusser's Road Town Pub.** Waterfront Dr. and Main St., Road Town. ☎ **284/494-3897.** Reservations recommended. Main courses $7–$19. AE, DISC, MC, V. Daily 10am–10pm. CARIBBEAN/ENGLISH PUB/MEXICAN.

Standing on the waterfront across from the ferry dock, the original Pusser's serves Caribbean fare, English pub grub, and good pizzas. This is not as fancy or as good as the Pusser's in the West End, but it's a lot more convenient and has faster service. The complete lunch and dinner menu includes English shepherd's pies and deli-style sandwiches. *Gourmet* magazine asked for the recipe for its chicken-and-asparagus pie. John Courage ale is on draft, but the drink to order here is the famous Pusser's Rum, the same blend of five West Indian rums that the Royal Navy has served to its men for more than 300 years. Thursday is nickel beer night.

HITTING THE BEACH

Beaches are rarely crowded on Tortola unless a cruise ship is in port. You can rent a car or a jeep to reach them, or take a taxi (but arrange for a time to be picked up).

Tortola's finest beach is ✪ **Cane Garden Bay,** on Cane Garden Bay Road directly west of Road Town (see "A Side Trip to Cane Garden Bay," below). These great sands are among the most popular in the B.V.I., and the lovely bay is beloved by yachties. There are some seven places here to eat, along with a handful of bars, plus outfitters that rent Hobie Cats, kayaks, and sailboards. Windsurfing is possible as well. Beware of crowds in high season.

Surfers like **Apple Bay,** west of Road Town, along North Shore Road. The beach isn't very big, but that doesn't diminish activity when the surf's up. Conditions are best in January and February. After enjoying the white sands here, you can have a drink at the Bomba Shack, at the water's edge. This dive is infamous for its "Full Moon Parties."

Site of a campground, **Brewers Bay,** reached along the long, steep Brewers Bay Road, is ideal for snorkelers and surfers. This clean, white-sand beach is a great place to enjoy walks in the early morning or at sunset. If you want to go "truly native," head here, sip a rum punch from the beach bar, and watch the world go by.

Smugglers Cove, known for its tranquillity and for the beauty of its sands, lies at the extreme western end of Tortola, opposite the offshore island of Great Thatch and just north of St. John. It's a lovely crescent of white sand, with calm turquoise waters. A favorite local beach, it's at the end of bumpy Belmont Road. Once you get here, a little worse for wear, you'll think the crystal clear water and the beautiful palm trees worth the effort. Snorkelers like this beach, which is sometimes called "Lower Belmont Bay."

The mile-long, white-sand beach at **Long Bay West**, reached along Long Bay Road, is one of the most beautiful in the B.V.I. Joggers run along the water's edge, and it's also a lovers' walk at dusk. Sunsets here, for some reason, seem more spectacular than usual. See "Where to Stay," above, for a review of the Long Bay Beach Resort, on the northeast side of the beach. Many visitors, even if they're not staying here, like to book a table at the resort's restaurant overlooking the water.

East of Tortola, **Long Bay East,** reached along Beef Island Road, is a great spot for swimming. Cross Queen Elizabeth Bridge to reach this mile-long beach with great views and white sands.

EXPLORING THE ISLAND

TOURS   Travel Plan Tours, Romasco Place, Wickhams Cay 1, Road Town (☎ 284/ 494-2872), organizes a 3½-hour tour that touches on the panoramic highlights of Tortola (a minimum of four participants is required). The cost is $25 per person, with a supplement of $5 per person if you want to extend the tour with a bout of hill-climbing in the rain forest. The company also offers 2½-hour snorkeling tours for $28 per person, or full-day snorkeling tours for $42 per person (with lunch included). A half-day sailing tour aboard a catamaran that goes from Tortola to either Peter Island or Norman Island costs $50 per person; a full-day tour, which goes as far afield as The Baths at Virgin Gorda and includes lunch, costs $80 per person. And if deep-sea fishing appeals to you, a half-day excursion, with equipment, for four fishers and up to two "nonfishing observers" will cost $520.

A **taxi tour** costs $45 for two passengers for 2 hours, or $55 for 3 hours. To call a taxi in Road Town, dial ☎ **284/494-2322;** on Beef Island, ☎ **284/495-2378.**

AN ANCIENT RAIN FOREST   No visit to Tortola is complete without a trip to ✪ **Sage Mountain National Park,** rising to an elevation of 1,780 feet. Here you'll find traces of a primeval rain forest, and you can enjoy a picnic while overlooking neighboring islets and cays. Go west from Road Town to reach the mountain.

Before you head out, stop by the tourist office and pick up the brochure called *Sage Mountain National Park.* It has a location map, directions to the forest (where there's a parking lot), and an outline of the main trails through the park.

Covering 92 acres, the park was established in 1964 to protect the remnants of Tortola's original forests not burned or cleared during the island's plantation era. From the parking lot, a trail leads to the main entrance to the park. The two main trails are the Rain Forest Trail and the Mahogany Forest Trail.

HORSEBACK RIDING   **Shadow's Ranch,** Todman's Estate (☎ **284/494-2262**), offers horseback rides through the national park or down to the shores of Cane Garden Bay. Call for details, Monday to Saturday from 9am to 4pm. The cost is from $25 per hour.

SNORKELING   If you plan on snorkeling by yourself, exercise due caution and consider driving or taking a taxi to **Marina Cay,** off Tortola's East End and known for its good snorkeling beach, or **Cooper Island,** across Sir Francis Drake Channel. Underwater Safaris (see box, below) leads dives and snorkel expeditions to both sites, weather permitting.

YACHT CHARTERS   Tortola boasts the largest fleet of bareboat sailing charters in the world. The best place for this is ✪ **The Moorings,** Wickhams Cay (P.O. Box 139, Road Town), B.V.I. (☎ **800/535-7289** in the U.S., or 284/494-2332), whose 8-acre waterside resort is also recommended in "Where to Stay," above. This outfit, along with a

The Wreck of the *Rhone* & Other Top Dive Sites

The one site in the British Virgin Islands that lures divers over from St. Thomas is ✪ **the wreck of the HMS *Rhone***, which sank in 1867 near the western point of Salt Island. *Skin Diver* magazine called this "the world's most fantastic shipwreck dive." It teems with marine life and coral formations and was featured in the 1977 movie *The Deep*, starring Nick Nolte and Jacqueline Bisset.

Although it's no *Rhone*, **Chikuzen** is another intriguing dive site off Tortola. It's a 270-foot steel-hulled refrigerator ship, which sank off the island's east end in 1981. The hull, still intact under about 80 feet of water, is now home to a vast array of tropical fish, including yellowtail, barracuda, black-tip sharks, octopus, and drum fish. The best way for novice and expert divers to see these and other great dive sites is with one of the following outfitters:

Baskin in the Sun (☎ **800/233-7938** in the U.S., or 284/494-2858), a PADI five-star facility on Tortola, is a good choice, with locations at the Prospect Reef Resort, near Road Town, and at Soper's Hole, on Tortola's West End. Baskin's most popular trip is the supervised "Half-Day Scuba Diving" experience for $95, catered to beginners, but there are trips for all levels of experience. Daily excursions are scheduled to the HMS *Rhone*, as well as "Painted Walls" (an underwater canyon, the walls of which are formed of brightly colored coral and sponges) and the "Indians" (four pinnacle rocks sticking out of the water, which divers follow 40 feet below the surface).

Underwater Safaris (☎ **284/494-3235**) takes you to all the best sites, including the HMS *Rhone*, "Spyglass Wall," and "Alice in Wonderland." It has two offices: "Safari Base" in Road Town and "Safari Cay" on Cooper Island. Get complete directions and information when you call. The center, connected with The Moorings (see below), offers a complete PADI and NAUI training facility. An introductory resort course and one dive costs $95, while an open-water certification, with 4 days of instruction and four open-water dives, goes for $385, plus $40 for the instruction manual.

---

handful of others, make the British Virgins the cruising capital of the world. You can choose from a fleet of sailing yachts, which can accommodate up to four couples in comfort and style. Depending on your nautical knowledge and skills, you can arrange a bareboat rental (with no crew) or a fully crewed rental with a skipper, a staff, and a cook. Boats come equipped with a portable barbecue, snorkeling gear, dinghy, linens, and galley equipment. The Moorings has an experienced staff of mechanics, electricians, riggers, and cleaners. If you're going out on your own, you'll get a thorough briefing session on Virgin Island waters and anchorages.

If you'd like sailing lessons, consider **Steve Colgate's Offshore Sailing School** (☎ **284/494-5119**) or Tortola's **Treasure Isle Hotel** (☎ **284/494-2501**), which offers courses in seamanship year-round. (One of their programs is exclusively on how to sail catamarans.)

SHOPPING

Most of the shops are on Main Street, Road Town, on Tortola, but know that the British Virgins have no duty-free shopping. British goods are imported without duty, and the wise shopper will be able to find some good buys among these imported items, especially in English china. In general, store hours are Monday to Friday from 9am to 4pm, Saturday from 9am to 1pm.

Sunny Caribbee Herb and Spice Company, Main Street, Road Town (☎ 284/ 494-2178), in an old West Indian building, was the first hotel on Tortola. It's now a shop specializing in Caribbean spices, seasonings, teas, condiments, and handcrafts. You can buy two world-famous specialties here: West Indian hangover cure and Arawak love potion. A Caribbean cosmetics collection, Sunsations, includes herbal bath gels, island perfume, and sunshine lotions. With its aroma of spices permeating the air, this factory is an attraction in itself. There's a daily sampling of island products—perhaps tea, coffee, sauces, or dips. Right next door is the **Sunny Caribbee Gallery,** featuring original paintings, prints, wood carvings, and hand-painted furniture, plus crafts from throughout the Caribbean.

Caribbean Corner Spice House Co., Soper's Hole (☎ 284/495-9567), offers the island's finest selection of spices and herbs, along with local crafts and botanical skincare products, which you may find useful in the fierce sun. There's also a selection of Cuban cigars, but you'll have to smoke them on island, as U.S. Customs does not allow their importation. **Flamboyance,** Soper's Hole (☎ 284/495-4099), is the best place to shop for perfume and upscale cosmetics.

Caribbean Fine Arts Ltd., Main Street, Road Town (☎ 284/494-4240), has one of the most unusual collections of art from the West Indies. It sells original watercolors and oils, limited-edition serigraphs and sepia photographs, and pottery and primitives. **Caribbean Handprints,** Main Street, Road Town (☎ 284/494-3717), features prints hand-done by local craftspeople. It also sells colorful fabric by the yard.

Fort Wines Gourmet, Main Street, Road Town (☎ 284/494-3036), is a storecum-cafe. For picnic provisions, you'd have to fly to the mainland to top this place. Sample its full line of Hediard pâté terrines along with a wide selection of chocolates, including some of the best from Paris. There's also an elegant showcase of glassware, lacquered boxes, and handmade Russian filigree items plated in 24-karat gold.

J. R. O'Neal, Upper Main Street, Road Town (☎ 284/494-2292), is across from the Methodist church. This home-accessories store has an extensive collection of terracotta pottery, wicker and rattan home furnishings, Mexican glassware, baskets, ceramics, fine crystal, china, and more, all at good prices.

Bargain hunters gravitate to **Sea Urchin,** Columbus Centre, Road Town (☎ 284/ 494-3129), for print shirts and shorts, T-shirts, bathing suits, and sandals. Good prices in swimwear are also available at **Turtle Dove Boutique,** Fleming Street, Road Town (☎ 284/494-3611), which has a wide selection. Women can purchase affordable linen and silk dresses here as well.

Pusser's Company Store, Main Steet and Waterfront Road, Road Town (☎ 284/ 494-2467), is for nautical memorabilia. There's a long, mahogany-trimmed bar accented with many fine nautical artifacts and a Pusser's Store selling a proprietary line of Pusser's clothing and gift items. Pusser's Rum is one of the best-selling items here, or perhaps you'd prefer a Pusser's ceramic flask as a memento.

TORTOLA AFTER DARK

Ask around to find out which hotel might have entertainment on any given evening. Steel bands and fungi or scratch bands (African-Caribbean musicians who improvise on locally available instruments) appear regularly, and nonresidents are usually welcome. Pick up a copy of *Limin' Times,* an entertainment magazine listing what's happening locally; it's usually available at hotels.

✪ **Bomba's Surfside Shack,** Cappoon's Bay (☎ 284/495-4148), is the oldest, most memorable, and most uninhibited nightlife venue on the island, sitting on a 20-foot-wide strip of unpromising coastline near the West End. By anyone's standards, this is the "junk palace" of the island, covered with Day-Glo graffiti and odds and ends of plywood, driftwood, and abandoned rubber tires. Despite its makeshift appearance, the shack has the sound system to create a really great party. Every month (dates vary), Bomba's stages a full moon party, with free house tea spiked with hallucinogenic mushrooms. (The tea is free because it's illegal to sell it.) The place is also wild on Wednesday and Sunday nights, when there's live music and a $7 all-you-can-eat barbecue. It's open daily from 10am to midnight (or later, depending on business).

The **Moorings/Mariner Inn,** Wickhams Cay (☎ **284/494-2332**), contains the preferred watering hole for some upscale yacht owners, but drink prices are low. Open to a view of its own marina, and bathed in a dim and flattering light, the place is nautical and relaxed. Another popular choice is **Spyglass Bar,** in the Treasure Isle Hotel, Road Town (☎ **284/494-2501**). The sunken bar on a terrace overlooks the pool and faraway marina facilities of this popular hotel.

The **Bat Cave,** Waterfront Drive, Road Town (☎ **284/494-4880**), is one of the newest hot spots, on the ground floor of Spaghetti Junction. The latest recorded hits are played nightly. On the last Friday of each month, the staff throws a big themed costume party—an island hit. **De Loose Mongoose,** Beef Island (☎ **284/495-2302**), is one of the funkiest beach bars in the Caribbean. Sailboats and yachts drop anchor at this laid-back haven overlooking Trellis Bay near the airport; the bar is set right on the water.

Other little hot spots, worth at least a stop on a bar-hopping jaunt, include **Bing's Drop in Bar,** Fat Hog's Bay in the East End (☎ **284/495-2627**), where the locals gather to listen to a DJ in winter. At **Jolly Roger,** West End (☎ **284/495-4559**), you can hear local or sometimes American bands, playing everything from reggae to blues. You can count on a jumping dance crowd at **Myett's,** Cane Garden Bay (☎ **284/495-9543**), on Friday and Saturday evenings and also after 3pm on Sunday afternoon, when the B.V.I. usually get pretty dull. In the same area, visit **Stanley's Welcome Bar,** Cane Garden Bay (☎ **284/495-4520**), where a rowdy fraternity-type crowd gathers to drink, talk, and drink some more. Finally, check out **Sebastians,** Apple Bay (☎ **284/495-4214**), especially on Saturday and Sunday when you can dance to live music under the stars—at least in winter.

A SIDE TRIP TO CANE GARDEN BAY

If you've decided to risk everything and navigate the roller-coaster hills of the B.V.I., then head to Cane Garden Bay, one of the choicest pieces of real estate on the island, its white-sand beach with sheltering palms long ago discovered by the sailing crowd.

Rhymer's, Cane Garden Bay (☎ **284/495-4639**), is the place to go for food and entertainment. Skippers of any kind of craft are likely to stock up on supplies here, but you can also order cold beer and refreshing rum drinks. If you're hungry, try the conch or lobster, black-bean gazpacho, or barbecued spareribs. The beach bar and restaurant is open daily from 8am to 9pm. On some nights, a steel-drum band entertains the mariners. Ice and freshwater showers are available (and you can rent towels). Ask about renting Sunfish and Windsurfers next door.

3 Virgin Gorda

In 1493, on his second voyage to the New World, Columbus named this island Virgin Gorda or "fat virgin" (from a distance, the island looks like a reclining woman with a protruding stomach). The second largest island in the cluster of British Virgin Islands, Virgin Gorda is 10 miles long and 2 miles wide, with a population of some 1,400. It's 12 miles east of Road Town and 26 miles from St. Thomas.

The island was a fairly desolate agricultural community until Laurance S. Rockefeller established the Little Dix Bay Hotel in the early 1960s, following his success with the Caneel Bay resort on St. John in the 1950s. He envisioned a "wilderness beach," where privacy and solitude would reign. In 1971, the Virgin Gorda Yacht Harbour opened. Operated by the Little Dix Bay Hotel, it accommodates 120 yachts today.

ESSENTIALS

The local **American Express** representative is **Travel Plan,** Virgin Gorda Yacht Harbour (☎ **284/494-2347**).

GETTING THERE   You can get to Virgin Gorda by air via St. Thomas in the U.S. Virgin Islands. **Air St. Thomas** (☎ **340/776-2722**) flies to Virgin Gorda daily from St. Thomas. A one-way trip (40 minutes) costs $68; round-trip, $139.

Speedy's Fantasy (☎ **284/495-5240**) operates a ferry service between Road Town and Virgin Gorda. Monday through Saturday, five ferries a day leave from Road Town, reduced to two on Sunday. The cost is $10 one-way or $19 round-trip. From St. Thomas to Virgin Gorda, there's service three times a week (on Tuesday, Thursday, and Saturday), costing $31 one-way or $50 round-trip.

You'll also find that the more luxurious services have their own boats to take you from the airport on Beef Island to Virgin Gorda.

GETTING AROUND   Independently operated open-sided **safari buses** run along the main road. Holding up to 14 passengers, these buses charge upwards from $3 per person to transport a passenger, say, from the Valley to the Baths.

If you'd like to rent a car, try one of the local firms, including **Mahogany Rentals,** The Valley, Spanish Town (☎ **284/495-5469**), across from the yacht harbor. This company is the least expensive on the island, beginning at around $50 daily for a Suzuki Samurai. An alternative choice is **Andy's Taxi and Jeep Rental** (☎ **284/ 495-5252**), 7 minutes from the marina in Spanish Town. Rates begin at $50 daily year-round. Representatives of either agency will meet you at the airport or ferry dock and do the paperwork there.

WHERE TO STAY
VERY EXPENSIVE

✪ **Biras Creek Estate.** North Sound (P.O. Box 54), Virgin Gorda, B.V.I. ☎ **800/608-9661** in the U.S., or 284/494-3555. Fax 284/494-3557. www.biras.com. 33 units. A/C. Winter $570 double; $870 two-bedroom villa for 2; $995 villa for 4. Off-season $425 double; $725 villa for 2; $800 villa for 4. Rates include all meals. AE, DISC, MC, V. Take the private motor launch from the Beef Island airport. Children 5 and under not accepted.

This private and romantic resort stands at the northern end of Virgin Gorda like a hilltop fortress, opening onto a decent beach, much of which is man-made. The hideaway has vastly improved after a major face-lift. On a 150-acre estate with its own marina, it occupies a narrow neck of land flanked by the sea on three sides. Units have well-furnished bedrooms and private patios. Most have king beds, with deluxe mattresses, plus spacious bathrooms with inviting garden showers and fluffy towels. There are no phones, radios, or TVs, but you do get such amenities as private safes, coffeemakers, fridges, and hair dryers. Even the latest editions of the *Wall Street Journal* and the *New York Times* are delivered daily.

Dining: The food has won high praise; the wine list is also excellent here. The hotel restaurant and drinking lounge are quietly elegant, and there's always a table with a view. A barbecued lunch is often served on the beach.

Amenities: Pool, snorkeling, Sunfish, paddleboards, tennis courts, kayaks, Hobie waves, and unlimited use of motor dinghies. Laundry, baby-sitting, taxi service for

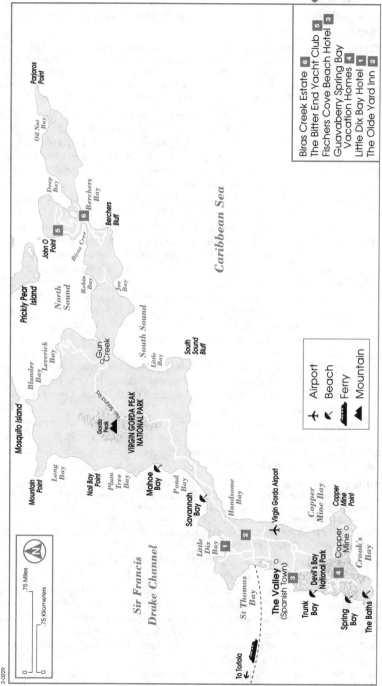

Virgin Gorda

Biras Creek Estate **6**
The Bitter End Yacht Club **5**
Fischers Cove Beach Hotel **3**
Guavaberry Spring Bay
Vacation Homes **4**
Little Dix Bay Hotel **1**
The Olde Yard Inn **2**

Airport ✈
Beach 🏖
Ferry ⛴
Mountain ▲

Caribbean Sea

Parjaros
Point

Oil Nut
Bay

Deep
Bay

Berchers
Bay

6 Berchers
Bluff

John O
Point **5**

Biras Cree

**Prickly Pear
Island**

North
Sound

Robin
Bay

Joe
Bay

South Sound

Blunder
Bay

Leverick
Bay

Gun
Creek

Little
Bay

South
Sound
Bluff

Mosquito Island

No Sound Rd

Gorda
Peak ▲

**VIRGIN GORDA
PEAK
NATIONAL PARK**

Mountain
Point

Long
Bay

Nail Bay
Point

Plum
Tree
Bay

Mahoe
Bay

Pond
Bay

Handsome
Bay

Savannah
Bay

Virgin Gorda Airport ✈

*Copper
Mine Bay*

Copper
Mine
Point

Little
Dix
Bay **1**

2

Copper
Mine

Crook's
Bay

*Sir Francis
Drake Channel*

St Thomas
Bay

The Valley
(Spanish Town)

Devil's Bay
National Park

3

4

Trunk
Bay

Spring
Bay

The Baths

To Tortola

.75 Miles
0

.75 Kilometers
0

N

2-0229

181

guests arriving in Virgin Gorda to the hotel's motor launch, free trips to nearby beaches.

✪ **The Bitter End Yacht Club.** John O'Point, North Sound (P.O. Box 46), Virgin Gorda, B.V.I. ☎ **800/872-2392** in the U.S. for reservations, or 284/494-2746. Fax 284/494-3557. www.beyc.com. 93 units, 3 yachts. Winter (double occupancy) $700 beachfront villa, Commodore Club suite, or yacht; $600 hillside villa. Off-season (double occupancy) $600 all units. Rates include meals. AE, DC, MC, V. Take the private ferry from the Beef Island airport.

This rendezvous point for the yachting set has hosted the likes of Jean-Michel Cousteau and treasure hunter Mel Fisher, but less well-known sailors or just lovers of the sea have also been drawn to this family-operated resort for the past 30 years. It opens onto one of the most unspoiled and secluded deep-water harbors in the Caribbean, offering the finest water-sports program in the U.S. or British Virgin Islands. Guests have unlimited use of the resort's million-dollar fleet, the Nick Trotter Sailing and Windsurfing School. The Bitter End offers an informal yet elegant experience, as guests settle into one of the hillside chalets or well-appointed beachfront and hillside villas overlooking the sound. Most units have varnished hardwood floors, sliding-glass doors, and wicker furnishings. The wraparound verandas also have hammocks large enough for two. All villas have either twin or king-size beds, each with a deluxe mattress, plus a large dressing area and a shower with sea views, along with ceiling fans, fluffy towels, a fridge, and a hair dryer. The Commodore Suites, the only units with air-conditioning, contain marble outdoor showers large enough for two.

For something novel, you can stay aboard one of the 30-foot yachts, yours to sail, with dockage and daily maid service, meals in the Yacht Club dining room, and overnight provisions. Yachts contain a shower with pressure water. Each yacht can accommodate four comfortably.

Dining/Diversions: Dining is in the Clubhouse Steak and Seafood Grille, the English Carvery, or the Pub. Evening entertainment is provided by "The Reflections," a steel-drum band who have performed for the late Princess Diana. On other nights, local reggae and soca bands perform.

Amenities: Unlimited use of Lasers, Sunfish, Rhodes 19s, windsurfing equipment, J-24s, Boston whalers, and outboard skiffs; reef snorkeling; scuba diving; sport fishing; fitness center; expeditions to neighboring cays; marine science participation; pool; laundry, free trips to nearby islands.

Little Dix Bay Hotel. On the northwest corner of the island (P.O. Box 70), Virgin Gorda, B.V.I. ☎ **800/928-3000** in the U.S., or 284/495-5555. Fax 284/495-5661. www.rosewood-hotels.com. E-mail: ldbhotel@caribsurf.com. 98 units. TEL. Winter $550–$750 double; $1,300 suite. Off-season $250–$575 double; $700–$900 suite. MAP (breakfast and dinner) $80 per person extra. Extra person $50. AE, DC, MC, V. Take the private ferry service from the Beef Island airport to the resort; $65 per person round-trip.

Completely renovated in 1996, this 1964 hotel is now run by the Dallas-based Rosewood chain of luxurious hotels. An embodiment of understated luxury, the Little Dix Bay Hotel is a resort discreetly scattered along a half-mile, crescent-shaped, private bay on a 500-acre preserve. Many guests find this resort pricey and stuffy, infinitely preferring the more casual elegance of Biras Creek Estate and the Bitter End Yacht Club. It has the same quiet elegance as Caneel Bay on St. John in the U.S. Virgins.

All rooms, built in the woods, have private terraces with views of the sea or gardens. Trade winds come through louvers and screens, and the units are further cooled by ceiling fans or air-conditioning (in 80% of the rooms). Some units are two-story rondavels (like tiki huts) raised on stilts to form their own breezeways. Accommodations are roomy, airy, and decorated with tropical flair. All guest rooms have been renovated with new furnishings and fabrics, evoking a Southeast Asian style with beautiful wicker or reed furniture, bamboo beds, Balinese boxes and baskets, and ceramic objets d'art. Comfort is the keynote here, with walk-in closets, twice-daily maid service, deluxe mattresses, and spacious bathrooms with hair dryers and fluffy towels.

Dining/Diversions: Four interconnected pyramids that face the sea comprise the roof of the Pavilion, the hotel venue for lunch buffets, afternoon teas, and candlelit dinners. The cuisine is international, with Caribbean seafood specialties like red snapper with ratatouille drizzled with a curry infusion. For drinks, guests can sit on the restaurant's terrace, where a band performs nightly. The Sugar Mill is elegant but casual, specializing in fresh grilled fish, lobster, and steaks. On the edge of the beach, the Beach Grill serves light lunches and dinners.

Amenities: Unequaled service with a "one-to-one" staff-guest ratio. Seven all-weather outdoor Laykold tennis courts, Sunfish sailboats, kayaks, snorkeling, scuba diving, waterskiing, boat rentals, deep-sea fishing, diving excursions, and the Virgin Gorda Yacht Harbor half a mile from the resort (owned and operated by Little Dix Bay). The lack of a pool may bother some guests, but there is a fitness center.

EXPENSIVE

✪ **The Olde Yard Inn.** The Valley (P.O. Box 26), Virgin Gorda, B.V.I. ☎ **800/653-9273** in the U.S., or 284/495-5544. Fax 284/495-5986. www.travelxn.com/oldeyard. E-mail: oldeyard@caribsurf.com. 14 units. Winter $195 double; $220 triple; $245 quad. Off-season $110 double; $130 triple; $150–$190 quad. MAP (breakfast and dinner) $50 per person extra. Honeymoon packages available. AE, MC, V.

This little charmer is a mile from the airport. Near the main house are two long bungalows with large renovated bedrooms, each with its own bathroom and patio. Four of the rooms are air-conditioned, and all have ceiling fans. Three of the rooms also contain minifridges. You can go for a sail on a yacht or embark on a snorkeling adventure at one of 16 beaches. Served under a cedarwood roof, the French-accented meals are one of the reasons for coming here. Lunch is served poolside at the Sip and Dip Grill. There's live entertainment three times a week in the dining room. Amenities include a Jacuzzi and a modern health club, one of the best hotel libraries in the Caribbean, a huge freshwater pool, and complimentary shuttle service to Savannah Bay Beach.

MODERATE

Fischers Cove Beach Hotel. The Valley (P.O. Box 60), Virgin Gorda, B.V.I. ☎ **284/495-5252.** Fax 284/495-5820. 20 units. A/C. Winter, $145–$150 double; $170–$285 studio cottage. Off-season, $100 double; $125–$205 studio cottage. MAP (breakfast and dinner) $40 per person extra. AE, MC, V.

There's swimming at your doorstep in this group of units nestled near the sandy beach of St. Thomas Bay. Erected of native stone, each of the eight cottages is self-contained, with one or two bedrooms and a combination living/dining room with a kitchenette. You can stock up on provisions at a food store near the grounds. There are also 12 pleasant but simple rooms with views of Drake Channel. Each has its own private bathroom (with hot and cold showers) and private balcony. Jeep rentals are available, as is a children's playground. Live entertainment is often presented.

Guavaberry Spring Bay Vacation Homes. Spring Bay (P.O. Box 20), Virgin Gorda, B.V.I. ☎ **284/495-5227.** Fax 284/495-5283. www.guavaberryspringbay.com. E-mail: gsbhomes@caribsurf.com. 18 houses. Winter $150 one-bedroom house for two; $210 two-bedroom house for four. Off-season $95 one-bedroom house for two; $140 two-bedroom house for four. Extra person $15–$20. No credit cards.

Staying in one of these hexagonal, white-roofed redwood houses built on stilts is like living in a treehouse, with screened and louvered walls to let in sea breezes. Each home, available for daily or weekly rental, has one or two bedrooms; all have private bathrooms, small kitchenettes, and dining areas. Each unique vacation house also has its own elevated sundeck overlooking Sir Francis Drake Passage. Within a few minutes of the cottage colony is the beach at Spring Bay, and the Yacht Harbour Shopping Centre is a mile away. It's also possible to explore "The Baths," nearby.

The owners provide a complete commissary for guests, and tropical fruits can be picked in season or bought at local shops. They will make arrangements for day charters for scuba diving or fishing, and will also arrange for island jeep tours and sailing.

WHERE TO DINE

Bath & Turtle Pub. Virgin Gorda Yacht Harbour, Spanish Town. ☎ 284/495-5239. Reservations recommended. Breakfast $4.50–$8.95; main courses $6.75–$9 lunch, $9–$20 dinner. AE, MC, V. Daily 7am–11pm. INTERNATIONAL.

At the end of the waterfront shopping plaza in Spanish Town sits the most popular pub on Virgin Gorda, packed with locals during happy hour from 4 to 6pm. Even if you don't care about food, you might join the regulars over midmorning guava coladas or peach daiquiris. There's live music every Wednesday and Sunday night, in summer only (no cover). From its handful of indoor and courtyard tables, you can order fried fish fingers, nachos, very spicy chili, pizzas, fresh pasta, barbecue chicken, steak, lobster, and daily seafood specials such as conch fritters from the simple menu here.

✪ **Pusser's Leverick Bay.** Leverick Bay, North Sound. ☎ 284/495-7369. Reservations recommended. Main courses $12.95–$24.95; lunch $5.95–$13.95; pizzas from $4.95. AE, MC, V. Daily 8:30am–10pm. CONTINENTAL.

Scattered throughout this restaurant are glass cases containing ship models; dark wooden beams and an antique English bar add just the right touch of quiet elegance. Although there are a few tables inside, the main dining area is on the deck overlooking North Sound. The menu selections range from the very simple to the more elaborate, such as tuna encrusted with sesame seed. The real bargains here are the meals served up until 6pm, when dinner begins. The breakfasts are hearty, lunches are filling, and to beat those higher prices at night, opt for an early dinner of pizza, which is served from 11am to 6pm every day.

Thelma's Hideout. The Valley. ☎ 284/495-5646. Reservations required for dinner. Dinner $13–$15; lunch $8–$9. No credit cards. Daily 7–10am, 11:30am–2:30pm, and (only upon notification before 3pm) 6–10pm. (Bar, daily 11am–midnight.) CARIBBEAN.

Mrs. Thelma King, one of the most outspoken grandes dames of Virgin Gorda (who worked in Manhattan for many years before returning to her native B.V.I.), runs this convivial gathering place for the island's local community. It's located in a concrete house whose angles are softened by ascending tiers of verandas. Food choices include grilled steaks, fish fillets, and West Indian stews containing pork, mutton, or chicken. Limeade or mauby are available, but many guests stick to rum or beer. Live music is presented on Saturday night in winter, and every other Saturday off-season.

Top of the Baths. The Valley. ☎ 284/495-5497. Reservations not necessary. Dinner from $18; sandwiches and salad plates $8–$12.50. AE, MC, V. Daily 8am–10pm. CARIBBEAN.

This aptly named green-and-white restaurant offers a patio with a swimming pool. Locals gather here to enjoy the food they grew up on. At lunch, you can order an array of appetizers, sandwiches, and salad plates. You're invited to swim in the pool either before or after dining. At night, the kitchen turns out good home-style cookery, including fresh fish, lobster, chicken, and steaks. Look for one of the daily specials. And save room for a piece of that rum cake! On Sunday, a DJ entertains from 10am to 3pm, and occasional live music is presented.

HITTING THE BEACH

The best beaches are at **The Baths** (see "A Great Snorkeling Spot," below), where giant boulders form a series of panoramic pools and grottoes flooded with sea water (nearby snorkeling is excellent). Scientists think the boulders were brought to the surface eons ago by volcanic activity. Neighboring The Baths is **Spring Bay,** one of the best of the island's beaches, with white sand, clear water, and good snorkeling. **Trunk Bay** is a wide sandy beach reachable by boat or along a rough path from Spring Bay. **Savannah Bay** is a sandy beach north of the yacht harbor, and Mahoe Bay, at the Mango Bay Resort, has a gently curving beach with neon-blue water.

EXPLORING THE ISLAND

The northern side of Virgin Gorda is mountainous, with Gorda Peak reaching 1,370 feet, the highest spot on the island. However, the southern half is flat, with large boulders appearing at every turn.

The best way to see the island if you're over for a day trip is to call **Andy Flax** at the Fischers Cove Beach Hotel. He runs the **Virgin Gorda Tours Association** (☎ 284/495-5252), which will give you a tour of the island for $20 per person. The tour leaves twice daily, or more often based on demand. You can be picked up at the ferry dock if you give 24-hour notice.

DIVING   Kilbrides Sunchaser Scuba is located at the Bitter End Resort at North Sound (☎ 800/932-4286 in the U.S., or 284/495-9638). Kilbrides offers the best diving in the British Virgin Islands at 15 to 20 dive sites, including the wreck of the ill-fated HMS *Rhone*. Prices range from $80 to $90 for a two-tank dive on one of the coral reefs. A one-tank dive in the afternoon costs $60. Equipment, except wet suits, is supplied at no charge, and videos of your dives are available.

A GREAT SNORKELING SPOT   **You'll find ✪ **The Baths on every Virgin Gorda to-do list, especially if snorkeling is involved (equipment can be rented on the beach). The Baths are a phenomenon of tranquil pools and caves formed by gigantic house-size boulders. As these boulders toppled over one another, they formed saltwater grottoes, suitable for exploring. The pools around The Baths are excellent for swimming.

Devil's Bay National Park can be reached by a trail from The Baths. The walk to the secluded coral-sand beach takes about 15 minutes through boulders and dry coastal vegetation.

The Baths and surrounding areas are part of a proposed system of parks and protected areas in the B.V.I. The protected area encompasses 682 acres of land, including sites at Little Fort, Spring Bay, The Baths, and Devil's Bay on the east coast.

HIKING   **Consider a trek up the stairs and hiking paths that crisscross Virgin Gorda's largest stretch of undeveloped land, the **Virgin Gorda Peak National Park. To reach the best departure point for your uphill trek, drive north of the Valley on the only road leading to North Sound for about 15 very hilly minutes (use of a four-wheel-drive vehicle is a good idea). Stop at the base of the stairway leading steeply uphill. There's a sign pointing to the Gorda Peak National Park.

Depending on your speed, you'll embark on a trek of between 25 and 40 minutes to reach the summit of Gorda Peak, the highest point on the island, where vistas of many scattered islets of the Virgin archipelago await you. There's a tower at the summit, which you can climb for enhanced views. Admire the flora and the fauna (birds, lizards, nonvenomous snakes) that you're likely to run across en route. Because the vegetation you'll encounter is not particularly lush, protect yourself from the intense noonday sun, and consider bringing a picnic, as tables are scattered along the hiking trails.

AN ABANDONED MINE   Another place of interest is **Copper Mine Point,** the site of an abandoned copper mine and smelter at the island's southeastern tip. Legend has it that the Spanish worked these mines in the 1600s; however, the only authenticated document reveals that the English sank the shafts in 1838 to mine copper.

SHOPPING

There isn't much here. Your best bet is the **Virgin Gorda Craft Shop** at Yacht Harbour (☎ 284/495-5137), which has some good arts and crafts, especially straw items. Some of the more upscale hotels have boutiques, notably the **Bitter End Yacht Club's Reeftique** (☎ 284/494-2745), with its selection of sportswear, including sundresses and logo wear. You can also purchase a hat here to protect you from the sun. You might also check **Island Silhouette in Flax Plaza,** near Fischer's Cove Beach Hotel (no phone), which has a good selection of resort wear hand-painted by local artists. **Pusser's Company Store,** Leverick Bay (☎ 284/495-7369), sells rum products, sportswear, and gift and souvenir items, a good selection. **Tropical Gift Collections,** The Baths (☎ 284/495-5380), is the best place to go for local crafts. Here you'll find island spices, bags, and pottery all at good prices.

VIRGIN GORDA AFTER DARK

There isn't a lot of action at night, unless you want to make some of your own. The **Bath & Turtle Pub,** at Yacht Harbour (☎ 284/495-5239), brings in local bands for dancing on Wednesday and Sunday at 8pm. Most evenings in winter, the **Bitter End Yacht Club** (☎ 284/494-2746) has live music. Reached only by boat, this is the best bar on the island. With its dark wood, it evokes an English pub and even serves British brews. Call to see what's happening at the time of your visit.

  Andy's Chateau de Pirate, at the Fischers Cove Beach Hotel, The Valley (☎ 284/495-5252), is a sprawling, sparsely furnished local hangout. It has a simple stage, a very long bar, and huge oceanfront windows which almost never close. The complex also houses the Lobster Pot Restaurant, the Buccaneer Bar, and the nightclub EFX. The **Lobster Pot,** open from 7am to 10pm, is a famous showcase for the island's musical groups, which perform Wednesday to Sunday from 8pm to midnight; lots of people congregate to listen and kibitz. There's a $5 cover Friday to Sunday nights. You might also check out **Pusser's at Leverick Bay,** which has live bands on Saturday night and Sunday afternoon. Call the **Olde Yard Inn** (☎ 284/495-5544) to see if its Sip and Dip Grill is staging live local bands at their Sunday night barbecues.

4 Jost Van Dyke

This rugged island off the west side of Tortola was named for a Dutch settler. In the 1700s, a Quaker colony settled here to develop sugarcane plantations. One of the colonists, William Thornton, won the worldwide competition to design the U.S. Capitol in Washington, D.C. Smaller islands surround the place, including Little Jost Van Dyke, the birthplace of Dr. John Lettsome, founder of the London Medical Society.

  About 150 people live on the 4 square miles of this mountainous island. On the south shore, **White Bay** and **Great Harbour** are good beaches. While there are only a handful of places to stay, there are several dining choices, as the island is a popular stopping-over point for the yachting set and many cruise ships, including Cunard (and often some all-gay cruises). The peace and tranquillity of yesteryear often disappear unless you're here when the cruise ships aren't.

GETTING THERE

Take the ferry from either St. Thomas or Tortola. (Be warned that departure times can vary widely throughout the year, and often don't adhere very closely to the printed timetables.) Ferries from St. Thomas depart from Red Hook 3 days a week (Friday, Saturday, and Sunday), usually twice daily. More convenient (and more frequent) are the daily ferryboat shuttles from Tortola's isolated West End. The latter departs three times a day for the 25-minute trip, and costs $8 one-way, $15 round-trip. Call the **Jost Van Dyke Ferryboat Service** (☎ **284/494-2997**) for information about departures from any of the above-mentioned points. If all else fails, carefully negotiate a transportation fee with one of the handful of privately operated water taxis.

WHERE TO STAY

Sandcastle Hotel. White Bay, Jost Van Dyke, B.V.I. ☎ **284/495-9888.** Fax 284/495-9999. www.sandcastle-bvi.com. E-mail: sandcastle@caribsurf.com. 6 units. Winter $170–$190 double. Off-season $100–$125 double. Extra person $35–$45. 3-night minimum. MC, V. Take the private motor launch from Tortola; it's a 20-minute ride.

A retreat for escapists who want few neighbors and absolutely nothing to do, these six cottages are surrounded by flowering shrubbery and bougainvillea and have panoramic views. Bedrooms are spacious, light, and airy, furnished in a tropical motif, with tile floors, local art, rattan furnishings, day beds, and king-size beds with excellent mattresses. There are large, tiled bathrooms, plus solar-heated showers outside. You mix your own drinks at the beachside bar, the Soggy Dollar, and keep your own tab. Visiting boaters often drop in to enjoy the beachside informality and order a drink called the "Painkiller." A line in the guest book proclaims, "I thought places like this only existed in the movies."

For reservations and information, call or write the Sandcastle, Suite 201, Red Hook Plaza, St. Thomas, U.S.V.I. 00802-1306 (☎ **340/495-9888**). Don't send mail to Jost Van Dyke, as it could take months to reach there.

Sandy Ground. East End (P.O. Box 594, West End), Tortola, B.V.I. ☎ **284/494-3391.** Fax 284/495-9379. www.bviwelcome.com/sandyground. E-mail: sandygroundsliz@ yahoo.com. 8 units. Weekly rates: Winter $1,650 villa for 2. Off-season $1,200 villa for 2. Extra person $300 per week in winter, $200 off-season. MC, V. Take a private water taxi from Tortola or St. Thomas.

These self-sufficient housekeeping units are on a 17-acre hill site on the eastern part of Jost Van Dyke. The complex rents two- and three-bedroom villas. One of our favorites was constructed on a cliff that seems to hang about 80 feet over a small beach. If you've come all this way, you might as well stay a week, which is the way the rates are quoted. The airy villas, each privately owned, are fully equipped with refrigerators and stoves. The interiors vary widely, from rather fashionable to bare bones. The living space is most generous, and extra amenities include a coffeemaker and an unstocked fridge, plus private balconies or terraces. Most rooms have showers only. The managers help guests with boat rentals and water sports. Diving, day sails, and other activities can also be arranged, and there are dinghies available. Snorkeling and hiking are among the more popular pastimes, and the beach is private.

WHERE TO DINE

Abe's by the Sea. Little Harbour. ☎ **284/495-9329.** Reservations recommended for groups of five or more. Dinner $12–$30; nightly barbecue $20. MC, V. Daily 8–11am, noon–3pm, and 7–10pm. Take the private motor launch or boat from Tortola; as you approach the east side of the harbor, you'll see Abe's on your right. CARIBBEAN.

In this local bar and restaurant, sailors are satisfied with a menu of fish, lobster, conch, and chicken. Prices are low, too, and it's money well spent, especially when a fungi band plays for dancing. For the price of the main course, you get peas and rice, coleslaw, and dessert. On some nights, a festive pig roast is served.

✪ **Foxy's Tamarind Bar.** Great Harbour. ☎ **284/495-9258.** Reservations recommended. Dinner $12–$35; lunch $7–$9. AE, MC, V. Daily 9am "until." CARIBBEAN.

Arguably the most famous bar in the B.V.I., this mecca of yachties and other boat people spins entirely around a sixth-generation Jost Van Dyke native, Philicianno ("Foxy") Callwood. He opened the place some three decades ago, and sailors and the world have been coming back ever since. A songwriter and entertainer, Foxy is part of the draw. He creates impromptu calypso—almost in the Jamaican tradition—around his guests. If you're singled out, he'll embarrass you, but all in good fun. He also plays the guitar and takes a profound interest in preserving the environment of his native island.

Thursday through Saturday nights, a live band entertains. On other evenings, it's rock-and-roll, perhaps reggae or soca. The food and drink aren't neglected, either—try Foxy's Painkiller Punch. During the day, flying-fish sandwiches, rotis, and the usual burgers are served, but evenings might bring freshly caught lobster, spicy steamed shrimp, or even grilled fish, depending on the catch of the day. No lunch is served on Saturday and Sunday.

Rudy's Mariner's Rendezvous. Great Harbour. ☎ **284/495-9282.** Reservations required by 6:30pm. Dinner $15–$25. MC, V. Daily 7pm–midnight. WEST INDIAN.

Rudy's, at the western end of Great Harbour, serves good but basic West Indian food—and plenty of it. The place looks and feels like a private home with a waterfront terrace for visiting diners. A welcoming drink awaits sailors and landlubbers alike, and the food that follows is simply prepared and inexpensive. Conch always seems to be available, and a catch of the day is featured.

The Sandcastle. On White Bay. ☎ **284/495-9888.** Reservations required for dinner by 5pm. Lunch main courses $6–$8; fixed-price dinner $32. MC, V. Daily 9:30am–3pm and one seating at 7:30pm. INTERNATIONAL/CARIBBEAN.

This hotel restaurant serves food that has often been frozen, but, even so, the flavors remain consistently good. Lunch is served in the open-air dining room, while lighter fare and snacks are available at the Soggy Dollar Bar. Dinner is by candlelight, featuring four courses, including such dishes as mahimahi Martinique (marinated in orange-lemon-lime juice and cooked with fennel, onions, and dill). Sandcastle hen is another specialty likely to appear on the menu: It's a grilled Cornish hen that's been marinated in rum, honey, lime, and garlic. But we'd skip all that for the sesame snapper, if available. Meals are served with seasonal vegetables and fresh pasta, along with a variety of salads and homemade desserts. Those desserts are luscious, including a piña-colada cheesecake and a mango mousse.

5 Anegada

The most northerly and isolated of the British Virgins, 30 miles east of Tortola, Anegada has a population of about 250, none of whom has found the legendary treasure from the more than 500 wrecks lying off its notorious Horseshoe Reef. It's different from the other British Virgins in that it's a coral-and-limestone atoll, flat, with a

2,500-foot airstrip. Its highest point reaches 28 feet, and it hardly appears on the horizon if you're sailing to it.

At the northern and western ends of the island are some good white-sand beaches, which might be your only reason for coming here. This is a remote little corner of the Caribbean: Don't expect a single frill, and be prepared to put up with some hardships, such as mosquitoes.

Most of the island has been declared off-limits to settlement and reserved for birds and other wildlife. The B.V.I. National Parks Trust has established a flamingo colony in a bird sanctuary, which is also the protected home of several different varieties of heron as well as ospreys and terns. It has also designated much of the interior of the island as a preserved habitat for Anegada's animal population of some 2,000 wild goats, donkeys, and cattle. Among the endangered species being given a new lease on life here is the rock iguana, a fierce-looking but quite harmless reptile that can grow to a length of 5 feet. Although rarely seen, these creatures have called Anegada home for thousands of years.

While you're here, you might want to drop in at **Pat's Pottery** (☎ **284/495-8031**), where islanders sell some interesting crafts, including dishes, plates, pitchers, and mugs in whimsical folk-art patterns.

ESSENTIALS

GETTING THERE   The only carrier flying from Tortola to Anegada, **Clair Aero Service** (☎ **284/495-2271**), uses six- to eight-passenger prop planes. It operates four times a week, on Monday, Wednesday, Friday, and Sunday, charging $59 per person round-trip. In addition, **Fly BVI** (☎ **284/495-1747**) operates a charter/sightseeing service between Anegada and Beef Island off Tortola. The one-way cost is $125 for two to three passengers.

GETTING AROUND   Limited taxi service is available on the island—not that you'll have many places to go. **Tony's Taxis,** which you'll easily spot when you arrive, will take you around the island. It's also possible to rent **bicycles**—ask around.

WHERE TO STAY & DINE

The Anegada Reef Hotel is the only major accommodation on the island. Neptune's Treasure, below, rents tents and basic rooms.

Anegada Reef Hotel. Setting Point, Anegada, B.V.I. ☎ **284/495-8002.** Fax 284/ 495-9362. 19 units. A/C. Winter $230–$250 double. Off-season $200–$230 double. Rates include all meals. MC, V.

The only major hotel on the island is 3 miles west of the airport, right on the beach-front. It's one of the most remote places covered in this guide—guests who stay here are, in effect, hiding out. It's a favorite of the yachting set, who enjoy the hospitality provided by Lowell Wheatley. He offers motel-like and very basic rooms with private porches, with either a garden or ocean view. Mattresses are adequate for the purpose—nothing more—and bathrooms are cramped, with shower stalls and rather thin towels. Come here for tranquillity, not for pampering.

You can arrange to go inshore fishing, deep-sea fishing, or bonefishing (there's also a tackle shop); they'll also set up snorkeling excursions and secure taxi service and jeep rentals. There's a beach barbecue nightly, the house specialty is lobster, and many attendees arrive by boat. Reservations for the 7:30pm dinner must be made by 4pm. Dinners begin at $18.50, $35 if you order the generous portion of lobster. Nonguests are also welcomed at breakfast or lunch. If you're visiting just for the day, you can use the hotel as a base. Call and they'll have a van meet you at the airport.

Neptune's Treasure. Between Pomato and Saltheap points, Anegada, B.V.I. ☎ **284/ 495-9439,** or VHF Channel 16 or 68. www.islandsonline.com. E-mail: neptunetreasure@ caribsurf.com. Reservations not necessary. Breakfast $7–$9; sandwiches $4–$9; fixed-price meals $16–$35. AE, MC, V. Daily 8am–10pm. INTERNATIONAL.

Set near its own 24-slip marina, near the southern tip of the island in the same cluster of buildings that includes the more high-priced Anegada Reef Hotel, this raffishly appealing bar and restaurant is known to off-island yacht owners who make it a point to mingle with local residents. Dining is in a spacious indoor area whose focal point is a bar and lots of nautical memorabilia. The drink of choice is a Pink Whopee, composed of fruit juices and rum. The Soares family and their staff serve platters of swordfish, lobster, fish fingers, chicken, steaks, and ribs; dispense information about local snorkeling sites; and generally maintain order and something approaching a (low-key) party atmosphere.

They also offer four simple bedrooms and about four tents for anyone looking for super-low-cost lodgings. Depending on the season, rooms with private bath rent for $70 to $85 double. Tents share the plumbing facilities of the restaurant and go for $25 a night for two. Continental breakfast is included in the rates, and discounts are offered for stays of a week or more.

6 Marina Cay

Near Beef Island, Marina Cay is a private 6-acre islet. Its only claim to fame: It served as the setting for the 1953 Robb White book *Our Virgin Isle,* which was later filmed with Sidney Poitier and John Cassavetes. For 20 years after Robb White's departure, the island lay uninhabited until the hotel (see below) opened. We only mention this tiny cay at all because of the Marina Cay Resort.

GETTING THERE

The island lies 5 minutes away by launch from Tortola's Trellis Bay, adjacent to Beef Island International Airport. The ferry running between Beef Island and Marina Cay is free. There are no cars on the island.

WHERE TO STAY & DINE

Pusser's Marina Cay Resort. Marina Cay (mailing address: P.O. Box 626, Road Town, Tortola), B.V.I. ☎ **284/494-2174.** Fax 284/494-4775. www.pussers.com. E-mail: marinacy@ caribsurf.com. 6 units. Winter $150 double; $350 villa. Off-season $95 double; $195 villa. Rates include continental breakfast. AE, MC, V.

Marina Cay is a tropical garden. This small cottage hotel, opened in 1960 and extensively renovated in 1995, attracts the sailing crowd. It houses guests in simply furnished double rooms overlooking a reef and Sir Francis Drake Channel, dotted with islands. Each room has a private balcony and light, airy furnishings. For privacy's sake, accommodations are set on a bluff, which makes them well ventilated. In lieu of air conditioning, the trade winds and ceiling fans are more than adequate.

Dining is casual in a beachside restaurant, with a cuisine featuring continental and West Indian dishes. Activities include snorkeling, Hobie Cat, scuba diving (with certification courses taught by a resident dive master), castaway picnics on secluded beaches, and kayaking.

7 Peter Island

Half of this island, boasting a good marina and docking facilities, is devoted to the yacht club. The other part is deserted. Beach facilities are found at palm-fringed

Deadman's Bay, which faces the Atlantic but is protected by a reef. All goods and services are at the one resort (see below).

The island is so private that except for an occasional mason at work, about the only company you'll encounter will be an iguana or a feral cat whose ancestors were abandoned generations ago by shippers (the cats are said to have virtually eliminated the island's rodent population).

GETTING THERE

A hotel-operated ferry, **Peter Island Boat** (☎ 284/495-2000), picks up any overnight guest who arrives at the Beef Island airport. It departs from the pier at Trellis Bay, near the airport. A round-trip costs $25. Other boats depart eight or nine times a day from Baughers Bay in Road Town. Passengers must notify the hotel 2 weeks before their arrival so transportation can be arranged.

WHERE TO STAY & DINE

✪ **Peter Island Resort.** Peter Island (P.O. Box 211, Road Town, Tortola), B.V.I. ☎ **800/346-4451** or 284/495-2000. Fax 284/495-2500. www.peterisland.com. 53 units. A/C MINIBAR TEL. Winter $705–$825 double; $1,180 two-bedroom villa; $5,500 four bedroom villa. Off-season $490–$595 double; $895 two-bedroom villa; $3,000 four-bedroom villa. Hawk's and Crow's Nest rates include all meals. MAP $75 per person extra. AE, MC, V.

This 1,800-acre tropical island is solely dedicated to Peter Island Resort guests and yacht owners who moor their crafts here. The island's tropical gardens and hillside are bordered by five private beaches, including Deadman's Beach (in spite of its name, it's often voted one of the world's most romantic beaches in travel-magazine reader polls).

The resort contains 30 rooms facing Sprat Bay and Sir Francis Drake Channel (ocean-view or garden rooms) and 20 larger rooms on Deadman's Bay Beach (beachfront). Designed with a casual elegance, each has a balcony or terrace, ceiling fan, and coffeemaker. Because of hurricane damage, the hotel was forced to close for major reconstruction and renovations. It reopened in the spring of 1999 better than ever, with fresh mattresses and fine new tropical-motif furnishings. The least desirable rooms are also the smallest and housed in two-story, A-frame structures next to the harbor. Baths range from standard motel-unit types to spectacular luxurious ones, depending on your room assignment. The Crow's Nest, a luxurious four-bedroom villa, overlooks the harbor and Deadman Bay and features a private swimming pool, full kitchen, maid, gardener, personal steward, and island vehicle. The Hawk's Nest villas are two 2-bedroom villas situated on a tropical hillside.

Dining/Diversions: The Tradewinds Restaurant serves breakfast and dinner throughout the year in fine Caribbean tradition. For a more casual setting, the Deadman's Beach Bar and Grill serves sandwiches and salads beside the ocean. The main bar, Drakes Channel Lounge, is also open throughout the day and evening.

Amenities: Fitness center, gift shop, freshwater pool with a stunning view of the sea, four tennis courts (two lit for night play), scuba-diving base, library, spa, conference facility, basketball, mountain bikes; complete yacht marina with complimentary use of Sunfish, snorkeling gear, sea kayaks, Windsurfers, and 19-foot Squib day-sailers, Hobie Cats, scuba, waterskiing, deep-sea fishing. Room service (breakfast only), laundry, massage, baby-sitting.

8 Mosquito Island (North Sound)

Sandy, 125-acre Mosquito Island, just north of Virgin Gorda, wasn't named for those pesky insects—it took its name from the Mosquito (or Moskito) tribe, who were the only known inhabitants of the small island before the Spanish conquistadors arrived in the 15th century. Archaeological relics of these peaceful people and their agricultural pursuits have been found here.

GETTING THERE

To get here, take a plane to the Virgin Gorda airport and **Speedy's Taxi** from there to Leverick Bay Dock. The taxi driver will radio ahead, and a boat will be sent from Drake's to take you on the 5-minute ride from the dock to the resort.

WHERE TO STAY & DINE

✪ **Drake's Anchorage Resort Inn.** North Sound (P.O. Box 2510, Virgin Gorda), B.V.I. ☎ **617/969-9913** in Massachusetts, or 284/495-7045. Fax 284/494-2254. For reservations, write to 1340 Centre St., Newton, MA 02159, or fax 617/969-1673. 12 units. Winter $505–$526 double cottage; $598 suite; $695 villa. Off-season $398–$425 double cottage; $515 suite; $595 villa. Rates include all meals. AE, MC, V.

The privately owned island is uninhabited except for Drake's Anchorage Resort Inn, which many patrons consider their favorite retreat in the British Virgins. Accommodations are in wood-frame cottages, trimmed in gingerbread and perched on stilts along the shoreline. The hotel has comfortable rooms and suites with private bathrooms and sea-view verandas. You don't get phones, radios, or TVs in the rooms here, and that's how the habitués like it. Natural materials and tiles went into the furnishings, which have a light, airy feel set against white walls. Accommodations are spacious, with roomy baths that contain sunken tubs and natural rock showers.

The resort's restaurant, attractively tropical in design, faces the water and offers a cuisine featuring local and continental dishes, including lobster and a fresh fish of the day. Guests have free use of Windsurfers, snorkeling equipment, and bicycles. For additional fees, you can go scuba diving, deep-sea fishing, sailing, or to The Baths on Virgin Gorda. The snorkeling and scuba here are so good that members of the Cousteau Society spend a month each year exploring local waters. There are four beaches on the island, each with different wave and water conditions.

9 Guana Island

This 850-acre island, a nature preserve and wildlife sanctuary, is one of the most private hideaways in the Caribbean. Don't come here looking for action; rather, consider vacationing here if you want to retreat from the world. This small island right off the coast of Tortola offers seven virgin beaches and nature trails ideal for hiking; it abounds in unusual species of plant and animal life. Arawak relics have been found here. Head up to the 806-foot peak of Sugarloaf Mountain for a panoramic view. It's said that the name of the island came from a jutting rock that resembled the head of an iguana.

GETTING THERE

The Guana Island Club will send a boat to meet arriving guests at the Beef Island airport (trip time is 10 minutes).

WHERE TO STAY & DINE

✪ **Guana Island Club.** P.O. Box 32, Road Town, Tortola, B.V.I. ☎ **800/544-8262** in the U.S., or 284/494-2354. 16 units. For reservations, write or call the Guana Island Club Reservations Office, 10 Timber Trail, Rye, NY 10580 (☎ **800/544-8262** in the U.S., or 914/967-6050; fax 914/967-8048). www.guana.com. E-mail: guana@guana.com. Winter $695 double; $1,390 cottage. Off-season $475–$535 double; $950–$1,070 cottage. Rent the island, $9,200–$11,800. Rates include all meals and drinks served with meals. No credit cards. Closed Sept–Oct.

Guana Island, the sixth or seventh largest of the British Virgin Islands, was bought in 1974 by Henry and Gloria Jarecki, dedicated conservationists who run this resort as a nature preserve and wildlife sanctuary. Upon your arrival on the island, a Land Rover will meet you and transport you up one of the most scenic hills in the region, in the northeast of Guana.

The cluster of white cottages was built as a private club in the 1930s on the foundations of a Quaker homestead. The stone cottages never hold more than 30 guests (and only two phones), and since the dwellings are staggered along a flower-dotted ridge overlooking the Caribbean and the Atlantic, the sense of privacy is almost absolute. The entire island can be rented by groups of up to 30. Although water is scarce on the island, each airy accommodation has a shower. The decor is rattan and wicker, and each unit has a ceiling fan. North Beach cottage, the most luxurious, is like renting a private home. The panoramic sweep from the terraces is spectacular, particularly at sunset. There are seven beaches, some of which require a boat to reach.

Dining: Guests will find a convivial atmosphere at the rattan-furnished clubhouse. Casually elegant dinners by candlelight are served on the veranda, with menus that include homegrown vegetables and continental and Stateside specialties. A buffet lunch is served every day. The self-service bars operate on the honor system.

Amenities: Two tennis courts (one clay and one all-weather), fishing, snorkeling, windsurfing, kayaks, small sailboats, waterskiing, laundry.

9

The Cayman Islands

Don't go to the Cayman Islands expecting fast-paced excitement. Island life focuses on the sea. Snorkelers will find a paradise, beach lovers will relish the powdery sands of Seven Mile Beach, but party-hungry travelers in search of urban thrills might be disappointed. Come to slow down and relax.

The Caymans, 480 miles due south of Miami, consist of three islands: **Grand Cayman, Cayman Brac,** and **Little Cayman.** Despite its name, Grand Cayman is only 22 miles long and 8 miles across at its widest point. The other islands are considerably smaller, of course, and contain very limited tourist facilities, in contrast to well-developed Grand Cayman. George Town on Grand Cayman is the capital and is therefore the hub of government, banking, and shopping.

English is the official language of the islands, although it's often spoken with an English slur mixed with an American southern drawl and a lilting Welsh accent.

1 Essentials

VISITOR INFORMATION

The **Cayman Islands Department of Tourism** has the following offices in the United States: 6100 Blue Lagoon Dr., 6100 Waterford Bldg., Suite 150, Miami, FL 33126 (☎ **305/266-2300**); 9525 W. Bryn Mawr, Suite 160, Rosemont, IL 60018 (☎ **847/678-6446**); Two Memorial City Plaza, 820 Gessner, Suite 170, Houston, TX 77024 (☎ **713/461-1317**); 3440 Wilshire Blvd., Suite 1202, Los Angeles, CA 90010 (☎ **213/738-1968**); 6100 Blue Lagoon Dr., Suite 150, Miami, FL 33126 (☎ **305/266-2300**); and 420 Lexington Ave., Suite 2733, New York, NY 10170 (☎ **212/682-5582**).

The Web site for the Cayman Islands is **www.caymanislands.ky.**

In Canada, contact Earl B. Smith, **Travel Marketing Consultants,** 234 Eglinton Ave. E., Suite 306, Toronto, ON M4P 1K5 (☎ **416 485-1550**).

In the United Kingdom, the contact is **Cayman Islands,** 100 Brompton Rd., London SW3 1EX (☎ **0171/581-9960**).

GETTING THERE

The Cayman Islands are easily accessible. Flying time from Miami is 1 hour 20 minutes; from Houston, 2 hours 45 minutes; from Tampa, 1 hour 40 minutes; and from Atlanta, 3 hours 35 minutes. Only a

Ahoy, Matey!

Cayman Islands Pirates' Week is held in late October. It's a national festival in which cutlass-bearing pirates and sassy wenches storm George Town, capture the governor, throng the streets, and stage a costume parade. The celebration, which is held throughout the Caymans, pays tribute to the nation's past and its cultural heritage. For the exact dates, contact the **Pirates Week Festival Administration** (☎ **345/949-5078**).

---

handful of nonstop flights are available from the heartland of North America to Grand Cayman, so many visitors use Miami as their gateway.

Cayman Airways (☎ **800/422-9626** in the U.S. and Canada, or 345/949-2311; www.caymanairways.com) offers the most frequent service to Grand Cayman, with three daily flights from Miami, four flights a week from Tampa, three flights a week from Orlando, and three nonstop flights a week from Houston and Atlanta. Once in the Caymans, the airline's subsidiary, **Island Air Ltd.** (☎ **345/949-5152**), operates frequent flights between Grand Cayman and Little Cayman and Cayman Brac. Round-trip fares between Grand Cayman and Cayman Brac begin at $154.

Many visitors also fly to Grand Cayman on **American Airlines** (☎ **800/ 433-7300;** www.aa.com), which operates three daily nonstop flights from Miami and from Raleigh/Durham. **Northwest Airlines** (☎ **800/447-4747;** www.nwa.com) flies to Grand Cayman from Detroit via Miami or Memphis, and from Memphis via Miami. **US Airways** (☎ **800/428-4322;** www.usairways.com) flies daily nonstop from Tampa, and offers three flights a week from Pittsburgh and also from Charlotte, N.C. **Delta** (☎ **800/221-1212;** www.delta-air.com) flies daily into Grand Cayman from its hub in Atlanta.

Fast Facts: The Cayman Islands

Business Hours   Normally, banks are open Monday to Thursday from 9am to 2:30pm, Friday from 9am to 1pm and 2:30 to 4:30pm. Shops are usually open Monday to Saturday from 9am to 5pm.

Currency   The legal tender is the Cayman Islands dollar (CI$), currently valued at U.S.$1.25 (U.S.$1 equals 80¢ CI). Canadian, U.S., and British currencies are accepted throughout the Cayman Islands, but you'll save money if you exchange your U.S. dollars for Cayman Islands dollars. The Cayman dollar breaks down into 100 cents. Coins come in 1¢, 5¢, 10¢, and 25¢. Bills come in denominations of $1, $5, $10, $25, $50, and $100 (there is no CI$20 bill). Most hotels quote rates in U.S. dollars. However, many restaurants quote prices in Cayman Islands dollars, which might lead you to think that food is much cheaper. Unless otherwise noted, *prices in this chapter are in U.S. dollars, rounded off.*

The cost of living in the Cayman Islands is about 20% higher than in the United States.

Documents   Citizens of the U.S. and Canada should carry a valid passport or else a birth certificate with a raised seal along with a government-issued photo ID. Citizens of the United Kingdom should have a valid passport. All visitors need a return or ongoing ticket.

Electricity   It's 110 volts AC (60 cycles), so American and Canadian appliances will not need adapters or transformers.

Emergencies   For medical or police emergencies, dial ☎ **911** or 555.

Hospital   On Grand Cayman, the only hospital is **George Town Hospital,** Hospital Road (☎ **345/949-4234**). On Cayman Brac, the only hospital is the 18-bed **Faith Hospital** (☎ **345/948-2243**).

Language   English is the official language of the islands.

Taxes   A government tourist tax of 10% is added to your hotel bill. A departure tax of CI$10 ($12.50) is collected when you leave the Caymans.

Telephone   The **Cable and Wireless,** Anderson Square, George Town, on Grand Cayman (☎ **345/949-7800**), is open Monday to Friday from 8:15am to 5pm, Saturday from 9am to 1pm, and Sunday from 9am to noon.

Time   U.S. eastern standard time is in effect all year; daylight saving time is not observed.

Tipping   Most restaurants add a 10% to 15% charge in lieu of tipping. Hotels also add a 10% service charge to your bill.

Water   The water in the Cayman Islands is safe to drink.

2 Grand Cayman

The largest of the three islands and a real diving mecca, Grand Cayman is one of the hottest tourist destinations in the Caribbean. With more than 500 banks, its capital, George Town, is the offshore banking center of the Caribbean. Retirees are drawn to the peace and tranquillity of this British Crown Colony, site of a major condominium development. Almost all the Cayman Islands' population of 32,000 live on Grand Cayman. The civil manners of the locals reflect their British heritage.

GRAND CAYMAN ESSENTIALS

VISITOR INFORMATION   The **Department of Tourism** is in the Pavilion Building, Cricket Square (P.O. Box 67), George Town, Grand Cayman, B.W.I. (☎ **345/ 949-0623**).

GETTING AROUND   All arriving flights are met by taxis. The fares are fixed by the director of civil aviation (☎ **345/949-7811**); typical one-way fares from the airport to Seven Mile Beach range from $10 to $12. Taxis (which can hold five people) will also take visitors on around-the-island tours. **Cayman Cab Team** (☎ **345/ 947-1173**) offers 24-hour service. You can also call **A.A. Transportation** at ☎ **345/949-7222.**

Several car-rental companies operate on the island, including **Cico Avis** (☎ **800/331-1212** in the U.S., or 345/949-2468), **Budget** (☎ **800/527-0700** in the U.S., or 345/949-5605), and **Ace Hertz** (☎ **800/654-3131** in the U.S., or 345/949-2280). Each will issue the mandatory Cayman Islands driving permit for an additional U.S. $7.50. All three require that reservations be made between 6 and 36 hours before pickup. At Avis drivers must be at least 21 and at Hertz, 25. Budget requires that drivers be between 25 and 70 years old. All three rental companies maintain kiosks within walking distance of the airport, although most visitors find it easier to take a taxi to their hotels and then arrange for the cars to be brought to them.

Remember to drive on the left and to reserve your car as far in advance as possible, especially in midwinter.

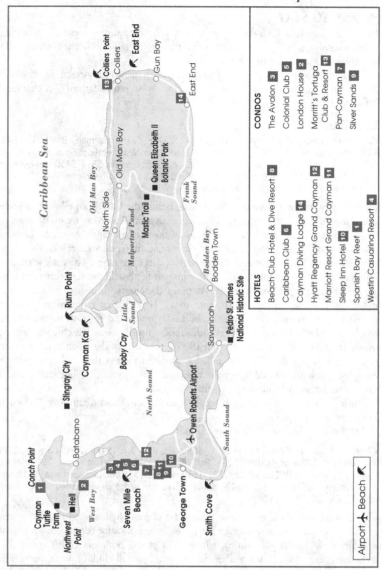

Grand Cayman Island

CONDOS

The Avalon `3`
Colonial Club `5`
London House `2`
Morritt's Tortuga Club & Resort `13`
Pan-Cayman `7`
Silver Sands `9`

HOTELS

Beach Club Hotel & Dive Resort `8`
Caribbean Club `6`
Cayman Diving Lodge `14`
Hyatt Regency Grand Cayman `12`
Marriott Resort Grand Cayman `11`
Sleep Inn Hotel `10`
Spanish Bay Reef `1`
Westin Casuarina Resort `4`

Caribbean Sea

Colliers Point `13` Colliers
East End Gun Bay
East End `14`

Old Man Bay
Old Man Bay
Old Man Bay
North Side

Malportas Pond

Queen Elizabeth II Botanic Park
Mastic Trail `■`

Frank Sound

Rum Point

Bodden Bay
Bodden Town

Cayman Kai

Booby Cay
Little Sound

Stingray City `■`

Savannah
Pedro St. James National Historic Site `■`

Conch Point

Batabano

`1`
Cayman Turtle Farm `■`
Hell `■`
Northwest Point
West Bay
`2`
Seven Mile Beach
`3`
`4`
`5`
`6`
`12`
`7`
`8` `11`
`9`
`10`
George Town
Smith Cove

North Sound

Owen Roberts Airport ✈

South Sound

Airport ✈ Beach ↖

Soto Scooters Ltd., Seven Mile Beach (☎ **345/945-4652**), located at Coconut Place, offers Honda Elite scooters for $30 daily, or bicycles for $15 daily. It also offers jeep and car rentals from $50 per day.

FAST FACTS   The largest pharmacy is **Island Pharmacy,** West Shore Centre, Seven Mile Beach (☎ **345/949-8987**), open Monday to Saturday from 8:30am to 5:30pm. In George Town, the **post office** and Philatelic Bureau is on Edward Street (☎ **345/949-2474**), open Monday to Friday from 8:30am to 5pm and on Saturday from 8:30am to noon. There's also a counter at the Seven Mile Beach Post Office, open the same hours.

WHERE TO STAY

Hotels, unlike many Caymanian restaurants, generally quote prices in U.S. dollars. When choosing a hotel, keep in mind that the quoted rates do not include the 10% government tax and the 10% hotel service tax.

Consider booking a package tour to make those expensive resorts more affordable! See the sections on "Package Deals" and "Tips on Accommodations," in chapter 2, before you book.

VERY EXPENSIVE

Caribbean Club. West Bay Rd. (P.O. Box 30499), Grand Cayman, B.W.I. ☎ **345/ 945-4099.** Fax 345/945-4443. www.caribclub.com. E-mail: reservations@caribclub.com. 18 units. A/C MINIBAR TV TEL. Winter $250–$420 one-bedroom villa; $335–$450 two-bedroom villa. Off-season $150–$300 one-bedroom villa; $240–$330 two-bedroom villa. AE, MC, V. Children under 10 not accepted Jan 3–Mar 15.

Located right at the midpoint of Seven Mile Beach, the Caribbean Club is an exclusive compound of well-furnished villas, each with a full-size living room, dining area, patio, and kitchen. When the owners are away, the units are rented to guests. The look is very Bermudian. Although it has a long list of faithful repeat visitors who would stay nowhere else, it's not as elegant as some hotels in its price range. The pink villas are 3 miles north of George Town, either on or just off the beach; the six oceanfront units are always more expensive, of course. Accommodations are furnished in each owner's individual taste (which may not be your own). They contain attractive tropical furnishings, open verandas (often with barbecues), spacious closets, firm mattresses, and combination baths (tub and shower) with a rack of fluffy towels. The club was last renovated in 1994, but was refurbished in 1996. At the core of the colony, the two-story club center, with tall, graceful arches, has picture windows that look out onto the grounds, which are planted with palm trees and flowering shrubs. The staff is one of the best and most helpful on the island.

Dining: Lantanas, the dining room, is open for lunch and dinner (see "Where to Dine," below).

Amenities: Tennis court, free guest laundry.

✪ **Hyatt Regency Grand Cayman.** West Bay Rd. (P.O. Box 1588), Grand Cayman, B.W.I. ☎ **800/233-1234** or 345/949-1234. Fax 345/949-8528. www.hyatt.com. 236 units, 55 villas. A/C MINIBAR TV TEL. Winter $305–$510 double; $575 one-bedroom villa; $735 two-bedroom villa. Off-season $220–$480 double; $315 one-bedroom villa; $440 two-bedroom villa. AE, CB, DC, DISC, MC, V.

This $80-million resort is the best managed and most stylish hotel in the Cayman Islands. Two miles north of George Town, the hotel is a major component in the 90-acre Britannia Resort community, which includes the Britannia Golf Course. Two acres front Seven Mile Beach and provide the setting for all kinds of water sports. This is definitely the choice for kids with well-heeled parents. The wide range of accommodations can meet the needs of families of almost any size.

The hotel's design combines neoclassicism with modern art and a sort of British colonial airiness. Dozens of Doric arcades are festooned with flowering vines that cascade beneath reflecting pools and comfortable teakwood settees. Low-rise buildings surround a large, landscaped courtyard that contains gardens, waterfalls, and the swimming pool.

Rooms are luxurious and have private verandas but are only moderate in size; they were last renovated in 1995. They have king or double beds, each with a quality mattress, plus spacious bathrooms in Italian marble with hair dryers and fluffy towels. Two buildings and 44 rooms are devoted to the Regency Club, which has concierge service from 5am to 11pm daily; these units cost about $100 more. The hotel also offers one- and two-bedroom luxury villas along the Britannia Golf Course or waterway; these have fully equipped kitchens and easy access to the resort's facilities. The villas have their own pool, whirlpool, laundry room, cabana, and patio area. By the time you arrive, Hyatt should have launched a new 5-story, 53-suite beachfront addition, with keyed elevator access for guests, plus everything from full kitchens to plush robes, even fax machines. This new facility has a rooftop sundeck, ice-cream cafe, water-sports center, and health center, plus a landscaped pool area.

Dining: The resort offers several dining choices, including the Garden Loggia Café, with Asian and Italian cuisine (and a buffet champagne brunch on Sunday). There's a seafood restaurant, Hemingway's (see "Where to Dine," below), and you can also have lunch or dinner daily at the Britannia Golf Club and Grille, a few steps away from the first tee. Hyatt's own ferry will take you on a 40-minute cruise to Rum Point where you can have lunch or dinner.

Amenities: The most complete array of water sports in the Caymans (see "Sports & Outdoor Pursuits," below), health club, four pools (with a whirlpool and swim-up bar), the Britannia Golf Course, tennis courts, room service, baby-sitting, laundry. The hotel recently added a spa, with European-trained therapists, a workout area, a 72-foot lap pool, and a juice bar. A Camp Hyatt program for children 3 to 12 costs $37 to $75 per day and has an activity-filled agenda.

Westin Casuarina Resort. Seven Mile Beach (P.O. Box 30620), Grand Cayman, B.W.I. ☎ **800/WESTIN-1** or 345/945-3800. Fax 345/949-5825. 345 units. A/C MINIBAR TV TEL. Winter $340–$525 double; from $1,100 suite. Off-season $200–$350 double; from $600 suite. AE, MC, V.

Desirable land on Seven Mile Beach is so sought after that when Westin wanted to build a luxury hotel, the largest on the island, it had to demolish the old Galleon Beach Hotel to make room for this $50-million investment. Completed late in 1995, and designed by eminent architect Edward D. Stone, Jr., with a postmodern gray facade and turquoise roofs, it was conceived as a direct competitor of the nearby Hyatt. Unlike the Hyatt, it lies directly on the sands of the beach on 8 acres of land-scaped gardens; it also has beautiful swimming pools and lots of sports facilities. The bedrooms are in five-story wings, each outfitted in a soothing color scheme. Most have French doors leading onto balconies, and all have in-room safes and ceiling fans. Units are a bit small for such a luxury hotel but are well equipped with coffeemakers, ironing boards, and quality mattresses and bed linens. Baths are very spacious, with oversize marble tubs, fluffy towels, and hair dryers.

Dining: The most upscale of the restaurants is Casa Havana, a dinner-only restaurant that evokes the glamour of pre-Castro Cuba. Ferdinand's is a middle-bracket restaurant serving breakfast, lunch, and dinner. Salads and sandwiches are served at the Courtyard Café poolside restaurant.

Amenities: One of the largest pools and poolside decks (5,000 square feet) in the Caymans, appealingly lined with palm and date trees, and centered around a swim-up bar. Swimming pools, designed as lazy ovals or lagoons, flank the north and south sides of the hotel, each with its own cascade/waterfall. An 18-hole championship golf course, The Links at Safehaven, is across the street from the resort. Illuminated tennis courts, an on-site branch of Red Sail Watersports for scuba and sailing, gift shop, hair and beauty salon, car rentals, 24-hour room service, concierge, limited programs for children, massage.

EXPENSIVE

Marriott Resort Grand Cayman. West Bay Rd. (P.O. Box 30371), Grand Cayman, B.W.I. ☎ **800/333-3333** or 345/949-0088. Fax 345/949-0288. 313 units. A/C TV TEL. Winter $230–$399 double; from $600 suite. Off-season $195–$295 double; from $600 suite. AE, DC, MC, V.

Opened in 1990, this five-story hotel has an enviable location beside Seven Mile Beach, a 5-minute drive (2 miles) north of George Town; there's good snorkeling 50 feet offshore. It's a favorite with large package-tour groups and conventions, and has good water-sports facilities. Its red-roofed, vaguely colonial design resembles a cluster of balconied town houses. Bedrooms were refurbished in the winter of 1996–97. Accommodations open onto the ocean or else the courtyard, and are decorated in cool Caribbean pastels. They have modern art, armoires, large closets, and private balconies; there are excellent mattresses on the large beds. Bathrooms are spacious, with combination tubs and showers, hair dryers, long vanities, plenty of shelf space, and fluffy towels.

Dining: Serving a standard international cuisine, an oceanfront restaurant offers three meals a day and guests a choice of dining inside or out in the open air overlooking the water. Choose this place more for the beach out front than for the cuisine.

Amenities: Pool ringed with a beach bar/cabana and sun parasols (located a few steps from the famous beach), fully equipped dive shop, Jacuzzi, health club, full range of water sports, room service, laundry, baby-sitting.

MODERATE

Beach Club Hotel & Dive Resort. West Bay Rd. (P.O. Box 903G), Grand Cayman, B.W.I. ☎ **800/330-8272** in the U.S., or 345/949-8100. Fax 345/945-5167. 41 units. A/C TV TEL. Winter $230 per person (nondiver); $280 per person (diver). Off-season $180 per person (nondiver); $240 per person (diver). Rates are all-inclusive. Children 6 and under stay free in parents' room; ages 7–17 $85 daily. Honeymoon and dive packages available. AE, MC, V.

Set 3 miles north of George Town, the Beach Club is one of the oldest and best located hotels on the island. Built in the early 1960s in a plain, single-story building along Seven Mile Beach, it has a scuba-diving center and has since attracted a loyal repeat clientele (although some guests complain that you pay a lot for what you get here). When cruise-ship passengers are in port, however, the beach space is overcrowded.

Designed like a large colonial plantation villa, it has a formal Doric portico, lots of lattices, and a popular bar that separates the hotel from the beach. Here, calypso music and rum flow freely for guests who seem to live in their bathing suits all day. The divers who opt for weeklong scuba packages usually take one of the tile-floored villas clustered amid trees at the edge of the beach. Otherwise, most accommodations are simple, nondescript, but comfortable bedrooms in the main hotel. The best units are the ocean-view rooms with four-poster beds. Each comes with a veranda and furniture ranging from Caribbean rattan to reproductions of English Sheraton. A final note: Housekeeping could be improved.

Spanish Bay Reef. West Bay Rd. (P.O. Box 30867), Grand Cayman, B.W.I. ☎ **800/482-3483** in the U.S., 800/424-5500 in Canada, or 345/949-3765. Fax 345/949-1842. www.caymanresorthotels.com. 66 units. A/C TV TEL. Winter $210–$255 per person (nondiver); $270–$325 per person (diver). Off-season $170–$205 per person (nondiver); $230–$265 per person (diver). Rates are all-inclusive. AE, MC, V.

A small, intimate resort set in an isolated location amid the scrublands of the northwestern tip of Grand Cayman, this was the island's first all-inclusive resort. Rather informally run, the pale-pink, two-story stucco units are favorites with divers who appreciate the marine life of the offshore reefs. The casual furnishings are in a

Caribbean motif. The accommodations, which are rather simple, have balconies or patios with garden or ocean views. Don't expect grand comfort here: Rooms appeal to divers but perhaps not those seeking resort-style accommodations and amenities. Beds are comfortable but the mattresses could be firmer, and bathrooms are a bit cramped, with rather thin towels.

Rates include all meals and beverages, island sightseeing, entertainment, use of bicycles, introductory scuba and snorkeling lessons, unlimited snorkeling or scuba diving from the shore (including tanks and weight belt), round-trip transfers, taxes, and service. If you're a diver, ask about Certified Divers Packages when making your reservations. There's a private coral beach, freshwater pool, and Jacuzzi. Guests lounge around Calico Jack's Poolside Bar, and later enjoy an array of food (with lots of fish) in the Spanish Main Restaurant. There's also a disco.

INEXPENSIVE

Cayman Diving Lodge. East End (P.O. Box 11), Grand Cayman, B.W.I. ☎ **800/852-3483** or 345/947-7555. Fax 345/947-7560. www.caymandivelodge.com. E-mail: divelodge@aol.com. 10 units. A/C. Winter 2-tank dives, $533 double for 3 nights, $900 for 5 nights, $1,251 for 7 nights; 3-tank dives, $563 double for 3 nights, $990 for 5 nights, $1,401 for 7 nights. Off-season 2-tank dives, $368 double for 3 nights, $626 for 5 nights, $884 for 7 nights; 3-tank dives, $423 double for 3 nights, $736 for 5 nights, $1,049 for 7 nights. Rates are all-inclusive. AE, DISC, MC, V.

This casual, laid-back place, in the southeast corner of the island, 20 miles east of George Town, offers good value to experienced divers. The horseshoe-shaped lodge is a two-story, half-timbered building set amid tropical trees on a private coral-sand beach with a live coral barrier reef just offshore. Scuba trips include a daily two-tank morning dive of 3½ hours. The resort owns two 45-foot Garcia dive boats that are very comfortable.

In the rooms, the view of the ocean is better than the somewhat plain decor and furnishings. Linoleum floors, shower-only bathrooms, and jalousies set the tone. A few units have balconies. The bedrooms have been slightly improved recently, with new beds, furnishings, dressers, and curtains. Bathrooms are a bit cramped, with stall showers. Chefs serve abundant meals and specialize in fish dishes; vegetarian food is also available. Guests can rent bikes to tour relatively flat Grand Cayman.

Sleep Inn Hotel. West Bat Rd. (P.O. Box 30111), Grand Cayman, B.W.I. ☎ **345/949-9111.** Fax 345/949-6699. 121 units. A/C TV TEL. Winter $120–$210 double; $170–$240 suite. Off-season $120–$140 double; $170–$190 suite. Rates include buffet breakfast. Children 12 and under stay free in parents' room. AE, DC, DISC, MC, V.

Opened in 1992, the Sleep Inn is the closest hotel on Seven Mile Beach to the center of George Town. On rather bleak grounds, it lies 250 feet from the sands and about a 5-minute drive from the international airport. It's one of the more reasonably priced hotels on the island, with great value for your money, and a good choice for families. A franchise of Choice Hotels International, it offers both smoking and no-smoking rooms and units that are accessible for persons with disabilities. Furnishings are rather nondescript but perfectly comfortable. The rooms have modern tropical furnishings and a small safe for valuables; the suites contain kitchenettes. Features include the Dive Shop, with a full-service dive and water-sports program, a swimming pool and Jacuzzi, a pool bar, and a pool grill.

CONDOS

The Avalon. West Bay Rd. (P.O. Box 31236), Grand Cayman, B.W.I. ☎ **345/945-4171.** Fax 345/945-4189. E-mail: avalon-c@candw.ky. 15 units. A/C TV TEL. Winter $620 apt for 4; $690 apt for 6. Off-season $415 apt for 4; $495 apt for 6. AE, MC, V.

One of Grand Cayman's best condo complexes is the Avalon, occupying prime real estate on Seven Mile Beach. It consists of 27 oceanfront three-bedroom/three-bathroom units, 15 of which can be rented. Only a short distance from restaurants, about a 5-minute drive from George Town, it has an architectural style and grace that's lacking in many beachfront properties. The well-appointed, spacious units have a tropical motif, plus king or twin beds with firm mattresses. Each condo has a fully equipped open kitchen and a large, screened lanai that overlooks a stretch of the beach. Oversized tubs and separate shower stalls are in each bathroom, along with fluffy towels. Facilities include a tennis court, fitness center, pool, and Jacuzzi. As a luxury touch, each condo unit has a private garage, and rooms have maid service every day but Tuesday.

Colonial Club. West Bay Rd. (P.O. Box 320W), Grand Cayman, B.W.I. ☎ **345/945-4660.** Fax 345/945-4839. 24 units. A/C TV TEL. Winter $470–$530 apt for 2; $520–$590 apt for 3–4; $570–$650 apt for 5–6. Off-season $260–$340 apt for 2; $310–$390 apt for 3–4; $360–$440 apt for 5–6. Minimum stay 5 nights Dec 16–Apr 15. AE, MC, V.

The pastel-pink Colonial Club occupies a highly desirable stretch of the famous Seven Mile Beach. Built in 1985, it's a three-story and rather standard condominium development about 4 miles north of George Town and some 10 minutes from the airport. First-class maintenance, service, and accommodations are provided in the apartments, all with kitchen fans, maid service, and laundry facilities. Usually only 12 of the 24 apartments are available for rent—the rest are privately owned and occupied but are sometimes rented out. You have a choice of units with two bedrooms and three bathrooms or units with three bedrooms and three bathrooms. Each unit has a firm mattress and a well-maintained bathroom with a stall shower. Facilities include a tennis court (lit at night), a Jacuzzi, and a freshwater pool. There's no on-site restaurant.

London House. Seven Mile Beach, Grand Cayman, B.W.I. ☎ **345/945-4060.** Fax 345/945-4087. 21 units. A/C TV TEL. Winter $315–$365 one-bedroom apt; $325–$425 two-bedroom apt; $850 three-bedroom apt. Off-season $220–$255 one-bedroom apt; $228–$298 two-bedroom apt; $550 three-bedroom apt. Extra person $20 per day. AE, MC, V.

At the more tranquil northern end of Seven Mile Beach, this hotel is a favorite for those seeking apartment living. The units have fully equipped kitchens, spacious living and dining areas, and private patios or balconies overlooking the water. Each was last renovated in 1996. Floral prints, rattan, tile floors, and Caribbean pastels set the tone in most units. Ceiling fans supplement the air-conditioning, and daily maid service is available. There are several different types of beds, but each comes with a good mattress; bathrooms are well maintained, with stall showers. The complex has its own seaside swimming pool (try to get a room away from the pool if you're bothered by noise, as house parties are sometimes staged on the patio). Many restaurants are nearby, although there's a stone barbecue for private poolside cookouts.

Morritt's Tortuga Club and Resort. East End (P.O. Box 496GT), Grand Cayman, B.W.I. ☎ **800/447-0309** or 345/947-7449. Fax 345/947-7449. www.morritt.com. E-mail: exchange@morritt.com. 169 units. A/C TV. Winter $185–$195 studio; $245–$270 one-bedroom apt; $310–$370 two-bedroom apt. Off-season $145–$155 studio; $160–$185 one-bedroom apt; $225–$280 two-bedroom apt. AE, DISC, MC, V.

Set on the grounds of the famed Tortuga Club, which was destroyed in 1989 by Hurricane Hugo, this condo cluster was built in the Antillean plantation style from the wreckage of the former hotel. The property sits on 8 beachfront acres on the East End, known for some of the island's best diving. Profiting from its position near offshore reefs teeming with marine life, it's the site of Cayman Windsurfing, which offers snorkeling and windsurfing, and rents sailboats and catamarans. Tortuga Divers, also on the premises, offers resort courses.

About a 26-mile drive from the airport, the club is composed of clusters of three-story beachfront condos opening onto the water. Many are rented as time-share units. There's also a swim-up bar around the pool. Each of the comfortably furnished apartments has a fully equipped kitchen, although many guests opt instead for meals in the complex's restaurant. The club's buildings and facilities are well maintained.

Pan-Cayman. West Bay Rd. (P.O. Box 440GT), Grand Cayman, B.W.I. ☎ **345/947-4002.** Fax 345/945-4011. 10 condos. A/C TV TEL. Winter $250–$350 two-bedroom apt; $410 three-bedroom apt. Off-season $190–$225 two-bedroom apt; $300 three-bedroom apt. Extra person $45. DISC, MC, V.

The Georgian-style facade of this popular beachfront choice was altered to suit its Caribbean setting, 4 miles north of George Town. It was last renovated in 1995. Each apartment has its own fully equipped kitchen, a private balcony or patio with an unrestricted view of the sea, and comfortable summer furniture. Hotel-type maid service is provided. This place is popular in winter, so reserve well in advance. The atmosphere is homey and welcoming, and people come for peace and tranquillity.

Silver Sands. West Bay Rd. (P.O. Box 205GT), Grand Cayman, B.W.I. ☎ **800/327-8777** in the U.S., or 345/949-3343. Fax 345/949-1223. www.cayman.org/silversands. E-mail: silsands@candw.ky. 15 condos. A/C TV. Winter $400 two-bedroom apt; $485 three-bedroom apt. Off-season $230–$260 two-bedroom apt; $320 three-bedroom apt. Additional person $25 extra. Children 10 and under stay free in parents' unit. Minimum stay 7 nights in winter, 3 nights in off-season. AE, MC, V.

A good choice for families, this modern eight-building complex is arranged horseshoe-fashion on the beach, 7 miles north of George Town. The well-maintained apartments are grouped around a freshwater pool. The eight apartment blocks contain either two-bedroom/two-bathroom or three-bedroom/three-bathroom units. The two-bedroom units can hold up to six people, while the three-bedroom units can house up to eight guests. Each apartment comes with a balcony, a fully equipped kitchen, and maid service. The resident manager will point out the two tennis courts and the utility rooms with washers and dryers. In all, this is a smoothly run operation, which, in spite of its high costs, satisfies most guests.

WHERE TO DINE

Make sure you understand which currency the menu is printed in. If it's not written on the menu, ask the waiter if the prices are in U.S. dollars or Cayman Island dollars. It will make a big difference when you get your final bill; each Cayman Island dollar is currently worth U.S $1.25. Also note that, since virtually everything must be shipped in, Cayman Islands restaurants are among the most expensive in the Caribbean. Even so-called moderate restaurants can quickly push you into the expensive category if you order steak or lobster. For the best taste and value, opt instead for West Indian fare—items such as conch and grouper, which are invariably at the lower end of the price scale.

EXPENSIVE

✪ **Grand Old House.** Petra Plantation, S. Church St. ☎ **345/949-9333.** Reservations required. Main courses CI$18.50–CI$32 (U.S.$23.15–$40). AE, MC, V. Mon–Fri 11:45am–2:30pm; daily 6–10pm. Closed Sept. AMERICAN/CARIBBEAN/PACIFIC RIM.

This former plantation house lies amid venerable trees a mile south of George Town, past Jackson Point. Built on bedrock near the edge of the sea, it stands on 129 ironwood posts that support the main house and a bevy of gazebos. The Grand Old House is the island's premier caterer and hosts everything from lavish weddings and political functions to informal family celebrations.

The restaurant was put on the Cayman culinary map by chef Tell Erhardt, and it's often called Chef Tell's. And though the former TV celebrity chef is long gone, the Grand Old House has suffered no fallout in either food or service. The same menu has been retained, but it's been slightly updated by the new chef, Indian-born Kandaphil Matahi. Appetizers remain the most delectable on the island, including home-smoked marlin and salmon or coconut beer-battered shrimp. Later, dig into the sautéed fresh snapper with shallots in a Chardonnay white-butter sauce, or else the potato-encrusted tuna.

Hemingway's. In the Hyatt Regency Grand Cayman, West Bay Rd. ☎ **345/949-1234.** Reservations recommended. Main courses CI$16.50–CI$34 (U.S.$20.65–$42.50); lunch CI$9.95–CI$16.75 (U.S.$12.45–$20.95). AE, CB, DC, DISC, MC, V. Daily 11:30am–2:30pm and 6–10pm. SEAFOOD/INTERNATIONAL.

The finest seafood on the island can be found 2 miles north of George Town at Hemingway's, which is named after the novelist and inspired by Key West, his one-time residence. You can dine in the open air with a view of the sea. The menu is among the more imaginative on the island. Appetizers include pepper-pot soup—a favorite of Papa's—and gazpacho served with a black-bean relish. The catch of the day, perhaps snapper or wahoo, emerges from the grill to your liking. You can also order roast rack of lamb served on a fruit compote with caramelized-onion mashed potatoes. Want something more imaginative? Try grouper stuffed with crabmeat, or Cuban-spiced tenderloin served on white bean and fennel ragoût.

✪ **Lantanas.** In the Caribbean Club, West Bay Rd. ☎ **345/945-5595.** Reservations recommended. Main courses CI$18–CI$36 (U.S.$22.50–$45). AE, DISC, MC, V. Daily 5:30–10pm. CARIBBEAN/AMERICAN.

In the middle of Seven Mile Beach is one of the best dining choices on Grand Cayman, with an imaginative menu. Begin, for example, with a jerk chicken quesadilla with jack cheese, black beans, roasted vegetables, and salsa, or roasted-garlic soup. The fish menu changes daily, offering only fresh and in-season seafood. Chances are that the seasonal menu will look like many others on the island—but look for a little more creativity here. The kitchen will even prepare an island-style jerk pork tenderloin with rice, black beans, plantains, and mango salsa. The Viennese apple strudel, called "apple pie" by the regulars, is still a specialty of the house prepared by the new chef, London-born, Cayman-settled Keith Griffin. The upstairs has a view of Seven Mile Beach, and the downstairs has a Caribbean tropical decor.

Lobster Pot. N. Church St. ☎ **345/949-2736.** Reservations required in winter. Main courses CI$18–CI$27 (U.S.$22.50–$33.75). AE, MC, V. Mon–Fri 11:30am–2:30pm; daily 5:30–10pm. SEAFOOD.

One of the island's best-known restaurants, the Lobster Pot overlooks the water from its second-floor perch at the western perimeter of George Town, near what used to be Fort George. True to its name, it offers lobster prepared in many different ways: Cayman style, bisque, and salad. Conch schnitzel and seafood curry are on the menu, together with turtle steak grown commercially at Cayman Island kraals. Sometimes the seafood is a bit overcooked for our tastes, but most dishes are right on the mark. The place is also known for its prime beef steaks. For lunch, you might like the English fish-and-chips or perhaps seafood jambalaya or a pasta. The Lobster Pot's pub is a pleasant place for a drink—you may find someone up for a game of darts, too.

Ottmar's Restaurant and Lounge. West Bay Rd. (side entrance of Grand Pavilion Hotel). ☎ **345/945-5879.** Reservations recommended. Main courses CI$15–CI$35 (U.S.$18.75–$43.75); Sun brunch CI$40 (U.S.$50). AE, MC, V. Daily 11:30am–2:30pm and 6–11pm. INTERNATIONAL/FRENCH/CARIBBEAN.

One of the island's top restaurants, Ottmar's is outfitted in a French Empire motif with lots of paneling, rich upholstery, and plenty of space between tables. There's a formal bar/lounge area decorated with deep-sea fishing trophies. This is the domain of an Austrian expatriate, Ottmar Weber, who has long abandoned the kitchen of his youth to roam the world, taking culinary inspiration wherever he finds it. The results are usually pleasing. You can order such dishes as Bavarian cucumber soup, bouillabaisse, French pepper steak, and Wiener schnitzel. Our favorite dish is chicken Trinidad, stuffed with grapes, nuts, and apples rolled in coconut flakes, sautéed golden brown, and served in orange-butter sauce. The menu includes an array of sophisticated desserts, plus a selection of vegetarian dishes. Lunch is served at the Waterfall Restaurant. There's a professional welcome and attentive service.

Ristorante Pappagallo. At Villas Pappagallo, Conch Point, Barkers (near the northern terminus of West Bay Rd. and Spanish Cove, 8 miles north of George Town). ☎ **345/949-1119.** Reservations required. Main courses CI$16–CI$32 (U.S.$20–$40). AE, MC, V. Daily 6–10:30pm. NORTHERN ITALIAN/SEAFOOD.

One of the island's most memorable restaurants lies on a 14-acre bird sanctuary overlooking a natural lagoon, 15 minutes north of George Town. Its designers incorporated Caymanian and Aztec weaving techniques in its thatched roof. Glass doors, black marble, and polished brass mix a kind of Edwardian opulence with a Tahitian decor. You dine on black tagliolini with lobster sauce, fresh crab ravioli with asparagus sauce, lobster in brandy sauce, or perhaps Italian-style veal and chicken dishes. An occasional dish may be beyond the reach of the chef to prepare well, but the veal and seafood are generally good bets. The place strikes some diners as too pricey for what you get; we like to stop in for a nightcap.

The Wharf. West Bay Rd. ☎ **345/949-2231.** Reservations recommended. Main courses CI$20–CI$30 ($25–$37.50). AE, MC, V. Mon–Fri noon–2:30pm; daily 6–10pm. CARIBBEAN/CONTINENTAL.

About 2 miles north of George Town, the 375-seat Wharf has been everything from a dinner theater to a nightclub. Try to catch the traditional 9pm feeding of the tarpon, which are kept in a large tank on the premises; it's quite a show. The restaurant is decorated in soft pastels and offers dining inside, out on an elevated veranda, or on a beachside terrace. The sound of the surf mingles with music from the strolling Paraguayan harpist and pan flute player and chatter from the Ports of Call Bar, located on the premises. Many diners begin with a Wharf salad of seasonal greens; others prefer the homemade black-bean soup or the home-smoked salmon. The main dishes feature everything from seafood potpourri, with lobster, shrimp, and scallops in a mild curry sauce, to veal Martinique, which is medallions of tender veal in a zesty citrus sauce. The kitchen makes a laudable effort to break away from the typical, dull menu items, and for the most part they succeed.

MODERATE

The Almond Tree. N. Church St. (near the corner of Eastern Ave.). ☎ **345/949-2893.** Reservations recommended. Main courses CI$14.95–CI$21.95 (U.S.$18.70–$27.45). AE, MC, V. Daily 5:30–10pm. SEAFOOD/INTERNATIONAL.

Likable and unpretentious, this restaurant is supported by poles and branches, and lined with reeds and thatch rising into a peak. It contains a bar area accented with Trader Vic's–style artifacts and a garden lined with palmettos and flowering shrubs. Many guests prefer to dine in the garden; others like a table in the building's interior. Simple, straightforward cuisine is served, including mango chicken, conch steak, catch of the day, lobster, and filet mignon. This is not the most imaginative array of dishes ever offered, but the kitchen concentrates on what it does well. If you've never ordered it (because it's banned Stateside), this might be the place to request turtle steak. It's grown commercially in the Caymans and not taken from the wild.

Benjamin's Roof. Coconut Place (off West Bay Rd.). ☎ **345/945-4080.** Reservations recommended. Main courses CI$10.95–CI$29.50 (U.S.$13.70–$36.90). AE, DC, MC, V. Daily 3–10:30pm. AMERICAN/INTERNATIONAL.

Set on the upper floor of a shopping center, this restaurant is decorated like the interior of a greenhouse, with a wealth of verdant plants. There's a bar set up in the corner of the place, and an accommodating staff serves food and drink to the accompaniment of live piano music and a singer/guitarist. Menu items might include blackened alligator tail, lobster bisque, a mixed grill of seafood, Austrian-style Wiener schnitzel, lobster fettuccine, blackened shrimp, and grilled lamb with herbs. This is a wholesome, family place, featuring a children's menu. Nothing is too spicy or overseasoned (a few dishes are even bland). But for the most part, the cookery is first-rate and well prepared.

Captain Brians. N. Church St. ☎ **345/949-6163.** Reservations recommended in winter for dinner. Main courses CI$9–CI$20 (U.S.$11.25–$25). AE, MC, V. Daily 8am–10pm (last order). Bar open till 1am. CARIBBEAN/ENGLISH.

On a plot of seafront land near the beginning of West Bay Road, this restaurant has a loyal following. In a low-slung cottage, whose verandas are vivid shades of pink, blue, and yellow, the place has an amusingly decorated pub and a Caribbean-inspired dining room open to a view of the harbor. In the pub, you can order such British staples as fish-and-chips or cottage pie and such drinks as a Snake Bite (equal parts hard English cider and English lager). Also available are all the foamy tropical drinks you'd expect.

The food is competently prepared and satisfying, though not a lot more. Dining choices include a Caesar salad topped with marinated conch or Cajun chicken, fresh catch of the day, shrimp, pastas, and seafood pastry stuffed with lobster, shrimp, and scallops, all of which are great values for the money. Don't overlook this as a possible site for breakfast, where you can devour huevos rancheros.

Cracked Conch by the Sea. West Bay Rd., near Turtle Bay Farm. ☎ **345/945-5217.** Reservations recommended. Main courses CI$15.95–CI25.95 (U.S.$19.95–$32.45). MC, V. Daily 11:30am–10pm. SEAFOOD.

Long a culinary landmark, this popular restaurant near the famous turtle farm in West Bay serves some of the island's freshest seafood and some of the most succulent turtle steak in the Caymans, along with burgers, chicken, steaks, and even a vegetarian pasta of the day. The menu is one of the largest on the island, and the inevitable namesake conch appears in various tasty combinations. Foods are freshly prepared—nothing frozen. The decor is a bit corny, including a cement floor made to look like "authentic" wood planking from a pirate ship. There's also a patio bar overlooking the sea, and a walkway built out so you can watch fish feeding at 8pm every evening.

Crow's Nest Restaurant. South Sound. ☎ **345/949-9366.** Reservations recommended. Main courses CI$15–CI$22 (U.S.$18.75–$27.50). AE, DISC, MC, V. Daily 11:30am–3pm and 5:30–10pm. CARIBBEAN.

With a boardwalk and terrace jutting onto the sands, this informal restaurant has a view of both Sand Cay and a nearby lighthouse. It's on the island's southwesternmost tip, a 4-minute drive from George Town. The restaurant is one of those places that evoke the Caribbean "the way it used to be." There's no pretense here—you get good, honest Caribbean cookery featuring grilled seafood. Try a daily special or perhaps sweet, tender Caribbean lobster. Other dishes include grilled tuna steak with ackee or

Jamaican chicken curry with roast coconut. For dessert, try the banana toffee pie, if it's available.

Island Taste. S. Church St. ☎ **345/949-4945.** Reservations recommended. Main courses CI$13–CI$27.95 (U.S.$16.25–$34.95). AE, MC, V. Mon–Sat 10:30am–4:30pm; daily 6–10pm. CARIBBEAN/MEDITERRANEAN.

Set beside the harbor front in George Town, this restaurant sits across from the head-quarters of the *Atlantis* submarine. There's an indoor and outdoor bar area and indoor tables, but the most popular seating area is on the wraparound veranda, one floor above street level. The restaurant has one of the largest starter selections on the island. Soups include both white conch chowder and turtle. Appetizers feature fresh oysters, Mexican ceviche, and calamari Vesuvio. At least seven pasta dishes are on the dinner menu, including linguine with small clams. You can also order T-bone steak and chicken parmigiana. However, most of the menu is devoted to seafood dishes. Dolphin (mahimahi) is served in different ways, and perennial favorites include the turtle steak and spiny lobster. This place caters more to large appetites than to picky gourmets.

INEXPENSIVE

Big Daddy's Restaurant and Sports Bar. West Bay Rd. ☎ **345/949-8511.** Reservations recommended at dinner. Main courses CI$10–CI$22.50 ($12.50–$28.15). AE, MC, V. Mon–Fri 8–1am, Sat–Sun 8am–midnight. INTERNATIONAL.

This bustling, big-windowed emporium of food and drink is set on the upper level of a concrete-sided building; look for the liquor store on the ground floor. One part of the restaurant is devoted to a woodsy, nautically decorated bar area, where TV screens broadcast either CNN or the day's big game. Three separate dining areas, more or less isolated from the activity at the bar, serve well-prepared food. Dishes include morning omelets, deli sandwiches, half-pound burgers, garlic shrimp, T-bone steaks, barbecued ribs, fresh catch of the day, country-fried steak, and such pasta dishes as fettuccine Alfredo.

✪ **Corita's Copper Kettle.** In Dolphin Center. ☎ **345/949-7078.** Reservations required. Main courses CI$6.75–CI$12 (U.S.$8.45–$15); lunch CI$6.50–CI$8.50 (U.S.$8.15–$10.65). No credit cards. Mon–Sat 7am–5pm, Sun 7am–3pm. CARIBBEAN/AMERICAN.

This place is generally packed in the mornings, when you can enjoy a full American breakfast or a wide selection of West Indian breakfast specialties, like green bananas served with fried dumplings, fried flying fish, and Corita's Special (ham, melted cheese, egg, and jelly all presented on a fried fritter). For lunch, the menu varies from salads to chicken and beef along with conch, turtle, or lobster prepared as burgers or served up in a hearty stew.

HITTING THE BEACH

One of the finest beaches in the Caribbean, Grand Cayman's ✪ **Seven Mile Beach,** which begins north of George Town, has sparkling white sands rimmed with Australian pines and palms. (Technically, it's called "West Bay Beach," but everybody just says "Seven Mile Beach.") Although it's not actually 7 miles long, it is still a honey, 5½ miles of white, white sands stretching all the way to George Town. It tends to be crowded near the big resorts, but the beach is so big you can always find some room to spread out your towel. There are no peddlers to hassle you, and the beach is beautifully maintained.

Because the beach is on the more tranquil side of Grand Cayman, there is no great tide and the water is generally placid and inviting, ideal for families, even those with small children. A sandy bottom slopes gently to deep water. The water's so clear, you can generally see what's swimming in it. It's great for snorkelers and swimmers of most ages and abilities.

From one end of the beach to the other, there are hotels and condos, many with beach-side bars that you can visit. All sorts of water-sports concessions can be found along this beach, including places that rent snorkel gear, boats, windsurfers, wave runners, paddlecats, and aqua trikes. Parasailing and waterskiing are also available.

Although they pale in comparison to Seven Mile Beach, Grand Cayman also has a number of minor beaches. Visit these if you want to escape the crowds. Beaches on the east and north coasts of Grand Cayman are good, filled with white sand and protected by an offshore barrier reef, so waters are generally tranquil.

One of our favorites is on the north coast, bordering the **Cayman Kai Beach Resort.** This beach is a Caribbean cliché of charm, with palm trees and beautiful sands, along with changing facilities. You can snorkel along the reef to Rum Point. The beach is also ideal as a Sunday-afternoon picnic spot. **Red Sail Sports** at Rum Point offers windsurfers, wave runners, sailboats, waterskiing, and even glass-bottom boat tours to see the stingrays offshore. They also offer scuba diving.

SPORTS & OUTDOOR PURSUITS

What they lack in nightlife, the Caymans make up for in water sports—the fishing, swimming, waterskiing, snorkeling, and especially diving are among the finest in the Caribbean. Coral reefs and coral formations encircle the islands and are filled with lots of marine life—which scuba divers are forbidden to disturb, by the way.

It's easy to dive close to shore, so boats aren't necessary, but there are plenty of boats and scuba facilities available. On certain excursions, we recommend a trip with a qualified divemaster. There are many dive shops for rentals, but they won't rent you scuba gear or supply air unless you have a card from one of the national diving schools, such as NAUI or PADI. Hotels also rent diving equipment to their guests, as well as arrange snorkeling and scuba-diving trips.

Universally regarded as the most up-to-date and best-equipped water-sports facility in the Cayman Islands, **Red Sail Sports** maintains its headquarters at the Hyatt Regency Grand Cayman, West Bay Road (☎ **800/255-6425** or 345/949-8745). Other locations are at the Westin Casuarina (☎ **345/949-8732**) and at Rum Point (☎ **345/947-9203**). They have a wide range of offerings, from deep-sea fishing to sailing, diving, and more. Red Sail can also arrange waterskiing for $75 per half hour (the cost can be divided among several people) and parasailing at $50 per ride.

What follows are the best options for a gamut of outdoor activities, arranged by subject.

CRUISES   **Red Sail Sports** (see above) has a number of inexpensive ways you can go sailing in Cayman waters, including a glass-bottom boat ride costing $25 without snorkeling equipment or $30 with snorkeling equipment. They also offer sunset cruises costing $27.50. A 10am-to-2pm sail to Stingray City, with snorkeling equipment and lunch included in the price of $65 per person, leaves once daily. Children under 12 pay half price.

FISHING   Grouper and snapper are most plentiful for those who bottom-fish along the reef. Deeper waters turn up barracuda and bonito. Sports people from all over the world come to the Caymans for the big ones: tuna, wahoo, and marlin. Most hotels can make arrangements for charter boats; experienced guides are also available. **Red Sail Sports,** in the Hyatt Regency Grand Cayman, West Bay Road (☎ **800/ 255-6425** or 345/947-5966), offers deep-sea-fishing excursions in search of tuna, marlin, and wahoo on a variety of air-conditioned vessels with an experienced crew. Tours depart at 7am and 1pm, last half a day, and cost $600 (a full day costs $800). The fee can be split among four to six people.

Into the Deep: Submarine Dives

So scuba diving's not enough for you? You want to see the real undiscovered depths of the ocean? On Grand Cayman, you can take the *Atlantis* reef dive. It's expensive, but it's a unique way to go underwater—and it might be the highlight of your trip.

One of the island's most popular attractions is the ***Atlantis XI,*** Goring Avenue (☎ **345/949-7700**), a submersible that's 65 feet long, weighs 80 tons, and was built at a cost of $3 million to carry 48 passengers. You can view the reefs and colorful tropical fish through the 26 large viewpoints 2 feet in diameter, as it cruises at a depth of 100 feet through the maze of coral gardens at a speed of 1½ knots; a guide keeps you informed.

There are two types of dives. The premier dive, *Atlantis* Odyssey, features such high-tech extras as divers communicating with submarine passengers by wireless underwater phone and moving about on underwater scooters. This dive, operated both day and night, costs $82. On the *Atlantis* Expedition dive, you'll experience the reef and see the famous Cayman Wall; this dive lasts 55 minutes and costs $72. Children 4 to 12 are charged half price (no children under 4 allowed). *Atlantis XI* dives Monday to Saturday, and reservations are recommended 3 days in advance.

GOLF   The only course on the island, the **Britannia Golf Club,** next to the Hyatt Regency on West Bay Road (☎ **345/949-8020**), was designed by Jack Nicklaus and is unique in that it incorporates three different courses in one: a 9-hole championship layout, an 18-hole executive setup, and a Cayman course. The last was designed for play with the Cayman ball, which goes about half the distance of a regulation ball. Greens fees are a pricey $100 to play 18 holes, or $60 for 9 holes. Car rentals are included, but club rentals cost $20 for 9 holes or $35 for 18 holes.

HIKING   **Mastic Trail** is a restored 200-year-old footpath through a 2-million-year-old woodland area in the heart of the island. The trail lies west of Frank Sound Road, about a 45-minute drive from the heart of George Town, and showcases the reserve's natural attractions, including a native mangrove swamp, traditional agriculture, and an ancient woodland area—home to the largest variety of native plant and animal life found in the Cayman Islands. Guided tours, lasting 2½ to 3 hours and limited to eight participants, are offered Monday to Friday at 8:30am and at 3pm, and again on Saturday at 8:30am. Reservations are required, and the cost is $50 U.S. per person. The hike is not recommended for children under 6, the elderly, or persons with physical disabilities. Wear comfortable, sturdy shoes and carry water and insect repellent. For reservations, call ☎ **345/945-6588** Monday to Friday from 7 to 9am.

✪ **SCUBA DIVING & SNORKELING**   The leading dive operation in the Cayman Islands is **Bob Soto's Diving Ltd.** (☎ **345/949-2022,** or 800/262-7686 to make reservations). Owned by Ron Kipp, the operation includes full-service dive shops at Treasure Island, the SCUBA Centre on North Church Street, and Soto's Coconut in the Coconut Place Shopping Centre. A full-day resort course, designed to teach the fundamentals of scuba to beginners who know how to swim, costs $99: The morning is spent in the pool and the afternoon is a one-tank dive from a boat. All necessary equipment is included. Certified divers can choose from a wide range of one-tank ($50) and two-tank ($75) boat dives daily on the west, north, and south walls, plus shore diving from the SCUBA Centre.

A one-tank night dive costs $50. Nondivers can take advantage of daily snorkel trips ($25), including Stingray City. The staff is helpful and highly professional.

Red Sail Sports (see above) offers beginners' scuba diving as well as excursions for the experienced. A two-tank morning dive includes exploration of two different dive sites at depths ranging from 50 to 100 feet, and costs $85. Beginners can take a daily course that costs $120 per person.

The offshore waters of Grand Cayman are home to one of the most unusual (and ephemeral) underwater attractions in the world, ✪ **Stingray City.** Set in the sun-flooded, 12-foot-deep waters of North Sound, about 2 miles east of the island's north-western tip, the site originated in the mid-1980s when local fishers cleaned their catch and dumped the offal overboard. They quickly noticed scores of stingrays (which usually eat marine crabs) feeding on the debris, a phenomenon that quickly attracted local divers and marine zoologists. Today, between 30 and 50 relatively tame stingrays hover in the waters around the site for daily handouts of squid and ballyhoo from increasing hordes of snorkelers and divers. To capitalize on the phenomenon, about half a dozen entrepreneurs lead expeditions from points along Seven Mile Beach, traveling around the landmass of Conch Point to the feeding grounds. One well-known outfit is **Treasure Island Divers** (☎ 345/949-4456), which charges divers $50 and snorkelers $30. Trips are made on Sunday, Wednesday, and Friday at 1:30pm. (Be warned that stingrays possess deeply penetrating and viciously barbed stingers capable of inflicting painful damage to anyone who mistreats them. Above all, the divers say, never try to grab one by the tail. Despite the dangers, divers and snorkelers seem amazingly adept at feeding, petting, and stroking the velvet surfaces of these batlike creatures while avoiding unpleasant incidents.)

You'll find plenty of concessions offering snorkel gear for rent along Seven Mile Beach. The snorkeling is great in the clear, warm waters here. Other popular sites are Parrot's Reef and Smith's Cove south of George Town. Lush reefs abound with parrot fish, coral, sea fans, and sponges. Also great for snorkelers is Turtle Farm Reef, a short swim from shore, offering a miniwall rising from a sandy bottom.

EXPLORING THE ISLAND

The capital, **George Town,** can easily be explored in an afternoon; stop by for its restaurants and shops (and banks!)—not sights. The town does offer a clock monument to King George V and the oldest government building in use in the Caymans today, the post office on Edward Street. Stamps sold here are avidly sought by collectors.

The island's premier museum, the **Cayman Islands National Museum,** Harbor Drive, in George Town (☎ 345/949-8368), is in a much-restored clapboard-sided antique building directly on the water. (The veranda-fronted building served until recently as the island's courthouse.) The formal exhibits include a collection of Caymanian artifacts collected by Ira Thompson beginning in the 1930s. Today the museum incorporates a gift shop, theater, cafe, and more than 2,000 items portraying the natural, social, and cultural history of the Caymans. Admission is CI$4 ($5) for adults and CI$2 ($2.50) for children 7 to 12 and seniors, free for children 6 and under. It's open Monday to Friday from 9am to 5pm and on Saturday from 10am to 2pm (last admission is half an hour prior to closing).

Elsewhere on the island, you might **go to Hell!** That's at the north end of West Bay Beach, a jagged piece of rock named Hell by a former commissioner. There the post-mistress will stamp "Hell, Grand Cayman" on your postcard to send back to the States.

The ✪ **Cayman Turtle Farm,** Northwest Point (☎ 345/949-3893), is the only green sea-turtle farm of its kind in the world. Once the islands had a multitude of turtles in the surrounding waters (which is why Columbus called the islands "Las Tortugas"), but today these creatures are sadly few in number (practically extinct elsewhere in the Caribbean), and the green sea turtle has been designated an endangered species (you cannot bring turtle products into the United States). The turtle farm has a twofold purpose: to provide the local market with edible turtle meat and to replenish the waters with hatchling and yearling turtles. Visitors today can look at 100 circular concrete tanks in which these sea creatures can be observed in every stage of development; the hope is that one day their population in the sea will regain its former status. Turtles here range in size from 6 ounces to 600 pounds. At a snack bar and restaurant, you can sample turtle dishes. The turtle farm is open daily from 8:30am to 5pm. Admission is $6 for adults, $3 for children 6 to 12, free for children 5 and under.

At **Batabano,** on the North Sound, fishers tie up with their catch, much to the delight of photographers. You can buy lobster (in season), fresh fish, even conch. A large barrier reef protects the sound, which is surrounded on three sides by the island and is a mecca for diving and sports fishing.

If you're driving, you might want to go along **South Sound Road,** which is lined with pines and, in places, old wooden Caymanian houses. After leaving the houses behind, you'll find good spots for a picnic.

On the road again, you reach **Bodden Town,** once the largest settlement on the island. At Gun Square, two cannons commanded the channel through the reef. They are now stuck muzzle-first into the ground.

On the way to the **East End,** just before Old Isaac Village, you'll see the onshore sprays of water shooting up like geysers. These are called blowholes, and they sound like the roar of a lion.

Later, you'll spot the fluke of an anchor sticking up from the ocean floor. As the story goes, this is a relic of the famous "Wreck of the Ten Sails" in 1788. A more modern wreck can also be seen—the *Ridgefield,* a 7,500-ton Liberty ship from New England, which struck the reef in 1943.

Old Man Bay is reached by a road that opened in 1983. From here you can travel along the north shore of the island to **Rum Point,** which has a good beach and is a fine place to end your island tour. Rum Point got its name from barrels of rum that once washed ashore here after a shipwreck. Today, it is dreamy and quaint, surrounded by towering causarina trees blowing in the trade winds. Most of these trees have hammocks hanging from their trunks, inviting you to enjoy the leisurely life. With its cays, reefs, mangroves, and shallows, Rum Point is a refuge that extends west and south for 7 miles. It divides the two "arms" of Grand Cayman. The sound's many spits of land and its plentiful lagoons are ideal for snorkeling, swimming, wading, and birding. It you get hungry, drop in to the Wreck Bar for a juicy hamburger. After visiting Rum Point, you can head back toward **Old Man Village,** where you can go south along a cross-island road through savannah country that will eventually lead you west to George Town.

On 60 acres of rugged wooded land off Frank Sound Road, North Side, the **Queen Elizabeth II Botanic Park** (☎ **345/947-9462**) offers visitors a 1-hour walk through wetland, swamp, dry thicket, mahogany trees, orchids, and bromeliads. The trail is eight-tenths of a mile long. You'll likely see chickatees, the freshwater turtles found only on the Caymans and in Cuba. Occasionally you'll spot the rare Grand Cayman parrot, or perhaps the anole lizard, with its cobalt-blue throat pouch. Even rarer is the endangered blue iguana. There are six rest stations with visitor information along the trail. The park is open daily from 7:30am to 5:30pm. Admission is CI$6 ($7.50) for adults, CI$3 ($3.75) for children, free for children 5 and under. There's a visitor center with changing exhibitions, plus a canteen for food and refreshments. It's set in a botanic park adjacent to the woodland trail and includes a heritage garden with a re-creation of a traditional Cayman home, garden, and farm; a floral garden with 1½ acres of flowering plants; and a 2-acre lake with three islands, home to many native birds.

Pedro St. James National Historic Site, Savannah (☎ 345/947-3329), is a restored great house dating from 1780 when only 400 people lived on the island. It outlasted all the hurricanes until 1970 but was destroyed by fire that year. Now it's been rebuilt and is the centerpiece of a new heritage park with a visitor center and an audio-visual theater with a laser light show. Because of its size, the great house was called "the Castle" by generations of Caymanians. Its primary historic importance dates back to December 5, 1831, when residents met here to elect Cayman's first legislative assembly. Therefore, Pedro St. James is the cradle of the island's democracy. The great house sits atop a limestone bluff with a panoramic view of the sea. Guests enter via a $1.5-million visitors center with a landscaped courtyard, a gift shop, and a cafe. Self-guided tours are possible. You can explore the house's wide verandas, rough-hewn timber beams, gabled framework, mahogany floors and staircases, and wide-beam wooden ceilings. Guides in 18th-century costumes are on hand to answer questions. Admission is $8 for adults and $4 for children (free for those 5 and under). Hours are daily from 9am to 5pm.

SHOPPING

The duty-free shopping in George Town encompasses silver, china, crystal, Irish linen, British woolen goods, and such local crafts as black-coral jewelry. However, we've found the prices on many items to be similar to U.S. prices. (Remember that you can't bring turtle products back to the U.S.) Below is the best shopping George Town has to offer.

Artifacts Ltd, Harbour Drive (across from the cruise-ship dock), George Town (☎ 345/949-2442), is the premier outlet for some of the rare stamps issued by the Caymanian government. Stamps range in price from 17¢ to $900, and the inventory includes the rare War Tax Stamp issued during World War II. Other items for sale include antique Dutch and Spanish coins unearthed from underwater shipwrecks, enameled boxes, and antique prints and maps.

Black Coral and . . ., Fort Street, George Town (☎ 345/949-0123), sells stunning black-coral creations of an internationally acclaimed sculptor, Bernard K. Passman. Connoisseurs of unusual fine jewelry and unique objets d'art are drawn here. Passman produced the Cayman Islands' wedding gift to Prince Charles and Lady Diana: a 97-piece cutlery set of sterling silver with black-coral handles. Another commission for the Cayman Islands was the creation of a black-coral horse and corgi dogs for Queen Elizabeth and Prince Philip. The gallery on Fort Street is a sightseeing attraction. Signed, limited-edition pieces are excellent investments.

Diamonds in Paradise, Harbour Drive (in front of the cruise-ship landing), George Town (☎ 345/949-2457), offers watches, black- and pink-coral jewelry, 14- and 18-karat jewelry, and, of course, diamonds, all with prices quoted in U.S. dollars. The shop is divided into two sections, one selling fine jewelry and the other hawking souvenirs. The **Jewelry Centre,** Cardinal Ave., George Town (☎ 345/949-0070), is a virtual department store of jewelry and has the largest selection on the island.

Kennedy Gallery, West Shore Centre, George Town (☎ 345/949-8077), in a shopping center on Seven Mile Beach, specializes in watercolors by local artists. Prices range from $15 to as high as $7,000. **Pure Art,** South Church Street (☎ 345/949-9133), is good for some local souvenirs. This is your best bet for art and crafts, including locally produced Christmas ornaments, art prints and note cards, carvings, ceramics, thatch work, and baskets.

Blackbeard's Liquors has several locations, the most convenient of which is at the Strand, opposite Foster's Food Fair (☎ 345/949-8763). These liquors are bottled in the Cayman Islands. Try various rum flavors such as banana, coconut, and mango, all based on original recipes. The **Tortgua Rum Company,** Selkirk Plaza (☎ 345/945-7655), not only sells rum but is also famous locally for its chocolate rum cake. Of course, most people come here for a bottle of its premium gold, 151-proof superb light rum, all at duty-free prices, costing $8.50 per liter.

Ayurvedic Concepts, Elizabethan Square (☎ 345/949-1769), is one of the most unusual stores in the Cayman Islands. It's been known for its natural herbal remedies which it has sold since 1930. Its products include MindCare, said to calm a "racing mind" and help enhance memory.

For tropical resort wear at reasonable prices, head for **Island Casuals,** Galleria Plaza, West Bay Road (☎ 345/949-8094). Casuals for both men and women, as well as children, are sold here.

Kayman Kids, Galleria Plaza on West Bay Road (☎ 345/945-2356), sells a vast array of items, mainly children's clothing, plus a large selection of bathing suits for boys and girls. They also sell dollhouses designed to look like a typical Caymanian cottage. A lot of specialty gifts are also hawked.

Kirk Freeport Plaza, Cardinal Avenue and Panton Street (☎ 345/949-7477), is the largest store of its kind on the Caymans, with a treasure trove of gold jewelry, watches, china, crystal, perfumes, and cosmetics. The store holds a Cartier franchise, with items priced 15% to 35% below suggested retail prices Stateside. Also stocked are crystal and porcelain from Wedgwood, Waterford, Lladró, and Baccarat, priced 30% to 50% less than recommended retail prices Stateside.

Tropical Trader Market & Bazaar, Edward Street (☎ 345/949-6538), is a good bet on an island of overpriced art galleries. You can pick up some typical Caymanian scenes here, not only paintings, but drawings and prints as well, for $15 and up. The outlet is a true bazaar, selling gold, silver, and black coral jewelry (the latter among the most inexpensive on the island). You can also purchase watches by Anne Klein, Casio, and Swiss Army, plus Tommy Bahama men's clothing. Bags and luggage by Kipling and Tumi are also sold.

An offbeat shopping adventure is found at **Caribbean Charlie's,** Hut Village, 4 miles from Rum Point (☎ 345/947-9452), on the north side of the island. This is the workshop and home of the remarkable Charlie Ebanks, who is known on the island for his brightly painted wooden waurie boards (a game that was believed to have been imported to the island by slaves). Everybody from Blackbeard to Ernest Hemingway has supposedly enjoyed playing this game. Charlie also makes birdhouses in the shape of the traditional Cayman cottages.

GRAND CAYMAN AFTER DARK

The **Lone Star Bar & Grill,** West Bay Road (☎ 345/945-5175), is a transplanted corner of the Texas Panhandle. You can enjoy juicy burgers in the dining room or head immediately for the bar in back. Here, beneath murals of Lone Star beauties, you can sip lime and strawberry margaritas and watch several sports events simultaneously on 15 different TV screens. Monday and Thursday are fajita nights, all-you-can-eat affairs at CI$12 (U.S.$15), and Tuesday is all-you-can-eat lobster at CI$34.95 (U.S.$43.70). There's also a new volleyball court.

The Planet (☎ 345/949-7169) lies about a block inland from West Bay Road, adjacent to the island's only cinema. This place has the island's largest dance floor, with the biggest indoor stage and four bars dispensing reasonably priced drinks along with bar food. The mix of locals and tourists form a wide age range—from 18 to 50. The club is closed Sunday and Monday and otherwise devoted to theme nights, such as reggae music on Friday and Saturday. Expect a $5 cover.

Coconuts Comedy Club, Cayman Falls Plaza, across from the Westin (☎ **345/949-6887**), is the chief comedy club in the island archipelago. There's a cover of $12; doors open Wednesday to Saturday at 9pm. Comedic talents are imported from all over the world. Seating is on a first-come, first-served basis. **Sharkey's,** Fall Shopping Center, Seven Mile Beach (☎ **345/947-5366**), is like "Back to the Future," filled with rock-and-roll paraphernalia from the 1950s. Music here ranges from karaoke to the big hits of the 1970s.

3 Cayman Brac

The "middle" island of the Caymans was given the name Brac (Gaelic for bluff) by 17th-century Scottish fishers who settled here. The bluff for which the 12-mile-long island was named is a towering limestone plateau rising to 140 feet above the sea, covering the eastern half of Cayman Brac. Caymanians refer to the island simply as Brac, and its 1,400 inhabitants, a hospitable bunch of people, are called Brackers. Perhaps their laid-back lifestyle speaks to the laissez-faire attitudes of their predecessors: In the early–18th century the Caymans were occupied by pirates, and Edward Teach, the infamous Blackbeard, is supposed to have spent quite a bit of time around Cayman Brac. The island is about 89 miles east of Grand Cayman.

There are more than 170 caves honeycombing the limestone heights of the island. Some of the caves are at the bluff's foot, whereas others can be reached only by climbing over jagged limestone rock. One of the biggest is Great Cave, which has a number of chambers. Harmless fruit bats cling to the roofs of the caverns.

On the south side of the bluff you won't see many people, and the only sounds are the sea crashing against the lava-like shore. The island's herons and wild green parrots are seen here. Most of the Brackers live on the north side, many in traditional wooden seaside cottages, some built by the island's pioneers. The islanders must all have green thumbs, as attested to by the variety of flowers, shrubs, and fruit trees in many of the yards. On Cayman Brac you'll see poinciana trees, bougainvillea, Cayman orchids, croton, hibiscus, aloe, sea grapes, cactus, and coconut and cabbage palms. The gardeners grow cassava, pumpkins, breadfruit, yams, and sweet potatoes.

There are no actual towns, only settlements, such as Stake Bay (the "capital"), Spot Bay, the Creek, Tibbitt's Turn, the Bight, and West End, where the airport is located.

GETTING THERE

Flights from Grand Cayman to Cayman Brac are operated by **Cayman Airways** (☎ **800/422-9626** in the U.S., or 345/949-2311). The airline uses relatively large 737 jets carrying 122 passengers each. There is an evening flight here, plus a morning return. The round-trip cost is $104 per person.

WHERE TO STAY

Brac Caribbean Beach Village. Stake Bay (P.O. Box 4), Cayman Brac, B.W.I. ☎ **800/791-7911** or 345/948-2265. Fax 345/948-1111. 16 units. A/C TV. Year-round $185 apt for 2; $245 apt for 4; $1,100 apt for 2 adults for 7 nights; $1,600 apt for 4 adults for 7 nights. Scuba packages from $325 for 6 dives. AE, MC, V.

The largest condo project on the island offers 16 two-bedroom/two-bathroom or two-bedroom/three-bathroom condos on a white sandy beach, along with a pool and scuba-diving program. Accommodations come with a full-size refrigerator with ice maker, microwave, and coffeemaker, and 12 of them open onto a private balcony. A variety of items, including breakfast food, is stocked before your arrival. The master bedroom is furnished with a queen-size bed, the guest bedrooms with twin beds. Each

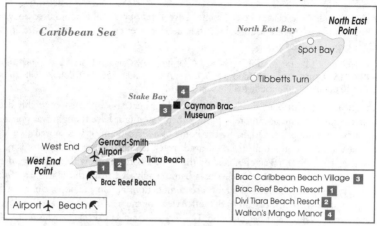

bedroom has a good, comfortable mattress. Bathrooms are medium in size. Maid service costs an extra $35 per day. The units are rather simply furnished in a Caribbean tropical motif, with rattan and chintz. The hotel offers some of the best dining on the island (see below).

Brac Reef Beach Resort. P.O. Box 56, Cayman Brac, B.W.I. ☎ **800/327-3835** in the U.S. and Canada, or 345/948-1323. 40 units. A/C TV. Winter $478–$703 per person double. Off-season $451–$676 per person double. Rates are for 3 nights and include MAP (breakfast and dinner) and 2 days of diving. Additional packages available. AE, DC, DISC, MC, V.

On a sandy plot of land on the south shore 2 miles east of the airport, near some of the best snorkeling in the region, this resort contains motel-style units comfortably furnished with carpeting, ceiling fans, and modern bathrooms. Beds are either king or double, each with a firm mattress. Once the location was little more than a maze of sea grapes, a few of whose venerable trunks still rise amid the picnic tables, hammocks, and boardwalks. On the premises are the rusted remains of a Russian lighthouse tower that was retrieved several years ago from a Cuban-made trawler.

    Dining: Lunches are informal affairs, while dinners are most often served buffet style under the stars. The food is not quite as good as that at the Divi Tiara (see below).

    Amenities: Pool, Jacuzzi, Reef Divers (a full-service operation providing instruction for both beginning and advanced divers, and the use of all rental gear, including masks, snorkels, fins, regulators, and weight belts), laundry, baby-sitting.

Divi Tiara Beach Resort. P.O. Box 238, Cayman Brac, B.W.I. ☎ **800/367-3484** in the U.S. and Canada, or 345/948-1553. Fax 345/948-1360. 71 units. A/C TV TEL. Winter $125–$200 double; $245–$255 suite. Off-season $95–$140 double; $180 suite. MAP (breakfast and dinner) $41 per person extra. Children under 12 stay free in parents' room. AE, MC, V.

Part of the Divi Divi hotel chain, the Tiara, about 2 miles east of the airport, attracts divers and honeymooners to its beachfront. Many newcomers respond at once to the landscaping, which incorporates croton, bougainvillea, and palms. All the rather basic accommodations are housed in motel-like outbuildings; 13 of the units are time-shares, each with an ocean view, Jacuzzi, and king-size bed with a firm mattress. Bathrooms, with combination tubs and showers, are well maintained.

    Dining/Diversions: At the bar, guests gaze out to sea while sipping their drinks before heading to the Poseidon dining room to enjoy Caribbean and American cuisine. There's entertainment at the hotel twice a week.

Amenities: An excellent Peter Hughes Dive Tiara operation, a pool raised above a white-sand beach where boardwalks run beneath groves of palms, tennis court lit for night play, laundry.

✪ **Walton's Mango Manor.** Stake Bay (P.O. Box 56), Cayman Brac. ☎ and fax **345/ 948-0518.** E-mail: waltons@condy.ky. 5 units. A/C. Winter $80–$90 double. Off-season $70–$80 double. Rates include full breakfast. AE, MC, V.

Unique on Cayman Brac, this is a personalized, intimate B&B that's more richly decorated, more elegant, and more appealing than you might have thought was possible in such a remote place. Originally the home of a sea captain, it was moved to a less exposed location and rebuilt from salvaged materials shortly after the disastrous hurricane of 1932. Set on 3 acres of land on the island's north shore, within a lush garden, it contains such intriguing touches as a banister salvaged from the mast of a 19th-century schooner. The most desirable accommodations are on the upper floor, partly because of their narrow balconies that offer views of the sea. Your hosts are Brooklyn-born Lynne Walton and her husband, George, a former USAF major who retired to his native Cayman Brac.

WHERE TO DINE

Captain's Table. Brac Caribbean Beach Village, Stake Bay. ☎ **345/948-1418.** Reservations recommended. Main courses $11.25–$22.50; lunch from $12. AE, MC, V. Mon–Sat 11:30am–3pm and 6–9:30pm; Sun noon–3pm. AMERICAN.

The decor is Caribbean cliché, vaguely nautical with oars over and around the bar and pieces of boats forming the restaurant's entryway. In the same building as a scuba shop and the hotel's reception desk, the restaurant offers both indoor and air-conditioned seating, along with outside dining by the pool. Begin with a captain's cocktail of shrimp and lobster or perhaps conch fritter, then follow with one of the soups such as black bean. Main dishes include everything from the catch of the day, often served pan-fried, to barbecue ribs. At lunch, you can order burgers and sandwiches.

FUN ON & OFF THE BEACH

The biggest lure to Cayman Brac is the variety of **water sports**—swimming, fishing, snorkeling, and some of the world's best diving to explore coral reefs. There are undersea walls on both the north and south sides of the island, with stunning specimens lining their sides. The big attraction for divers is the M.V. *Tibbetts,* a 330-foot-long Russian frigate resting in 100 feet of water, a relic of the Cold War sunk in September of 1996. It is complete with guns both fore and aft. Hatches into the ship have been barred off to ensure diver safety. Marine life is becoming more pronounced on this relic which now rests in a watery grave far, far from its home. The best dive center is **Peter Hughes Dive Tiara** at the Divi Tiara Beach Resort (☎ **800/367-3484** or 345/948-1553).

History buffs might check out the **Cayman Brac Museum,** in the former Government Administration Building, Stake Bay (☎ **345/948-2622**), which has an interesting collection of Caymanian antiques, including pieces rescued from shipwrecks and items from the 18th century. Hours are Monday to Friday from 9am to noon and 1 to 4pm, Saturday from 9am to noon, and Sunday from 1 to 4pm. Admission is free.

4 Little Cayman

The smallest of the Cayman Islands, cigar-shaped Little Cayman has only about 40 permanent inhabitants. Little Cayman is 10 miles long and about a mile across at its widest point. It lies about 75 miles northeast of Grand Cayman and some 5 miles from Cayman Brac. The entire island is coral and sand.

The islands of the Caymans are mountaintops of the long-submerged Sierra Maestra Range, which runs north and into Cuba. Coral formed layers over the underwater peaks, eventually creating the islands. Beneath Little Cayman's Bloody Bay is one of the mountain's walls—a stunning sight for snorkelers and scuba divers.

The island seems to have come into its own now that fishing and diving have taken center stage; this is a near-perfect place for such pursuits. The waters around the little island were hailed by the late Jacques Cousteau as one of the three finest diving spots in the world. The flats on Little Cayman are said to offer the best bonefishing in the world, and a brackish inland pool can be fished for tarpon. Even if you don't dive or fish, you can row 200 yards off Little Cayman to isolated and uninhabited Owen Island, where you can swim at the sandy beach and picnic by a blue lagoon.

There may still be pirate treasure buried on the island, but it's in the dense interior of what is now the largest bird sanctuary in the Caribbean. In addition to having the largest population of rock iguanas in the entire Caribbean, which you will easily see, Little Cayman is also home to one of the oldest species of reptiles in the New World—the tree-climbing *Anulis maynardi* (which is known by no other name). This rare lizard is difficult to spot, however, because the females are green, the males brown, and, as such, they blend into local vegetation.

Blossom Village, the island's "capital," is on the southwest coast.

GETTING THERE

Most visitors fly from Grand Cayman to Little Cayman. **Cayman Airways** (☎ **800/ 323-3345** in the U.S., or 345/949-5252 on Grand Cayman) is the reservations agent for Island Air, a charter company that charges $154 (U.S.) round-trip.

WHERE TO STAY

✪ **Little Cayman Beach Resort.** Blossom Village, Little Cayman, Cayman Islands, B.W.I. ☎ **800/327-3835** in the U.S. and Canada, or 345/948-1033. Fax 345/948-1040. www. braclittle.com. E-mail: bestdiving@aol.com. 40 units. A/C TV. Winter $565–$696 per person double (diver), $415–$546 per person double (nondiver). Off-season $510–$641 per person double (diver), $360–$491 per person double (nondiver). Rates are for 3 nights and include MAP (breakfast and dinner). Longer packages are available. AE, MC, V.

Lying on the south coast, this resort is close to many of the island's diving and sporting attractions, including bonefishing in the South Hole Sound Lagoon. It's popular with fisherfolk, divers, bird watchers, and adventurous types. The hotel, owned by the Tibbetts family, lies only three-quarters of a mile from the Edward Bodden Airport (really a grass airstrip), and it has a white-sand beach fringing a shallow, reef-protected bay. No-smoking units are available, and the rooms have ceiling fans. They are divided into two pastel coral, two-story buildings with gingerbread trim. The most desirable units are the four luxurious oceanfront rooms, which go fast, since, in spite of their added comfort, they're booked at the same rate as the less preferred rooms. Ceiling fans and tropical colors make for an inviting, airy atmosphere, and units have one king or two double beds, each with a good mattress, plus a combination bath (tub and shower). The hotel has a tennis court, pool overlooking the sea, Jacuzzi, and complete watersports facilities, including a dive shop. Its bar and restaurant are among the most popular on the island.

✪ **Pirates Point Resort, Ltd.** Little Cayman, Cayman Islands, B.W.I. ☎ **345/948-1010.** Fax 345/948-1011. 10 units, 2 without A/C. Winter $230 per person double (diver), $170 per person double (nondiver). Off-season $210 per person double (diver), $150 per person double (nondiver). Rates are all-inclusive (nondiver rates do not include bar tab); triple rates are slightly lower. MC, V. Children 5 and under not accepted.

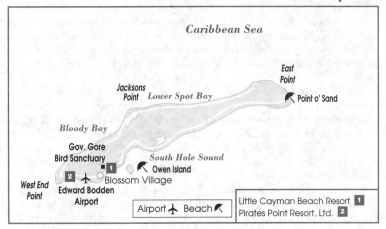

For water activities or just relaxing, this resort near West End Point offers a family environment with gourmet cuisine. The owner and manager, Gladys Howard, a graduate of Cordon Bleu in Paris, who has studied with such stars as Julia Child and the late James Beard, has written several cookbooks. In her menus, she uses fresh fruits and vegetables grown locally, as well as local seafood.

The place has remodeled rooms, and a non–air-conditioned family cottage of two large rooms, each suitable for three or four people. In addition, it has four recently built seaside cottages, with balconies overlooking Preston Bay. The bathrooms are well maintained, with a set of fluffy towels. The resort's packages include room, three excellent meals per day with appropriate wines and all alcoholic beverages, and two-tank boat dives daily featuring tours of the Bloody Bay Wall, the Cayman trench, and Jackson Reef. Nondiving activities include snorkeling, bird watching, and exploring. Recent facilities added include a swimming pool and Jacuzzi. Bonefishing, tarpon fishing, and an Owen Island picnic are available for an additional charge. Prince Charles himself, sailing by on his yacht, selected Owen Island for a picnic.

WHERE TO DINE

Birds of Paradise. At Little Cayman Resort. ☎ **345/948-1033.** Reservations recommended for dinner. Dinner CI$25 (U.S.$31.25); lunch CI$15 (U.S.$18.75); breakfast CI$12 (U.S.$15). AE, MC, V. Daily 7:30–8:30am, 12:30–1:30pm, and 6:30–7:30pm. AMERICAN/CONTINENTAL.

The best buffet dinners on the island—the kind your parents might have enjoyed back in the golden 1950s or 1960s—are served at this little spot that caters primarily to hotel guests, but welcomes outsiders. The best night to show up is Tuesday, which features the island's most generous barbecue spread—all the ribs, fish, and Jamaican-inspired jerk chicken you'd want. On other nights, try the prime rib, fresh fish Caribbean style (your best bet), or chicken either Russian style (Kiev) or French style (cordon bleu). There's a freshly made salad bar, and homemade desserts are yummy, especially the Key lime pie. At night, opt for an outdoor table under the stars.

The Hungry Iguana. Paradise Resort. ☎ **345/948-0007.** Reservations recommended. Dinner CI$14.95–CI$23.95 (U.S.$18.70–$29.95); lunch CI$7.25–CI$9.95. (U.S.$9.05–$12.45). AE, MC, V. Daily noon–9:30pm. (Bar, Mon–Fri noon–1am, Sat–Sun noon–midnight.) AMERICAN/CARIBBEAN.

At the beach, you'll spot this place immediately with its mammoth iguana mural. The island's tastiest dishes are served here, a winning combination of standard American fare along with some zesty flavors from the islands south of here. It's the most macho place on the island, especially the sports bar with its satellite TV in the corner, a sort of TGI Friday's atmosphere. Lunch is the usual burgers and fries along with some well-stuffed sandwiches. We always prefer the grilled chicken salad. Dinner gets a little more elaborate—there's usually a special meat dish of the day, depending on the market (supplies are shipped in once a week by barge). The chef always seems willing to prepare a steak as you like it. Try one of the seafood platters. Marinated shrimp with rémoulade is a tasty choice as well.

SPORTS & OUTDOOR PURSUITS

The **Governor Gore Bird Sanctuary** is home to some 5,000 pairs of red-footed boobies. As far as it is known, this is the largest colony of such birds in the western hemisphere. The sanctuary, lying near the small airport, is also home to dramatic colonies of snowy egrets and black frigates. Many bird watchers from the States fly into Little Cayman just to see these bird colonies.

The best **fishing** is at Bloody Bay, lying off the island's north coast. It is especially noted for its bonefishing and tarpon catches. For fishing, contact **Sam McCoy's Diving and Fishing Lodge** (☎ **800/626-0496**).

The Bloody Bay Wall is also the best dive site on island, lying just 20 minutes off shore and reached by boat. The drop here begins at only 20 feet but plunges to more than 1,200 feet. This is one of the great dive spots in the Caymans. For more information about how to enjoy it, call **Paradise Divers** at ☎ **800/450-2084**, or 345/948-0004. You can also make arrangements at Sam McCoy's as well.

10 Curaçao

Just 35 miles north of the coast of Venezuela, Curaçao, the "C" of the Dutch ABC islands of the Caribbean, is the most populous of the Netherlands Antilles. Visitors are attracted to its distinctive culture, warm people, duty-free shopping, lively casinos, and water sports. Fleets of tankers head out from its harbor to bring refined oil to all parts of the world.

A self-governing part of the Netherlands, Curaçao was spotted not by Columbus, but by two of his lieutenants, Alonso de Ojeda and Amerigo Vespucci, in 1499. The Spaniards exterminated all but 75 members of a branch of the peaceful Arawaks. However, they in turn were ousted by the Dutch in 1634, who also had to fight off French and English invasions.

The Dutch made the island a tropical Holland in miniature. Pieter Stuyvesant, stomping on his peg leg, ruled Curaçao in 1644. The island was turned into a Dutch Gibraltar, bristling with forts. Thick ramparts guarded the harbor's narrow entrance; the hilltop forts (many now converted into restaurants) protected the coastal approaches.

In the 20th century, it remained sleepy until 1915, when the Royal Dutch/Shell Company built one of the world's largest oil refineries to process crude from Venezuela. Workers from some 50 countries poured onto the island, turning Curaçao into a polyglot, cosmopolitan community.

The largest of the Netherlands Antilles, Curaçao is 37 miles long and 7 miles across at its widest point. Because of all that early Dutch building, Curaçao is the most important island architecturally in the entire West Indies, with more European flavor than anywhere else. After leaving the capital, **Willemstad,** you plunge into a strange, desertlike countryside that evokes the American Southwest. The relatively arid landscape is studded with three-pronged cactus, spiny-leafed aloe, and divi-divi trees, with their windblown foliage. Classic Dutch-style windmills are scattered in and around Willemstad and in parts of the countryside.

Curaçao, together with Bonaire, St. Eustatius, St. Maarten, and Saba, is in the Kingdom of the Netherlands as part of the Netherlands Antilles. Curaçao has its own governmental authority, relying on the Netherlands only for defense and foreign affairs. Its population of 171,000 represents more than 50 nationalities.

Curaçao

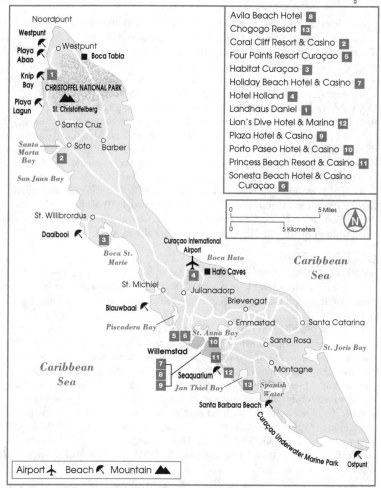

Avila Beach Hotel **8**
Chogogo Resort **13**
Coral Cliff Resort & Casino **2**
Four Points Resort Curaçao **5**
Habitat Curaçao **3**
Holiday Beach Hotel & Casino **7**
Hotel Holland **4**
Landhaus Daniel **1**
Lion's Dive Hotel & Marina **12**
Plaza Hotel & Casino **9**
Porto Paseo Hotel & Casino **10**
Princess Beach Resort & Casino **11**
Sonesta Beach Hotel & Casino Curaçao **6**

Airport ✈ Beach ⚓ Mountain ▲▲

1 Essentials

VISITOR INFORMATION
In the United States, contact the **Curaçao Tourist Board** at 475 Park Ave. S., Suite 2000, New York, NY 10016 (☎ **800/270-3350** or 212/683-7660); or 330 Biscayne Blvd., Suite 330, Miami, FL 33132 (☎ **305/374-5811**). You can also point your Web browser to **www.curacao-tourism.com**.

Once you're on the island, go to the **Curaçao Tourist Board,** Pietermaai (☎ **599/9-616000**).

GETTING THERE
The air routes to **Curaçao International Airport,** Plaza Margareth Abraham (☎ **599/9-682288**), are still firmly linked to those leading to nearby Aruba. In recent years, however, some airlines have initiated direct or nonstop routings into Curaçao from such international hubs as Miami.

American Airlines (☎ 800/433-7300; www.aa.com) offers a daily nonstop flight to Curaçao from its hub in Miami; it departs late enough in the day to permit easy connections from cities all over the Northeast. American also offers flights to Curaçao's neighbor, Aruba, from New York, Miami, and San Juan, Puerto Rico. Once on Aruba, many travelers transfer on to Curaçao on any of ALM's many shuttle flights. American Airlines also offers discounted hotel/airfare packages.

Air Aruba (☎ 800/88-ARUBA; www.interknowledge.com/air-aruba) flies daily from Newark, New Jersey, to Aruba, with two flights on Saturday and Sunday. The same airline also offers daily nonstop flights to Aruba from Miami and Tampa, and direct service from Baltimore. On Aruba, regardless of their points of origin, Curaçao-bound passengers either remain on the same plane for its continuation on to Curaçao, or transfer to another aircraft after a brief delay.

ALM (☎ 800/327-7230; www.alm-airlines.com) is Curaçao's national carrier. It flies 14 times a week from Miami to Curaçao. Although 10 of these flights stop on Aruba, Bonaire, or Haiti, the others are nonstop. ALM also flies two times a week to Curaçao from Atlanta, usually with a stop on Bonaire en route.

GETTING AROUND

BY RENTAL CAR Since all points of interest on Curaçao are easily accessible via paved roads, you may want to rent a car. U.S., British, and Canadian visitors can use their own licenses, if valid. *Note: Traffic moves on the right.* International road signs are observed.

Avis (☎ 800/331-2112) and **Budget** (☎ 800/472-3325) offer some of the lowest rates. Budget usually offers the best deal if it has compact cars with manual transmission in stock; rates begin at $228 per week with unlimited mileage. At Avis, the lowest rate is around $256 a week with unlimited mileage. The cheapest car at **Hertz** (☎ 800/654-3001 in the U.S., or 599/9-8681182) is $228 per week, an especially good value as it includes air-conditioning. Rentals are often cheaper if you reserve from North America at least a week before your departure.

Local car-rental firms include **Rent a Yellow,** Santa Rosa 9 (☎ 599/9-7673777), whose cars are painted like a yellow cab. The lowest rates are for vehicles without air-conditioning, costing from $30 daily, rising to $33.50 with air-conditioning. Tariffs include tax and insurance.

BY TAXI Since taxis don't have meters, ask your driver to quote a rate before you get in. Drivers are supposed to carry an official tariff sheet, which they'll produce upon request. Charges go up by 25% after 11pm. Generally, there's no need to tip, unless a driver helps you with your luggage. The charge from the airport to Willemstad is about $15, and the cost can be split among four passengers. If a piece of luggage is so big that the trunk lid won't close, you'll be assessed a surcharge of $1.

In town, the best place to get a taxi is on the Otrabanda side of the floating bridge. To summon a cab, call ☎ 599/9-8690747. Cabbies will usually give you a tour of the island for around $20 per hour for up to four passengers.

BY BUS Some hotels operate a free shuttle that takes you from the suburbs to the shopping district of Willemstad. A fleet of DAF yellow buses operates from Wilhelmina Plein, near the shopping center, to most parts of Curaçao. Some limousines function as "C" buses. If you see one listing your destination, you can hail it at any of the designated bus stops.

Fast Facts: Curaçao

Banking Hours Bank hours are Monday to Friday from 8:30am to noon and 1:30 to 4:30pm. However, the Banco Popular and the Bank of America remain open during the lunch hour, doing business Monday to Friday from 9am to 3pm.

Currency While Canadian and U.S. dollars are accepted for purchases on the island, the official currency is the Netherlands Antillean florin (NAf), also called a guilder, which is divided into 100 NA (Netherlands Antillean) cents. The exchange rate is $1 U.S. to 1.77 NAf (1 NAf = 56¢ U.S.). Shops, hotels, and restaurants usually accept most major U.S. and Canadian credit and charge cards.

Documents To enter Curaçao, U.S. or Canadian citizens need proof of citizenship, such as a birth certificate or a passport, along with a return or continuing airline ticket out of the country and photo ID. British subjects need a valid passport.

Electricity The electricity is 110 to 130 volts AC (50 cycles), the same as in North America, although many hotels will have transformers if your appliances happen to be European.

Hospital The **St. Elisabeth Hospital,** Breedestraat 193 (☎ **599/9-4624900**), near Otrabanda in Willemstad, is one of the most up-to-date facilities in the Caribbean.

Language Dutch, Spanish, and English are spoken on Curaçao, along with Papiamento, a patois that combines the three major tongues with Amerindian and African dialects.

Police The police emergency number is ☎ **114.**

Safety While Curaçao is not plagued with crime, it's wise to safeguard your valuables.

Taxes Curaçao levies a room tax of 7% on accommodations, and most hotels add 12% for room service. There's a departure tax of $12.50 for international flights, or $5.65 for flights to other islands in the Netherlands Antilles.

Telephone To call Curaçao from the United States, dial **011** (the international access code), then **599** (the country code for Curaçao), and then **9** (the area code) and the local number (the number of digits in the local number varies). Once on Curaçao, to call another number on the island, only the local number is necessary; to make calls to an off-island destination, dial **021** and then the area code and number.

Time Curaçao is on Atlantic standard time year-round, 1 hour ahead of eastern standard time and the same as eastern daylight saving time.

Water The water comes from a modern desalination plant and is safe to drink.

Weather Curaçao has an average temperature of 81°F; trade winds keep the island fairly cool. It's flat and arid, with an average rainfall of only 22 inches per year.

2 Where to Stay

Your hotel will be in Willemstad or in one of the suburbs, which lie only 10 to 15 minutes from the shopping center. The bigger hotels often have free shuttle buses running into town, and most of them boast their own beaches and pools.

Curaçao is a bustling commercial center, and the downtown hotels often fill up fast with business travelers as well as visitors from neighboring countries such as Venezuela, here on a shopping holiday. Therefore, reservations are always important.

When making reservations, ask if the 7% room tax and 12% service charge are included in the price you're quoted. There is also a $3 daily (per room) energy tax in all hotels. Be sure to take a look at our section on package tours in chapter 2!

VERY EXPENSIVE

Habitat Curaçao. Rif St. Marie, Curaçao, N.A. ☎ **800/327-6709** in the U.S., or 599/9-8648800. Fax 599/9-8648464. 76 units. A/C. Winter $776–$858 double; $1,025 cottage for 2. Off-season $407–$543 double; $633 cottage for 2. Rates include buffet breakfast, airport transfers, unlimited 24-hour shore diving on 5-day and 4-night package. AE, DC, MC, V.

The diving legend of the ABC Islands, Captain Don Stewart, longtime operator of Captain Don's Habitat on Bonaire, has invaded Curaçao. About 20 minutes from Willemstad, this new oceanfront resort provides environmentally sensitive dive vacations. Facilities include a PADI five-star instruction center, offering dive courses from novice to instructor levels. The resort, set in manicured gardens, opens onto a private beach and also has a pool. Accommodations include junior suites, which are tastefully furnished with two queen-size beds with fine mattresses, a fully equipped kitchenette, a large balcony or patio, and a full bathroom. Cottages each have two bedrooms, a living room, a kitchen, a bathroom, and a large patio.

EXPENSIVE

Princess Beach Resort & Casino. Dr. Martin Luther King Blvd., Willemstad, Curaçao, N.A. ☎ **800/992-2015** in the U.S. and Canada, or 599/9-7367888. Fax 599/9-4617025. www.princessbeach.com. E-mail: lconmarketing@prooigy.net. 349 units. A/C MINIBAR TV TEL. Winter $210 double; from $340 suite. Off-season $145 double; from $230 suite. MAP $50 per person extra. AE, DC, MC, V.

The island's largest resort is a modern, low-rise, condominium-style beachfront property in front of the Curaçao Underwater Park and close to the Seaquarium (a complimentary shuttle ride away from Willemstad). This high-energy hotel has the only half-kilometer-long beach on the island. Many people assume that it's operated by the Princess Cruise Line because of its name; actually, it's a Holiday Inn Crowne Plaza Resort. The hotel is Sonesta's only serious rival on the island, but we give the edge to Sonesta for superior amenities. Many of the refurbished bedrooms here look out over the beach, and all have balconies or patios shielded by tropical plants. The most modern—and most sought-after—units are in a wing completed in 1993. Most rooms are quite spacious, with excellent mattresses, king or queen beds, combination shower/tubs, and hair dryers. Some of the accommodations are wheelchair accessible.

Dining/Diversions: There's an outdoor dining area, an air-conditioned gourmet restaurant with an international dinner menu, nightly entertainment, and the best casino on Curaçao.

Amenities: Docking facilities for deep-sea fishing, windsurfing center, two tennis courts, two freshwater pools (one with a swim-up bar). Room service, laundry, dry cleaning, baby-sitting.

✪ **Sonesta Beach Hotel & Casino Curaçao.** Piscadera Bay (P.O. Box 6003), Willemstad, Curaçao, N.A. ☎ **800/766-3782** in the U.S., or 599/9-7368800. Fax 599/9-4627502. 248 units. A/C MINIBAR TV TEL. Winter $255–$340 double; from $375 suite. Off-season $180–$255 double; from $285 suite. MAP $60 per person extra. Extra person $40. AE, DC, MC, V.

This is the most glamorous and most prominent hotel on the island. Operated by Boston-based Sonesta Hotels (a chain known for the original artworks throughout its properties), it's set beside the largest and most popular beach on Curaçao, 10 minutes from both the airport and the capital of Willemstad. The hotel is arranged into a low-lying cluster of three-story buildings whose distinctive shape and ocher color were adapted from traditional Dutch colonial architecture. The open-sided lobby was designed for optimum views of the resort's beach and its many fountains. Scattered throughout the property are unusual, often monumental, artworks by local and international artists, and a collection of unfussy, overstuffed furniture.

Each fuchsia-and-turquoise unit offers a view of the ocean and contains either one king or two queen beds with quality mattresses, plus a spacious bathroom with a combination tub/shower, fluffy towels, and a hair dryer.

Dining/Diversions: The open-air, American/Caribbean Palm Café serves breakfast and lunch; on Wednesday, it hosts a limbo/fire-eating show. The clublike Emerald Bar & Grill serves grilled continental specialties and light appetizers. The Portofino, open for dinner only, features northern Italian specialties in an airy setting inspired by a Mediterranean resort. There's also a casino.

Amenities: Two tennis courts lit at night, lagoon-shaped pool with swim-up bar, two open-air Jacuzzis patterned after Roman models, duty-free shopping arcade, a variety of land and water sports. Room service (from 6am to 1am), concierge, beauty salon, massage, children's program for kids 5 to 12.

MODERATE

✪ **Avila Beach Hotel.** Penstraat 130 (P.O. Box 791), Willemstad, Curaçao, N.A. ☎ 599/9-4614377. Fax 599/9-4611493. www.Avilahotel.com. E-mail: info@avilahotel.com. 108 units. TV TEL. Winter $110–$235 double; $280 suite. Off-season $100–$195 double; $230–$240 suite. MAP $50 per person extra. AE, DC, MC, V. From the airport, follow signs to Punda; turn left after the second traffic light in town; stay on the right side of the Plaza Smeets road and go straight. The hotel is on the right-hand side.

This is the only beachfront hotel in Willemstad proper, set on its own private sandy beach that offers year-round ocean swimming. It consists of a beautifully restored 200-year-old mansion and a large extension, called La Belle Alliance. In 1997, the addition of the Blues Wing further expanded the size of the hotel. Each of the new rooms has air-conditioning, TV, private bathroom with tub, minifridge, and a balcony with an ocean view; some also contain kitchenettes. The rooms in the main mansion, though rather basic and small, have charm. Most units have a king-size bed or two twins, each fitted with a good mattress. The hotel lies on the shore road leading east out of the city from the shopping center. The core of the Avila Beach remains the historic mansion, which was built by the English governor of Curaçao during the British occupation of the island at the time of the Napoleonic wars. The mansion was converted into a hotel in 1949, and today attracts the royals of the Netherlands.

The romantic, open-air Belle Terrace, shaded by huge trees, features a full à la carte menu. Blues, an elevated restaurant/bar at the end of the pier, caters to small, informal parties with a taste for jazz, swing, and, of course, blues. (See "Where to Dine," below, for reviews.) There's also Antillean nights with local cuisine and live music, plus Saturday-night barbecues. Amenities include tennis courts, baby-sitting, and laundry service.

Coral Cliff Resort & Casino. Santa Martha Bay (P.O. Box 3782), Curaçao, N.A. ☎ 599/9-641610. Fax 599/9-641781. 56 units. A/C TV TEL. Winter $135 double; from $150 suite. Off-season $115 double; from $135 suite. AE, MC, V.

On the western part of the island, this resort is surrounded and isolated by 18 acres of grounds, cliffs, mountains, and bays. Renovated in 1994, it offers rooms overlooking the Caribbean Sea. This is not a plushly decorated place—in fact, it's rather rustic, with wood beams. Tourists from the Netherlands view it as an offbeat Antillean retreat; others seeking first-class accommodations may find the rooms a bit austere and ready for some rejuvenation. Beds are reasonably comfortable, although mattresses have known many visitors before you, and the bathrooms are a bit cramped. The location is on a natural beach attracting scuba divers and snorkelers. Scuba and other water-sports equipment is available at the hotel's beachside water-sports center, and other facilities include day and night tennis, minigolf, volleyball, and a children's playground.

The hotel staff will pick you up at the airport and provide complimentary shuttle service into town, as well as laundry and baby-sitting on request. You can relax with drinks at the open-air Cliffhanger Bar as you watch the sun set. The open-air Terrace Restaurant, overlooking the water, offers international-style, but sometimes rather bland, meals. A small and lackluster casino also overlooks the sea.

Four Points Resort Curaçao. Piscadera Bay, John F. Kennedy Blvd. (P.O. Box 2133), Willemstad, Curaçao, N.A. ☎ **800/537-8483** in the U.S., or 599/9-4625000. Fax 599/9-4625846. www.ccresort.com. E-mail: curesort@cura.net. 196 units. A/C TV TEL. Winter $120–$135 double; $140–$155 triple; $160–$175 quad. Off-season $115–$125 double; $135–$145 triple; $155–$165 quad. Suites from $180 year-round. AE, DC, MC, V.

Taken over by Tour Star Hotels and completely renovated in 1998, this formerly stale property is now better than ever. The five-story resort on the northern outskirts of Willemstad opens onto a tiny beach, and has free bus service to take you shopping in town. A self-contained concrete complex, it's set among rocky bluffs with all rooms either on the ocean or a garden. Glass-enclosed elevators clinging to the exterior walls of the hotel offer a panoramic view as you're whisked to your room. The guest rooms have traditional furnishings, good mattresses, private balconies, and bathrooms with big towels. Although not stylish, the rooms are comfortably furnished and well maintained. An Executive Floor offers amenities such as direct-dial phones and fax machines.

The wide-open lower lounge area, with a windswept view of Piscadera Bay, is most impressive. The Pisca Terrace bar/restaurant opens onto a star-shaped pool and the ruins of a fort 2 centuries old; you can enjoy a buffet breakfast on this terrace. Other choices include La Garuda for Indonesian cuisine, Pirates Restaurant for seafood, and the Coco Steak House. Mexican nights are popular, as are Antillean nights with folklore shows. The casino is a major attraction. The Seascape dive shop offers the best water-sports program on the island (including skin diving, sailing, deep-sea fishing, and sea jeeps). There's also two Grasstex tennis courts (lit at night), a well-stocked shopping complex, room service (from 7am to 11pm), laundry, baby-sitting, and free bus service to town.

Holiday Beach Hotel & Casino. Pater Euwensweg 31 (P.O. Box 2178), Willemstad, Curaçao, N.A. ☎ **599/9-4625400.** Fax 599/9-4625409. 200 units. A/C TV TEL. Winter $150–$165 double. Off-season $120 double. MAP $33 per person extra. AE, DC, MC, V.

Along a sandy beach dotted with palm trees, this four-story establishment, no longer a Holiday Inn, sits near a grassy peninsula jutting out to sea about a mile from the capital. It boasts all the facilities of a resort hotel, a crescent-shaped beach against a backdrop of palms, and exceptionally reasonable rates. The main part of the complex houses the Casino Royale, one of the largest casinos on the island, and the property contains a handful of tennis courts.

Guest rooms are in two four-story wings, centering around a U-shaped garden with a large freshwater pool. The 30-year-old bedrooms have recently been refurbished, opening onto private balconies. A few front the water; others face the parking lot or pool. Wall-to-wall carpeting and big tile bathrooms are just two of the comforts. Laundry, baby-sitting, and room service are available. A water-sports concession operates on the grounds, and there's also a supervised children's program.

Lion's Dive Hotel & Marina. Bapor Kibrá, Willemstad, Curaçao, N.A. ☎ **599/9-4618100.** Fax 599/9-4618200. www.lionsdive.com/facts.html. 72 units. A/C TV TEL. Winter $150 double. Off-season $130 double. AE, DC, MC, V.

On the island's largest white-sand beach, a 30-minute taxi ride southeast of the airport, this complete dive resort features programs supervised by the Underwater Curaçao staff. Each of its comfortable though routinely standard accommodations has a sea view, a balcony or terrace, two queen-size beds, and a safety-deposit box. Other facilities include a freshwater pool, a restaurant specializing in steak and seafood, and a beach bar and restaurant open for lunch and dinner. Introductory dives and resort and certification courses are offered, and a fully equipped dive shop is on site. Seven boat dives are conducted daily; waterskiing, windsurfing, and sailing can also be arranged. Additional amenities include massage, laundry, baby-sitting, a health club, and a seaquarium complex with marine-life encounters.

Plaza Hotel & Casino. Plaza Pier (P.O. Box 813), Willemstad, Curaçao, N.A. ☎ **800/447-7462** in the U.S., or 599/9-4612500. Fax 599/9-4618347. www.plazahotelcuracao.com. E-mail: info@plazahotelcuracao.com. 245 units. A/C TV TEL. Winter $150 double; $180 suite. Off-season $105 double; $135 suite. Rates include breakfast. AE, MC, V.

Standing guard over the Punda side of St. Anna Bay, the Plaza is nestled in the ramparts of an 18th-century waterside fort on the eastern tip of the harbor entrance, a 20-minute drive south of the airport. In fact, it's one of the harbor's two "lighthouses." (The hotel has to carry marine collision insurance, the only accommodation in the Caribbean with that distinction.) The original part of the hotel was built in 1954, long before the wave of tourist interest swept the island, and followed the style of the arcaded fort. However, now there's a tower of rooms stacked 15 stories high. Each of the bedrooms—your own crow's nest—is comfortably furnished and contains a personal safe, although the room decor may strike you as garish.

The pool, with a bar and suntanning area, is inches away from the parapet of the fort. The Waterfort Grill serves American and continental dishes. The more formal Tournesol, which features French cuisine for dinner only, offers a panoramic view from its location on the top floor of the hotel. Amenities include laundry, baby-sitting, room service (from 7:30am to 11pm), and a small casino.

INEXPENSIVE

Chogogo Resort. Jan Thiel Bay, Curaçao, N.A. ☎ **599/9-7472844.** Fax 599/9-7472424. www.chogogo.com. E-mail: chogogo@cura.net. 54 units. A/C TV TEL. Year-round rates per week: $487 studio for 2; $557 one-bedroom apt for 2–4. Two-bedroom bungalows: $700 for 2; $766 for 3; $870 for 4. Supplemental charges for water and electricity average about $10 a day per unit, depending on usage. MC, V.

Named after a species of local flamingo, and set within an arid landscape between the oceanfront beaches and a shallow saltwater bay southeast of Willemstad, this resort caters largely to European (mostly Dutch) families who check in for at least a week and prepare their own meals. Housed within several dozen party-colored buildings of either one or two stories, each unit contains a kitchenette and airy, unpretentious furniture. On the premises are a free-form swimming pool (complete with its own waterfall), a grocery store, a bar, and a restaurant. Don't expect a lot of amenities or services here, as the resort was conceived for independent travelers looking to escape urban life and to relax with little or no input from a social director. The activities revolve around the in-house bar and restaurant, as well as the reefs, white sands, and marine life of a nearby beach club. Although clean towels are provided daily, apartments are cleaned only three times a week; stays of less than a week are not encouraged.

Hotel Holland. F. D. Rooseveltweg 524, Curaçao, N.A. ☎ **599/9-8688044.** Fax 599/9-688114. 45 units. A/C TV TEL. Year-round $79 double; from $117 suite. AE, DC, MC, V.

A 2-minute drive from the airport, the Hotel Holland contains the Flying Dutchman Bar, a popular gathering place, plus a casino that opened in 1991. For a few brief minutes of every day, you can see airplanes landing from your perch at the edge of the poolside terrace, where well-prepared breakfasts, lunches, and dinners from the Cockpit Restaurant are served in good weather (see "Where to Dine," below, for a review). This property is the domain of former Navy frogman Hans Vrolijk and his family. Hans still retains his interest in scuba and arranges dive packages for his guests. The comfortably furnished accommodations have VCRs, fridges, and balconies. Laundry, baby-sitting, and room service are available.

Landhaus Daniel. Wegnaar, Westpunt, Curaçao, N.A. ☎ and fax **599/9-8648400.** 7 units. TV TEL. Winter $45–$55 double. Off-season $40–$50 double. AE, DC, MC, V.

A mile south of Westpunt, near the island's most northwestern tip, this mustard-colored plantation house is most often visited by locals for its on-site restaurant (see "Where to Dine," below). If you don't mind a location away from the beach, it offers the best value on the island. The nearest worthwhile beach is Porto Marie or Habitat Curaçao, which are a 7- to 10-minute drive away.

Very simple but comfortable bedrooms, located a floor above the restaurant, are tidily maintained and have small private bathrooms. Only two rooms are air-conditioned, but all units have ceiling fans—or you can rely on the trade winds to keep cool. Ask for a room in the main house: The converted slave quarters are small, but charming. This place's basic rooms and communal TV room give it something of the aura of a youth hostel; guests also play billiards and darts.

✪ **Porto Paseo Hotel & Casino.** De Rouvilleweg 47, Willemstad, Curaçao, N.A. ☎ **599/9-4627878.** Fax 599/9-4627969. E-mail: ppaseo@cura.net. 47 units. Year-round with breakfast $95 double, $150 suite for two; without breakfast $110 one- or two-bedroom apt. 7-night minimum for apts. AE, MC.

Set on the Otrabanda side of Willemstad's harbor front, this is one of the capital's most beautiful and stylish restorations of a historic building, and one of the island's best hotel values. If you stay here, you'll get a sense of Dutch colonial life of long ago. Completed in 1992, the hotel incorporates what was originally constructed in the 1870s as the island's first hospital with a sprawling garden and clusters of modern, low-rise buildings that each contain four or five units. One of the centerpieces of the estate is a flagstone-covered courtyard, illuminated with streetlamps, and a simple brasserie, the Bon Bini, open for lunch. On the premises are a casino and a bar with views over St. Anna Bay. Bedrooms are severely dignified, airy, and comfortable.

3 Where to Dine

EXPENSIVE

✪ **Bistro Le Clochard.** Riffort, on the Otrabanda side of the pontoon bridge. ☎ **599/9-4625666.** Reservations recommended. Main courses $22–$28. AE, DISC, MC, V. Mon–Fri noon–2pm; Mon–Sat 6:30–10:45pm (Harborside Terrace, Mon–Sat 6–11pm.). FRENCH/SWISS.

Bistro Le Clochard snugly fits into the northwestern corner of the grim ramparts of Fort Rif, at the gateway to the harbor. Its entrance is marked with a canopy, which leads to a series of rooms, each built under the 19th-century vaulting of the old Dutch fort. Several tables have a view of the Caribbean Sea. More panoramic is the establishment's outdoor terrace, built directly at the edge of the water, with a view of the sparkling lights of the nearby town.

To begin, you might order bouillabaisse *à notre façon*, a fresh local fish soup. Among the alpine specialties are raclette (melted Swiss cheese served with boiled potatoes, onions, and pickles) and a fondue bourguignonne. Of course, critics maintain that food such as this is best served at a ski resort in the Alps. One section of the menu is called "Romancing the Stone": The stone is heated in the oven and brought directly to your table; then, without using oil or fat, your choice from the menu—tournedos, sirloin, T-bone, boneless chicken breast, or fresh fish—is cooked on the stone. Heavy or light, the food is consistently reliable and good, although we wish the prices weren't so high.

De Taveerne. Landhuis Groot Vavelaar, Silena. ☎ **599/9-7370669.** Reservations recommended. Main courses $20–$28; set-price menus $29–$35. AE, DC, MC, V. Mon–Fri noon–2pm; Mon–Sat 7–11pm. FRENCH/INTERNATIONAL.

One of the most historic buildings in the district is this brick-sided manor house, which was originally built by a Venezuelan revolutionary in exile in Curaçao during the mid-1800s. Capped with an octagonal cupola, it also contains an art gallery that exhibits photos, paintings, and sculpture by mostly Curaçaon artists. Furnishings in the restaurant evoke an old Curaçao farmhouse, complete with polished brass, white stucco walls, dark woods, and terra-cotta tiles. Menu items make use of as much local produce as possible, albeit with goodly numbers of ingredients imported from Miami. Main courses include a well-seasoned version of medallions of monkfish with a fluffy sauce made from champagne and fresh oysters, lobster bisque spiked with Armagnac, carpaccio of salmon, and roasted rack of lamb marinated with garlic, thyme, and rosemary, and served with a balsamic ratatouille.

Fort Nassau. Near Point Juliana, a 5-minute drive from Willemstad. ☎ **599/9-4613086.** Reservations recommended. Main courses $22.30–$28.45. AE, DC, MC, V. Mon–Fri noon–3pm; daily 6:30–11pm. INTERNATIONAL.

This restored restaurant and bar is built on a hilltop overlooking Willemstad in the ruins of a buttressed fort dating from 1796. Inside, it has retained an 18th-century decor; outside, from the Battery Terrace, a 360-degree panorama of the sea, the harbor, and Willemstad unfolds. You'll even have a distant view of the island's vast oil refinery and a signal tower on the cliff, which sends out beacons to approaching ships. You can stop by the fashionably decorated bar just to enjoy a drink and watch the sunset; happy hour is Monday through Friday from 6 to 7pm.

Queen Beatrix and Crown Prince Claus have dined here, and rumor has it they were more captivated by the view than by the food. Some of the more imaginative dishes on the menu perhaps should never have been conjured up. However, we were impressed with the goat cheese in puff pastry and a cold terrine with layers of salmon and sole. The cream of mustard (yes, that's right) soup seems an acquired taste. Opt for the breast of duck with sun-dried tomatoes and basil, or even a well-prepared steak.

La Pergola. In the Waterfront Arches, Waterfort Straat. ☎ **599/9-4613482.** Reservations recommended. Main courses $18–$34. AE, MC, V. Mon–Sat noon–11pm, Sun 6–11pm. ITALIAN.

Of the quintet of restaurants nestled into the weather-beaten core of the island's oldest fort, this is the only one focusing on the cuisine and traditions of Italy, and it has thrived here for more than a decade. As the name implies, the decor is enhanced by a replica of a pergola evocative of the Renaissance. The kitchen and one of the three dining areas are in the cellar, while two others benefit from streaming sunlight and a view over the seafront. Menu items change virtually every day, and are as authentic to Italian (non-Americanized) traditions as anything else in Curaçao. Examples include gnocchi of chicken, fettuccine Giulio Cesare (with ham, cream, and mushrooms), a succulent version of *grigliata mista*, seafood salad, and a topnotch version of exotic mushrooms, in season, garnished with Parmesan cheese and parsley. Looking for an unusual form of pasta? Ask for *maltagliata* (pasta cut at random angles and lengths) served with either Gorgonzola sauce or Genoan-style pesto.

Wine Cellar. Ooststraat/Concordiastraat. ☎ **599/9-4612178.** Reservations required. Main courses $18–$37. AE, DC, MC, V. Tues–Fri noon–2pm and 6pm–midnight, Sat–Sun 6pm–midnight. INTERNATIONAL.

Opposite the cathedral in the center of town is the domain of Nico and Angela Cornelisse and their son, Daniel, who offer one of the most extensive wine lists on the island. The Victorian atmosphere is reminiscent of an old-fashioned Dutch home. The kitchen turns out an excellent lobster salad and a sole meunière in a butter-and-herb sauce. You might also try, if featured, fresh red snapper or U.S. tenderloin of beef with goat cheese sauce. Game dishes, imported throughout the year from Holland, are likely to include venison roasted with mushrooms, hare, or roast goose. After years of dining here, we have found the food commendable in every way—dishes are flavorful and hearty, and there are selections for lighter appetites as well. Of course, the food never matches the impressive wine list.

MODERATE

Belle Terrace. In the Avila Beach Hotel, Penstraat 130. ☎ **599/9-4614377.** Reservations required. Main courses $15–$25; menu dégustation $27 for two courses, $32 for three courses; Sat barbecue $25. AE, DC, MC, V. Daily 7–10am, noon–2:30pm, and 7–10pm. From the airport, follow signs to Punda; turn left after the second traffic light in town; stay on the right side of the Plaza Smeets road and go straight. The hotel is on the right-hand side. INTERNATIONAL/DANISH.

This open-air restaurant, in a 200-year-old mansion on the beachfront of Willemstad, offers superb dining in a relaxed and informal atmosphere. The Schooner Bar, where you can enjoy a rum punch, is shaped like a weather-beaten ship's prow looking out to sea. The restaurant, sheltered by an arbor of flamboyant branches, features Scandinavian, continental, and local cuisine with such specialties as pickled herring, smoked salmon, and a Danish lunch platter. Local dishes, such as *keshi yena* (baked Gouda cheese with a spicy meat filling), are also on the menu. On Saturday night, there's a mixed grill and a help-yourself salad bar. Fish is always fresh at Belle Terrace, and the chef prepares a seafood platter to perfection: grilled, poached, or meunière. Desserts include Danish pastry and cakes, as well as a large selection of homemade ice creams.

Blues. In the Avila Beach Hotel, Penstraat 130. ☎ **599/9-4614377.** Reservations recommended. Main courses $15–$25; two-course menu $30; three-course menu $35. AE, DC, MC, V. Daily 11am–2:30pm and 7–10pm. From the airport, follow signs to Punda; turn left after the second traffic light in town; stay on the right side of the Plaza Smeets road and go straight. The hotel is on the right-hand side. SEAFOOD/INTERNATIONAL.

Few other restaurants in Curaçao convey as strong an association with the sea as this one, thanks to its location on a pier jutting far out from the beachfront of the Avila Beach Hotel, water that ripples beneath your seat, and heaping platters of fresh seafood that sometimes challenge even the heartiest of appetites. Examples include blue mussels cooked in wine sauce with shallots and herbs, dorado with mustard-flavored beurre blanc (white butter), fillets of flounder with an herb-flavored Chablis sauce and beurre blanc, braised lamb with blackberry sauce, and imported Maine lobster prepared with Creole herbs in a style inspired by the cuisine of New Orleans. An especially impressive dish is a "seafood challenge" that combines whatever fresh fish is available that day into a single huge dinner. When we visited, it included flavorful portions of tuna, salmon, squid, langoustine, and scallops. A dessert that manages to please everybody is the "Jam Session": A hefty sampling of every sweet offered on the menu is assembled onto a large platter and served to two diners at a time. See also "Curaçao After Dark," below.

Fisherman's Wharf. Dr. Martin Luther King Blvd. 91–93. ☎ **599/9-4657558.** Reservations recommended. Main courses $16–$25. AE, MC, V. Mon–Sat 5–11pm. SEAFOOD/ INTERNATIONAL.

This restaurant, only a few yards from the sea, offers an authentic island-style dining experience. Fish lovers gravitate to it, knowing it has perhaps the freshest fish in Curaçao. In simple and casual surroundings, Fisherman's Wharf serves a cuisine based on recent purchases from the fishermen who set out daily in search of such catches as mula (similar to kingfish) and tuna. Some of the fish brought in here reach a length of 5.3 feet, weighing as much as 80 pounds. The kitchen also offers Japanese-inspired sashimi.

We recommend starting with the seafood soup, which is the most consistently reliable appetizer, or a tartar of local poached marlin, intriguingly prepared with a compote of mango. Shrimp bisque is served with old Cuban rum, or else you might opt for giant mussels in a cheese sauce. The catch of the day is likely to be barracuda prepared with fresh pine nuts or pan-fried tuna with a homemade tapenade of black olives and anchovy. Some meat dishes are available for those who don't like fish. A local "ice chef" on the island prepares a tropical surprise for dessert: piña colada ice cream.

Fort Waakzaamheid Bistro. Seru di Domi, Otrabanda. ☎ **599/9-4623633.** Reservations recommended. Main courses $17–$26. AE, MC, V. Wed–Mon 5–10pm. Bar until 1am weekdays, later on weekends. INTERNATIONAL/STEAK.

Captain Bligh, of *Bounty* fame, captured this old fort in 1804 and laid siege to Willemstad for almost a month. A stone-and-hardwood tavern and restaurant have been created in the fort, which opens onto a view of Otrabanda and the harbor entrance. Try to arrive in time to watch the panoramic sunset from this country tavern–like setting. You can stop in for just drinks and munchies, or stick around for a dinner of steak or barbecued fish along with generous helpings from the salad bar. This isn't a venue for overly elaborate cuisine: Your best bet might be the fresh fish, perhaps Curaçao snapper. Prime rib, garlic shrimp (a bit overcooked for our taste), and a notable conch platter may also be on the menu. This fort is often patronized by those wishing to escape the hordes who occasionally descend on Fort Nassau (see above).

Landhaus Daniel. Wegnaar, Westpunt, Curaçao. ☎ **599/9-8648400.** Reservations recommended. Lunch main courses $6–$45; set-price lunch $20; dinner main courses $20–$45. AE, DC, MC, V. Daily noon–5pm and 8–11pm. INTERNATIONAL.

Surrounded by arid scrubland about a mile south of Westpunt, near the island's most northwesterly tip, this establishment occupies what was originally built in 1711 as an inn and tavern. Today, its mustard-colored facade, white columns, terra-cotta roof, and old-timey green-and-yellow dining room are carefully preserved as one of the most historically authentic buildings in the northern tier of Curaçao. Menu items are cooked slowly, to order, in a setting filled with sea breezes and sunlight streaming in the big windows. Worthwhile starters here include the mixed mesclun salad with blue cheese, assorted nuts, and raspberry-flavored vinaigrette; New Zealand oysters; stuffed crabs with a coulis of tomatoes and blue cheese; and spicey Cajun shrimp. Main courses include sirloin steak with pepper sauce, a succulent tenderloin of lamb in a red port sauce, and several kinds of fresh fish. Only the latter is very, very expensive (see the high end of the price ranges, above).

Pisces Seafood. Caracasbaaiweg 476. ☎ **599/9-7672181.** Reservations recommended. Main courses $16–$33. MC, V. Fri–Wed 6–10pm. CREOLE/SEAFOOD.

This West Indian restaurant may be difficult to find, as it's on a flat, industrial coastline near a marina and an oil refinery, about 20 minutes from the capital on the island's southernmost tip. There's been a restaurant here since the 1930s, when sailors and workers from the oil refinery came for home-cooked meals. Today, the simple frame building offers seating near the rough-hewn bar or in a breeze-swept inner room. Pisces's menu depends on the catch of the day. Main courses, served with rice, vegetables, and plantains or potatoes, might include sopi, "seacat" (squid), mula (similar to kingfish), or red snapper; if you wish, the Pisces platter combines any of these in copious quantities for two or more people. Shrimp and conch are each prepared three different ways: with garlic, with curry, or Creole style. Essentially, this place offers food the way the locals used to eat long before the cruise ships started arriving and the sprawling resorts opened. It's simple, straightforward, affordable, and often quite good.

✪ **Rijstaffel Restaurant Indonesia and Holland Club Bar.** Mercuriusstraat 13, Salinja. ☎ **599/9-4612606.** Reservations recommended. Main courses $14–$43; rijstaffel $22 for 16 dishes, $27 for 20 dishes, $42.85 for 25 dishes; all vegetarian $22.85 for 16 dishes. AE, DC, MC, V. Mon–Sat noon–2pm and 6–9:30pm, Sun 6–9:30pm. Take a taxi to this villa in the suburbs near Salinja, near the Princess Beach Resort & Casino southeast of Willemstad. INDONESIAN.

This is the best place on the island to sample the Indonesian rijstaffel, the traditional rice table with all the zesty side dishes. At lunchtime, the selection of dishes is more modest, but for dinner, Javanese cooks prepare the specialty of the house—a rijstaffel consisting of 16, 20, or 25 dishes. There's even an all-vegetarian rijstaffel. Warming trays are placed on your table; the service is buffet style. You're allowed to season your plate with peppers rated hot, very hot, and palate-melting. It's best to go with a party so that all of you can share in the feast. The spicy food is a good change of pace when you tire of seafood and steak.

INEXPENSIVE

The Cockpit. In the Hotel Holland, F. D. Rooseveltweg 524. ☎ **599/9-8688044.** Reservations required. Main courses $10–$25. AE, DC, MC, V. Daily 7am–10pm. DUTCH/INTERNATIONAL.

The restaurant's dining room has an aeronautical flavor, with the nose of an airplane cockpit as the focal point; there's also seating outside around the pool. Located on the scrub-bordered road leading to the airport, a few minutes from the landing strips, the Cockpit serves international cuisine with an emphasis on Dutch and Antillean specialties. Guests enjoy fresh fish in season (served Curaçao style), Dutch-style steak, Caribbean curried chicken, split-pea soup, and various pasta dishes, such as shrimp linguine della mama in a lobster sauce. All dishes are accompanied by fresh vegetables and Dutch-style potatoes. No one pretends the food is gourmet fare—it's robust, hearty, and filled with good country flavor, nothing else. But on some occasions, nothing else will do, and this place is also one of the best dining values on an island where food prices often climb to dizzying heights.

✪ **Golden Star.** Socratesstraat 2. ☎ **599/9-4618741.** Reservations not necessary. Main courses $7.50–$25.70. AE, DC, MC, V. Daily 9am–1am. At the corner of Dr. Hugenholtzweg and Dr. Maalweg, southeast of Willemstad. CREOLE.

The best place to go on the island for *criollo* (local) food is inland from the coast road leading southeast from St. Anna Bay. Evoking a roadside diner, the air-conditioned restaurant is quite simple, but it has a large menu of very tasty Antillean dishes, such as carco stoba (conch stew), bestia chiki (goatmeat stew), bakijauw (salted cod), and concomber stoba (stewed meat and marble-size spiny cucumbers). Other specialties include criollo shrimp (kiwa) and sopi carni (meat stew). Everything is served with a side order of funchi, the cornmeal staple. The Golden Star has a large local following, with an occasional tourist dropping in.

4 Beaches

Its beaches aren't the best in the Dutch Leewards, but Curaçao does have nearly 40 of them, ranging from hotel sands to secluded coves. Beaches are called *playas* or *bocas*. Playas are the larger, classic sandy beaches, whiles bocas are small inlets placed between two large rock formations. The northwest coast is generally rugged and difficult for swimming, but the more tranquil waters of the west coast are filled with sheltered bays, offering excellent swimming and snorkeling.

About 30 minutes from town, in the Willibrordus area on the west side of Curaçao, **Daaibooi** is a good beach. It's free, but there are no changing facilities. Shade is provided by wooden umbrellas. Snorkelers are attracted to the sides of the bay, as the cliffs rise out of the surf. Small rainbow-hued fish are commonplace, and many varying corals cover the rocks. This beach gets very crowded on Sunday with locals.

A good private beach on the eastern side of the island is **Santa Barbara Beach.** It's between the open sea and the island's primary water-sports and recreational area known as Spanish Water. A mining company owns this land, which also contains Table Mountain, a remarkable landmark, and an old phosphate mine. The natural beach has pure-white sand and calm water. A buoy line protects swimmers from boats. Facilities include rest rooms, changing rooms, a snack bar, and a terrace; water bicycles and small motorboats are available for rent. The beach, open daily from 8am to 6pm, has access to the Curaçao Underwater Park.

Blauwbaai (Blue Bay) is the largest and most frequented beach on Curaçao, with enough white sand for everybody. Along with showers and changing facilities, there are plenty of shady places to retreat from the noonday sun. To get here, follow the road that goes past the Holiday Beach Hotel, heading in the direction of Juliandorp. Follow the sign that tells you to bear left for Blauwbaai and the fishing village of San Michiel.

Westpunt, a public beach on the northwestern tip of the island, is known for the Sunday divers who jump from its gigantic cliffs into the ocean below. You can spot rainbow-hued little boats and fishermen's nets hanging out to dry here. There are no facilities at this beach, which tends to be exceptionally hot and has no shade trees (bring sun protection). Nonetheless, the calm waters offer excellent swimming. They're not good for snorkeling, however, as the bay is too wide. **Knip Bay,** just south of Westpunt, has white sands, rocky sides, and beautiful turquoise waters, making it suitable for snorkeling, swimming, and sunbathing. The beach tends to be crowded on weekends, often with locals. Manzanilla trees provide some shade, but their fruit is poisonous; never seek shelter under the trees when it rains, as drops falling off the leaves will cause major skin irritation. Changing facilities and refreshments are available.

Playa Abao, with crystal turquoise waters, is at the northern tip of the island. One of Curaçao's most popular strands, this is often called Playa Grandi ("Big Beach"). It can get very, very hot at midday, but pergolas (thatched shade umbrellas) provide some protection. A stairway and ramp lead down to the excellent white sands. There's a snack bar in the parking lot. Near the large cove at Playa Abao is **Playa Kenepa,** which is much smaller but gets our nod as one of the island's most beautiful strips. Partially shaded by trees, it's a good place for sunbathing, swimming, and shore diving. A 10-minute swim from the beach leads to a reef where visibility is often 100 feet. Baby sea turtles are often spotted here. A snack bar is open on weekends.

A beach popular with families and a base for fishing boats, **Playa Lagun** lies well concealed in the corner of the village of Lagun as you approach from Santa Cruz. The narrow cove is excellent for swimming because of the tranquil, shallow water. Rainbow-hued fish appear everywhere, so the beach is also a favorite with snorkelers. Some concrete huts provide shelter from the scorching sun; a snack bar is open on weekends. The man-made **Seaquarium Beach,** near the center of Willemstad, charges a fee of $2.50 for access to its complete facilities, including two bars, two restaurants, a water-sports shop, beach-chair rentals, changing facilities, and showers. The calm waters make this beach ideal for swimming, but you have to dive outside the breakwaters.

A word of caution to swimmers: The seawater remains an almost-constant 76°F year-round, with good underwater visibility, but beware of stepping on the spines of the sea urchins that sometimes abound in these waters. To give temporary first aid for an embedded urchin's spine, try the local remedies of vinegar or lime juice or, as the natives advise, a burning match if you're tough. While the urchin spines are not fatal, they can cause several days of real discomfort.

5 Sports & Outdoor Pursuits

BOAT TOURS   Taber Tours, Dokweg (☎ **599/9-7376637**), offers a handful of seagoing options, such as an 8-hour snorkel/barbecue trip to Port Marie, which includes round-trip transportation to excellent reef sites, use of snorkel equipment, and a barbecue; cost is $60 per person, $30 for children 9 and under. A 2-hour sunset cruise, with wine and cheese, leaves at dusk on Friday; it costs $30 for adults and $20 for children 11 and under.

Travelers looking for an experience similar to the sailing days of yore should book a trip on the ***Insulinde,*** Handelskade (☎ **599/9-5601340;** note that this is a cellular phone and the connection may be poor). The 120-foot traditionally rigged sail clipper is available for day trips and chartering. Every Thursday (or by special arrangement), the ship sails north from its berth beside Willemstad's main pier to the island's northwestern shore. Here, at Porto Marie (also referred to as Boca St. Marie), guests disembark onto the white sands of a beach, beside a private beach house. Included in the $55 cost is lunch and use of snorkel equipment. Advance reservations are necessary. Outbound transit is by sail; the return is by the ship's engines. Departure from the pier is at 8:30am every Thursday; return to the pier is around 6pm the same day. Longer trips to Bonaire or Venezuela are also possible.

Like a ghost ship from ancient times, a dual-masted, five-sailed wooden schooner cruises silently through the waters of Curaçao. It carries a name steeped in history—the ***Bounty*** (☎ **599/9-5601887**), though it's not a replica of its famous namesake. On Friday, the 90-foot, gaff-rigged schooner heads to the secluded white-sand beach of Porttomarie Bay. On Sunday, the ship sets out for Klein Curaçao, a desert island that's a favorite of snorkelers. Each Monday, the *Bounty* visits Spanish Bay, a coastal community surrounded by terraced hills. The Friday and Sunday trips cost $50, with the Monday cruise going for $30; all prices include a buffet lunch.

GOLF   The **Curaçao Golf and Squash Club,** Wilhelminalaan, in Emmastad (☎ **599/9-7373590**), is your best bet. Greens fees are $30, and both clubs and carts can be rented upon demand. The nine-hole course (the only one on the island) is open to nonmembers Friday through Wednesday from 8am to noon, Thursday from 10am to sundown.

HORSEBACK RIDING   At Christoffel National Park, **Rancho Christof** (☎ **599/9-8640535**) specializes in private trips along unspoiled trails, riding smooth-gaited "paseo" horses suitable even for nonriders. Most trail rides cost $49, with departures daily at 9am. Call for reservations daily between 8am and 4pm.

TENNIS   Most of the deluxe hotels have tennis courts. Another option is the **Santa Catherine Sports Complex,** Club Seru Coral, Koraal Partier 10 (☎ **599/9-7677028**), where court costs are $20 per hour.

WATER SPORTS   Most hotels offer their own water-sports programs. If your hotel isn't equipped, we suggest heading for one of the most complete water-sports facilities on Curaçao, **Seascape Dive and Watersports,** at the Four Points Resort Curaçao (☎ **599/9-4625000**). Specializing in snorkeling and scuba diving to reefs and underwater wrecks, it operates from a hexagonal kiosk set on stilts above the water, just offshore from the hotel's beach.

Open from 8am to 5pm daily, the company offers snorkeling excursions for $25 per person in an underwater park offshore from the hotel, waterskiing for $40 per half hour, and jet ski rentals for $50 per half hour. A Sunfish can be rented for $20, and an introductory scuba lesson, conducted by a competent dive instructor with PADI certification, goes for $45; four-dive packages cost $124.

One trip enthusiastically endorsed by visitors departs from the hotel at 7am (when participation warrants) for Little Curaçao, midway between Curaçao and Bonaire. Swimwear is skimpy once you get to the sugar-white sands of the island. Highlights include fishing, snorkeling, and the acquisition of a "topless tan." The price is $70 per person for the full-day excursion.

Seascape can also arrange deep-sea fishing for $336 for a half-day tour carrying a maximum of six people, $560 for a full-day tour. Drinks and equipment are included, but you'll have to get your hotel to pack your lunch.

Underwater Curaçao, in Bapor Kibrá (☎ **599/9-4618131**), has a complete PADI-accredited underwater-sports program. A fully stocked modern dive shop offers retail and rental equipment. Individual dives and dive packages are offered, costing $33 per dive for experienced divers. An introductory dive for novices is priced at $65, and a snorkel trip costs only $20, including equipment.

Scuba divers and snorkelers can expect spectacular scenery in waters with visibility often exceeding 100 feet at the ✪ **Curaçao Underwater Park,** which stretches along 12½ miles of Curaçao's southern coastline. Although the park technically begins at Princess Beach and extends all the way to East Point, the island's most southeasterly tip, some scuba aficionados and island dive operators are aware of other excellent dive sites outside the official boundaries of this park. Lying beneath the surface of the water are steep walls, at least two shallow wrecks, gardens of soft coral, and more than 30 species of hard coral. Although access from shore is possible at Jan Thiel Bay and Santa Barbara Beach, most people visit the park by boat. For easy and safe mooring, there are 16 mooring buoys, placed at the best dive and snorkel sites. A snorkel trail with underwater interpretive markers is laid out just east of the Princess Beach Resort &

Casino and is accessible from shore. Spearfishing, anchoring in the coral, and taking anything from the reefs, except photographs, are strictly prohibited.

WINDSURFING   At Seaquarium Beach you'll find **Top Watersports Curaçao** (☎ 599/9-4617343), the best windsurfing center on the island. It offers both rentals and instruction. The cost for windsurfing equipment is $15 per hour, plus a refundable $60 deposit. This is a tranquil section of the coast, which makes it more suitable for beginners.

6 Exploring the Island

Most cruise-ship passengers see only Willemstad—or, more accurately, the shops—but you may want to get out into the *cunucu,* or countryside, and explore the towering cacti and rolling hills topped by *landhuizen* (plantation houses) built more than 3 centuries ago.

WILLEMSTAD

Willemstad was originally founded as Santa Ana by the Spanish in the 1500s. Dutch traders found a vast natural harbor, a perfect hideaway along the Spanish Main, and they renamed it Willemstad in the 17th century. Not only is Willemstad the capital of Curaçao, but it's also the seat of government for the Netherlands Antilles. Today it boasts rows of pastel-colored, red-roofed town houses in the downtown area. After 10 years of restoration, the historic center of Willemstad and the island's natural harbor, Schottegat, have been inscribed on UNESCO's World Heritage List.

The city grew up on both sides of the canal. It's divided into **Punda** (Old World Dutch ambience and the best shopping) and **Otrabanda** ("the other side," the contemporary side). Both sections are connected by the **Queen Emma Pontoon Bridge,** a pedestrian walkway. Powered by a diesel engine, it swings open many times a day to let ships from all over the globe pass in and out of the harbor.

From the bridge, there's a view of the old **gabled houses** in harmonized pastel shades. The bright colors, according to legend, are a holdover from the time when one of the island's early governors had eye trouble, and flat white gave him headaches. The colonial-style architecture, reflecting the Dutch influence, gives the town a storybook look. The houses, built three or four stories high, are crowned by steep gables and roofed with orange Spanish tiles. Hemmed in by the sea, a tiny canal, and an inlet, the streets are narrow, and they're crosshatched by still narrower alleyways.

Except for the pastel colors, Willemstad may remind you of old Amsterdam. It has one of the most intriguing townscapes in the Caribbean. But don't let the colors deceive you: The city can be rather dirty, in spite of its fairy-tale appearance.

A **statue of Pedro Luis Brion** dominates the square known as Brionplein right at the Otrabanda end of the pontoon bridge. Born in Curaçao in 1782, he became the island's favorite son and best-known war hero. Under Simón Bolívar, he was an admiral of the fleet and fought for the independence of Venezuela and Colombia.

In addition to the pontoon bridge, the **Queen Juliana Bridge** opened to vehicular traffic in 1973. Spanning the harbor, it rises 195 feet, which makes it the highest bridge in the Caribbean and one of the tallest in the world.

The Waterfront originally guarded the mouth of the canal on the eastern or Punda side, but now it has been incorporated into the Plaza Hotel. The task of standing guard has been taken over by **Fort Amsterdam,** site of the Governor's Palace and the 1769 Dutch Reformed church. The church still has a British cannonball embedded in it. The arches leading to the fort were tunneled under the official residence of the governor.

A corner of the fort stands at the intersection of Breedestraat and Handelskade, the starting point for a plunge into the island's major shopping district. A few minutes' walk from the pontoon bridge, at the north end of Handelskade, is the **Floating Market,** where scores of schooners tie up alongside the canal, a few yards from the main shopping area. Docked boats arrive from Venezuela and Colombia, as well as other West Indian islands, to sell tropical fruits and vegetables—a little bit of everything, in fact, including handcrafts. The modern market under its vast concrete cap has not replaced this unique shopping expedition, which is fun to watch; arrive early or stay late.

At some point, save time to visit the **Waterfort Arches,** stretching for a quarter mile. They rise 30 feet high and are built of barrel-vaulted 17th-century stone set against the sea. At Waterfort, you can explore boutiques, have film developed quickly, cash a traveler's check, or purchase fruit-flavored ice cream. You can walk through to a breezy terrace on the sea for a local Amstel beer or a choice of restaurants. The grand buildings and cobbled walkways are illuminated at night.

Between the I. H. (Sha) Capriles Kade and Fort Amsterdam, at the corner of Columbusstraat and Hanchi di Snoa, stands the **Mikve Israel-Emanuel Synagogue** (☎ **599/9-4611067**), the oldest in the western hemisphere. Consecrated on the eve of Passover in 1732, it antedates the first U.S. synagogue (in Newport, Rhode Island) by 31 years and houses the oldest Jewish congregation in the New World. Joaño d'Illan led the first Jewish settlers (13 families) to the island in 1651, almost half a century after their expulsion from Portugal by the Inquisition. The settlers came via Amsterdam to Curaçao. This synagogue, a fine example of Dutch colonial architecture, covers about a square block in the heart of Willemstad; it was built in a Spanish-style walled courtyard, with four large portals. Following a Portuguese Sephardic custom, sand covers the sanctuary floor, representing the desert where Israelites camped when the Jews passed from slavery to freedom. The highlight of the east wall is the Holy Ark, rising 17 feet; a raised banca, canopied in mahogany, is on the north wall.

Adjacent to the synagogue courtyard is the **Jewish Cultural Historical Museum,** Kuiperstraat 26–28 (☎ **599/9-4611633**), housed in two buildings dating back to 1728. They were originally the rabbi's residence and the bathhouse. The 250-year-old mikvah (bath for religious purification purposes) was in constant use until around 1850, when this practice was discontinued and the buildings sold. They have since been reacquired through the Foundation for the Preservation of Historic Monuments and turned into the present museum. On display are ritual, ceremonial, and cultural objects, many of which date back to the 17th and 18th centuries and are still in use by the congregation for holidays and events.

The synagogue and museum are open to visitors Monday through Friday from 9 to 11:45am and 2:30 to 4:45pm; if there's a cruise ship in port, also on Sunday from 9am to noon. Services are Friday at 6:30pm and Saturday at 10am. Visitors are welcome, with appropriate dress required. There's a $2 entrance fee to the museum.

WEST OF WILLEMSTAD

You can walk to the tiny **Curaçao Museum,** Van Leeuwenhoekstraat (☎ **599/9-4626051**), from the Queen Emma Pontoon Bridge. Built in 1853 by the Royal Dutch Army Corps of Engineers as a military quarantine hospital for victims of yellow fever, the building was carefully restored from 1946 to 1948 and is a fine example of 19th-century Dutch architecture. Equipped with paintings, objets d'art, and furniture crafted in the 19th century by local cabinetmakers, it re-creates the atmosphere of an era gone by. There's also a large collection from the Caiquetio tribes, the early inhabitants described by Amerigo Vespucci as 7-foot-tall giants, and a reconstruction of a traditional music pavilion in the garden, where Curaçao musicians give regular performances. It's open Monday to Saturday from 9am to noon and 2 to 5pm, Sunday from 10am to 4pm. Admission is $2.50 for adults, $1.25 for children 13 and under.

The **Maritime Museum,** Van De Brandhof Straat 7 (☎ 599/9-4652327), is in the historic Scharloo neighborhood of Willemstad, just off the old harbor of St. Ana Bay. More than 40 permanent displays trace the story of Curaçao, beginning with the arrival of the island's original inhabitants in 600 B.C. Video presentations cover the development of Curaçao's harbor and the role of the island as one of the largest slave depots in the Caribbean. There's also five oral histories (one from a 97-year-old Curaçaoan who served on the cargo vessel *Normandie*), antique miniatures, 17th-century ship models, and a collection of maps. Admission is $6 for adults, $4 for children; hours are Monday to Saturday from 10am to 5pm.

The **Curaçao Underwater Marine Park** (☎ 599/9-4624242), established in 1983 with the financial aid of the World Wildlife Fund, stretches from the Princess Beach Resort & Casino to the east point of the island, a strip of about 12½ miles of untouched coral reefs. For information on snorkeling, scuba diving, and trips in a glass-bottom boat to view the park, see "Sports & Outdoor Pursuits," above.

The **Country House Museum,** 12 miles west of Willemstad at Doktorstuin 27 (☎ 599/9-8642742), is a small-scale restoration of a 19th-century manor house that boasts thick stone walls, a thatched roof, and artifacts that represent the old-fashioned methods of agriculture and fishing. It's open Tuesday to Friday from 9am to 4pm, Saturday and Sunday from 9am to 5pm. Admission is $2.

En route to Westpunt, you'll come across a seaside cavern known as **Boca Tabla,** one of many such grottoes on this rugged, uninhabited northwest coast. In the Westpunt area, a 45-minute ride from Punda in Willemstad, **Playa Forti** is a stark region characterized by soaring hills and towering cacti, along with 200-year-old Dutch land houses, the former mansions that housed slave owners.

Out toward the western tip of Curaçao, a high-wire fence surrounds the entrance to the 4,500-acre **Christoffel National Park** in Savonet (☎ 599/9-8640363), about a 45-minute drive from the capital. A macadam road gives way to dirt, surrounded on all sides by abundant cactus and bromeliads. In the higher regions you can spot rare orchids. Rising from flat, arid countryside, 1,230-foot-high St. Christoffelberg is the highest point in the Dutch Leewards. Donkeys, wild goats, iguanas, the Curaçao deer, and many species of birds thrive in this preserve, and there are some Arawak paintings on a coral cliff near the two caves. The park has 20 miles of one-way trail-like roads, with lots of flora and fauna along the way. The shortest trail is about 5 miles long and, because of the rough terrain, takes about 40 minutes to drive through. There are also various walking trails; one takes you to the top of **St. Christoffelberg** in about 1½ hours. (Come early in the morning when it isn't too hot.) The park is open Monday to Saturday from 8am to 4pm, Sunday from 6am to 3pm. The entrance fee is $13.50 per person and includes admission to the museum.

The park's **museum** has varying exhibitions year-round, set in an old storehouse left over from plantation days. Call to arrange a guided tour. Next door, the park has opened the **National Park Shete Boka** (Seven Bays). This turtle sanctuary contains a cave with pounding waves off the choppy north coast. Admission to this park is $1.50 per person.

NORTH & EAST OF WILLEMSTAD

Just northeast of the capital, **Fort Nassau** was completed in 1797 and christened by the Dutch as Fort Republic. Built high on a hill overlooking the harbor entrance to the south and St. Anna Bay to the north, it was fortified as a second line of defense in case the waterfront gave way. When the British invaded in 1807, they renamed it Fort George in honor of their own king. Later, when the Dutch regained control, they renamed it Orange Nassau in honor of the Dutch royal family. Today, diners have replaced soldiers (see "Where to Dine," above).

The **Curaçao Liqueur Distillery,** Landhuis Chobolobo, Saliña Arriba (☎ 599/9-4613526), offers a chance to visit and taste at Chobolobo, the 17th-century land-huis where the famous Curaçao liqueur is made. The cordial is a distillate of dried peel of a particular strain of orange found only on Curaçao. Several herbs are added to give it an aromatic bouquet. One of the rewards of a visit here is a free snifter of the liqueur, offered Monday to Friday from 8am to noon and 1 to 5pm.

On Schottegatweg West, northwest of Willemstad, past the oil refineries, lies the **Beth Haim Cemetery,** the oldest Caucasian burial site still in use in the western hemisphere. Meaning "House of Life," the cemetery was consecrated before 1659. There are some 2,500 graves on about 3 acres here. The carving on some of the 17th- and 18th-century tombstones is exceptional.

Landhuis Brievengat, Brievengat (☎ 599/9-7378344), gives visitors a chance to visit a Dutch version of an 18th-century West Indian plantation house. This stately building, in a scrub-dotted landscape on the eastern side of the island, contains a few antiques, high ceilings, and a gallery facing two entrance towers, said to have been used to imprison slaves. The plantation was originally used for the cultivation of aloe and cattle, but an 1877 hurricane caused it to cease operation. It's open daily from 9:15am to 12:15pm and 3 to 6pm; admission is $1.

Hato Caves, F. D. Rooseveltweg (☎ 599/9-8680379), have been called mystical. Every hour, professional local guides take visitors through this Curaçao world of stalagmites and stalactites, found in the highest limestone terrace of the island. Actually, they were once old coral reefs, which were formed when the ocean water fell and the landmass was lifted up over the years. Over thousands of years, limestone formations were created, some mirrored in an underground lake. After crossing the lake, you enter the Cathedral, an underground cavern. The largest hall of the cave is called La Ventana ("The Window"). Also on display are samples of ancient Indian petroglyph drawings. The caves are open daily from 10am to 4pm; admission is $6.25 for adults and $4.75 for children 4 to 11.

Curaçao Seaquarium, off Dr. Martin Luther King Boulevard at a site called Bapor Kibrá (☎ 599/9-4616666), has more than 400 species of fish, crabs, anemones, sponges, and coral on display in a natural environment. A rustic boardwalk connects the low-lying hexagonal buildings of the Seaquarium complex, which sits near a point where the *Oranje Nassau* hit the rocks and sank in 1906 (the name of the site, Bapor Kibrá, means "sunken ship"). Located a few minutes' walk along the rocky coast from the Princess Beach Resort & Casino, the Seaquarium is open daily from 8:30am to 6pm. Admission is $12.50 for adults, $7 for children 14 and under.

A special feature of the aquarium is a "shark and animal encounter," which costs $55 for divers or $30 for snorkelers. Divers, snorkelers, and experienced swimmers can feed, film, and photograph sharks, which are separated from them by a large window with feeding holes. In the animal-encounters section, swimmers can swim among stingrays, lobsters, tarpons, parrotfish, and other marine life, feeding and photographing these creatures in a controlled environment where safety is always a consideration. The Seaquarium is also home to Curaçao's only full-facility, palm-shaded, white-sand beach.

The *Seaworld Explorer* is a semi-submersible submarine that departs daily at 4:30pm on hour-long journeys into the deep. You're taken on a tour of submerged wrecks off the shores of Curaçao and treated to close encounters of coral reefs with rainbow-hued tropical fish. The *Explorer* has a barge top that submerges only 5 or so feet under the water, but the submerged section has wide glass windows allowing passengers underwater views, which can extend 110 feet. Reservations must be made a day in advance by calling ☎ **599/9-5604892.** It costs $33 for adults, $19 for children 11 and under.

SIGHTSEEING TOURS

Taber Tours, Dokweg (☎ **599/9-7376637**), offers several trips to points of interest on Curaçao. The tour through Willemstad, to the Curaçao Liqueur distillery, through the residential area and the Bloempot shopping center, and to the Curaçao Museum (the admission fee is included in the tour price) costs $12.50 for adults, $6.25 for children 11 and under.

The easiest way to go exploring is to take a 1¼-hour **trolley tour,** visiting the highlights of Willemstad. The open-sided cars, pulled by a silent "locomotive," make two trips each week—Monday at 11am and Wednesday at 4pm. The tour begins at Fort Amsterdam near the Queen Emma Pontoon Bridge. The cost is $15.90 for adults, $10.90 for children 2 to 12. Call ☎ **599/9-4628833** for more information.

7 Shopping

Curaçao is a shopper's paradise. Some 200 shops line the major shopping malls of such streets as Heerenstraat and Breedestraat. Right in the heart of Willemstad is the 5-block **Punda** shopping district. Most stores are open Monday through Saturday from 8am to noon and 2 to 6pm (some, from 8am to 6pm). When cruise ships are in port, stores are also open for a few hours on Sunday and holidays. To avoid the cruise-ship crowds, do your shopping in the morning.

Look for good buys on French perfumes, Dutch Delft blue souvenirs, finely woven Italian silks, Japanese and German cameras, jewelry, silver, Swiss watches, linens, leather goods, liquor, and island-made rum and liqueurs, especially Curaçao liqueur, some of which has a distinctive blue color. The island is famous for its 5-pound wheels of Gouda and Edam cheeses. You'll also see wooden shoes, although we're not sure what you'd do with them. Some of the stores also stock some deals on intricate lacework imported from Portugal, China, and everywhere in between. If you're a street shopper and want something colorful, consider one of the wood carvings or flamboyant paintings from Haiti or the Dominican Republic. Both are hawked by street vendors at any of the main plazas.

Incidentally, Curaçao is not technically a free port, but its prices are often inexpensive because of its low import duty.

Curaçao Creations, Schrijnwerkerstraat 14, off Breedestraat (☎ **599/9-4624516**), is a showcase for authentic handcrafts made within the walls of a 150-year-old storefront in Otrobanda. On a narrow side street, it's within easy walking distance of the Queen Emma Bridge, the bus stop, and the cruise-ship terminal. A workshop and souvenir outlet are combined, so you can see how your purchases were created. This is one of the few shops on the island to offer authentic, handmade Curaçao crafts; most stores sell imported items.

Kas di Arte Kursou, Breedestraat 126, Otrabanda (☎ **599/9-8642516**), in a 19th-century mansion in Otrobanda near the cruise-ship terminal, sells unique souvenirs such as one-of-a-kind T-shirts, all handmade by local artists. The gallery also has changing exhibits of paintings, plus a sculpture gallery.

Every garment sold in **Bamali,** Breedestraat 2 (☎ **599/9-4612258**), is designed and, in many cases, crafted by the store owners. Influenced largely by Indonesian patterns, the airy attire includes V-neck cotton pullovers perfect for a casual, hot-weather climate, as well as linen shifts, often in batik prints, appropriate for a glamorous cocktail party. Most pieces here are for women; all are made from all-natural materials, such as cotton, silk, and linen, and there's also a limited array of sandals and leather bags. **Benetton,** Madurostraat 4 (☎ **599/9-4614619**), has invaded Curaçao with all its many colors. Some items are marked down by about 20% off Stateside prices (this is done to get rid of surplus stock from the previous season); in-season clothing is available as well.

Bert Knubben Black Koral Art Studio, in the Princess Beach Resort & Casino, Dr. Martin Luther King Blvd. (☎ **599/9-4652122**), is a name synonymous with craftsmanship and quality. Although collection of black coral has been made illegal by the Curaçao government, an exception was made for Bert, a diver who has been harvesting corals and fashioning them into fine jewelry and objets d'art for more than 35 years. Collectors avidly seek out this type of coral, not only for the quality of its craftsmanship, but also because it's becoming increasingly rare and may one day not be offered for sale at all. The jewelry here is rivaled only by Bernard I. Passman's Black Coral and . . . shops in George Town in the Cayman Islands and in Charlotte Amalie on St. Thomas.

Gandelman Jewelers, Breedestraat 35, Punda (☎ **599/9-4611854**), is the island's best and most reliable choice for jewelry. It's well stocked with a large selection of fine jewelry, often exquisitely designed and set with diamonds, rubies, emeralds, sapphires, and other gemstones. You'll also find famous-maker timepieces and the unique line of Prima Classe leather goods with the world map. Gandelman Jewelers has eight other stores in the Dutch Caribbean.

Little Holland, Braedestraat 37, Punda (☎ **599/9-4611768**), is the main branch of a chain of stores with outlets in Bonaire and Aruba. This masculine-looking enclave specializes in silk neckties, Nautica shorts and shirts, and, most important, a sophisticated array of cigars. Crafted in Cuba, the Dominican Republic, and Brazil, they include some of the most prestigious names in smoke, including Montecristos, Cohiba, and Churchills. *Warning:* At this writing, it's illegal to bring Cuban cigars into the mainland U.S.

Electronics are a good buy on Curaçao, as they can be sold duty free; we recommend the very reliable **Boolchand's,** Heerenstraat 4B, Punda (☎ **599/9-4612262**), in business since 1930. If you can't find what you're looking for, try **Palais Hindu,** Heerenstraat 17 (☎ **599/9-4616897**), which sells a wide range of video and cassette recorders, photographic equipment, and watches.

Penha & Sons, Heerenstraat 1 (☎ **599/9-4612266**), in the oldest building in town (1708), has a history dating to 1865. It has long been known for its perfumes, cosmetics, and designer clothing (for both men and women), one of the finest collections in the ABC islands. It distributes such names as Calvin Klein, Yves Saint Laurent, Elizabeth Arden, Clarins, and Estée Lauder, among others. There are 10 other branches in the Caribbean.

The Yellow House (La Casa Amarilla), Breedestraat 46 (☎ **599/9-4613222**), in a yellow-and-white 19th-century building and operating since 1887, sells an intriguing collection of perfume and cosmetics from all over the world and is an agent of Christian Dior, Guerlain, Cartier, and Van Cleef & Arpels. It has the widest and best selection of scents on Curaçao, although it isn't a "cut-rate" discount house.

At **Landhuis Groot Santa Martha,** Santa Martha (☎ **599/9-8641559**), craftspeople with disabilities fashion unusual handcrafts, some evoking those found in South America. **Yoqui,** De Rouvilleweg 9A (☎ **599-9-4627533**), sells an unusual collection of artifacts from the Incas and the Mayan Indians, most made of clay and onyx. There's also contemporary tribal paintings done on leather and bark.

8 Curaçao After Dark

Most of the action spins around the island's **casinos:** the **Sonesta Beach Hotel & Casino,** Piscadera Bay (☎ 599/9-7368800); **Holiday Beach Hotel & Casino,** Otrabanda, Pater Euwensweg 31 (☎ 599/9-4625400); **Plaza Hotel & Casino,** Plaza Piar, in Willemstad (☎ 599/9-4612500); **Porto Paseo Hotel & Casino,** De Rouvilleweg 47 in Willemstad (☎ 599/9-4627878); and **Princess Beach Resort & Casino,** Martin Luther King Blvd. 8 (☎ 599/9-7367888).

The **Emerald Casino** at the Sonesta is especially popular, designed to resemble an open-air courtyard. It features 143 slot machines, six blackjack tables, two roulette wheels, two Caribbean stud poker tables, a craps table, a baccarat table, and a mini-baccarat table. The casino at the **Princess Beach Hotel** is the liveliest on the island. These hotel gaming houses usually start their action at 2pm, and some of them remain open until 4am. The Princess Beach serves complimentary drinks.

The historic **Landhuis Brievengat** (see "Exploring the Island," above), in addition to being a museum with island artifacts, is also the site of Wednesday, Friday, and Sunday rijsttafel parties. They begin at 7:30pm, require an admission fee of $8 (which includes the first drink), and feature heaping portions of rijsttafel that start at $16.50 each. Although the Landhuis itself is not directly connected with the dancing and drinking, there's a platform set up amid the flamboyant trees nearby, and two bands that alternate with each other to provide a pleasant ambience. It's wise to phone before going, as the event is very popular, especially on Friday night.

The landlocked, flat, and somewhat dusty neighborhood of **Salinja** is now the nightlife capital of Curaçao, with many drinking and dancing outlets. Among the best of them is **Blues,** in the Avila Beach Hotel, Penstraat 130 (☎ **599/9-4614377**). Don't overlook this restaurant (see "Where to Dine," above) as an option for nightlife: Its bar is active with couples and singles every night of the week except Monday. Live music, performed by U.S.-based jazz musicians, is offered Thursday from 7pm to midnight and Saturday from 9pm to 1:30am. There's no cover charge, ever.

Studio 99, Lindbergweg (☎ **599/9-4655433**), in a sprawling building set inland from the coast, in the heart of the Salinja district, is the leading and most attractive disco on Curaçao. The jungle motif is enhanced by masses of coconut palms, a dance floor where rhythms seem to pulsate out of the floor, and a copious bar area where more than a usual number of drinks seem to be tinted blue. Although hours vary with the season and according to the number of foreign visitors on the island, it's usually open Wednesday to Sunday from 9:30pm to 2am. The cover is $6 to $7.

Club Façade, Lindbergweg 8 (☎ **599/9-4614640**), in the Salinja district, is one of the most popular discos on the island. Spread over several different levels of a modern building, it has a huge bar, three dance floors, and live music nightly. It's open Wednesday to Sunday from 8pm to 3am. The cover is $5 to $10.

Dominica 11

The meager beaches aren't worth the effort to get here, but the landscape and rivers are. Nature lovers who visit Dominica (pronounced *dom-in-EE-ka*) experience a wild Caribbean setting, as well as the rural life that has largely disappeared on the more developed islands. Dominica is, after all, one of the poorest and least developed islands in the Caribbean, where many of its citizens make a subsistence living from fishing or working the land. Come to Dominica for the beauties of nature more than for *la dolce vita.* There are no casinos and no megaresort hotels—and hardly any road signs. In fact, some have suggested that it's the only island in the Caribbean that Columbus would still recognize.

Hiking and mountain climbing are good reasons to visit Dominica, and the flora is extremely lush and often rare. Covered by a dense tropical rain forest that blankets its mountain slopes, including cloud-wreathed Morne Diablotin at 4,747 feet, it has vegetation unique in the West Indies and remains the most rugged of the Caribbean islands. The mountainous island is 29 miles long and 16 miles wide, with a total land area of 290 square miles, much of which has never been seen by explorers. Should you visit, you'll find clear rivers, waterfalls, hot springs, and boiling lakes. According to myth, Dominica has 365 "rivers," one for each day of the year.

With a population of 75,000, Dominica lies in the eastern Caribbean, between Guadeloupe to the north and Martinique to the south. English is the official language, but a French patois is widely spoken. The Caribs, the indigenous people of the Caribbean whose numbers have dwindled to 3,000, live as a community on the northeast of the island, where the art of traditional basketry is still practiced.

Alec Waugh, the travel writer, wrote in 1948: "There is only one way to understand Dominica. You have to walk across it and along it. Range after range with its leaf-domed summit merges into the background of successive ranges, with each shade of green merging into another." That observation still holds true today.

Because of the pristine coral reefs, dramatic drop-offs, and shipwrecks found in the crystal-clear waters (with visibility of 100-plus feet), scuba diving is becoming increasingly popular, particularly off the west coast, site of Dominica's two dive operations.

Yearly rainfall varies from 50 inches along the dry west coast to as much as 350 inches in the tropical rain forests of the mountainous interior, where downpours are not uncommon.

Clothing is casual, including light summer wear for most of the year. However, take along walking shoes for those trips into the mountains and a sweater for cooler evenings. Locals, who are rather conservative, frown on bikinis and swimwear when worn on the streets of the capital city, **Roseau,** or in the villages.

1 Essentials

VISITOR INFORMATION

Before you go, you can contact the **Dominica Tourist Office** at 10 E. 21st St., Suite 600, New York, NY 10010 (☎ 212/475-7542; www.dominica.dm).

In England, information is available from the **Office of the Dominica High Commission London,** 1 Collingham Gardens, London SW5 0HW (☎ 0171/370-5194).

On the island, the **Dominica Tourist Information Office** is on the Old Market Plaza, Roseau, with administrative offices at the National Development Corporation offices, Valley Road (☎ 767/448-2186); it's open Tuesday through Friday from 8am to 4pm, Monday from 8am to 5pm.

There are also information bureaus at **Melville Hall Airport** (☎ 767/445-7051) and **Canefield Airport** (☎ 767/449-1242).

GETTING THERE

BY PLANE There are two airports on Dominica, neither of which is large enough to handle a jet; therefore, there are no direct flights from North America. The **Melville Hall Airport** (☎ 767/445-7100) is on the northeastern coast, almost diagonally across the island from the capital, Roseau, on the southwestern coast. Melville Hall is a 1½ -hour taxi ride from Roseau, a tour across the island through the forest and coastal villages; the fare is $18 per person, and drivers have the right to gather up at least four passengers. By private taxi, the fare could be $50.

The newer **Canefield Airport** (☎ 767/449-1199) is about a 15-minute taxi ride north of Roseau. The 2,000-foot airstrip accommodates smaller planes than those that can land at Melville Hall. From here, the typical taxi fare into town is $15. There's also a public bus (with an *H* that precedes the number on the license plate) that costs only $2 per person; buses come every 20 minutes and hold between 15 and 18 passengers.

For many Americans, the easiest way to reach Dominica is via the daily **American Eagle** (☎ 800/433-7300) flight from San Juan (Thursday through Sunday, there are two flights daily). From Antigua, you can board one of the five daily **LIAT** (☎ 800/468-0482 in the U.S. and Canada, or 767/448-2422) flights to Dominica. Another possibility would be to fly via St. Maarten. From there, LIAT offers one nonstop flight daily and two other daily flights with intermediary stops.

You can also fly to Guadeloupe and make a connection on **Air Guadeloupe** (☎ 767/448-2181), which has two flights a day to Dominica except on Sunday, when there is no morning flight (flying time is 30 minutes). If you're in Fort-de-France on Martinique, you can take a LIAT flight to Dominica.

Two minor airlines also serve Dominica: **Helen Air** (☎ 767/448-2181) flies in from Barbados and St. Lucia, arriving twice daily at both the Canefield and Melville Hall airports; and **Cardinal Airlines** (☎ 767/449-0600) wings in from the islands of Antigua, Barbados, and Dutch St. Maarten, arriving at Canefield daily.

BY BOAT The *Caribbean Express* (☎ 596/63-12-11, or 767/448-2181 on Dominica), sailing from the French West Indies, runs between Guadeloupe in the north to Martinique in the south; Dominica is a port of call along the way. Departures are Friday to Wednesday; call for exact schedules.

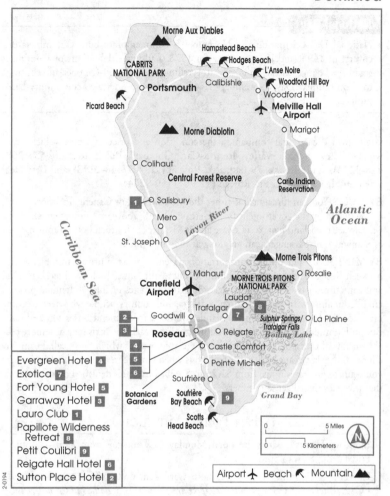

Evergreen Hotel **4**
Exotica **7**
Fort Young Hotel **5**
Garraway Hotel **3**
Lauro Club **1**
Papillote Wilderness
  Retreat **8**
Petit Coulibri **9**
Reigate Hall Hotel **6**
Sutton Place Hotel **2**

In addition, car-ferries sail from Pointe-à-Pitre to Roseau five to seven times a week, depending on demand. For schedule information, contact **White Church Travel,** 5 Great Marlborough St., Roseau (☎ **767/448-2181**). A one-way fare costs EC$224.50 ($83.05).

GETTING AROUND

The capital of Dominica is Roseau, and many of the places to stay are found here or very close by.

BY RENTAL CAR   If you rent a car, there's a fee of EC$30 ($11.10) to obtain a driver's license, which is available at the airports. The island has 310 miles of newly paved roads, and only in a few areas is a four-wheel-drive vehicle necessary. *Note: Driving is on the left.*

Most U.S. vacationers reserve their car in advance from the local representative of **Avis,** 4 High St., Roseau (☎ **800/331-1212** in the U.S., or 767/448-2481), although we've found the service here poor. There are also a handful of small, usually

National Day celebrations on November 3 commemorate both Columbus's discovery, in 1493, and independence, in 1978. Cultural celebrations of Dominica's traditional dance, music, song, and storytelling begin in mid-October and continue to Community Day, November 4, when people undertake community-based projects.

family-owned car-rental companies, the condition and price of whose vehicles vary widely. They include **Valley Rent-a-Car,** Goodwill Road, Roseau (☎ 767/448-3233); **Wide Range,** 79 Bath Rd., Roseau (☎ 767/448-2198); and **Best Deal Car Rental,** 15 Hanover St., Roseau (☎ 767/449-9204).

BY TAXI   You can hire a taxi at either the Melville Hall or Canefield Airport. Prices are regulated by the government (see "Getting There," above, for airport fares). If you want to see the island by taxi, rates are about $18 per car for each hour of touring, and as many as four passengers can go along at the same time.

BY MINIBUS   The public transportation system consists of private minibus service between Roseau and the rest of Dominica. These minibuses, each of which is painted and sometimes garishly decorated according to the tastes of their individual owners, are filled mainly with schoolchildren, workers, and country people who need to come into Roseau. On most Caribbean islands, we don't recommend buses too zealously. But on Dominica, buses afford the best insight into local life. Taxis may be a more reliable means of transport for visitors, but there are hotels at which buses call during the course of the day. You can also just hail a bus when you see it, and tell the driver where you want to go. Fares range from $1.25 to $3.35. Buses are identified by the letter *H* that precedes their license numbers.

Fast Facts: Dominica

Banking Hours   Banks are open Monday to Thursday from 8am to 3pm, Friday from 8am to 5pm.

Currency   Dominica uses the Eastern Caribbean dollar (EC$), worth about EC$2.70 to U.S $1. *Prices in this chapter are given in U.S. dollars unless otherwise indicated.*

Customs   Dominica is lenient, allowing you to bring personal and household effects, plus 200 cigarettes, 50 cigars, and 40 ounces of liquor or wine per person.

Documents   To enter, U.S. and Canadian citizens must have proof of citizenship, such as a passport or birth certificate along with a photo ID. In addition, an ongoing or return ticket must be shown. British visitors should have a valid passport.

Drugstores   See "Pharmacies," below.

Electricity   The electricity is 220–240 volts AC (50 cycles), so both adapters and transformers are necessary for U.S.-made appliances. It's smart to bring a flashlight with you, in case of power outages.

Emergencies   To call the police, report a fire, or summon an ambulance, dial ☎ 999.

Hospital   The island hospital is **Princess Margaret Hospital,** Federation Drive, Goodwill (☎ 767/448-2231). However, those with serious medical complications may want to forgo a visit to Dominica, as island medical facilities are often inadequate.

Language   English is the official language. Locals often speak a Creole-French patois.

Pharmacies   The island's best-stocked drugstore is **Jolly's Pharmacy,** in Roseau at 37 Great George St., and 12 King George V St. Both branches share the same phone number and hours (☎ **767/448-3388**). They're open Monday to Thursday from 8am to 4:30pm, Friday from 8am to 5pm, and Saturday from 8am to 1:30pm. They also have a 24-hour prescription service available at the same number for after-hours needs.

Safety   Although crime is rare here, you should still safeguard your valuables. Never leave them unattended on the beach or in a locked car.

Taxes   A 10% government room tax is added on accommodations, and a 3% tax on alcoholic drinks and food items. Anyone who remains on Dominica for more than 24 hours must pay a $12 (U.S.) departure tax.

Telephone   International direct dialing is available on Dominica, as well as U.S. direct service through AT&T. To call Dominica from the United States, dial **1**, then **767** (the country code for Dominica) and the local number. To call Dominica from another island within the Caribbean, just dial **767,** plus the seven-digit local number.

Time   Dominica is on Atlantic standard time, 1 hour ahead of eastern standard time in the United States. Dominica does not observe daylight saving time, so when the United States changes to daylight time, clocks in Dominica and the U.S. East Coast tell the same time.

Tipping   Most hotels and restaurants add a 10% service charge to all bills. If this charge has not been included, tipping is up to you.

Water   The water is drinkable from the taps and in the high mountain country. Pollution is hardly a problem here.

Weather   Daytime temperatures average between 70° and 85°F. Nights are much cooler, especially in the mountains. The rainy season is June to October, when there can be warnings of hurricane activity. Regrettably, Dominica lies in the "hurricane path," and fierce storms have taken their toll on the island over the years.

2 Where to Stay

The government imposes a 10% tax on hotel rooms and a 3% tax on beverages and food, which will be added to your hotel bill. Unless otherwise noted, the rates given below are year-round and in U.S. dollars. Before you book your hotel, see the section on "Package Deals," in chapter 2.

IN ROSEAU & CASTLE COMFORT

Evergreen Hotel. P.O. Box 309, Castle Comfort, Dominica, W.I. ☎ **767/448-3288.** Fax 767/448-6800. www.delphis.dm/evergreen.htm. E-mail: evergreen@cwdom.dm. 22 units. A/C TV TEL. Year-round $110–$150 double. Extra person $30. Rates include full breakfast. AE, DC, DISC, MC, V.

Built in 1986, this pleasant, family-run hotel looks a bit like a Swiss chalet from the outside, although once inside you're greeted with an open-air restaurant with bright jungle prints, crystal teardrop chandeliers, and an art-deco bar. The newer annex, though sterile looking, has better rooms than the main building. A few units have access to wraparound tile-floored verandas; all have stone accents. Accommodations are bright and airy, with paired double beds, decent mattresses, and ample storage space; bathrooms have showers only. The Evergreen sits amid a cluster of other hotels about a mile south of Roseau. A stony beach is visible a few steps beyond the garden. Inside and out, the airy, comfortably modern place is trimmed with local gommier wood. Mena Winston, the Dominican-born owner, assists in preparing your meals, which are well done and cost $20 to $25. Laundry service and scuba diving can be arranged. There's a pool on site.

Fort Young Hotel. Victoria St. (P.O. Box 519), Roseau, Dominica, W.I. ☎ **800/223-1588** in the U.S., 800/544-7631 in Canada, or 767/448-5000. Fax 767/448-5006. www. fortyounghotel.com. E-mail: fortyoung@cwdom.dm. 53 units. A/C TV TEL. Winter $95–$145 double; $210 suite. Off-season $85–$135 double, $210 suite. AE, MC, V.

Occupying a cliffside setting, this modern hotel grew from the ruins of the 1770 Fort Young, once the island's major military installation. Traces of its former historic role remain, including cannons at the entrance. Once a domain of business travelers to Roseau, it's attracting more and more tourists, drawn to the comfortable bedrooms with ceiling fans and balconies. Here you are elevated far above the "mosquito line," so you can actually sit out and enjoy the balmy Caribbean air without being attacked by these pests, the curse of the West Indies. The hotel recently added 21 new ocean-front guest rooms and a trio of one-bedroom suites at the base of a cliff below the existing fort. Ask for one of these new units, which have direct ocean views facing west toward the Caribbean, plus a sitting area and two queen beds with firm mattresses. Another new addition is a swimming pool with waterfalls and shade pergola, at the edge of the sea in lieu of a beach. Adjacent to the pool is a fitness room containing exercise equipment. Laundry service and tours can be arranged.

The Fort Young Hotel Restaurant, a candlelit room with stone walls and a ceiling of wood rafters, is better than ever. The Jamaican chef not only draws upon his homeland for inspiration, but is also an expert at regional dishes. Much of his repertoire evokes a continental flair.

Garraway Hotel. Place Heritage, The Bayfront (P.O. Box 789), Roseau, Dominica, W.I. ☎ **767/449-8800.** Fax 767/449-8807. www.dephis.dm/garraway.htm. E-mail: garraway@ cwdom.dm. 31 units. A/C TV TEL. Year-round $130 double; $140–$170 suite. AE, DC, MC, V.

This hotel opened in 1994 adjacent to the home of its owners, the Garraway family, who cater largely to a business clientele, although it's a perfectly acceptable choice for leisure travelers as well. If you normally book into a Ramada on your travels, this is the closest thing you'll find on Dominica. It offers spacious guest rooms in seashell colors, most with vistas stretching all the way to Dominica's southernmost tip. The higher the floor, the more colorful the views of the rooftops of Roseau. Each unit is outfitted with rattan furniture and pastel floral-print fabrics, one king or two double beds, good mattresses, a combination tub/shower bathroom, and a hair dryer. Don't faint at the news, but Dominica now has a hotel with an elevator. Some locals like to visit just to ride up in it, but Garraway rises only five floors. Public rooms are given an authentic island touch with artwork and locally made vetiver-grass mats. On the premises is the Balisier restaurant (see "Where to Dine," below) and, adjacent to the sea, the Pavement Café. Room service and laundry service are available; baby-sitting can be arranged.

Reigate Hall Hotel. Mountain Rd. (P.O. Box 200, Reigate), Dominica, W.I. ☎ **767/ 448-4031.** Fax 767/448-4034. E-mail: reigate@cwdom.dm. 19 units. A/C TEL. Winter $95 double; $150 suite; $180 cottage apt. Off-season $80 double; $125 suite; $135 cottage apt. Rates include breakfast. AE, MC, V.

On a steep hillside about a mile east of Roseau, this hotel was originally built in the 18th century as a plantation house. It was once one of the finest hotels on the island, but it now faces increased competition and has slipped a bit in terms of maintenance and service. It still has its admirers, though, especially those drawn to its lofty setting and panoramic views. Some parts of the original structure are left, but the building has been substantially altered. The hotel has a comfortably airy design, with hardwood floors and exposed stone. Guest rooms curve around the sides of a rectangular pool and offer ocean vistas. Two deluxe one-bedroom suites each have a fridge, wet bar, and private in-room Jacuzzi. Reigate also offers one two-bedroom apartment (without cooking facilities) that can accommodate three comfortably. Facilities include a tennis court, a good restaurant, laundry, baby-sitting, and room service.

✪ **Sutton Place Hotel.** 25 Old St., Roseau, Dominica, W.I. ☎ **767/449-8700.** Fax 767/448-3045. www.delphis.dm/sutton.htm. E-mail: sutton2@cwdom.dm. 8 units. A/C TV TEL. Year-round $95 double; $135 suite. AE, DISC, MC, V.

If former visitors Alec Waugh, Noël Coward, or Princess Margaret were to show up today, chances are they would head for this little retreat. A small, historic property in the center of town, it was once a 1930s guest house run by "Mother" Harris, a matriarch who became a local legend. Destroyed by Hurricane David in 1979, the new Sutton Place was rebuilt in a traditional Caribbean style by the same Harris family, who continue the old traditions but with far greater style. Rooms are tastefully furnished with antique-style pieces, including four-poster beds with great mattresses, brass desk lamps, and teak bathroom furnishings along with fluffy towels and a hair dryer. Suites contain fully equipped kitchenettes. The staircase and floors of the suites are laid with a fine hardwood, tauroniro from South America. Stylized floral arrangements, exotic prints, and luxurious fabrics contribute to the upscale style. The Cellar, housing a bar, is the only part of the original structure that survived the hurricane. The restaurant is now one of the choice places to dine in Roseau, with a Creole/international menu that also embraces some dishes from Italy, China, and India. The nearest beach is about a mile or so away.

AT SALISBURY

✪ **Lauro Club.** Grande Savane, Salisbury (P.O. Box 483, Roseau), Dominica, W.I. ☎ **767/449-6602.** Fax 767/449-6603. 10 units. Winter $73–$205 double. Off-season $58–$164 double. AE, DC, MC, V.

Built in 1991, a short walk uphill from the island's west coast, this rustic villa complex lies about half a mile from the town of Salisbury (pop. 2,000), midway between Roseau and Portsmouth. Owned and operated by a Swiss expatriate couple, Roland and Laurence Pralong, it's a simple but neat compound of white-sided concrete buildings with green, red, and gray roofs. This is a small, nonresorty hotel with few amenities or diversions other than the beach and the local botany; it definitely offers an escapist mood favored by Europeans. The studios come two to a cottage, while the one-bedroom units stand alone. None have TVs or phones, but each has a covered veranda, floral draperies and upholstery, queen beds with firm mattresses, and views of the water. You pay for what you get here, as bedrooms range from standard doubles—rather small—to spacious deluxe seafront units. Tile floors and mahogany furnishings add to the tropical motif. Bathrooms are small but efficiently organized, with stall showers and sufficient shelf space. Although the sea is nearby, it takes a 5-minute walk and a climb down a long, serpentine staircase to get to a beach that's suitable for swimming. On the premises is a restaurant, the Lauro Club, serving Creole and international dishes. Table tennis, scuba diving, snorkeling, and guided tours of Dominica are available through the reception desk.

IN THE RAIN FOREST

✪ **Papillote Wilderness Retreat.** Trafalgar Falls Rd. (P.O. Box 2287), Roseau, Dominica, W.I. ☎ **767/448-2287.** Fax 767/448-2285. www.papillote.dm. E-mail: papillote@cwdom. dm. 7 units. Year-round $85 double; $90 suite; $180 two-bedroom cottage (sleeps up to 4). MAP $35 per person extra. AE, MC, V. Closed Aug 15–Oct 15.

This property is run by the Jean-Baptistes: Cuthbert, who handles the restaurant, and his wife, Anne Grey, who was a marine scientist. Their unique resort, 4 miles east of Roseau, stands right in the middle of Papillote Forest, at the foothills of Morne Macaque. In this remote setting, you can lead an Adam and Eve life, surrounded by exotic fruits, flowers, and herb gardens. The rooms have a rustic, log-cabin atmosphere. Laundry and room service are both available.

Don't expect constantly sunny weather, since this part of the jungle is known for its downpours; their effect, however, keeps the orchids, begonias, and brilliantly colored bromeliads lush. The 12 acres of sloping and forested land are pierced with a labyrinth of stone walls and trails, beside which flows a network of freshwater streams, a few of which come from hot mineral springs. Natural hot mineral baths are available, and you'll be directed to a secluded waterfall where you can swim in the river. The Jean-Baptistes also run a boutique that sells Dominican products, including appliquéd quilts made by local artisans. Even if you don't stay here, it's an experience to dine on the thatch-roofed terrace.

NEAR SOUFRIÈRE

✪ **Petit Coulibri.** Petit Coulibri Estate, near Soufrière (P.O. Box 331), Dominica, W.I. ☎ **767/446-3150.** Fax 767/446-3153. www.delphis.dm/petit.htm. E-mail: barnardm@ cwdom.dm. 5 units. Winter $115 studio; $225 cottage. Off-season $100 studio; $180 cottage. AE, DC, DISC, MC, V.

After much publicity in travel magazines, this escapist Shangri-la is emerging as a famous local spot that makes for an exceptional and affordable vacation experience. That is, if you can get here: It takes a bumpy 10-minute drive from Soufrière in a four-wheel-drive vehicle, but it's worth the effort. This is really a retreat in the wilderness—so expect comfort, not deluxe living. U.S. expats Loye and Barney Barnard have created a trio of two-bedroom cottages, each with large verandas and a kitchen, plus two small, rather basic-looking studios, each with a large bedroom and small veranda. The Barnards built the solar-powered cottages from stone and wood and added artful decorative touches, including stained glass. Dominican crafts help create a homey island ambience. The cottages aren't air-conditioned, as nights are cool at this high elevation. Beds are doubles or twins, draped in mosquito netting, and bathrooms are small. Supplies can be purchased in Roseau, although shopping is very basic; the hotel will also stock your kitchen if asked. Even better, let the owners prepare a home-cooked breakfast ($12) or a delectable dinner ($30). The pool overlooks a 1,000-foot drop and a view over the Martinique Channel.

AT MORNE ANGLAIS

✪ **Exotica.** Morne Anglais (P.O. Box 109), Roseau, Dominica, W.I. ☎ **767/448-8839.** Fax 767/448-8829. www.delphis.dm/eiexotic.htm. E-mail: exotica@cwdom.dm. 8 units. Winter $132.25 double. Off-season $125.35 double. Extra person $23. Children under 12 stay free in parents' room. Breakfast and dinner $35 per person extra. AE, DISC, MC, V.

In 1995, one of Dominica's best-known couples, Fae and Altherton Martin, erected this cluster of cottages on the western slope of Morne Anglais in the southern half of the island. This tropical setting is home to what's called an "agro-eco" resort, with some 38 different flowers and fruit trees on the 4-acre organic farm. Once you finally reach the place after a harrowing ride, you can enjoy the cool mountain breezes at 1,600 feet above sea level, at a point some 5 miles from Roseau. The resort's cottages are constructed from hardwoods, cured pine, and stone to blend into their natural surroundings. Accommodations are comfortable and tastefully furnished, each with a private porch, spacious living room, kitchen, large bedroom with two double beds, and private bathroom. The best swimming is in a nearby river, a 5-minute walk away. Guests can prepare their own meals or dine at the Sugar Apple Café, enjoying such delights as steamed local fish or apricot-glazed chicken with savory rice.

3 Where to Dine

It's customary to dine at your hotel, although Dominica has a string of independent restaurants. Dress is casual. If you're going out in the evening, always call to make sure your dining choice is actually open. You'll also have to arrange transportation there and back because of the bad lighting and awful roads.

IN ROSEAU

Balisier. In the Garraway Hotel, Place Heritage, The Bayfront. ☎ **767/449-8800.** Reservations recommended. Main courses EC$35–EC$80 ($12.95–$29.60); lunch EC$45–EC$80 ($16.65–$29.60); Fri lunch buffet EC$25 ($9.25). AE, MC, V. Daily noon–2:30pm and 6:30–10pm. CREOLE/INTERNATIONAL.

Named after a small red flower that thrives in the jungles of Dominica, this restaurant occupies the ground floor of the Garraway hotel and was designed to maximize the views over Roseau's harbor. We highly recommend the food, which might include shrimp mousse; chicken Garraway (breast of chicken stuffed with plantain and sweet corn); loin of pork with pineapple, mushrooms, and onions; and a choice of steak, vegetarian, or lobster entrees. Favorite local dishes include crab backs and Creole-style mountain chicken (frog's legs). End your meal with a slice of homemade coconut-cream pie. Lunches are simpler than dinners and might feature West Indian curries, fish Creole, or several kinds of salads.

✪ **Guiyave.** 15 Cork St. ☎ **767/448-2930.** Reservations recommended. Lunch EC$25–EC$55 ($9.25–$20.35); dinner EC$35–EC$75 ($12.95–$27.75). AE, MC, V. Mon–Fri 8:30am–3pm, Sat 9am–2:30pm; Mon–Sat 5:30pm–midnight. CREOLE.

This airy restaurant occupies the second floor of a wood-frame West Indian house. Rows of tables almost completely fill the narrow balcony overlooking the street outside. You can enjoy a drink at the stand-up bar on the second floor. Specialties include different preparations of conch, octopus, and lobster, spareribs, chicken, pork chops, and various grills for dinner. On Saturday, rotis and "goat water" are available. The place is known for its juices, including refreshing glasses of soursop, tamarind, sorrel, cherry, and strawberry. One part of the establishment is a pâtisserie specializing in French pastries.

✪ **La Robe Creole.** 3 Victoria St. ☎ **767/448-2896.** Reservations required. Main courses $25–$30. DISC, MC, V. Mon–Sat noon–9:30pm. CREOLE/SEAFOOD.

The best independent restaurant in the capital, La Robe Creole sits on the second floor of a colonial house, beside a sunny plaza on a slope above the sea. The staff, dressed in madras Creole costumes, serve food in a long, narrow dining room capped with heavy beams and filled with relics from the 19th century. You can enjoy pumpkin-pimiento soup, callaloo with cream of coconut soup, crab backs (in season), pizzas, mountain chicken (frog's legs) in beer batter, and shrimp in coconut with garlic sauce.

The food is in the spicy Creole style. One patron found the cuisine "seductive." For dessert, try banana or coconut cake or ice cream.

A street-level section of the restaurant, **The Mouse Hole,** is a good place for food on the run. You can take out freshly made sandwiches and salads, or good Trinidad-inspired rotis (Caribbean burritos: wheat pancakes wrapped around beef, chicken, or vegetables). On Dominica, these rotis are often flavored with curry. The Mouse Hole is open Monday to Saturday from 8am to 9:30pm.

✪ **Pearl's Cuisine.** 50 King George V St., Rouseau. ☎ 767/448-8707. Reservations not needed. EC$5–EC$30 ($1.85–$11.10) lunch, EC$20–EC$60 ($7.40–$22.20) dinner. AE, DC, MC, V. Daily 9am–9pm. CARIBBEAN.

In this restored Creole house with a veranda, Chef Pearl is the hearty empress, and enjoys a certain celebrity in town for her island delicacies. Come here for a true taste of Dominica likely to be unequaled anywhere else. Begin with one of her tropical fruit juices, then go on to sample mountain chicken (frog's legs) or perhaps freshly caught crayfish. Whenever lobster is available, it's served at dinner any way you want it. She also makes some mean pork chops, and her curried goat will make a man of you, even if you're a woman. Try the rice and spareribs or the codfish and plantains if you want to see what delights the local patronage. What's Pearl's favorite dish? Souse or pickled pigs' feet.

World of Food Restaurant and Bar. In Vena's Hotel, 48 Cork St. ☎ **767/448-3286.** Main courses EC$28–EC$58 ($10.35–$21.45). No credit cards. Daily 7:30am–10:30pm. CREOLE.

If you want to reach the restaurant without passing through Vena's Hotel (which is really a guest house), its entrance is on Field's Lane. In the 1930s, the garden containing this restaurant belonged to the novelist Jean Rhys, author of *Wide Sargasso Sea.* Today it's the patio for one of the most charming Creole restaurants in Roseau. Some say that its owner, Vena McDougal, is the best Creole cook in town. You can have a drink at the stone-walled building at the far end of the garden if you want, but many guests select one of the tables in the shadow of a large mango tree. Specialties include steamed fish or fish steak, curried goat, chicken-filled roti, black pudding, breadfruit puffs, conch, and tee-tee-ree (fried fish cakes). Vena also makes the best rum punches on the island.

IN THE RAIN FOREST

Papillote Wilderness Retreat. Trafalgar Falls Rd. ☎ 767/448-2287. Reservations recommended for lunch, required for dinner. Main courses EC$25–EC$60 ($9.25–$22.20). AE, DISC, MC, V. Daily 7:30am–10pm; dinner served at 7:30pm. CREOLE/CARIBBEAN.

Previously recommended for its lodgings, Papillote is an alluring Eden-esque restaurant. It would certainly be Tarzan's favorite. Even if you're not staying here, come by taxi for lunch; it's only 4 miles east of Roseau. For dinner, you'll need to make arrangements. Amid nature trails laced with exotic flowers, century-old trees, and filtered sunlight, you dine overlooking rivers and mountains. The array of healthful food includes flying fish and truly delectable freshwater prawns known as *bookh.* Mountain chicken (frog's legs) appears in season, as does kingfish. Breadfruit or dasheen puffs merit a taste if you've never tried them, and tropical salads are filled with flavor. Our favorite dishes include "the seafood symphony" and chicken rain forest (sautéed with orange, papaya, and banana, and wrapped in a banana leaf). Near the dining terrace is a Jacuzzi-size pool, which is constantly filled with the mineral-rich waters of a hot spring. Nonguests may use the pool for EC$5 ($1.85). Bring sturdy walking shoes in addition to a bathing suit.

NEAR SOUFRIÈRE

✪ **Forest Bistro.** Soufrière. ☎ **767/448-7104.** Reservations required. Main courses EC$25–EC$35 ($9.25–$12.95). Daily 11am–9pm. No credit cards. CARIBBEAN.

This bistro is aptly named. It's your best bet if you're hiking, diving, or driving in the Soufrière area of Dominica. On the southwestern coast, Forest Bistro is set in a lush tropical section of the island, cozy and secluded, with cliffs as a backdrop and a panoramic vista of the Caribbean from the tables. Cows roam among the acres of lime trees, and the whole place has such a bucolic setting, you'd want to come here even if the food weren't good. But the cuisine is excellent, well prepared, and made whenever possible with the freshest of ingredients, often grown by your hosts, Andre and Joyce Charles. The restaurant on this 5-acre dairy farm is actually the top floors of the Charles' home. Joyce is a top-notch chef, having worked at some of the island's finest restaurants. Her talent is particularly obvious in her fresh fish dishes. The farm also provides an endless source of refreshing drinks, including lime squash, passion fruit, grapefruit, and fresh coconut water. At lunch, you can order some of the island's most delightful soups, either made with peas, pumpkin, callaloo, or papaya. Stick to the fish unless you're a total vegetarian, in which case you might opt for one of the delicious Creole-style vegetarian dishes such as a savory eggplant.

4 Sports & Outdoor Pursuits

BEACHES If you're a true beach buff and you demand great beaches as part of your Caribbean vacation, you should choose another island. Dominica has some of the worst beaches in the Caribbean; most are rocky with gray-black volcanic sand. Some beaches, even though they don't have great sand or shade, are still good for diving or snorkeling in the turquoise waters surrounding the island.

The best beach on the island lies on the northwest coast. **Picard Beach** stretches for about 2 miles, a strip of grayish sand with palm trees as a backdrop. It's ideal for snorkeling or windsurfing, but not much else. You can drop in for food and drink at one of the hotels along the beach.

On the northeast coast, a quartet of beaches—**L'Anse Noire, Hodges Beach, Woodford Hill Bay,** and **Hampstead Beach**—are among the island's most beautiful, although none are ideal for swimming. Divers and snorkelers seek them out, however at times the water becomes too turbulent. Be duly warned about the strong currents here.

The southwest coast also has some beaches, but the sand here is black and studded with rocks. Nonetheless, snorkelers and scuba divers flock to **Soufrière Bay Beach** and **Scotts Head Beach** for the clear waters and the stunning underwater walls.

HIKING Wild and untamed Dominica offers very experienced and physically fit hikers some of the most bizarre geological oddities in the Caribbean. Sights include scalding lava covered with a hot, thin, and not-very-stable crust; a boiling lake where mountain streams turn to vapor as they come into contact with super-heated volcanic fissures; and a barren wasteland known as the "Valley of Desolation."

All these attractions are in the 17,000 heavily forested acres of the ✪ **Morne Trois Pitons National Park,** in the island's south-central region. You should go with a guide—they're in plentiful supply, waiting for your business in the village of Laudat. Few markers appear en route, but the trek, which includes a real assortment of geological oddities, stretches 6 miles in both directions from Laudat to the Boiling Lake. Hikers walk cautiously, particularly in districts peppered with bubbling hot springs. Regardless of where you turn, you'll run into streams and waterfalls, the inevitable result of an island whose mountaintops receive up to 400 inches of rainfall a year. Winds on the summits are strong enough to have pushed one recreational climber to her death several years ago, so be careful. Ferns, orchids, trees, and epiphytes create a tangle of underbrush; insect, bird, and reptilian life is profuse.

On your trek, pay a visit to the **Titou Gorge,** a deep and very narrow ravine whose depths were created as lava flows cooled and contracted. En route, you might spot rare Sisserou and Jacquot parrots, monkeys, and vines whose growth seems to increase visibly on an hourly basis. The hill treks of Dominica have been described as "sometimes easy, sometimes hellish," and if it should happen to rain during your climb (and it rains very frequently on Dominica), your path is likely to become very slippery. But botanists, geologists, and experienced hikers all agree that climbs through the jungles of Dominica are the most rewarding in the Caribbean.

Locals warn that to proceed along the island's badly marked trails into areas that can be physically treacherous is not a good idea; climbing alone or even in pairs is not advisable. Guides should be used for all unmarked trails. You can arrange for a guide by going to the office of the **Dominica National Park,** in the Botanical Gardens in Roseau (☎ 767/ 448-2401), or the Dominica Tourist Board. Forestry officials recommend **Ken's Hinterland Adventure Tours & Taxi Service,** 10A Old St., Roseau (☎ 767/448-4850). Depending on the destination and the featured attractions, treks cost $25 to $50 per person for up to four participants and require 4 to 8 hours round-trip. Usually included in the price is minivan transportation from Roseau to the starting point of your hill climb.

KAYAKING There is no greater kayaking adventure in all the Caribbean like that possible in Dominica. You can rent a kayak for $25 for a half day, then go on a unique adventure around the rivers and coastline of the lushest island in the West Indies. **Nature Island Dive,** in Roseau (☎ 767/449-8181), offers rentals and gives the best advice. You can combine bird watching, swimming, and snorkeling as you glide along. Consider Soufrière Bay, a marine reserve in southwest Dominica. Off the west coast, you can discover tranquil Caribbean waters with rainbow-hued fish along the beaches in Mero, Salisbury, and in the region of the Layou and Macoucherie Rivers.

SCUBA DIVING Diving holidays in Dominica are becoming more and more popular. The underwater terrain is spectacular, extending into the ocean. Most of the diving is on the southwestern end of the island, with its dramatic drop-offs, walls, and pinnacles. These volcanic formations are interwoven with cuts, arches, ledges, and overhangs, home to a myriad of sponges, gorgonians, and corals. An abundance of invertebrates, reef fish, and unusual sea creatures such as sea horses, frog-fish, batfish, and flying gunards attract the underwater photographer.

Dive Dominica, in the Castle Comfort Diving Lodge (P.O. Box 2253, Roseau), Castle Comfort, Dominica, W.I. (☎ 767/448-2188), gives open-water certification (both NAUI and PADI) instruction. Two diving catamarans and a handful of smaller boats get you to the dive sites in relative comfort. The dive outfit is closely linked to its on-site hotel, a 15-room lodge where at least 90% of the clientele check in as part of a dive package. A 7-night dive package, double occupancy, begins at $949 per person, including breakfasts and dinners, five two-tank dives, and one night dive. A single tank dive goes for $45, a two-tank dive for $75, and a night dive for $50. All rooms in the lodge are air-conditioned, and about half have TVs and phones. On the premises is a bar (for residents and their guests only) and a Jacuzzi.

Divers from all over the world patronize the **Dive Centre,** at the Anchorage Hotel in Castle Comfort (☎ 767/448-2638). A fully qualified PADI and NAUI staff awaits you. A single-tank dive costs $50; a double-tank dive, $65; and a one-tank night dive, $55. A unique whale and dolphin watch from 2pm to sunset is a popular attraction.

The price for a 3½-hour experience of communal straining to catch sight of the animals is $45 per person. On the way home (and not before), rum punches are served. With a pool, classrooms, a private dock, a miniflotilla of dive boats, and a well-trained and alert staff, this is the most complete dive resort on Dominica.

SNORKELING   Snorkel sites are never very far away, regardless of where you are on Dominica. The western side of the island, where nearly all of the snorkeling takes place, is the leeside, meaning the waters are tranquil. In all, there are some 30 separate and first-rate snorkeling areas immediately off the coast. You can explore the underwater hot springs at Champagne and Toucari, the Coral Gardens off Salisbury, and the southern shoreline of Scotts Head Beach, with more than 190 species of flamboyantly colored fish. The closeness of the reefs to shore makes snorkeling here among the best in the Caribbean, although it isn't a highly organized operation.

SWIMMING   The beaches may be lousy, but Dominica has some of the best river swimming in the Caribbean. Some say the little island has 365 rivers, one for every day of the year. The best places for swimming are under a waterfall, and there are dozens of them on the island. Almost all waterfalls have a refreshing pond at the base of them, ideal for a dip. Your best bets are on the west coast at the **Picard** or the **Machoucherie Rivers.** On the east coast, the finest spot is **White River,** near the hamlet of La Plaine. Consider also the **Layou River** and its gorges. Layou is the island's largest river, ranging from tranquil beach-lined pools ideal for swimming to deep gorges and turbulent rapids. All the rivers are unpolluted, and make nice spots for a little sunbathing or perhaps a picnic lunch to enjoy along their banks.

5 Exploring the Island

Those making day trips to Dominica from other Caribbean islands will want to see the ✪ **Carib Indian Reservation,** in the northeast. In 1903, Britain got the Caribs to agree to live on 3,700 acres of land. Hence, this is the last remaining turf of the once-hostile tribe for whom the Caribbean was named. Their look is Mongolian, and they are no longer "pure-blooded," as they have married outside their tribe. Today they survive by fishing, growing food, and weaving baskets and vetiver-grass mats, which they sell to the outside world. They still make dugout canoes as well.

It's like going back in time when you explore ✪ **Morne Trois Pitons National Park,** a primordial rain forest. Mists rise gently over lush, dark-green growth, drifting up to blue-green peaks that have earned Dominica the title "Switzerland of the Caribbean." Framed by banks of giant ferns, rivers rush and tumble. Trees sprout orchids, green sunlight filters down through trees, and roaring waterfalls create a blue mist.

One of the best starting points for a visit to the park is the village of **Laudat,** 7 miles from Roseau. Exploring the heart of Dominica is for serious botanists and only the most skilled hikers, who should never penetrate unmarked trails without a very experienced guide. (See also "Hiking" under "Sports & Outdoor Pursuits," above.)

Deep in the park is the **Emerald Pool Trail,** a half-mile circuit loop that passes through the forest to a pool with a beautiful waterfall. Downpours are frequent in the rain forest, and at high elevations cold winds blow. It lies 3½ miles northeast of Pont Casse.

Five miles up from the **Roseau River Valley,** in the south-central sector of Dominica, **Trafalgar Falls** can be reached after you drive through the village of Trafalgar. Here, however, you have to approach on foot, as the slopes are too steep for vehicles. After a 20-minute walk past ginger plants and vanilla orchids, you arrive at the base, where a trio of falls converge into a rock-strewn pool.

Searching for Moby Dick

More sperm whales, pilot whales, killer whales, and dolphins can be seen on
✪ **whale- and dolphin-watching trips** off Dominica than any other island in the
Caribbean. A pod of sperm whales can often be spotted just yards from your boat, since
there are no laws here regarding the distance which you can go to "meet the whales." The
best tours are offered by the **Anchorage Hotel,** at Castle Comfort (☎ **767/448-2638**);
a 4-hour trip costs $40 (children under 12 pay half price). The vessels leave the dock
every Wednesday and Sunday at 2pm. Locals refer to these jaunts as "searching for Moby
Dick."

The **Sulphur Springs,** and the Boiling Lake east of Roseau as well, are evidence of
the island's volcanic past. Jeeps or Land Rovers can get quite close. This seemingly
bubbling pool of gray mud sometimes belches smelly sulfurous fumes. Only the very
fit should attempt the 6-hour round-trip to **Boiling Lake,** the world's second-largest
boiling lake. Go only with an experienced guide, as, according to reports, some
tourists lost their lives in the **Valley of Desolation;** they stumbled and fell into the
boiling waters.

Finally, **Titou Gorge** is a deep and narrow gorge where it's possible to swim under
a waterfall. You can get warm again in a hot sulfur spring close by. Again, a visit here
is best attempted only with an experienced guide (arranged at the tourist office). The
guide will transport you to the gorge and let you know if swimming is dangerous,
which it can be after heavy rainfall.

On the northwestern coast, **Portsmouth** is Dominica's second-largest settlement.
Once here, you can row up the Indian River in native canoes, visit the ruins of old
Fort Shirley in Cabrits National Park, and bathe at Sandy Beach on Douglas Bay and
Prince Rupert Bay.

Cabrits National Park, on the northwestern coast, 2 miles south of Douglas Bay
(☎ 767/448-2732), is a 1,313-acre protected site containing mountain scenery, tropical forests, swampland, volcanic-sand beaches, coral reefs, and the ruins of a fortified,
18th-century garrison of British, then French, construction. The park's land area is a
panoramic promontory formed by twin peaks of extinct volcanoes, overlooking
beaches, with Douglas Bay on one side and Prince Rupert Bay across the headland.
Part of Douglas Bay forms the marine section of the park. Fort Shirley, the large garrison last used as a military post in 1854, is being wrested from encroaching vegetation. A small museum highlights the natural and historic aspects of the park. The
name *Cabrits* comes from the Spanish-Portuguese-French word for goat, because of
the animals left here by early sailors to provide fresh meat on future visits. Entrance is
EC$5.30 ($1.95).

6 Shopping

Store hours are usually Monday to Friday from 8am to 5pm and Saturday from 9am
to 1pm.

In Roseau, the **Old Market Plaza,** of historical significance as a former
slave-trading market and more recently the site of a Wednesday-, Friday-, and
Saturday-morning vegetable market, now houses three craft shops, each specializing in
coconut, straw, and Carib craft products.

Tropicrafts Island Mats, 41 Queen Mary St. and Turkey Lane (☎ 767/
448-2747), offers the well-known grass rugs handmade and woven in several intricate

patterns at Tropicrafts' factory. They also sell handmade dolls, shopping bags, and place mats, all appliquéd by hand. The Dominican vetiver-grass mats are known throughout the world, and you can watch the weaving process during store hours. There's another outlet on Bay Street opposite Burroughs Square in Portsmouth (☎ 767/445-5956).

Caribana, 31 Cork St. (☎ 767/448-7340), displays Dominica's arts and crafts. This is the latest manifestation of the old Caribana Handicrafts, established by the late Iris Joseph, who is credited with creating the straw-weaving industry on the island. The staff is usually pleased to explain the dyeing processes that turn the straw into one of three different earth tones.

Other outlets for crafts include **Dominica Pottery,** Bayfront Street at Kennedy Avenue, Roseau (no phone), run by a local priest. An array of pottery made from local clays is on sale, as well as other handcrafts. **Balisier's,** 35 Great George St., Roseau (no phone), is run by a young and talented artist, Hilroy Fingol, an expert in airbrush painting. The shop also has some of the most original T-shirts on the island as well as an assortment of Carnival dolls and handmade jewelry .

A medley of goods from all over the Caribbean is featured at the **Rainforest Shop,** 17 Old St., Roseau (☎ 767/448-8834). Many of the gifts and souvenirs are hand-painted, often in flamboyant colors. The shop honors the rain forest of Dominica by contributing one dollar from every purchase to protecting the fragile environment.

7 Dominica After Dark

It's not very lively, but there is some evening activity. A couple of the major hotels, such as the **Castaways Beach Hotel,** at Mero (☎ 767/449-6244), and **Reigate Hall Hotel** on Mountain Road (☎ 767/448-4031), have entertainment on weekends, usually a combo or "jing ping" (traditional local music). In the winter season, the Castaways sponsors a weekend barbecue on the beach with live music. The **Anchorage Hotel** at Castle Comfort (☎ 767/448-2638) also has live entertainment and a good buffet on Thursday. Call for details.

The Warehouse, Checkhall Estate (☎ 767/449-1303), a 5-minute drive north of Roseau, adjacent to Canefield Airport, is the island's major dance club, a social magnet open on Saturday. Recorded disco, reggae, and other music is played from 11pm to 5am in this 200-year-old stone building, once used to store rum. The cover is EC$10 ($3.70); beer costs EC$4 ($1.50).

If you're seeking more action, such as it is, head for **Wykie's Tropical Bar,** 51 Old St. (☎ 767/448-8015), in Roseau. This is little more than a cramped hole-in-the-wall, yet curiously enough it draws the power brokers of the island. Happy hour on Friday is the time to show up. You might be offered some black pudding or stewed chicken to go with your local tropical drink. A homegrown calypso band is likely to entertain. You'll definitely hear some "jing ping." The **Dominica Club,** 49 High St. (☎ 767/448-2995), in Roseau, is another choice. It has two tennis courts, a lively bar, and live music on Friday night.

Other hot spots include **QClub,** corner of Bath Road and High Street, Roseau (☎ 767/448-2995), the place to be on a Friday night. Records, both local and American, are played 'til dawn breaks. If you get bored here, head for **Symes Zee's,** 34 King George V St., Roseau (☎ 767/448-2494), the domain of Symes Zee, the island's best blues man. A local band entertains with blues, jazz, and reggae. Here's your chance to smoke a reasonably priced Cuban cigar. They're sold here, but remember that you can't bring them back into the United States.

12 The Dominican Republic

Sometimes called "the fairest land under heaven" because of its sugar-white beaches and mountainous terrain, the Dominican Republic has long attracted visitors not only for its natural beauty but also for its rich colonial heritage. At the same time, many travelers shy away from this region because of its not-so-fair reputation for high crime, poverty, and social unrest. But despite these issues, the Dominican Republic has become one the fastest-growing destinations in the Caribbean. Its Latin flavor is a sharp contrast to the character of many nearby islands, especially the British- and French-influenced ones.

The 54-mile-wide Mona Passage separates the Dominican Republic from Puerto Rico, and many poverty-stricken Dominicans risk their lives crossing this channel every day, hoping to slip into Puerto Rico and then illegally into the United States. Crime, especially muggings and robberies of visitors, is on the rise. Still, the island holds such fascination that travelers often return again and again. Canadians are especially fond of the Dominican Republic because their dollar buys more here than on any other Caribbean island. Although often mistakenly referred to as "just a poor man's Puerto Rico," the Dominican Republic has its own distinctive cuisine and cultural heritage.

Columbus sighted its coral-edged Caribbean coastline on his first voyage to the New World and pronounced: "There is no more beautiful island in the world." The first permanent European settlement in the New World was founded here on November 7, 1493, and its ruins still remain near Montecristi in the northeast part of the island. Natives called the island Quisqueya, "Mother Earth," before the Spaniards arrived to butcher them.

Nestled amid Cuba, Jamaica, and Puerto Rico, the island of Hispaniola (Little Spain) consists of Haiti, on the westernmost third of the island, and the Dominican Republic, which has a lush landmass equal to that of Vermont and New Hampshire combined. In the Dominican interior, the fertile Valley of Cibao (rich sugarcane country) ends its upward sweep at Pico Duarte, formerly Pico Trujillo, the highest mountain peak in the West Indies, which soars to 10,417 feet.

Much of what Columbus first saw still remains in a natural, unspoiled condition, but that may change: The country is building and expanding rapidly. In the heart of the Caribbean archipelago, the Dominican Republic has an 870-mile coastline, about a third of which is devoted to beaches (the best are in Puerto Plata and La

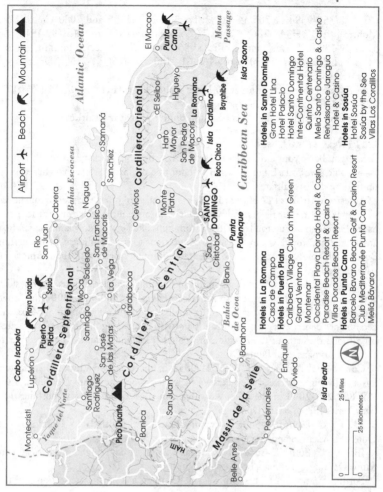

Legend: Airport ✈ Beach ↙ Mountain ◀

Hotels in Santo Domingo
Gran Hotel Lina
Hotel Palacio
Hotel Santo Domingo
Inter-Continental Hotel
Quinto Centenario
Meliá Santo Domingo & Casino
Renaissance Jaragua
Hotel & Casino

Hotels in Sosúa
Hotel Sosúa
Sosúa by the Sea
Villas Los Corallillos

Hotels in La Romana
Casa de Campo

Hotels in Puerto Plata
Caribbean Village Club on the Green
Grand Ventana
Montemar
Occidental Playa Dorado Hotel & Casino
Paradise Beach Resort & Casino
Villas Dorados Beach Resort

Hotels in Punta Cana
Barceló Bávaro Beach Golf & Casino Resort
Club Mediterranée Punta Cana
Meliá Bávaro

Map labels: Atlantic Ocean, Mona Passage, El Macao, Punta Cana, Isla Saona, Higüey, Bayahibe, La Romana, Isla Catalina, El Seibo, Caribbean Sea, Hato Mayor, San Pedro de Macorís, Boca Chica, Cordillera Oriental, Samaná, Sanchez, Bahía Escocesa, Nagua, Cabrera, Rio San Juan, Cevicos, Monte Plata, SANTO DOMINGO, Punta Palenque, San Francisco de Macoris, Salcedo, Moca, La Vega, Jarabacoa, Central, San Cristobal, Baní, Banio, Bahía de Ocoa, Cordillera Septentrional, Playa Dorada, Sosúa, Puerto Plata, Lupéron, Cabo Isabela, Santiago, Santiago Rodriguez, San José de las Matas, Cordillera, San Juan, Barahona, Enriquillo, Oviedo, Isla Beata, Montecristi, Banica, Pico Duarte, Yaque del Norte, Massif de la Selle, Pedernales, HAITI, Belle Anse

25 Miles / 25 Kilometers

Romana), and near-perfect weather year-round. So why did it take so long for the country to be discovered by visitors? The answer is largely political. The Dominican Republic has been steeped in misery and bloodshed almost from its beginning, and it climaxed with the infamous reign of Rafael Trujillo (1930 to 1961) and the civil wars that followed.

Today the Dominican Republic is being rebuilt and restored, and it offers visitors a chance to enjoy the sun and sea as well as to learn about the history and politics of a developing society.

1 Essentials

VISITOR INFORMATION

Before your trip, contact any of the following **Dominican Republic Tourist Information Centers:** 136 E. 57th St., Suite 803, New York, NY 10022 (☎ **888/ 374-6361** or 212/575-4966); 2355 Salzedo St., Suite 307, Coral Gables, FL 33134

(☎ **888/358-9594** or 305/444-4592; fax 305/444-4845); and 2080 Crescent St., Montréal, PQ, H3A, 2B6, Canada (☎ **800/563-1611** or 514/499-1918; fax 514/499-1393). There's another office at 35 Church St., Unit 53, Toronto, Ontario M5E 1TE (☎ **888/494-5050** or 416/361-2130; fax 416/361-2130). Don't expect too many specifics.

In England there's an office at 20 Hand Court, High Holborn, W.C.1 (☎ **0171/723-1552;** fax 0171/723-9877).

The Dominican Republic can be found on the Web at **www.drl.com**.

GETTING THERE

Before you book your airline tickets, read the section on "Package Deals" in chapter 2—it could save you a bundle! Even if you don't book a package, see that chapter's tips on finding the best airfare.

American Airlines (☎ **800/433-7300;** www.aa.com) offers the most frequent service, at least a dozen flights daily from cities throughout North America to either Santo Domingo or Puerto Plata. Flights from hubs like New York, Miami, or San Juan are usually nonstop. You can also make connections to the Dominican Republic from Boston, Chicago, Los Angeles, and other cities through Miami. Ask about American's package deals.

If you're heading to one of the Dominican Republic's smaller airports, your best bet is to catch a connecting flight with **American Eagle** (☎ **800/433-7300**), the American-affiliated local commuter carrier. Its small-scale (up to a maximum of 64 passengers) planes depart every day from San Juan (with connecting flights from Mayagüez) for airports throughout the Dominican Republic, including Santo Domingo, Puerto Plata, La Romana, and Punta Cana.

Continental Airlines (☎ **800/231-0856** in the U.S.; www.flycontinental.com) has a daily flight between New Jersey's Newark airport and Santo Domingo. **TWA** (☎ **800/221-2000** in the U.S.; www.twa.com) flies nonstop every morning from New York's JFK to Santo Domingo.

ALM (☎ **809/687-4569;** www.alm-airlines.com) links Santo Domingo with Dutch St. Maarten and Curaçao, both part of the Netherlands Antilles.

Iberia (☎ **800/772-4642;** www.iberia.com) offers daily flights from Madrid to Santo Domingo, making a brief stop in San Juan.

For information on flights into Casa de Campo/La Romana, see section 3 of this chapter.

Be warned: Arriving at Santo Domingo's Las Américas International Airport is confusing and chaotic. Customs officials tend to be rude and overworked and give you a very thorough check. Stolen luggage is not uncommon here; beware of "porters" who offer to help with your bags. Arrival at La Unión International Airport, 23 miles east of Puerto Plata on the north coast, is generally much smoother and safer, but you should still be cautious.

GETTING AROUND

This is not always easy if your hotel is in a remote location. The most convenient modes of transport are shuttle flights, taxis, rental cars, *públicos* (multipassenger taxis), or *guaguas* (public buses).

BY PLANE The quickest and easiest way to get across a difficult landscape is on one of the shuttle flights offered by **Air Santo Domingo** (☎ **809/687-4569**), flying from Santo Domingo to Puerto Plata, Punta Cana, La Romana, Samaná, and Santiago, among other towns. Each one-way flight generally costs about $50.

BY RENTAL CAR   The best way to see the Dominican Republic is to drive. Unlike many Caribbean islands, *motorists drive on the right here.* Although major highways are relatively smooth, the country's secondary roads, especially those in the east, are riddled with potholes and ruts. Roads also tend to be badly lit and poorly marked in both the city and the countryside. Drive carefully and give yourself plenty of time when traveling between island destinations. Watch out for policemen who may flag you down and accuse you (often wrongly) of some infraction. Many locals give these low-paid policemen a $5 *regalo,* or gift "for your children," and are then free to go.

The high accident and theft rate in recent years has helped to raise car-rental rates here. Prices vary, so call around for last-minute quotes. Make sure you understand your insurance coverage (or lack thereof) before you leave home. Your credit-card issuer may already provide you with this type of insurance; call to find out.

For reservations and more information, call the rental companies at least a week before your departure: **Avis** (☎ **800/331-1212** or 809/535-7191), **Budget** (☎ **800/527-0700** or 809/562-6812), and **Hertz** (☎ **800/654-3001** or 809/221-5333) all operate in the Dominican Republic. Although the cars may be not as well maintained as the big three above, you can often get a cheaper deal at one of the local firms, notably **Nelly Rent-a-Car** (☎ **809/544-1800**) or **McBeal** (☎ **809/688-6518**). If you want seat belts, you must ask. Your Canadian or American driver's license is suitable documentation, along with a valid credit card or a substantial cash deposit.

BY TAXI   Taxis aren't metered, and determining the fare in advance (which you should do) may be difficult if you and your driver have a language problem. Taxis can be hailed in the streets, and you'll definitely find them at the major hotels and at the airport. The minimum fare within Santo Domingo is $6, but most drivers try to get more. In Santo Domingo, the most reliable taxi companies are **Tecni-Taxi** (☎ **809/567-2010**) and **El Conde Taxi** (☎ **809/563-6131**). In Puerto Plata, call **Tecni-Taxi** at 809/320-7621. Don't get into an unmarked street taxi. Many visitors, particularly in Santo Domingo, have been assaulted and robbed by doing just that.

BY PUBLIC TRANSPORTATION   *Públicos* are unmetered multipassenger taxis that travel along main thoroughfares, stopping often to pick up people waving from the side of the street. A público is marked by a white seal on the front door. You must tell the driver your destination when you're picked up to make sure the público is going there. A ride is usually RD$2 (15¢).

Public buses, often in the form of minivans or panel trucks, are called *guaguas.* For about the same price, they provide the same service as públicos, but they're generally more crowded. Larger buses provide service outside the towns. Beware of pickpockets on board.

Fast Facts: The Dominican Republic

Currency   The Dominican monetary unit is the **peso (RD$),** made up of 100 centavos. Coin denominations are 1, 5, 10, 25, and 50 centavos, and 1 peso. Bill denominations are RD$5, RD$10, RD$20, RD$50, RD$100, RD$500, and RD$1,000. Price quotations in this chapter appear sometimes in American and sometimes in Dominican currency, depending on the policy of the establishment. The use of any currency other than Dominican pesos is technically illegal, but few seem to bother with this mandate. At press time, we got about RD$14.05 to U.S.$1. (RD$1 equals about 7.1¢). Bank booths at the international airports and major hotels will change your currency at the prevailing free-market rate.

Documents   To enter the Dominican Republic, citizens of the United States, Canada, and the U.K. need a valid passport. Upon your arrival at the airport in the Dominican Republic, you must purchase a tourist card for U.S. $10. You can avoid waiting in line by purchasing this card when checking in for your flight to the island.

Electricity   The country generally uses 110 volts AC (60 cycles), so adapters and transformers are usually not necessary for U.S.-made appliances.

Emergencies   In the event of an emergency, call ☎ **911.**

Embassies   All embassies are in Santo Domingo, the capital. The embassy of the **United States** is on Calle Cesar Nicholas Penson at the corner of Leopold Navarro (☎ **809/221-2171**). The embassy of the **United Kingdom** is at Febrero 27 (☎ **809/472-7111**). The embassy of **Canada** is at Avenida Máximo Gómez 39 (☎ **809/685-1136**).

Language   The official language is Spanish; many people also speak some English.

Safety   The Dominican Republic has more than its fair share of crime (see "Getting There," above, for a warning about crime at airports). Avoid unmarked street taxis, especially in Santo Domingo; you could be targeted for assault and robbery. While strolling around the city, beware of hustlers selling various wares; pickpockets and muggers are common here, and visitors are easy targets. Don't walk in Santo Domingo at night. Locals like to offer their services as guides, and it is often difficult to decline. Hiring an official guide from the tourist office is your best bet.

Taxes & Service Charges   A departure tax of U.S. $10 is assessed and must be paid in U.S. currency. The government imposes a 13% tax on hotel rooms, which usually is configured in conjunction with a 10% service charge that's automatically added onto your hotel bill for a total surcharge of 23%, a sum so staggering it helps support the country.

Telephone   To call the Dominican Republic from the United States, dial **1,** then **809** and the local seven-digit number.

Time   Atlantic standard time is observed year-round. When New York and Miami are on eastern standard time and it's noon there, it's 1pm in Santo Domingo. However, during daylight saving time, when it's noon on the U.S. East Coast, it's noon in Santo Domingo too.

Tipping   In most restaurants and hotels, a 10% service charge is added to your check. Most people usually add 5% to 10% more, especially if the service has been good.

Water   It's recommended that you stick to drinking bottled water in the Dominican Republic.

Weather   The average temperature is 77°F. August is the warmest month and January the coolest month, although even then it's warm enough to swim.

2   Santo Domingo

Bartholomeo Columbus, brother of Christopher, founded the city of New Isabella (later renamed Santo Domingo) on the southeastern Caribbean coast in 1496. It's the

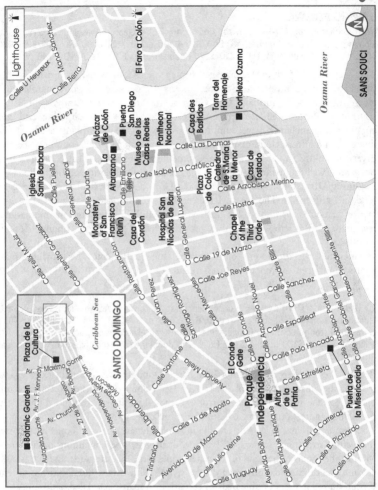

oldest city in the New World and the capital of the Dominican Republic. Santo Domingo has had a long, sometimes glorious, more often sad, history. At the peak of its power, Diego de Valásquez sailed from here to settle Cuba, Ponce de León went forth to conquer and settle Puerto Rico and Florida, and Cortés set out for Mexico. The city today still reflects its long history—French, Haitian, and especially Spanish.

ESSENTIALS

In Santo Domingo, **24-hour drugstore** service is provided by San Judas Tadeo, Av. Independencia 57 (☎ **809/689-6664**). An emergency room operates at the **Centro Médico Universidad,** Av. Máximo Gómez 68, on the corner of Pedro Enrique Urena (☎ **809/221-0171**). For the **police,** call ☎ **911.**

WHERE TO STAY

Remember that taxes and service charges will be added to your bill, which will make the rates 23% higher. When making reservations, ask if they're included in the rates quoted—usually they aren't.

VERY EXPENSIVE

Inter-Continental Hotel Quinto Centenario. Av. George Washington 218, Santo Domingo, Dominican Republic. ☎ **800/327-0200** or 809/221-0000. Fax 809/221-2020. 300 units. A/C MINIBAR TV TEL. $250–$270 double; from $335 suite. AE, DC, MC, V.

This soaring, 15-story tower, managed by the Inter-Continental group since 1994, caters to business travelers and conventioneers. Inside, acres of white marble add a glossy dignity to the formal lobby. Guest rooms are airy and sunny, each with a seafront view and well-selected furniture. Rooms have rich carpeting and nice appointments, including large, sumptuous areas, with one or two king-size beds, fine linens, firm mattresses, and marble-clad bathrooms with generous counter space, hair dryers, and fluffy towels. If you don't see something you want, just call for it: The first-rate staff is well trained in managing a large and sophisticated international hotel.

Dining/Diversions: The Bambu Bar and Grill, beside the pool, serves Caribbean food and stiff drinks. The Tasca Mar specializes in Spanish food such as *zarzuelas* (a savory seafood stew) and grilled medleys of shellfish. There's also an international restaurant, La Brasserie, and a casino, providing lots of glitter amid ringing bells and whistles.

Amenities: Meeting rooms, outdoor pool, sauna, tennis court, health club, squash courts. Concierge, car-rental, hairdresser, and gift shops.

EXPENSIVE

✪ **Hotel Santo Domingo.** Av. Independencia (at the corner of Av. Abraham Lincoln), Santo Domingo, Dominican Republic. ☎ **800/877-3643** or 809/221-1511. Fax 809/535-4050. www.hotel.stodgo.com.do. E-mail: reservations@hotel.stodgo.coh.do. 335 units. A/C MINIBAR TV TEL. $153 double; $172 Excel Club double; $246 executive suite. Rates include American breakfast. AE, MC, V.

Run by Premier Resorts & Hotels, the Santo Domingo has a tasteful extravagance without the glitzy overtones of the Jaragua (see below). This ocher stucco structure opens onto the sea and sits on 14 tropical acres, 15 minutes from downtown. The prestigious address often attracts Latin American diplomats.

Oscar de la Renta helped design the interior. The average-size rooms occupy two three-story structures, framed by latticework loggias, one containing orange trees. Most of the rooms have views of the water, while some face the garden, which is quite charming. Accommodations have deluxe styling with bright floral carpets, tasteful Caribbean fabrics, and double beds fitted with firm mattresses. Tiled bathrooms have efficient showers, adequate shelf space, and fluffy towels. Guests in the superior Excel Club rooms get ocean-view balconies and other amenities, plus access to a private lounge featuring continental breakfast, afternoon hors d'oeuvres, and cocktails.

Dining/Diversions: Guests can enjoy dinner at El Alcázar or El Cafetal; Las Brisas serves a poolside lunch. The piano bar, Las Palmas, and its neighbor, Marrakesh Bar, draw a lively crowd at night.

Amenities: Three pro tennis courts (lit at night), Olympic-size pool, sauna, 24-hour room service, laundry, baby-sitting, rental cars.

✪ **Renaissance Jaragua Hotel & Casino.** Av. George Washington 367, Santo Domingo, Dominican Republic. ☎ **800/228-9898** in the U.S. and Canada, or 809/221-2222. Fax 809/686-0528. www.renaissancehotels.com. E-mail: h.jaragua@codetel.net.do. 300 units. A/C MINIBAR TV TEL. Year-round $221 double; from $500 suite. MAP (breakfast and dinner) $65 per person extra. AE, DC, MC, V.

Often referred to as the "the pride of the Dominican Republic," this hotel was built on the 14-acre site of the old Jaragua (*ha-RA-gwa*) Hotel, which was popular in Trujillo's day. Open since 1988, it's a splashy, candy-pink waterfront palace that doesn't quite have the dignity and class of the Hotel Santo Domingo (though it does have the island's finest gym and spa facilities). Instead, the Jaragua offers a more ostentatious and flashy Latin flavor, and was appropriately featured on *Lifestyles of the Rich and Famous*. Located off the Malecón and convenient to the city's major attractions and shops, this Las Vegas–style hotel consists of two separate buildings: the 10-story Jaragua Tower and the two-level Jaragua Gardens Estate. Although the hotel took a direct hit during the 1998 hurricanes, everything should be up and running by the time you check in.

The luxurious rooms, the largest in Santo Domingo, feature marble bathrooms with large makeup mirrors, fluffy towels, and hair dryers; multiple phones; fridges; and other posh amenities. Wicker headboards crown king or double beds, each with a deluxe mattress and fine linen.

Dining/Diversions: The Jaragua boasts the largest casino in the Caribbean, a 1,000-seat Las Vegas–style showroom, a cabaret theater, and a disco. Among the more intriguing dining choices are the Manhattan Grill and El Latino, both open for dinner only. Café Jaragua is open 24 hours and serves a lavish lunch buffet for RD$225 ($15.95) in addition to a full menu.

Amenities: Pool with 12 private cabanas, snack bar, and outdoor bar; one of the best tennis centers in Santo Domingo, with four clay courts (lit at night) and a pro shop; beauty parlor and barber; the finest spa/health club in the Dominican Republic; 24-hour room service; laundry and dry cleaning; doctor on 24-hour call.

MODERATE

Gran Hotel Lina Avs. Máximo Gómez and 27 de Febrero, Santo Domingo, Dominican Republic. ☎**800/942-2461** or 809/563-5000. Fax 809/686-5521. www.barcelo.com. E-mail: h-lina@codetel.net.do. 217 units. A/C MINIBAR TV TEL. Year-round $111 double. Extra person $28. Rates include breakfast. AE, DC, MC, V.

Rising 15 floors in the heart of the capital in a sterile cinder-block design, the Lina offers a wide range of amenities. All the units contain fridges; at least a third overlook the Caribbean. Bedrooms are comfortable and many of them quite spacious, but the decor is the standard motel style, not exactly stylish. The best are on the 11th floor, as these have balconies. The tiled bathrooms have combination shower/tubs and spacious marble vanities.

The hotel boasts one of the best-known restaurants in the Caribbean (see "Where to Dine," below), a cafeteria and snack bar, and a nightclub. Amenities include 24-hour room service, laundry, pool, Jacuzzi, solarium, gym, sauna, and shopping arcade.

Meliá Santo Domingo & Casino Av. George Washington 365, Santo Domingo, Dominican Republic. ☎ **800/211-8572** in the U.S., or 809/221-6666. Fax 809/687-8150. www.solmelia.es. E-mail: meliasdb@codetel.net.do. 254 units. A/C MINIBAR TV TEL. Year-round $120–$130 double; $170–$450 suite. AE, DC, MC, V.

Originally built as a Sheraton, this hotel was acquired by the Spanish hotel chain Meliá in 1997. A high-rise set back from the Malecón and designed in a neutral international style, it's perched at the end of a tree-lined drive, and boasts a very large lobby whose big windows give it a greenhouse feel. Except for those on the third floor, each unit has a sea view, and some are equipped for travelers with disabilities. The bedrooms are a bit bigger than you might expect, and floor by floor, each was renovated in 1998 and 1999. Now they're better than ever, with new mattresses, quality tropical furnishings, and spacious closets, plus combination baths (tub and shower) with marble vanities, fluffy towels, and hair dryers.

On site are the Petit Café; Yarey's Lounge, a piano bar; La Terraza coffee shop, with a terrace surrounding a large pool; La Canasta, featuring Dominican food; the Omni

Disco; and a casino. Amenities include a complete business center, health club, outdoor pool, tennis courts, gift and sundries shops, boutique, tour desk, 24-hour room service, baby-sitting, laundry, dry cleaning, 24-hour medical service, and in-room safes. There's a golf course nearby.

INEXPENSIVE

✪ **Hotel Palacio.** Calle Duarte 106 (at Calle Solomé Ureña), Santo Domingo, Dominican Republic. ☎ **809/682-4730.** Fax 809/687-5535. E-mail: h.palacio@codetel.net.do. 16 units. A/C TV TEL. $63–$71 double. Children 12 and under stay free in parents' room. AE, MC, V.

This severely dignified stone-and-stucco building is a stripped-down reminder of the grander aspects of the city's colonial past. It lies in the heart of Santo Domingo's historic zone, 2 blocks from the cathedral. Built in the 1600s, it was the family home of a former president of the Dominican Republic, Buenaventura Báez, and still retains its original iron balconies and high ceilings. In the early 1990s, kitchenettes and simple, warm-weather furniture were added to all rooms. Since this was designed as a private home, not all rooms are the same size. You can always request a more spacious unit, which are assigned on a first-come, first-served basis. Many bathrooms were tacked onto the rooms and tend to be small. Your fellow residents are likely to be visiting business travelers from other parts of the Latin Caribbean, as well as other tourists. There's a small gym, with its own Jacuzzi on the rooftop.

WHERE TO DINE

Most of Santo Domingo's restaurants stretch along the seaside, bordering Avenida George Washington, popularly known as the Malecón. Some of the best restaurants are in hotels. It's safer to take a taxi when dining out at night.

In most restaurants, casual dress is fine, although shorts are frowned upon at the fancier, more expensive spots. Many Dominicans prefer to dress up when dining out, especially in the capital.

EXPENSIVE

La Briciola. Calle Arzobispo Merino 152-A at Calle Padre Bellini. ☎ **809/688-5055.** Reservations recommended. Main courses RD$175–RD$275 ($12.40–$19.50). AE, DC, MC, V. Mon–Sat 7pm–midnight. ITALIAN/INTERNATIONAL.

This restaurant was established in 1994 as the Dominican branch of a chain of restaurants based in Milan. It occupies a once run-down trio of colonial houses whose 16th-century foundations were built very close to the Catedral de Santa María la Menor. Careful renovations retained the buildings' historic character and produced one air-conditioned dining room with a vaulted ceiling and a series of arcade-covered dining rooms, cooled by ceiling fans. Each overlooks an interior courtyard whose masonry and accents evoke colonial Spain.

The menu represents all of Italy's culinary regions, with an emphasis on fresh pastas and the classics, including tortellini with pesto cream sauce, gnocchi, flavorful risottos, osso buco, and plenty of fresh fish and meat main courses. Chances are you won't be disappointed when sampling these savory dishes.

✪ **Lina Restaurant.** In the Gran Hotel Lina, Avs. Máximo Gómez and 27 de Febrero. ☎ **809/563-5000,** ext. 7250. Reservations recommended. Main courses RD$120–RD$350 ($8.50–$24.85). AE, DC, DISC, MC, V. Daily noon–4pm and 6:30pm–1am. INTERNATIONAL/SPANISH.

Set on the lobby level of the Gran Hotel Lina is one of the most prestigious restaurants in the Caribbean. Spanish-born Lina Aguado originally came to Santo Domingo as the personal chef of the dictator Trujillo, whom she served until opening her own restaurant. Today, four master chefs, to whom Dona Lina taught her secret recipes, rule the kitchen of this modern hotel restaurant. The cuisine is international with an emphasis on Spanish dishes, and the service is first rate. Try the paella Valenciana, the sea bass flambéed with brandy, or perhaps mixed seafood au Pernod, cooked casserole style. We found the cooks extremely professional in both their preparation and presentation of meals. Lina's cuisine even wins the approval of visiting and hard-to-please Madrileños we know, who are a bit contemptuous of Spanish food served outside Spain.

Pappalapasta. Calle Dr. Baez 23. ☎ **809/689-4849.** Reservations recommended. Pastas RD$140–RD$225 ($9.95–$15.95); main courses RD$200–RD$300 ($14.20–$21.30). AE, DC, MC, V. Daily noon–3pm and 7pm–1am. ITALIAN/INTERNATIONAL.

Housed within an 80-year-old building that was once a private home, this restaurant is just a short walk from the presidential palace, and so is known for its chaotic lunch scene. The dining rooms are accented with modern art, cut-glass windows, and varnished hardwoods. Frankly, the staff is not as attentive as they should be, which is ironic considering the restaurant's high-powered clientele of lawyers and other professionals. The food, when it finally arrives, is far better than the service. You can order from a variety of Italian dishes such as sea bass grilled with Creole sauce or meunière (lightly floured and sautéed in butter); fillet of beef with a brandy and mushroom cream sauce; red snapper with garlic, olives, and capers; and an assortment of pastas, gnocchis, and raviolis in savory sauces.

Reina de España. Calle Cervantes 103. ☎ **809/685-2588.** Reservations required Fri–Sat. Main courses RD$160–RD$350 ($11.35–$24.85). AE, MC, V. Daily noon–midnight. SPANISH/CREOLE/INTERNATIONAL.

One of the best independent (nonhotel) restaurants in Santo Domingo, Reina de España lies near the Meliá Santo Domingo & Casino in a once-private villa. The chef draws inspiration from many regions of Spain, including roast suckling pig from Castile. The paellas are excellent, frog's legs are prepared à la Romana, and the quail stew with herbs is as fine as that served in Toledo. However, the roast duck with mango sauce and the Dominican shrimp soup are definitely locally inspired. Lobster is prepared almost any way you like it, and most fish dishes are solid, including the seafood casserole. Meals here are among the most expensive in the capital, but patrons are usually satisfied. Imported meat is used.

✪ **Vesuvio I.** Av. George Washington 521. ☎ **809/221-3333.** Reservations recommended Fri–Sat. Main courses RD$170–RD$350 ($12.05–$24.85). AE, DC, MC, V. Daily noon–1am. ITALIAN.

Along the Malecón, the most famous Italian restaurant in the Dominican Republic draws crowds of visitors and local businesspeople. What to order? That's always a problem here, as the Neapolitan owners, the Bonarelli family, have worked since 1954 to perfect and enlarge their menu. Their homemade soups are excellent. Fresh red snapper, sea bass, and oysters are prepared in interesting ways. Recent menu additions include pappardelle al Bosque (with porcini mushrooms, rosemary, and garlic), kingfish carpaccio (thin-sliced cured fish, olive oil, chopped onion, and freshly ground black pepper), and black tallarini with shrimp à la crema. They also serve lobster Mediterráneo (chopped cold lobster with fresh tomatoes, onion, olive oil, and basil) and risotto tricolor (sun-dried tomatoes, basil, and mozzarella). Specialties include Dominican crayfish à la Vesuvio (topped with garlic and bacon).

The owner claims to be the pioneer of pizza in the Dominican Republic, and he makes a unique one next door in **Pizzeria Vesuvio**—a yard-long pizza pie! If you want to try his other Italian place, go to **Vesuvio II,** Av. Tiradentes 17 (☎ **809/562-6060**).

MODERATE/INEXPENSIVE

Coco's. Calle Padre Billini 53, Zona Coloniale. ☎ **809/687-9624.** Reservations recommended. Main courses RD$105–RD$225 ($7.45–$15.95); Sun buffet RD$225 ($15.95). AE, MC, V. Tues–Sun noon–2:30pm and 6:30–10:30pm. ENGLISH/INTERNATIONAL.

The clientele here is almost exclusively local, including Europeans who live in the colonial zone. In 1992, it fell under the control of Colin Leslie, a native of South London, who promotes old-fashioned English cookery in the heart of the Spanish-speaking New World. The nerve center of the site is the Johnny Walker bar, which provides an English pub atmosphere with a Spanish accent. Menu items are unabashedly British or international, and include steak and kidney pie, Indian curries, fried Camembert with cranberry sauce, several kinds of pâté, grilled steaks and chicken, and a dessert specialty of pears stuffed with Stilton and served with walnuts. Feeling nostalgic for Merrie Olde Things? Consider dropping in for Sunday lunch, when a traditional set-price meal of roast beef with potatoes and Yorkshire pudding is served.

✪ **La Bahía.** Av. George Washington 1. ☎ **809/682-4022.** Main courses RD$70–RD$250 ($4.95–$17.75). AE, MC, V. Daily 9am–2am. SEAFOOD.

You'd never know that this unprepossessing place right on the Malecón serves some of the best, and freshest, seafood in the Dominican Republic. One predawn morning as we passed by, fishermen were waiting outside to sell the chef their latest catch. Rarely in the Caribbean will you find a restaurant with such a wide range of seafood dishes. To start, you might try ceviche, sea bass marinated in lime juice, or lobster cocktail. Soups usually contain big chunks of lobster as well as shrimp. Specialties include king-fish in coconut sauce, sea bass Ukrainian style, baked red snapper, and seafood in the pot. Conch is a special favorite with the chef. Desserts are superfluous. The restaurant will stay open until the last customer departs.

Mesón de la Cava. Av. Mirador del Sur 1. ☎ **809/533-2818.** Reservations required. Main courses RD$125–RD$300 ($8.90–$21.30). AE, DC, MC, V. Daily noon–4pm and 6pm–1:30am. DOMINICAN/INTERNATIONAL.

You descend a perilous, open-backed iron stairway into an actual cave with stalactites and stalagmites—at first we thought this was a mere gimmicky club, but the cuisine is among the finest in the capital. Recorded music (merengue, Latin jazz, blues, and salsa) gives the place a festive ambience. For an appetizer, try the shrimp cocktail, onion soup, gazpacho, or our favorite, the red-snapper chowder. The chefs take justifiable pride in their meats, especially the gourmet beefsteak, but you can also order fresh fish. Try, if featured, the sea bass in red sauce.

Spaghettissimo. Paseo de Los Locubres 13. ☎ **809/565-3708.** Main courses RD$145–RD$365 ($10.30–$25.90). AE, DC, MC, V. Daily noon–3pm and 7–11pm. ITALIAN.

Convivial and unpretentious, this restaurant manages to convey the sense that a chef somewhere in a steamy kitchen will be genuinely disappointed if you don't manage to actually finish your pasta. You might begin your meal with a drink in the bar near the entrance, then move to the simple but dignified dining room, where you may be distracted by the sight of a generously appointed antipasti buffet (most of the selections are fish or grilled vegetables that have been succulently marinated in olive oil and herbs). Starters might include shellfish, fish soup, foie gras, and the inevitable pastas such as penne with artichokes, which can be configured as main courses if you prefer. Meats and fish are often grilled, well seasoned, and redolent of the traditions of far-away Italy.

OUTDOOR PURSUITS & SPECTATOR SPORTS

BEACHES   The Dominican Republic has some great beaches, but they aren't in Santo Domingo. The principal beach resort near the capital is at **Boca Chica,** less than 2 miles east of the international airport and about 19 miles from the center of Santo Domingo. Here you'll find clear, shallow blue water, a white-sand beach, and a natural coral reef. The east side of the beach, known as "St. Tropez," is popular with Europeans. In recent years, the backdrop of the beach has become rather tacky, with an array of pizza and fast-food stands (some selling Dominican fried chicken), beach cottages, chaise longues, water-sports concessions, and plastic beach tables.

Slightly better maintained is the narrow white-sand beach of **Juan Dolio,** a 20-minute drive east of Boca Chica. Several resorts have recently located here. The beach used to be fairly uncrowded, but with all the hotels now lining it, it's likely to be as crowded as Boca Chica any day of the week.

BASEBALL   Baseball is the national sport. The Dominican team is always a popular draw at the summer Olympics, and many of the country's native-born sons have gone on to the U.S. major leagues, including Yankee shortstop Tony Fernandez, Braves outfielder Luís Polonia, and the most famous, Tony Peña, a standout defensive catcher for many teams in the 1980s and 1990s. From October to February, games are played at stadiums in Santo Domingo and elsewhere. Check the local newspaper for schedules and locations.

HORSE RACING   Santo Domingo's racetrack, **Hipódromo V Centenario,** on Avenida Las Américas (☎ **809/687-6060**), schedules races daily. You can spend the day here and have lunch at the track's restaurant. Admission is free.

TENNIS   Budget hotels rarely have courts, but you can often play on the courts of major resorts if you ask your hotel desk to call in advance for you and make arrangements.

SEEING THE SIGHTS

Prieto Tours, Av. Francia 125 (☎ **809/685-0102**), one of the capital's leading tour operators, offers a 3-hour tour of the Colonial Zone, leaving most mornings at 9am and again at 3pm if there's sufficient demand; it costs $32. On Wednesday and Friday, a 6-hour tour visits the Colonial Zone, the Columbus Lighthouse, the Aquarium, and the city's modern neighborhoods; the $50 cost includes lunch and entrance to several well-known museums and monuments. About an hour of the tour is devoted to shopping. Note that this full-day tour is available only if eight participants show signs of attending.

THE RELICS OF COLUMBUS & A COLONIAL ERA

Santo Domingo, a treasure trove of historic, sometimes crumbling buildings, is undergoing a major government-sponsored restoration. The old town is still partially enclosed by remnants of its original city wall. The narrow streets, old stone buildings, and forts are like nothing else in the Caribbean, except perhaps Old San Juan. The only thing missing is the clank of the conquistadors' armor.

Old and modern Santo Domingo meet at the **Parque Independencia,** a big city square whose most prominent feature is its Altar de la Patria, a shrine dedicated to Duarte, Sanchez, and Mella, who are all buried here. These men led the country's fight for freedom from Haiti in 1844. As in provincial Spanish cities, the square is a popular family gathering place on Sunday afternoon. At the entrance to the plaza is **El Conde Gate,** named for the count (El Conde) de Penalva, the governor who resisted the forces of Admiral Penn, the leader of a British invasion. It was also the site of the March for Independence in 1844, and holds a special place in the hearts of Dominicans.

In the shadow of the Alcázar, **La Atarazana** is a fully restored section that once centered around one of the New World's finest arsenals. It extends for a city block, a catacomb of shops, art galleries, boutiques, and some good regional and international restaurants.

Just behind river moorings is the oldest street in the New World, **Calle Las Damas** (Street of the Ladies). Some visitors assume that this was a bordello district, but it was actually named for the elegant ladies of the viceregal court who used to promenade here in the evening. It's lined with colonial buildings.

Just north is the chapel of **Our Lady of Remedies,** where the first inhabitants of the city used to attend mass before the cathedral was erected.

Try to see the **Puerta de la Misericordia.** Part of the original city wall, this "Gate of Mercy" was once a refuge for colonists fleeing hurricanes and earthquakes. To reach it, head 4 blocks west along Calle Padre Billini and turn left onto Calle Palo Hincado.

The **Monastery of San Francisco** is but a mere ruin, lit at night. That any part of it is still standing is a miracle; it was destroyed by earthquakes, pillaged by Drake, and bombarded by French artillery. To get here, go along Calle Hostos and across Calle Emiliano Tejera; continue up the hill, and about midway along you'll see the ruins.

You'll see a microcosm of Dominican life as you head east along **Calle El Conde** from Parque Independencia to **Columbus Square,** which has a large bronze statue honoring the discoverer, made in 1882 by a French sculptor, and the **Catedral de Santa María la Menor** (see below).

✪ **Alcázar de Colón.** Calle Emiliano Tejera (at the foot of Calle Las Damas). ☎ **809/ 689-4363.** Admission RD$20 ($1.40). Mon and Wed–Fri 9am–5pm, Sat 9am–4pm, Sun 9am–1pm.

The most outstanding structure in the old city is the Alcázar, a palace built for the son of Columbus, Diego, and his wife, the niece of Ferdinand, king of Spain. Diego became the colony's governor in 1509, and Santo Domingo rose as the hub of Spanish commerce and culture in America. Constructed of native coral limestone, it stands on the bluffs of the Ozama River. For more than 60 years, it was the center of the Spanish court and entertained such distinguished visitors as Cortés, Ponce de León, and Balboa. The nearly two dozen rooms and open-air loggias are decorated with paintings and period tapestries, as well as 16th-century antiques.

Casa del Cordón (Cord House). At Calle Emiliano Tejera and Calle Isabel la Católica. No phone. Free admission. Tues–Sun 8:30am–4:30pm.

Near the Alcázar de Colón, the Cord House was named for the cord of the Franciscan order, which is carved above the door. Francisco de Garay, who came to Hispaniola with Columbus, built the casa from 1503 to 1504, which makes it the oldest stone house in the western hemisphere. It once lodged the first royal audience of the New World, which performed as the Supreme Court of Justice for the island and the rest of the West Indies. On another occasion, in January 1586, the noble ladies of Santo Domingo gathered here to donate their jewelry as ransom demanded by Sir Francis Drake in return for his promise to leave the city.

✪ **Catedral de Santa María la Menor.** Calle Arzobispo Meriño (on the south side of Columbus Sq.). ☎ **809/689-1920.** Free admission. Cathedral, Mon–Sat 9am–4pm, Sun masses begin at 6am; treasury, Mon–Sat 9am–4pm.

The oldest cathedral in the Americas was begun in 1514 and completed in 1540. With a gold coral limestone facade, it's a stunning example of the Spanish Renaissance style, with elements of Gothic and baroque. The cathedral, visited by Pope John Paul II in 1979 and again in 1984, was the center for a celebration of the 500th anniversary of the European Discovery of America in 1992. An excellent art collection of retables (raised shelves above the altar, used for holding candles), ancient wood carvings, furnishings, funerary monuments, and silver and jewelry can be seen in the treasury.

El Faro a Colón (Columbus Lighthouse). Av. España (on the water side of Los Tres Ojos, near the airport in the Sans Souci district). ☎ **809/591-1492.** Admission RD$10 (70¢) adults, RD$5 (35¢) children 11 and under. Tues–Sun 10am–5pm.

Built in the shape of a pyramid cross, the towering El Faro a Colón monument is both a sightseeing attraction and a cultural center. In the heart of the structure is a chapel containing the Columbus tomb, and perhaps his mortal remains. The "bones" of Columbus were moved here from the Cathedral of Santa María la Menor (see above). (It should be pointed out that other locations, including the Cathedral of Seville, also claim to possess the remains of the explorer.) Adjacent to the chapel is a series of museums representing more than 20 countries, plus a museum dedicated to the history of Columbus and the lighthouse itself. The most outstanding and unique feature is the lighting system composed of 149 xenon Skytrack searchlights and a 70-kilowatt beam that circles out for nearly 44 miles. When illuminated, the lights project a gigantic cross in the sky that can be seen for miles beyond, even as far as Puerto Rico.

While the concept of the memorial dates back 140 years, the first stones were not laid until 1986, following the design submitted in 1929 by J. L. Gleave, the winner of the worldwide contest held to choose the architect. The monumental lighthouse was inaugurated on October 6, 1992, the day Columbus's "remains" were transferred from the Santo Domingo cathedral, the oldest in the Americas. The multimillion-dollar monument stands 688 feet tall (taller than the Washington Monument) and 131 feet wide with sloping sides from 56 feet at the top to 109 feet at the bottom.

Museo de las Casas Reales (Museum of the Royal Houses). Calle Las Damas (at Calle Las Mercedes). ☎ **809/682-4202.** Admission RD$10 (70¢). Tues–Sat 9am–4:45pm, Sun 10am–1pm.

Through artifacts, tapestries, maps, and re-created halls, including a courtroom, this museum traces Santo Domingo's history from 1492 to 1821. Gilded furniture, arms and armor, and other colonial artifacts make it the most interesting of all museums of Old Santo Domingo. It contains replicas of the three ships commanded by Columbus, and one exhibit is said to hold part of the ashes of the famed explorer. You can see, in addition to pre-Columbian art, the main artifacts of two galleons sunk in 1724 on their way from Spain to Mexico, along with remnants of another 18th-century Spanish ship, the *Concepción.*

OTHER ATTRACTIONS

In total contrast to the colonial city, modern Santo Domingo dates from the Trujillo era. A city of broad, palm-shaded avenues, its seaside drive is called **Avenida George Washington,** more popularly known as the **Malecón.** This boulevard is filled with restaurants, hotels, and nightclubs. Use caution at night—there are pickpockets galore.

We also suggest a visit to the **Paseo de los Indios,** a sprawling 5-mile park with a restaurant, fountain displays, and a lake.

About a 20-minute drive from the heart of the city, off the Autopista de las Américas on the way to the airport and the beach at Boca Chica, is **Los Tres Ojos** or "The Three Eyes," which stare at you across the Ozama River from Old Santo Domingo. There's a trio of lagoons set in scenic caverns, with lots of stalactites and stalagmites. One lagoon is 40 feet deep, another 20 feet, and yet a third—known as

"Ladies Bath"—only 5 feet. A Dominican Tarzan will sometimes dive off the walls of the cavern into the deepest lagoon. The area is equipped with walkways.

Jardín Botánico, Avenida República de Colombia, at the corner of de los Proceres (☎ 809/867-6211), sprawls over 445 acres in the northern sector of the Arroyo Hondo, making it among the largest gardens in Latin America. It emphasizes the flowers and lush vegetation native to the Dominican Republic, and requires at least 2 hours to even begin to explore. A small, touristy-looking train makes a circuit through the park's major features, which include a Japanese park, the Great Ravine, and a floral clock. Admission is RD$10 (70¢) for adults, RD$5 (35¢) for children; the train tour costs RD$15 ($1.05) for adults, RD$7 (50¢) for children. Hours are Tuesday through Sunday from 9am to 5pm.

The former site of the Trujillo mansion has been turned into a park, which contains the **Museo de Arte Moderno,** Plaza de la Cultura, Calle Pedro Henríquez Ureña (☎ 809/685-2153). It displays national and international works (the emphasis is, of course, on native-born talent). Admission is RD$20 ($1.40); hours are Tuesday through Saturday from 9am to 5pm. Also in the Plaza de la Cultura are the **National Library** (☎ 809/688-4086) and the **National Theater** (☎ 809/687-3191), which sponsors, among other events, folkloric dances, opera, outdoor jazz concerts, traveling art exhibits, and classical ballet.

SHOPPING

The best buys are handcrafted native items, especially amber jewelry. **Amber,** petrified tree resin that has fossilized over millions of years, is the national gem. Look for pieces of amber with trapped objects, such as insects and spiders, inside the enveloping material. Colors range from a bright yellow to black, but most of the gems are golden in tone. Fine-quality amber jewelry, along with lots of plastic fakes, is sold throughout the country.

A semiprecious stone of light blue (sometimes a dark-blue color), **larimar** is the Dominican turquoise. It often makes striking jewelry, and is sometimes mounted with wild boar's teeth.

Ever since the Dominicans presented John F. Kennedy with what became his favorite rocker, visitors have wanted to take home a **rocking chair.** To simplify transport, these rockers are often sold unassembled.

Other good buys include Dominican rum, hand-knit articles, macramé, ceramics, and crafts in native mahogany. Always haggle over the price, particularly in the open-air markets; no stallkeeper expects you to pay the first price asked.

The best shopping streets are **El Conde,** the oldest and most traditional shop-flanked avenue, and **Avenida Mella.** In the colonial section, **La Atarazana** is filled with galleries and gift and jewelry stores, charging inflated prices. Duty-free shops are found at the airport, in the capital at the **Centro de los Héroes,** and at both the Hotel Santo Domingo and the Hotel Embajador. Shopping hours are generally Monday to Saturday from 9am to 12:30pm and 2 to 5pm.

Head first for the National Market, ✪ **El Mercado Modelo,** Avenida Mella, filled with stall after stall of crafts, spices, and produce. The merchants will be most eager to sell, and you can easily get lost in the crush. Remember to bargain. You'll see a lot of tortoise-shell work here, but exercise caution, since many species, especially the hawksbill, are on the endangered-species list and could be impounded by U.S. Customs if discovered in your luggage. Also for sale here are rockers, mahogany, sandals, baskets, hats, and clay braziers for grilling fish.

Ambar Marie, Caonabo 9, Gazcue (☎ 809/682-7539), is a trustworthy source for amber. Look for the beautiful necklaces, as well as the earrings and pins; you can even design your own setting here. **Amber World Museum,** Arzobispo Meriño 452 (☎ **809/682-3309**), lives up to its name. In the wake of the film *Jurassic Park,* more and more visitors are flocking here to see plants, insects, and even scorpions fossilized in resin millions of years ago. Although some of the displays are not for sale, in an adjoining salon you can watch craftspeople at work, polishing and shaping raw bits of ancient amber for sale.

Another reliable source for stunning amber, as well as coral and larimar, is **Ambar Nacionale,** Calle Restauración 110 (☎ **809/686-5700**). In general, prices here are a bit less expensive than those at the more prestigious Amber World Museum around the corner. In the colonial section of the old city, **Ambar Tres,** La Atarazana 3 (☎ **809/688-0474**), sells jewelry made from amber and black coral, as well as mahogany carvings, watercolors, and oil paintings.

In the center of the most historical section of town is the well-known **Galería de Arte Nader,** Rafael Augusto Sanchez 22 (☎ **809/687-6674**), which sells so many Latin paintings that they're sometimes stacked in rows against the walls. Many of these paintings appear quite worthy, and works by some leading artists are displayed here. But others, especially those shipped in by the truckload from Haiti, seem to be mere tourist junk. In the ancient courtyard in back, you can get a glimpse of how things looked in the Spanish colonies hundreds of years ago.

Although the name implies that it's new, **Novo Atarazana,** La Atarazana 21 (☎ **809/689-0582**), is actually one of the longest-established shops in town. If you don't have much time to shop around for local art and crafts, you'll find a wide selection here, including amber, black coral, leather goods, wood carvings, and Haitian paintings. **Arawak Gallery,** Avenida Pasteur 104 (☎ **809/685-1661**), features not only pre-Columbian artifacts but also modern art and ceramics.

Plaza Criolla, at the corner of Avenidas 27 de Febrero and Anacaona, is a modern shopping complex. Its shops are set amid gardens with tropical shrubbery and flowers, facing the Olympic Center. A covered wooden walkway links the stalls.

SANTO DOMINGO AFTER DARK
DANCE CLUBS

La Guácara Taína, Calle Mirador, in Parque Mirador del Sur (☎ **809/533-1051**), is the best *discoteca* in the country. Set in an underground cave within a verdant park, the specialty is merengue, salsa, and other forms of music. There are three bars, two dance floors, and banquettes and chairs nestled into the rocky walls. The cover is RD$150 ($10.65).

Neon Discotheque, in the Hispaniola Hotel, Avenida Independencia (☎ **809/221-1511**), is one of the town's best-established dance clubs, popular for its disco music and flashing lights, as well as its Latin jazz with different guest stars each week. The clientele tends to be very young, and includes many university students. There's a cover of RD$80 ($5.70) unless you're a guest of the hotel.

Omni Disco/Diamante Bar, in the Meliá Santo Domingo Hotel & Casino, Av. George Washington 361 (☎ **809/221-6666**), is a hot spot along the Malecón. You can spend an intriguing evening by dividing your time between these two watering holes. The Omni Disco is one of the most artfully decorated discos in town. If you consider yourself older and a bit more sedate (at least by D.R. standards), avoid the place on Tuesday nights, when it's college night. After a while, many visitors move on to the Diamante Bar, the showcase bar in the Sheraton's casino, in an annex building adjacent to the hotel itself. Here, live bands perform merengue, salsa, and other music, often with zest and flair. Both bars are open daily from 8pm to 4am. The disco charges a cover of RD$60 ($4.25).

Adventures in the National Parks

This island nation has 16 national parks and seven nature reserves, which is remarkable for a country so small. Outdoor opportunities range from **mountain climbing**—Pico Durate in J. Armando Bermúdez National Park is the highest peak in the West Indies at 10,700 feet—to **cascading,** an eco-sport involving climbing to the top of a waterfall, then rappelling down the middle of the cascade. In the southwestern tip of the country, **Parque Nacional Jaragua** is the largest national park in the country and one of the largest in the Caribbean, with everything from offshore islands to inland deserts. Home to turtles and reptiles, it also has more than half of all the bird species found on the island. Dominican tourist offices can provide complete details about how to tour these parks on your own.

In the colonial zone, the best club is **Bachata Rosa,** La Atarazana 9 (☎ **809/688-0969**), which takes its name from a popular song on the island. In fact, Juan Luís Guerra, the Dominican merengue megastar who made the song a hit, is part owner. Currently, this is the island's best dance club, with action taking place on three floors. There's also a typical restaurant here serving local specialties. A trio of wide screens show videos.

The country's leading gay dance club is **Disco Free,** Avenida Ortega y Gaset (☎ 809/565-8100), open Thursday to Sunday only. It has some of the best music in town, and is known for its salsa and merengue.

PUBS & BARS

Many of the chic stops are in the big hotels. **Las Palmas,** in the Hotel Santo Domingo, Avenida Independencia (☎ **809/221-7111**), is adjacent to the lobby, in premises that were originally decorated by Oscar de la Renta. It's a cross between a conventional bar and a disco, with an emphasis on the bar trade between 6 and 9:30pm, shifting to live music, such as salsa and merengue, from 9:30pm to 4am. When someone isn't performing, large-screen TVs broadcast music videos from the U.S. mainland. Drink prices are reduced from 6 to 8pm.

Merengue Bar, in the Renaissance Jaragua Resort & Casino, Av. George Washington 367 (☎ 809/221-2222), has a party atmosphere that often spills out into the sophisticated casino. High-ceilinged and painted in dark, subtly provocative colors, it includes a sprawling bar area, a sometimes overcrowded dance floor, and rows of banquettes and tables that face a brightly lit stage. Here, animated bands from as far away as the Philippines perform daily, from 4pm to the wee hours of the morning. The joint really gets jumping around 10pm, when this bar/nightclub seems to forget that it operates in a jangling casino.

ROLLING THE DICE

Santo Domingo has several major casinos, all of which are open nightly until 4 or 5am. The most spectacular is the **Renaissance Jaragua Resort & Casino,** Av. George Washington 367 (☎ 809/221-2222), whose brightly flashing sign is the most dazzling light along the Malecón at night. The most glamorous casino in the country is fittingly housed in the capital's poshest hotel, and offers blackjack, baccarat, roulette, and slot machines. You can gamble in either Dominican pesos or U.S. dollars.

Another casino is at the **Hispaniola Hotel,** Avenida Independencia (☎ 809/221-7111). One of the most stylish choices is the **Omni Casino,** in the Meliá Santo Domingo Hotel & Casino, Av. George Washington 361 (☎ 809/221-6666). Its bilingual staff will help you play blackjack, craps, baccarat, and keno, among other games. There's also a piano bar.

3 La Romana & Altos de Chavón

On the southeast coast of the Dominican Republic, La Romana was once a sleepy sugarcane town that specialized in cattle raising. Visitors didn't come near the place, but when Gulf & Western Industries opened a luxurious tropical paradise resort, the Casa de Campo, La Romana soon began drawing the jet set. Just east of Casa de Campo is Altos de Chavón, a re-creation of a 15th-century village built specially for artists.

GETTING THERE

BY PLANE   The easiest route to Casa de Campo from almost anywhere in North America is through San Juan, Puerto Rico (see "Getting There" in chapter 18). **American Eagle** (☎ **800/433-7300** in the U.S.) operates at least two (and in busy seasons, at least three) daily nonstop flights to Casa de Campo/La Romana from San Juan. Each flight takes a little over an hour and departs late enough in the day to permit transfers from other flights.

BY CAR   If you're already in Santo Domingo, you can drive here in about an hour and 20 minutes from the international airport, along Las Américas Highway. (Allow another hour if you're in the center of the city.) Of course, everything depends on traffic conditions. Watch for speed traps—low-paid police officers openly solicit bribes whether you're speeding or not.

LA ROMANA
WHERE TO STAY

✪ **Casa de Campo**. La Romana, Dominican Republic. ☎ **800/877-3643** in the U.S., Canada, Puerto Rico, and the Virgin Islands; or 809/523-3333. Fax 809/523-8548. www.casadcampo.com. E-mail: res@pwmonline.com. 450 units. A/C MINIBAR TV TEL. Winter $250–$522 casita for 2; $237 per person two-bedroom villa for 4. Off-season $336–$400 casita for 2; $184 per person two-bedroom villa for 4. Rates are all-inclusive. AE, MC, V.

Translated as "House in the Country," Casa de Campo is the greatest resort in the entire Caribbean, bringing a whole new dimension to a holiday. Gulf & Western took a vast hunk of coastal land, more than 7,000 acres in all, and carved out this chic resort, today owned and operated by Premier Resorts & Hotels and known as one of the best golf resorts in the world. Miami architect William Cox helped create it, and Oscar de la Renta provided the original style and flair. Dominican paintings, louvered doors, and flamboyant fabrics decorate the interior.

Accommodations are divided into red-roofed, two-story casitas near the main building and more upscale villas that dot the edges of the golf courses, the gardens near the tennis courts, and the Atlantic shoreline. Some are clustered in a semi-private hilltop compound with views overlooking the meadows, the sugarcane, and the fairways down to the distant sea. The resort's numerous recreational facilities and programs lure many types of travelers, including families. Children's programs (for ages 3 to 12) include full-day camping with horseback riding, aerobics, swimming, sack races, and treasure hunts.

Dining: Around the four pools, each on a different level, are thatch huts on stilts serving beverages and light meals. La Caña is the two-level bar and lounge, with a thatch roof but no walls. For dinner, guests enjoy some of the best food in the Dominican Republic on a rustic roofed terrace. There's sometimes a pig roast right on the beach; most of the beef used is raised on the plains of La Romana. See "Where to Dine," below, for reviews of El Patio, the Lago Grill, and the Tropicana Steakhouse.

Amenities: One of the most complete fitness centers on the island, with weight and exercise machines, whirlpool and sauna, aerobics classes, and massage. See "Sports &

Outdoor Pursuits," below, for details on golf, tennis, water sports, fishing, and polo and horseback-riding facilities. Room service (from 7am to midnight), laundry, baby-sitting.

WHERE TO DINE

El Patio. In Casa de Campo. ☎ **809/523-3333.** Main courses RD$155–RD$330 ($11–$23.45); buffet RD$236 ($16.75). AE, DC, MC, V. Daily 7am–2:30pm and 3–10pm. CARIBBEAN/AMERICAN.

El Patio is technically a glamorized bistro, with a shield of lattices, banks of plants, and checkerboard tablecloths. It specializes in all-you-can-eat buffets which are remarkable in value, considering the quality of both the cooking and the first-class ingredients. You can also feast on selections from the constantly changing à la carte menu. Try such pleasing dishes as grilled snapper in a savory lime sauce or fillet of salmon with a per-fectly prepared vinaigrette. The fettuccine in seafood sauce also wins approval. If you like your dishes plainer, opt for half a roast chicken or the classic beef tips in a mush-room and onion sauce.

✪ **Lago Grill.** In Casa de Campo. ☎ **809/523-3333.** Buffet RD$300 ($21.30) at lunch, RD$400 ($28.40) at dinner. AE, DC, MC, V. Daily 7–11am, noon–4pm, and 7–11pm. CARIBBEAN/AMERICAN.

The Lago Grill is ideal for breakfast; in fact, it has one of the best-stocked morning buffets in the country. Your view is of a lake, a sloping meadow, and the resort's pri-vate airport, with the sea in the distance. At the fresh-juice bar, an employee in colo-nial costume will extract juices from 25 different tropical fruits in any combination you prefer. Then you can select your ingredients for an omelet, which an employee will whip up while you wait. The buffet includes sandwiches, burgers, *sancocho* (the famous Dominican stew), and fresh conch chowder. There's also a well-stocked salad bar. A changing array of dinner buffets here might feature Chinese, Italian, or Dominican food.

Tropicana Steakhouse. In Casa de Campo. ☎ **809/523-3333,** ext. 3000. Reservations required. Main courses RD$175–RD$600 ($12.40–$42.60). AE, MC, V. Daily 6–11pm. CARIBBEAN/STEAKS.

One of the most glamorous restaurants in the resort complex, the Tropicana is a breezy pavilion known for its innovative Caribbean flair and a wide range of seafood and exotic West Indian dishes. Its steaks, especially the T-bone and New York sirloin, are the best in this part of the country. You can also order char-grilled pork chops and some delectable spareribs. There's a vegetarian menu as well.

HITTING THE BEACH

A large, palm-fringed sandy crescent, **Bayahibe** is a 20-minute launch trip or a 30-minute drive from La Romana. In addition, **La Minitas** is a tiny, but nice, immac-ulate beach and lagoon. Transportation is provided on the bus, or you can rent a horse-drawn buckboard. Finally, **Catalina** is a turquoise beach on a deserted island just 45 minutes away by motorboat.

SPORTS & OUTDOOR PURSUITS

FISHING   You can charter a boat for deep-sea fishing—Casa de Campo maintains eight charter vessels, with a minimum of eight people required per outing. Only three can fish at a time. Some of the biggest snook ever recorded have been caught here. Deep-sea fishing costs $300 for 4 hours (from 8:30am to 12:30pm or 1:30 to 5:30pm), or $400 for 8 hours (from 9am to 5pm). The hotel can also arrange fresh-water river fishing trips on the Chavón.

GOLF The Casa de Campo courses are known to dedicated golfers everywhere; in fact, *Golf* magazine declared it "the finest golf resort in the world." The course called ✪ **Teeth of the Dog** has also been described as "a thing of almighty beauty," and we agree. The ruggedly natural terrain has seven holes skirting the ocean. Opened in 1977, ✪ **The Links** is an inland course modeled after some of the seaside courses of Scotland and built on sandy soil away from the beach. Most golf passes are sold as unlimited memberships for either 3 days ($195) or 7 days ($330). Extra days cost $65 each. Golf-cart rentals are $25 per person per round. To play 18 holes, the cost is $125 for Teeth of the Dog, $85 for the Links (including cart). Hours are daily from 7am to 7pm.

HORSEBACK RIDING Trail rides at Casa de Campo cost $20 for 1 hour, $40 for 2. The resort's stables shelter 250 horses.

POLO Ever since the grand days when Dominican playboy Porfirio Rubirosa mounted some of the finest horses in the world, the Dominican Republic has been a mecca for polo players. Today Casa de Campo is the ideal venue in the Caribbean for playing, learning, and watching the fabled sport. There are three full-size polo fields (one for practice only), a horse-breeding farm, and scores of polo ponies, as well as a small army of veterinarians, grooms, and polo-related employees. If a polo match is scheduled during your visit, by all means go.

Most serious polo players arrive with their own equipment, but beginners learn by watching more experienced players and participating in trail rides (which last 1 to 3 hours), as well as taking riding lessons at the resort's dude ranch. If polo players are present, they can play polo for $45 per player per match per chukker. Polo lessons are $40 per hour.

SNORKELING Casa de Campo has one of the most complete water-sports facilities in the Dominican Republic. Reservations and information on any seaside activity can be arranged through the resort's concierge. You can charter one of the resort's eight vessels, with a minimum of eight people required per outing. Full-day snorkeling trips to Isla Catalina are offered Wednesday through Monday; the cost is about $30 and includes lunch.

TENNIS Some 13 clay courts at Casa de Campo are lit for night play. The courts are available daily from 7am to 10pm. Charges are $17 per hour during the day or $20 at night. Tennis lessons are $50 per hour with a tennis pro, $42 with an assistant pro, and $35 with a junior pro.

ALTOS DE CHAVÓN: AN ARTISTS' COLONY

In 1976, a plateau 100 miles east of Santo Domingo was selected by Charles G. Bluhdorn, then chairman of Gulf & Western Industries, as the site for a remarkable project. Dominican stonecutters, woodworkers, and ironworkers began the task that would create ✪ **Altos de Chavón,** today a flourishing art center set above the canyon of the Río Chavón and the Caribbean Sea.

A walk down one of the cobblestone paths of this combination living museum and artisans' colony reveals at every turn architecture reminiscent of another era. Coral block and terra-cotta brick buildings house artists' studios, craft workshops, galleries, stores, and restaurants. Mosaics of black river pebbles, sun-bleached coral, and red sandstone spread out to the plazas. The ornate stone **Church of St. Stanislaus** is centered on the main plaza, with its fountain of the four lions, colonnade of obelisks, and panoramic views.

The **School of Design** at Altos de Chavón has offered a 2-year Associate in Applied Science degree, in the areas of communication, fashion, environmental studies, product design, and fine arts/illustration since its inauguration in 1982. The school is affiliated with the Parsons School of Design in New York and Paris, providing local and international graduates with the opportunity to acquire the advanced skills needed for placement in design careers.

From around the world come artists-in-residence, both the established and the aspiring. Altos de Chavón provides them with lodging, studio space, and a group exhibition at the culmination of their 3-month stay.

The three **galleries** offer a varied and engaging mix of exhibits, showcasing the work of well-known and emerging Dominican and international artists. In a consignment space, finely crafted silk screens and other works are available for sale.

Altos de Chavón's *talleres* are craft ateliers, where local artisans have been trained to produce ceramic, silk-screen, and woven-fiber products. From the clay apothecary jars with carnival devil lids to the colored tapestries of Dominican houses, the richness of island myth and legend, folklore, and handcraft tradition is much in evidence. The posters, note cards, and printed T-shirts that come from the silk-screen workshops are among the most sophisticated in the Caribbean. All the products of Altos de Chavón's *talleres* are sold at **La Tienda,** the foundation village store.

Bugambilia (☎ **809/523-3333,** ext. 2355) is one of Altos de Chavón's best shops. The staff will explain the origins of dozens of ceramic figures on display. The female figures are crafted in the industrial city of Santiago as part of a long tradition of presenting peasant women without faces. Look, however, for an expression of dignity in the bodies of the figurines. The store also has a winning collection of grotesque papier-mâché carnival masks. The jewelry at **Everett Designs** (☎ **809/523-3333,** ext. 8331) is so original that many visitors mistake this place for a museum. Each piece is hand-crafted in a mini-factory at the rear of the shop. The collection includes Dominican larimar and amber, 17th-century Spanish pieces-of-eight from sunken galleons, and polished silver and gold.

Thousands of visitors per year view the **Regional Museum of Archaeology,** which houses the objects of Samuel Pion, an amateur archaeologist and collector of treasures from the vanished Taíno tribes, the island's first settlers. The timeless quality of some of the museum's objects makes them seem strangely contemporary in design—some sculptural forms recall the work of Brancusi or Arp. The museum is open daily from 9am to 9pm.

At the heart of the village's performing-arts complex is the 5,000-seat, open-air **amphitheater.** Since its inauguration over a decade ago by Carlos Santana and the late Frank Sinatra, the amphitheater has hosted renowned concerts, symphonies, theater, and festivals, including concerts by Julio Iglesias and Gloria Estefan. The annual **Heineken Jazz Festival** has brought together such diverse talents as Dizzy Gillespie, Toots Thielmans, Tania Maria, and Randy Brecker.

WHERE TO DINE

Café del Sol. Altos de Chavón. ☎ **809/523-3333,** ext. 2346. Pizza $8–$14. AE, MC, V. Daily 11am–11pm. To reach the cafe, climb a flight of stone steps to the rooftop of a building whose ground floor houses a jewelry shop. ITALIAN.

The pizzas at this stone-floored indoor/outdoor cafe are the best on the south coast. The favorite seems to be *quattro stagioni,* made with tomato, mozzarella, mushrooms, artichoke hearts, cooked ham, and olives. You can also order such antipasti as a Mediterranean salad with tuna and ratatouille or a pasta primavera. The chef makes a soothing minestrone in the true Italian style, served with freshly made bread.

Casa del Río. Altos de Chavón. ☎ **809/523-3333,** ext. 2345. Reservations required. Main courses $16–$22.50. AE, MC, V. Daily 6–11pm. FRENCH/CARIBBEAN.

The most romantic restaurant at Altos de Chavón occupies the basement of an Iberian-style 16th-century castle whose towers, turrets, tiles, and massive stairs are entwined with strands of bougainvillea. Inside, brick arches support oversized chandeliers, suspended racing sculls, and wine racks. Amid this bucolic atmosphere, you can indulge in some of the best seafood dishes on the south coast. Although the food has a slight French flair, and often a few Thai twists, everything tastes and looks firmly West Indian. Any of the seafood choices, perhaps a lobster lasagna, is worthy of your attention. Lobster might also appear glazed with a vanilla vinaigrette that tastes a lot better than it sounds. You'll encounter innovative cuisine here, especially in dishes involving lemongrass or coriander. Two particular favorites include sautéed salmon, served on a bed of leeks with oyster mushrooms and a spicy black currant sauce, and sautéed tenderloin of beef with Roquefort cheese and almonds. Finally, we just can't seem to forget the hearts of palm vichyssoise we once ordered here.

El Sombrero. Altos de Chavón. ☎ **809/523-3333.** Reservations recommended. Main courses RD$155–RD$250 ($11–$17.75). AE, MC, V. Daily 6–11pm. MEXICAN.

In this thick-walled, colonial-style building, the jutting hand-hewn timbers and roughly textured plaster evoke a corner of Old Mexico. There's a scattering of dark, heavy furniture and an occasional genuine antique, but the main draw is the spicy cuisine. Most guests dine outside on the covered patio, within earshot of a group of wandering minstrels wearing sombreros. A margarita is an appropriate accompaniment to the nachos, enchiladas, black-bean soup, skillet-hot pork chops, grilled steaks, and brochettes.

La Piazzetta. Altos de Chavón. ☎ **809/523-3333.** Reservations required. Main courses RD$150–RD$354 ($10.65–$25.15). AE, MC, V. Daily 3–10pm. ITALIAN.

La Piazzetta snuggles in the 16th-century–style "village" set high above the Chavón River. Well-prepared Italian dinners might begin with an antipasto misto, followed with fillet of sea bass with artichokes-and-black-olive sauce, chicken saltimbocca (with ham), or beef brochette with a walnut-and-arugula sauce. Your fellow diners are likely to be guests from the deluxe Casa de Campo nearby.

4 Punta Cana

Continuing east from La Romana, you reach Punta Cana, site of several major vacation developments, including Club Med, with more scheduled to arrive in the near future. Perhaps this easternmost tip of the Dominican Republic will one day rival Puerto Plata.

Known for its white-sand beaches and clear waters, Punta Cana is an escapist's retreat. When you've had enough sun, you can head inland to the typical Dominican city of Higüey, 27 miles from Punta Cana, which has yet to be built up for tourism's sake. Here, you can see the **Basilica Nuestra Señora de la Altagracia,** with the largest carillon in the Americas.

Higüey was founded in 1494 by the conqueror of Jamaica, Juan de Esquivel, with immigrants brought in between 1502 and 1508 by Ponce de León to populate the land. It was from the castle he built here that the tireless seeker of the Fountain of Youth set out in 1509 to conquer Puerto Rico and in 1513 to explore Florida.

Toward the southern coast is **Saona Island,** where some 1,000 people live on 80 square miles of land, surviving primarily by fishing and hunting for pigeons and wild hogs. It must be a healthy way to live, for Saona has the lowest mortality rate in the Dominican Republic.

GETTING THERE

American Eagle (☎ 800/433-7300) offers two to four daily nonstop flights to Punta Cana from San Juan; flying time is 57 minutes. You can also opt for one of American Eagle's two or three (depending on the season) daily flights from San Juan to La Romana and then make the 90-minute drive to Punta Cana.

WHERE TO STAY & DINE

Barcelo Bavaro Beach Golf & Casino Resort. Apdo Postal 1, Punta Cana, Higüey, Dominican Republic. ☎ **888/228-2761** or 809/686-5797. Fax 809/656-5680. E-mail: bavaro@codetel.net.do. 1,960 units. A/C TV TEL. Winter $200–$300 double; $290–$340 junior suite for two. Off-season $154–$196 double; $196–$270 junior suite for two. Rates are all-inclusive. Discounts of 45% to 65% for children 2–12 staying in parents' room. AE, DC, MC, V.

This is one of the most ambitious resort colonies in the Dominican Republic, a project whose scope hasn't been equaled here since the early days of Casa de Campo. Built between 1985 and 1996, it occupies almost 4½ square miles of land, including a 2-mile beach that has some of the best seafront property on the island. Developed by the Spain-based Barcelos Group, it consists of five separate low-rise hotels: Bavaro Beach Hotel, Bavaro Garden Hotel, Bavaro Golf Hotel, Bavaro Casino Hotel, and the newest contender, the Bavaro Palace Hotel. Arranged in the shape of a horseshoe, most of the buildings lie parallel to the beachfront for maximum exposure to the sun. The overall effect is an unhurried, somewhat anonymous, and sometimes disorganized vacation village dotted with recreational facilities.

Accommodations in all five hotels are roughly equivalent. (The Bavaro Palace's rooms are somewhat more comfortable than the others.) Units, which are fairly compact but not too small for comfort, have private verandas or terraces, tile floors, and simple, summery Dominican furniture painted red and green. Bathrooms are a bit small, equipped in routine motel style. The all-inclusive plan includes meals, snacks, most domestic (i.e., native Dominican) drinks, and most nonmotorized sports, although a bewildering array of packages (with a focus on golf, tennis, or scuba) are also available. Most of the rooms are booked through as many as 60 different tour operators scattered throughout the world, so consider the prices listed above merely as guidelines. The clientele consists primarily of chartered tour groups from Italy, Spain, Germany, and South America, especially Argentina. Despite the resort's vast size and abundant recreational and dining facilities, expect the sense that the complex is evolving and growing; it never really seems to be either finished or particularly well staffed.

Dining/Diversions: The resort contains 14 restaurants and 16 bars. Although each of them participates to some degree in the resort's all-inclusive program, you might be charged supplements for some items. Every evening, two of the bars become nightclubs, one specializing in disco, the other in Latin music. The resort has one of the largest casinos in the region, open every evening from 5pm until the last casino chip hits the roulette table.

Amenities: Five pools, an 18-hole golf course, daily aerobics sessions, scuba diving, snorkeling, sailing, windsurfing, waterskiing, deep-sea fishing, tennis, horseback riding, beauty salon, whirlpool baths big enough for 30 people at a time, medical facilities, on-site bank. Laundry, baby-sitting, massage.

Club Mediterranée Punta Cana. Apdo. Postal 106, Provincia La Altagracia, Dominican Republic. ☎ **800/CLUB-MED** in the U.S. and Canada, or 809/686-5500. Fax 809/687-2896. 334 units. A/C. Winter $819–$1,379 per person per week. Off-season $889–$959 per person per week. Rates are all-inclusive. Children 11 and under stay in parents' room for $679 to $889 per week in winter, $679 per week in summer, or else free during certain weeks of summer. Every guest is charged an annual membership fee of $50 per adult, $20 per child, plus a one-time initiation fee of $30 per family. AE, MC, V.

Some 145 miles east of Santo Domingo, this family-oriented Club Med opened in 1981 and put the far-eastern tip of the island of Hispaniola on the tourism map. The village, designed in a series of multistoried concrete buildings that might remind you of many conventional beachfront hotels, lies along a reef-protected white-sand beach, off of which are some spectacular dive sites. It was here that the crews of the *Niña*, *Pinta*, and *Santa Maria* are believed by some to have put ashore. Three-story clusters of bungalows are strung along the beach; each contains twin beds with good mattresses, a private safe, and a small, compact bathroom, and opens onto either the beach or a coconut grove. Frankly, if you're single and looking for an environment with other singles and the possibility of some romantic action, select another Club Med village that's better suited to your needs.

Dining/Diversions: The heart of the village is a combined dining room/bar/dance floor and theater complex facing the sea. There are also three restaurants and a disco beside the sea. You get the usual Club Med activities here, including picnics, boat rides, nightly dancing, shows, and optional excursions.

Amenities: Sailing, windsurfing, snorkeling, waterskiing, swimming, archery, seven tennis courts (six lit at night), laundry service. Preteen entertainment and child-care facilities at this resort are particularly emphasized. The Petit Club is for infants ages 2 to 3, the Mini-Club is for juniors ages 4 to 7, and the Kids Club is for kids ages 8 to 11. All three offer circus training, makeup classes, arts and crafts, communal sports, and more.

Meliá Bávaro. Playa El Cortecito, Punta Cana, Higüey, Dominican Republic. ☎ **800/ 336-3542** or 809/221-2311. Fax 809/686-5427. www.solmelia.es. E-mail: melia.bavaro@ codetel.net.do. 82 units. Christmas to New Year's holidays $179 suite for 2. Other times $77–$147 suite for 2. MAP (breakfast and dinner) $70 per person extra. AE, DC, MC, V.

The most glamorous addition to the resort scene in Punta Cana when it opened in 1992, this hotel transformed all of its rooms into junior suites in 1995. The Spanish-born architect, Alvaro Sanz, retained most of the palms and mangrove clusters on the property and installed freshwater reservoirs, creating an oasis not only for vacationers, but also for the many species of birds that call the resort home. Owned by Meliá Hotels, the Spain-based giant, this resort drew at least part of its architectural inspiration from the company's successful hostelry in Bali.

All accommodations are suites that lie within earshot of the resort's mile-long private beach. Most of the units occupy a compound of two-story bungalows; the rest are adjacent to the resort's headquarters, a high-ceilinged, open-air pavilion. The split-level suites contain refrigerators and king or twin beds, each fitted with a good mattress. The small bathrooms have combination tub/showers and marble counters.

Dining/Diversions: The most appealing of the resort's seven choices is El Trapiche, a seafood restaurant built on an island in the middle of one of the swimming pools. An international restaurant, El Licey, sits on a pier jutting over a freshwater lake, adjacent to an open-air disco. The resort's main restaurant serves an array of buffets. There's a handful of bars, one a pub/disco floating atop a lake, another a swim-up pool bar.

Amenities: Two pools, land and water-sports facilities, shopping arcade, four lit tennis courts. 24-hour room service, concierge, baby-sitting, car and scooter rentals.

5　Puerto Plata

Columbus wanted to establish a city at Puerto Plata and name it La Isabela. Unfortunately, a tempest detained him, and it wasn't until 1502 that Nicolás de Ovando founded Puerto Plata ("port of silver"), 130 miles northwest of Santo Domingo. The port became the last stop for ships going back to Europe, their holds laden with treasures taken from the New World. Puerto Plata appeals to a mass-market crowd that shuns those pricey, pampering hotels in favor of the less expensive, all-inclusive resorts that keep popping up here; some hotels are booked solid almost year-round. Unfortunately, some excellent restaurants have been forced to close because of the all-inclusive trend; in fact, the most popular dining choice along the coast now is Pizza Hut.

Most of the hotels are not actually in Puerto Plata itself but in a tourist zone called Playa Dorada, which consists of major hotels, a scattering of secluded condominiums and villas, a Robert Trent Jones, Jr.–designed golf course, and a riding stable with horses for each of the major properties.

Note that it rains a lot in Puerto Plata during the winter (whereas the southern region and Punta Cana are drier).

ESSENTIALS

GETTING THERE　By Plane　The international airport is actually not in Puerto Plata but is east of Playa Dorado on the road to Sosúa. For information about flights from North America, see "Getting There," at the beginning of this chapter.

By Car　From Santo Domingo, the 3½-hour drive directly north on Autopista Duarte passes through the lush Cibao Valley, home of the tobacco industry and Bermudez rum, and through Santiago de los Caballeros, the second-largest city in the country, 90 miles north of Santo Domingo.

GETTING AROUND　For information on renting a car, see "Getting Around" at the beginning of this chapter. You might find that a motor scooter will be suitable for transportation in Puerto Plata or Sosúa, although the roads are potholed.

By Motoconcho　The cheapest way of getting around is on a *motoconcho,* found at the major corners of Puerto Plata and Sosúa. The motorcycle concho (taxi) offers a ride to practically anywhere in town. You can also go from Puerto Plata to Playa Dorada (site of most of the hotels). Fares range from RD$20 to RD$25 ($1.40 to $1.80).

By Minivan　Minivans are another means of transport, especially if you're traveling outside town. They leave from Puerto Plata's Central Park and will take you all the way to Sosúa. Determine the fare before getting in. Usually a shared ride between Puerto Plata and Sosúa costs RD$15 ($1.05) per person. Service is daily from 6am to 9pm.

By Taxi　Agree with the driver on the fare before your trip starts, as cabs are not metered. You'll find taxis on Central Park at Puerto Plata. At night, it's wise to rent your cab for a round-trip. If you go in the daytime by taxi to any of the other beach resorts or villages, check on reserving a vehicle for your return trip. Note that a taxi from Puerto Plata to Sosúa will cost around RD$250 ($17.75) each way, and it will hold up to four occupants.

By Organized Tour　Two of the town's best-valued tour operators include **Apollo Tours,** Calle John F. Kennedy 15 (☎ **809/586-6610**), and **Turissimo,** Avenida Manolo Tavares Justo (☎ **809/586-3497**). Both conduct half-day tours of Puerto Plata aboard minibuses that contain between 15 and 33 passengers, visiting the seafront, sites of historic interest (including Fort San Felipe), some of the town's more visible shops, and the Amber Museum. The cost is RD$300 ($21.30) per person.

FAST FACTS Round-the-clock **drugstore** service is offered by **Farmacía Deleyte,** Calle John F. Kennedy 89 (☎ **809/586-2583**). Emergency medical service is provided by **Clínica Dr. Brugal,** Calle José del Carmen Ariza 15 (☎ **809/586-2519**). To summon the **police** in Puerto Plata, call ☎ **809/586-2331.** Tourist information is available in Puerto Plata at the **Office of Tourism,** Playa Long Beach (☎ **809/586-3676**).

WHERE TO STAY

Caribbean Village Club on the Green. Playa Dorada, Puerto Plata, Dominican Republic. ☎ **809/320-1111,** or 305/269-5909 in Miami. Fax 809/320-5386. 336 units. A/C TV TEL. Winter $130 per person double. Off-season $80 per person double. Rates are all-inclusive. AE, MC, V.

Upgraded in 1996 by a hotel chain, this modern low-rise property is near a cluster of competitors east of the airport and 10 minutes by foot to the nearest good beach. The all-inclusive rates cover accommodations in comfortable but simple rooms, three meals a day, all beverages, and some water sports. Surprisingly, their so-called suites aren't much different from the regular doubles—and don't cost any more. Units are decorated in tropical Caribbean colors, with private safes, two queen beds with firm mattresses (some rooms have king beds), and excellently maintained medium-size bathrooms.

Standard Dominican and international food is offered at El Pilon, Italian pastas at Firenze, and fresh seafood and local beef at La Miranda. At that last restaurant, you may want to sample some of the excellent Chilean vintages, all at reasonable prices. Amenities include water-sports facilities, seven all-weather tennis courts, a gym, a sauna, and a pool with a swim-up bar.

Grand Ventana. Playa Dorada (Apdo. Postal 22), Puerto Plata, Dominican Republic. ☎ **809/320-2111.** Fax 809/320-4017. 556 units. A/C TV TEL. May–June and Oct–Nov $120 double; $195 suite for two. Other months $170 double; $245 suite for two. AE, MC, V.

One of Puerto Plata's newest hotels is this attractive trio of ochre-colored beachfront buildings inspired by the traditional architecture of Spain's American colonies. Each three-story building is trimmed with ornate, Victorian-inspired gingerbread, and each unit offers mahogany furniture, ceiling fans, a balcony or patio, and, in all but a few rooms, views of the sea. Bedrooms are compact but efficiently designed; most have new mattresses. Baths are a bit small but have up-to-date plumbing. The gardens and lawns surrounding the site are dotted with gazebos, flowering shrubs, and tropical plants and palms. Everyone here checks in on the all-inclusive plan, which includes lots of beach or pool time, but a relatively limited one hour per day per client of snorkeling, windsurfing, sailing, horseback riding, kayaks, and scuba diving.

Some form of musical entertainment is presented nightly in the four bars, and food is offered in one way or another, at one outlet or another, almost continuously from 7am to 10:30pm. Guests looking for gambling or a disco have unlimited access to the facilities at the Playa Dorada Hotel & Casino, a 5-minute walk away. The resort's more formal restaurant, Octopus, which offers seating only to guests of the hotel, requires advance reservations and cannot be visited more than once in the context of any 1-week holiday. The most recent addition is Sapore di Mare, an upscale Italian eatery. Other amenities include separate pools for adults and children, a gymnasium/sauna, a nursery, tennis courts, conference rooms, shops, a beauty parlor/massage facility, concierge, water-sports facilities, and baby-sitting for a small additional charge.

Occidental Playa Dorada Hotel & Casino. Playa Dorada (Apdo. Postal 272), Puerto Plata, Dominican Republic. ☎ **800/545-8089** or 809/320-3988. Fax 809/320-2775. www.

occidental-hotels.com. 351 units. A/C TV TEL. Year-round $220 double; $310 suite for two. Extra person $70–$125. Children ages 2–12 pay $50. AE, MC, V.

This theatrically designed hotel east of the airport is one of the few in all the Caribbean that can boast nearly full occupancy during most of the year. The reception area is an air-conditioned oasis of Victorian latticework set beneath the soaring ceiling. The guest rooms are arranged along rambling corridors. More than two-thirds of the hotel's units are set in red-roofed wings that face the 1½-mile-long beach. As for the rooms, once a Holiday Inn, always a Holiday Inn (the former name of this hotel). They recently received a long overdue renovation, but they're so compact, they have been compared to everything from a bunker to a shoebox. Each has a king or two queen beds with decent mattresses, plus small bathrooms. As a grace note, some units have sliding-glass doors opening onto private balconies. The hotel is recommended to those who plan to spend most of their time outdoors instead of lounging around in their rooms. The hotel also has specially designed rooms for travelers with disabilities.

In addition to La Palma restaurant, the many bars and entertainment facilities include a cocktail lounge and disco. Las Brisas has an ongoing series of buffets. Around the pool, the management hosts barbecues, buffet suppers, and weekly entertainment, including singers and dancers known throughout the Spanish-speaking world. A sports package is included in the rates, so all the facilities are free. They include boating, water sports, golf, three tennis courts (lit at night), and one of the largest pools in the area. Baby-sitting, laundry, and valet services are all available. At press time, the resort planned to add an extra 150 rooms, three new restaurants, an additional pool, and a new disco. During the construction progress, expect some areas of the resort to be partially shut down, although management hopes to keep disruption to a minimum during the enlargement process.

✪ **Paradise Beach Resort & Casino.** Playa Dorada (Apdo. Postal 337), Puerto Plata, Dominican Republic. ☎ **800/752-9236** or 809/586-3663. Fax 809/320-4858. 440 units. A/C TV TEL. Winter $270 double; $330 suite for two. Off-season $210 double; $270 suite for two. Rates are all-inclusive. AE, DC, MC, V.

This all-inclusive resort is the best-positioned of all the Playa Dorada hotels, with superior amenities and a well-trained staff. It also boasts an eco-friendly design: a cluster of Caribbean-Victorian low-rises with white-tile roofs and lattice-laced balconies. Brick paths cut through the well-manicured, tropical grounds. Accommodations are neatly furnished with tile floors, twin or queen beds with excellent mattresses, fridges (in most cases), and large closets. Most rooms have French doors leading to private patios or balconies. Only the suites have views opening onto the water. Bathrooms are compact, but efficiently organized with adequate shelf space.

The food under the all-inclusive plan is above average for the Playa Dorada area, and there's always plenty of it at the three restaurants. Bars seem to be in all the right places, and there's also a disco, plus a casino open daily from 10am to 4pm.

Facilities include a water-sports center, two tennis courts, an 18-hole golf course nearby, and horseback riding nearby.

Villas Doradas Beach Resort. Playa Dorada (Apdo. Postal 1370), Puerto Plata, Dominican Republic. ☎ **809/320-3000.** Fax 809/320-4790. 244 units. A/C TV TEL. Year-round $60–$80 per person double. Rates are all-inclusive. AE, MC, V.

This collection of town houses east of the airport is arranged in landscaped clusters, most of them around a courtyard. There's no beachfront here. Each unit is pleasantly furnished with louvered doors and windows and sleek tropical styling (tile floors, rattan and bamboo furnishings, wooden ceilings). Most rooms have queen or twin beds, each with firm mattresses that are replaced regularly. Many also have tiny kitchenettes, as well as balconies or patios. Bathrooms are small but tidy.

Personal service from the lackadaisical staff seems at a minimum here. A focal point of the resort is the restaurant Las Garzas, where shows entertain guests every evening. The management also offers barbecues around the pool area, where a net is sometimes set up for volleyball games. Of course, it would be tempting never to leave the shade of the cone-shaped thatch-roofed pool bar, one of the most popular parts of the whole resort. El Pescador features seafood beside the beach, Pancho serves Mexican dishes, and Jardín de Jade offers Chinese cuisine. Facilities include a pool, a kiddie pool, tennis courts, and horseback riding. Sand beaches and golf facilities are within walking distance.

WHERE TO DINE

✪ **Acuarela.** Calle Certal 3 at Calle Presidente Vasquez. ☎ **809/586-5314.** Main courses $10–$30. Tues–Sun 6–11pm or midnight, depending on business. AE, MC, V. CARIBBEAN.

The best and most appealing restaurant in Puerto Plata occupies the rose-colored wood-sided walls of what was built 150 years ago as a private house, and which was later the birthplace and home of the nation's most famous watercolorist, Rafi Vasquez, a living artist who is widely acknowledged for his contributions to Dominican painting. Today, the site is maintained as a restaurant by the artist's son, Rafael Vasquez, and daughter-in-law, Linda. You'll dine within an old-fashioned setting dominated by at least 20 of the artist's oversized watercolors, some of which are for sale at prices that range from $750 to $3,000. Menu items are steeped in the tenets of nouvelle cuisine, but with a definite Caribbean twist. Well-crafted starters include Camembert tropicale, wrapped in prosciutto and served with guava and orange slices, and shrimp Acuarela, breaded in yucca flour and served with a tropical fruit chutney. Main courses include a confit of crispy duck with Asian hoisin sauce; New Zealand lamb chops with chutney, tomatoes, onions, and rosemary; and a mixed seafood platter with lobster, shrimp, and calamari.

Another World/Otro Mundo. km 7, Hwy. Puerto Plata–Sosúa. ☎ **809/320-4400** or 809/543-8019. Reservations recommended. Main courses RD$95–RD$300 ($6.75–$21.30). DC, MC, V. Daily 6pm–midnight. INTERNATIONAL.

This is the most prosperous and unusual independent restaurant in Puerto Plata; it attracts diners from the nearby all-inclusive hotels. About a mile east of the Playa Dorada tourist zone, in a green-sided Victorian building, it has a benign resident ghost that some readers claim to have spotted, an indoor/outdoor format accented with tropical touches, and an ersatz zoo whose residents (a tiger, monkeys, a honey bear, and wild birds) were all once abused before finding a home with the restaurant's kind-hearted owner. That owner is Stuart Ratner, a New York–born singer and actor who appeared in some productions during the 1970s with Barbra Streisand. Precede a meal here with the place's most popular drink, a "cocolobo, guaranteed to make you fly." Follow with food that by local standards is almost incomprehensibly exotic, including frog's legs, deep-water Caribbean crab, river prawns, Châteaubriand, and beef Wellington. Also featured is fresh local fish, particularly snapper. Live music is sometimes featured.

Hemingway's Café. Playa Dorado Plaza. ☎ **809/320-2230.** Reservations not necessary. Burgers RD$55–RD$88 ($3.90–$6.25); Mexican platters, steaks, and seafood RD$90–RD$250 ($6.40–$17.75). AE, MC, V. Daily noon–1:30am. INTERNATIONAL.

The most theme-conscious restaurant in Puerto Plata celebrates the macho braggadocio of everybody's favorite red-blooded role model, Papa Ernesto. Inside, you'll find photographs of the writer fishing, drinking, womanizing, bullfighting, or whatever, and lots of rough-and-ready memorabilia in a place that may remind you of a dockside restaurant in Key West. Menu items include at least four kinds of burgers, grilled fish, two-fisted man-size portions of New York strip steak or pepper steak, and a full complement of Mexican nachos, burritos, and tacos. Drinks include a half-dozen kinds of beer from virtually everywhere, priced at from RD$35 ($2.50) per bottle. After around 9pm, a karaoke machine cranks out romantic or rock-and-roll favorites so that anyone can be a star.

Porto Fino. Av. Las Hermanas Mirabal. ☎ **809/586-2858.** Main courses RD$50–RD$210 ($3.55–$14.90). AE, MC, V. Daily 10am–11pm. ITALIAN/DOMINICAN.

This popular restaurant serves up generous helpings of parmesan breast of chicken, eggplant parmesan, ravioli, and pizzas, and such regional dishes as *arroz con pollo* (chicken with rice). You'll get off cheap if you order only pizza. Locals and visitors mingle freely here. This is a place to go for a casual meal in casual clothes, and not for some major gastronomic experience.

Roma II. Calle Emilio Prud'homme 45, at Calle Beller. ☎ **809/586-3904.** Main courses RD$75–RD$285 ($5.30–$20.25); pizza RD$57–RD$175 ($4.05–$12.40). AE, MC, V. Daily 11am–midnight. INTERNATIONAL.

This air-conditioned restaurant in the corner of town is staffed by an engaging crew of well-mannered young employees who work hard to converse in English. You can order from 13 varieties of pizza, including shrimp and garlic. Seafood dishes include paella and several preparations of lobster and sea bass. The menu is unfussy, as is the preparation. Don't look for any new taste sensations (except for octopus vinaigrette, one of the chef's specialties). The meat dishes are less successful than the fish offerings.

HITTING THE BEACH

Although they face the sometimes turbulent waters of the Atlantic, and it rains a lot in winter, beaches put the north coast on the tourist map. The beaches at **Playa Dorada** are centered around the resort of Puerto Plata, which is called the "Amber Coast" for all the deposits of amber that have been discovered here. Playa Dorada has one of the highest concentrations of hotels on the north coast, so the beaches here, though good, are likely to be crowded at any time of the year. The beaches are lovely with either white or beige powdery sand. The Atlantic waters here are very popular for waterskiing and windsurfing. Many concession stands along the beach rent equipment.

Another good choice in the area, **Luperón Beach** lies about a 60-minute drive to the west of Puerto Plata. This is a wide beach of powdery white sand, set amid palm trees that provide wonderful shade when the noonday sun grows too fierce. It's more ideal for windsurfing, scuba diving, and snorkeling than for general swimming. Various water-sports concessions can be found here, along with several snack bars.

SPORTS & OUTDOOR PURSUITS

The north coast is a water-sports scene, although the sea here tends to be rough. Snorkeling is popular, and the windsurfing is among the best in the Caribbean. The resort of **Cabarete,** east of Puerto Plata, hosts an annual windsurfing tournament.

GOLF Robert Trent Jones, Jr. designed the par-72, 18-hole **Playa Dorada** championship golf course (☎ 809/320-3803), which surrounds the resorts and runs along the coast. Even nongolfers can stop at the clubhouse for a drink or a snack to enjoy the views. Greens fees are RD$450 ($31.95) for 18 holes. It's best to make arrangements at the activities desk of your hotel.

Hanging Out at Samaná

For an offbeat, laid-back look at how the Caribbean used to be before the big developers moved in, head for the peninsula of Samaná along the east coast of the Dominican Republic. Settled in the 1820s by thousands of escaped American slaves who established new lives here in little fishing villages, Samaná is just awakening to tourism. You can meet and talk to many of the descendants of the runaway slaves, who still speak English in a Spanish-speaking country. Las Terrenas, on the north coast of the peninsula, boasts 17 miles of virgin beach. Samaná is 168 miles east of the Puerto Plata airport, across rugged terrain.

The 4,888-yard, par-72 **Playa Grande Golf Course** at Playa Grande, kilometer 9, Carretera Rio San Juan-Cabrera (☎ **800/858-2258** or 809/223-0768), is generating a lot of excitement. Some pros have already hailed it as one of the best courses in the Caribbean. Its design consultant was Robert Trent Jones, Jr. Ten of its holes border the Atlantic, and many of these are also set atop dramatic cliffs overlooking the turbulent waters. When you're not concentrating on your game of golf, you can take in the panoramic views of the ocean and of Playa Grande Beach. Greens fees are $50 year-round; carts cost $25.

TENNIS   Nearly all the major resort hotels have tennis courts. If yours doesn't, there are seven all-weather courts at the **Caribbean Village Club on the Green** (see "Where to Stay," above), although guests at the resort have first dibs.

SEEING THE SIGHTS

Fort San Felipe, the oldest fort in the New World, is a popular attraction. Philip II of Spain ordered its construction in 1564, a task that took 33 years to complete. Built with 8-foot-thick walls, the fort was virtually impenetrable, and the moat surrounding it was treacherous—the Spaniards sharpened swords and embedded them in coral below the surface of the water to discourage use of the moat for entrance or exit purposes. The doors of the fort are only 4 feet high, another deterrent to swift passage. During Trujillo's rule, Fort San Felipe was used as a prison. Standing at the end of the Malecón, the fort was restored in the early 1970s. Admission is RD$10 (70¢). It's open Thursday to Tuesday from 8am to 4pm.

Isabel de Torres (no phone), a tower with a fort built when Trujillo was in power, affords a panoramic view of the Amber Coast from a point near the top, 2,595 feet above sea level. You reach the observation point by cable car (*teleférico*), a 7-minute ascent. Once here, you're also treated to 7 acres of botanical gardens. The round-trip costs RD$80 ($5.70) for adults, RD$20 ($1.40) for children 12 and under. The aerial ride is operated Thursday to Tuesday from 8am to 5pm. There's often a long wait in line for the cable car, and at certain times it's closed for repairs, so check at your hotel before you head out.

You can see a collection of rare amber specimens at the **Museum of Dominican Amber,** Calle Duarte 61 (☎ **809/586-2848**), near Puerto Plata's Central Park. It's open Monday to Saturday from 9am to 5pm. Guided tours in English are offered. Admission is RD$20 ($1.40) for adults, RD$5 (35¢) for children.

SHOPPING

The neoclassical house sheltering the Museum of Dominican Amber (see above) also contains the densest collection of **boutiques** in Puerto Plata. Many of the paintings here are from neighboring Haiti, but the amber, larimar, and mahogany wood carvings are from the Dominican Republic.

A Break from the Beach in the Dominican Alps

Most visitors to the Dominican Republic are concerned with the coastlines and the white sandy beaches—but for an offbeat adventure, head inland to the resort towns of Jarabacoa and Constanza, the heartland of what's known as the Dominican Alps. These resorts are unexpected on a tropical island, offering cool evenings and chalets rather than humidity and beach houses. That lover of nature and other things, former dictator Trujillo preferred these towns among all others on the island. Located 90 miles north of Santo Domingo, and easily reached by car, the beauty of the forests, the towering "Alps," and the rushing waterfalls await you.

The **Plaza Turisol Complex,** the largest shopping center on the north coast, has about 80 different outlets. You may want to make this your first stop so you can get an idea of the merchandise available in Puerto Plata. It's about 5 minutes from the centers of Puerto Plata and Playa Dorada, on the main road heading east. Nearby is a smaller shopping center, **Playa Dorada Plaza,** with about 20 shops, selling handcrafts, clothing, souvenirs, and gifts. Both centers are open daily from 9am to 9pm.

The **Centro Artesanal,** Calle John F. Kennedy 3 (☎ 809/586-3724), is a nonprofit school for the training of future Dominican craftspeople, and it's also a promotional center for local crafts and jewelry. Selected student projects are for sale.

The **Plaza Isabela,** in Playa Dorada about 500 yards from the entrance to the Playa Dorada Hotel complex, is a collection of small specialty shops constructed in the Victorian gingerbread style, although much of its inventory has a Spanish inspiration and/or flair. Here you'll find the main branch of the Dominican Republic's premier jeweler, **Harrison's** (☎ 809/586-3933), a specialist in platinum work. Although there are almost two dozen branches of Harrison's in the Dominican Republic, the chain—at least as yet—has no outlets anywhere else in the world. Madonna, Michael Jackson, and Keith Richards have all been spotted wearing Harrison's jewelry. The store has a special clearance area; tours are available. There's another branch in the Playa Dorada Plaza (☎ 809/320-2219) in the Playa Dorada Hotel complex.

PUERTO PLATA AFTER DARK

Puerto Plata has two casinos, both open daily until 5am. **Allegro's Jack Tar Village,** Playa Dorada (☎ 809/320-3800), joins the gaming flock with a casino and disco, along with a European-style restaurant and five bars. It's built in Spanish Mediterranean colonial style with a terra-cotta roof. **Playa Dorada Casino,** in the Playa Dorada Hotel, Playa Dorada (☎ 809/586-3988), has an entrance flanked by columns which leads to an airy garden courtyard. Inside, mahogany gaming tables are reflected in the silver ceiling. No shorts are permitted inside the premises after 7pm, and beach attire is usually discouraged.

The Playa Dorada Hotel complex contains about 20 hotels, five of which have **discos** that welcome anyone, guest or not, into their confines. None charge a cover, and the almost-universal drink of choice, Presidente Beer, costs around RD$40 ($2.85) a bottle. The best spots in the Playa Dorado Hotel complex are **Andromeda,** in the Hotel Heaven (☎ 809/320-5250), a high-voltage club off the lobby that opens nightly at 10pm; and **Crazy Moon,** in the Paradise Hotel (☎ 809/320-3663), outfitted in a colonial Caribbean style, with open-air balconies. You can also stop by **Crystal,** a ground-floor disco at the corner of Avenida Las Hermanas Mirabel and the Malecón (☎ 809/586-3752), which charges a cover of RD$100 ($7.10).

6 Sosúa

About 15 miles east of Puerto Plata is one of the finest beaches in the Dominican Republic, **Sosúa Beach.** A strip of white sand more than half a mile wide, it's tucked in a cove sheltered by coral cliffs. The beach connects two communities, which together make up the town known as Sosúa. But, regrettably, you may not be able to enjoy a day on the beach in peace, as vendors, and often beggars, frequently pursue visitors aggressively.

At one end of the beach is **El Batey,** an area with residential streets, gardens, restaurants, shops, and hotels. Real-estate transactions have been booming in El Batey and its environs, where many streets have been paved and villas constructed.

At the other end of Sosúa Beach lies the typical village community of **Los Charamicos,** a sharp contrast to El Batey. Here you'll find tin-roofed shacks, vegetable stands, chickens scrabbling in the rubbish, and warm, friendly people.

Sosúa was founded in 1940 by European Jews seeking refuge from Hitler. Trujillo invited 100,000 of them to settle in his country on a banana plantation, but only 600 or so Jews were actually allowed to immigrate, and of those, only about a dozen or so remained. However, there are some 20 Jewish families living in Sosúa today, and for the most part they are engaged in the dairy and smoked-meat industries which the refugees began during the war. Biweekly services are held in the local one-room synagogue. Many of the Jews intermarried with Dominicans, and the town has taken on an increasingly Spanish flavor; women of the town are often seen wearing both the Star of David and the Virgin de Altagracia. Nowadays many German expatriates are also found in the town.

To get here from Puerto Plata, take the autopista east for about 30 minutes. If you venture off the main highway, anticipate enormous potholes. Taxis, charter buses, and públicos from Puerto Plata and Playa Dorada let passengers off at the stairs leading down from the highway to Sosúa beach.

WHERE TO STAY

✪ **Hotel Sosúa.** Calle Dr. Alejo Martínez, El Batey, Sosúa, Dominican Republic. ☎ **809/571-2683.** Fax 809/571-2180. E-mail: hotel.sosua@net.do. 40 units. A/C TV TEL. Winter $50 double. Off-season $40 double. Rates include continental breakfast. AE, MC, V.

Although this has been one of the best choices for affordable accommodations in Sosúa for at least a decade, it was made even better in 1994 after the owners completely renovated the interior. It's in a suburban community about a 2-minute drive from the center of town. The hotel's simple and attractive layout includes a reception area designed to conceal a flagstone-rimmed pool from the street outside. The medium-size guest rooms are strung along a wing extending beside the pool. Units contain simple furniture (for the most part crafted locally), ceiling fans, minifridges, and the occasional pinewood balcony. The bathrooms are a bit cramped. On the premises is the Caballo Blanco restaurant, a minigym, a bar, and a shop selling the day-to-day necessities that tourists might need.

Sosúa by the Sea. Sosúa Beach, Sosúa (Apdo. Postal 361), Puerto Plata, Dominican Republic. ☎ **809/571-3222.** Fax 809/571-3020. 81 units. A/C MINIBAR TV TEL. Year-round $92 double; $105 suite. AE, MC, V.

The blue-and-white main building here is softened with inviting wooden lattices. The resort stands on a coral cliff above the beach, and its pool area opens onto Sosúa Bay. From the open-air rooftop lounge, you have a view of Mount Isabel de Torres. The accommodations are situated along meandering paths through tropical gardens. Reached by elevator, the airy but rather basic guest rooms are generous in size. They contain light tropical furnishings, often cane, plus quilted bedspreads, firm mattresses, private safes, kitchenettes, and wet bars. The oceanfront units open onto views but lack balconies; the French windows allow the trade winds to drift in if you don't like air-conditioning. Bathrooms are routine and a bit cramped.

A formal restaurant serves both Dominican specialties and an international cuisine with live entertainment; you can lunch at the poolside bar and grill. The hotel has many amenities, including a massage parlor and a beauty salon.

Villas los Coralillos. Alejo Martínez 1, Sosúa (Apdo. Postal 851), Puerto Plata, Dominican Republic. ☎ **809/571-2645.** Fax 809/571-2095. 53 units. A/C. Year-round $90 studio for two; $120 villa for one to four. AE, DC, MC, V.

The well-furnished accommodations here are in a series of terra-cotta–tiled Iberian villas cantilevered over a bougainvillea-draped hillside. The action centers around the pool and main restaurant overlooking Sosúa Bay. Guests can request one- or two-bedroom villas, some of which boast the most panoramic views in Sosúa. Each good-size unit has twin beds and a small veranda. Villas have TVs; studios don't. Dining is at the hotel's El Coral restaurant (see "Where to Dine," below); you can also get pizzas daily from 8am to 3am at La Bahía, directly on the beach. This is the only hotel in town with direct access to the main Sosúa beach; if you tire of the pool, you can stroll to the sea through century-old mahogany and almond trees.

WHERE TO DINE

El Coral. El Batey. ☎ **809/571-2645.** Reservations recommended. Main courses RD$75–RD$250 ($5.30–$17.75). AE, DC, MC, V. Daily 7am–10:30pm. CARIBBEAN/SEAFOOD.

The best and arguably the most pleasant restaurant in town is El Coral, in a Spanish-style building set at the bottom of the garden near the end of the Sosúa beach. It offers a spacious area with terra-cotta tiles, wooden accents, and stark-white walls opening onto a panoramic ocean view. A bar adjoins the dining room. The specialties include conch or octopus Creole style, pork chops with pineapple, and shrimp with garlic. Dishes are tasty and filled with flavor, especially the seafood. The cooks long ago fine-tuned their cooking, and they like to keep turning out the dishes they already know best without any experimentation.

✪ **La Puntilla de Piergiorgio.** Calle La Puntilla. ☎ **809/571-2215.** Main courses RD$175–RD$295 ($12.40–$20.95). AE, MC, V. Daily noon–4pm and 6pm–midnight. ITALIAN.

Set a 10-minute walk west of Sosúa's center, this place serves the best Italian food in town, thus attracting an animated clientele of Europeans looking for a change from Creole and Dominican cuisine. Architecturally, the place might remind you of a garden-style veranda, perched over low cliffs at the edge of the sea. Everybody's drink of choice here seems to be mimosas, a homemade version that delectably precedes such dishes as veal cutlets Milanese, spaghetti with marinara or clam sauce, or spaghetti prepared Sicilian style with eggplant and tomatoes. Also look for at least five different preparations of fresh fish, including a barbecued version that's especially succulent.

Morua Mai. Pedro Clisante 5, El Batey. No phone. Main courses RD$95–RD$275 ($6.75–$19.50). AE, MC, V. Daily 8am–midnight. CONTINENTAL/DOMINICAN.

The patio here, which faces a popular intersection in the center of town, is the closest thing to a European sidewalk cafe in town. Inside, where occasional live entertainment is a featured attraction, is a high-ceilinged, double-decked, and stylish space filled with touches of neo-Victorian gingerbread, upholstered banquettes, and wicker furniture. Consider this place for a sun-washed drink or cup of afternoon tea in the side court-yard, where a cabaña bar serves drinks from beneath a palm-thatched roof. Pasta, pizzas, and sandwiches, along with light meals, are available at lunch. Full dinners include such dishes as charcoal-grilled lobster, seafood platters, lots of locally caught fish, and an excellent paella. All meats and seafood are specially selected by the owner for freshness. The cookery isn't outstanding, but it's solidly good.

Sunset Place Restaurant. At Sosúa by the Sea, Sosúa. ☎ **809/571-3222.** Reservations required in winter. Main courses RD$142–RD$450 ($10.10–$31.95). AE, MC, V. Daily 7:30–11am, noon–4pm, and 6:30–10:30pm. INTERNATIONAL/DOMINICAN.

Rooftop gourmet dining entices both guests and nonguests of this previously recom-mended hotel. The restaurant serves soups, salads, and sandwiches at lunch, although dinner is when the chef's talents really shine. After watching the sun go down, choose from a selection of appetizers that might include soup, pâté, or perhaps vol-au-vent seafood pastry shell. Main dishes usually feature grilled lobster or tuna with bacon and mushrooms. You might also try the pepper steak, spaghetti carbonara, or chicken with pineapple, each of which had a zesty flavor on our most recent visit. For dessert, choose from a collection of fresh pastries or order a continental favorite like crêpes Suzette or sabayon.

13 Grenada

Its political troubles long over, this sleepy island offers fairly friendly people and the lovely and popular white sands of Grand Anse Beach. Exploring its lush interior, especially Grand Etang National Park, is also worthwhile. Crisscrossed by nature trails and filled with dozens of secluded coves and sandy beaches, Grenada has moved beyond the turbulence of the 1980s. It's not necessarily for the serious party person and definitely not for those seeking action at the casino. Instead, it attracts visitors who like snorkeling, sailing, fishing, and doing nothing more invigorating than lolling on a beach under the sun.

The "Spice Island," Grenada is an independent, three-island nation that includes Carriacou, the largest of the Grenadines, and Petite Martinique. Grenada is imbued with the fragrance of various spices and exotic fruits. It has more spices per square mile than any other place in the world—cloves, cinnamon, mace, cocoa, tonka beans, ginger, and a third of the world's supply of nutmeg. "Drop a few seeds anywhere," the locals will tell you, "and you have an instant garden." The central area is like a jungle of palms, oleander, bougainvillea, purple and red hibiscus, crimson anthurium, bananas, breadfruit, birdsong, ferns, and palms.

Beefed up by financial aid from the United States, this island of some 100,000 people has revived a sagging tourist industry. Following the election of Nicholas Braithwaite as prime minister in 1990, the present government of Grenada is regarded as U.S.-friendly. Many improvements, including a workable phone system and better roads, have been made with the benefit of U.S. aid.

1 Essentials

VISITOR INFORMATION

In the United States, the **Grenada Tourist Office** is at 800 Second Ave., Suite 400K, New York, NY 10017 (☎ **800/927-9554** or 212/687-9554).

In Canada, contact the **Grenada Board of Tourism,** 439 University Ave., Suite 820, Toronto, ON M5G 1Y8 (☎ **416/ 595-1339**).

In London, contact the **Grenada Board of Tourism,** 1 Collingham Gardens, Earl's Court, London, SW5 0HW (☎ **0171/ 370-5164**).

Blue Horizons Cottage Hotel **1**
Calabash **7**
Coyaba Beach Resort **2**
Grenada Grand Beach Resort **3**
La Sagesse Nature Center **11**
La Source **6**
No Problem Apartment Hotel **10**
Rex Grenadian **5**
Secret Harbour **9**
Spice Island Inn **4**
Twelve Degrees North **8**

Levera Beach and National Park

Sauteurs

Victoria

Mt. St. Catherine

Gouyave (Charlottetown)

Douglaston Estate

Pearl's Beach

Grand Etang National Park

Grand Roy

Grenville

Caribbean Sea

Mt. Qua Qua

Grand Etang

Grenville Bay

Marquis

Annandale Falls

Constantine

Mt. Sinai

Beaulieu

St. George's

St. David's

Grand Anse Beach

Woburn

Atlantic Ocean

Morne Rouge Bay

L'Anse aux Epines

La Sagesse Beach

Point Salines

Pink Gin Beach

0   5 Miles
0   5 Kilometers

Airport ✈ Beach ⚓ Mountain ▲▲

2-0195

On the island, pick up maps, guides, and general information at the **Grenada Board of Tourism,** the Carenage, in St. George's (☎ **473/440-2279**), open Monday to Friday from 8am to 4pm.

You can find Grenada information on the Web at **www.grenada.org**.

GETTING THERE

The **Point Salines International Airport** lies at the southwestern toe of Grenada. The airport is a 5- to 15-minute taxi ride from most of the major hotels.

American Airlines (☎ **800/433-7300**; www.aa.com) offers daily flights from New York to Grenada. If you live in one of the cities of the southeast, such as Atlanta, the better connection is via Miami.

BWIA (☎ **888/538-2942**; www.bwee.com) has direct service from New York on Thursday and Sunday. The rest of the week, flights from New York to Grenada stop over on Antigua, St. Lucia, or Barbados.

LIAT (☎ **800/468-0482** in the U.S. and Canada, or 268/462-0700) has scheduled service between Barbados and Grenada (at least four flights daily, though flights are sometimes canceled with little notice). We've often spent hours and hours waiting in the Barbados airport for a plane. Through either LIAT or BWIA, you can connect on Barbados with several international airlines, including British Airways, Air Canada, American Airlines, and Air France.

British Airways (☎ **0345/222-111** in England; www.british-airways.com) flies to Grenada every Wednesday and Friday from London's Gatwick Airport, making a single stop at Antigua en route.

The second weekend of August brings colorful Carnival parades, music, and dancing. The festivities begin on a Friday, continuing practically nonstop to Tuesday. Steel bands and calypso groups perform at Queen's Park. Jouvert, one of the highlights of the festival, begins at 5am on Monday with a parade of Djab Djab/Djab Molassi, devil-costumed figures daubed with a black substance. (*Be warned:* Don't wear nice clothes to attend this event—you may get sticky from close body contact.) The carnival finale, a gigantic "jump-up" (like a hoedown), ends with a parade of bands from Tanteen through the Carenage into town.

GETTING AROUND

BY TAXI   Rates are set by the government. Most arriving visitors take a cab at the Point Salines International Airport to one of the hotels near St. George's, at a cost of $12. Add a third to the fare from 6pm to 6am. You can also use most taxi drivers as a guide for a day of sightseeing; the cost can be negotiated, depending on what you want to do, and divided among three or four passengers.

BY RENTAL CAR   First, remember to *drive on the left.* A U.S., British, or Canadian driver's license is valid on Grenada; however, you must obtain a local permit, costing EC$30 ($11.10). These permits can be obtained either from the car-rental company or from the traffic department at the Carenage in St. George's.

Avis (☎ **800/331-1212** or 473/440-3936) operates out of a Shell station on Lagoon Road, on the southern outskirts of Saint George's. Avis will meet you at the airport, but requires at least 24-hour notice to guarantee availability. To get the best deal, it pays to shop around; try **Dollar Rent-a-Car,** at the Point Salines Airport (☎ **473/444-4786**), or a local concern such as **McIntyre Brothers Ltd.,** in the True Blue area (☎ **473/444-3944**).

A word of warning about local drivers: There's such a thing as Grenadian driving machismo: The drivers take blind corners with abandon. An extraordinary number of accidents are reported in the lively local paper. Gird yourself with nerves of steel, and be extra alert for children and roadside pedestrians when driving at night. Many foreign visitors, in fact, find any night driving hazardous.

BY BUS   Minivans, charging EC$1 to EC$6 (40¢ to $2.20), are the cheapest way to get around. The most popular run is between St. George's and Grand Anse Beach. Most minivans depart from Market Square or from the Esplanade area of St. George's.

Fast Facts: Grenada

Banking Hours   Banks in St. George's, the capital, include **Barclays,** at Church and Halifax streets (☎ 473/440-3232); **Scotiabank,** on Halifax Street (☎ 473/440-3274); the **National Commercial Bank (NCB),** at the corner of Halifax and Hillsborough streets (☎ 473/440-3566); the **Grenada Bank of Commerce,** at the corner of Halifax and Cross streets (☎ 473/440-3521); and the **Grenada Cooperative Bank,** on Church Street (☎ 473/440-2111). Hours are usually Monday through Friday from 8am to 1:30 or 2pm, Friday from 2:30 to 5pm.

Currency   The official currency is the **Eastern Caribbean dollar (EC$),** worth about EC$2.70 to U.S $1. Always determine which dollars, EC or U.S., you're talking about when someone on Grenada quotes you a price.

Documents   A valid passport is required of U.S., British, and Canadian citizens entering Grenada, plus a return or ongoing ticket.

Drugstores   See "Pharmacies," below.

Electricity   Electricity is 220 to 240 volts AC (50 cycles), so transformers and adapters will be needed for U.S.-made appliances.

Embassies & High Commissions   The **U.S. Embassy** is at Point Salines, St. George's (☎ **473/444-1173**). The **British High Commission** is on Church Street, St. George's (☎ **473/440-3536**).

Emergencies   Dial ☎ **911** to summon the police, report a fire, or call an ambulance.

Hospital   There's a general hospital, **St. George's Hospital** (☎ **473/440-2051**), with an X-ray department and operating room. Private doctors and nurses are available on call.

Language   English is commonly spoken due to long years of British influence. Creole English, a mixture of several African dialects, English, and French, is spoken informally by the majority.

Pharmacies   Try **Gittens Pharmacy,** Halifax Street, St. George's (☎ **473/440-2165**), open Monday, Tuesday, Wednesday, and Friday from 8am to 6pm, Thursday from 8am to 5pm, and Saturday from 8am to 3pm.

Post Office   The general post office, at the Pier, St. George's, is open Monday to Friday from 8am to 3:30pm.

Safety   Street crime occurs here, tourists have been victims of armed robbery in isolated areas, and thieves frequently steal U.S. passports and alien registration cards in addition to money. Muggings, purse-snatchings, and other robberies occur in areas near hotels, beaches, and restaurants, particularly after dark. Don't leave valuables unattended at the beach. Exercise appropriate caution when walking after dark, or rely on taxis. You may wish to consult with local authorities, your hotel, and/or the U.S. embassy for current information. The loss or theft of a U.S. passport should be reported immediately to the local police and the nearest U.S. embassy or consulate.

Taxes   A 10% VAT (value-added tax) is imposed on food and beverages, and there's an 8% room tax. Upon leaving Grenada, you must fill out an immigration card and pay a departure tax of $14.

Telephone   International telephone service is available 24 hours a day from pay phones. Public telegraph, Telex, and fax services are also provided from the Carenage offices of **Grenada Telecommunications (Grentel)** in St. George's (☎ **473/440-1000** for all Grentel offices), open Monday to Friday from 7:30am to 6pm, Saturday from 7:30am to 1pm, and Sunday and holidays from 10am to noon. To call another number on Grenada, dial all seven digits, as the island is divided among four telephone exchanges: 440, 442, 443, and 444. The most commonly used is 440.

Time   Grenada is on Atlantic standard time year-round, which means it's usually one hour ahead of the U.S. East Coast—except during daylight saving time, when the clocks are the same.

Tipping   A 10% service charge is added to most restaurant and hotel bills.

Water   On Grenada, we recommend sticking to bottled water.

Weather Grenada has two distinct seasons, dry and rainy. The dry season is from January to May; the rest of the year is the rainy season, although the rainfall doesn't last long. The average temperature is 80°F. Because of constant trade winds, there's little humidity.

2 Where to Stay

Your hotel or inn will probably add a service charge of 10% to your bill—ask in advance about this. Also, there's an 8% government tax on rooms.

VERY EXPENSIVE

✪ **Calabash.** L'Anse aux Epines (P.O. Box 382, St. George's), Grenada, W.I. ☎ **800/ 528-5835** in the U.S. and Canada, or 473/444-4334. Fax 473/444-5050. www. calabashhotel.com. E-mail: calabash@caribsurf.com. 30 units. A/C MINIBAR TEL. Winter $390–$595 suite for 2. Off-season $235–$320 suite for 2. Extra person $130–$160 in winter, $95–$115 in off-season. MAP (breakfast and dinner) $35 per person extra. Children staying in parents' room pay $35 a day, including all meals. AE, MC, V. Children 12 and under not permitted in winter.

Built in the early 1960s, the Calabash is today the leading hotel on Grenada. Five miles south of St. George's and only minutes from the Point Salines airport, it occupies a landscaped 8-acre beach along an isolated section of Prickly Bay (L'Anse aux Epines). Many of the shrubs on the grounds practically dwarf the stone outbuildings. Foremost among the plants are the scores of beautiful calabashes (gourds) for which the resort was named. The social center of the place is a low-slung, rambling building whose walls are chiseled from blocks of dark-gray stone. The eight private plunge-pool suites and 22 whirlpool-bath suites all have verandas and either one king bed (which can be split and made up as two twins) or two double beds, with firm mattresses. Extras include fridges and coffeemakers. Bathrooms are very spacious, with big stall showers, oversized tubs, bidets, and thick towels.

Dining/Diversions: The restaurant serves an excellent West Indian and continental menu. Entertainment, ranging from piano music to steel bands, is provided 4 or 5 nights a week.

Amenities: Tennis court, outdoor pool, sailboat rentals. Room service, laundry, baby-sitting.

✪ **La Source.** Pink Gin Beach (P.O. Box 852, St. George's), Grenada, W.I. ☎ **800/ 544-2883** in the U.S. and Canada, or 473/444-2556. Fax 473/444-2561. www.lasource. com.gd. E-mail: lasource@cariburf.com. 100 units. A/C TEL. Winter $530–$580 double; $520–$630 suite for 2. Off-season $420–$500 double; $520–$550 suite for 2. Rates are all-inclusive. AE, DISC, MC, V.

The first completely all-inclusive hotel on Grenada opened in 1993, covering 40 acres of a former cocoa and nutmeg plantation, with two white-sand beaches separated from each another by a rocky knoll. Within a 5-minute drive of the island's international airport and associated with two St. Lucian resorts, La Source stresses revitalization of the body and mind through spa treatments and experiences with nature. Meals, drinks, water sports, entertainment, and most (but not all) spa treatments are included in the all-inclusive price. In a hillside compound of white-walled, terra-cotta–roofed buildings, the resort is floored with multicolored marble tiles and furnished for the most part with mahogany and greenheart furniture imported from Venezuela. The guest rooms, with mahogany four-poster beds, Italian marble floors, and ceiling fans, evoke a dignified colonial plantation house. The marble-clad bathrooms are extremely roomy with plenty of shelf space, hair dryers, and fluffy towels.

Dining/Diversions: The plush Great Room serves one of the island's best cuisines; less formal is the open-sided Terrace Restaurant. Live piano music is presented during the cocktail hour in one bar, while a small stage in the other offers live bands for dancing.

Amenities: Concierge; two free-form swimming pools; a nonregulation "mashie" golf course (known Stateside as a par-3 course), with very short distances between the holes (outings to a regulation nine-hole golf course in the area can be arranged); instruction in fencing, windsurfing, calypso dancing, and weight training. The Oasis offers massages, saunas, land and water aerobics, yoga, stress-management treatments, and salt loofah rubs.

✪ **Spice Island Inn.** Grand Anse (P.O. Box 6, St. George's), Grenada, W.I. ☎ **800/ 742-4276** in the U.S., 212/251-1800 in New York City, or 473/444-4258. Fax 473/444-4807. E-mail: spiceisl@caribsurf.com. 56 units. A/C MINIBAR TEL. Winter $395–$750 suite for 2; $565–$835 suite for 3. Off-season $315–$575 suite for 2; $345–$660 suite for 3. Rates include MAP (breakfast and dinner). AE, MC, V.

On an estate overlooking the Caribbean, this inn is built along 1,200 feet of Grand Anse Beach, directly north of the airport. The main house, reserved for dining and dancing, has a tropical feel and lots of tasteful touches. Some 32 units are beach suites, which we prefer. Second-floor suites have terraces overlooking the ocean and the garden; 17 units have their own private plunge pools where guests can go skinny-dipping. Room furnishings are casual, outdoor-type pieces in wicker or rattan. The light-wood beds are fitted with deluxe mattresses and fine linens. The bathrooms are the largest and most luxurious on Grenada, with fluffy white towels (enough to please Frank Sinatra during his road days) and Jacuzzis.

Dining/Diversions: Chefs not only prepare an international cuisine, but also deftly turn out good Grenadian food, including soursop or nutmeg ice cream, breadfruit vichyssoise, and Caribbean lobster (see "Where to Dine," below). There's sometimes live music for dancing.

Amenities: Beach, private pools, fitness center, tennis courts (lit at night). Bikes, nonmotorized water sports, and greens fees for the Grenada Golf Course are complimentary. Room service for all three meals.

EXPENSIVE

Coyaba Beach Resort. Grand Anse Beach (P.O. Box 336, St. George's), Grenada, W.I. ☎ 473/444-4129. Fax 473/444-4808. www.coyaba.com. E-mail: coyaba@caribsurf.com. 70 units. A/C TV TEL. Winter $200 double. Off-season $120 double. Extra person $45 in winter, $22 in off-season. MAP (breakfast and dinner) $40 per person extra. AE, DC, MC, V.

On a 5½-acre site on Grand Anse Beach next to the medical school, this resort, whose name means "heaven" in Arawak, is 6 miles from St. George's and 3 miles north of the international airport. Opened in 1987, the hotel has views of the town and of St. George's harbor. All units have double beds with good mattresses, verandas and patios, and spacious bathrooms with hair dryers. For persons with disabilities, this is the best choice on the island, with its widened doorways, ramps, and three wheelchair-accessible guest rooms. Amenities include two open-air restaurants, two bars (one at poolside), a Laykold tennis court, volleyball, water sports offered by Grand Anse Aquatics on the premises (see "Sports & Outdoor Pursuits," below), laundry, room service, and baby-sitting.

Grenada Grand Beach Resort. P.O. Box 441, Grand Anse Beach, Grenada, W.I. ☎ 473/444-4371. Fax 473/444-4800. 186 units. A/C TV TEL. Winter $207–$271 double; $414–$600 suite. Off-season $142–$202 double; $414–$600 suite. MAP (breakfast and dinner) $55.65 per person extra. AE, DISC, MC, V.

Last renovated in 1991, and rather short on island atmosphere, this hotel stands on a desirable stretch of white sandy beachfront, 3 miles north of the airport. The cedar-shingled facade might have been inspired by an 18th-century plantation house. Guests register beneath the octagonal roof of the entrance hall, then are ushered between a pair of manicured formal gardens to their (often small) rooms, which are tiled and furnished with mahogany pieces. Each has a balcony or patio. Twin or king beds are fitted with excellent mattresses, and the combination bathrooms (tub and shower) contain a set of good-size towels and a hair dryer. The beach-view rooms are the most desirable, naturally.

Dining/Diversions: You can dine indoors or out at the Terrace Restaurant, which has a passable international cuisine. Entertainment is usually offered at night.

Amenities: Beach, pool, fitness center, tennis courts, water-sports kiosk (renting snorkeling and scuba-diving equipment, sailboats, Windsurfers, Sailfish, and jet skis). Room service, laundry, baby-sitting.

Rex Grenadian. Point Salines, about a quarter of a mile from the international airport (P.O. Box 893, St. George's), Grenada, W.I. ☎ **473/444-3333.** Fax 473/444-1111. www.rexcaribbean.com/index/html E-mail: grenrex@caribsurf.com. 212 units. TEL. Winter $175–$260 double; $280–$360 suite. Off-season $115–$200 double; $220–$300 suite. MAP (breakfast and dinner) $49 per person extra. AE, DC, MC, V.

Opened late in 1993, this is the largest and most important hotel on the island, though not the best. It's a convention-group favorite, set on 12 rocky, partially forested acres that slope steeply down to a pair of white-sand beaches. Each of the wintergreen and pale-blue units is uniquely configured from its neighbors, and each is outfitted in rattan, wicker, and muted tropical fabrics. Eighty-four units offer ocean views, but not all are air-conditioned. Beds are exceedingly comfortable with fine mattresses and good linens, and the more expensive rooms contain combination baths (tub and shower) with hair dryers and fluffy towels. The bathrooms in other units are smaller and more compact. Adjacent to the accommodations is a 2-acre artificial lake strewn with islands that are connected to the "mainland" with footbridges and paddleboats.

Dining/Diversions: Drinking and dining options include the International, specializing in buffets with foods from around the world, and the far better Oriental, for Asian cuisine. The Tamarind Lounge offers cabaret singing and disco music.

Amenities: Water-sports options include scuba, snorkeling, sailing, and deep-sea fishing; other diversions can be arranged. There's a fitness center in an outlying annex (the Pavilion) and the most dramatic pool on the island, drilled and blasted directly into the volcanic rock of a stony promontory jutting out toward the open ocean, and graced with a water cascade and its own bar and restaurant. Room service, baby-sitting, laundry.

✪ **Secret Harbour.** Mount Hartman Bay, L'Anse aux Epines (P.O. Box 11, St. George's), Grenada, W.I. ☎ **800/437-7880** in the U.S. and Canada, or 473/444-4439. Fax 473/444-4819. www.secretharbour.com. E-mail: secret@caribsurf.com. 20 units. A/C TEL. Winter $230 suite for 2. Off-season $130 suite for 2. Extra person $20. MAP (breakfast and dinner) $41 per person extra. AE, MC, V. No children under 12 accepted.

Seen from the water of Mount Hartman Bay, Secret Harbour reminds us of a Mediterranean complex on Spain's Costa del Sol—a tasteful one, that is, with white stucco arches, red-tile roofs, and wrought-iron light fixtures, with steps leading down to a good beach. From all over Grenada, including some island plantation homes, antiques were purchased, restored, and installed here. Guest rooms have generous closet space, fridges, and mahogany four-poster beds fitted with quality mattresses and crisp white spreads. Each of the suites has wide windows with harbor views, a dressing room, living area, and patio overlooking the water. The bathrooms are luxurious, with fluffy towels, hair dryers, and sunken tubs lined with Italian tiles.

Secret Harbour is a favorite of the yachting set. While many guests reside at the hotel, others stay on yachts anchored off the property. Owned by the Moorings, an international hotel and yacht-charter company based in Clearwater, Florida, Secret Harbour is located about 20 minutes from Point Salines International Airport and 15 minutes from St. George's.

Dining: The antique-filled Mariners Restaurant features a good international menu, often prepared with fresh produce from Grenada. Guests enjoy the lobby/bar/terrace in the evening, savoring the tranquillity—there's no loud, rowdy entertainment.

Amenities: Marina, wide range of water sports (including snorkeling and windsurfing), sailing, and boating programs (including bareboat charters and "Learn to Cruise" lessons), tennis court, pool. Room service, laundry.

Twelve Degrees North. L'Anse aux Epines, 3 miles east of the airport (P.O. Box 241, St. George's), Grenada, W.I. ☎ and fax **473/444-4580** (call collect to make reservations). E-mail: 12degrsn@caribsurf.com. 8 units. Winter $195 one-bedroom apt for 2; $300 two-bedroom apt for 4. Off-season $130 one-bedroom apt for 2; $225 two-bedroom apt for 4. Extra person $60–$70. MC, V. No children under 15 accepted.

On a very private beach, this cluster of spotlessly clean efficiency apartments is owned and operated by Joseph Gaylord, a former commercial real-estate broker from New York, who greets visitors in front of a large flame tree on his front lawn. Many of the staff members have been with Mr. Gaylord since he opened the place many years ago. They'll cook breakfast, prepare lunch (perhaps pumpkin soup and flying fish), do the cleaning and laundry, and fix regional specialties for dinner (which you can heat up for yourself later). A housekeeper/cook, assigned to each unit, arrives at 8am to perform the thousand small kindnesses that make Twelve Degrees North a favorite lair for repeat guests from the United States and Europe. All units are equipped with efficiency kitchens, large beds with firm mattresses (which can be separated or pushed together), and shower-only bathrooms with robes. The owner prefers to rent by the week because, as he says, "a few days aren't enough to get to know Grenada." Amenities include a grass-roofed beach bar facing the water, a pool, a double-seat kayak, snorkeling equipment, a tennis court, and two Sunfish—all free for guests' use.

MODERATE/INEXPENSIVE

✪ **Blue Horizons Cottage Hotel.** P.O. Box 41, Grand Anse, Grenada, W.I. ☎ **800/223-9815** or 473/444-4316. Fax 473/444-4807. E-mail: spiceisl@caribsurf.com. 32 cottages. A/C TV TEL. Winter $155–$170 single; $160–$180 double. Off-season $105–$115 single; $110–$120 double. Extra person $50 in winter, $35 in off-season. AE, DC, DISC, MC, V.

Co-owners Royston and Arnold Hopkin purchased this place from a bankrupt estate and transformed the neglected property into one of the finest on the island. Grand Anse Beach is only a 5-minute walk away. The medium-sized units are spread throughout a flowering garden of 6¼ acres. Rates depend on the category of the cottage: superior or deluxe. The deluxe suites come with a separate living and dining area along with two king or double beds with firm mattresses. Superior studios contain a small dining alcove and a king-size bed. Each has an efficiency kitchen and comfortable, solid mahogany furniture. Baths, though small, are well maintained and equipped with hair dryers and generous towels. Children are welcome; they might enjoy watching the 21 varieties of native birds said to inhabit the grounds.

On the grounds is one of the best restaurants on the island, La Belle Creole. Lunch is served around a pool bar. Guests who prefer to cook in their rooms can buy supplies from a Food Fair at Grand Anse, a 10-minute walk away. Laundry, baby-sitting, and room service are provided.

No Problem Apartment Hotel. True Blue (P.O. Box 280, St. George's), Grenada, W.I. ☎ **800/74-CHARMS** in the U.S., or 473/444-4634. Fax 473/444-2803. 20 units. A/C TV TEL. Winter $75–$85 double. Off-season $55–$65 double. Extra person $20. MAP (breakfast and dinner) $30 per person extra. AE, MC, V.

An all-suite hotel 5 minutes from the airport and Grand Anse Beach, these small one-bedroom apartments are housed in a two-story motel unit. They offer one of the best deals on the island. The simply furnished suites open onto a pool and bar area; each is equipped with satellite TV, phones, good beds, and fully equipped kitchenettes. Baby-sitting can be arranged, and laundry service is provided. Thoughtful extras include a help-yourself coffee bar and free use of bicycles, plus a shuttle to and from the beach. There's also a reading room. The place has one of the most helpful staffs on the island.

✪ **La Sagesse Nature Center.** St. David's (P.O. Box 44), St. George's, Grenada, W.I. ☎ **473/444-6458.** Fax 473/444-6458. E-mail: tsnature@caribsurf.com. 6 units. MINIBAR TV TEL. Winter $95–$105 double. Off-season $75–$80 double. AE, MC, V.

On a sandy, tree-lined beach 10 miles from Point Salines International Airport, La Sagesse consists of a seaside guest house, restaurant, bar, and art gallery, with water sports and satellite TV. Nearby are trails for hiking and exploring, a haven for wading and shore birds, hummingbirds, hawks, and ducks. Rivers, mangroves, and a salt pond sanctuary enhance the natural beauty of the place. The original great house of what was once La Sagesse plantation contains two apartments, one with a fully equipped kitchen, and each with high ceilings and comfortable beds. Guests also have a choice of a two-bedroom beach cottage, with well-used but comfortable furnishings and a wraparound porch. The least desirable accommodations are two small, economy-priced bedrooms in back of the inn's patio restaurant. The restaurant/bar specializes in lobster, fresh fish, and salads. You must book early in winter.

3 Where to Dine

EXPENSIVE

✪ **Canboulay.** Morne Rouge. ☎ **473/444-4401.** Reservations recommended. 4-course fixed-price meal (in winter) EC$80–EC$100 ($29.60–$37); main courses (off-season) EC$74–EC$90 ($27.40–$33.30). AE, MC, V. Mon–Sat 6:30–9:30pm. CARIBBEAN.

This restaurant has a gracious West Indian formality, an elegant Caribbean-colonial decor, and some of the most unusual Antillean food on Grenada. Set on a hilltop with a view of Grand Anse Beach, it occupies a clapboard house painted in vibrant Caribbean colors. Throughout the winter, the only evening option available is a fixed-price menu. Specialties include coconut crêpes stuffed with crabmeat and served with callaloo relish, cornmeal baked or fried in coconut milk (the result is a traditional starch known as *coo coo*), blackened flying fish, grilled or baked chicken with a sauce of tomatoes and local herbs, and many kinds of steak. The owners are sorcerers in the kitchen.

Coconut's Beach Restaurant. Grand Anse Beach, about half a mile north of St. George's. ☎ **473/444-4644.** Reservations recommended. Lunch platters EC$15–EC$35 ($5.60–$13); main courses EC$35–EC$75 ($13–$27.80). AE, DISC, MC, V. Wed–Mon noon–10pm. FRENCH/CREOLE.

Raffish and informal, this restaurant occupies a pink-and-green clapboard house set directly on the sands of the beach. From the dining room, you can watch the staff at work in the exposed kitchen. They'll definitely be making a callaloo soup, made with local herbs and blended to a creamy smoothness. The kitchen specializes in various kinds of lobster, including one made with spaghetti, although the lobster stir-fry with ginger chili is more imaginative. Fish predominates, including a catch of the day served with mango chutney. Chicken and meats are also savory, especially breast of chicken cooked in local herbs and lime juice.

Warning: Because of the restaurant's close proximity to at least four major hotels, many people opt to walk along the beach to reach it. Don't! Tourists have been attacked by machete-carrying thugs who've robbed them and threatened their lives. Even though it might be only a short ride, take a taxi to the door instead.

✪ **La Belle Creole.** At Blue Horizons, Grand Anse Beach. ☎ **473/444-4316.** Reservations required for non-hotel guests. 5-course fixed-price dinner $40. AE, DC, MC, V. Daily 12:30–2:30pm and 7–9pm. CREOLE/SEAFOOD.

One of the best restaurants on Grenada is run by Arnold and Royston Hopkin, sons of "Mama" Audrey Hopkin, long considered the best cook on the island if you're seeking West Indian specialties. Lunch, which can be taken poolside, features soup and chicken, fish, or lobster salad. Dinner can be a fixed-price menu, with a variety of choices from continental recipes with West Indian touches. The chefs prepare one of the most creative cuisines on the island, as exemplified by their choice of appetizers and soups. To get you going, try chilled conch mousse if it's featured; it's tasty and smoothly delectable in every way. The lobster Creole is a classic and it's served in a shell, but even better is the spicy ginger pork chops with local seasonings, heightened with a touch of white wine. Another longtime favorite of ours is the deviled fish with curry and local seasonings. Three local vegetables fresh from the lush countryside are served with each meal. Desserts, however, are nothing special.

Spice Island Inn. Grand Anse Beach. ☎ **473/444-4258.** Reservations required for nonguests. Fixed-price dinner $40. AE, DC, DISC, MC, V. Daily 7:30–9:30am, 12:30–2:30pm, and 7–9:30pm. CREOLE/SEAFOOD.

Want to dine on an uncrowded beachfront in the full outdoors, with a parapet over your head to protect you from sudden tropical showers? The parapet here, built of imported pine and cedar, looks like a Le Corbusier rooftop. Some of the best hotel food on the island is served in this winning setting. The view here is of one of the finest beaches in the Caribbean—miles of white sand sprouting an occasional grove of sea grape or almond trees. You can even eat your lunch in a swimsuit. Local seafood is featured on the constantly changing menu. The most generous buffet on the island, a real Grenadian spread, is served on Wednesday, along with live entertainment. Friday is barbecue night with a steel band, and on Saturday seafood is the specialty.

MODERATE/INEXPENSIVE

The Boatyard. L'Anse aux Epines, Prickly Bay. ☎ **473/444-4662.** Main courses EC$25–EC$60 ($9.25–$22.20). AE, MC, V. Daily 8:30am–midnight. INTERNATIONAL.

A favorite hangout of the island's medical students, this restaurant is situated on the water overlooking the marina where the yachts are moored. Lunch consists of a Caribbean daily special, and may include stewed pork or Creole chicken served in a tomato-based sauce with rice. Some of the featured dishes include stewed and barbe-cued chicken, baked conch parmesan, and grilled steak; most are served with rice, salad, and fresh vegetables. Mexican specialties and Italian pastas also appear on the menu. On Friday nights a steel-drum band plays, and when they're done the sound system is cranked up for indoor-outdoor dancing to the wee hours.

✪ **Mamma's.** Lagoon Rd., St. George's. ☎ **473/440-1459.** Reservations required a day in advance. Fixed-price meal EC$50 ($18.50). MC, V. Daily 8am–midnight. CREOLE.

Mamma's is situated on the road leading to Grenada Yacht Services. Every trip to the Caribbean should include a visit to an establishment like this. Serving copious meals, this Mamma became particularly famous during the United States intervention in Grenada, as U.S. servicepeople adopted her as their own island mama. Mamma (Insley Wardally) is now deceased, but her daughter, Cleo, carries on.

Meals include such dishes as callaloo soup with coconut cream, shredded cold crab with lime juice, freshwater crayfish, fried conch, rôtis made of curry and yellow chickpeas, and a casserole of cooked bananas, yams, and dasheen, along with ripe baked plantain, and followed by sugar-apple ice cream for dessert. The seafood offerings are likely to include crab backs, octopus in a hot-and-spicy sauce, and even turtle steak, although the latter could be an endangered species. Mamma is also known for her "wild meats," which may include (depending on availability) armadillo, opossum, monkey (yes, that's right), game birds, and even the endangered iguana. The specialty drink of the house is rum punch—the ingredients are a secret.

✪ **Morne Fendue.** St. Patrick's, 25 miles north of St. George's. ☎ **473/442-9330.** Reservations required. Fixed-price lunch EC$45 ($16.45). No credit cards. Mon–Sat 12:30–3pm. CREOLE.

As you're touring north from the beach at Grand Anse, one memorable place is the late Betty Mascoll's Morne Fendue. This 1912 plantation house, constructed the year she was born, is her ancestral home. It was built of carefully chiseled river rocks held together with a mixture of lime and molasses. Although Miss Mascoll died in June of 1998, her loyal staff carries on in her same tradition. Of course, they need time to prepare food for your arrival, so it's imperative to give them a call to let them know you're coming by. Lunch is likely to include yam and sweet-potato casserole, curried chicken with lots of hot spices, and a hot pot of pork and oxtail. Because this is very much a private home, tipping should be done with the greatest tact. Nonetheless, the hardworking cook and maid seem genuinely appreciative of a gratuity.

The Nutmeg. The Carenage, St. George's. ☎ **473/440-2539.** Main courses EC$16–EC$45 ($5.90–$16.65) lunch, EC$18–EC$55 ($6.65–$20.35) dinner. AE, DISC, MC, V. Mon–Sat 8am–11pm, Sun 2–11pm. SEAFOOD/CREOLE.

Right on the harbor, The Nutmeg is above the Sea Change Shop, where you can pick up paperbacks and souvenirs. A rendezvous point for the yachting set and a favorite with just about everybody, it's suitable for a snack or a full-fledged dinner in an informal atmosphere. The drinks are very good; try one of the Grenadian rum punches made with Angostura bitters, grated nutmeg, rum, lime juice, and syrup. There's always fresh fish, and usually callaloo or pumpkin soup, plus potato croquettes. Lambi (that ubiquitous conch) is done very well here. A small wine list has some California, German, and Italian selections, and you can drop in just for a glass of beer to enjoy the sea view. Sometimes, however, you'll be asked to share a table.

Pier 1. At the extreme tip of the northern edge of the Carenage. St. George's. ☎ **473/440-9747.** Main courses EC$18–EC$28 ($6.65–$10.35). MC, V. Mon–Sat 8am–11pm. INTERNATIONAL/WEST INDIAN.

This place was originally built as a warehouse, but when someone added a waterfront veranda to the boxy, unimaginative building, it was immediately transformed into the most desirable perch along the waterfront. The cool breezes that blow in off the port make this place best suited for a midday pick-me-up, with or without alcohol. Drinks include U.S. bombers, mango daiquiris, and an especially potent concoction the owners refer to as "navy grog." Menu items include such West Indian dishes as lambi (conch) chowder, sandwiches, and the most popular dish, lobster cooked in a coconut cream sauce. We wouldn't say it's the best cooking in town, but it's quite competent and a good value.

Portofino. The Carenage, St. George's. ☎ **473/440-3986.** Reservations recommended. Pastas and pizzas EC$17–EC$40 ($6.30–$14.80); main courses EC$20–EC$60 ($7.40–$22.20). AE, MC, V. Mon–Sat 11am–11pm, Sat–Sun 6–11pm. PIZZA/SEAFOOD.

The venue is spartan and simple, with hints of Italy's Portofino. It's not a bad choice for its fine, unpretentious pastas, veal, chicken, and Italian-style beef. Portofino serves the best pizzas in the capital, Italian-style antipasti such as eggplant parmesan, and a good bowl of minestrone. However, the fish and meat dishes are more ordinary, although the catch of the day—served with pasta and fresh vegetables—is usually available, as are shrimp and lobster. The finest pasta dish is the linguine with fresh fish. The menu also caters to vegetarians, with choices like vegetarian lasagna. Live jazz is presented every Friday night, and on Sunday night there's a festival of Caribbean music, along with candlelight dining and dancing (no cover).

The Red Crab. L'Anse aux Epines. ☎ **473/444-4424.** Reservations required in winter. Main courses EC$45–EC$96 ($16.65–$35.50). AE, MC, V. Mon–Sat 11am–2pm and 6–10:30pm. WEST INDIAN/INTERNATIONAL.

The Red Crab, a popular place with visitors and locals alike, is only a short taxi ride from the major hotels. The place is especially popular with students from the medical college. Patrons can dine inside or out under the starry night. The beefsteaks, especially the pepper steak, are among Grenada's finest. Other offerings include local lobster tail; lambi (conch); and locally caught fish such as snapper, dolphin (mahimahi), and grouper, though other island chefs prepare better versions of these seafood dishes. Dessert might be a homemade cheesecake. It's not sublime cuisine, but come here for the convivial atmosphere and the good times.

✪ Rudolf's. The Carenage, St. George's. ☎ **473/440-2241.** Reservations recommended. Main courses EC$26–EC$60 ($9.60–$22.20). MC, V. Mon–Sat 10am–midnight. INTERNATIONAL.

A longtime favorite and an excellent value for your money, Rudolf's overlooks St. George's deep, U-shaped harbor. On the north center of the Carenage, it's a good spot for lethal rum drinks in the late afternoon. Austrian-born Rudolf is very charming, and he has a hardworking and genteel staff. The restaurant does a busy lunch business; ceiling fans cool patrons off at midday. The ceiling is sheathed in a layer of corrugated egg cartons, which adds an unconventional, appealing touch and also muffles the noise from the sometimes very crowded bar area. The menu is the most extensive on the island, the food is well prepared, and the steaks are the best in the capital. Flying fish and dolphin (mahimahi), prepared in several different ways, deserve the most praise. There's even a classic Wiener schnitzel in honor of the chef's origins.

4 Beaches

The best of the 45 beaches on Grenada are in the southwestern part of the island. The daddy of them all is ✪ **Grand Anse Beach,** 2 miles of sugar-white sand fronting a sheltered bay, only a 10-minute ride from St. George's and the site of major resort hotels. This beach is really the stuff of dreams, and many visitors on short jaunts to Grenada never leave it to explore the interior of the island. Protected from strong winds and currents, the waters here are relatively safe, making Grand Anse a family favorite. The clear, gentle waters are populated with schools of rainbow-hued fish. Water-sports concessions are found here, offering water-skiing, parasailing, windsurfing, and scuba diving; palms and sea-grape trees offer shade; and vendors peddle coral jewelry, local crafts, and the inevitable T-shirts.

The beach at **Morne Rouge Bay** is less frequented but just as desirable, with its white sands bordering clear waters. Morne Rouge is noted for its calm waters and some of the best snorkeling in Grenada. It's about a mile south of Grand Anse Bay.

Pink Gin Beach lies near the airport at Point Salinas, bordering two large resorts, La Source and Rex Grenadian (see "Where to Stay," above, for reviews). This is also a beach of white sand with clear waters, ideal for swimming and snorkeling. You'll find a restaurant and kayak rentals here.

Also on Grenada's southern coast, **La Sagesse Beach** is part of La Sagesse Nature Center. This especially powdery strip of white sand is a lovely, tranquil area; in between time spent on the beach, you can go for nature walks in most directions. A small restaurant opens onto the beach.

If you like your waters more turbulent, visit the dramatic **Pearl's Beach,** north of Grenville on the Atlantic coast. The light grey sand stretches for miles and is lined with palm trees. You'll practically have the beach to yourself.

Part of Levera National Park, **Levera Beach,** at the northeastern tip of the island, is one of the most beautiful on Grenada. Its sands front the Atlantic, which most often means rough waters. Many locals come here for Sunday picnics.

5 Sports & Outdoor Pursuits

DEEP-SEA FISHING   Fishers come here from November to March in pursuit of both blue and white marlin, yellowfin tuna, wahoo, sailfish, and more. Most of the bigger hotels have a sports desk that will arrange fishing trips for you. The **Annual Game Fishing Tournament,** held in January, attracts a number of regional and international participants.

GOLF   At the **Grenada Golf Course and Country Club,** Woodlands (☎ 473/444-4128), you'll find a nine-hole course. Greens fees are $16 for 9 holes, or $23 if you want to play 18 holes on the nine-hole course. Hours are Monday to Saturday from 8am to 7pm, Sunday from 8am to 1:30pm. The course offers a view of both the Caribbean Sea and the Atlantic.

HIKING   Grenada's lushness and beauty make it one of the best Caribbean islands for hiking. The best trails wind through **Grand Etang National Park and Forest Preserve** (☎ 473/440-6160). You can take a self-guided nature trail around Crater Lake or a more elaborate jaunt, perhaps to the peak of Mount Qua Qua at 2,373 feet. The latter should be done with a guide, costing $25 per person for a 4-hour hike. A guided hike to Mount St. Catherine, at 2,757 feet, costs $35. For information, call **Telfor Bedeau Hiking Tours** (☎ 473/442-6201) or **Arnold's Tours** (☎ 473/440-0531).

SCUBA DIVING & SNORKELING   Grenada offers divers an underwater world rich in submarine gardens, exotic fish, and coral formations, sometimes with visibility stretching to 120 feet. Off the coast is the wreck of the ocean liner *Bianca C,* which is nearly 600 feet long. Novice divers might want to stick to the west coast of Grenada, while more experienced divers might search out the sights along the rougher Atlantic side.

Daddy Vic's Watersports, in the Grenada Renaissance, Grand Anse Beach (☎ 473/444-4371, ext. 638), is directly on the sands. The premier dive outfit on the island, it has night dives or two-tank dives for $65, and PADI instructors offer an open-water certification program for $350 per person. This is also the best center for other water sports, offering snorkeling trips for $18 (1½ to 2 hours) or windsurfing with board rentals for $16 per hour. Sunfish rentals are $16 per hour, parasailing is $30 per 10 minutes, and waterskiing is $15 per run. Even deep-sea-fishing arrangements can be made.

Giving the center serious competition is **Grand Anse Aquatics,** at the Coyaba Beach Resort on Grand Anse Beach (☎ **473/444-7777**). A Canadian-run place, it's welcoming and inviting to divers, and there's a PADI instructor on site. The dive boat is well equipped with well-maintained gear. Both scuba-diving and snorkeling jaunts to panoramic reefs and shipwrecks teeming with marine life are offered. A single dive costs $35, a resort course $75, and a night dive $55. A snorkeling trip can be arranged for $20 in winter or $15 in off-season. Diving instruction, including a resort course, is available.

If you'd rather strike out on your own, take a drive to Woburn and negotiate with a fisher for a ride to **Glovers Island,** an old whaling station, and snorkel away. Glovers Island is an uninhabited rock spit a few hundred yards offshore from the hamlet of Woburn.

Warning: Divers should know that Grenada doesn't have a decompression chamber. If you should get the bends, you'll have to take an excruciatingly painful air trip to Trinidad.

SAILING   Two large "party boats," designed for 120 and 250 passengers, respectively, operate out of St. George's harbor. The ***Rhum Runner*** and ***Rhum Runner II,*** ℅ Best of Grenada, P.O. Box 188, St. George's, Grenada, W.I. (☎ **473/440-4FUN**), make shuttle-style trips, three times a day, with lots of emphasis on strong liquor, steel-band music, and good times. Four-hour tours, conducted every morning and afternoon, coincide with the arrival of cruise ships, but will carry independent travelers if space is available. Rides cost $20 per person and include snorkeling stops at reefs and beaches along the way. Evening tours are much more frequently attended by island locals, and are more bare-boned, louder, and usually less restrained. They cost $7.50 per person.

TENNIS   For the most part, the big resorts have tennis courts for their guests. If you're staying at a small inn, you won't find such facilities. There are public courts, however, both at Grand Anse and in Tanteen in St. George's.

6 Exploring the Island

ST. GEORGE'S & VICINITY

The capital city of Grenada, **St. George's** is the prettiest harbor town in the West Indies. Its landlocked inner harbor is actually the deep crater of a long-dead volcano—or so one is told. In the town, you'll see some of the most charming Georgian colonial buildings in the Caribbean, still standing in spite of a devastating hurricane in 1955. The steep, narrow hillside streets are filled with houses of ballast bricks, with wrought-iron balconies and sloping, red-tile roofs. Many of the pastel warehouses date back to the 18th century. Frangipani and flamboyant trees add to the palette of color.

The port, which some have compared to Portofino, Italy, is flanked by old forts and bold headlands. Among the town's attractions is an 18th-century pink **Anglican church,** on Church Street, and the **Market Square,** where colorfully attired farm women offer even more colorful produce for sale. **Fort George,** on Church Street, built by the French, stands at the entrance to the bay, with subterranean passageways and old guardrooms and cells.

Everyone strolls along the waterfront of the **Carenage** on the inner harbor, or relaxes on its pedestrian plaza, with seats and hanging planters providing shade from the sun.

On this side of town, the **Grenada National Museum,** at the corner of Young and Monckton streets (☎ 473/440-3725), is set in the foundations of an old French army barrack and prison built in 1704. Small but interesting, it houses finds from archaeological digs, including the petroglyphs, native fauna, the first telegraph installed on the island, a rum still, and memorabilia depicting Grenada's history. The most comprehensive exhibit traces the native culture of Grenada. One of the exhibits shows two bathtubs—the wooden barrel used by the fort's prisoners and the carved marble tub used by Joséphine Bonaparte during her adolescence on Martinique. Hours are Monday to Friday from 9am to 4:30pm, Saturday from 10am to 1pm. Admission is $2.

The Outer Harbour, fronting the Caribbean, is also called the **Esplanade.** It's connected to the Carenage by the Sendall Tunnel, which is cut through the promontory known as St. George's Point, dividing the two bodies of water.

You can take a drive up to Richmond Hill and **Fort Frederick,** begun by the French in 1779 and completed by the English in 1791. From its battlements, you'll have a superb view of the harbor and of the yacht marina.

An afternoon tour of St. George's and its environs takes you into the mountains northeast of the capital. A 15-minute drive delivers you to ✪ **Annandale Falls,** a tropical wonderland, with a cascade about 50 feet high. You can enjoy a picnic surrounded by liana vines, elephant ears, and other tropical flora and spices. The **Annandale Falls Centre** (☎ 473/440-2452) offers gift items, handcrafts, and samples of the indigenous spices of Grenada. Nearby, an improved trail leads to the falls where you can enjoy a refreshing swim. Swimmers can use the changing cubicles at the falls free. The center is open daily from 8am to 4pm.

A SPECTACULAR RAIN FOREST & MORE

If you head north out of St. George's along the western coast, you can take in beaches, spice plantations, and the fishing villages that are so typical of Grenada.

You'll pass through **Gouyave,** a spice town, the center of the nutmeg and mace industry. Before reaching the village, you can stop at the **Dougaldston Estate,** where you'll witness the processing of nutmeg and mace.

At the **Grenada Cooperative Nutmeg Association** (☎ 473/444-8337), near the entrance to Gouyave, huge quantities of the spice are aged, graded, and processed. Workers sit on stools in the natural light from the open windows of the aging factory, and laboriously sort the raw nutmeg and its by-product, mace, into different baskets for grinding, peeling, and aging. Jams, jellies, syrups, and more are all for sale. Hours are Monday to Friday from 10am to 1pm and 2 to 4pm; admission is $1.

Proceeding along the coast, you reach **Sauteurs,** at the northern tip of Grenada. This is the third-largest town on the island. It was from this great cliff that the Caribs leaped to their deaths instead of facing enslavement by the French.

To the east of Sauteurs is the palm-lined **Levera Beach,** an idyll of sand where the Atlantic meets the Caribbean. This is a great spot for a picnic lunch, but swimming can sometimes be dangerous. On the distant horizon you'll see some of the Grenadines.

Opened in 1994, the 450-acre **Levera National Park** has several white-sand beaches for swimming and snorkeling, although the surf is rough here where the Atlantic meets the Caribbean. It's also a hiker's paradise, and offshore are coral reefs and seagrass beds. The park contains a mangrove swamp, a lake, and a bird sanctuary. Perhaps you'll see a rare tropical parrot. Its interpretative center (☎ 473/442-1018) is open Monday to Friday from 8am to 4pm, Saturday from 9am to 4pm, and Sunday from 9am to 5pm.

Heading down the east coast of Grenada, you reach **Grenville,** the island's second city. If you pass through on a Saturday morning, you can enjoy the hubbub of the native produce market. There's also a fish market along the waterfront. A nutmeg factory here welcomes visitors.

From Grenville, you can cut inland into the heart of Grenada. Here you're in a world of luxuriant foliage, passing along nutmeg, banana, and cocoa plantations.

In the center of the island, reached along the major interior road between Grenville and St. George's, is ✪ **Grand Etang National Park,** containing the island's spectacular rain forest, which has been made more accessible by hiking trails. Beginning at the park's forest center, the short hike on the **Morne LeBaye Trail** affords a view of the 2,309-foot Mount Sinai and the east coast. Down the **Grand Etang Road,** trails lead to the 2,373-foot summit of Mount Qua Qua and the Ridge, and the **Lake Circle Trail,** taking hikers on a 30-minute trek along Grand Etang Lake, the crater of an extinct volcano lying in the midst of a forest preserve and bird sanctuary. You're likely to see the yellow-billed cuckoo and the emerald-throated hummingbird. The park is also a playground for Mona monkeys. Guides for the park trails are available, but arrangements must be made in advance. After a rainfall the trails can be very slippery; hikers should wear shoes with good traction, and carry drinking water as well. Much of the rain falls on Grenada between June and November. The park's **Grand Etang Interpretation (Nature) Centre,** on the shores of Grand Etang Lake (☎ 473/440-6160), is open Monday to Friday from 8am to 4pm, featuring a video about the park. Admission is $1.

On your descent from the mountains, you'll pass hanging carpets of mountain ferns. Going through the tiny hamlets of Snug Corner and Beaulieu, you eventually come back to the capital.

On yet another day, you can drive south from St. George's to the beaches and resorts spread along the already much-mentioned **Grand Anse,** which is one of the most beautiful beaches in the West Indies. Water taxis can also take you from the Carenage in St. George's to Grand Anse.

Point Salines, where the airport is located, is at the southwestern tip of the island, where a lighthouse stood for 56 years. A sculpture of the lighthouse has been constructed on the grounds just outside the airport terminal building. A panoramic view ranging from the northwest side of Grenada to the green hills in the east to the undulating plains in the south can be seen from a nearby hill.

Along the way you'll pass through the village of **Woburn,** which was featured in the film *Island in the Sun,* and go through the sugar belt of **Woodlands,** with its tiny sugarcane factory.

7 Shopping

Everybody who visits Grenada goes home with a basket of **spices,** better than any you're likely to find in your local supermarket. These hand-woven panniers of palm leaf or straw are full of items grown on the island, including the inevitable nutmeg, as well as mace, cloves, cinnamon, bay leaf, vanilla, and ginger. The local stores also sell a lot of luxury imports, mainly from England, at prices that are almost (not quite) duty free. Of course, Grenada is no grand merchandise mart of the Caribbean like St. Thomas and St. Maarten, but you may locate some local handcrafts, gifts, and even art; wherever you go you'll be besieged by spice vendors.

Some shoppers consider **Arawak Islands,** Upper Belmont Road, St. George's (☎ 473/444-3577), a celebration of the best scents produced on an island that's legendary for its spices. Look for fragrances distilled from such island plants as frangipani, wild lilies, cinnamon, nutmeg, and cloves; an all-natural insect repellent that some clients insist is the most effective (and safest) they've ever used; caffeine-free teas distilled from local plants; bitters that will perk up any rum-based drink; and soaps made in small batches and scented with nutmeg. Especially interesting is the root of the khus-khus plant, pulverized and stuffed into potpourri bags.

✪ **Spice Island Perfumes,** the Carenage, near the harbor entrance and close to the Ministry of Tourism (☎ 473/440-2006), is a treasure trove of perfumes made from all those herbs and spices grown on Grenada. If you're a collector of exotic scents, this is your store. The workshop produces perfumes, potpourri, and teas made from locally grown flowers and spices. Scents include island flower, spice, frangipani, jasmine, patchouli, and wild orchid.

Art Fabrik, Young Street, St. George's (☎ 473/440-0568), conveys a vivid impression of the labor and detail that go into the manufacture of the boldly patterned cloth known as batik. Make time for a quick visit to the studio, where you can see the hot wax applications and multiple dyeing rituals that go into the psychedelic patterns of the shirts, shifts, shorts, skirts, and T-shirts sold in the showroom. You can also buy the dyed fabric in bolts.

Bon Voyage, the Carenage (☎ 473/440-4217), is the island's leading purveyor of diamonds, precious stones, and gold and silver jewelry, plus china and crystal that includes such world-renowned names as Wedgwood, Blue Delft, Royal Doulton, Royal Brierley, and Coalport. Of course, if you're going on to Aruba, St. Maarten, or St. Thomas, you may want to wait and make serious purchases there. Bon Voyage also sells sunglasses, scarves, and accessories.

Gift Remembered, Cross Street, St. George's (☎ 473/440-2482), in the center of town a block from the water, sells handcrafts, straw articles, jewelry, batiks, film, beach wear, postcards, high-quality T-shirts, books, and wood carvings.

Tikal, Young Street, St. George's (☎ 473/440-2310), is in an early-18th-century brick building off the Carenage, next to the museum. You'll find an array of tastefully chosen handcrafts from around the world, as well as the finest selection of crafts made on Grenada, including batiks, ceramics, wood carvings, paintings, straw work, and clothing. The owner, Jeanne Fisher, is the designer of the local crafts.

Yellow Poui Art Gallery, Cross Street, a 2-minute walk from Market Square (☎ 473/440-3001), is the most interesting shop for souvenirs and artsy items. Here you can see oil paintings and watercolors, sculpture, prints, photography, antique maps, engravings, and woodcuts, with prices beginning at $10 and up. There's also a comprehensive display of newly acquired works from Grenada, the Caribbean area, and other parts.

If you're in the Grand Anse Beach area and would like to break up your time in the sun, **Imagine,** Grand Anse Shopping Centre (☎ 473/444-4028), is your best bet. The resort wear isn't the most fashionable, but if you're seeking a small gift, the handcrafts (dolls, ceramic, straw items) are an excellent value.

Sea Change Bookstore, the Carenage (☎ 473/440-3402), is cramped and crowded, but it's the largest repository of British and American newspapers on Grenada. There's also a collection of paperback books, island souvenirs, postcards, and film.

8 Grenada After Dark

Regular evening entertainment is provided by the resort hotels and includes steel bands, calypso, reggae, folk dancing, and limbo—even crab racing. Ask at your hotel desk to find out what's happening at the time of your visit.

CatBam, Grand Anse Beach, next to the Coyaba Beach Resort (☎ 473/ 444-2050), offers dancing to calypso and reggae, and dining on rotis and Carib beer on its open terrace. This is one of the best places on the island for a sundowner, and it stays open late. You can also try **Boatyard,** Prickly Bay, L'Anse aux Epines (☎ 473/444-4662), down by the marina. Friday night after 11pm, a local DJ spins dance music until dawn.

The island's most popular nightspot is **Fantazia 2001,** Morne Rouge Beach (☎ 473/444-2288). It's air-conditioned, with state-of-the-art equipment, good acoustics, and fantastic disco lights, and plays the best in regional and international sounds. Theme nights are frequent; live shows are presented on Friday and Saturday. The cover is EC$10 to EC$35 ($3.70 to $12.95), depending on the entertainment.

Le Sucrier, Sugar Mill, Grand Anse (☎ 473/444-1068), has comedy acts, golden oldies, and a disco scene. A young local crowd, both visitors and residents, shows up any time after 9pm, Wednesday through Saturday nights.

Casablanca, Grand Anse (☎ 473/444-1631), is the island's major sports bar. It's also a piano bar. You can enjoy good music and good company, and watch games on a big-screen TV. The **Beachside Terrace** at the Flamboyant Hotel, Grand Anse (☎ 473/444-4247), is a laid-back spot featuring crab races on Monday, a steel band on Wednesday and Saturday, and, our favorite, a beach barbecue with live calypso music on Friday.

For those seeking culture, the 200-seat **Marryshow Folk Theatre,** Herbert Blaize Street near Bain Alley, St. George's (☎ 473/440-2451), offers performances of Grenadian, American, and European folk music, drama, and West Indian interpretative folk dance. This is a project of the University of the West Indies School of Continuing Studies. Check with the theater or the tourist office to see what's on. Tickets cost EC$15 to EC$20 ($5.60 to $7.40).

One of our favorite bars is **The Aquarium** at Point Salines (☎ 473/444-1410), which also serves delectable food. A vaulted wooden roof shelters an array of bamboo stools, fake marble pillars, wooden tables, and a sprawl of decks, all open to the trade winds. You can enjoy the lights of St. George's Harbour here at night.

14

Guadeloupe

"The time is near, I believe, when thousands of American tourists will come to spend the winter among the beautiful countryside and friendly people of Guadeloupe." So Theodore Roosevelt accurately predicted on February 21, 1916. Guadeloupe isn't the same place it was when the Rough Rider rode through, but the natural beauty he observed is still here.

Guadeloupe is part of the Lesser Antilles, about 200 miles north of Martinique, closer to the United States than to its cousin island. Guadeloupe is actually formed by two different islands, separated by a narrow seawater channel known as the Rivière Salée. **Grande-Terre,** the eastern island, is typical of the charm of the Antilles, with its rolling hills and sugar plantations. **Basse-Terre,** to the west, is a rugged mountainous island, dominated by the 4,800-foot volcano, La Soufrière, which is still alive. Its mountains are covered with tropical forests, impenetrable in many places. Bananas grown on plantations are the main crop, and the island is ringed by beautiful white-sand beaches, which have attracted much tourism.

1 Essentials

VISITOR INFORMATION

For advance information, contact the **French Government Tourist Office** at one of the following locations: 444 Madison Ave., **New York, NY** 10022; 9454 Wilshire Blvd., Suite 715, **Beverly Hills, CA** 90212; or 676 N. Michigan Ave., Suite 3360, **Chicago, IL** 60611. For all information in the United States, you can call ☎ **202/ 659-7779.**

You can also contact the **Guadeloupe Tourist Office,** 161 Washington Valley Rd., Suite 205, Warren, NJ 07059 (☎ **732/302-1223;** fax 732/302-0809).

Guadeloupe is on the Web at **www.fgtousa.org**.

On the island, the major tourist office is the **Office Départemental du Tourisme,** Square de la Banque 5, in Pointe-à-Pitre (☎ **0590/ 82-09-30**).

GETTING THERE

Most flights into Guadeloupe are tied in with air connections to Martinique. See "Getting There," in chapter 16.

Guadeloupe

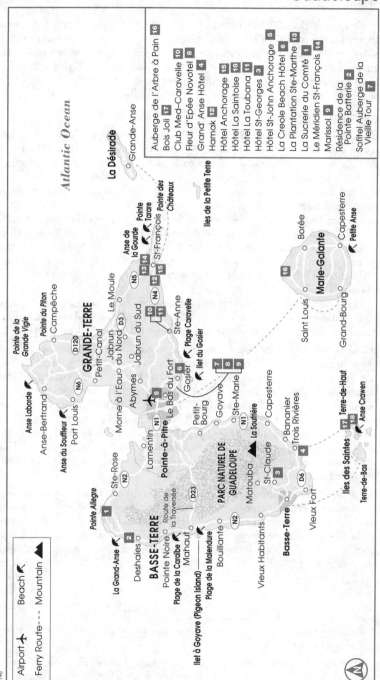

Airport ✈   Beach ⤸   Mountain ▲

Ferry Route ----

Auberge de l'Arbre à Pain **16**
Bois Joli **17**
Club Med-Caravelle **10**
Fleur d'Epée Novotel **8**
Grand' Anse Hôtel **4**
Hamak **12**
Hôtel Anchorage **15**
Hôtel La Saintoise **18**
Hôtel La Toubana **11**
Hôtel St-Georges **3**
Hôtel St-John Anchorage **5**
La Creole Beach Hôtel **6**
La Plantation Ste-Marthe **13**
La Sucrerie du Comté **1**
Le Méridien St-François **14**
Marissol **9**
Résidence de la Pointe Batterie **2**
Sofitel Auberge de la Vieille Tour **7**

Atlantic Ocean

La Désirade

311

Air Canada (☎ **800/268-7240** in Canada, or 800/776-3000 in the U.S.; www.aircanada.ca) flies between Montréal and Guadeloupe (but not Martinique) every Saturday year-round. When this isn't convenient, passengers from throughout Canada can route themselves through Toronto on one of the daily nonstop flights to Barbados. From there, passengers can transfer onto other carriers (usually LIAT) making the ongoing journey to points within the French West Indies.

GETTING AROUND

BY RENTAL CAR   Having a car enables you to circumnavigate Basse-Terre, which is one of the most panoramic drives in the Caribbean. Car-rental kiosks at the airport are open to meet international flights. Rental rates at local companies might appear lower, but several readers have complained of mechanical problems, billing irregularities, and difficulties in resolving insurance disputes in the event of accidents. So we recommend reserving a car in advance through North America's largest car-rental companies: **Hertz** (☎ **800/654-3001** or 0590/21-09-35), **Avis** (☎ **800/331-1212** or 0590/21-13-54), and **Budget** (☎ **800/527-0700** or 0590/21-13-48), each of which is represented on the island and has its headquarters at the airport. In addition to the rental rates, you'll have to pay a one-time airport surcharge of 100 F ($17) and VAT (value-added tax) of 9.5%. Prices are usually 20% to 25% lower between March and early December.

As in France, *driving is on the right-hand side of the road,* and there are several gas stations along the island's main routes. Because of the distance between gas stations away from the capital, try not to let your gas gauge fall below the halfway mark.

BY TAXI   You'll find taxis when you arrive at the airport, but no limousines or buses. From 9pm until 7am, cabbies are legally entitled to charge you 40% more. In practice, either day or night, they charge you whatever they think the market will bear, although technically fares are regulated by the government. Always agree on the price before getting in. Approximate fares are 120 F to 130 F ($20.40 to $22.10) from the airport to Gosier hotels, or 70 F ($11.90) from the airport to Pointe-à-Pitre. **Radio taxis** can be called at ☎ **0590/82-99-88.** On Basse-Terre, call ☎ **0590/81-79-70.**

If you're traveling with more than two people, it's possible to sightsee by taxi. Usually the concierge at your hotel will help you make this arrangement. Fares are usually negotiated, but are around 800 F ($136) per day.

BY BUS   Buses link almost every hamlet to Pointe-à-Pitre. However, you may need to know some French to use the system. From Pointe-à-Pitre, you can catch one of these jitney vans, either at the Gare Routière de Bergevin if you're going to Basse-Terre, or the Gare Routière de Mortenol if Grande-Terre is your destination. Service is daily from 5:30am to 7:30pm. The fare from the airport to the Pointe-à-Pitre terminal on rue Peynier is 7 F ($1.20).

Fast Facts: Guadeloupe

Banking Hours   Banks on Guadeloupe are usually open Monday through Friday from 9am to 3pm.

Currency   The official monetary unit is the **French franc (F),** although some shops will take U.S. dollars. The exchange rate used to calculate the dollar values given in this chapter is 5.90 F to U.S.$1 (1 F = 17¢ U.S.). As this is sure to fluctuate a bit, use this rate for general guidance only.

Customs   Items for personal use "in limited quantities" can be brought in tax free.

Documents   For stays of less than 21 days, U.S., British, or Canadian residents need a passport, plus a return or ongoing plane ticket.

Drugstores   See "Pharmacies," below.

Electricity   The local electricity is 220 volts AC (50 cycles), which means that those using U.S.-made appliances will need a transformer and an adapter. Some of the big resorts lend these to guests, but don't count on it.

Emergencies   Call the **police** at ☎ **17.** To report a **fire** or summon an **ambulance,** dial ☎ **18.**

Hospitals   There are five modern hospitals on Guadeloupe, plus 23 clinics. Hotels and the Guadeloupe tourist office can assist in locating English-speaking doctors. There's a 24-hour emergency room at the **Centre Hôpitalier de Pointe-à-Pitre,** Abymes (☎ **0590/89-10-10**).

Language   The official language is French; Creole is the unofficial second language. As on Martinique, English is spoken only in the major tourist centers, rarely in the countryside.

Pharmacies   The pharmacies carry French medicines, and most over-the-counter American drugs have French equivalents. Prescribed medicines can be purchased if you have the prescription with you. At least one drugstore is always open; the tourist office can tell you what pharmacies are open at what time.

Police   In an emergency, call ☎ **17.** Otherwise, call ☎ **0590/93-00-66.**

Safety   Like Martinique, Guadeloupe is relatively free of serious crime. But don't go wandering alone at night on the streets of Pointe-à-Pitre; by nightfall they are relatively deserted and might be dangerous. Purse-snatching by fast-riding motorcyclists has been reported, so exercise caution.

Taxes   A departure tax, required on scheduled flights, is included in the airfares. Hotel taxes are included in all room rates.

Telephone   To call Guadeloupe from the United States, dial **011** (the international access code), then **590** (the country code for Guadeloupe) and the rest of the local number, which will be six digits. Once you're on Guadeloupe—at least for purposes of phoning the other islands of the French Antilles—be aware that St. Barts, French St. Martin, and offshore dependencies of Guadeloupe such as Ile des Saints or La Désirade are all directly linked to the phone network of Guadeloupe. Consequently, no telephone prefix is required, and you'll be connected to points on any of those islands simply by dialing the six-digit local phone number. But if you're on Guadeloupe and want to dial someone in Martinique, you'll have to punch in the prefix for Martinique (0596), followed by the six-digit local number.

Time   Guadeloupe is on Atlantic standard time year-round, 1 hour ahead of eastern standard time (when it's 6am in New York, it's 7am on Guadeloupe). When daylight saving time is in effect in the States, clocks in New York and Guadeloupe show the same time.

Tipping   Hotels and restaurants usually add a 10% to 15% service charge. Most taxi drivers who own their own cars do not expect a tip.

Water   While on Guadeloupe, stick to bottled water only.

2 Pointe-à-Pitre

The port and chief city of Guadeloupe, Pointe-à-Pitre lies on Grande-Terre. Unfortunately, it doesn't have the old-world charm of Fort-de-France on Martinique, and what beauty it does possess is often hidden behind closed doors.

Having been burned and rebuilt so many times, the port now lacks character. Modern apartments and condominiums form a high-rise backdrop over jerry-built shacks and industrial suburbs. The rather narrow streets are jammed during the day with a colorful crowd that creates a permanent traffic jam. However, at sunset the town becomes quiet again and almost deserted. The only raffish charm left is around the waterfront, where you might expect to see Bogie or Sydney Greenstreet sipping rum at a cafe table.

The real point of interest in Pointe-à-Pitre is **shopping.** It's best to visit the town in the morning—you can easily cover it in half a day—taking in the waterfront and outdoor market (the latter is livelier in the early hours).

The town center is **place de la Victoire,** a park shaded by palm trees and poincianas. Here you'll see some old sandbox trees said to have been planted by Victor Hugues, the mulatto who organized a revolutionary army of both whites and blacks to establish a dictatorship. In this square he kept a guillotine busy, and the death-dealing instrument stood here—but not in use—until modern times.

With the recent completion of the **Centre St-John-Perse,** a $20-million project that had been on the drawing boards for many years, the waterfront of Pointe-à-Pitre has been transformed from a bastion of old warehouses and cruise-terminal buildings into an architectural complex comprising a hotel, three restaurants, 80 shops and boutiques, a bank, and the expanded headquarters of Guadeloupe's Port Authority.

Named for Saint-John Perse, the 20th-century poet and Nobel Laureate who was born just a few blocks away, the center is designed in contemporary French Caribbean style, which blends with the traditional architecture of Pointe-à-Pitre. It offers an array of French Caribbean attractions: duty-free shops selling Guadeloupean rum and French perfume, small tropical gardens planted around the complex, and a location near the open-air markets and small shops. For brochures and maps, the Guadeloupe tourist office is just minutes away.

WHERE TO STAY

Hôtel St-John Anchorage. Centre Saint-John-Perse, rue Frébaut (at the harborfront), 97110 Pointe-à-Pitre, Guadeloupe, F.W.I. ☎ **0590/82-51-57.** Fax 0590/82-52-61. 44 units. A/C TV TEL. Year-round 523 F ($88.90) double. Rates include continental breakfast. MC, V.

This hotel rises four stories above the harborfront, near the quays. The small rooms are clean, simple, and furnished with locally crafted mahogany pieces. Very few units have views over the sea. Bathrooms are small with no frills. Once you check in, the laissez-faire staff might leave you alone until the end of your stay. There's a simple coffee shop/cafe on street level. Stay here if you want to be in the capital and don't have convenient transportation to go elsewhere. To reach a beach, you'll have to travel 2 miles to the east to Le Bas du Fort and the Grosier area (see below).

WHERE TO DINE

Le Big Steak House. 2 rue Delgrès (at quai Lardenoy). ☎ **0590/82-12-44.** Main courses 92 F–128 F ($15.65–$21.75). AE, MC, V. Mon–Sat noon–3pm. STEAKS/SEAFOOD.

Virtually every shopkeeper and office worker in Pointe-à-Pitre is familiar with this well-managed restaurant, which offers some of the best midday meals in town.

Outfitted in wood paneling and a Wild West decor that evokes a steakhouse some-where west of the Mississippi, it imports its meats from the mainland of France, and prepares them any way you prefer, usually with a choice of five different sauces. Anyone who wants more than one sauce as a garnish is cheerfully obliged—examples include versions with mustard, shallots, peppercorns, and chives. Fish culled from local waters is also popular, and includes red snapper cooked *en papillote,* or grilled daurade with Creole sauce. As you'd expect, the wine cellar holds a wide array of French wines. The site is especially suitable for cruise-ship day-trippers, as it's virtually adjacent to the piers where cruise ships are tethered.

Restaurant Sucré-Salé. Bd. LéGitimus. ☎ **0590/21-22-55.** Reservations recommended. Main courses 60 F–120 F ($10.20–$20.40). AE, DC, MC, V. Mon–Sat noon–4:30pm; Tues–Sat 7–9:30pm. FRENCH.

Set in the heart of Pointe-à-Pitre, adjacent to an Air France office and near several international banks, this restaurant was established in 1995 and has been filled at lunchtime ever since with dealmakers and office workers from throughout the city. The decorative theme revolves around jazz, with an emphasis on portraits of such American greats as Billie Holliday and Miles Davis. A covered terrace overlooking the busy boulevard serves as an animated singles bar every evening after work. The charming Marius Pheron, the Guadeloupe-born owner who did an 18-year stint in Paris, offers such menu items as fillets of snapper served with pommes soufflés and black pepper, meal-sized salads, entrecôte steaks, sweetbreads in orange sauce, and an impressive medley of grilled fish. The restaurant is host to a jazz concert one evening a month, when posters announcing the event appear all over town.

SHOPPING

Frankly, we suggest that you skip a shopping tour of Pointe-à-Pitre if you're going to Fort-de-France on Martinique, as you'll find far more merchandise there, and perhaps friendlier service. If you're not, however, we recommend the following shops, some of which line rue Frébault.

Your best buys will be anything French–perfumes from Chanel, silk scarves from Hermès, cosmetics from Dior, crystal from Laique and Baccarat. Though they're expensive, we've found (but not often) some of these items discounted as much as 30% below U.S. or Canadian prices. While most shops will accept U.S. dollars, they'll give these discounts only for purchases made by traveler's check. Purchases are duty free if brought directly from store to plane. In addition to the places below, there are also duty-free shops at **Raizet Airport** (☎ **0590/21-14-66**) selling liquor, rums, per-fumes, crystal, and cigarettes.

Most shops open at 9am, close at 1pm, then reopen between 3 and 6pm. They're closed on Saturday afternoon, Sunday, and holidays. When the cruise ships are in port, many eager shopkeepers stay open longer and on weekends.

One of the best places to buy French perfumes, at prices often lower than those charged in Paris, is **Phoenicia,** 8 rue Frébault (☎ **0590/83-50-36**). The shop also has a good selection of imported cosmetics. U.S. traveler's checks will get you further dis-counts.

Other leading perfume shops include **Au Bonheur des Dames,** 49 rue Frébault (☎ **0590/82-00-30**), which is also known for its skin-care products. **L'Artisan Par-fumeur,** Centre St-John Perse (☎ **0590/83-80-25**), carries not only top French per-fumes but also leading American brands at discounted prices. Sample one of their bottles of "tropical scents."

Rosébleu, 5 rue Frébault (☎ **0590/82-93-44**), sells fine crystal, fine porcelain, and tableware from all the grand chic names of Europe's leading manufacturers, including

Christofle, Kosta Buda, and Villeroy & Bosch, always at prices 20% less than on the French mainland.

Vendôme, 8–10 rue Frébault (☎ **0590/83-42-84**), has imported fashions for both men and women, as well as a large selection of gifts and perfumes, including the big names. Usually you can find someone who speaks English to sell you a Cardin watch.

If you're interested in French foodstuffs imported from France—everything from cheese to chocolate—head for **Delice Shop,** 45 rue Achille René-Boisneuf (☎ **0590/82-98-24**).

The **Distillerie Bellevue,** rue Bellevue-Damoiseau, Le Moule (☎ **0590/23-55-55**), caters to those who want to purchase "the essence of the island." On Guadeloupe that essence is *rhum agricole,* a pure rum that's fermented from sugarcane juice. Savvy locals say that the rum here (whose brand name is Rhum Damoiseau) is the only kind you can drink without suffering the devastation of a rum hangover the next morning. You're allowed to taste the product.

If you're adventurous, you may want to seek out some native goods in little shops along the backstreets of Pointe-à-Pitre. Collector's items are the straw hats or **salacos** made in Les Saintes islands. They look distinctly related to Chinese coolie hats and are usually well designed, often made of split bamboo. Native **doudou dolls** are also popular gift items.

Open-air stalls surround the **covered market** (Marché Couvert) at the corner of rue Frébault and rue Thiers. Here you can discover the many fruits, spices, and vegetables that are fun to look at as well as to taste. In madras turbans, local Creole women make deals over their strings of fire-red pimientos. The bright fabrics they wear compete with the rich colors of oranges, papayas, bananas, mangos, and pineapples.

MOVING ON

Saint-John Perse once wrote about the fine times sailors had in Pointe-à-Pitre, as a stopover on the famous route du Rhum. But since those days are long gone, you may not want to linger; you can take a different route instead, this one to the "South Riviera," from Pointe-à-Pitre to Pointe des Châteaux. The hotels recommended below grew up on Grande-Terre because of the long stretches of white sand lying between Bas du Fort and Gosier. These beaches, however, are not spectacular, but often narrow and artificially created.

3 Le Bas du Fort

The first tourist complex, just 2 miles east of Pointe-à-Pitre, is called **Le Bas du Fort,** near Gosier.

The **Aquarium de la Guadeloupe,** place Créole, Marina Bas-du-Fort (☎ **0590/90-92-38**), is rated as one of the three most important of France and is the largest and most modern in the Caribbean. Just off the highway near **Bas-du-Fort Marina,** the aquarium is home to tropical fish, coral, underwater plants, huge sharks, and other sea creatures. Hours are daily from 9am to 7pm. Admission is 38 F ($6.45) for adults, 20 F ($3.40) for children 6 to 12, free for kids 5 and under.

WHERE TO STAY

Fleur d'Epée Novotel. Bas-du-Fort Coralia. Le Bas du Fort, 97190 Gosier, Guadeloupe, F.W.I. ☎ **800/221-4542** in the U.S., or 0590/90-40-00. Fax 0590/90-99-07. www.intel-media.fr/ im-caraibes/accor.htm. E-mail: novotel@outremer.com. 190 units. A/C TV TEL. Winter 1,245 F–1,860 F ($211.65–$316.20) double. Off-season 870 F–1,015 F ($147.90–$172.55) double. Rates include buffet breakfast. AE, DC, MC, V.

This is Guadeloupe's most prominent branch of the successful French hotel chain. Even though it has a rather laid-back staff and is architecturally undistinguished, the hotel is still popular with young people from the French mainland who turn up here in bikini-clad droves. It stands beside a pair of crescent-shaped bays whose narrow, cramped white sands are shaded by palms and sea-grape trees. Geared for the resort-lovers, the hotel has only three floors. Each guest room is a well-scrubbed, modern, tiled enclave with private bathroom and a simple motel-style floor plan; 100 units were recently renovated, with new mattresses installed. Although the rooms are medium-size and no better than a good roadside motel in the United States, they're well maintained. The compact bathrooms have combination tub/showers and hair dryers.

There's a breeze-filled restaurant, Le Jardin des Tropiques, on site, plus about a dozen indoor/outdoor restaurants within walking distance, many with views of the beach.

Marissol. Le Bas du Fort, 97190 Gosier, Guadeloupe, F.W.I. ☎ **800/221-4542** in the U.S., or 0590/90-84-44. Fax 0590/90-83-32. www.intel-media.fr/im-caraibes/accor.htm. E-mail: novotel@outreme.com. 195 units. A/C TV TEL. Winter 1,145 F–1,920 F ($194.65–$326.40) double. Off-season 795 F–935 F ($135.15–$158.95) double. Rates include continental breakfast. AE, DC, MC, V.

Associated with the France-based Accor group, with accommodations and amenities that are usually compared to those within a Novotel, this secluded bungalow colony of two- and three-story structures sits near the entrance to the tourist complex of Bas du Fort. Set a soothing distance back from the main road, the Marissol occupies the grounds between a secondary route and the shoreline. In 1997, its bedrooms underwent a long-overdue renovation, bringing them up to spiffy, albeit simple, standards of summer-inspired comfort. The well-maintained rooms open onto views of the grounds or the water. The furnishings are sober and modern (nothing special), the floors are tiled, and all units have either twin or double beds, each with a firm mattress.

Dining/Diversions: In the mid–1990s, lack of interest from the dining public forced this hotel to close its deluxe restaurant, Le Grand Baie, focusing instead on its moderately priced bistro, Sicali, an open grill lying halfway between the beach and the pool. Next to the pool is a circular bar. The in-house disco is open only to hotel guests and their guests, and only in winter on Friday and Saturday.

Amenities: Small artificial beach, large pool, beauty and fitness center, water-sports kiosk (with windsurfing, sailing, and snorkeling). Scuba diving can be arranged. Laundry, massage, baby-sitting, concierge.

WHERE TO DINE

✪ **Rosini.** La Porte des Caraïbes, Bas-du-Fort. ☎ **0590/90-87-81.** Reservations recommended. Main courses 52 F–175 F ($8.85–$29.75). AE, DC, MC, V. Daily noon–2:30pm and 6:30–10:30pm. NORTHERN ITALIAN.

This is the best Italian restaurant in the French West Indies, thanks to a sophisticated father-in-law/son-in-law team of Venice-born Luciano Rosini and Provence-derived Christophe Giraud. It's contained within two air-conditioned dining rooms on the ground floor of a well-heeled condo complex across from the Novotel in Bas-du-Fort. Recorded opera music provides a background for succulent versions of tournedos layered with foie gras, osso buco, and freshwater prawns served diavolo style in a tomato, garlic, and parsley sauce with freshly made fettucine. Ravioli comes stuffed either with veal and herbs or with lobster, according to the whims of the chef and the availability of shellfish. At least five types of pizza are also available, although they're usually proposed for the small children of the adult clientele, who, frankly, tend to find the restaurant's more substantial fare more appealing. Thanks to Mr. Giraud's long apprenticeship at a restaurant within Washington, D.C.'s Watergate complex, English is readily understood.

4 Gosier

Some of the biggest and most important hotels of Guadeloupe are found at Gosier, with its nearly 5 miles of sandy but narrow beach, stretching east from Pointe-à-Pitre. All the hotels below are in easy proximity to the sands below.

For an excursion, you can climb to the semi-ruined heights of **Fort Fleur-d'Epée,** dating from the 18th century. Its dungeons and battlements are testaments to the ferocious fighting between the French and British armies in 1794. The well-preserved ruins command the crown of a hill, which affords good views over the bay of Pointe-à-Pitre. On a clear day, you can see the neighboring offshore islands of Marie-Galante and Iles des Saintes.

Gosier is a good place to shop for souvenirs and some Haitian paintings. Try **Boutique de la Plage,** Bd. Général de Gaulle (☎ **0590/84-52-51**), which has all sorts of handcrafts. Many are quite junky, but some are amusing. The island's best selection of Haitian art is at **Centre d'Art Haitien,** 65 Montauban (☎ **0590/84-32-60**).

WHERE TO STAY

La Creole Beach Hôtel. Pointe de la Verdure, 97190 Gosier, Guadeloupe, F.W.I. ☎ **800/322-2223** or 0590/90-46-46. Fax 0590/90-46-66. www.leader-hotel.gp. E-mail: creolebeach@leader-hotel.gp. 315 units. Winter 713 F–1,386 F ($121.20–$235.60) double. Off-season 598 F–998 F ($101.65–$169.65) double. Year-round 1,400 F–1,600 F ($238–$272) duplex for 1–4. Rates include continental breakfast. AE, DC, MC, V.

This is the largest resort on Guadeloupe, but because of the way it's divided into three distinct sections, you'll get a sense of isolation and privacy. It's located alongside two beaches within a setting of lawns, trees, hibiscus, and bougainvillea, with a strong French Creole flavor. The establishment suits both budget-conscious guests, who might want to cook their own meals, and to somewhat more upmarket guests who have no interest whatsoever in preparing their own meals. The entire compound attracts both young couples and families with children, often from France.

The most upscale of the resort's subdivisions include Le Creole, a brown-and-white three-story building with verandas influenced by French colonial architecture. Its approximate equal in terms of desirability is Le Mahogany, a comfortable blue-and-white compound which contains a high percentage of oceanfront rooms (most without kitchens). Le Yucca houses the budget-category units, painted in cheerful pastel tones; each contains a cramped and ultra-simple kitchenette. All units in all three subdivisions were renovated in 1994, and almost all have a patio or veranda large enough for a breakfast retreat. Most rooms are spacious and contain two double beds. Baths are small and very basic.

Dining: Les Alizés, attractively decorated with plants, serves many local specials along with a more familiar international cuisine. Guests can enjoy drinks at the poolside bar or lunch at the beach snack bar. Another restaurant, Le Zawag, lies just on the rocks by the sea, offering fresh fish and seafood along with lobster. There's also a simple snack bar ("Pizza Beach") and a bar.

Amenities: Pool, tennis courts, scuba diving, waterskiing, sailboat rentals, deep-sea fishing. Laundry, baby-sitting.

Sofitel Auberge de la Vieille Tour. Montauban, 97190 Gosier, Guadeloupe, F.W.I.
☎ **800/221-4542** or 0590/84-23-23. Fax 0590/84-33-43. E-mail: 1345h@accor-hotel.com.
180 units. A/C MINIBAR TV TEL. Winter 1,345 F–3,200 F ($228.65–$544) double; 1,680
F–3,200 F ($285.60–$544) duplex suite for 2–4. Off-season 1,090 F–1,730 F ($185.30–
$294.10) double; 1,600 F–2,200 F ($272–$374) duplex suite for 2–4. Rates include breakfast.
AE, DC, MC, V.

Though it became a Sofitel in 1995, this place grew from a family inn that was originally built around the shadow of an old sugar mill. Today, the former mill's stone-
sided tower serves as the resort's reception area. Despite some improvements made by
Sofitel, the personal service and attention to detail are not particularly noticeable. If
you don't mind the relative anonymity of a chain hotel, this is an appropriate choice
for guests who don't expect a lot of pampering and are adept at creating their own
good times regardless of the setting.

The older guest rooms are relatively short on charm, and some contain vestiges of
battered and ill-equipped kitchens that most guests use only for storing cold drinks.
The better maintained units, none of which ever contained kitchens, are within La
Résidence, a series of town house–style accommodations set near the pool. Their desirability is rivaled only by units referred to as "luxury-class," set close to the water near
the beach. Some units have balconies that overlook the gardens or the small, semiprivate, and often rather crowded beach. Rooms have comfortable French mattresses and
compact bathrooms with hair dryers.

Dining: The Restaurant de la Vieille Tour and Zagaya serve French and Creole
food, respectively, in relatively elegant, semi-formal settings. Less structured, and more
closely tuned to the weather and the vagaries of temperature, is L'Ajoupa, a grill-style
indoor-outdoor affair that specializes in salads, sandwiches, steaks, fish, and party-
colored drinks.

Amenities: Tennis court (lit at night), pool, water sports (including snorkeling,
sailing, and windsurfing) from a booth set up on the hotel's small and narrow beach.
Laundry, concierge.

WHERE TO DINE

Chez Violetta. Perinette Gosier. ☎ **0590/84-10-34.** Main courses 88 F–95 F
($14.95–$16.15); fixed-price meal 75 F–160 F ($12.75–$27.20). AE, DC, MC, V. Daily
noon–3:30pm and 7:30–11pm. FRENCH/CREOLE.

At the far-eastern end of Gosier village, en route to Ste-Anne, this is the most formally
decorated of all the Creole restaurants on the island. The interior combines Creole
madras patterns with touches of French style. This was originally the domain of a
high priestess of Creole cookery, Violetta Chaville, whose skill became a legend on
the island. Today, her polite and well-mannered brother, Josef Galaya, carries on in
her tradition. Still missing are her personality and style, but she must have recorded
her recipes before she passed on, as you can still find the same dishes and flavors
here.

On the à la carte menu, try stuffed crabs, *blaff of seafood*, or fresh fish of the day
(perhaps red snapper). For an appetizer, ask for cod fritters or *accra* (beignets). The
classic blood sausage, boudin, is also served here. In addition, the chef does a fine fricassée of conch, superb in texture and flavor; it's best when served with hot chiles grown
on Guadeloupe. On occasion, he'll even prepare a brochette of shark, if available.
Fresh pineapple makes an ideal dessert, or you can try the banana cake.

✪ **Le Bananier.** Rue Principale de Gosier, Montauban. ☎ **0590/84-34-85.** Reservations
recommended. Main courses 72 F–170 F ($12.25–$28.90). AE, DC, MC, V. Tues–Sun
noon–2:30pm and 7–10pm. CREOLE.

Well-established Guadeloupe-born entrepreneurs Élixe Virolan (maître-d'hôtel) and chef Yves Clarus joined forces years ago to create a restaurant where some of the most imaginative dishes in the Creole repertoire are handled with finesse and charm. Within a 50-year-old clapboard-sided cottage, whose dining room is air-conditioned, you'll find a handful of old-fashioned staples, such as stuffed crab backs and *accras* (beignets) of codfish. Much more appealing, however, are such modernized dishes as filet mignon served with pulverized blood sausage, port wine, and a reduction of crayfish bisque; a *clafoutis* (gratinated medley) of shellfish; and a *tourtière d'oeufs aux crabes* (an omelet that combines breaded and baked crabmeat, fresh tomatoes, and reduction of callaloo leaves). The menu's most appealing dessert is a flambéed banana whose alcoholic afterglow results from a use of *Schrubb*, an obscure Guadeloupian liqueur made from fermented orange peels that was prized by the owners' grandparents.

5 Ste-Anne

About 9 miles east of Gosier, little Ste-Anne is a sugar town and a resort offering many fine beaches and lodgings. In many ways, it's the most charming village of Guadeloupe, with its pastel-colored town hall, its church, and its principal square, Place de la Victoire, where a statue of Schoelcher commemorates the abolition of slavery in 1848.

All the rainbow colors of the Caribbean are for sale at **La Case à Soie** in Ste-Anne (☎ **0590/88-11-31**), known for its flamboyantly colored scarves and its flowing silk dresses.

WHERE TO STAY & DINE

Club Med–Caravelle. 97180 Ste-Anne, Guadeloupe, F.W.I. ☎ **800/CLUB-MED** in the U.S., or 0590/85-49-50. Fax 0590/85-49-70. 329 units. A/C TEL. Nov–Apr $1,029–$1,239 weekly. May–Oct $1,029–$1,169 weekly. Rates are per person based on double occupancy. Rates are all-inclusive. Children 4–12 are charged 75% of the adult rate. Single supplement 20%–40% above the per person double rate. AE, MC, V. Children 3 and under not accepted.

Ste-Anne's best-known resort is Club Med–Caravelle, covering 45 acres along a peninsula dotted with palm trees. Its beach is one of the finest in the French West Indies. The guest rooms tend to be small, but have good beds. Tiled baths are compact and short on amenities. The building known as Marie-Galante contains the resort's largest and most comfortable rooms (each with a terrace or veranda), costing about 20% more than the smaller, bland standard rooms. Don't expect massive doses of Gallic charm at this somewhat time-weary resort—it simply isn't that kind of place.

Note that during the summer (but a bit less so during the winter), this resort markets itself almost exclusively to a French clientele through its sales outlets in Paris. Though North Americans are welcome, almost all midsummer activities here are conducted in French.

Dining/Diversions: When it comes to dining here, the emphasis is on quantity, not quality. The breakfast and lunch buffet tables groan with French, continental, and Creole food. Dinner is served in the main dining room or in the candlelit, more romantic annex restaurant beside the sea. At the weekly folklore night, the Guadeloupe folklore ballet performs, and the dinner features specialties of the region. There's also a bar, dance floor, and midnight disco.

Amenities: Windsurfing, sailing, snorkeling trips (leaving daily from the dock), sea excursions to explore the island's coastline, six tennis courts, archery, calisthenics, volleyball, basketball, table tennis. Laundry. Children 4 and over are welcome, but special supervision and "child-amusing" programs are in place only at specific times of the year, usually during school vacations.

Hôtel La Toubana. Durivage (B.P. 63), 97180 Ste-Anne, Guadeloupe, F.W.I. ☎ **800/ 322-2223** or 0590/88-25-78. Fax 0590/88-38-90. www.toubana.gp. E-mail: toubana@ leaderhotels.gp. 32 units. A/C TEL. Winter 708 F–1,316 F ($120.35–$223.70) double. Off-season 612 F–826 F ($104.05–$140.40) double. Rates include American breakfast. AE, CB, DC, MC, V.

Built on 4 acres of sloping land close to the beach (a 5-minute walk on a path carved into the cliff side), Hôtel La Toubana is centered around a low-lying stone building on a rocky cliff overlooking the bay and Ste-Anne Beach. Many guests come here just for the view, which on a clear day encompasses Marie-Galante, Dominica, La Désirade, and the Iles des Saintes, but you'll quickly learn that there's far more to this charming place than just a panorama. The red-roofed bungalows lie scattered among the tropical shrubs along the adjacent hillsides (*toubana* means "small house" in Arawak). Each unit contains a kitchenette, comfortable beds fitted with fine French mattresses, and a rather compact bathroom.

Dining: Le Baobab, which was renovated and enlarged in 1995, offers both indoor and alfresco dining in a site overlooking the pool. It serves the best lobster on the island.

Amenities: Pool, tennis court. Deep-sea fishing and other water sports can be arranged. Laundry, baby-sitting.

6 St-François

Continuing east from Ste-Anne, you'll notice many old round towers named for Father Labat, the Dominican founder of the sugarcane industry. These towers were once used as mills to grind the cane. St-François, 25 miles east of Pointe-à-Pitre, used to be a sleepy fishing village, known for its native Creole restaurants. Then Air France discovered it and opened a Méridien hotel with a casino. That was followed by the promotional activities of J. F. Rozan, a native who invested heavily to make St-François a jet-set resort. Now the once sleepy village has first-class accommodations, as well as an airport available to private jets, a golf course, and a marina.

WHERE TO STAY

Hamak. 97118 St-François, Guadeloupe, F.W.I. ☎ **800/633-7411** in the U.S., or 0590/ 88-59-99. Fax 0590/88-41-92. www.caribbean-inn.com. E-mail: inns4carib@aol-com. 54 units. A/C MINIBAR TV TEL. Winter $345–$450 double. Off-season $250–$320 double. Rates include continental breakfast. AE, MC, V.

One of the most prestigious and stylish resorts in Guadeloupe, Hamak lies 25 miles east of Pointe-à-Pitre and a quarter of a mile from the Méridien. Its private, white-sand beach along a saltwater lagoon, as well as its proximity to golf and a tiny airport, once made it the most popular place on the island for jet-setters. Despite its sometimes illustrious clientele, it maintains a simple and unpretentious style of management, with few dress-code restrictions and a friendly approach to newcomers. Spread on a 250-acre estate, about half of which is devoted to the island's only golf course, are the villas, each housing two individual tropical suites opening onto a walled garden patio where you can sunbathe au naturel. The bungalows house two visitors comfortably, although some readers have found the rooms cramped and simple for the price. Units contain twins or king-size beds, each fitted with a firm mattress. Each compact bathroom has a shower stall, tile floors, and usually a hair dryer.

Dining: Hamak maintains a day bar and a night bar, plus a dining room that opens onto views of both the beach and the garden. Nonguests can dine here if they reserve in advance.

Amenities: The island's top golf course, the Robert Trent Jones, Sr.–designed Golf Municipale de St-François, is a short walk from the hotel. On site are tennis courts, facilities for windsurfing and other water sports, a fitness center, and a beauty salon. There's no pool, but few guests seem to mind with the private beach nearby. Room service, laundry, baby-sitting.

Hotel Anchorage. Domaine de l'Anse des Rochers, 97118 St-François, Guadeloupe, F.W.I. ☎ **0590/93-90-00.** Fax 0590/93-91-00. 356 units. A/C TV TEL. Year-round 570 F–975 F ($96.90–$165.75) double. MAP (breakfast and dinner) 155 F ($26.35) per person extra. AE, MC, V.

The largest hotel on Guadeloupe, opened in 1995, sprawls across 27 acres of sloping land in St-François. Accommodations are within either a half-dozen multileveled, hotel-style buildings, each of which contains 39 units, or 32 party-colored bungalows (four units per bungalow). Decor is airy, summery, and uncluttered. Bedrooms are fairly routine, most often small. Despite the size of the resort (it's quite a hike to the beach), guests still feel a sense of isolation and intimacy, thanks to the way the place is configured into smaller blocks. The focal point of everything is an enormous (almost 4,000 square feet of surface area) pool—one of the largest anywhere. Expect lots of young families with children, honeymooners, and large-scale, reduced-price European package-tour groups.

Dining/Diversions: Three restaurants include Titolo, a snack-style beachfront eatery; Le Blan Mangé, with an oft-replenished series of buffets; and the most formal of the three, La Villa Romaine. There's some form of entertainment, often a reggae or calypso band performing danceable music, every night, somewhere on the premises.

Amenities: Huge pool, areas landscaped for games of *pétanques,* two tennis courts, beachfront volleyball, archery, mini-mart for groceries and sundries. Car rental, limited concierge services.

✪ **La Plantation Ste-Marthe.** 97118 St-François, Guadeloupe, F.W.I. ☎ **800/223-5695** or 0590/93-11-11. Fax 0590/88-72-47. 120 units. A/C MINIBAR TV TEL. Winter 880 F–1,600 F ($149.60–$272) double; 2,000 F ($340) duplex suite for 2. Off-season 666 F ($113.20) double; 1,600 F ($272) duplex suite for 2. Rates include buffet breakfast. AE, MC, V.

Built on the site of a 19th-century sugar plantation in 1992, this is one of Guadeloupe's finest major hotels. Although the manor house that once stood on the premises is now in ruins, vestiges of the site's original function are still visible in the stables, the ruined rum distillery, and the molasses factory, whose crumbling walls still evoke a sense of the French colonial empire. All buildings that are associated with a vacation, however, are new, scattered amid the vegetation of a landscaped garden centered around a large pool. Beachgoers are shuttled to and from the nearby seacoast by minivan.

Accommodations are in a quartet of three-story structures, whose architecture was inspired by the Creole buildings of Louisiana. Each unit has lots of exposed wood and boldly patterned tiles, plus a large terrace or balcony that many visitors end up using as an extension of their living quarters. The duplex suites feature a sleeping loft designed in a style that may remind you of a big-city apartment, and the furnishings are modernized versions of antique French designs, utilizing lots of woven cane. Most units are spacious, with king-size beds and firm French mattresses, plus tiled bathrooms with hair dryers, bidets, shower stalls, and fluffy towels.

Dining/Diversions: The hotel's restaurant, La Vallée d'Or, is informal and unpretentious throughout the day, when it might remind you of a poolside snack bar that serves salads, sandwiches, and light grills. The evening brings a series of all-you-can-eat buffets. There are also two bars, one of which offers live music virtually every night.

Amenities: Two tennis courts, one of the largest pools on the island, health club, water sports. Concierge, baby-sitting, minivan transfers to and from the beach (La Plage du Lagon).

Le Méridien St-François. 97118 St-François, Guadeloupe, F.W.I. ☎ **800/543-4300** in the U.S., or 0590/88-51-00. Fax 0590/88-40-71. www.lemeridien-hotel.com. 265 units. A/C MINIBAR TV TEL. Winter 1,600 F–2,300 F ($272–$391) double; 3,200 F ($544) suite. Off-season 900 F–1,100 F ($153–$187) double; from 1,500 F–2,200 F ($255–$374) suite. Rates include continental breakfast. AE, DC, MC, V.

At five stories, this is one of the tallest buildings in the area. It stands alongside one of the best beaches on Guadeloupe on 150 acres of land at the southernmost tip of the island, a 10-minute walk from the village of St-François. The climate, quite dry here, is refreshed by trade winds. Rooms, renovated in the early 1990s, each overlook the sea or the Robert Trent Jones, Sr.–designed golf course. Each contains many amenities and modern-style furnishings with Creole overtones. Most of the medium-size bedrooms contain twin beds, each fitted with a quality mattress. Each unit has a small but tidily maintained bathroom with a shower stall and good-sized towels.

Dining: Guests dine at Balaou, a terraced restaurant with an evening buffet and an à la carte lunch. Other dining choices include the Casa Zomar, serving lunch only, the Bambou snack bar for sandwiches and salads, and the Lele bar.

Amenities: Pool, two tennis courts, Windsurfers, small airport for anyone wanting to charter flights to such neighboring islands as La Désirade, golf available for an extra charge at the course next door, nearby marina, access to additional water sports. Room service (breakfast only), massage, baby-sitting, laundry.

WHERE TO DINE

La Louisiane. Quartier Ste-Marthe, about 1½ miles east of St-François. ☎ **0590/88-44-34.** Main courses 88 F–150 F ($14.95–$25.50). MC, V. Tues–Sun noon–2pm and 6–10pm. Closed 2 weeks in Sept. FRENCH/CARIBBEAN.

The oldest building in the neighborhood, this century-old former plantation house is sheltered from the road by trees and shrubbery. The restaurant evokes the France of long ago, in an environment streaming with Caribbean sunlight and vegetation. Launch yourself into a fine repast with a duck pâté studded with pistachios and served with old rum jelly. The "crazy and rich salad" might attract your attention. (It's actually chicken with a shaving of foie gras, grapes, almond mousse, and quail egg.) Cream of pumpkin soup appears with savory spices and bits of smoked fish. For a main course, opt for grilled crayfish from the fish tank or scallops in onion compote with a spicy shellfish sauce. Among the meat selections, the roast lamb flavored with hazelnuts and garlic, pineapple, and tomato chutney is a sure-fire palate pleaser. Save room for one of the exotic sorbets made with fresh fruit.

Les Oiseaux. Anse des Rochers, about 3½ miles from St-François. ☎ **0590/88-56-92.** Reservations recommended. Main courses 80 F–180 F ($13.60–$30.60). MC, V. Sun noon–2:30pm, Mon–Sat 7–10pm. Closed Sept. FRENCH/ANTILLEAN.

The best evocation of a Provençal farmhouse on the island stands beside a seaside road, resting on a scrub-covered landscape whose focal point is the sea and the island of Marie-Galante. The walled-in front garden frames a stone-sided, low-slung building that emits an aroma of a southern French and Antillean cuisine worth the detour.

This is the domain of Arthur Rollé and his French-born wife, Claudette. Together they serve delectable dishes, each homemade, including Creole-style beef, a cassoulet of seafood, and the island's finest sea urchins. Try also the marmite Robinson, inspired by Robinson Crusoe, a tasty fondue of fish and vegetables that you cook for yourself in a combination of bubbling coconut and corn oil. Dessert might be a composite of four exotic sherbets or a crêpe.

7 Pointe des Châteaux

Seven miles east of St-François is the rocky headland of Pointe des Châteaux, the easternmost tip of Grand-Terre, where the Atlantic meets the Caribbean. Here, where crashing waves sound around you, you'll see a cliff sculpted by the sea into dramatic castle-like formations, the erosion typical of France's Brittany coast. The view from here is panoramic. At the top is a cross erected in the 19th century.

You might want to walk to **Pointe des Colibris,** the extreme end of Guadeloupe. From here you'll have a view of the northeastern sector of the island, and to the east a look at La Désirade, another island that has the appearance of a huge vessel anchored far away (see section 13, "Side Trips from Guadeloupe").

Pointe des Châteaux has miles of coved white-sand beaches. Most of these are safe for swimming, except at the point where the waves of the turbulent Atlantic encounter the tranquil Caribbean Sea, churning up the waters. There's a nudist enclave at **Pointe Tarare.**

WHERE TO DINE

Restaurant Les Châteaux. Pointe des Châteaux. ☎ **0590/88-43-53.** Fixed price menu 100 F–150 F ($17–$25.50). Tues–Sun noon–2pm; Sat 7:30–10pm. CREOLE.

Many visitors make this gazebo-style restaurant the final destination of a drive to the extreme eastern tip of Grande-Terre. Lunches are informal affairs, with at least some guests showing up in bathing suits. Dinner, served only Saturday night, is a bit more formal, but still permeated by a barefoot kind of charm that's heightened by the isolation you may feel on Guadeloupe's flat, sandy, scrub-covered eastern tip. For savory local fare, try squid in Creole sauce, a court bouillon of fish (a version that's been simmering on the stove all day), several preparations of lobster, or an unusual *salade de coffre* that's concocted from the tenderized and grilled flesh of a local fish (*le coffre*) whose armor is so tough that local fishers compare it to a crustacean.

A STOP IN LE MOULE

To go back to Pointe-à-Pitre from Pointe des Châteaux, you can use an alternative route, N5 from St-François. After a 9-mile drive, you'll reach the village of **Le Moule,** which was founded at the end of the 17th century and known long before Pointe-à-Pitre. It used to be a major shipping port for sugar. Now a tiny coastal fishing village, it never regained its importance after it was devastated in the hurricane of 1928, like so many other villages of Grand-Terre. Because of its more than 10 miles of crescent-shaped beach, it's developing as a holiday center; in recent years, modern hotels have opened to accommodate visitors.

Specialties of this Guadeloupean village are *palourdes,* the clams that thrive in the semi-salty mouths of freshwater rivers. Known for being more tender and less "rubbery" than saltwater clams, they often, even when fresh, have a distinct sulfur taste not unlike that of overpoached eggs. Local gastronomes prepare them with saffron and aged rum or cognac.

Nearby, the sea unearthed some skulls, grim reminders of the fierce battles fought among the Caribs, French, and English. It's called the "Beach of Skulls and Bones."

Three miles from Le Moule heading toward Campêche, the **Edgar Clerc Archaeological Museum La Rosette,** Parc de la Rosette (☎ **0590/23-57-57**), shows a collection of both Carib and Arawak artifacts gathered from various islands of the Lesser

Antilles. Hours are Thursday to Tuesday from 9am to 12:30pm and 2 to 5pm. Admission is 10 F ($1.70).

To return to Pointe-à-Pitre, we suggest that you use route D3 toward Abymes. The road winds around as you plunge deeply into Grand-Terre. As a curiosity, about halfway along the way a road will bring you to **Jabrun du Nord** and **Jabrun du Sud.** These two villages are inhabited by Caucasians with blond hair, said to be survivors of aristocrats slaughtered during the Revolution. Those members of their families who escaped found safety by hiding out in Les Grands Fonds. The most important family here is named Matignon, and they gave their name to the colony known as "les Blancs Matignon." These citizens are said to be related to Prince Rainier of Monaco. Pointe-à-Pitre lies only 10 miles from Les Grand Fonds.

8 A Drive Around the Northern Coast of Grande-Terre

From Pointe-à-Pitre, head northeast toward Abymes, passing next through Morne à l'Eau; you'll reach **Petit Canal** after 13 miles. This is Guadeloupe's sugarcane country, and a sweet smell fills the air.

PORT LOUIS

Continuing northwest along the coast from Petit Canal, you come to Port Louis, well known for its beautiful beach, **La Plage du Souffleur.** We like it best in spring, when the brilliant white sand is effectively shown off against a contrast of the flaming red poinciana. During the week, the beach is an especially quiet spot. The little port town has some good restaurants.

WHERE TO DINE

✪ **Le Poisson d'Or.** 2 rue Sadi-Carnot, Port Louis. ☎ **0590/22-88-63.** Reservations required. Main courses 65 F–85 F ($11.05–$14.45); fixed-menu 85 F–150 F ($14.45–$25.50). AE, MC, V. Daily 11:30am–4pm; dinner by reservation only. Drive northwest from Petit Canal along the coastal road. CREOLE.

You'll enter this white-sided Antillean house by walking down a narrow corridor and emerging into a rustic dining room lined with varnished pine. Despite the simple setting, the food is well prepared and satisfying. Don't even think of coming here at night without an advance reservation—you might find the place locked up and empty. The establishment's true virtue, however, is evident during the lunch hour, when, depending on the season, it's likely to shelter a mixture of local residents and tourists from the French mainland. Try the stuffed crabs or the court bouillon, topped off by coconut ice cream, which is homemade and tastes it. The place is a fine choice for an experience with Creole cookery, complemented by a bottle of good wine.

ANSE BERTRAND

About 5 miles from Port Louis is Anse Bertrand, the northernmost village of Guadeloupe. What is now a fishing village was the last refuge of the Carib tribes, and a reserve was once created here. Everything now, however, is sleepy.

WHERE TO DINE

✪ **Chez Prudence (Folie Plage).** Anse Laborde, Anse Bertrand. ☎ **0590/22-11-17.** Reservations not required for lunch, recommended for dinner. Main courses 70 F–153 F ($11.90–$26); fixed-price menu 100 F–180 F ($17–$30.60). AE. Daily noon–3pm and 7–10pm. CREOLE.

About a mile north of Anse Bertrand at Anse Laborde, this place is owned by Prudence Marcelin, a *cuisiniére patronne* who enjoys much local acclaim for her Creole cookery. She draws people from all over the island, especially on Sunday. Island children frolic in the saltwater pool, while in between courses, diners shop for crafts, clothes, and souvenirs sold by a handful of nearby vendors. Her court bouillon is excellent, as is the goat or chicken colombo (curried). The *palourdes* (clams) are superb, and she makes a zesty sauce to serve with fish. The place is relaxed and casual.

Chez Prudence also rents half a dozen very basic motel-style bungalows priced at 250 F ($42.50), single or double occupancy.

✪ **Le Château de Feuilles.** Campêche, Anse Bertrand. ☎ **0590/22-30-30.** Reservations required, especially in summer (when meals are prepared only in anticipation of your arrival). Main courses 115 F–165 F ($19.55–$28.05). V. Winter Tues–Sun 11:30am–4pm; at night, at least 10 diners must reserve before they will open. Closed June. FRENCH/CARIBBEAN.

Set inland from the sea, amid 8 rolling acres of greenery and blossoming flowers, this gastronomic hideaway is owned and run by a Norman-born couple, Jean-Pierre and Martine Dubost, whose main goal in moving to this outpost was to escape the detrimental effects of civilization. To reach their place, which is 9 miles from Le Moule, near the eastern tip of Grande-Terre, motorists must pass the ruins of La Mahaudière, an 18th-century sugar mill. A gifted chef making maximum use of local ingredients, Monsieur Dubost prepares pâté of warm sea urchins, sautéed conch with Creole sauce, a cassoulet of crayfish, and a traditional version of magret of duckling with fresh sugarcane. One unusual taste sensation is a *pavé of tazar* (a local fish) served with a fresh garlic sauce. We've had some of our finest meals on Guadeloupe at this restaurant.

CONTINUING AROUND THE NORTHERN TIP

From Anse Bertrand, you can drive along a gravel road heading for **Pointe de la Grande Vigie,** the northernmost tip of the island, which you'll reach after 4 miles of what we hope will be cautious driving. Park your car and walk carefully along a narrow lane that will bring you to the northernmost rock of Guadeloupe. The view of the sweeping Atlantic from the top of rocky cliffs is remarkable—you stand about 280 feet above the sea.

Afterward, a 4-mile drive south on a good road will bring you to the **Porte d'Enfer** or "gateway to hell," where the sea rushes violently against two narrow cliffs.

After this awesome experience in the remote part of the island, you can head back, going either to Morne à l'Eau or Le Moule before connecting to the road taking you back to Pointe-à-Pitre.

9 Around Basse-Terre

Leaving Pointe-à-Pitre by Route N1, you can explore the lesser windward coast. Here you'll find views as panoramic as those along the corniche along the French Riviera, but without the heavy traffic and crowds. After 1½ miles you cross the Rivière Salée at Pont de la Gabarre. This narrow strait separates the two islands that form Guadeloupe. For the next 4 miles the road runs straight through sugarcane fields.

At the sign, on a main crossing, turn right on Route N2 toward **Baie Mahault.** Don't confuse this with the town of Mahault, which is a different entity on Basse-Terre's westernmost coast. Leaving that town, head northwest to **Lamentin.** This village was settled by *corsairs* (pirates) at the beginning of the 18th century. Scattered about are some colonial mansions.

STE-ROSE

From Lamentin, you can drive for 6½ miles to Ste-Rose, where you'll find several good **beaches.** On your left, a small road leads to **Sofaia,** from which you'll have a panoramic view over the coast and forest preserve. The locals claim that a sulfur spring here has curative powers.

WHERE TO STAY

La Sucrerie du Comté. Comté de Loheac, 97115 Ste-Rose, Guadeloupe, F.W.I. ☎ **0590/28-60-17.** Fax 0590/28-65-63. 50 units. A/C. Winter 500 F ($85) double. Off-season 320 F ($54.40) double. Rates include breakfast. AE, MC, V.

Although you'll see the ruins of a 19th-century sugar factory (including a rusting loco-motive) on the 8 acres of forested land overlooking the sea, most of the resort is modern (it opened in 1991). The medium-size accommodations are in 26 pink-toned bungalows. Each cozy bungalow comes with chunky and rustic handmade furniture and a bay window overlooking either the sea or a garden. (Each bungalow contains two units, both with ceiling fans; none have TVs or phones.) The firm mattresses will put you to sleep; bathrooms are tiny but tidy. Scuba diving, snorkeling, and fishing can be arranged. There's a restaurant on site, open daily for lunch and dinner, and a bar set beneath a veranda-style roof near a pool. The nearest major beach is Grand Anse, a 10- to 15-minute drive from the hotel, but there's a small, unnamed beach within a 10-minute walk, although the swimming isn't very good.

WHERE TO DINE

✪ **Restaurant Clara.** Ste-Rose. ☎ **0590/28-72-99.** Reservations recommended. Main courses 45 F–120 F ($7.65–$20.40). MC, V. Mon–Tues and Thurs–Sat noon–2:30pm and 7–10pm, Sun noon–2:30pm. CREOLE.

On the waterfront near the center of town is the culinary statement of Clara Lesueur. Clara lived for 12 years in Paris as a member of an experimental jazz dance troupe, but she returned to Guadeloupe, her home, to set up this breeze-cooled restaurant, which she rebuilt in 1990 after hurricane damage. Try for a table on the open patio, where palm trees complement the color scheme.

Clara artfully melds the French style of fine dining with authentic Creole cookery. Specialties include *ouassous* (freshwater crayfish), brochette of swordfish, *palourdes* (small clams), several different preparations of conch, sea-urchin omelets, and *crabes farcis* (red-orange crabs with a spicy filling). The "sauce chien" that's served with many of the dishes is a blend of hot peppers, garlic, lime juice, and "secret things." The house drink is made with six local fruits and ample quantities of rum. Your dessert sherbet might be guava, soursop, or passion fruit.

DESHAIES/GRAND ANSE

A few miles farther along, you reach Pointe Allegre, the northernmost point of Basse-Terre. At **Clugny Beach,** you'll be at the site where the first settler landed on Guade-loupe.

A couple of miles farther will bring you to **Grand Anse,** one of the best beaches on Guadeloupe, which is very large and still secluded, sheltered by many tropical trees.

At **Deshaies,** snorkeling and fishing are popular pastimes. The narrow road winds up and down and has a corniche look to it, with the blue sea underneath, and the view of green mountains studded with colorful hamlets.

Nine miles from Deshaies, **Pointe Noire** comes into view, its name coming from black volcanic rocks. Look for the odd polychrome cenotaph in town.

WHERE TO STAY

Grand'Anse Hôtel. Grand Anse, 97114 Trois-Rivières, Guadeloupe, F.W.I. ☎ **0590/92-92-21.** Fax 0590/92-93-69. 16 bungalows. A/C TV TEL. Winter 400 F ($68) double. Off-season 300 F–400 F ($51–$68) double. Rates include breakfast. MC, V.

Built in the 1970s but renovated in 1996, this secluded hotel is removed from all the tourist hordes. Although it's near the ferryboat piers of the hamlet of Trois-Rivières, you'll appreciate the distance from the crowds and the unpretentious, polite staff. The hotel is made up of interconnected bungalows set in a garden with a view of the mountains and, in some cases, the sea. The small accommodations are mostly modern, with sliding-glass doors, vague hints of French colonial styling, and mahogany furniture. The bar and Creole restaurant are well recommended. The closest beach, Plage Grand'Anse (with black volcanic sand), is three-quarters of a mile away, but there's a rectangular swimming pool on site. The hotel's location near the ferryboat departures for the Iles des Saintes makes day trips there both convenient and easy.

Résidence de la Pointe Batterie. 97126 Pointe Batterie Deshaies, Guadeloupe, F.W.I. ☎ **800/322-2223** in the U.S., or 0590/28-57-03. Fax 0590/28-57-28. 24 units. A/C TV TEL. Winter 890 F ($151.30) one-bedroom villa without pool (for up to 4); 1,300 F ($221) one-bedroom villa with pool (for up to 4); 1,420 F ($241.40) two-bedroom villa with pool (for up to 6). Off-season 540 F ($91.80) one-bedroom villa without pool; 690 F ($117.30) one-bedroom villa with pool, 890 F ($151.30) two-bedroom villa with pool. MC V.

This is neither the most elegant nor the simplest villa compound on the island. Built in 1996 on steeply sloping land near the edge of both the rain forest and the sea, its all-wood villas each contain a veranda, an American-built kitchen, ceiling fans, good beds with firm mattresses, and summery furniture made from rattan, local hardwoods, and wicker. On the premises is a well-managed, indoor-outdoor restaurant, Les Canons de la Baie. The nearest beach, Grand Anse, is a 3-minute drive away. If you opt for this hotel, be warned that you'll face a lot of hiking between your villa and the sea, thanks to a rugged uphill-sloping terrain whose upper stretches afford very good views.

WHERE TO DINE

Chez Jacky. Anse Guyonneau, Pointe Noire. ☎ **0590/98-06-98.** Reservations recommended at dinner. Main courses 50 F–135 F ($8.50–$22.95); fixed-price menu 65 F–120 F ($11.05–$20.40). MC, V. Daily 9am–10pm. CREOLE.

Named after its owner, the grande dame Creole matriarch Jacqueline Cabrion, this establishment has gained a loyal following since it first appeared on the restaurant scene in 1981. In a French-colonial house about 30 feet from the sea, it features lots of exposed wood, verdant plants, tropical furniture, and a bar that sometimes does a respectable business in its own right. Menu items include colombo of conch, fricassée of conch, or freshwater crayfish, several preparations of grilled fish, lobster, ragoût of lamb, and a dessert specialty of bananas flambé. Lighter fare includes a limited choice of sandwiches and salads, which tend to be offered only during daylight hours.

Les Gommiers. Rue Baudot, Pointe Noire. ☎ **0590/98-01-79.** Main courses 70 F–150 F ($11.90–$25.50). AE, MC, V. Daily 11:30am–3pm; Tues–Sat 7–10pm. CREOLE.

Named after the large rubber trees (*les gommiers*) that grow nearby, this popular Creole restaurant serves up well-flavored platters in a dining room lined with plants. You can order such Creole staples as *accras de morue* (codfish), *boudin Creole* (blood pudding), fricassée of freshwater crayfish, seafood paella, and a custardlike dessert known as *flan coucou*. Dishes inspired by mainland France include fillet of beef with Roquefort sauce and veal scallops.

Le Karacoli. Grand Anse (1¼ miles north of Deshaies). ☎ **0590/28-41-17.** Reservations recommended. Main courses 80 F–150 F ($13.60–$25.50). MC, V. Daily noon–2pm; Fri–Sat 5–9:30pm. CREOLE.

It's the best-signposted restaurant in town, with at least three large signs indicating its position at the edge of the region's most famous beach. The setting is as airy and tropical as you'd expect, with streaming sunlight, tables set outdoors in a garden, and a bar area that's sheltered from storms. No one will mind if you drop in just for a drink, but if you want lunch, consider ordering any of such dishes as a boudin Creole (blood pudding), stuffed crab backs, scallops prepared "in the style of the chef," court bouillon of fish, a fricassée of octopus, and fried chicken. Sunday is usually more popular than most other days.

PARC NATUREL DE GUADELOUPE: A TROPICAL FOREST

Four miles from Pointe Noire, you reach **Mahaut.** On your left begins the ✪ **Route de la Traversée,** the Transcoastal Highway. This is the best way to explore the scenic wonders of **Parc Naturel de Guadeloupe,** passing through a tropical forest as you travel between the capital, Basse-Terre, and Pointe-à-Pitre.

To preserve the Parc Naturel, Guadeloupe has set aside 74,100 acres, about one-fifth of its entire terrain. Easily accessible via modern roads, this is a huge tract of mountains, tropical forests, and panoramic scenery, and one of the largest and most spectacular parks in the Caribbean.

The park is home to a variety of tame animals, including *titi* (a raccoon adopted as its official mascot) and such birds as the wood pigeon, turtledove, and thrush. Small exhibition huts, devoted to the volcano, the forest, or to coffee, sugarcane, and rum, are scattered throughout the park. The Parc Naturel has no gates, no opening or closing hours, and no admission fee.

You can hike for only 15 minutes or stretch out the adventure to all day, as there are 180 miles of trails here, taking in rain forests and the wooded slopes of the 4,813-foot-high Soufrière volcano, passing by hot springs, rugged gorges, and rushing streams (see also "Hiking" under "Sports & Outdoor Pursuits," below).

From Mahaut, you climb slowly in a setting of giant ferns and luxuriant vegetation. Four miles after the fork, you reach **Les Deux Mamelles (The Two Breasts),** where you can park your car and go for a hike. Some of the trails are for experts only; others, such as the **Pigeon Trail,** will bring you to a summit of about 2,600 feet, where the view is impressive. Expect to spend at least 3 hours going each way. Halfway along the trail, you can stop at **Forest House;** from that point, many lanes, all signposted, branch off on trails that will take anywhere from 20 minutes to 2 hours. Try to find the **Chute de l'Ecrevisse,** the "Crayfish Waterfall," a little pond of very cold water at the end of a quarter-mile path.

After the hike, the main road descends toward **Versailles,** a hamlet about 5 miles from Pointe-à-Pitre. However, before taking this route, while still traveling between Pointe Noire and Mahaut on the west coast, you might consider the following lunch stop.

WHERE TO DINE

Chez Vaneau. Mahaut/Pointe Noire. ☎ **0590/98-01-71.** Main courses 50 F–150 F ($8.50–$25.50). AE, MC, V. Daily noon–4pm and 7–10:30pm. CREOLE.

Set in an isolated pocket of forest about 18 miles north of Pointe Noire, far from any of its neighbors, Chez Vaneau offers a wide, breeze-filled veranda overlooking a gully, the sight of neighbors playing cards, and steaming Creole specialties coming from the kitchen. This is the well-established domain of Vaneau Desbonnes, who is assisted by his wife, Marie-Gracieuse, and their children. Specialties include oysters with a piquant sauce, crayfish bisque, ragoût of goat, fricassée of conch, different preparations of octopus, and roast pork. In 1995, they installed a saltwater tank to store lobsters, which are now featured heavily on their menu.

BOUILLANTE

If you don't take the route de la Traversée at this time but wish to continue exploring the west coast, you can head south from Mahaut until you reach the village of Bouillante, which is exciting for only one reason: You might encounter the former French film star and part-time resident, Brigitte Bardot.

Try not to miss seeing the small island called **Ilet à Goyave** or **Ilet du Pigeon.** Jacques Cousteau often explored the silent depths around it.

After a meal, you can explore the area around the village of Bouillante, the country known for its **thermal springs.** If you scratch the ground for only a few inches in some places, you'll feel the heat.

WHERE TO DINE

✪ **Chez Loulouse.** Malendure Plage. ☎ **0590/98-70-34.** Reservations required for dinner. Main courses 50 F–200 F ($8.50–$34). Fixed-price menu 80 F ($13.60). AE, MC, V. Daily noon–3:30pm and 7–10pm. CREOLE.

A good choice for lunch, this staunchly matriarchal establishment, with plenty of offhanded charm, stands beside the sands of the well-known beach, opposite Pigeon Island. Many guests prefer their rum punches on the panoramic veranda, overlooking a scene of loaded boats preparing to depart and merchants hawking their wares. A quieter oasis is the equally colorful dining room inside, just past the bar. Here, beneath a ceiling of palm fronds, is a wraparound series of Creole murals that go well with the reggae music emanating loudly from the bar.

This is the creation of one of the most visible and charming Creole matrons on this end of the island, Mme Loulouse Paisley-Carbon. Assisted by her children, she offers house-style Caribbean lobster, spicy versions of conch, octopus, accras (codfish), gratin of christophine (squash), and savory colombos (curries) of chicken or pork.

Le Rocher de Malendure. Malendure Plage, Pointe Batterie, Bouillante. ☎ **0590/98-70-84.** Reservations recommended. Main courses 78 F–350 F ($13.25–$59.50). MC, V. Daily 11am–2pm; Mon–Sat 7–10pm. FRENCH/CREOLE.

This restaurant's position, on a rocky peninsula 30 feet above the rich offshore reefs near Pigeon Island, allows for panoramic views over the land and seascape. Each table is sheltered from direct sunlight (and rain) by a shed-style roof, which also affords a greater sense of privacy. Much of the cuisine served here is seafood caught in offshore waters. Examples include grilled red snapper, fondues of fish, marinated marlin steaks, and different preparations of lobster and conch. Meat dishes include veal in raspberry vinaigrette and fillet of beef with any of three different sauces.

Although most of the energy here is devoted to the food, the restaurant also maintains 11 bungalows, which cost 350 F ($59.50) per night, single or double occupancy. Each small unit has a sea view, a tiny bathroom, and a simple kitchenette, where many visitors cook most of their meals.

BASSE-TERRE

The winding coast road brings you to **Vieux Habitants** (Old Settlers), one of the oldest villages on the island, founded in 1636. The name comes from the people who settled it: After serving in the employment of the West Indies Company, they retired here, but they preferred to call themselves inhabitants, so as not to be confused with slaves.

Another 10 miles of winding roads bring you to **Basse-Terre,** the capital of Guadeloupe. This sleepy town of some 14,000 inhabitants lies between the water and La Soufrière, the volcano. Founded in the 1640s, it's the oldest town on the island and still has a lot of charm; its market squares are shaded by tamarind and palm trees.

The town suffered heavy destruction at the hands of British troops in 1691 and again in 1702. It was also the center of fierce fighting during the French Revolution, when the political changes that swept across Europe caused explosive tensions on Guadeloupe. As it did in France, the guillotine claimed many lives on the island during the infamous Reign of Terror.

In spite of the town's history, there isn't much to see in Basse-Terre except for a 17th-century **cathedral** and **Fort St-Charles,** which has guarded the city (not always well) since it was established. On the narrow streets, you can still see old clapboard buildings, upper floors of shingle-wood tiles, and wrought-iron balconies. For the most interesting views, seek out the **place du Champ d'Arbaud** and the **Jardin Pichon.** At the harbor on the southern tier of town, you can see **Fort Delgrès,** which once protected the island from the English. There are acres of ramparts to be walked with panoramic vistas in all directions.

Originally selected as Guadeloupe's capital because of its prevailing breezes and its altitudes above the steaming lowlands of Pointe-à-Pitre, Basse-Terre is today a city that's curiously removed from other parts of the French Antilles that it governs, and, when the business of the day is concluded, it's an almost bizarrely calm and quiet town. The neighboring municipality of **St-Claude,** in the cool heights above the capital, was always where the island's oldest families proudly maintained their ancestral homes, and where they continue to live today. These families, direct descendants of the white, slave-owning former plantation owners who originally hailed from such major French Atlantic ports as Bordeaux and Nantes, tend to live quietly, discreetly, and separately from both the island's blacks and the French *métropolitains* whose tourist ventures have helped change the face of Guadeloupe.

WHERE TO STAY

Hotel St-Georges. Rue Gratien, Parize, 97120 St-Claude, Guadeloupe, F.W.I. ☎ **0590/ 80-10-10.** Fax 0590/80-30-50. www.pro-wanadoo.fr/hotel.st.georges. E-mail: hotel-st-georges@wanadoo.fr. 40 units. A/C TV TEL. Year-round 660 F–690 F ($112.20–$117.30) double; 890 F ($151.30) suite. MAP (breakfast and dinner) 120 F ($20.40) per person extra. AE, DC, MC, V.

In 1996, the civic authorities of Basse-Terre alleviated a sorry lack of accommodations within the town by financing the construction of this tastefully modern inn, set on a hill with sweeping views over the town and the sea. A series of three-story buildings is centered around a large swimming pool. The medium-size bedrooms are outfitted, Creole style, with dark-grained and rattan furniture, beige-and-salmon-colored floor tiles, and small bathrooms trimmed with touches of marble. Overall, this place has the feel of a business-related hotel, since many rooms are occupied by dignitaries visiting Guadeloupe from the French mainland and other islands of the Caribbean. Expect lots of amiable goodwill from the 20 or 30 students registered at the hotel training school that's associated with this establishment, as part of their diplomas depend on the hands-on training received on the premises.

The on-site restaurant, Lamasure (the name of the surrounding region), is open daily for lunch and dinner, charging from 175 F to 215 F ($29.75 to $36.55) for fixed-price menus, and from 85 F to 180 F ($14.45 to $30.60) for main courses. Dishes are French-derived but concocted from Caribbean ingredients, and include *Roi des Sources* (*ouassous,* or freshwater crayfish, served with yellow bananas), a confit of duckling with caramelized Caribbean spices, and a fricassee of spiny lobster with pink peppercorns and ginger.

WHERE TO DINE

Restaurant Lamasure, at the Hotel St-Georges (see above), also serves good food.

✪ **L'Orangerie.** Lieu-dit Desmarais, Basse-Terre. ☎ **0590/81-01-01.** Reservations recommended. Main courses 109 F–145 F ($18.55–$24.65); set-price lunch 130 F ($22.10). Sun–Fri noon–2:30pm; Thurs–Sat 7–10pm. MC, V. CREOLE.

L'Orangerie reigns as the finest restaurant in Basse-Terre, and as such, it's always filled with representatives from the city's many legal offices, government agencies, hospitals, and cultural organizations. It occupies what was originally built in 1823 as the home of a slave-owning French aristocrat, and it's known as one of the most beautiful colonial buildings in Basse-Terre, with its sweeping verandas, masonry walls, and wide-plank floors. Award-winning French chef Christophe Moreau prepares upscale and modern interpretations of old-timey Creole recipes. Examples include a *gâteau* of octopus and smoked chicken, served with rondelles of leeks marinated in starfruit-enhanced vinaigrette; a moussaka of conch served with a reduction of tomatoes, lentils, and smoked fish; and a fillet of beef roasted with black Jamaican pepper and flambéed with aged rum. Tables fill both the Creole-inspired interior and the verandas; most have views of a sprawling French-Caribbean garden loaded with tropical fruit trees.

AROUND LA SOUFRIÈRE

The big attraction of Basse-Terre is the famous sulfur-puffing **La Soufrière** volcano, which is still alive, but dormant—for the moment at least. Rising to a height of some 4,800 feet, it's flanked by banana plantations and lush foliage.

After leaving the capital at Basse-Terre, you can drive to **St-Claude,** a suburb, 4 miles up the mountainside at a height of 1,900 feet. It has a reputation for its perfect climate and tropical gardens.

Another option, instead of going to St-Claude, is to head for idyllic **Matouba,** in a country of clear mountain-spring water. The only sounds you're likely to hear are birds and the running water of dozens of springs. The village was settled long ago by Hindus.

From St-Claude, you can begin the climb up the narrow, winding road the Guadeloupeans say leads to hell—that is, **La Soufrière.** The road ends at a parking area at La Savane à Mulets, at an altitude of 3,300 feet. This is the ultimate point to be reached by car. Hikers are able to climb right to the mouth of the volcano. However, in 1975, the appearance of ashes, mud, billowing smoke, and earthquakelike tremors proved that the old beast was still alive.

In the resettlement process that followed the eruption, 75,000 inhabitants were relocated to safer terrain in Grande-Terre. No deaths were reported, but the inhabitants of Basse-Terre still keep a watchful eye on the smoking giant.

Even in the parking lot, you can feel the heat of the volcano merely by touching the ground. Steam emerges from fumaroles and sulfurous fumes from the volcano's "burps." Of course, fumes come from its pit and mud cauldrons as well.

WHERE TO DINE

Chez Paul de Matouba. Rivière Rouge. ☎ **0590/80-01-77.** Main courses 55 F–150 F ($9.35–$25.50); fixed-price menu 100 F ($17). No credit cards. Daily noon–3pm. Follow the clearly marked signs—it's beside a gully close to the center of the village. CREOLE/ INTERNATIONAL.

You'll find good food in this family-run restaurant, which sits beside the banks of the small Rivière Rouge (Red River). The dining room on the second floor is enclosed by windows, allowing you to drink in the surrounding dark-green foliage of the mountains. The cookery is Creole, with a specialty of crayfish dishes. However, because of the influence of the region's early settlers, East Indian meals are also available. By all means, drink the mineral or spring water of Matouba. What one diner called "an honest meal" might include stuffed crab, colombo (curried) of chicken, and an array of French, Creole, and Hindu specialties. You're likely to find the place overcrowded in winter with the tour-bus crowd.

THE WINDWARD COAST

From Basse-Terre to Pointe-à-Pitre, the road follows the east coast, called the Windward Coast. The country here is richer and greener than elsewhere on the island.

To reach **Trois Rivières** you have a choice of two routes: One goes along the coastline, coming eventually to Vieux Fort, from which you can see Les Saintes archipelago. The other heads across the hills, Monts Caraïbes.

Near the pier in Trois Rivières you'll see the pre-Columbian petroglyphs carved by the original inhabitants, the Arawaks. They're called merely **Roches Gravées,** or "carved rocks." In this archaeological park, the rock engravings are of animal and human figures, dating most likely from A.D. 300 or 400. You'll also see specimens of plants, including cocoa, pimento, and banana, that the Arawaks cultivated long before the Europeans set foot on Guadeloupe. From Trois Rivières, you can take boats to Les Saintes.

After leaving Trois Rivières, continue on Route 1. Passing through the village of Bananier, you turn on your left at Anse Saint-Sauveur to reach the famous **Chutes du Carbet,** a trio of waterfalls. The road to two of them is a narrow, winding one, along many steep hills, passing through banana plantations as you move deeper into a tropical forest.

After 3 miles, a lane, suitable only for hikers, brings you to **Zombie Pool.** If you drive a half mile farther, a fork to the left takes you to **Grand Etang,** or large pool. At a point 6 miles from the main road, there's a parking area, but you'll have to walk the rest of the way on an uneasy trail toward the second fall, **Le Carbet.** Expect to spend around 20 to 30 minutes walking, depending on how slippery the lane is. You'll then be at the foot of this second fall, where the water drops from 230 feet. The waters here average 70°F, which is pretty warm for a mountain spring.

The first fall is the most impressive, but it takes 2 hours of rough hiking to get to it. The third fall is reached from **Capesterre** on the main road by climbing to **Routhiers.** This fall is less impressive in height, only 70 feet. When the Carbet water runs out of La Soufrière, it's almost boiling.

After Capesterre, a 4½-mile drive brings you to **Ste-Marie;** in the town square, you can see the statue of the first visitor who landed on Guadeloupe. That visitor was Christopher Columbus, who anchored a quarter of a mile from Ste-Marie on November 4, 1493. In the journal of his second voyage, he wrote: "We arrived, seeing ahead of us a large mountain which seemed to want to rise up to the sky, in the middle of which was a peak higher than all the rest of the mountains from which flowed a living stream."

However, when the Caribs started shooting arrows at him, he left quickly.

After Ste-Marie, you pass through Goyave, then Petit-Bourg, seeing on your left the route de la Traversée before reaching Pointe-à-Pitre. You'll have just completed the most fascinating scenic tour Guadeloupe has to offer.

10 Beaches

Chances are, your hotel will be right on a beach, or no more than 20 minutes from a good one. Plenty of natural beaches dot the island, from the surf-brushed dark strands of western Basse-Terre to the long stretches of white sand encircling Grande-Terre. Public beaches are generally free, but some charge for parking. Unlike hotel beaches, they have few facilities. Hotels welcome nonguests, but charge for changing facilities, beach chairs, and towels.

Sunday is family day at the beach. Topless sunbathing is common at hotels, less so on village beaches.

Most of the best beaches lie between Gosier and St-François on Grande Terre. Visitors usually head for the hotel beaches at **Gosier.** Stone jetties were constructed here to protect the beaches from erosion. Since this area has the largest concentration of tourists, it's likely to be crowded.

These beaches are not peas-in-a-pod; each one is different. There's no shade at the **Creole Beach** fronting Creole Beach Hotel, although you can retreat to the bar there for a drink. The sands on this beach appear mainly on a stone jetty. A stone retaining wall blocks access to the water. Nearby, the **Salako Beach** has more sand and is set against a backdrop of palms that offer some shade. Part of this beach also leads up to a jetty. This is a fine sandy beach, although a little too crowded at times, and it also contains a snack bar.

Also nearby, **Arawak Beach** is that cliché of a tropical beach with plenty of palm trees, beige sand, and shade. Like the others, it too is protected by jetties. Close at hand, **Callinago Beach** is smaller than Arawak's but is still sought out for its pleasant crescent of beige sand and palms. **Ilet du Gosier** is a little speck of land lying off the shore of Gosier. It attracts mainly French tourists, who sunbathe and swim in the buff.

Le Bas du Fort, 2 miles east of Pointe-à-Pitre and close to Gosier, is another much-frequented area. Its beaches, also protected by jetties, are shared by guests at the Hotels Fleu d'Epee and Marissol. This is a picture-postcard tropical beach with tranquil waters, plenty of sand, and palms for shade. There are hotel bars as well as snack bars, and vendors, too—some of whom are rather aggressive.

Some of Grande-Terre's best beaches are in the **Ste-Anne** area, site of a Club Med. **Plage Caravelle** is heaped with white sand, attracting crowds of sunbathers; snorkelers, too, are drawn to the beach's reef-protected waters.

The French tourists here often like to go nude, and there is no finer nude beach than **Pointe Tarare,** a 45-minute drive from Gosier. This beach lies east of St-François at Pointe des Chateaux. It's one of the island's most pristine, tranquil beaches, but there's no shade to protect you from the fierce noonday sun. You can snorkel here if the water's not too turbulent. There's a good restaurant by the car park. *Warning:* The tourist office doesn't recommend that women come here unaccompanied.

If you're not a nudist, you can enjoy the lovely strip of white sand at **Anse de la Gourde,** lying between St-François and Pointe des Chateaux. It has good sand, but tends to become crowded on weekends.

The eastern coast of Grande-Terre is less desirable for swimming, as it fronts the more turbulent Atlantic. Nonetheless, the sands at **Le Moule** make for an idyllic beach because a reef protects the shoreline. There are also beach bars here—and the inevitable crowds, especially on weekends. You'll find a more secluded strip of sand north of here at **La Porte d'Enfer.**

There are two other excellent beaches on the northwestern coast—one at **Anse Laborde** just outside the hamlet of Anse-Bertrand, the other called **Anse du Souffleur** at Port-Louis. We especially like the beach at Souffleur for its brilliant flamboyant trees that bloom in the summer. There are no facilities here, but you can pick up provisions in the shops in the little village, then enjoy a picnic on the beach.

In Basse-Terre, a highly desirable beach is **La Grande-Anse,** just outside Deshaies, reached by heading west from Sainte Rose along N2. You won't find any facilities here, but we think you'll enjoy the powdery sands, tranquil waters, and palm trees. Another desirable beach is **Plage de la Malendure,** on the west coast (the more tranquil side) of Basse-Terre across from Pigeon Island. This is a major center for scuba diving, but the sand tends to be dark here.

If you want to escape the crowds, seek out the spurs and shoulders produced by the mountains of Basse-Terre. In the northwest is a string of fine sandy beaches. Although small, these are highly desirable enclaves for sunbathing and swimming. Favorites include **La Plage de Cluny** (near Pointe Allegre), **Plage de la Tillette,** and **Plage de la Perle.**

South of Pointe Noire, also on the west coast, is **Plage de La Caraïbe,** with its calm waters and sandy strip. This beach has picnic facilities, a shower, and toilets.

Warning: The beaches on the north coast of Basse-Terre are exceedingly dangerous for swimming. **Plage de Clugny** is especially treacherous, and there have been several deaths by drowning.

Other good beaches are found on the offshore islands, **Iles des Saintes** and **Marie-Galante** (see below).

11 Sports & Outdoor Pursuits

DEEP-SEA FISHING   Whereas blue marlin, wahoo (known locally as *thazar*), and yellowfin tuna can be bagged throughout the year, the season for such fish as dorado is limited to December through March. Hotels can recommend outfitters, who may or may not be moored at bases nearby; one of the most universally well-recommended is **Franck Mouÿ** (☎ **0590/55-49-33**), whose 33-foot Bertram is moored at Le Rocher de Malendure, Bouillante, on Basse-Terre, a 50-minute drive from the hotel complex at Gosier. Brittany-born Mouÿ will assemble up to eight fishers per trip, providing all the necessary equipment. A half-day excursion costs 800 F ($136) per person; a full-day excursion costs 1,100 F ($187) per person.

GOLF   Guadeloupe's only public golf course is the well-known ✪ **Golf de St-François** (☎ **0590/88-41-87**), opposite the Hôtel Méridien. The course runs alongside an 800-acre lagoon where windsurfing, waterskiing, and sailing prevail. Designed by Robert Trent Jones, Sr., it's a challenging 6,755-yard, par-71 course, with water traps on six of the 18 holes, not to mention massive bunkers, prevailing trade winds, and a particularly fiendish 400-yard, par-4 ninth hole. The par-5 sixth is the toughest hole on the course; its 450 yards must be negotiated in the constant easterly winds. Greens fees are 250 F ($42.50) per day per person, which allows a full day of playing time. You can rent clubs for 100 F ($17) a day; a cart costs 220 F ($37.40) for 18 holes. Hours are daily from 7:30am to 6:30pm.

HIKING   The 74,100-acre **Parc Naturel de Guadeloupe** is riddled with marked trails, making it the best hiking grounds in the Caribbean (see the touring notes on Route de la Traversée in section 9, "Around Basse-Terre," above). The 180 miles of trails cut through the deep foliage of rain forest, passing waterfalls and cool mountain pools, hot springs, and rugged gorges along the way. The big excursion country, of course, is around the volcano, La Soufrière. Another highlight is Chutes du Carbet, one of the tallest waterfalls in the Caribbean, with a drop of 800 feet.

Hiking brochures are available from the tourist office. Hotel tour desks can make arrangements. For information about this and other hikes in the national park, contact **Organisation des Guides de Montagne de la Caraïbe,** Maison Forestière, Matouba (☎ **0590/94-29-11**).

Warning: Hikers may experience heavy downpours. The annual precipitation on the higher slopes is 250 inches per year, so be prepared.

SAILING   Sailboats of varying sizes, crewed or bareboat, are plentiful. Information can be secured at any hotel desk. Sunfish sailing can be arranged at almost every beachfront hotel.

SCUBA DIVING   Scuba divers are drawn more to the waters off Guadeloupe than to any other point in the French-speaking islands. The allure is the relatively calm seas and **La Réserve Cousteau,** a kind of French national park with many intriguing dive sites, where the underwater environment is rigidly protected. Jacques Cousteau once described the waters off Guadeloupe's Pigeon Island as "one of the world's 10 best diving spots." During a typical dive, sergeant majors become visible at a depth of 30 feet, spiny sea urchins and green parrot fish at 60 feet, and magnificent stands of finger, black, brain, and star coral at 80 feet. Despite the destruction of some branch coral in a 1995 hurricane, the reserve is still one of the most desirable underwater sites in the French-speaking world.

The most popular dive sites include Aquarium, Piscine, Jardin de Corail, Pointe Carrangue, Pointe Barracuda, and Jardin Japonais. Although scattered around the periphery of the island, many are in the bay of Petit Cul-de-Sac Marin, south of Rivière Salée, the channel that separates the two halves of Guadeloupe. North of the Salée is another bay, Grand Cul-de-Sac Marin, where the small islets of Fajou and Caret also boast fine diving.

Reacting to the rich diversity of underwater flora and fauna, which thrive at relatively shallow, and relatively safe, depths, several entrepreneurs have set up shop as a means of exposing divers of all degrees of expertise to the glories of the underwater ecology. One of these is **Les Heures Saines,** Rocher de Malendure, Pigeon-Malendure (☎ **0590/98-86-63**), whose trio of dive boats departs three times a day for explorations of the waters within the reserve. With all equipment included, dives cost 250 F ($42.50) each. Novices, at least for the very first time they engage in the sport, pay 280 F ($47.60) for what is referred to as a *baptême* (baptism). Les Heures Saines maintains its own 11-room hotel, **Le Paradis Creole** (☎ **0590/98-71-62**), where simple, motel-style accommodations rent for between 400 F and 600 F ($68 and $102), with breakfast included. Rooms, which are occupied almost exclusively by avid divers on holiday from the French mainland, are air-conditioned, but contain few other amenities.

This outfit's slightly larger competitor, located a short distance away, is **Centre International de la Plongée (C.I.P.),** B.P. 4, Lieu-Dit Poirier, Malendure Plage, Pigeon, Bouillante (☎ **0590/98-81-72**). It's acknowledged as the most professional dive operation on the island. In a wood-sided house on Malendure Plage, close to a well-known restaurant, Chez Loulouse, it's well-positioned at the edge of the Cousteau Underwater Reserve. Certified divers pay 220 F ($37.40) for a one-tank dive. What the Americans usually refer to as a "resort course" for first-time divers (the French refer to it as a *baptême*) costs 280 F ($47.60) and is conducted one-on-one with an instructor. Packages of six or 12 dives are offered for 1,100 F and 2,000 F ($187 and $340), respectively.

A miniresort, **Le Jardin Tropical** (☎ **0590/98-77-23**), patronized almost exclusively by dive enthusiasts from France, lies adjacent to this school. Here, 16 rooms—each with air-conditioning and phone—rent for 556 F ($94.50) per person, including breakfast, dinner, and two dives, with lots of price breaks for divers who purchase accommodations as part of a hotel-dive package.

TENNIS   All the large resort hotels have tennis courts, many lit at night. (The noonday sun is often too hot for most players.) If you're a guest, tennis is free at most of these hotels, but you'll be charged for night play. If your hotel doesn't have a tennis court of its own, consider an outing to the public court at **St-François Plage,** in St-François, a durable but somewhat weathered facility that is often unused despite the fact that access is free to whoever happens to show up. For information, contact **La Mairie** (Town Hall) of St-François (☎ **0590/88-71-37**).

WATERSKIING & WINDSURFING   Each of the large-scale hotels on Guadeloupe provides facilities and instructions for both sports, but if you prefer to strike out on your own, or if your hotel doesn't provide it, head for **Surfing Club,** Plage de St-François, St-François (☎ **0590/88-72-04**). A 30-minute windsurfing lesson goes for around 120 F ($20.40) per hour, and rentals, depending on the size and make of the board you rent, average 150 F ($25.50) per hour.

If you want in-depth exposure to windsurfing, or perhaps a weeklong deep immersion in the sport, head for **UCPA** (*Union National des Centres Sportifs de Plein-Air*), St-François (☎ **0590/88-64-80**). Sojourns and use of the facilities at this 60-room resort are available only by the week, where rates include all meals and sports. A week's sojourn, double occupancy, costs 2,830 F ($481.10) per person, and includes a focus on windsurfing, surfing and surfboard-riding, golf, and physical fitness.

12 Guadeloupe After Dark

Guadeloupeans claim that the *beguine* was invented here, not on Martinique, and they dance it as if it truly were their own. Of course, calypso and the merengue move rhythmically along as well—the islanders are known for their dancing.

Ask at your hotel for details on the folkloric **Ballets Guadeloupeans** performances. This troupe makes frequent appearances at the big resorts, although they don't enjoy the fame of the **Ballets Martiniquais,** the troupe on Guadeloupe's neighbor island.

An important casino, one of only two on the island, **Casino Gosier-les-Bains,** 43 Pointe de la Verdure, Gosier, is in the resort community (☎ **0590/84-79-68**). Although dress tends to be casually elegant, coat and tie for men are not required. The bulk of the establishment is open nightly from 7:30pm to 3am (until 4am on Friday and Saturday), although an area containing only slot machines is open daily from 10am to 3 or 4am, depending on the night of the week. There's no cover, and no ID requested, for admission to the area with the slot machines, but entrance to the gaming tables and roulette wheels costs 69 F ($11.75), and requires the presentation of a photo ID or passport.

A smaller casino, with fewer slot machines, is **Casino de la Marina,** avenue de l'Europe (☎ **0590/88-41-31**), near the Hotel Méridien in St-François. Slot machines begin whirring every day at noon, continuing until 2am from Sunday to Thursday, and until 3am on Friday and Saturday. The more interesting main core of the casino, containing tables devoted to blackjack, roulette, and chemin-de-fer, doesn't open until 8pm. Entrance costs 69 F ($11.75). Dress codes are the same as those at the casino at Gosier-les-Bains, and both casinos contain bars.

If you don't like casino action, you'll find other nighttime diversions in Guadeloupe, although these tend to be seasonal, with more offerings in the winter. **Lele Bar,** at Le Méridien in St-François (☎ **0590/88-51-00**), is the most active on the island, attracting Guadeloupeans along with visitors. **Le Figuier Vert,** Mare Gallaird in Gosier (☎ **0590/85-85-51**), presents live jazz on most Friday and Saturday nights. At the marina, **Le Jardin Bresilien,** Bas-du-Fort (☎ **0590/90-99-31**), is known for its live music. The island's dance clubs charge a uniform cover of 48 F ($8.15), unless some special entertainment is being presented.

If you'd like to dance the night away, head for **New Land,** route Riviera (☎ **0590/84-34-91**); **Caraïbes 2,** Carrefour de Blanchard, Bas-du-Fort (☎ **0590/ 90-97-16**); or **Le Plantation,** Gourbeyre (☎ **0590/81-23-37**), the latter on Basse-Terre.

If you want to escape all the tourist joints and find some real local color, make it ✪ **Les Tortues,** off the N2 near Bouillante, signposted near the main road on Basse-Terre's western coast (☎ **0590/98-82-83**). This bar is a local hangout, often filled with scuba divers downing Corsaire beer and telling tall tales of the deep. The bartender's specialty is *ti punch,* made with the strongest rum on the island, cut with lime and cane syrup. You can also dine here on good food, especially the catch of the day (marlin, kingfish, ray, snapper, or Caribbean lobster). Les Tortues is closed all day Sunday and on Monday night.

13 Side Trips from Guadeloupe

THE ILES DES SAINTES

A cluster of eight islands off the southern coast of Guadeloupe, the Iles des Saintes are certainly off the beaten track. The two main islands and six rocks are Terre-de-Haut, Terre-de-Bas, Ilet-à-Cabrit, La Coche, Les Augustins, Grand Ilet, Le Redonde, and Le Pâté; only Terre-de-Haut ("land of high") and, to a lesser extent, Terre-de-Bas ("land below") attract visitors.

If you're planning a visit, **Terre-de-Haut** is the most interesting Saint to call upon. It's the only one with facilities for overnight guests.

Some claim that Les Saintes has one of the nicest bays in the world, a lilliput Rio de Janeiro with a sugarloaf. The isles, just 6 miles from the main island, were discovered by Columbus (who else?) on November 4, 1493, who named them "Los Santos."

The history of Les Saintes is very much the history of Guadeloupe itself. In years past, the islands have been heavily fortified, as they were Guadeloupe's Gibraltar. The climate is very dry, and until the desalination plant opened, water was often rationed.

The population of Terre-de-Haut is mainly Caucasian, all fisherfolk or sailors and their families who are descended from Breton corsairs. The very skilled sailors maneuver large boats called *saintois* and wear coolielike headgear called *salacos,* which are shallow and white, with sun shades covered in cloth built on radiating ribs of thick bamboo. Frankly, the hats look like small parasols. If you want to take a photograph of these sailors, please make a polite request (in French, no less; otherwise they won't know what you're talking about). Visitors often like to buy these hats (if they can find them) for use as beach wear.

Terre-de-Haut is a place for nature lovers, many of whom stake out their exhibitionistic space on the nude beach at Anse Crawen.

Some visitors over for the day like to go scuba diving. **Centre Nautique des Saintes,** Plage de la Colline, at Bourg in Terre-de-Haut (☎ **0590/99-54-24**), rents gear and will direct you to the dozen or so top dive sites around the island.

ESSENTIALS

GETTING THERE   By Plane   The fastest way to get here is by plane. The "airport" is a truncated landing strip that accommodates nothing larger than 20-seat Twin Otters. **Air Guadeloupe** (☎ **0590/82-47-00** on Guadeloupe, or 0590/99-51-23 on

Terre-de-Haut) has two round-trip flights daily from Pointe-à-Pitre, which take 15 minutes and cost around 360 F ($61.20) per person, round-trip.

By Ferry   Most islanders reach Terre-de-Haut via one of the several ferryboats that travel from Guadeloupe every day. Visitors opt for one of the two boats that depart daily from Pointe-à-Pitre's Gare Maritime des Iles, on quai Gatine, across the street from the well-known open-air market. The trip is 60 minutes each way, and costs 180 F ($30.60) round-trip. The most popular departure time for Terre-de-Haut from Pointe-à-Pitre is Monday to Saturday at 8am, or Sunday at 7am, with returns scheduled every afternoon at 4pm. Be at the ferryboat terminal at least 15 minutes prior to the anticipated departure. Pointe-à-Pitre is not the only departure point for Terre-de-Haut: Other ferryboats (two per day) also depart from Trois Rivières, and one additional boat leaves daily from the island's capital of Basse-Terre. Transit from either of these last two cities requires 25 minutes each way, and costs 100 F ($17) round-trip.

For more information and last-minute departure schedules, contact **Frères Bru-dey** (☎ **0590/90-04-48**) or **Trans Antilles Express,** Gare Maritime, quai Gatine, Pointe-à-Pitre (☎ **0590/83-12-45**).

GETTING AROUND   On an island that doesn't have a single car-rental agency, you get about by walking or riding a bike or motor scooter, which can be rented at hotels and in town near the pier. **Localizé,** at Bourg in Terre-de-Haut (☎ **0590/ 99-51-99**), rents both motorboats and scooters.

There are also minibuses called **Taxis de l'Ile** (eight in all), which take six to eight passengers.

WHERE TO STAY ON TERRE-DE-HAUT

Bois Joli. 97137 Terre-de-Haut, Les Saintes, Guadeloupe, F.W.I. ☎ **800/233-9815** in the U.S., or 0590/99-50-38. Fax 0590/99-55-05. E-mail: boisjoli@wanadoo.fr. 31 units. A/C TEL. Winter 915 F ($155.55) double; 1,380 F ($234.60) bungalow for 2. Off-season 800 F ($136) double; 1,175 F ($199.75) bungalow for 2. Rates include MAP (breakfast and dinner). MC, V.

On the western part of the island, 2 miles from the village, this hotel overlooks a fine beach. Renovated in 1996, Bois Joli is a stucco structure set on a palm-studded rise of a slope. The accommodations include bedrooms in the main house and eight bungalows (two with kitchenettes) on the hillside. (Note that bungalows with kitchens don't cost more than those without.) The rooms have bold-patterned fabrics, comfortable beds, and modern but bland furnishings; bathrooms are small. All but two of the units are air-conditioned, with various combinations of shower and tub arrangements. Most rooms have private phones. Because of the bungalows' isolation and increased sense of privacy, they may appeal to families. Food served in the dining room is based on conservative and relatively uninspired Creole traditions. M. Blandin, the French owner, can arrange for waterskiing, sailing, boat trips to some of the islets or rocks that form Les Saintes, and snorkeling. In winter, reservations are suggested at least 6 months in advance.

Hôtel La Saintoise. Place de la Mairie, 97137 Terre-de-Haut, Les Saintes, Guadeloupe, F.W.I. ☎ **0590/99-52-50.** 8 units. A/C. Year-round 370 F ($62.90) double. Rates include continental breakfast. MC, V.

Originally built in the 1960s, La Saintoise is a modern two-story building set near the almond trees and widespread poinciana of the town's main square, near the ferryboat dock, across from the town hall. As in a small French village, the inn places tables and chairs on the sidewalk, where you can sit and observe what action there is. The owner will welcome you and show you through the uncluttered lobby to one of his modest, second-floor bedrooms, each outfitted with a small tile bathroom. Housekeeping is good, beds have firm mattresses, and the comfort level is suitable. This is a friendly and unpretentious place.

WHERE TO DINE ON TERRE-DE-HAUT

✪ **Chez Jeannine (Le Casse-Croûte).** Fond-de-Curé, Terre-de-Haut. ☎ **0590-99-53-37.** Reservations recommended for large groups only. Fixed-price three-course meal 75 F ($12.75). V. Daily 9–10am, noon–3pm, and 7pm–midnight. CREOLE.

The creative statement of Mme Jeannine Bairtran, originally from Guadeloupe, this restaurant is a 3-minute walk south of the town center in a simple Creole house decorated with modern Caribbean accents. Only a fixed-price meal is served, and it includes avocado stuffed with crabmeat, a *gâteau de poissons* (literally "fish cake"), and several different curry-enhanced stews (including one made with goat). Crayfish and grilled fish (the ubiquitous catch of the day) appear daily on the menu. Local vegetables are used. The ambience is that of a Creole bistro—in other words, a hut with nautical trappings and bright tablecloths.

Les Amandiers. Place de la Mairie. ☎ **0590/99-50-06.** Reservations recommended. Fixed-price menu 70 F–90 F ($11.90–$15.30). AE, MC, V. Daily 8am–3pm and 6:30–9:30pm. CREOLE.

Across from the town hall on the main square of Bourg is the most traditional Creole bistro on Terre-de-Haut. Monsieur and Madame Charlot Brudey are your hosts in this beige-painted building, with tables and chairs on the upper balconies for open-air dining. A TV set (at loud volumes) might be providing entertainment in the bar when you stop in. Conch (*lambi*) is prepared either in a fricassée or a colombo, a savory curry stew. Also offered are a court bouillon of fish, a gâteau (terrine) of fish, and a seemingly endless supply of grilled crayfish, a staple of the island. The catch of the day is also grilled the way you like it. You'll find an intriguing collection of stews, concocted from fish, bananas, and christophine (chayote). A knowledge of French is helpful around here.

EXPLORING THE ISLAND

On Terre-de-Haut, the main settlement is at **Le Bourg,** a single street that follows the curve of the harbor. A charming but sleepy hamlet, it has little houses with red or blue doorways, balconies, and Victorian gingerbread. Donkeys are the beasts of burden, and everywhere you look, you'll see fish nets drying in the sun. You can also explore the ruins of **Fort Napoléon,** which is left over from those 17th-century wars, including the naval encounter known in European history books as "The Battle of the Saints." You can see the barracks and prison cells, as well as the drawbridge and art museum. Occasionally you'll spot an iguana scurrying up the ramparts. Directly across the bay, atop Ilet-à-Cabrit, sits the fort named in honor of empress Joséphine.

You might also get a sailor to take you on his boat to the other main island, **Terre-de-Bas,** which has no accommodations. Or you can stay on Terre-de-Haut and hike to **Le Grand Souffleur,** with its beautiful cliffs, and to **Le Chameau,** the highest point on the island, rising to a peak of 1,000 feet.

Scuba diving is not limited to mainland Guadeloupe. The underwater world off Les Saintes has attracted deep-sea divers as renowned as Jacques Cousteau, but even the less experienced may explore its challenging depths and multicolored reefs. Intriguing underwater grottoes can be found near Fort Napoléon on Terre-de-Haut.

SHOPPING

Few come here to shop, but there is one offbeat choice at **Kaz an Nou Gallery** on Terre-de-Haut (☎ **0590/99-52-29**), where a local artist, Pascal Fay, makes carved wooden house facades, all candy colored and trimmed in gingerbread. Naturally, they're in miniature. The most popular reproduction graces the cover of the best-selling picture book *Caribbean Style*. Mr. Fay will point the way to the real house a few blocks away, which has become a sightseeing attraction all on its own due to the book's popularity. The "houses" measure about 16 by 13 inches and sell for $100 to $400 each.

If you're looking for an authentic salaco hat, head to **José Beaujour** at Terre-de-Bas (☎ **0590/99-80-20**). At **Mahogany Artisanat,** Bourg in Terre-de-Haut (☎ **0590/ 99-50-12**), you'll find Yves Cohen's batik and hand-painted T-shirts.

MARIE-GALANTE

This offshore dependency of Guadeloupe is an almost-perfect circle of about 60 square miles. Almost exclusively French-speaking, it lies 20 miles south of Guadeloupe's Grand-Terre and is full of rustic charm.

Columbus noticed it before he did Guadeloupe, on November 3, 1493. He named it for his own vessel, but didn't land here. In fact, it was 150 years later that the first European came ashore.

The first French governor of the island was Constant d'Aubigne, father of the marquise de Maintenon. Several captains from the West Indies Company attempted settlement, but none of them succeeded. In 1674, Marie-Galante was given to the Crown, and from that point on its history was closely linked to that of Guadeloupe.

However, after 1816, the island settled down to a quiet slumber. You could hear the sugarcane growing on the plantations—and that was about it. Many windmills were built to crush the cane, and lots of tropical fruits were grown.

Today, some 30,000 inhabitants live here, making their living from sugar and rum, the latter said to be the best in the Caribbean. The island's climate is rather dry, and there are many good beaches. One of these stretches of brilliantly white sand covers at least 5 miles. However, swimming can be dangerous in some places. The best beach is at **Petite Anse,** 6½ miles from **Grand-Bourg,** the main town, with an 1845 baroque church. You can visit the 18th-century Grand Anse **rum distillery** and the historic fishing hamlet of **Vieux Fort.**

ESSENTIALS

GETTING THERE   Air Guadeloupe (☎ **0590/82-74-00**) will bring you to the island in just 20 minutes from Pointe-à-Pitre, landing at Les Basse Airport on Marie-Galante, about 2 miles from Grand-Bourg. Round-trip passage costs 360 F ($61.20).

Antilles Trans Express (Exprès des Iles), Gare Maritime, quai Gatine, Pointe-à-Pitre (☎ **0590/83-12-45** or 0590/91-13-43), operates boat service to the island with three daily round-trips between Point-à-Pitre and Grand-Bourg. The round-trip costs 170 F ($28.90). Departures from Pointe-à-Pitre are daily at 8am, 12:30pm, and 5pm, with returns from Grand-Bourg at 6am, 9am, and 3:45pm.

GETTING AROUND   A limited number of **taxis** are available at the airport, but the price should be negotiated before you drive off.

WHERE TO STAY

There are only a few little accommodations on the island, which, even if they aren't very up-to-date in amenities, are clean and hearty, and often fully booked throughout the winter. The hosts are friendly, but their greetings may be bewildering if you speak no French. Even if you do, be prepared for some very unusual grammar.

Auberge de l'Arbre à Pain. Rue Jeanne-d'Arc 34, 97112 Grand-Bourg, Marie-Galante, Guadeloupe, F.W.I. ☎ **0590/97-73-69.** 7 units. A/C. Year-round 300 F ($51) double. V. At the harbor, take the first street going toward the church.

Set behind a clapboard facade close to the street, about a 5-minute stroll from the harborfront, this establishment was named after the half-dozen breadfruit trees (*les arbres à pain*) that shelter its courtyard and its simple but pleasant bedrooms from the blazing sun. You'll get a taste of Old France at this respectable auberge, which has easy access to nearby beaches. Each room has uncomplicated furnishings and a private bathroom.

The hotel's restaurant is a favorite with many town residents. Meals are served daily from noon to 2pm and 7 to 11pm. Main courses cost 65 F to 100 F ($11.05 to $17), and include fresh fish and shellfish. No reservations are required for the restaurant, although advance reservations for overnight stays are important.

WHERE TO DINE

In addition to the following choice, the **Auberge de l'Arbre à Pain** has a popular restaurant (see above).

Le Touloulou. Plage de Petite Anse, Marie-Galante, Guadeloupe, F.W.I. ☎ **0590/97-32-63.** Fax 0590/97-33-59. Main courses 45 F–150 F ($7.65–$25.50); set menu 90 F–120 F ($15.30–$20.40). MC, V. Tues–Sun noon–2:30pm; Tues–Sat 7–9:30pm. Closed Sept 15–Oct 15. CREOLE.

Its French-speaking owners will tell you, if you ask them, about one of the recent hurricanes blowing the relatively rare bamboo walls of this 30-year-old house away (they were later replaced with conventional boards). Set adjacent to the beach, with a hardworking staff and a hyper-casual clientele, Le Touloulou specializes in shellfish and crayfish culled from local waters. If sea urchins or lobster are your passion, you'll find them here in abundance, prepared virtually any way you want. Other standbys include a savory, and highly ethnic, version of *bébélé* (cow tripe enhanced with breadfruit, dumplings, and plantains) and conch served either as fricassée or in puff pastry.

The inn has also added five very basic units, each with air-conditioning and a small private bathroom. In winter, a double costs 250 F ($42.50); a double with kitchenette, 280 F ($47.60). A two-bedroom bungalow with kitchenette, suitable for four, rents for 400 F ($68). In the off-season, a double ranges from 220 F to 280 F ($37.40 to $47.60), with the bungalow going for 350 F ($59.50).

LA DÉSIRADE

The ubiquitous Columbus spotted this *terre désirée* or "sought-after land" after his Atlantic crossing in 1493. Named La Désirade, the island, just 5 miles off the eastern tip of Guadeloupe proper, is less than 7 miles long and about 1½ miles wide, and has a single potholed road running along its length.

The island has fewer than 1,700 inhabitants, including the descendants of Europeans exiled here by royal command. Tourism has hardly touched the place, if you can ignore those day-trippers. Most visitors opt to spend only a day on La Désirade, sunbathing or perhaps touring the island's barren expanses. There are, however, a handful of exceptionally simple guest houses charging from 300 F ($51) for overnight accommodations for two. Don't expect anything grand.

The main hamlet is **Grande Anse,** which has a small church with a presbytery and flower garden, and the homes of the local inhabitants. **Le Souffleur** is a village where boats are constructed, and at **Baie Mahault** are the ruins of the old leper colony (including a barely recognizable chapel) from the early–18th century.

The best **beaches** are Souffleur, a tranquil oasis near the boat-building hamlet, and Baie Mahault, a small quintessentially Caribbean beach with white sand and palm trees.

ESSENTIALS

GETTING THERE   From Pointe-à-Pitre, **Air Guadeloupe** (☎ 0590/82-47-00) offers flights to La Désirade from Guadeloupe's Le Raizet Airport three times a week on aircraft containing passengers only. The round-trip costs 360 F ($61.20); trip time is between 15 to 20 minutes each way. Unless a respectable number of passengers shows up, the flight may be cancelled, leaving passengers to fend for themselves and find other means of transport.

As a result, some visitors opt to charter a three-passenger plane, suitable for daytime flights only, from a local school that's devoted to the training of pilots and aviators, **Ailes Guadeloupiennes** (☎ 0590/82-24-66). Its accredited pilots, and planes, are occasionally available for chartered flights from Guadeloupe to La Désirade for a one-way fare of 700 F ($119), the cost of which is divided among the three passengers.

Because of the infrequency of flights and the expense, most passengers opt for transit to La Désirade by **ferry,** which leaves St-François every day at 8am and 5pm (and sometimes at 3pm as well, depending on the season) from the wharves at St-François, near Guadeloupe's eastern tip. Returns from La Désirade for St-François include a daily departure at 3pm, allowing convenient access for day-trippers. Trip time is around 50 minutes each way, depending on conditions at sea. Round-trip passage on the ferryboat costs 170 F ($28.90). Call ☎ 0590/83-12-45 for schedules.

GETTING AROUND   On La Désirade, three or four **minibuses** run between the airport and the towns. To get around, you might negotiate with a local driver. **Bicycles** are also available at the hotels.

WHERE TO STAY

If you'd like to spend the night, call **L'Oasis** (☎ 0590/20-02-12) or **Le Mirage** (☎ 0590/20-01-08;** fax 0590/20-07-45). Both are at Beauséjour, half a mile from the airport. Oasis has six plain rooms, charging 280 F ($47.60) for a double, including breakfast. Built in 1990 of concrete, it's simple and boxy, lying a short walk from a good beach. Le Mirage offers seven rather drab rooms, also charging 300 F ($51) for a double, including breakfast. Built of concrete around the same time as Oasis, it offers a simple bar and restaurant, and lies a bit closer to the sea than its competitor.

15 Jamaica

Most visitors already have a mental image of this English-speaking nation before they arrive, picturing its boisterous culture of reggae and Rastafarianism; its white, sandy beaches; and its jungles, rivers, mountains, and clear waterfalls. Jamaica's art and cuisine are also remarkable.

Jamaica can be a tranquil and intriguing island, but there's no denying that it's plagued by crime, drugs, and muggings. There is also palpable racial tension here. But many visitors are unaffected; they're escorted from the airport to their heavily patrolled hotel grounds and venture out only on expensive organized tours. These vacationers are largely sheltered from the more unpredictable and sometimes dangerous side of Jamaica. Those who want to see "the real Jamaica," or at least see the island in greater depth, had better be prepared for some hassle. Vendors on the beaches and in the markets can be particularly aggressive.

Most Jamaicans, in spite of economic hard times, have unrelenting good humor and genuinely welcome visitors to the island. Others, certainly a minority, harbor hostility toward tourists; many visitors vow never to return. Jamaica's appealing aspects have to be weighed against its poverty and problems, the legacy of a history of slavery and colonization common to the region, combined with more recent traumatic political upheavals, beginning in the 1970s.

Should you go? By all means, yes. Be prudent and cautious, just as if you were visiting New York, Miami, or Los Angeles. Jamaica is definitely worth it! The island has fine hotels and a zesty cuisine. It's well geared to couples who come to tie the knot or celebrate their honeymoon. As for sports, Jamaica boasts the best golf courses in the West Indies, and its landscape offers lots of outdoor activities like rafting and serious hiking. The island has some of the finest diving waters in the world, with an average diving depth of 35 to 95 feet, and visibility of usually 60 to 120 feet. Most of the diving is done on coral reefs, which are protected by underwater parks where fish, shells, coral, and sponges are plentiful.

Jamaica lies 90 miles south of Cuba and is the third largest of the Caribbean islands, with some 4,400 square miles of predominantly green land, a mountain ridge peaking at 7,400 feet above sea level, and, on the north coast, many white-sand beaches with clear blue waters.

1 Essentials

VISITOR INFORMATION

Before you go, you can get information from the **Jamaica Tourist Board** at the following U.S. addresses: 500 N. Michigan Ave., Suite 1030, **Chicago, IL** 60611 (☎ 312/527-1296); 1320 S. Dixie Hwy., Suite 1101, **Coral Gables, FL** 33146 (☎ 305/665-0557); 3440 Wilshire Blvd., Suite 805, **Los Angeles, CA** 90010 (☎ 213/384-1123); 801 Second Ave., **New York, NY** 10017 (☎ 212/856-9727). In **Atlanta,** information can be obtained by phone only (☎ 770/452-7799).

In **Canada,** contact 1 Eglinton Ave. E., Suite 616, Toronto, ON M4P 3A1 (☎ 416/482-7850). Brits can contact the **London** office: 1–2 Prince Consort Rd., London SW7 2BZ (☎ 0171/224-0505).

Once on the island, you'll find tourist offices at 2 St. Lucia Ave., **Kingston** (☎ 876/929-9200); Cornwall Beach, St. James, **Montego Bay** (☎ 876/952-4425); Shop no. 29, Coral Seas Plaza, **Negril** (☎ 876/957-4243); in the Ocean Village Shopping Centre, **Ocho Rios** (☎ 876/974-2582); in City Centre Plaza, **Port Antonio** (☎ 876/993-3051); and in Hendriks Building, 2 High St., **Black River** (☎ 876/965-2074).

Jamaica is on the Internet at **www.jamaicatravel.com**.

GETTING THERE

Before you book your own airfare, read the sections on "Package Deals" and "Finding the Best Airfare" in chapter 2—you may save a bundle!

There are two **international airports** on Jamaica: Donald Sangster in Montego Bay (☎ **887/952-3124**) and Norman Manley in Kingston (☎ **876/924-8235**). The most popular flights to Jamaica are from New York and Miami. Remember to reconfirm all flights, coming and going, no later than 72 hours before departure. Flying time from Miami is 1¼ hours; from Los Angeles, 5½ hours; from Atlanta, 2½ hours; from Dallas, 3 hours; from Chicago and New York, 3½ hours; and from Toronto, 4 hours.

Some of the most convenient service to Jamaica is provided by **American Airlines** (☎ **800/433-7300** in the U.S.; www.aa.com) through its hubs in New York and Miami. Throughout the year, three daily nonstop flights depart from New York's Kennedy airport for Montego Bay, continuing on to Kingston. Return flights to New York usually depart from Montego Bay, touch down briefly in Kingston, then continue nonstop back to Kennedy. From Miami, at least two daily flights depart for Kingston and two daily flights for Montego Bay.

US Airways (☎ **800/428-4322;** www.usairways.com) has two daily flights from New York, stopping in Charlotte or Philadelphia. It also offers two daily flights out of Baltimore, also stopping in either Charlotte or Philadelphia before continuing to Jamaica. **Northwest Airlines** (☎ **800/225-2525;** www.nwa.com) flies directly to Montego Bay daily from Minneapolis and Tampa.

Air Jamaica (☎ **800/523-5585** in the U.S.; www.airjamaica.com) operates about 14 flights a week from New York, most of which stop at both Montego Bay and Kingston, and even more frequent flights from Miami. The airline has connecting service within Jamaica through its reservations network to **Air Jamaica Express,** whose planes usually hold between 10 and 17 passengers. Air Jamaica Express flies from the island's international airports at Montego Bay and Kingston to small airports around the island, including Port Antonio, Boscobel (near Ocho Rios), Negril, and Tinson Pen (a tiny airport near Kingston).

Jamaica

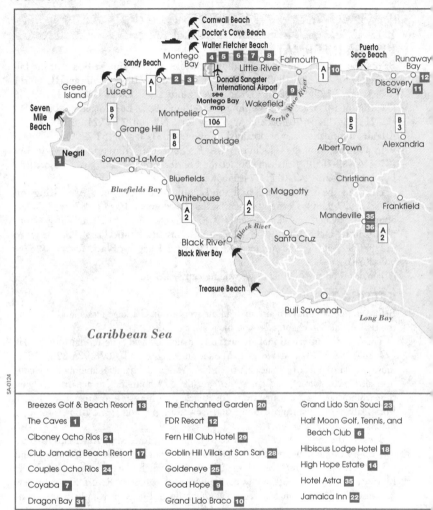

Breezes Golf & Beach Resort **13**

The Caves **1**

Ciboney Ocho Rios **21**

Club Jamaica Beach Resort **17**

Couples Ocho Rios **24**

Coyaba **7**

Dragon Bay **31**

The Enchanted Garden **20**

FDR Resort **12**

Fern Hill Club Hotel **29**

Goblin Hill Villas at San San **28**

Goldeneye **25**

Good Hope **9**

Grand Lido Braco **10**

Grand Lido San Souci **23**

Half Moon Golf, Tennis, and Beach Club **6**

Hibiscus Lodge Hotel **18**

High Hope Estate **14**

Hotel Astra **35**

Jamaica Inn **22**

Air Canada (☎ **800/268-7240** in Canada, or 800/776-3000 in the U.S.; www.air-canada.ca) flies from Toronto to Jamaica daily in winter, on Saturday and Sunday in the off-season. All this is subject to change, depending on demand, so check with the airline. **British Airways** (☎ **0345/222-111** in England; www.british-airways.com) has four nonstop flights weekly to Montego Bay and Kingston from London's Gatwick Airport.

GETTING AROUND

BY PLANE   Most travelers enter the country via Montego Bay. If you want to fly elsewhere, you'll need to use the island's domestic air service, which is provided by Air Jamaica Express. Reservations are handled by **Air Jamaica** (☎ **800/523-5585** in the U.S., or 876/923-8680), which has consolidated its reservation system. You can also reserve before you leave home through a travel agent or through Air Jamaica.

Air Jamaica Express offers 30 scheduled flights daily, covering all the major resort areas. For example, there are 11 flights a day between Kingston and Montego Bay and

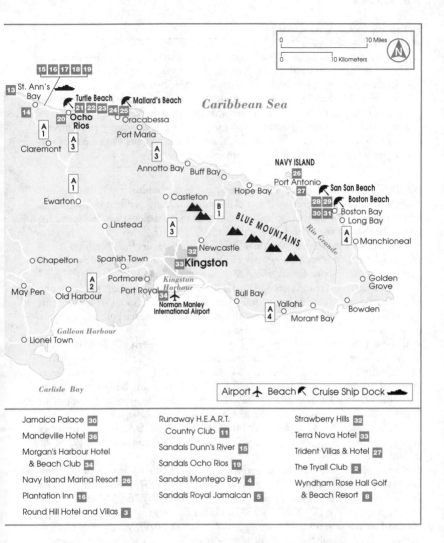

Airport ✈ Beach ☂ Cruise Ship Dock 🚢

Jamaica Palace **30**

Mandeville Hotel **36**

Morgan's Harbour Hotel & Beach Club **34**

Navy Island Marina Resort **26**

Plantation Inn **16**

Round Hill Hotel and Villas **3**

Runaway H.E.A.R.T. Country Club **11**

Sandals Dunn's River **15**

Sandals Ocho Rios **19**

Sandals Montego Bay **4**

Sandals Royal Jamaican **5**

Strawberry Hills **32**

Terra Nova Hotel **33**

Trident Villas & Hotel **27**

The Tryall Club **2**

Wyndham Rose Hall Golf & Beach Resort **8**

three flights a day between Negril and Port Antonio. (Incidentally, Tinson Pen Airport in the heart of downtown Kingston is for domestic flights only.) Car-rental facilities are available only at the international airports at Kingston and Montego Bay.

Air SuperClub (☎ **876/940-7746**) also provides shuttle service between Montego Bay and Ocho Rios and between Montego Bay and Negril. **Tropical Airlines** (☎ **876/968-2473** in Kingston, or **876/979-3565** in Montego Bay) flies between Montego Bay and Kingston and also between Montego Bay and Cuba. Although travel to Cuba is still restricted, many Americans fly this route for a look at Castroland.

BY TAXI & BUS   Kingston has no city taxis with meters, so agree on a price before you get in. In Kingston and on the rest of the island, special taxis and buses for visitors are operated by **JUTA** (Jamaica Union of Travellers Association) and have the union's emblem on the side of the vehicle. All prices are controlled, and any local JUTA office will supply a list of rates. JUTA drivers handle nearly all the ground transportation, and some offer sightseeing tours.

Digging into Jerk Pork

Wherever you go in Jamaica, you'll encounter ramshackle stands selling jerk pork. There is no more authentic local experience than to stop at one of these stands and order a lunch of jerk pork, preferably washed down with a Red Stripe beer. Jerk is a special way of barbecuing highly spicy meats on slats of pimento wood, over a wood fire set in the ground. One is never sure what goes into the seasoning, but the taste is definitely of peppers, pimento, and ginger. You can also order jerk chicken, sausage, fish, even lobster. The cook will haul out a machete and chop the meat into bite-size pieces for you, then throw them into a paper bag.

BY RENTAL CAR   Jamaica is big enough, and public transportation is unreliable enough, that a car is a necessity if you plan to do much independent sightseeing. In lieu of this, you can always take an organized tour to the major sights and spend the rest of the time on the beaches near your hotel.

Depending on road conditions, driving time for the 50 miles from Montego Bay to Negril is 1½ hours; from Montego Bay to Ocho Rios, 1½ hours; from Ocho Rios to Port Antonio, 2½ hours; from Ocho Rios to Kingston, 2 hours.

Unfortunately, car-rental rates on Jamaica have skyrocketed recently, making it one of the most expensive rental scenes in the Caribbean. There's also a 15% government tax on rentals. Equally unfortunate are the unfavorable insurance policies that apply to virtually every car-rental agency on Jamaica.

It's best to stick to branches of U.S.-based rental outfits. **Avis** (☎ **800/331-1212** in the U.S.) maintains offices at the international airports in both Montego Bay (☎ **876/952-4543**) and Kingston (☎ **876/924-8013**). The company's least-expensive car requires a 24-hour advance booking. There's also **Budget Rent-a-Car** (☎ **800/527-0700** in the U.S., 876/952-3838 at the Montego Bay Airport, or 876/924-8762 in Kingston); with Budget, a daily collision-damage waiver is mandatory and costs another $15. **Hertz** (☎ **800/654-3001** in the U.S.) operates branches at the airports at both Montego Bay (☎ **876/979-0438**) and Kingston (☎ **876/924-8028**).

If you'd like to shop for a better deal with one of the local companies in Montego Bay, try **Jamaica Car Rental,** 23 Gloucester Ave. (☎ **876/952-5586**), with a branch at the Sangster International Airport at Montego Bay (☎ **876/952-9496**), plus a branch in Ocho Rios (☎ **876/974-2505**). Daily rates begin at $70. You can also try **United Car Rentals,** 49 Gloucester Ave. (☎ **876/952-3077**), which rents Mazdas, Toyotas, Hondas, and Suzuki Jeeps, costing from $48 per day for a two-door car without air-conditioning.

In Kingston, try **Island Car Rentals,** 17 Antigua Ave. (☎ **876/926-5991**), with a branch at Montego Bay's Sangster International Airport (☎ **876/952-5771**). It rents Hondas and Samurais with rates beginning at $115 daily in winter, $96 in the off-season.

Driving is on the left, and you should exercise more than your usual caution here because of the unfamiliar terrain. Be especially cautious at night. Speed limits in town are 30 m.p.h., and 50 m.p.h. outside towns. Gas is measured in the Imperial gallon (a British unit of measure that will give you 25% more than a U.S. gallon), and the charge is payable only in Jamaican dollars; most stations don't accept credit cards. Your own valid driver's license from back home is acceptable for short-term visits to Jamaica.

BY BIKE & SCOOTER These can be rented in Montego Bay; you'll need a valid driver's license. **Montego Honda/Bike Rentals,** 21 Gloucester Ave. (☎ **876/952-4984**), rents Honda scooters for $30 to $35 a day (24 hours), plus a $300 deposit. Bikes cost $10 a day, plus a $150 deposit. Deposits are refundable if the vehicles are returned in good shape. Hours are daily from 7:30am to 5pm.

Fast Facts: Jamaica

Business Hours Banks islandwide are open Monday to Friday from 9am to 5pm. Shop hours vary widely, but as a general rule, most establishments are open Monday to Friday from 8:30am to 4:30 or 5pm. Some shops are open on Saturday until noon.

Currency The unit of currency on Jamaica is the **Jamaican dollar,** and it uses the same symbol as the U.S. dollar ($). There is no fixed rate of exchange for the Jamaican dollar. Subject to market fluctuations, it's traded publicly. Visitors to Jamaica can pay for any goods in U.S. dollars. *Be careful!* Ask whether a price is being quoted in Jamaican or U.S. dollars.

In this guide we've generally followed the price-quotation policy of the establishment, whether in Jamaican dollars or U.S. dollars. The symbol "J$" denotes prices in Jamaican dollars; the conversion into U.S. dollars follows in parentheses. ***When dollar figures stand alone, they are always U.S. currency.***

Jamaican currency is issued in banknotes of J$10, J$20, J$50, J$100, and J$500. Coins are available in denominations of 5¢, 10¢, 25¢, 50¢, J$1, and J$5. Five-dollar banknotes and one-cent coins are also in circulation, but are increasingly rare. At press time (but subject to change), the exchange rate of Jamaican currency is J$36 to U.S.$1 (J$1 equals about 2.8¢ U.S. cents). There are 58 Jamaican dollars in one pound sterling (or, stated differently, J$1 to 1.7 pence).

There are Bank of Jamaica exchange bureaus at both international airports (Montego Bay and Kingston), at cruise-ship piers, and in most hotels.

Customs Do *not* bring in or take out illegal drugs from Jamaica. Your luggage will be searched; marijuana-sniffing police dogs are stationed at the airport. Otherwise, you can bring in most items intended for personal use.

Documents U.S. and Canadian residents need a passport and a return or ongoing ticket. In lieu of a passport, an original birth certificate plus photo ID will do. Always check, however, with your airline in case document requirements have changed. Other visitors, including British subjects, need passports, good for a maximum stay of 6 months.

Immigration cards, needed for bank transactions and currency exchange, are given to visitors at the airport arrival desks.

Drugstores See "Pharmacies," below.

Electricity Most places have the standard 110 volts AC (60 cycles), as in the United States. However, some establishments operate on 220 volts AC (50 cycles). If your hotel is on a different current from your U.S.-made appliance, ask for a transformer and adapter.

Embassies, Consulates & High Commissions Calling embassies or consulates in Jamaica is a challenge. Phones will ring and ring before being picked up, if they are answered at all. Extreme patience is needed to reach a live voice on

A Word on Marijuana

You will almost certainly be approached by someone selling ganja (marijuana), and, to be frank, that's why many travelers come here. However, we should warn you that drugs (including marijuana) are illegal, and imprisonment is the penalty for possession. Don't smoke pot openly in public. Of course, hundreds of visitors do and get away with it, but you may be the one who gets caught—the person selling to you might even be a police informant. Above all, don't consider for a second bringing marijuana back into the United States. There are drug-sniffing dogs stationed at the Jamaican airports, and they will check your luggage. U.S. Customs agents, well aware of the drug situation on Jamaica, have also easily caught and arrested many who have tried to take a chance on bringing some home.

---

the other end. The embassy of the **United States** is at the Jamaica Mutual Life Centre, 2 Oxford Rd., Kingston 5 (☎ **876/929-4850**). The High Commission of **Canada** is in the Mutual Security Bank Building, 30–36 Knutsford Blvd., Kingston 5 (☎ **876/926-1500**), and there's a consulate at 29 Gloucester Ave., Montego Bay (☎ **876/952-6198**). The High Commission of the **United Kingdom** is at 28 Trafalgar Rd., Kingston 10 (☎ **876/926-9050**).

Emergencies For the **police** and air rescue, dial ☎ **119;** to report a **fire** or call an **ambulance,** dial ☎ **110.**

Hospitals In Kingston, the **University Hospital** is at Mona (☎ **876/ 927-1620**); in Montego Bay, the **Cornwall Regional Hospital** is at Mount Salem (☎ **876/952-5100**); and in Port Antonio, the **Port Antonio General Hospital** is at Naylor's Hill (☎ **876/993-2646**).

Language The language spoken on Jamaica is English.

Pharmacies In Montego Bay, try **Overton Pharmacy,** 49 Union St., Overton Plaza (☎ **876/952-2699**); in Ocho Rios, **Great House Pharmacy,** Brown's Plaza (☎ **876/974-2352**); and in Kingston, **Moodie's Pharmacy,** in the New Kingston Shopping Centre (☎ **876/926-4174**). Prescriptions are accepted by local pharmacies only if issued by a Jamaican doctor. Hotels have doctors on call. If you need any particular medicine or treatment, bring evidence, such as a letter from your own physician.

Safety Major hotels have security guards who protect the grounds, so most vacationers don't have any real problems. It's not wise to accept an invitation to see "the real Jamaica" from some stranger you meet on the beach. Exercise caution when traveling around Jamaica. Safeguard your valuables, and never leave them unattended on a beach. Likewise, never leave luggage or other valuables in a car, or even the trunk of a car. The U.S. State Department has issued a travel advisory about crime rates in Kingston, so don't walk around alone at night. Caution is also advisable in many north-coast tourist areas, especially remote houses and isolated villas that can't afford security.

Taxes The government imposes a 12% room tax. You'll be charged a J$750 ($21.40) departure tax at the airport, payable in either Jamaican or U.S. dollars. There's also a 15% government tax on rental cars and a 15% tax on all overseas phone calls.

Time Jamaica is on eastern standard time year-round. However, when the United States is on daylight saving time, at 6am in Miami it's 5am in Kingston.

Tipping   Tipping is customary. A general 10% or 15% is expected in hotels and restaurants on occasions when you would normally tip. Some places add a service charge to the bill. Tipping is not allowed in the all-inclusive hotels.

Water   It's usually safe to drink piped-in water, islandwide, as it's filtered and chlorinated. But, as always, it's more prudent to drink bottled water if it's available.

Weather   Expect temperatures around 80° to 90°F on the coast. Winter is a little cooler. In the mountains it can get as low as 40°F. There is generally a breeze, which in winter is noticeably cool. The rainy periods generally are October and November (although it can extend into December) and May and June. Normally rain comes in short, sharp showers; then the sun shines.

2 Montego Bay

Situated on the northwestern coast of the island, Montego Bay first attracted tourists in the 1940s when Doctor's Cave Beach became popular with wealthy vacationers, who bathed in the warm water fed by mineral springs. It's now Jamaica's second-largest city.

Despite the large influx of visitors, Montego Bay still retains its own identity as a thriving business and commercial center, and functions as the market town for most of western Jamaica. It has cruise-ship piers and a growing industrial center at the free port.

Since Montego Bay has its own airport, those who vacation here have little need to visit Kingston, the island's capital. You'll have everything you need in Mo Bay, the most cosmopolitan of Jamaica's resorts.

WHERE TO STAY

Most of the big, full-service resorts are frequently included in package tours. Booking a package will make the rates much more reasonable. See "Package Deals" and "Tips on Accommodations" in chapter 2.

VERY EXPENSIVE

Breezes Montego Bay. Gloucester Ave., Montego Bay, Jamaica, W.I. ☎ **800/859-SUPER** or 876/940-1150. Fax 876/940-1160. www.superclubs.com/resorts/reezes/MontegoBay/accommodations.html. E-mail: info@superclubs.com. 124 units. A/C TV TEL. All-inclusive rates for 3 nights: Winter $1,584 double. Off-season $1,446 double. AE, MC, V. No children under 16 accepted.

Built in 1995 in a boomerang-shaped five-story complex that contains a pool and a cluster of bars and boutiques, this is one of the newest members of Jamaica's Super-Club chain. Defined as "a sandbox for your inner child," it's the only major hotel perched directly on the sands of Montego Bay's most popular public beach, Doctor's Cave. Guests here experience more of the street and beach life of Jamaica than those who stay at the more secluded resorts set off within compounds of their own. The venue is adult and indulgent, but without the emphasis on raucous partying that's the norm at Hedonism II (a member of the same chain). Bedrooms are simply furnished and breezy, overlooking either the beach or the garden that separates the hotel from the traffic of Montego Bay's main commercial boulevard, Gloucester Avenue. Rooms range from intimate cabins to lavish suites. The cabin rooms, 31 in all, are similar to a ship's cabin, very intimate with a queen bed. Slightly larger are the deluxe rooms, with twins or a king bed. The best are the deluxe oceanfront rooms, with king beds, and the oceanfront suites. All units come with such extras as irons and ironing boards,

Montego Bay

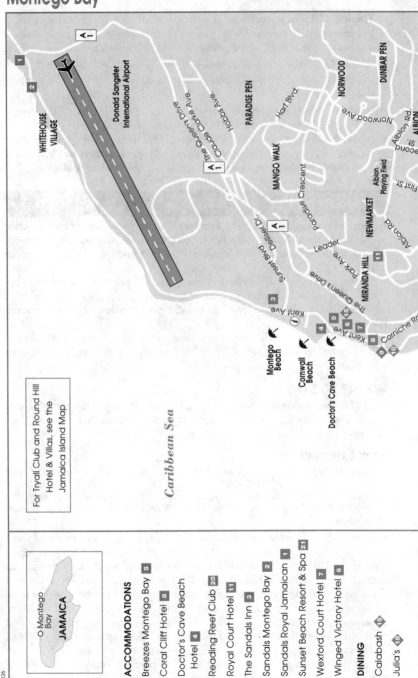

For Tryall Club and Round Hill Hotel & Villas, see the Jamaica Island Map

Caribbean Sea

JAMAICA
O Montego Bay

ACCOMMODATIONS

Breezes Montego Bay **5**

Coral Cliff Hotel **8**

Doctor's Cave Beach Hotel **4**

Reading Reef Club **20**

Royal Court Hotel **11**

The Sandals Inn **3**

Sandals Montego Bay **2**

Sandals Royal Jamaican **1**

Sunset Beach Resort & Spa **21**

Wexford Court Hotel **7**

Winged Victory Hotel **6**

DINING

Calabash **15**

Julia's **18**

SA-0126

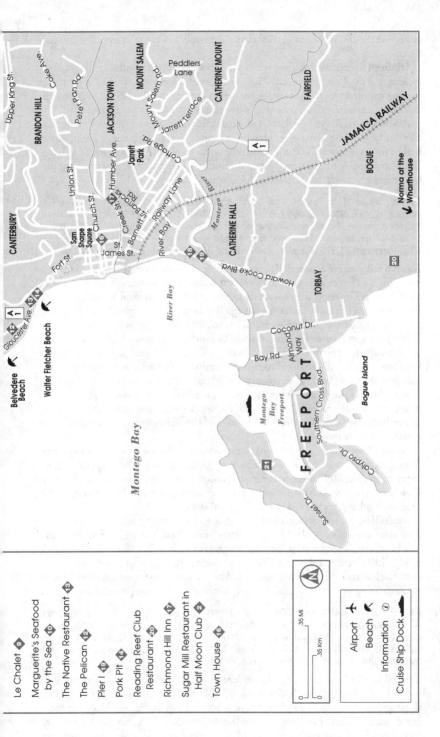

Le Chalet 9

Marguerite's Seafood by the Sea 8

The Native Restaurant 13

The Pelican 12

Pier I 19

Pork Pit 14

Reading Reef Club Restaurant 20

Richmond Hill Inn 11

Sugar Mill Restaurant in Half Moon Club 2

Town House 6

Airport ✈

Beach ◣

Information ⓘ

Cruise Ship Dock ◣

.35 Mi

.35 Km

coffeemakers, and private safes. Bathrooms are small, but come equipped with a hair dryer.

Dining/Diversions: Informal meals are served at Jimmy's Buffet, a terrace overlooking the pool and the beach. The more formal, candlelit Martino's is an Italian rooftop restaurant. A poolside snack bar serves burgers and hot dogs throughout the day, and there are four bars, one with a live pianist, to quench your thirst.

Amenities: Freshwater pool; rooftop Jacuzzi; full range of water sports with instruction on how to use water skis, Hobie Cats, and Windsurfers; tennis courts (lit at night); fitness center with Nautilus equipment and aerobics and water-aerobics classes. The staff works hard to provide group diversions, games, toga parties, mingling parties, mixology classes, steel bands, and reggae lessons.

✪ **Half Moon Golf, Tennis, and Beach Club.** Rose Hall (P.O. Box 80), Montego Bay, Jamaica, W.I. ☎ **800/626-0592** in the U.S., or 876/953-2211. Fax 876/953-2731. www. halfmoon.com.jm. E-mail: reservation@halfmoonclub.com. 418 units. A/C TV TEL. Winter $330–$480 double; from $530 suite; from $1,650 villa. Off-season $220–$280 double; from $320 suite; from $1,320 villa. MAP (breakfast and dinner) $65 per person extra. AE, MC, V.

About 8 miles east of Montego Bay's city center and 6 miles from the international airport, this is a classic, and one of the 300 best hotels in the world, according to *Condé Nast Traveler.* The resort is set on a mile-long beach and has incredible sports facilities. From here, you can easily taxi into Montego Bay to sample the nightlife and shopping.

Attracting distinguished guests over the years, such as George Bush and Queen Elizabeth, the resort complex consists of spacious hotel rooms, suites, and private five- to seven-bedroom villas (many with a private pool) scattered over 400 acres of fertile landscape, all carefully arranged to provide maximum privacy. Each unit is comfortably furnished with an English colonial/Caribbean motif. Rooms here are so vast and varied, you can live in almost any style your purse will allow. Queen Anne–inspired furniture is set off by bright Jamaican paintings, and many units have mahogany four-poster beds. Bathrooms are totally up-to-date with state-of-the-art plumbing, hair dryers, and fluffy towels.

Dining/Diversions: The Sugar Mill restaurant is set beside a working water wheel from a bygone sugar estate (see "Where to Dine," below). The Seagrape Terrace (named after the 80-year-old sea-grape trees on the property) offers meals alfresco. Il Giardino serves savory Italian cuisine. Evening entertainment includes music from a resident band and nightly folklore and musical shows.

Amenities: Sailing, windsurfing, snorkeling, scuba diving, deep-sea fishing, 51 freshwater swimming pools, 13 tennis courts (seven floodlit at night), four lit squash courts, outstanding 18-hole golf course designed by Robert Trent Jones, Sr., horseback riding, fitness center, and sauna. Shopping village (with a pharmacy, Japanese restaurant, English-style pub, and boutiques) and beauty salon. Room service (from 7am to midnight), laundry, baby-sitting, massage, instruction in various water sports.

✪ **Round Hill Hotel and Villas.** Rte. A1 (P.O. Box 64), Montego Bay, Jamaica, W.I. ☎ **800/972-2159** in the U.S., or 876/956-7050. Fax 876/956-7505. www.roundhilljamaica. com. E-mail: roundhill@cwjamaica.com. 74 units. A/C TEL. Winter $390–$470 double; $570–$780 villa. Off-season $240–$290 double; $340–$510 villa. Extra person $65. MAP (breakfast and dinner) $70 per person extra. AE, DC, MC, V.

Opened in 1953 and now a Caribbean legend, this is one of the most distinguished hotels in the West Indies. It stands on a lushly landscaped 98-acre peninsula that slopes gracefully down to a sheltered cove, where the elegant reception area and social center stand. Guests have included the Kennedys, Cole Porter, and more recently, Steven Spielberg and Harrison Ford. Most evenings are informal, except Saturday, when a jacket and tie or black tie are required for men. Likewise, it's preferred that tennis players wear all white on the courts.

Surrounded by landscaped tropical gardens, Round Hill accommodates some 200 guests, who enjoy its private beach, the views of Jamaica's north shore and the mountains, and the colonial elegance of the resort. There are full spa services, lots of water sports, and fine tennis facilities. The guest rooms are in a richly appointed seaside building known as the Pineapple House, and each opens onto views of the water and beach. Each unit has a plantation-style decor with refinished antique furniture and twin beds with luxury mattresses, plus spacious bathrooms with fluffy towels. The most deluxe rooms are upstairs. There are also privately owned villas dotting the hillside, most available for rental when the owners are not in residence. Each contains two to four individual suites with a private living area and/or patio; 19 of the villas have their own pools. Each is individually decorated, sometimes lavishly so, and rates include the services of a uniformed maid, a cook, and a gardener. Deluxe villas have virtually everything, depending on the expensive tastes of their owners. In other words, you might live as Ralph Lauren (one of the villa owners) does when he's on vacation.

Dining/Diversions: Informal luncheons are held in an intimate straw hut with an open terrace in a little sandy bay. Jamaican and continental dishes are served on a candlelit terrace or in the Georgian colonial room overlooking the sea. The entertainment is varied.

Amenities: Pool, fitness center (with aerobics classes), top-quality tennis courts (lit at night), safety-deposit boxes, windsurfing, glass-bottomed-boat rides, scuba diving, horseback riding, sailing, paddleboats, rubber-sided inflatable boats, waterskiing. Room service (from 7:30am to 9:30pm), concierge, laundry, baby-sitting, valet service. You can have someone come and prepare breakfast in your villa.

The Sandals Inn (formerly Carlyle on the Bay). Kent Ave. (P.O. Box 412), Montego Bay, Jamaica, W.I. ☎ **800/SANDALS** in the U.S. and Canada, or 876/952-4140. Fax 876/952-6913. www.sandals.com. 52 units. A/C TV TEL. All-inclusive rates for 4 days/3 nights: Winter $1,335–$1,600 double. Off-season $1,160–$1,300 double. AE, MC, V.

The Sandals Inn is a couples-only (male-female) hotel built around a large pool and patio, with a beach a short walk across a busy highway. This is the least expensive, least glamorous, least spacious, and least attractive of the Sandals all-inclusive resorts scattered across Jamaica. But it's a trade-off: You don't get luxury, but you do get proximity to downtown Montego Bay, reasonable rates, and free day passes (including free transportation) to both of the Sandals resorts of Montego Bay.

Thirty-eight rooms open onto the pool; all units contain king beds with good mattresses. There is now so-called environmentally friendly linen service, so that sheets and towels are not changed unless you request it. Bathrooms are small but equipped with hair dryers.

Dining/Diversions: Food is served in bountiful portions in the resort's only dining room, and there's nightly entertainment. A specialty restaurant, Caryle, specializing in flambé dishes, breaks the routine of the main dining room.

Amenities: Recreational and sports program, exercise room, saunas, Jacuzzi, tennis courts, pool, room safes. Room service (from 9am to 10pm), free round-trip airport transfers.

Sandals Montego Bay. Kent Ave. (P.O. Box 100), Montego Bay, Jamaica, W.I. ☎ **800/ SANDALS** in the U.S. and Canada, or 876/952-5510. Fax 876/952-0816. www.sandals.com. 244 units. A/C TV TEL. All-inclusive rates for 4 days/3 nights: Winter $1,660–$2,000 double; $1,780–$3,000 suite for 2. Off-season $1,380–$1,640 double; $1,780–$3,120 suite for 2. AE, MC, V.

Located 5 minutes northeast of the airport, this honeymoon haven next to White-house Village is always booked solid (reserve as far ahead as possible). The 19-acre site is a couples-only (male-female), all-inclusive resort. Everything is covered in the price—meals, snacks, nightly entertainment (including those notorious toga parties), unlimited drinks night or day at one of four bars, tips, and round-trip airport transfers and baggage handling from the Montego Bay airport. Lots of entertainment and sports facilities are available on the property, so many guests never leave. In contrast to its somewhat more laid-back nearby counterpart (the Sandals Royal Jamaican), this resort offers many different activities for a clientele and staff who tend to be extroverted and gregarious; the Playmakers, as staff members are called, keep everybody amused and the joint jumping. If you want peace, quiet, and seclusion, it's not for you.

The accommodations are either in villas spread along 1,700 feet of white-sand beach or in the main house, where all bedrooms face the sea and contain private balconies. Try to avoid booking into a room over the dining room; these don't have balconies and may be noisy. Most rooms have king beds, private safes, and coffeemakers. The best are the grande luxe ocean or beachfront units, with private balconies or patios. Each medium-size bathroom has a combination tub/shower and a hair dryer.

Dining/Diversions: Options include the main dining room; Tokyo Joe's, serving six-course Asian meals; the Beach Grill; and the Oleander Deck, with "white-glove service," featuring Jamaican and Caribbean cuisine. The Oleander offers the finest dining in the Sandals chain. The late-night disco often has rum and reggae nights.

Amenities: Waterskiing, snorkeling, sailing, scuba diving daily with a certification program (PADI or NAUI), windsurfing, paddleboats and a glass-bottom boat, two freshwater pools, three Jacuzzis, tennis courts (lit at night), fully equipped fitness center. Free shuttle bus to the resort's twin, the Sandals Royal Jamaican, whose facilities are open without charge to residents here.

✪ **Sandals Royal Jamaican.** Mahoe Bay (P.O. Box 167), Montego Bay, Jamaica, W.I. ☎ **800/SANDALS** in the U.S. and Canada, or 876/953-2231. Fax 876/953-2788. www. sandals.com. 190 units. A/C TV TEL. All-inclusive rates for 4 days/3 nights: Winter $1,960–$2,600 per couple; $2,800–$3,940 suite for 2. Off-season $1,800–$2,280 per couple; $2,420–$3,440 suite for 2. AE, MC, V.

This all-inclusive, couples-only (male-female) resort is a reincarnation of a prestigious colonial-style Montego Bay hotel. The building lies on its own private beach (which, frankly, isn't as good as the one at the Sandals Montego Bay). Some of the British colonial atmosphere remains (e.g., the formal tea in the afternoon), but there are modern touches as well, including a private, clothing-optional island reached by boat.

The spacious rooms come in a wide range of categories, from standard to superior to deluxe, but each has a king bed with a luxury mattress, a private safe, and a coffeemaker. Most desirable are the grand luxe beachfront rooms with private patios or balconies. Each unit has a small but well-equipped private bathroom with fluffy towels and a hair dryer.

Dining/Diversions: The Regency Suite and Deck is the Jamaican-inspired main dining room. Bali Hai is an Indonesian restaurant on the previously mentioned offshore island. The Courtyard Grill serves such items as grilled sirloin, grilled snapper, and smoked marlin. There are four bars, food and drink available throughout the day, and live music by a local reggae band.

Amenities: Scuba diving, windsurfing, sailing, three tennis courts, pool. Laundry, massage, free shuttle bus to the resort's twin Sandals (whose facilities are available without charge to any resident).

Sunset Beach Resort & Spa. Montego Freeport Peninsula, P.O. Box 1168, Montego Bay, Jamaica. ☎ **876/979-8800.** Fax 876/953-6744. E-mail: sunsetbeach@cwjamaica.com. 420

Catch a Fire: Jamaica's Reggae Festivals

Every August, Jamaica comes alive with the pulsating sounds of **Reggae Sunsplash,** the world's largest annual reggae festival. This weeklong music extravaganza has featured some of the most prominent reggae groups and artists, including Ziggy Marley, Cocoa Tea, and the Melody Makers. Sunsplash takes place at different venues; check with Jamaican tourist boards for the latest details. Some time during the second week of August, **Reggae Sunfest** takes place in Montego Bay. Usually this is a 4-day musical event. Some of the biggest names in reggae, both from Jamaica and worldwide, perform. Many local hotels are fully booked for the festival, so advance reservations are necessary.

The Jamaican Tourist Board's U.S. and Canadian offices can give you information about packages and group rates for the festivals and fill you in on other reggae concerts and events held throughout the year on Jamaica.

units. A/C TV TEL. Winter $566–$706 double; $1,190 suite for 2. Off-season $526–$776 double; $1,152 suite for 2. Rates include accommodations, all meals, drinks, entertainment, and most land and water sports. A 3-night minimum stay is usually required, except in very slow seasons when space is not a problem. AE, MC, V.

The newest all-inclusive hotel in Jamaica opened in 1998 on the grounds of what was originally the Seawind Resort. It aims for a marketing niche less glamorous (and less expensive) than that occupied by the Beaches and Sandals Group, to which it is frequently compared. The complex consists of three separate beaches, two pale-pink, 11-story towers containing a total of 300 units, plus a 120-room annex, the Beach Inn, whose low-rise design allows guests closer and more immediate access to the sands. Guests appreciate the location within a residential neighborhood on a peninsula that forms the southern edge of Montego Bay's harbor, far enough from other hotels to allow a sense of relative privacy. Accommodations are outfitted in a subdued motif that includes vague references to tropical design, but which tends to be more soothing, even blander, than the decor of many of its competitors. Rooms are fairly spacious with excellent mattresses on comfortable beds, plus medium-size bathrooms with tubs and shower stalls.

Dining/Diversions: Meals at each of the property's four restaurants are included in the all-inclusive rates. The Silk Road offers Pacific Rim cuisine, Botticelli serves Italian cuisine, and the Sunset Grill is an indoor/outdoor pool and beach restaurant. The Banana Walk is the resort's all-purpose dining room, with an ongoing roster of buffets, served in a style that might remind you of Club Med. There's nightly entertainment.

Amenities: Three pools, four tennis courts, a frilly gazebo that's sometimes used as a site for weddings, shuffleboard courts, jogging trails, giant chess and checker boards, beachfront volleyball, fitness center, supervised children's program.

✪ **The Tryall Club.** St. James (P.O. Box 1206), Montego Bay, Jamaica, W.I. ☎ **800/ 238-5290** in the U.S., or 876/956-5660. Fax 876/956-5673. www.tryallclub.com. E-mail: tryallclub@cwjamaica.com. 68 units. A/C TEL. Winter $500 double; from $857 villa. Off-season $350 double; from $429 villa. Extra person $70 in winter, $55 in off-season. MAP (breakfast and dinner) $66 per person extra. AE, MC, V.

With more spacious grounds than almost any other hotel on Jamaica, this stylish and upscale resort sits 12 miles west of town on the site of a 2,200-acre former sugar plantation. It doesn't have the fine beach that Half Moon does, nor the house-party atmosphere of Trident at Port Antonio, but it's noteworthy nevertheless. Known as one of the grandest resorts of Jamaica, the property lies along a 1½-mile seafront and is presided over by a 165-year-old Georgian-style great house. It's a top choice for vacationers who are serious about their golf game.

The accommodations, in either modern wings or luxurious villas, are decorated in cool pastels with English colonial touches. All contain ceiling fans and air-conditioning, along with picture windows framing sea and mountain views. Guest rooms are exceedingly spacious with luxurious beds, safes, coffeemakers, private patios or terraces, and tile floors. Bathrooms are roomy, with plenty of counter space, combination tub/showers, hair dryers, and plenty of fluffy towels. The resort's famous villas are set amid lush foliage and are designed for privacy. Each villa comes with a full-time staff, including a cook, maid, laundress, and gardener. All have private pools.

Dining/Diversions: The most formal of the resort's dining areas is in the great house. More casual meals are served in a beachside cafe. A resident band plays everything from reggae to slow-dance music every night during dinner. Afternoon tea is served in the great house.

Amenities: Championship 18-hole par-71 golf course (site of many world-class golf competitions and the pride of this elegant property), nine Laykold tennis courts, 2-mile jogging trail, pool with a swim-up bar, windsurfing, snorkeling, deep-sea fishing, paddleboats, glass-bottom boats. Room service, baby-sitting, laundry, massage; lessons given in golf, tennis, and water sports.

EXPENSIVE

✪ **Coyaba.** Mahoe Bay, Little River, Montego Bay, Jamaica, W.I. ☎ **800/237-3237** or 876/953-9150. Fax 876/953-2244. www.coyabajamaica.com. E-mail: coyaba@n5.com.jm. 50 units. A/C TV TEL. Winter $240–$340 double. Off-season $150–$210 double. All meals $70 per person extra. Children 11 and under get a 50% discount. AE, MC, V.

With only 50 rooms, and a graceful British colonial atmosphere, this is one of the smaller and more elegant all-inclusive resorts, an oceanfront retreat that is intimate and inviting, evoking a country inn. It was established in 1994 by American/Jamaican-Chinese entrepreneurs, the Robertson family, and built from scratch at a cost of $4 million. Set on a lovely strip of beachfront, a 15-minute drive east of the center of Montego Bay, it's centered around an adaptation of a 19th-century great house.

Accommodations in the main building overlook the garden; those in the pair of three-story outbuildings lie closer to the beach and are somewhat more expensive. The decor is British colonial, with traditional prints, expensive chintz fabrics, French doors leading onto private patios or verandas, carved mahogany furniture, and other reminders of the plantation age. Hand-carved bedsteads, often four-posters, are fitted with luxury mattresses. Most rooms open onto the Caribbean or else the Ironshore Golf Course. Recently added to all units were such amenities as irons and ironing boards, VCRs, and coffeemakers. The roomy bathrooms have combination shower/tubs, hair dryers, and fluffy towels. The establishment, which welcomes children but hasn't yet built them any special facilities, is less rowdy and raucous than other Jamaican resorts geared to singles and young couples; it prides itself on its peaceful and somewhat staid atmosphere. The owners are usually on hand to ensure that the operation runs smoothly.

Dining/Diversions: The hotel's main and most formal restaurant, the Vineyard, serves first-rate Jamaican and continental dinners. Less upscale is Docks Caribbean Bar & Grill, where there's a daily salad bar. Three bars are scattered about the grounds.

Amenities: Tennis court lit at night, rectangular pool, exercise room, outdoor hot tub, water-sports center, gift shop. Afternoon teas, room service, massage, laundry, and nanny service for care and feeding of children.

Wyndham Rose Hall Golf & Beach Resort. Rose Hall (P.O. Box 999), Montego Bay, Jamaica, W.I. ☎ **800/624-7326** in the U.S., or 876/953-2650. Fax 876/953-2617. www.wyndham.com. 489 units. A/C TV TEL. Winter $185–$220 double; from $425 suite. Off-season $130–$155 double; from $390 suite. MAP (breakfast and dinner) $50.60 per person extra. AE, DC, MC, V.

Wyndham Rose Hall sits at the bottom of a rolling 30-acre site along the north-coast highway 9 miles east of the airport. On a former sugar plantation that once covered 7,000 acres, the hotel abuts the 200-year-old home of the legendary "White Witch of Rose Hall," now a historic site, and has a thin strip of sandy beach. Although it's popular as a convention site, the hotel also caters to a family market (children are an important part of the clientele) and has serious golf and tennis facilities. The staff stays busy organizing games and social events. The seven-story H-shaped structure features a large and attractive lobby on the ground floor; upstairs, guest rooms all have sea views and rather unremarkable furnishings. Most units have two queen beds, and each accommodation has a small private balcony. The tiled bathrooms are well maintained, with a hair dryer and a combination tub/shower. Although the rooms all have paintings by local artists depicting typical Caribbean scenes, what's missing here is real Jamaican style and ambience.

Dining/Diversions: There are four restaurants, and it's never more than a short walk to one of the many bars scattered around the property. Wednesday nights in winter feature a poolside buffet and a Caribbean variety show with dancers, fire-eaters, and calypso and reggae performances.

Amenities: Three pools (one for small children), complimentary sailboats, top-rated golf course meandering over part of the grounds, tennis complex (with six lit all-weather Laykold courts) headed by pros who offer a complete tennis program, air-conditioned fitness center. Room service (from 7am to 11pm), baby-sitting, laundry, massage. The "Kids Klub" has an array of supervised activities that are included in the rate.

MODERATE/INEXPENSIVE

✪ **Coral Cliff Hotel.** 165 Gloucester Ave. (P.O. Box 253), Montego Bay, Jamaica, W.I. ☎ **876/952-4130.** Fax 876/952-6532. www.montego-bay-jamaica.com/coralcliff/index. html.jtm. E-mail: coralclif@usa.net. 32 units. A/C TEL. Winter $85–$95 double; $97–$115 triple; from $160 suite. Off-season $80–$90 double; $92–$105 triple; from $140 suite. MC, V.

For good value, the Coral Cliff may be your best bet in Montego Bay. The hotel grew from a colonial-style building that was once the private home of Harry M. Doubleday (of the famous publishing family). It's located about a mile west of the center of town but only 2 minutes from Doctor's Cave Beach. The Coral Cliff also offers its own luxurious pool. Many of the light, airy, and spacious bedrooms open onto a balcony with a view of the sea. The rooms, as befits a former private house, come in a wide variety of shapes and sizes, most of them containing old colonial furniture, wicker, and rattan. Most units also have twin beds with firm mattresses. The bathrooms are small in the older bedrooms, but more spacious in the newer wing out back. Each is tidily maintained and has a combination tub/shower. The hotel's breeze-swept restaurant overlooking the bay is appropriately called the Verandah Terrace, specializing in Jamaican and international dishes, with succulent tropical fruit. The food features local produce and fresh seafood whenever available.

✪ **Doctor's Cave Beach Hotel.** Gloucester Ave. (P.O. Box 94), Montego Bay, Jamaica, W.I. ☎ **800/44-UTELL** in the U.S., or 876/952-4355. Fax 876/952-5204. www.doctorscave.com.

E-mail: info@doctorscave.com. 90 units. A/C TEL. Winter $130–$140 double; $160 suite for 2. Off-season $105–$115 double; $140 suite for 2. Extra person $30. MAP (breakfast and dinner) $29 per person extra. AE, DISC, MC, V.

Across the street from the well-known Doctor's Cave Beach in the bustle of the town's commercial zone, this three-story property offers great value. It has its own gardens, a pool, a Jacuzzi, and a small gymnasium, all set on 4 acres of tropical gardens. The rooms are simply but comfortably furnished, and suites have kitchenettes. Rooms are rented standard or superior, the latter more spacious with balconies opening onto a view. All units have tile floors; floral spreads on queen or twin beds, each fitted with a good mattress; and small but efficiently organized tiled bathrooms with combination tub/showers. Hair dryers are available upon request from the front desk.

The two restaurants are the Coconut Grove, whose outdoor terrace is floodlit at night, and the less formal Greenhouse. In the Cascade Bar, where a waterfall tumbles down a stone wall, you can listen to a piano duo during cocktail hours.

Reading Reef Club. Rte. A1, on Bogue Lagoon, at the bottom of Long Hill Rd. (P.O. Box 225), Reading, Montego Bay, Jamaica, W.I. ☎ **800/315-0379** in the U.S., or 876/952-5909. Fax 876/952-7217. www.montego-bay-jamaica.com/jhta/reefclub. E-mail: rrc@n5.com.jm. 34 units. A/C TEL. Winter $100–$165 double; $250 two-bedroom suite, $300 three-bedroom suite. Off-season $75–$125 double; $200 two-bedroom suite; $250 three-bedroom suite. AE, MC, V.

This pocket of posh reflects the sense of style and flair for cuisine possessed by its American creator, former fashion designer JoAnne Rowe. Located on 2½ acres, the hotel is a 15-minute drive west of Montego Bay, on a 350-foot sandy beach where people relax in comfort, undisturbed by beach vendors. The complex of four buildings overlooks beautiful reefs once praised by Jacques Cousteau for their aquatic life.

The accommodations, which include two- and three-bedroom suites, open onto a sea view. All have air-conditioning and ceiling fans and a light Caribbean motif. The luxury rooms contain minibars, and the two- and three-bedroom suites offer kitchenettes. Quality mattresses and fine linens are found on the most comfortable beds, and the medium-size bathrooms contain adequate shelf space. See "Where to Dine," below, for details on the restaurant. There's also a bar/lounge and a beachside luncheon barbecue specializing in Jamaican (jerk) sausages, English sausages, and Tex-Mex food. Services include laundry, valet, and drivers for island tours. Guests also enjoy the freshwater pool and free water sports, including snorkeling, windsurfing, and sailing in a 12-foot sailboat; scuba diving costs extra.

Royal Court Hotel. Sewell Ave. (P.O. Box 195), Montego Bay, Jamaica, W.I. ☎ **876/952-4531.** Fax 876/952-4532. 20 units. A/C TEL. Winter $80–$90 double; $150 suite. Off-season $70 double; $100 suite. AE, MC, V.

This reasonable choice is located on the hillside overlooking Montego Bay, above Gloucester Avenue and off Park Avenue. The small rooms are outfitted in bright, tasteful colors, and all have patios and decent beds; the larger ones have fully equipped kitchenettes. This hotel is clean and attractive, has a charming atmosphere, and is a good value. Meals are served in the Pool Bar and Eatery. Its restaurant, Leaf of Life, specializes in vegetarian food, among other selections. Free transportation is provided to the town, the beach, and the tennis club. New amenities and facilities include massage, gym, steam room, Jacuzzi, TV room, conference room, and a doctor on the premises. There's also a "Wellness Center," offering holistic health consultations, hypnotherapy sessions, and other personalized programs.

Wexford Court Hotel. 39 Gloucester Ave. (P.O. Box 108), Montego Bay, Jamaica, W.I. ☎ **800/237-3421** in the U.S., or 876/952-2854. Fax 876/952-3637. www.

montego-bay-jamaica.com/wexford. E-mail: wexford@cwjamaica.com. 67 units. A/C TV TEL. Winter $137.50 double; $143 apt. Off-season $104.50–$115.50 double; $115.50 apt. MAP (breakfast and dinner) $33 per person extra. AE, MC, V.

Stay here for economy, not style. About 10 minutes from downtown Mo Bay, near Doctor's Cave Beach, this hotel has a small pool and a patio (where calypso is enjoyed in season). The apartments have living/dining areas and kitchenettes, so you can cook for yourself. All the back-to-basics rooms contain patios shaded by gables and Swiss chalet–style roofs. The Wexford Grill includes a good selection of Jamaican dishes, such as chicken deep-fried with honey. Guests can enjoy drinks in a bar nearby.

Winged Victory Hotel. 5 Queen's Dr., Montego Bay, Jamaica, W.I. ☎ **800/74-CHARMS** in the U.S., or 876/952-3892. Fax 876/952-5986. 24 units. A/C. Winter $90–$110 double; $175–$225 suite. Off-season $80–$100 double; $110–$150 suite. MAP (breakfast and dinner) $30 per person extra. AE, MC, V.

On a hillside road in Montego Bay, in the Miranda Hill District, this tall and modern hotel delays revealing its true beauty until you pass through its comfortable public rooms into a Mediterranean-style courtyard in back. Here, urn-shaped balustrades enclose a terraced garden, a pool, and a veranda looking over the faraway crescent of Montego Bay. The veranda's best feature is the Calabash Restaurant. The owner, Roma Chin Sue, added hotel rooms to her already well-known restaurant in 1985. All but five have a private balcony or veranda, along with an eclectic decor that's part Chinese, part colonial, and part Iberian. The bedrooms are of generous size and are well maintained with firm mattresses renewed as frequently as needed, along with average-size bathrooms.

WHERE TO DINE

The Montego Bay area has some of the finest—and most expensive—dining on the island. But if you're watching your wallet and don't have a delicate stomach, you'll find lots of terrific street food. On **Kent Avenue** you might try authentic jerk pork or seasoned spareribs grilled over charcoal fires and sold with extra-hot sauce; order a Red Stripe beer to go with it. Cooked shrimp are also sold on the streets of Mo Bay; they don't look it, but they're very spicy, so be warned. And if you have an efficiency unit with a kitchenette, you can buy fresh lobster or the catch of the day from Mo Bay fishers and make your own dinner.

EXPENSIVE

Julia's. Julia's Estate, Bogue Hill. ☎ **876/952-1772.** Reservations required. Fixed-price dinner $35–$45. AE, MC, V. Daily 5:30–10:30pm. Private van transportation provided; ask when you reserve. ITALIAN.

The winding jungle road you take to reach this place is part of the before-dinner entertainment. After a jolting ride to a setting high above the city and its bay, you pass through a walled-in park that long ago was the site of a private home built in 1840 for the duke of Sutherland. Today, the focal point is a long, low-slung modern house with fresh decor and sweeping views. The chefs prepare chicken Parmesan, breaded cutlet Milanese with tomato sauce and cheese, fillet of fresh fish with lime juice and butter, and 10 different kinds of pasta. Lobster, veal, and shrimp are also regularly featured. The food, although competently prepared with fresh ingredients whenever possible, can hardly compete with the view. The homemade breads and desserts, however, are always winning accompaniments.

✪ **Norma at the Wharfhouse.** Reading Rd. ☎ **876/979-2745.** Reservations required. Main courses $26–$32. MC, V. Tues–Wed 6:30–10pm, Thurs–Sun noon–3:30pm and 6:30–10pm. Drive 15 minutes west of the town center along Rte. A1. NOUVELLE JAMAICAN.

Set in a coral-stone warehouse whose 2-foot-thick walls are bound together with molasses and lime, this is the finest restaurant in Montego Bay, a favorite of many of Jamaica's visiting celebrities. Built in 1780, it was restored by Millicent Rogers, heiress of the Standard Oil fortune, and now serves as the north-shore domain of Norma Shirley, one of Jamaica's foremost restaurateurs. Request a table either on the large pier built on stilts over the coral reef (where a view of Montego Bay glitters in the distance) or in the elegantly formal early-19th-century dining room illuminated only with flickering candles. Before- or after-dinner drinks are served in the restaurant or in the Wharf Rat, an informal bar in a separate building, much favored by locals.

The restaurant's service is impeccable, and the food is praised throughout the island. Menu specialties include grilled deviled crab backs, smoked marlin with papaya sauce, chicken breast with callaloo, nuggets of lobster in a mild curry sauce, and Châteaubriand larded with pâté in a peppercorn sauce. Dessert might be a rum-and-raisin cheesecake or a piña-colada mousse. Look also for the daily specials.

Sugar Mill Restaurant. At the Half Moon Club, Half Moon Golf Course, Rose Hall, along Rte. A1. ☎ **876/953-2314.** Reservations required. Main courses $18.50–$39.50. AE, MC, V. Daily noon–2:30pm and 7–10pm. A minivan can be sent to most hotels to pick you up. INTERNATIONAL/CARIBBEAN.

This restaurant, near a stone ruin of what used to be a water wheel for a sugar plantation, is reached after a drive through rolling landscape. Guests dine by candlelight either indoors or on an open terrace with a view of a pond, the water wheel, and plenty of greenery. Lunch can be a relatively simple affair, perhaps an ackee burger with bacon, preceded by Mama's pumpkin soup and followed with homemade rum-and-raisin ice cream. For dinner, try one of the chef's zesty jerk versions of pork, fish, or chicken. He also prepares the day's catch with considerable flair. Smoked north-coast marlin is a specialty. On any given day, you can ask the waiter what's cooking in the curry pot. Chances are, it will be a Jamaican specialty such as goat, full of flavor and served with island chutney. Top your meal with a cup of unbeatable Blue Mountain coffee.

MODERATE

Ambrosia. Across from the Wyndham Rose Hall Resort, Rose Hall. ☎ **876/953-2650.** Reservations recommended. Main courses $15–$29. AE, MC, V. Thurs–Tues 6:30–10pm. MEDITERRANEAN.

Ambrosia sits across from one of the largest hotels in Montego Bay. With its cedar-shingled design and trio of steeply pointed roofs, it has the air of a country club. Once you enter the courtyard, complete with a set of cannons, you find yourself in one of the loveliest restaurants in the area. You'll enjoy a sweeping view over the rolling lawns leading past the hotel and down to the sea, interrupted only by Doric columns. Not everything is ambrosia on the menu, but the cooks turn out a predictable array of good pasta and seafood dishes. Many of the flavors are Mediterranean, especially the lobster tails and other seafood dishes. The chefs handle the Long Island duckling expertly, although it arrives frozen on the island.

Day-O Plantation Restaurant. Barnett Estate Plantation, Lot 1, Fairfield, P.O. Box 6, Granville P.O., Montego Bay. ☎ **876/952-1825.** Reservations required. Main courses $15–$28. AE, DC, DISC, MC, V. Tues–Sun 7-11pm. It's an 8-minute drive west of town off the A-1 highway leading toward Negril; minivan service will pick up diners at any of the Montego Bay hotels, and return them after their meal. INTERNATIONAL/JAMAICAN.

This place was originally built in the 1920s as the home of the overseer of one of the region's largest sugar producers, the Barnett Plantation. Established as a restaurant in

1994, it occupies a long, indoor/outdoor dining room that's divided into two halves by a dance floor and a small stage. Here, owner Paul Hurlock performs as a one-man band, singing and entertaining the crowd while his wife, Jennifer, and their three children manage the dining room and kitchen.

Every dish is permeated with Jamaican spices and a sense of tradition. Try the chicken made plantation style, with red wine sauce and herbs; fillet of red snapper in Day-O style, with olives, white wine, tomatoes, and peppers; or, even better, one of the best versions of jerked snapper in Jamaica. We also like the grilled rock lobster with garlic butter sauce.

Marguerite's Seafood by the Sea and Margueritaville Sports Bar & Grill. Gloucester Ave. ☎ **876/952-4777.** Reservations recommended only for Marguerite's Seafood by the Sea. Main courses (in restaurant) $18.75–$28; platters, sandwiches, and snacks (in sports bar) $5–$21. AE, DC, MC, V. Restaurant daily 6–11pm; sports bar daily 10am–3am. INTERNATIONAL/SEAFOOD.

This two-in-one restaurant across from the Coral Cliff Hotel specializes in seafood served on a breeze-swept terrace overlooking the sea. There's also an air-conditioned lounge with an adjoining "Secret Garden." The chef specializes in exhibition cookery at a flambé grill. The menu is mainly devoted to seafood, including fresh fish, but there's also a number of innovative pastas and rather standard meat dishes. The changing dessert options are homemade, and a reasonable selection of wines is served. The sports bar and grill features a 110-foot Hydroslide, live music, satellite TV, water sports, a sundeck, a CD jukebox, and a straightforward menu of seafood, sandwiches, pasta, pizza, salads, and snacks—nothing fussy. Naturally, the bartenders specialize in margaritas.

Pier 1. Howard Cooke Blvd. ☎ **876/952-2452.** Main courses $9–$21. AE, MC, V. Daily 11am–11pm (even later on Sat–Sun if business warrants it). A private minivan will pick you up and return you to your hotel. SEAFOOD.

Pier 1, one of the major dining and entertainment hubs of Mo Bay, was built on a landfill in the bay. Fisherfolk bring fresh lobster to the restaurant, which the chef prepares in a number of ways, including Creole style or curried. You might begin with one of the typically Jamaican soups, such as conch chowder or red pea (which is actually red bean). At lunch, the hamburgers are the juiciest in town, or you might find the quarter-decker steak sandwich with mushrooms equally tempting. The chef also prepares such famous island dishes as jerk pork and chicken, and Jamaican red snapper. (The jerk dishes, however, are better at the Pork Pit, reviewed below.) Finish your meal with a slice of moist rum cake. You can drink or dine on the ground floor, open to the sea breezes, but most guests seem to prefer the more formal second floor. Although this place remains a local favorite and its waterfront setting is appealing, service is very laid-back.

○ Reading Reef Club Restaurant. On Bogue Lagoon, on Rte. A1 at the bottom of Long Hill Rd. (4 miles west of the town center). ☎ **876/952-5909.** Reservations required. Pastas $8–$11; main courses $10–$22. AE, MC, V. Daily 7am–11pm. ITALIAN/CONTINENTAL/CARIBBEAN.

There are those, and Lady Sarah Churchill was among them, who claim that the food served here is the finest in Montego Bay. The menu is the creative statement of JoAnne Rowe, who has a passion for cooking and party planning. In this second-floor terrace overlooking Bogue Lagoon, the offerings include perfectly prepared scampi, imaginative pasta dishes, and a catch of the day, usually snapper, yellowtail, kingfish, or dolphin (mahimahi). JoAnne also imports quality New York sirloin steaks, but whenever possible likes to use local produce. Dinner might begin with Jamaican soup, such as pepper pot or pumpkin, and end with the restaurant's well-known lime pie. Lunches are low-key, with a more limited menu.

Richmond Hill Inn. 45 Union St. ☎ **876/952-3859.** Reservations recommended. Main courses $16.50–$28.50. AE, MC, V. Daily 7:30am–9:30pm. Take a taxi (a 4-minute ride uphill, east of the town's main square) or ask the restaurant to have you picked up at your hotel. INTERNATIONAL/CONTINENTAL.

This plantation-style house was originally built in 1806 by owners of the Dewar's whiskey distillery, who happened to be distantly related to Annie Palmer, the "White Witch of Rose Hall." Today it's run by an Austrian family, who prepare well-flavored food for an appreciative clientele. Dinners include a shrimp-and-lobster cocktail, an excellent house salad, different preparations of dolphin (mahimahi), breaded breast of chicken, surf-and-turf, Wiener schnitzel, filet mignon, and a choice of dessert cakes. Many of the dishes are of a relatively standard international style, but others, especially the lobster, are worth the trek up the hill.

Town House. 16 Church St. ☎ **876/952-2660.** Reservations recommended. Main courses $15–$30. AE, DC, MC, V. Mon–Sat 11:30am–3:30pm; daily 6–10:30pm. Free limousine service to and from many area hotels. JAMAICAN/INTERNATIONAL.

Housed in a red-brick building dating from 1765, the Town House is a tranquil luncheon choice. It offers sandwiches and salads, or more elaborate fare if your appetite demands it. At night, it's flood-lit, with outdoor dining on a veranda overlooking an 18th-century parish church. You can also dine in what used to be the cellars, where old ship lanterns provide a warm atmosphere. Soups, which are increasingly ignored in many restaurants, are a specialty here. The pepper pot or pumpkin is a delectable start to a meal. The chef offers a wide selection of main courses, including the local favorite, red snapper en papillote (wrapped in parchment paper). We're fond of the chef's large rack of barbecued spareribs, with the owners' special Tennessee sauce. The pasta and steak dishes are also good, especially the homemade fettuccine with whole shrimp and the perfectly aged New York strip steak. The restaurant often attracts the rich and famous.

INEXPENSIVE

Calabash Restaurant. In the Winged Victory Hotel, 5 Queen's Dr. ☎ **876/952-3892.** Reservations recommended. Main courses $6–$25. AE, MC, V. Daily 7:30am–10pm. INTERNATIONAL/JAMAICAN.

Perched on the hillside road in Montego Bay 500 feet above the distant sea, this well-established restaurant has amused and entertained Peter O'Toole, Robert McNamara, Leonard Bernstein, Francis Ford Coppola, and Roger Moore. The restaurant was opened more than 25 years ago in this Mediterranean-style courtyard and elegantly simple eagle's-nest patio. The menu of seafood, international favorites, and Jamaican classics includes curried goat, lobster dishes, and the house specialty—baked stuffed Jamaican she-crab, plus a year-round version of a Jamaican Christmas cake.

Le Chalet. 32 Gloucester Ave. ☎ **876/952-5240.** Main courses $3–$16 lunch, $5–$16 dinner. AE, MC, V. Mon–Sat 11am–10:30pm, Sun 4–10:30pm. INTERNATIONAL/JAMAICAN.

Set in the densest concentration of stores and souvenir shops of Montego Bay's "tourist strip," this high-ceilinged restaurant lies across Gloucester Avenue from the sea, and looks somewhat like a Howard Johnson's. Food is served in copious portions, and includes a lunchtime menu of burgers, sandwiches, barbecued ribs, and salads, and a more substantial selection of evening platters. These might include chicken, steak, fresh fish, and lobster, which seems to taste best here if prepared with Jamaican curry.

The staff is articulate and helpful, and proud of their straightforward and surprisingly well-prepared cuisine.

The Native Restaurant. 29 Gloucester Ave. ☎ **876/979-2769.** Reservations recommended. Main courses J$270–J$1,100 ($7.70–$31.35). AE, MC, V. Daily 7:30am–10pm. JAMAICAN/INTERNATIONAL.

Open to the breezes, this casual restaurant with panoramic views serves some of the finest Jamaican dishes in the area. Appetizers include jerk reggae chicken and ackee and saltfish, or smoked marlin. This can be followed by such old favorites as steamed fish, or fried or jerk chicken. The most tropical offering is "goat in a boat" (that is, a pineapple shell). A more recent specialty is Boononoonoos; billed as "A Taste of Jamaica," it's a big platter with a little bit of everything—meats and several kinds of fish and vegetables. Although fresh desserts are prepared daily, you may prefer to finish with a Jamaican Blue Mountain coffee.

The Pelican. At the Pelican, Gloucester Ave. ☎ **876/952-3171.** Reservations recommended. Main courses $5–$25. AE, DC, MC, V. Daily 7am–11pm. JAMAICAN.

A Montego Bay landmark, the Pelican has been serving good food at reasonable prices for more than a quarter of a century. Most of the dishes are at the lower end of the price scale, unless you order shellfish. It's ideal for families, as it keeps long hours. Many diners come here at lunch for one of the well-stuffed sandwiches, juicy burgers, or barbecued chicken. You can also choose from a wide array of Jamaican dishes, including stewed peas and rice, curried goat, Caribbean fish, fried chicken, and curried lobster. A "meatless menu" is also featured, and includes such dishes as a vegetable plate or vegetable chili. Sirloin and seafood are available as well, and the soda fountain serves old-fashioned sundaes with real whipped cream, making it one of the best choices for kids in the area.

✪ **Pork Pit.** 27 Gloucester Ave. ☎ **876/952-1046.** 1 pound of jerk pork $11. No credit cards. Daily 11am–11:30pm. JAMAICAN.

The Pork Pit is the best place to go for the famous Jamaican jerk pork and jerk chicken, and the location is right in the heart of Montego Bay, near Walter Fletcher Beach. In fact, many beach buffs head over here for a big, reasonably priced lunch. Picnic tables encircle the building, and everything is open-air and informal. A half-pound of jerk meat, served with a baked yam or baked potato and a bottle of Red Stripe, is usually sufficient for a meal. The menu also includes steamed roast fish.

HITTING THE BEACH

Cornwall Beach (☎ **876/952-3463**) is a long stretch of white sand with dressing rooms, a bar, and a cafeteria. The grainy sand has made Cornwall a longtime favorite. Unlike some of Jamaica's remote, hard-to-get-to beaches, this one is near all the major hotels, especially the moderately priced ones. Regrettably, especially in winter, there isn't a lot of room for seclusion. Swimming is excellent all year, although we've noticed that the waters are coolest in January and February. As swimming is safe, the beach is often a playground for children—but parents should watch that their children don't venture out too far. The ocean bottom is shallow, gently sloping down to deeper waters. The beach is almost always occupied by tourists; it doesn't seem to be popular with the Jamaicans themselves. It's open daily from 9am to 5pm. Admission is $2 for adults, $1 for children.

Across from the Doctor's Cave Beach Hotel is **Doctor's Cave Beach,** on Gloucester Avenue (☎ **876/952-2566**). This beach, arguably the loveliest stretch of sand bordering Montego Bay, helped launch the resort area in the 1940s. Its gentle surf, golden sands, and fresh turquoise water make it one of the most inviting places to swim. Popular with families (the placid waters rarely become turbulent unless a storm is brewing), it's the best all-around beach in Montego Bay, although some prefer Cornwall or Walter Fletcher. Sometimes schools of tropical fish weave in and out of the waters, but usually the crowds of frolicking people scare them away. Since it's almost always packed, especially in winter, you must go early to stake out a beach-blanket-sized spot. Admission is $2 for adults, $1 for children 12 and under. Dressing rooms, chairs, umbrellas, and rafts are available from 8:30am to 5pm daily.

One of the premier beaches of Jamaica, **Walter Fletcher Beach** (☎ 876/ 979-9447), in the heart of Mo Bay, is noted for its tranquil waters, which makes it a particular favorite for families with children. This is one of the most beautiful beaches along the southern coast of Jamaica. Easy to reach, it's generally crowded in winter, and enjoyed by visitors and locals alike. Some people bring a picnic, but you must be careful not to litter, or else face a fine. From December to March, there seems to be a long-running beach party here. Somehow, regardless of how many people show up, there always seems to be a place in the sun for them. Visitors show up in almost anything (or lack of anything), although actual nudity is prohibited. There are changing rooms, a restaurant, and lifeguards. Hours are daily from 9am to 5pm. Admission is $2 for adults, $1 for children.

Frankly, you may want to skip all these public beaches entirely and head instead for the **Rose Hall Beach Club** (☎ 876/953-2323), on the main road 11 miles east of Montego Bay. The club offers half a mile of secluded white-sand beach with crystal-clear water, plus a restaurant, two bars, a covered pavilion, an open-air dance area, showers, rest rooms, changing rooms, beach volleyball courts, beach games, a full water-sports program, and live entertainment. Admission is $8 for adults, $5 for children. Hours are daily from 10am to 6pm. This beach club is far better equipped than any of the beaches previously recommended.

SPORTS & OUTDOOR PURSUITS

DEEP-SEA FISHING   Seaworld Resorts, whose main office is at the Cariblue Hotel, Rose Hall Main Road (☎ 876/953-2180), operates flying-bridge cruisers, with deck lines and outriggers, for fishing expeditions. A half-day fishing trip costs $350 for up to six participants.

DIVING, SNORKELING & OTHER WATER SPORTS   Seaworld Resorts (see above) also operates scuba-diving excursions, plus sailing, windsurfing, and more. Its dives plunge to offshore coral reefs, among the most spectacular in the Caribbean. There are three certified dive guides, one dive boat, and all the necessary equipment for both inexperienced and already-certified divers. One-tank dives cost $35; night dives are $50.

In Montego Bay, the waters right on the beach are fine for snorkeling. However, it's more rewarding to go across the channel to Cayaba Reef, Seaworld Reef, and Royal Reef, which are full of barjacks, blue and brown chromis, yellow-headed wrasses, and spotlight parrot fish. You must have a guide here, as the currents are strong and the wind picks up in the afternoon. If you're not staying at a resort offering snorkeling expeditions, then Seaworld is your best bet. For a cost of usually $25 per hour, the guide swims along with you and points out the various tropical fish.

GOLF   ✪ Wyndham Rose Hall Golf & Beach Resort, Rose Hall (☎ 876/ 953-2650), has a noted course with an unusual and challenging seaside and mountain layout, built on the shores of the Caribbean. Its eighth hole skirts the water, then doglegs onto a promontory and a green thrusting 200 yards into the sea. The back nine are the most scenic and interesting, rising up steep slopes and falling into deep ravines on Mount Zion. The 10th fairway abuts the family burial grounds of the Barretts of Wimpole Street, and the 14th passes the vacation home of singer Johnny Cash. The 300-foot-high 13th tee offers a rare panoramic view of the sea and the roof of the hotel, and the 15th green is next to a 40-foot waterfall, once featured in a James Bond movie. Amenities include a fully stocked pro shop, a clubhouse, and a professional staff. Guests at the Wyndham pay $70 for 18 holes, $50 for 9 holes. Nonguests pay $80 for 18 holes, $60 for 9 holes. Mandatory cart rental is $33 for 18 holes, and the use of a caddy (also mandatory) is another $14 for 18 holes.

The excellent course at the ✪ **Tryall** (☎ **876/956-5660**), 12 miles from Montego Bay, is so regal, it's often been the site of major golf tournaments, including the Jamaica Classic Annual and the Johnnie Walker Tournament. For 18 holes, guests of Tryall are charged $80 in winter, $40 the rest of the year. In winter, the course is usually closed to nonguests; the rest of the year, they pay a steep $150.

Half Moon, at Rose Hall (☎ **876/953-2560**), features a championship course designed by Robert Trent Jones, Sr., with manicured and diversely shaped greens. Half Moon hotel guests pay $100 for 18 holes; nonguests pay $130. Carts cost $35 for 18 holes, and caddies (which are mandatory) are hired for $15.

The ✪ **Ironshore Golf & Country Club,** Ironshore, St. James, Montego Bay (☎ **876/953-3681**), is another well-known 18-hole, 72-par course. Privately owned, it's open to all golfers who show up. Greens fees for 18 holes are $57.50.

HORSEBACK RIDING   A good program for equestrians is offered at the **Rocky Point Riding Stables,** at the Half Moon Club, Rose Hall, Montego Bay (☎ **876/953-2286**). Housed in the most beautiful barn and stables in Jamaica, built in the colonial Caribbean style in 1992, it offers around 30 horses and a helpful staff. A 90-minute beach or mountain ride costs $50, while a 2½-hour combination ride (including treks along hillsides, forest trails, and beaches, and ending with a salt-water swim) goes for $70.

RAFTING   **Mountain Valley Rafting,** 31 Gloucester Ave. (☎ **876/956-4920**), offers excursions on the Great River, which depart from the Lethe Plantation, about 10 miles south of Montego Bay. Rafts are available for $36 for up to two people. Trips last 45 minutes and operate daily from 8am to 5pm. The rafts are composed of bamboo trunks with a raised dais to sit on. In some cases, a small child can accompany two adults on the same raft, although due caution should be exercised if you choose to do this. Ask about pickup by taxi at the end of the rafting run to return you to your rented car. For $45 per person, a half-day experience will include transportation to and from your hotel, an hour's rafting, lunch, a garden tour of the Lethe property, and a taste of Jamaican liqueur.

TENNIS   **Wyndham Rose Hall Golf & Beach Resort,** Rose Hall (☎ 876/953-2650), outside Montego Bay, is an outstanding tennis resort, though it's not the equal of Half Moon or Tryall (see below). Wyndham offers six hard-surface courts, each lit for night play. As a courtesy, nonguests are sometimes invited to play for free, but permission has to be obtained from the manager. You cannot play unless you're invited. The resident pro charges $55 per hour for lessons, or $35 for 30 minutes.

Half Moon Golf, Tennis, and Beach Club, outside Montego Bay (☎ 876/953-2211), has the finest courts in the area, even outclassing Tryall. Its 13 state-of-the-art courts, seven of which are lit for night games, attract tennis players from around the world. Lessons cost $20 to $30 per half hour, $35 to $55 per hour.

Residents play free, day or night. The pro shop, which accepts reservations for court times, is open daily from 7am to 9pm. If you want to play after those hours, you switch on the lights yourself. If you're not a hotel guest, you must purchase a day pass ($50 per person) at the front desk; it allows access to the resort's courts, gym, sauna, Jacuzzi, pools, and beach facilities.

Tryall Golf, Tennis, and Beach Club, St. James (☎ 876/956-5660), offers nine hard-surface courts, three lit for night play, near its great house. Day games are free for guests; nonguests pay $30 per hour. All players are assessed $10 per hour for night-time illumination. Four on-site pros provide lessons for $15 to $30 per half hour, or $20 to $50 per hour.

SEEING THE SIGHTS
TOURS & CRUISES

The **Croydon Plantation,** P.O. Box 1348, Catadupa, St. James (☎ 876/979-8267), is a 25-mile ride from Montego Bay. It can be visited on a half-day tour from Montego Bay (or Negril) on Wednesday and Friday. Included in the $45 price are round-trip transportation from your hotel, a tour of the plantation, a taste of tropical fruits in season, and a barbecued-chicken lunch. Most hotel desks can arrange this tour.

To see plantations, go on a **Hilton High Day Tour,** through Beach View Plaza (☎ 876/952-3343). The tour includes round-trip transportation on a scenic drive through historic plantation areas. Your day starts with continental breakfast at an old plantation house. You can roam the 100 acres of the plantation and visit the German village of Seaford town or St. Leonards village nearby. Calypso music is played throughout the day, and a Jamaican lunch is served at 1pm. The cost is $55 per person for the plantation tour, breakfast, lunch, and transportation. Tour days are Tuesday, Wednesday, Friday, and Sunday.

Day and evening cruises are offered aboard the **Calico,** a 55-foot gaff-rigged wooden ketch that sails from Margaritaville on the Montego Bay waterfront. An additional vessel, **Calico B,** also carries another 40 passengers. You can be transported to and from your hotel for either cruise. The day voyage, which departs at 10am and returns at 1pm, offers a day of sailing, sunning, and snorkeling (with equipment supplied). The cruise costs $35 and is offered daily. On the **Calico's** evening voyage, which goes for $25 and is offered Wednesday to Saturday from 5 to 7pm, cocktails and wine are served as you sail through sunset. For information and reservations, call Capt. Bryan Langford, **North Coast Cruises** (☎ 876/952-5860). A 3-day notice is recommended.

MEETING SOME FEATHERED FRIENDS

Rocklands Wildlife Station. Anchovy, St. James. ☎ **876/952-2009.** Admission J$300 ($8.55). Daily 2:30–5pm.

It's a unique experience to have a Jamaican doctor bird perch on your finger to drink syrup, to feed small doves and finches millet from your hand, and to watch dozens of other birds flying in for their evening meal. Don't take children 5 and under to this sanctuary, as they tend to bother the birds. Rocklands is about a mile outside Anchovy on the road from Montego Bay.

THE GREAT HOUSES

Occupied by plantation owners, each great house of Jamaica was always built on high ground so that it overlooked the plantation itself and was in sight of the next house in the distance. It was the custom for the owners to offer hospitality to travelers crossing the island by road; travelers were spotted by the lookout, and bed and food were given freely.

Barnett Estates and Bellfield Great House. Barnett Estates. ☎ **876/952-2382.** Admission $10. Daily 9:30am–5pm.

Once a totally private estate sprawled across 50,000 acres, this great house has hosted everybody from John F. Kennedy to Winston Churchill and even Queen Elizabeth II over the years. Now anybody who pays the entrance fee can come in and take a look. The domain of the Kerr–Jarret family during 300 years of high society, this was once the seat of a massive sugar plantation. At its center is the 18th-century Bellfield Great House. Restored in 1994, it is a grand example of Georgian architecture, though not as ornate as Rose Hall (see below). Guides in costumes offer narrated tours of the property. After the tour, drop in to the old Sugar Mill Bar for a tall rum punch.

Greenwood Great House. On Rte. A1, 14 miles east of Montego Bay. ☎ **876/953-1077.** Admission $12 adults, $6 children under 12. Daily 9am–6pm.

Some people find the 15-room Greenwood even more interesting than Rose Hall (see below). Erected on its hillside perch between 1780 and 1800, the Georgian-style building was the residence of Richard Barrett (cousin of poet Elizabeth Barrett Browning). Elizabeth Barrett Browning herself never visited Jamaica, but her family used to be one of the largest landholders here. An absentee planter who lived in England, her father once owned 84,000 acres and some 3,000 slaves. On display is the original library of the Barrett family, with rare books dating from 1697, along with oil paintings of the family, Wedgwood china, rare musical instruments, and a fine collection of antique furniture. The house today is privately owned but open to the public.

✪ **Rose Hall Great House.** Rose Hall Hwy., 9 miles east of Montego Bay. ☎ **876/953-2323.** Admission $15 adults, $10 children. Daily 9am–5:15pm.

The legendary Rose Hall is the most famous great house on Jamaica. The subject of at least a dozen Gothic novels, it was immortalized in the H. G. deLisser book *White Witch of Rose Hall.* The house was built from 1778 to 1790 by John Palmer, a wealthy British planter. At its peak, this was a 6,600-acre plantation, with more than 2,000 slaves. However, it was Annie Palmer, wife of the builder's grandnephew, who became the focal point of fiction and fact. Called "Infamous Annie," she was said to have dabbled in witchcraft. She took slaves as lovers and then killed them off when they bored her. Servants called her "the Obeah woman" (*Obeah* is Jamaican for voodoo). Annie was said to have murdered several of her husbands while they slept and eventually suffered the same fate herself. Long in ruins, the house has now been restored and can be visited by the public. Annie's Pub is on the ground floor.

SHOPPING

Be prepared for aggressive vendors. Since selling a craft item may mean the difference between having a meal or going hungry, there's often a feverish attempt to peddle goods to potential customers, all of whom are viewed as rich. Therefore, prepare yourself for being pursued persistently.

Warning: Some so-called "duty-free" prices are actually lower than Stateside prices, but then the government hits you with a 10% "general consumption tax" on all items purchased. But you can still find good duty-free items here, including Swiss watches, Irish crystal, Italian handbags, Indian silks, and liquors and liqueurs. Appleton's rums are an excellent value. Tía Maria (coffee-flavored) and Rumona (rum-flavored) are the best liqueurs. Khus Khus is the local perfume. Jamaican arts and crafts are available throughout the resorts and at the Crafts Market (see below).

The main shopping areas are at **Montego Freeport,** within easy walking distance of the pier; **City Centre,** where most of the duty-free shops are, aside from those at the large hotels; and **Holiday Village Shopping Centre.**

The **Old Fort Craft Park,** a shopping complex with 180 vendors (all licensed by the Jamaica Tourist Board), fronts Howard Cooke Boulevard (up from Gloucester Avenue in the heart of Montego Bay, on the site of Fort Montego). A market with a varied assortment of handcrafts, it's grazing country for both souvenirs and more serious purchases. You'll see wall hangings, hand-woven straw items, and wood sculpture. You can even get your hair braided. Vendors can be very aggressive, so be prepared for major hassles. If you want something, also be prepared for some serious negotiation, as persistent bargaining on your part will lead to substantial discounts.

At the **Crafts Market,** near Harbour Street in downtown Montego Bay, you can find the best selection of handmade souvenirs of Jamaica, including straw hats and bags, wooden platters, straw baskets, musical instruments, beads, carved objects, and toys. That *jipijapa* hat is important if you're going to be out in the island sun.

One of the newest and most intriguing places for shopping is an upscale minimall, **Half Moon Plaza,** on the coastal road about 8 miles east of the commercial center of Montego Bay. It caters to the shopping and gastronomic needs of guests of one of the region's most elegant hotels, the Half Moon Club. On the premises are a bank and about 25 shops, each arranged around a central courtyard and selling a wide choice of carefully selected merchandise.

Ambiente Art Gallery, 9 Fort St. (☎ 876/952-7919), is housed in a 100-year-old clapboard cottage set close to the road. The Austrian-born owner, Maria Hitchins, is one of the doyennes of the Montego Bay art scene. She has personally encouraged and developed scores of fine artworks and prints by local artists. **Neville Budhai Paintings,** Budhai's Art Gallery, Reading Main Road, Reading, 5 miles east of town on the way to Negril (☎ 876/979-2568), is the art center of a distinguished artist, Neville Budhai, the president and co-founder of the Western Jamaica Society of Fine Arts. He has a distinct style, and his work captures the special flavor of the island and its people.

Things Jamaican, 44 Fort St. (☎ 876/952-5605), is a showcase for the artisans of Jamaica. On display is a wealth of products, including wood sculptures, hand-woven baskets, rums and liqueurs, jerk seasoning, and orange-pepper jelly. Look for Busha Browne's fine Jamaican sauces, especially spicy chutneys or planters' spicy piquant sauce. Also look for reproductions of the Port Royal collection. Port Royal was buried by an earthquake and tidal wave in 1692. After resting underwater for 275 years, beautiful pewter items, such as a spoon with the heads of the monarchs William and Mary, were recovered and are reproduced here. **Klass Kraft Leather Sandals,** 44 Fort St. (☎ 876/952-5782), next door to Things Jamaican, offers sandals and leather accessories made on location by a team of Jamaican craftspeople.

At **Blue Mountain Gems Workshop,** at the Holiday Village Shopping Centre (☎ 876/953-2338), you can take a tour to see the raw stone turned into finished pieces. Wooden jewelry, local carvings, and one-of-a-kind ceramic figurines are also sold. **Golden Nugget,** 8 St. James Shopping Centre, Gloucester Ave. (☎ 876/952-7707), is a duty-free shop with an impressive collection of watches for both women and men and a fine assortment of jewelry, especially gold chains. The shop also carries leading brand-name cameras and a wide assortment of French perfumes.

MONTEGO BAY AFTER DARK
There's a lot more to do here at night than go to the dance clubs, but the area certainly has those, too. Much of the entertainment is offered at the various hotels.

Pier 1, Howard Cooke Boulevard (☎ 876/952-2452), reviewed above as a restaurant, might also be your choice for a night on the town. Friday night, there's disco action from 10pm to 5am, with a J$300 ($8.55) cover, and cheap Red Stripe beer.

Cricket Club, at Wyndham Rose Hall (☎ 876/953-2650), is more than just a sports bar; it's where people go to meet and mingle with an international crowd. Televised sports, karaoke sing-alongs, tournament darts, and backgammon are all part of the fun. It's open daily from 7pm to 1am; there's no cover.

We've enjoyed the atmosphere at **Walter's,** 39 Gloucester Ave. (☎ 876/952-9391), which has an authentic Jamaican laid-back feel—complete with a constant flow of calypso and reggae music from as early as 10am daily (for the diehards) until 2am. There's never a cover, and they have live bands on the weekends.

If you want to stick to the more familiar, try **Witches Nightclub,** Holiday Inn Sunspree Resort (☎ 876/953-2485). Nonguests of the hotel can pick up a pass at the front desk for $50, which allows them all-inclusive privileges at the nightclub. The pass includes a buffet and all the drinks and dancing you can handle. We found their policy to be a bit restrictive, but the house/disco/jazz music is as imaginative as what you'll find at a club in the United States. It's open daily from 6pm to 2am.

Whereas Walter's is definitely a Jamaican experience, and Witches definitely has an American feel, **Margueritaville,** Gloucester Avenue (☎ 876/952-4777), is a hybrid of the two. It's entirely Jamaican in feel—but be aware that you are as likely to hear country and western as reggae. In addition to the $3 nightly entrance charge and $10 cover on Saturday night, there is only one other requirement of its patrons—"Just have a good time, mon."

When you tire of your fellow visitors and want to escape to a place where time has stood still—the way Jamaica used to be—head for the appropriately named ✪ **Time 'n' Place,** just east of Falmouth (☎ 876/954-4371). From Montego Bay, you'll spot the sign by the side of the road before you reach Falmouth, reading, "If you got the time, then we got the place." On an almost deserted 2-mile beach sits this raffish beach bar, built of driftwood and looking like it's just waiting for the next hurricane to blow it away. Sit back in this relaxed, friendly place and listen to the reggae from the local stations. You can order the island's best daiquiries, made from fresh local fruit, or stick around for peppery jerk chicken or lobster. Time 'n' Place isn't as completely undiscovered as we've made it out to be: Somehow the fashion editors of *Vogue* have swooped down on the place, using it as a backdrop for beach fashion shots.

3 Negril

This once sleepy village has turned into a tourist mecca, with visitors drawn to its beaches along three well-protected bays: Long Bay, Bloody Bay (now Negril Harbour), and Orange Bay. Negril became famous in the late 1960s when it attracted laid-back American and Canadian youths, who liked the idea of a place with no phones and no electricity; they rented modest digs in little houses on the West End where the local people extended their hospitality. But those days are long gone. Today, more sophisticated hotels and all-inclusive resorts, such as Hedonism II and Sandals Negril, draw a better-heeled and less rowdy crowd, including Europeans.

On the western tip of the island, Negril is now famous for its ✪ **Seven Mile Beach.** The town is 50 miles and about a 2-hour drive from Montego Bay's airport, along a winding road and past ruins of sugar estates and great houses. At some point you'll want to explore **Booby Cay,** a tiny islet off the Negril coast. Once it was featured in the Walt Disney film *20,000 Leagues Under the Sea,* but now it's overrun with nudists from Hedonism II.

Chances are, however, you'll stake out your own favorite spot along Negril's Seven Mile Beach. You don't need to get up for anything, as somebody will be along to serve you. Perhaps it'll be the "banana lady," with a basket of fruit perched on her head. Maybe the "ice-cream man" will set up a stand right under a coconut palm. Surely the "beer lady" will find you as she strolls along the beach with a carton of Jamaican beer on her head, and hordes of young men will peddle illegal ganja (marijuana), whether you smoke it or not.

There are really two Negrils: The West End is the site of many little local restaurants, and cottages that still receive visitors. The other Negril is on the east end, the first you approach on the road coming in from Montego Bay. Here are the upscale hotels, with some of the most panoramic beachfronts.

GETTING THERE

BY PLANE If you're going to Negril, you will fly into **Donald Sangster Airport** in Montego Bay. Some hotels, particularly the all-inclusive resorts, will arrange for airport transfers from that point. Be sure to ask when you book.

If your hotel does not provide transfers, you can fly to Negril's small airport on the independent carrier **Air Jamaica Express,** booking your connection through Air Jamaica (☎ **800/523-5585** in the U.S.). The airfare is $45 one-way.

BY BUS The 2-hour bus trip costs $20. We recommend **Tour Wise** (☎ **876/979-1027** in Montego Bay, or 876/974-2323 in Ocho Rios) or **Caribic Vacations** (☎ **876/953-9874** in Montego Bay, or 876/974-9106 in Ocho Rios). The bus will drop you off at your final destination once you reach Negril.

BY RENTAL CAR & TAXI Negril is a 76-mile, 2-hour drive east of Montego Bay. For information on car rentals, see "Getting Around" in section 1, "Essentials," at the beginning of this chapter. By taxi, a typical one-way fare from Montego Bay to Ocho Rios is $50 to $60. Always negotiate and agree on a fare *before* getting into the cab.

WHERE TO STAY
VERY EXPENSIVE

The Caves. P.O. Box 15, Lighthouse Station, Negril, Jamaica, W.I. ☎ **800/OUT-POST** in the U.S., or 876/957-0270. Fax 876/957-4930. www.islandoutpost.com. 9 units. Winter $450 double; $500–$625 one-bedroom apt for 2; $700–$900 two-bedroom apt for 2; $950 two-bedroom apt for 4. Off-season $425 double; $500 one-bedroom apt for 2; $575–$775 two-bedroom apt for 2; $825 two-bedroom apt for 4. Rates are all-inclusive. AE, MC, V.

This small-scale hotel was established in 1990 on 2 acres of land perched above a honeycombed network of cliffs, 32 feet above the surf at a point near Negril's lighthouse, close to Jamaica's westernmost tip. Accommodations are summer-style units within a quintet of cement and wood-sided cottages, each with a thatched roof and sturdy furniture. None have air-conditioning, but a TV and VCR can be brought in upon request. The medium-size cottages are colorfully West Indian, with an abundance of batik fabrics, hand-carved furnishings inlaid with Jamaican plant motifs, and four-posters draped with mosquito netting over fine linen and quality mattresses. These rooms are more suitable for romantic couples, and small children will not be happy here. Bathrooms come with hair dryers and thick towels. Suites contain a limited supply of cooking equipment. You get a vivid sense that this place is well-suited for those who opt to rent the entire compound for reunions of friends and family.

Dining: Sumptuous meals are prepared only for guests, not for outsiders, and are included, along with domestic Jamaican drinks from the bar, as part of the all-inclusive price.

Negril

JAMAICA

O Montego Bay
O Negril
Kingston

Accommodations
The Caves **16**
Charela Inn **10**
Grand Lido **2**
Hedonism II **3**
Negril Beach Club Hotel **13**
Negril Cabins **1**
Negril Gardens Hotel **12**
Negril Inn **11**
Negril Tree House **8**
Sandals Negril **4**
Sea Splash Resort **5**
Swept Away **6**

Dining
Chicken Lavish **15**
Cosmo's Seafood
  Restaurant & Bar **7**
Le Vendôme **10**
Margueritaville **9**
Mariners Inn &
  Restaurant **14**
Restaurant Tan-Ya's/
  Calico Jack's **5**
Rick's Café **17**

Airport ✈ Beach ☂

0   1 Mile
0   1 Kilometer
N

To **Montego Bay**

Bloody Bay

Norman Manley Blvd.

Negril Airport

THE GREAT MORASS

Booby Cay

Hedonism II Beach

S E V E N   M I L E   B E A C H

A1

PARISH OF HANNOVER
PARISH OF WESTMORELAND

Long Bay

Norman Manley Blvd.

Caribbean Sea

South Negril River

Crafts Market

Negril
Yacht Club

Post Office

Jamaica
Tourist Board

Plaza
de Negril

Police
Station

Sheffield Rd.

West End Rd.

Whitehall Rd.

WHITE HALL

WEST END

2-0145

Amenities: Spa treatments, sauna, bikes available, airport transfers, snorkeling equipment. Many sports, such as horseback riding, kayaking, scuba, and golf, can be arranged. There's a saltwater pool and Jacuzzi on site, but unless you're interested in snorkeling in the rocky waters offshore, you'll have to drive into Negril for a sandy beach.

✪ **Grand Lido.** Negril Bloody Bay (P.O. Box 88), Negril, Jamaica, W.I. ☎ **800/859-7873** in the U.S., 800/553-4320 in Canada, or 876/957-5010. Fax 876/957-5517. www. superclubs.com. 210 units. A/C MINIBAR TV TEL. All-inclusive rates for 4 days/3 nights: Winter $2,360–$3,140 suite for 2. Off-season $1,700–$2,580 suite for 2. Minimum stay of 4 days/3 nights. AE, MC, V. Children not accepted.

The grandest and most architecturally stylish hotel of its chain, the Grand Lido sits on a flat and lushly landscaped stretch of beachfront adjacent to Hedonism II. It's much more subdued than its neighbor. This is the most upscale and deliciously luxurious of the string of resorts known as Jamaica's SuperClubs. Each spacious suite contains either a patio or a balcony that (except for a few) overlooks the beach. The hotel recently added 10 luxury suites to its impressive roster of accommodations, which lie in modern wings running parallel to the beach. Most units are bilevel, with stereos, coffeemakers, private safes, king or twin beds (each with a quality mattress and fine linen), and large bathrooms with tub/showers and hair dryers. The elegant hardwood furniture in the rooms was handmade in Jamaica. The smaller of the resort's two beaches is reserved for nudists. If you don't like looking at nude bathers outside your window, ask for a "swimwear-side" unit. Only adults are welcome, but unlike many other all-inclusive resorts, especially Club Med, there's no resistance here to giving a room to a single occupant.

Dining/Diversions: In addition to the cavernous and airy main dining room, a trio of restaurants serve nouvelle, continental, and Italian cuisines. Guests also enjoy an all-night disco, a piano bar, pool tables, and nine bars. Even after the four restaurants close, there are three different dining enclaves that remain open throughout the night, each with a bubbling Jacuzzi nearby.

Amenities: Four tennis courts, two pools, four Jacuzzis, gym/sauna/health club, spa facility, and one of the most glamorous yachts in the West Indies, the *M-Y Zein*, given by Aristotle Onassis to Prince Rainier and Princess Grace of Monaco as a wedding present. 24-hour room service, concierge, laundry, free airport transfers, tour desk that arranges visits to other parts of Jamaica, instructors to teach tennis and sailing.

Hedonism II. Negril Beach Rd. (P.O. Box 25), Negril, Jamaica, W.I. ☎ **800/859-7873** in the U.S., or 876/957-5200. Fax 876/957-4289. E-mail: info@superclubs.com. 280 units. A/C. All-inclusive rates for 4 days/3 nights: Winter $1,450–$2,310 double, $2,640–$3,630 suite for 2. Off-season $1,164–$1,980 double, $2,100–$3,180 suite for 2. AE, MC, V. Children not accepted.

Devoted to the pursuit of pleasure, Hedonism II packs the works into a one-package deal, including all the drinks and partying anyone could want. There's no tender of any sort, and tipping is not permitted. Of all the members of the SuperClubs chain, this is the most raucous. It's a meat market, deliberately inviting its mainly single guests to go wild for a week. To provide a sense of the ambience, we'll tell you that one manager boasted that the resort holds the record for the most people in a Jacuzzi at once. The rooms are stacked in two-story clusters dotted around a sloping 22-acre site about 2 miles east of the town center. Most of the guests, who must be at least 18 years of age, are Americans. Closed to the general public, this is not a couples-only resort; singles are both accepted and encouraged. The hotel will find you a roommate if you'd like to book on the double-occupancy rate. Accommodations don't have balconies, but

A Note on Nudity

Nude bathing is allowed at a number of hotels, clubs, and beaches (especially in Negril), but only where there are signs stating "swimsuits optional." Elsewhere, the law will not even allow topless sunbathing.

---

are very spacious, with such extras as coffeemakers and irons and ironing boards. Each has a king or twin beds, fitted with firm mattresses and fine linen, with mirrors hanging over the beds. Bathrooms have combination tub/showers and hair dryers.

On one section of this resort's beach, clothing is optional. It's called the "Nude" section; the other is known as "the Prude." The resort also has a secluded beach on nearby Booby Cay, where guests are taken twice a week for picnics.

Dining/Diversions: There's nightly entertainment, along with a live band, a high-energy disco, and a piano bar. International cuisine is served in daily buffets. There's also a clothing-optional bar, a prude bar, and a grill.

Amenities: Sailing, snorkeling, waterskiing, scuba diving, windsurfing, glass-bottom boat, clothing-optional Jacuzzi, pool, six tournament-class tennis courts (lit at night), two badminton courts, basketball court, two indoor squash courts, volleyball court, table tennis, Nautilus and free-weight gyms, aerobics, indoor games room, massage, free airport transfers.

Sandals Negril. Norman Manley Blvd., Negril, Jamaica, W.I. ☎ **800/SANDALS** in the U.S. and Canada, or 876/957-5216. Fax 876/957-5338. www.sandals.com. E-mail: sng@ cw.jamaica.com. 215 units. A/C TV TEL. All-inclusive rates for 4 days/3 nights: Winter $1,780–$2,220 double; $2,360–$3,100 suite. Off-season $1,640–$2,000 double; $2,100–$2,820 suite. Minimum stay of 4 days/3 nights. AE, MC, V. Children not accepted.

Sandals Negril is an all-inclusive, couples-only (male-female) resort, part of the expanding empire of the enterprising local businessman Gordon "Butch" Stewart, who pioneered similar operations in Montego Bay. If you're the wildest of raunchy party types, you'd be better off at Hedonism II—life isn't exactly subdued at Sandals, but it's tamer. The resort occupies some 13 acres of prime beachfront land a short drive east of Negril's center, on the main highway leading in from Montego Bay. It's about a 1½-hour drive (maybe more) from the Montego Bay airport. The developers linked two older hotels into a unified whole, and most guests never leave the property. The crowd is usually convivial, informal, and young. The casual, well-furnished rooms have a tropical motif. Recently renovated, they come in a wide range of styles, but are generally spacious, with such extras as coffeemakers, private safes, and hair dryers. The best units open directly on the beach. Honeymooners usually end up in a Jamaican-built four-poster mahogany bed. For a balcony and sea view, you have to pay the top rates.

Dining/Diversions: Rates include all meals; snacks; unlimited drinks, day and night, at one of four bars (including two swim-up pool bars); and nightly entertainment, including theme parties. Coconut Cove is the main dining room, but guests can also eat at one of the specialty rooms, including the Sundowner, offering white-glove service and Jamaican cuisine, with low-calorie health food served beside the beach. Kimono features Japanese cuisine.

Amenities: Three freshwater pools, tennis courts (lit at night), scuba diving, snorkeling, Sunfish sailing, windsurfing, canoeing, aerobics classes, glass-bottom boat, fitness center with saunas and Universal exercise equipment. Laundry, massage, airport transfers.

✪ **Swept Away.** Norman Manley Blvd. (P.O. Box 77), Negril, Jamaica, W.I. ☎ **800/545-7937** in the U.S. and Canada, or 876/957-4061. Fax 876/957-4060. 134 units. A/C TEL. All-inclusive rates for 3 nights: Winter $1,500–$1,875 per couple. Off-season $1,380–$1,710 per couple. AE, DC, MC, V. Children not accepted.

Another member of the SuperClubs, this is one of the best-equipped hotels in Negril—it's certainly the one most conscious of both sports and relaxation. All-inclusive, it caters to male-female couples eager for an ambience with all possible diversions available but absolutely no organized schedule and no pressure to participate if you just want to relax. As a staff member told us (privately, of course), "We get the health and fitness nuts, and Sandals or Hedonism get the sex-crazed." The resort occupies 20 flat and sandy acres, which straddle both sides of the highway leading in from Montego Bay. The accommodations (the hotel defines them as "veranda suites" because of their large balconies) are in 26 two-story villas clustered together and accented with flowering shrubs and vines, a few steps from the 7-mile beachfront. Each lovely, airy, and spacious unit has a ceiling fan, a king-size bed, and (unless the vegetation obscures it) sea views. Twenty of the units contain a combination tub/shower, the rest showers only; all have hair dryers.

Dining/Diversions: The resort's social center is its international restaurant, Feathers, which lies inland, across the road from the sea. There's also an informal beachfront restaurant and bar, and four bars scattered throughout the property, including a "veggie bar."

Amenities: Racquetball, squash, and 10 lit tennis courts; fully equipped gym; aerobics; yoga; massage; steam; sauna; whirlpool; billiards; bicycles; beachside pool; scuba diving; windsurfing; reef snorkeling. Room service (for continental breakfast only), laundry, tour desk for arranging visits to other parts of Jamaica, airport transfers.

EXPENSIVE/MODERATE

✪ **Charela Inn.** Norman Manley Blvd. (P.O. Box 33), Negril, Jamaica, W.I. ☎ **800/423-4095** in the U.S., or 876/957-4648. Fax 876/957-4414. www.negrilbiz.com/charela. 39 units. A/C TEL. Winter $154–$210 double. Off-season $118–$148 double. MAP (breakfast and dinner) $38 per person extra. 5-night minimum stay in winter, 3-night minimum in summer. MC, V.

A seafront inn reminiscent of a Spanish hacienda, this place sits on the main beach strip on 3 acres of landscaped grounds. The building's inner courtyard, with a tropical garden and a round, freshwater pool, opens onto one of the widest (250 feet) sandy beaches in Negril. The inn attracts a loyal following of visitors seeking a home away from home. Try for one of the 20 or so rooms with a view of the sea, as these are the most desirable. Accommodations are generally spacious, often with a bit of Jamaican character with their wicker furnishings and ceiling fans. All the rooms have either private patios or balconies. Most of the good-sized bathrooms have combination tub/showers, though some have shower stalls only.

Le Vendôme, facing the sea and the garden, offers both an à la carte menu and a five-course fixed-price meal that changes daily (see "Where to Dine," below). Sunsets are toasted on open terraces facing the sea. Sunset cruises, lasting 3½ hours, are offered, along with Sunfish sailing, windsurfing, and kayaking. Thursday and Saturday nights, there's live entertainment. Simplicity, a quiet elegance, and excellent value for the money are the hallmarks of the inn.

Negril Beach Club Hotel. Norman Manley Blvd. (P.O. Box 7), Negril, Jamaica, W.I. ☎ **800/526-2422** in the U.S. and Canada, or 876/957-4220. Fax 876/957-4364. 85 units. A/C. Winter $189 double; $210 suite. Off-season $108 double; $138 suite. MAP (breakfast and dinner) $30 per person extra. AE, MC, V.

This casual, informal resort, where topless bathing is the norm, has many admirers, although it will be too laid-back and too basically furnished and maintained for those who want some vacation comfort and pampering. The resort is designed around a series of white stucco cottages with exterior stairways and terraces. The entire complex is clustered like a horseshoe around a rectangular garden that abuts a sandy beach. The accommodations range from simply furnished rooms, rented either as singles or doubles, to one- and two-bedroom suites, each with a kitchenette. The well-appointed rooms each have a private bathroom; the less expensive units don't have balconies. Because some of the units are time-shares, not all of the accommodations are available at all times.

There's easy access to a full range of sporting facilities, including snorkeling, a pool, volleyball, table tennis, and windsurfing. Other activities can be organized nearby, and beach barbecues and buffet breakfasts are ample and frequent. The Seething Cauldron Restaurant on the beach serves barbecues and seafood.

Negril Gardens Hotel. Norman Manley Blvd. (P.O. Box 58), Negril, Jamaica, W.I. ☎ **800/752-6824** in the U.S. or 876/957-4408. Fax 876/957-4374. www.negrilgardens.com. E-mail: negrilgardens@cwjamaica.com. 66 units. A/C TV TEL. Winter $165–$225 double; $280 one-bedroom suite; $350 two-bedroom suite. Off-season $145 double; $175 one-bedroom suite; $275 two-bedroom suite. Extra person $40. Two children under 12 stay free in parents' room. MAP (breakfast and dinner) $40 per person extra. AE, MC, V.

Attracting a young, international clientele, Negril Gardens rests amid tropical greenery on the famous 7-mile stretch of beach. The two-story Georgian-style villas are well furnished, and rooms open onto a front veranda or a balcony with either a beach or a garden view. The cheaper garden-side units face the pool, pool bar, and tennis court. A quartet of beachside rooms is the most requested. Even though small, most units contain two double beds, each fitted with a firm mattress. All come with private safes and furnished balconies or patios.

Directly on the beach is a Tahitian-style bar, and right behind it stands an alfresco restaurant, the Orchid Terrace, serving some of the best food in Negril, including international and authentically Jamaican dishes. Nonguests are welcome to dine here.

Negril Inn. Norman Manley Blvd. (P.O. Box 59), Negril, Jamaica, W.I. ☎ **876/957-4209.** Fax 876/957-4365. 46 units. A/C. Winter $280 double; $390 triple. Off-season $220 double; $270 triple. Rates are all-inclusive, including airport transfers. AE, MC, V. Children not accepted in winter.

Located about 3 miles east of the town center in the heart of the 7-mile beach stretch, this is one of the smallest all-inclusive resorts in Negril. Because of its size, the atmosphere is much more low-key than what you'll find at its larger competitors, such as Hedonism II. The resort, not confined to couples only, offers very simple but comfortably furnished guest rooms with private balconies, in a series of two-story structures in a garden setting. The helpful staff offers a host of activities, day and night.

Included in the package are all meals, all alcoholic drinks (except champagne), and nightly entertainment (including a disco). Meals are consumed in the resort's only restaurant, which serves pretty good food; there are also bars in the disco and beside the pool. Amenities include a range of water sports (windsurfing, waterskiing, scuba diving, snorkeling, hydrosliding, and aqua bikes), two floodlit tennis courts, a Jacuzzi, a piano room, a Universal weight room, and a freshwater pool. Room service (for breakfast only), laundry, round-trip transfers to and from the airport at Montego Bay, and filtered water are also available.

Negril Tree House. Norman Manley Blvd. (P.O. Box 29), Negril, Jamaica, W.I. ☎ **800/NEGRIL-1** in the U.S. and Canada, or 876/957-4287. Fax 876/957-4386. www.negrilbiz.com.

E-mail: jacksonj@cwjamaica.com. *67 units. A/C TV TEL. Winter $145.31–$180.19 double; $296.44–$331.30 family suite for up to 4. Off-season $104.63–$139.50 double; $174.38–$197.63 family suite. AE, MC, V.*

Negril Tree House is a desirable little hideaway with an ideal beachfront location. Simply furnished units, including 12 suites, each with very small tiled bathrooms, are scattered across the property in 11 octagonal buildings. Rooms come with terrazzo floors, ceiling fans, and private safes; suites also have kitchenettes. The plumbing is hardly state-of-the-art with a dripping faucet here and there. This rather rustic resort features a number of water sports, including parasailing, snorkeling, and jet-skiing. The Tree House also has a pool, a Jacuzzi, and beach volleyball.

Sea Splash Resort. Norman Manley Blvd. (P.O. Box 123), Negril, Jamaica, W.I. ☎ **800/ 254-2786** in the U.S., or 876/957-4041. Fax 876/957-4049. E-mail: seasplash@mail. cwjamaica.com. *15 units. A/C TV TEL. Winter $199 suite for 2. Off-season $135 suite for 2. Extra person $20. Full board $33 per person extra. AE, CB, DC, MC, V.*

Partly because of its small size, this beachfront resort often has a friendly, personable feeling. In deliberate contrast to the megaresorts nearby, it lies on a small but carefully landscaped sliver of beachfront land planted with tropical vegetation. The suites are spacious and stylishly decorated with wicker furniture and fresh pastel colors. All are the same size and contain the same amenities—a kitchenette, a balcony or patio, large closets, and either a king-size bed or twin beds—although those on the upper floor have higher ceilings and feel more spacious. Living areas contain sofa beds, ideal for small families. The small bathrooms come with hair dryers.

The resort contains two different restaurants, Calico Jack's and the more elaborate Tan-Ya's (see "Where to Dine," below). There's also a poolside bar, a small gym, a Jacuzzi, and a pool. Amenities include baby-sitting, laundry, and room service.

INEXPENSIVE

✪ Negril Cabins. Ruthland Point, Negril, Jamaica, W.I. ☎ **876/957-5350.** Fax 876/957-5381. www.negrilcabins.com. E-mail: negrilcabins@cwjamaica.com. *70 units. Winter $150–$176 cabin for 2; $192 cabin for 3. Off-season $130–$154 cabin for 2; $162 cabin for 3. Children 12 and under stay free in parents' room. AE, MC, V.*

Except for the palm trees and the sandy beach, you might imagine yourself at a log-cabin complex in the Maine woods. In many ways, this is the best bargain in Negril, suitable for the budget-conscious traveler eager to get away from it all. The cabins are in a forest, across the road from a beach called Bloody Bay (where the infamous 18th-century pirate, Calico Jack, was captured by the British). The 9 acres of gardens are planted with royal palms, bull thatch, and a rare variety of mango tree.

The unadorned cabins are really small timber cottages, none more than two stories high, rising on stilts. Each accommodation offers two spacious and comfortable bedrooms, plus a balcony. Many units have been recently upgraded and improved. The best are rented as "executive suites," with a sunken living and dining area, plus a pull-out queen-size sofa bed for small families. All have private safes; the executive ones also come with air-conditioning and an iron and ironing board. Bathrooms are small but well maintained. The bar and restaurant serve tropical punch, a medley of fresh Jamaican fruits, and flavorful but unpretentious Jamaican meals. A children's program is also available, and live entertainment is offered on some nights.

✪ Rockhouse. West End Rd. (P.O Box 24), Negril, Jamaica, W.I. ☎ and fax **876/957-4373.** *28 units. MINIBAR. Winter $100 studio; $165 villa. Off-season $85 studio; $120 villa. Extra person $25. Children 11 and under stay free in parents' unit. AE, MC, V.*

This boutique inn stands in stark contrast to the hedonistic all-inclusive resorts, evoking both a South Seas island retreat and an African village, with thatched roofs capping stone-and-pine huts. A team of enterprising young Aussies recently restored and expanded this place, which was one of Negril's first hotels (the Stones hung out here in the 1970s). The rooms have minibars, ceiling fans, and fridges. You'll really feel you're in Jamaica when you go to bed in a mosquito-draped four-poster or take a shower in the open air (mercifully, the toilet facilities are inside). One cottage is divided into two studios; other units contain queen-size beds; and four cottages have sleeping lofts with extra queen-size beds. A quarter mile from the beach, Rockhouse has a ladder down to a cove where you can swim and snorkel; equipment is available for rent. After a refreshing dip in the cliffside pool, you can dine in the open-sided restaurant pavilion serving spicy local fare three times a day.

WHERE TO DINE
EXPENSIVE

Le Vendôme. In the Charela Inn, Negril Beach. ☎ **876/957-4648.** Reservations recommended for Sat dinner. Continental breakfast $5; English breakfast $10; main courses $20–$30; fixed-price meal $24–$35. MC, V. Daily 7:30am–10pm. JAMAICAN/FRENCH.

This place some 3½ miles from the town center enjoys a good reputation. You don't have to be a hotel guest to sample the cuisine, which owners Daniel and Sylvia Grizzle describe as a "dash of Jamaican spices" with a "pinch of French flair." Dine out on the terra-cotta terrace, where you can enjoy a view of the palm-studded beach. Start off with a homemade pâté, or perhaps a vegetable salad, and then follow with baked snapper, duckling à l'orange, or a seafood platter. You may have had better versions of these dishes at other places, of course, but the food is quite satisfying here, and there's rarely an unhappy customer. The wines and champagnes are imported from France.

Rick's Café. Lighthouse Rd. ☎ **876/957-0380.** Reservations accepted for parties of 6 or more. Main courses $12–$28. MC, V. Daily 2–10pm. SEAFOOD/STEAKS.

At sundown, everybody in Negril heads toward the lighthouse along the West End strip to Rick's Café, whether or not they want a meal. Of course, the name was inspired by the old watering hole of Bogie's *Casablanca*. There was a real Rick (Richard Hershman), who first opened this bar back in 1974, but he's long gone. This laid-back cafe was made famous in the '70s as a hippie hangout, and ever since it's attracted the bronzed and the beautiful (and some who want to be). The sunset here is said to be the most glorious in Negril, and after a few fresh-fruit daiquiris (pineapple, banana, or papaya), you'll give no argument. Casual dress is the order of the day, and reggae and rock comprise the background music.

There are several Stateside specialties, including imported steaks along with a complete menu of blackened dishes, Cajun style. You might begin with the smoked marlin platter. The fish—red snapper, fresh lobster, or grouper—is always fresh. The food is rather standard fare, and expensive for what you get, but that hardly keeps the crowds away. You can also buy plastic bar tokens at the door, which you can use instead of money, à la Club Med.

MODERATE/INEXPENSIVE

✪ **Chicken Lavish.** West End Rd. ☎ **876/957-4410.** Main courses $5–$13. MC, V. Daily 10am–10pm. JAMAICAN.

We've found that Chicken Lavish, whose name we love, is the best of the low-budget eateries. Just show up on the doorstep of this place along the West End beach strip, and see what's cooking. Curried goat is a specialty, as is fresh fried fish. The red snapper is caught in local waters. But the big draw is the restaurant's namesake, the chef's special Jamaican chicken. He'll tell you, and you may agree, that it's the best on the island. What to wear here? Dress as you would to clean up your backyard on a hot August day.

✪ **Cosmo's Seafood Restaurant & Bar.** Norman Manley Blvd. ☎ **876/957-4784.** Main courses J$200–J$620 ($5.70–$17.65). AE, MC, V. Daily 9am–10pm. SEAFOOD.

One of the best places to go for local seafood is centered around a Polynesian thatched bohío (beach hut) open to the sea and bordering the main beachfront. This is the dining spot of Cosmo Brown, who entertains locals as well as visitors. You can order his famous conch soup, or conch in a number of other ways, including steamed or curried. He's also known for his savory kettle of curried goat, or you might prefer freshly caught seafood or fish, depending on what the catch turned up. It's a rustic establishment, and prices are among the most reasonable at the resort.

Margueritaville. Norman Manley Blvd. ☎ **876/957-4467.** Burgers and sandwiches $5.75–$7.75; main courses $7.75–$25.95. AE, MC, V. Daily 10am–11pm. AMERICAN/INTERNATIONAL.

From its open, breeze-filled windows and veranda, it's only a short walk across the sand, past hundreds of sunbathing bodies, to the sea. Set in the center of Negril, adjacent to the Beachcomber Hotel, this restaurant combines a gift shop, an art gallery, and a bar into one high-energy, well-managed, and sometimes very crowded place. Look for at least 50 variations of margaritas. Menu items include burgers, sandwiches, lobster, grilled chicken and fish, and conch. Most of the paintings in the on-site art gallery, incidentally, were executed by a long-time resident of Negril, American-born Geraldine Robbins. Every evening, beginning around 9pm, there's live, usually loud, music. Artists include local reggae stars Cowboys on Pebbles and Fathers & Sons. On Saturday night, there's old-time Jamaican music known as *mentho,* whose style most locals remember from their childhoods. Sunday and Wednesday, everyone can be a star, thanks to a karaoke setup.

Mariners Inn & Restaurant. West End Rd. ☎ **876/957-0392.** Pizzas $6.60–$10.20; main courses $14–$20; all-you-can-eat dinner buffet $11. AE, MC, V. Daily 8am–10:30pm. JAMAICAN/AMERICAN/CONTINENTAL.

Many guests escaping from their all-inclusive dining rooms head here, looking for some authentic Jamaican flavor. The bar is shaped like a boat, and there's an adjoining restaurant, entered through a tropical garden. As you drink or dine, the sea breezes waft in, adding to the relaxed atmosphere. The one appetizer is a bacon-wrapped banana, not everybody's favorite way to begin a meal, but the food picks up considerably after that. The chef knows how to use curry effectively in the lobster and chicken dishes, and even the goat. The *coq au vin* (chicken in wine) has never been to France, so you're better off sticking to such dishes as pan-fried snapper or fried chicken.

Restaurant Tan-Ya's/Calico Jack's. In the Sea Splash Resort, Norman Manley Blvd. ☎ **876/957-4041.** Reservations recommended. Breakfast from $3; lunch $4–$7.50; dinner main courses $10–$23. AE, MC, V. Daily 11am–3pm and 6:30–10pm. JAMAICAN/INTERNATIONAL.

Set within the thick white walls of this resort, these two restaurants provide well-prepared food and the charm of a small, family-run establishment. Informal and very affordable lunches are served at Calico Jack's, whose tables are in an enlarged gazebo, near a bar and the pool. The resort's gastronomic showcase, however, is Tan-Ya's. Here, specialties include lemon-flavored chicken, Tan-Ya's snapper with herb butter, three different preparations of lobster, and deviled crab backs sautéed in butter. On many nights these dishes are filled with flavor and well prepared; on some occasions they're slightly off the mark.

HITTING THE BEACH

Beloved by the hippies of the 1960s, ✪ **Seven Mile Beach** is still going strong, but it's no longer the idyllic retreat it once was. Resorts now line this beach, attracting an international crowd. Nudity, however, is just as prevalent, especially along the stretch near Cosmo's (see "Where to Dine," above). Seven Mile Beach promotes a laid-back lifestyle and carefree ambience more than any other on Jamaica, perhaps even in the Caribbean. On the western tip of the island, the white powdery sand stretches from Bloody Bay in Hanover to Negril Lighthouse in Westmoreland; clean, tranquil aquamarine waters, coral reefs, and a backdrop of palm trees add to the appeal. When you tire of the beach, you'll find all sorts of resorts, clubs, beach bars, open-air restaurants, and the like. Vendors will try to sell you everything from Red Stripe beer to ganja (see "A Word on Marijuana," on p. 350).

Many of the big resorts have nude beaches as well. The hottest and most exotic is found at **Hedonism II,** although **Grand Lido** next door draws its fair share. Nude beaches at each of these resorts are in separate and "private" areas of the resort property. Total nudity is required for strolling the beach, and security guards keep Peeping Toms at bay. Photography is not permitted. Most of the resorts also have a nude bar, a nude hot tub, and a nude swimming pool.

SCUBA DIVING & SNORKELING

The **Negril Scuba Centre,** in the Negril Beach Club Hotel, Norman Manley Boulevard (☎ **800/818-2963** or 876/957-9641), is the most modern, best-equipped scuba facility in Negril. A professional staff of internationally certified scuba instructors and dive masters teach and guide divers to Negril's colorful coral reefs. Beginner's dive lessons are offered daily, as well as multiple-dive packages for certified divers. Full scuba certifications and specialty courses are also available.

A resort course, designed for first-time divers with basic swimming abilities, costs $75 and includes all instruction, equipment, a lecture on water and diving safety, and one open-water dive. It begins at 10am daily and ends at 2pm. A one-tank dive costs $30 per dive plus $20 for equipment rental (not necessary if divers bring their own gear). More economical is a two-tank dive, which must be completed in one day. It costs $55, plus the (optional) $20 rental of all equipment. This organization is PADI-registered, although it accepts all recognized certification cards.

One of the best-recommended dive facilities in Negril is **Scuba World,** a PADI-approved five-star dive shop at Orange Bay (☎ **876/957-6290**). It's open daily from 8am to 5pm. A 4-day certification course costs $350, a resort course for beginners is $70, and a one-tank dive for already-certified divers goes for $30, plus $20 for the rental of the necessary equipment. A two-tank dive costs $55, plus only $10 for equipment rental.

The best area for snorkeling is off the cliffs in the West End. The coral reef here is extremely lively with marine life at a depth of about 10 to 15 feet. The waters are so clear and sparkling that just by wading in and looking down, you'll see lots of marine life. The fish are small but extremely colorful. Along West End Road are dozens of shops that rent snorkeling equipment for about $10 per day. There is no snorkeling on the beachfront.

NEGRIL AFTER DARK

Although smaller than Mo Bay, Negril is not without nightspots, though you're likely to spend most evenings enjoying the entertainment in your own resort. Fun places are easy to find, as nearly *everything* is on Norman Manley Boulevard, the only major road in Negril.

Alfred's (☎ 876/957-4735) is a neat Jamaican experience where travelers will still feel welcome. There's no cover, and in addition to grabbing a drink, you can also order a bite to eat until midnight. Particularly interesting is the beach-party area, with a stage for live reggae and jazz acts. You can also boogie on the dance floor inside, shaking to hits you'll hear at clubs Stateside.

For more Jamaican/American nightclub experiences, try **De Buss** (☎ 876/957-4405). The cover depends on special events or live acts, so call ahead to see what's planned.

4 Falmouth

This port town lies on the north coast of Jamaica, only about 23 miles east of Montego Bay. The **Trelawny Beach Hotel** originally put it on the tourist map (though we no longer recommend staying here, as it's a bit worn down). The town itself is interesting but ramshackle. There's talk about fixing it up for visitors, but no one has done anything yet. If you leave your car at Water Square, you can explore the town in about an hour. The present courthouse was reconstructed from the early 19th-century building, and fisherfolk still congregate on Seaboard Street. You'll pass the Customs Office and a parish church dating from the late 18th century. Later, you can go on a shopping expedition outside town to Caribatik.

WHERE TO STAY

✪ **Good Hope.** P.O. Box 50, Falmouth, Jamaica, W.I. ☎ **876/954-3289.** Fax 876/954-3289. www.goodhope.com.jm. 10 units. Winter $150–$190 double. Off-season $125–$150 double. Rates include continental breakfast. AE, MC, V.

This beautifully restored 1755 Georgian great house in the mountains of Cockpit Country exemplifies the romantic living that can be found in the more rural parts of Jamaica. Some 5 miles south of Falmouth and the beach, and set on a 2,000-acre plantation with the Martha Brae River running through, the estate features lush gardens and country trails, horseback riding, tennis, and swimming. This is the closest you can get to enjoying the rich life of the grand planters of long ago—but with all the modern conveniences.

Don't despair as you traverse the unmarked potholed road getting here (call for directions). The house at the end is worth the effort. The main house, which contains four spacious guest rooms, is furnished with antiques, all evocative of the plantation era. The former coach house has five medium-size rooms and can be rented as a self-contained unit. In the rear is an antique guest house with a wrought-iron canopy bed, ideal for honeymooners. Six rooms are air-conditioned. All meals, including afternoon tea, are prepared in the classic Jamaican style and served in the main house. Even if you can't stay here, call and see if you can come for dinner.

Market Day

On Wednesday morning, Falmouth hosts the biggest flea market in the country, with hundreds of booths linking the marketplace and overflowing into the streets. Buyers from all over the island flock here to pick up bargains (later sold at inflated prices). Take time out to buy a loaf of *bammy* (cassava bread) and pick up the makings of a picnic.

WHERE TO DINE

Glistening Waters Inn and Marina. Rock Falmouth (between Falmouth and the Trelawny Beach Hotel). ☎ **876/954-3229.** Main courses $8–$22. AE, MC, V. Daily 10am–9pm. SEAFOOD.

Residents of Montego Bay often make the 28-mile drive out here, along Route A1, just to sample the ambience of Old Jamaica. This well-recommended restaurant, with a veranda overlooking the lagoon, is housed in what was originally a private clubhouse for the aristocrats of nearby Trelawny. The furniture here may remind you of a stage set for *Night of the Iguana*. Menu items usually include local fish dishes, such as snapper or kingfish, served with bammy (a form of cassava bread). Other specialties are three different lobster dishes, three different preparations of shrimp, three different conch viands, fried rice, and pork chops. The food is just what your mama would make (if she came from Jamaica).

The waters of the lagoon contain a rare form of phosphorescent microbe, which, when the waters are agitated, glows in the dark. Ask about evening booze cruises, which cost $10 per person, including one drink. Departures are nightly at about 6:30pm.

RIVER RAFTING NEAR FALMOUTH

Rafting on the **Martha Brae** is an adventure. To reach the starting point from Falmouth, drive approximately 3 miles inland to **Martha Brae's Rafters Village** (☎ 876/952-0889). The rafts are similar to those on the Río Grande, near Port Antonio; you sit on a raised dais on bamboo logs. The cost is $40, with two riders allowed on a raft, plus a small child if accompanied by an adult (but use caution). The trips last 1¼ hours and operate daily from 9am to 4pm. Along the way, you can stop and order cool drinks or beer along the banks of the river. There's a bar, a restaurant, and two souvenir shops in the village.

SHOPPING

Two miles east of Falmouth on the north-coast road is **Caribatik Island Fabrics,** at Rock Wharf on the Luminous Lagoon (☎ 876/954-3314). You'll recognize the place easily, as it has a huge sign painted across the building's side. This is the private domain of Keith Chandler, who established the place with his late wife, Muriel, in 1970. Today, the batiks Muriel Chandler created before her death in 1990 are viewed as stylish and sensual garments by the chic boutiques in the States.

The shop has a full range of fabrics, scarves, garments, and wall hangings, some patterned after such themes as Jamaica's doctor bird and various endangered animal species of the world. The gallery continues to sell a selection of Muriel's original batik paintings. Either Keith or a member of the staff will be glad to describe the intricate process of batiking during their open hours of Tuesday to Saturday from 9am to 4pm. They're closed in September and on national holidays.

5 Runaway Bay

Once this resort was a mere western satellite of Ocho Rios. However, with the opening of some large resort hotels, plus a colony of smaller hostelries, Runaway Bay is now a destination in its own right.

This part of Jamaica's north coast has several distinctions: It was the first part of the island seen by Columbus, the site of the first Spanish settlement on the island, and the point of departure of the last Spaniards leaving Jamaica following their defeat by the British.

Jamaica's most complete equestrian center is the **Chukka Cove Farm and Resort,** at Richmond Llandovery, St. Ann (☎ **876/972-2506**), less than 4 miles east of Runaway Bay. A 1-hour trail ride costs $30, while a 2-hour mountain ride goes for $40. The most popular ride is a 3-hour beach jaunt which involves riding over trails to the sea, then swimming in the surf. The $55 cost includes refreshments. A 6-hour beach ride, complete with picnic lunch, goes for $130. Polo lessons are also available, costing $50 for 30 minutes.

WHERE TO STAY & DINE

Breezes Golf and Beach Resort. P.O. Box 58 (6 miles west of Ocho Rios), Runaway Bay, Jamaica, W.I. ☎ **800/GO-SUPER** or 876/973-2436. Fax 876/973-2352. www.superclubs. com. E-mail: breezesgolf@cwjamaica.com. 238 units. A/C TEL. All-inclusive rates for 3 nights: Winter $1,618–$1,778 double; from $1,900 suite for 2. Off-season $1,258–$1,518 double; from $1,500 suite for 2. AE, DC, MC, V. Children under 15 not accepted.

This stylish resort operates on a plan that includes three meals a day, all free drinks, and a galaxy of other benefits. Its clubhouse is approached by passing through a park filled with tropical trees and shrubbery. The lobby is the best re-creation of the South Seas on Jamaica, with hanging wicker chairs and totemic columns. Guest rooms are spacious with a light, tropical motif. They're fitted with local woods, cool tile floors, and private balconies or patios. The most elegant are the suites, with Jamaican-made four-poster beds. The good-sized bathrooms have combination tub/showers and generous marble counters. There's a minijungle with hammocks and a nearby nude beach.

Dining/Diversions: Live music emanates from the stylish Terrace every evening at 7pm, and a nightclub offers live shows 6 nights a week at 10pm. Dine either in the beachside restaurant or in the more formal Italian restaurant, Martino's.

Amenities: Gym filled with Nautilus equipment, pool, sports-activities center (featuring scuba diving, windsurfing, and a golf school), 18-hole championship golf course. Reggae exercise classes held twice daily.

✪ **FDR (Franklyn D. Resort).** Main St. (P.O. Box 201), Runaway Bay, St. Ann, Jamaica, W.I. ☎ **800/654-1FDR** in the U.S., or 876/973-4591. Fax 876/973-3071. www.fdrholidays.com. E-mail: fdr@fdrholidays.com. 76 units. A/C TV TEL. Winter $620–$690. Off-season $510– $530. Rates are all-inclusive. Children 15 and under stay free in parents' suite. AE, MC, V.

Located on Route A1, 17 miles west of Ocho Rios, FDR is geared to families with children and is dedicated to including all meals and activities in a net price. The resort, named after its Jamaican-born owner and developer (Franklyn David Rance), is on 6 acres of flat, sandy land dotted with flowering shrubs and trees, on the main seaside highway. Each of the Mediterranean-inspired buildings has a terra-cotta roof, a loggia or outdoor terrace, Spanish marble in the bathrooms, a kitchenette, and a personal attendant—called a vacation nanny—who cooks, cleans, and cares for children. Although neither the narrow beach nor the modest pools are the most desirable on the island, and most rooms lack a sea view, many visitors appreciate the spacious units and the resort's wholehearted concern for visiting kids.

Dining/Diversions: Two restaurants on the property serve free wine with lunch and dinner (and offer special children's meals), a piano bar provides music every evening, and a handful of bars keep the drinks flowing. There's live music nightly.

Amenities: An attendant baby-sits for free every day between 9:30am and 4:45pm, after which she can be hired privately for $3 an hour. There's a children's supervisor in attendance at "Kiddies' Centre" (where a computer center, a kiddies' disco, and even kiddies' dinners are regular features). Adults appreciate the scuba lessons, picnics, photography lessons, arts and crafts, and donkey rides that keep the kids entertained. Water sports, lit tennis courts, satellite TV room, disco, gym, free use of bicycles for getting around the neighborhood, free tours to Dunn's River Falls and Ocho Rios shopping.

Grand Lido Braco. Rio Bueno P.O., Trelawny, Jamaica. ☎ **800/859-7873** or 876/954-0000. Fax 876/954-0020 or -0021. 178 units. A/C TV TEL. All-inclusive rates for 3 nights: Winter $1,788–$2,220 double; from $1,954 suite for 2. Off-season $1,572–$1,780 double; from $1,422 suite for 2. AE, DC, DISC, MC, V. Children under 16 not accepted.

Established in 1995, this is one of the most historically evocative all-inclusive resorts in Jamaica. Set on 85 acres of land near Buena Vista, a 15-minute drive west of Runaway Bay, it's a re-creation of a 19th-century Jamaican Victorian village, adjacent to an impressive stretch of prime beachfront. A stately copy of a courthouse hosts meetings and entertainment, benches and flowering trees line the symmetrical borders of the town square, and meals are served in four separate venues inspired by an idealized version of Old Jamaica. Employees, most of whom come from the nearby hamlet of Rio Bueno, are encouraged to mingle with guests and share their personal and community stories. You get vivid insights into Jamaican life here that wouldn't be possible at the more cloistered and remote all-inclusive resorts. This is not a place for children; the venue is primarily adult, relaxed, and reasonably permissive.

The predominant color scheme throughout the resort is pink and yellow. Accommodations are in 12 blocks of three-story buildings, each trimmed in colonial-style gingerbread and filled with wicker furniture. All units have private patios or verandas and face the ocean, although blocks one through six are closer to the beachfront, while blocks five and six face a strip of sand designated as a "clothing-optional" area. Beds are most comfortable, with extremely good mattresses and fine linen; the bathrooms are well maintained.

Dining/Diversions: Separate dining areas serve Jamaican cuisine, pizza and pasta, and international fare; the Piacere Restaurant serves upscale dinners and has a dress code. Four bars make getting a drink relatively easy.

Amenities: A soccer field where a local Jamaican team sometimes volunteers to play with (or against) aficionados from the village, a fitness center, a nine-hole golf course, a disco, three fishing ponds, bike and jogging trails, four tennis courts, use of a glass-bottom boat for snorkeling tours, and one of the largest pools in Jamaica. The staff keeps conversations and good times rolling along.

✪ **Runaway H.E.A.R.T. Country Club.** Ricketts Ave. (P.O. Box 98), Runaway Bay, St. Ann, Jamaica, W.I. ☎ **876/973-2671.** Fax 876/973-2693. 20 units. A/C TV TEL. Winter $138 double. Off-season $99–$124 double. Rates include MAP (breakfast and dinner). AE, MC, V.

Called "the best-kept secret in Jamaica," this place is located on the main road, and it practically wins hands-down as the bargain of the north coast. One of Jamaica's few training and service institutions, the club and its adjacent academy are operated by the government to provide a high level of training for young Jamaicans interested in the hotel trade. The helpful staff of both professionals and trainees offers the finest service of any hotel in the area.

The good-sized rooms are bright and airy. Bathrooms have generous shelf space and good towels. The accommodations open onto private balconies with views of well-manicured tropical gardens or vistas of the bay and golf course. Laundry is available, and facilities include a pool and golf course. Guests enjoy having a drink in the piano bar (ever had a cucumber daiquiri?) before heading for the dining room, the Cardiff Hall Restaurant, which serves Jamaican and continental dishes. Nonguests can also enjoy dinner, served nightly from 7 to 10pm; a well-prepared meal costs around $25. The academy has won awards for some of its dishes, including "go-go banana chicken" and curried codfish.

BEACHES & WATER SPORTS

The two best beaches at Runaway Bay are **Paradise Beach** and **Cardiffall Lot Public Beach.** Both wide, white-sand strips are clean and well maintained—ideal spots for a picnic. There is a great natural beauty to this part of Jamaica, and many foreigners, especially Canadians, seek it out, preferring its more raffish look to the well-publicized tourist meccas of Ocho Rios. If you're staying in Ocho Rios and want to escape the crowds, come here. You don't get a lot of facilities, however, so you'd better bring along whatever you need.

The waters are calm almost all year, but the noonday sun is quite fierce. Prevailing trade winds will keep you cool in the mornings and late afternoon. Since there are no lifeguards, be especially careful if you're with children.

Runaway Bay offers some of the best areas for snorkeling in Jamaica. The reefs are close to shore and extremely lively with marine life, including enormous schools of tropical fish such as blue chromis, triggerfish, small skate rays, and snapper. Since boats and fishing canoes can be a problem close to shore, go on a snorkeling excursion with the best diving facility at Runaway Bay: **Resort Divers** (☎ 876/974-5338), along the beach. This five-star PADI facility takes you out to one of several protected reefs where the water currents aren't dangerous, and where fishing boats are required to stay at least 200 yards away from snorkelers. Resort Divers also provides sport-fishing jaunts as well as scuba-diving certification and equipment. A resort dive costs $75, with a one-tank dive going for $35 or a two-tank dive for $65. Parasailing is also available, costing $40 per half hour.

EXPLORING THE AREA

Columbus Park Museum, on Queens Highway, in Discovery Bay (☎ 876/973-2135), is a large, open area between the main coast road and the sea at Discovery Bay. Just pull off the road and walk among the fantastic collection of exhibits; admission is free. There's everything from a canoe made from a solid piece of cottonwood (the way Arawaks did it more than 5 centuries ago) to a stone cross that was originally placed on the Barrett estate at Retreat (9 miles east of Montego Bay) by Edward Barrett, brother of poet Elizabeth Barrett Browning. You'll see a tally, used to count bananas carried on men's heads from plantation to ship, as well as a planter's strongbox with a weighted lead base to prevent its theft. Other items are 18th-century cannons, a Spanish water cooler and calcifier, a fish pot made from bamboo, a corn husker, and a water wheel. Pimento trees, from which allspice is produced, dominate the park, which is open daily from 8:30am to 4:30pm.

You can also visit the **Seville Great House,** Heritage Park (☎ 876/972-2191). Built in 1745 by the English, it contains a collection of artifacts once used by everybody from the Amerindians to African slaves. In all, you're treated to an exhibit of 5 centuries worth of Jamaican history. Modest for a great house, it has a wattle-and-daub construction. A small theater presents a 15-minute historical film about the house. It's open daily from 9am to 5pm; admission is $4

6 Ocho Rios

This north-coast resort is a 2-hour drive east of Montego Bay or west of Port Antonio. Ocho Rios was once a small banana and fishing port, but tourism became the leading industry long ago. Short on charm, it's now Jamaica's cruise-ship capital. The bay is dominated on one side by a bauxite-loading terminal and on the other by a range of hotels with sandy beaches fringed by palm trees.

Ocho Rios and neighboring Port Antonio have long been associated with Sir Noël Coward (who invited the world to his doorstep) and Ian Fleming, creator of James Bond (see below for details about their homes here).

Frankly, unless you're a cruise passenger, you may want to stay away from the major attractions when a ship is in port. The duty-free markets are overrun then, and the hustlers become more strident in pushing their crafts and junk souvenirs. Dunn's River Falls becomes almost impossible to visit at those times.

However, Ocho Rios has its own unique flavor and offers the usual range of sports, including a major fishing tournament every fall, in addition to a wide variety of accommodations.

GETTING THERE

BY PLANE If you're going to Ocho Rios, you will fly into the **Donald Sangster Airport** in Montego Bay. Some hotels, particularly the larger resorts, will arrange for airport transfers from that point. Be sure to ask when you book.

BY BUS If your hotel does not provide transfers, you can go by bus for a $25 one-way fare. We recommend two private companies: **Tour Wise** (☎ 876/979-1027 in Montego Bay, or 876/974-2323 in Ocho Rios) or **Caribic Vacations** (☎ 876/953-9874 in Montego Bay, or 876/974-9016 in Ocho Rios). The bus will drop you off at your hotel. The trip takes 2 hours.

BY RENTAL CAR & TAXI You can rent a car for the 67-mile drive east along Highway A1 (see "Getting Around" in section 1, "Essentials," at the beginning of this chapter). Or you can take a taxi; the typical one-way fare from Montego Bay is $70, but always negotiate and agree upon a fare *before* you get into the taxi.

WHERE TO STAY
VERY EXPENSIVE

✪ **Goldeneye.** Oracabessa, St. Mary's, Jamaica, W.I. ☎ **800/688-7678** or 876/974-3354. Fax 876/975-3679. www.islandoutpost.com. E-mail: goldeneye@cwjamaica.com. 5 villas. Year-round $1,000 one-bedroom villa for 2; $1,650 two-bedroom villa for up to 4; $2,000 three-bedroom villa for up to 6; $5,000 Ian Fleming's three-bedroom house for up to 6; $10,000 for entire property of 11 bedrooms (sleeping up to 22). Rates are all-inclusive. AE, MC, V.

It was here that the most famous secret agent in the world, James Bond (007) was created in 1952 by then-owner Ian Fleming. Fleming built the imposing but simple house in 1946, and within its solid masonry walls, wrote each of the 13 original James Bond books. During its heyday, Noël Coward was a frequent guest, along with Graham Greene, Truman Capote, and Evelyn Waugh. In the early 1990s, music publisher Christopher Blackwell bought and restored the by-then dilapidated property to its original, somewhat spartan dignity, retaining the large bronze pineapples on its entrance gates. Fleming's original desk remains, and the overall decor of oversized Indonesian furniture is enhanced, Hollywood-style, with memorabilia from what later became the most famous spy movies in the world.

Unless you opt to rent the main house, you'll have to settle for any of the relatively simple bungalows set adjacent to the beach. Outfitted in tones of forest green and burgundy, with appealing but undistinguished furniture, they're cozy, comfortable, idiosyncratic, and glamorous in a way that might appeal to a rock star on an off-the-record weekend. Each villa has a good-sized bathroom with a shower stall.

There's no pool on the premises, but considering the splendors of the nearby beach, no one seems to mind. The configuration of the site is conducive to privacy within each cluster of units. The nearest town, Oracabessa, is completely devoid of the tourist amenities that abound in nearby Ocho Rios, a fact that adds considerably to its somewhat seedy and run-down charm.

✪ **Grand Lido Sans Souci.** Rte. A3 (P.O. Box 103), Ocho Rios, Jamaica, W.I. ☎ **800/ 859-7873** in the U.S., or 876/974-2353. Fax 876/974-2544. 111 units. A/C MINIBAR TV TEL. All-inclusive rates for 3 nights: Winter $2,304 double; from $2,430 suite for 2; $3,426 penthouse for 2. Off-season $1,860–$1,956 double; from $2,064 suite for 2; from $2,886 penthouse for 2. AE, DC, MC, V.

If a cookie-cutter Sandals resort is the last thing you want, don your best resort finery and head for a classier joint: this one. Sans Souci is a pink, cliffside fantasy that recently completed a $7-million renovation, turning it into an all-inclusive Jamaica SuperClub. This is one of the finest spas in the Caribbean and has fabulous sports facilities. It's located 3 miles east of town on a forested plot of land whose rocky border abuts a good beach. A cliffside elevator brings guests to an outdoor bar. There's a freshwater pool, a mineral bath big enough for an elephant, and a labyrinth of catwalks and bridges stretching over rocky chasms filled with surging water.

Each unit features a veranda or patio, copies of Chippendale furniture, plush upholstery, and subdued colonial elegance. Some contain Jacuzzis. Accommodations range from rather standard bedrooms to vast suites with large living and dining areas, plus kithens. Deluxe touches include glazed tile floors, luxurious beds, and marble bathrooms with whirlpool tubs, stall showers, and hair dryers.

Dining/Diversions: See "Where to Dine," below, for a review of the Casanova restaurant. There's also the Ristorante Palazzina by the beach. The Balloon Bar tries to bring back some 1920s style, and there are several terraces for drinking.

Amenities: Established in 1987, Charlie's Spa is the best place on Jamaica for a health-and-fitness vacation, not to mention one of the finest in the entire Caribbean. Sports lovers appreciate the hotel's three Laykold tennis courts (two lit) and the nearby croquet lawn. Scuba diving, snorkeling, windsurfing, deep-sea fishing, and Sunfish and catamaran sailing are available at the beach. Guests can golf on an 18-hole course and watch polo matches while they take afternoon tea at the St. Ann Polo Club, Drax Hall. 24-hour room service, laundry/valet, massages.

✪ **Jamaica Inn.** Main St. (P.O. Box 1), Ocho Rios, Jamaica, W.I. ☎ **800/837-4608** in the U.S., or 876/974-2514. Fax 876/974-2449. www.jamaicainn.com. E-mail: jaminn@intochan. com. 45 units. A/C TEL. Winter, including all meals $525–$700 double; from $725 suite for 2. Off-season, including MAP (breakfast and dinner) $275–$375 double; from $345 suite for 2. AE, MC, V. Children 13 and under not accepted.

Built in 1950, the Jamaica Inn is a series of long, low, buildings set in a U-shape near the sea, 1½ miles east of town. Noël Coward, arriving with Katharine Hepburn or Claudette Colbert, was a regular, and Errol Flynn and Ian Fleming used to drop in from time to time. It's an elegant anachronism, a true retro hotel, and has remained little changed in 4 decades, avoiding the brass and glitter of all-inclusives like Sandals. Lovely patios open onto the lawns, and the bedrooms are reached along garden paths. This gracious, family-run inn, long a Jamaican landmark, underwent a $4-million upgrade to all its rooms in 1993. The old charm, including the antique furniture, remains. Guest rooms are very spacious, with colonial two-poster beds, quality carved-wood period pieces, and balustraded balconies opening onto views. Bathrooms are elegant and roomy, gleaming with marble vanities, combination shower/tubs, robes, and deluxe toiletries. The beach is a wide, champagne-colored strip; close to the shore, the sea is almost too clear to make snorkeling an adventure, but farther out it's rewarding.

Dining: The European-trained chef prepares both international and Jamaican dishes. The emphasis is on cuisine that uses fresh local produce. Men must wear a jacket and tie at night in winter.

Amenities: Pool, tennis court, comfortable lounge with books, games room with cards and jigsaw puzzles; Upton Golf Course nearby. Room service, laundry.

EXPENSIVE

✪ **Ciboney Ocho Rios.** Main St. (P.O. Box 728), Ocho Rios, St. Ann, Jamaica, W.I. ☎ **800/333-3333** in the U.S. and Canada, or 876/974-1027. Fax 876/974-7148. www.ciboney.com. E-mail: ciboney@infochan.com. 254 units. A/C MINIBAR TV TEL. All-inclusive rates per couple: Winter $500–$520 double; $550 junior suite; $590–$670 one-bedroom villa suite; $1,140 honeymoon villa; $1,240 two-bedroom villa for 4. Off-season $424–$440 double; $480 junior suite; $500–$580 one-bedroom villa suite; $1,000 honeymoon villa; $1,024 two-bedroom villa for 4. AE, DC, MC, V. Children 15 and under not accepted.

This all-inclusive Radisson franchise is a 1½-mile drive southeast of town, set on 45 acres of a private estate dotted with red-tile villas. A great house in the hills overlooks the Caribbean Sea. Across from the imposing gate near the resort's entrance are the white sands of a private beach. All but a handful of the accommodations are in one-, two-, or three-bedroom villas, each with a pool, a fully equipped kitchen, and a shaded terrace. Honeymoon villas have their own whirlpools. Thirty-six units are traditional single or double rooms on the third floor of the great house. Regardless of their location, accommodations are high-ceilinged, roomy, and decorated in Caribbean colors. They're well furnished, with particularly fine beds, and bathrooms are well maintained. Throughout the property, stone retaining walls frame the sloping grounds, which include carefully landscaped beds of flowering trees and vines.

Dining/Diversions: The Manor Restaurant & Bar offers indoor and outdoor patio dining (classic Jamaican food) and entertainment. The Marketplace Restaurant has a contemporary American and Jamaican menu, while Alfresco Casa Nina highlights Italian cuisine. Orchids is a restaurant developed in collaboration with the Culinary Institute of America, with a menu based on haute cuisine, as well as healthy food. Late-night entertainment and dancing are featured at Nicole.

Amenities: European-inspired beauty spa with its own health-and-fitness center, several different conference rooms, six tennis courts (lit for night play), beach club offering an array of water sports, two main pools with swim-up bars (plus 90 other semiprivate pools on the grounds), spa with 20 Jacuzzis, golf course nearby. Complimentary manicure, pedicure, and 25-minute massage.

Club Jamaica Beach Resort. P.O. Box 343, Turtle Beach, Ocho Rios, Jamaica, W.I. ☎ **800/818-2964** or 876/974-6632. Fax 876/974-6644. 95 units. TEL. Winter $290 double. Off-season $220 double. Rates are all-inclusive. AE, DC, MC, V.

The area's newest all-inclusive resort is near the geographical heart of Ocho Rios, adjacent to its crafts market and Turtle Beach. Don't expect a particularly pulled-together staff, as the ambience here is very laid-back and, at least to the observer, not overwhelmingly organized. The completely unpretentious, motel-style bedrooms are outfitted with white tile, bright colors, and contemporary, airy-looking furniture. Bathrooms, a bit small, have shower stalls.

The resort offers three bars, a pool, a restaurant, and lots of local color and live music that starts up at the cocktail hour. Amenities include a glass-bottom boat, snorkeling equipment that's dispensed from a kiosk on the sands of the public beach, lots of options for hanging out with other guests at the hotel's bars, and easy access to the goings-on around the property.

Couples Ocho Rios. Tower Isle, along Rte. A3 (P.O. Box 330), Ocho Rios, Jamaica, W.I. ☎ **800/268-7537** in the U.S., or 876/975-4271. Fax 876/975-4439. www.couples.com. E-mail: couplesresort@couples.com. 212 units. A/C TEL. All-inclusive rates for 3 nights: Winter $1,520–$2,210 per couple. Off-season $1,320–$1,915 per couple. AE, MC, V. The hotel usually accepts bookings for a minimum of any 3 nights of the week, though most guests book by the week; a 4-day stay is sometimes required at certain peak periods, such as over the Christmas holidays. No one 17 or under accepted.

Don't come here alone—you won't get in! The management defines couples as "any *man and woman* in love," and this is a couples-only resort. Most visiting couples are married, and many are on their honeymoon. Everything is in pairs, even the chairs by the moon-drenched beach. Some guests slip away from the resort, which is an 18-minute drive (5 miles) east of town, to Couples' private island to bask in the buff. In general, this is a classier operation than the more mass-market Sandals (the Dunn's River and the Ocho Rios versions). Once you've paid the initial all-inclusive rate, you're free to use all the facilities. There will be no more bills—even the whiskey is free, in addition to the three meals a day and all the wine you want; breakfast is bountiful. Tips aren't permitted. The bedrooms have either a king-size bed or two doubles, pleasantly traditional furnishings, and a patio fronting either the sea or the mountains. Good-sized bathrooms have showers and hair dryers.

Guests have a choice of six restaurants. Five-course dinners are followed by dancing on the terrace every evening, with entertainment. Amenities include five tennis courts (three lit at night), a Nautilus gym, scuba diving, snorkeling, windsurfing, sailing, waterskiing, room service (for breakfast only), and laundry.

High Hope Estate. Box 11, St. Ann's Bay, near Ocho Rios, Jamaica W.I. ☎ **876/972-2277.** Fax 876/972-1607. www.highhopeestate.com. E-mail: info@highhopeestate.com. 6 units. TEL. Year-round $174–$270 double. Rates include breakfast. MC, V.

Because of the small size of this upscale hotel, your happiness, and the success of your holiday here, will depend a lot on whether you click with the owner and the other guests. It's conceived as a tranquil, private home that accepts paying guests, in the style of the British colonial world at its most rarefied. It was built for a socially prominent heiress, Kitty Spence, granddaughter of prairie-state populist William Jennings Bryan, and later served as the home and laboratory of a horticulturist who successfully bred 560 varieties of flowering hibiscus. Consequently, the estate's 40 acres, set 550 feet above the coast and 7 miles west of Ocho Rios, thrive with flowering plants as well as memories of such luminaries as Noël Coward, who used to play the grand piano that graces one of the public areas. There are absolutely no planned activities here. Basically, it's an upscale private home, the domain of U.S. entrepreneur Dennis Rapaport, whose staff is on hand to help with supervising children, maintaining the property, and preparing meals for anyone who gives advance notice. Bedrooms are a delight—spacious, well thought out, and exceedingly comfortable. The excellent bathrooms have combination shower/tubs. On the premises is a pool, a tennis court, a communal TV room, and a semi-enclosed courtyard modeled on a 15th-century villa. There are sweeping views out over the Jamaican coastline; the nearest beach is a 10-minute ride away. You could rent the entire villa with a group of friends.

✪ **Plantation Inn.** Main St. (P.O. Box 2), Ocho Rios, Jamaica, W.I. ☎ **800/752-6824** in the U.S., or 876/974-5601. Fax 876/974-5912. E-mail: plantationinn@cwjamaica.com. 70 units. A/C TEL. Winter $225–$335 double; $385–$870 suite; $4,375–$5,800 villa for up to 4 (7-night minimum). Off-season $150–$210 double; $230–$550 suite; $2,700–$5,100 villa (7-night minimum). MAP (breakfast and dinner) $55 per person extra. Children under 13 stay free in parents' room. AE, MC, V.

This hotel evokes an antebellum southern mansion. At any moment, you expect Vivien Leigh as Scarlett to come rushing down to greet you. You'll drive up a sweeping driveway and enter through a colonnaded portico, set in gardens, 1½ miles east of town. Two private beaches are reached via 36 steps down from the garden; seats on the way provide resting spots. All bedrooms open off balconies and have their own patios overlooking the sea. The rooms are attractively decorated with chintz and comfortable furnishings. Beds are elegantly outfitted with fine linens, and the spacious bathrooms come with hair dryers. Apart from the regular hotel, the Plantana Villa above the eastern beach sleeps two to six people, while the Blue Shadow Villa on the west side accommodates up to eight guests.

Dining: There's an indoor dining room, but most of the action takes place under the tropical sky. You can have breakfast on your balcony and lunch outdoors. English tea is served on the terrace every afternoon.

Amenities: Jungle gym with exercise equipment, sauna, two tennis courts, snorkeling, Sunfish sailing, windsurfing, scuba diving, kayaking, glass-bottom boat; an 18-hole golf course is a 15-minute drive away. Room service, facials, massages, waxing.

Sandals Dunn's River. Rte. A3 (P.O. Box 51), Ocho Rios, Jamaica, W.I. ☎ **800/SANDALS** in the U.S. and Canada, or 876/972-1610. Fax 876/972-1611. www.sandals.com. E-mail: sdrinet@cwjamaica.com. 266 units. TV TEL. All-inclusive rates per couple for 4 days/3 nights: Winter $1,800–$2,300 double; $2,460–$3,140 suite. Off-season $1,640–$2,000 double; $2,140–$2,430 suite. Minimum stay of 4 days/3 nights. AE, MC, V.

Having been through various incarnations as the Jamaica Hilton and Eden II, this luxury resort has now found its latest identity as a member of Jamaican entrepreneur Butch Stewart's rapidly expanding Sandals empire. Located on a wide, sugary beach, this is the finest of the Sandals resorts, at least in the opinion of some guests who have sampled them all. Only male-female couples are allowed.

Set on the beachfront between Ocho Rios and St. Ann's Bay, the resort is very sports-oriented. It occupies 25 well-landscaped acres, offering attractively furnished and often quite spacious accommodations. All the rooms were reconstructed after the Sandals takeover and given an Italianate/Mediterranean motif. The elegant guest rooms are scattered among the six-story main building, two lanai buildings, and a five-story west wing. Extras include coffeemakers, spacious balconies, private safes, walk-in closets, king-size beds, and hair dryers.

Dining/Diversions: Before retreating to the disco, guests can choose among several dining options. The International Room is elegant, with fabric-covered walls and rosewood furniture. West Indian Windies serves Caribbean specialties. D'Amore offers Italian cuisine, and Restaurant Teppanyaki serves Chinese, Polynesian, and Japanese dishes.

Amenities: Three Jacuzzis, two whirlpool baths, fitness center, jogging course, beach bar, pitch-and-putt golf course, one of the most spectacular swim-up bars on Jamaica in the lagoon-shaped pool; transport to the Sandals Golf and Country Club. Tours to Dunn's River Falls, shuttles to Sandals Ocho Rios, massages.

Sandals Ocho Rios Resort & Golf Club. Main St. (P.O. Box 771), Ocho Rios, Jamaica, W.I. ☎ **800/SANDALS** in the U.S. and Canada, or 876/974-5691. Fax 876/974-5700. www. sandals.com. 237 units. TV TEL. All-inclusive rates per couple for 4 days/3 nights: Winter $1,600–$2,020 double; $2,140–$2,260 suite. Off-season $1,460–$1,800 double; $1,940–$2,060 suite. AE, MC, V.

Another Jamaican addition to the ever-expanding couples-only empire of Gordon "Butch" Stewart, Sandals Ocho Rios attracts a mix of coupled singles and married folk, including honeymooners. At times the place seems like a summer camp for grown-ups (or others who didn't quite grow up). The resort uses the same formula: one price per male-female couple, including everything. This is the most low-key of the Sandals properties. Is it romantic? Most patrons think so, although we've encountered other couples here whose relationship didn't survive the 3-night minimum stay.

On 13 well-landscaped acres a mile west of the town center, it offers comfortably furnished but uninspired rooms with either ocean or garden views, plus some cottage units. All units are reasonably large, with king-size beds for loving couples, private safes, coffeemakers, and good-size bathrooms with hair dryers.

Dining/Diversions: You can sip free drinks at an oceanside swim-up bar. Nightly theme parties and live entertainment take place in a modern amphitheater. A unique feature of the resort is an open-air disco. The resort's main dining room is St. Anne's; Michelle's serves Italian food, and the Reef Terrace Grill does gourmet Jamaican cuisine and fresh seafood. A new addition is the Arizona Steak House.

Amenities: Three freshwater pools, private artificial beach, sporting equipment and instruction (including waterskiing, windsurfing, sailing, snorkeling, and scuba diving), paddleboats, kayaks, glass-bottom boat, Jacuzzi, saunas, fully equipped fitness center, two tennis courts. Round-trip transfers from the airport, tours to Dunn's River Falls, massages, laundry.

MODERATE

✪ **The Enchanted Garden.** Eden Bower Rd. (P.O. Box 284), Ocho Rios, Jamaica, W.I. ☎ **800/847-2535** in the U.S. and Canada, or 876/974-1400. Fax 876/974-5823. www.interknowledge.com/jamaica/enchanted/encho3.htm. 113 units. A/C TV TEL. All-inclusive rates per couple: Winter $330–$370 double; from $440 suite. Off-season $270–$310 double; from $370 suite. AE, DC, MC, V.

This most verdant of Jamaican resorts sits on a secluded hilltop high above the commercial center of town. Owned and developed by Edward Seaga, former Jamaican prime minister, the land includes 20 acres of rare botanical specimens, nature trails, and 14 cascading waterfalls much loved by such former visitors as Mick Jagger. The lobby is housed in a pink tower accented with white gingerbread; the interior sports marble floors, big windows, and enormous potted palms. Bisected by the Turtle River, the place is of particular interest to botanists and bird watchers.

The bedrooms are contained in eight different low-rise buildings amid the resort's carefully landscaped grounds. All of the roomy, elegantly furnished units have sturdy rattan furniture, queen or king beds, and private patios or balconies; some contain kitchens. The spacious bathrooms have combination tub/showers and hair dryers.

Dining: The resort's restaurants serve continental, Thai, Japanese, Indonesian, and regional Chinese cuisines. A pasta bar is designed like a treehouse in a tropical forest. The Seaquarium offers a cold buffet in a setting surrounded by tropical fish. Annabella's nightclub provides after-dinner entertainment in a setting like something out of the *Arabian Nights*.

Amenities: Spa, beauty salon, pool, two lit tennis courts, walk-in aviary with hundreds of exotic birds (feeding time is every afternoon around 4pm), fitness center. Seaquarium with 15 aquariums for marine-life exotica. Daily transportation to the Beach Club, shuttle for shopping.

INEXPENSIVE

✪ **Hibiscus Lodge Hotel.** 87 Main St. (P.O. Box 52), Ocho Rios, St. Ann, Jamaica, W.I. ☎ **876/974-2676.** Fax 876/974-1874. 27 units. A/C TV. Winter $105 double; $150 triple. Off-season $99 double; $135 triple. Rates include breakfast. AE, CB, DC, MC, V.

The Hibiscus Lodge Hotel offers more value for your money than any resort at Ocho Rios. The intimate little inn, perched precariously on a cliff along the shore 3 blocks from the Ocho Rios Mall, has both character and charm. All medium-size bedrooms, either doubles or triples, have small, tidy private bathrooms, ceiling fans, and verandas opening to the sea. Singles can be rented for the double rate.

After a day spent in a pool suspended over the cliffs, or lounging on the large sun-deck, guests can enjoy a drink in the unique swinging bar. Also on the 3-acre site are a Jacuzzi, tennis court, and conference facilities. The owners provide dining at the Almond Tree (see below).

WHERE TO DINE
EXPENSIVE

The Casanova. In the Grand Lido Sans Souci, along Rte. A3, 3 miles east of Ocho Rios. ☎ **876/974-2353.** Reservations required except Tues and Fri. Nonguest evening pass (7pm–2am) of $75 per person includes dinner (beach buffet Tues and Fri), entertainment, and drinks. AE, DC, MC, V. Daily 6:30–9:30pm. FRENCH.

The suave Casanova is one of the most elegant enclaves along the north coast, a super choice when you feel like dressing up. Meals are included for guests of the hotel, but nonguests who purchase a pass can also enjoy dinner and entertainment here. All drinks are included. Jazz wafting in from a lattice-roofed gazebo might accompany your meal.

In the late 1960s, Harry Cipriani (of Harry's Bar fame in Venice) taught the staff some of his culinary techniques, and a little more care seems to go into the cuisine here, as opposed to the mass-market chow-downs at some of the other all-inclusives. Salads, vegetarian dishes, and soups are made fresh daily. Typical dishes include an appetizer of smoked chicken breast in a continental berry sauce, or a small vegetable mousse with a fontina cheese sauce. For your main course, you might prefer osso buco (braised veal shanks) or roast Cornish hen with citrus and mild spice. Follow the sumptuous desserts with one of the house's four special coffees.

✪ **Plantation Inn Restaurant.** In the Plantation Inn, Main St. ☎ **876/974-5601.** Reservations required. Main courses $20–$35; fixed-price dinner $38. AE, DC, MC, V. Daily 7:30–10am, 1–2:30pm, 4:30–5:30pm (afternoon tea), and 7–10pm. JAMAICAN/ CONTINENTAL.

You'll think you've arrived at Tara in *Gone With the Wind*. An evening spent here, dining and dancing by candlelight, offers one of the most romantic experiences in Ocho Rios. You're seated at beautifully set tables with crisp linen, either indoors in the dining room or outdoors on the Bougainvillea Terrace. A few steps away is an annex, the Peacock Pavilion, where afternoon tea is served daily. After the dinner plates are cleared, a band plays for dancing. This is definitely the pampered life.

The continental cuisine is spiced up a bit by Jamaican specialties. Appetizers are always spicy and tangy; our favorite is "Fire & Spice," a chicken and beef kebab with a ginger-pimiento sauce. For the main course, we always ask the chef to prepare a whole roast fish from the catch of the day. The perfectly cooked fish is served bone-less and seasoned with island herbs and spices. It's slowly roasted in the oven and pre-sented with fresh country vegetables. Since the place attracts a lot of meat eaters, the chefs always prepare the classics, lamb chops Provençale, and the like. The fixed-price menu offered every evening is also a good value. Opt for the banana cream pie for dessert, if featured—it's creamy and tasty.

MODERATE

Almond Tree Restaurant. In the Hibiscus Lodge Hotel, 87 Main St. ☎ **876/974-2813.** Reservations recommended. Main courses $15.50–$37. AE, DC, MC, V. Daily 7am–2:30pm and 6–9:30pm. INTERNATIONAL.

The Almond Tree is a two-tiered patio restaurant with a tree growing through the roof, overlooking the Caribbean at the Hibiscus Lodge Hotel (see "Where to Stay," above). Lobster Thermidor is the most delectable item on the menu, but we also like the bouillabaisse (made with conch and lobster). Other excellent choices are the roast suckling pig, medallions of beef Anne Palmer, and a fondue bourguignonne. Jamaican plantation rice is a local specialty. The wine list offers a variety of vintages, including Spanish and Jamaican. Have an aperitif in the unique "swinging bar" (swinging chairs, that is).

Evita's Italian Restaurant. Eden Bower Rd. ☎ **876/974-2333.** Reservations recommended. Main courses $11–$24. AE, MC, V. Daily 11am–11pm. ITALIAN.

Located a 5-minute drive south of the commercial heart of Ocho Rios, in a hillside residential neighborhood that enjoys a panoramic view over the city's harbor and beachfronts, this is the premier Italian restaurant of Ocho Rios—and one of the most fun restaurants along the north coast of Jamaica. Its soul and artistic flair come from Eva Myers, the convivial former owner of some of the most legendary bars of Montego Bay, who established her culinary headquarters in this white gingerbread Jamaican house in 1990. An outdoor terrace adds additional seating and enhanced views. More than half the menu is devoted to pastas, including almost every variety known in northern and southern Italy. If you don't want pasta, the fish dishes are excellent, especially the snapper stuffed with crabmeat and the lobster and scampi in a buttery white cream sauce. Italian (or other) wines by the bottle might accompany your entree. The restaurant lies a few steps from the Enchanted Gardens, an all-inclusive resort.

Little Pub Restaurant. 59 Main St. ☎ **876/974-2324.** Reservations recommended. Main courses $13–$28. AE, MC, V. Daily 7pm–midnight. JAMAICAN/INTERNATIONAL.

Located in a red-brick courtyard with a fish pond and a waterfall in the center of town, this indoor-outdoor pub's centerpiece is a restaurant in the dinner-theater style. Top local and international artists are featured, as are Jamaican musical plays. No one will mind if you just enjoy a drink while seated on one of the pub's barrel chairs. But if you want dinner, proceed to one of the linen-covered tables topped with cut flowers and candles. Menu items include barbecued chicken, stewed snapper, grilled kingfish, and the inevitable and overpriced lobster.

✪ **Toscanini's.** Harmony Hall, Tower Isles on Rte A3, 4 miles east of Ocho Rios. ☎ **876/975-4785.** Main courses $11–$22; pastas $9–$16. Daily noon–2:30pm and 7–10:30pm. AE, MC, V. ITALIAN.

Parma, Italy, is the birthplace of the trio of partners behind this restaurant set at an art gallery along the coast. Hailing from the city of a marvelous ham, a peerless cheese, and one of Italy's finest cuisines are Emanuele and Lella Guilivi and her brother, chef Pierluigi Ricci. Coming from a long line of restaurateurs, they bring style and a continental sophistication to their food service and preparation. The menu offers many classic Italian dishes, supplemented by ever-changing specials, depending on what's fresh at the market. Specialties include marinated marlin, various homemade pastas, carpaccio, gnocchi, and a strong emphasis on fresh lobster and seafood. The chef also caters to the vegetarian palate. All this good food is backed up by a fine wine list. For dessert, the chef makes a "wicked" tiramisu.

INEXPENSIVE

✪ **Ocho Rios Village Jerk Centre.** Da Costa Dr. ☎ **876/974-2549.** Jerk pork $3 quarter-pound, $11 1 pound. Whole jerk chicken $14. MC, V. Daily 10am–11pm. JAMAICAN.

At this open-air restaurant, you can get the best jerk dishes along this part of the coast. When only a frosty Red Stripe beer can quench your thirst, and your stomach is growling for the fiery taste of Jamaican jerk seasonings, head here—and don't dress up. Don't expect anything fancy: It's the food that counts, and you'll find fresh daily specials posted on a chalkboard menu on the wall. The dishes are hot and spicy, but not *too* hot; hot spices are presented on the side for those who want to go truly Jamaican. The barbecue ribs are especially good, and fresh fish is a delight, perfectly grilled—try the red snapper. Vegetarian dishes are also available on request, and if you don't drink beer you can wash it all down with natural fruit juices. If a cruise ship is in port, wait until the evening, as the place is likely to be swamped with passengers during the day.

Parkway Restaurant. 60 DaCosta Dr. ☎ **876/974-2667.** Main courses $8–$20. AE, MC, V. Daily 8am–11:30pm. JAMAICAN.

Come here to eat as Jamaicans eat. This popular spot in the commercial center of town couldn't be plainer or more unpretentious, but it's always packed. Locals know they can get some of Ocho Rios's best-tasting and most affordable dishes here. It's the local watering and drinking joint and is a bit disdainful of all those Sandals and Couples resorts with their contrived international food. Hungry diners dig into straightforward fare such as Jamaican-style chicken, curried goat, sirloin steak, and fillet of red snapper, topping it all off with banana cream pie. Lobster and fresh fish are usually featured. The restaurant recently renovated its third floor to offer entertainment and dancing. Tuesday's Reggae Night lets local bands do their best "to let the groove ooze," as they say here.

HITTING THE BEACH

The most idyllic sands are at the often-overcrowded **Mallards Beach,** in the center of Ocho Rios and shared by hotel guests and cruise-ship passengers. Locals may steer you to the white sands of **Turtle Beach** in the south, between the Renaissance Jamaica Grande and Club Jamaica.

The most frequented (and to be avoided when cruise ships are in port) is **Dunn's River Beach,** located below the famous falls. Another great spot is **Jamaica Grande's Beach,** which is open to the public. Parasailing is a favorite sport here.

Many exhibitionistic couples check into the famous but pricey **Couples Resort,** which is known for its private au natural island. A shuttle boat transports visitors offshore to this beautiful little island with a fine sandy beach. A bar, pool, and hot tub are just a few hundred yards offshore from Couples. Security guards keep the gawkers from bothering guests here.

Our favorite is none of the above. We always follow the trail of 007 and head for ✪ **James Bond Beach** (☎ **876/975-3663**), east of Ocho Rios at Oracabessa Beach. Chris Blackwell, the entrepreneur, reopened writer Ian Fleming's former home, Goldeneye. For $5, nonguests can enjoy its sand strip any day except Monday. Admission includes a free drink (beer or soda) and use of the changing rooms. There's a water-sports rental center here as well.

SPORTS & OUTDOOR PURSUITS

GOLF   **SuperClub's Runaway Golf Club,** at Runaway Bay near Ocho Rios on the north coast (☎ **876/973-4820**), charges no fee to guests who stay at any of Jamaica's affiliated SuperClubs. For nonguests, the price is $80 year-round. Any player can rent carts for $35 for 18 holes; clubs are $14 for 18 holes.

Sandals Golf & Country Club (☎ **876/975-0119**), a 15-minute ride from the center of the resort, is a 6,500-yard course, known for its panoramic scenery some 700 feet above sea level. From the center of Ocho Rios, travel along the main by-pass for 2 miles until you reach Mile End Road. A Texaco station is located at the corner of Mile End Road. Turn right and drive for another 5 miles until you come to the Sandals course on your right. The 18-hole, par-71 course was designed by P. K. Saunders and opened in 1951 as the Upton Golf Club. Rolling terrain, lush vegetation, and flowers and fruit trees dominate the 120-acre course. A putting green and driving range are available for those who wish to hone their skills first. Sandals guests play free; nonguests pay $50 for 9 holes or $70 for 18 holes.

SCUBA DIVING & SNORKELING The best outfitter is **Resort Divers Shop,** Main Street, Turtle Beach (☎ **876/974-6632**), at the Club Jamaica Resort. The skilled staff here can hook you up for dive trips or snorkeling. The best spot for either of these sports is 200 yards offshore (you'll be transported there). A boat leaving daily at 1pm goes to Paradise Reef, where tropical fish are plentiful.

TENNIS **Ciboney Ocho Rios,** Main Street, Ocho Rios (☎ **876/974-1027**), focuses more on tennis than any other resort in the area. It offers three clay-surface and three hard-surface courts, all lit for night play. Guests play free, day or night, but nonguests must call and make arrangements with the manager. An on-site pro offers lessons for $25 an hour. Ciboney also sponsors twice-a-day clinics for both beginners and advanced players. Frequent guest tournaments are also staged, including handicapped doubles and mixed doubles.

EXPLORING THE AREA

A scenic drive south of Ocho Rios along Route A3 will take you inland through **Fern Gully.** This was originally a riverbed, but now the main road winds up some 700 feet among a profusion of wild ferns, a tall rain forest, hardwood trees, and lianas. There are hundreds of varieties of ferns, and roadside stands offer fruits and vegetables, carved-wood souvenirs, and basketwork. The road runs for about 4 miles; at the top of the hill, you come to a right-hand turn onto a narrow road leading to Golden Grove, a small Jamaican community of no tourist interest.

Head west when you see the signs pointing to Lyford, a small community southwest of Ocho Rios. To approach it, take A3 south (the Fern Gully Road) until you come to a small intersection directly north of Walkers Wood. Follow the signpost west to Lyford. You'll pass the remains of the 1763 **Edinburgh Castle,** the lair of one of Jamaica's most infamous murderers, a Scot named Lewis Hutchinson, who used to shoot passersby and toss their bodies into a deep pit. The authorities got wind of his activities, and although he tried to escape by canoe, he was captured by the navy and hanged. Rather proud of his achievements (evidence of at least 43 murders was found), he left £100 and instructions for a memorial to be built. It never was, but the castle ruins remain.

Continue north on Route A1 to **St. Ann's Bay,** the site of the first Spanish settlement on the island, where you can see the **statue of Christopher Columbus,** cast in his hometown of Genoa and erected near St. Ann's Hospital on the west side of town, close to the coast road. There are a number of Georgian buildings in the town—the **Court House** near the parish church, built in 1866, is the most interesting.

Brimmer Hall Estate. Port Maria, St. Mary's. ☎ **876/994-2309.** Tours $15. Tours Mon–Fri at 11am, 1:30pm, and 3pm.

Some 21 miles east of Ocho Rios, in the hills 2 miles from Port Maria, this 1817 estate is an ideal place to spend a day. You can relax beside the pool and sample a wide variety of brews and concoctions. The Plantation Tour Eating House offers typical Jamaican dishes for lunch, and there's a souvenir shop with a good selection of ceramics, art, straw goods, wood carvings, rums, liqueurs, and cigars. All this is on a working plantation where you're driven around in a tractor-drawn jitney to see the tropical fruit trees and coffee plants; the knowledgeable guides will explain the various processes necessary to produce the fine fruits of the island.

Coyaba River Garden and Museum. Shaw Park Rd. ☎ **876/974-6235.** Admission $4.50, free for children 12 and under. Daily 8:30am–5pm. Take the Fern Gully–Kingston road, turn left at St. John's Anglican Church, and follow the signs to Coyaba, just half a mile farther.

A mile from the center of Ocho Rios, at an elevation of 420 feet, this park and museum were built on the grounds of the former Shaw Park plantation. The word *coyaba* comes from the Arawak name for paradise. Coyaba is a Spanish-style museum with a river and gardens filled with native flora, a cut-stone courtyard, fountains, and a crafts shop and bar. The museum boasts a collection of artifacts from the Arawak, Spanish, and English settlements in the area.

✪ **Dunn's River Falls.** Rte. A3. ☎ **876/974-2857.** Admission $6 adults, $3 children 2–11, free for children under 2. Daily 8:30am–5pm (8am–5pm on cruise-ship arrival days). From St. Ann's Bay, follow Route A3 east back to Ocho Rios, and you'll pass Dunn's River Falls; there's plenty of parking.

For a fee, you can relax on the beach or climb with a guide to the top of the 600-foot falls. You can splash in the waters at the bottom of the falls or drop into the cool pools higher up between the cascades of water. The beach restaurant provides snacks and drinks, and dressing rooms are available. If you're planning to climb the falls, wear old tennis shoes to protect your feet from the sharp rocks and to prevent slipping.

Firefly. Grants Pen, in St. Mary, 20 miles east of Ocho Rios above Oracabessa. ☎ **876/997-7201.** Admission $10. Daily 8:30am–5:30pm.

Firefly was the home of Sir Noël Coward and his longtime companion, Graham Payn, who, as executor of Coward's estate, donated it to the Jamaica National Heritage Trust. The recently restored house is more or less as it was on the day Sir Noël died in 1973. His Hawaiian-print shirts still hang in the closet of his austere bedroom, with its mahogany four-poster. The library contains a collection of his books, and the living room is warm and comfortable, with big armchairs and two grand pianos (where he composed several famous tunes). When the Queen Mother was entertained here, the lobster mousse Coward planned on serving melted, so, with a style and flair that was the stuff of legend, he opened a can of pea soup instead. Guests were housed at Blue Harbour, a villa closer to Port Maria; they included Evelyn Waugh, Winston Churchill, Errol Flynn, Laurence Olivier, Vivien Leigh, Claudette Colbert, Katharine Hepburn, and Mary Martin. Paintings by the noted playwright/actor/author/composer adorn the walls. An open patio looks out over the pool and the sea. Across the lawn, his plain, flat white marble gravestone is inscribed simply: "Sir Noël Coward, born December 16, 1899, died March 26, 1973."

Harmony Hall. Tower Isles on Rte A3, 4 miles east of Ocho Rios. ☎ **876/975-4222.** Free admission. Gallery Mon–Sat 10am–6pm; restaurant/cafe daily 10am–10pm.

Harmony Hall was built near the end of the 19th century as the centerpiece of a sugar plantation. Today it has been restored and is now the focal point of an art gallery and restaurant that showcases the painting and sculpture of Jamaican artists as well as a tasteful array of arts and crafts. Among the featured gift items are Sharon McConnell's Starfish Oils, which contain natural additives harvested in Jamaica. The gallery shop also carries the "Reggae to Wear" line of sportswear, designed and made on Jamaica.

Harmony Hall is also the setting for one of the best Italian restaurants along the coast, Toscanini's (see "Where to Dine," above).

Prospect Plantation. Rte. A3, 3 miles east of Ocho Rios, in St. Ann. ☎ **876/994-1058.**
Tours $12 adults, free for children 12 and under; 1-hour horseback ride $20. Tours Mon–Sat
at 10:30am, 2pm, and 3:30pm; Sun at 11am, 1:30pm, and 3pm.

This working plantation adjoins the 18-hole Prospect Mini Golf Course. A visit to this
property is an educational, relaxing, and enjoyable experience. On your leisurely ride
by covered jitney through the scenic beauty of Prospect, you'll readily see why this section of Jamaica is called "the garden parish of the island." You can view the many trees
planted by such visitors as Winston Churchill, Henry Kissinger, Charlie Chaplin,
Pierre Trudeau, Noël Coward, and many others. You'll learn about and observe
pimento (allspice), bananas, cassava, sugarcane, coffee, cocoa, coconut, pineapple, and
the famous leucaena "Tree of Life." You'll see Jamaica's first hydroelectric plant and
sample some of the exotic fruit and drinks.

Horseback riding is available on three scenic trails at Prospect. The rides vary from
1 to 2¼ hours. Advance booking of 1 hour is necessary.

SHOPPING

For many, Ocho Rios provides an introduction to Jamaica-style shopping. After surviving the ordeal, some visitors may vow never to go shopping again. Literally hundreds of Jamaicans pour into Ocho Rios hoping to peddle items to cruise-ship
passengers and other visitors. Be prepared for aggressive vendors. Pandemonium greets
many an unwary shopper, who must also be prepared for some fierce haggling. Every
vendor asks too much at first, which gives them the leeway to "negotiate" until the
price reaches a more realistic level. Is shopping fun in Ocho Rios? A resounding no.
Do cruise-ship passengers and land visitors indulge in it anyway? A decided yes.

SHOPPING CENTERS & MALLS   There are seven main shopping plazas. We've
listed them because they're here, not because we heartily recommend them. The originals are Ocean Village, Pineapple Place, and Coconut Grove. Newer ones include the
New Ocho Rios Plaza, in the center of town, with some 60 shops. Island Plaza is
another major shopping complex, as is the Mutual Security Plaza with some 30 shops.
Opposite the New Ocho Rios Plaza is the Taj Mahal, with 26 duty-free stores.

Ocean Village Shopping Centre (☎ **876/974-2683**)   This shopping area contains
numerous boutiques, food stores, a bank, sundries purveyors, travel agencies, service
facilities, and what have you. The **Ocho Rios Pharmacy** (☎ **876/974-2398**) sells
most proprietary brands, perfumes, and suntan lotions, among its many wares.

Pineapple Place Shopping Centre   Just east of Ocho Rios, this is a collection of
shops in cedar-shingle-roofed cottages set amid tropical flowers.

Ocho Rios Craft Park   You can browse some 150 stalls here. A vendor will weave a
hat or a basket while you wait, or you can buy a ready-made hat, hamper, handbag,
place mats, or lampshade. Other stands stock hand-embroidered goods and will make
small items while you wait. Wood carvers work on bowls, ashtrays, statues, and cups.

Coconut Grove Shopping Plaza   This collection of low-lying shops is linked by
walkways and shrubs. The merchandise consists mainly of local craft items. Many of
your fellow shoppers may be cruise-ship passengers.

Island Plaza   Right in the heart of Ocho Rios is some of the best Jamaican art, all
paintings by local artists. You can also purchase local handmade crafts (be prepared to
do some haggling), carvings, ceramics, kitchenware, and the inevitable T-shirts.

SPECIALTY SHOPS   In general, the shopping is better in Montego Bay. If you're
not going there, wander the Ocho Rios crafts markets, although much of the merchandise has the same monotony. We list the places that deserve special mention.

Swiss Stores, in the Ocean Village Shopping Centre (☎ 876/974-2519), sells jewelry and all the big names in Swiss watches, including Juvenia, Tissot, Omega, Rolex, Patek Philippe, and Piaget. The Rolex watches here are real, not those fakes touted by hustlers on the streets.

One of the best bets for shopping is **Soni's Plaza,** 50 Main St., the address of all the shops recommended below. **Casa dé Oro** (☎ 876/974-5392) specializes in duty-free watches, fine jewelry, and classic perfumes. **Chulani's** (☎ 876/974-2421) sells a goodly assortment of quality watches and brand-name perfumes, although some of the leather bags might tempt you as well. There's also a wide variety of 14-karat and 18-karat settings with diamonds, emeralds, rubies, and sapphires.

Gem Palace (☎ 876/974-2850) is the place to go for diamond solitaires and tennis bracelets. The shop specializes in 14-karat gold chains and bracelets. **Mohan's** (☎ 876/974-9270) offers one of the best selections of 14-karat and 18-karat gold chains, rings, bracelets, and earrings. Jewelry studded with precious gems such as diamonds and rubies is sold here as well.

Soni's (☎ 876/974-2303) dazzles with gold, but also cameras, French perfumes, watches, china and crystal, linen tablecloths, and even the standard Jamaican souvenirs. **Taj Gift Centre** (☎ 876/974-9268) has a little bit of everything: Blue Mountain coffee, film, cigars, and hand-embroidered linen tablecloths. For something different, look for Jamaican jewelry made from hematite, a mountain stone. **Tajmahal** (☎ 876/974-6455) beats most competition with its name-brand watches, jewelry, and fragrances. It also has Paloma Picasso leather wear and porcelain by Lladró.

We generally ignore hotel gift shops, but the **Jamaica Inn Gift Shop,** in the Jamaica Inn, Main Street (☎ 876/974-2514), is better than most, selling everything from Blue Mountain coffee to Walkers Wood products, even guava jelly and jerk seasoning. If you're lucky, you'll find marmalade from an old family recipe, plus Upton Pimento Dram, a unique liqueur flavored with Jamaican allspice. Local handcrafts include musical instruments for kids, brightly painted country cottages of tin, and intricate jigsaw puzzles of local scenes. The store also sells antiques and fine old maps of the West Indies.

OCHO RIOS AFTER DARK

The **Sports Bar** at the Little Pub Restaurant (see above) is open daily from 10am to 3am, and Sunday is disco night. Most evenings are devoted to some form of entertainment, including karaoke.

Hotels often welcome nonguests to their live entertainment. Ask at your hotel desk where the action is on any given night. Otherwise, you may want to stop by **Silks Discothèque,** in the Shaw Park Hotel, Cutlass Bay (☎ 876/974-2552), which has a smallish dance floor and a sometimes-animated crowd of drinkers and dancers. If you're not a guest of the hotel, you can enter for an all-inclusive price of J$200 ($5.70).

Jamaic'N Me Crazy, at the Jamaican Grande Hotel (☎ 876/974-2201), is an all-inclusive spot that's more like a New York nightclub than a Jamaican one. It has the best lighting and sound system in Ocho Rios (and perhaps Jamaica), and the crowd includes everyone from the passing yachter to the curious tourist, who may be under the mistaken impression that he or she is seeing an authentic Jamaican nightclub. It charges nonguests $30 to cover everything you can shake or drink, nightly from 10pm to 3am.

For more of the same without an overbearing Americanized atmosphere, try the **Acropolis,** 70 Main St. (☎ 876/974-2633). The adventurous traveler can rest assured that this is a lot closer to an authentic Jamaican nightclub than Jamaic'N Me

Crazy. Cover is required only on nights with a live band, and it's rarely any higher than J$200 ($5.70).

7 Port Antonio

Port Antonio, sometimes called the Jamaica of 100 years ago, is a verdant and sleepy seaport on the northeast coast, 63 miles northeast of Kingston. It's the mecca of the titled and the wealthy, including European royalty and stars like Whoopi Goldberg and Peter O'Toole.

This small, bustling town is like many on the island: clean but untidy, with sidewalks around a market filled with vendors, and tin-roofed shacks competing with old Georgian and modern brick and concrete buildings. At the market, you can browse for local craftwork, spices, and fruits.

Travelers used to arrive by banana boat and stay at the Titchfield Hotel (which burned down). Captain Bligh landed here in 1793 with the first breadfruit plants, and Port Antonio claims that the ones grown in this area are the best on the island. Visitors still arrive by water, but now it's in cruise ships that moor close to Navy Island, and the passengers come ashore just for the day.

Navy Island and the long-gone Titchfield Hotel were owned for a short time by film star Errol Flynn. The story is that after suffering damage to his yacht, he put into Kingston for repairs, visited Port Antonio by motorbike, fell in love with the area, and in due course acquired Navy Island (some say he won it in a bet). Later, he either lost or sold it and bought a nearby plantation, Comfort Castle, still owned by his widow, Patrice Wymore Flynn, who spends most of her time there. He was much loved and admired by the Jamaicans and was totally integrated into the community. They still talk of him in Port Antonio—his reputation for womanizing and drinking lives on.

GETTING THERE

BY PLANE   If you're going to Ocho Rios, you will fly into the **Donald Sangster Airport** in Montego Bay or the **Norman Manley International Airport** in Kingston. Some hotels, particularly the larger resorts, will arrange for airport transfers from that point. Be sure to ask when you book.

If your hotel does not provide transfers, you can fly to Port Antonio's small airport aboard **Air Jamaica Express,** booking your connection through Air Jamaica (☎ 800/523-5585 in the U.S.). The one-way fare is $45 from Kingston, $60 from Montego Bay.

BY BUS   The bus costs $25 one-way. We recommend two private companies: **Tour Wise** (☎ 876/979-1027) or **Caribic Vacations** (☎ 876/953-9874). The bus will drop you off at your hotel. The trip takes 2 hours, but for safety's sake, we only recommend this option if you fly into Montego Bay.

BY RENTAL CAR & TAXI   You can rent a car for the 133-mile drive east along Route A1 (see "Getting Around" in section 1, "Essentials," at the beginning of this chapter), but we don't advise this 4-hour drive for safety's sake, regardless of which airport you land at. If you take a taxi, the typical one-way fare from Montego Bay is $100, but always negotiate and agree upon a fare *before* you get into the cab.

WHERE TO STAY
VERY EXPENSIVE

Fern Hill Club Hotel. Mile Gully Rd., San San (P.O. Box 100), Port Antonio, Jamaica, W.I. ☎ 876/993-7374. Fax 876/993-7373. 31 units. A/C TV. Winter $300 double; $310–$390 suite. Off-season $209–$220 double; $231–$253 suite. Rates are all-inclusive. AE, MC, V. Drive east along Allan Ave. and watch for the signs.

Attractive, airy, and panoramic, Fern Hill occupies 20 forested acres high above the coastline, attracting primarily a British and Canadian clientele. This is a far less elegant choice than its main competitor, Goblin Hill (see below). Technically classified as a private club, the establishment is comprised of a colonial-style clubhouse and three outlying villas, plus a comfortable annex at the bottom of the hill. The accommodations come in a wide range of configurations, including standard rooms, junior suites, spa suites, and villas with cooking facilities. All units are highly private and attract many honeymooners. Bathrooms are adequate with plenty of shelf space.

Dining: See "Where to Dine," below, for a review of the hotel restaurant, which offers an international menu. There's also the Blue Mahoe Bar and a patio for dining.

Amenities: Three pools, tennis court. A shuttle bus makes daily trips down the steep hillside to the beach.

✪ **Trident Villas and Hotel.** Rte. A4 (P.O. Box 119), Port Antonio, Jamaica, W.I. ☎ **876/993-2602.** Fax 876/993-2960. 22 units. A/C TV TEL. Winter $385 double; from $620 suite. Off-season $220 double; from $340 suite. Rates include MAP (breakfast and dinner). AE, MC, V.

This elegant rendezvous of the rich and famous is about 2½ miles east of Port Antonio along Allan Avenue, on the coast toward Frenchman's Cove. It's one of the most tasteful and refined hotels on the north shore. Sitting regally above jagged coral cliffs with a seaside panorama, it's the personal and creative statement of Earl Levy, scion of a prominent Kingston family. Nearby, he has erected a multimillion-dollar replica of a European château, known as Trident Castle, which can be rented as one unit; guests are grandly housed in eight large bedrooms beautifully furnished in plantation style.

The hotel's main building is furnished with antiques, and flowers decorate the lobby, which is cooled by sea breezes. Your accommodations will be a studio cottage or tower, reached by a path through the gardens. In the cottages, a large bedroom with ample sitting area opens onto a private patio with a sea view. All units have ceiling fans, plenty of storage space, and tasteful Jamaican antiques and colorful chintzes. Beds are most comfortable with deluxe mattresses, while tiled bathrooms have combination tub/showers and hair dryers. Jugs of ice and water are constantly replenished. There's a small, private sand beach, and the gardens surround a pool and a gingerbread gazebo. Lounges, tables, chairs, and bar service add to your pleasure.

Dining: The main building has two patios, one covered, where breakfast and lunch are served. You can also have breakfast on your private patio, served by your own butler. Men are required to wear jackets and ties at dinner, when silver service, crystal, and Port Royal pewter sparkle on the tables. Dinner is a multicourse, fixed-price meal, so if you have dietary restrictions, make your requirements known early.

Amenities: Pool, tennis courts, and such water sports as sailing and snorkeling. Room service, laundry, baby-sitting.

EXPENSIVE/MODERATE

Dragon Bay. P.O. Box 176, Port Antonio, Jamaica, W.I. ☎ **876/993-8751.** Fax 876/993-3284. 97 units in 33 bungalows. A/C TEL. Winter $145–$160 double; $220 one-bedroom suite for 2; $330 two-bedroom suite for up to 4; $450 three-bedroom suite for 6–8. Off-season $120 double; $150–$230 one-bedroom suite for 2; $230 two-bedroom suite for up to 4; $320 three-bedroom suite for 6–8. AE, MC, V.

Established in 1969 on 55 acres of forested land that slopes down to a sandy beach, this resort has changed hands frequently during its lifetime, and gone through a series of ups and downs. Today, it's a well-managed, carefully designed compound of bungalows and villas that caters to a mostly European clientele, most of whom check in for relatively long stays of 2 weeks or more. Accommodations are within about 30 pink-and-white, two-story bungalows, some built on flatlands beside the beach, others on the steeply sloping terrain leading uphill to the resort's "clubhouse." Furnishings are durable but comfortable; the efficiently organized bathrooms have shower stalls. All but the smallest units contain kitchens, a fact that's appreciated by guests who prepare at least some of their own meals with supplies purchased at neighborhood grocery stores.

There are two restaurants, one beside the beach, the other a more substantial eatery. There are three bars—our favorite is the "Cruise Bar," which was used as a set for Tom Cruise in *Cocktail*. Amenities include an on-site dive shop, which will provide instruction; a pool adjacent to the beach; two tennis courts; hiking paths through the forest; and aerobics classes.

Goblin Hill Villas at San San. San San (P.O. Box 26), Port Antonio, Jamaica, W.I. ☎ **876/993-7443.** Fax 876/925-6248. 28 units. A/C. Winter $110–$195 one-bedroom villa; $185–$245 two-bedroom villa. Off-season $90–$165 one-bedroom villa; $145–$195 two-bedroom villa. Rates include airport transfers and rental car. AE, MC, V.

This green and sun-washed hillside—once said to shelter goblins—is now filled with Georgian-style vacation homes on San San Estate. The pool is surrounded by a vine-laced arbor, which lies just a stone's throw from an almost impenetrable forest. A long flight of steps leads down to the crescent-shaped sands of San San beach. This beach is now private, but guests of the hotel receive a pass. The accommodations are townhouse style; some have ceiling fans and king-size beds, but none have phones or TVs. The generally roomy units are filled with handmade pine pieces, along with a split-level living and dining area with a fully equipped kitchen. Housekeepers prepare and serve meals and attend to chores in the villas. There's also a restaurant and bar on the premises, serving a rather good international/Jamaican menu. Facilities include two Laykold tennis courts and a pool. Dragon Bay, about a 5- to 10-minute drive away, offers a variety of water sports, including snorkeling, windsurfing, and scuba diving.

Jamaica Palace. Williamsfield (P.O. Box 277), Port Antonio, Jamaica, W.I. ☎ **800/ 472-1149** in the U.S., or 876/993-7720. Fax 876/993-7759. www.in-site.com/jampal. E-mail: jampal@in-site.com. 80 units. A/C TEL. Winter $140–$200 double; $230–$400 suite. Off-season $140–$180 double; $210–$355 suite. MAP (breakfast and dinner) $60 per person extra in winter, $50 in off-season. AE, MC, V. It's 5 miles east of Port Antonio.

Rising like a stately mansion from a hillock surrounded by 5 tropically landscaped acres, this property strives to combine the elegance of a European hotel with the relaxed atmosphere of a Jamaican resort. The public rooms are filled with furnishings and art from Europe, including a 6-foot Baccarat crystal candelabrum and a pair of Italian ebony-and-ivory chairs from the 15th century. Outside, the Palace offers white marble columns, sun-filled patios and balconies, and an unusual 114-foot pool shaped like the island of Jamaica.

Most accommodations are large, with 12½-foot ceilings and oversize marble bathrooms. Some, however, are rather small, but still elegantly furnished. Suites are individually furnished with crystal chandeliers, Persian rugs, and original works of art. All units have excellent beds, often sleigh beds. TVs are available upon request.

Both continental and Jamaican food are served in the main dining room with its lighted "waterwall" sculpted from Jamaican cave stones. Men are requested to wear jackets and ties. There's also a poolside cafe with a barbecue area, live dance music and calypso bands, a pool, and a boutique (operated by Patrice Wymore Flynn, widow of Errol Flynn). Other amenities include room service, laundry, baby-sitting, massage facilities, and complimentary shuttle service to the private San San Beach, to which hotel guests are admitted.

INEXPENSIVE

Navy Island Marina Resort. Navy Island (P.O. Box 188), Port Antonio, Jamaica, W.I. ☎ **876/993-2667.** 7 units. Year-round $80 double; $100 one-bedroom villa for two; $130 one-bedroom villa for three; $225 two-bedroom villa for three; $250 two-bedroom villa for four. Rates include breakfast. Children 11 and under stay free in parents' villa. AE, MC, V.

Jamaica's only private island getaway, this resort and marina is on that "bit of paradise" once owned by the actor Errol Flynn. Today, this cottage colony and yacht club is one of the best-kept travel secrets in the Caribbean. To reach the resort, you'll have to take a ferry from the dockyards of Port Antonio on West Street for a short ride across one of the most beautiful harbors of Jamaica (hotel guests travel free). One of the resort's beaches is a secluded clothing-optional stretch of sand known as Trembly Knee Cove. You can leisurely explore the island, whose grounds are dotted with hybrid hibiscus, bougainvillea, and palms (many of which were originally ordered planted by Flynn himself).

Each accommodation is designed as a studio cottage or villa branching out from the main club. Ceiling fans and trade winds keep the cottages cool, and mosquito netting over the comfortable beds adds a plantation touch. Bathrooms are fairly small and routine, but at least the plumbing in this remote location is workable. At night, after enjoying drinks in the H.M.S. *Bounty* Bar, you can dine in the Bounty. There's also a pool, two beaches, and snorkeling.

WHERE TO DINE

All hotels welcome outside guests for dinner, but reservations are required.

Fern Hill Club. Mile Gully Rd. ☎ **876/993-7374.** Reservations recommended. Main courses $5–$10 lunch, $12–$20 dinner. AE, MC, V. Daily 7:30am–9:30pm. Head east on Allan Ave. INTERNATIONAL/JAMAICAN.

One of the finest dining spots in Port Antonio has a sweeping view of the rugged coastline—the sunsets here are the best at the resort. Well-prepared specialties are served: jerk chicken, jerk pork, grilled lobster, and Creole fish. Depending on who's in the kitchen, the food here can be quite satisfactory, though once in a while, especially off-season, the cuisine might be a bit of a letdown. The club also offers entertainment, with a calypso band and piano music during the week and disco music on weekends.

✪ **Trident Hotel Restaurant.** Rte. A4. ☎ **876/993-2602.** Reservations required. Jackets and ties required for men. Fixed-price dinner $44. AE, MC, V. Daily 8am–4pm and 8–10pm. Head east on Allan Ave. INTERNATIONAL.

Trident Hotel Restaurant has long been sought out by travelers in search of fine cuisine on Jamaica. Part of the main hotel building, the restaurant has an air of elegance. The high-pitched wooden roof set on white stone walls holds several ceiling fans that gently stir the air. The antique tables are set with old china, English silver, and Port Royal pewter. The formally dressed waiters will help you choose your wine and whisper the name of each course as they serve it: Jamaican salad, dolphin (mahimahi) with mayonnaise-and-mustard sauce, steak with broccoli and sautéed potatoes, and peach Melba and Blue Mountain coffee with Tía Maria, a Jamaican liqueur. The six-course dinner menu changes daily. The cuisine is always fresh and prepared with first-class ingredients, though the setting and the white-gloved service are generally more memorable than the food.

Remember Brooke Shields, way back before she tried to become a TV-sitcom star? She made the film *The Blue Lagoon* in this calm, protected cove. The water is so deep, nearly 20 feet or so, that it turns a cobalt blue. There's almost no more scenic spot in all of Jamaica. The Blue Lagoon, with its small, intimate beach, lies 10 miles to the east of Port Antonio. It's a great place for a picnic; you can pick up plenty of the famous peppery delicacy, jerk pork, smoked at various shacks along the Boston Bay Beach area.

Yachtsman's Wharf. 16 West St. ☎ **876/993-3053.** Main courses $7–$15. No credit cards. Daily 7:30am–10pm. INTERNATIONAL.

This restaurant beneath a thatch-covered roof is at the end of an industrial pier, near the departure point for ferries to Navy Island. The rustic bar and restaurant is a favorite of the expatriate yachting set. Crews from many of the ultra-expensive boats have dined here and have pinned their ensigns on the roughly textured planks and posts. The kitchen opens for breakfast and stays open all day, serving up menu items such as burgers, ceviche, curried chicken, and ackee with saltfish. Main dishes include vegetables. Come here for the setting, the camaraderie, and the usual array of tropical drinks; the food is only secondary.

HITTING THE BEACH

Port Antonio has several white-sand beaches, including the famous **San San Beach,** which has recently gone private, although guests of certain hotels are admitted with a pass.

Boston Beach is free, and often has light surfing; there are picnic tables as well as a restaurant and snack bar. On your way here, stop and get the makings for a picnic lunch at the most famous center for peppery jerk pork and chicken on Jamaica. These rustic shacks also sell the much rarer jerk sausage. It's 11 miles east of Port Antonio and the Blue Lagoon.

Also free is **Fairy Hill Beach** (Winnifred), with no changing rooms or showers. **Frenchman's Cove Beach** attracts a chic crowd to its white-sand beach combined with a freshwater stream. Nonguests are charged a fee.

Navy Island, once Errol Flynn's personal hideaway, is a fine choice for swimming (one beach is clothing optional) and snorkeling (at **Crusoe's Beach**). Take the boat from the Navy Island dock on West Street across from the Exxon station. It's a 7-minute ride to the island; a one-way fare is 30¢. The ferry runs 24 hours a day. The island is the setting for the Navy Island Marina Resort (see above).

SPORTS & OUTDOOR PURSUITS

DEEP-SEA FISHING   Northern Jamaican waters are world renowned for their game fish, including dolphin (mahimahi), wahoo, blue and white marlin, sailfish, tarpon, barracuda, and bonito. The Jamaica International Fishing Tournament and Jamaica International Blue Marlin Team Tournaments run concurrently at Port Antonio every September or October. Most major hotels from Port Antonio to Montego Bay have deep-sea-fishing facilities, and there are many charter boats.

A 30-foot-long **sport-fishing boat** (☎ **876/993-3209**) with a tournament rig is available for charter rental. Taking out up to six passengers at a time, it charges $250 per half day or $450 per day, with crew, bait, tackle, and soft drinks included. It docks at Port Antonio's Marina, off West Palm Avenue, in the center of town. Call for bookings.

RAFTING   Rafting started on the Río Grande as a means of transporting bananas from the plantations to the waiting freighters. In 1871, a Yankee skipper, Lorenzo Dow Baker, decided that a seat on one of the rafts was better than walking, but it was not until Errol Flynn arrived that the rafts became popular as a tourist attraction. Flynn used to hire the craft for his friends, and he encouraged the rafters to race down the Río Grande. Bets were placed on the winner. Now that bananas are transported by road, the raft skipper makes one or maybe two trips a day down the waterway. If you want to take a trip, contact **Río Grande Attractions Limited,** c/o Rafter's Restaurant, St. Margaret's Bay (☎ **876/993-5778**).

The rafts, some 33 feet long and only 4 feet wide, are propelled by stout bamboo poles. There's a raised double seat about two-thirds of the way back. The skipper stands in the front, trousers rolled up to his knees, the water washing his feet, and guides the craft down the lively river, about 8 miles between steep hills covered with coconut palms, banana plantations, and flowers, through limestone cliffs pitted with caves, through the "Tunnel of Love," a narrow cleft in the rocks, then on to wider, gentler water.

The day starts at the Rafter's Restaurant, west of Port Antonio, at Burlington on St. Margaret's Bay. Trips last 2 to 2½ hours and are offered from 8am to 4pm daily at a cost of $45 per raft, which holds two passengers. From the restaurant, a fully insured driver will take you in your rented car to the starting point at Grants Level or Berrydale, where you board your raft. The trip ends back at the Rafter's Restaurant, where you can collect your car, which has been returned by the driver. If you feel like it, take a picnic lunch, but bring enough for the skipper, too, who will regale you with lively stories of life on the river.

SNORKELING & SCUBA DIVING   The best outfitter is **Lady Godiva's Dive Shop** in Dragon Bay (☎ **876/993-8988**), 7 miles from Port Antonio. Full dive equipment is available. Technically, you can snorkel off most of the beaches in Port Antonio, but you're likely to see much more farther offshore. The very best spot is San San Bay by Monkey Island. The reef here is extremely active and full of a lot of exciting marine life. Lady Godiva offers two excursions daily to this spot for $10 per person. Snorkeling equipment costs $9 for a full day's rental.

EXPLORING THE AREA

Athenry Gardens and Cave of Nonsuch. Portland. ☎ **876/993-3740.** Admission (including guide for gardens and cave) $5 adults, $2.50 children 11 and under. Daily 9am–5pm (last tour at 4:30pm). From Harbour St. in Port Antonio, turn south in front of the Anglican church onto Red Hassel Rd. and proceed approximately a mile to Breastworks community (fork in road); take the left fork, cross a narrow bridge, go immediately left after the bridge, and proceed approximately 3½ miles to the village of Nonsuch.

Twenty minutes from Port Antonio, it's an easy drive and an easy walk to see the stalagmites, stalactites, fossilized marine life, and evidence of Arawak civilization in Nonsuch. The cave is 1.5 million years old. From the Athenry Gardens, there are panoramic views over the island and the sea. The gardens are filled with coconut palms, flowers, and trees, and complete guided tours are given.

Crystal Springs. Buff Bay, Portland. ☎ **876/996-1400.** Admission J$100 ($2.85) adults, J$50 ($1.45) children. Daily 9am–5pm.

Crystal Springs is a tract of forested land whose borders were originally specified in 1655. It was then attached to a nearby plantation, whose great house is now under separate (and private) ownership. Visitors can still trek through the organization's 156 acres of forest, whose shelter is much beloved by birds and wildlife. A simple restaurant is on the premises, as well as a series of cottages erected in the early 1990s. These are usually rented to visiting ornithologists who don't care for the amenities or distractions of a traditional resort.

Folly Great House. On the outskirts of Port Antonio on the way to Trident Village, going east along Rte. A4. Free admission.

This house was reputedly built in 1905 by Arthur Mitchell, an American millionaire, for his wife, Annie, daughter of Charles Tiffany, founder of the famous New York store. Seawater was used in the concrete mixtures of its foundations and mortar, and the house began to collapse only 11 years after they moved in. Because of the beautiful location, it's easy to see what a fine great house it must have been.

Somerset Falls. 8 miles west of Port Antonio, just past Hope Bay on Rte. A4. ☎ **876/913-0108.** Tour $3. Daily 9am–5pm.

Here the waters of the Daniels River pour down a deep gorge through a rain forest, with waterfalls and foaming cascades. You can take a short ride in an electric gondola to the hidden falls. A stop on the daily Grand Jamaica Tour from Ocho Rios, this is one of Jamaica's most historic sites; the falls were used by the Spanish before the English captured the island. At the falls, you can swim in the deep rock pools and buy sandwiches, light meals, soft drinks, beer, and liquor at the snack bar. The guided tour includes the gondola ride and a visit to both a cave and a freshwater fish farm.

8 Kingston & Vicinity

Kingston, the largest English-speaking city in the Caribbean, is the capital of Jamaica and its cultural, industrial, and financial center. It's home to more than 650,000 people, including those living on the plains between Blue Mountain and the sea.

The buildings here are a mixture of the modern, graceful, old, and just plain ramshackle. It's a busy city, as you might expect, with a natural harbor that's the seventh largest in the world. The University of the West Indies has its campus on the edge of the city.

WHERE TO STAY

Remember to ask if the 12% room tax is included in the rate quoted when you make your reservation. The rates listed below are year-round unless otherwise noted. All leading hotels in security-conscious Kingston have guards.

✪ **Strawberry Hill.** Irish Town, Blue Mountains, Jamaica, W.I. ☎ **800/OUTPOST** or 876/944-8400. Fax 876/944-8408. E-mail: strawberry@cwjamaica.com. 16 units. TV TEL. Year-round $280–$590 double. AE, DC, MC, V. Guests are personally escorted to the hotel in a customized van or via a 7-minute helicopter ride. It's a 50-minute drive from the Kingston airport or 30 minutes via mountain roads from the center of the city.

The best place to stay in Kingston is out of Kingston. Strawberry Hill, in the Blue Mountains, lies 3,100 feet above the sea, overlooking this turbulent city, which seems far removed in this lush setting. A self-contained facility with its own power and water-purification system, Strawberry Hill also has elaborate botanical gardens. This cottage complex was built on the site of a great house from the 1600s, which Hurricane Gilbert disposed of in 1988. The property was conceived by multimillionaire Christopher Blackwell, the impresario who launched Bob Marley into reggae fame through Island Records. One former guest described this exclusive resort as a "home away from home for five-star Robinson Crusoes." Activities include coffee-plantation tours, hiking and mountain biking through the Blue Mountains, and even such spa services as massages.

Local craftspeople fashioned the cottages and furnished them in classic plantation style, with canopied four-poster beds and louvered windows. In one case, a doorway was carved with figures inspired by Madonna's book, *Sex*. The elegant bathrooms come with hair dryers and combination shower/tubs.

The food here is better than you'll find in Kingston, with such Jamaican dishes as grilled shrimp with fresh cilantro, or fresh grilled fish with jerk mango and sweet-pepper salsa. It's called "new Jamaican cuisine," and so it is. There's no pool or tennis court, but there is a gym/spa/sauna/steam room.

Terra Nova Hotel. 17 Waterloo Rd., Kingston 10, Jamaica, W.I. ☎ **876/926-2211.** Fax 876/929-4933. www.cariboutpost.com. 35 units. A/C TV TEL. Year-round $132 double. AE, MC, V.

This house is on the western edge of New Kingston, near West Kings House Road. Built in 1924 as a wedding present for a young bride, it was converted into a hotel in 1959. Set in 2½ acres of gardens with a backdrop of greenery and mountains, it's now one of the best small Jamaican hotels, although the rooms are rather basic and not at all suited for those who want a resort ambience. Most of the bedrooms are in a new wing. The Spanish-style El Dorado Room, with a marble floor, wide windows, and spotless linen, offers local and international food. Your buffet breakfast is served on the coffee terrace, and there's a pool at the front of the hotel, with a pool bar and grill.

IN NEARBY PORT ROYAL

Morgan's Harbour Hotel & Beach Club. Port Royal, Kingston 1, Jamaica, W.I. ☎ **800/44-UTELL** in the U.S., or 876/967-8030. Fax 876/967-8073. 51 units. A/C MINIBAR TV TEL. Year-round $150 double; $170–$200 suite. AE, DC, MC, V. Take the public ferryboat that departs every 2 hours from near Victoria Pier on Ocean Blvd.; many visitors arrive by car or taxi.

The yachtie favorite, this hotel is in Port Royal, once believed to be the wickedest city on earth. Rebuilt after 1988's Hurricane Gilbert, Morgan's lies near the end of a long sand spit whose rocky and scrub-covered length shelters Kingston's harbor. On the premises is a 200-year-old red-brick building once used to melt pitch for His Majesty's navy, a swimming area defined by docks and buoys, and a series of wings whose eaves are accented with hints of gingerbread. Set on 22 acres of flat and rock-studded seashore, the resort contains the largest marina facility in Kingston, plus a breezy waterfront restaurant and a popular bar (where ghost stories about the old Port Royal seem especially lurid as the liquor flows on Friday night). Longtime residents quietly claim that the ghosts of soldiers killed by a long-ago earthquake are especially visible on hot and very calm days, when British formations seem to march out of the sea.

The well-furnished bedrooms are laid out in an 18th-century Chippendale-Jamaican style. Medium-size bathrooms are tidily maintained, with a rack of good-sized towels, hand-held showers, and brass fittings. The Buccaneer Scuba Club organizes dives to some of the 170-odd wrecks lying close to shore. Deep-sea-fishing charters and trips to outlying cays can also be arranged.

WHERE TO DINE

✪ **Blue Mountain Inn.** Gordon Town Rd. ☎ **876/927-1700.** Reservations required. Jackets required for men (ties optional). Main courses $12–$30 lunch, $14–$35 dinner. AE, DC, MC, V. Mon–Fri noon–2pm; Mon–Sat 7–9:30pm. Head north on Old Hope Rd. into the mountains. CARIBBEAN/INTERNATIONAL.

About a 20-minute drive north from downtown Kingston is an 18th-century coffee-plantation house set high on the slopes of Blue Mountain. Surrounded by trees and flowers, it rests on the bank of the Mammee River. On cold nights, log fires blaze, and

Climbing Blue Mountain

Jamaica has some of the most varied and unusual topography in the Caribbean, including a mountain range laced with rough rivers, streams, and waterfalls. The 192,000-acre **Blue Mountain–John Crow Mountain National Park** is maintained by the Jamaican government. The mountainsides are covered with coffee fields, producing a blended version that's among the leading exports of Jamaica. But for the nature enthusiast, the mountains reveal an astonishingly complex series of ecosystems that change radically as you climb from sea level into the fog-shrouded peaks.

The most popular climb begins at **Whitfield Hall,** a high-altitude hostel and coffee estate about 6 miles from the hamlet of **Mavis Bank.** Reaching the summit of Blue Mountain Peak (3,000 feet above sea level) requires between 5 and 6 hours, each way. En route, hikers pass through acres of coffee plantations and forest, where temperatures are cooler than you might expect, and where high humidity encourages thick vegetation. Along the way, watch for an amazing array of bird life, including hummingbirds, many species of warblers, rufous-throated solitaires, yellow-bellied sapsuckers, and Greater Antillean pewees.

Dress in layers and bring bottled water. If you opt for a 2am departure in anticipation of watching the sunrise from atop the peak, carry a flashlight as well. Sneakers are usually adequate, although many climbers bring their hiking boots. Be aware that even during the "dry" season (from December to March), rainfall is common. During the "rainy" season (the rest of the year), these peaks can get up to 150 inches of rainfall a year, and fogs and mists are frequent.

You can opt to head out alone into the Jamaican wilderness, but considering the dangers of such an undertaking, and the crime you might encounter en route, it isn't completely advisable. A better bet involves engaging one of Kingston's best-known specialists in eco-sensitive tours, **Sunventure Tours,** 30 Balmoral Ave., Kingston 10 (☎ **876/960-6685**). The staff here can always arrange an individualized tour for you and/or your party, but offers a mainstream roster of choices as well. The **Blue Mountain Sunrise Tour** involves a camp-style overnight in one of the most remote and inaccessible areas of Jamaica. For a fee of $140 per person, participants are retrieved at their Kingston hotels, driven to an isolated ranger station, Wildflower Lodge, that's accessible only via four-wheel-drive vehicle, in anticipation of a two-stage hike that begins at 4:30pm. A simple mountaineer's supper is served at 6pm around a campfire at a ranger station near Portland Gap. At 3am, climbers hike by moonlight and flashlight to a mountaintop aerie that was selected for its view of the sunrise over the Blue Mountains. Climbers stay aloft until around noon that day, then head back down the mountain for an eventual return to their hotels in Kingston by 4pm.

A second popular offering involves an excursion from Kingston **"Y's Waterfall"** on the Black River, in southern Jamaica's Elizabeth Parish. Participants congregate in Kingston at 6:30am for a transfer to a raft and boating party near the hamlet of Lacovia, and an all-day waterborne excursion to a region of unusual ecological interest. Depending on the number of participants, fees range from $80 to $100 per person, including lunch.

the dining room gleams with silver and sparkling glass. The inn is one of Jamaica's most famous restaurants, not only for its food but also for its atmosphere and service. The effort of dressing up is worth it, and the cool night air justifies it; women are advised to take a wrap.

Ever since Olivia della Costa took over the restaurant in 1994, the cuisine has been considerably upgraded, especially the fresh seafood and vegetables from the gardens of Jamaica. It's not so old-fashioned in preparation any more, and menus change monthly. Top off your meal with one of the fresh-fruit desserts or homemade ice creams.

HITTING THE BEACH

You don't really come to Kingston for beaches, but there are some here. To the southwest of the sprawling city are black sandy **Hellshire Beach** and **Fort Clarence.** Both of these beaches are very popular with the locals on weekends. Both have changing rooms, heavy security, and numerous food stands. The reggae concerts at Fort Clarence are legendary on the island.

Just past Fort Clarence, the fisherman's beach at **Naggo Head** is an even hipper destination, or so Kingston beach buffs claim. After a swim in the refreshing waters, opt for one of the food stands selling "fry fish" and bammy (cassava bread). The closest beach to the city (although it's not very good) is **Lime Cay,** a little island on the outskirts of Kingston Harbour, approached after a short boat ride from Morgan's Harbour at Port Royal.

SEEING THE SIGHTS

Even if you're staying at Ocho Rios or Port Antonio, you may want to visit Kingston for brief sightseeing and for trips to nearby Port Royal and Spanish Town.

IN TOWN

One of the major attractions, **Devon House,** 26 Hope Rd. (☎ **876/929-7029**), was built in 1881 by George Stiebel, a Jamaican who made his fortune mining in Latin America, becoming one of the first black millionaires in the Caribbean. A striking classical building, the house has been restored to its original beauty by the Jamaican National Trust. The grounds contain crafts shops, boutiques, two restaurants, shops that sell the best ice cream in Jamaica (in exotic fruit flavors), and a bakery and pastry shop with Jamaican puddings and desserts. The main house also displays furniture of various periods and styles. Admission to the main house is J$110 ($3.15); hours are Tuesday to Saturday from 9:30am to 5pm. Admission to the grounds (the shops and restaurants) is free.

Almost next door to Devon House are the sentried gates of **Jamaica House,** residence of the prime minister, a fine, white-columned building set well back from the road.

Continuing along Hope Road, at the crossroads of Lady Musgrave and King's House roads, turn left and you'll see a gate on the left with its own personal traffic light. This leads to **King's House,** the official residence of the governor-general of Jamaica, the queen's representative on the island. The outside and front lawn of the gracious residence, set in 200 acres of well-tended parkland, is sometimes open for viewing, Monday to Friday from 10am to 5pm. The secretarial offices are housed next door in an old wooden building set on brick arches. In front of the house is a gigantic banyan tree in whose roots, legend says, *duppies* (ghosts) take refuge when they're not living in the cotton trees.

Between Old Hope and Mona roads, a short distance from the Botanical Gardens, is the **University of the West Indies** (☎ 876/927-1660), built in 1948 on the Mona Sugar Estate. Ruins of old mills, storehouses, and aqueducts are juxtaposed with modern buildings on what must be the most beautifully situated campus in the world. The chapel, an old sugar-factory building, was transported stone by stone from Trelawny and rebuilt. The remains of the original sugar factory here are well preserved and give a good idea of how sugar was made in slave days.

The **National Library of Jamaica** (formerly the West India Reference Library), Institute of Jamaica, 12 East St. (☎ 876/922-0620), a storehouse of the history, culture, and traditions of Jamaica and the Caribbean, is the finest working library for West Indian studies in the world. It has the most comprehensive, up-to-date, and balanced collection of materials on the region, including books, newspapers, photographs, maps, and prints. Exhibits highlight different aspects of Jamaica and West Indian life. It's open Monday to Thursday from 9am to 5pm, Friday from 9am to 4pm.

The **Bob Marley Museum** (formerly Tuff Gong Studio), 56 Hope Rd. (☎ 876/927-9152), is the most-visited sight in Kingston, but if you're not a Marley fan, it may not mean much to you. The clapboard house with its garden and high surrounding wall was the famous reggae singer's home and recording studio until his death. You can tour the house and view assorted Marley memorabilia, and you may even catch a glimpse of his children, who often frequent the grounds. Hours are Monday to Saturday from 9am to 4pm. Admission is J$350 ($10) for adults, J$175 ($5) for children 4 to 12. It's reached by bus no. 70 or 75 from Halfway Tree, but take a cab to save yourself the hassle of dealing with Kingston public transport.

IN PORT ROYAL

From West Beach Dock, Kingston, a ferry ride of 20 to 30 minutes will take you to Port Royal, which conjures up visions of swashbuckling pirates led by Henry Morgan, swilling grog in harbor taverns. This was once one of the largest trading centers of the New World, with a reputation for being the wickedest city on earth. Blackbeard stopped here regularly on his Caribbean trips. But it all came to an end on June 7, 1692, when a third of the town disappeared underwater as the result of a devastating earthquake. Nowadays, Port Royal, with its memories of the past, has been designated by the government for redevelopment as a tourist destination.

Buccaneer Scuba Club, Morgan's Harbour, Port Royal, outside Kingston (☎ 876/967-8061), is one of Jamaica's leading dive and water-sports operators. It offers a wide range of sites to accommodate various divers' tastes, from the incredible Texas Wreck to the unspoiled beauty of the Turtle Reef. PADI courses are also available. A wide array of water sports are offered, including waterskiing, bodyboarding, ring-skiing, and even a banana-boat ride. One-tank dives begin at $28, while a 1-hour boat-snorkeling trip goes for $15, including equipment.

As you drive along the Palisades, you arrive first at **St. Peter's Church.** It's usually closed, but you may persuade the caretaker, who lives opposite, to open it if you want to see the silver plate, said to be spoils captured by Henry Morgan from the cathedral in Panama. In the ill-kept graveyard is the tomb of Lewis Galdy, a Frenchman swallowed up and subsequently regurgitated by the 1692 earthquake.

Fort Charles (☎ 876/967-8438), the only one remaining of Port Royal's six forts, has withstood attack, earthquake, fire, and hurricane. Built in 1656 and later strengthened by Morgan for his own purposes, the fort was expanded and further armed in the 1700s, until its firepower boasted more than 100 cannons, covering both the land and the sea approaches. In 1779, Britain's naval hero, Horatio Lord Nelson, was commander of the fort and trod the wooden walkway inside the western parapet as he kept watch for the French invasion fleet. Scale models of the fort and ships of past eras are on display. The fort is open daily from 9am to 5pm; admission is J$140 ($4).

Part of the complex, **Giddy House,** once the Royal Artillery storehouse, is another example of what the earth's movements can do. Walking across the tilted floor is an eerie and strangely disorienting experience.

IN SPANISH TOWN

From 1662 to 1872, Spanish Town was the capital of the island. Originally founded by the Spaniards as Villa de la Vega, it was sacked by Cromwell's men in 1655, and all traces of Roman Catholicism were obliterated. The English cathedral, surprisingly retaining a Spanish name, **St. Jago de la Vega,** was built in 1666 and rebuilt after being destroyed by a hurricane in 1712. As you drive into the town from Kingston, the ancient cathedral catches your eye with its brick tower and two-tiered wooden steeple, which was not added until 1831. Since the cathedral was built on the foundation and remains of the old Spanish church, it is half English and half Spanish, and displays two distinct styles: Romanesque and Gothic. Of cruciform design and built mostly of brick, it's one of the most interesting buildings on the island. The black-and-white marble stones of the aisles are interspersed with ancient tombstones, and the walls are heavy with marble memorials that are almost a chronicle of Jamaica's history, dating back as far as 1662.

Beyond the cathedral, turn right; 2 blocks along, you'll reach Constitution Street and the **Town Square.** This little square is surrounded by towering royal palms. On the west side is old **King's House,** gutted by fire in 1925, although the facade has been restored. This was the residence of Jamaica's British governors until 1872, when the capital was transferred to Kingston.

Beyond the house is the **Jamaica People's Museum of Craft & Technology,** Old King's House, Constitution Square (☎ **876/922-0620**), open Monday to Friday from 10am to 4pm. Admission is J$10 (30¢) for adults, J$5 (15¢) for children. The garden contains examples of old farm machinery, an old water-mill wheel, a hand-turned sugar mill, a fire engine, and more. An outbuilding houses a museum of crafts and technology, together with a number of smaller agricultural implements. In the small archaeological museum are old prints, models, and maps of the town's grid layout from the 1700s.

The streets around the old Town Square contain many fine Georgian town houses intermixed with tin-roofed shacks. Nearby is the **market,** so busy in the morning that you'll find it difficult, almost dangerous, to pass through. It provides, however, a bustling scene of Jamaican life.

SHOPPING

Downtown Kingston, the old part of the town, is centered around Sir William Grant Park, formerly Victoria Park, a showpiece of lawns, lights, and fountains. Cool arcades lead off from King Street, but everywhere is a teeming mass of people going about their business. There are some beggars and the inevitable hucksters who sidle up and offer "hot stuff, mon," frequently highly polished brass lightly dipped in gold and offered at high prices as real gold.

For many years, the richly evocative paintings of Haiti were viewed as the most valuable contribution to the arts in the Caribbean. There is on Jamaica, however, a rapidly growing perception of itself as one of the artistic leaders of the Third World. An articulate core of Caribbean critics is focusing the attention of the art world on the unusual, eclectic, and sometimes politically motivated paintings being produced here.

Frame Centre Gallery, 10 Tangerine Place (☎ 876/926-4644), is one of the most important art galleries on Jamaica. Its founder and guiding force, Guy McIntosh, is widely respected today as a patron of the Jamaican arts. There are three viewing areas and a varied collection of more than 300 works. **Mutual Life Gallery,** in the Mutual Life Centre, 2 Oxford Rd. (☎ 876/926-9025), one of the country's most prominent galleries, is in the corporate headquarters of a major insurance company. After you pass a security check, you can climb to the corporation's mezzanine level for an insight into the changing face of Jamaican art.

Kingston Crafts Market, at the west end of Harbour Street (reached via Straw Avenue, Drummer's Lane, or Cheapside), is a large, covered area of small stalls, selling all kinds of island crafts: wooden plates and bowls; pepper pots made from mahoe (the national wood of the island); straw hats, mats, and baskets; batik shirts; banners for wall decoration, inscribed with the Jamaican coat-of-arms; and wood masks with elaborately carved faces. Apart from being a good place to buy worthwhile souvenirs, the market is where you can learn the art of bargaining and ask for a *brawta* (a free bonus). However, be aware that bargaining is *not* a Jamaican tradition. Vendors will take something off the price, but not very much.

The **Shops at Devon House,** 26 Hope Rd. (☎ 876/929-7029), ring the borders of a 200-year-old courtyard once used by slaves and servants. Associated with one of the most beautiful and historic mansions on Jamaica, a building operated by the Jamaican National Trust, 4 of these 10 or so shops are operated by Things Jamaican, a nationwide emporium dedicated to the enhancement of the country's handcrafts. Shops include the Cookery, offering island-made sauces and spices, and the Pottery, selling crockery and stoneware. Look for pewter knives and forks, based on designs of pewter items discovered in archaeological digs in the Port Royal area in 1965. Other outlets include a children's shop, a leather shop, a stained-glass shop, and a gallery.

9 Mandeville

The "English Town," Mandeville lies on a plateau more than 2,000 feet above the sea, in the tropical highlands. The small commercial part of the town is surrounded by a sprawling residential area popular with the large North American expatriate population (mostly involved with the bauxite-mining industry). Much cooler than the coastal resorts, it's a possible base from which to explore the entire island.

Shopping in the town is a pleasure, whether in the old center or in one of the modern complexes, such as **Grove Court.** The **market** in the center of town teems with life, particularly on weekends when the country folk bus into town for their weekly visit. Among the several interesting old buildings, the square-towered **church** built in 1820 contains fine stained glass, and the little churchyard has an interesting history. The **Court House,** built in 1816, is a fine old Georgian stone-and-wood building with a pillared portico reached by a steep, sweeping double staircase. There's also **Marshall's Pen,** one of the great houses in Mandeville.

WHERE TO STAY & DINE

Hotel Astra. 62 Ward Ave., Mandeville, Jamaica, W.I. ☎ 876/962-3725. Fax 876/962-1461. www.access-ja.com/countrystyle. E-mail: comtours@cwjamaica.com. 22 units. TV TEL. Year-round $65 double; $150 suite. Rates include continental breakfast. AE, MC, V.

Our top choice in this area is the family-run Astra, operated by Diana McIntyre-Pike, known to her family and friends as Thunderbird. She's always coming to the rescue of guests, happily picks up people in her own car and takes them around to see the sights, and organizes introductions to people of the island. The accommodations are mainly in two buildings reached along open walkways. Units are spartan with well-worn beds, but they're well maintained and have basic comforts, such as small private bathrooms. Amenities include a pool, a sauna, and therapeutic massages. You can spend the afternoon at the Manchester Country Club, where tennis and golf are available. Horses can be provided for cross-country treks.

The Country Fresh Restaurant offers excellent meals. Lunch or dinner is a choice of homemade soup such as red pea or pumpkin, followed by local fish and chicken specialties. The kitchen is under the personal control of Diana, who's always collecting awards in Jamaican culinary competitions. A complete meal costs $12 to $20, with some more expensive items such as lobster and steak. Thursday is barbecue night, when guests and townsfolk gather around the pool. The Revival Room is the bar, where everything including the stools is made from rum-soaked barrels. Try the family's own homemade liqueur and "reviver," a pick-me-up concocted from Guinness, rum, egg, condensed milk, and nutmeg.

Mandeville Hotel. 4 Hotel St. (P.O. Box 78), Mandeville, Jamaica, W.I. ☎ **876/962-2460.** Fax 876/962-0700. 56 units. TV TEL. Year-round $65–$125 double; from $95 suite. AE, MC, V.

This ornate hotel was established around the turn of the century, and for a while housed part of the British military garrison. In the 1970s, the venerable hotel was replaced with a modern structure, which was completely refurbished in 1982. It lies in the heart of Mandeville, across from the police station. It offers an outdoor and indoor bar and a spacious lounge, and good food and service. Activity centers mainly around the pool and the coffee shop, where substantial meals are served at moderate prices. Bedrooms, which range in size from small to spacious, are furnished with Jamaican styling, often including a four-poster and mahogany furniture. Bathrooms are old-fashioned but tidily maintained, although towels are a bit skimpy. There are attractive gardens, and you can play golf or tennis at the nearby Manchester Country Club.

Popular with local businesspeople, the hotel restaurant offers a wide selection of sandwiches, plus milk shakes, tea, and coffee. The à la carte menu features Jamaican pepper pot, lobster Thermidor, fresh snapper, and kingfish. Potatoes and vegetables are included in the main-dish prices. There is no pretension to the food at all. It's homemade and basic, almost like that served in the house of a typical Jamaican family. From the dining room, you'll have a view of the pool and the green hills of central Jamaica. Main courses range from $12 to $30; reservations are recommended.

EXPLORING THE AREA

Mandeville is the sort of place where you can become well acquainted with the people and feel like part of the community.

One of the largest and driest **caves** on the island is at Oxford, about 9 miles northwest of Mandeville. Signs direct you to it after you leave Mile Gully, a village dominated by St. George's Church, some 175 years old.

Manchester Country Club, Brumalia Road (☎ **876/962-2403**), is Jamaica's oldest golf course, but has only nine holes. Beautiful vistas unfold from 2,201 feet above sea level. Greens fees are J$750 ($21.40), with caddy fees running J$500 ($14.25). The course also has a clubhouse. The club is also one of the best venues in central Jamaica for tennis.

Marshall's Pen is one of the great houses, a coffee-plantation home some 200 years old. It has been in the hands of the Sutton family since 1939; they farm the 300 acres and breed Jamaican Red Poll cattle. This is very much a private home and should be treated as such, although guided tours can be arranged. A contribution of $10 is requested for a minimum of four people. For information or an appointment to see the house, contact Ann or Robert Sutton, **Marshall's Pen,** Great House, P.O. Box 58, Mandeville, Jamaica, W.I. (☎ 876/904-5454).

At Marshall's Pen **cattle estate** and **private nature reserve,** near Mandeville, guided **bird watching** tours of the scenic property and other outstanding birding spots on Jamaica may be arranged in advance. Six persons are taken on a tour for $200. Self-catering accommodation is sometimes available for bird watchers only, but arrangements must be made in advance. For information, contact Ann or Robert Sutton, Marshall's Pen, P.O. Box 58, Mandeville, Jamaica, W.I. (☎ 876/904-5454). Robert Sutton is coauthor of *Birds of Jamaica,* a photographic field guide published by Cambridge University Press.

Martinique 16

With beautiful white-sand beaches and a culture full of French flair, Martinique is part of the Lesser Antilles and lies in the semitropical zone; its western shore faces the Caribbean and its eastern shore fronts the more turbulent Atlantic. The surface of the island is only 420 square miles—50 miles at its longest and 21 miles at its widest point.

The terrain is mountainous, especially in the rain-forested northern part where Mount Pelée, a volcano, rises to a height of 4,656 feet. In the center of the island the mountains are smaller, with Carbet Peak reaching a 3,960-foot summit. The high hills rising among the peaks or mountains are called *mornes*. The southern part of Martinique has only big hills, reaching peaks of 1,500 feet at Vauclin and 1,400 feet at Diamant. The irregular coastline of the island provides five bays, dozens of coves, and miles of sandy beaches. Almost a third of the island's year-round population of 360,000 lives in the capital and largest city, Fort-de-France.

The climate is relatively mild, with the average temperature in the 75° to 85°F range. At higher elevations, it's considerably cooler. The island is cooled by a wind the French called *alizé*, and rain is frequent but doesn't last very long. Late August to November might be called the rainy season. April to September are the hottest months.

The early Carib peoples, who gave Columbus such a hostile reception, called Martinique "the island of flowers," and indeed it has remained so. The lush vegetation includes hibiscus, poinsettias, bougainvillea, coconut palms, and mango trees. Almost any fruit can sprout from Martinique's soil: pineapples, avocados, bananas, papayas, and custard apples.

Bird-watchers are often pleased at the number of hummingbirds, and visitors can also see the mountain whistler, the blackbird, and the mongoose. Multicolored butterflies flit about, and after sunset, there's a permanent concert of grasshoppers, frogs, and crickets.

1 Essentials

Before you go, you can contact the **French Government Tourist Office** at 444 Madison Ave., **New York, NY** 10022; 9454 Wilshire Blvd., Suite 715, **Beverly Hills, CA** 90212; and 676 N. Michigan Ave., Suite 3360, **Chicago, IL** 60611. To call for information in the United States, dial ☎ **800/391-4909.**

In Canada, contact the **Martinique Tourist Office,** 2159 rue Mackay, Montréal, Quebec H3G 2J2 (☎ **800/361-9099** or 514/844-8566).

On the Web, go to **www.martinique.org**.

On the island, the **Office Départemental du Tourisme** (tourist office) is on Boulevard Alfassa in Fort-de-France, across the waterfront boulevard from the harbor (☎ **0596/63-79-60**); it's open Monday to Friday from 8am to 5pm, Saturday from 8am to noon. The information desk at Lamentin Airport is open daily until the last flight comes in.

GETTING THERE

BY PLANE   Before you book your own airfare, read the sections on "Package Deals" and "Finding the Best Airfare" in chapter 2—you may save a bundle!

Lamentin International Airport is outside the village of Lamentin, a 15-minute taxi ride east of Fort-de-France and a 40-minute taxi ride northeast of the island's densest concentration of resort hotels (the Trois Islets peninsula). Most flights to Martinique and Guadeloupe require a transfer on a neighboring island—usually Puerto Rico, but occasionally Antigua. Direct or nonstop flights to the French islands from the U.S. mainland are rare: **Air France** (see below) offers only one flight per week, on Sunday, which leaves from Miami and stops at each of the two islands.

American Airlines (☎ 800/433-7300; www.aa.com) flies into its busy hub in San Juan, and from here passengers transfer to one of usually two daily **American Eagle** (same phone number) flights heading to both Martinique and Guadeloupe. The Eagle flights usually take between 1½ and 2 hours. Off-season, the evening flights to both islands are sometimes combined into a single flight, landing first on one island before continuing on to the next. Return flights to San Juan usually depart separately from both islands twice a day. Ask an American Airlines reservations clerk about booking your hotel simultaneously with your flight, since substantial discounts may apply.

Air France (☎ 800/237-2747; www.airfrance.com), an outfit that's heavily subsidized by the French government as its airborne ambassador to the world, flies from Miami to Martinique, sometimes with a touchdown in Guadeloupe en route, every Tuesday, Thursday, and Saturday year-round. Committed to its role of binding together the country's far-flung overseas *départements,* it also operates separate nonstop flights from Paris to both Martinique and Guadeloupe. These depart at least once a day, and in some cases, depending on the season and the day of the week, twice a day. The airline also maintains three weekly flights from Port-au-Prince, Haiti, to Martinique, and three flights a week, depending on the season, between Cayenne, in French Guyana, and Martinique.

Antigua-based **LIAT** (☎ 800/468-0482 in the U.S. and Canada, 268/462-0700, or through the reservations department of American Airlines) flies from Antigua and Barbados to both Martinique and Guadeloupe several times a day. Depending on the season, flights to the two islands are either separate or combined into a single flight, with touchdowns en route. Both Antigua and Barbados are important air-terminus links for such larger carriers as American Airlines (see above).

Another option for reaching either Martinique or Guadeloupe involves flying **BWIA** (☎ 800/538-2942; www.bwee.com), the national airline of Trinidad and Tobago, from either New York or Miami nonstop to both Barbados and Antigua, and from there, transferring onto a LIAT flight to either of the French-speaking islands.

British Airways (☎ 800/247-9297 in the U.S., or 0345/222-111 in England; www.british-airways.com) flies separately to both Antigua and Barbados three times a week from London. From either of those islands, LIAT connects to either Guadeloupe or Martinique.

Martinique

Airport ✈ Beach 🏖 Mountain 🔺

Martinique Passage

Macouba
Grand' Rivière
Basse-Pointe **1**
Leyritz
Le Lorrain
N1
Montagne Pelée
Ajoupa-Bouillon
Le Marigot **2**
N1
Le Prêcheur

Atlantic Ocean

Morne Rouge
Ste-Marie
Tartane
Morne des Esses
■ Caravelle Nature Preserve
St-Pierre
Caravelle Peninsula
Trinité **3**
■ Musée Gaugin
Gros-Morne
Le Carbet
N2
N3
Balata
N4
Bellefontaine
🔺 Carbet Peak
St-Joseph
Case-Pilote
N1
Schoelcher **18**
15
N1
Lamentin
4
16
Le François
Fort-de-France
✈ Lamentin International Airport
Pointe du Bout 🏖 **10**
11
Mt. Vauclin 🔺
N6
Anse Mitan 🏖 **12 13**
14
N5
Vauclin
Anse-à-l'Ane 🏖
Les Trois-Ilets **D7**
Grande Anse
Anses-d'Arlets
8 9 **D7**
Rivière-Pilote
D37
Le Diamant
Le Marin
🏖 Diamond Beach
Ste-Luce
D18A
■ Diamond Rock
Cap Chevalier 🏖
5
6
Ste-Anne
7
Les Salines 🏖
■ Petrified Forest
Caribbean Sea
Pointe des Salines
St. Lucia Channel

Ⓝ

Auberge de l'Anse Mitan **14**
Club Med Les Boucaniers **5**
Frégate Bleue **4**
Habitation LaGrange **2**
Hôtel Bakoua-Sofitel **13**
Hotel Diamant Les Bains **9**
Hôtel La Batelière **18**
Hôtel L'Impératrice **16**
Hôtel Méridien Trois-Ilets **11**

Hôtel Plantation de Leyritz **1**
La Dunette **6**
La Pagerie **12**
Le Lafayette **15**
Manoir de Beauregard **7**
Novotel Carayou **10**
Novotel Le Diamant **8**
Saint-Aubin Hôtel **3**

BY FERRY You can travel between Guadeloupe and Martinique by boat in a leisurely 3¾ hours with an intermediate stop on Dominica or Les Saintes. **Exprès des Iles** operates at least one (sometimes two) modern, comfortable ferryboat a day between the French West Indies' two largest islands. Morning departures from Pointe-à-Pitre for Fort-de-France are usually at 8am, and departures from Fort-de-France for Pointe-à-Pitre are usually at 2pm, although the schedule can vary unexpectedly according to the season and the day of the week. One-way fares are 340 F to 535 F ($57.80 to $90.95) round-trip. For details and reservations, contact **Exprès des Iles,** Gare Maritime, qui Gatine, 97110 Pointe-à-Pitre, Guadeloupe (☎ **0590-83-12-45**), or Terminal Inter-Iles, Bassin de Radoub, 97200 Fort-de-France, Martinique (☎ **0596/63-12-11**).

GETTING AROUND

BY RENTAL CAR The scattered nature of Martinique's geography makes renting a car especially tempting. Martinique has several local car-rental agencies, but clients have complained of mechanical difficulties and billing irregularities. We recommend renting from one of the U.S.-based "big three" (Hertz, Budget, and Avis). You must be 21 and have a valid driver's license to rent a car for up to 20 days. After that, an International Driver's License is required. *Note that traffic moves on the right side of the road.*

Budget has an office at 12 rue Félix-Eboué, Fort-de-France (☎ **800/527-0700** in the U.S., or 0596/63-69-00); **Avis** is at 4 rue Ernest-Deproge, Fort-de-France (☎ **800/331-1212** in the U.S., or 0596/70-11-60); and **Hertz** is at Lamentin Airport (☎ **800/654-3001** or 0596/51-01-01). Although each of these rental companies also maintains a kiosk at Lamentin Airport with staffs willing to transport prospective renters to pickup depots a short drive away, prices are usually lower if you reserve a car in North America at least 2 business days before your arrival.

Remember that regardless of which company you choose, you'll be hit with a value-added tax (VAT) of 9.5% on top of the final car-rental bill. (VATs for some luxury goods, including jewelry, on Martinique can go as high as 14%.) Collision-damage waivers (CDWs), an excellent idea in a country where the populace drives somewhat recklessly, cost 60 F to 127 F ($10.20 to $21.60) per day.

BY TAXI Travel by taxi is popular but can be expensive. Most of the cabs aren't metered, and you'll have to agree on the fare before getting in. Most visitors arriving at Lamentin Airport head for one of the resorts along the peninsula of Pointe du Bout—a ride that costs about 170 F ($28.90) during the day, about 255 F ($43.35) in the evening. Night fares are in effect from 7pm to 6am, when 40% surcharges are added. You can call for a **radio taxi** (☎ **0596/63-63-62**).

If you want to rent a taxi for the day, expect to pay from 700 F to 850 F ($119 to $144.50) and up for a 5-hour tour, depending on the itinerary you negotiate with the driver. Generally, four passengers sharing a cab are charged 200 F ($34) per hour.

BY BUS & TAXI COLLECTIF There are two types of buses operating on Martinique. Regular buses, called *grands busses,* hold about 40 passengers and cost 5 F to 8 F (85¢ to $1.35) to go anywhere within the city limits of Fort-de-France. To travel beyond the city limits, *taxis collectifs* are used. These are privately owned minivans that traverse the island and bear the sign *TC.* Their routes are flexible and depend on passenger need. A one-way fare from Fort-de-France to Ste-Anne is 30 F ($5.10). Taxis collectifs depart from the heart of Fort-de-France from the parking lot of Pointe Simon. There's no phone number to call for information about this unpredictable means of transport, and there are no set schedules. Traveling in a taxi collectif is for the adventurous visitor—they're crowded and not very comfortable.

Carnival

If you like masquerades and dancing in the streets, you should be here in January or February to attend ✪ **Carnival,** or *Vaval,* as it's known here. It begins right after the New Year, as each village prepares costumes and floats. Weekend after weekend, frenzied celebrations take place, reaching fever pitch just before Lent. Fort-de-France is the focal point for Carnival, but the spirit permeates the whole island. On Ash Wednesday, the streets of Fort-de-France are filled with *diablesses,* or she-devils (portrayed by members of both sexes). Costumed in black and white, they crowd the streets to form King Carnival's funeral procession. As devils cavort about and the rum flows, a funeral pyre is built at La Savane. When it's set on fire, the dancing of those "she-devils" becomes frantic (many are thoroughly drunk at this point). Long past dusk, the cortège takes the coffin to its burial, ending Carnival until next year.

BY FERRY   The least expensive way to go between quai d'Esnambuc in Fort-de-France and Pointe du Bout is by ferry (*vedette*), costing 15 F ($2.55) one-way, 30 F ($5.10) round-trip. Schedules for the ferryboats, which usually run daily from 6am to midnight, are printed in the free visitor's guide *Choubouloute,* which is distributed by the tourist office. For information, call ☎ **0596/73-05-53.** If the weather is bad or the seas are rough, all ferryboat services may be canceled.

There is also a smaller ferryboat that runs between Fort-de-France and the small-scale, unpretentious resorts of Anse Mitan and Anse-à-l'Ane, both across the bay and home to many two- and three-star hotels and modest Creole restaurants. A boat departs from quai d'Esnambuc in Fort-de-France at 30-minute intervals, daily between 6am and 6:30pm. The trip takes about 20 minutes. A one-way fare is 20 F ($3.40); for more information, call ☎ **0596/63-06-46.**

BY BICYCLE & MOTORBIKE   You can rent motor scooters from **Funny,** 80 rue Ernest-Deproge, Fort-de-France (☎ **0596/63-33-05**). The new 18-speed VTT (*velo tout terrain,* or all-terrain bike) is gradually making inroads from mainland France into the rugged countryside of Martinique, although there aren't many places to rent one. **St. Luce Location,** 14 rue Schoelcher, St-Luce (☎ **0596/62-49-66**), about a 30-minute drive from Fort-de-France, rents scooters as well; a deposit of 3,500 F ($595) is required. **Jacques-Henry Vartel,** VT Tilt, Anse Mitan (☎ **0596/66-01-01**), has moved away from rentals but operates bike tours around Martinique based on demand. Call for more information.

Fast Facts: Martinique

Banking Hours   Banks are open Monday to Friday from 7:30am to noon and 2:30 to 4pm.

Currency   The **French franc (F)** is the legal tender here. Prices in this chapter are in both U.S. dollars and French francs. Currently, 1 franc is worth about 17¢ (5.90 F = U.S. $1). Banks give much better exchange rates than hotels, and there's a money-exchange service, **Change Caraïbes** (☎ **0596/42-17-11**), available at Lamentin Airport. Its downtown branch is at 4 rue Ernest-Deproge (☎ **0596/60-28-40**).

Customs   Items for personal use, such as tobacco, cameras, and film, are admitted without formalities or tax if not in excessive quantity.

Documents   U.S., British, and Canadian citizens need a valid passport. A return or ongoing ticket is also necessary.

Drugstores   See "Pharmacies," below.

Electricity   Electricity is 220 volts AC (50 cycles), the same as that used on the French mainland. However, check with your hotel to see if they have converted the electrical voltage and outlets in the bathrooms (some have). If they haven't, bring your own transformer and adapter for U.S. appliances.

Emergencies   Call the **police** at ☎ **17,** report a **fire** by dialing ☎ **18,** and summon an **ambulance** at ☎ **0596/75-15-75.**

Hospitals   There are 18 hospitals and clinics on the island, and a 24-hour emergency room at **Hôpital Pierre Zobda Quikman,** Châteauboeuf, right outside Fort-de-France (☎ **0596/55-20-00**).

Language   French, the official language, is spoken by almost everyone. The local Creole patois uses words borrowed from France, England, Spain, and Africa. In the wake of increased tourism, English is occasionally spoken in the major hotels, restaurants, and tourist organizations—but don't count on driving around the countryside and asking for directions in English.

Pharmacies   Try the **Pharmacie de la Paix,** at the corner of rue Perrinon and rue Victor-Schoelcher in Fort-de-France (☎ **0596/71-94-83**), open Monday to Friday from 7:15am to 6:15pm and on Saturday from 7:45am to 1pm.

Safety   Crime is hardly rampant on Martinique, yet there are still those who prey on unsuspecting tourists. Follow the usual precautions here, especially in Fort-de-France and in the tourist-hotel belt of Pointe du Bout. It's wise to protect your valuables and never leave them unguarded on the beach.

Taxes & Service Charges   Most hotels include a 10% service charge in the bill; all restaurants include a 15% service charge. There's also a resort tax; this varies from place to place, but never exceeds $1.50 per person per day.

Telephone   To call Martinique from the United States, dial **011** (the international access code), then **596** (the country code for Martinique), and finally the six-digit local number. When making a call from one place on Martinique to another on the island, you'll have to add a **0** (zero) to the country code: dial **0596** plus the six-digit local number—in all, 10 digits for calls made on the island.

Time   Martinique is on Atlantic standard time year-round, 1 hour earlier than eastern standard time except when daylight saving time is in effect. Then, Martinique time is the same as on the East Coast of the United States.

Water   Potable water is found throughout the island.

Weather   The climate is relatively mild—the average temperature is in the 75° to 85°F range.

2 Fort-de-France

With its iron-grillwork balconies overflowing with flowers, Fort-de-France, the largest town on Martinique, reminds us of a cross between New Orleans and a town on the French Riviera. It lies at the end of a large bay surrounded by evergreen hills.

The proud people of Martinique are even more fascinating than the town, although today the Creole women are likely to be seen in jeans instead of their traditional turbans and Empress Joséphine–style gowns, and they rarely wear those massive earrings that used to jounce and sway as they sauntered along.

Narrow streets climb up the steep hills, where houses have been built to catch the overflow of the capital's more than 100,000 inhabitants.

WHERE TO STAY

Rates are sometimes advertised in U.S. dollars, sometimes in French francs, and sometimes in a combination of both. Be sure to check out our "Package Deals" and "Tips on Accommodations" sections, in chapter 2.

Don't stay in town if you want a hotel near a beach (see the hotels listed below for beach resorts). If you do opt to stay in Fort-de-France, you'll have to take a ferryboat to reach the beaches at **Pointe du Bout** (see section 3, below). The one exception to this is the Hôtel La Batelière, which opens onto a small beach, but it's in the suburb of Schoelcher.

Hôtel La Batelière. 20 rue des Alizés, 97233 Schoelcher, Martinique, F.W.I. ☎ **0596/ 61-49-49.** Fax 0596/61-70-57. 198 units. A/C TV TEL. Winter 1,000 F–1,600 F ($170–$272) double; 1,900 F–3,500 F ($323–$595) duplex or suite. Off-season 800 F–1,200 F ($136–$204) double; 1,800 F–3,300 F ($306–$561) duplex or suite. Rates include buffet breakfast. AE, DC, MC, V.

This five-story, waterside, French-modern hotel isn't superglamorous, but it offers many social activities and dining options, and is the best choice in the Fort-de-France area, standing on 7 acres of tropically landscaped grounds north of town. It's a pink-and-green stucco structure set back in a garden from a small beach that's sheltered from the waves by a breakwater. Each spacious unit has a wide glass door that opens onto your own water-view terrace, although some views are blocked by the roof of the dining terrace. Rooms come with private safes, French double or twin beds, and firm mattresses.

In the Bleu Marine dining room, French, international, and Creole cuisine is served, and there's a beach restaurant near the pool. Tennis is free at the six courts (the island's best), except at night when there's a surcharge. On the premises are a pool, a casino, a disco, a beauty salon, a barbershop, and a handful of boutiques. The hotel's small beach is sheltered from the waves by a breakwater.

Hôtel L'Impératrice. 15 place de la Savane, rue de la Liberté, 97200 Fort-de-France, Martinique, F.W.I. ☎ **0596/63-06-82.** Fax 0596/72-66-30. 42 units. A/C TEL. Year-round 360 F–450 F ($61.20–$76.50) double. Rates include breakfast. AE, DC, MC, V.

Favored by businesspeople, this stucco-sided, five-story hotel faces a landscaped mall in the heart of town, near the water's edge. L'Impératrice was originally built in the 1950s and named in honor of one of Martinique's most famous exports, Joséphine. Its balconies overlook the traffic at the western edge of the sprawling promenade known as the Savane. The small- to medium-size guest rooms are modern and functional, and many contain TVs. The front rooms tend to be noisy, but do offer a look into life along the Savane. Bathrooms are compact, with shower stalls. Don't expect outstanding service here. Almost no one on staff speaks English, and they all seem a bit jaded. But despite the confusion in the very noisy lobby, and the unremarkable decor of the simple bedrooms, you might end up enjoying the unpretentiousness of this place.

The hotel's restaurant, Le Joséphine, does a brisk business with local shoppers in town for the day. The more popular of the two lounges has large, white wicker chairs and an adjoining bar.

Le Lafayette. 5 rue de la Liberté, 97200 Fort-de-France, Martinique, F.W.I. ☎ **0596/73-80-50.** Fax 0596/60-65-79. 24 units. A/C MINIBAR TV TEL. Year-round 400 F ($68) double. AE, MC, V.

You'll enter this modest downtown hotel, located right on La Savane, through rue Victor-Hugo; the reception hall is up a few terra-cotta steps. The dark-brown wooden doors are offset by soft beige walls. Japanese wall tapestries decorate the cramped and slightly dowdy bedrooms; most units contain comfortable twin beds, with small pure-white bathrooms. The overall impression is neat but simple and unpretentious. The inn is the oldest continuously operating hotel on Martinique, originally built in the 1940s with quasi–art deco hints that are now slightly dowdy. There's no on-site restaurant, but several eateries are within a short walk.

WHERE TO DINE

La Mouina. 127 rte. de Redoute. ☎ **0596/79-34-57.** Reservations recommended for Sat–Sun dinner. Main courses 85 F–225 F ($14.45–$38.25). MC, V. Mon–Fri noon–2:30pm; Mon–Sat 7:30–9:30pm. FRENCH/CREOLE.

La Mouina, Creole for a meeting house, is a venerable restaurant established some 20 years ago by members of the French-Swiss-Hungarian Karschesz family. Next to the police station in the suburb of Redoute, about 1½ miles north of Fort-de-France, this 65-year-old colonial house is the culinary domain of one of the island's most experienced groups of chefs. You might begin with *crabes farcis* (stuffed crabs) or *escargots de Bourgogne,* then follow with tournedos Rossini, *rognon de veau entier grillé* (whole grilled veal kidneys), or duckling in orange sauce. The owners are particularly proud of their version of red snapper baked in parchment. Ask at your hotel for good directions before setting out (or even better, take a taxi), as it's hard to find.

✪ **La Plantation.** In Martinique Cottages, Pays Mélé Jeanne-d'Arc, Lamentin. ☎ **0596/50-16-08.** Reservations required. Main courses 110 F–200 F ($18.70–$34); fixed-price lunch 200 F ($34). AE, MC, V. Mon–Fri noon–2pm; Mon–Sat 7:30–9:30pm. FRENCH.

Near the airport, a 20-minute drive south of Fort-de-France, this is one of the finest restaurants on the island. In a small French Antillean hotel designed a quarter of a century ago to resemble a 19th-century private home, La Plantation is run by a hard-working staff and a chef who aims to serve an imaginative cuisine. The foie gras come from France, but the herbs flavoring it are Antillean. We found a traditional version of rack of lamb perfectly cooked and herby. Everything we've sampled here has been noteworthy, especially a soup of gargantuan crayfish. A salad served here was worth getting *Gourmet* magazine on the phone. It was filled with crab, hearts of palm, conch, and baby octopus—all bathed in a champagne vinaigrette with a confetti of pecans, carrots, red bell peppers, diced sweet prunes, and parsley.

Le Planteur. 1 rue de la Liberté. ☎ **0596/63-17-45.** Reservations recommended. Main courses 30 F–140 F ($5.10–$23.80); set menus 80 F ($13.60) and 180 F ($30.60). AE, MC, V. Mon–Fri noon–2:30pm; daily 7–10:30pm. FRENCH/CREOLE.

A growing number of local fans and members of the island's business community appreciate this restaurant's location on the southern edge of La Savane, in the commercial core of Fort-de-France. Established in 1997, it contains several somewhat idealized painted depictions of colonial Martinique, flowered napery with accents of red and white that dress up a series of small rectangular tables, and a hardworking, somewhat distracted staff who run around hysterically trying to be all things to all diners. Menu items are fresh, flavorful, and usually received with approval. They include a hot *velouté* (soup) concocted from shrimp and *giraumons,* a green-skinned tropical fruit with a succulent yellow core; a cassoulet of minced conch; fillet of *daurade* with coconut; and a *blanquette* (white, slow-simmered stew) of shellfish that's available only when the local catch makes such a dish possible.

✪ **Le Second Souffle.** 27 rue Blénac. ☎ **0596/63-44-11.** Main courses 38 F–45 F ($6.45–$7.65); fixed-price four-course lunch or dinner 75 F ($12.75). No credit cards. Mon–Fri 11am–3:30pm. VEGETARIAN.

This restaurant prides itself on being the only vegetarian restaurant on Martinique that prepares its dishes exclusively from local ingredients. Set in a woodsy and rustic dining room close to Fort-de-France's cathedral, it employs a staff of health-conscious local residents. You can admire a series of wall murals as you wait for medium- and large-sized platters of *crudités,* casseroles concocted from such vegetables as eggplant and christophine, vegetarian soups, and salads. Dessert might be a *filet de tinain* (miniature green bananas) served with chocolate sauce.

✪ **Marie-Sainte.** 160 rue Victor-Hugo. ☎ **0596/70-00-30.** Main courses 80 F–180 F ($13.60–$30.60); fixed-price lunch 70 F ($11.90). AE, V. Mon–Sat noon–4pm. CREOLE.

In its way, this is one of the most evocative restaurants in town, the kind of place you'd expect to find in remote areas of the island but not right in the capital. Your host is Agnés Marie-Sainte, a venerable Creole cook whose recipes for *boudin Créole, daube de poisson,* and *colombo* of mutton were derived from her ancestors. In a simple dining room that's likely to be crowded with locals, she offers fixed-price lunches with a strong emphasis on fresh fish (grilled or fried), and perhaps a fricassée of conch, always accompanied by a medley of such *legumes de pays* as fresh beans, dasheen, breadfruit, and christophine. This is about as authentic as it gets, and also as inexpensive as you're likely to find for meals of such quality and authenticity.

SPORTS & OUTDOOR PURSUITS

If it's a beach you're looking for, take the ferry to **Pointe du Bout** (see section 3, below). The island's only **golf course** is located in Les Trois-Ilets, also discussed in the next section.

DEEP-SEA FISHING   Most hotels maintain a list of the yachts and skippers who will take groups out for a day of *la pêche à la ligne* on the wide blue sea. If yours doesn't offer such arrangements, call the staff at **Caribtours,** B.P. 292, Lamentin (☎ **0596/50-93-49**). The cost of renting such a boat, in which all equipment is usually included, is 700 F ($119) for a half-day charter for up to six anglers. Most game fish tend to be most active very early in the morning, and many experienced fishers claim that it's not worth going after 10am, so departures tend to leave before breakfast, around 6am. Note, however, that this sport is in decline in waters around Martinique due to overfishing.

HIKING   Inexpensive guided excursions for tourists are organized year-round by the personnel of the **Parc Naturel Régional de la Martinique,** Excollège Agricole de Tivoli, B.P. 437, Fort-de-France (☎ **0596/64-42-59**); special excursions can be arranged for small groups.

SAILING   If you want to see the waters around Martinique, it's better to go on one of the sailboat excursions in the bay of Fort-de-France. Ask at your hotel desk what boats are taking passengers on cruises in Martinique waters. These vessels tend to change from season to season.

EXPLORING FORT-DE-FRANCE

At the heart of town is **La Savane,** a broad garden with many palms and mangos, playing fields, walks, and benches, plus shops and cafes lining its sides. In the middle of this grand square stands a statue of Joséphine, "Napoléon's little Creole," made of white marble by Vital Debray. With the grace of a Greek goddess, the statue poses in a Regency gown and looks toward Trois-Ilets, where she was born. The statue was beheaded, though, in 1991, probably because islanders felt she championed slavery. Near the harbor, at the edge of the park, you'll find vendors' stalls with handmade crafts, including baskets, beads, bangles, wood carvings, and straw hats.

Your next stop should be the 1875 **St. Louis Roman Catholic Cathedral,** on rue Victor-Schoelcher. The religious centerpiece of the island, it's an extraordinary iron building, which someone once likened to "a sort of Catholic railway station." A number of the island's former governors are buried beneath the choir loft.

A statue in front of the Palais de Justice is of the island's second main historical figure, **Victor Schoelcher** (you'll see his name a lot on Martinique), who worked to free the slaves more than a century ago. The **Bibliothèque Schoelcher,** 21 rue de la Liberté (☎ 0596/70-26-67), also honors this popular hero. Functioning today as the island's central government-funded library, the elaborate structure was first displayed at the Paris Exposition of 1889. The Romanesque portal, the Egyptian lotus-petal columns, even the turquoise tiles were imported piece by piece from Paris and reassembled here. This is one of the most stringently protected historic buildings in the French West Indies. It's open Monday from 1 to 5:30pm, Tuesday through Thursday from 8:30am to 5:30pm, Friday from 8:30am to 5pm, and Saturday from 8:30am to noon.

Guarding the port is **Fort St-Louis,** built in the Vauban style on a rocky promontory. In addition, **Fort Tartenson** and **Fort Desaix** stand on hills overlooking the port.

Musée Départemental de la Martinique, 9 rue de la Liberté (☎ 0596/71-57-05), the one bastion on Martinique that preserves its pre-Columbian past, has relics left from the early settlers, the Arawaks, and the Caribs. The era the museum celebrates is from 3000 B.C to A.D. 1635. Everything here stops shortly after the arrival of the first French colonials on the southern tip of Martinique in the early 1600s. In other words, it's mostly an ethnological museum, which was enlarged and reorganized into a more dynamic and up-to-date place in 1997. The museum faces La Savane and is open Monday to Friday from 8am to 5pm and on Saturday from 9am to noon; admission is 15 F ($2.55) for adults, 10 F ($1.70) for students, and 5 F (85¢) for children.

Sacré-Coeur de Balata Cathedral, at Balata, overlooking Fort-de-France, is a copy of the one looking down from Montmartre upon Paris—and this one is just as incongruous, maybe more so. It's reached by going along route de la Trace (route N3). Balata is 6 miles northwest of Fort-de-France.

A few minutes away on route RN3, **Jardin de Balata** (☎ 0596/64-48-73) is a tropical botanical park, created by Jean-Philippe Thoze on land that the jungle was rapidly reclaiming around a Creole house that belonged to his grandmother. He has also restored the house, furnishing it with antiques and historic engravings. The garden contains a profusion of flowers, shrubs, and trees, offering a vision of tropical splendor. It's open daily from 9am to 5pm. Admission is 40 F ($6.80) for adults, 15 F ($2.55) for children 7 to 12, and free for children under 6.

SHOPPING

Your best buys on Martinique are French luxury imports, such as perfumes, fashions, Vuitton luggage, Lalique crystal, or Limoges dinnerware. Sometimes (but don't count on it) prices are as much as 30% to 40% below those in the United States.

If you pay in dollars, store owners supposedly will give you a 20% discount; however, the exchange rates vary considerably from store to store, and almost invariably they are far less favorable than the rate offered at one of the local banks. You're actually better off shopping in the smaller stores, where prices are 8% to 12%

lower on comparable items, and paying in francs that you have exchanged at a local bank.

The main shopping street in town is **rue Victor-Hugo.** The other two leading shopping streets are **rue Schoelcher** and **rue St-Louis.** However, the most boutique-filled streets, where you'll find the latest French designs, are **rue Antione Siger, rue de la Liberté, rue Lamartine,** and **rue Moreau de Jones.** Facing the tourist office and alongside **quai d'Esnambuc** is an open market where you can purchase local hand-crafts and souvenirs (though many of these are tacky).

Far more interesting is the display of vegetables and fruit at the **open-air stalls** along **rue Isambert.** It's full of local flavor and you can't help but smell the **fish market** alongside the Levassor River. Gourmet chefs will find all sorts of spices in the open-air markets, or such goodies as tinned pâté or canned quail in the local *super-marchés.*

For the ubiquitous local fabric, **madras,** there are shops on every street with bolts and bolts of it, all colorful and inexpensive.

Note: Try to postpone your shopping trip if a cruise ship is in town, to avoid the stampede.

La Case à Rhum, in the Galerie Marchande, 5 rue de la Liberté (☎ **0596/73-73-20**), is the place to go for the local brew. Aficionados consider Martinique rum to be one of the world's finest distilled drinks. This shop offers all the brands manufactured on Martinique (at least 12), as well as several others famous for their age and taste. Prices range from 35 F to 5,400 F ($5.95 to $918) for a connoisseur's delight—a bottle distilled by the Bally Company in 1924. Samples are offered; we suggest trying Clement, a mellow Old Mahogany, or a blood-red liqueurlike rum bottled by Bally.

Cadet-Daniel, 72 rue Antoine-Siger (☎ **0596/71-41-48**), offers Lalique crystal and Christofle silver flatware, although by far the most visible merchandise is the 18-karat gold jewelry, some of it inset with precious stones. Most of it is manufactured on Martinique, and much of it is fashioned into traditional patterns inspired by the Creoles.

Centre des Métiers d'Art, rue Ernest Deproges (☎ **0596/70-25-01**), adjacent to the tourist office, has a mixture of valuable and worthless local handmade artifacts, including bamboo, ceramics, painted fabrics, and patchwork quilts suitable for hanging.

Galeries Lafayette, 10 rue Victor-Schoelcher, near the cathedral (☎ **0596/71-38-66**), is a small-scale branch (a pale version) of what is the most famous department store in Paris. Specializing in fashion for men, women, and children, it also offers leather goods, jewelry, watches, and perfume. It offers 20% off for purchases made with U.S. dollar traveler's checks or a credit card.

Galeries St-Louis, 87 rue Lamartine (☎ **0596/63-04-60**), is another large depart-ment store, stocked with a downscale assortment of housewares. Despite the many workaday items, it's also known for its toys, luggage, accessories, china, and crystal. Come here to look for occasional bargains. The emphasis is French with Caribbean overtones.

Roger Albert, 7–9 rue Victor-Hugo (☎ **0596/71-71-71**), is the largest emporium of luxury goods on Martinique, a department store for both locals and cruise passen-gers. It's one of five different branches on the island, but this one is by far the busiest. You'll find watches, perfumes, sportswear by LaCoste and Tacchini, Lladró and Limoges porcelain, and crystal by Swarovski. Anyone with a non-French passport gets a reduction of 20% off what a local resident would pay, plus discounts of an additional 20%, depending on seasonal discounts and promotions. Even better, value-added tax is not added to the price of your purchases.

Begin the Beguine

The sexy and rhythmic beguine was *not* an invention of Cole Porter. It's a dance of the islands—though exactly which island depends on whom you ask. Popular wisdom and the encyclopedia give the nod to Martinique. Guadeloupeans claim it for their own, and to watch them dance it, you might be convinced. Of course, calypso and the merengue move rhythmically along, too—these islanders are known for their dancing.

On Guadeloupe, the folkloric troupe **Ballets Guadeloupeans** makes frequent appearances at the big hotels, whirling and moving to the rhythms of island music in colorful costumes and well-choreographed routines. Some resorts, including the Club Med—Caravelle, use their weekly visit to set the theme for the evening, serving up a banquet of traditional island dishes to accompany the dance, music, and costumes.

Ask at your hotel where the Ballets Guadeloupeans will be appearing during your stay, as their schedule tends to vary as they tour the island. You can catch them as they rotate through the hotels Arawak, Salako, L'Auberge de le Vieille Tour, and Fleur d'Epée Novotel, as well as the Club Med—Caravelle. On the night of any of these performances, you can order a drink at the bar for 30 F ($5.10) or more and witness the show, or partake of a hotel buffet for 180 F ($30.60). Buffets usually start around 8pm, with the show beginning at 8:30pm. The troupe also performs on some cruise ships.

More famous than the dancers on Guadeloupe, however, is the touring group **Les Grands Ballets Martiniquais.** Everybody who goes to Martinique wants to see the show performed by this bouncy group of about two dozen dancers, along with musicians, singers, and choreographers. This interesting program of folk dances in the Caribbean was launched in the early 1960s, and the performances of the traditional dances of Martinique have been acclaimed in both Europe and the States. With a swoosh of gaily striped skirts and clever acting, the dancers capture all the exuberance of the island's soul. The group has toured abroad with great success, but they perform best on their home ground, presenting tableaux that tell of jealous brides and faithless husbands, demanding overseers and toiling cane cutters. Dressed in traditional costumes, the island women and men dance the spirited mazurka, which was brought from the ballrooms of Europe, and, of course, the exotic beguine.

Les Grands Ballets Martiniquais perform Monday at the Hôtel Diamant-Novotel, Wednesday at the Novotel Carayou, Thursday at the Méridien Trois-Ilets, Friday at the Bakoua Beach, and Saturday at Hôtel La Batalière, but this, too, can vary, so check locally. In addition, the troupe gives miniperformances aboard visiting cruise ships. The cost of dinner and the show is usually 260 F ($44.20). Most performances are at 8:30pm, with dinners at the hotels beginning at 7:30pm.

Whoever performs it for you, on whichever island, you'll soon realize that the beguine is more than a dance—it's a way of life. See it for yourself, or dance it, if you think you can.

La Galleria, route de Lamentin, midway between Fort-de-France and the airport, is the most upscale and elegant shopping complex on Martinique. On the premises are more than 60 different vendors, a handful of cafes and simple restaurants, and an outlet or two for the local pastries and sweets.

Paradise Island, 20 rue Ernest-Deproges (☎ **0596/63-93-63**), features the most stylish and upscale T-shirts on Martinique, each displayed as a kind of couture-conscious art form. Whatever you like will be available in about a dozen different colors.

FORT-DE-FRANCE AFTER DARK

The most exciting after-dark activity is seeing a performance of the folkloric troupe **Grand Ballets de Martinique** (see "Begin the Beguine," above).

Jazz sessions are a regular feature at **Westindies,** Boulevard Alfassa (☎ **0596/ 63-63-77**).

The popularity of dance clubs rises and falls almost monthly. Most of them charge a cover of 48 F ($8.15). Current favorites, drawing both locals and visitors, are **L'Alibi,** Morne Tartenson, (☎ **0596/63-45-15**), and **Zenith,** 24 Blvd. Allègre (☎ **0596/ 60-20-22**). Another local hot spot is **Le Queen,** Hôtel La Batelière, at Schoelcher, outside Fort-de-France (☎ **0596/61-49-49**), which draws disco devotees.

For casino action, head for Martinique's newest, **Casino Batelière Plaza,** at Schoelcher (☎ **0596/61-91-51**), outside Fort-de-France. You'll need a passport and 70 F ($11.90) to enter. A jacket and tie are also required for men. You can play French baccarat, roulette, and blackjack, or dispense with the formalities and the entrance fee to play the slots, which are found on the left as you enter. Slots are open Monday to Saturday from noon to 3am. The more formal gambling is daily from 8pm to 3am.

As for the gay scene, Martinique remains fairly conservative. Although you'll often see same-sex couples dancing together in the local discos, the only gay bar is **Daly's,** Route de Ravine Vilaine (☎ **0596/79-66-26**), in an affluent suburb of Fort-de-France. It's open only on Friday and Saturday nights, offering two dance floors and both indoor and alfresco bars. Head out of Fort-de-France in the direction of St-Joseph and look for the signs.

3 Pointe du Bout & Les Trois-Ilets

Pointe du Bout is a narrow peninsula across the bay from the busy capital of Fort-de-France. It's the most developed resort area of Martinique, with at least four of the island's largest hotels, an impressive marina, about a dozen tennis courts, pools, and facilities for horseback riding and all kinds of water sports. There's also a handful of independent restaurants, a gambling casino, boutiques, and in nearby Trois-Ilets, a Robert Trent Jones, Sr.–designed golf course. Except for the hillside that contains the Hôtel Bakoua, most of the district is flat and verdant, with gardens and rigidly monitored parking zones. All the hotels listed below are near the clean white-sand beaches of Pointe du Bout. Some of the smaller properties are convenient to the white sandy beaches of Anse Mitan. Nearby is also Les Trois-Ilets, the birthplace of Joséphine, the wife of Napoléon Bonaparte and Empress of France.

GETTING THERE

BY CAR   If you're driving from Fort-de-France, take Route 1, which crosses the plain of Lamentin—the industrial area of Fort-de-France and the site of the international airport. Often the air is filled with the fragrance of caramel, from the large sugarcane factories in the surrounding area. After 20 miles, you reach Trois-Ilets, Joséphine's hometown. Three miles farther on your right, take Route D38 to Pointe du Bout.

BY FERRY   The ferry service runs all day long until midnight from the harbor front (quai d'Esnambuc) in downtown Fort-de-France. Round-trip fare is 30 F ($5.10). See "Getting Around" in section 1, above, for details.

WHERE TO STAY
EXPENSIVE

Hôtel Bakoua-Sofitel. Pointe du Bout, 97229 Trois-Ilets, Martinique, F.W.I. ☎ **800/ 221-4542** in the U.S., 0181/283-4500 in London, or 0596/66-02-02. Fax 0596/66-00-41. 142 units. A/C MINIBAR TV TEL. Winter 1,115 F–3,200 F ($189.55–$544) double; from 4,500 F ($765) suite. Off-season 920 F–1,680 F ($156.40–$285.60) double; from 3,700 F ($629) suite. Rates include continental breakfast. MAP (breakfast and dinner) 240 F ($40.80) per person extra. AE, DC, MC, V.

Its reputation for French chic now seems from yesterday, but this is still the area's finest hotel, even if airline crews fill up many of its rooms today. It's known for the beauty of its landscaping and its somewhat isolated hillside location, and it's the only really upscale hotel on the island. Run by the Sofitel chain, it consists of three low-rise buildings in the center of a garden, plus another pair of bungalow-type buildings set directly on the beach. Accommodations come in a wide range of sizes, from small to spacious. Rooms have balconies or patios, private safes, extra-comfortable beds, and small tiled bathrooms with hair dryers. We'd choose this hotel over Hôtel Méridien (see below).

Dining: A dramatically engineered bar, crafted into a perfect circle out of exotic Caribbean hardwood, is one of the ideal rendezvous points of Pointe du Bout. The most upscale and elegant restaurant, Le Chateaubriand, serves French and Caribbean cuisine every night. La Sirene is a beachfront restaurant specializing in Caribbean cuisine.

Amenities: Pool, active sports program (including golf and scuba-diving lessons), diving center, waterskiing, jet-skiing, golf; horseback riding nearby. Concierge, laundry, baby-sitting, free twice-daily shuttle bus to the golf course.

Hôtel Méridien Trois-Ilets. Pointe du Bout, Trois-Ilets (B.P. 894, 97245 Fort-de-France), Martinique, F.W.I. ☎ **800/543-4300** in the U.S. and Canada, or 0596/66-00-00. Fax 0596/66-00-74. www.lemeridien-hotels.com. 295 units. A/C TV TEL. Winter 1,500 F–2,400 F ($255–$408) double; from 2,300 F ($391) suite. Off-season 850 F–1,300 F ($144.50–$221) double; from 1,500 F ($255) suite. Rates include buffet breakfast. AE, DC, MC, V.

This is the largest and tallest (at seven stories) building in the resort community of Pointe du Bout, and offers extensive facilities. But despite its prominence, we definitely don't find it the most desirable place to stay—it needs renovations, and some readers have complained about dingy rooms. The bedrooms remain a patchwork of hasty repairs. In spite of this, many visitors wind up here, especially convention groups.

The hotel has a slightly shabby reception area that opens onto the palm-fringed pool, the waters of the bay, and the faraway lights of Fort-de-France. The hotel is slightly angled to follow the contours of the shoreline, so each bedroom overlooks either the Caribbean or the bay. Each unit contains a private balcony and conservatively modern furnishings with tropical accents. Rooms have comfortable beds, most often doubles, plus roomy tiled bathrooms containing bidets, hair dryers, combination tub/showers, and toiletries.

Dining/Diversions: La Capitane offers buffet dinners and a view of the sea, the latter its best feature. Less expensive is Le Cocoterais, beside the beach. Thursdays, the hotel hosts the Grands Ballets Martiniquais in a pavilion near the pool. There's also a casino (see "Pointe du Bout After Dark," below) and a dull disco.

Amenities: Waterside garden, 100-foot marina, pool, two tennis courts, sauna. Extensive water-sports facilities, including scuba diving (see "Sports & Outdoor Pursuits," below), sailing, snorkeling, waterskiing, and windsurfing. Laundry, concierge, massage.

Novotel Carayou. Pointe du Bout, 97229 Trois-Ilets, Martinique, F.W.I. ☎ **800/221-4542** in the U.S., or 0596/66-04-04. Fax 0596/66-00-57. 201 units. A/C TV TEL. Winter 1,305 F–2,165 F ($221.85–$368.05) double. Off-season 885 F–1,025 F ($150.45–$174.25) double. Rates include American buffet. AE, DC, MC, V.

A member of France's biggest hotel chain, the Accor Group, this hotel, popular with families and groups, has always prided itself on its lush gardens and glamorous garden setting. Radically renovated in late 1994 and early 1995, it reopened with yellow-beige exterior walls and an almost completely rebuilt physical plant. The accommodations aren't the most attractive in the area, but they are housed in a series of three-story out-buildings, each encircled by large lawns dotted with coconut or palm trees and flow-ering shrubs. The seaside rooms are the best, and some of the units are air-conditioned. Against a setting of wood trim and whitewashed walls, the rooms are generally small but well maintained. Bathrooms are equipped with a combination tub/shower, bidet, toiletries, and large mirrors. The property has a small beach.

Dining/Diversions: There are three different dining areas, including a formal French and Creole restaurant, Le Boucaut, and a beachfront grill for sandwiches and salads. Creole cookery is prepared with flair, especially the seafood items. One appealing bar, La Paillote, sports a view of the sea.

Amenities: Pool, water sports (including windsurfing, scuba diving, waterskiing, sailboat rentals, and snorkeling). 24-hour concierge, laundry.

MODERATE

La Pagerie. Pointe du Bout, 97229 Trois-Ilets, Martinique, F.W.I. ☎ **800/221-4542** in the U.S., or 0596/66-05-30. Fax 0596/66-00-99. 94 units. A/C TV TEL. Winter 870 F–940 F ($147.90–$159.80) double. Off-season 560 F–720 F ($95.20–$122.40) double. Rates include buffet breakfast. AE, DC, MC, V.

The facilities here are relatively modest compared to those in some of the larger and more expensive hotels of Pointe du Bout, but its guests can compensate by visiting the many restaurants, bars, and sports facilities in the area. Set close to the gardens of the Hôtel Bakoua-Sofitel, a 16-mile drive from the airport, this hotel offers comfortably modern bedrooms, although walls are thin. The units are neat and uncomplicated, with tile floors, small fridges, and balconies with views opening onto the bay; about two-thirds contain tiny kitchenettes at no extra charge. The accommodations are out-fitted with floral prints, low-slung furnishings, and louvered closets. The tiled bath-rooms have combination tub/showers, marble vanities, bidets, and wall-mounted showerheads. The hotel has a small pool and a tiny bar, open only in the evening, plus a bar and restaurant, L'Hibiscus. Guests usually walk the short distance to the Novotel Carayou for other facilities, including water sports and access to the beach.

INEXPENSIVE

Auberge de L'Anse Mitan. Anse Mitan, 97229 Trois-Ilets, Martinique, F.W.I. ☎ **0596/ 66-01-12.** Fax 0596/66-01-05. 25 units. A/C TEL. Winter 420 F ($71.40) double; 400 F ($68) studio for one or two. Off-season 330 F ($56.10) double; 300 F ($51) studio for one or two. Room (but not studio) rates include breakfast. AE, DC, MC, V.

Many guests like this hotel's location at the isolated end of a road whose more com-mercial side is laden with restaurants and a bustling nighttime parade. The hotel was built in 1930, but it has been renovated several times since by the hospitable Athanase family. What you see today is a three-story concrete box–type structure. Six of the units are studios with kitchens and TVs; all have private showers. Rooms are boxy, but the beds are comfortable with firm mattresses. Bathrooms are very small and cramped, but tidy. You don't get anything special here, but few object to the price.

WHERE TO DINE

In the words of one longtime expatriate, "We have some really crummy restaurants in Pointe du Bout." Here's the pick of the litter.

Au Poisson d'Or. L'Anse Mitan. ☎ **0596/66-01-80.** Reservations recommended. Main courses 80 F–140 F ($13.60–$23.80); fixed-price menu 130 F–190 F ($22.10–$32.30). AE, MC, V. Tues–Sun noon–2:30pm and 7–9:30pm. Closed July. CREOLE.

Its position near the entrance of the resort community of Pointe du Bout makes it easy to find. There's no view of the sea and the traffic runs close to the edge of the veranda and terrace, but the reasonable prices and the complete change of pace make up for that. The rustic dining room offers such menu items as grilled fish, grilled conch scallops sautéed in white wine, poached local fish, and flan. These ordinary dishes are prepared with a certain flair and served with style.

Pignon sur Mer. Anse-à-l'Ane. ☎ **0596/68-38-37.** Main courses 55 F–170 F ($9.35–$28.90). MC, V. Tues–Sun 12:15–4pm; Tues–Sat 7–9:30pm. CREOLE.

Simple and unpretentious, this is a small-scale Creole restaurant containing about 15 tables, set within a rustically dilapidated building beside the sea (it's a 12-minute drive from Pointe du Bout). Menu items are island-inspired, and might include *delices du Pignon*, a platter of shellfish, or whatever grilled fish or shellfish was hauled in that day. *Lambi* (conch), shrimp, and crayfish are almost always available, and brochettes of chicken are filling and flavorful.

✪ **La Villa Creole.** L'Anse Mitan. ☎ **0596/66-05-53.** Reservations recommended. Main courses 85 F–150 F ($14.45–$25.50); set menus 160 F–400 F ($27.20–$68). AE, MC, V. Tues–Sat noon–2pm; Tues–Sun 7–10:30pm. CREOLE/FRENCH.

This restaurant, a 3- or 4-minute drive from the hotels of Pointe du Bout, has thrived since the late 1970s, offering a colorful, small-scale respite from the island's high-rise resorts. Set within a simple but well-maintained Creole house, with no particular views other than the small garden that surrounds it, the restaurant serves fairly priced set-price menus of such staples as *accras de morue* (beignets of codfish), *boudin creole* (blood sausage), and *un féroce* (a local form of pâté concocted from fresh avocados, pulverized codfish, and manioc flour). Especially flavorful is the red snapper prepared either with tomato sauce or grilled. Owner Guy Bruère-Dawson, a singer and guitarist, entertains as you dine.

HITTING THE BEACH

The clean white-sand beaches of **Pointe du Bout,** site of the major hotels of Martinique, were created by developers and tend to be rather small. Most of the tourists head here, so the narrow beaches are among the island's most crowded. It doesn't help that Pointe du Bout is also the site of several marinas lining the shore, as well as the docking point for the ferry from Fort de France. Even if you don't find a lot of space on the beach, with its semiclear waters, you will find toilets, phones, restaurants, and cafes galore. The waters suffer from industrial usage, although apparently the pollution is not severe enough to prevent people from going in. You'll often see the French standing deep in the water, conversing and smoking cigarettes—perhaps not your idea of an idyllic beach holiday.

To the south, however, the golden-sand beaches at **Anse Mitan** have always been welcoming visitors, including many snorkelers. The beaches here are far less crowded and more inviting, with cleaner waters. However, the steepness of Martinique's shoreline leaves much to be desired by its swimmers and snorkelers. The water declines steeply into depths, no reefs ring the shores, and fish are rarely visible. Nonetheless, beaches here are ideal for sunbathing.

The neighboring beach to Anse-Mitan is **Anse-à-l'Ane**, an ideal place for a picnic on the white sands. There's also a little shell museum here of passing interest.

SPORTS & OUTDOOR PURSUITS

GOLF In 1976, the famous golf-course designer Robert Trent Jones, Sr., visited Martinique and left behind the 18-hole **Golf de l'Impératrice-Joséphine,** at Trois-Ilets (☎ **0596/68-32-81**), a 5-minute drive from Pointe du Bout and about 18 miles from Fort-de-France. The only golf course on Martinique, the greens slope from the birthplace of Empress Joséphine (for whom it's named) across rolling hills with scenic vistas down to the sea. Amenities include a pro shop, a bar, a restaurant, and three tennis courts. Greens fees are 270 F ($45.90) for 18 holes.

HORSEBACK RIDING The premier riding facility on Martinique is **Ranch Jack,** Morne Habitué, Trois-Ilets (☎ **0596/68-37-69**). It offers morning horseback rides for both experienced and novice riders, at a cost of 350 F ($59.50) for a 3½- to 4-hour ride. Jacques and Marlene Guinchard make daily promenades across the beaches and fields of Martinique, with a running explication of the history, fauna, and botany of the island. Cold drinks are included in the price, and transportation is usually free to and from the hotels of nearby Pointe du Bout. Four to 15 participants are needed to book a tour. This is an ideal way to discover both botanical and geographical Martinique.

SCUBA DIVING & SNORKELING The beachfront of the Hôtel Méridien (at Pointe du Bout) is the headquarters for the island's best-recommended dive outfit, **Espace Plongée Martinique** (☎ **0596/66-00-00**), which welcomes anyone who shows up, regardless of where they happen to be staying. Daily dive trips, depending on demand, leave from Hôtel Méridien's pier every day at 9am, returning at noon, and at 2:30pm, returning at 6pm. Popular dive sites within a reasonable boat ride, with enough diversity and variation in depth to appeal to divers of all degree of proficiency, include *La Baleine* (The Whale) and *Cap Solomon*. A dive shop stocks everything you'll need to take the plunge, from weight belts and tanks to wet suits and underwater cameras. Divers pay between 220 F and 250 F ($37.40 and $42.50) per session. Pool instruction for novice divers, which is conducted in the Méridien's pool every day from 11:30am to noon, is free.

Snorkeling equipment is usually available free to hotel guests, who quickly learn that coral, fish, and ferns abound in the waters around the Pointe du Bout hotels.

TENNIS Tennis pros at Bathy's Club at the **Hôtel Méridien**, Pointe du Bout (☎ **0596/66-00-00**), usually allow nonguests to play for free if the courts are otherwise unoccupied, except at night, when the charge is almost always imposed.

You can also play on one of the three courts at **Golf de l'Impératrice-Joséphine,** at Trois-Ilets (☎ **0596/68-32-81**). The setting here is one of the most beautiful on Martinique. It costs 70 F ($11.90) per hour to play. No racquet rentals are available.

WINDSURFING An enduringly popular sport in the French West Indies, windsurfing (*"la planche à voile"*) is available at most of the large-scale hotels. One of the best equipped is the **Cabane des Sports,** the beachfront facilities at the Hotel Méridien, Pointe du Bout (☎ **0596/66-00-00**). Lessons cost 100 F ($17) for 1 hour, and boards rent for about 60 F ($10.20) an hour.

A VISIT TO TROIS-ILETS

Marie-Josèphe-Rose Tascher de la Pagerié was born here in 1763. As Joséphine, she was to become the wife of Napoléon I and empress of France from 1804 to 1809. Six years older than Napoléon, she pretended that she'd lost her birth certificate so he wouldn't find out her true age. Although many historians call her ruthless and selfish, she is still revered by some on Martinique as an uncommonly gracious lady. Others have less kind words for her—because Napoléon is said by some historians to have "reinvented" slavery, they blame Joséphine's influence.

Twenty miles south of Fort-de-France, you reach Trois-Ilets, a charming little village. A mile outside the hamlet, turn left to La Pagerie, where the small **Musée de la Pagerie** (☎ 0596/68-33-06), has been installed in the former estate kitchen, where Joséphine gossiped with her slaves and played the guitar. Along with her childhood bed, you'll see a passionate letter from Napoléon and other mementos. The collection was compiled by Dr. Robert Rose-Rosette.

Still remaining are the partially restored ruins of the Pagerié sugar mill and the church (in the village itself) where she was christened in 1763. The plantation was destroyed in a hurricane. The museum is open Tuesday through Friday from 9am to 5:30pm, Saturday and Sunday from 9am to 1pm and 2:30 to 5:30pm. Admission is 20 F ($3.40).

A botanical garden, the **Parc des Floralies,** is adjacent to the golf course (see above), as is the museum devoted to Joséphine (see above).

Maison de la Canne, Pointe Vatable (☎ 0596/68-32-04), is on the road to Trois-Ilets. (From Fort-de-France, you can take a taxi or shuttle bus to La Marina, Pointe du Bout; from here, an unnumbered bus heads for Pointe Vatable.) It was created in 1987 on the premises of an 18th-century distillery; its permanent exhibitions tell the story of sugarcane and the sweeping role it played in the economic and cultural development of Martinique. Displays include models, tools, a miniature slave ship, an ancient cart tethered to life-size models of two oxen, and a restored carriage. It's open Tuesday to Sunday from 9am to 5:30pm, charging an admission of 20 F ($3.40) for adults, 5 F (85¢) for children 5 to 12 (free 4 and under).

SHOPPING

The Marina complex has a number of interesting boutiques; several sell handcrafts and curios from Martinique. They're sometimes of good quality, but are quite expensive, particularly the enameled jewel boxes and some of the batiks of natural silk.

At Christmastime, many of the island's traditional foie gras and pastries are presented in crocks made by Martinique's largest earthenware factories, the **Poterie de Trois-Ilets,** Quartier Poterie, Trois-Ilets (☎ 0596/68-03-44). At least 90% of its production is devoted to brick-making. However, one small-scale offshoot of the company devotes itself to producing earth-toned stoneware and pottery whose colors and shapes have contributed to the folklore of Martinique. In theory, the studios are open Monday to Saturday from 7am to 2:30pm, but call before you set out to make sure they'll accept visitors.

POINTE DU BOUT AFTER DARK

Martinique has one of the dullest casinos in the French West Indies, **Casino Trois-Ilets,** Hotel Méridien Trois-Ilets, Pointe du Bout (☎ 0596/66-00-30), open daily from 10pm to 3am. It costs 70 F ($11.90) to play roulette or blackjack; entrance to the slot-machine room is free. A picture ID is required.

A mellow piano bar atmosphere is found at **L'Amphore,** in the rear of Le Bakoua Hotel, Pointe du Bout (☎ 0596/66-03-09). Another piano bar is **Le Cotton Club** (☎ 0596/66-03-09), at Trois-Ilets, taking its name from the once-fabled club in New York's Harlem.

4 The South Loop

We now leave Pointe du Bout and head south for more sun and beaches. Resort centers here include Le Diamant and Ste-Anne.

From Trois-Ilets, you can follow a small curved road that brings you to **Anse-à-l'Ane, Grande Anse,** and **Anses d'Arlets.** At any of these places, you'll find small beaches, quite safe and usually not crowded.

ANSES D'ARLETS

The scenery is beautiful here. Brightly painted fishing boats (*gommiers*) draw up on the white-sand beach, and the nets are spread out to dry in the sun. Children swim and oldsters fish from the good-size pier. The waters off Anses d'Arlets are a playground for divers, with a wide variety of small tropical fish and colorful corals.

The area itself has been for many years a choice spot for weekend "second homes," and is now beginning to develop touristically. The charming little village features a pretty steepled church, a bandstand for holiday concerts, and a smattering of modest little dining spots.

From Anses d'Arlets, Route D37 takes you to Diamant, along a panoramic road.

LE DIAMANT

Set on the island's southwestern coast, this village offers a good beach, open to the prevailing southern winds. The village is named after one of Martinique's best-known geological oddities, ✪ **Le Rocher du Diamant** (Diamond Rock), a barren offshore island that juts upward from the sea to a height of 573 feet. Sometimes referred to as the Gibraltar of the Caribbean, it figured prominently in a daring British-led invasion in 1804, when British mariners carried a formidable amount of ammunition and 110 sailors to the top. Despite frequent artillery bombardments from the French-held coastline, the garrison held out for 18 months, completely dominating the passageway between the rock and the coast of Martinique. Intrepid foreigners sometimes visit Diamond Rock, but the access across the strong currents of the channel is risky.

✪ **Diamond Beach,** on the Martinique mainland, offers a sandy bottom, verdant groves of swaying palms, and many different surf and sunbathing possibilities. The entire district has developed in recent years into a resort, scattered with generally small hotels.

WHERE TO STAY

Hotel Diamant Les Bains. 97223 Le Diamant, Martinique. F.W.I. ☎ **0596/76-40-14.** Fax 0596/76-27-00. 27 units. A/C TV TEL. Winter 550 F ($93.50) double; 600 F ($102) bungalow. Off-season 380 F ($64.60) double; 450 F ($76.50) bungalow. Rates include continental breakfast. MAP (breakfast and dinner) 120 F–160 F ($20.40–$27.20) per person extra. MC, V. Closed 10 days in June, and Sept 1 to early Oct.

Capably managed by resident owners Hubert and Marie-Yvonne Andrieu, this is a simple, unpretentious, family-style hotel. From the edge of the resort's pool, you can enjoy a view of the offshore island of Diamond Rock. Twenty units are in outlying motel-style bungalows set either in a garden or beside the beach; the others are in the resort's main building, which also houses the dining and drinking facilities. Two rooms are outfitted for travelers with disabilities. Accommodations generally have furnished terraces or patios, white-tile floors, small fridges, and built-in furniture made from polished fruitwoods. Most rooms are medium in size except for the small units on the second floor of the main building, which are often rented to business travelers from the French mainland. The most ideal are the 10 rustic bungalows directly above the beach. Bathrooms, which are aging but still work just fine, are accented with blue tiles and equipped with such extras as bidets; each has a shower stall.

The main building houses the restaurant, where Mr. Andrieu works as the chef. Full lunches and dinners are served Thursday through Tuesday. The cuisine is for the most part Creole, with some French dishes thrown in. A fixed-price meal at 125 F ($21.25) might include specialties such as crab salad, spicy black pudding, and a fish blaff, with coconut flan for dessert. Locally caught fish often appears on the menu.

Novotel Le Diamant. 97223 Le Diamant, Martinique, F.W.I. ☎ **800/221-4542** in the U.S., or 0596/76-42-42. Fax 0596/76-22-87. 181 units. A/C TV TEL. Winter 895 F–2,090 F ($152.15–$355.30) double; 1,345 F–2,590 F ($228.65–$440.30) suite. Off-season 845 F ($143.65) double; 1,345 F ($228.65) suite. Rates include breakfast. AE, CB, DC, MC, V.

On 6 acres of forested land, 2 miles outside the village and 18 miles south of Fort-de-France, this low-rise building is in one of the most beautiful districts on Martinique. It's the ultimate in laissez-faire management—guests, often tour groups from France, are basically left to fend for themselves. Guest rooms, housed in four three-story wings, face either the pool or the coast, with its view of Diamond Rock. From many of the rooms, the views are more evocative of the South Pacific than of the Caribbean. The inviting units have tropical decor, white-tile floors, whitewashed walls, roomy closets, and rattan furnishings, plus adequate desk space. Bathrooms have combination tub/showers, full-length mirrors, and hair dryers.

The reception opens onto a large pool that you traverse via a Chinese-style wooden bridge to get to the dining facilities. These include Le Flamboyant, La Cabana du Pêcheur, Les Alizés, and a poolside cafe. Outside the hotel, the neighboring beaches aren't too crowded, as they aren't too good. Lawns and gardens, as well as tennis courts, surround the property. Water sports are also available. The taxi ride from the airport should take about 40 minutes.

WHERE TO DINE

Chez Christiane. Rue Principale, Bourg Le Diamant. ☎ **0596/76-49-55.** Main courses 70 F–120 F ($11.90–$20.40); set menu 50 F ($8.50). AE, DC, V. Mon–Sat 7–11pm. CREOLE.

On the main street of Bourg Le Diamant, in a dining room decorated with varnished bamboo and slats of local hardwood, you can taste the Creole specialties of Christiane Ravin, who has earned the respect of her colleagues after almost a dozen years at her trade. Friday night, live music gives the dining room an ambience more like a nightclub than a restaurant. Otherwise, it's a worthy choice for such menu items as fricassée of chicken or conch, curried shrimp, octopus with Creole sauce, and well-seasoned fillets of fish that include local, freshly caught snapper.

STE-ANNE

From Le Marin, a 5-mile drive brings you to Ste-Anne, at the extreme southern tip of Martinique. This sleepy little area is known for the white-sand beaches of **Les Salines** (those to the north are more grayish in color). In many ways, these are Martinique's finest. The climate is arid like parts of Arizona, and the beaches are almost always sunny, perhaps too much so at midday. The name comes from Étang des Salines, a large salt pond forming a backdrop to the strip of sand. Manchineel trees are found at the southeastern end of the beach. Under no circumstances should you go under these trees for protection in a rainfall. When it's sunny you can seek shade here, but when it rains, drops falling from the poisonous tree will be like acid on your tender skin.

Holidays and weekends tend to be crowded, as many islanders and their families flock to this beach. Regrettably, it's not big enough to handle the hordes, and you'd be wise to seek out other beaches at these times.

Salines is also the site of Martinique's only real **gay beach.** Drive to the far end of the parking lot, near the sign labeled Petite Anse des Salines. Here you'll find a trail leading through thick woods to a sun-flooded beach often populated by naked gay men, with an occasional lesbian couple or two. Technically, there are no legal nudist beaches on Martinique, so it's possible you could be arrested for going nude, although authorities don't seem to enforce this law. Throughout the island, however, the European custom of topless bathing is not uncommon on any of the beaches or even around hotel pools.

Ste-Anne opens onto views of the Sainte Lucia Canal, and nearby is the Petrified Savanna Forest, which the French call **Savane des Pétrifications.** It's a field of petrified volcanic boulders in the shape of logs. The eerie, desertlike site is studded with cacti.

WHERE TO STAY

Club Med Les Boucaniers (Buccaneer's Creek). Pointe Marin, 97227 Ste-Anne, Martinique, F.W.I. ☎ **800/CLUB-MED** in the U.S., or 0596/76-76-13. Fax 0596/76-72-02. 313 units. A/C. All-inclusive weekly rates: Winter 798 F–959 F ($135.65–$163.05). Off-season 819 F ($139.25). Rates are per person and based on double occupancy. AE, MC, V. No children under 12 accepted.

Set on a peaceful cove at the southernmost tip of Martinique, about a 50-minute drive from the airport, this resort is designed as a series of scattered outbuildings reminiscent of a Creole village. The club is on the 48-acre site of a former pirate's hideaway at Buccaneer's Creek, amid a forest of coconut palms. Bedrooms are a bit spartan with rather thin mattresses; baths are compact with shower stalls. Although many Club Meds welcome children, this particular one does not accept kids 11 and under, and is geared more toward single guests or couples, some of whom like the au naturel beach nearby. The emphasis is often on group activities.

Dining/Diversions: In a domed two-level building in the heart of the resort, you'll find an amusement center, theater, dance floor, and bar. A walk along rue du Port (the main street of Club Med) leads to Tour du Port, a bar that overlooks the sailboat fleet anchored in the marina. The resort contains a communal dining room (Le Grand Restaurant) and a well-recommended, less formal restaurant (La Maison Creole) specializing in Antillean cuisine. Meals are served at long tables whose seating plans are conducive to meeting other guests (even if you don't want to). The disco stays open until the wee hours.

Amenities: Sailing, waterskiing, snorkeling; part of the beach is reserved for nude sunbathing. Social director, massage.

La Dunette. 97227 Ste-Anne, Martinique, F.W.I. ☎ **0596/76-73-90.** Fax 0596/76-76-05. 18 units. A/C TV TEL. Winter 600 F ($102) double. Off-season 500 F ($85) double. Rates include continental breakfast. MC, V.

A motel-like stucco structure directly beside the sea, this hotel appeals to guests who appreciate its simplicity and its isolation from the more built-up resort areas of other parts of Martinique. A three-story building originally constructed in the late 1960s, it's near the Club Med and the white-sand beaches of the Salines. Best defined as an unpretentious seaside inn with a simple, summery decor, the hotel is accented with a garden filled with flowers and tropical plants. The furnishings are casual and modern, and although some rooms are quite small, each benefited from a complete renovation in 1993. The private bathrooms, although small, are well maintained. Drinks are served every night on the terrace above the sea. The in-house restaurant is better than you might expect, thanks to the culinary finesse of the Tanzania-born owner, Gerard Kambona. Main courses may include a succulent version of red snapper stuffed with sea urchins, or a wide selection of shellfish plucked from local waters.

✪ **Manoir de Beauregard.** Chemins des Salines (a 10-minute walk south of Ste-Anne), 97227 Ste-Anne, Martinique, F.W.I. ☎ **0596/76-73-40.** Fax 0596/76-93-24. E-mail: manoirbeauregard@cgit.com. 11 units. A/C TEL. Winter 900 F–1,300 F ($153–$221) double. Off-season 750 F–950 F ($127.50–$161.50) double. AE, MC, V.

One of the most venerable and historic hotels on Martinique lies within the massive walls of a manor house that once administered many acres of surrounding sugarcane fields. It was originally built between 1720 and 1800 by a prominent French family, and almost resembles a medieval church. A tragic fire in 1990 completely gutted the building's interior and led to 4 years of restoration. Today, there are three bedrooms on the upper floors of the original house, and another eight within a modern, less inspired one-story annex, built a few steps from the main house in 1975. Rooms within the annex, although not as dignified, have direct views over the garden and antique West Indian beds. Most units are roomy with double or twin beds, plus a compact tiled bathroom with a combination tub/shower. A truly superb beach, Plage des Salines, is a 5-minute drive to the south, and a slightly less appealing beach, Plage de Sainte-Anne, is within a 15-minute walk.

Meals here are conservative, traditional, and similar to the tried-and-true Creole cuisine that flourished at this place throughout the early 20th century. Examples include codfish fritters, boudin Creole, grilled fish in Creole sauce, curries, and fresh lobster.

WHERE TO DINE

✪ **Aux Filets Bleus.** Pointe Marin, Ste-Anne. ☎ **0596/76-73-42.** Reservations required. Fixed-price menu 59 F–260 F ($10.05–$44.20). MC, V. Daily noon–3:30pm and 7–10:30pm. CREOLE/FRENCH.

This family-run blue-and-white restaurant is a 30-minute drive south of the airport. The seaside exposure of the alfresco dining room and its terrace makes you feel as if you're in an isolated tropical retreat, where the only sound is the splash of waves and the tinkling of ice in glasses. What appears to be a glass-covered reflecting pool set into the floor is actually a lobster tank, supposedly one of only a few on Martinique. The restaurant offers one of the island's cheapest fixed-price menus. Specialties include *bouillabaisse de la mer,* three types of fish covered with a tomato and onion sauce; crab-meat salad with a coulis of tomato, basil, and olive oil; and *pavé de daurade aux senteurs des îles,* white fish with a coriander-and-fennel sauce. You can go for a swim before or after your meal.

Restaurant Frédéric. Domaine de Belfond, Ste-Anne. ☎ **0596/76-95-84.** Reservations recommended. Main courses 105 F–165 F ($17.85–$28.05); set menu 150 F ($25.50). MC, V. Tues–Sun 7:15–10:30pm. Closed 3 weeks June–July. FRENCH/CREOLE.

One of the most talked-about and oft-visited restaurants on the island is the result of native son Fréderic Cadasse's return to Martinique, after nearly 20 successful years at a restaurant in St-Tropez. His restaurant lies within a 2-minute walk of the Hotel Anchorage, in a graceful 5-year-old villa that was designed to emulate much older models. You can enjoy an aperitif on one of the rocking chairs in any of three salons before heading to your table, where there's a view over the tropical garden outside. Menu items combine local ingredients with time-honored tenets of French cuisine. Examples include a mousseline of lobster with chive sauce, conch in puff pastry with crabmeat marinated in coconut milk, and medallions of *sarde* (a local whitefish) with crayfish. Also look for an *émincé* of red snapper with rum-based vinegar and a saffron-and-rum sauce, and breast of duckling served with acacia-flavored honey. Dessert might be a house-style frozen nougat. By all means try his famous Punch le Zombi de l'Amour, an acclaimed aphrodisiac on the island.

5 The North Loop

As we swing north from Fort-de-France, our main targets are Le Carbet, St-Pierre, Montagne Pelée, and Leyritz. However, we'll sandwich in many stopovers along the way.

From Fort-de-France, there are three ways to head north to Montagne Pelée. The first is to follow Route N4 up to St-Joseph. There you take the left fork for 3 miles after St-Joseph and turn onto Route D15 toward Marigot.

Another way to Montagne Pelée is to take Route N3 through the vegetation-rich *mornes* (hills) until you reach Le Morne Rouge. This road is known as "route de la Trace" and is now the center of the Parc Naturel de la Martinique.

Yet a third route to Montagne Pelée is via Route N2 along the coast. This is the route we'll follow, and the order in which we'll list the towns along the way. Near Fort-de-France, the first town you reach is **Schoelcher.** Farther along Route N2 is **Case-Pilote,** and then Bellefontaine. This portion, along the most frequented tourist route in Martinique—that is, Fort-de-France to St-Pierre—is very reminiscent of the way the French Riviera used to look. **Bellefontaine** is a small fishing village, with boats stretched along the beach. Note the many houses also built in the shape of boats.

LE CARBET

Leaving Bellefontaine, a 5-mile drive north will deliver you to Le Carbet. Columbus landed here in 1502, and the first French settlers arrived in 1635. In 1887, Gauguin lived here for 4 months before going on to Tahiti. You can stop for a swim at an Olympic-size pool set into the hills, or watch the locals scrubbing clothes in a stream. The town lies on the bus route from Fort-de-France to St-Pierre.

The **Centre d'Art Musée Paul-Gauguin,** Anse Turin, Le Carbet (☎ **0596/78-22-66**), is near the beach represented in the artist's *Bord de Mer.* The landscape hasn't changed in 100 years. The museum, housed in a five-room building, commemorates the French artist's stay on Martinique in 1887, with books, prints, letters, and other memorabilia. There are also paintings by René Corail, sculpture by Hector Charpentier, and examples of the work of Zaffanella. Of special interest are faïence mosaics made of once-white pieces that turned pink, maroon, blue, and black in 1902 when the fires of Montagne Pelée devastated St-Pierre. There are also changing exhibits of works by local artists. Hours are daily from 9am to 5:30pm; admission is 20 F ($3.40) for adults, 5 F (85¢) for children under 8.

ST-PIERRE

At the beginning of this century, St-Pierre was known as the "Little Paris of the West Indies." Home to 30,000 inhabitants, it was the cultural and economic capital of Martinique. On May 7, 1902, the citizens read in their daily newspaper that "Montagne Pelée does not present any more risk to the population than Vesuvius does to the Neapolitans."

However, on May 8, at 8am, the southwest side of Montagne Pelée exploded into fire and lava. At 8:02am, all 30,000 inhabitants were dead—that is, all except one. A convict in his underground cell was saved by the thickness of the walls. When islanders reached the site, the convict was paroled and left Martinique to tour in Barnum and Bailey's circus.

St-Pierre never recovered its past splendor. It could now be called the Pompeii of the West Indies. Ruins of the church, the theater, and some other buildings can be seen along the coast.

Photo Ops

Martinique lends itself to photography, almost more than any other island in the Caribbean. That's why French fashion magazines often come here for photo shoots. The most picturesque sites are La Savane, in Fort-de-France; St-Pierre, the best place to photograph towering Mount Pelée; La Pagerie, with its decaying ruins of a sugar factory; and from the panoramic overlooks along La Trace, the serpentine road winding through the entire rain forest. If you want some snapshots of local residents, they usually don't mind being photographed, providing you ask first.

One of the best ways to get an overview of St-Pierre involves riding a rubber-wheeled "train," the **CV Paris Express** (☎ 0596/78-31-41), which departs on tours from the base of the Musée Volcanologique. Tours cost 50 F ($8.50) for adults, 25 F ($4.25) for children, and run Monday through Friday from 10:30am to 1pm and 2:30 to 7pm. In theory, tours depart about once an hour, but they only leave when there are enough people to justify a trip.

The **Musée Volcanologique,** rue Victor-Hugo, St-Pierre (☎ 0596/78-10-32), was created by the American volcanologist Franck Alvard Perret, who turned the museum over to the city in 1933. Here, in pictures and relics dug from the debris, you can trace the story of what happened to St-Pierre. Dug from the lava is a clock that stopped at the exact moment the volcano erupted. The museum is open daily from 9am to 5pm; admission is 10 F ($1.70) for adults, free for children 7 and under.

WHERE TO DINE

La Factorerie. Quartier Fort, St-Pierre. ☎ **0596/78-12-53.** Reservations recommended. Main courses 72 F–150 F ($12.25–$25.50). AE, MC, V. Daily noon–2pm. CREOLE.

This eatery is midway between St-Pierre and Le Prêcheur, near the ruins of a 19th-century church, the Eglise du Fort. It's a ramshackle-looking cottage within a grove of mango trees and coconut palms. The restaurant is a bit battered, but if you're in the neighborhood around noontime, it makes a convenient stop. You'll enjoy such dishes as chicken with coconut, fricassée of conch, chicken with prawns, a freshwater crayfish served with a piquant tomato sauce, and a dessert flan made with fresh coconuts and sweet potatoes. At least some of the staff have been trained at Martinique's nearby agricultural training school.

LE PRÊCHEUR

From St-Pierre, you can continue along the coast north to Le Prêcheur. Once the home of Madame de Maintenon, the mistress of Louis XIV, it's the last village along the northern coast of Martinique. Here you can see hot springs of volcanic origin and the **Tombeau des Caraïbes (Tomb of the Caribs),** where, according to legend, the collective suicide of many West Indian natives took place after they returned from a fishing expedition and found their homes pillaged by the French.

MONTAGNE PELÉE

A panoramic and winding road (Route N2) takes you through a tropical rain forest. The curves are of the hairpin variety, and the road is not always kept in good shape. However, you're rewarded with tropical flowers, baby ferns, plumed bamboo, and valleys so deeply green you'll think you're wearing cheap sunglasses.

The village of **Morne Rouge,** right at the foot of Montagne Pelée, is a popular vacation spot for Martiniquais. From here on, a narrow and unreliable road brings you to a level of 2,500 feet above sea level, 1,600 feet under the round summit of the volcano that destroyed St-Pierre. Montagne Pelée itself rises 4,575 feet above sea level.

If you're a serious mountain climber and you don't mind 4 or 5 hours of hiking, you can scale the peak, though you should hire an experienced guide to accompany you. Realize that this is a real mountain, that rain is frequent, and that temperatures drop very low. Tropical growth often hides deep crevices in the earth, and there are other dangers. The park service maintains more than 100 miles of trails. Although the hikes up from Grand-Rivière or Le Prêcheur are generally the less arduous of the three options leading to the top, most visitors opt for departures from Morne Rouge, a land-locked village set to the south of the summit, because it doesn't take as long to finish the trip. It's steeper, rockier, and more exhausting, but you can make it in just 2½ hours versus the 5 hours it takes from the other two towns. There are no facilities other than these villages, so it's vital to bring water and food with you. Your arduous journey will be rewarded at the summit with sweeping views over the sea and panoramas that sometimes stretch as far as mountainous Dominica to the south. As for the volcano, its deathly eruption in 1902 apparently satisfied it—at least for the time being!

Upon your descent from Montagne Pelée, drive down to **Ajoupa-Bouillon,** one of the most beautiful towns on Martinique. Abounding in flowers and shrubbery with bright yellow and red leaves, this little village is the site of the remarkable **Gorges de la Falaise.** These are mini-canyons on the Falaise River, up which you can travel to reach a waterfall. Ajoupa-Bouillon also makes a good lunch stop.

WHERE TO DINE

Le Fromager. Route de Fonds-St-Denis, St-Pierre. ☎ **0596/78-19-07.** Reservations recommended. Fixed-price menu 100 F–150 F ($17–$25.50); main courses 80 F–130 F ($13.60–$22.10). AE, DC, MC, V. Daily noon–3pm. CREOLE/FRENCH.

Set about a half mile uphill (east) of the center of St-Pierre, this indoor-outdoor villa, owned by the René family, welcomes guests with a humor and charm that's half French, half Martiniquais. The restaurant, which resembles a covered open-air pavilion, has a sweeping view of the town. Good-tasting menu items include marinated octopus, grilled conch or lobster, curried goat or chicken, and whatever grilled fish is available that day. This is a good lunch stopover during your tour of the island.

LEYRITZ

Continue east toward the coast, near the town of Basse-Pointe in northeastern Martinique. A mile before Basse-Pointe, turn left and follow a road that goes deep into sugarcane country to Leyritz, where you'll find one of the best-restored plantations on Martinique.

WHERE TO STAY & DINE

✪ **Hôtel Plantation de Leyritz.** 97218 Basse-Pointe, Martinique, F.W.I. ☎ **0596/78-53-92.** Fax 0596/78-92-44. www.fwinet.com/leyritz.htm. E-mail: hyleyritz@cgit.com. 67 units. A/C TV TEL. Winter 700 F ($119) double. Off-season 520 F ($88.40) double. Rates include continental breakfast. AE, MC, V.

This hotel, which offers spa facilities, was built around 1700 by a plantation owner, Bordeaux-born Michel de Leyritz. It's still a working banana plantation which has been restored to its original character. It was the site of the "swimming-pool summit meeting" in 1974 between Presidents Gerald Ford and Valéry Giscard d'Estaing. Today, instead of politicians, you're likely to meet a stampede of cruise-ship passengers. There are 16 acres of tropical gardens, with views that sweep across the Atlantic and take in fearsome Montagne Pelée. At the core of the grounds is an 18th-century great house, with rugged stone walls (20 inches thick), beamed ceilings, and tile and flagstone floors. The interior is cozy, with mahogany tables, overstuffed sofas, and gilt mirrors. About half the accommodations are in a series of small outbuildings scattered around the property; others are in a newer annex adjacent to the spa. The guest rooms come in a variety of different sizes; some have sundecks. The bathrooms, though tiny, are tidy. Don't expect well-polished luxury—that's not the style here. Laundry service and an outdoor pool are pluses.

The dining room is in a former rum distillery, incorporating the fresh spring water running down from the hillside. You may want to begin your meal with the traditional lanter's punch. Tour-bus crowds predominate at lunch, when a fixed-price menu (127 F/$21.60) may include such authentic Creole items as grilled chicken in coconut-milk sauce, *oussous* (a freshwater crayfish) in an herb sauce, sautéed breadfruit, and sautéed bananas. Dinner is more elaborate and dramatic, with both French and Creole dishes, such as duck with pineapple, *boudin* (blood pudding) Creole, colombo or curry of lamb, *accras de morue* (codfish fritters), and a surprising sauerkraut that substitutes shredded papaya for the traditional cabbage. The fixed-price dinner goes for 150 F ($25.50).

BASSE-POINTE

At the northernmost point on the island, Basse-Pointe is a land of pineapple and banana plantations, covering the Atlantic-side slopes of Mount Pelée volcano.

WHERE TO DINE

✪ **Chez Mally Edjam.** Route de la Côte Atlantique. ☎ **0596/78-51-18.** Reservations required. Main courses 70 F–180 F ($11.90–$30.60); fixed-price menu 70 F ($11.90). MC, V. Daily noon–3pm; dinner by special arrangement only. Closed mid-July to mid-Aug. FRENCH/CREOLE.

This local legend operates from a modest house beside the main road in the center of town, 36 miles from Fort-de-France. Appreciating its exotic but genteel charm, many visitors prefer to drive all the way from Pointe du Bout to dine here instead of at the Leyritz Plantation. You can sit at one of a handful of tables on the side porch or in the somewhat more formal dining room. Grandmotherly Mally Edjam (who is ably assisted by France-born Martine Hugé) is busy in the kitchen turning out her Creole delicacies. Both women are adept at preparing all the dishes for which the island is known: stuffed land crab with a hot seasoning, small pieces of conch in a tart shell, and a classic colombo de porc (the Creole version of pork curry). Equally acclaimed are the lobster vinaigrette, the papaya soufflé (which must be ordered in advance), and the highly original confitures—tiny portions of fresh island fruits, such as pineapple and guava, that have been preserved in a vanilla syrup.

GRAND' RIVIÈRE

After Basse-Pointe, the town you reach on your northward trek is Grand' Rivière. From here you must turn back, but before doing so, you may want to stop at a good restaurant right at the entrance to the town.

WHERE TO DINE

Yva Chez Vava. Blvd. Charles-de-Gaulle. ☎ **0596/55-72-72.** Reservations recommended. Main courses 60 F–130 F ($10.20–$22.10); fixed-price menu 80 F ($13.60). AE, DC, MC, V. Daily noon–6pm. FRENCH/CREOLE.

Directly west of Basse-Pointe, in a low-slung building painted the peachy-orange of a paw-paw fruit, Yva Chez Vava is a combination private home and restaurant. It represents the hard labor of three generations of Creole women. Infused with a simple country-inn style, it was established in 1979 by a well-remembered, long-departed matron, Vava, whose daughter, Yva, is now assisted by her own daughter, Rosy. Family recipes are the mainstay of this modest bistro. À la carte items include Creole soup, a blaff of sea urchins, lobster, and various colombos or curries. Local delicacies have changed little since the days of Joséphine and her sugar fortune, and include *z'habitants* (crayfish), *vivaneau* (red snapper), *tazard* (kingfish), and *accras de morue* (cod fritters).

LE MARIGOT

After passing back through Basse-Pointe and Le Lorrain, you come to a small village that was relatively ignored by tourists until hotelier Jean-Louis de Lucy used France's tax-shelter laws to restore a landmark plantation and turn it into one of the finest hotels on the island. True, the nearest good beach is at Trinité, a 30-minute drive from the hotel, but guests of the Habitation LaGrange don't seem to mind.

WHERE TO STAY & DINE

Habitation LaGrange. 97225 Le Marigot, Martinique, F.W.I. ☎ **0596/53-60-60.** Fax 0596/53-50-58. (For reservations, contact Caribbean Inns, P.O. Box 7411, Hilton Head Island, SC 29983; ☎ **800/633-7411** in the U.S.) 15 units. A/C MINIBAR TEL. Winter 1,600 F–1,750 F ($272–$297.50) double; 2,100 F ($357) suite. Off-season 1,200 F–1,400 F ($204–$238) double; 1,750 F ($297.50) suite. Rates include breakfast. MAP (breakfast and dinner) 180 F ($30.60) per person extra. AE, MC, V.

One of the more unusual and historic properties of Martinique, this hotel lies in isolation about a mile north of the village of Le Marigot. It's set on 6 acres of land whose edges are engulfed by acres of banana fields. About 1½ miles inland from the coast, it was originally built in 1928 as part of the last sugar plantation and rum distillery on Martinique. Today, the ruins of that distillery rise a short distance from the Louisiana-style main house.

Rooms are either in the main house or in a comfortable annex, which was erected in 1990. Each unit is different, and contains antique or reproduction furniture crafted from mahogany, baldaquin-style beds with good mattresses, and accessories steeped in the French colonial style. All units have verandas or patios, with ample vistas over a tropical landscape of gardens and faraway banana groves. As a conscious effort to preserve the calm and quiet, no units contain TVs or radios. Bathrooms are among the island's finest, with wood paneling, four-footed tubs, and pedestal sinks.

Meals are prepared in the Creole style by local chefs, then served in the Ajoupa, an open-sided pavilion. Three-course fixed-price lunches or dinners cost 195 F to 300 F ($33.15 to $51), without wine. The property also offers a pool, tennis court, concierge (who can arrange car or boat rentals and sports activities around the island), and pickup service from the airport (on request).

STE-MARIE

Heading south along the coastal road, you'll pass Le Marigot en route to the little town of Ste-Marie. The ✪ **Musée du Rhum Saint-James,** route de l'Union at the Saint James Distillery (☎ **0596/69-30-02**), displays engravings, antique tools and machines, and other exhibits tracing the history of sugarcane and rum from 1765 to the present. When inventories of rum are low and the distillery is functioning (February to July), guided tours of both the museum and its distillery are offered. Tours depart four times a day (at 10am, 11:30am, 1pm, and 2:30pm), cost 20 F ($3.40) per person, and include a rum tasting. Admission to the museum (open daily from 9am to 6pm, regardless of whether the distillery is functioning) is free. Rum is available for purchase on site.

From here you can head out the north end of town and loop inland a bit for a stop at Morne des Esses, or continue heading south straight to Trinité.

WHERE TO DINE

✪ **Restaurant La Découverte/Chez Tatie Simone.** Fôret la Philippe, Route du marigot, Ste-Marie. ☎ **0596/69-44-04.** Reservations recommended. Main courses 80 F–160 F ($13.60–$27.20). AE, DC, MC, V. Daily 11am–11pm. CREOLE.

Set near Martinique's northeastern tip, 2½ miles north of Ste-Marie, this restaurant prepares superb versions of traditional Creole cuisine. The cement-sided house, built in the early 1980s, is the showcase for the cuisine of "Auntie" (*Tatie*) Simone Adelise. In a dining room accented with white wainscoting and folkloric paintings, you'll enjoy her *boudin rouge* (blood sausages, in this case accented with habañera peppers and cinnamon), *boudin blanc* (sausages made from pulverized conch and spices), couscous with *fruits de mer* (garnished with shrimp, crayfish, sea urchins, clams, and octopus), and a succulent array of grilled fish.

A member of the staff may propose a short promenade after your meal, along a well-marked trail dotted with signs that give the names of specific trees and plants. At its end, you'll be rewarded with sweeping panoramas over sea and coastline. Estimated round-trip time for the hike, not counting stops to admire the view, is 40 minutes.

MORNE DES ESSES

This is the *vannerie* (basket-making) capital of Martinique, and you can pick up a sturdy straw food basket in any of the small village shops.

WHERE TO DINE

Le Colibri (The Hummingbird). Allée du Colibri. ☎ **0596/69-91-95.** Main courses 100 F–250 F ($17–$42.50). AE, DC, MC, V. Daily noon–3pm and 7–10pm. CREOLE.

One of the longest-running restaurants on Martinique, this rustic-looking spot was established by the well-respected Mme Clotilde Paladino, who is assisted by her children, Marie-José, Marie-Joseph, and Joël. The site, which was enlarged and embellished in the mid-1990s with a series of paintings by local artists, lies in the heart of town. The interior dining room is supplemented by two outdoor terraces, one of which overlooks the busy kitchen. The cuisine, deeply rooted in Creole traditions, usually includes steaming bowlfuls of callaloo soup, Creole-style *boudin* (blood sausage), *accras* of codfish, and less conventional fare such as stuffed pigeon, chicken with coconut, conch tarts, avocado stuffed with crabmeat, and roast suckling pig. Especially appealing is a *salade de Colibri* loaded with seafood, which some diners select as a main course, and *tourte des oursins* (sea-urchin pie). Interestingly, whenever there's a surplus of local sea urchins—usually in December—they're removed from their own spiney shells and, for aesthetic reasons, artfully served in the shells of *St-Jacques* (scallops).

TRINITÉ

If you're in Morne-des-Esses, continue south, then turn east, or from Ste-Marie head south along the coastal route (N1), to reach Trinité. The town is the gateway to the Carvalle peninsula, where **Presqu'île de la Caravelle Nature Preserve,** a well-protected peninsula jutting into the Atlantic Ocean from the town of Trinité, has safe beaches and well-marked trails through tropical wetlands and to the ruins of historic Château Debuc. It offers excellent hiking and one of the only safe beaches for swimming on the Atlantic coast. It would hardly merit an actual stop were it not for the Saint-Aubin Hôtel.

WHERE TO STAY

✪ Saint-Aubin Hôtel. 97220 Trinité, Martinique, F.W.I. ☎ **0596/69-34-77.** Fax 0596/69-41-14. 15 units. A/C TEL. Winter 480 F–580 F ($81.60–$98.60) double. Off-season 380 F ($64.60) double. Rates include continental breakfast. AE, DC, MC, V.

A former restaurant owner, Normandy-born Guy Forêt has sunk his fortune into restoring this three-story Victorian house and turning it into a three-star hostelry, one of the loveliest inns in the Caribbean. Painted a vivid pink with fancy gingerbread, the hotel was originally built in 1920 of brick and poured concrete as a replacement for a much older wood-sided house, which served as the seat of a large plantation. It sits on a hillside above sugarcane fields and Trinité's bay, 2 miles from the village of Trinité itself. It was named after the uninhabited islet of St-Aubin, which lies offshore and is visible from the hotel. There are 800 yards of public beach, plus a pool on the grounds. All the good-size bedrooms sport wall-to-wall carpeting and modern (not antique) furniture; views are of either the garden or the sea. There are some family rooms as well. The restaurant and bar are reserved for use by hotel guests. Dinners are offered Monday through Saturday, and might include avocado vinaigrette, Creole black pudding, grilled fresh fish, stuffed crab, and fish poached in court bouillon. After dinner, you can relax on the verandas on the first and second floors.

LE FRANÇOIS

Continuing your exploration of the east coast of Martinique, you can stop over in Le François to visit the **Musée Rhum Clement** at the Domaine de l'Acajou (☎ **0596/54-62-07**), about 1½ miles south of the village center. The distillery is in the cellar of an 18th-century mansion with period furnishings. The house commemorates the summit meeting of Presidents Mitterrand and Bush in 1992. A Christopher Columbus exhibit is set up in caves, and other exhibits trace the institution of slavery in the islands. The museum is located in a botanic park; you could easily spend 2 or 3 hours exploring the exhibits and grounds. It's open daily from 9am to 6pm. Admission is 40 F ($6.80).

WHERE TO STAY

Frégate Bleue. Route de Vauclin, Le François 97240, Martinique, F.W.I. ☎ **800/633-7411** or 0596/54-54-66. Fax 0596/54-78-48. E-mail: fregatebleue@cgit.com. 7 units. Winter 700 F–1,400 F ($119–$238) double. Off-season 500 F–600 F ($85–$102) double. Extra person 120 F ($20.40). AE, MC, V.

This is the closest thing to a European B&B on the island. It's a calm and quiet choice with touches of personal, old-fashioned charm. It's not the place for vacationers looking for nightlife and lots of activities—it's for escapists who don't mind the 10-minute drive to the beaches of St-François or the prevailing sense of isolation. Much of this ambience is the work of owner Yveline de Lucy de Fossarieu, an experienced veteran of the hotel industry. Her house is a 5-minute drive inland from the sea, and it overlooks several chains of deserted offshore islands (including Les Ilets de St-François and Les Ilets de l'Imperatrice). Bedrooms are small but cozy, each with a compact bathroom with a shower stall.

Breakfast is served en famille, and three nights a week, between December and April, Mme de Fossarieu (who speaks perfect English) prepares an evening meal, served to whomever requests it in advance, for around 150 F ($25.50) per person.

17 | Nevis

A local once said that the best reason to go to Nevis was to practice the fine art of *limin'*. To him, that meant doing nothing in particular. Limin' might still be the best reason to venture over to Nevis, a small volcanic island. Once here, you can stay at the lovely Four Seasons, or find lodging in one of the old plantation houses, now converted to inns, and experience the calm still found here. If you want to lie out in the sun, head for reef-protected Pinney's Beach, a 3-mile strip of dark-gold sand set against a backdrop of palm trees, with panoramic views of St. Kitts.

Two miles south of St. Kitts, Nevis (*NEE-vis*) was sighted by Columbus in 1493. He called it Las Nieves, Spanish for "snows," because its mountains reminded him of the snow-capped range in the Pyrenees. When viewed from St. Kitts, the island appears like a perfect cone, rising gradually to a height of 3,232 feet. A saddle joins the tallest mountain to two smaller peaks, Saddle Hill (1,250 feet) in the south and Hurricane Hill (only 250 feet) in the north. Coral reefs rim the shoreline, and there's mile after mile of palm-shaded white-sand beaches.

Settled by the British in 1628, the volcanic island is famous as the birthplace of Alexander Hamilton, the American statesman who wrote many of the articles contained in the Federalist Papers and was Washington's secretary of the treasury. Nevis is also the island on which Admiral Horatio Lord Nelson married a local woman, Frances Nisbet, in 1787. The historical facts are romanticized, but this episode is described in James Michener's *Caribbean*.

In the 18th century, Nevis, the "Queen of the Caribees," was the leading spa of the West Indies, made so by its hot mineral springs. The island was also once peppered with prosperous sugarcane estates, but they're gone now—many have been converted into some of the most intriguing hotels in the Caribbean. Sea Island cotton is the chief crop today.

As you drive around the island, through tiny villages such as Gingerland (named for the spice it used to export), you'll reach the heavily wooded slopes of Nevis Peak, which offers views of the neighboring islands. Nevis is an island of beauty and has remained relatively unspoiled. Its people, in the main, are descendants of African slaves.

On the Caribbean side, **Charlestown,** the capital of Nevis, was fashionable in the 18th century, when sugar planters were carried around in carriages and sedan chairs. Houses are of locally quarried volcanic stone, encircled by West Indian fretted verandas. A town of wide, quiet streets, this port only gets busy when its major link to the world, the ferry from St. Kitts, docks at the harbor.

If Nevis succeeds in breaking from St. Kitts, with which it forms a two-island nation, it will become one of the smallest capitals in the world. But that doesn't mean it will necessarily be a Caribbean backwater: Already it has some 9,000 offshore businesses registered, or about one per inhabitant.

More than half of these businesses, operating under strict secrecy laws, have opened since the mid-1990s. Many of these are presumably just fronts to launder money for drug traffickers and other criminal enterprises, despite denials by certain Nevis officials. In fact, it was a spat with St. Kitts about controls over offshore banking activities that may lead to a breakup of this Caribbean ministate.

1 Essentials

VISITOR INFORMATION

Information is available from the St. Kitts and Nevis tourist board's offices at 414 E. 75th St., **New York, NY** 10021 (☎ **800/582-6208** or 212/535-1234); or 1464 Whippoorwill Way, **Mountainside, NJ** 07092 (☎ **208/233-6701**).

In **Canada,** an office is at 365 Bay St., Suite 806, Toronto, ON, M5H 2V1 (☎ **416/376-6707**), and in the **United Kingdom,** at 10 Kensington Court, London, W8 5DL (☎ **0171/376-0881**).

The Web site for both St. Kitts and Nevis is **www.stkitts-nevis.com**.

The best source for information on the island is the **Tourist Bureau,** on Main Street in Charlestown (☎ **869/469-1042**).

GETTING THERE

BY PLANE   You can fly to Nevis on **LIAT** (☎ **800/468-0482** in the U.S. and Canada, or 869/469-9333), which offers regularly scheduled service to the island. Flights from St. Kitts and Antigua are usually nonstop, while flights from St. Thomas, St. Croix, San Juan, Barbados, and Caracas, Venezuela, usually require at least one stop before reaching Nevis. It's only a 7-minute hop from St. Kitts.

Nevis Express (☎ **869/469-9755**) operates a daily shuttle service between St. Kitts and Nevis. A round-trip ticket from St. Kitts to Nevis costs $40. Call for reservations and information.

Any of North America's larger carriers, including **American Airlines** (☎ **800/433-7300**; www.aa.com), can arrange ongoing passage to Nevis on LIAT through such hubs as Antigua, San Juan, or St. Maarten, connecting with your flight from North America.

The airport lies half a mile from Newcastle in the northern part of the island.

BY FERRY   You can also use the interisland ferry service from St. Kitts to Charlestown, Nevis, aboard the government passenger ferry **M.V.** *Caribe Queen.* It departs from each island between 7 and 7:30am on Monday, Tuesday, Wednesday, Friday, and Saturday, returning at 4 and 6pm (check the time at your hotel or the tourist office). The cost is $4 each way. You can also take the air-conditioned, 110-passenger ferry **M.V.** *Spirit of Mount Nevis,* which sails twice daily on Thursday and Sunday, costing $6 one-way. Call **Nevis Cruise Lines** (☎ **869/469-9373**) for more information.

GETTING AROUND

BY TAXI Taxi drivers double as guides, and you'll find them waiting at the airport for the arrival of every plane. The fare between Charlestown and Newcastle Airport is EC$40 ($14.80); between Charlestown and Old Manor Estate, EC$30 ($11.10); and from Charlestown to Pinney's Beach, EC$13 ($4.80). Between 10pm and 6am, 50% is added to the prices for Charlestown trips. Call ☎ **869/469-5621** for more information.

BY RENTAL CAR If you're prepared to face the winding, rocky, potholed roads of Nevis, you can arrange for a rental car from a local firm through your hotel. Or you can check with **Skeete's Car Rental,** Newcastle Village, near the airport (☎ **869/ 469-9458**).

To drive on Nevis, you must obtain a permit from the traffic department, which costs EC$50 ($18.50) and is valid for a year. Car-rental companies will handle this for you. Remember, *drive on the left side of the road.*

Fast Facts: Nevis

Business Hours Banks are open Monday to Saturday from 8am to noon; most are also open on Friday from 3:30 to 5:30pm. Normal store hours are Monday to Friday from 8am to noon and 1 to 4pm, but on Thursday some places close in the afternoon, and on Saturday some stay open to 8pm. Most are closed Sunday.

Currency The local currency is the **Eastern Caribbean dollar (EC$),** valued at about $2.70 to the U.S. dollar. Many prices, however, including those of hotels, are quoted in U.S. dollars. Always determine which "dollar" locals are talking about.

Documents U.S. and Canadian citizens can enter with proof of citizenship, such as a passport or birth certificate with a raised seal, along with a photo ID. British subjects also need a passport, but not a visa. A return or ongoing ticket is also mandatory. Of course, if you clear customs in St. Kitts, you don't need to clear customs again in Nevis.

Drugstores See "Pharmacies," below.

Electricity As on St. Kitts, an electrical transformer and adapter will be needed for most U.S. and Canadian appliances as the electricity is 230 volts AC (60 cycles). However, check with your hotel to see if it has converted its voltage and outlets.

Emergencies For the police, call ☎ **911.**

Hospitals There's a 24-hour emergency room at **Alexandra Hospital**, Government Road, in Charlestown (☎ **869/469-5473**).

Language English is the language of the island and is spoken with a decided West Indian patois.

Pharmacies Try **Evelyn's Drugstore,** Charlestown (☎ **869/469-5278**), open Monday to Friday from 8am to 5:30pm (closes at 5pm on Thursday), Saturday from 8am to 7pm, and Sunday for only 1 hour, from 7 to 8pm, to serve emergency needs.

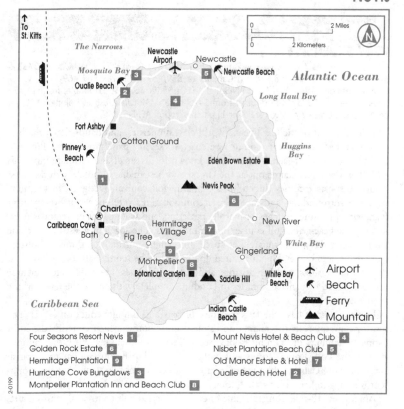

Four Seasons Resort Nevis **1**
Golden Rock Estate **6**
Hermitage Plantation **9**
Hurricane Cove Bungalows **3**
Montpelier Plantation Inn and Beach Club **8**

Mount Nevis Hotel & Beach Club **4**
Nisbet Plantation Beach Club **5**
Old Manor Estate & Hotel **7**
Oualie Beach Hotel **2**

Post Office The post office, on Main Street in Charlestown, is open Monday to Wednesday and on Friday from 8am to 3pm, Thursday from 8 to 11am, and Saturday from 8am to noon.

Safety Although crime is rare here, protect your valuables and never leave them unguarded on the beach.

Taxes The government imposes a 7% tax on hotel bills, plus a departure tax of EC$27 ($10) per person. You don't have to pay the departure tax on Nevis if you're returning to St. Kitts.

Telephone Telegrams and telexes can be sent from the **Cable & Wireless office,** Main Street, Charlestown (☎ **869/469-5000**). International phone calls, including collect calls, can also be made from the cable office. It's open Monday to Friday from 8am to 5pm, Saturday from 8am to noon.

Time As with St. Kitts, Nevis is on Atlantic standard time year-round, which means it's usually 1 hour ahead of the U.S. East Coast, except when the mainland goes on daylight saving time and clocks are the same.

Tipping A 10% service charge is added to your hotel bill. In restaurants, it's customary to tip 10% to 15% of the tab.

Water In the 1700s, Lord Nelson regularly brought his fleet to Nevis just to collect water, and Nevis still boasts of having Nelson spring water.

2 Where to Stay

VERY EXPENSIVE

✪ **Four Seasons Resort Nevis.** Pinney's Beach, Charlestown, Nevis, W.I. ☎ **800/332-3442** in the U.S., 800/268-6282 in Canada, or 869/469-1111. Fax 869/469-1112. www.fourseasons.com. 196 units. A/C MINIBAR TV TEL. Winter $625–$685 double; from $1,175 suite. Off-season $275–$485 double; from $475 suite. MAP (breakfast and dinner) $80 per person extra. Up to 2 children stay free in parents' room. AE, DC, MC, V.

This hotel is one of the Caribbean's world-class properties, and hands-down the best choice on the island. Located on its west coast, it's set in a palm grove beside Pinney's, Nevis's finest sandy beach. On an island known for its small and intimate inns, this 1991 low-rise resort stands out as the largest and best-managed hotel, with the most complete sports facilities (including a fabulous golf course). Designed in harmony with the surrounding landscape, the accommodations offer rich but conservative mahogany furniture, touches of marble, carpeting, and wide patios or verandas overlooking the beach, the golf course, or Mount Nevis. The spacious guest rooms come with coffeemakers, generous closet space, full-length mirrors, luxurious upholstery and fabrics, and queen, king, or paired double beds. The roomy bathrooms have hair dryers, double sinks, makeup mirrors, and Bulgari toiletries. The public areas include rooms inspired by paneled libraries in London, complete with one of the few working fireplaces on Nevis.

Dining: Guests have the largest choice of bars and dining venues on Nevis. The resort's centerpiece is the plantation-inspired great house, which contains the most formal restaurant, the Dining Room (see "Where to Dine," below). Other options include the Grill Room (steaks and barbecues), the Tap Room (similar to a British pub), the Pool Cabaña, the Ocean Terrace (drinks and light fare), and the most opulent watering hole on Nevis, the Library Bar.

Amenities: 18-hole Robert Trent Jones, Jr.–designed golf course, 10 tennis courts with three different surfaces, on-site scuba department, massage facilities, health club, sauna, whirlpool, beauty salon, two pools. 24-hour room service, laundry, babysitting. Employees can arrange diving, deep-sea fishing, boating, hiking, or shopping excursions. A flotilla of yachts is on hand to ferry guests to and from the international airport on St. Kitts. "Kids for All Seasons" is one of the most carefully planned youth programs in the Caribbean; there's a supervised children's hour at 6pm daily in the Grill Room.

Hermitage Plantation. Hermitage Village, St. John's Parish, Nevis, W.I. ☎ **800/682-4025** in the U.S., or 869/469-3477. Fax 869/469-2481. www.hermitagenevis.com. E-mail: nevherm@caribsurf.com. 15 units, 1 manor house. Winter $325–$450 double; $790 manor house. Off-season $170–$260 double; $650 manor house. AE, MC, V. Take the main island road 4 miles from Charlestown.

This much-photographed, frequently copied historians' delight is said to be the oldest all-wood house in the Antilles and was built amid the high-altitude plantations of Gingerland in 1740. Some believe it welcomed Alexander Hamilton and Horatio Nelson at one time. Today, former Philadelphian Richard Lupinacci and his wife, Maureen, have assembled one of the best collections of antiques on Nevis. Wide-plank floors, intricate latticework, and high ceilings add to the hotel's beauty. The accommodations are in nine glamorous outbuildings designed like small plantation houses. Many contain huge four-poster beds, antique accessories, and colonial louvered windows. Extras include private safes, fridges, and coffeemakers. The spotlessly maintained private bathrooms contain hair dryers and combination tub/showers. The most luxurious and expensive unit is a yellow manor house on a half acre of private gardens with its own ceramic-tile pool, two large bedrooms furnished with antique canopy beds, oversize bathrooms with dressing rooms, a comfortable living room, dining room, full kitchen, and laundry. Gently sloping inland from the sea, the property is protected by rows of retaining walls.

Amenities include a pool, tennis court, thoroughbred stables, and laundry service. Complimentary beach transportation is provided; the best nearby beach is a 15-minute drive.

✪ **Montpelier Plantation Inn & Beach Club.** St. John Figtree (P.O. Box 474), Montpelier, Nevis, W.I. ☎ **800/223-9832** in the U.S., 869/469-3462, or 212/252-1818 in New York City. Fax 869/469-2932. www.montpeliernevis.com. E-mail: montpinn@caribsurf.com. 17 units. TEL. Winter $310 double. Off-season $210 double. Year-round $360 suite. Rates include breakfast. MC, V. Children under 8 not accepted in winter. Closed mid-Aug to Sept.

One of the Plantation Inns of Nevis, the Montpelier stands in the hills, 700 feet high, with grandstand views of the ocean. It's owner-managed, and a house-party atmosphere prevails. Diana, the late Princess of Wales, made the inn her choice during a 1993 visit. The 18th-century plantation is in the center of its own 100-acre estate, which contains 10 acres of ornamental gardens that surround the cottage units. Accommodations are generally spacious and brightened with fresh flowers, along with amenities ranging from desk space to coffeemakers, comfortable chairs to excellent mattresses, dressing tables to private safes. Bathrooms, with glass-enclosed tubs and hair dryers, are kept sparkling clean. Everything here is done with style and grace.

Dining/Diversions: Montpelier focuses on the standards of its food, wine, and service. Much use is made of fresh local produce (see "Where to Dine," below). Breakfast is served in the garden room, dinner on a covered terrace overlooking the garden. In season, a steel or string band is brought in about every 10 days.

Amenities: Huge pool with pool bar, hard tennis court, transportation to a private beach 4 to 5 miles away, windsurfing, horseback riding, hiking, ecorambles. Laundry, baby-sitting (evenings), room service (for continental breakfast only).

Nisbet Plantation Beach Club. Newcastle, St. James's Parish, Nevis, W.I. ☎ **800/742-6008** in the U.S. and Canada, or 869/469-9325. Fax 869/469-9864. E-mail: nisbethbc@caribsurf.com. 38 units. Winter $425–$515 double; from $525 suite. Off-season $255–$295 double; from $325 suite. Rates include MAP (breakfast and dinner). AE, DISC, MC, V. Turn left out of the airport and go 1 mile.

A respect for fine living prevails in this gracious estate house on a coconut plantation. This is the former home of Frances Nisbet who, at the age of 22, married Lord Nelson. Although enamored of Miss Nisbet when he married her, Lord Nelson later fell in love with Lady Hamilton (as detailed in the classic film *That Hamilton Woman*).

The present main building was rebuilt on the foundations of the original 18th-century great house. The ruins of a circular sugar mill stand at the entrance, covered with bougainvillea, hibiscus, and poinciana. Guest cottages are set in the palm grove. All rooms are brightly decorated and beautifully appointed, with king-size beds and firm mattresses. The bathrooms, with combination tub/showers, are tidily maintained.

Dining/Diversions: Breakfast and lunch are served at the Coconuts Beach and Poolside Restaurant, where a Thursday evening barbecue features a live band. Dinner is offered inside the great house. Local fish and lobster are featured, along with continental and American cuisine. Among the complimentary extras are afternoon tea and a rum-punch party.

Amenities: Pool, tennis court, snorkeling opportunities off the beach, 3 miles of beachcombing right in front of the hotel. Scuba diving, sport fishing, sailing, horseback riding, ecorambles, mountain hiking, and golf at the Four Seasons can be arranged. Laundry.

EXPENSIVE

Golden Rock Estate. P.O. Box 493, Gingerland, Nevis, W.I. ☎ **869/469-3346**. Fax 869/469-2113. 16 units. Winter $260 double; $295 suite. Off-season $190 double; $225 suite. Rates include MAP (breakfast and dinner). Children under 2 stay free in parents' room. AE, MC, V.

This former sugar estate was built in 1815, high in the hills of Nevis. A 15-minute drive east of Charlestown, Golden Rock is one of the most charming and atmospheric inns in the Caribbean, set on 100 lushly tropical acres and fronted by a 25-acre garden. The original windmill, a stone tower, has been turned into a duplex honeymoon suite (or accommodations for a family of four), with a four-poster bed. Cottages are scattered about the garden, and each has a four-poster king-size bed made of bamboo. Rooms have large porches with views of the sea as well. Fabrics are island made, with tropical flower designs. Guests live in fairly spacious surroundings here, in a setting of pineapple friezes, island crafts, family heirlooms, and tile flowers. Bathrooms are a bit small, with shower stalls, but each comes with a generous set of good-sized towels.

There's access to one beach on the leeward side (part of Pinney's Beach) and another beach on the windward side, where there's surfing. The hotel also lies at the beginning of a rain-forest walk; it takes about 3 to 4 hours to follow the trail round-trip (the hotel provides a map).

Dining/Diversions: Dinner is likely to be a West Indian meal served at the 175-year-old "long house." Saturday night from December to June, there's a West Indian buffet, served plantation style, while a string band plays outside under the stars. Before dinner you can enjoy a drink in the hotel's bar. A separate facility at Pinney's Beach, the Old Fort, serves lobster, shrimp, grilled fish, and hamburgers with coconut-husk flavor; it's open daily in winter. Picnic lunches can be prepared in the hotel's kitchen.

Amenities: Freshwater pool with a shady terrace (where tropical rum punches are served), tennis court, nature trail through the rain forest. Scuba, snorkeling, windsurfing, and horseback riding, along with day sailing, can be arranged. Laundry, baby-sitting, free round-trip shuttles to both beaches (with stops in Charlestown if requested).

Mount Nevis Hotel & Beach Club. Newcastle (P.O. Box 494), Charlestown, Nevis, W.I. ☎ **800/75-NEVIS** in the U.S. and Canada, 869/469-9373, or 212/874-4276 in New York City. Fax 869/469-9375. www.mountnevishotel.com. E-mail: mountnevis@aol.com. 32 units. A/C TV. Winter $210–$235 double; $300 junior suite. Off-season $145–$165 double; $210 junior suite. Rates include continental breakfast. Extra person $35. AE, MC, V.

This family-owned and -run resort dating from 1989 is on the slopes of Mount Nevis, a 5-minute drive southwest of Newcastle Airport. It's known for the quality of its accommodations, for its panoramic views, and for serving some of the best food on Nevis. Near the historic fishing village of Newcastle, it offers standard rooms and junior suites, the latter with fully equipped kitchens and space enough to accommodate at least four guests comfortably, making it an ideal family choice. The rooms have such amenities as VCRs and ceiling fans, and are furnished in a tropical motif, with wicker and colorful island prints. The tidily maintained private bathrooms are well equipped with hair dryers, a shower stall, and a set of thick towels.

Dining/Diversions: See "Where to Dine," below, for a review of the hotel's main restaurant. Just a 5-minute drive from the hotel, the Mount Nevis Beach Club offers a site on Newcastle Bay and features a beach pavilion, bar, and restaurant. It pretty much introduced pizza to the island. The club is open November to June, daily from 10am to 10pm. Occasional entertainment is offered.

Amenities: Outdoor 60-foot pool. Water sports such as windsurfing, waterskiing, snorkeling, and deep-sea fishing can be arranged. Beach shuttle, exercise room.

Old Manor Estate & Hotel. P.O. Box 70, Gingerland, Nevis, W.I. ☎ **800/892-7093** or 869/469-3445. Fax 869/469-3388. 13 units. Winter $230–$250 double. Off-season $165–$195 double. Rates include continental breakfast. AE, MC, V.

East of Charlestown and north of Gingerland, at a cool and comfortable elevation of 800 feet, the Old Manor Estate & Hotel has an old-world grace, lying a 15- to 20-minute drive from Pinney's Beach, where the hotel operates its own beach bar and grill. When Nevis was originally colonized, the forested plot of land on which the hotel sits was granted to the Croney family in 1690 by the king of England. The estate thrived as a working sugar plantation until 1936. Today, the stately ruins of its great house, once described by British historians as "the best example of Georgian domestic architecture in the Caribbean," complement the hotel's outbuildings. The rusted fly-wheels of cane-crushing machines are scattered around the property. Since its acquisition by new owners in 1995, the hotel has been renovated and now has a far more cheerful, tropical appearance. The color scheme of green and light peach blends beautifully with the cut stonework of the plantation buildings. Ongoing improvements are being made, since the property had fallen into decline. Accommodations contain wide-plank floors of tropical hardwoods, reproduction furniture, and high ceilings. Bathrooms come with hair dryers; some are shower-only.

The Cooperage dining room (see "Where to Dine," below) is among the best on the island. Facilities include a beach and town shuttle, a pool, and a Jacuzzi.

MODERATE

Hurricane Cove Bungalows. Oualie Beach, Nevis, W.I. ☎ and fax **869/469-9462.** E-mail: hcove@caribsurf.com. 11 units. Winter $145–$225 one-bedroom bungalow; $225–$265 two-bedroom bungalow; $445 three-bedroom villa. Off-season $95–$180 one-bedroom bungalow; $155–$200 two-bedroom bungalow; $225–$325 three-bedroom villa. DISC, MC, V.

This cluster of self-contained bungalows is set on a hillside with a world-class view, a far better sight than the complex's rather ramshackle facade. It's located on the northernmost point of Nevis, a 5-minute drive west of the airport. Each bungalow is wood-sided and vaguely Scandinavian in design, with a tile roof and a massive foundation that anchors it into the rocky hillside. No meals are served, but each unit has a full kitchen; guests can dine out every night or prepare meals themselves, either in their own kitchens or at a poolside barbecue grill. Each bungalow contains a queen-size bed with a firm mattress, a covered porch, a ceiling fan, and a coffeemaker. The small, compact bathrooms are efficiently organized with adequate shelf space, a shower stall, and a set of medium-size towels. There's a freshwater pool built into the foundation of a 250-year-old fortification, and the beach lies at the bottom of a steep hillside. The three-bedroom villa has its own small, but private, pool.

Oualie Beach Hotel. Oualie Bay, Nevis, W.I. ☎ **800/682-5431** or 869/469-9735. Fax 869/469-9176. www.oualie.com. E-mail: oualie@oualie.com. 28 units. A/C TV TEL. Winter $195–$225 double; $255 studio. Off-season $140–$155 double; $205 studio. AE, MC, V.

This place is often fully booked several months in advance by European sun-worshipers. Set on low-lying flatlands adjacent to the white sands of the island's second-most-famous beach (Oualie Beach), the hotel consists of four concrete outbuildings. Each medium-size unit is clean and simple, with tiled floors and small fridges; 18 rooms are air-conditioned, and a few have kitchenettes. Extras include full-length mirrors, irons and ironing board, mahogany furnishings, and double or four-poster queen-size beds. Baths are small with shower only. The resort's centerpiece is its well-recommended restaurant and bar, where doors open directly onto a view of the beach (see "Where to Dine," below).

3 Where to Dine

VERY EXPENSIVE

✪ **The Dining Room.** In the Four Seasons Resort Nevis, Pinney's Beach. ☎ **869/469-1111.** Reservations recommended. Main courses $26–$45. AE, DC, MC, V. Daily 6:30–10pm. INTERNATIONAL/WEST INDIAN/ASIAN.

Set beneath a soaring, elaborately trussed ceiling, this is the largest and most formal dining room on Nevis, and the island's best and most expensive restaurant. Decorated in a Caribbean interpretation of French Empire design, it offers rows of beveled-glass windows on three sides, massive bouquets of flowers, hurricane lamps with candles, a fireplace, a collection of unusual paintings, and impeccable service.

The fusion cuisine, with lots of nouvelle touches, roams the world for inspiration. Only quality ingredients are used, and some dishes are low in fat and calories. The menu changes nightly, but appearing with frequency are savory seafood gumbo, or Cuban black-bean soup with applewood-smoked bacon. The pan-seared salmon with a curried fruit relish is incomparably fragrant, although the grilled mahimahi with a wasabi-mango sauce is equally tempting. Vegetarians also have options here, perhaps vegetable cannelloni gratiné with a purple-basil–tomato sauce. Dessert might be a flaming meringue "Mount Nevis." The service and the wine selection are the island's best.

Hermitage Plantation. Hermitage Village, St. John's Parish. ☎ **869/469-3477.** Reservations required. Lunch $20, dinner $50. AE, MC, V. Daily 8–10am, noon–3pm, and dinner at 8pm. Go south on the main island road from Charlestown. INTERNATIONAL.

At this restaurant, you can combine an excellent dinner with a visit to the oldest house on Nevis, now one of the island's most unusual hotels (see "Where to Stay," above). Meals are served on the latticed porch of the main house, amid candles and good cheer. Maureen Lupinacci, who runs the place with her husband, Richard, combines continental recipes with local ingredients. Enjoy a before-dinner drink in the colonial-style living room, then move on to the likes of snapper steamed in banana leaves, carrot-and-tarragon soup, brown-bread ice cream, and a delectable version of rum soufflé. Many people turn up on Wednesday for the roast-pig dinner.

✪ **Miss June's.** Jones Bay. ☎ **869/469-5330.** Reservations required. Fixed-price meal $50–$65. MC, V. 3 to 5 evenings a week, depending on business, beginning around 7:30pm. CARIBBEAN/INTERNATIONAL.

This charming venue, midway between the Four Seasons Resort and the airport, is the private home of June Mestier, a Trinidad-born grande dame, and probably wouldn't exist if it had not been for an enthusiastic visit from Oprah Winfrey. On a recent trip, Oprah heard that Ms. Mestier was the finest cook on the island and arranged a private dinner; after being served an excellent meal, Oprah urged her to open a restaurant.

A dinner in Mestier's home, which is adorned with latticework and Victorian gingerbread, requires advance reservations; some visitors call before they even arrive on Nevis. Guests at these dinner parties assemble for canapés and drinks in an airy living room, then sit down for soup and sherry. The tables hold from 2 to 10 diners, and the silver and porcelain are quaintly elegant and charmingly mismatched. Fish and wine follow. All of this is followed with samples of about 20 to 30 buffet dishes that hail from Trinidad, New Orleans, India, and the French isles. Ms. Mestier's comments on the food are one of the evening's most delightful aspects. After dinner, guests retire to a lounge for dessert and port. Many visitors find the meal to be one of the highlights of their visit to Nevis.

Montpelier Plantation Inn and Beach Club. Montpelier. ☎ **869/469-3462.** Reservations recommended for lunch, required for dinner. Fixed-price dinner $45–$55. MC, V. Daily 12:30–2pm and dinner at 8pm. Closed mid-Aug to Sept. INTERNATIONAL.

This hotel, a mile off the main island road to Gingerland, provides some of the finest dining on the island. You sit by candlelight on the verandas of a grand old West Indian mansion, overlooking floodlit gardens, the lights of Charlestown, and the ocean. Lobster and fish are served the day the catch comes in, and the foreign and Nevisian chefs conspire to produce delectable tropical dishes. Menu items might include Cajun prawns, fresh tuna salad, mussels Provençale, curried ackee, suckling pig, and soursop-and-orange mousse for dessert. There's one seating for dinner, so try to show up on time. An excellent and well-balanced wine list is available.

EXPENSIVE/MODERATE

✪ **The Cooperage.** In the Old Manor Estate, Gingerland. ☎ **869/469-3445.** Reservations recommended, especially for nonguests. Main courses $16–$30. AE, MC, V. Daily 6:30am–9:30pm. INTERNATIONAL/CARIBBEAN.

Directly east of Charlestown and north of Gingerland, the Cooperage is set in a reconstructed 17th-century building where "coopers" once made barrels for the sugar mill. The dining room has a high, raftered ceiling and stone walls. The food doesn't even try to compete with that at the Four Seasons, but it's good and reliable. Some of the appetizers are those 1950s favorites: French onion soup or shrimp cocktail. For a main course, you can order a 12-ounce New York strip steak or charcoal-grilled filet mignon with a béarnaise sauce. The grilled Caribbean lobster is also appealing, as is the Nevisian pork. The menu harkens back to the days when appetites were more robust—main dishes are served with fresh vegetables of the day and your choice of twice-baked potato, rice, or pasta. Few leave hungry, especially after finishing with Old Manor's cheesecake, which has been sampled by all the movers and shakers on the island.

Mount Nevis Hotel Restaurant. Newcastle. ☎ **869/469-9373.** Reservations recommended for dinner. Main courses $10–$13 lunch, $18–$32 dinner. AE, MC, V. Daily 8–10am and 11:30am–2:30pm; Mon–Sat 6:30–8:30pm. CARIBBEAN/CONTINENTAL.

The restaurant in this previously recommended hotel is a discovery, serving some of the finest cuisine on Nevis with menus that change every night. New chef Daryl Basse, of the Citranel Restaurant in Washington, D.C., has done a wonderful job of embracing the local tastes with a big-city gourmet twist. Just steps above the pool, the restaurant offers vistas of palm groves and the Caribbean Sea from its bar and dining terrace. You never know what's likely to be featured: A very smooth yet spicy conch chowder might get you going, or an equally delectable coconut-fried lobster with grilled pineapple and green-chili salsa, providing a sweet island flavor. The standard fillet of grouper, snapper, or mahimahi that occupies every menu in the Caribbean is also here, as chef Basso tends to prepare only what he can obtain locally. A lamb shank, another fairly standard menu item, is also delectable here, with an array of local vegetables. A worthy specialty is the roast duck breast, raised locally, and served with wild mushrooms and leek. The duck confit salad is also worth a try. The lunch menu is more limited but still filled with some surprises—tannia fritters (instead of conch), for example. In addition to pita pockets and club sandwiches (including a delicious lobster club), you can even order a West Indian rôti, the traditional Caribbean crêpe.

Oualie Beach Hotel. Oualie Bay. ☎ **869/469-9735.** Reservations recommended for dinner. Breakfast $6–$11; lunch $7–$16; dinner main courses $18–$24.50. AE, MC, V. Daily 7–10am, noon–4pm, and 7–11pm. INTERNATIONAL/NEVISIAN.

This restaurant is the centerpiece of the Oualie Beach Hotel (see "Where to Stay," above), the only lodging adjacent to Oualie Beach. An airy, open-sided building with a pleasant staff and a setting a few steps from the ocean, it contains a bar area, a screened-in veranda, and a chalkboard menu with the day's special. Depending on the catch that day, it might be broiled wahoo. The chef also prepares several lobster dishes, and the Creole conch stew is the island's best. Pastas appear frequently on the menu, along with some fairly bland international dishes such as spinach-stuffed chicken breast. Every day, however, the chef prepares a creative menu with real Caribbean flair, so you may want to study it closely before ordering. Any of an array of brightly colored rum drinks is available, and you can get a reasonably priced breakfast or lunch here, too.

INEXPENSIVE

✪ **Eddy's.** Main St., Charlestown. ☎ **869/496-5958.** Main courses EC$28–EC$50 ($10.35–$18.50). AE, MC, V. Mon–Wed and Fri–Sat 11:45am–3pm and 7–9:30pm. INTERNATIONAL.

Set on the upper floor of a plank-sided Nevisian house in the center of Charlestown, this local restaurant is open on three sides to the prevailing winds and offers an eagle's-eye view of street life in the island's capital. Its balcony juts out over the pedestrian traffic below, and the clean and airy interior contains a tuckaway bar, lattices and gingerbread, and lots of tropical color. The menu items, posted on one of several signs, are among the best prepared in Charlestown. Featured are such dishes as Eddy's fish cioppino with roasted garlic-mayonnaise croutons and juicy tandoori-sauced chicken. For a new twist on a traditional favorite, try the lime-glazed seafood kebabs with black-bean salsa. No one will mind if you arrive only for a drink at the corner bar, but you'll be missing out on a tasty meal.

Muriel's Cuisine. Upper Happyhill Dr., Charlestown. ☎ **869/469-5920.** Reservations recommended. Lunch EC$15–EC$30 ($5.55–$11.10); dinner EC$25–EC$65 ($9.25–$24.05). AE, MC, V. Daily 8–10am and 11:30am–7pm. WEST INDIAN.

This restaurant is in the back of a concrete building whose front is devoted to a store, Limetree. It's a 6-minute walk from Charlestown's waterfront and set in an outlying neighborhood of low-rise commercial buildings. Head here for a slice of real island life, and for a West Indian cuisine that's typical of what the locals eat. Muriel's curries are the best in town, ranging from the simple goat or chicken to the more elaborate lobster. She also turns out some fabulous chicken or seafood rôtis, and even a lobster Creole for those who want to get fancy. Her jerk pork or chicken would win the approval of a Jamaican, and her preparations of conch, stewed or curried, are worth the trip. If you want to go native all the way, ask for saltfish or goatwater stew.

Tequila Sheila's. Cades Bay. ☎ **869/469-8139.** Reservations recommended. Main courses EC$20–EC$35 ($7.40–$12.95) lunch, EC$28–EC$60 ($10.35–$22.20) dinner. Daily noon–3:30pm and 7–10pm. WEST INDIAN/INTERNATIONAL.

Named after one of its owners, a soft-spoken woman who isn't nearly as raucous as her name would imply, this restaurant is on the premises of the Inn at Cades Bay. Set on a wooden platform less than 60 feet from the seafront, with a covered parapet but without walls, it offers panoramic views as far away as St. Kitts, and a menu that incorporates West Indian, Mexican, and international cuisine. Lunchtime brings dishes such as rôti, enchiladas, grilled or jerk chicken, and lobster quesadillas. Dinner platters include vegetable-stuffed chicken, lobster, New York strip steak with horse-radish sauce or béarnaise sauce, and fish. Flying fish, wahoo, and mahimahi are very fresh here, and prepared as simply as possible—usually grilled with lemon juice and herbs—as a means of allowing the flavors to shine. The bar, fashioned from an over-turned fishing boat, offers margaritas, various brands of tequila, and all the usual party-colored drinks you'd expect.

4 Beaches

The best beach on Nevis—in fact, one of the best in the Caribbean—is the reef-protected ✪ **Pinney's Beach,** which has gin-clear water, golden sands, and a gradual slope; it's just a short walk north of Charlestown on the west coast. You'll have 3 miles of sand (often virtually to yourself) that culminates in a sleepy lagoon, set against a backdrop of coconut palms. It's almost never crowded, and its calm, shallow waters are perfect for swimming. It's also ideal for wading, which makes it a family favorite. The chic and super-expensive Four Seasons Resort lies in the middle of this beach. It's best to bring your own sports equipment; the hotels are stocked with limited gear that may be in use by its guests. You can go snorkeling or scuba diving here among damselfish, tangs, grunts, blue-headed wrasses, and parrot fish, among other species. The beach is especially beautiful in the late afternoon, when flocks of cattle egrets fly into its north end to roost at the freshwater pond at Nelson's Spring.

If your time on Nevis is limited, go to Pinney's. But if you're going to be around for a few more days, you might want to search out the other beaches, notably beige-sand **Oualie Beach,** known especially for its diving and snorkeling. The location is north of Pinney's, and just south of Mosquito Bay. The beach is well maintained and rarely crowded; you can purchase food and drink, as well as rent water-sports equipment, at the Oualie Beach Hotel.

Indian Castle Beach, at the very southern tip of Nevis, is rarely sought out. It has an active surf and a swath of fine-gray sand. Indian Castle is definitely for escapists—chances are you'll have the beach all to yourself except for an indigenous goat or two, who may be very social and interested in sharing your picnic lunch.

Newcastle Beach is by the Nisbet Plantation, at the northernmost tip of the island on the channel that separates St. Kitts and Nevis. Snorkelers flock to this strip of soft, beige sand set against a backdrop of coconut palms.

The beaches along the east coast aren't desirable. They front Long Haul Bay in the north and White Bay in the south. These bays spill into the Atlantic ocean and are rocky and too rough for swimming, although rather dramatic to visit if you're sightseeing. Of them all, **White Bay Beach** (sometimes called Windward Beach), in the southeastern section, east of Gingerland, is the most desirable. If you want some chillier Atlantic swimming, head here—but be careful, as the waters can suddenly turn turbulent.

5 Sports & Outdoor Pursuits

BOATING   Scuba Safaris, an outfit that operates independently on the premises of the Oualie Beach Hotel (☎ **869/469-9518**), offers boat charters to Banana Bay and Cockleshell Bay, which can make for a great day's outing; it costs $50 round-trip.

FISHING   Nevis Water Sports (☎ **869/469-9060**) offers the best deep-sea fishing aboard its custom 31-foot fishing boat. Holding up to six fishers, it charges $350 for 4 hours or $700 for 8 hours.

GOLF The ✪ **Four Seasons Golf Course,** Pinney's Beach (☎ 869/469-1111), has one of the most challenging and visually dramatic golf courses in the world. Designed by Robert Trent Jones, Jr. (who called it "the most scenic golf course I've ever designed"), this 18-hole championship course wraps around the resort and offers panoramic ocean and mountain views at every turn. From the first tee (which begins just steps from the well-accessorized sports pavilion), through the 660-yard, par-5, to the 18th green at the ocean's edge, the course is, in the words of one avid golfer, "reason enough to go to Nevis." Guests of the hotel pay $125 for 18 holes; nonguests are charged $150. Rental clubs are available, costing $40 for 18 holes.

HIKING & MOUNTAIN CLIMBING Hikers can climb **Mount Nevis,** 3,232 feet up to the extinct volcanic crater, and enjoy a trek to the rain forest to watch for wild monkeys. This hike is strenuous and is recommended only to the stout of heart. Ask your hotel to pack a picnic lunch and arrange a guide (who will charge about $35 per person). The hike takes about 5 hours, and once at the summit you'll be rewarded with views of Antigua, Saba, Statia, St. Kitts, Guadeloupe, and Montserrat. Of course, you've got to reach that summit, which means scrambling up near-vertical sections of the trail requiring handholds on not-always-reliable vines and roots. It's definitely not for acrophobes! Guides can also be arranged at the **Nevis Historical and Conservation Society,** based at the Museum of Nevis History, Main Street, Charlestown (☎ 869/469-5786).

Eco-Tours Nevis (☎ 869/469-2091) offers three uniquely different walking tours of the 36-mile island. The expeditions explore the shore, tropical forests, and historic ruins. They're taken at a leisurely pace, requiring only an average level of fitness. The 2½-hour "Eco-Ramble," on the windswept, uninhabited east coast, covers the 18th-century New River and Coconut Walk Estates. Participants will see the diverse ecology of Nevis, discover archaeological evidence of pre-Colombian Amerindian settlers, and visit the remains of the last working sugar factory on Nevis. The cost is $20.

The easy, 2½-hour "Mountravers Hike" takes a close look at Montraverse House, one of the hidden secrets of Nevis. These great-house ruins are spectacular. The cost for this walk is $20.

"Historic Charlestown," 1½ hours, takes you through the charming, Victorian-era capital to explore its rich and turbulent past: 300 years of fire, earthquake, hurricanes, and warfare. The cost is $10.

Shorts, socks, and closed shoes are suitable for all three walking tours. A hat is a welcome addition; suitable casual attire is appreciated in Charlestown (no swim suits). The "Eco-Ramble" is recommended for children over 12; the other tours are not suitable for kids. All walking tours are offered on a reservation-only basis.

HORSEBACK RIDING Horseback riding is available at the **Nisbet Plantation Beach Club,** Newcastle (☎ 869/469-9325). You can ride English saddle, and the cost is $45 per person for 45 minutes. A guide takes you along mountain trails to visit sites of long-forgotten plantations.

SCUBA DIVING & SNORKELING Some of the best dive sites on Nevis include **Monkey Shoals,** 2 miles west of the Four Seasons. This is a beautiful reef starting at 40 feet, with dives up to 100 feet in depth. Angelfish, turtles, nurse sharks, and extensive soft coral can be found here. **The Caves** are on the south tip of Nevis, a 20-minute boat ride from the Four Seasons. A series of coral grottoes with numerous squirrelfish, turtles, and needlefish make this ideal for both certified and resort divers. **Champagne Garden,** a 5-minute boat ride from the Four Seasons, gets its name from bubbles created from an underwater sulfur vent. Because of the warm water temperature, large numbers of tropical fish are found here. Finally, **Coral Garden,** 2 miles west of the

Four Seasons, is another beautiful coral reef with schools of Atlantic spadefish and large sea fans. The reef is at a maximum depth of 70 feet and is suitable for both certified and resort divers.

Snorkelers should head for Pinney's Beach. You might also try the waters of Fort Ashby, where the settlement of Jamestown is said to have slid into the sea; legend has it that the church bells can still be heard, and the undersea town can still be seen when conditions are just right. So far, no diver, to our knowledge, has ever found the conditions "just right."

Scuba Safaris, Oualie Beach (☎ **869/469-9518**), on the island's north end, offers PADI scuba diving and snorkeling in an area rich in dive sites. It also offers resort and certification courses, dive packages, and equipment rental. A one-tank scuba dive costs $45; a two-tank dive, $80. Full certification courses cost $450 per person. Snorkeling trips cost $35 per person. Boat charters to Banana Bay and Cockleshell Bay are offered.

TENNIS   Some of the big hotels have tennis courts, but you must call in advance and see if nonguests are allowed to play. They may charge a fee. Outside of the posh Four Seasons resort, the best courts are at **Pinney's Beach hotel**, Pinney's Beach, just outside Charlestown (☎ **869/469-5207**); **Golden Rock**, Gingerland (☎ **869/ 469-3346**); and **Nisbet Plantation**, Newcastle Beach (☎ **869/469-9325**).

WINDSURFING   The waters here are often ideal for this sport, especially for beginners and intermediates. **Windsurfing Nevis** at the Oualie Beach Hotel (☎ **869/ 469-9682**), offers the best equipment, costing $25 for 30 minutes.

6 Exploring the Island

Negotiate with a taxi driver to take you around Nevis. The distance is only 20 miles, but you may find yourself taking a long time if you stop to see specific sights and talk to all the people who will want to chat with you. A 3-hour sightseeing tour around the island will cost $60; the average taxi holds up to four people. No sightseeing bus companies operate on Nevis, but a number of individuals own buses that they use for taxi service. Call **All Seasons Streamline Tours** (☎ **869/469-5705** or 869/ 469-1138) for information.

The major attraction is the **Museum of Nevis History,** in the house where Alexander Hamilton was born, on Main Street in Charlestown (☎ **869/469-5786**), overlooking the bay. Hamilton was the illegitimate son of a Scotsman and Rachel Fawcett, a Nevisian of Huguenot ancestry. The family immigrated to St. Croix, and from there Alexander made his way to the North American colonies, where he became the first secretary of the U.S. Treasury. His picture, of course, appears on the U.S. $10 bill. The lava-stone house by the shore has been restored. The museum, dedicated to the history and culture of Nevis, houses the island's archives. Hours are Monday to Friday from 8am to 4pm, Saturday from 10am to noon. Admission is $2 for adults, $1 for children.

The **Eden Brown Estate,** about 1½ miles from New River, is said to be haunted. Once, it was the home of a wealthy planter, whose daughter was to be married, but her husband-to-be was killed in a duel at the prenuptial feast. The mansion was then closed forever and left to the ravages of nature. A gray solid stone still stands. Only the most adventurous come here on a moonlit night.

At one time, Sephardic Jews who came from Brazil made up a quarter of the island's population, and it's believed that Jews introduced sugar production into the Leewards. Outside the center of Charlestown, at the lower end of Government Road, the **Jewish**

Cemetery has been restored and is the resting place of many of the early shopkeepers of Nevis. Most of the tombstones date from between 1690 and 1710.

An archaeological team from the United States believes that an old stone building in partial ruin on Nevis is probably the oldest **Jewish synagogue** in the Caribbean. Preliminary findings in 1993 traced the building's history to one of the two oldest Jewish settlements in the West Indies, and current work at the site plus historic documents in England establish its existence prior to 1650. The site is located adjacent to the government administration building in Charlestown.

One of the island's newest attractions is the 8-acre **Botanical Garden of Nevis** (☎ 869/469-3509), 3 miles south of Charlestown on the Montpelier Estate. Rainforest plants grow in re-created Mayan ruins on a hillside site overlooking the Caribbean. The on-site restaurant serves an English tea with scones and double Devon cream. You can also order a Plowman's Lunch (French bread, pickled onions, and cheese). If you patronize the restaurant and gift shop, the admission of $8 to the gardens is eliminated. The garden is open daily from 10am to 6pm.

A bit incongruous for Nevis, **Caribbean Cove**, Stoney Grove (☎ 869/469-1286), is an amusement park which is just as popular with locals as visitors. A 2-acre, multimillion-dollar facility, it was created by Joseph Murphy, a Philadelphia businessman, who wanted to create a slice of Walt Disney World. Among the attractions is an 18-hole miniature golf course loosely following the history of Nevis, focusing on times when pirates ruled the seas, complete with sculptured caves, waterfalls, a lagoon, blasting cannons, and even a simulated rain forest. An on-site deli offers sandwiches as well as Philly cheese steaks in honor of Murphy's hometown. There's a gift shop, restaurant, and live entertainment, including bands, comedians, and fashion shows. Admission is $4; hours are daily from 10am to 10pm.

The **Nevis Jockey Club** organizes and sponsors thoroughbred races every month. Local horses as well as some brought over from other islands fill out a typical five-race card. If you want to have a glimpse at what horse racing must have been like a century or more ago, you'll find the Nevis races a memorable experience. For information, contact Richard Lupinacci, a Jockey Club officer and owner and operator of the Hermitage Plantation (☎ 869/469-3477).

7 Shopping

For original art, visit **Eva Wilkins's Studio,** Clay Ghaut, Gingerland (☎ 869/469-2673). Wilkins was the island's most famous artist; even Prince Charles showed up to look at her work. Until her death in 1989, she painted island people, local flowers, and scenes of Nevis life. Prints are available in some of the local shops, but originals sell for $100 and up. You can visit her former atelier, on the grounds of an old sugar-mill plantation near Montpelier.

In a stone building about 200 feet from the wharf, near the marketplace, **Nevis Handicraft Cooperative Society,** Cotton House, Charlestown (☎ 869/469-1746), contains locally made gift items, including unusual objects of goatskin, local wines made from a variety of fruits grown on the island, hot-pepper sauce, guava cheese, jams, and jellies.

Hand-painted or tie-dyed cotton along with batik clothing are featured at **Island Hopper,** in the T.D.C. Shopping Mall, Main Street, Charlestown (☎ 869/469-0893), which also has locations on St. Kitts and Antigua. From beach wraps to souvenirs, a wide selection of products is available.

The **Sandbox Tree,** Evelyn's Villa, Charlestown (☎ 869/469-5662), housed in a clapboard house that was built in 1836, is the most appealing gift shop on Nevis, with artwork from Haiti and Nevis, books for adults and children, hand-painted clothing, sheets, napkins, antique furniture, and spices, relishes, and exotic chutneys. It also sells 100% cotton hand-silk-screened fabrics and a complete line of clothing.

Those interested in stamp collecting can go to **Nevis Philatelic Bureau,** Head Post Office, Market Street (next to the public market), Charlestown (☎ 869/469-5535), to see the wide range of colorful stamps. They feature butterflies, shells, birds, and fish.

8 Nevis After Dark

Nightlife is not the major reason to visit Nevis. Summer nights are quiet, but there's organized entertainment in winter, often steel bands performing at the major hotels.

Most action takes place at the **Four Seasons Resort,** Pinney's Beach (☎ 869/ 469-1111), on Friday and Saturday nights. The **Old Manor Estate,** Gingerland (☎ 869/469-3445), often brings in a steel band on Friday nights. On Saturday, the action swings over to the **Golden Rock,** Gingerland (☎ 869/469-3346), where a string band enlivens the scene. Friday and Saturday nights can get raucous at **Eddy's,** on Main Street (see "Where to Dine," above), when West Indian buffets are served and live bands entertain.

The best place on a Wednesday night is **Pinney's Beach Hotel**, Pinney's Beach (☎ 869/469-5207), which stages a dinner and dance. The **Oualie Beach Hotel,** Oualie Beach (☎ 869/469-9735), offers a Saturday buffet with a live string band entertaining guests. Disco reigns supreme at **Tequila Sheila's** at Cades Bay (see "Where to Dine," above) on Saturday night.

One of the best beach bars on island is the **Beachcomber**, Pinney's Beach (☎ 869/469-1192), known for its happy hour and barbecues. Sometimes live bands appear. Another favorite in winter only is **Sunset Terrace at Cliff Dwellers,** on Tamarind Bay (☎ 869/469-0262). This is the best place for a sundowner, except you must take a not-always reliable tram ride up the side of a sheer cliff. In all of Nevis, there's no more dramatic perch for a tropical punch.

18 Puerto Rico

No one has ever suffered from boredom on Puerto Rico, which offers a huge variety of resorts, activities, and entertainment. It has hundreds of beaches, a mind-boggling array of water sports, acres of golf courses, miles of tennis courts, and casinos galore. It has more discos than any other place in the Caribbean, and shopping bargains to equal St. Thomas. And all this fun comes with a much more reasonable price tag than it does on many of the other islands.

Lush, verdant Puerto Rico is only half the size of New Jersey and is located some 1,000 miles southeast of the tip of Florida. With 272 miles of Atlantic and Caribbean coastline and a culture dating back 2,000 years, Puerto Rico is packed with attractions. Old San Juan is its greatest historic center, with 500 years of history, as reflected in its restored Spanish colonial architecture.

It's also a land of contrasts. There are 79 cities and towns on Puerto Rico, each with a unique charm and flavor. The countryside is dotted with centuries-old coffee plantations, sugar estates still in use, a fascinating tropical rain forest, and foreboding caves and enormous boulders with mysterious petroglyphs carved by the Taíno peoples, the original settlers.

Dorado Beach, Cerromar Beach, and Palmas del Mar are the chief centers for those who've come for golf, tennis, and beaches. San Juan's hotels on the Condado/Isla Verde coast also have, for the most part, a complete array of water sports. The continental shelf, which surrounds Puerto Rico on three sides, contributes to an abundance of coral reefs, caves, sea walls, and trenches for scuba diving and snorkeling.

San Juan is the world's second-largest home port for cruise ships, and the old port of San Juan recently underwent a $90-million restoration.

In this chapter, we start out in San Juan, and then move west, counterclockwise around the island, until we reach Ponce. Then we'll turn our attention to attractions east of San Juan, and head clockwise around the island. Keep in mind that you can base yourself at one resort and still do a lot of exploring elsewhere if you don't mind driving for a couple of hours. It's possible to branch out and see a lot of the island even if you're staying in San Juan.

If you choose Puerto Rico and would like even more comprehensive coverage, consider getting yourself a copy of *Frommer's Puerto Rico.*

Puerto Rico

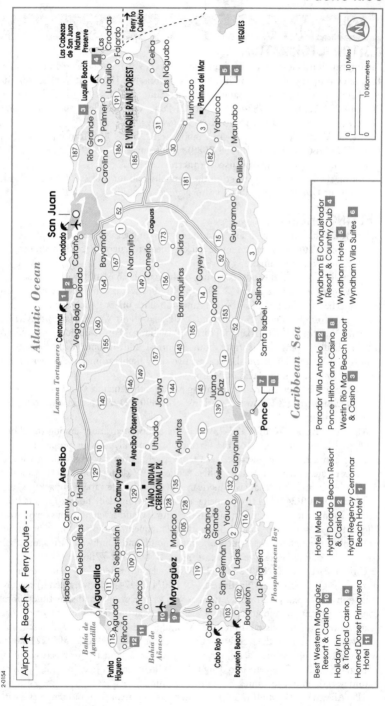

Airport ✈ Beach ⚑ Ferry Route - - -

Atlantic Ocean

Caribbean Sea

Best Western Mayagüez Resort & Casino 10

Holiday Inn & Tropical Casino 9

Horned Dorset Primavera Hotel 11

Hotel Meliá 7

Hyatt Dorado Beach Resort & Casino 2

Hyatt Regency Cerromar Beach Hotel 1

Parador Villa Antonio 12

Ponce Hilton and Casino 8

Westin Rio Mar Beach Resort & Casino 3

Wyndham El Conquistador Resort & Country Club 4

Wyndham Hotel 5

Wyndham Villa Suites 6

2-0154

1 Essentials

VISITOR INFORMATION

For information before you leave home, contact one of the following **Puerto Rico Tourism Company** offices: 575 Fifth Ave., New York, NY 10017 (☎ **800/223-6530** or 212/586-6262); 3575 W. Cahuenga Blvd., Suite 405, Los Angeles, CA 90068 (☎ **800/874-1230** or 213/874-5991); or 901 Ponce de León Blvd., Suite 604, Coral Gables, FL 33134 (☎ **800/815-7391** or 305/445-9112).

In Canada you can stop by 41–43 Colbourne St., Suite 301, Toronto, ON M5E 1E3 (☎ **800/667-0394** or 416/368-2680) for information.

The official Web site is **www.discoverpuertorico.com**.

Out on the island, it's best to go to the local city hall for tourist information. Ask for a copy of *Qué Pasa,* the official visitors' guide.

GETTING THERE

Before you book your own airfare, read the section on package tours in chapter 2—it can save you a bundle! There are more package deals to Puerto Rico than almost any other island except for Jamaica.

Puerto Rico is by far the most accessible of the Caribbean islands, with frequent airline service. **American Airlines** (☎ 800/433-7300; www.aa.com) has designated San Juan as its hub for the entire Caribbean. American alone offers 39 nonstop daily flights to San Juan from Baltimore, Boston, Chicago, Dallas—Fort Worth, Hartford, Miami, Newark, New York (JFK), Orlando, Philadelphia, Tampa, Fort Lauderdale, and Washington (Dulles), plus flights from both Montréal and Toronto with changes in Chicago or Miami. There are also at least two daily flights from Los Angeles to San Juan that touch down in Dallas or Miami.

American also offers many money-saving packages that include your hotel or resort; call **American Airlines FlyAway Vacations** at ☎ **800/321-2121,** and ask about their current offerings.

American Eagle (☎ 800/433-7300) is the undisputed leader among the short-haul local commuter flights of the Caribbean. It usually flies in propeller planes carrying between 34 and 64 passengers. Collectively, American Eagle, along with its larger associate, American Airlines, offers service to 37 destinations on 31 islands of the Caribbean and the Bahamas. American also offers a wide variety of packages.

Delta (☎ **800/241-4141;** www.delta-air.com) has four daily nonstop flights from Atlanta Monday to Friday, nine nonstops on Saturday, and seven nonstops on Sunday. Flights into Atlanta from around the world are frequent, with excellent connections from points throughout Delta's network in the South and Southwest. Ask about their packages by calling **Delta Dream Vacations** at ☎ **800/872-7786.**

United Airlines (☎ **800/241-6522;** www.ual.com) offers daily nonstop flights from Chicago to San Juan. **Northwest** (☎ **800/447-4747;** www.nwa.com) has one daily nonstop to San Juan from Detroit, as well as at least one (and sometimes more) connecting flights to San Juan from Detroit. That airline also offers flights to San Juan, some of them nonstop, from both Memphis and Minneapolis, with a schedule that varies according to the season and the day of the week. **TWA** (☎ **800/221-2000;** www.twa.com) offers three daily nonstop flights throughout the year between New York and San Juan. There are also daily nonstop flights to San Juan from St. Louis on Saturday and Sunday in winter, but none in summer.

US Airways (☎ **800/428-4322;** www.usairways.com) also competes, with daily connecting flights between Baltimore and San Juan, where flights make an

Great Discounts Through the LeLoLai VIP Program

For the $10 it will cost you to join Puerto Rico's ✪ **LeLoLai VIP** (Value in Puerto Rico) program, you can enjoy the equivalent of up to $250 in travel benefits. You'll get discounts on admission to folklore shows, guided tours of historic sites and natural attractions, lodgings, meals, shopping, activities, and more. Of course, most of the experiences linked to LeLoLai are of the rather touristy type, but it can still be a good investment.

With membership, the *paradores puertorriqueños,* the island's modestly priced network of country inns, give cardholders 10% to 20% lower room rates Monday to Thursday. Discounts of 10% to 20% are offered at many restaurants, from San Juan's toniest hotels to several *mesones gastronómicos,* government-sanctioned restaurants serving Puerto Rican fare. Shopping discounts are offered at many stores and boutiques and, best yet, cardholders get 10% to 20% discounts at many island attractions.

The card also entitles you to free admission to some of the island's folklore shows. At press time, the pass included *Jolgorio,* presented every Wednesday at 8:30pm at the Caribe Terrace of the Caribe Hilton, although the specifics might change by the time of your arrival in Puerto Rico.

For more information about this card, call ☎ 787/723-3135 or go to the El Centro Convention Center at Ashford Avenue on the Condado. Although you can call for details before you leave home, you can only sign up for this program once you reach Puerto Rico. Many hotel packages include participation in this program as part of their offerings.

---

intermediate stop in Charlotte, North Carolina, before continuing nonstop to San Juan. The airline also offers three daily nonstop flights to San Juan from Philadelphia, and one daily nonstop from Pittsburgh. You can also ask about packages offered by **US Airways Vacations** (☎ 800/455-0123).

Finally, **Iberia** (☎ 800/772-9642; www.iberia.com) has two weekly flights from Madrid to San Juan, leaving on Tuesday and Saturday.

GETTING AROUND

BY PLANE   American Eagle (☎ 787/749-1747) flies from Luís Muñoz International Airport to Mayagüez, which can be your gateway to the west of Puerto Rico. Fares vary widely according to the season, the restrictions associated with your ticket, and whatever special promotion might be in effect at the time of your booking, but expect to pay between $124 and $176 round-trip, per person, and try to book your passage as early as possible prior to your flight.

BY RENTAL CAR   Some local car-rental agencies may tempt you with slashed prices, but if you're planning to tour the island, you won't find any local branches should you run into car trouble. Plus, some of the agencies advertising low-cost deals don't take credit cards and want cash in advance. You also have to watch out for hidden extras and the insurance problems that sometimes proliferate among the smaller and not very well known firms.

The old reliables include **Avis** (☎ 800/331-1212 or 787/791-2500), **Budget** (☎ 800/527-0700 or 787/791-3685), or **Hertz** (☎ 800/654-3001 or 787/791-0840). Each of the "big-three" companies offers minivan transport to its office and car depot from the San Juan airport. Another alternative is **Kemwel Holiday Auto** (☎ 800/678-0678). None of these companies rents jeeps, four-wheel-drive vehicles, or convertibles.

The annual **Casals Festival** in June is the Caribbean's most celebrated cultural event. The bill at San Juan's Performing Arts Center includes a glittering array of international guest conductors, orchestras, and soloists who come to honor the memory of Pablo Casals, the renowned cellist who was born in Spain to a Puerto Rican mother, and who died in Puerto Rico in 1973. Tickets range from $20 to $40; a 50% discount is offered to students, seniors, and persons with disabilities. Call ☎ 787/721-7727 for tickets.

The island's **Carnival** celebrations feature float parades, dancing, and street parties; the festivities in **Ponce** are marked by masqueraders wearing brightly painted horned masks, the crowning of a Carnival queen, and the closing "burial of the sardine." For more information, call ☎ **787/840-4141.**

Added security comes from an antitheft double-locking mechanism that has been installed in most of the rental cars available on Puerto Rico. Car theft is high on Puerto Rico, so extra precaution is always needed.

Distances are often posted in kilometers rather than miles (a kilometer is 0.62 miles), but speed limits are in miles per hour.

BY PUBLIC TRANSPORTATION *Públicos* are cars or minibuses that provide low-cost transportation and are designated with the letters *P* or *PD* following the numbers on their license plates. They usually operate only during daylight hours, carry up to six passengers at a time, and charge rates that are loosely governed by the Public Service Commission. Although prices are low, this option is slow, with frequent stops, often erratic routing, and lots of inconvenience. The choice is yours.

Locals are adept at figuring out their routes along rural highways, and in some cases, simply wave at a moving *público* that they suspect might be headed in their direction. Unless you're fluent in Spanish, and feeling adventurous, we suggest phoning either of the numbers below, describing where and when you want to go, and agreeing to the prearranged price between specific points. Then, be prepared to wait. Although, at least in theory, a *público* might be arranged between most of the towns and villages of Puerto Rico, by far the most popular routes are between San Juan and Ponce and San Juan and Mayagüez. Fares vary according to whether a *público* will make a detour to pick up or drop off a passenger at a specific locale. If you want to deviate from the predetermined routes, you'll pay more than if you wait for a *público* at vaguely designated points beside the main highway, or at predefined points that include airports and, in some cases, the main plaza (central square) of a town.

Information about *público* routes between San Juan and Mayagüez is available from **Lineas Sultana,** Calle Esteban González 898, Urbanización Santa Rita, Rio Piedras (☎ 787/765-9377). Information about *público* routes between San Juan and Ponce is available from **Choferes Unidos de Ponce,** terminal de carros públicos, Calle Vive in Ponce (☎ **787/722-3275,** or 787/764-0540). Fares from San Juan to Ponce cost $20.

SIGHTSEEING TOURS   If you want to see more of the island but you don't want to rent a car or deal with public transportation, perhaps an organized tour is for you. If you're based in San Juan, the following options will help you see more of the island.

Castillo Sightseeing Tours & Travel Services, Calle Laurel 2413, Punta La Marias, Santurce (☎ **787/791-6195**), maintains offices at some of San Juan's major hotels. They can also arrange pickup at other accommodations in one of their six air-conditioned buses. One of the most popular half-day tours runs from San Juan to El

Yunque Rain Forest; it departs in the morning, lasts 4 to 5 hours, and costs $30 per person. The company also offers a 4-hour city tour of San Juan that costs $32 and includes a stopover at the Bacardi rum factory. Full-day snorkeling tours to the reefs near the coast of a deserted island off Puerto Rico's eastern edge aboard one of two sail-and motor-driven catamarans go for $69, with lunch, snorkeling gear, and piña coladas included.

For a full-day excursion to the best islands, beaches, reefs, and snorkeling in the area, contact **Bill and Donna Henry** at the Puerto Del Rey Marina in Fajardo, on the east coast (☎ **787/860-4401**). They offer tours aboard their 50-foot Gulfstar, where two to six passengers pay $75. A barbecue chicken meal is cooked onboard. Donna will prepare vegetarian or kosher food if notified. Sunset cruises for $55 per person are also offered, including drinks and hors d'oeuvres; a minimum of four passengers must sign up for this.

Fast Facts: Puerto Rico

Banking Hours Most major U.S. banks have branches in San Juan, and are open Monday to Friday from 8:30am to 2:30pm.

Currency The **U.S. dollar** is the coin of the realm. Canadian currency is accepted by some big hotels in San Juan, although reluctantly.

Documents Since Puerto Rico is part of the United States, American citizens do not need a passport or visa. Canadians, however, should carry some form of identification, such as a birth certificate and photo ID, though we always recommend carrying your passport. Citizens of the United Kingdom should have a passport.

Electricity The electricity is 110 volts AC (60 cycles), as it is in the continental United States and Canada.

Emergencies In an emergency, call ☎ **911.**

Language English is understood at the big resorts and in most of San Juan, though it's polite to at least greet people in Spanish and ask if they speak English before you make assumptions. Out in the island, Spanish is still *numero uno.*

Safety Use common sense and take precautions. Muggings are commonly reported on the Condado and Isla Verde beaches in San Juan, so you might want to confine your moonlit-beach nights to the fenced-in and guarded areas around some of the major hotels. The countryside of Puerto Rico is safer than San Juan, but caution is always the rule. Avoid small and narrow little country roads and isolated beaches, either by night or day.

Taxes There's a government tax of 7% in regular hotels or 9% in hotels with casinos. The airport departure tax is included in the price of your ticket.

Telephone To call Puerto Rico from the United States, simply dial **1,** then **787** (the area code for Puerto Rico), and the seven-digit local number.

Time Puerto Rico is on Atlantic standard time year-round, putting it 1 hour ahead of U.S. eastern standard time. In winter, when it's noon in Miami, it's 1pm in San Juan. But from April until late October (during daylight saving time on the East Coast), Puerto Rico and the East Coast keep the same time.

Tipping Some hotels add a 10% service charge to your bill. If they don't, you're expected to tip for services rendered. Tip as you would in the United States (15% to 20%).

Water   The water in Puerto Rico is generally safe to drink, although you may prefer bottled water.

Weather Puerto Rico is cooler than most of the other Caribbean islands because of its northeast trade winds. Sea, land, and mountain breezes also help keep the temperatures at a comfortable level. The climate is fairly stable all year, with an average temperature of 76°F. The only variants are found in the mountain regions, where the temperature fluctuates between 66° and 76°F, and on the north coast, where the temperature ranges from 70° to 80°F. There is no real rainy season, but August is the wettest month.

2 San Juan

San Juan, the capital of Puerto Rico, is a major city—actually an urban sprawl of several municipalities that lie along the island's north coast. Its architecture ranges from classic colonial buildings that recall the Spanish empire to modern beachfront hotels reminiscent of Miami Beach.

SAN JUAN ESSENTIALS

ARRIVING—If you're not traveling on a package deal that includes transfers to your hotel, you'll see lots of options after landing at the San Juan airport. A wide variety of vehicles refer to themselves as *limosinas* (their Spanish name).

Dozens of taxis line up outside the airport to meet arriving flights, so you rarely have to wait. The island's **Public Service Commission** (☎ 787/751-5050) sets flat rates between the Luís Muñoz Marin Airport and major tourist zones as follows: From the airport to any hotel in Isla Verde, $8; to any hotel in the Condado district, $12, and to any hotel in Old San Juan, $16. Tips of between 10% and 15% of that fare are expected.

One company with a sign-up desk in the international airport, near the American Airlines arrival facilities, is the **Airport Limousine Service** (☎ 787/791-4745). It offers minivan transport from the airport to various neighborhoods of San Juan for prices that are lower than for similar routings offered by taxis. Whenever 8 to 10 passengers can be accumulated, the fare for transport, with luggage, to any hotel in Isla Verde is $50 per van; to the Condado, $60 for the van; and to Old San Juan, also $60 per van.

For conventional limousine service, **Bracero Limousine** (☎ 787/253-5466) offers upholstered cars with drivers to meet you at the arrivals terminal for luxurious and strictly private transport to your hotel or anywhere you specify in Puerto Rico. This luxury and convenience will cost you, though; the price for going anywhere in San Juan ranges from $85 to $105, and transport to points throughout the island vary from $150 to $275, depending on the time and distance.

VISITOR INFORMATION   Tourist information is available at the **Luís Muñoz Marín Airport** (☎ 787/791-1014). Another office is at **La Casita,** Pier 1, Old San Juan (☎ 787/722-1709).

ORIENTATION   San Juan breaks down into several divisions: **San Juan Island,** containing the city center and the old walled city (Old San Juan); **Santurce,** a large peninsula that's linked to San Juan Island by causeway; **Condado,** a narrow peninsula that stretches between San Juan Island and Santurce; **Puerto de Tierra,** the section east of Old San Juan that contains many government buildings; **Miramar,** a lagoon-front section south of Condado; and **Isla Verde,** which is detached from the rest of San Juan by an isthmus.

GETTING AROUND   The best way to save your feet in Old San Juan is to board one of the free open-air trolleys that slowly make their way through the narrow, often cobblestoned, old streets. You can board a trolley at any point along its route (either side of the Calle Fortaleza or Calle San Jos are good bets), or you can go to either the marina or La Puntilla for departures.

The **Metropolitan Bus Authority** (☎ 787/250-6064) operates buses in the greater San Juan area. Bus stops are marked by upright metal signs or yellow posts, reading *parada*. Bus terminals in San Juan are in the dock area and at Plaza de Colón. A typical fare is 25¢ to 50¢. The higher fee is for the faster buses that make fewer stops; call for more information about routes and schedules.

Taxis are metered; tips between 10% and 15% of the fare are customary. The initial charge for destinations in the city is $1, plus 10¢ for each ¹/₁₀ mile and 50¢ for every suitcase, with a minimum fare of $3. Taxis are invariably lined up outside the entrance to most of the island's hotels, and if not, a staff member can almost always call one for you. If you want to arrange a taxi on your own, call the **Mejor Cab Company** (☎ 787/723-2460). If you want to take a cab to a destination outside the city, you must negotiate a flat fee with the driver. For complaints or questions, contact the **Public Service Commission** (☎ 787/751-5050), which regulates cabs.

FAST FACTS   One of the most centrally located **pharmacies** is the **Puerto Rico Drug Co.,** Calle San Francisco 157 (☎ 787/725-2202), in Old San Juan; open Monday to Friday from 7am to 9:30pm, Saturday from 8am to 9:30pm, and Sunday from 8:30am to 7:30pm. **Walgreen's,** 1130 Ashford Ave., Condado (☎ 787/725-1510), is a 24-hour pharmacy.

In a **medical emergency,** call ☎ 787/721-2116. Ashford Memorial Community Hospital, 1451 Ashford Ave. (☎ 787/721-2160) maintains a 24-hour emergency room.

American Express services are handled by the **Travel Network,** 1035 Ashford Ave., Condado (☎ 787/725-0960). The office is open Monday to Friday from 9am to 5pm and on Saturday from 9 to 11:30am.

WHERE TO STAY

All hotel rooms on Puerto Rico are subject to a 7% to 9% tax, which is not included in the rates listed in this chapter. Most hotels also impose a 10% service charge.

Before you book a hotel, refer back on the section on "Package Deals" in chapter 2. Packages can save you a lot of money, especially if you want to stay at one of the big resorts.

IN OLD SAN JUAN

El Convento. 100 Cristo St., San Juan, PR 00901. ☎ **800/468-2779** or 787/723-9020. Fax 787/721-2877. www.elconvento.com. E-mail: elconvento@ad.com. 57 units. A/C TV TEL. Winter $285–$375 double. Off-season $220–$280 double. Year-round from $500 suite. AE, DC, DISC, MC, V. Bus: A7, T1, or 21.

Puerto Rico's most famous (though not its best) hotel had deteriorated into a shabby version of its former self, but it came back to life when it was restored and reopened in 1997. Built in 1651, this hotel in the heart of the old city was once the New World's first Carmelite convent. Over the years El Convento played many roles when it ceased being a convent—everything from dance hall to flop house to a parking lot for garbage trucks. Rescued from ruin, it opened as a hotel in 1962 but didn't make money and was seized by the government for back taxes.

Now restored at the cost of around $275,000 per room, El Convento offers roomy accommodations on its third to fifth floors, with a concierge-style reception and

San Juan

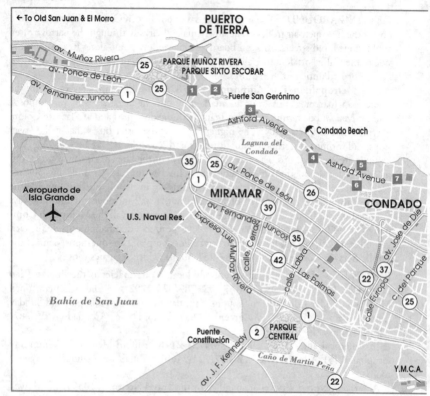

check-in and a club lounge. Handcrafted in Spain, room furnishings are in traditional Spanish style, with mahogany beams and handmade tile floors. Each room contains doubles or twins, each fitted with a good mattress and fine linen, and such extras as VCRs and stereos, coffeemakers, irons, and ironing boards. The small bathrooms, with combination tubs and showers, contain scales, second phones, and hair dryers. The interior courtyard is again open to the sky, as it was in the 1600s.

Dining/Diversions: The lower two floors feature artists and artisans in residence, with galleries, specialty shops, restaurants, and cafes. Breakfast is served in an outdoor garden terrace. There's also an intimate casino.

Amenities: Pool, Jacuzzi, indoor fitness center, massage.

Gallery Inn at Galería San Juan. Calle Norzagaray 204–206, San Juan, PR 00901. ☎ **787/ 722-1808.** Fax 787/724-7360. www.thegalleryinn.com. E-mail: reservations@galleryinn.com. 22 units. Year-round $95–$350 double; $200–$350 suite. Rates include continental breakfast. AE, MC, V. There are 3 free parking spaces, plus parking on the street. Bus: Old Town trolley.

This hotel's location and ambience are unbeatable. We suggest booking one of the least expensive doubles here—even the cheapest units are fairly roomy and attractively furnished with good beds and small but adequate bathrooms. Set on a hilltop in the Old Town, with a sweeping sea view, this unusual hotel contains a maze of verdant courtyards. In the 1700s, it was the home of an aristocratic Spanish family. Today, it's one of the most whimsically bohemian hotels in the Caribbean. All courtyards and rooms are adorned with hundreds of sculptures, silk-screens, or original paintings, usually for sale. The nearest beach is a 15-minute ride away, though.

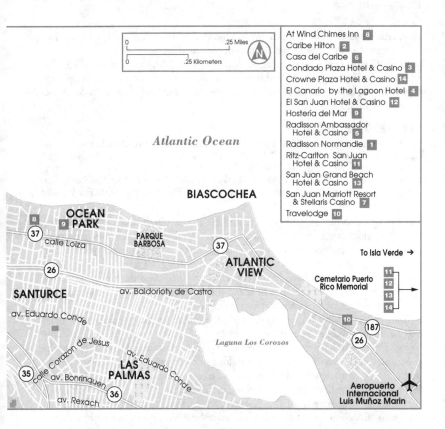

Atlantic Ocean

BIASCOCHEA

OCEAN PARK

8 **9**

37 calle Loíza

PARQUE BARBOSA

37

26

ATLANTIC VIEW

To Isla Verde →

SANTURCE

av. Baldorioty de Castro

av. Eduardo Conde

Cemeterio Puerto Rico Memorial

11
12
13
14

Calle Corazon de Jesus

av. Eduardo Conde

Laguna Los Corozos

10

187

26

35 av. Bonriquen

LAS PALMAS

36

av. Rexach

Aeropuerto Internacional Luis Muñoz Marin ✈

Wyndham Old San Juan Hotel & Casino. 100 Brumbaugh St., San Juan, PR 00901.
☎ **800/996-3426** or 787/721-5100. Fax 787/721-1111. www.windham.com. 240 units.
A/C TV TEL. Winter $315 double; from $550 suite. Off-season $225 double; from $375 suite.
AE, CB, DC, DISC, MC, V. Free parking; valet parking $15. Bus: A7.

Opened in 1997, this nine-story waterfront hotel was conceived as part of a $100-
million renovation of San Juan's cruise-port facilities. Its position between buildings
erected by the Spanish monarchs in the 19th century and the city's busiest and most
modern cruise-ship terminals is both unusual and desirable. Most (but not all) of the
major cruise ships dock nearby, making this a great choice is you want to spend time
in San Juan before boarding a ship.

Great care was taken to create a pastel-colored building whose iron railings and
exterior detailing convey a sense of colonial San Juan, an effect that's enhanced by the
expensive mahogany trim inside the hotel. Its triangular floor plan encircles an inner
courtyard that floods light into the tasteful and comfortable, beige-and-white bedrooms, each of which has two phone lines and a modem connection for laptop com-
puters. Other than that, the rooms lack character and are a bit bandboxy and small,
although each comes with a comfortable mattress, plus a compact bathroom with a
shower stall. Think of a typical Holiday Inn geared for business travelers instead of a
luxury resort.

Dining/Diversions: About 80% of the lobby level is devoted to a 10,000-square-
foot casino, with slot machines and poker and roulette tables. There's an upscale
dining room that also functions as the breakfast area; it serves perfectly fine if

unremarkable international cuisine with some Puerto Rican regional specialties. Two bar/lounges, one with live music, round out the entertainment.

Amenities: A conference center, within an early-20th-century historic building known as *Isla Bonita,* is connected to the hotel by an aerial catwalk. A rooftop pool, fully equipped health club, and Jacuzzi overlook the harbor and cruise-ship docks. 24-hour room service, concierge.

IN PUERTO DE TIERRA

Caribe Hilton. Calle Los Rosales, San Juan, PR 00902. ☎ **800/HILTONS** in the U.S. and Canada, or 787/721-0303. Fax 787/725-8849. www.caribehilton.com. E-mail: info@ CaribeHilton.com. 670 units. A/C MINIBAR TV TEL. Winter $280–$390 double. Off-season $190–$290 double. Year-round $350–$1,000 suite. Children 16 and under stay free in parents' room (maximum 4 people per room). AE, CB, DC, DISC, MC, V. Self-parking $7; valet parking $14. Bus: A7.

The Hilton, with the only private beach on the island, stands near the old Fort San Jerónimo, which has been incorporated into its complex. If there is one party hotel along the San Juan beachfront, this is it, and it often attracts conventions and tour groups. Only the Condado Beach and Hotel El San Juan rival it for nonstop activity. Set on San Juan Bay, the hotel is also convenient to the walled city of San Juan. You can walk to the 16th-century fort or spend the day on a tour of Old San Juan, then come back and enjoy the beach and swimming cove.

Built in 1949 in a 17-acre tropical park, the Hilton recently underwent a major $40-million renovation. Rooms are housed in an old 10-story building or a 20-story tower, although all have the same amenities such as twin or doubles, each fitted with good linen and a quality mattress. If you don't mind skipping the view, you can stay in the most recently renovated Garden Wing, with spacious rooms, picture windows, big desks, king-size beds, and large bathrooms. The Cabana Wing is also choice, as it curves along the oceanfront in a single-story format. Some rooms are suitable for persons with disabilities, and others are set aside for nonsmokers. All bathrooms are equipped with a generous set of good-sized towels and a hair dryer.

Dining/Diversions: The dining options at the Hilton, although not as exciting as at the El San Juan Hotel, are some of the best and most varied of any hotel in San Juan. The Hilton hires some of the most imaginative chefs on the island, who use fine ingredients and often change their menus. The Caribe Terrace restaurant complex features an international cuisine with a different menu each night. Other venues include El Batey del Pescador, a seafood restaurant; La Rôtisserie Il Giardino, devoted to northern Italian cuisine; and the Peacock Paradise Chinese Restaurant. In the Caribe Terrace Bar, you can order the bartender's celebrated piña colada, which was once enjoyed by the likes of movie legends Joan Crawford and Errol Flynn. The 12,400-square-foot casino, adjacent to the lobby atrium area, is open daily from noon to 4am, featuring blackjack, craps, baccarat, roulette, and slot machines.

Amenities: Spa Caribe, two freshwater pools, health club, aerobics, beach activities, children's playground, play room, six lit tennis courts, business center, room service (from 6am to 1am), laundry/valet, baby-sitting.

Radisson Normandie. Av. Muñoz-Rivera (at the corner of Calle Los Rosales), San Juan, PR 00902. ☎ **800/333-3333** in the U.S., or 787/729-2929. Fax 787/729-3083. 180 units. A/C MINIBAR TV TEL. Winter $220–$250 double; $490 suite. Off-season $175–$205 double; $410 suite. Rates include full American breakfast. AE, DC, DISC, MC, V. Outdoor parking $5. Bus: A7.

Geared to the upscale business traveler, but also good for independent vacationers, the Normandie first opened in 1939 and reopened in 1989 after a $20-million renovation

Old San Juan

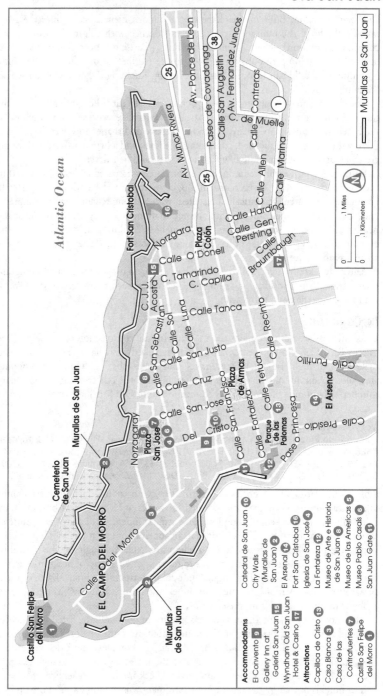

Atlantic Ocean

Castillo San Felipe del Morro

Cemeterio de San Juan

EL CAMPO DEL MORRO

Murallas de San Juan

Calle del Morro

Murallas de San Juan

Fort San Cristobal

Norzgara

Plaza Colón

Calle O'Donell

C. Tamarindo

C. Capilla

C. J. J. Acosta

Calle San Sebastian

Calle Sol

Calle Luna

Calle Tanca

Calle San Justo

Calle Cruz

Plaza de Armas

Calle San Francisco

Calle San Jose

Del Cristo

Calle Tetuan

Calle Recinto

Calle Harding

Calle Gen. Pershing

Calle Braumbaugh

Norzagaray

Plaza San Jose

Calle Fortaleza

Parque de las Palomas

Calle San Cristo

Pase o Princesa

Calle Puntillo

El Arsenal

Calle Presidio

Av. Ponce de Leon

Paseo de Covadonga

Calle San Augustin

Av. Fernandez Juncos

Av. Munoz Rivera

Calle Hard

Calle Allen

Calle Contreras

C. de Muelle

Calle Marina

Murallas de San Juan

Accommodations

El Convento 9
Gallery Inn at Galería San Juan 15
Wyndham Old San Juan Hotel & Casino 17

Attractions

Capilloa de Cristo 13
Casa Blanca 3
Casa de las Contrafuertes 7
Castillo San Felipe del Morro 1
Catedral de San Juan 10
City Walls (Murallas de San Juan) 2
El Arsenal 14
Fort San Cristobal 16
Iglesia de San José 4
La Fortaleza 12
Museo de Arte e Historia de San Juan 8
Museo de las Americas 5
Museo Pablo Casals 6
San Juan Gate 11

Murallas de San Juan

471

and reconstruction. Built in the shape of the famous French ocean liner the *Normandie,* the hotel is a monument to art deco. Adorned with columns, cornices, and countless decorations, it was originally built for a Parisian cancan dancer (who was married to a building tycoon). Next door to the Caribe Hilton, the hotel lies only 5 minutes from Old San Juan, its beachside setting adjoining the noted Sixto Escobar Stadium.

The elegant and elaborate rooms are spacious and well furnished with all the amenities, including coffeemakers; the more expensive units are executive rooms. Because of the hotel's triangular shape, many of the rooms have odd shapes and sizes, but each is fitted with a king or double bed, containing fine linen and a firm mattress. Bathrooms are spacious and well appointed, with thick towels and hair dryers.

Dining: A continental menu, including some items prepared tableside, is served in the elegant Normandie Restaurant. Although the food at the Radisson is perfectly acceptable, and often is artistically presented, with a strong reliance on fresh ingredients, the hotel cannot compete with the international culinary razzle-dazzle of the nearby Hilton. So Radisson guests can often be seen dining at the Hilton in the evening and taking advantage of its entertainment possibilities. The Atrium Lounge is set in a swirl of greenery.

Amenities: Freshwater pool with a bar; hair salon; an on-site water-sports program offers scuba diving, snorkeling, sailing—all the usual stuff; room service (to 11pm), laundry, concierge desk, baby-sitting.

In Condado

Once this was a wealthy residential area, but with the construction of El Centro, the Puerto Rico Convention Center, all that changed. Private villas were torn down to make way for high-rise hotels, restaurants, and nightclubs. The Condado shopping area, along Ashford and Magdalena avenues, became the center of an extraordinary number of boutiques. There are bus connections into Old San Juan, or you can take a taxi.

Very Expensive

✪ **Condado Plaza Hotel & Casino.** 999 Ashford Ave., San Juan, PR 00907. ☎ **800/468-8588** in the U.S., or 787/721-1000. Fax 787/721-4613. www.williamshosp.com. 555 units. A/C MINIBAR TV TEL. Winter $350–$1,000 double; $375–$1,000 suite. Off-season $200–$1,000 double; $225–$1,000 suite. AE, CB, DC, DISC, MC, V. Valet parking $15. Bus: A7.

This is one of the busiest hotels on Puerto Rico, with enough facilities, restaurants, and distractions to keep a visitor occupied for weeks. It's a favorite of business travelers, tour groups, and conventions, but also attracts independent travelers because of its wide array of amenities. The Hilton is its major rival, but we prefer this hotel's style and flair, especially after its recent $40-million overhaul. Although not the most intimate of San Juan's hotels, it is the most prominent, set on a strip of beachfront at the beginning of the Condado. The original buff-colored structure is linked by an elevated passageway above Ashford Avenue to its annex, the Laguna Wing, which has its own lobby with direct access from the street.

All units have private terraces and are spacious, bright, and airy, fitted with deluxe beds and mattresses, either king-size or doubles, but most often twins. The good-sized bathrooms contain thick towels and hair dryers. The complex's most deluxe section, the Plaza Club, has 80 units (including five duplex suites), a VIP lounge reserved exclusively for the use of its guests, and private check-in/check-out service.

The hotel is owned by the same consortium that owns the somewhat more upscale El San Juan Hotel & Casino. Use of the facilities at one hotel can be charged to a room at the other.

Dining/Diversions: Only the Hotel El San Juan has a more dazzling array of dining options. This place is known for creating charming restaurants with culinary diversity that many local residents flock to sample. The newest restaurants are Mandalay, which blends Chinese cuisine with a sushi bar and teppanyaki tables, and Cobia, a tapas bar and seafood grill specializing in American dishes along with Pacific Rim and Caribbean flavors. Ristorante Capriccio has northern Italian cuisine, and Las Palmas and Tony Roma's are other choices. La Posada, next to the casino and open 24 hours a day, is known for its New York deli fare. For nighttime entertainment, La Fiesta offers live Latin music.

Amenities: Five pools, water sports, Plaza Spa, fitness center in the Laguna Wing, two lit Laykold tennis courts, 24-hour room service, fresh towels at beach and pools, laundry.

San Juan Marriott Resort & Stellaris Casino. 1309 Ashford Ave., San Juan, PR 00907. ☎ **800/464-5005** or 787/722-7000. Fax 787/722-6800. www.marriott.com/marriott/ SJUPR. E-mail: sjmarbc@tld.net. 538 units. A/C MINIBAR TV TEL. Winter $325–$430 double; from $550 suite. Off-season $205 double; from $550 suite. AE, DC, DISC, MC, V. Parking $8. Bus: B21.

It's the tallest building on the Condado, a 21-story landmark that Marriott spent staggering sums to renovate in a radically different format after a tragic fire gutted the premises in 1989. The current building packs in lots of postmodern style, and one of the best beaches on the Condado is right outside. Furnishings in the soaring lobby were inspired by Chippendale. If there's a flaw, it's the decor of the comfortable but bland bedrooms, with pastel colors that look washed out when compared to the rich mahoganies and jewel tones of the rooms in the rival Condado Plaza Hotel. Nonetheless, the units here boast one of the most advanced telephone networks on the island, carefully maintained security and fire-prevention systems, safes, and in-room VCRs. They're generally spacious, with good views of the water. Extras include two phones with voice mail, plus an iron and ironing board. Some of the accommodations are suitable for those with disabilities. Bathrooms have excellent plumbing, hair dryers, and shower/tub combinations.

Dining/Diversions: We suggest having only one dinner in-house (at Tuscany's; see "Where to Dine," below), then dining out for the rest of your stay, unless you want just a fresh salad or a sandwich. There's live music in the lobby every evening from 6 to 9pm; two bands perform here Thursday to Saturday from 9pm to 3am. La Vista offers buffet lunches and dinners, and a poolside grill serves tropical drinks, sandwiches, and salads. The Stellaris Casino, which isn't as glitzy as some of its competitors, is next to the main lobby.

Amenities: Two tennis courts; two pools (whose mosaic bottoms glow luminously when viewed from the hotel's observatory-style 21st floor); a health club with many massage and spa treatments. 24-hour room service, concierge, beauty salon, shopping kiosks, tour desk, car-rental facilities.

Expensive

Radisson Ambassador Hotel & Casino. 1369 Ashford Ave., San Juan, PR 00907. ☎ **800/468-8512** in the U.S., or 787/721-7300. Fax 787/723-6151. www.radisson.com. 320 units. A/C TV TEL. Winter $245–$275 double; $275–$385 suite. Off-season $220–$250 double; $250–$320 suite. AE, CB, DC, DISC, MC, V. Self-parking $6; valet parking $10. Bus: A7.

In the heart of the Condado, but a short walk from the beach, the Ambassador emerged as a star-studded hotel after entrepreneur Eugene Romano poured more than $40 million into its restoration in 1990. The hotel offers theatrical drama and big-time pizzazz, with Czech and Murano chandeliers; hand-blown wall sconces; Turkish,

Greek, and Italian marble; and yards of exotic hardwoods. What's missing (especially at these prices) are the resort amenities associated with the Hilton and the Condado Plaza.

Accommodations are in a pair of high-rise towers, one of which is devoted to suites. The decors are inspired variously by 18th-century Versailles, 19th-century London, imperial China, and art-deco California. However, in spite of the gaudy, glitzy overlay, know that the hotel used to be a Howard Johnson, and you can tell from the size of the standard rooms. Each unit has pay-per-view movies and a balcony with outdoor furniture. The beds, twins or doubles, are fitted with fine linen and quality mattresses, and the bathrooms have generous shelf space, a combination tub/shower, and a rack of thick towels.

Dining/Diversions: La Scala's northern Italian cuisine is the hotel's culinary high-light. The newest offering is Sweeney's, a "Scotch & Sirloin" grill with fine steaks. The casino (open from noon to 4am) has more slot machines than any other on the Con-dado, and a singer/pianist performs from a quiet corner bar. There are four bar/lounges, one of which has live local dance music.

Amenities: Penthouse-level fitness and health club, beauty salon, rooftop pool, Jacuzzi, business center (staffed with typists, translators, guides, and stenographers), room service (from 6:30am to midnight), baby-sitting, laundry, 24-hour concierge, VIP floors with extra amenities and enhanced services, a social programmer who offers a changing array of daily activities.

Moderate

El Canario by the Lagoon Hotel. Calle Clemenceau 4, Condado, San Juan, PR 00907. ☎ **800/533-2649** in the U.S., or 787/722-5058. Fax 787/723-8590. www.canariohotels. com. E-mail: canariopr@aol.com. 40 units. A/C TV TEL. Winter $100–$110 double. Off-season $80–$90 double. Rates include continental breakfast and morning newspaper. AE, DC, DISC, MC, V. Bus: B-21 or C-10.

A relaxing, informal European-style hotel, El Canario is in a quiet residential neigh-borhood just a short block from Condado Beach. This is one of the better B&Bs in the area, although it still charges affordable rates. The hotel is very much in the Con-dado styling, which evokes Miami Beach in the 1960s. The bedrooms are generous in size and have balconies. Most of them have twin beds, each with a firm mattress. Bath-rooms are sleek and contemporary, with generous towels and enough space to spread out your stuff. Extra amenities include an in-room safe and a complimentary tropical breakfast with the morning newspaper. Free coffee is also available in the lobby. Hotel amenities include a tour desk and a self-service Laundromat; the staff can make arrangements for you to have access to a nearby health club. If the hotel doesn't have room for you, it can book you into its sibling properties, either El Canario Inn or El Canario by the Sea.

Inexpensive

At Wind Chimes Inn. 1750 Ashford Ave., Condado, San Juan, PR 00911. ☎ **800/946-3244** or 787/727-4153. Fax 787/726-5321. 13 units. A/C TV TEL. Winter $65–$95 double. Off-season $55–$85 double. Rates include continental breakfast. AE, DC, DISC, MC, V. Parking $5. Bus: B-21 or AS.

This restored and renovated Spanish manor, one short block from the beach and 3½ miles from the airport, is one of the best guest houses on the Condado. Upon entering a tropical patio, you'll find tile tables surrounded by palm trees and bougainvillea. There's plenty of space on the deck and a covered lounge for relaxing, socializing, and eating breakfast. Dozens of decorative wind chimes add melody to the daily breezes. The good-sized rooms offer a choice of size, beds, and kitchens; all contain ceiling fans and air-conditioning. Beds have firm mattresses, and bathrooms, though small, are efficiently laid out. The inn has recently added a pool.

Casa del Caribe. Calle Caribe 57, San Juan, PR 00907. ☎ **787/722-7139.** Fax 787/723-2575. 11 units. A/C TV TEL. Winter $65–$95 double. Off-season $55–$85 double. Rates include continental breakfast. AE, DISC, MC, V. Parking $5. Bus: B-21 or C-10.

Don't expect the Ritz, but if you're looking for a bargain on the Condado, this is it. Formerly known as Casablanca, this renovated guest house was built in the 1940s, later expanded, then totally refurbished with a tropical decor late in 1995. A very Puerto Rican ambience has been created, with emphasis on Latin hospitality and comfort. On a shady side street just off Ashford Avenue, behind a wall and garden, you'll discover Casa del Caribe's wraparound veranda. The small but cozy guest rooms have ceiling fans and air-conditioners, and most feature original Puerto Rican art. The bedrooms are most inviting, with firm mattresses and efficiently organized bathrooms. The front porch is a social center for guests. You can also cook out at a barbecue area. The beach is a 2-minute walk away, and the hotel is also within walking distance of some megaresorts with their glittering casinos.

IN OCEAN PARK

✪ **Hostería del Mar.** 1 Tapia St., Ocean Park, Santurce, San Juan, PR 00911. ☎ or fax **787/727-3302.** E-mail: hosteria@taribe.net. 21 units. A/C TV TEL. Winter $150 double; $175 apt. Off-season $98 double; $150 apt. Children 11 and under stay free in parents' room. AE, DC, DISC, MC, V.

Lying a few blocks from the Condado casinos are the white walls of this distinctive landmark. It's located between Isla Verde and Condado in a residential seaside community that's popular with locals looking for beach action on weekends. The hotel boasts medium-size ocean-view rooms. Those on the second floor have balconies; those on the first floor open onto patios. The guest-room decor is invitingly tropical, with wicker furniture, good beds, pastel prints, and ceiling fans, plus small but efficient bathrooms. There's no pool, but a full-service restaurant here is known for its vegetarian, macrobiotic, and Puerto Rican plates, all freshly made. The place is simple, yet with its own elegance, and the hospitality is warm.

IN ISLA VERDE

Isla Verde, right on the beach, is closer to the airport than the other sections of San Juan, but farther from Old Town. Some of the Caribbean's most upscale hotels are located here. If you plan to spend most of your time on the beach rather than exploring the city, consider one of the following hotels.

Very Expensive

✪ **El San Juan Hotel & Casino.** 6063 Isla Verde Ave., San Juan, PR 00902. ☎ **800/468-2818** or 787/791-1000. Fax 787/791-0390. 389 units. A/C MINIBAR TV TEL. Winter $330–$490 double; from $575 suite. Off-season $205–$335 double; from $450 suite. AE, DC, DISC, MC, V. Self-parking $8; valet parking $13. Bus: A7, M7, or T1.

For dozens of reasons, this is the best hotel on Puerto Rico—some say it's the best in the entire Caribbean basin, evoking Havana in its heyday. Built in the 1950s, it was restored with an infusion of millions—some $80 million in 1997 and 1998 alone. It's also a great choice for (well-to-do) families, with more activities for children than any other property on Puerto Rico.

The beachfront hotel is surrounded by 350 palms, century-old banyans, and gardens. Its 700-yard-long sandy beach is the finest in the San Juan area. The hotel's river pool, with its currents, cascades, and lagoons, evokes a jungle stream, and the lobby is the most opulent and memorable in the Caribbean. Entirely sheathed in red marble and hand-carved mahogany paneling, the public rooms stretch on almost endlessly.

The large, well-decorated rooms have intriguing touches of high-tech; each contains a dressing room, three phones, and a VCR. Bedrooms are the ultimate in luxury in San Juan with honey-hued woods and rattans, private safes, and deluxe mattresses on the king or double beds. Bathrooms have all the amenities, from robes to hair dryers to thick towels; a few feature Jacuzzis. About 150 of the units, designed as comfortable bungalows, are in the outer reaches of the garden. Known as *casitas,* they include Roman tubs, atrium showers, and access to the fern-lined paths of a tropical jungle a few steps away. A 17-story, $60 million wing with 120 suites, all oceanfront, was completed late in 1998. The ultra-luxury tower features 103 one- or two-bedroom units, eight garden suites, five governor's suites, and four presidential suites.

Dining/Diversions: There is no hotel in the entire Caribbean that offers such a rich diversity of dining options and such high-quality food, often made with the finest and most expensive of ingredients. Even if you're not a guest, consider at least one dinner here. It's a sightseeing attraction in its own right, and its cuisine is worth the trip. La Veranda Restaurant, near the beach, is open 24 hours, serving American and Caribbean food. Yamato, a Japanese restaurant, is one of the best at the hotel. Good Italian food is served at La Piccola Fontane. Or you can promenade down a re-creation of a Hong Kong waterfront to a Chinese restaurant, Back Street Hong Kong. The Palm Restaurant is a branch of the fabled midtown Manhattan steakhouse, an exact replica of the New York dining room, right down to the cartoons and celebrity caricatures (see "Where to Dine," below). At the new rooftop Ranch Restaurant, you can chow down on barbecued ribs and chicken. (Waiters greet guests with a "buenas noches, y'all.") Tequila Bar & Grill is known for its Mexican food, mighty margaritas, and sunset views. Finally, the main lobby now sports a trendy Cigar Bar (see "San Juan After Dark," below). The in-house casino is open daily from noon to 4am.

Amenities: Rooftop health club, Penthouse Spa, two pools, water sports, steam room, sauna, tennis court, table tennis, 24-hour room service, dry cleaning, babysitting, massage service. The supervised Kids Klub has daily activities ranging from face painting to swimming lessons—all for children 5 to 12. There will also be a three-floor underground parking garage, plus four new tennis courts and a pro shop.

✪ **Ritz-Carlton San Juan Hotel & Casino.** 6961 State Rd., #187, Isla Verde, Carolina, PR 00979. ☎ **800/241-3333,** or 787/253-1777. Fax 787/253-0700. www.ritzcarlton.com/ location/caribbean/55.main.htm. 414 units. A/C MINIBAR TV TEL. Winter $400–$475 double; from $950 suite. Off-season $300–$360 double; from $825 suite. AE, DC, DISC, MC, V. Valet parking $10. Bus: A7, M7, or T1.

Only a couple of years old, the Ritz-Carlton immediately took its place among the most spectacular deluxe hotels in Puerto Rico (though we still give a slight edge to El San Juan). The beachfront hotel is only 15 minutes from the airport on 8 acres of prime ocean-view property. Appealing to both business travelers and vacationers, it's a trail-blazer in tropical elegance. The hotel decor reflects Caribbean flavor and the Hispanic culture of the island, with artwork from well-known local artists, wrought-iron chandeliers, and tropical plants; beveled and leaded glass throughout the building captures views of the ocean.

Beautifully furnished guest rooms open onto ocean views or green mountains. Rooms have rattan furniture, contemporary artwork, excellent mattresses, fine linen, and tasteful fabrics, plus honor bars and dataports. The luxurious bathrooms have hair dryers, fluffy towels, scales, terry bathrobes, and deluxe personal toiletries. Some rooms are accessible for guests with disabilities. The preferred accommodations are in the upper-floor Ritz-Carlton Club, which has the added benefit of a private lounge and personal concierge staff, accessed by a key-activated elevator only.

Dining/Diversions: The dining here is second only to the El San Juan. The Ritz-Carlton premier venue, the Vineyard Room, rates a separate recommendation (see below). The Caribbean Grill offers alfresco dining and ocean views; it specializes in Caribbean market buffets, but also offers an à la carte menu. The Ocean Bar and Grill is also alfresco, with panoramic views of the beach and ocean, often complemented by a live steel band. "The Bar," as it's called, has dark paneling and deep burgundy leather club chairs, offering drinks and cigars. The Lobby Lounge, also with panoramic ocean views and live entertainment nightly, is especially noted for its afternoon tea. The hotel has the Caribbean's largest casino (see below).

Amenities: The 12,000-square foot spa, the largest and most sophisticated of its kind on Puerto Rico, has panoramic ocean views; it offers yoga, fitness programs, aerobics, and aqua-aerobics in the pool. Upstairs, there are 11 treatment rooms, offering facials, massages, manicures, pedicures, hydrotherapy, body wraps, and more. Healthful cuisine is available to serious spa-goers, too. Two lit tennis courts, 7,200-square-foot outdoor pool overlooking the beach, twice-daily maid service, 24-hour room service, laundry service, baby-sitting, beauty salon, programs for children. Arrangements can be made for golf, snorkeling, fishing, waterskiing, sailing, and horseback riding.

San Juan Grand Beach Hotel & Casino. 187 Isla Verde Ave., Isla Verde, PR 00979. ☎ **800/443-2009** in the U.S., or 787/791-6100. Fax 787/791-8525. www.sjgrand.com. E-mail: sjgrand@coqui.net. 420 units. A/C TV TEL. Winter $295–$525 double; from $525 suite. Off-season $235–$315 double; from $395 suite. AE, DC, DISC, MC, V. Self-parking $5; valet parking $12. Bus: A7, M7, or T1.

In January 1998, this four-star resort reopened on the site of the former Sands hotel, following an extensive $15.2-million restoration. It is still outclassed by the far swankier El San Juan Hotel next door, but amid tropical gardens and with a beachfront setting, it enjoys a high occupancy rate, and is often featured in package tours. Most of the comfortable, medium-size rooms have balconies and terraces. All units have the same amenities but are priced differently based on exposure, the most expensive being on the top floor, even though they lack balconies. Extras include coffeemakers, second phones, irons and ironing boards, and luxury beds with deluxe mattresses, tasteful fabrics, and fine linen. Bathrooms have power showerheads, deep tubs, thick towels, hair dryers, and scales. The most desirable units are in the Plaza Club, a mini-hotel within the hotel that sports a private entrance, concierge service, complimentary food and beverage buffets, and suite/spa and beach facilities.

Dining/Diversions: Although this hotel's restaurants don't equal those of the nearby El San Juan, it's still got fine restaurants. In fact, Giuseppe offers some of the beachfront's best northern Italian food, and Ruth's Chris Steak House serves the juiciest steaks in Puerto Rico. On the boardwalk, Ciao offers breakfast and light Mediterranean fare. In the lobby area is a teppanyaki and sushi bar. At the Grand Market, you can buy a picnic basket for a day on the beach. The in-house nightclub offers revue-style spoofs of Hollywood legends and glittery, Vegas-inspired shows. The casino is also popular.

Amenities: The resort boasts the Caribbean's largest free-form swimming pool, complete with waterfalls, rockscapes, and a swim-up bar; business center; scuba diving; room service (6am to 2pm and 5pm to 2am), baby-sitting, laundry, limousine service, massage service.

Expensive

Crown Plaza Hotel & Casino. Rte. 187, km 1.5 Isla Verde, San Juan, PR 00979. ☎ **800/ 2-CROWN** in the U.S. and Canada, or 787/253-2929. Fax 787/253-0079. 254 units. A/C TV TEL. Winter $199–$239 double; $239–$369 suite. Off-season $169–$209 double; $199–$269 suite. AE, DC, DISC, MC, V. Self-parking $6; valet parking $10. Bus: T1.

This is the easternmost of the grand modern hotels of San Juan, and the leading Caribbean showcase of the Holiday Inn chain. Severely battered by Hurricane Georges in 1998, it should be fully functional by the time of your arrival, following massive restorations (ask when you reserve, though). A preferred choice for business travelers, it's set on a landscaped plot of beachfront near the airport. The hotel incorporates tropical themes and colors in its decor, and rises 12 stories above a great sandy beach studded with palm trees and sea grapes.

The bedrooms—each of a standard motel size—offer some kind of ocean view and are bright and inviting in spite of the standard decor. They have either king or double beds, each fitted with a quality mattress and fine linen. The bathrooms are more modest, though well maintained. Each room is double-insulated against noises from the nearby airport. Units on the concierge floors have free continental breakfast and evening hors d'oeuvres.

Dining/Diversions: An acceptable (but not great) Italian cuisine is offered at La Dolce Vita. The food isn't a major reason to stay here, but you can always take a taxi over to the El San Juan Hotel. There's also a large casino.

Amenities: Large free-form pool with swim-up bar, car-rental facilities, tour desk, children's games room, children's pool, fitness center, gift shop, and both a sports club and a beach club devoted to land and water sports. Room service (from 6:30am to midnight), baby-sitting, laundry.

Moderate

Travelodge. Av. Isla Verde (P.O. Box 6007, Loiza Station), Santurce, San Juan, PR 00914. ☎ **800/578-7878** or 787/728-1300. Fax 787/268-7150. 90 units. A/C TV TEL. Winter $135 double; $175 suite. Off-season $93 double; $150 suite. AE, MC, V.

Rising eight stories above the busy traffic of Isla Verde, this chain hotel offers comfortable but small bedrooms furnished simply with bland, modern furniture. They're done in typical motel style, with small but serviceable bathrooms. Many guests carry a tote bag to the beach across the street, then hit the bars and restaurants of the expensive hotels nearby. There's only one restaurant (the Country Kitchen), one pool, and one bar (the Escort Lounge), which features live dance music every Wednesday to Saturday night. In 1997, about a third of the hotel's rooms were renovated; more are set to be spruced up. Though it's simple and not very personal, this is a good choice for the money.

WHERE TO DINE
IN OLD SAN JUAN
Very Expensive

✪ **Chef Marisoll.** Calle del Cristo 202. ☎ **787/725-7454**. Reservations required. Main courses $24–$32. AE, MC, V. Tues–Sat noon–2:30pm; Tues–Sun 7–10:30pm. Bus: A7, T1, or 2. CONTEMPORARY.

Marisoll Hernández is one of the top chefs of Puerto Rico. Trained in Hilton properties, including one in London, she broke away to become an independent restaurateur in the Old Town of San Juan. In a Spanish colonial building, with a courtyard patio for dining, her eight-table restaurant is warm and intimate. Service is low-key and slightly formal, though a bit distracted. Two of her soups are worthy of appearing in

Gourmet magazine, including a cream of exotic wild mushrooms with an essence of black truffles, and her butternut-squash soup with crisp ginger. Caesar salads might appear garnished with duck or lobster. There's usually a catch of the day, such as dorado with a medley of sauces—whatever strikes the chef's fancy. You can also sample her risotto with shrimp, lobster, and scallops in a saffron sauce. A truly elegant and beautifully flavored tenderloin with foie gras is another specialty.

La Chaumière. Calle Tetuán 367. ☎ **787/722-3330.** Reservations recommended. Main courses $22–$34. AE, DC, MC, V. Mon–Sat 6pm–midnight. Closed July–Aug. Bus: A7, T1, or 2. FRENCH.

Behind the famous Tapía Theater, this restaurant with a cafe-style decor has a loyal following of foodies drawn to its classic cuisine. The setting is almost like a greenhouse. You might begin with a hearty country pâté, then follow with a rack of baby lamb Provençale. A tender Châteaubriand is served only for two. Two old standbys, veal Oscar and oysters Rockefeller, also regularly appear.

Expensive

Il Perugino. Calle del Cristo 105. ☎ **787/722-5481.** Reservations required. Main courses $18–$32. AE, MC, V. Daily 6:30–11pm. Bus: A7, T1, or 2. TUSCAN/UMBRIAN.

This is one of the most elegant Italian restaurants in San Juan, with a courtyard containing covered tables. It's located in a 200-year-old town house, a short walk uphill from the cathedral. The entire setting is painted in shades of ochre and umber, reminiscent of Perugia, the homeland of owner/chef Franco Seccarelli. Dishes and flavors are perfectly balanced. Examples include shrimp salad (usually a mundane dish, but quite special here), a carpaccio of scallops, a perfectly marinated fresh salmon, veal entrecôte with mushrooms, and medaillons of beef flavored with balsamic vinegar. Want something more adventurous? Try the "black pasta" with crayfish and baby eels.

✪ Parrot Club. Calle Fortaleza 363. ☎ **787/725-7370.** Reservations not accepted. Main courses $9–$24 lunch, $9–$16 brunch, $16–$24 dinner. MC, V. Tues–Fri 11:30am–3pm, Sat noon–3pm; Tues–Wed 6–11pm, Thurs–Sat 6pm–midnight; Sun noon–4pm and 6:30–10pm. Closed 2 weeks in July. Bus: A7, T1, or 2. MODERN PUERTO RICAN.

The hottest restaurant in Old San Juan at the moment is this bistro and bar serving a Nuevo Latino cuisine that blends traditional Puerto Rican cookery with Spanish, Taíno, and African influences, heightened by rich, contemporary touches. It's set in a neighborhood known as SOFO (South of Fortaleza Street), within a stately looking 1902 building that was originally a hair-tonic factory. Today, you'll find a cheerful-looking dining room where Gloria Vanderbilt, San Juan's mayor, and the governor of Puerto Rico can sometimes be spotted, and a verdantly landscaped courtyard where tables for at least 200 diners are scattered amid potted ferns, palms, and orchids. Live music, either Brazilian, salsa, or Latino jazz, is offered every night of the week, as well as during the popular Sunday brunches.

Menu items are updated interpretations of old-fashioned Puerto Rican specialties. They include ceviche of halibut, salmon, tuna, and mahimahi that's marinated in lime juice and seasonings; delicious crab cakes; *criolla*-style flank steak; and pan-seared tuna served with a sauce made from dark rum and essence of oranges. Everybody's favorite drink is a "parrot passion," made from lemon-flavored rum, triple sec, oranges, and passion fruit.

Moderate

✪ Amadeus. Calle San Sebastián 106 (across from the Iglesia de San José). ☎ **787/722-8635.** Reservations recommended. Main courses $8–$24. AE, MC, V. Mon 6pm–2am, Tues–Sun noon–2am (kitchen closes at 12:30am). Bus: M2, M3, or T1. CARIBBEAN.

Housed in a brick-and-stone building that was constructed in the 18th century by a wealthy merchant, Amadeus offers Caribbean ingredients with a nouvelle twist. The appetizers alone are worth the trip here, especially the Amadeus dumplings with guava sauce and arrowroot fritters. The chef will even prepare a smoked-salmon-and-caviar pizza. While receiving a cordial welcome, you can enjoy dishes *de la tierra* (from the land) or *del mar* (from the sea), including a fresh catch of the day. One zesty specialty is pork scaloppini with sweet-and-sour sauce.

El Patio de Sam. Calle San Sebastián 102 (across from the Iglesia de San José). ☎ **787/723-1149.** Sandwiches, burgers, salads $8.95–$12; main courses $10.95–$22.95. AE, DC, DISC, MC, V. Sun–Thurs 11am–midnight, Fri–Sat 11am–1:30am. Bus: A7, T1, or 2. AMERICAN/PUERTO RICAN.

This is a popular gathering spot for American expatriates, newspeople, and shopkeepers, and is known for having the best burgers in San Juan. Even though the dining room is not outdoors, it has been transformed into a patio. You'll swear you're dining alfresco: Every table is placed near a cluster of potted plants, and canvas panels and awnings cover the skylight. For a satisfying lunch, try the black-bean soup, followed by the burger platter, and top it off with a Key lime tart. Except for the hamburgers, some other items on the menu have not met with favor among many visitors, who have written us that the food was overpriced and the service confused. Nevertheless, it remains Old Town's most popular dining room. There's now live entertainment, Tuesday through Saturday, with a guitarist playing Spanish music some nights, giving way to a classical pianist on other nights.

Inexpensive
Butterfly People Café. Calle Fortaleza 152. ☎ **787/723-2432.** Reservations not required. Main courses $5.50–$13. AE, DC, MC, V. Mon–Sat 11am–5pm. Bus: Old Town trolley. CONTINENTAL/AMERICAN.

This butterfly venture with gossamer wings (see "Shopping," below) is on the second floor of a restored mansion in Old San Juan. Next to the world's largest gallery devoted to butterflies, you can dine in the cafe, which overlooks a patio and has 15 tables inside. The cuisine is tropical and light European fare made with fresh ingredients. You might begin with gazpacho or vichyssoise, follow with quiche or a daily special, and finish with chocolate mousse or the tantalizing raspberry chiffon pie with fresh raspberry sauce. Wherever you look are lovely framed butterflies.

Hard Rock Café. Calle Recinto Sur 253. ☎ **787/724-7625.** Reservations recommended. Main courses $6.99–$17.99. AE, MC, V. Daily 11:30am–midnight. (Bar daily 11am–2am.) Bus: A7, T1, or 2. AMERICAN.

Serving a "classic" American cuisine against a backdrop of loud rock music, the Hard Rock is here to stay, packing in the crowds for drinks, burgers, and T-shirts. You've seen it all before, but there's a decent memorabilia collection in this one, including one of Elton John's wigs, John Lennon's jacket, a Pink Floyd guitar, and Phil Collins's drumsticks.

✪ La Bombonera. Calle San Francisco 259. ☎ **787/722-0658.** Reservations recommended. American breakfast $7; main courses $6.55–$18. AE, DISC, MC, V. Daily 7:30am–8pm. Bus: M2, M3, or T1. PUERTO RICAN.

Offering exceptional value, this place has been offering homemade pastries, well-stuffed sandwiches, and endless cups of coffee since 1902. Its atmosphere evokes turn-of-the-century Castile transplanted to the New World. The food is authentically Puerto Rican, homemade, and inexpensive, with regional dishes like rice with squid, roast leg of pork, and seafood *asopao*. For dessert, you might select an apple, pineapple, or prune pie, or one of many types of flan. Service is polite, if a bit rushed, and the place fills up quickly at lunchtime.

La Mallorquina. Calle San Justo 207. ☎ **787/722-3261.** Reservations not accepted at lunch, recommended at dinner. Dinner main courses $13.95–$25.95. AE, MC, V. Mon–Sat 11:30am–10pm. Bus: A7, T1, or 2. PUERTO RICAN.

San Juan's oldest restaurant was founded in 1848. It's in a three-story, glassed-in courtyard with arches and antique wall clocks. Even if you've already eaten, you might want to stop by for a drink at the old-fashioned wooden bar. Begin with garlic soup or gazpacho. The chef specializes in the most typical Puerto Rican rice dish: *asopao.* You can have it with either chicken, shrimp, or lobster and shrimp. *Arroz con pollo* (rice with chicken) is almost as popular. Other recommended dishes are grilled pork chop with fried plantain, beef tenderloin Puerto Rican style, and assorted seafood stewed in wine. Lunch is busy; dinners are sometimes quiet. The food seems little changed over the decades; visit here for tradition and exceptional value rather than innovation.

IN CONDADO
Very Expensive
La Scala. In the Radisson Ambassador Plaza Hotel & Casino, 1369 Ashford Ave. ☎ **787/ 721-7300.** Reservations recommended. Main courses $17–$40. AE, MC, V. Tues–Fri noon–3pm; daily 5:30–11:30pm. Bus: A7. NORTHERN ITALIAN.

One of the most sophisticated Italian restaurants in San Juan caters to discerning diners who appreciate the nuances of fine cuisine and service. The decor includes neutral colors, stucco arches, and murals. The menu lists just about the entire repertoire of northern Italian cuisine. You'll find a specialty version of Caesar salad, fresh mushrooms in garlic sauce, and a succulent, half-melted version of fresh mozzarella in carozza. The fresh fish and seafood are flown in from New York and Boston. Specialties include fresh halibut cooked in parchment, rigatoni with shiitake mushrooms and ricotta, and rack of lamb in a red-wine sauce. Most meals here are memorable, and the cooking, for the most part, is creative and delicate. Service is attentive.

✪ **Pikayo.** In the Comfort Inn Tanama Princess Hotel, Calle Joffre 1. ☎ **787/721-6194.** Reservations recommended. Main courses $26–$49. AE, MC, V. Mon–Sat 6–10:30pm. Closed 2 weeks in Dec. Bus: T1. PUERTO RICAN/CAJUN.

This is an ideal place to go for a new generation of Puerto Rican cooking, with a touch of Cajun thrown in for spice and zest. This place not only keeps up with the latest culinary trends, it often sets them. Set on the lobby level of a hotel on the Condado, the restaurant occupies a dining room lined with mahogany, varnished cherry, and light pastel shades of turquoise and green. Formal but not stuffy, it configures itself as a specialist in the *criolla* cuisine of colonial Puerto Rico, emphasizing the Spanish, Indian, and African elements that contributed to its unusual recipes. A staff member, perhaps chef Wilo Benet or his wife, Lorraine, will answer your questions about such traditional dishes as *mofongo* (plantains layered with shrimp and served with saffron-flavored broth), *viandas* (mashed tropical tubers), *tostones* (fritters made from green plantains) stuffed with codfish or cheese, or crabmeat stew. One innovative main course is fresh red snapper with a plantain crust flavored with a white-wine reduction. Especially delicious is seared yellowfin tuna with fresh onions.

✪ **Ramiro's.** Av. Magdalena 1106. ☎ **787/721-9049.** Reservations recommended off-season, required in winter. Main courses $23–$37. AE, DC, MC, V. Sun–Fri noon–3pm; Mon–Thurs 6:30–10:30pm, Fri–Sat 6:30—11pm, Sun 6–10pm. Bus: A7, T1, or 2. SPANISH/INTERNATIONAL.

In a half-century-old building near the Marriott Hotel, you'll find a refined cuisine and a touch of Old Spain. This restaurant prepares "New Creole" cooking, a style pioneered by owner and chef Jesús Ramiro. The menu is the most imaginative on the Condado. You might begin with breadfruit *mille-feuille* with local crabmeat and avocado. For your main course, any fresh fish or meat can be charcoal-grilled for you on request. Some of the latest menu specialties include paillard of lamb with spiced root vegetables and guava sauce, char-grilled black Angus steak with shiitake mushrooms, or grilled striped sea bass with a citrus sauce. Among the many homemade desserts are caramelized mango on puff pastry with strawberry-and-guava sauce, and "four seasons" chocolate.

Expensive

Chayote. In the Olimpo Hotel, Av. Miramar 603. ☎ **787/722-9385.** Reservations recommended. Main courses $16–$24. AE, MC, V. Tues–Fri noon–2:30pm; Tues–Sat 7–10:30pm. Bus: 5. PUERTO RICAN/INTERNATIONAL.

Chayote's cuisine is among the most innovative in San Juan. It draws local business leaders, government officials, and film stars such as Sylvester Stallone and Melanie Griffith. It's an artsy, modern, basement-level bistro in a surprisingly obscure hotel (the Olimpo). The restaurant changes its menu every three months, but you might find appetizers like a yuca turnover stuffed with crabmeat and served with a mango and papaya chutney, or a ripe plantain stuffed with chicken and served with a fresh tomato sauce. For a main dish, you might try a red snapper fillet with a citrus vinaigrette made of passion fruit, orange, and lemon. An exotic touch appears in the pork fillet seasoned with dried fruits and spices in a tamarind sauce and served with a green banana and taro root timbale. To finish off your meal, there's nothing better than the mango flan served with macerates strawberries.

✪ **Compostela.** Av. Condado 106. ☎ **787/724-6088.** Reservations required. Main courses $19–$34. AE, DC, MC, V. Mon–Fri noon–3pm; Mon–Sat 6:30–10:30pm. Bus: 2. SPANISH/PUERTO RICAN.

This restaurant offers formal service from a battalion of well-dressed waiters. Established by a Galician-born family, the pine-trimmed restaurant has gained a reputation as one of the best in the capital. The chef made his name on the roast peppers stuffed with salmon mousse. Equally delectable is duck with orange and ginger sauce or baby rack of lamb with fresh herbs. Of course, any shellfish grilled in a brandy sauce is a sure winner. The chef also makes two different versions of paella, both savory. The wine cellar, comprised of some 10,000 bottles, is one of the most impressive in San Juan.

Ristorante Tuscany. In the San Juan Marriott Resort, 1309 Ashford Ave. ☎ **787/722-7000.** Reservations recommended. Main courses $10–$30. AE, DC, DISC, MC, V. Daily 6–11pm. Bus: B21. NORTHERN ITALIAN.

This is the showcase restaurant of one of the most elaborate hotel reconstructions in the history of Puerto Rico, and the kitchen continues to rack up culinary awards. You'll have lots of choices here, including a range of gourmet pizzas prepared in a wood-burning oven. The chef doesn't skimp on ingredients, preparing such elegant selections as a veal chop with a Brunnello Tuscan red-wine sauce or seafood casserole with shrimp, scallops, and prawns with tomato sauce. There are several appealing pastas, such as ravioli filled with lobster and herbs (served with a leek and saffron sauce), or a trio of risottos that can be ordered as an appetizer or main course. Sirloin steak Florentine style arrives perfectly cooked.

Moderate

Ajili Mójili. 1052 Ashford Ave. (at the corner of Calle Joffre). ☎ **787/725-9195.** Reservations recommended. Main courses $13–$28. AE, MC, V. Sun–Thurs 6–10pm, Fri–Sat 6–11pm, Sun 12:30–4pm. Bus: B21. PUERTO RICAN/CREOLE.

This is the only restaurant in San Juan's tourist zone that's devoted exclusively to *la cucina criolla*, the starchy, down-home cuisine that developed on the island a century ago. It's set in the heart of the Condado's tourist strip, across from the convention center. Though the building housing it is quite modern, look for artful replicas of the kind of crumbling brick walls you'd expect in Old San Juan, and a bar that evokes Old Spain. The staff will willingly describe menu items in colloquial English. Locals come here for a taste of the food they enjoyed at their mother's knee, like *mofongos* (green plantains stuffed with veal, chicken, shrimp, or pork), *arroz con pollo* (stewed chicken with saffron rice), *medallones de cerdo encebollado* (pork loin sautéed with onions), *carne mechada* (beef rib eye stuffed with ham), and *lechon asado con maposteado* (roast pork with rice and beans). Wash it all down with an ice-cold bottle of local beer, such as Medalla.

In Santurce

✪ **La Casona.** Calle San Jorge 609 (at the corner of Av. Fernández Juncos). ☎ **787/727-2717.** Reservations required. Main courses $24–$45. AE, DC, MC, V. Mon–Fri noon–3pm; Mon–Sat 6–11pm. Bus: 1. SPANISH/INTERNATIONAL.

La Casona, in a turn-of-the-century mansion surrounded by gardens, offers the kind of dining usually found in Madrid, complete with a strolling guitarist. The much-renovated but still charming place draws some of the most fashionable diners on Puerto Rico. Paella marinara, prepared for two or more, is a specialty, as is *zarzuela de mariscos* (seafood medley). Or you might select fillet of grouper in Basque sauce, octopus vinaigrette, osso buco (veal shanks), or a rack of lamb. Grilled red snapper is a specialty, and you can order it with almost any sauce you want, although the chef recommends one made from olive oil, herbs, lemon, and pulverized toasted garlic. The cuisine here has both flair and flavor.

In Ocean Park

✪ **Pamela's.** In the Número Uno Guest House, Calle Santa Ana 1, Ocean Park. ☎ **787/726-5010.** Reservations recommended. Main courses $18–$29. AE, MC, V. Sat–Sun noon–3pm; Mon–Fri 7–10:30pm. CARIBBEAN FUSION.

This guest house in Ocean Park is a surprising place to find one of the finest chefs in the Caribbean, Pamela Hope Yahn. But that's what you get at Pamela's. For starters, we recommend her stuffed shrimp with a ginger mousse or one of her delectable and original soups—perhaps spiced South American turkey, corn, and potato, served with an aji sauce, avocado, and sour cream. Move on to a main dish of red snapper with baked stuffed mango, hearts of palm, and both portobello and button mushrooms—Caribbean dining at its finest. You might also opt for the Jamaican-style roast loin of pork with candied ginger, dark rum, cloves, lime, and garlic, accompanied by nutmeg-scented sweet potatoes. The desserts are equally yummy. Hours may change during the life of this edition, so call for the latest schedules.

In Isla Verde

Very Expensive

The Palm. In the El San Juan Hotel, 6063 Isla Verde Rd., Carolina. ☎ **787/791-1000.** Reservations recommended. Main courses $16–$35, except lobster, which is priced by the pound, and can easily cost $80 per person. AE, DC, MC, V. Daily 6–10pm. STEAKS/SEAFOOD.

The management of San Juan's most elegant hotel invited the Palm, a legendary New York steakhouse, to open a branch on the premises. The setting includes a stylish, masculine-looking saloon, where drinks are stiff, and artfully simple linen-covered tables set in a room decorated with caricatures of local personalities, politicians, artists, and personalities-about-town. If you've hit it big at the nearby casino, maybe you'll want to celebrate with the Palm's famous and famously pricey lobster (the lobster and all the shellfish can be shockingly expensive). Otherwise, there's a tempting number of options, all served in gargantuan portions: jumbo lump crabmeat cocktail, Caesar salad, lamb chops with mint sauce, grilled halibut steak, prime porterhouse steak, and steak "à la stone," which finishes cooking on a sizzling platter directly atop your table. One thing is certain—you'll never go hungry here.

✪ **Vineyard Room.** In The Ritz-Carlton, 6961 State Rd. #187, Isla Verde, Carolina. ☎ **787/ 253-1700.** Reservations required. Main courses $30–$45. AE, DC, MC, V. Daily 7pm– midnight. CALIFORNIA/MEDITERRANEAN.

The Ritz-Carlton's fine restaurant offers dinner in a charming setting reminiscent of a Napa Valley winery. The room's decor features rich red and gold fabrics, Frette linens, and dark etimoe-wood paneling. The California-Mediterranean cuisine is complemented by an extensive selection of California, French, German, South American, and additional Stateside wines. The menu is forever refreshing and will excite you with its possibilities. The staff is the best trained on the island.

We've made an entire menu from the cold and hot appetizers. Start off with Bacardi-marinated salmon in a cucumber dill salad that manages to wed Puerto Rican and Scandinavian culinary traditions. The salad of sesame, seaweed, and seared scallops was only surpassed by the black truffle and sweetbread medaillons. Always count on two tempting soups a night, perhaps cream of frog's legs with sweet garlic petals. Main dishes are wisely limited but exquisite, going from a braised leg of rabbit with wild mushrooms and sultanas to fillet of turbot with a saffron cracked wheat crush and crayfish. Save room for dessert, which might be a trio of crème brûlées or else green lime sabayon with a light tuile and berries.

Expensive

Back Street Hong Kong. In El San Juan Hotel & Casino, Isla Verde Ave. ☎ **787/791-1000,** ext. 1758. Reservations recommended. Main courses $16.50–$34. AE, MC, V. Daily 6pm–midnight. Bus: M4 or T1. MANDARIN/SZECHUAN/HUNAN.

To reach this restaurant, you head down a re-creation of a backwater street in Hong Kong—disassembled from its original home at the 1964 New York World's Fair, and rebuilt here with its original design intact. A few steps later, you enter one of the best Chinese restaurants in the Caribbean, serving consistently good food, filled with fragrance and flavor. Beneath a soaring redwood ceiling, you can enjoy pineapple fried rice served in a real pineapple, a version of scallops with orange sauce, Szechuan beef with chicken, or a Dragon and Phoenix (lobster mixed with shrimp).

✪ **La Piccola Fontana.** In El San Juan Hotel & Casino, Isla Verde Ave. ☎ **787/791-1000,** ext. 1271. Reservations required. Main courses $18–$36. AE, MC, V. Daily 6pm–midnight. Bus: T1. NORTHERN ITALIAN.

Right off the luxurious Palm Court in the El San Juan Hotel, this restaurant takes classic northern Italian cuisine seriously and delivers plate after plate of delectable food nightly. From its white linen to its classically formal service, it enjoys a fine reputation. The food is straightforward, generous, and extremely well prepared. You'll dine in one of two neo-Palladian rooms whose wall frescoes depict Italy's ruins and landscapes. Menu items range from the appealingly simple (grilled fillets of fish or grilled veal chops) to more elaborate dishes such as tortellini San Daniele, made with veal, prosciutto, cream, and sage; or *linguine scogliere*, with shrimps, clams, and seafood. Grilled medaillons of filet mignon are served with braised arugula, Parmesan cheese, and balsamic vinegar.

Inexpensive

✪ **Metropol.** Av. Isla Verde. ☎ **787/791-4046.** Reservations not necessary. Main courses $5.50–$28.90. AE, MC, V. Daily 11am–7pm. CUBAN/PUERTO RICAN/INTERNATIONAL.

This is part of a restaurant chain known for serving the island's best Cuban food, although the chefs prepare a much wider range of dishes. Metropol is the happiest blend of Cuban and Puerto Rican cuisine we've ever had. The black-bean soup is among the island's finest, served in the classic Havana style with a side dish of rice and chopped onions. Endless garlic bread accompanies most dinners, likely to include Cornish game hen stuffed with Cuban rice and beans or perhaps marinated steak topped with a fried egg (reportedly Castro's favorite). Smoked chicken or chicken fried steak are also heartily recommended; portions are huge. Plantains, yucca, and all that good stuff accompany most dishes. Finish with a choice of thin or firm custard. Most dishes are at the low end of the price scale.

IN MIRAMAR

Augusto's Cuisine. In the Hotel Excelsior, 101 Av. Ponce de León, Miramar. ☎ **787/ 725-7700.** Reservations recommended. Main courses $25–$32; set menu $66–$96. AE, MC, V. Tues–Fri noon–3pm; Tues–Sat 7–9:30pm. FRENCH/INTERNATIONAL.

This is one of the most elegant and glamorous restaurants of Puerto Rico, with a European flair. Austrian-born owner/chef Augusto Schreiner, assisted by a partly French-born staff, operates from a gray-and-green dining room set on the lobby level of a 15-story hotel in Miramar, a suburb near the island's main airport. Menu items are concocted from strictly fresh ingredients, and include such dishes as lobster risotto, rack of lamb with aromatic herbs and fresh garlic, an oft-changing cream-based soup of the day (one of the best is corn and fresh oyster soup), and a succulent version of medaillons of veal Rossini style, prepared with foie gras and Madeira sauce. The wine list is one of the most extensive on the island.

HITTING THE BEACH

Some public stretches of shoreline around San Juan are overcrowded, especially on Saturday and Sunday; others are practically deserted. If you find that secluded, hidden beach of your dreams, proceed with caution. On unguarded beaches you'll have no way to protect yourself or your valuables should you be approached by a robber or mugger, which has been known to happen. For more information about the island's many beaches, call the **Department of Sports and Recreation** (☎ 787/721-2500).

All beaches on Puerto Rico, even those fronting the top hotels, are open to the public, although you will be charged for parking and for use of *balneario* facilities, such as lockers and showers. Public beaches shut down on Monday; if Monday is a holiday, the beaches are open for the holiday but close the next day, Tuesday. Beach hours are from 9am to 5pm in winter, to 6pm off-season. Major public beaches in the San Juan area have changing rooms and showers; Luquillo also has picnic tables.

Famous with beach buffs since the 1920s, ✪ **Condado Beach** put San Juan on the map as a tourist resort. Backed up by high-rise hotels, it seems more like Miami Beach than any other in the Caribbean. From parasailing to sailing, all sorts of water sports can be booked at kiosks along the beach or at the activities desk of the various hotels. There are also plenty of outdoor bars and restaurants when you tire of the sands. Condado is especially busy wherever a high-rise resort is located. People watching seems a favorite sport along these golden strands.

At the end of Puente Dos Hermanos, the westernmost corner of the Condado is the most popular strip. This section of the beach is small and shaded by palms, and a natural rock barrier calms the turbulence of the waters rushing in, making for protected, safe swimming in gin-clear waters. The lagoon on the other side of the beach is ideal for windsurfing and kayaking. The lagoon runs east to west, and its waters are tranquil with steady parallel winds.

A favorite of San Juaneros themselves, golden-sand **Isla Verde Beach** is also ideal for swimming, and it, too, is lined with high-rise resorts à la Miami Beach. Many luxury condos are also on this beachfront. Isla Verde has picnic tables, so you can pick up the makings of a lunch and make it a day at the beach. This strip is also good for snorkeling because of its calm, clear waters, and many kiosks will rent you equipment. Isla Verde Beach extends from the end of Ocean Park to the beginning of a section called Boca Cangrejos. The best beach at Isla Verde is at the Hotel El San Juan. Most sections of this long strip have separate names, such as El Alambique, which is often the site of beach parties, and Punta El Medio, bordering the new Ritz-Carlton, also a great beach and very popular even with the locals. If you go past the luxury hotels and expensive condos behind the Luís Muñoz Marín International Airport, you arrive at the major public beach at Isla Verde. Here you'll find a balneario with parking, showers, fast-food joints, and water-sports equipment. The sands here are whiter than the golden sands of the Condado, and are lined with coconut palms, sea-grape trees, and even almond trees, all of which provide shade from the fierce noonday sun.

One of the most attractive beaches in the Greater San Juan area is **Ocean Park,** a mile of fine gold sand in a neighborhood east of Condado. This beach attracts both young people and a big gay crowd. Access to the beach at Ocean Park has been limited recently, but the best place to enter is from a section called El Ultimo Trolley. This area is also ideal for volleyball, paddleball, and other games. The easternmost portion, known as Punta Las Marias, is best for windsurfing. The waters at Ocean Park are fine for swimming, although they can get rough at times.

Rivaling Condado and Isla Verde beaches, ✪ **Luquillo Public Beach** is the grandest in Puerto Rico and one of the most popular. It's 30 miles east of San Juan near the town of Luquillo. Here you'll find a mile-long half-moon bay set against a backdrop of coconut palms. This is another of the dozen or so balnearios of Puerto Rico. Saturday and Sunday are the worst times to go, as hordes of San Juaneros head here for fun in the sun. Water-sports kiosks are available, offering everything from windsurfing to sailing. Facilities include lifeguards, an emergency first-aid station, ample parking, showers, and toilets. You can easily have a local lunch here at one of the beach shacks offering cod fritters and tacos.

SPORTS & OUTDOOR PURSUITS

CRUISES   For the best cruises of San Juan Bay, go to Caribe **Aquatic Adventures** (see "Scuba Diving," below). Bay cruises start at $20 per person.

DEEP-SEA FISHING   It's top-notch! Allison tuna, white and blue marlin, sailfish, wahoo, dolphin (mahimahi), mackerel, and tarpon are some of the fish that can be caught in Puerto Rican waters, where 30 world records have been broken. Charter arrangements can be made through most major hotels and resorts.

Capt. Mike Benitez, who has chartered out of San Juan for more than 40 years, is one of the most qualified sport-fishing captains in the world. Past clients have included Jimmy Carter. **Benitez Fishing Charters** can be contacted directly at P.O. Box 9066541, Puerto de Tierra, San Juan, PR 00906 (☎ **787/723-2292** until 9pm). The captain offers a 45-foot air-conditioned deluxe Hatteras, the *Sea Born*. Fishing tours for parties of up to six cost $450 for a half-day excursion and $750 for a full day, with beverages and all equipment included.

HORSE RACING   Great thoroughbreds and outstanding jockeys compete all year at **El Comandante,** Avenida 65 de Infantería, Route 3, kilometer 15.3, at Canovanas (☎ **787/724-6060**), Puerto Rico's only racetrack, a 20-minute drive east of the center of San Juan. Post time varies from 2:15 to 2:45pm on Monday, Wednesday, Friday, Saturday, and Sunday. Entrance to the clubhouse costs $3, although no admission is charged for the grandstand.

SCUBA DIVING   In San Juan, the best outfitter is **Caribe Aquatic Adventures,** P.O. Box 9024278, San Juan Station, San Juan, PR 00902 (☎ **787/724-1882** or 787/765-7444), which operates a dive shop in the rear lobby of the Radisson Normandie Hotel. The company offers diving certification from both PADI and NAUI as part of 40-hour courses priced at $465 each. A resort course for first-time divers costs $97. Also offered are local daily dives in San Juan or windsurfing (see below), and a choice of full-day diving expeditions to various reefs off the east coast of Puerto Rico. If time is severely limited, the outfitter will take you to sites in San Juan where diving is best—but since the best dive sites are out on the island's coasts, the serious scuba diver will want to take a full-day tour.

SNORKELING   Snorkeling is better in the outlying portions of the island instead of in overcrowded San Juan. But if you don't have time to explore greater Puerto Rico, you'll find that most of the popular beaches, such as Luquillo and Isla Verde, have pretty good visibility and kiosks renting equipment. Snorkeling equipment generally costs $15. If you're on your own in the San Juan area, one of the best places is the San Juan Bay marina near the Caribe Hilton.

Water-sports desks at the big San Juan hotels at Isla Verde and Condado can generally make arrangements for instruction and equipment rental and can also lead you to the best places for snorkeling, depending on where you are in the sprawling metropolis. If your hotel doesn't offer such services, you can also contact **Caribe Aquatic Adventures** (see "Scuba Diving," above), which caters to both snorkelers and scuba divers. Other possibilities for equipment rentals are at **Caribbean School of Aquatics,** Taft No. 1, Suite 10F, in San Juan (☎ **787/728-6606**), and **Mundo Submarino,** Laguna Gardens Shopping Center, Isla Verde (☎ **787/791-5764**).

TENNIS   In San Juan, the **Caribe Hilton & Casino,** Puerta de Tierra (☎ **787/ 721-0303**), and the **Condado Plaza Hotel & Casino,** 999 Ashford Ave. (☎ **787/ 721-1000**), have courts. Nonguests can use these hotel courts if they make reservations. There's also 17 public courts, lit at night, at **San Juan Central Municipal Park,** at Calle Cerra (exit on Route 2; ☎ **787/722-1646**). Fees are $3 an hour from 8am to 6pm, going up to $4 per hour from 6 to 10pm.

WINDSURFING   A favorite spot it the sheltered waters of the Condado Lagoon in San Juan. Throughout the island, many of the companies featuring snorkeling and scuba diving also offer windsurfing equipment and instruction, and dozens of hotels offer facilities on their own premises.

One of the best places in San Juan to go windsurfing is at the Radisson Normandie Hotel, where **Caribe Aquatic Adventures** has its main branch (☎ **787/724-1882** or 787/765-7444). Board rentals cost $25 per hour, with a lesson costing $45.

STEPPING BACK IN TIME:
EXPLORING THE HISTORIC SITES OF SAN JUAN

The Spanish moved to Old San Juan in 1521, and the city played an important role as Spain's bastion of defense in the Caribbean. Today, the streets are narrow and teeming with traffic, but a walk through Old San Juan (El Viejo San Juan) is like a stroll through 5 centuries of history. You can do it in less than a day. In a

7-square-block landmark area in the westernmost part of the city, you can see many of Puerto Rico's chief historical attractions, and do some shopping along the way.

You can explore on your own, but if you'd like to be guided by an expert, consider the walking tours offered by **Colonial Adventures,** Calle Recinto Sur 201, in Old San Juan (☎ 787/729-0114), for which you'll need a reservation. They're usually conducted Monday through Saturday at 10am, 2pm, and 4pm; last for 2 hours; and begin and end at Pier 1, near the Plaza Darsena, in Old San Juan. The price is $20 for a 2-hour tour.

CHURCHES

Capilla de Cristo. Calle del Cristo (directly west of Paseo de la Princesa). Free admission. Tues 10am–2pm. Bus: Old Town trolley.

The Cristo Chapel was built to commemorate what legend says was a miracle. In 1753, a young rider lost control of his horse in a race down this very street during the fiesta of St. John's Day, plunging over the precipice. Moved by the accident, the secretary of the city, Don Mateo Pratts, invoked Christ to save the youth, and had the chapel built when his prayers were answered. Today it's a landmark in the old city and one of its best-known monuments. The chapel's gold-and-silver altar can be seen through its glass doors. Since the chapel is open only one day a week, most visitors have to settle for a view of its exterior.

Catedral de San Juan. Calle del Cristo 153 (at Caleta San Juan). ☎ **787/722-0861.** Free admission. Daily 8:30am–4pm. Bus: Old Town trolley.

San Juan Cathedral was begun in 1540 and has had a rough life. Restoration today has been extensive, so it hardly resembles the thatch-roofed structure that stood here until 1529, when it was wiped out by a hurricane. Hampered by lack of funds, the cathedral slowly added a circular staircase and two adjoining vaulted Gothic chambers. But then, in 1598, along came the Earl of Cumberland to loot it, and a hurricane in 1615 to blow off its roof. In 1908, the body of Ponce de León was disinterred from the nearby Iglesia de San José and placed here in a marble tomb near the transept, where it remains. Since 1862, the cathedral has contained the wax-covered mummy of St. Pio, a Roman martyr persecuted and killed for his Christian faith. To the right of the mummy, you might notice a bizarre wooden statue of Mary with four swords stuck in her bosom. Although the cathedral's great treasures, including gold and silver, were looted long ago, many beautiful stained-glass windows remain. The cathedral faces Plaza de las Monjas (the Nuns' Square), a shady spot where you can rest and cool off.

Iglesia de San José. Plaza de San José, Calle del Cristo. ☎ **787/725-7501.** Free admission. Church and Chapel of Belém, Mon–Wed and Fri 7am–3pm, Sat 8am–1pm. Bus: Old Town trolley.

Initial plans for this church were drawn in 1523, and Dominican friars supervised its construction in 1532. Before entering, look for the statue of Ponce de León in the adjoining plaza—it was made from melted-down British cannons captured during Sir Ralph Abercromby's unsuccessful attack on San Juan in 1797.

Both the church and its monastery were closed by decree in 1838, and the property was confiscated by the royal treasury. Later, the Crown turned the convent into a military barracks. The Jesuits restored the badly damaged church. This was the place of worship for Ponce de León's descendants, who are buried here under the family's coat-of-arms. The conquistador, killed by a poisoned arrow in Florida, was interred here until his removal to the Catedral de San Juan in 1908.

Although badly looted, the church still has some treasures, including *Christ of the Ponces,* a carved crucifix presented to Ponce de León; four oils by José Campéche, the leading Puerto Rican painter of the 18th century; and two large works by Francisco Oller, the stellar artist of the late 19th and early 20th centuries. Many miracles have been attributed to a painting in the Chapel of Belém, a 15th-century Flemish work called *The Virgin of Bethlehem.*

FORTS

✪ **Castillo San Felipe del Morro.** At the end of Calle Norzagaray. ☎ **787/729-6960.** Admission $2 adults, $1 ages 13–17, free for children 12 and under. Daily 9am–5pm. Bus: A-5, B-21, or B-40.

Called "El Morro," this fort stands on a rocky promontory dominating the entrance to San Juan Bay. Constructed in 1540, the original fort was a round tower, which can still be seen deep inside the lower levels of the castle. More walls and cannon-firing positions were added, and by 1787, the fortification attained the complex design you see today. This fortress was attacked repeatedly by both the English and the Dutch.

The National Park Service protects the fortifications of Old San Juan, which have been declared a World Heritage Site by the United Nations. With some of the most dramatic views in the Caribbean, you'll find El Morro an intriguing labyrinth of dungeons, barracks, vaults, lookouts, and ramps. Historical and background information is provided in a video in English and Spanish. The nearest parking is the underground facility beneath the Quincentennial Plaza at the Ballajá barracks (Cuartel de Ballajá) on Calle Norzagaray. Sometimes park rangers lead hour-long tours for free, although you can also visit on your own. With the purchase of a ticket here, you don't have to pay the admission for Fort San Cristóbal (see below) if you visit during the same day.

✪ **Fort San Cristóbal.** In the northeast corner of Old San Juan (uphill from Plaza de Colón on Calle Norzagaray). ☎ **787/729-6960.** Admission $2 adults, $1 ages 13–17, free for children 12 and under. Daily 9am–5pm. Bus: A-5, B-21 or B-40; then the free trolley from Covadonga station to the top of the hill.

This huge fortress, begun in 1634 and re-engineered in the 1770s, is one of the largest ever built in the Americas by Spain. Its walls rise more than 150 feet above the sea, a marvel of military engineering. San Cristóbal protected San Juan against attackers coming by land as a partner to El Morro, to which it is linked by a half-mile of monumental walls and bastions filled with cannon-firing positions. A complex system of tunnels and dry moats connects the center of San Cristóbal to its "outworks," defensive elements arranged layer after layer over a 27-acre site. You'll get the idea if you look at the scale model on display. Like El Morro, the fort is administered and maintained by the National Park Service. Be sure to see the Garita del Diablo, or the Devil's Sentry Box, one of the oldest parts of San Cristóbal's defenses, and famous in Puerto Rican legend. The devil himself, it is said, would snatch away sentinels at this lonely post at the edge of the sea. In 1898, the first shots of the Spanish-American War in Puerto Rico were fired by cannons on top of San Cristóbal during an artillery duel with a U.S. Navy fleet. Sometimes park rangers lead hour-long tours for free, although you can visit on your own.

Fort San Jerónimo. Calle Rosales, east of the Caribe Hilton, at the entrance to Condado Bay. ☎ **787/724-1844.** Free admission. Wed–Sat 9am–3pm. Bus: T1.

Completed in 1608, this fort was damaged in the English assault of 1797. Reconstructed in the closing year of the 18th century, it has now been taken over by the Institute of Puerto Rican Culture. Anyone wanting to see the view from the inside must call the Caribe Hilton; security here will open the gate to let you inside, but a special request has to be made.

OTHER HISTORIC SITES

The **city walls** around San Juan were built in 1630 to protect the town against both European invaders and Caribbean pirates, and indeed were part of one of the most impregnable fortresses in the New World. Even today, they're an engineering marvel. At their top, notice the balconied buildings that served for centuries as hospitals and also residences of the island's various governors. The thickness of the walls averages 20 feet at the base and 12 feet at the top, with an average height of 40 feet. Between Fort San Cristóbal and El Morro, bastions were erected at frequent intervals. The walls come into view as you approach from San Cristóbal on your way to El Morro. To get here, take the T1 bus.

San Juan Gate, Calle San Francisco and Calle Recinto Oeste, built around 1635, just north of La Fortaleza, several blocks downhill from the cathedral, was the main gate and entry point into San Juan—that is, if you arrived by ship in the 18th century. The gate is the only one remaining of the several that once pierced the fortifications of the old walled city. To get here, take the B-21 bus.

El Arsenal. La Puntilla. ☎ **787/724-0700.** Free admission. Wed–Sun 8:30am–4:30pm. Bus: B-21.

The Spaniards used shallow craft to patrol the lagoons and mangroves in and around San Juan. Needing a base for these vessels, they constructed El Arsenal in the 19th century. It was at this base that they staged their last stand, flying the Spanish colors until the final Spaniard was removed in 1898, at the end of the Spanish-American War. Changing art exhibitions are held in the building's three galleries.

Casa Blanca. Calle San Sebastián 1. ☎ **787/724-4102.** Admission $2. Tues–Sat 9am–noon and 1–4:30pm. Bus: B-21.

Ponce de León never lived here, although construction of the house (built in 1521) is sometimes attributed to him. The house was erected 2 years after the explorer's death, and work was ordered by his son-in-law, Juan García Troche. The parcel of land was given to Ponce de León as a reward for services rendered to the Crown. Descendants of the explorer lived in the house for about 2½ centuries, until the Spanish government took it over in 1779 for use as a residence for military commanders. The U.S. government also used it as a home for army commanders. On the first floor, the Juan Ponce de León Museum is furnished with antiques, paintings, and artifacts from the 16th through the 18th centuries. In back is a garden with spraying fountains, offering an intimate and verdant respite from the monumental buildings of old San Juan.

La Fortaleza. Calle Fortaleza, overlooking San Juan Harbor. ☎ **787/721-7000,** ext. 2211. Free admission. 30-minute tours of the gardens and building (conducted in English and Spanish) given Mon–Fri, every hour 9am–4pm. Bus: B-21.

The office and residence of the governor of Puerto Rico is the oldest executive mansion in continuous use in the western hemisphere, and it has served as the island's seat of government for more than 3 centuries. Yet its history goes back farther, to 1533, when construction began on a fortress to protect San Juan's Spanish settlers during raids by Carib tribesmen and pirates. The original medieval towers remain, but as the edifice was subsequently enlarged into a palace, other modes of architecture and ornamentation were also incorporated, including baroque, Gothic, neoclassical, and Arabian. La Fortaleza has been designated a national historic site by the U.S. government. Informal but proper attire is required.

MUSEUMS

Museo de las Américas. Cuartel de Ballajá. ☎ **787/724-5052.** Free admission. Tues–Fri 10am–4pm, Sat–Sun 11am–5pm. Bus: Old Town trolley.

A Side Trip to El Yunque Tropical Rain Forest

Some 25 miles east of San Juan lies the Caribbean National Forest, known as El Yunque, the only tropical forest in the U.S. National Forest Service system. It was given its status by President Theodore Roosevelt. With 28,000 acres, it contains some 240 tree species (only half a dozen of which are found on the mainland United States). In this world of cedars and satinwood, draped in tangles of vines, you'll hear chirping birds, see wild orchids, and perhaps hear the song of the tree frog, the coquí. The entire forest is a bird sanctuary and may be the last retreat of the rare Puerto Rican parrot.

El Yunque is situated high above sea level, and the peak of El Toro rises to 3,532 feet. You can be fairly sure you'll encounter at least a brief shower, as more than 100 billion gallons of rain falls here annually—but the rain is usually over quickly and there are lots of shelters.

El Yunque offers a number of walking and hiking trails. The most scenic is the rugged El Toro Trail, which passes through four different forest systems en route to the 3,523-foot Pico El Toro, the highest peak in the forest. The signposted El Yunque Trail leads to three of the recreation area's most spectacular lookouts, and the Big Tree Trail is an easy walk to panoramic La Mina Falls. Just off the main road is La Coca Falls, a sheet of water cascading down mossy cliffs.

Nearby, the Sierra Palm Interpretive Service Center offers maps and information and arranges for guided tours of the forest.

A 45-minute drive southeast from San Juan (near the intersection of Route 3 and Route 191), El Yunque is a popular half-day or full-day outing. Major hotels provide guided tours.

El Portal Tropical Forest Center, Route 191, Rio Grande (☎ 787/ **888-1810**), an $18-million exhibition and information center, opened its doors in the tropical rain forest, with 10,000 square feet of exhibition space. Three pavilions offer exhibits and bilingual displays. The actor Jimmy Smits narrates a documentary called *Understanding the Forest.* The center is open daily from 9am to 5pm, charging an admission of $3.

One of the major new museums of San Juan, Museo de las Americas showcases the artisans of North, South, and Central America, featuring everything from carved figureheads from New England whaling ships to dugout canoes carved by Carib Indians in Dominica. It is unique in Puerto Rico and well worth a visit. Also on display is a changing collection of paintings by artists from throughout the Spanish-speaking world, some of which are for sale, and a permanent collection called "Puerto Rican *Santos,*" which includes a collection of wood saints (carved wooden depictions of saints) donated by Dr. Ricardo Alegría.

Museo Pablo Casals. Plaza de San José, Calle San Sebastián 101. ☎ **787/723-9185.** Admission $1 adults, 50¢ children. Tues–Sat 9:30am–5pm. Bus: Old Town trolley.

Adjacent to Iglesia de San José, this museum is devoted to the memorabilia left to the people of Puerto Rico by the musician Pablo Casals. The maestro's cello is here, along with a library of videos (played upon request) of some of his festival concerts. This small 18th-century house also contains manuscripts and photographs of Casals. The annual Casals Festival draws worldwide interest and attracts some of the greatest performing artists; it's still held during the first two weeks of June.

Museo de Arte e Historia de San Juan. Calle Norzagaray 150. ☎ **787/724-1875.** Free admission. Wed–Sun 10am–5pm. Bus: B-21 to Old San Juan terminal; then a trolley car from the terminal to the museum.

Located in a Spanish colonial building at the corner of Calle MacArthur, this cultural center was the city's main marketplace in the mid–19th century. Local art is displayed in the east and west galleries, and audiovisual materials reveal the history of the city. Sometimes major cultural events are staged in the museum's large courtyard. English- and Spanish-language audiovisual shows are presented Monday to Friday every hour on the hour from 9am to 4pm.

SHOPPING

U.S. citizens don't pay duty on items brought back to the United States. And you can still find great bargains on Puerto Rico, where the competition among shopkeepers is fierce.

The streets of **Old Town,** such as Calle San Francisco and Calle del Cristo, are the major venues for shopping. Note, however, that most stores in Old San Juan are closed on Sunday.

Local handcrafts can be good buys, including needlework, straw work, ceramics, hammocks, papier-mâché fruits and vegetables, and paintings and sculptures by Puerto Rican artists. Puerto Rican *santos* (saints) are sought by collectors. These carved wooden religious idols vary greatly in shape and size, and devout locals believe they have healing powers—often the ability to perform *milagros* or miracles. Santos have been called Puerto Rico's greatest contribution to the plastic arts.

The biggest and most up-to-date shopping plaza in the Caribbean Basin is **Plaza Las Americas,** in the financial district of Hato Rey, right off the Las Americas Expressway. The complex, with its fountains and advanced architecture, has more than 200 mostly upscale shops. Although many city residents shop here, you might want to skip it unless you need specific items, like clothing. Prices are about comparable to what they are Stateside, and the goods and stores are about what you'd find in a big mall back home.

If you're interested in acquiring Puerto Rican art, there are many possibilities. **Galería Botello,** Calle del Cristo 208 (☎ **787/723-2879**), is a contemporary Latin American gallery, a living tribute to the late Angel Botello, one of Puerto Rico's most outstanding artists. His paintings and bronze sculptures, evocative of his colorful background, are done in a style uniquely his own. This galería is his former home, and he restored the colonial mansion himself. On display are his and other local artists' paintings and sculptures, as well as a large collection of Puerto Rican antique *santos.* **Galería Palomas,** Calle del Cristo 207 (☎ **787/725-2660**), is another leading choice. Works range from $75 to $35,000, include some of the leading painters of the Latin American world, and are rotated every 2 to 3 weeks. The setting is a 17th-century colonial house. Of special note are works by such local artists as Homer, Moya, and Alicea.

San Juan is also a center for fashion. Try **Lindissima Shop,** Calle Fortaleza 300 (☎ **787/721-0550**), offering contemporary women's sportswear and dresses. If you want an outfit for a formal evening aboard ship, you're likely to find it here.

Nono Maldonado, 1051 Ashford Ave. (☎ **787/721-0456**), is named after its owner, a Puerto Rican designer who worked for many years as the fashion editor of *Esquire* magazine. This is one of the most fashionable and upscale haberdashers in the Caribbean. Selling both men's and women's clothing, it has everything from socks to dinner jackets, as well as ready-to-wear versions of Maldonado's twice-a-year collections. Although this is the designer's main store (midway between the Condado Plaza and the Ramada Hotel), there is also a Maldonado boutique in the El San Juan Hotel in Isla Verde.

The **Polo Ralph Lauren Factory Store,** Calle del Cristo 201 (☎ 787/722-2136), has prices that are often 35% to 40% less what you'd find on the U.S. mainland. You can find even greater discounts on irregular or slightly damaged garments. One upstairs room is devoted to home furnishings. The town's best factory outlet for clothing is **London Fog,** Calle del Cristo 156 (☎ 787/722-4334). The last thing you need in steamy San Juan is a winter overcoat or parka, but the prices here are usually so low that a purchase is often well worth it. Prices are between 30% and 35% less than for equivalent garments on the U.S. mainland.

Butterfly People, Calle Fortaleza 152 (☎ 787/723-2432), is a gallery/cafe in a handsomely restored building in Old San Juan. Butterflies, preserved forever in artfully arranged boxes, range from $20 for a single mounting to thousands of dollars for whole-wall murals. Most of these butterflies come from farms around the world, some of the most beautiful from Indonesia, Malaysia, and New Guinea. Tucked away, on the same premises, is **Malula Antiques.** Specializing in tribal art from the Moroccan sub-Sahara and Syria, it contains a sometimes startling collection of primitive and timeless crafts and accessories.

Barrachina's, Calle Fortaleza 104, between Calle del Cristo and Calle San José (☎ 787/725-7912), is more than a jewelry store. This is also the birthplace, in 1963, of the piña colada. It's a favorite of cruise-ship passengers, offering one of the largest selections of jewelry, perfume, cigars, and gifts in San Juan. There's a patio for drinks, plus a Bacardi rum outlet selling bottles cheaper than Stateside, but at the same prices as the Bacardi distillery. You'll also find a costume-jewelry department, a gift shop, a restaurant, and a section for authentic silver jewelry.

El Artesano, Calle Fortaleza 314 (☎ 787/721-6483), is a curiosity. You'll find Mexican and Peruvian icons of the Virgin Mary; charming depictions of fish and Latin American birds in terra-cotta and brass; all kinds of woven goods; painted cupboards, chests, and boxes; and mirrors and Latin dolls. **Galería Bóveda,** Calle del Cristo 209 (☎ 787/725-0263), is a long narrow space crammed with exotic jewelry, clothing, greeting cards of images of life in Puerto Rico, some 100 handmade lamps, antiques, Mexican punched tin and glass, and art-nouveau reproductions, among other items.

Olé, Calle Fortaleza 105 (☎ 787/724-2445), deserves an Olé. Browsing this store is a learning experience. Practically everything comes from Puerto Rico or Latin America. If you want a straw hat from Ecuador, hand-beaten Chilean silver, Christmas ornaments, or Puerto Rican *santos,* this is the place.

✪ **Puerto Rican Arts & Crafts,** Calle Fortaleza 204 (☎ 787/725-5596), set in a 200-year-old colonial building, is one of the premier outlets on the island for authentic artifacts. Of particular interest are papier-mâché carnival masks from Ponce. Taíno designs inspired by ancient petroglyphs are incorporated into most of the sterling silver jewelry sold here. There's an art gallery in back, with silk-screened serigraphs by local artists, and a gourmet Puerto Rican food section with such items as coffee, rum, and hot sauces. The store also exhibits and sells small carved *santos,* representations of the Catholic saints and the infant Jesus laboriously carved by artisans in private studios around the island.

Bared & Sons, Calle Fortaleza 65 (at the corner of Calle San Justo; ☎ 787/724-4811), now in its fourth decade, is the main outlet of a chain of at least 20 upscale jewelry stores on Puerto Rico. On the ground floor, cruise-ship passengers shop for gemstones, gold, diamonds, and watches. One floor up, there's a monumental collection of porcelain and crystal. It's a great source for hard-to-get and discontinued patterns discounted from Christofle, Royal Doulton, Wedgwood, Limoges, Royal Copenhagen, Lalique, Lladró, Herend, Baccarat, and Daum.

The **Gold Ounce,** Plaza los Muchachos, Calle Fortaleza 201 (☎ 787/724-3102), is the direct factory outlet for the oldest jewelry factory on Puerto Rico, the Kury Company. Don't expect a top-notch jeweler here: Many of the pieces are replicated in endless repetition. But don't overlook the place for 14-karat-gold ornaments. Some of the designs are charming, and prices are about 20% less than at retail stores in the U.S. In addition, the outlet has opened an art store, called **Arts and More,** featuring regional works, plus a cigar store called **The Cigar Shop.**

Joyería Riviera, Calle La Cruz 205 (☎ 787/725-4000), is an emporium of 18-karat gold and diamonds, the island's leading jeweler. Adjacent to Plaza de Armas, the shop has an impeccable reputation. This is the major distributor of Rolex watches on Puerto Rico. **200 Fortaleza,** Calle Fortaleza 200 (at the corner of Calle La Cruz) (☎ 787/723-1989), is known as a leading value-priced place to buy fine jewelry in Old San Juan.

Yas Mar, Calle Fortaleza 205 (☎ 787/724-1377), sells convincing, glittering fake diamonds for those who don't want to wear or can't afford the real thing. It also stocks real diamond chips, emeralds, sapphires, and rubies, too. **Leather & Pearls,** Calle Tanca 252 (at the corner of Calle Tetuán; ☎ 787/724-8185), are two products that don't always go together, but at this outlet form a winning combination. Majorca pearls and fine leather garments (bags, shoes, suitcases, briefcases, and accessories) are sold here from manufacturers that include Gucci and Fendi.

The Linen House, Calle Fortaleza 250 (☎ 787/721-4219), specializes in napery, bed linens, and lace, including embroidered shower curtains, lace doilies, bun warmers, and tablecloths that took weeks for seamstresses to complete. Some astonishingly beautiful items are available for around $30 each. The aluminum/pewter serving dishes have strikingly beautiful Spanish colonial designs.

For Puerto Rican coffee, which is gaining an increasingly fine reputation among aficionados, and for those hot spicy sauces of the Caribbean, head for **Spicy Caribbee,** Calle Cristo 154 (☎ 787/725-4690).

For travel guides, maps, and just something to read on the beach, there are two good bookstores. Try **Bell, Book & Candle,** 102 de Diego Ave., Santurce (☎ 787/728-5000), a large general-interest bookstore that carries fiction and classics in both Spanish and English, plus a huge selection of postcards. **The Book Store,** Calle San José 255 (☎ 787/724-1815), is the leading choice in the old town, with the largest selection of titles. It sells a number of books on Puerto Rican culture as well as good maps of the island.

SAN JUAN AFTER DARK
THE PERFORMING ARTS

Qué Pasa, the official visitor's guide to Puerto Rico, lists cultural events, including music, dance, theater, film, and art exhibits. It's distributed free by the tourist office.

A major cultural venue in San Juan is **Teatro Tapía,** Avenida Ponce de León (☎ 787/723-2079), across from Plaza de Colón, one of the oldest theaters in the western hemisphere (built about 1832). Much of Puerto Rican theater history is connected with the Tapía, named after the island's first prominent playwright, Alejandro Tapía y Rivera. Various productions, some musical, are staged here throughout the year and include drama, dance, and cultural events. You'll have to call the box office (open Monday to Friday from 10am to 6pm) for specific information. Tickets generally range in price from $15 to $38.

THE CLUB & MUSIC SCENE

Modeled after an artist's rendition of the once-notorious city of Mesopotamia, **Babylon,** in El San Juan Hotel & Casino, 6063 Isla Verde, Isla Verde (☎ 787/791-1000), is circular, with a central dance floor and a wraparound balcony where onlookers can scope out the action below. The crowd is usually in the 25-to-45 age group. This place has one of the best sound systems in the Caribbean. You might want to make a night of it, stopping into the El San Juan's bars and casino en route. The club is open from Thursday to Saturday from 9:30pm to 3am. Guests of the hotel enter free; otherwise there's a $10 cover.

Cafe Matisse, Ashford Avenue (☎ 787/723-7910), is a hot spot for Latin sounds. Although it's also a restaurant, it's best known as a bar where live music—often salsa—is usually part of the ambience. Depending on the night of the week, you can also hear rumba, merengue, blues, jazz, or rock-and-roll. Overall, the site is convivial, has a sense of Big Apple cool, and plays hot music that makes everyone want to dance, dance, dance. It's open Tuesday to Saturday from 5pm to around 2am or later, depending on the crowd. The only time a $3 cover is imposed is on a night when an expensive band is brought in.

Egipto, Av. Roberto H. Todd 1 (☎ 787/725-4664), is a busy nightclub attracting young, upwardly mobile singles. There's a dance floor well worn by years of boogying, although many visitors just come for drinks at the long and very accommodating bar. The decor is inspired by ancient Egypt, and the sound system is great. There's live music Thursday and Friday. Its transformation from a bar to a crowded disco usually begins around 10 or 11pm. It seems that everybody under 35 in San Juan has probably been to Egipto at least once, and many of them are regulars. You'll find the place in the Condado district, about 3 blocks south of Ashford Avenue. The club is open nightly from 8pm to either 2am or 5am, depending on business. A $10 cover is charged.

Laser, Calle del Cruz 251 (☎ 787/725-7581), is set in the heart of the old town near the corner of Calle Fortaleza. This disco is especially crowded when cruise ships pull into town. Once inside, you can wander over the three floors, listening to whatever music happens to be hot, with lots of additional merengue and salsa thrown in as well. Depending on the night, the age of the crowd varies. Usually, it's open daily from 8pm to 4am. Women enter free after midnight on Saturday. The cover ranges from $6 to $10.

Millennium, in the Condado Plaza Hotel, 999 Ashford Ave. (☎ 787/721-1900), is another favorite. Its entrance is adjacent to the main entrance ramp of the Condado Plaza Hotel, which also has a popular casino. You'll find a pleasant and highly accommodating cigar bar and a sound system made for techno music, Latin merengues, and disco classics from the 1970s. The crowds here tend to be in their late 20s and early 30s, but in the animated setting, folks in their 40s and 50s won't feel out of place. The club is open nightly from 7pm to 2am, with most dance-a-holics arriving around 10:30pm. After 9pm, a whopping $25 cover is charged.

Two of the most dramatic bars in San Juan are at **El San Juan Hotel & Casino,** 6063 Isla Verde Ave., Isla Verde (☎ 787/791-1000). There is no more beautiful bar in the Caribbean than the **Palm Court** here, which never closes. Set in an oval wrapped around a sunken bar area, amid marble and burnished mahogany, it offers a view of one of the world's largest chandeliers. After 9pm Monday to Saturday, live music, often salsa and merengue, emanates from an adjoining room (the El Chico Bar). There's also a fine **Cigar Bar,** with a magnificent repository of the finest cigars in the world. Some of the most fashionable women in San Juan—and men, too—can be seen puffing away in this chic rendezvous, while sipping a cognac.

Ireland and its ales meet the tropics at **Shannon's Irish Pub,** Calle Bori 46, Río Piedras (☎ 787/281-8466). This is definitely a Gallic pub with a Latin beat. A sports bar, it's the regular watering hole of many university students, a constant supplier of high-energy rock-n-roll and 10 TV monitors. There's live music Wednesday through Sunday—everything from rock to jazz to Latin. There are pool tables, and a simple cafe serves inexpensive food daily from 11:30am to 10pm. A $3 cover is infrequently imposed.

Violeta's, Calle Fortaleza 56, 2 blocks from the Gran Hotel Convento (☎ 787/723-6804), is stylish and comfortable, occupying the ground floor of a 200-year-old beamed house. Because of its location in the old town, the bar draws an equal mixture of visitors and locals, usually in their 20s and 30s. Sometimes a pianist performs. An open courtyard out back provides additional seating for sipping margaritas or other drinks.

HOT NIGHTS IN GAY SAN JUAN

The Barefoot Bar, Calle Vendig 2 (☎ 787/724-7230), along with the bar at the Atlantic Beach Hotel, just across the street, is the hippest gay bar in Puerto Rico. It occupies a blue building whose terrace extends out over the sands of the same beach shared by the Marriott Hotel, which is almost next door. At least 98% of the clientele is gay and male, and lots of airline and cruise-ship staff members drop in when they're in town.

The Beach Bar, in the Atlantic Beach Hotel, Calle Vendig 1 (☎ 787/721-6900), has the island's most popular tea-dance on Sunday, and there's also a happy hour nightly. Its layout and location are roughly equivalent to those of the Barefoot Bar, which is just across the street.

Cups, Calle San Mateo 1708, Santurce (☎ 787/268-3570), is a Latin tavern, the only place in San Juan that caters almost exclusively to lesbians. Men—of any sexual persuasion—aren't particularly welcome. Although the club is open Wednesday through Sunday from 7pm to 4am, entertainment such as live music or cabaret is presented only on Wednesday at 9pm, Friday at 10pm, and Sunday at 8pm.

Eros, 1257 Ponce de León, Santurce (☎ 787/722-1131), is the town's most popular gay disco, with strippers and shows. Most of the crowd is in its late 20s. Rumbased drinks, merengue, and the latest dance tunes are on tap; the place really gets going after around 10:30pm. It's open Wednesday through Sunday from 9pm to 5am. A cover, including two free drinks, is imposed only on Friday and Saturday nights.

CASINOS

Many visitors come to Puerto Rico on package deals and stay at one of the posh hotels at the Condado or Isla Verde just to gamble.

The casino generating all the excitement today is the 18,500-square-foot **Casino at The Ritz-Carlton,** 6961 State Rd., Isla Verde (☎ 787/253-1700), the largest in Puerto Rico. It combines the elegant decor of the 1940s with tropical fabrics and patterns. This is one of the plushest and most exclusive entertainment complexes in the Caribbean. You almost expect to see Joan Crawford arrive beautifully frocked and on the arm of Clark Gable. It features traditional games such as blackjack, roulette, baccarat, craps, and slot machines.

One of the splashiest of San Juan's casinos is at the **Wyndham Old San Juan Hotel & Casino,** Calle Brumbaugh 100 (☎ 787/721-5100). Five-card stud competes with some 240 slot machines and roulette tables. You can also try your luck at the **Caribe**

Hilton (one of the better ones), Puerta de Tierra (☎ 787/721-0303), **El San Juan Hotel & Casino** on Isla Verde Avenue (☎ 787/791-1000) in Isla Verde (one of the most grand), and the **Condado Plaza Hotel & Casino,** 999 Ashford Ave. (☎ 787/721-1000). There are no passports to flash or admissions to pay, as in European casinos.

The **Radisson Ambassador Plaza Hotel and Casino,** 1369 Ashford Ave. (☎ 787/721-7300), is another deluxe hotel noted for its casino action. The Stellaris Casino at the **San Juan Marriott Resort,** 1309 Ashford Ave. (☎ 787/722-7000), is one of the island's newest, as is El Tropical Casino at **Crown Plaza Hotel & Casino,** Route 187, km. 1.5, Isla Verde (☎ 787/253-2929). El Tropical is open 24 hours a day and is the only theme casino in San Juan, re-creating El Yunque Tropical Rain Forest.

The **San Juan Grand Beach Hotel & Casino,** 187 Isla Verde Ave. (☎ 787/791-6100) in Isla Verde, is open continuously from noon to 4am daily. This 10,000-square-foot gaming facility is an elegant spot (one of its Murano chandeliers is longer than a bowling alley). The casino offers 207 slot machines, 16 blackjack tables, 3 dice tables, 4 roulette wheels, and a minibaccarat table.

Most casinos are open daily from noon to 4pm and again from 8pm to 4am. Jackets for men are requested after 6pm.

3 Dorado

Along the north shore of Puerto Rico, about a 40-minute (22-mile) drive west of San Juan, a world of luxury resorts and villa complexes unfolds. The big properties of the Hyatt Dorado Beach Hotel and Hyatt Regency Cerromar Beach Hotel sit on the choice white sandy beaches here. Many guests of these hotels only pass through San Juan on arrival and departure, though if you're a first-time visitor to Puerto Rico, you may want to spend a day or so sightseeing and shopping in San Juan before heading for one of these complete resort properties, since, chances are, once you're at the resort you'll never leave the grounds.

GETTING THERE

If you don't have a car, and need to use public transportation, call **Dorado Transport Corp.,** which is on the site shared by the Hyatt Hotels (☎ 787/796-1234). Using 18-passenger minibuses, it offers frequent shuttle service between the Hyatt Hotels and the San Juan airport. It operates at frequent intervals, every day between 11am and 10pm. The charge is only $15 per person, but a minimum of three passengers must make the trip for the bus to operate.

WHERE TO STAY

Either Hyatt resort is a good choice for families. These Dorado twins offer family getaway packages at Camp Coquí, the Puerto Rican version of Camp Hyatt, featuring professionally supervised day and evening programs for children 3 to 12. Children also receive a 50% discount on meals.

✪ **Hyatt Dorado Beach Resort & Casino.** Dorado, PR 00646. ☎ **800/233-1234** in the U.S., or 787/796-1234. Fax 787/796-6560. www.hyatt.com/pages/d/dorado.html. 298 units, 17 casitas. A/C MINIBAR TV TEL. Winter $495–$655 double; $785 casita for 2. Off-season $170–$325 double; $385–$450 casita for 2. MAP (mandatory in winter) $65 extra per day for adults, $35 extra per day for children. AE, DC, DISC, MC, V.

While the Cerromar is more like a conventional resort hotel, the Dorado Beach's low-rise buildings sprawl across a former plantation, amidst palms, pine trees, purple bougainvillea, all within a short walk of a 2-mile sandy beach. Its fans appreciate the emphasis on natural landscaping. Families interested in massive facilities and the best sports-oriented program in Puerto Rico gravitate to the Cerromar Beach; those interested in a more peaceful, relaxing ambience cast their vote for the Dorado Beach. We like it better than the Cerromar (see below), especially since a shuttle bus runs back and forth between the two resorts every half hour, allowing you to use the Cerromar's fabulous pool area even if you stay here.

Hyatt has spent millions on improvements. The renovated guest rooms have marble bathrooms and terra-cotta floors throughout. Accommodations are available on the beach or in villas tucked in and around the lushly planted grounds. They're fairly spacious, with a lot of extras such as irons and ironing boards. Bathrooms have everything from hair dryers to bathrobes, thick towels to power showers. The casitas are a series of private beach or poolside houses.

Dining/Diversions: Breakfast can be taken on your private balcony, and lunch on an outdoor ocean terrace. Dinner is served in a three-tiered main dining room where you can watch the surf. Hyatt Dorado chefs have won many awards, and the food at the hotel restaurants and Su Casa Restaurant (not included in the MAP) is among the most appealing in the Caribbean. The Beach Grill and Pro Shop are for casual meals. And don't forget the casino.

Amenities: Two 18-hole championship golf courses designed by Robert Trent Jones, Sr. (see below); seven all-weather tennis courts; a full-service spa; two pools; children's camp; one of the best windsurfing schools in Puerto Rico; 24-hour room service; baby-sitting; laundry/dry cleaning.

Hyatt Regency Cerromar Beach Hotel. Dorado, PR 00646. ☎ **800/233-1234** or 787/796-1234. Fax 787/796-4647. www.hyatt.com/pages/c/cerroa.html. 506 units. A/C MINIBAR TV TEL. Winter $350–$480 double; from $770 suite. Spring and fall $245–$325 double; from $570 suite. Summer $190–$230 double; from $435 suite. MAP (breakfast and dinner) $65 extra for adults, $35 extra for children. AE, DC, DISC, MC, V.

Near the more elegant Hyatt Dorado Beach Hotel, the bustling Cerromar stands on its own beach and boasts a wealth of sports facilities and resort amenities. The name Cerromar is a combination of two Spanish words—*cerro* (mountain) and *mar* (sea)—and true to its name, it's surrounded by mountains and ocean. Approximately 22 miles west of San Juan, the high-rise hotel shares the 1,000-acre former Livingston estate with the Dorado, so guests can enjoy the Robert Trent Jones, Sr., golf courses and other facilities at the next-door hotel; a shuttle bus runs back and forth between the two resorts every half hour. This property is more action-packed than the Dorado Beach, and attracts more convention groups and families with kids.

All rooms have first-class appointments and are well maintained; most have private balconies. The floors throughout are tile, the furnishings casual tropical, in soft colors and pastels. All rooms have honor bars, in-room safes, and good mattresses. Many units are wheelchair accessible, and some are reserved for nonsmokers. Bathrooms are equipped with thick towels and power showers; the Regency Club units also have robes and hair dryers.

Dining/Diversions: The outdoor Swan Café has three levels connected by a dramatic staircase; some tables overlook a lake populated by swans and flamingos. Other dining choices include Sushi Wong's and the hotel's pride and joy, Medici's. The Flamingo bar offers a wide, open-air expanse overlooking the sea and the water playground. The resort also has a casino and dance club.

Amenities: The water playground contains the world's longest freshwater swimming pool: a 1,776-foot-long fantasy pool with a riverlike current in five connected free-form pools. It takes 15 minutes to float from one end of the pool to the other.

There are also 14 waterfalls, tropical landscaping, a subterranean Jacuzzi, water slides, walks, bridges, and a children's pool. A full-service spa and health club provide services for all manner of body and skin care, including massages. In addition to tennis courts and two golf courses (see below), there's also a children's day camp for ages 3 to 12, open year-round and known as Camp Hyatt. 24-hour room service, laundry/dry cleaning, baby-sitting.

WHERE TO DINE

El Malecón. Rte. 693, km 8.2. ☎ **787/796-1645.** Reservations not necessary. Main courses $7.25–$35.95. AE, MC, V. Daily 11am–11pm. PUERTO RICAN.

If you'd like to discover an unpretentious local place serving good Puerto Rican cuisine, then head for El Malecón, a simple concrete structure one minute from a small shopping center. It has a cozy family ambience and is especially popular on weekends. Some members of the staff speak English, and the chef is best with fresh seafood, which most diners order. The chef might also prepare a variety of items not listed on the menu. Most of the dishes are at the lower end of the price scale (see above); only the lobster is expensive.

Steak Co. In the Hyatt Regency Cerromar. ☎ **787/796-1234,** ext. 3240. Reservations required. Main courses $18–$38. AE, DC, DISC, MC, V. Daily 6:30–9:30pm. STEAKS/NORTHERN ITALIAN.

This is the best of the three upscale restaurants in the two Hyatt hotels. Frequented by an upscale, usually well-dressed clientele, it occupies a soaring, two-story room whose marble and Italian-tile floors can be observed from the lobby above through plate-glass windows. Diners enjoy views of venerable trees draped in Spanish moss, a landscaped pond, and a waterfall while dining on well-conceived cuisine. The best steaks and prime ribs in this part of Puerto Rico are served here—tender and grilled or cooked to your specifications. Most dishes are accompanied by large, perfectly baked (not soggy) potatoes and great sourdough bread. In the highly unlikely possibility you have room for dessert, you'll be glad you do.

SPORTS & OUTDOOR PURSUITS

GOLF   The **Hyatt Resorts Puerto Rico** at Dorado (☎ 787/796-1234), with 72 holes of golf, offers the greatest number of options in the Caribbean.

The Robert Trent Jones, Sr.–designed courses at the Hyatt Regency Cerromar and the Hyatt Dorado Beach match the finest anywhere. The two original courses—east and west (☎ 787/796-8961), both of which are associated with the Hyatt Dorado Beach Resort—were carved out of a jungle and offer tight fairways bordered by trees and forests, with lots of ocean holes. The somewhat newer and less noted north and south courses (☎ 787/796-8915), which fall under the jurisdiction of the Hyatt Regency Cerromar, feature wide fairways with well-bunkered greens and an assortment of lakes, water traps, and tricky wind factors. Each of the four has a 72 par. The longest course is the south course at 7,047 yards.

Guests of the Hyatt hotels get preferred tee times and lower fees than nonguests. For the north and south courses, Hyatt guests pay $65 for greens fees, while nonguests are charged $85. At the east and west courses, Hyatt guests are charged $110 for greens fees, rising to $160 for nonguests. Golf carts at any of the courses rent for $20, whether you play 9 or 18 holes. The north and south, and the east and west courses each maintain separate pro shops, each with a bar and snack-style restaurant. Both are open daily from 7am until dusk.

TENNIS   Again, the twin Hyatt resorts of **Dorado** and **Cerromar** (☎ 787/ 796-1234) have the monopoly in this area, with a total of 15 courts between them. The charge is $15 an hour, rising to $18 from 6 to 10pm. Lessons are available for $60 per hour. Nonguests can't use the courts, however.

WINDSURFING & OTHER WATER SPORTS   The best place on the island's north shore is along the well-maintained beachfront of the Hyatt Dorado Beach Hotel near the 10th hole of the hotel's famous east golf course. Here, **Penfield Island Adventures** (☎ 787/796-1234, ext. 3200, or 787/796-2188) offers 90-minute **windsurfing lessons** for $60 each; board rentals cost $50 per half day. Well-supplied with a wide array of Windsurfers, including some designed specifically for beginners and children, the school benefits from the almost uninterrupted flow of the north shore's strong, steady winds and an experienced crew of instructors. A **kayaking/snorkeling** trip (☎ 787/796-4645), departing daily at 9:15am and 11:45am, and lasting 1½ hours, costs $45. Two-tank boat **dives** go for $119 per person. **Waverunners** can be rented for $60 per half hour for a single rider, and $75 for two riders. A **Sunfish** rents for $45 for 1 hour, $65 for 2 hours.

4 Highlights in Northwestern Puerto Rico

Dubbed "an ear to heaven," the **Arecibo Observatory** (☎ 787/878-2612) contains the world's largest and most sensitive radar/radiotelescope. The telescope features a 20-acre dish or radio mirror set in an ancient sinkhole. It's 1,000 feet in diameter and 167 feet deep, and allows scientists to examine the ionosphere, the planets, and the moon with powerful radar signals and to monitor natural radio emissions from distant galaxies, pulsars, and quasars. It's being used by scientists as part of the Search for Extraterrestrial Intelligence (SETI). This research effort speculates that advanced civilizations elsewhere in the universe might also communicate via radio waves. The 10-year, $100-million search for life in space was launched on October 12, 1992, the 500-year anniversary of the New World's discovery by Columbus.

Unusually lush vegetation flourishes under the giant dish—ferns, wild orchids, and begonias. Assorted creatures like mongooses, lizards, and dragonflies have also taken refuge there. Suspended in outlandish fashion above the dish is a 600-ton platform that resembles a space station.

Tours at $3.50 are available at the observatory Wednesday to Friday from noon to 4pm and Saturday and Sunday from 9am to 4pm. There's a souvenir shop on the grounds. The observatory is a 90-minute drive west of San Juan, outside the town of Arecibo. From Arecibo, it's a 35-minute drive via routes 22, 134, 635, and 625 (the site is signposted).

✪ **Río Camuy Cave Park** is 1 hour and 20 minutes west of San Juan on Route 129, at km 18.9 (☎ 787/898-3100), and contains the third-largest underground river in the world. It runs through a network of caves, canyons, and sinkholes that have been cut through the island's limestone base over the course of millions of years. Known to the pre-Columbian Taíno peoples, the caves came to the attention of speleologists in the 1950s. They were opened to the public in 1986.

Visitors first see a short film about the caves, then descend into the caverns in open-air trolleys. The trip takes you through a 200-foot-deep sinkhole and a chasm where tropical trees, ferns, and flowers flourish, along with birds and butterflies. The trolley then goes to the entrance of Clara Cave of Epalme, one of 16 in the Camuy caves network, where visitors begin a 45-minute walk, viewing the majestic series of rooms rich in stalagmites, stalactites, and huge natural "sculptures" formed over the centuries. The park has added the Tres Pueblos Sinkhole and the Spiral Sinkhole to its slate of attractions.

The caves are open Tuesday to Sunday from 8am to 4pm. Tickets are $10 for adults, $7 for children 2 to 12, $5 for seniors. Parking is $2. For more information, phone the park.

5 Rincón

100 miles W of San Juan

At the westernmost point of the island, Rincón, 6 miles north of Mayagüez, has one of the most exotic beaches on the island, which draws surfers from around the world. In and around this small fishing village are some unique accommodations.

GETTING THERE   If you rent a car at the San Juan airport, it will take approximately 2 1/2 hours to drive here via the busy northern Route 2, or 3 hours via the scenic mountain route (no. 52) to the south. We recommend the southern route through Ponce.

In addition, there are 4 flights daily from San Juan to Mayagüez on **American Eagle** (☎ 800/433-7300). These flights take 40 minutes, and round-trip air fares range from $85 to $133. From the Mayagüez airport, Rincón is a 30-minute drive to the north on Route 2 (go left or west at the intersection with Route 115).

WHERE TO STAY

✪ **Horned Dorset Primavera Hotel.** Rte. 429 (P.O. Box 1132), Rincón, PR 00677. ☎ **800/633-1857** or 787/823-4030. Fax 787/823-5580. www.relaischateau.fr. 31 units. A/C. Winter $430 double; $530–$850 suite for 2. Off-season $280 double; $420–$650 suite for 2. MAP (breakfast and dinner) $80.45 per person extra. AE, MC, V. Children under 12 not accepted.

This is the most sophisticated hotel on Puerto Rico, and one of the most exclusive and elegant small properties anywhere in the Caribbean. It was built on the massive breakwaters and seawalls erected by a local railroad many years ago. Guests here enjoy a secluded semiprivate beach.

The hacienda evokes an aristocratic Spanish villa, with wicker armchairs, hand-painted tiles, ceiling fans, seaside terraces, and cascades of flowers. This is really a restful place. Accommodations are in a series of suites that ramble uphill amid lush gardens. The decor is tasteful, with four-poster beds and brass-footed tubs in marble-sheathed bathrooms. Rooms are spacious and luxurious, with Persian rugs over tile floors, queen sofa beds in the sitting areas, and deluxe mattresses, fine linen, and tasteful fabrics on the elegant beds. Bathrooms are equally roomy and luxurious, with hair dryers and thick towels.

The eight-suite Casa Escondida villa, set at the edge of the property, adjacent to the sea, is decorated with an accent on teakwood and marble. Some of the units have private plunge pools; others offer private verandas or sundecks. Each contains high-quality reproductions of colonial furniture by Baker.

Dining/Diversions: The hotel's restaurant is one of the finest on Puerto Rico (see "Where to Dine," below). There's a bar open throughout the day that serves delectable rum punches. Guitarists and singers often perform during cocktail and dinner hours.

Amenities: The best hotel library on Puerto Rico, pool, deep-sea fishing, room service (at breakfast and lunch only), concierge, laundry, massage, limousine and touring services. A gym, tennis courts, golf, and scuba diving are available nearby.

Parador Villa Antonio. Rte. 115, km 12.3 (P.O. Box 68), Rincón, PR 00677. ☎ **800/443-0266** in the U.S., or 787/823-2645. Fax 787/823-3380. www.villa-antonio.com. E-mail:

pva@villa-antonio.com. 55 units. A/C TV TEL. Year-round $80.25–$107 double. AE, DC, MC, V.

Ilia and Hector Ruíz offer apartments by the sea in this privately owned and run parador. The beach outside is nice, but we've seen litter here; it's not kept as clean as it should be by the local authorities. Facilities include a children's playground, games room, two tennis courts, and a pool. Surfing and fishing can be enjoyed just outside your front door, and you can bring your catch right into your cottage and prepare a fresh seafood dinner in your own kitchenette (there's no restaurant). Be aware that the air-conditioning doesn't work properly here, and in general better maintenance is needed. Nonetheless, this is a popular destination with families from Puerto Rico who crowd in on the weekends, occupying the motel-like rooms with balconies or terraces. Furnishings are well used but offer reasonable comfort. Bathrooms are small.

WHERE TO DINE

✪ **Horned Dorset Primavera.** In the Horned Dorset Primavera Hotel, Rte. 429. ☎ **787/ 823-4030.** Reservations recommended. Fixed-price dinner $64 for 5 courses, $88 for 11 courses. AE, MC, V. Daily noon–2:30pm and 7–9:30pm. FRENCH/CARIBBEAN.

This is the finest restaurant in western Puerto Rico, so romantic that people sometimes come from San Juan just for an intimate dinner. A masonry staircase sweeps from the garden to the second floor, where soaring ceilings and an atmosphere similar to that within a private villa awaits you.

The menu, which changes virtually every night based on the inspiration of the chef, might include chilled parsnip soup, a fricassée of wahoo with wild mushrooms, grilled loin of beef with peppercorns, and medaillons of lobster in an orange-flavored beurre-blanc (white butter) sauce. The grilled breast of duckling with bay leaves and raspberry sauce is also delectable. Dorado (mahimahi), on another occasion, was grilled and served with a ginger-cream sauce on a bed of braised Chinese cabbage. It was delicious, as was grilled squab with tarragon sauce.

HITTING THE BEACH (& THE LINKS)

One of Puerto Rico's most outstanding surfing beaches is at **Punta Higuero,** on Route 413 near Rincón. In the winter months especially, uninterrupted Atlantic swells with perfectly formed waves averaging 5 to 6 feet in height roll shoreward, and rideable swells sometimes reach 15 to 25 feet.

Punta Borinquén Golf Club, Route 107 (☎ **787/890-2987**), 2 miles north of Aguadilla's center, across the highway from the city's airport, was originally built by the U.S. government as part of the Ramey Air Force Base. Today, its 18 holes function as a public golf course, open daily from 7am to 6:30pm. Greens fees are $20 for an all-day pass, and rental of a golf cart that can carry two passengers is $24 for 18 holes, or $12 for 9 holes. Clubs can be rented for $10. The clubhouse contains a bar and a simple restaurant.

6 Mayagüez

98 miles SW of San Juan

This port city, not architecturally remarkable, is the third largest city on Puerto Rico. It was once the needlework capital of the island, and there are still craftspeople who sew fine embroidery. Mayagüez is also the honeymoon capital of Puerto Rico. The tradition dates from the 16th century; it's said that when local fathers needed husbands for their daughters, they kidnapped young Spanish sailors who were en route to Latin America.

GETTING THERE   **American Eagle** (☎ 800/433-7300) flies four times daily throughout the year between San Juan to Mayagüez. Flight time is 40 minutes, although there are often delays on the ground at either end of the itinerary. Depending on restrictions and the season you book your flight, round-trip fares ranges from $85 to $133 per person.

If you rent a car at the San Juan airport and want to drive to Mayagüez, it's faster and more efficient to take the northern route that combines sections of the newly widened Route 22 with the older Route 2. Estimated driving time for a local resident is about 90 minutes, although newcomers usually take about 30 minutes longer. The southern route, which combines the modern Route 52 with a transit across the outskirts of historic Ponce, and a final access into Mayagüez via the southern section of Route 2, requires a total of about 3 hours and affords some worthwhile scenery across the island's mountainous interior.

WHERE TO STAY

Best Western Mayagüez Resort & Casino. Rte. 104 (P.O. Box 3629), Mayagüez, PR 00709. ☎ **888/689-3030** or 787/832-3030. Fax 787/834-3475. www.mayaguezresort. com. E-mail: sales@mayaguezresort.com. 148 units. A/C MINIBAR TV TEL. Year-round $145–$175 double; $250 suite. AE, MC, V. Parking $4.50.

In 1995, this former Hilton was bought by a consortium of local investors, who poured $5.5 million into a radical renovation. Since its reopening in 1996, the hotel has benefited more than ever from its redesigned casino, country-club format, and position on 20 acres of tropical gardens at the northern approach to the city, 3 miles from the airport. The carefully landscaped grounds have been designated an adjunct to the nearby Mayagüez Institute of Tropical Agriculture by the U.S. Department of Agriculture. There are five species of palm trees, eight kinds of bougainvillea, and numerous species of rare flora, set adjacent to the Institute's collection of tropical plants, which range from a pink torch ginger to a Sri Lankan cinnamon tree.

The hotel's well-designed bedrooms open onto views of the swimming pool, and many units have private balconies. Guest rooms tend to be small, but have good beds and mattresses. Some units are suitable for nonsmokers, while others are accessible for persons with disabilities. Bathrooms have hair dryers, makeup mirrors, thick towels, and scales.

Dining/Diversions: For details about El Castillo, the hotel's restaurant, see "Where to Dine," below. The hotel functions as the major entertainment center of Mayagüez. Its casino has free admission and is open daily from noon to 4am. You can drink and dance at the Victoria Lounge Wednesday to Sunday from 8:30pm to 3am; entrance is also free.

Amenities: Olympic-size pool, children's pool, playground, Jacuzzi, mini-gym, three tennis courts, room service (from 6:30am to 11pm), laundry, baby-sitting. Deep-sea fishing, skin-diving, surfing, and scuba diving can be arranged. A golf course is a 30-minute drive from the hotel.

Holiday Inn & Tropical Casino. 2701 Rte. 2, km 149.9, Mayagüez, PR 00680-6328. ☎ **800/HOLIDAY** in the U.S. and Canada, or 787/833-1100. Fax 787/833-1300. www. holiday-inn.com. 151 units. A/C TV TEL. Year-round $109.50–$152 double; $210–$260 suite. AE, DC, MC, V.

This place competes with the Best Western Mayagüez Resort & Casino, though we like the Best Western better. Set 2 miles north of Mayagüez's city center, behind a parking lot and a well-maintained lawn that simply isn't as dramatically landscaped as the Mayagüez Resort's surrounding acreage, it's a six-story hotel. Clean, contemporary, and comfortable, it has a marble-floored, high-ceilinged lobby, an outdoor pool with its own waterside bar, and a big, glittery casino. Bedrooms are comfortably but functionally outfitted in motel style; they've recently been refurbished. The hotel's social center is Holly's Café, an airy, stylish place that's open daily for breakfast, lunch, and dinner.

WHERE TO DINE

El Castillo. In the Best Western Mayagüez Resort & Casino, Rte. 104. ☎ **787/832-3030.** Breakfast buffet $11.25. Mon–Sat buffet lunch $14; Sun brunch buffet $21.95; main courses $17.30. AE, MC, V. Daily 6:30am–11pm. INTERNATIONAL/PUERTO RICAN.

This is the best-managed large-scale dining room in western Puerto Rico, the main restaurant for the largest hotel and casino in the area. Known for its generous lunch buffets, it serves only à la carte items at dinner, including seafood stew served on beds of linguine with marinara sauce, grilled salmon with a mango-flavored Grand Marnier sauce, and fillets of sea bass with a cilantro, white wine, and butter sauce. Steak and lobster are served on the same platter, if you want it. The food has real flavor and flair, and isn't the typical bland hotel fare so often dished up.

EXPLORING THE AREA: BEACHES & TROPICAL GARDENS

Along the western coastal bends of Route 2, north of Mayagüez, lie the best surfing **beaches** in the Caribbean. Surfers from as far away as New Zealand come to ride the waves. You can also check out panoramic **Punta Higuero** beach, nearby on Route 413, near Rincón.

The chief sight is the ✪ **Tropical Agriculture Research Station** (☎ 787/831-3435), which is located on Route 65, between Post Street and Route 108, adjacent to the University of Puerto Rico at Mayagüez campus and across the street from the **Parque de los Próceres** (Patriots' Park). At the administration office, ask for a free map of the tropical gardens, which contain a huge collection of tropical species useful to people, including cacao, fruit trees, spices, timbers, and ornamentals. The grounds are open Monday to Friday from 7am to 5pm, and there is no admission charge.

Mayagüez might also be the jumping-off point for a visit by chartered boat to **Mona Island**, "the Galápagos of the Caribbean," which enjoys many legends of pirate treasure and is known for its white-sand beaches and marine life. The island is virtually uninhabited, except for two policemen and a director of the institute of natural resources. The island attracts hunters seeking pigs and wild goats, along with big-game fishers. But mostly it's intriguing to anyone who wants to escape civilization. **Playa Sardinera** on Mona Island was a base for pirates. On one side of the island, at **Playa de Pajaros,** are caves where the Taíno people left their mysterious hieroglyphs. Everything needed, including water, must be brought in, and everything, including garbage, must be taken out. For further information, call the **Puerto Rico Department of Natural Resources** at ☎ 787/723-1616.

Encantos Ecotours (☎ 787/272-0005) offers bare-bones but ecologically sensitive camping tours to Mona Island at sporadic intervals that vary according to the demand of clients who are interested. The experience includes ground transport to and from San Juan, sea transport departing from Cabo Rojo, use of camping and snorkeling gear, all meals (expect the equivalent of K-rations cooked over a campfire), and fees. Three nights and 4 days of outdoor life, which doesn't come without its share of discomforts and inconveniences, sells for around $600.

7 Ponce

75 miles SW of San Juan

Puerto Rico's second-largest city, Ponce ("The Pearl of the South") was named after Loíza Ponce de León, grandson of Ponce de León. Today it's Puerto Rico's principal shipping port on the Caribbean Sea. The city is well kept and attractive, with many plazas, parks, and public buildings. It has the air of a provincial Mediterranean town. Look for the *rejas* (framed balconies) of the handsome colonial mansions. Ponce is a city—not a beach resort—and should be visited mainly for its sights.

ESSENTIALS

VISITOR INFORMATION   Maps and information can be found at the **tourist office,** Fox Delicias Mall, on plaza de las Delicias (☎ **787/840-5695**).

GETTING THERE   Ponce is 75 miles southwest of San Juan and is reached by Route 52. Allow at least 1½ hours if you drive.

American Eagle (☎ **800/433-7300**) offers one daily flight between San Juan and Ponce (flight time is approximately 35 minutes) for $85 to $176 round-trip, depending on the ticket. Prices are known to fluctuate, so call for last-minute details.

WHERE TO STAY

Meliá. Calle Cristina 2, Ponce, PR 00731. ☎ **800/742-4276** in the U.S., or 787/842-0260. Fax 787/841-3602. E-mail: melia@coqui.net. 78 units. A/C TV TEL. Year-round $75–$95 double. Rates include continental breakfast. AE, DC, MC, V. Parking $3.

A city hotel with southern hospitality, the Meliá, which has no connection with the international hotel chain, often attracts businesspeople. The location is a few steps away from the Cathedral of Our Lady of Guadalupe and from the Parque de Bombas (the red-and-black firehouse). Although this old and somewhat tattered hotel was long ago outclassed by the more expensive Hilton, many people who could afford more upscale accommodations still prefer to stay here for its old-time atmosphere. The lobby floor and all stairs are covered with Spanish tiles of Moorish design. The desk clerks speak English. The small rooms are comfortably furnished and pleasant enough, and most have a balcony facing either busy Calle Cristina or the old plaza. In some rooms, the mattresses are a bit tired, but others are new. Bathrooms are tiny. Breakfast is served on a rooftop terrace with a good view of Ponce, and Mark's Restaurant thrives under separate management (see below). You can park your car in the lot nearby.

✪ **Ponce Hilton and Casino.** 1150 Avenida Caribe (P.O. Box 7419), Ponce, PR 00732. ☎ **800/HILTONS** in the U.S. and Canada, or 787/259-7676. Fax 787/259-7674. www.hiltons.com. 153 units. A/C MINIBAR TV TEL. $220–$230 double; $495 suite. Extra person $20. AE, CB, DC, DISC, MC, V. Self-parking $4.50; valet parking $10.

On an 80-acre tract of land right on the beach at the western end of Avenida Santiago de los Caballeros, about a 5-minute (7-mile) drive from the center of Ponce, this is the most glamorous hotel in southern Puerto Rico. Designed like a miniature village, with turquoise-blue roofs, white walls, and lots of tropical plants, ornamental waterfalls, and gardens, it welcomes conventioneers and individual travelers alike. Accommodations contain tropically inspired furnishings, ceiling fans, and terraces or balconies. All the rooms are medium to spacious, with adequate desk and storage place, tasteful fabrics, good upholstery, and fine linen and quality mattresses. The ground-floor rooms are the most expensive. Each bathroom is equipped with thick towels and a hair dryer.

Dining/Diversions: The food is the most sophisticated and refined on the south coast of Puerto Rico. Chefs use only the freshest ingredients, and combine them with imagination. Everyone on the waitstaff seems to have an extensive knowledge of the menu and will aid and guide you through some exotic dishes—of course, you'll find familiar fare, too. The more glamorous of the hotel's two restaurants is La Cava, whose cuisine is some of the most intricate and thoughtful around. The less formal La Terraza specializes in well-organized and sometimes lavish buffets. (See separate reviews under "Where to Dine," below.) El Bohemio cocktail lounge offers sunset-colored drinks and live music every evening, and the hotel's casino, an appropriately glittery showcase, is open daily from noon to 4am.

Amenities: Lagoon-shaped pool ringed with gardens, business center, fitness center, video arcade, bike rentals, playground, summer camp for children; water sports available. Room service (from 7am to midnight), laundry, baby-sitting (if arranged in advance).

WHERE TO DINE

El Ancla. Av. Hostos Final 9, Playa Ponce. ☎ **787/840-2450.** Main courses $10.95–$35. AE, DC, MC, V. Sun–Thurs 11am–10pm, Fri–Sat 11am–midnight. PUERTO RICAN/SEAFOOD.

This is one of Ponce's best restaurants, with a lovely location 2 miles south of the city center on soaring piers that extend from the rocky coastline out over the surf. As you dine, the sound of the sea rises literally from beneath your feet.

Menu items are prepared with real Puerto Rican zest and flavor. An old favorite here is red snapper stuffed with lobster and shrimp, served either with fried plantain or mashed potatoes. Other specialties are fillet of salmon in a caper sauce, and a seafood medley of lobster, shrimp, octopus, and conch. Most of the dishes are reasonably priced, especially the chicken and conch. One corner of the menu is reserved for lobster, which tops the price scale. The side orders are also delectable, including crabmeat rice or yucca in garlic.

✪ **La Cava.** In the Ponce Hilton, 1150 Avenida Caribe. ☎ **787/259-7676.** Reservations recommended. Main courses $18–$32. AE, DISC, DC, MC, V. Mon–Sat noon–3pm and 6:30–10:30pm. INTERNATIONAL.

Designed like a network of venerable rooms within a 19th-century coffee plantation, this is the most appealing and elaborate restaurant in Ponce. There's a well-trained staff, a sense of antique charm, well-prepared cuisine, and a champagne and cigar bar where the bubbly sells for around $6 a glass. Menu items change every 6 weeks, but might include duck foie gras with toasted brioche, Parma ham with mango, cold poached scallops with mustard sauce, a fricassee of lobster and mushrooms in a pastry shell, grilled lamb sausage with mustard sauce on a bed of couscous, and a sophisticated seafood grill. Dessert could be a black-and-white soufflé, or a trio of tropical sorbets.

La Montserrate. Sector Las Cucharas, Rte. 2. ☎ **787/841-2740.** Main courses $15–$20. AE, DC, DISC, MC, V. Daily 11am–10pm. PUERTO RICAN/SEAFOOD.

Beside the seafront, in a residential area about 4 miles west of the town center, this restaurant draws a loyal following from the surrounding neighborhood. A culinary institution in Ponce since it was established 20 years ago, it occupies a large, airy, modern building divided into two different dining areas. The first of these is slightly more formal than the next. Most visitors, however, head for the large room in back, where windows on three sides encompass a view of some offshore islands. Specialties, concocted from the catch of the day, might include octopus salad, four different kinds of asopao, a whole red snapper in Creole sauce, or a selection of steaks and grills. Nothing is innovative, but the cuisine is typical of the south of Puerto Rico, and it's a family favorite. The fish dishes are better than the meat selections.

La Terraza. In the Ponce Hilton, 1150 Avenida Caribe. ☎ **787/259-7676.** Lunch buffet $18; dinner buffet $19–$28. AE, DC, DISC, MC, V. Daily noon–3pm and 6:30–10:30pm. INTERNATIONAL.

This is an appealing, well-laid-out buffet restaurant. Featuring an impressive array of salads, soups, breads, meats, fish, and desserts, the buffet is more formal and elaborate, and a bit more expensive, at dinner than at lunch, but overall, this is one of the best values in Ponce. At dinner, a waitstaff will bring your main course to your table, although appetizers, salads, desserts, and garnishes are retrieved at the buffet. A different theme is emphasized every night of the week: Monday is devoted to variations on traditional Puerto Rican *mofongos* (plantains layered with various combinations of meat or seafood); Tuesday, Wednesday, and Thursday feature Mexican fajitas, barbecued ribs, and lobster, respectively. Friday is fish night, Saturday is steak, and Sunday is most festive of all, devoted to Caribbean versions of paella.

✪ **Mark's at the Meliá.** In the Meliá Hotel, calle Cristina. ☎ **787/842-0260.** Reservations recommended. Main courses $18–$28; lunch $12–$28. AE, MC, V. Wed–Sun noon–3pm and 5–10pm. INTERNATIONAL.

The hot restaurant excitement in Ponce is generated by Mark and Melody French, who took over what was a rather dull restaurant in this landmark hotel. This elegantly appointed setting provides a showcase for chef Mark's classical cookery with fresh local ingredients and Melody's expertise in wine and service. At lunch, you can be tantalized by tostone skins with plantains, or tempura jumbo shrimp with an Oriental salad. Soups are likely to feature cream of pumpkin, followed by such main dishes as corn-crusted red snapper with a yucca purée. At night, you get the best French signature dishes in Ponce, including roast rack of lamb with a mint crust, country veal chop flavored with horseradish, and duck breast with summer berries. Spectacular desserts include vanilla flan layered with rum sponge cake and topped with caramelized banana.

SEEING THE SIGHTS

A $40-million project is restoring more than 1,000 buildings in town to their original turn-of-the-century charm. Architectural styles that combine neoclassical with "Ponce Creole" and art deco give the town a distinctive ambience.

Any of the Ponceños will direct you to their ✪ **Museo de Arte de Ponce,** Avenida de las Americas 25 (☎ **787/848-0505**), which has a fine collection of European and Latin American art, the best on the island. Among the nearly 400 paintings, sculptures, and artworks on display are exceptional pre-Raphaelite and Italian baroque paintings. The building was designed by Edward Durell Stone, and has been called the "Parthenon of the Caribbean." It's open daily from 10am to 5pm. Adults pay $4; children 11 and under are charged $1.

Most visitors head for the **Parque de Bombas,** Plaza de las Delicias (☎ **787/ 284-4141**), the main plaza of Ponce. This fantastic old black-and-red firehouse was built for a fair in 1883. It's open Wednesday through Monday from 9:30am to 6pm.

Around the corner from the firehouse, a trail will lead you to the **Cathedral of Our Lady of Guadalupe,** Calle Concordia/Calle Union (☎ **787/842-0134**). Designed by architects Francisco Porrata Doría and Francisco Trublard in 1931, featuring a pipe organ installed in 1934, it remains an important place for prayer. It's open Monday to Friday from 6am to 3:30pm and on Saturday and Sunday from 6am to noon and 3 to 8pm.

El Museo Castillo Serrallés, El Vigía 17 (☎ **787/259-1774**), the largest and most imposing building in Ponce, was built high on a hilltop above town by the Serrallés family (owners of a local rum distillery) in the 1930s. This is one of the architectural gems of Puerto Rico and the best evidence of the wealth produced by the turn-of-the-century sugar boom. Guides will escort you through the Spanish Revival house, where Moorish and Andalusian details include panoramic courtyards, a baronial dining room, and a small cafe and souvenir shop. Hours are Tuesday through Sunday from 10am to 5pm. Admission is $3 for adults, $2 for seniors over 62, and $1.50 for students and children 15 and under.

The oldest cemetery in the Antilles, excavated in 1975, is near Ponce on Route 503 at kilometer 2.7. The **Tibes Indian Ceremonial Center** (☎ **787/840-2255**) contains some

186 skeletons, dating from A.D. 300, as well as pre-Taíno plazas from A.D. 700. Guided tours in English and Spanish are conducted through the grounds. Shaded by trees are seven rectangular ball courts and two dance areas. The arrangements of stone points on the dance grounds, in line with the solstices and equinoxes, suggest a pre-Columbian Stonehenge. A re-created Taíno village includes not only the museum but also an exhibition hall where you can see a documentary about Tibes; you can also visit the cafeteria and souvenir shop. The museum is open Wednesday to Sunday from 9am to 4pm. Admission is $2 for adults and $1 for children.

Hacienda Buena Vista, Route 10, kilometer 16.8 (☎ **787/848-7020** or 787/ 722-5882), is a 30-minute drive north of Ponce. Built in 1833, it preserves an old way of life, with its whirring waterwheels and artifacts of 19th-century farm production. Once it was one of the most successful plantations on Puerto Rico, producing coffee, corn, and citrus. It was a working coffee plantation until the 1950s, and 86 of the original 500 acres are still part of the estate. The rooms of the hacienda have been furnished with authentic pieces from the 1850s.

Tours, lasting 2 hours, are conducted Wednesday to Sunday at 8:30am, 10:30am, 1:30pm, and 3:30pm (in English only at 1:30pm). Reservations are required. Tours cost $5 for adults, $2 for children. The hacienda lies in the small town of Barrio Magüeyes, on Route 10 between Ponce and Adjuntas.

SHOPPING

If you feel a yen for shopping, head for the **Fox-Delicias Mall,** at the intersection of calle Reina Isabel and plaza de Las Delicias, the city's most innovative shopping center.

The best outlet for souvenirs and artisan work is in the very center of town: **El Palacio del Coquí Inc.** (Palace of the Tree Frog), Fox Delicias Mall (☎ **787/ 841-0216**). This is the place to buy the grotesque masks (viewed as collectors' items) that are used at carnival time. Ask the owner to explain the importance and significance of these masks.

BEACHES & OUTDOOR PURSUITS

There is little in the way of organized sports, but a 10-minute drive west of Ponce will take you to **Playa de Ponce,** a long strip of white sand opening onto the tranquil waters of the Caribbean. This beach is usually better for swimming than the Condado in San Juan.

Scuba divers can go to the best dive sites along the southern coast with **Gregory's Dive Center** (☎ **787/840-6424**). The center can also make arrangements for fishing and sailing in the Ponce area.

The city owns two **tennis complexes**, one at Poly Deportivos, with nine hard courts and another at Rambla, with six courts. Both are open from 9am to 10pm and are lit for night play. You can play free.

To golf, you have to go to **Aguirre Golf Course**, Route 705, Aguirre (☎ **787/ 853-4052**), 30 miles east of Ponce (take Highway 52). This nine-hole course, open from 7:30am to sunset daily, charges greens fees of $15 Monday through Friday, going up to $18 on weekends and holidays. Another course, **Club Zeportivo,** Carretera 102, km 15.4, Barrio Jogudas, Cabo Rojo (☎ **787/254-3748**), is 30 miles west of Ponce. This course is a nine-holer, open daily from 7am to 6pm. Greens fees are $30 daily.

A SIDE TRIP TO HISTORIC SAN GERMÁN

Only an hour's drive from Ponce or Mayagüez and the beaches of the southern coast, and just over 2 hours from San Juan, San Germán, Puerto Rico's second-oldest town, is a little museum piece. It was founded in 1512 and destroyed by the French in 1528.

Rebuilt in 1570, it was named after Germain de Foix, the second wife of King Ferdinand of Spain. Once the rival of San Juan, Sam Germán harbored many pirates, who pillaged the ships that sailed off the nearby coastline. Indeed, many of today's residents are descended from the smugglers, poets, priests, and politicians who lived here.

Although the pirates and sugar plantations are long gone, the city retains many colorful reminders of those former days. Today it has settled into a slumber, albeit one that has preserved the feel of the Spanish colonial era. Flowers brighten the patios here as they do in Seville. Also as in a small Spanish town, many of the inhabitants stroll in the plaza in the early evening. Nicknamed "Ciudad de las Lomas," or City of the Hills, San Germán boasts scenery that provides a pleasant backdrop to a variety of architectural styles—Spanish colonial (1850s), criollo (1880s), neoclassical (1910s), art deco (1930s), and international (1960s)—depicted in the gracious old-world-style buildings that line its streets. So significant are these buildings that San Germán is only the second Puerto Rican city (the other is San Juan) to be included in the National Register of Historic Places.

The city's 249 noteworthy historical treasures are within easy walking distance of one another. Regrettably, you must view most of them from the outside. If some of them are actually open, count yourself fortunate, as they have no phones, keep no regular hours, and are staffed by volunteers who rarely show up.

One building you can enter is ✪ **Iglesia Porta Coeli** (Gate of Heaven), on a knoll at one end of town. Dating from 1606, this is the oldest church in the New World. Restored by the Institute of Puerto Rican Culture, it contains a museum of religious art with a collection of ancient *santos*, the carved figures of saints that have long been a major branch of Puerto Rican folk art. Look for the 17th-century portrait of St. Nicholas de Bari, the French Santa Claus. Inside, the original palm-wood ceiling and tough, brown ausobo-wood beams draw the eyes upward. Along the sides of the chapel are treasures gathered from all over the world, including early choral books from Santo Domingo, a primitive carving of Jesus, and 19th-century Señora de la Monserrate Black Madonna and Child statues. Further restoration work is now being done by Porta Coeli. Admission is $1. Open Tuesday through Sunday from 9am to 4:15pm. Call ☎ **787/264-4258** for more information.

Across the street, the **Tomás Vivoni House** is San Germán's most popular and widely recognized house. Named after the local architect who designed it, it was built in 1913; the home boasts a Queen Anne style, with a tower and gables that are key elements in the town's urban profile.

Next door is **Parque de Santo Domingo**, one of San Germán's two main plazas. Originally a marketplace, the plaza is now bordered with black iron and wooden park benches and features busts of some of the prominent figures in the town's history. The park also is the site of the Farmacia Martin, a Spanish colonial building converted to a pharmacy, which still operates today, and the Old City Hall.

San Germán de Auxerre Church is the centerpiece of Plaza Mariano Quiñones, the town's other main plaza. Built in the 19th century, its wooden vault features a beautiful trompe-l'oeil painting in blue and gray. The original pattern on the ceiling was restored in 1993.

Acosta y Forés and **Juán Ortiz Perichi houses**, nearby, are among the most beautiful homes in Puerto Rico. The Acosta y Forés House, a stunning example of criollo architecture, built in 1917, features traditional wood construction. Inside, the house has floor-to-ceiling stenciled designs painted over the walls of each room. Constructed in the 1920s and designed by Luis Pardo Fradera, the Juán Ortiz Perichi House is a fine example of Puerto Rican ornamental architecture. It features a multilevel design with a curved balcony and pitched roofs.

WHERE TO STAY & DINE

Parador El Oasis. Calle Luna 72, San Germán, PR 00683. ☎ **787/892-1175.** Fax 787/
892-1156. 52 units. A/C TV TEL. Year-round $69.50 double. Extra person $10. Children 11
and under stay free in parents' room. AE, DC, DISC, MC, V.

Although not state-of-the-art, this hotel has some Spanish colonial charm. If you'd like
to anchor into this quaint old town, far removed from the beaches, it's a fine place to
stay. A three-story building constructed around a pool and patio area, the hotel used
to be a family mansion some 200 years ago. With its mint-green walls and white
wicker furniture, some of the old grace remains. Right off the lobby, the older rooms
show the wear and tear of the years, but are still preferred by some. The more modern
rooms in the back are without character—plain, functional, clean, but more spacious
than the older units. Three of the units have private balconies.

The rather standard restaurant has a full bar and serves three reasonably priced
meals a day. There's also a small gym and sauna.

8 Las Croabas & Luquillo Beach

31 miles E of San Juan

Now that we've covered the western portion of Puerto Rico, we'll begin heading east
from San Juan. From the capital, Route 3 leads toward the fishing town of Fajardo,
where you'll turn north to Las Croabas, about 31 miles from the capital.

You'll be near ✪ **Luquillo Beach,** one of the island's best and most popular public
stretches of sand. From here, you can also easily explore El Yunque Rain Forest. See section
2 of this chapter for details on both.

GETTING THERE Private limousine from the San Juan airport costs $255 per car-
load to either the El Conquistador or the Westin Rio Mar Beach resort. A taxi will cost
approximately $70. Hotel buses make trips to and from the San Juan airport at 30-
minute intervals throughout the day for $55 per person, round-trip for transport to
El Conquistador; $23 per person, one-way to the Westin.

If you are driving, pass the San Juan airport, following the signs to "Carolina,"
which will lead to Route 3 going east. Go all the way until you see signs for El Yunque
(the rain forest). At this marker, the Westin is signposted.

WHERE TO STAY

Both of the resorts reviewed below are frequently featured in package deals. See
chapter 2 for details.

✪ **Westin Rio Mar Beach Resort & Casino.** 6000 Rio Mar Blvd. (19 miles east of Luis
Muñoz Marin International Airport, with entrance off Puerto Rico Hwy. 3), Rio Grande, PR
00745. ☎ **800/4 RIOMAR** or 787/888-6000. Fax 787/888-6600. www.westinriomar.com/
reservations.html. 600 units. A/C MINIBAR TV TEL. Winter $375–$650 double; $500–$3,350
suite. Off-season $275–$420 double; $365–$3,350 suite. AE, CB, DC, DISC, MC, V.

Marking Westin's debut entry into the Caribbean, this $180-million, 481-acre resort
opened in 1996 onto a relatively uncrowded neighbor (Rio Mar Beach) of the
massively popular Luquillo Beach, a 5-minute drive away. (El Yunque Rain Forest is
only a 15-minute drive from here.) One of the three largest hotels in Puerto Rico, it
was designed to compete with the Hyatt hotels at Dorado and El Conquistador, with
which it's frequently compared. The Westin's centerpiece, and site of all of its accommodations, is a seven-story Spanish/Caribbean-style ochre-colored building whose
U-shaped floor plan opens onto views of the sea.

Landscaping includes lots of Jacuzzis, grottoes, fountains, and tropical gardens.
More than 60% of the guest rooms look out over palm trees to the Atlantic. Other

units open onto gardens and forests. Throughout, the style is Spanish hacienda with nods to the surrounding jungle, incorporating massive murals of tropical vegetation, alternating with dark woods, deep colors, rounded archways, big windows, and tile floors. Muted earth tones, wicker, rattan, and painted wood furniture add to the ambience. Bedrooms are spacious, with balconies or terraces, good mattresses, irons and ironing boards, and coffeemakers. Bathrooms are equally luxurious with thick towels, hair dryers, and deluxe toiletries.

Dining/Diversions: You'll never go hungry here. The resort boasts 12 restaurants and lounges, everything from Marbella (a relatively casual indoor/outdoor all-day restaurant) to Palio, an upmarket Italian gourmet spot that serves the most elegant food in the most formal setting. There's also a beachfront pool grill and bar, and a lobby bar with prolonged bouts of live merengue and salsa. In the evening, guests usually gather to enjoy the recorded music in an outdoor nightclub, or else try their luck in the 6,500-square-foot casino.

Amenities: The resort encompasses the Rio Mar Country Club, site of two important golf courses. The older of the two, the Ocean Course, was designed by George and Tom Fazio as part of the original resort. In 1997, Westin opened the property's second 18-holer, the slightly more challenging River Course, designed as the first Greg Norman–designed course in the Caribbean. Par for both courses is 72. Thirteen tennis courts, a beach club with equipment rentals, health club with aerobics classes, a spa offering massage and other treatments, 24-hour room service, laundry/dry cleaning. The Iguana Kid's Club keeps children 4 to 12 amused during morning and evening sessions. The activities staff will help you arrange any sport or activity, including nearby horseback riding, hiking, deep-sea game fishing, sailing, and boating.

✪ **Wyndham El Conquistador Resort & Country Club.** Las Croabas (P.O. Box 70001, Fajardo), PR 00738. ☎ **800/468-5228** in the U.S., or 787/863-1000. Fax 787/863-6500. www.wyndham.com. 908 units. A/C MINIBAR TV TEL. Winter $350–$545 double; $1,400–$1,950 suite for 1–4; $1,075–$2,095 casita for 1–6. Off-season $175–$350 double; $1,075–$1,600 suite for 1–4; $985–$1,600 casita for 1–6. Additional bed for 3rd or 4th occupant $40 extra. MAP (breakfast and dinner) $82 extra per adult per day, $42 extra per child 12 and under. Children 15 and under stay free in parents' room. AE, DC, DISC, MC, V. Parking $10 per day.

One of the most impressive resorts anywhere in the tropics, El Conquistador is a destination unto itself, with an incredible array of facilities. Rebuilt in 1993 at a cost of $250 million by Kumagai/Mitsubishi, it boasts a million dollars' worth of art and encompasses 500 acres of forested hills sloping down to the sea. Accommodations are divided into five separate sections that share a common theme of Mediterranean architecture and lush landscaping. Most of them lie several hundred feet above the sea, within two sections (Las Brisas and La Vista) of the bulky main building. At the same altitude, a bit off to the side, is a replica of an Andalusian hamlet, Las Casitas Village, which seems straight of out of the south of Spain; these plush, pricey units are an enclave unto themselves. If money is no object, join the likes of John Travolta and Janet Jackson, who have checked into the casitas to enjoy peace and pampering. A short walk downhill is a circular cluster of tastefully modern accommodations, Las Olas Village. And at sea level, adjacent to an armada of pleasure craft bobbing at anchor, is La Marina Village, whose balconies seem to hang directly over the water. The accommodations are outfitted with comfortable and stylish furniture, excellent mattresses, soft tropical colors, bathrobes, ironing boards, coffeemakers, hair dryers, and thick towels. All the far-flung elements of the resort are connected by serpentine, landscaped walkways, and by a railroad-style funicular that makes frequent trips up and down the hillside. Throughout, gardens mingle with murals, paintings, and sculptures.

In the winter, you see fewer children and more older couples; younger people and families are more evident in summer. Expect crowds. If you want a quieter, more romantic getaway, consider the Horned Dorset Primavera in Rincón (see section 5 of this chapter).

Dining/Diversions: The resort contains 16 different restaurants and lounges, one of which is a tropical deli; some of the others are highlighted in "Where to Dine," below. There's also a casino, a piano bar, and bars. Drake's Library is outfitted with books, mahogany, and a billiards table, while the disco, Amigos Bar and Lounge, offers live merengue and salsa.

Amenities: The hotel is sole owner of a "fantasy island" (Palomino Island), with caverns, nature trails, horseback riding, and water sports such as scuba diving, windsurfing, and snorkeling. About half a mile offshore, the island is connected by private ferries to the main hotel at frequent intervals. There's also a 25-slip marina where some of the boats are for rent, six pools, many Jacuzzi tubs, a fitness center, and state-of-the-art conference facilities. Seven tennis courts are lit for night play, and there's an 18-hole championship golf course designed by Arthur Hills with unbelievable views; greens fees are $95 to $155 per person. Arcade of 22 retail shops, room service (from 7am to 11:30pm), baby-sitting, men's and women's beauty salon, laundry/dry cleaning, massages, spa services, special activities area and games room for kids. Camp Coquí provides for children 3 to 12, for $38 per day (from 9am to 3:30pm). Activities may include fishing, sailing, arts and crafts, nature walks, or treasure hunts.

WHERE TO DINE

✪ **Cassava.** In the El Conquistador Resort, Las Croabas. ☎ **787/863-1000.** Reservations recommended. Main courses $28–$35. AE, DISC, MC, V. Daily 6–10pm. PUERTO RICAN/ CARIBBEAN.

This is the most experimental and most unusual restaurant in El Conquistador. You'll find it within earshot of the casino, in a super-colorful setting. Flavors really explode on your palate. Starters include an herbed version of beef carpaccio, Cajun crab cakes, French onion soup, and lobster bisque. Main courses include relatively conservative and time-tested versions of New York strip steak, prime rack of lamb, and extra-thick veal chops, or more experimental dishes like grilled salmon with passion-fruit sauce, or asopao of lobster and cassava in a saffron-flavored broth. The most alluring dessert is a beautifully presented crème brûlée.

Isabela's Grill. In the El Conquistador Resort, Las Croabas. ☎ **787/863-1000.** Reservations recommended. Main courses $29–$36. AE, DISC, MC, V. Daily 6–11pm. AMERICAN STEAK-HOUSE.

Of all the restaurants in El Conquistador Resort, this is the most "American." If Ike were to miraculously return, he'd feel comfortable with this '50s menu. The severe baroque room was inspired by an aristocratic monastery in Spain. The massive gates are among the most spectacular pieces of wrought iron on Puerto Rico. The service is impeccable, the steaks tender, and the seafood fresh.

Special care is taken with the beef dishes, even though the meat has to be imported frozen. You can begin with the lobster bisque or French soup, then move on to the thick cut of veal chop or the perfectly prepared rack of lamb. Prime rib of beef is a feature, as are the succulent steaks, especially the New York strip or the porterhouse.

TO THE LIGHTHOUSE: EXPLORING LAS CABEZAS DE SAN JUAN NATURE RESERVE

Better known as El Faro or "The Lighthouse," this preserve in the northeastern corner of the island, north of Fajardo off Route 987, is one of the most beautiful and important areas on Puerto Rico—a number of different ecosystems flourish in the vicinity.

Surrounded on three sides by the Atlantic Ocean, the 316-acre site encompasses forestland, mangroves, lagoons, beaches, cliffs, offshore cays, and coral reefs. El Faro serves as a research center for the scientific community. It's home to a vast array of flora and fauna, including sea turtles and other endangered species.

The nature reserve is open Wednesday to Sunday; reservations are required, so call before going. For reservations throughout the week, call ☎ **787/722-5882;** for reservations on Saturday and Sunday, ☎ **787/860-2560** (reservations on weekends can be made only on the day of your intended visit). Admission is $5 for adults, $2 for children 11 and under, and $2.50 for seniors. Guided tours are conducted at 9:30am, 10am, 10:30am, and 2pm (in English at 2pm).

9 Palmas del Mar

45 miles E of San Juan

On the Caribbean side of Puerto Rico, the residential resort community of Palmas del Mar lies on the island's eastern shore, outside the town of Humacao. It's about an hour's drive from the San Juan airport.

You'll find plenty to do: golf, tennis, scuba diving, sailing, deep-sea fishing, horseback riding, whatever. Hiking on the resort's grounds is another favorite activity, and there's a forest preserve with giant ferns, orchids, and hanging vines. There's even a casino. In fact, the Palmas del Mar resort has one of the most action-packed sports programs in the Caribbean, rivaled only by Hyatt's Cerromar at Dorado.

One of the largest and most ambitious real-estate projects in the Caribbean, **Wyndham Palmas del Mar,** 170 Candelero Dr., Humacao, PR 00792 (☎ **800/ 725-6273** in the U.S., or 787/852-6000), manages 2,700 rolling acres of what used to be a coconut plantation but is now a development that mixes private homes, villa rentals, a hotel, an impressive golf facility, and 3 miles of sandy beaches. The complex attracts both conventions and vacationers in search of horseback riding, tennis, golf, and R&R. It's more tranquil here than in sprawling resorts of El Conquistador and Westin Rio Mar Beach. Because of this resort's sheer land mass, there are more places to retreat away from the hordes.

Once you arrive at Palmas del Mar, you can depend on the free shuttle-bus service that interconnects the far-flung aspects of this community at 20- to 30-minute intervals. The complex offers families an activities program year-round. Children ages 3 to 13 are divided into compatible age groups, and enjoy arts and crafts, tennis and swimming lessons, mini-golf, and water polo.

GETTING THERE   The **Humacao Regional Airport** is 3 miles from the northern boundary of Palmas del Mar. Its 2,300-foot strip will accommodate private planes; no regularly scheduled airline currently serves the Humacao airport.

Palmas del Mar will arrange minivan or bus transport from Humacao to the San Juan airport for $25 each way. Call the resort if you want to be met at the airport.

WHERE TO STAY

Wyndham Hotel. 170 Candalero Dr., Wyndham Palmas del Mar, Humacao, PR 00791. ☎ **800/725-6273** in the U.S., or 787/852-6000. Fax 787/852-6320. www.palmasdelmar. com. 101 units. A/C TV TEL. Winter $230–$263 double. Off-season $166–$191 double. MAP (breakfast and dinner) $34.50 per person extra. AE, DC, MC, V.

Although the acreage within the Palmas del Mar development contains thousands of privately owned villas, many of which can be rented by vacationers, this is the only conventional, full-service hotel. It was radically renovated in 1997. None of the well-furnished bedrooms overlooks the sea, but many have private patios or verandas, and most are roomier than you might expect. Rooms have tile floors, tropical furnishings, large closets, fine linens, and good mattresses. Bathrooms are small but have adequate shelf space and thick towels. The beach, tennis center, and golf courses are close at hand, and the staff will help you enjoy the many diversions available within the Palmas del Mar compound.

Wyndham Villa Suites. 170 Candelero Dr., Wyndham Palmas del Mar, Humacao PR 00792. ☎ **800/725-6273** in the U.S., or 787/852-6000. Fax 787/852-6320. www.palmasdelmar. com. 135 units. A/C TV TEL. Winter $386–$520 one-bedroom suite; $562–$682 two-bedroom suite; $723–$858 three-bedroom suite. Off-season $232–$312 one-bedroom suite; $337–$410 two-bedroom suite; $434–$515 three-bedroom suite. Minimum stay, ranging from 3 to 7 nights, required during some peak seasons.

Set almost adjacent to the Wyndham Hotel, this complex of red-roofed, white-walled, Iberian-inspired town houses would be a good choice for a family vacation. Divided into three separate clusters, and carefully landscaped with tropical plants, each unit—within reason—is furnished and decorated according to the taste of its individual owner. Regardless of the individual decor, each contains a kitchen, a comfortable bed, and a well-equipped, well-maintained private bathroom with a hair dryer. You'll enjoy a sense of privacy, and views of either the ocean or the gardens. Rental fees depend on the unit's proximity to the beachfront or golf course; an additional handful of villas built against a steep hillside overlook the resort's 21 tennis courts.

WHERE TO DINE

All the restaurants are open during the winter season; however, in summer only three or four may be fully functional. For a complete rundown, ask when you make your booking.

Chez Daniel/Le Grill. Marina de Palmas del Mar. ☎ **787/850-3838.** Reservations required. Main courses $22–$32. AE, MC, V. Fri–Sun noon–3pm; daily 6:30–10pm. Closed June and Tues (Apr–Dec only). FRENCH.

It's French, it's fun, and it's the favorite of the folks who tie up their yachts at the adjacent pier. Normandy-born Daniel Vasse, the owner, along with his French Catalonian wife, Lucette, maintain twin dining rooms that in their way are the most appealing at Palmas del Mar. Le Grill is a steakhouse with a Gallic twist and lots of savory flavor in the form of béarnaise, garlic, peppercorn sauce, or whatever else you specify. Chez Daniel shows a more faithful allegiance to the tenets of classical French cuisine, placing an emphasis on such dishes as the bouillabaisse (both the Catalonian and Marseillaise versions), onion soup, and snails, as well as lobster and chicken dishes. For dessert, consider a soufflé au Cointreau.

Toco Coco's. In the Wyndham Hotel. ☎ **787/852-6000,** ext. 50. Reservations required only for groups of 6 or more. Main courses $15–$30. AE, DISC, MC, V. Daily 6:30–11am, noon–2:30pm, and 6–10:30pm. INTERNATIONAL.

Cooled by trade winds, this restaurant overlooking a courtyard and pool is an ideal choice for any casual meal. Lunch always includes sandwiches and burgers; if you want heartier fare, ask for the Puerto Rican specialty of the day, perhaps red snapper in garlic butter, preceded by black-bean soup. Dinner is more elaborate—begin with stuffed jalapeños or chicken tacos, followed by Caribbean lobster, New York sirloin, paella, or the catch of the day. The cooking, although of a high standard, is never quite gourmet—it's just good, hearty food. Every night in winter is a virtual theme night here, ranging from an Italian festival on Monday to a Puerto Rican night on Saturday.

SPORTS, ON & OFF THE WATER

Nonguests of the Palmas del Mar resorts can still use these hotel facilities, but should call ahead first. The main office can help you arrange deep-sea diving and other activities.

Coral Head Divers & Water Sports Center (☎ **800/635-4529** in the U.S., or 787/850-7208), operates out of a building on the harbor at the Palmas del Mar Resort. The dive center owns two fully equipped boats, measuring 26 and 48 feet. The center offers daily two-tank open-water dives for certified divers, plus snorkeling trips to Monkey Island and Vieques. The two-tank dive includes tanks, weights, and computer for $80. A snorkeling trip to Monkey Island includes use of equipment and a beverage for $45 per person.

The Gary Player–designed, par-72 **golf course** (☎ **800/725-6273** in the U.S., or 787/852-6000) is one of the most impressive anywhere. Its botanical highlights include thousands of mature palm trees and carefully maintained sections of tropical rain forest. The course is so good that many golf-playing retirees have bought homes adjacent to the fairways. The most challenging holes? Numbers 11 through 16, although many beginners have lost their tempers over number 18 as well. Lessons are offered to players of all different levels.

The **Tennis Center** at Palmas del Mar (☎ **787/852-6000,** ext. 51), the largest on Puerto Rico, features 15 hard courts and five clay courts. Court fees for hotel guests are $18 per hour, or $22 for nonguests. Special tennis packages, which include accommodations, are available. Call for more information.

PALMAS DEL MAR AFTER DARK

The **casino** in the Palmas del Mar complex, near the Palmas Inn (☎ **787/852-6000,** ext. 10142), has 12 blackjack tables, two roulette wheels, a craps table, and dozens of slot machines. The casino is open daily year-round, Sunday through Thursday from 6pm to 2am and Friday and Saturday from 6pm to 3am. Under Puerto Rican law, drinks cannot be served in a casino.

19

Saba

An extinct volcano, with no beaches or flat land, cone-shaped Saba is 5 square miles of rock carpeted with lush foliage such as orchids, giant elephant ears, and Eucharist lilies. At its zenith, Mount Scenery, it measures 2,900 feet. Under the sea, the volcanic walls that form Saba continue a sheer drop to great depths, making for some of the most panoramic dives in the Caribbean.

Unless you're a serious hiker or diver, you might confine your look at Saba to a day trip from St. Maarten (and flee as the sun sets). If you're a self-sufficient type who demands almost no artificial amusement, then sleepy Saba might be your hideaway.

Saba is 150 miles east of Puerto Rico and 90 miles east of St. Croix. Most visitors fly from St. Maarten, 28 miles to the north.

Sabans were known to take advantage of their special topography—they pelted invaders from above with rocks and boulders. Because of the English missionaries and Scottish seamen from the remote Shetland Islands who settled on the island, Saba has always been English-speaking. The official language, however, is Dutch. Also, because of those early settlers from Europe, 60% of the population is Caucasian, many with red hair and freckled fair skin.

1 Essentials

VISITOR INFORMATION

Before you go, you can get information from the **Saba Tourist Office,** P.O. Box 6322, Boca Raton, FL 33427 (☎ **800/722-2394** or 561/ 394-8580).

On the island, the **Saba Tourist Board** is at Lambees Place in the heart of Windwardside (☎ **599/4-62231**). It's open Monday through Thursday from 8am to noon and 1 to 5pm, Friday from 8am to noon and 1 to 4:30pm.

Saba is on the Web at **www.turq.com/saba**.

GETTING THERE

BY PLANE Direct flights to St. Maarten are offered on **American Airlines** (☎ **800/433-7300** in the U.S.; www.aa.com), from New York's JFK, and **Continental Airlines** (☎ **800/231-0856;** www. flycontinental.com), flying out of Newark (see chapter 24 for other airlines with connections through San Juan). From Queen Juliana

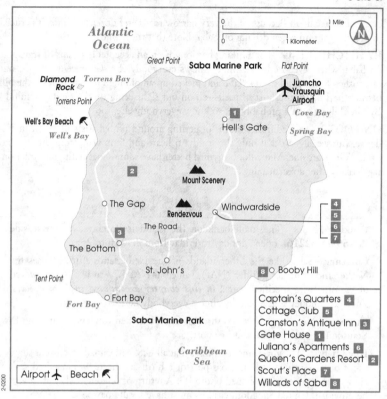

Atlantic
Ocean

Great Point **Saba Marine Park** *Flat Point*

Diamond *Torrens Bay*
Rock

Torrens Point Juancho
Yrausquin
Airport

Cove Bay

Well's Bay Beach ○
Hell's Gate *Spring Bay*

Well's Bay

☐2

▲▲
Mount Scenery

○ The Gap

▲▲
Rendezvous Windwardside 4
5
☐3 *The Road* 6
7
The Bottom ○

○
St. John's 8 ○ Booby Hill

Tent Point

○ Fort Bay

Fort Bay **Saba Marine Park**

Caribbean
Sea

Captain's Quarters	4
Cottage Club	5
Cranston's Antique Inn	3
Gate House	1
Juliana's Apartments	6
Queen's Gardens Resort	2
Scout's Place	7
Willards of Saba	8

Airport ✈ Beach ○

Airport on St. Maarten, you can take the 12-minute hop to Saba on **Winair** (Windward Islands Airways International) (☎ **599/4-62255**).

Arriving by air from St. Maarten, travelers step from Winair's 20-passenger planes onto the tarmac of the **Juancho Yrausquin Airport** (☎ **599/4-62255**). The airstrip is one of the shortest landing strips in the world, stretching only 1,312 feet along the aptly named Flat Point, one of the few level areas on the island.

Many guests at hotels on St. Maarten fly over to Saba on the morning flight, spend the day sightseeing, then return to St. Maarten on the afternoon flight. Winair connections can also be made on Saba to both St. Kitts and St. Eustatia.

GETTING AROUND

BY TAXI Taxis meet every flight. Up to four persons are allowed to share a cab. The fare from the airport to Windwardside is $8, or $12.50 to the Bottom. A taxi from Windwardside to the Bottom costs $6.50. There is no central number to call for service

BY RENTAL CAR None of the "big three" car-rental companies maintains a branch on Saba, partly because most visitors opt to get around by taxi. In the unlikely event that you should dare to drive a car on Saba, locally operated companies include **Johnson's Rental,** Windwardside (☎ **599/4-62269**), renting about six Mazdas, starting at $40 per day and including a full tank of gas and unlimited mileage. Some insurance is included in the rates, but you might be held partly responsible in the event of an accident. Because of the very narrow roads and dozens of cliffs, it's crucial to exercise caution when driving on Saba. Note that traffic moves on the right.

BY HITCHHIKING   Hitchhiking has long been an acceptable means of transport on Saba, where everybody seemingly knows everybody else. On recent rounds, our taxi rushed a sick child to the plane and picked up an old man to take him up the hill because he'd fallen and hurt himself—all on our sightseeing tour! (We didn't mind.) By hitchhiking, you'll probably get to know everybody else, too.

ON FOOT   The traditional means of getting around on Saba is still much in evidence. But we suggest that only the sturdy in heart and limb walk from the Bottom up to Windwardside. Many do, but you'd better have some shoes with good traction, particularly after a recent rain.

Fast Facts: Saba

Banking Hours   The main bank on the island is **Barclays,** Windwardside (☎ **599/4-62216**), open Monday to Friday from 8:30am to 2pm.

Currency   Saba, like the other islands of the Netherlands Antilles, uses the **Netherlands Antilles guilder (NAf),** valued at NAf 1.77 to U.S.$1. However, unless otherwise specified, *rates in this chapter are quoted in U.S. dollars,* since U.S. money is accepted by almost everybody here.

Customs   You don't have to go through Customs when you land at Juancho E. Yrausquin Airport, as this is a free port.

Documents   The government requires that all U.S. and Canadian citizens show proof of citizenship, such as a passport or a birth certificate with a raised seal, along with a government-issued photo ID. A return or ongoing ticket must also be provided. United Kingdom citizens must have a valid passport.

Electricity   Saba uses 110 volts AC (60 cycles), so most U.S.-made appliances don't need transformers or adapters.

Hospital   Saba's hospital complex is the A. M. Edwards Medical Centre, the Bottom (☎ **599/4-63289**).

Language   The official language on Saba is Dutch, but you'll find English widely spoken.

Pharmacies   Try **The Pharmacy,** the Bottom (☎ **599/4-63289**), open Monday to Friday from 7:30am to 5:30pm.

Police   Call ☎ **599/4-63237** for the police.

Safety   Crime on this island, where everyone knows everyone else, is practically nonexistent. But who knows? A tourist might rob you. It would be wise to safeguard your valuables.

Taxes   The government imposes an 8% tourist tax on hotel rooms. If you're returning to St. Maarten or flying over to Statia, you must pay a $5 departure tax. If you're going anywhere else, however, a $10 tax is imposed.

Telephone   International phone calls can be placed at **Antelecon,** the Bottom (☎ **599/4-63211**).

To call Saba from the United States, dial **011** (the international access code), then **599** (the country code for the Netherlands Antilles), and finally **4** (the area code for all of Saba) and the five-digit local number. To make a call within Saba, only the five-digit local number is necessary.

Time   Saba is on Atlantic standard time year-round, 1 hour earlier than eastern standard time. When the United States is on daylight saving time, clocks on Saba and the U.S. East Coast read the same.

Water   The water on Saba is generally safe to drink.

2 Where to Stay

If you're looking for a hotel on the beach, you've come to the wrong island. Saba's only beach, Well's Bay Beach, is tiny and can be reached from most hotels via a $10 taxi ride.

Captain's Quarters. Windwardside, Saba, N.A. ☎ **800/446-3010** or 599/4-62201. Fax 599/4-62377. www.saba-online.com. E-mail: sabacq@megatropic.com. 12 units. MINIBAR TV. Winter $175 double. Off-season $160 double. Rates include American breakfast. Extra person $35. AE, DISC, MC, V.

A restored 1850s sea captain's house has been converted into a hideaway for royalty, celebrities, and other visitors. Just off the village center of Windwardside, it's a complex of several guest houses surrounding the main house, with its traditional verandas and covered porches. You make your way here by going down a narrow, steep lane. Thrust out toward the water is a freshwater swimming pool surrounded by a terrace, where you can sunbathe or order refreshments from an open-air bar.

The first floor of the main house contains the library, sitting room, and kitchen, with two private accommodations above (one is a "honeymoon" room). The house is furnished with antiques gathered from many ports of the world, and everywhere are quaint reminders of New England. Well-designed and cozy studio units are set in the garden. About half the bedrooms contain four-poster beds, and each has a balcony overlooking the sea and Mount Scenery. Dutch visitors often request room no. 1, where Queen Juliana once slept. The small bathrooms have shower stalls.

Cottage Club. Windwardside, Saba, N.A. ☎ **599/4-62486.** Fax 599/4-62476. E-mail: cottageclub@megatropic.com. 10 units. TV TEL. Winter $115 studio apt for two. Off-season $100 studio apt for two. Third and fourth person $20 extra. MC, V.

Small, intimate, and immersed in the architectural and aesthetic traditions of Saba, this hotel complex occupies about a half acre of steeply sloping and carefully landscaped terrain, a 2-minute walk of the center of the island's capital. Only its lobby evokes a historic setting: Designed of local stone, and set at an altitude above the other buildings of the complex, it's the focal point for a collection of island antiques, lace curtains, and a round-sided swimming pool. The medium-size studio apartments each contain a kitchenette, a semiprivate patio, ceiling fans, a living-room area, and a queen-size bed with a firm mattress. These units are housed in clapboard replicas of antique cottages—two studios per cottage—with red roofs, green shutters, white walls, and yellow trim. The interiors are breezy, airy, and comfortable. If you'd like a room with an ocean view, request nos. 1 or 2. Bathrooms have showers and are well maintained. There's no bar or restaurant on the premises, but a nearby supermarket will deliver supplies on request. The owners of the establishment are three Saban brothers (Gary, Mark, and Dean) whose extended families all seem to assist in the construction and maintenance of the place.

♦ **Cranston's Antique Inn.** The Bottom, Saba, N.A. ☎ **599/4-63203.** Fax 599/4-63469. 6 units. Winter $99 double. Off-season $129 double. A/C TV. DISC, MC, V.

Everyone congregates for rum drinks and gossip on the front terrace of this inn near the village roadway, on the west coast north of Fort Bay. It's an old-fashioned house, more than 100 years old, with antique four-poster beds in all the rooms. Mr. Cranston, the owner, will gladly rent you the same bedroom where Queen Juliana once spent a holiday in 1955. Aside from the impressive wooden beds, the furnishings are mostly hit or miss, and not much has changed since the Queen checked in oh so long ago. The bedrooms are quite tiny, although the floral spreads jazz them up a bit. Come here for the old-timey atmosphere and the cheap prices, not for any grand style. The biggest improvement is that all the rooms now have private—and extremely cramped—bathrooms, as well as new mattresses.

Mr. Cranston has a good island cook, who makes use of locally grown spices. Island dishes include goat meat, roast pork from Saba pigs, red snapper, and broiled grouper. Meals begin at $15 to $20 and are served on a covered terrace in the garden or inside. The house is within walking distance of Ladder Bay.

The Gate House. Hell's Gate, Saba, N.A. ☎ **599/4-62416** or 708/354-9641 (reservations only). Fax 599/4-62550. www.members.aol.com/travel/saba. E-mail: sabagate@aol.com. 6 units. Winter $95 double. Off-season $85 double. Rates include continental breakfast. MC, V. Closed Sept.

Named for its position at the gateway to Saba, almost adjacent to the airport, this hotel sits on steep terrain that's about 5 minutes from the coast. Built in 1990, it consists of three two-story, cement-sided replicas of Saban town houses surrounded by a wraparound veranda. There's also an oval-shaped pool on the premises. The red roofs, green shutters, and white walls evoke old Saba; inside, floors are either wooden or tile. Guest rooms are small, but still comfortable and efficiently arranged. Some units have private balconies, while those on the top share a common porch with a distant view of the islands of St. Maarten, St. Kitts, and Anguilla. Bathrooms are strictly functional affairs, most with a shower stall—although our favorite room, no. 1, has twin beds and a real bathtub (a rarity on this island). Your hosts are an American-Dutch couple, Jim Siegel and Manuela Doey, who devote much of their time and attention to running the popular in-house restaurant (see "Where to Dine," below).

Juliana's Apartments. Windwardside, Saba, N.A. ☎ **599/4-62269.** Fax 599/4-62389. www.julianas-hotel.com. E-mail: julianas@megatropic.com. 10 units. Winter $115 double; $135 apt or cottage. Off-season $90 double; $115 apt or cottage. Extra person $20. Dive packages available. AE, MC, V.

Built in 1985 near the Captain's Quarters, this hostelry is set on a hillside. Each guest room is modern, immaculate, and simply but comfortably furnished. All have access to a sundeck and balconies opening onto beautiful views of the Caribbean, except nos. 1 to 3 in the rear. Opt for one of the trio of upper-level rooms (nos. 7, 8, or 9), as they offer the best views. Bathrooms are small but adequate, and housekeeping wins high marks here. Also available are a 2½-room apartment, complete with kitchenette, and a renovated original Saban cottage, with two bedrooms, a spacious living room, a dining room, a TV, and a fully equipped kitchen. The property also contains a recreation room, a pool, and a simple restaurant. Unless you specifically like the old-fashioned ambience of Scout's Place, a stay here would be a superior upgrade.

Queen's Gardens Resort. P.O. Box 4, Troy Hill, The Bottom, Saba, N.A. ☎ **800/599-9407** or 599/4-63494. Fax 599/4-63495. www.gobeach.com/saba/queens/htm. E-mail: queens@ gobeach.com. 12 units. TV TEL. Winter $150 double; $200 one-bedroom suite for 2; $300 two-bedroom suite for up to 4. Off-season $128 double; $170 one-bedroom suite for 2; $255 two-bedroom suite for up to 4. AE, DC, MC, V.

One of the most massive engineering projects in Saba's recent memory included the placement of a rock-sided terrace on this plot of forested, steeply sloping land 1,200 feet above the sea. The result, early in 1997, was a well-conceived cluster of white-walled, red-roofed bungalows angled for sweeping views, and clustered around the semicircular edges of the largest pool on Saba, with north-facing views over the island's capital and the sea. From a distance, the compound might remind you of a fortified village in Iberia; close-up, it's charming and much, much more comfortable. Accommodations are simple, modern, airy, and clean, each decorated in pastel colors. Most units are split-level, with large living rooms; all have kitchenettes and fine double or twin beds. Bathrooms are large but shower only. On the premises is a restaurant, the Mango Royale (see "Where to Dine," below), and a dive shop.

Scout's Place. Windwardside, Saba, N.A. ☎ **599/4-62205.** Fax 599/4-62388. 15 units. Winter $85 double; $100 apt for two. Off-season discounts of around 20%. Rates include continental breakfast. DISC, MC, V.

Right in the center of the village, Scout's Place is hidden from the street and set on the ledge of a hill. With only 15 rooms, it's still the second-largest inn on the island. The old house has a large covered but open-walled dining room, where every table has a view of the sea. Owner Diana Medora makes guests feel right at home in this informal place, with a decor ranging from Surinam hand-carvings to red-and-black wicker peacock chairs to silver samovars. Guest rooms open onto an interior courtyard filled with flowers, and each has a view of the sea. The rooms are small and rather plain, except for the four-poster beds; many have linoleum floors and tiny TVs. The best units are on the lower floor, as they have French doors opening onto balconies fronting the ocean. Furniture is haphazard, while mattresses, although much used, are still comfortable. Bathrooms are also small, with showers only. The apartment with kitchenette is suitable for up to five occupants; an extra person is charged $20.

✪ **Willards of Saba.** Windwardside, Saba, N.A. ☎ **599/4-62498.** Fax 599/4-62482. E-mail: willard@sintmaarten.net. 7 units. Winter $250 double; $300–$450 bungalow; $500 honeymoon suite. Off-season discounts of around 20%. Extra person $50. AE, DISC, MC, V. Children 11 and under not accepted.

Until Brad Willard arrived, Saba never had anything remotely related to posh. Willard is the great-grandson of Henry Augustus Willard, who built his namesake hotel in Washington, D.C. The Saba hotel opened in 1994 and became an immediate sellout, attracting visitors, often celebrities, who might not have set foot on the island before. Five units are in a concrete building designed in the island's distinctive style, with red roofs, white walls, and green shutters. Guest rooms have *Casablanca*-like ceiling fans; furnishings are not of the highest standard, but are still comfortable. The least expensive units are the two rooms in the main building, which are quite spacious. For the most luxurious living, ask for the VIP Room overlooking the pool, with its own large balcony. Lower Cliffside units are the smallest, but have good views from their private balconies. The Room in the Sky is the choice of honeymooners. Bathrooms are small, with shower only. Much care went into the design of this place, making use of everything from cedar from the Northwest to original island paintings. No more than a dozen or so guests are ever found here at one time. Because of its position in a garden high on a hill overlooking the island's southwestern coastline, each accommodation has sweeping views and access to almost constant ocean breezes.

Young children are not accepted here because the railings on upper floors are not safe for them, though occasionally an exception may be made for older children; you should definitely ask before you make a reservation. From the pool or hot tub, guests can look over the waters to at least five neighboring islands on a clear day. Corazon's restaurant and its bar are recommended in "Where to Dine," below. Facilities include tennis courts, a hot tub/Jacuzzi, and a large pool.

3 Where to Dine

⊘ Brigadoon Pub & Eatery. Windwardside. ☎ **599/4-62380.** Main courses $11.95–$27.95. MC, V. Wed–Mon 6:30–9:30pm. CARIBBEAN/AMERICAN.

An array of Caribbean, American, and other international flavors combine to form a savory cuisine in this century-old colonial building with an open front. It's the island's best dining choice. Whenever possible, fresh local ingredients are used, including herbs, spices, fruits, and farm-fresh vegetables. Fresh local fish is generally the preferred course, or you can order live local lobster from the island's only live lobster tank (prices on this delicacy are likely to vary). Steaks are flown in weekly. You might also prefer the Saba fish pot, a variety of fresh catch from Saba's waters in a basil-and-tomato sauce. Other main courses include mahimahi with citrus butter sauce (justifiably very popular) and Thai shrimp in a coconut-curry sauce.

Corazon. In Willards of Saba Hotel, Windwardside. ☎ **599/4-62498.** Reservations required. Main courses $25–$50. AE, DISC, MC, V. Daily 11:30am–3pm and 7–9:30pm. ANTILLEAN/ASIAN/INTERNATIONAL.

This restaurant features a breezy island decor; a sweeping, high-altitude view of Saba's southeastern coastline; and some of the freshest fish and lobster on the island. Most of the catch featured on the "island-inspired" menu comes from the boats of local fisherfolk. Entrees change with the availability of the ingredients, although grouper, snapper Florentine, and lobster Thermidor are usually featured, as are two recently sampled and truly savory dishes: pork loin with a champagne-and-caper sauce or Chinese-style beef with oyster sauce. You can cool down with a crêpe stuffed with banana and jackfruit, then fried and served with homemade ice cream. The restaurant takes its name from Corazon de Johnson, manager and chef. Although born in the Philippines, she doesn't limit her inspiration to her homeland, but roams the world for ideas for her fusion cuisine. There's a pleasant bar on the premises where you might enjoy a round of before-dinner drinks.

The Gate House. Hells Gate. ☎ **599/4-62416.** Reservations recommended. Fixed-price three-course meal $25. MC, V. Thurs–Tues 6:30–9:30pm. Closed Sept. CARIBBEAN.

Set on one of the upper floors of a previously recommended hotel, this popular and lively place is closer to the island's only airport than any other restaurant. Views from its premises encompass the coastline, the hotel pool, and the arrival and departure of virtually every plane that lands on Saba. Staff members might be from the U.S. mainland, Holland, or St. Vincent, depending on whomever happens to be here on the night of your arrival. The menu changes every night, depending on what's available on-island and the inspiration of the chef. Staples that virtually always appear include curried conch, coconut shrimp, and grilled flank steak, whereas items that come and go include pan-fried grouper, grilled mahimahi with jerk sauce or with lemon-butter-garlic sauce, and grilled chicken with Creole sauce.

Mango Royale. In the Queen's Gardens Resort, Troy Hill, The Bottom. ☎ **599/4-63494.** Reservations recommended. Lunch platters $12–$18; dinner main courses $14–$25. AE, DC, MC, V. Daily 11am–3pm and 5:30–11pm. INTERNATIONAL.

Part of this restaurant's allure results from its placement beside the largest pool on Saba, its high-altitude views that sweep northward over the sea, and its flaming torches that add a flickering glamour to the site during the dinner hour. You can dine on an indoor/outdoor terrace, or—for more privacy—within a lattice-covered structure inspired by a gazebo. Menu items at lunch include salads, sandwiches, and relatively simple versions of grilled fish. Evening meals are more elaborate, with offerings such as goatmeat with mint sauce, lobster bisque, Saba spiced shrimp with Peking dumplings, grilled chicken with tropical herbs, barbecued beef kebabs, and fettuccine with cream sauce.

Saba Chinese Bar & Restaurant (Moo Goo Gai Pan). Windwardside. ☎ **599/4-62353.** Main courses $7–$17. DISC, MC, V. Tues–Sun 11am–midnight. CHINESE.

Amid a cluster of residential buildings on a hillside above Windwardside, this place is operated by a family from Hong Kong. It offers some 120 dishes, an unpretentious decor of plastic tablecloths and folding chairs, and food so popular that many residents claim this is their most frequented restaurant. Meals include an array of Cantonese and Indonesian specialties—lobster Cantonese, Chinese chicken with mushrooms, sweet-and-sour fish, conch chop suey, several curry dishes, roast duck, and nasi goreng. If you've sampled the great Chinese restaurants of New York, San Francisco, and Hong Kong, you may find these dishes bland, but it's good, change-of-pace fare.

Scout's Place. Windwardside. ☎ **599/4-62205.** Reservations required 2 to 3 hours in advance. Lunch $13; fixed-price dinner $17–$32. MC, V. Lunch daily at 12:30pm; dinner daily at 7:30pm. INTERNATIONAL.

This is a popular dining spot among day-trippers to the island, but you should have your driver stop by early to make a reservation for you. Lunch at Scout's is simple, good, and filling, and the prices are low, too. Dinner is more elaborate, with tables placed on an open-sided terrace, the ideal spot for a drink at sundown. Fresh seafood is a specialty, as is curried goat. The sandwiches are the island's best, and they're made with freshly baked bread. Locals come from all over the island to sample them. Each day, a selection of homemade soups is also offered, perhaps pumpkin or pigeon pea. Scout's chef is proud of his ribs as well. Fresh local fruits and vegetables are used whenever possible. Even if you don't like the food, it's the best place on the island to catch up on the latest gossip.

4 Sports & Outdoor Pursuits

If it's beaches you're seeking, forget it: It's better to remain on the sands of St. Maarten. Sports here are mostly do-it-yourself, but visitors are still attracted to Saba for its underwater scenery.

DIVING

Dive sites around Saba, all protected by the Saba Marine Park, have permanent moorings and range from shallow to deep. Divers see pinnacles, walls, ledges, overhangs, and reefs—all with abundant coral and sponge formations and a wide variety of both reef and pelagic marine life. There's also a fully operational decompression chamber/hyperbaric facility located in the Fort Bay harbor.

Saba Deep Dive Center, P.O. Box 22, Fort Bay, Saba, N.A. (☎ **599/4-63347**), is a full-service dive center that offers scuba diving, snorkeling, equipment rental/repair, and tank fills. Whether one diver or 20, novice or experienced, Mike Myers and his staff of NAUI and PADI instructors and dive masters make an effort to provide personalized service and great diving. The **In Two Deep Restaurant** and the **Deep Boutique** offer air-conditioned comfort, a view of the harbor area and the Caribbean Sea, good food and drink, and a wide selection of clothes, swimwear, lotions, and sunglasses. The restaurant is open for breakfast and lunch. A certification course goes for $375. A single-tank dive costs $50; a two-tank dive, $90. Night dives are $65. The center is open daily from 8am to 6pm.

The Coral Gardens

Circling the entire island and including four offshore underwater mountains (seamounts), the **Saba Marine Park,** Fort Bay (☎ **599/4-63295**), preserves the island's coral reefs and marine life. The park is zoned for various pursuits. The all-purpose recreational zone includes Well's Bay Beach, Saba's only beach, but it's seasonal—it disappears with the winter seas, only to reappear in late spring. There are two anchorage zones for visiting yachts and Saba's only harbor. The five dive zones include a coastal area and four seamounts, a mile offshore. In these zones are more than two dozen marked and buoyed dive sites and a snorkeling trail. You plunge into a world of coral and sponges, swimming with parrot fish, doctorfish, and damselfish. The snorkel trail, however, is not for the neophyte. It can be approached from Well's Bay Beach but only from May to October. Depths of more than 1,500 feet are found between the island and the seamounts, which reach a minimum depth of 90 feet. There's a $3 per dive visitor fee. Funds are also raised through souvenir sales and donations. The park office at Fort Bay is open Monday to Friday from 8am to 5pm, Saturday from 8am to noon, and Sunday from 10am to 2pm.

Sea Saba Dive Center, Windwardside (☎ **599/4-62246**), has nine experienced instructors eager to share their knowledge of Saba Marine Park: famous deep and medium-depth pinnacles, walls, spur-and-groove formations, and giant boulder gardens. Their two 40-foot, uncrowded boats are best suited for a comfortable day on Saba's waters. Daily boat dives are made between 9:30am and 1:30pm, allowing a relaxing interval for snorkeling. Courses range from resort through dive master. Extra day and night dives can be arranged. A one-tank dive costs $50, a two-tank dive $90.

Saba Reef Divers, Fort Bay Harbour, Windwardside (☎ **599/4-62541**), a long-established dive center, is a PADI resort and ANDI training facility. The staff guides divers through the shoals, walls, shelves, reefs, pinnacles, and seamounts that surround the volcanic cone of the landmass of Saba, including the "Pinnacles" and Diamond Rock, where divers can spot barracuda, stingrays, grouper, and snapper lurking near its lush, sloping walls. Tent Reef, a long, underwater fault crisscrossed with crevasses and drop-offs ranging from 40 to 130 feet, is another unusual option for adventurous divers. Packages are available; a single-tank dive costs around $50, a two-tank dive $90.

HIKING

Saba is as beautiful above the water as it is below. It offers many trails, both for the neophyte and the more experienced hiker, all reached by paths leading off from "The Road." There's nothing more dramatic than the hike to the top of ✪ **Mount Scenery,** a volcano that erupted 5,000 years ago. Allow at least 3 hours and take your time climbing the 1,064 sometimes-slippery concrete steps up to the cloud-reefed, 2,855-foot mountain. You'll pass through a lush rain forest of palms, bromeliads, elephant ears, heliconia, mountain raspberries, lianas, and tree ferns. Queen Beatrix of the Netherlands climbed these steps in her pumps and, upon reaching the summit, declared: "This is the smallest and highest place in my kingdom." On a clear day, you can see the neighboring islands of St. Kitts, St. Eustatius, St. Maarten, and even St. Barthélemy. Ask your inn to pack you a picnic lunch, and bring water. The higher you climb, the cooler it grows, about a drop of 1°F every 328 feet; on a hot day this can be an incentive.

One of our favorite hikes—with some of Saba's most panoramic views—is the **Crispeen Track,** reached from Windwardside as the main road descends to the hamlet of St. John's. Once at St. John's, the track heads northeast going through a narrow but dramatic gorge covered in thick tropical foliage. The vegetation grows lusher and lusher, taking in banana and citrus fields. As you reach the higher points of a section of the island called Rendezvous, the fields are no longer cultivated and resemble a rain forest, covered with such flora as philodendron, anthurium, and the wild mammee. Hiking time to Rendezvous is about an hour.

If you don't want to explore the natural attractions of the island on your own, the **Saba Tourist Office,** P.O. Box 527, Windwardside (☎ **599/4-62231**), can arrange tours of the tropical rain forests. Jim Johnson (☎ **599/4-63307**), a fit, forty-ish Sabian guide, conducts most of these tours, and knows the terrain better than anyone else on the island (he's sometimes difficult to reach, however). Johnson will point out orchids, golden heliconia, and other flora and fauna as well as the rock formations and bromeliads you're likely to see. Tours can accommodate one to eight hikers and usually last about half a day; depending on your particular route and number of participants, the cost can be anywhere from $40 to $80. Actual prices, of course, are negotiated.

5 Exploring the Island

Tidy white houses cling to the mountainside, and small family cemeteries adjoin each dwelling. Lace-curtained, gingerbread-trimmed cottages give a Disneyland aura.

The first jeep arrived on Saba in 1947. Before that, Sabans went about on foot, climbing from village to village. Hundreds of steps had been chiseled out of the rock by the early Dutch settlers in the 1640s.

Engineers told them it was impossible, but Sabans spent two decades or so building a single, 19-mile-long, cross-island road by hand. Nothing else in the Caribbean compares with "The Road." Filled with hairpin turns, it zigzags from Fort Bay, where a deep-water pier accommodates large tenders from cruise ships, to a height of 1,600 feet and the lush interior. Along the way are fortresslike supporting walls.

Past storybook villages, the road goes over the crest to **the Bottom.** Derived from the Dutch word *botte,* which means "bowl-shaped," this village is nestled on a plateau and surrounded by rocky volcanic domes. It occupies about the only bit of ground, 800 feet above the sea. It's also the official capital of Saba, a charming Dutch village of chimneys, gabled roofs, and gardens.

From the Bottom, you can take a taxi up the hill to the mountain village of **Windwardside,** perched on the crest of two ravines about 1,500 feet above sea level. This village of red-roofed houses, the second most important on Saba, is the site of the two biggest inns and most of the shops.

From Windwardside, you can climb steep steps cut in the rock to yet another village, **Hell's Gate,** teetering on the edge of a mountain. There's also a serpentine road from the airport to Hell's Gate, where you'll find the island's largest church. Only the most athletic climb from here to the lip of the volcanic crater.

6 Shopping

After lunch, you can go for a stroll in Windwardside and stop at the boutiques, which often look like someone's living room—and sometimes they are. Most stores are open Monday to Saturday from 9am to noon and 2 to around 5:30pm; some are also open shorter hours on Sunday.

The traditional **drawn threadwork** of the island is famous. Sometimes this work, introduced by a local woman named Gertrude Johnson in the 1870s, is called Spanish work, because it was believed to have been perfected by nuns in Caracas. Selected threads are drawn and tied in a piece of linen to produce an ornamental pattern. It can be expensive if a quality linen has been used.

Try to go home with some **"Saba Spice,"** an aromatic blend of 150-proof cask rum, with such spices as fennel seed, cinnamon, cloves, and nutmeg, straight from someone's home brew. It's not for everyone (too sweet), but it will make an exotic bottle to show off at home.

Most streets in Windwardside have no names, but because it's so small, shops are easy to find.

Ex-Manhattanite Jean Macbeth runs **Around the Bend,** at Scout's Place, Windwardside (☎ 599/4-62519), a classy little boutique featuring gift items and what she calls "pretties," all one-of-a-kind. Charming, locally made, wooden Saba cottage wall plaques are sold along with magnets, switchplates, bright parrot and Toucan pinwheels, Caribbean perfumes, and spices. Naturally, there is a collection of hand-painted silk-screened T-shirts as well.

Saba Tropical Arts, Windwardside (☎ 599/4-62373), is the place to go to watch hand silk-screening, and perhaps even buy some wares. Designer Mieke van Schadewijk has produced some catchy patterns, all of which are displayed at her workshop boutique.

In recent years, the **Saba Artisan Foundation,** the Bottom (☎ 599/4-63260), has made a name for itself with its hand-screened resort fashions. The clothes are casual and colorful. Among the items sold are men's bush-jacket shirts, numerous styles of dresses and skirts, napkins, and place mats, as well as yard goods. Island motifs are used in many designs. Also popular are the famous Saba drawn-lace patterns. The fashions are designed, printed, sewn, and marketed by Sabans. Mail-order as well as wholesale-distributorship inquiries are invited.

7 Saba After Dark

If you're thinking about going to Saba to do some partying, you might want to consider another island. Saba is known for is tucked-away, relaxed, and calm atmosphere. However, don't be too dismayed; there's still something to do at night.

Scout's Place, Windwardside (☎ 599/4-62205), is the place to hang out if you want to relax, enjoy a drink, and have a laugh, especially on the weeknights. A hotel and restaurant, Scout's Place moonlights as a local watering hole, entertaining tourists and locals alike with a distinct Saban/Caribbean atmosphere. You won't do much dancing (well, that actually depends on how much you've had to drink), but it's much better than the weeknight alternative: nothing. It's open daily from noon to around midnight (but actual closing hours depend on business or the lack of it). There's no cover.

Normally a pizzeria, **Guido's,** near Scout's Place in Windwardside (☎ 599/4-62230), serves simple food and drinks weeknights, but becomes the most happening place on the island on Friday and Saturday nights, as it's really your only option to get a drink *and* boogie down. As a disco, it's known as Mountain High Club. There's a dance floor, a sound system, and even a disco ball. Get yourself a white polyester suit, and you'll be ready for fun. Weeknights are similar to Scout's Place: a simple dining crowd. Hours are Monday through Thursday from 6pm to midnight, and Friday and Saturday from 6pm to 2am. There's no cover.

St. Barthélemy

20

For luxury with minimum hassle, although at a high price tag, St. Barts is rivaled only by Anguilla. It's the ultimate in sophistication in the tropics: chic, rich, and very Parisian. Forget such things as historic sites or ambitious water-sports programs here, and come for the relaxation, the ultimate level of comfort, the French cuisine, and the white-sand beaches.

New friends call it "St. Barts," while old-time visitors prefer "St. Barths." Either way, it's short for St. Barthélemy, named by its discoverer Columbus in 1493 and pronounced *San Bar-te-le-MEE.* The uppermost corner of the French West Indies, it's the only Caribbean island with a touch of Sweden.

For the most part, St. Bartians are descendants of Breton and Norman fisherfolk. Many are of French and Swedish ancestry, the latter evident in their fair skin, blond hair, and blue eyes. The mostly Caucasian population is small, about 3,500 living in some 8 square miles, 15 miles southeast of St. Martin and 140 miles north of Guadeloupe.

Occasionally you'll see St. Bartians dressed in the provincial costumes of Normandy; when you hear them speak Norman French, you'll think you're back in the old country, except for the temperature. In little **Corossol,** more than anywhere else, people sometimes follow traditions brought from 17th-century France. You might see elderly women wearing the starched white bonnets, at least on special occasions. This headgear, brought from Brittany, was called *quichenotte,* a corruption of "kiss-me-not," and served as protection from the close attentions of English or Swedish men on the island. The bonneted women can also be spotted at local celebrations, particularly on August 25, **St. Louis's Day.** Many of these women are camera-shy, but they offer their homemade baskets and hats for sale to visitors.

For a long time, the island was a paradise for a few millionaires, such as David Rockefeller, who has a hideaway on the northwest shore, and Edmond de Rothschild, who occupies some fabulous acres at the "other end" of the island. Nowadays, however, St. Barts is developing a broader base of tourism as it opens more hotels. Nevertheless, the island continues to be a celebrity favorite in the Caribbean, attracting the likes of Tom Cruise, Harrison Ford, and Mikhail Baryshnikov.

It also attracts a lot of star-seeking paparazzi, who stalk celebrities not only at their private villas, but also at the beach, including Grand Saline beach, where John F. Kennedy, Jr., was photographed bathing in the nude (which is common and legal at this beach). On another occasion, the paparazzi caught Brad Pitt sunning in the nude at his private villa, with then-girlfriend Gwyneth Paltrow. In February, the island guest list reads like a roster from *Lifestyles of the Rich and Famous.*

The island's capital is **Gustavia,** named after a Swedish king. It's St. Barts's only town and seaport. A sheltered harbor, it has the appearance of a little dollhouse-scale port.

1 Essentials

VISITOR INFORMATION

For information before you go, contact the **French Government Tourist Office** at 444 Madison Ave., **New York, NY** 10022; 9454 Wilshire Blvd., Suite 715, **Beverly Hills, CA** 90212; or 676 N. Michigan Ave., Suite 3360, **Chicago, IL** 60611. For all information in the United States, you can call ☎ **202/659-7779.**

Information on the Web is available at **www.fgtousa.org**.

On the island, go to the **Office du Tourisme,** in the commercial heart of Gustavia, adjacent to La Capitanerie (the Port Authority Headquarters), quai du Général-de-Gaulle (☎ **0590/27-87-27**).

GETTING THERE

BY PLANE Before you book your own airfare, read the section on package tours in chapter 2—it can save you a bundle!

From the United States, the principal gateways are St. Maarten (see chapter 24), St. Thomas (see chapter 27), and Guadeloupe (see chapter 14). At any of these islands, you can connect to St. Barts via interisland carriers.

It's just a 10-minute flight from Queen Juliana Airport on Dutch-held St. Maarten. Your best bet is **Windward Islands Airways International (Winair)** (☎ **0590/27-61-01**), which offers 18 daily flights to St. Barts. Round-trip passage costs $97.50.

If you're on Guadeloupe, you can fly **Air Guadeloupe** (☎ **0590/27-61-90**); trip time is 55 minutes, and flights depart four or five times a day from Pointe-à-Pitre's Le Raizet Airport. Round-trip passage from Guadeloupe to St. Barts costs $200 one-way. Air Guadeloupe also offers regular service, about three flights a day, to St. Barts from the small Espérance Airport on the French side of St. Martin. A one-way fare costs $83.

Air St. Thomas (☎ **800/522-3084** or 0590/27-71-76) offers two flights a day to St. Barts from both San Juan and St. Thomas. However, customers have complained that the airline's schedule is unpredictable. The fare from St. Thomas to St. Barts is $248 round-trip; from San Juan to St. Barts, $335 round-trip.

The makeshift landing strip on St. Barts has been the butt of many jokes. It's short and accommodates only small aircraft; the biggest plane it can land is a 19-seater. In addition, no landings or departures are permitted after dark.

Flying Tips

Always reconfirm your return flight from St. Barts with your interisland airline. If you don't, your reservation will be canceled. Also, don't check your luggage all the way through to St. Barts or you may not see it for a few days. Instead, check your bags to your gateway destination (whatever island you're connecting through, most often St. Maarten), then take your luggage to your interisland carrier and recheck your bags to St. Barts.

Airport ✈ Beach 🏖 Mountain ▲▲ Ferry Route ----

Carl Gustaf **13**	François Plantation **1**	Le P'tit Morne **2**
Christopher Hôtel **10**	Hôtel Guanahani **11**	Le Toiny **12**
Eden Rock **5**	Hôtel Manapany Cottages **4**	Le Village St-Jean **7**
El Sereno Beach Hotel **12**	Hôtel Normandie **9**	St. Barth Isle de France **3**
Filao Beach **6**	La Banane **8**	Tropical Hôtel **5**

BY BOAT   If you want to arrive on St. Barts by sea, there are several options for waterborne transit from such neighboring islands as St. Maarten/St. Martin. We recommend the *Voyager* vessels (☎ **0590/27-77-24**), which operate from a base in Gustavia harbor and make frequent (usually daily) runs between St. Barts and either side of St. Maarten/St. Martin. Although the exact configuration changes with the season and the marketing priorities of the owners, *Voyager II* (a catamaran with room for 150 passengers) usually departs from Marigot Harbor for St. Barts every morning at 9am, arriving in Gustavia at 10:30am. *Voyager I,* a single-hulled sailboat with room for 110 passengers, travels from Philipsburg Harbour to Gustavia every day at approximately the same hours. Both vessels charge around $60 round-trip, plus a $7 departure tax. Advance reservations are a good idea, particularly since the departure points and hours for both of these vessels is likely to change several times during the lifetime of this edition.

GETTING AROUND

BY TAXI   Taxis meet all flights and are not superexpensive, mostly because destinations aren't far from one another. Dial ☎ **0590/27-66-31** for taxi service. A typical rate, St-Jean to Cul-de-Sac, is 85 F ($14.45). Night fares between 7pm and midnight are 50% higher. Except under rare circumstances, taxi service isn't available from midnight until around 7am.

Virtually every cab driver is aware of the official prices that the island government imposes on tours by taxi. Taxi tours that last between 45 and 90 minutes can be arranged through **St. Barth Voyages,** rue Duquesne, Gustavia (☎ **0590/27-79-79**). But many travelers simply approach a likely looking taxi driver, or ask someone at their hotel to contact a taxi driver, for island tours whose rates are officially designated as follows: Island tours for between one and three passengers cost 150 F ($25.50) for 45 minutes, 200 F ($34) for 60 minutes, and 250 F ($42.50) for 90 minutes. If there are between four and eight persons in your party, add 50 F ($8.50) to each of the above-mentioned prices.

BY RENTAL CAR   The hilly terrain, and the sense of adventure of the residents, combine to form a car-rental situation unique in the Caribbean. Never have we seen as many open-sided Mini-Mokes and Suzuki Samurais as we have on St. Barts. You'll enjoy driving one, too, as long as you're handy with a stick shift and don't care about your coiffure.

Budget (☎ **800/527-0700** or 0590/27-66-30) offers the least stringent terms for its midwinter rentals, and some of the most favorable rates. It rents Suzuki Samurais and Mitsubishi Mini-Mokes for $60 a day or $420 a week, with unlimited mileage. A collision-damage waiver (CDW; in French, *une assurance tous-risques*), absolving renters of all but 2,500 F ($425) of responsibility in the event of an accident, costs 68 F ($11.55) a day. For the lowest rate, you should reserve at least 3 business days before your arrival.

Hertz (☎ **800/654-3001**) operates on St. Barts through a local dealership, **Henry's Car Rental,** with branches at the airport and in St-Jean (☎ **0590/27-71-14**). It offers open-sided Suzuki Samurais for 2,160 F ($367.20) a week, and more substantial Suzuki Sidekicks for 2,520 F ($428.40) per week. A CDW sells for around $10 per day, although you'll still be responsible for the first $500 worth of damage if you have an accident. To guarantee the availability of a car in winter, Hertz insists that a deposit of $100 (payable in the form of a cashier's check or a debit held against a valid credit or charge card) be phoned or mailed directly to the local rental agent 3 weeks before your arrival on the island.

At **Avis** (☎ **800/331-1212** or 0590/27-71-43), you'll need a reservation a full month in advance during high season, plus the advance payment of a $100 deposit. In the winter, cars range from $60 to $70 a day, with weekly rentals going from $390 to $455. In the off-season, rentals are $30 to $50 a day, with weekly rentals from $292 to $325. The CDW costs $10 extra per day, but even if you agree to buy the extra insurance, you'll still be liable for the first $500 worth of damage to your rented vehicle in the event of an accident.

Gas is extra. Tanks hold enough to get you to one of the island's two gas stations. Never drive with less than half a tank of gas; you might regret it if you do, especially since the Shell station near the airport is closed every Sunday; the rest of the week, it's open only from 7:30am to noon and 2 to 5:30pm. (Fortunately, the pumps here are automated, and accept Visa cards, a fact that might allow you to avoid running out of gas over a long weekend.) The island's only other gas station is a Shell station near L'Orient. All valid foreign driver's licenses are honored. Honk your horn furiously while going around the island's blind corners, a practice that avoids many sideswiped fenders.

BY MOTORBIKE & SCOOTER   Denis Dufau operates **Rent Some Fun,** rue Gambetta (☎ **0590/27-70-59**), as well as its affiliate, **La Boutique Harley Davidson,** at the aéroport St-Jean (☎ **0590/27-54-83**). Both maintain the same inventories of vehicles and charge equivalent prices for rentals. A helmet is provided, and renters must either leave an imprint of a valid credit card or pay a 3,000 F ($510) deposit. Rental fees vary from 145 F to 175 F ($24.65 to $29.75) per day, depending on the size of the bike. For all but the smallest models, presentation of a valid driver's license is required.

Fast Facts: St. Barthélemy

Banking Hours   The two best-established banks are both in Gustavia. The **Banque Française Commerciale,** rue du Général-de-Gaulle (☎ **0590/27-62-62**), is open Monday through Friday from 8am to 12:30pm and 2 to 4:30pm; it's closed Wednesday afternoon. The **Banque Nationale de Paris,** rue du Bord-de-Mer (☎ **0590/27-63-70**), is open Monday through Friday from 8am to noon and 2 to 3:30pm.

Currency   The official monetary unit is the **French franc (F),** but most stores and restaurants prefer payment in U.S. dollars. Most hotels also quote their rates in American currency at a discount from the rates quoted in francs. At press time, the current exchange rate is 5.90 F to U.S. $1 (1 F = 17¢ U.S.), and this is the rate that was used to convert prices in this chapter. As this is sure to fluctuate a bit, use this rate for general guidance only.

Customs   You're allowed to bring in items for personal use, including tobacco, cameras, and film.

Documents   If you're flying in, you'll need to present your return or ongoing ticket. U.S., British, and Canadian citizens need only a passport.

Drugstores   See "Pharmacies," below.

Electricity   The electricity is 220 volts AC (50 cycles); U.S.-made appliances will require adapter plugs and transformers.

Emergencies   Dial ☎ **16** for police or medical emergencies, ☎ **18** for fire emergencies.

Hospital   St. Barts is not the greatest place to find yourself in a medical emergency. Except for vacationing doctors escaping their own practices in other parts of the world, it has only seven resident doctors and about a dozen on-call specialists. The island's only hospital, with the only emergency facilities, is the **Hôpital de Bruyn,** rue Jean-Bart (☎ **0590/27-60-35**), about a quarter of a mile north of Gustavia. Serious medical cases are often flown out to St. Martin, Martinique, Miami, or wherever the accident victim or his/her family specifies.

Language   The official language is French, but English is widely spoken.

Pharmacies   The **Pharmacie de Saint-Barth** is on quai de la République, Gustavia (☎ **0590/27-61-82**). Its only competitor is the **Pharmacie de l'Aéroport,** adjacent to the airport (☎ **0590/27-66-61**). Both are open Monday to Saturday from 8:30am to 7:30pm; on Sunday, one or the other remains open for at least part of the day.

Safety   Although crime is rare here, it would be wise to protect your valuables. Don't leave them unguarded on the beach or in parked cars, even if locked in the trunk.

Taxes & Service Charges   An airport departure tax of 30 F ($5.10) is assessed. Hotels don't add a room tax, though they usually levy a service charge of 10% to 15%.

Telephone St. Barts is linked to the Guadeloupe telephone system. To call St. Barts from the United States, dial **011** (the international access code), then **590** (the country code for Guadeloupe), and finally the six-digit local number. To make a call to anywhere in St. Barts from within St. Barts, dial only the six-digit local number, and ignore the prefix "0590."

Time When standard time is in effect in the United States and Canada, St. Barts is 1 hour ahead of the U.S. East Coast. Thus, when it's 7pm on St. Barts, it's 6pm in New York. When daylight saving time is in effect in the United States, clocks in New York and St. Barts show the same time.

Water The water on St. Barts is generally safe to drink.

Weather The climate of St. Barts is ideal: dry with an average temperature of 72° to 86°F.

2 Where to Stay

With the exception of a few of the really expensive hotels, most places here are homey, comfortable, and casual. Everything is small, as tiny St. Barts is hardly in the mainstream of tourism. In March, it's often hard to stay on St. Barts unless you've made reservations far in advance. Accommodations throughout the island, with some exceptions, tend to be exceptionally expensive, and a service charge of between 10% and 15% is usually added to your bill. Some hotels quote their rates in U.S. dollars, others in French francs.

St. Barts has a sizable number of villas, beach houses, and apartments for rent by the week or month. Villas are dotted around the island's hills—very few are on the beach. Instead of an oceanfront bedroom, you get a panoramic view. One of the best agencies to contact for villa, apartment, or condo rentals is **St. Barth Properties,** 2 Master Dr., Franklin, MA 02038 (☎ **800/421-3396** in the U.S. and Canada, or 508/528-7727). Peg Walsh, a longtime aficionado of St. Barts, assisted by her capable son, Tom Smyth, will let you know what's available; she can also make arrangements for car rentals and air travel to St. Barts, and when you arrive, she can book babysitters and restaurant reservations. Rentals can range from a one-room "studio" villa away from the beach, for $875 per week off-season, up to $32,000 per week for a minipalace at Christmas. Yes, that $32,000 is right, but it's for a very unusual, antique-furnished luxury home. Most rentals are far cheaper, averaging between $2,500 and $3,200 a week between mid-December and mid-April, with discounts of between 30% and 50% the rest of the year. In addition to villas, Ms. Walsh can also arrange accommodations in all categories of St. Barts's hotels.

VERY EXPENSIVE

✪ **Carl Gustaf.** Rue des Normands, 97099 Gustavia, St. Barthélemy, F.W.I. ☎ **800/322-2223** in the U.S., or 0590/27-82-83. Fax 0590/27-82-37. 14 units. A/C MINIBAR TV TEL. Winter $820–$1,025 one-bedroom suite; $1,130–$1,300 two-bedroom suite. Off-season $510 one-bedroom suite; $740 two-bedroom suite. Rates include continental breakfast. AE, MC, V.

The most glamorous hotel in Gustavia rises above the town's harbor from its position on a steep hillside. Each state-of-the-art unit is in one of a dozen pink or green, red-roofed villas whose facilities include a private kitchenette, two phones, a fax machine, two stereo systems, a private terrace, a private pool, two TVs, and comfortably plush rattan furniture. Access to each building is via a central staircase, which tests the stamina of even the most active of guests. The wood-frame units are angled for maximum views of the boats bobbing far below in the bay and panoramic sunsets. Bedrooms aren't large, as might be expected at such prices, but they are exceedingly well furnished, especially suite nos. 30 to 33. You'll walk across Italian marble floors under a pitched ceiling to reach your luxurious bed with elegant fabrics and a deluxe mattress. Bathrooms are also well equipped, with mosaic-clad showers (no tubs), makeup mirrors, and luxuriously thick towels. Beach facilities are within a 10-minute walk. The mood is French, not unlike what you'd find on the coast of Provence.

Dining/Diversions: There's a restaurant set on the uppermost level of the hotel, plus a small but charming bar. The cuisine is French and Creole. Often a well-known chef from Paris appears in winter. There's also a sunset bar, featuring a different cocktail every day.

Amenities: Sauna, exercise room, two yachts that can be privately chartered at a rate of 4,000 F to 8,500 F ($680 to $1,445) a day for up to 10 participants. 24-hour room service, concierge, massage.

Christopher Hôtel. Pointe Milou (B.P. 571), 97133 St. Barthélemy, F.W.I. ☎ **800/ 221-4542** in the U.S., or 0590/27-63-63. Fax 0590/27-92-92. E-mail: christopherhotel@ compuserve.com. 41 units. A/C MINIBAR TV TEL. Winter $420–$630 double; from $850 suite. Off-season $280–$340 double; $580 suite. Rates include American breakfast. One child under 12 can stay free in parents' room. AE, DC, MC, V. Closed Sept–Oct 15.

Set on a dramatic promontory above the ocean, this is a full-service hotel offering views of St. Martin and nearby islets. It required major renovations in 1995 following hurricane damage. Built and managed by Sofitel, it offers a French-colonial decor and a low-rise design that incorporates four slate-roofed, white-sided buildings arranged in a semicircle above a rocky coastline. Although the hotel is not adjacent to the water, guests usually drive about 10 minutes to reach a good beach, Plage de l'Orient. Most of the resort's activities revolve around the swimming pool. The roomy accommodations, with king-size beds fitted with luxury mattresses, fall into two categories—deluxe oceanfront with patio or deluxe ocean view with terrace. All are furnished in a Creole style with ceiling fans. The differences between the two categories of rooms are most pronounced in the bathrooms. The oceanfront rooms have separate showers, while the ocean views have small garden areas opening directly off the bathrooms to the open air.

Dining: Breakfast and gourmet French dinners are served at L'Orchidée, while lunch is a poolside affair, featuring platters, light snacks, and low-calorie or dietetic meals.

Amenities: The resort's pool, a 4,500-square-foot pair of interconnected ovals with a bridge, is the largest on the island. Nearby, a fitness center/health club offers nutritional counseling, massage, and relaxation therapy. Room service (from 7am to 9:30pm). A concierge can arrange horseback riding, scuba diving, or deep-sea fishing.

Filao Beach. Baie de St-Jean (B.P. 667), 97099 St. Barthélemy, F.W.I. ☎ **0590/27-64-84.** Fax 0590/27-62-24. www.st-barths.com/filao-beach. E-mail: failao@compuserve.com. 30 units. A/C MINIBAR TV TEL. Winter 1,900 F–3,200 F ($323–$544) double. Off-season 1,000 F–2,200 F ($170–$374) double. Rates include continental breakfast and airport transfers. AE, DC, MC, V. Closed Aug 31–Oct 16.

This white-stucco bungalow hotel is set on 4 flat acres, 4 minutes from the airport, next to one of the island's most important beaches, the oh-so-chic St. Jean Beach. Established in 1982, and permeated with a sense of Gallic nostalgia and style, this is one of the few Relais & Châteaux hotels in the Caribbean. Each room is named after a château in France. Although the staff is charming and the setting is supremely comfortable, the hotel simply isn't able to maintain the standards of a Relais & Châteaux property in France. The accommodations, many of which suggest a nice motel room, were refitted with new floor tiles and upholsteries after the hurricanes of 1995; all are modern and fitted with large closets, private safes, ceiling fans, and sun-flooded terraces, where you can enjoy a leisurely breakfast. Some units are subject to traffic noise; only a few open right onto the beach. The staff is most welcoming, providing a bottle of rum, slippers, and a robe in each bedroom. Bathrooms are small but well appointed with oversize tubs, deluxe toiletries, and thick towels. Critics maintain that despite the management's efforts, the place has a subtle dowdiness that prevents it from being one of St. Barts's avidly sought-out hotels.

A bar and restaurant overlook St. Jean Beach, serving both French and international cuisine. On site is a freshwater swimming pool; scuba diving, snorkeling, windsurfing, and waterskiing can be arranged. Laundry and baby-sitting can be arranged as well.

Hôtel Guanahani. 97098 Anse de Grand Cul-de-Sac, St. Barthélemy, F.W.I. ☎ **800/ 223-6800** in the U.S., or 0590/27-66-60. Fax 0590/27-70-70. 77 units. A/C MINIBAR TV TEL. Winter $440–$800 double; $800–$1,400 suite. Off-season $250–$530 double; $530–$800 suite. Rates include continental breakfast and round-trip airport transfers. AE, DC, MC, V. Closed Sept.

Hôtel Guanahani, isolated in the northeast part of the island, has been the largest hotel on St. Barts ever since its much-publicized opening in 1986. Much of its charm is also the root of much of its inconvenience: On its own peninsula, it's spread over 7 steeply sloping acres dotted with a network of 50 Lilliputian cottages trimmed in gingerbread and painted in playland versions of bold, tropical colors. Don't consider this place if you are immobile, use a wheelchair, or hate puffing up and down steep slopes. If that's not a problem, the views over the sea from each unit are broad and sweeping, and the exercise you'll get might contribute to your overall health. Most units, at least those on the resort's upper slopes, are self-contained in their own individual cottages. The bungalows closer to the beach, a private white-sand strip on a reef-protected bay, sometimes contain two units each. Regardless of the layout, each roomy accommodation has a private patio, a fridge, ceiling fans, and a private patio or balcony. Queen Anne–style desks and tables, tasteful upholstery, and four-poster beds spell deluxe living, as do the fine linen and comfortable beds. Bathrooms are brightly tiled with excellent plumbing, a hair dryer, and a set of thick towels.

Dining: The Guanahani has two restaurants. The more formal is a Provençal hideaway, Bartolomeo (see "Where to Dine," below). Indigo is the more casual poolside cafe.

Amenities: Two freshwater pools, a Jacuzzi with a good view of Grand Cul-de-Sac, two hard-surface tennis courts (lit at night), a fitness center, a beauty salon, water sports (some at an additional charge). Room service, laundry, baby-sitting, massages.

✪ **Hôtel Manapany Cottages.** Anse des Cayes (B.P. 114), 97133 St. Barthélemy, F.W.I. ☎ **800/847-4249** in the U.S., or 0590/27-66-55. Fax 0590/27-75-28. www. lemanapany.com. E-mail: manapany@st-barths.com. 46 units. A/C TV TEL. Winter $440–$825 double; $595–$960 junior suite; $960–$1,645 cottage. Off-season $260–$420 double; $365–$460 junior suite; $365–$665 cottage. Rates include continental breakfast. AE, DC, MC, V.

Hôtel Manapany climbs a steep, well-landscaped hillside on the northwestern side of the island, a 10-minute taxi ride north of the airport. This is one of the most stylish hotels on St. Barts, last renovated in 1997. It's small, intimate, and accommodating. The name, translated from Malagese, means "small paradise," and the place was designed as a minivillage of gingerbread-trimmed Antillean cottages, set either on a steeply sloping hillside or beside the water. They have red roofs and rambling verandas open to the sea, air-conditioned bedrooms with sliding-glass doors, and open-sided living rooms that allow you to enjoy the trade winds. Units can be reconfigured depending on your needs. The furnishings include both white rattan and Caribbean colonial pieces carved from mahogany and imported from the Dominican Republic. Mosquito netting covers most of the four-poster beds for a romantic touch. Rooms come with large-screen TVs with in-house video movies, ceiling fans, kitchenettes, ceiling fans, safes, and beds fitted with fine mattresses. Bathrooms are tiled or clad in marble, each quite luxurious with state-of-the-art plumbing and a rack of thick towels.

Dining: The restaurant, Ouanalao, is a crescent-shaped terrace overlooking the sea and the pool, featuring casual Italian dining with light lunches and candlelit romantic dinners.

Amenities: Small-scale spa facility for massages and stress reduction. Concierge, 24-hour room service, laundry, baby-sitting.

La Banane. 97133 Lorient, St. Barthélemy, F.W.I. ☎ **0590/27-68-25.** Fax 0590/27-68-44. www.st-barths.com/labanane.fr.html. E-mail: labanane@wanadoo.fr. 9 units. A/C MINIBAR TV TEL. Winter $280–$480 double. Off-season $150–$180 double. MAP (breakfast and dinner) $40 per person extra. AE, MC, V.

About a mile from the airport, on the outskirts of the village of Lorient, is this small, intimate, and well-furnished hotel. Because of its size and carefully restricted access, many aspects of this place might remind you of a private, and very Parisian, house party, particularly since the in-house restaurant is reserved only for residents or their guests. It's filled with some of the most stylish antiques on the island. Set on a flat, low-lying, and somewhat steamy landscape, the hotel grounds are richly planted with bananas, flowering shrubs, and palms. It's about a 3-minute walk from the beach. The accommodations here are delightful and quite roomy. Our favorite contains a large mahogany four-poster bed whose trim was made from a little-known Central and South American wood called *angelique.* The other units are less spacious, but each has some Haitian art, a mixture of antique and modern designs, a fridge, a private terrace, and louvered windows overlooking the garden; some are air-conditioned. Decorated in Mexican tiles, bathrooms are open to private gardens with alfresco tubs and showers; thick towels and hair dryers are provided. Frankly, this is a very French, rather blasé setting where the staff seems happiest if you quietly enjoy your holiday and basically leave them alone.

Dining: There's a small, informal restaurant, closed to most nonguests, where a French/Caribbean cuisine is prepared using fresh local ingredients. Dinner might include grilled snapper with herbs and citrus sauce, steak au poivre, or sautéed calamari.

Amenities: Two freshwater pools; room service.

✪ **Le Toiny.** Anse de Toiny, 97133 St. Barthélemy, F.W.I. ☎ **0590/27-88-88** or 800/278-6469. Fax 0590/27-89-30. E-mail: letoiny@saint-barths.com. 12 suites. A/C MINIBAR TV TEL. Winter $920 one-bedroom suite for 2; $1,800 three-bedroom suite for up to 6. AE, MC, V. Closed Sept 1–Oct 20.

One of the most glamorous and chillingly expensive resorts on St. Barts contains only a dozen suites, which are scattered among a half-dozen buildings clinging to a gently sloping hillside near Plage des Gouverneurs. The nearest beach for swimming is a 5-minute drive away at Saline, the only sanctioned nude beach on the island. The resort was established in the early 1990s, and immediately gained the kind of international cachet that has appealed to such clients as Brad Pitt and the late Princess of Wales. (She was turned away, much to the regret of management, simply because there was no room at the inn on the day she wanted to arrive.) Pitt might have wished he were turned away: He was photographed in the nude with Gwyneth Paltrow by cliff-climbing paparazzi. All the suites here have floors of either wide planks or terra-cotta tiles, neocolonial mahogany or teakwood furniture, kitchenettes, mahogany four-posters draped with mosquito netting, and much subdued glamour. Each provides plenty of privacy, thanks to thoughtful positioning of shrubs and tropical plants, and lots of space between units.

St. Barth Isle de France. 97098 Anse des Flamands, St. Barthélemy, F.W.I. ☎ **800/ 810-4691** in the U.S., or 0590/27-61-81. Fax 0590/27-86-83. www.isle-de-france.com. E-mail: isledefr@saint-barths.com. 30 units. A/C MINIBAR TV TEL. Winter $450–$680 double; $840 suite; $450–$680 bungalow. Off-season $345–$520 double; $700 suite; $345–$460 bungalow. Rates include continental breakfast. AE, MC, V.

Set adjacent to one of the island's finest and prettiest beaches, this resort opened in 1992 but was devastated by Hurricane Luis in 1995, which led to massive renovations. Centered around a re-creation of a colonial plantation house, the hotel is small, family run, and completely isolated from a chain-hotel mentality, with unusually spacious guest rooms for St. Barts. Each top-notch unit contains a private patio or terrace, a private safe, a coffeemaker, a fridge, and an individual decor with antique mahogany and rattan furniture and engravings collected from neighboring islands. Beds are luxurious, fitted with fine linen and quality mattresses. Clad in marble, bathrooms are spacious and well equipped with dual basins, large tubs (in some cases with whirlpool jets), thick towels, and hair dryers.

Dining: The restaurant, La Case de L'Isle, is on the beachside opening onto views of Baie de Flamands. Meals are charming, and despite their informality, show a commitment to tenets of sophisticated international cuisine with strong French overtones. Grilled fresh fish and fillet of lamb with red wine or parsley sauce are especially popular.

Amenities: Air-conditioned squash court, two pools a few steps from the beach, tennis court, exercise room, gift shop.

EXPENSIVE

Eden Rock. 97133 St-Jean, St. Barthélemy, F.W.I. ☎ **0590/27-72-94.** Fax 0590/27-88-37. www.edenrockhotel.com. E-mail: info@edenrockhotel.com. 13 units. A/C MINIBAR TV TEL. Winter $275–$780 double. Off-season $185–$450 double. Rates include buffet breakfast. AE, MC, V.

When the quartzite promontory this hotel sits on was purchased many years ago by the island's former mayor, Rémy de Haenen, the seller was an old woman who laughed at him for paying too many francs for it. Today, it's part of island lore, and the single most spectacular building site on St. Barts, flanked by two perfect beaches. The building capping its pinnacle looks like an idealized version of a Provençal farmhouse amid a landscape of rocks, scrub, and pines. Offering some of the best panoramas on the island, it's surrounded on three sides by the waters of St. Jean Bay, allowing views from the terra-cotta terrace of frigatebirds wheeling and diving for fish in the turquoise waters below. In 1995, the building was sold to English expatriates David Matthews and family, who emptied the contents of their manor house in Nottinghamshire to fill it. Regrettably, shortly after the transfer of title, Hurricane Luis struck in full fury, delaying the opening of the hotel for a few months and requiring repairs to the terraces and wraparound decks. Today, the stone house contains a collection of French antiques and paintings left over from the de Haenen family, plus English antiques and paintings imported by the new owners. New annex buildings were set directly adjacent to the sands of the nearby beach, Plage de St-Jean. They include a scattering of cement-sided bungalows and a stylish restaurant with a big veranda. The decor in each guest room includes a stylish mixture of tasteful antiques and reproductions, and fabrics and accessories pulled together with an undeniable European flair. All the roomy accommodations have VCRs, private safes, and superb mattresses. Some are situated on the rock, while others are on the beach with their own access to the sand. The best and most expensive are the ocean suites with private balconies. The least expensive are the cabins, small and cozy, better for young couples with children and teenagers. Bathrooms are compact and come with a hair dryer. Staff members are usually bilingual and often eccentric in a congenial kind of way.

Dining: Eden Rock maintains three restaurants, the most glamorous of which occupies a panoramic aerie in the site's original house. Perched high above the sea and the beaches below, it's more upscale than the resort's newer dining enclave, a modern pavilion built close to the beach. Frankly, although the owners had devoted lots of time and attention to launching this place, the staff seems somewhat disorganized, and at least at this writing, hadn't made enough of an impact on the island's dining scene to really evaluate.

El Sereno Beach Hôtel. Grand Cul-de-Sac (B.P. 19), 97133 St. Barthélemy, F.W.I. ☎ **800/322-2223** in the U.S., or 0590/27-64-80. Fax 0590/27-75-47. 32 units. A/C MINIBAR TV TEL. Winter $220–$420 double; $460–$800 suite. Off-season $180–$220 double; $350–$460 suite. Rates include continental breakfast. Extra person $60. AE, DC, MC, V. Closed Sept–Oct 15.

Sereno's low-slung pastel facade and its isolated location (4 miles east of Gustavia) create the aura of St-Tropez in the Antilles. The Riviera crowd is attracted to its location on a good beach with calm waters. More of the units overlook the gardens than the sea, although in view of their relaxed informality and comfort, no one seems to mind. Each unit contains two beds with firm mattresses, a safe, and a fridge. The compact, shower-only bathrooms are tidily maintained with a hair dryer and a rack of medium-size towels. Video movies are available.

Dining: The feeling is a bit like a private compound, whose social center is an open-air bar and poolside restaurant, the West Indies Café (see "Where to Dine," below).

Amenities: Freshwater pool, in the center of which is a verdant island.

✪ **François Plantation.** Colombier, 97133 St. Barthélemy, F.W.I. ☎ **800/932-3223** in the U.S., or 0590/29-80-22. Fax 0590/27-61-26. www.st-barths.com/franplant.html. E-mail: fplantation@compuserve.com. 12 units. A/C MINIBAR TV TEL. Winter $300–$500 bungalow for 2. Off-season $180–$280 bungalow for 2. Rates include American breakfast and free use of a rental car in summer only. AE, MC, V. Closed Aug 15–Oct 20.

This complex, 2 miles northwest of Gustavia and a 10-minute ride from the airport, re-creates the plantation era, standing on a steep hill with panoramic views of the beach below. The management skillfully compensates for its position inland from the beach by including, during off-season only, the use of a Mini-Moke or equivalent car. Newly arrived guests drive themselves from the airport to the hotel, then enjoy maximum independence during their stay. The resort consists of a tropical garden, a central administrative center, and 12 bungalows, decorated in an elegant West Indian style. Eight of the units open onto sea views, while the others look out over a garden. Spacious bedrooms contain mahogany four-posters, ceiling fans, and safes. Moroccan rugs on marble or tile floors make the places extra cozy. Marble bathrooms come with bidets, open showers, dual basins, and a rack of fluffy towels. The owners are Françoise and François (you heard right) Beret, longtime residents of St. Barts.

Dining: The hotel has an exceptional restaurant, La Route des Epices, featuring food that's more exotic than many of its competitors.

Amenities: Swimming pool with a view over the sea several hundred feet below. Laundry.

MODERATE/INEXPENSIVE

Hôtel Normandie. 97133 Lorient, St. Barthélemy, F.W.I. ☎ **0590/27-61-66.** Fax 0590/27-98-83. 8 units. A/C. Winter 450 F ($76.50) double; 750 F ($127.50) triple. Off-season 400 F ($68) double; 600 F ($102) triple. No credit cards.

Modest, unassuming, and completely without chic, this is what the French call an *auberge antillaise.* Set near the intersection of two major roads, about 100 yards from the sands of Lorient Beach and 3 miles east of the airport, it offers motel-inspired bedrooms of casual comfort. The more expensive units are larger, lie adjacent to the hotel's modest pool, and contain TVs. The less expensive, smaller rooms are next to the highway. Mattresses are a bit thin, and the bathrooms are really too small but well kept, each with a shower and a set of just adequate towels. A family-owned hotel, there are virtually no facilities here other than the clean but somewhat dreary accommodations. It's one of the least expensive places to stay on St. Barts.

Le P'tit Morne. Colombier, P.O. Box 14, 97098 St. Barthélemy, F.W.I. ☎ **0590/27-62-64.** Fax 0590/27-84-63. www.st-barths.com/ptitmorne.html. E-mail: leptitmorne@wanadoo.fr. 14 units. A/C TV TEL. Winter 900 F ($153) double. Off-season 630 F ($107.10). Off-season rates include daily breakfast and unlimited use of a car. Closed June. AE, MC, V.

This is hardly the most luxurious or stylish lodging on an island that's legendary for its glamour and its five-star hotels. But the hotel's three-star format, its relatively low rates, and the warm welcome extended by its island-born owner, Marie-Joëlle, make it a worthy vacation site where you won't have to mortgage your home to pay for it. Set about 250 feet above sea level, on sloping and verdantly planted terrain, it's a buff-colored three-story concrete building from 1975. The guest rooms are usually beige, green, or pink, and filled with completely unpretentious furniture and generally comfortable beds, although don't expect deluxe living. There's plenty of elbow room, however, and units were built to catch the trade winds. Bathrooms are compact with rather thin towels and shower stalls.

✪ **Le Village St-Jean.** Baie de Saint-Jean (B.P. 623), 97098 St. Barthélemy CEDEX, F.W.I. ☎ **800/651-8366** in the U.S., or 0590/27-61-39. Fax 0590/27-77-96. www. st-barths.com/village-st-jean. E-mail: vsjhotel@compuserve.com. 31 units. A/C TEL. Winter $150 double; $170–$330 one-bedroom cottage; $450 two-bedroom cottage; $395 suite. Off-season $99 double; $120–$230 one-bedroom cottage; $295 two-bedroom cottage; $230 suite. Room rates include continental breakfast. Extra person $65 for cottages and the suite. AE, CB, MC, V.

Over the years, this cottage colony hideaway, a mile from the airport toward St-Jean, has attracted a distinguished clientele. Lying in the most central part of St. Barts, a 5-minute drive uphill from Plage de Saint-Jean, it offers one of the best values on this high-priced resort island. Its stone-and-wood cottages contain kitchens, sundecks or gardens, terraced living rooms, balconies, and ceiling fans. Furnishings are modest but comfortable, and the living space is generous. The tiled bathrooms are compact and have hair dryers and showers only; some come with bidets. Although the rates here are modest compared to other places on the island, don't be surprised to see a media headliner here; after all, some of them like to save money, too.

The complex has a well-managed restaurant and bar, Le Patio, with a sprawling terrace on a platform above the sloping terrain (see "Where to Dine," below). The pool has two decks overlooking the bay, cascading water, and a Jacuzzi. Founded in the early 1960s, this was the first inn of its kind on St. Barts, and it's still administered by the Charneau family.

Tropical Hôtel. St-Jean (B.P. 147), 97095 St. Barthélemy, F.W.I. ☎ **800/223-9815** or 0590/27-64-87. Fax 0590/27-81-74. E-mail: tropicalhotel@compuserve.com. 20 units. A/C TV

TEL. Winter $200–$320 double. Off-season $135–$165 double. Rates include continental breakfast. AE, MC, V.

Small and unpretentious, with a facade that looks like a postcard of a Caribbean colonial inn, this hotel was designed in a rectangle, with an open center that contains a well-maintained and verdant green space that serves as the hotel's core. Originally built in 1981, and repainted and restored in 1997, it's perched on a hillside about 50 yards above St. Jean Beach (a mile from the airport and a mile and a half from Gustavia). Each room contains a private shower-only bathroom, a king-size bed with a good mattress, tile floors, and a fridge to cool your tropical drinks. Nine units come with a sea view and balcony, and no. 11 has a porch opening onto a garden that's so lush it looks like a miniature jungle.

There's a hospitality center where guests read, listen to music, or order drinks at a paneled bar surrounded by antiques. The freshwater swimming pool is small, but water sports are available on the beach. Breakfast is served on the poolside terrace.

3 Where to Dine

IN GUSTAVIA
EXPENSIVE

Au Port. Rue Sadi-Carnot. ☎ **0590/27-62-36.** Reservations recommended, especially for veranda tables. Main courses 100 F–175 F ($17–$29.75); menu Creole 190 F ($32.30). AE, MC, V. Mon–Sat 6:30–10pm. Closed July–Aug. FRENCH/CREOLE.

This restaurant is one of the culinary staples of the island, having survived for many years, thanks to a straightforward and unpretentious ambience that focuses on good cooking, generous portions, and an utter lack of snobbery. Set one floor above street level, in the center of town, separated from a view of the water by the island's new post office, it features a neocolonial decor with models of sailboats, antique accessories, and the flavorful cuisine of Alain Bunel. Menu items include foie gras of duckling, a *boudin* of conch and lobster, crayfish in green curry sauce, lobster tail with morels, and magret of duckling with a honey-flavored butter sauce. The fish soup makes a worthwhile beginning.

✪ **La Mandala.** Rue Courbet. ☎ **0590/27-96-96.** Reservations recommended. Main courses 105 F–150 F ($17.85–$25.50). Daily 5pm–midnight; tapas and cocktails daily 5–7pm. AE, DC, MC, V. THAI/EUROPEAN.

Established shortly after the hurricanes of 1995, this is one of the most exciting restaurants on St. Barts. It occupies a house on the steepest street in Gustavia, high above the harbor. If you drive your own car up to the entrance, a valet will park it for you. Its name derives from the Mandala, symbol of Buddhist harmony, whose design of a square within a circle is duplicated by the position of the dining deck above a swimming pool visible from above. The owners and chefs are partners Kiki and Boubou (Christophe Barjetta and Olivier Megnin), whose nicknames disguise their formidable training at some of the grandest restaurants of France. Gastronomes on St. Barts have watched the menu here make many sophisticated detours from the Mediterranean theme that was the norm during its earliest years. Today, the cuisine is Thai and European. Examples include tempura of crayfish with mango salad and coriander sauce; a traditional Thai dish, *tataki,* composed of deliberately undercooked fish with a ginger-flavored vinaigrette, shallots, and sesame oil; dorado with mushroom risotto; and rack of lamb with exotic spices and a cold purée of cucumbers and mint. A specialty here is Spanish-style tapas. Everybody's favorite dessert is the warm chocolate tart.

Le Rivage. In the St. Barth Beach Hotel, Grand Cul de Sac. ☎ **0590/27-82-42.** Reservations recommended. Main courses 88 F–300 F ($14.95–$51). AE, MC, V. Daily noon–6pm and 7–10pm. FRENCH/CARIBBEAN.

Sunflooded and insouciant, this restaurant offers the kind of offhanded charm and oversized Gallic egos that you'd expect in a chic but somewhat disorganized beach resort in the south of France. It's set on a covered veranda built on piers above the waters of the lagoon. About half the tables are open to views of the stars; the others are sheltered from rainfall by an open-sided roof. During the day, no one objects to bathing suits at the table; at night, fashionably casual is the preferred dress. Menu items that merit raves include carpaccio of beef and a tempting roster of "super-salads," the most justifiably popular of which combines shrimp with smoked salmon and melted goat cheese. There's also a seafood platter of raw shellfish (scallops, clams, and crayfish), artfully arranged on a bed of seaweed; grilled crayfish, *daurade*, snapper, and tuna; and a full complement of such Creole specialties as *boudin noir* (blood sausage), *accras de morue* (beignets of codfish), and *court bouillon* of fish.

✪ **Le Sapotillier.** Rue Sadi-Carnot. ☎ **0590/27-60-28.** Reservations required. Main courses 140 F–220 F ($23.80–$37.40). AE, DISC, MC, V. Tues–Sun 6:30–10:30pm; daily Christmas–Easter. Closed mid-May to Oct. FRENCH/SEAFOOD.

This West Indian house beside the less frequented part of Gustavia's harbor is the domain of Austrian-born Adam Rajner, who runs one of the best-known restaurants in Gustavia. Le Sapotillier is near the top of the list for every visiting gourmet. Named after a gnarled and wind-blown sapodilla tree in the courtyard, the restaurant offers diners a choice of seating locations—outside on the candlelit patio or inside the clapboard-covered Antillean bungalow that was transported from the outlying village of Corossol.

Mr. Rajner, in the best tradition of European innkeeping, pays strict attention to the quality and presentation of his food. Your meal might begin with a homemade duck-liver pâté, or perhaps the fish soup. Among the more interesting meat dishes are a whole young pigeon imported from Bresse, France, and a fillet of young lamb with ratatouille. Try the couscous made with large spicy shrimp, or you might order steamed stingray with a horseradish sauce. A casserole of sea scallops and prawns is flavored with balsamic vinegar and served with Creole sauce.

L'Escale. Rue Jeanne-d'Arc, La Pointe. ☎ **0590/27-81-06.** Reservations required in high season. Main courses 110 F–180 F ($18.70–$30.60). AE, MC, V. Daily 11am–midnight. ITALIAN/FRENCH.

Some villa owners cite L'Escale, a hip, sometimes raucous, and always irreverent hangout for the raffish and wealthy, as their favorite restaurant on the island. It's set in a simple, industrial-looking building on the relatively unglamorous south side of Gustavia's harbor, adjacent to dozens of moored yachts. You can dine lightly and inexpensively here, or spend a lot of money, depending on your menu selections and appetite. Typical fare might include one of about a half-dozen pizzas or meal-size salads, as well as such well-received pastas as lasagna (a perennial favorite here), *penne a l'arrabiata,* or any of several gnocchis. Also available are carpaccio of raw marinated fish and beef, Milanese-style veal, and a wide roster of grilled meats and fish (such as a whole snapper, grilled and served with Creole sauce and rondelles of lemon). Thursday nights feature Canadian lobster, flown in specially from Newfoundland. The dessert specialty is the island's most theatrical version of flambé bananas: Lights are dimmed and the shooting flames of the ritual's burning rum illuminate the entire restaurant.

Le Toiny. Anse de Toiny. ☎ **0590/27-88-88.** Reservations required. Main courses 130 F–150 F ($22.10–$25.50) lunch, 145 F–270 F ($24.65–$45.90) dinner. AE, MC, V. Daily noon–3pm and 7–11pm. Closed Sept 1–Oct 20. FRENCH.

Set within the confines of St. Bart's most upscale and expensive hotel, this restaurant opens its doors to folks who aren't willing to pay $920 a day for a room, but who still might want dinner and a quick overview of the lifestyles of the jaded, the very rich, and the sometimes famous. Guests dine in an open-air pavilion adjacent to the resort's pool, with a view that sweeps out over the wide blue sea. The emphasis is French, casually stylish, and offhanded in a way that might remind you of a particularly rich version of bohemian Paris. At lunchtime, menu items might include eggplant ravioli with tomato coulis and parmesan, a *tarte fine* with tomatoes and feta, or prawns in "an oriental nest" with sage and onion sauce. After dark, choices are most *recherché* and even more esoteric. Examples include crabmeat salad with fennel, ravioli stuffed with conch and served with a garlicky cream sauce, sea bass with cauliflower and caramelized balsamic vinegar, and roasted rack of lamb with truffle sauce and parmesan. The cuisine, the setting, the first-rate ingredients: Everything works to make a memorable meal here.

L'Iguane. Carré d'Or, quai de la République. ☎ **0590/27-88-46.** Reservations recommended for dinner. Continental breakfast 35 F ($5.95); sushi 15.50 F–18 F ($2.65–$3.05) per piece; main courses 155 F–180 F ($26.35–$30.60). AE, MC, V. Mid-Nov to Aug, cafe daily 8–11am; restaurant daily 11am–11pm. Off-season, cafe Mon–Sat 8–11am; restaurant Mon–Sat 11am–3pm, daily 7–11pm. Closed Sept–Oct. JAPANESE/INTERNATIONAL.

Set adjacent to three upscale shops, this restaurant and cafe offers an international menu that includes sushi, American breakfasts, and California-style sandwiches and salads. The walls are ocher and blue, and the lighting fixtures are filtered to flatter even the most weather-beaten skin. The sometimes-glamorous clients all seem to be watching their waistlines. The ambience grows more Asian as the evening progresses. Sushi, imported twice a week from suppliers in Miami and served according to time-honored Japanese techniques, is the main allure here, with special emphasis on tuna, snapper, salmon, and eel. Cosmopolitan owner Mario Giorno Dupont maintains that this is the only site in the French West Indies specializing exclusively in this form of cuisine.

Wall House Restaurant. La Pointe, Gustavia. ☎ **0590/27-71-83.** Reservations recommended for dinner. Lunch platters 55 F–90 F ($9.35–$15.30); dinner main courses 130 F–165 F ($22.10–$28.05); dinner set menus 195 F–295 F ($33.15–$50.15). AE, MC, V. Daily 11:30am–3pm and 6:45–10pm. AE, MC, V. FRENCH/INTERNATIONAL.

Boasting one of the best views of any restaurant in Gustavia, this restaurant sits adjacent to the island's public library and municipal museum, on a peninsula that forms the less congested edge of Gustavia's busy harbor. Its name derives from a nearby ruin ("The Wall") that was originally built during the island's Swedish occupation, and which in recent years was carefully incorporated into newer buildings by St. Barts's government. Lunches here are unpretentious, sun-flooded affairs where diners enjoy the views and such lighthearted fare as burgers, simple grills, salads, and sandwiches. Dinners are more elaborate and ritualized, prepared by French-born owner Gérard Pagan and a chef who was brought in from upscale kitchens in such fashionable resorts as La Baule. A set-price "lobster menu," priced at 295 F ($50.15), includes lobster ravioli and a delicious version of parmentier of lobster in a crispy thyme crust. The à la carte menu features foie gras of duckling, shellfish salads, a gratin of scallops with vanilla, and noisettes of lamb with a *brunoise* of baby vegetables and turnip chips. A

Picnic Fare on St. Barts

St. Barts is so expensive that many visitors opt to buy at least one of their meals—perhaps a "gourmet lunch to go" package—from a take-out deli. The most centrally located of the island's epicurean delis is **La Rôtisserie,** rue Oskar-II (☎ **0590/27-63-13**), which is proud of its endorsement by Fauchon, the world-famous food store in Paris. On display are bottles of wine, crocks of mustard, pâté, herbs, and exotic oils and vinegars, as well as take-out (and very French) platters sold by the gram. *Plats du jour* cost around 50 F to 65 F ($8.50 to $11.05) for a portion suitable for one. Set on a narrow street behind the eastern edge of Gustavia's harbor, the place is open Monday through Saturday from 6:30am to 7pm, Sunday from 7am to 1pm. American Express, MasterCard, and Visa are accepted.

worthy ending is the hot and cold chocolate-based desserts, served with coffee sauce and vanilla ice cream, artfully arranged on the same platter.

IN THE ST-JEAN BEACH AREA

✪ **Le Patio.** Le Village St-Jean. ☎ **0590/27-70-67.** Reservations required. Main courses 110 F–170 F ($18.70–$28.90). CB, MC, V. Thurs–Tues 6:30–10pm. Closed mid-June to late July. ITALIAN/PIZZA.

Proudly positioned as the centerpiece of a charming and not particularly expensive hotel (see "Where to Stay," above), Le Patio has a deserved reputation for well-conceived food that's the creative statement of Turin-born chef Luca San Giuliano. Examples of his cuisine include spaghetti with squid ink and gorgonzola, ravioli stuffed with spiny crayfish meat, *saltimbocca* (veal and ham) alla Romana, an unusual version of spaghetti *en papillote* with fresh vegetable sauce, and one of our personal favorites, chicken breast layered with pancetta. There's a rotating choice of unusual pizzas as well, including versions that feature asparagus or freshwater crayfish with parsley. Desserts usually include a *cassata Siciliana* (candied fruits with ice cream).

✪ **Vincent Adam.** Carenage de St-Jean. ☎ **0590/27-93-22.** Reservations recommended, especially in winter. Set menus 190 F–250 F ($32.30–$42.50). AE, MC, V. Daily 6:30–10pm. CONTINENTAL/CARIBBEAN.

Set in a 50-year-old converted Creole house, high in the hills above the bay of St. Jean, this is one of the finest restaurants in St. Barts. Expect to sit in one of two indoor/outdoor dining areas where groves of banana plants frame a sweeping view of the seacoast below. Ironically, the restaurant's namesake is no longer associated with the place, but the new owner, Gilles Malfroid, retains the name purely for PR purposes. The innovative menu changes every Friday night, and might include items like mille-feuille of foie gras and potatoes, fillet of lamb in puff pastry with a duxelle of mushrooms, or a Provence-derived *barigoule* of red snapper and shrimp cooked on a brochette and served on a bed of artichoke hearts and herbs. The set menu priced at 250 F ($42.50) features different preparations of lobster, served both as an appetizer and as a main course. All wines are from France.

AT MORNE LURIN

Santa Fe Restaurant. Morne Lurin. ☎ **0590/27-61-04.** Burgers 30 F–50 F ($5.10–$8.50); meal platters 70 F–110 F ($11.90–$18.70). No credit cards. Mon–Tues and Thurs–Sat noon–2pm and 5–10pm, Sun 5–10pm. Closed for lunch Apr–Oct. AMERICAN.

Set inland from the sea, atop one of the highest elevations on the island, this burger house and sports bar has carved out a formidable niche for itself with the island's

English-speaking clientele. Named after a romantic song popular at the time of its establishment in 1966 (and having nothing to do with the city in New Mexico), it features wide-screen TVs that show events like the Super Bowl to as many as 450 viewers. After the hurricanes of 1995, its roof, wraparound decks, and bar tops were completely rebuilt of teakwood, and a more nautical flair was introduced. You can take in the view of the surrounding landscapes for free, but most clients stop for one of the well-recommended hamburgers or steak, shrimp, or barbecued-chicken dishes. This place earned its reputation on its burgers, cheeseburgers, and fresh-made fries, which some diners compare to the best available in the States.

AT COLOMBIER

✪ **La Route des Epices.** In the François Plantation, Colombier. ☎ **0590/29-80-22.** Reservations required. Main courses 200 F–300 F ($34–$51). AE, MC, V. Daily 6:30–10pm. Closed May 31–Oct 30. FRENCH.

In 1995, Françoise and François Beret decided to initiate a cuisine that many diners consider an enjoyable departure from the ubiquitous French/Creole. Their dining room, adapted from part of the old plantation that stood here, makes a point of flavoring many dishes with spices not usually seen in the French repertoire. Exact components change frequently, but might include *boeuf de coutancie* (a "core" of entrecôte prepared in the traditional style), an aromatic, highly spicy version of fish soup; a stir-fry of jumbo shrimp with lime-and-ginger sauce; or local red snapper roasted in its own skin and served with vinegar-marinated algae pods and cumin. The food is as cerebral as it is satisfying. The wine, the service, and the quality of ingredients used in the dishes presented are top-notch.

ANSE DU GRAND CUL-DE-SAC

Bartolomeo. In the Hôtel Guanahani, Anse du Grand Cul-de-Sac. ☎ **0590/27-66-60.** Reservations required, especially for nonguests. Main courses 160 F–250 F ($27.20–$42.50). AE, DC, MC, V. Daily 7:30–10pm. Closed Sept. PROVENÇAL/NORTHERN ITALIAN.

Despite its role as the deluxe dining choice for one of the most exclusive and expensive hotels on the island, this place works hard to be unthreatening, informally sophisticated, and gracefully upscale. Soothed with music from a live pianist, it features a menu that changes frequently, with food items that are interestingly spiced, sauced, and served. Examples include lobster cannelloni on a bed of spinach with lobster sauce, sea scallops with Szechuan peppers and crêpe-studded risotto, filet mignon with green peppercorns and a gratin of *pommes dauphinoise,* and roasted rack of lamb with goat-cheese ravioli. Two unusual variations on the casually formal routine occur during the twice-per-week buffets. Wednesday features a sweeping array of cold antipasti, and the chef will prepare any pasta you want from an artfully arranged display of seafoods, meats, herbs, wines, and cream.

GRANDE SALINE

Le Tamarin. Plage de Saline. ☎ **0590/27-72-12.** Reservations required for dinner. Main courses 130 F–180 F ($22.10–$30.60). MC, V. Nov 1–May 30, daily 12:30–4pm and Fri–Sun 7–9:30pm. Closed May 15–Nov 10. FRENCH/CREOLE.

One of the island's genuinely offbeat restaurants is Le Tamarin, a deliberately informal bistro that caters to a clientele from the nearby Plage de Saline. It's isolated amid rocky hills and forests east of Gustavia, in a low-slung cottage whose eaves are accented with gingerbread. Inside, a teak-and-bamboo motif prevails. Lunch is the more popular and animated meal here, with most customers dining in T-shirts and bathing suits. If you have to wait, you can order an aperitif in one of the hammocks stretched under a tamarind tree (hence the name of the restaurant). The menu focuses on light, summery meals that go well with the streaming sunlight and tropical heat. Examples include gazpacho, a *pavé* of Cajun-style tuna with Creole sauce and baby vegetables, a carpaccio of fish that includes very fresh portions of marinated salmon and tuna, and chicken roasted with lemon and ginger. There's a broad-based wine list, plus a dessert specialty (chocolate cake) that seems to appeal to dyed-in-the-wood chocoholics. Service can be hectic, but if you're in a rush, you shouldn't be here. It's the perfect place for a lazy afternoon on the beach.

GRAND CUL-DE-SAC

Club Lafayette. Grand Cul-de-Sac. ☎ **0590/27-62-51.** Reservations recommended. Main courses 195 F–350 F ($33.15–$59.50). AE, MC, V. Daily noon–4pm and 7–10pm. Closed May–Oct. FRENCH/CREOLE.

Come here for a sun-flooded, wine-soaked lunch in the sun amid beach-loving clients who shrug at the idea that their *maillots de bain* are revealing. Lunching here, at a cove on the eastern end of the island, east of Marigot, is like taking a meal at your own private beach club—and a very expensive beach club at that. After a dip in the ocean or pool, you can order a *planteur* in the shade of a sea grape, and later proceed to lunch itself. You might begin with a *tarte fine aux tomates, mozzarelle, et herbes de Provence* that's lighter and more flavorful than most pizzas. Be warned that the congenial owners and chefs, Toulouse-born Nadine and Georges Labau, would be horrified to hear it compared to a pizza. There's also warm foie gras served with apples, grilled chicken breast with mushroom sauce, an *émincé* of lobster served with basil-flavored pasta, and one of the best meal-size lobster salads on the island. Desserts include a *croustillant au chocolate* that manages to be warm, crisp, and unctuous all at the same time. As you can tell by now, this is no fast-food beach joint. After your meal, have a refreshing citrus-flavored sherbet.

West Indies Café. In El Sereno Beach Hôtel, Grand Cul-de-Sac. ☎ **0590/27-64-80.** Reservations recommended. Main courses 145 F–170 F ($24.65–$28.90). AE, MC, V. Daily noon–2:30pm and 7:30–8:30pm (last dinner order). Closed Sept–Oct 25. FRENCH/INTERNATIONAL.

Four miles east of Gustavia, one of the most endearing restaurants on the island manages to incorporate aspects of a Parisian cabaret with simple but well-prepared meals served on a breeze-filled tropical terrace. At lunch, you'll be shaded from the sun by a wooden roof that might remind you of a giant parasol. The design allows for a 360-degree view that overlooks a lagoon, a pool, and, at night, a small stage where five professional dancers are joined in their singing and dancing by members of the restaurant's kitchen staff. Shows, configured as part of the Café Chow de la Banane, begin Tuesday through Saturday between 9 and 9:30pm, last for about 75 minutes, and may remind you of a Gallic version of Las Vegas, with a choreography conceived by Paris's well-respected impresario Marie Rivière. Menu items are deliberately geared to the midmarket price range, but are actually more carefully prepared than you might have expected. Examples include fish tartare, eggplant mousse, grilled lobster, and grilled tuna and snapper. Guests who are dining pay no cover for the cabaret; bar patrons who drop in for just drinks, however, pay a cover of 50 F ($8.50).

VITET

Hostellerie des Trois Forces. Vitet. ☎ **0590/27-61-25.** Reservations required. Main courses 120 F–210 F ($20.40–$35.70); fixed-price menu 230 F ($39.10). AE, MC, V. Mon–Sat noon–3pm and 6–10:30pm. FRENCH/CREOLE/VEGETARIAN.

Isolated from the bulk of St. Barts's tourism, this restaurant is located midway up the island's highest mountain (Morne Vitet). The place has a resident astrologer, a French provincial decor, terraces accented with gingerbread, and food that in 1995 won its owner/chef an award from France's prestigious Confrérie de la Marmite d'Or. The heart and soul of the place is Hubert de la Motte, who arrived from Brittany with his wife to create a hotel where happiness, good food, comfort, and conversation are a way of life. Even if you don't stay here, you might want to drive out for a meal. The setting is a compound that contains seven pastel-colored, gingerbread-trimmed cottages, each named after a different sign of the zodiac, in a high-altitude setting of bucolic charm. Although the same menu is available throughout the day and evening, dinners are more formal than lunches, and might include fish pâté, beef shish kebab with curry sauce, grilled fresh lobster, veal kidneys flambé with cognac, a cassoulet of snails, and desserts such as crêpes Suzette flambé. "Each dish takes time," in the words of the owner, as it's prepared fresh. Count on a leisurely meal and a well-informed host who has spent years studying astrology.

PUBLIC

Maya's. Public. ☎ **0590/27-75-73.** Reservations required. Main courses 165 F–205 F ($28.05–$34.85). AE, V. Mon–Sat 6–10pm. Closed Sept to mid-Oct. CREOLE.

It's the most surprising restaurant on St. Barts, thanks to its artful simplicity and glamorous clients. A much-rebuilt green-and-white Antillean house with almost no architectural charm, it attracts crowds of luminaries from the worlds of media, fashion, and entertainment between New York and Hollywood. This is the kind of place you might find on Martinique, because that's where its French-Creole chef, Maya Beuzelin-Gurley, grew up. Assisted by her Massachusetts-born husband, Randy Gurley, it stresses "clean, simple" food with few adornments other than its freshness and a flavorful sprinkling of island herbs and lime juice. You might begin with the salad of tomatoes, arugula, and endive, then follow with grilled fish in sauce *chien* (hot) or a grilled fillet of beef. Maya also prepares what she calls "sailor's chicken," a marinated version made with fresh chives, lime juice, and hot peppers. Almost no cream is used in any dish, a fact that makes the place beloved by the fashion models and actors who hang out here. You'll find the place directly west of Gustavia, close to the island's densest collection of factories and warehouses. Views face west and south, ensuring glorious sunset-watching.

4 Beaches

St. Barts has 14 white-sand beaches. Few are ever crowded, even in winter; all are public and free. Topless sunbathing is quite common. The most famous beach is ✪ **St-Jean,** which is actually two beaches divided by the Eden Rock promontory. It offers water sports, restaurants, and a few hotels, as well as some shady areas. **Flamands,** to the west, is a very wide, long beach with a few small hotels and some areas shaded by lantana palms. In winter, the surf here can be a bit rough, although it is rarely hazardous. For a beach with hotels, restaurants, and water sports, **Grand Cul-de-Sac,** on the northeast shore, fits the bill. This is a narrow beach protected by a reef.

Gouverneur Beach, on the south, can be reached by driving through Gustavia and up to Lurin. Turn at the Santa Fe Restaurant (see "Where to Dine," above) and head down a narrow road. The beach is gorgeous and completely uncrowded, but there's no shade. **Grande Saline,** to the east of Gouverneur, is reached by driving up the road from the commercial center in St-Jean; a short walk over the sand dune and you're here. Like Gouverneur, Saline offers some waves but no shade. This beach is full of beautiful sunbathers, all in the nude.

Lorient, on the north shore, is quiet and calm, with shady areas. It's popular with both local families and surfers. **Marigot,** also on the north shore, is narrow but offers good swimming and snorkeling.

Colombier is difficult to get to but well worth the effort. It can only be reached by boat or by taking a rugged goat path from Petite Anse past Flamands, a 30-minute walk. Shade and snorkeling are found here, and you can pack a lunch and spend the day. Locals call it Rockefeller's Beach, because for many years David Rockefeller owned the property surrounding it.

South of Gustavia, **Shell Beach** or **Grand Galet** is awash with seashells. Snorkeling around the rocks, you'll find some wonderful shells, and rocky outcroppings protect this beach from strong waves. It's also the scene of many a weekend party.

North of the commercial port at Gustavia, the rather unromantic sounding **Public Beach** is a combination of sand and pebbles. This beach is more popular with boaters than swimmers, as it's the location of the St. Barts Sailing School. There is no more beautiful place on the island, however, to watch the boats at sunset. Located near a small fishing village, **Corossol Beach** offers a typical glimpse of French life, St. Barts style. This is a calm, protected beach, with a charming little **seashell museum.**

5 Sports & Outdoor Pursuits

FISHING   People who like fishing are fond of the waters around St. Barts. From March to July, they catch dolphin (the fish, also commonly known as mahimahi, not the mammal); in September, wahoo. Atlantic bonito, barracuda, and marlin also turn up with frequency. **Marine Service,** quai du Yacht-Club, Gustavia (☎ **0590/ 27-70-34**), rents a 30-foot Phoenix that is specifically outfitted for big-game fishing. A full day for four fishers costs 4,100 F ($697), which includes a captain and first mate. The outfitter also offers shore fishing on a 21-foot day cruiser, which tends to remain close to the island's shoreline, searching for tuna, barracuda, and other fish. A full-day excursion, with fishing and scuba gear for up to four participants, costs 2,400 F ($408).

SCUBA DIVING   **Marine Service,** quai du Yacht-Club, in Gustavia (☎ **0590/ 27-70-34**), is the most complete water-sports facility on the island. It operates from a one-story building set directly on the water at the edge of a marina, on the opposite side of the harbor from the more congested part of Gustavia. Tailoring its dives for both beginners and advanced divers, the outfit is familiar with at least 20 unusual sites scattered at various points offshore. The most interesting of these include the Grouper, a remote reef west of St. Barts, close to the rich reef life surrounding the uninhabited cay known as Ile Forchue. Almost as important are the reefs near Roche Rouge, off the opposite (i.e., eastern) edge of St. Barts. The island has only one relatively safe wreck dive, the rusting hulk of *Kayali,* a trawler that sank offshore in 1994. Set in deep waters, it's recommended only for experienced divers. A *baptême* (baptism, or resort course), including two open-water dives for persons who are strong swimmers but inexperienced divers, costs 650 F ($110.50). A "scuba review," for already-certified divers who are out of practice, goes for 350 F ($59.50), while a one-tank dive for already-certified divers begins at 300 F ($51). If you purchase a package that combines several dive experiences, the per-dive price goes down.

SNORKELING   You can test your luck at hundreds of points offshore, simply by donning a mask, fins, and a snorkel. Ask a local where a worthy and relatively safe site might be. If you want a complete immersion into experiences that show off the marina fauna of St. Barts at its most densely populated, consider one of the daily snorkeling expeditions conducted by **Marine Services,** quai du Yacht-Club, Gustavia (☎ **0590/ 27-70-34**). A 7-hour excursion (from 9am to 4pm), including a full French-style picnic, all equipment, and exploration of two separate snorkeling sites, costs 530 F ($90.10). Access to the snorkeling sites is aboard any of several different sailing vessels, a fact that allows you to combine a sailing trip with your snorkeling.

WINDSURFING   Windsurfing is one of the most popular sports here. Try **Wind Wave Power,** Grand Cul de Sac (☎ **0590/27-82-57**), open daily from 9am to 5pm. Windsurfing costs 130 F ($22.10) per hour, and professional instructors are on hand.

6 Shopping

You don't pay any duty on St. Barts, so it's a good place to buy liquor and French perfumes, at some of the lowest prices in the Caribbean—often cheaper than in France itself. St. Barts is the only completely free-trading port in the world, with the exception of French St. Martin and Dutch St. Maarten. The only trouble is, selections are limited. However, you'll find good buys in sportswear, crystal, porcelain, watches, and other luxuries.

If you're in the market for island crafts, try to find the fine straw hats St. Bartians like to wear. *Vogue* once featured this high-crown headwear in its fashion pages. You may also see some interesting block-printed resort clothing in cotton.

La Maison de Free Mousse, Carré d'Or, quai de la République (☎ **0590/27-63-39**), is the most unusual gift shop on St. Barts, with an intensely idiomatic range of wood carvings and handcrafts from throughout Europe, especially Italy, and such countries as Nepal, Thailand, Brazil, Mexico, Indonesia, and the Philippines. Italy-born Tina Palla seems to select her merchandise intuitively, focusing on whatever she thinks might look exotic or mysterious in a well-conceived private home.

Diamond Genesis/Kornérupine, 12 rue du Général-de-Gaulle/Les Suites du Roi-Oskar-II (☎ **0590/27-66-94**), a well-recommended gold, gemstone, and diamond shop, maintains an inventory of designs strongly influenced by European tastes. Although the prices can go as high as $60,000, a particularly appealing best-seller is an 18-karat-gold depiction of St. Barts, which sells for around $20. It's one of the few shops on the island where jewelry is handcrafted on the premises. You can also peruse the selection of watches by Corum and Jaeger Lecoultre (both of which are available only through this store), as well as Brietling and Tag Heuer.

Little Switzerland, rue de la France (☎ **0590/27-64-66**), is the largest purveyor of luxury goods on St. Barts, a glittering tribute to the good life of conspicuous consumption. The entire second floor is devoted to perfumes and crystal, the street level to jewelry and all kinds of watches. Prices are usually 15% to 20% less than equivalent retail goods sold Stateside, and since the island is a duty-free port, some good buys can be found. Smart shoppers immediately ask what sales promotions are in effect at the time of their visit.

The elegant, upscale **Le Comptoir du Cigare,** 6 rue du Général-de-Gaulle (☎ **0590/27-50-62**), is designed exclusively for the tastes of gentlemen. Elegantly sheathed in exotic hardwood, and enhanced with a glass-sided, walk-in humidor for the storage of thousands of cigars, it caters to the December-to-April crowd of villa and yacht owners who flock to St. Barts. Cigars hail from Cuba and the Dominican Republic; the connoisseur-quality rums come from Martinique, Cuba, and Haiti. Cuban cigars, however, cannot be brought into the United States. There's also a worthy collection of silver ornaments suitable for adorning the desk of a CEO, artisan-quality Panama hats from Ecuador, and the most beautiful collection of cigar boxes and humidors in the Caribbean. Accessories are by Davidoff, DuPont, and Dunhill.

La Boutique Couleur des Îles, 8 rue du Général-de-Gaulle (☎ **0590/27-51-66**), tucked off a courtyard adjacent to one of the main streets of Gustavia, sells shirts and blouses with hand-embroidered references to the flora and fauna of St. Barts. Suitable for both men and women to wear to a "casually elegant" onboard cocktail party, they sell for between $30 and $50. Also available are what might be the most elegant beach towels in the world, each a thirsty mass of terry cloth embroidered in gold letters.

Laurent Eiffel, rue du Général-de-Gaulle (☎ **0590/27-54-02**), is for fashion. Despite the elegance of this store and the tact of its employees, nothing sold here is original—everything is either "inspired by" or crafted "in imitation of" designer models that usually cost 10 times as much. Look for belts, bags, and accessories that are copies of Versace, Prada, Hermès, Gucci, and Chanel, sold at prices much lower than what you'd pay in Paris.

St. Barts Style, rue Lafayette, near rue du Port (☎ **0590/27-76-17**), is staffed by a crew who schizophrenically interchange doses of Parisian *froideur* with *Franglais* and American slang. It offers racks of beachwear by such makers as Jams World and Vicidomine in citrus colors of lemon, lime, grapefruit, and orange, and psychedelic-looking T-shirts from about a dozen different manufacturers.

Sud, Etc., Galerie du Commerce, St-Jean (☎ **0590/27-98-75**), is set within a cluster of shops adjacent to the airport. It's known for its stylish clothing, both day and evening wear. Most of the inventory is for women, although a selection of swim trunks and Bermuda shorts are stocked for men. If you're a high-fashion model, or an heiress who's trying to look like one, chances are this boutique will have something whimsical, light-textured, and insouciant that might appeal.

Versace, Carré d'Or, quai de la République (☎ **0590/27-99-30**), is chic and relentlessly upscale. This stylish boutique pays homage to the semi-tropical climate of St. Barts—don't even think about seeing Versace's winter collections, as the inventory here focuses almost exclusively on the warm-weather collections for both men and women.

7 St. Barts After Dark

Most guests consider a French Creole dinner under the stars enough of a nocturnal adventure. After that, there isn't a lot of excitement.

In Gustavia, the most popular gathering place is **Le Select,** rue de la France (☎ **0590/27-86-87**), apparently named after its more famous granddaddy in the Montparnasse section of Paris. It's utterly simple: Tables are set on the gravel in the open-air garden, near the port, and a game of dominoes might be under way as you walk in. At the outdoor grill, Jimmy Buffet found inspiration for "Cheeseburger in Paradise." Need we say more? You never know who might show up here—perhaps Mick Jagger. Beer begins at 10 F ($1.70), and the place is open Monday to Saturday from 10am to 11pm. The locals like it a lot; outsiders are welcomed but not necessarily embraced until they get to know you a bit. If you want to spread a rumor and have it travel fast across the island, start it here.

La Cantina, rue du Bord-de-Mer (☎ **0590/27-55-66**), is one of the more charming watering holes in Gustavia. It's set along the waterfront, with a decor that includes artifacts from Mexico. Part of its offbeat allure stems from its "Côte d'Azur in the 1970s" mood (before it was ruined by tour operators). The menu is set up like something aboard a cruise ship, and is very, very simple, featuring only sandwiches, salads, and drinks. Don't expect gourmet fare, but come to check out the scenery and sociology from this portside perch in the heart of Gustavia. Salads and platters range from 50 F to 125 F ($8.50 to $21.25); it's open daily from 7am to 10pm.

Bar de l'Oubli, 5 rue de la République (☎ **0590/27-70-06**), occupies the most prominent corner in Gustavia, at the intersection of streets that are so well known that most local residents don't even know their names—they refer to it simply as "Centre-Ville." The setting is hip and Gallic, the color scheme is marine blue and white, and the background music might be the Rolling Stones. Sandwiches and salads are served. It's open daily from 8am (when breakfast is served to clients recovering from various stages of their hangovers) to 10 or 11pm, depending on business.

21

St. Eustatius

Called "Statia," this Dutch-held island is a mere 8-square-mile pinpoint in the Netherlands Antilles, still basking in its 18th-century heritage as the "Golden Rock." One of the true backwaters of the West Indies, it's just awakening to tourism.

It might be best to visit first on a day trip from St. Maarten to see if you'd like it for an extended stay. As Caribbean islands go, it's rather dull here, with no nightlife, and the volcanic, black-sand beaches aren't especially alluring. Some pleasant strips of beach exist on the Atlantic side, but the surf here is dangerous for swimming.

If you're a hiker or a diver, the outlook improves considerably. You can hike around the base of the Quill, an extinct volcano on the southern end of the island. Wandering through a tropical forest, you'll encounter wild orchids, philodendron, heliconia, anthurium, fruit trees, ferns, wildlife, and birds, along with the inevitable oleander, hibiscus, and bougainvillea.

The island's reefs are covered with corals and enveloped by marine life. At one dive site, known as Crack in the Wall, or sometimes "the Grand Canyon," pinnacle coral shoots up from the floor of the ocean. Darting among the reefs are barracudas, eagle rays, black-tip sharks, and other large ocean fish.

Statia is located 150 miles east of Puerto Rico, 38 miles south of St. Maarten, and 17 miles southeast of Saba. The two extinct volcanoes, the Quill and "Little Mountain," are linked by a sloping agricultural plain known as De Cultuurvlakte, where yams and sweet potatoes grow.

Overlooking the Caribbean on the western edge of the plain, **Oranjestad** (Orange City) is the capital and the only village, consisting of both an Upper and Lower Town, connected by stone-paved, dogleg Fort Road.

Statia was sighted by Columbus in 1493, on his second voyage, and the island was claimed for the Netherlands by Jan Snouck in 1640. The island's history was turbulent before it settled down to peaceful slumber under Dutch protection; from 1650 to 1816, Statia changed flags 22 times! Once the trading hub of the Caribbean, Statia was a thriving market, both for goods and for slaves.

Before the American Revolution, the population of Statia did not exceed 1,200, most of whom were slaves engaged in raising sugarcane. When war came and Britain blockaded the North American coast, Europe's trade was diverted to the Caribbean. Dutch neutrality lured many traders, which led to the construction of 1½ miles of warehouses in Lower Town. The American revolutionaries obtained gunpowder and ammunition through Statia—perhaps one of the first places anywhere to recognize as a country the newly declared United States of America.

1 Essentials

VISITOR INFORMATION

The U.S.-based representative of the St. Eustatius Tourist Bureau is **Classic Communications International,** P.O. Box 6322, Boca Raton, FL 33427 (☎ **800/722-2394** or 561/394-8580).

The Internet address for Statia is **www.turq.com/statia**.

On the island, the **Tourist Bureau** is at 3 Fort Oranjestrat (☎ **599/3-82213**), open Monday through Thursday from 8am to noon and 1 to 5pm, Friday from 8am to noon and 1 to 4:30pm.

GETTING THERE

St. Eustatius can be reached from Dutch St. Maarten's Queen Juliana Airport via the 20-seat planes of **Windward Islands Airways International (Winair)** (☎ **599/ 5-54230** on St. Maarten). The five flights a day take only 20 minutes to hop the waters to Statia's Franklin Delano Roosevelt Airport (☎ **599/3-82362**). From here you can also make connections for flights to Saba or St. Kitts, two flights a day to Saba, and two a week to St. Kitts.

The little airline, launched in 1961, has an excellent safety record and has flown such passengers as David Rockefeller. Always reconfirm your return passage once you're on Statia.

GETTING AROUND

BY TAXI   Taxis are your best bet. They meet all incoming flights, and on the way to the hotel your driver may offer himself as a guide during your stay on the island. Taxi rates are low, probably no more than $3.50 to $5 from the airport to your hotel. If you book a 2- to 3-hour tour (and in that time you should be able to cover all the sights on Statia), the cost is about $40 per vehicle. To summon a taxi, call **Rainbow Taxis** (☎ **599/3-82811**) or **Josser Daniel** (☎ **599/3-82358**).

BY RENTAL CAR   **Avis** (☎ **800/331-1212** in the U.S., or 599/3-82421), offering unlimited mileage, is your best bet if you want to reserve a car in advance. Drivers must be 21 years old and present a valid license and credit or charge card. Avis is located at the airport. You can also search for a cheaper deal at one of the local companies, although don't expect cars to be too well maintained. Try **Rainbow Car Rental** (☎ **599/3-82811**) or **Walter's** (☎ **599/3-82719**). Walter's rents both cars and jeeps.

Fast Facts: St. Eustatius

Banking Hours   **Barclay's Bank,** Wilhelminastraat, Oranjestad (☎ **599/ 3-82392**), the only bank on the island, is open Monday to Thursday from 8:30am to 3:30pm, Friday from 8:30am to 12:30pm and 2 to 4:30pm. On weekends, most hotels will exchange money.

Currency   The official unit of currency is the **Netherlands Antilles guilder (NAf,** at NAf 1.77 to each U.S.$1, but nearly all places will quote you prices in U.S. dollars.

Customs   There are no Customs duties since the island is a free port.

Documents   U.S. and Canadian citizens need proof of citizenship, such as a passport or a birth certificate with a raised seal and a government-authorized photo ID, along with an ongoing ticket. British subjects need a valid passport.

Electricity   It's 100 volts AC (60 cycles), the same as in the United States.

Hospital   A licensed physician is on duty at the **Queen Beatrix Medical Center,** 25 Princessweg, in Oranjestad (☎ **599/3-82211**).

Language   Dutch is the official language, but English is commonly spoken as well.

Safety   Although crime is rare here, it's wise to secure your valuables and take the kind of discreet precautions you would anywhere. Don't leave valuables unguarded on the beach.

Taxes & Service Charges   There's a $5 tax if you're returning to the Dutch-held islands of St. Maarten or Saba; if you're going elsewhere, the tax is $10. Hotels on Statia collect a 7% government tax. Most hotels, guest houses, and restaurants add a 10% service charge.

Telephone   St. Eustatius maintains a 24-hour-a-day telephone service—and sometimes it takes about that much time to get a call through!

To call Statia from the States, dial **011** (the international access code), then **599** (the country code for the Netherlands Antilles), and finally **3** (the area code for Statia) and the five-digit local number. To make a call within Statia, only the five-digit local number is necessary.

Time   St. Eustatius operates on Atlantic standard time year-round. Thus in winter, when the United States is on standard time, if it's 6pm in Oranjestad it's 5pm in New York. During daylight saving time in the United States, the island keeps the same time as the U.S. East Coast.

Water   The water here is safe to drink.

Weather   The average daytime temperature ranges from 78° to 82°F. The annual rainfall is only 45 inches.

2 Where to Stay

Don't expect deluxe hotels or high-rises—Statia is strictly for escapists. Guests are sometimes placed in private homes. A 15% service charge and 7% government tax are added to hotel bills.

Airport View Apartments. Golden Rock, St. Eustatius, N.A. ☎ **599/3-82474.** Fax 599/3-82517. 9 units. A/C TV TEL. Year-round $66 apt for two. AE, MC, V.

Airport View Apartments has two locations: Most units are in the Golden Rock area near the airport, while four others are on Princessweg in Upper Town, Oranjestad. The accommodations in the Golden Rock area all have compact fridges, coffeemakers, and private baths. They consist of five one-bedroom apartments for one or two people and four two-bedroom apartments for up to four. On the premises are a bar/restaurant and an outdoor patio with a pool and barbecue facilities.

In Upper Town, the accommodations consist of two three-bedroom units holding up to nine guests and two two-bedroom apartments for up to four. All have kitchens, living rooms, cable TV, dining rooms, and small baths. Check into here for economy, not grand comfort. Mattresses are a bit lumpy and the towels a little too thin, but nobody complains when it comes time to pay the bill.

Airport View Apartments 2
Golden Era Hotel 4
Kings Well Resort 3
Talk of the Town Hotel 1

Airport ✈ Beach ↖ Mountain ▲▲

Golden Era Hotel. Lower Town, Oranjestad, St. Eustatius, N.A. ☎ **599/3-82345.** Fax 599/3-82445. 20 units. Winter $88 double; $104 triple. Off-season $75 double; $90 triple. MAP (breakfast and dinner) $30 per person extra. AE, DISC, MC, V.

Set directly on the water, this modern hotel is clean, serviceable, and comfortable. Built in stages between 1968 and 1975, the establishment, including its simply decorated bar and dining room, is operated by Hubert Lijfrock and Roy Hooker. Eight units lack water views, but the remaining rooms offer a full or partial exposure to the sea (the most stunning panorama is from no. 205). All accommodations are tasteful and spacious, with king or queen beds. Regrettably, the bathrooms are so tiny that it's hard to maneuver. You can, if you wish, sit on the toilet and wash your face at the same time. Lunch and dinner are served daily. The fruit punch, with or without the rum, is delectable. The hotel also has a pool.

Kings Well Resort. Oranje Bay, Oranjestad, St. Eustatius, N.A. ☎ and fax **599/3-82538.** 8 units. TV. Winter $60–$90 double; $90 efficiency. Off-season $50–$75 double; $75 efficiency. Rates include breakfast. DISC, MC, V.

Set on the western (Caribbean Sea) side of the island, about half a mile north of Oranjestad, this simple, secluded choice occupies about two-thirds of an acre perched on an oceanfront cliff. The surf is some 60 feet below. Construction on the hotel started in 1994 and has progressed slowly ever since. If you're looking for a laid-back, escapist vacation, this is your place. (Your nearest neighbors will be in the local cemetery.) Most views look out to the southwest, ensuring colorful sunsets that tend to be enhanced by drinks served from the bar of the in-house restaurant (see "Where to Dine," below). There are no room keys, so don't expect much security around here. The accommodations are small and rather sparsely furnished, but each is somewhat different. Beds are draped with mosquito netting; room nos. 1 and 4 contain waterbeds. The rooms in the rear are larger and face the sea, while those in front open onto a shared sea-view balcony. You'll have to leave your windows open, as there's no air-conditioning. Bathrooms are small, with showers only. There's no pool, and the entire resort contains few amenities, other than the peace and calm that reign here.

Talk of the Town Hotel. L. E. Sadlerweg, Golden Rock, St. Eustatius, N.A. ☎ **599/ 3-82236.** Fax 599/3-82640. www.tradereps.com/tot/talk.html. E-mail:tottown@ megatropic.com. 20 units. A/C TV TEL. Year-round $90 double. AE, DISC, MC, V.

Badly damaged by the hurricane of 1998 but recovering, this inn lies in the hamlet of Golden Rock in the heart of the island. It's in a flat area between the hills in the north and the volcano (the Quill) to the south, convenient to both the airport and the historic old capital at Oranjestad, though the beaches (such as they are) are a good trek away. There is, however, a swimming pool on site. The bedrooms are generally spacious, with mattresses replaced after the hurricane, along with small private bathrooms that are well maintained. You get no more comfort here than you would at a standard motel, but the price is right. The well-known restaurant which operated on this site was shut down by the 1998 hurricane; perhaps in the lifetime of this edition, it will open once again.

3 Where to Dine

Blue Bead Bar & Restaurant. Bay Rd., Lower Town, Oranjestad. ☎ **599/3-82873.** Main courses $6.50–$8.50 lunch, $13–$18 dinner. No credit cards. Daily 11:30am–2:30pm and 6–9:45pm. Bar daily 10am–10:30pm. INTERNATIONAL.

Set beside the beach, in a wood-sided Antillean house brightly painted in neon shades of blue and yellow, this restaurant combines West Indian raffishness with a polite staff and cuisine that's well prepared by a crew of Dutch and California-born entrepreneurs. Menu items are international, whimsical, and charming, and rely on culinary inspiration from around the world. Examples include grilled chicken salads, spicy Thai-style fish, beef skewers in a peanut-based satay, and grilled steaks and fish. The restaurant's name, incidentally, derives from the blue-glazed ceramic beads, originally used as money by Statia's slaves, that sometimes wash up on the island's beaches after severe storms.

Fruit Tree Restaurant. 484 Prinses Weg, Upper Town, Oranjestad. ☎ **599/3-82584.** Main courses $8.25–$9.90. No credit cards. Mon–Thurs 8am–9pm, Fri 8am–5pm, Sat 6–9pm, Sun 7am–9pm. CARIBBEAN.

Authentically West Indian, this restaurant, in a wood-sheathed antique house, offers one of the simplest formats on Statia. Named after the fruit trees (mango, papaya, banana, and soursop) that grow in its garden, it serves earthy and ethnic specialties that include roasted goat with Caribbean herbs, baked chicken, goatwater stew, braised oxtail, stewed beef, and fish. Most dishes are accompanied by peas and rice and cornmeal johnnycakes. No alcoholic drinks are served here, although management won't interfere if you bring a bottle of wine. Otherwise, preferred drinks include ginger beer, guava juice, sorrel juice, and lime juice.

Kings Well Restaurant. Oranje Bay, Oranjestad. ☎ **599/3-82538.** Lunch platters $5–$12; dinner main courses $10–$18. DISC, MC, V. Daily 11:30am–2pm and 6–8:30pm. INTERNATIONAL.

It's more successful and more complete than the simple hotel in which its housed (see "Where to Stay," above). Set about a half mile north of Oranjestad, and perched on a cliff about 60 feet above the surf, it features wooden columns and panels, an open kitchen, and great sunset panoramas. Enjoy a fruity drink from the rustic bar before ordering lunch or dinner. Lunches feature deli-style sandwiches and a selection of platters from the dinner menu, which is more elaborate. Dishes might include grilled Colorado beefsteaks, fresh lobster, pan-fried grouper or snapper with parsley-butter sauce, plus a few German meat dishes like *Sauerbraten.*

L'Etoile. 6 Van Rheeweg, northeast of Upper Town. ☎ **599/3-82299.** Reservations required. Main courses $10–$20. AE, MC, V. Mon–Fri 9am–1pm and 5–9pm, Sat 9am–1pm and 5–10pm. CREOLE.

Caren Henríquez has had this second-floor restaurant with a few simple tables for some time. She's well known on Statia for her local cuisine, but you don't run into too many tourists here. Favored main dishes include the ubiquitous "goatwater" (a stew), stewed whelks, mountain crab, tasty spareribs, and Caribbean-style lobster. Caren is also known for her *pastechis*—deep-fried turnovers stuffed with meat. Expect a complete and very filling meal.

4 Beaches

Most of the beaches of Statia are small narrow strips of sand, either volcanic black or else a dull mudlike gray. Regrettably, the preferred beaches are on the Atlantic side instead of the more tranquil Caribbean side, which means the waters are often too rough for swimming.

Beachcombers delight, however, in their search for the fabled **blue-glass beads,** which were manufactured in the 1600s by a Dutch West Indies Company. These beads were used in lieu of money for the trading of such products as tobacco, cotton, and rum. They were even used to purchase slaves. These beads—real collector's items—often are unearthed after a heavy rainfall or tropical storm.

On the Atlantic side, **Zeelandia Beach** is 2 miles long and filled with either a dark, dark beige or volcanic-black sand. One tourist promotion speaks of its "exciting Atlantic surf and invigorating trade winds," but fails to warn of the dangerous undertow. Only one small designated section is safe for swimming. The beach is suitable, however, for wading, hiking, and sunbathing. The place is nearly always deserted.

Orange Beach is also called Smoke Alley Beach. On the leeward side of the island, it lies directly off Lower Town. This is one of the small volcanic beaches on the southwest shore, with beige or black sands and waters suitable for a leisurely swim. You virtually have the beach to yourself until late afternoon, when locals start to arrive for a dip.

Also on the leeward or Caribbean side is **Crooks Castle Beach,** south of Oranjestad. The waters, filled with giant yellow sea fans, sea whips, and pillar coral, attract snorkelers, while beachcombers are drawn to the many blue beads that have been unearthed here.

On the southeast Atlantic side of the island, **Corre Corre Bay** has a strip of dark golden sand. It's about half an hour down Mountain Road and is worth the trip to get here, although the waters are often too churned up for comfortable swimming. Two bends north of this beach, the light-brown-sand **Lynch Bay Beach** is more sheltered from the wild swells of the Atlantic. Nonetheless, the surf here is still almost always rough, plus there's a dangerous undertow; this beach is better used for sunbathing than swimming.

5 Sports & Outdoor Pursuits

HIKING   This is the most popular outdoor activity on the island. Those with the stamina can climb the slopes of the Quill, the highest point on Statia. Its extinct volcanic cone harbors a crater filled with a dense tropical rain forest, containing towering kapok trees and a dozen or more species of wild orchids, some quite rare. It's also home to at least 50 species of birdlife, including the rare blue pigeon, known to frequent the breadfruit and cottonwood trees here. Islanders once grew cocoa, coffee, and cinnamon in the crater's soil, but today bananas are the only crop. The tourist office (☎ 599/3-82433) will supply you with a list of a dozen trails of varying degrees of difficulty and can also arrange for a guide. You'll have to negotiate the fee; it's usually $20 and up.

WATER SPORTS   On the Atlantic side of the island, at Concordia Bay, the **surfing** is best. However, there's no lifeguard protection.

Snorkeling is available on the Caribbean side; you can explore the remnants of an 18th-century man-of-war and the walls of warehouses, taverns, and ships that sank below the surface of Oranje Bay more than 200 years ago.

Dive Statia is a full PADI diving center on Fishermen's Beach in Lower Town (☎ 599/3-82435), offering everything from beginning instruction to dive master certification. Its professional staff guides divers of all levels of experience to spectacular walls, untouched coral reefs, and historic shipwrecks. Dive Statia offers one- and two-tank boat dives, costing $40 to $75, including equipment. Night dives and snorkel trips are also available.

Many adventurers come to Statia to enjoy **waterskiing,** but it's expensive. **Scubagua,** operating out of the Golden Era Hotel, Bay Road, Lower Town (☎ 599/3-82345), will hook you up with the sport for $90 per hour.

TENNIS   Statia maintains two courts at the **Community Center,** Rosemary Laan in Upper Town (☎ 599/3-82249), costing only $2 per hour. You'll have to bring your own rackets and balls, but there is a changing room.

6 Exploring the Island

Oranjestad stands on a cliff looking out on a beach and the island's calm anchorage, where in the 18th century you might have seen 200 vessels offshore. **Fort Oranje** was built in 1636 and restored in honor of the U.S. Bicentennial celebration of 1976. Perched atop the cliffs, its terraced rampart is lined with the old cannons.

St. Eustatius Historical Foundation Museum, Upper Town (☎ 599/3-82288), is also called the de Graaff House in honor of its former tenant, Johannes de Graaff. After British Admiral Rodney sacked Statia for its tribute to the United States, he installed his own headquarters in this 18th-century house. Today a museum, the house stands in a garden, with a 20th-century wing crafted from 17th-century bricks. There are exhibits on the process of sugar refining and shipping and commerce, a section devoted to the pre-Columbian period, archaeological artifacts from the colonial period, and a pair of beautiful rooms furnished with 18th-century antiques. In the wing annex is a massive piece of needlework by an American, Catherine Mary Williams, showing the flowers of Statia. The museum is open Monday to Friday from 9am to 5pm, Saturday and Sunday from 9am to noon; admission is $2 for adults, $1 for children.

A few steps away, a cluster of 18th-century buildings surrounding a quiet courtyard is called **Three Widows' Corner.**

Nearby are the ruins of the first **Dutch Reformed church,** on Kerkweg or Church Way. To reach it, turn west from Three Widows' Corner onto Kerkweg. Tilting headstones record the names of the characters in the island's past. The St. Eustatius Historical Foundation recently completed restoration of the church. Visitors may climb to the top level of the tower and see the bay as lookouts did many years before.

Once, Statia had a large colony of Jewish traders, and you can explore the ruins of **Honen Dalim,** the second oldest Jewish synagogue in the western hemisphere. Built around 1740 and damaged by a hurricane in 1772, the synagogue stands beside Synagogpad, a narrow lane whose entrance faces Madam Theatre on the square.

The walls of a *mikvah* (ritual bath) rise beside the **Jewish burial ground** on the edge of town. Most poignant is the memorial of David Haim Hezeciah de Lion, who died in 1760 at the age of 2 years, 8 months, 26 days; carved into the baroque surface is an angel releasing a tiny songbird from its cage.

You can also visit **Lynch Plantation Museum** at Lynch Bay (☎ 599/3-82209), but you'll have to call to arrange a tour. Donations are accepted; otherwise admission is free. Locals still call this place the Berkel Family Plantation, although today it's a museum depicting life on Statia a century ago, through antiques, fishing and farming equipment, pictures, and old Bibles. Usually Ismael Berkel is on hand to show you around. This is still very much a place of residence, rather than some dead, dull museum.

7 Shopping

At **Mazinga Giftshop,** Fort Oranje Straat, Upper Town (☎ 599/3-82253), you'll find an array of souvenirs, T-shirts, liquor, costume jewelry, 14-karat-gold jewelry, cards, drugstore items, beachwear, children's books, handbags, and paperback romances. You may have seen more exciting stores in your life, but this is without parallel for Statia. A selection of souvenirs and crafts, mainly toys, is found at the **Fun Shop,** Van Tonningenweg in Upper Town (☎ 599/3-82253), and you can also purchase books and magazines at the **Paper Corner,** Van Tonningenweg, Upper Town (☎ 599/3-82208).

8 Statia After Dark

Las Vegas it isn't. Nightlife pickings here are among the slimmest in the Caribbean. Even though most visitors are satisfied by drinks and dinner, there are a few spots to wander after hours. Weekends are the best and busiest time to go out on Statia. Check to see if there's any action at **Talk of the Town** (see "Where to Stay," above), which often has live music on Sunday. **Exit Disco** (☎ 599/3-82543), at the Stone Oven Restaurant, 16A Feaschweg, Upper Town, Oranjestad, often has dancing and local bands on weekends; you can enjoy simple West Indian fare here. For local flavor, try **Cool Corner** (☎ 599/3-82523), across from the St. Eustatius Historical Foundation Museum, in the center of town.

22 St. Kitts

St. Kitts has become a resort mecca in recent years. Its major crop is sugar, a tradition dating from the 17th century. But tourism may overwhelm it in the years to come, as its southeastern peninsula, site of the best white-sand beaches, has been set aside for massive resort development. Most of the island's other beaches are of gray or black volcanic sand.

Far more active and lively than Nevis, its companion island, St. Kitts is still fairly sleepy itself—but go now before its lifestyle changes forever.

At some point during your visit you should eat sugar directly from the cane. Any farmer will sell you a huge stalk, and there are sugarcane plantations all over the island—just ask your taxi driver to take you to one. Strip off the hard exterior of the stalk, bite into it, chew on the tasty reeds, and swallow the juice. It's best with a glass of rum.

The Caribs, the early settlers, called the island Liamuiga, or "fertile isle." Its mountain ranges reach up to nearly 4,000 feet, and its interior contains virgin rain forests, alive with hummingbirds and wild green vervet monkeys. The monkeys were brought in as pets by the early French settlers and were turned loose in the forests when the island became British in 1783. These native African animals have proliferated and can be seen at the Estridge Estate Behavioral Research Institute. Another import, this one British, is the mongoose, brought in from India as an enemy of rats in the sugarcane fields. However, the mongooses and rats operate on different time cycles—the rats ravage while the mongooses sleep. Wild deer are found in the mountains.

Sugarcane climbs right up the slopes, and there are palm-lined beaches around the island. As you travel around St. Kitts, you'll notice ruins of old mills and plantation houses, as well as lots of trees and rich vegetation.

Once a British colony, St. Kitts was given self-government in 1967, and, along with Nevis, to which it's tied politically, it became a state in association with Britain. Anguilla, included in this associated state at the time, eventually broke away. In 1983, the Federation of St. Kitts and Nevis became a totally independent nation, complete with U.N. membership. However, that alliance, by the time you read this, may have dissolved.

St. Kitts and Nevis are so small they are more accurately called a "ministate" instead of a country. But even so small a geographic area is in danger of being broken. The five-person Nevis legislature voted unanimously in October 1997 to secede from its federation with St. Kitts. The vote to secede must stand the test of a referendum, which is expected to be ratified easily. The national government of St. Kitts and Nevis, based in Basseterre, has promised to honor the wishes of the people of Nevis, many of whom feel that the government has ignored their island and has neglected to bring them vital services.

The capital of St. Kitts, **Basseterre,** lies on the Caribbean shore near the southern end of the island, about a mile from Robert L. Bradshaw Golden Rock Airport. With its white colonial houses with toothpick balconies, it looks like a Hollywood version of a West Indian port.

For decades St. Kitts and Nevis slumbered as backwaters of the Caribbean, but in recent years celebrities have been spotted here, almost for the first time. This doesn't mean, of course, that St. Kitts and Nevis are playgrounds for the rich and famous— not yet. But people who can go anywhere have selected St. Kitts and Nevis as their vacation choice, including the late Princess Di, Oprah Winfrey, Sylvester Stallone, Danny Glover, Robert DeNiro, Michael J. Fox, and Gerald and Betty Ford. Sharon Stone herself has expressed interest in acquiring a getaway house here.

1 Essentials

VISITOR INFORMATION

Information is available from the tourist board's **Stateside offices** at 414 E. 75th St., New York, NY 10021 (☎ **800/582-6208** or 212/535-1234).

In **Canada,** an office is at 365 Bay St., Suite 806, Toronto, ON, M5H 2V1 (☎ **416/376-0881**), and in the **United Kingdom** at 10 Kensington Court, London, W8 5DL (☎ **0171/376-0881**).

St. Kitts is on the Web at **www.stkitts-nevis.com**.

On the island, the local **tourist board** operates at Pelican Mall, Bay Road in Basseterre (☎ **869/465-4040**). It's open Monday and Tuesday from 8am to 4:30pm and Wednesday through Friday from 8am to 4pm.

GETTING THERE

Dozens of daily flights on **American Airlines** (☎ **800/800/433-7300;** www.aa.com) land in San Juan. From here, **American Eagle** (same phone) makes four daily nonstop flights into St. Kitts.

If you're already on St. Maarten and want to visit St. Kitts (with perhaps a side trip to Nevis), you can do so aboard one of the most remarkable little airlines in the Caribbean. Known by its nickname, **Winair** (Windward Islands Airways International) (☎ **869/465-8010**), it makes three to four flights a week from St. Maarten to St. Kitts, with easy connections to or from such other Dutch islands as Saba, St. Eustatius, and about a dozen other destinations throughout the Caribbean.

Another possibility involves transfers into St. Kitts or Nevis through Antigua, St. Maarten, or San Juan on the Antigua-based carrier, **LIAT** (☎ **800/468-0482** in the U.S. and Canada, or 869/465-8613). Likewise, LIAT can also be used for Canadians and British, as the LIAT flies in from Antigua. **Air Canada** (☎ **800/268-7240**, or 800/776-3000 in the U.S.; www.aircanada.ca) flies from Toronto to Antigua, and **British Airways** (☎ **800/247-9297;** www.british-airways.com) flies from London to Antigua.

GETTING AROUND

BY TAXI Since most taxi drivers are also guides, this is the best means of getting around. You don't even have to find a driver at the airport—one will find you. Drivers also wait outside the major hotels. Before heading out, however, you must agree on the price, since taxis aren't metered. Also, ask if the rates quoted to you are in U.S. or Eastern Caribbean dollars. The fare from Robert L. Bradshaw Golden Rock Airport to Basseterre is about EC$16 ($5.90); to Sandy Point, EC$37 ($13.70) and up. For more information, call **St. Kitts Taxi Association** (☎ **869/465-8487**).

BY RENTAL CAR **Avis,** South Independence Square (☎ **800/331-1212** in the U.S., or 869/465-6507), charges from $50 per day, $300 per week, plus $10 per day for collision damage, with a $250 deductible. Tax is 5% extra, and a week's rental allows a seventh day for free. The company offers free delivery service to either the airport or to any of the island's hotels, and drivers must be between ages 25 and 75. **Budget,** at Golden Rock Airport (☎ **869/466-5585**), now offers comparable service, vehicles, and prices to Avis.

Delisle Walwyn & Co., Liverpool Row, Basseterre (☎ **869/465-8449**), is a local company offering cars and jeeps. This might be your best deal on the island. You can also check two other local companies: **Sunshine,** Cayon Street in Basseterre and a kiosk at the Golden Rock Airport (☎ **869/465-2193**), and **TDC Rentals**, West Independence Square in Basseterre (☎ **869/465-2991**).

Remember: *Driving is on the left!* You'll need a local driver's license, which can be obtained at the **Traffic Department,** on Cayon Street in Basseterre, for EC$50 ($18.50). Usually a member of the staff at your car-rental agency will drive you to the Traffic Department to get one.

Fast Facts: St. Kitts

Banking Hours Banks are open Monday to Thursday from 8am to noon and on Friday from 8am to noon and 3 to 5pm.

Currency The local currency is the **Eastern Caribbean dollar (EC$),** valued at about $2.70 to the U.S. dollar. Many prices, however, including those of hotels, are quoted in U.S. dollars. Always determine which "dollar" locals are talking about.

Customs You are allowed in duty-free with your personal belongings. Sometimes luggage is subjected to a drug check.

Documents U.S. and Canadian citizens can enter with proof of citizenship, such as a passport or birth certificate with a raised seal accompanied by a government-issued photo ID. British subjects need a passport, but not a visa.

Drugstores See "Pharmacies," below.

Electricity St. Kitt's electricity is 230 volts AC (60 cycles), so you'll need an adapter and a transformer for U.S.-made appliances.

Emergencies Dial ☎ **911** for emergencies.

Hospital In Basseterre, there's a 24-hour emergency room at **Joseph N. France General Hospital,** Cayon Street (☎ **869/465-2551**).

Language English is the language of the island and is spoken with a decided West Indian patois.

Pharmacies Try **Parris Pharmacy,** Central Street at Basseterre (☎ **869/ 465-8569**), open Monday to Wednesday from 8am to 5pm, Thursday from 8am to 1pm, Friday from 8am to 5:30pm, and Saturday from 8am to 6pm. You can also try **City Drug,** Fort Street in Basseterre (☎ **869/465-2156**), open Monday

to Wednesday and Friday to Saturday from 8am to 7pm, Thursday from 8am to 5pm, and Sunday from 8 to 10am.

Safety This is still a fairly safe place to travel. Most crimes against tourists—and there aren't a lot—are robberies on Conaree Beach, so exercise the usual precautions. It's wise to safeguard your valuables, and women should not go jogging alone along deserted roads.

Taxes The government imposes a 7% tax on rooms and meals, plus another EC$27 ($10) airport departure tax (though not to go to Nevis).

Telephone Telegrams and Telexes can be sent from **Skantel,** Cayon Street, Basseterre (☎ **869/465-1000**), Monday to Friday from 8am to 6pm, Saturday from 7:30am to 1pm, and Sunday and holidays from 6 to 8pm. International telephone calls, including collect calls, can also be made from this office.

Time St. Kitts is on Atlantic standard time all year. This means that in winter, when it's 6am in Basseterre, it's 5am in New York. When the U.S. goes on daylight saving time, St. Kitts and the East Coast are on the same time.

Tipping Most hotels and restaurants add a service charge of 10% to cover tipping. If not, tip 10% to 15%.

Water The water on St. Kitts and Nevis is so good that Baron de Rothschild's chemists selected St. Kitts as their only site in the Caribbean to distill and produce CSR (Cane Sugar Rothschild), a pure sugarcane liqueur.

Weather   St. Kitts lies in the tropics, and its warm climate is tempered by the trade winds. The average air temperature is 79°F; the average water temperature, 80°F. Dry, mild weather is usually experienced from November to April; May to October it's hotter and rainier.

2 Where to Stay

VERY EXPENSIVE

✪ **Golden Lemon.** Dieppe Bay, St. Kitts, W.I. ☎ **869/465-7260.** Fax 869/465-4019. 22 units. Winter $300–$395 double; $465–$765 suite. Off-season $245–$300 double; $390–$640 suite. Rates include American breakfast. Extra person $100. 4-night minimum stay required in winter. Honeymoon packages available. AE, DC, MC, V. Children 15 and under not usually accepted.

Arthur Leaman, one-time decorating editor of *House & Garden* magazine, has used his taste and background to create a hotel of great charm in this once-busy shipping port. The 1610 French manor house with an 18th-century Georgian upper story is set back from a coconut grove and a black volcanic-sand beach beyond St. Paul's, on the northwest coast of St. Kitts. Flanking the great house are the Lemon Court and Lemon Grove Condominiums, where you can rent luxuriously furnished suites surrounded by manicured gardens; most have private pools. The spacious rooms are furnished with antiques and always contain fresh flowers, but are not air-conditioned. Bedrooms have recently been redecorated with new fabrics, rugs, and accessories. The names of rooms evoke their themes: Victorian, Paisley, or Lemon. Many beds are raised four-posters draped in mosquito netting in the old plantation style; each is equipped with fine linen and a luxury mattress. Most of the tiled bathrooms are huge; they contain deluxe toiletries, combination shower/tubs, and dressing areas. The larger villas even have sunken tubs, kitchens, and dishwashers. Sophisticated and elegant describe both the Golden Lemon and its clientele.

Dining: The Golden Lemon Restaurant serves a fine continental and Caribbean cuisine (see "Where to Dine," below).

Amenities: Pool, tennis, snorkeling, rain-forest trips, horseback riding, catamaran trips, scuba diving, day trips to other islands. Massage, laundry, duty-free shopping.

Jack Tar Village St. Kitts Beach Resort & Casino. Frigate Bay (P.O. Box 406), St. Kitts, W.I. ☎ **800/858-2258** in the U.S., or 869/465-8651. Fax 869/465-1031. 242 units. A/C TV TEL. Winter $300–$360 double. Off-season $250–$270 double. Rates include meals, golf fees, drinks, and most water sports. AE, MC, V. Children accepted only around the Christmas holidays.

The largest hotel on St. Kitts, and the showcase of the much-touted Frigate Bay development, this all-inclusive chain resort lies 1½ miles east of the airport. It's set on a flat, sandy isthmus between the sea and a saltwater lagoon. It seems a lot like a frenetic private country club, and it's almost completely self-contained. Each unit has a patio or balcony and very simple tropical furniture. Most visitors prefer the second-floor rooms, which have higher ceilings. The bandbox rooms are hardly the island's most glamorous, but they are comfortable with double or king beds, safes, combination tub/showers, and hair dryers. When you check in, ID tags are issued for security purposes.

Dining/Diversions: The resort has two restaurants, serving a cuisine more bountiful than gourmet, a number of bars, and the island's only casino. Organized activities include Scrabble and shuffleboard tournaments, scuba lessons, and toga contests.

Amenities: Two pool areas (one for quiet reading, another for active sports), four tennis courts (two lit at night); golf course nearby. Laundry, baby-sitting.

✪ **Ottley's Plantation Inn.** Ottley's (P.O. Box 345, Basseterre), St. Kitts, W.I. ☎ **800/ 772-3039** in the U.S., or 869/465-7234. Fax 869/465-4760. www.ottleys.com. E-mail: ottleys@caribsurf.com. 17 units. A/C. Winter $295–$435 double; $695 suite. Off-season $220–$335 double; $505 suite. Rates include breakfast. Wedding, honeymoon, and other packages available. AE, MC, V. Children under 9 discouraged.

North of Basseterre on the east coast, beyond Hermitage Bay, Ottley's became one of the most desirable places to stay on the island shortly after it opened in 1989. Six miles north of the airport, and near a rain forest, it occupies a 35-acre site on a former West Indian plantation founded in the 18th century. Those seeking charm and tranquillity will like the nine rooms in an 1832 great house, plus the units divided among three cottages, with air-conditioning and overhead fans. In the winter of 1997, two cottages with four new suites were constructed, each with modern amenities and luxuries, including private pools and panoramic views. Two of the suites are truly deluxe, with their own Jacuzzis. Rooms are elegantly appointed and very spacious, with private safes, queen or king beds, and bathrooms with combination tub/showers and deluxe toiletries.

Dining: The plantation operates one of the best restaurants on the island, the Royal Palm (see "Where to Dine," below). There's a Sunday champagne brunch. With a day's advance notice, the kitchen will prepare a box lunch with directions on how to reach one of many secluded beaches on the southeastern peninsula.

Amenities: Spring-fed, granite-tiled, 65-foot pool in an old sugar factory; extensive tropical gardens and an on-site rain-forest ravine with walking trails. Room service for continental breakfast, laundry, baby-sitting, massage; daily shuttle to the beach, tennis, shops, golf course. The great house contains a sitting room and library with an extensive collection of classic books and videos.

✪ **Rawlins Plantation.** P.O. Box 340, Mount Pleasant, St. Kitts, W.I. ☎ **800/346-5358** in the U.S., 0171/730-7144 in London, or 869/465-6221. Fax 869/465-4954. www. rawlinsplantation.com. E-mail: rawplant@caribsurf.com. 10 units. Winter $420 double. Off-season $285 double. Rates include MAP (breakfast and dinner) and afternoon tea. AE, MC, V. Closed Sept–Oct.

This hotel near Dieppe Bay is situated among the remains of a muscovado sugar factory just outside St. Paul's, on the northeast coast, with a good sandy beach just a short drive away. The rather isolated former plantation is 350 feet above sea level and enjoys cool breezes from both ocean and mountains. Behind the grounds, the land rises to a rain forest and Mount Liamuiga.

A 17th-century windmill has been converted into a charming accommodation, complete with private bathroom and sitting room, while the boiling houses, which formerly housed caldrons of molasses, have been turned into a cool courtyard, where guests dine amid flowers and tropical birds. Other accommodations are in pleasantly decorated cottages equipped with modern facilities. There's no air-conditioning, but ceiling fans and cross ventilation keep the place cool. Each unit, generous in size, is decorated in a Caribbean country-house style with antiques, stone or white walls, floral prints, local art, and rattan furnishings. Bedrooms often have mahogany four-posters; all have luxury mattresses and fine linen. Bathrooms are superb with plenty of shelf space, toiletries, thick towels, and a hair dryer.

Dining: A $25 West Indian buffet lunch is served daily. One critic called the food here "a mix of Kittitian, serious Cordon Bleu, and love and inspiration." In the evening, elegant dinners are offered at a fixed price of $45 for nonguests; reservations are required. Afternoon tea is also served.

Amenities: Spring-fed pool, grass tennis court, croquet lawn. Free laundry.

The White House. P.O. Box 436, St. Peter's, St. Kitts, W.I. ☎ **800/223-1108** in the U.S. and Canada, or 869/465-8162. Fax 869/465-8275. 10 units. Winter $375 double. Off-season $250 double. Rates include full breakfast and afternoon tea. AE, MC, V. Closed July–Aug.

Small and special, the White House boasts a plantation great house ambience. Set at the foot of Monkey Hill, overlooking Basseterre, it's directly west of Golden Rock Airport. The beach at Frigate Bay is a 10-minute ride away. Set in stone cottages, the guest rooms are bright and airy, with four-poster beds and Laura Ashley fabrics. Each spacious unit is individually decorated and has real Caribbean charm, with hardwood floors, chaise longues, four-poster beds, and well-maintained bathrooms with thick towels and combination shower/tubs. There's ceiling fans and cross ventilation, but no air-conditioning.

Dining: The zesty international cuisine with West Indian overtones capitalizes on fresh fish in particular, as well as locally grown ingredients. Since the hoteliers here own the Georgian House restaurant (see Mango's Garden Bar & Bistro in "Where to Dine," below), arrangements can be made for MAP to dine there as well.

Amenities: Pool, room service, laundry, shuttle to the beach (15 minutes away).

MODERATE/INEXPENSIVE

Bird Rock Beach Hotel. P.O. Box 227, Basseterre, St. Kitts, W.I. ☎ **800/621-1270** in the U.S., or 869/465-8914. Fax 869/465-1675. E-mail:birdrock@caribbeans.com. 38 units. A/C TV TEL. Winter $150 double; $165 efficiency apt; $175 studio suite for two; $295 one-bedroom apt; $425 three-bedroom apt. Off-season $75 double; $80 efficiency apt; $90 studio suite for two; $125 one-bedroom apt; $170 three-bedroom apt. AE, MC, V.

Set on a secluded, half-moon-shaped beach 2 miles southeast of Basseterre, this small resort is clean, uncomplicated, and easygoing. Views from the balconies of most of the bedrooms are either of the Bay of Basseterre and the capital or of the ocean stretching toward Nevis. Each of the units is in a two-story cottage containing four to eight rooms. All have private patios or balconies and rather bland furniture inspired by the tropics. Showing signs of wear and tear, the bedrooms carry out the Caribbean motif with flowery fabrics and paintings of birds. Mattresses are aging but still firm, and bathrooms are small but adequate. Amenities include louvered windows, ceiling fans, and cable TV. The superior rooms have one king or two double beds, while studio suites offer a queen bed plus a sofa bed and a full kitchen. The efficiency apartments have two double beds, a microwave, a toaster, a coffeemaker, and a small fridge. Facilities include a pool with its own swim-up bar, a tennis court, a beachfront snack bar with a well-attended happy hour, and an evening restaurant with a well-prepared international cuisine.

Coconut Beach Club. Frigate Bay (P.O. Box 1198, Basseterre), St. Kitts, W.I. ☎ **800/345-0271** in the U.S., or 869/465-8597. Fax 869/466-7085. 60 units. Winter $100–$125 double; $150 studio suite; $175 one-bedroom apt for up to 4; $275 two-bedroom apt for up to 6. Off-season $75–$90 double; $105 studio suite; $120 one-bedroom apt for up to 4; $190 two-bedroom apt for up to 6. AE, MC, V.

Located at the foot of a green mountain, this resort, a family favorite, is the only hotel on Caribbean Beach at Frigate Bay. It's located 3 miles east of Basseterre. Though short on island atmosphere, it opens onto one of the finest beaches on St. Kitts. Naturally, the most sought-after units in this one- and two-bedroom condo complex are those opening directly onto the beach, with swimming, sailing, and water sports at your doorstep. There's also a pool, and it's just a short drive from an 18-hole golf course. The rooms are furnished in a Caribbean motif, and the larger accommodations have kitchens. Units here are time-shares, so there are no routine amenities. Most have decent mattresses and a medium-size bathroom. Accommodations house from two to six people; there are no singles rented as such.

Guests are booked in on the European plan (no meals), but they can patronize the increasingly popular Banana Tree Restaurant, which features informal beachfront dining. Dinners at the cafe are particularly restful, and fresh grilled seafood is a specialty.

Frigate Bay Resort. Frigate Bay (P.O. Box 137, Basseterre) St. Kitts W.I. ☎ **869/465-8935.** Fax 869/465-7050. www.frigatebay.com. E-mail: Frigbay@caribsurf.com. 64 units. A/C TV TEL. Winter double $125–$175; from $267 suite. Off-season $85–$120 double; from $190 suite. MAP (breakfast and dinner) $40 per person extra. Packages available. A/C TEL. AE, MC, V.

On a verdant hillside east of Basseterre, Frigate Bay has standard rooms and condo suites administered as hotel units for their absentee owners. The older units are more spacious than the newer accommodations. Rooms are nicely furnished to the taste of the owners and painted in an array of pastel colors. They have both air-conditioning and ceiling fans. Nautical prints, tile floors, flowery prints, and private terraces or balconies make the place more alluring. Mattresses are frequently renewed, and the small bathrooms are well maintained. Many units contain fully equipped kitchens with breakfast bars. The central core of the resort has a large pool and a cabana bar where you can enjoy a drink while partially immersed. The Garden Room Restaurant, overlooking the pool and featuring its own swim-up bar, serves both a continental and Caribbean cuisine. An 18-hole golf course and tennis courts are within walking distance, and the beach is a 4-minute walk from the hotel.

Ocean Terrace Inn. P.O. Box 65, Fortlands, St. Kitts, W.I. ☎ **869/465-2754.** Fax 869/ 465-1057. 53 units. A/C TV TEL. Winter $116–$225 double; $165 studio; $242–$346 one- or two-bedroom apt. Off-season $101–$164 double; $138 studio; $177–$235 one- or two-bedroom apt. Dive, honeymoon, and eco-safari packages available. AE, DC, DISC, MC, V. Go west along Basseterre Bay Rd. past the Cenotaph.

Ocean Terrace Inn is affectionately known as the "OTI" by its mainly business clients. If you want to be near Basseterre, it's the best hotel around the port, with oceanfront verandas and a view of the harbor and the capital. It's so compact that a stay here is like a house party on a great liner. Terraced into a landscaped hillside above the edge of Basseterre, the hotel also has gardens and well-kept grounds. All the handsomely decorated rooms have a light, tropical feel and overlook a well-planted terrace. Beds are a wide variety of sizes, but all fitted with good mattresses. Bathrooms, with shower stalls, are compact and tidily maintained. The hotel also offers apartments at the Fisherman's Wharf and Village, a few steps from the nearby harbor. These units are filled with most of the comforts of home.

The flagstone-edged pool has a row of underwater stools where you'll be served drinks while still immersed. Our favorite of the four bars is in the shadow of an elaborate aviary. (For details on the cuisine here, see "Where to Dine," below.) Amenities include room service, laundry, baby-sitting, two pools, a Jacuzzi, water sports, and scuba diving. Rain-forest safaris, historic-plantation tours, deep-sea fishing, snorkeling adventures, and island tours are available through the hotel reception. A free shuttle hauls you to Turtle Beach, a 25-minute drive away.

3 Where to Dine

EXPENSIVE

✪ **The Golden Lemon.** Dieppe Bay. ☎ **869/465-7260.** Reservations usually required; walk-ins accepted if space available. Lunch main courses $3.50–$20; fixed-price dinner

$30–$55; Sun brunch $24. AE, MC, V. Mon–Sat noon–3pm and 6:30–10:30pm, Sun noon–3pm and 6:30–10:30pm. CONTINENTAL/CREOLE.

If you're touring St. Kitts, the best lunch stop is at the Golden Lemon, a 17th-century house that's been converted into a fine hotel on the northern coast beyond St. Paul's (see "Where to Stay," above). The food is very good, and the service polite. Dinner is served in an elegant, candlelit dining room, in the garden, or on the gallery. The cuisine features Creole, continental, and American dishes, with locally grown produce. Many of the recipes were created by the hotel's sophisticated owner. The menu changes daily, but is likely to include baked Cornish hen with ginger, fresh fish of the day, and Creole sirloin steak with a spicy rum sauce. Vegetarian dishes are also available. Dress is casually chic.

✪ **The Patio.** Frigate Bay Beach. ☎ **869/465-8666.** Reservations required. Main courses $28–$38. MC, V. Mon–Sat 7–9pm. Closed May 31–Dec 15. CARIBBEAN/INTERNATIONAL.

The Patio is at the private home of a Kittitian family, the Mallalieuses, 6 minutes southwest of the airport. Complimentary drinks are served in the flower garden just a few feet from the house. The family's high-ceilinged modern living room has been transformed into a dining room with antique furniture, tablecloths, and kerosene lanterns. Meals include home-grown vegetables and a fresh seafood menu that changes nightly. Fresh lobster is cooked perfectly, never overdone; the Black Angus beef is well flavored and tender. The orange-rum sauce certainly adds zest to the Long Island duckling, and the plantation roast loin of pork is spiked with ginger sauce for a tantalizing flavor. If you have any special menu requests, Peter Mallalieu will probably follow them; each dish is prepared to order. Dress is casual but elegant—no shorts, please.

✪ **The Royal Palm.** In Ottley's Plantation Inn, north of Basseterre, on the east coast. ☎ **869/465-7234.** Reservations required. Lunch main courses $8.95–$17.95; Sun champagne brunch $25; fixed-price dinner from $65. AE, MC, V. Mon–Sat noon–3pm, Sun brunch noon–2pm; daily dinner seating 7:30–8:30pm. CARIBBEAN FUSION.

On the grounds of Ottley's Plantation Inn, the Royal Palm is an island favorite, serving the most creative cuisine on St. Kitts. It also has a colorful setting: Gaze through the ancient stone arches to the ocean on one side and Mount Liamuiga and the inn's great house on the other. The restaurant is set beside the pool, and many diners prefer to visit it at night. The menu changes daily, so you won't know what the inspiration of the moment will be. You might start with Brazilian gingered-chicken soup or chili-flavored shrimp corn cakes, each equally tempting. If featured, the lobster quesadillas—made with local lobster—are worth crossing the island to sample. The dinner menu, wandering the globe for inspiration, is more elaborate, beginning perhaps with a white cheddar and green chili bisque. The main courses tend to be impeccably prepared, especially the French roast of lamb or the breast of chicken Molyneux with almonds, country ham, mozzarella, and mushroom stuffing.

MODERATE

Ballahoo Restaurant. The Circus, Fort St., Basseterre. ☎ **869/465-4197.** Reservations recommended. Main courses EC$25–EC$65 ($9.25–$24.05). AE, MC, V. Daily 8am–10pm. CARIBBEAN.

Overlooking the town center's Circus Clock, the Ballahoo is about a block from the sea, on the second story of a traditional stone building. Its open-air dining area is one of the coolest places in town on a hot afternoon, thanks to the sea breezes. One of the best and most reliable dishes to order is Blue Parrot fish fillet. The chef also makes some of the best chili and baby back ribs in town. Seafood platters, such as chili shrimp or fresh lobster, are served with a coconut salad and rice, and, for more elegant fare, there's Italian-style chicken breast topped with pesto tomatoes and cheese and served with a pasta and salad. The service is casual. Because of its central location, this restaurant draws the cruise-ship crowd.

Fisherman's Wharf Seafood Restaurant and Bar. Fortlands, Basseterre. ☎ **869/465-6623.** Reservations recommended. Main courses $12–$28. AE, DISC, MC, V. Daily 7–11pm. SEAFOOD/CARIBBEAN.

At the west end of Basseterre Bay Road, the Fisherman's Wharf is between the sea and the white picket fence of the Ocean Terrace Inn. Near the busy buffet grill, hard-working chefs prepare fresh seafood. An employee will take your drink order, but you personally place your food order at the grill. It's a bit like eating at picnic tables, but the fresh fish selection is excellent, caught locally and grilled to order over St. Kitts chosha coals. Spicy conch chowder is a good starter; grilled lobster is an elegant main course choice, but you may prefer the grilled catch of the day, often snapper. Grilled swordfish steak is always a pleaser, as is the combination platter, which includes lobster, barbecued shrimp kebab, and calypso chicken breast.

Mango's Garden Bar & Bistro. S. Independence Sq., Basseterre. ☎ **869/465-4049.** Reservations recommended. Lunch main courses EC$19–EC$55 ($7.05–$20.35); dinner main courses EC$36–EC$75 ($13.30–$27.75). AE, MC, V. Mon–Sat 7–9:30pm. INTERNATIONAL.

Mango's is the best place in town for lunch. Begin with conch ceviche (marinated in lime juice and flavored with cilantro) or opt for the freshly made soup of the day. House salads are always a winner here, especially the Caesar or the grilled chicken salad. From the grill emerges a classic burger or the catch of the day, prepared as you like it. At dinner, the cuisine is more elaborate and always filled with flavor. One section of the menu, called "hot and spicy," includes Thai shrimp curry. Pastas are succulent, and the chef specializes in lobster and steaks from the grill. The menu uses quality ingredients in familiar dishes, including the likes of New York strip, grilled pork chop, and lobster Thermidor.

Next door, you can visit the Georgian House & Coffee Shop, both a library and a reading room, serving all kinds of tea and coffee. This property is one of the most historic on the island, erected "shortly after 1727." It was used as a backdrop for the island's slave market, whose victims were purchased and sold in the square outside.

Ocean Terrace Inn. Fortlands. ☎ **869/465-2754.** Reservations recommended. Main courses $18–$29; fixed-price lunch $15; fixed-price dinner $35. AE, DC, DISC, MC, V. Daily 7–10am, noon–2pm, and 7–9:30pm. Drive west on Basseterre Bay Rd. to Fortlands. CARIBBEAN/INTERNATIONAL.

Some of the finest cuisine in Basseterre is found here, along with one of the best views, especially at night when the harbor is lit up. Dinner might include tasty fish cakes, accompanied by breaded carrot slices, creamed spinach, a stuffed potato, johnnycake, a cornmeal dumpling, and a green banana in a lime-butter sauce, topped off by a tropical fruit pie and coffee. The kitchen also prepares French or English dishes along with some flambé specialties, including Arawak chicken, Châteaubriand, steak Diane, and veal Fantasia. The kitchen is best when preparing the real down-home dishes of the island instead of the blander international specialties. The special night to attend is Friday, which features a Caribbean night with an all-you-can-eat buffet and a steel band at a cost of $21. Some form of entertainment is often presented. Dining is on an open-air veranda.

Stonewalls. Princes St. ☎ **869/465-5248.** Reservations recommended. Main courses EC$38–EC$60 ($14.05–$22.20). AE, MC, V. Mon–Sat 5–11pm. CARIBBEAN/INTERNATIONAL.

Surrounded by ancient stone walls, this casual, open-air bar in a tropical garden in Basseterre's historical zone is cozy and casual. It's the type of Caribbean bar you think exists, but can rarely find. In a garden setting of banana, plantain, lime, and bamboo trees, Wendy and Garry Speckles present an innovative and constantly changing menu. The fare might be Caribbean, with fresh kingfish or tuna and a zesty gumbo, or an authentic, spicy Dhansak-style curry. Hot-off-the-wok stir-fries are served along with sizzling Jamaican-style jerk chicken. Appetizers might include piquant conch fritters. A small but carefully chosen wine list is available. The bar here is one of the most convivial places on the island for a drink.

Turtle Beach Bar & Grill. Southeastern Peninsula. ☎ **869/469-9086.** Reservations recommended. Main courses $10–$24. AE, MC, V. Daily noon–5pm. Follow the Kennedy Simmonds Hwy. over Basseterre's Southeastern Peninsula; then follow the signs. SEAFOOD.

Set directly on the sands above Turtle Beach, this airy, sun-flooded restaurant is one of the most popular lunch stops for those doing the whirlwind tour of St. Kitts. Many guests spend the hour before their meal swimming or snorkeling beside the offshore reef; others simply relax on the verandas or in hammocks under the shade trees, perhaps with a drink in hand. Scuba diving, ocean kayaking, windsurfing, and volleyball are available, and a flotilla of rental sailboats moor nearby. Menu specialties are familiar stuff, but prepared with an often scrumptious flavor. Typical dishes might be stuffed broiled lobster, conch fritters, barbecued swordfish steak, prawn salads, and barbecued honey-mustard spareribs.

INEXPENSIVE

The Atlantic Club. At the Morgan Heights Condominiums, Canada Estate. ☎ **869/465-8633.** Reservations recommended for dinner. Main courses EC$15–EC$45 ($5.60–$16.70). AE, MC, V. Mon–Sat 11am–11pm. SEAFOOD/WEST INDIAN.

A Nevisian, Genford Gumbs, who worked at the deluxe Golden Lemon for 15 years, struck out on his own and opened this enterprise in the early 1990s. Set on the east coast, a 5-minute drive from the center of Basseterre and a 3-minute drive from the airport, it overlooks the Atlantic Ocean. The cuisine is West Indian, with some seafood such as fresh fish, conch, and lobster usually available. The atmosphere is relaxed and casual, and the portions are large. A lot of locals show up on Saturday for the special, goatwater and souse. Some foreigners may want to skip this treat and instead order the burgers, soups, salads, and sandwiches, or even a Black Angus steak.

Glimbara Diner. In the Glimbara Guest House, Cayon St., Basseterre. ☎ **869/465-1786.** Reservations not necessary. Main courses EC$12–EC$18 ($4.45–$6.65). AE, MC, V. Daily 7am–11pm. CARIBBEAN.

Don't expect grand cuisine from this workaday but honest eatery. Established in 1998 in a simple family-run guest house in the heart of town, it promises to become a local favorite, thanks to the hardworking staff and down-to-earth cuisines. Small and cozy, and painted in shades of pink and white, it serves Creole cuisine that varies with the mood and inspiration of the cook, plus conventional American-style platters, including hamburgers and hot dogs, usually served with fries and soda. Examples might include large or small portions of the stewlike goatwater, pumpkin or bean soup, and several kinds of fried or grilled fish, which might be accompanied by coleslaw or green salad. Ask for a local fruit punch known as *fairling* or the bottled sugary drink called Ting.

4 Beaches

Beaches are the primary concern of most visitors. The narrow peninsula in the southeast that contains the island's salt ponds also boasts the best white-sand beaches. All beaches, even those that border hotels, are open to the public. However, if you use the beach facilities of a hotel, you must obtain permission first and will probably have to pay a small fee.

For years, it was necessary to take a boat to enjoy the beautiful, unspoiled beaches of the southeast peninsula. But in 1989, the Dr. Kennedy Simmonds Highway, a 6-mile road beginning in the Frigate Bay area, opened to the public. To traverse this road is one of the pleasures of a visit to St. Kitts. Not only will you take in some of the island's most beautiful scenery, but you'll also pass lagoon-like coves and fields of tall guinea grass. If the day is clear (and it usually is), you'll have a panoramic vista of Nevis. The best beaches along the peninsula are **Frigate Bay, Friar's Bay, Sand Bank Bay, White House Bay, Cockleshell Bay,** and **Banana Bay.** Of all these, Sand Bank Bay gets our nod as the finest strip of sand.

Both **Cockleshell Bay** and **Banana Bay** also have their devotees. These two beaches run a distance of 2 miles, all with powder-white sands. So far, in spite of several attempts, this area isn't filled with high-rise resorts.

For excellent snorkeling, head to the somewhat rocky **White House Bay,** which opens onto reefs. Schools of rainbow-hued fish swim around a sunken tugboat from long ago—a stunning sight.

Friar's Bay is lovely, although its pristine qualities may be forever disturbed by the construction of a new Hyatt. Friar's has powder-fine sand as well, and many locals consider it their favorite.

Frigate Bay, with its powder-white sand, is ideal for swimming as well as windsurfing and waterskiing.

As a curiosity, you may want to visit **Great Salt Pond** at the southern end of St. Kitts. This is an inland beach of soft white sand, opening onto the Atlantic Ocean in the north and the more tranquil Caribbean Sea in the south.

The beaches in the north of St. Kitts are numerous but are of gray volcanic sand and much less frequented than those of the southeast peninsula. Many beachcombers like to frequent them, and they can be ideal for sunbathing, but swimming is much better in the southeast, as waters in the north, sweeping in from the Atlantic, can often be turbulent.

The best beach on the Atlantic side is **Conaree Bay,** with a narrow strip of gray-black sand. Bodysurfing is popular here. **Dieppe Bay,** also a black-sand beach on the north coast, is good for snorkeling and windsurfing but not for swimming. This is the site of the island's most famous inn, the Golden Lemon, which you might want to visit for lunch. If you should be on this beach during a tropical shower, do not seek shelter under the dreaded manicheel trees, which are poisonous. Rain falling off the leaves will feel like acid on your skin.

5 Sports & Outdoor Pursuits

BOATING   Most outfitters are found at Frigate Bay on the southeast peninsula. The best of these is the provocatively named **Mr. X Watersports** (☎ 869/465-0673), where you can rent kayaks for $15 an hour, arrange windsurfing for the same price, rent a Sunfish for $20 per hour, or else hook up with a snorkeling tour lasting 2 hours and costing $25 per person.

GOLF The **Royal St. Kitts Golf Course,** Frigate Bay (☎ **869/465-8339**), is an 18-hole championship course that opened in 1976, covering 160 acres. It's bounded on the south by the Caribbean Sea and on the north by the Atlantic Ocean, and features 10 water hazards. The course rating is 72 and can be 5,349, 6,033, 6,476, or 6,918 yards, depending on which tees are used. It's open daily from 7am to 7pm. Greens fees are $40 for 18 holes. Cart rentals cost $50 for 18 holes, plus another $15 for clubs. A bar and on-site restaurant opens daily at 7am.

HIKING **Kris Tours** (☎ **869/465-4042**) takes small groups into the crater of Mount Liamuiga, through a rain forest to enjoy the lushness of the island, or to Verchild's Mountain, which isn't a difficult trek. A half-day tour costs $50 per person.

HORSEBACK RIDING **Trinity Stables** (☎ **869/465-3226**) charges $35 for a half-day tour through a rain forest. You might also get to see the wild lushness of the North Frigate Bay area and the rather desolate Conaree Beach. You must call for a reservation; you'll then be told where to meet and offered any advice, including what to wear.

SCUBA DIVING, SNORKELING & OTHER WATER SPORTS Some of the best dive spots include **Nag's Head,** at the south tip of St. Kitts. This is an excellent shallow-water dive starting at 10 feet and extending to 70 feet. A variety of tropical fish, eagle rays, and lobster are found here. The site is ideal for certified divers. Another good spot for diving is **Booby Shoals,** lying between Cow 'n' Calf Rocks and Booby Island, off the coast of St. Kitts. Booby Shoals has abundant sea life, including nurse sharks, lobster, and stingrays. Dives are up to 30 feet in depth, ideal for both certified and resort divers.

A variety of activities are offered by **Pro-Divers,** at Turtle Beach (☎ **869/465-3223** or 869/469-9086). You can swim, float, paddle, or go on scuba-diving and snorkeling expeditions from here. A two-tank dive costs $50 to $60; night dives are $50. A PADI certification is available for $300, and a resort course costs $75. Three-hour snorkeling trips are $35; day trips to Nevis cost $25.

WINDSURFING See "Boating," above.

6 Exploring the Island

The British colonial town of **Basseterre** is built around a so-called **Circus,** the town's round square. A tall green Victorian clock stands in the center of the Circus. After Brimstone Hill Fortress, this **Berkeley Memorial Clock** is the most photographed landmark of St. Kitts. In the old days, wealthy plantation owners and their families used to promenade here.

At some point, try to visit the **marketplace,** especially on a Saturday morning. Here, country people bring baskets brimming with mangos, guavas, soursop, mammy apples, and wild strawberries and cherries just picked in the fields, and tropical flowers abound.

Another major landmark is **Independence Square.** Once an active slave market, it's surrounded by private homes of Georgian architecture.

You can negotiate with a taxi driver to take you on a tour of the island for about $60 for a 3-hour trip; most drivers are well versed in the lore of the island. Lunch can be arranged either at the Rawlins Plantation Inn or the Golden Lemon. For more information, call the **St. Kitts Taxi Association,** the Circus, Basseterre (☎ **869/465-8487** during the day, or 869/465-7818 at night).

Into the Volcano

Mount Liamuiga was dubbed "Mount Misery" long ago, but it sputtered its last gasp around 1692. This dormant volcano on the northeast coast is today one of the major highlights for hikers on St. Kitts. The peak of the mountain often lies under cloud cover.

The ascent to the volcano is usually made from the north end of St. Kitts at Belmont Estate. The trail winds through a rain forest and travels along deep ravines up to the rim of the crater at 2,625 feet. The actual peak is at 3,792 feet. Figure on 5 hours of rigorous hiking to complete the round-trip walk, with 10 hours required from hotel pickup to return.

The caldera itself is some 400 feet from its rim to the crater floor. Many hikers climb or crawl down into the dormant volcano. However, the trail is steep and slippery, so be careful. At the crater floor is a tiny lake along with volcanic rocks and various vegetation.

Greg's Safaris, P.O. Box Basseterre (☎ **869/465-4121**), offers guided hikes to the crater for $60 per person (a minimum of six needed), including breakfast and a picnic at the crater's rim. The same outfit also offers half-day rain-forest explorations for $35 per person.

The ✪ **Brimstone Hill Fortress** (☎ **869/465-6211**), 9 miles west of Basseterre, is the major stop on any tour of St. Kitts. This historic monument, among the largest and best preserved in the Caribbean, is a complex of bastions, barracks, and other structures ingeniously adapted to the top and upper slopes of a steep-sided 800-foot hill. The fortress dates from 1690, when the British attempted to recapture Fort Charles from the French.

Today, the fortress is the centerpiece of a national park of nature trails and a diverse range of plant and animal life, including the **green vervet monkey.** It's also a photographer's paradise, with views of mountains, fields, and the Caribbean Sea. On a clear day, you can see six neighboring islands.

Visitors will enjoy self-guided tours among the many ruined or restored structures, including the barrack rooms at Fort George, which comprise an interesting museum. The gift shop stocks prints of rare maps and paintings of the Caribbean. Admission is $5, half price for children. The Brimstone Hill Fortress National Park is open daily from 9:30am to 5:30pm.

In the old days, a large tamarind tree in the hamlet of **Half-Way Tree** marked the boundary between the British-held sector and the French half, and you can visit the site.

It was near the hamlet of **Old Road Town** that Sir Thomas Warner landed with the first band of settlers and established the first permanent colony to the northwest at Sandy Point. Sir Thomas's grave is in the cemetery of St. Thomas Church.

A sign in the middle of Old Road Town points the way to **Carib Rock Drawings,** all the evidence that remains of the former inhabitants. The markings are on black boulders, and the pictographs date from prehistoric days.

Most visitors to St. Kitts or Nevis like to spend at least one day on the neighboring island. **LIAT** provides twice daily flights to and from Nevis. Make reservations at the LIAT office on Front Street in Basseterre (☎ **869/465-8613**) rather than at the airport.

If you'd rather not fly, the government passenger ferry **M.V. *Caribe Queen*** departs from each island between 7 and 7:30am on Monday, Tuesday, Wednesday, Friday, and

Saturday, returning at 4 and 6pm (check the schedule at your hotel or the tourist office). The cost is $4 each way.

7 Shopping

The good buys here are in local handcrafts, including leather items made from goatskin, baskets, and coconut shells. Some good values can also be found in clothing and fabrics, especially Sea Island cottons. Store hours vary, but are likely to be Monday to Saturday from 8am to noon and 1 to 4pm.

If your time is limited, head first for the **Pelican Shopping Mall,** Bay Road, which contains some two dozen shops. Opened in 1991, it also offers banking services, a restaurant, and a philatelic bureau. Some major retail outlets in the Caribbean, including Little Switzerland, have branches here. Also check out the offerings along the quaintly named **Liverpool Row,** which has some unusual merchandise, and **Fort Street.**

The **Linen and Gold Shop,** in the Pelican Mall (☎ 869/465-9766), offers a limited selection of gold and silver jewelry, usually in bold modern designs. But the real appeal of this shop is the tablecloths, doilies, and napkins, laboriously handcrafted in China from cotton and linen. The workmanship is as intricate as anything you'll find in the Caribbean.

Ashburry's, the Circus/Liverpool Row, Basseterre (☎ 869/465-8175), is a local branch of a chain of luxury-goods stores based on St. Maarten. This well-respected emporium sells fragrances, fine porcelain, Baccarat crystal, Fendi handbags, watches, and jewelry, at prices 25% to 30% below what you might pay in retail stores in North America, although the selection is similar to dozens of equivalent stores throughout the Caribbean.

Cameron Gallery, 10 N. Independence Sq., Basseterre (☎ 869/465-1617), is a leading art gallery. On display are scenes of St. Kitts and Nevis by Brit Rosey Cameron-Smith, along with works by 10 to 15 other artists. Rosey is well known on the island for her paintings of Kittitian Carnival clowns, and she also produces greeting cards, postcards, and calendars. The finest gallery on St. Kitts is **Kate Design,** Mount Pleasant (☎ 869/465-7740), set in an impeccably restored West Indian house, on a hillside below the Rawlins Plantation. Virtually all the works on display are by English-born Kate Spencer, who is well known throughout North America and Europe. Her paintings of island scenes range in price from $200 to $3,000 and have received critical acclaim. Also for sale are a series of Ms. Spencer's silk-screened scarves, each crafted from extra-heavy stone-washed silk.

The Palms, in the Palms Arcade, Basseterre (☎ 869/465-2599), specializes in island things, including handcrafts; larimar, sea opal, and amber jewelry; West Indies spices, teas, and perfumes; tropical clothes by Canadian designer John Warden; and Bali batiks by Kisha.

Island Hopper, the Circus, below the popular Ballahoo Restaurant, Basseterre (☎ 869/465-1640), is one of St. Kitts's most patronized shops, with the biggest inventory of any store on the island. Notice the all-silk, shift-style dresses from China and the array of batiks made on St. Kitts. About half of the merchandise is from the islands.

✪ **Romney Manor,** Old Road, 10 miles west of Basseterre (☎ 869/465-6253), is the most unusual factory in St. Kitts. It was built around 1625 as a manor house for sugar baron Lord Romney. For years, it has been used as the headquarters and manufacturing center for a local clothier, Caribelle Batik, whose tropical cottons sell widely to cruise-ship passengers and tourists from at least three outlets in the eastern Caribbean. The merchandise ranges from scarves to dresses, along with an extensive collection of wall hangings. In 1995, a tragic fire and hurricane completely gutted the historic building. The manor has now been rebuilt and extended. Consider a stopover here if only to admire the 5 acres of lavish gardens, where 30 varieties of hibiscus, rare orchids, huge ferns, and a 250-year-old saman tree still draw horticultural enthusiasts. Entrance to the gardens is free.

8 St. Kitts After Dark

The **Ocean Terrace Inn's Fisherman's Wharf,** Fortlands, has a live band every Friday from 8 to 10pm and a DJ from 10pm. The **Turtle Beach Bar and Grill,** Turtle Bay on the southeast peninsula, has a popular seafood buffet on Sunday with a live steel band from 12:30 to 3pm; on Saturday, it's beach disco time. There's no cover at either place.

If you're in the mood to gamble, St. Kitts's only casino is at the **Jack Tar Village,** Frigate Bay (☎ **869/465-8651**). It's open to all visitors, who can try their luck at roulette, blackjack, poker, craps, and slot machines. The casino is open daily from 10:30am to 2am. There's no cover.

A few other night spots come and go (mostly go). Currently, **Henry's Night Spot,** Dunn's Cottage, Lower Cayon Street, in Basseterre (☎ **869/465-3508**), is one of the island's most frequented dance clubs. **Bayembi Cultural Entertainment Bar & Café,** just off the Circus in Basseterre (☎ **869/466-5280**), couldn't look junkier, but it's a hot and happening place with a jazz guitarist on Wednesday and the inevitable karaoke on Saturday. Its daily happy hours pack them in at sunset.

On Friday and Saturday nights, locals often head for **J's Place,** Romney Grounds across from Brimstone Hill (☎ **869/465-6264**). The place is often jumping until the early hours. Another fun joint is **Doo-Wop Days,** Memory Lane, Frigate Bay (☎ **869/465-1960**), painted in sherbet colors. The place looks like a junkyard, with its old 1940s photos of such singers as Frank Sinatra and Chuck Berry. Note the velvet Elvis paintings and guitar-shaped pillows. Many nights there's live music, especially from doo-wop groups of yesterday. Saturday is karaoke night.

23 St. Lucia

In very recent years, St. Lucia (pronounced *LOO-sha*), second largest of the Windward Islands, has become one of the most popular destinations in the Caribbean, with some of its finest resorts. The heaviest tourist development is concentrated in the northwest, between the capital of Castries and the northern end of the island, where there's a string of white-sand beaches.

The rest of St. Lucia remains relatively unspoiled, a checkerboard of green-mantled mountains, valleys, banana plantations, a bubbling volcano, wild orchids, and fishing villages. There's a hint of the South Pacific about the island, as well as a mixed French and British heritage.

A mountainous island of some 240 square miles, St. Lucia has about 120,000 inhabitants. The capital, **Castries,** is built on the southern shore of a large harbor surrounded by hills. The approach to the airport is very impressive.

Native son Derek Walcott was born in Castries. His father was an unpublished poet who died when Walcott was just a year old, and his mother was a former headmistress at the Methodist school on St. Lucia. In 1992, Walcott won the Nobel Prize for literature. He prefers, however, not to tout the charms of St. Lucia, telling the press, "I don't want everyone to go there and overrun the place." His warning has come too late.

1 Essentials

VISITOR INFORMATION

In the **United States,** the St. Lucia Tourist Board office is at 820 Second Ave., New York, NY 10017 (☎ **800/456-3984** or 212/867-2950).

In the **United Kingdom,** contact the tourist office at 421A Finchley Rd., London NW3 6HJ (☎ **0171/431-3675**).

St. Lucia information is on the Web at **www.st-lucia.com**.

On the island, the main tourist office is at Point Seraphine, Castries Harbour (☎ **758/452-4094**). In Soufrière, there's a branch on Bay Street (☎ **758/459-7200**).

GETTING THERE

Before you book your own airfare, read the section on package tours in chapter 2—it can save you a bundle!

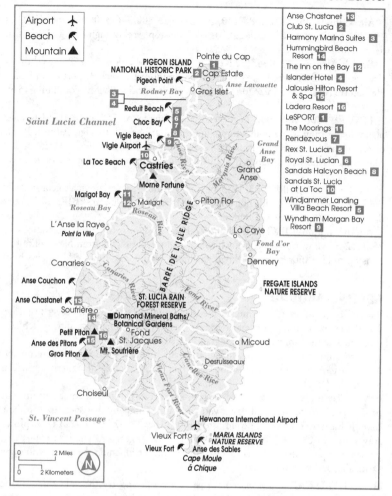

Airport ✈
Beach ⚓
Mountain ▲

Anse Chastanet **13**
Club St. Lucia **2**
Harmony Marina Suites **3**
Hummingbird Beach Resort **14**
The Inn on the Bay **12**
Islander Hotel **4**
Jalousie Hilton Resort & Spa **15**
Ladera Resort **16**
LeSPORT **1**
The Moorings **11**
Rendezvous **7**
Rex St. Lucian **5**
Royal St. Lucian **6**
Sandals Halcyon Beach **8**
Sandals St. Lucia at La Toc **10**
Windjammer Landing Villa Beach Resort **5**
Wyndham Morgan Bay Resort **9**

The island maintains two separate airports, whose different locations cause endless confusion to many newcomers. Most international long-distance flights land at **Hewanorra International Airport** (☎ 758/454-6249) in the south, 45 miles from Castries. If you arrive here and you're booked into a hotel in the north, you'll have to spend about an hour and a half traveling along the potholed East Coast Highway. The average taxi fare is $50 for up to four passengers.

Flights from other parts of the Caribbean usually land at the somewhat antiquated **Vigie Airport** (☎ 758/452-2596), in the northeast. Its location just outside Castries affords much more convenient access to the capital and most of the island's hotels.

You'll probably have to change planes somewhere else in the Caribbean to get to St. Lucia. **American Eagle** (☎ 800/433-7300 or 758/452-1820) serves both of the island's airports with nonstop flights from San Juan. Connections from all parts of the North American mainland to the airline's enormous hub in San Juan are frequent and convenient. American also offers some good package deals.

Air Canada (☎ **800/268-7240** in Canada, 800/776-3000 in the U.S., or 758/454-6038; www.aircanada.ca) has one nonstop weekly flight to St. Lucia that departs from Toronto.

British Airways (☎ **0345/222-111** in England, or 758/452-3778; www.british-airways.com) offers three flights a week from London's Gatwick Airport to St. Lucia's Hewanorra Airport. All these touch down briefly on Antigua before continuing to St. Lucia.

LIAT (☎ **800/468-0482** in the U.S. and Canada, or 758/452-3015) has small planes flying from many points throughout the Caribbean into Vigie Airport. Points of origin include such islands as Barbados, Antigua, St. Thomas, St. Maarten, and Martinique. Know in advance that LIAT flights tend to island-hop en route to St. Lucia.

Air Jamaica (☎ **800/523-5585** or 758/454-8869; www.airjamaica.com) serves the Hewanorra Airport with nonstop service from either New York's JFK or Newark daily, except Wednesday and Friday.

Another option is **BWIA** (☎ **800/292-1183** for North American reservations, or 758/452-3778; www.bwee.com), which has two weekly flights from New York's JFK nonstop to Hewanorra, two weekly flights from Miami, and two weekly flights from London's Gatwick Airport.

GETTING AROUND

BY TAXI   Taxis are ubiquitous on the island, and most drivers are eager to please. The drivers have to be quite experienced to cope with the narrow, hilly, switchback roads outside the capital. Special programs have trained them to serve as guides. Their cabs are unmetered, but tariffs for all standard trips are fixed by the government. Always determine if the driver is quoting a rate in U.S. dollars or Eastern Caribbean dollars (EC$).

Most day tours of the island cost $120, which can be divided among up to four people, and also cut to a half day if you wish. One company that specializes in these tours is **Barnard's Travel**, Micoud Street in Castries (☎ **758/452-2214**). **Explorer Adventure,** in Castries (☎ **758/450-8356**), can arrange a jeep safari for your party, perhaps a trip to the rain forest followed by a barbecue lunch on the beach with some snorkeling and swimming.

BY RENTAL CAR   *Remember to drive on the left,* and try to avoid some of the island's more obvious potholes. Drive carefully and honk your horn while going around the blind hairpin turns. You'll need a St. Lucia driver's license, which can easily be purchased at either airport when you arrive or at the car-rental kiosks when you pick up your car. You'll present a valid driver's license from home to the counter attendant or government official and pay a fee of $12.

All three of the big U.S.-based car-rental companies maintain offices on St. Lucia: **Budget** (☎ **800/527-0700** or 758/452-0233), **Avis** (☎ **800/331-1212** or 758/452-2700), and **Hertz** (☎ **800/654-3001** or 758/452-0679). All three have offices at (or will deliver cars to) both of the island's airports. Each also has an office in Castries and, in some cases, at some of the island's major hotels.

You can sometimes get lower rates by booking through one of the local car-rental agencies, where rates begin at $55 per day. Try **C.T.L. Rent-a-Car,** Grosislet Highway, Rodney Bay Marina (☎ **758/452-0732**). **Cool Breeze Car Rental,** New Development, Soufrière (☎ **758/454-7729**), is also a good bet if you're staying in the south.

BY BUS   Minibuses (with names like "Lucian Love") and jitneys connect Castries with such main towns as Soufrière and Vieux Fort. They're generally overcrowded and often filled with produce on the way to market—but at least they're cheap, unlike taxis. Buses for Cap Estate, in the northern part of the island, leave from Jeremy Street in Castries, near the market. Buses going to Vieux Fort and Soufrière depart from Bridge Street in front of the department store.

Fast Facts: St. Lucia

Banking Hours   Banks are open Monday to Thursday from 8am to 1pm and on Friday from 8am to noon and 3 to 5pm.

Currency   The official monetary unit is the **Eastern Caribbean dollar (EC$).** It's about 37¢ in U.S. currency. *Most of the prices quoted in this section will be in American dollars,* as they are accepted by nearly all hotels, restaurants, and shops.

Customs   At either airport, Customs may be a hassle if there's the slightest suspicion, regardless of how ill-founded, that you're carrying illegal drugs.

Documents   U.S., British, and Canadian citizens need a valid passport, plus an ongoing or return ticket.

Drugstores   See "Pharmacies," below.

Electricity   Visitors from the U.S. will need to bring an adapter and transformer, as St. Lucia runs on 220 to 230 volts AC (50 cycles).

Emergencies   Call the police at ☎ **999.**

Hospitals   There are 24-hour emergency rooms at **St. Jude's Hospital,** Vieux Fort (☎ **758/454-7671**), and **Victoria Hospital,** Hospital Road, Castries (☎ **758/452-2421**).

Language   Although English is the official tongue, St. Lucians probably don't speak it the way you do. Islanders also speak a French-Creole patois, similar to that heard on Martinique.

Pharmacies   The best is **William Pharmacy,** Williams Building, Bridge Street, in Castries (☎ **758/452-2797**), open Monday through Thursday from 8am to 4:30am, Friday from 8am to 5:30pm, and Saturday from 8am to 1pm.

Safety   St. Lucia has its share of crime, like every other place these days. Use common sense and protect yourself and your valuables. If you've got it, don't flaunt it! Don't pick up hitchhikers if you're driving around the island. Of course, the use of narcotic drugs is illegal, and their possession or sale could lead to stiff fines or jail.

Taxes & Service Charges   The government imposes an 8% occupancy tax on hotel rooms, and there's an $11 departure tax for both airports. Most hotels and restaurants add a 10% service charge.

Telephone   On the island, dial all seven digits of the local number. Faxes may be sent from your hotel or from **Cable & Wireless,** in the NAS Building on the waterfront in Castries (☎ **758/452-3301**).

Time   St. Lucia is on Atlantic standard time year-round, placing it 1 hour ahead of New York. However, when the United States is on daylight saving time, St. Lucia matches the clocks of the U.S. East Coast.

Water   Water here is generally considered safe to drink; if you're prudent, however, you'll stick to bottled water.

Weather   This little island, lying in the path of the trade winds, has year-round temperatures of 70° to 90°F.

2 Where to Stay

Most of the leading hotels on this island are pretty pricey; you have to really search for the bargains or else book a package, as many of the big resorts here are frequently featured in such deals (see the section on "Package Deals," in chapter 2). Once you reach your hotel, chances are you'll feel pretty isolated, but that's exactly what most guests want. Many St. Lucian hostelries have kitchenettes where you can prepare simple meals. Prices are usually quoted in U.S. dollars. As mentioned above, an 8% hotel tax and a 10% service charge are added to your bill.

VERY EXPENSIVE

✪ **Anse Chastanet.** Anse Chastanet Beach (P.O. Box 7000, Soufrière), St. Lucia, W.I. ☎ **800/223-1108** in the U.S., or 758/459-7000. Fax 758/459-7700. www.ansechastanet. com. E-mail: ansechastanet@candw.lc. 48 units. Winter $410–$690 double; $495–$858 triple. Off-season $180–$420 double; $234–$495 triple. Winter rates include MAP (breakfast and dinner). AE, MC, V.

One of the few places that merits the cliché "tropical paradise," this is not only St. Lucia's premier dive resort but also an exceptional Caribbean inn. It offers warm service, excellent food, a beach location, and first-class facilities. It lies 18 miles north of Hewanorra International Airport (a 50-minute taxi ride), 2 miles north of Soufrière on a forested hill, and a 103-step climb above palm-fringed Anse Chastanet Beach. You're surrounded by coffee trees, mangos, papayas, banana plants, breadfruit, grapefruit, coconut palms, flamboyants, and hibiscus. The core of the house is a main building decorated in a typical island style, with a relaxing bar and dining room.

Guests can stay on the beach in spacious accommodations styled like West Indian plantation villas. Other units, constructed like octagonal gazebos and cooled by ceiling fans, have views of the Pitons, St. Lucia's famous twin peaks. The spacious rooms are comfortably appointed with locally made furniture crafted from island woods. They have tropical hardwood floors, wooden jalousie louvers, ceiling fans, king beds, and roomy private bathrooms with shower stalls and dual sinks. There are no phones or TVs to disturb you—and no air-conditioning.

Dining: You can dine or drink on a wind-cooled terrace, built like a tree house over the tropical landscape, in the Pitons Bar and Restaurant. Even if you're not a guest of the hotel, consider a stop at the beachside restaurant, Trou au Diable, offering West Indian cuisine and a barbecue grill, plus a twice-weekly Creole dinner buffet.

Amenities: Five-star PADI dive operation, waterskiing, sailboat rentals. Laundry, baby-sitting (no children under 4), transfers from the airport (available with advance notification).

✪ **Jalousie Hilton Resort & Spa.** P.O. Box 251, Soufrière, St. Lucia, W.I. ☎ **800/HILTONS** in the U.S. for reservations only, or 758/459-7666. Fax 758/459-7667. www. jalousie-hilton.com. E-mail: jar_sales&mkt@candw.lc. 112 units. A/C TV TEL. Winter $400 Sugar Mill double; $500 villa; $600 villa suite. Off-season $250 Sugar Mill double; $300 villa; $350 villa suite. MAP (breakfast and dinner) $75 per person extra. Honeymoon, dive, and spa packages available. AE, CB, DC, DISC, MC, V. Small pets allowed.

For visitors to St. Lucia's southwest coast who require a bit more luxury than can be found at Ladera or Anse Chastanet, Hilton has recently refurbished (for $6 million) this sprawling resort. Among other improvements, Hilton has added an inviting, gently sloping white-sand beach. The location, between the Pitons, is one of the most scenic in the Caribbean. The property is so large that vans constantly circulate to ferry guests around. Set on 325 acres, most of the resort's accommodations are in individual villas or villa suites (slightly larger, with separate sitting rooms) that dot the hillside. All the tile-floored villa rooms have four-star amenities, including remote-control air-conditioning, satellite TV, VCRs, excellent mattresses, fold-out sofas, in-room safes, coffeemakers, and fluffy bathrobes. All villas and suites also have private plunge pools. Our only complaint is that the degree of privacy is not always enough to allow, say, nude sunbathing. In addition to the villas, 12 Sugar Mill double rooms are in two buildings; they're slightly smaller, but still have private terraces. The staff here is especially friendly and helpful.

Dining/Diversions: Breakfast is served at the Verandah; the Bayside Bar & Grill is an inviting, informal buffet lunch spot on the beach; the Pier Restaurant, which features seafood and Creole specialties, offers live entertainment most nights; the Plantation Restaurant is the formal room. Chef Frederic Maigrot's inventive cuisine is ambitious but best when he concentrates on flavorful, locally available ingredients. Desserts are uniformly divine.

Amenities: Full-service spa with sauna and Jacuzzi, plus exquisite views of the Pitons; fully equipped fitness center (aerobic classes offered daily); air-conditioned squash court; four Laykold tennis courts; complimentary water sports (kayaks, paddleboats, snorkeling, Sunfish, aquacycle, windsurfing); PADI-approved scuba center; par-3 "executive" golf course; nearby nature trails; excellent full program of children's activities; business center; tour desk; beauty salon; room service.

✪ **Ladera Resort.** P.O. Box 225, Soufrière, St. Lucia, W.I. ☎ **800/738-4752** in the U.S. and Canada, or 758/459-7323. Fax 758/459-5156. http://ladera-resort.com. E-mail: reservtions@ladera.stlucia.com. 24 units. Winter $330–$475 suite; $505–$690 villa. Off-season $195–$295 suite; $325–$490 villa. Extra person $15–$40. MAP (breakfast and dinner) $48 per person extra. 7-night minimum stay Dec 18–Jan 4. AE, DISC, MC, V.

The Ladera is an exercise in luxurious simplicity on St. Lucia's southwest end, a frequent retreat for the rich and famous who seek total privacy from the outside world: There are no phones or TVs in the rooms. Outside the town of Soufrière, this hideaway is perched on a hillside 1,100 feet above sea level. Sandwiched between the Pitons, the resort has views of Jalousie Bay—perhaps the most stunning vistas you are likely to find on St. Lucia. The villas and suites are completely open to the views of the Pitons and cooling breezes (units are not air-conditioned). You don't come here for the beach—it's a complimentary 15- to 20-minute shuttle ride away—but for the lovely setting, gracious service, and privacy.

Accommodations are constructed of tropical hardwoods, stone, and tile, and are furnished with 19th-century French furniture, wicker, and accessories built by local craftspeople. You'll find interesting touches in all the rooms—sinks made of shells, or open, rock-walled showers. All units afford total privacy and have indoor gardens and plunge pools; some have two terraces so that you can still sit outside when the afternoon sun sets behind the bay. Many rooms have four-poster queens draped in mosquito netting, and most have fridges. To get in here in winter, reserve 4 months in advance.

Dining: The Dasheene Restaurant & Bar offers fine dining, specializing in a local Creole and continental cuisine. The seafood is caught fresh daily. Guests enjoy high tea in Ladera's botanical garden.

Amenities: Large pool and deck below the restaurant and bar, horseback riding, scuba-diving and snorkel trips, sailboating, fishing charters. Shuttle service to the beach at Anse de Pitons, complimentary transportation to and from the town of Soufrière and Hewanorra International Airport.

LeSPORT. P.O. Box 437, Cariblue Beach, St. Lucia, W.I. ☎ **800/544-2883** in the U.S. and Canada, or 758/450-8551. Fax 758/450-0368. E-mail: reservations@lesportstlucia.com. 102 units. A/C TEL. Winter $580–$670 double; $750 suite. Off-season $450–$530 double; $700 suite. Children 6–15 get a 50% discount, ages 5 and under $20 per day. Rates are all-inclusive. AE, DISC, MC, V.

LeSPORT cares for your body with first-class pampering, but it isn't a hotel for jocks, as the name suggests. It's set on a 1,500-acre estate at the northernmost tip of the island, an 8-mile run from Castries; guests seem to prefer this isolation.

The resort makes a promise faithfully kept: Everything you "do, see, enjoy, drink, eat, and feel" is included in the price. That means not only accommodations, three meals a day, all refreshments, and bar drinks, but also use of sports equipment, facilities, and instruction, plus airport transfers. Units are in a four-story building on a hill site fronting a long palm-fringed beach. Bedrooms are roomy and beautifully appointed, with fridges, white wicker furnishings, and king or paired twin beds. Bathrooms are spacious, with tubs and showers, dual basins, and hair dryers. The resort offers a full fitness program and a selection of relaxation classes, such as stress management, tai chi, and yoga.

Dining/Diversions: Meals are served in an open-air restaurant overlooking the Caribbean. Breakfast and lunch are buffet style; dinner offers a choice between lighter-style dishes and "not-so-light" options. Nonguests are welcome to dine here. The food is arguably the best of that offered by the all-inclusive resorts. There's live entertainment, and a piano bar that's popular until late at night.

Amenities: Full program of daily scuba diving, windsurfing, waterskiing, snorkeling, sailing, fencing, archery, and bike riding; pool; floodlit tennis court; rather basic exercise room; emphasis on European body tonics based on thalassotherapy, involving seawater massage, thermal jet baths, toning, and beauty treatments for both sexes. Room service (for breakfast), transfers to and from the airport. Laundry, babysitting, and salon available at additional charge.

Rendezvous. P.O. Box 190, Malabar Beach, St. Lucia, W.I. ☎ **800/544-2883** in the U.S. and Canada, or 758/452-4211. Fax 758/452-7419. www.rendezvous.com.lc. E-mail: rendezvous@candw.lc. 100 units. A/C TEL. Winter $380–$455 double; $485–$510 suite for 2. Off-season $340–$410 double; $440–$475 suite for 2. Rates are all-inclusive. AE, DISC, MC, V. Children not accepted.

On Malabar Beach, Rendezvous (formerly Couples, St. Lucia) is an unusual hotel, where all meals, drinks, entertainment, and most incidental expenses are included in the initial price. There are several price categories, depending on the season and the accommodation; top rates are charged for oceanfront luxury suites for two. A recent major refurbishment has involved the installation of marble floors, replacement of furnishings (including mattresses), and a general upgrading. Many beds are four-poster kings draped in mosquito netting. The bathrooms are small but have combination shower/tubs, lighted makeup mirrors, dual basins, and hair dryers. Balconies and terraces are common to all units. The resort is north of Vigie Airport, near Castries, set within a 7-acre tropical garden on the edge of a beach. The center of the complex is under a gridwork of peaked, terra-cotta-tile ceilings. Only male/female couples are accepted.

Dining/Diversions: The Trysting Place, a classical colonial-style dining room, is highlighted by polished brass chandeliers. The informal, open-air Terrace Restaurant features pastas as well as traditional favorites. For live entertainment 6 nights a week, guests frequent the Piano Bar.

Amenities: Two freshwater outdoor pools, swim-up bar at the free-form pool with landscaped island, fitness center, sauna, scuba-diving facilities, waterskiing, tennis courts, prearranged picnics, windsurfing, beach volleyball, fitness classes, bicycle tours. A member of the staff will meet your plane at the airport.

Royal St. Lucian. P.O. Box 512, Reduit Beach, St. Lucia. W.I. ☎ **800/255-5859** in the U.S. and Canada, or 758/452-9999. Fax 758/452-9639. www.rexcaribbean.com. 96 suites. A/C TV TEL. $475–$725 double; $625–$975 triple. Off-season $390–$640 double; $530–$880 triple. AE, MC, V.

Built in the late 1980s in a low-rise beachfront format, this hotel is a classy joint— which you'll know as you enter its reception area, built to resemble an Italian palazzo with marble walls, bubbling fountains, a regal staircase, and a vaulted atrium. Set 7 miles north of Castries, the complex is surrounded by beautiful gardens of royal palms and tropical flowers. The all-suite accommodations are plush and spacious, with louvered shutters separating bedrooms from sunken living areas, tile floors covered with rich toned rugs, private safes, king or twin beds, and well-equipped bathrooms with hair dryers, scales, and luxury toiletries. The most idyllic rooms are five suites with private sundecks, one with its own small plunge pool. Much of the room decor evokes Palm Beach rather than the Caribbean.

Dining/Diversions: Three in-house restaurants include the upper-bracket l'Epicure; the seafood emporium, La Nautique; and a beachfront veranda within view of the waves, Le Mirage. An assortment of cozy bars, one of which features live entertainment, are scattered throughout the property, always with comfortable seats and unusually stiff drinks.

Amenities: A rectangular pool lined with deck chairs and chaise longues; access to four tennis courts.

Sandals Halcyon Beach. Choc Bay (P.O. Box GM 910, Castries), St. Lucia, W.I. ☎ **800/ SANDALS** or 758/453-0222. Fax 758/451-8435. www.sandals.com. 170 units. TV TEL. All-inclusive rates for 3 nights: Winter $920–$1,210 per person double. Off-season $820–$1,040 per person double. AE, MC, V.

Within walking distance of Palm Beach and a 15-minute drive northeast of Castries, this is the smaller of the two Sandals properties on St. Lucia (see below), with fewer facilities. Many cost-conscious guests choose this 22-acre resort and take advantage of the free, 15-minute minibus rides to its larger twin, Sandals St. Lucia, to use its nine-hole golf course and extensive amenities. Guest rooms come in a wide range of categories, usually with a king-size bed or a mahogany four-poster. Private safes, coffeemakers, and ceiling fans are standard features. Bathrooms have hair dryers and combination shower/tubs. All food, drink, and diversions are included in the all-inclusive price. The food is copious, but not of the highest quality. The best place to dine here is the Pier Restaurant, a West Indian–style restaurant atop a 150-foot pier. Other choices include Mario's, for Italian cuisine, and Bay Side, for international fare. There's also three pools (one with a swim-up bar) and a piano bar, plus a wide array of water sports and diversionary activities. Only male-female couples are welcome.

Sandals St. Lucia at La Toc. La Toc Rd. (P.O. Box 399, Castries), St. Lucia, W.I. ☎ **800/ SANDALS** in the U.S. and Canada, or 758/452-3081. Fax 758/452-1012. www.sandals.com. E-mail: sandalslu@candw.lc. 273 units. A/C TV TEL. All-inclusive rates for 3 nights: Winter $980–$1,970 per person double; $1,400–$1,970 per person suite. Off-season $900–$1,720 per person double; $1,210–$1,720 per person suite. AE, DC, MC, V. Children not accepted.

The Jamaica-based Sandals opened this clone on a forested 155-acre site that slopes steeply down to the sea. The hotel is a 10-minute drive west of Castries on the island's northwestern coast. Centered around a gazebo-capped pool that incorporates an artificial waterfall, a swim-up bar, and a dining pavilion, the resort offers larger-than-expected guest rooms that contain king-size four-poster beds with mahogany headboards, balconies or patios, coffeemakers, safes, and pastel tropical decor. Bathrooms are spacious with combination shower/tubs and hair dryers. Only male/female couples are accepted.

Dining/Diversions: The resort's five restaurants are infinitely superior to the cuisine served at Sandals Halcyon Beach (see above). The most upscale, La Toc, features French cuisine. Kimonos offers Japanese food cooked on a heated table top, teppanyaki style. The main dining room serves continental fare; Les Pitons offers St. Lucian specialties. The Arizona Restaurant, as befits its name, features the cuisine of the American Southwest. After dark, guests gravitate to Jaime's, the nightclub/disco, or to Herbie's Piano Bar.

Amenities: Nine-hole golf course, five tennis courts (lit at night), health club, a series of "neighborhood Jacuzzis" that appear unexpectedly in different areas of the resort. Massage, hairdresser/manicurist, currency exchange, tour desk.

Wyndham Morgan Bay Resort. Choc Bay (P.O. Box 2167, Gros Islet), St. Lucia, W.I. ☎ **800/822-4200** in the U.S., or 758/450-2511. Fax 758/450-1050. 238 units. A/C TV TEL. Winter $470–$540 double. Off-season $380–$440 double. Year-round $630 suite for 2. Rates are all-inclusive. Winter children 13–18 staying in parents' room pay $80, children 3–12 pay $55, children under 3 stay free. Off-season children 17 and under stay free in parents' room. AE, DC, DISC, MC, V.

Set a 10-minute drive north of Castries, on 45 landscaped acres partially shaded with trees and flowering shrubs, this all-inclusive resort draws more Europeans than Americans. Opened in 1992 and operated by the Wyndham chain, it offers guest rooms in six different annexes. Standard features include patios or verandas, rattan and wicker furnishings, safes, fridges, coffeemakers, and single queen or paired twin beds. The spacious marble-trimmed bathrooms contain hair dryers and combination shower/tubs. Unlike some other all-inclusive hostelries on the island, this one welcomes children. The beach here is small, with murky water.

Dining/Diversions: You can dine by candlelight at the resort's premier restaurant, the Trade Winds, overlooking the garden. Palm Grill, the snack bar and grill, overlooks the beach and offers a nightly buffet dinner, often a theme night. The cuisine is resort standard, nothing more. Local musicians, steel bands, and calypso singers often perform live in the Sundowner Bar.

Amenities: A heart-shaped freshwater pool, four tennis courts (two lit at night), fitness center (with saunas, Jacuzzis, and steam room), archery, croquet, water sports. Car-rental kiosk, tour desk, Kids Club (for ages 5 to 12).

EXPENSIVE

Club St. Lucia. Smugglers Village (P.O. Box 915), St. Lucia, W.I. ☎ **800/777-1250** in the U.S., or 758/450-0551. Fax 758/450-0281. www.clubsinternational.com. E-mail: rmichelin@clubsinternational.com. 372 units. TV TEL. Winter $284–$337 double; $344–$399 triple. Off-season $257–$312 double; $319–$372 triple. Rates are all-inclusive. AE, DC, MC, V.

The most economical but also the least luxurious all-inclusive resort on the island sits in Cap Estate on a 50-acre site, an area near LeSPORT. It's 8 miles north of Vigie Airport at the northern tip of the island. Very sports- and entertainment-oriented, the hotel opens onto a curved bay where smugglers used to bring in brandies, cognacs, and cigars from Martinique. The club's core is a wooden building with decks overlooking a free-form pool. The accommodations are in simple bungalows scattered over landscaped grounds. Each features one king-size or two twin beds, air-conditioning and/or ceiling fans, and patios or terraces. Bathrooms have recently been upgraded, with makeup mirrors, marble vanities, and excellent showers. Thoughtful extras include irons and ironing boards and coffeemakers. Your fellow guests are likely to be vacationing Brits, Germans, or Swiss.

Dining/Diversions: The inclusive package is impressive, offering all meals, even snacks, along with unlimited beer, wine, and mixed drinks both day and night. The food is standard resort fare, but you'll never go hungry here. Guests can dine in the regular restaurant, Lakatan; sample the seafood at Lambi's; or head to the pizza parlor. To break the monotony, guests are often transported to the Great House, a restaurant at Cap Estate, where they receive a discount on meals. Other activities include free movies and nightly entertainment.

Amenities: Day or night tennis, unlimited water sports (waterskiing, Sunfish sailing, windsurfing, snorkeling, and paddleboats), three pools, two beaches, children's Mini Club with a playground and a supervised activities program. Laundry, baby-sitting, shuttle bus to Rodney Bay and Reduit Beach.

✪ **Windjammer Landing Villa Beach Resort.** Labrelotte Bay (P.O. Box 1504, Castries), St. Lucia, W.I. ☎ **800/743-9609** in the U.S., 800/267-7600 in Canada, 0171/234-0600 in the United Kingdom, or 758/452-0913. Fax 758/452-9454. www.wlv-resort.com. E-mail: windjammer@candw.lc. 210 units. A/C TV TEL. Winter $240–$280 double; $360–$450 one-bedroom villa for two; $580 two-bedroom villa for four. Winter rates are 15%–20% higher Dec 20–Jan 3. Off-season $160–$190 double; $260–$320 one-bedroom villa for two; $400 two-bedroom villa for four. Up to two extra occupants are allowed in the villas (but not in the double rooms) at $45 each per night. MAP (breakfast and dinner) $55 extra. AE, DC, MC, V.

Windjammer, set on 55 tropical acres north of Reduit Beach, about a 15-minute drive from Castries, is a quiet, luxurious retreat, one of the most glamorous in the West Indies. The resort was designed with a vaguely Moorish motif heavily influenced by Caribbean themes; pastel colors predominate. It's composed of a cluster of white villas climbing a forested hillside above a desirable beach. This is an all-suite/villa resort (the larger villas have private plunge pools), making it a good choice for families or anyone who likes a lot of space. Standard features include coffeemakers, ceiling fans, fridges, private safes, and queen or paired twin beds. The roomy villas offer separate living and dining rooms, full kitchens, cassette players, and VCRs upon request. All bedrooms adjoin private bathrooms and open onto sun terraces. Some bathrooms have showers only.

Dining: The resort contains more restaurants per capita than most of its competitors. The most elegant of the lot is Mango Tree. Josephine's serves breakfast and a three-times-per-week evening barbecue. Papa Don's is an Italian trattoria specializing in pizza and pasta. Jammer's restaurant and bar is a nautically styled, informal bar/steakhouse/grill.

Amenities: Water sports, horseback riding, greens fees, tennis courts. Largest freshwater pool on the island, with built-in waterfalls. Fitness center, children's program, health and beauty club. Room service, baby-sitting.

MODERATE/INEXPENSIVE

✪ **Harmony Marina Suites.** Rodney Bay Lagoon (P.O. Box 155, Castries), St. Lucia, W.I. ☎ **758/452-0336.** Fax 758/452-8677. E-mail: harmony@candw.lc. 30 units. A/C TV TEL. Winter $127–$169 double. Off-season $105–$148 double. Extra person $20. AE, MC, V.

Between 1992 and 1993, this set of two-story buildings, a short walk from one of the island's finest beaches at Reduit, was renovated and upgraded. Originally built in 1980, the complex now offers well-maintained accommodations at reasonable rates. The suites, decorated in rattan, wicker, and florals, sit adjacent to a saltwater lagoon, where boats find refuge from the rough waters of the open sea. Each unit offers a patio or balcony with views of moored yachts, the lagoon, and surrounding hills. All suites, except the VIP/honeymoon units, have sofa beds. Each VIP suite features a double Jacuzzi, a four-poster queen bed on a pedestal, a sundeck, white rattan furnishings, and a bidet. Eight of the suites contain kitchenettes, complete with coffeemakers, fridges, and wet bars—ideal for families on a budget. Bathrooms are small, of the routine motel variety, but are tidily maintained.

Hummingbird Beach Resort. Soufrière, (P.O. Box 280) St. Lucia, W.I. ☎ **758/459-7232.** Fax 758/459-7033. www.best-caribbean.com/hummingbird. E-mail: hbr@candw.lc. 11 units. Winter $135 double; $145 suite; $250 cottage for 2–4. Off season $80 double; $95 suite; $150 cottage for 2–4. AE, DISC, MC, V.

Set on three-quarters of an acre of verdantly landscaped grounds, this is a small, charming, and carefully maintained inn that enjoys direct access to a sandy strip of beachfront, on the northern edge of Soufrière on St. Lucia's southwest coast. Originally conceived as the private vacation home of a Canadian investor, it was transformed in the mid-1970s into this hotel, thanks to the enlargement of the original building. There's a restaurant—the Hummingbird—on the premises (see "Where to Dine," below), plus a bar and a pool. Bedrooms are sheathed in white stucco, accented with varnished hardwoods such as mahogany, and usually angled for views over the water or the soaring nearby heights of Petit Titon and the rugged landscape of southern St. Lucia. Each has a ceiling fan and mosquito netting that's artfully draped over the sometimes elaborately carved bedsteads. Regrettably, the low wattage in the bedside lamps makes nighttime reading difficult. Bathrooms are very compact, but have combination shower/tubs and adequate shelf space.

The Inn on the Bay. Seaview Ave., Marigot Bay (P.O. Box 387, Castries), St. Lucia, BWI. ☎ **758/451-4260.** Fax 758/451-4264. www.saint-lucia.com. E-mail: info@saint-lucia.com. 4 units. Winter $135 double. Off-season $115 double. AE, MC, V. Closed Aug 15–Sept 15. Children under 18 not accepted.

Although it was established as recently as 1995 with only four units, this small-scale inn has already attracted a healthy percentage of repeat clients. Perched 300 feet above the waters of Marigot Bay on a site that required massive retaining walls to buttress, it's the creative statement of Montréal-born Normand Viau and his wife, Louise Boucher. Abandoning careers as a lawyer and social worker, respectively, they designed the hotel themselves, modeling its blue roof and veranda-ringed style on the island's plantation-house tradition. Today, the centerpiece of their establishment is an open-air terrace, site of a small pool and semiprivate dinners available only to hotel guests. Conducted twice a week and priced at $35, they contribute to the establishment's aura of a small and charming house party. Bedrooms, with 10-foot ceilings, are spacious, comfortably furnished, and airy. By conscious design, none is air-conditioned, although each has a ceiling fan and ample windows for cross-ventilation. Some bathrooms are shower only, but each comes with a hair dryer. This makes for a great romantic escape.

✪ Islander Hotel. Rodney Bay Marina (P.O. Box 907, Castries), St. Lucia, W.I. ☎ **800/ 223-9815** in the U.S., 800/468-0023 in Canada, 212/545-8469 in New York City, or 758/452-8757. Fax 758/452-0958. 64 units. A/C TV TEL. Winter $85 double; $90 studio for one; $95 studio for two; $240 two-bedroom apt for six. Off-season $70 double; $75 studio for one; $85 studio for two; $175 two-bedroom apt for six. Extra person $20. MAP (breakfast and dinner) $28 per person extra. AE, DC, DISC, MC, V.

North of Castries, near the St. Lucian Hotel and Reduit Beach, this well-recommended hotel has an entrance festooned with hanging flowers. A brightly painted fishing boat serves as a buffet table near the pool, and there's a spacious covered bar area perfect for socializing with the owner, Greg Glace. Overlooking a grassy courtyard sheltered with vines and flowers, all guest rooms have good mattresses and well-kept bathrooms. The regular rooms have showers and small bars with minifridges; slightly more expensive are the 20 studios, with kitchenettes and tubs or showers. Four two-bedroom apartments are in an annex across the street. A network of walkways leads to a convivial restaurant. Guests walk a few hundred feet to the beach or take a courtesy bus, a 3-minute ride.

The Moorings. Marigot Bay (P.O. Box 101, Castries), St. Lucia, W.I. ☎ **800/437-7880** in the U.S., or 758/451-4357. Fax 758/451-4353. E-mail: yacht@moorings.com. 16 units. Winter $135 cottage for 2. Off-season $85 cottage for 2. Extra person $15. MAP (breakfast and dinner) $51 per person extra. AE, MC, V.

Operated by a company famous for chartering yachts, the Moorings is at the southern edge of a symmetrically shaped lagoon that author James Michener described as "the most beautiful bay in the Caribbean." The resort consists of a wood-sided, heavily timbered main building and a series of veranda-fronted accommodations that extend over a steeply sloping hillside. A ferryboat makes frequent runs across the bay to a neighboring resort, Marigot Beach Club. Well known in yachting circles for the safe haven provided by Marigot Bay, the Moorings offers an opportunity to swim and sail, or to simply relax and read amid the palm and banana groves. The decor is inspired by the West Indies, with lots of rattan, pastel tones, and open-sided patios. All the spacious rooms have king-size beds; bathrooms are small and compact, equipped with shower stalls. The hotel's restaurant, the Hurricane Hole, is reviewed separately (see "Where to Dine," below). Amenities include a pool, laundry, and baby-sitting. The harbor serves as a base for the Moorings Yacht Charter fleet.

3 Where to Dine

IN CASTRIES

Green Parrot. Red Tape Lane, Morne Fortune. ☎ **758/452-3399.** Reservations recommended. Lunch main courses EC$35–EC$80 ($12.95–$29.60); fixed-price dinner EC$95–EC$115 ($35.15–$42.55). AE, MC, V. Daily 7am–midnight. EUROPEAN/WEST INDIAN.

About 1½ miles east of the center, Green Parrot overlooks Castries Harbour and remains the local hot spot for visitors, expats, and locals. It takes about 12 minutes to walk from downtown, but the effort is worth it. This elegant place is run by chef Harry, who had many years of training in prestigious restaurants and hotels in London, including Claridges. Guests take their time and make an evening of it; many enjoy a before-dinner drink in the Victorian-style salon. You might like to try a Grass Parrot (made from coconut cream, crème de menthe, bananas, white rum, and sugar). The price of a meal in the English-colonial dining room usually includes entertainment, which might be a limbo contest or a fire-eating show. All this may sound gimmicky, but the food doesn't suffer for all the activity. There's an emphasis on St. Lucian specialties and home-grown produce. Try the *christophine au gratin* (a Caribbean squash with cheese) or the Creole soup made with callaloo and pumpkin. There are five kinds of curry with chutney, as well as a selection of omelets and sandwiches at lunch.

Green Parrot also offers some of the island's least expensive lodging; rooms come with air-conditioning and phones. In winter, doubles are $100; in off-season, $80.

San Antoine. Morne Fortune. ☎ **758/452-4660.** Reservations recommended. Main courses EC$50–EC$110 ($18.50–$40.70). AE, MC, V. Mon–Fri 11:30am–2:30pm and 6:30–10:30pm, Sat 6:30–10:30pm. CONTINENTAL/WEST INDIAN.

Constructed in the 19th century as a great house, this restaurant is up the Morne and offers vistas over the capital and the water. Sometime in the 1920s, it was turned into the first hotel on St. Lucia by Aubrey Davidson-Houston, the British portrait painter whose subjects included W. Somerset Maugham. Begin your meal with the classic callaloo soup of the island, then follow with fettuccine Alfredo, or perhaps fresh fish *en papillote.* Lobster Thermidor might also be featured. Frankly, many visitors have found the view and ambience far more stunning than the cuisine, but if you order grilled fish and fresh vegetables, you should have a most satisfying meal.

AT MARIGOT BAY

Hurricane Hole. In the Moorings, Marigot Bay. ☎ **758/451-4357.** Reservations recommended for nonguests. Dinner EC$52–EC$75 ($19.25–$27.75). AE, MC, V. Daily 7:30–10am and 7–10pm. INTERNATIONAL/ST. LUCIAN.

Cozy, candlelit, and nautical, this is the restaurant of the Marigot Bay Resort, which charters yachts to clients from around the hemisphere. The congenial bar does a brisk business before dinner, when the Marigot Hurricane (rum, banana, grenadine, and apricot brandy) is especially popular. Ceiling fans spin languidly as you peruse the menu, which is geared in part to fresh fish fans, as well as dishes with genuine island flavor, especially at dinner. Okra adds zest to the callaloo soup with crab, though we're equally fond of the pumpkin soup blended with herbs and cream. A stuffed crab back is an alluring appetizer, followed by the freshest available fish of the day, which can be served in any number of ways—we prefer au natural with herbs, fresh butter, lemon, and garlic. Meats and poultry range from a spicy Indian curried chicken to smoked pork chops that are grilled to perfection.

IN THE SOUFRIÈRE AREA

Camilla's. 7 Bridge St., Soufrière. ☎ **758/459-5379.** Main courses $10–$33. AE, MC, V. Mon–Sat 8am–11pm. WEST INDIAN.

Set a block inland from the waterfront, one floor above street level, this is a clean and decent Caribbean-style restaurant with simple, unpretentious food. It's operated by a local matriarch, Camilla Alcindor, who will welcome you for coffee, a soda, or Perrier, or for full-fledged dinners that include Caribbean fish Creole, lobster Thermidor, and prime loin of beef with garlic sauce. The food is straightforward but flavorful. Opt for the fish and shellfish instead of the beef, although the chicken curry is a savory choice as well. Lunches are considerably less elaborate and include an array of sandwiches, salads, omelets, and burgers. Our favorite tables are the pair that sit on a balcony overlooking the energetic activities in the street below. Otherwise, the inside tables can get a bit steamy on a hot night, as there's no air-conditioning.

✪ **Dasheene Restaurant & Bar.** In the Ladera Resort, between Gros and Petit Piton. ☎ **758/459-7323.** Reservations recommended. Main courses EC$65–EC$100 ($24.05–$37). AE, MC, V. Daily 8–10am, 11:30am–2:30pm, and 6:30–9pm. CARIBBEAN/CALIFORNIAN.

One of the most widely heralded restaurants on St. Lucia, and definitely the one with the most dramatic setting, this mountaintop hideaway offers some of the most refined and certainly the most creative cuisine on St. Lucia, taking as inspiration the best of the Caribbean/Creole kitchen plus the innovations of California. Start with a garden salad of locally grown greens or the christophene and coconut soup. We're especially fond of the chilled Creole seafood soup, which is reminiscent of gazpacho. Moving on to main dishes, the chef has a special flair for seafood pasta or marinated sirloin steak, and chicken appears stuffed with bread crumbs, sweet peppers, and onions. But the best bet is the catch of the day, likely to be kingfish or red snapper, and grilled to perfection. The chocolate soufflé flambée for dessert makes the night out all the more festive.

The Hummingbird. At the Hummingbird Beach Resort, on the waterfront just north of the main wharf at Soufrière. ☎ 758/459-7232. Platters EC$40–EC$62 ($14.80–$22.95). AE, DC, MC, V. Daily noon–3:30 and 7–11pm. WEST INDIAN/INTERNATIONAL.

The complex that contains this outdoorsy, beach-oriented restaurant consists of about a half-dozen wood-sided buildings. Originally built in the mid-1970s, this simple resort is most appropriately recommended for its restaurant, a raffish-looking veranda that's perched adjacent to the sands of Hummingbird Beach. The cuisine focuses on such West Indian dishes as Creole-style conch, lobster, burgers, steaks, and fillets of both snapper and grouper, punctuated with such American staples as burgers and BLTs. A tiny gift shop on the premises sells batik items crafted by members of the staff.

The Still. Soufrière. ☎ **758/459-7224.** Main courses EC$20–EC$45 ($7.40–$16.65). AE, DC, DISC, MC, V. Daily 8am–5pm. CREOLE.

The first thing you'll see as you drive up the hill from the harbor is a very old rum distillery set on a platform of thick timbers, the home of this restaurant less than a mile east of Soufrière. The site is a working cocoa and citrus plantation that has been in the same St. Lucian family for four generations. The front blossoms with avocado and breadfruit trees, and a mahogany forest is a few steps away. The bar near the front veranda is furnished with tables cut from cross-sections of mahogany tree trunks. In the more formal and spacious dining room, you can feast on excellently prepared St. Lucian specialties, depending on what's fresh at the market that day. Try to avoid the place when it's overrun with cruise-ship passengers or tour groups. There are far better restaurants on St. Lucia, but if it's lunchtime and you're near Diamond Falls, you don't have a lot of choices.

IN RODNEY BAY

The Bistro (On the Waterfront). Rodney Bay. ☎ **758/452-9494.** Reservations recommended. Main courses EC$35–EC$75 ($12.95–$27.75). AE, MC, V. Fri–Wed 5:30–10:30pm. SEAFOOD/INTERNATIONAL.

Operated by Nick and Pat Bowden, a husband-and-wife team of English expatriates, this popular restaurant was designed as a long, thin veranda; it offers more waterfront tables than any other place on the island. The owners may be English, but their bistro has a decidedly French cafe atmosphere, with a comfortable bar area. Many of the owners of the luxury yachts moored alongside the restaurant dine here, knowing that the Bowdens provide the freshest ingredients available. Look to the chalkboards for daily specials. Our favorite appetizer is scallops, lobster, shrimp, and crab au gratin, chopped finely and baked in a creamy sauce with cheese. The seafood bisque is excellent, as are any of the homemade pastas, including a fettuccine with shrimp, mussels, and calamari. In honor of the owners' origins, pub grub such as steak-and-kidney pie is featured as well. And here's your chance to sample a traditional hot and spicy West Indian pepper pot, with beef, lamb, and chicken. Finally, the potato-crusted snapper in a tomato-basil sauce is sublime.

Capone's. Reduit Beach, Rodney Bay. ☎ **758/452-0284.** Reservations recommended. Main courses EC$35–EC$85 ($12.95–$31.45). AE, MC, V. Tues–Sun 6:30–10:30pm. ITALIAN/CARIBBEAN.

Capone's could have been inspired by *Some Like It Hot.* Actually, this is a rendition of a Miami Beach speakeasy from the 1930s. North of Reduit Beach, near the lagoon, it's brightly lit at night. At the entrance is a self-service pizza parlor that also serves burgers and well-stuffed pita-bread sandwiches daily from 11am to 1pm. However, we recommend that you head to the back for a really superb Italian or Caribbean meal, beginning with a drink, perhaps "Prohibition Punch" or a "St. Valentine's Day Massacre," served by "gangster" barmen, who will later present the check in a violin case. A player piano enlivens the mood. If you feel all this atmosphere is a little too cute and gimmicky, rest assured that the dishes here are well prepared, with fresh, quality ingredients. The "Little Caesar" salad leads off many a meal, and the creamy lasagna is a special favorite. The safest bet is the fresh local charcoal-grilled fish or some of the best steaks on the island.

The Charthouse. Reduit Beach, Rodney Bay. ☎ **758/452-8115.** Reservations recommended. Main courses EC$45–EC$100 ($16.65–$37). AE, MC, V. Mon–Sat 6–10:30pm. AMERICAN/CREOLE.

In a large building with a skylit ceiling and a mahogany bar, the Charthouse is one of the oldest restaurants in the area and one of the island's most popular dining venues. It was built several feet above the bobbing yachts of the lagoon, without walls, to allow an optimal view of the water. The helpful staff serves simple, honest, good food in large portions. The specialties might include callaloo soup, St. Lucian crab backs, "meat-falling-off-the-bone" baby back spareribs, and fresh local lobster (from September to April, you can often witness the live lobster being delivered from the boat at around 5pm). If you fancy a well-cooked charcoal-broiled steak, you'll see why this dish made the restaurant famous. Of course, traditionalists always visit the Charthouse for one reason only—its roast prime rib of beef, which is never better on St. Lucia than here.

✪ The Lime. Rodney Bay. ☎ **758/452-0761.** Reservations recommended for dinner. Main courses EC$35–EC$75 ($12.95–$27.75). MC, V. Daily 11am–2pm and 6:30–11pm. AMERICAN/CREOLE.

The Lime stands north of Reduit Beach in an area that's known as restaurant row. Some of these places are rather expensive, but the Lime continues to keep its prices low, its food good and plentiful, and its service among the finest on the island. Both locals and visitors come here for "limin'," or hanging out. West Indian in feeling and open-air in setting, the restaurant features a "lime special" drink in honor of its namesake. Specialties include stuffed crab backs and fish steak Creole, as well as shrimp, steaks, lamb and pork chops, and rôti (Caribbean burritos). The steaks are done over a charcoal grill. Nothing is fancy, nothing is innovative, and nothing is nouvelle—just like the savvy local foodies like it. It's cheaper than the more touristy Capone's.

The Mortar & Pestle. In the Harmony Marina Suites, Rodney Bay Lagoon. ☎ **758/ 452-8711.** Reservations recommended, especially for dinner. Main courses EC$50– EC$95 ($18.50–$35.15). MC, V. Daily 7:30am–2:30pm and 3–11pm. CARIBBEAN/ INTERNATIONAL.

Set on the waterfront of Rodney Bay Lagoon, in a previously recommended hotel, this restaurant offers indoor-outdoor dining with a view of the boats moored at the nearby marina. The menu includes select recipes from the various islands of the southern Caribbean, with their rich medley of African, British, French, Spanish, Portuguese, Dutch, Indian, Chinese, and even Amerindian influences. To get you going, try the rich and creamy conch chowder, followed by crab *farci* (a delicious stuffed crab in the shell). Trinidad *rule Jol* (salt codfish with tomatoes, onions, peppers, and lime juice, with pepper sauce), an unusual dish and an acquired taste for some, is also available. To sample something truly regional, try the Barbados *souse*, with marinated pieces of lean cooked pork. A steel band or some other local band sometimes accompanies the meals.

Razmataz! Rodney Bay Marina. ☎ **758/452-9800.** Reservations recommended. Main courses EC$24–EC$55 ($8.90–$20.35). MC, V. Fri–Wed 4pm until the last customer leaves. INDIAN.

Across from the Royal St. Lucian Hotel, this welcome entry into the island cuisine features delectable tandoori dishes, among other offerings. It's in an original Caribbean colonial timbered building with lots of gingerbread, decorated in a medley of colors and set in a garden, a 2-minute walk from the beach. A tempting array of starters greets you, everything from fresh local fish marinated in spicy yogurt and cooked in the tandoor to mulligatawny soup (made with lentils, herbs, and spices). Tandoori delights include shrimp, fresh fish such as snapper or mahimahi, chicken, and mixed grill, not to mention the best assortment of vegetarian dishes on the island. There's live music on weekends, and the owner is often the entertainer.

IN GROS ISLET

Great House. Cap Estate. ☎ **758/450-0450.** Reservations recommended. Main courses $20–$32. AE, DC, DISC, MC, V. Daily 7–10:30pm. FRENCH/CREOLE/INTERNATIONAL.

Built on the foundation stones of the original plantation house of Cap Estate, this restaurant lies under a canopy of ampeche and cedar trees. The inviting ambience extends to the formal dining room, which opens onto a tranquil patio overlooking the sea. French cuisine is served here with Caribbean flair. The service, food, and wine are first rate. The menu is adjusted frequently so that only the freshest of ingredients are used. Begin with a callaloo cream soup or local crab back, with chives and a vinaigrette sauce. Creatively prepared main courses include a seafood casserole with coconut milk. To go local, try the St. Lucian beef, savory chicken, or pork pepper pot. For dessert, the coconut cheesecake with a tropical fruit topping is without equal.

4 Beaches

Since most of the island hotels are built right on the beach, you won't have far to go for swimming. All beaches are open to the public, even those along hotel properties. However, if you use any of the hotel's beach equipment, you must pay for it. We prefer the beaches along the western coast, as a rough surf on the windward (east) side makes swimming there potentially dangerous.

Leading beaches include **Pigeon Island** off the north shore, part of the Pigeon Island National Historic Park. The small beach here has white sand and picnic facilities; it's an ideal place for a picnic. Pigeon Island is joined to the "mainland" of St. Lucia by a causeway, so it's easy to reach. Cleared of its natural growth long ago, the island has since been replanted with palm trees among other tropical trees and shrubs.

The most frequented beach is **Reduit Beach** at Rodney Bay, a mile of soft beige sand fronting very clear waters, a 20-minute drive from Castries. Many water-sports kiosks can be found along the strip bordering Rex St. Lucian Hotel. With all its restaurants and bars, you'll find plenty of refueling stops.

Choc Bay is a long stretch of sand and palm trees on the northwestern coast, convenient to Castries and the big resorts. Its tranquil waters lure swimmers and especially families, including locals, who have small children.

The 2-mile white-sand **Malabar Beach** runs parallel to the Vigie Airport runway, in Castries, to the Rendezvous resort. **Vigie Beach,** north of Castries Harbour, is also popular. It has fine sands, often a light beige in color, sloping gently into crystalline water. **La Toc Beach,** just south of Castries, opens onto a crescent-shaped bay containing golden sand.

Marigot Bay is the quintessential Caribbean cove, framed on three sides by steep emerald hills and skirted by palm trees. There are some small but secluded beaches here. The bay itself is an anchorage for some of the most expensive yachts in the Caribbean.

One of the most charming and hidden beaches of St. Lucia is the idyllic cove of **Anse Chastanet,** north of Soufrière. This is a beach connoisseur's delight. Towering palms provide shade from the fierce noonday sun, while lush hills provide a refreshing contrast to the dark sandy strip. Heading south on the windward side of the island is **Anse des Sables,** opening onto a shallow bay swept by tradewinds that make it great for windsurfing.

The dramatic crescent-shaped bay of **Anse des Pitons** is at the foot of and between the twin peaks of the Pitons, south of Soufrière. The Jalousie Hilton transformed the natural black-sand beach by covering it with white sand; walk through the resort to get to it. It's popular with divers and snorkelers. While here, you can ask about a very special beach reached only by boat, the black volcanic sands and tranquil waters of **Anse Couchon.** With its shallow reefs, snorkeling possibilities, and picture-postcard charm, this beach has become a hideaway for lovers. It's south of Anse-le-Raye.

Finally, you'll discover miles of white sand at the beach at **Vieux Fort,** at the southern end of the island. Reefs protect the gin-clear waters here, making them tranquil and ideal for swimming.

5 Sports & Outdoor Pursuits

BOATING   The most dramatic trip offered is aboard the 140-foot **Brig** *Unicorn* (☎ 758/452-6811), used in the filming of the famous *Roots* TV miniseries. Passengers sail to Soufrière and the twin peaks of the Pitons, among other natural attractions of the island. A full-day sail costs $70. The ship is moored at Vigie Cove in Castries.

CAMPING   Camping is now possible on St. Lucia courtesy of the **Environmental Educational Centre,** a division of the St. Lucia National Trust (☎ 758/452-5005). This reserve, opened in 1998, features 12 campsites (with many more to be added) along a beautiful stretch of beach on historic Anse Liberté, in the fishing town of Canaries, 25 miles southwest of Castries and 8 miles north of Soufrière. Beachfront campsites, available for around $20 per night, offer a view of the harbor and of Martinique on a clear day. There are nearby community bathrooms and community cooking areas. The reserve has 5 miles of hiking trails; staff members give tours of the area and explain the rich emancipation history of the Anse Liberté, which literally translated means "freedom harbor." Camping equipment is available for rent.

DEEP-SEA FISHING   The waters around St. Lucia are known for their game fish, including blue marlin, sailfish, mako sharks, and barracuda, with tuna and kingfish among the edible catches. Most hotels can arrange fishing expeditions. Call **Mako Watersports** (☎ 758/452-0412), which offers half-day fishing trips for $360, full-day trips for $720. **Captain Mike's** (☎ 758/452-7044) also conducts fishing trips, renting boats by the half day for $400 to $550, or a whole day in the $800 to $1,100 price range.

GOLF   St. Lucia has a nine-hole golf course at the **Cap Estate Golf Club,** at the northern end of the island (☎ 758/450-8523). Greens fees are $40 for 18 holes, $30 for 9 holes; there are no caddies. Carts cost from $15 to $25, and clubs can be rented for $10. Hours are from 8am to sunset daily.

HIKING   A tropical rain forest covers a large area in the southern half of St. Lucia, and the St. Lucia Forest & Lands Department has proven to be a wise guardian of this resource. This forest reserve divides the western and eastern halves of the island. Although there are several trails, one of the most popular is the **Barre De L'Isle Trail,** located almost in the center of St. Lucia, southeast of Marigot Bay; it's a fairly easy trail that even children can handle. There are four panoramic lookout points, where you'll have a dramatic view of the sea where the Atlantic Ocean meets the Caribbean. It takes about an hour to walk this mile-long trail, which lies about a 30-minute ride from Castries. Guided hikes can usually be arranged through the major hotels or through the **Forest and Lands Department** (☎ 758/450-2231 or 758/450-2078).

HORSEBACK RIDING North of Castries, you can ride at **Cas-En-Bas.** To make arrangements, call René Trim (☎ **758/450-8273**). The cost is $40 for 1 hour, $50 for 2 hours. Ask about a picnic trip to the Atlantic, with a barbecue lunch and drinks included, for $60. Departures on horseback are at 8:30am, 10am, 2pm, and 4pm.

PARASAILING Some say the most panoramic view of the northwest coast is from a point high over Rodney Bay. Parasailing is the key to this, and it's available at the water-sports kiosk at the **Rex St. Lucian Hotel** at Rodney Bay (☎ **758/452-8351**). The cost is $40.

SCUBA DIVING In Soufrière, **Scuba St. Lucia,** in the Anse Chastanet Hotel (☎ **758/459-7000**), offers one of the world's top dive locations at a five-star PADI dive center. At the southern end of Anse Chastanet's quarter-mile-long, secluded beach, it features premier diving and comprehensive facilities for divers of all levels. Some of the most spectacular coral reefs of St. Lucia, many only 10 to 20 feet below the surface, lie a short distance from the beach and provide shelter for many marine denizens and a backdrop for schools of reef fish.

Many professional PADI instructors offer four dive programs a day. Photographic equipment is available for rent (film can be processed on the premises), and instruction is offered in picture taking. Experienced divers can rent the equipment they need on a per item basis. The packages include tanks, backpacks, and weight belts. PADI certification courses are available. A 2- to 3-hour introductory lesson costs $75 and includes a short theory session, equipment familiarization, development of skills in shallow water, a tour of the reef, and all equipment. Single dives cost $35. Hours are from 8am to 5:45pm daily.

Another full-service scuba center is now available on St. Lucia's southwest coast at the new **Jalousie Hilton,** at Soufrière (☎ **758/459-7666**). The PADI center offers dives in St. Lucia's National Marine Park; there are numerous shallow reefs near the shore. The diver certification program is available to hotel guests and other visitors ages 12 and up. Prices range from a single dive for $55 to a certification course for $425. Monday through Saturday, there's a daily resort course for noncertified divers that includes a supervised dive from the beach; it costs $70. All prices include equipment, tax, and service charges.

Rosamond Trench Divers, at the Marigot Beach Club, Marigot Bay (☎ 758/451-4761), is adjacent to the waters of the most famous bay on St. Lucia. The outfit takes both novices and experienced divers to shallow reefs or to some of the most challenging trenches in the Caribbean. A resort course designed for novices (including theory, a practice dive in sheltered waters, and one dive above a reef) costs $75. A one-tank dive for certified divers, with all equipment included, goes for $50; a two-tank dive, $70; and a night dive, $65. A six-dive package is $190; a 10-dive package, $300.

TENNIS The best place for tennis on the island is the **St. Lucia Racquet Club,** adjacent to Club St. Lucia (☎ **758/450-0551**). It opened in 1991 and quickly became one of the finest tennis facilities in the Lesser Antilles. Its seven courts are maintained in state-of-the-art condition, and there's also a good pro shop on site. You must reserve 24 hours in advance. Guests of the hotel play for free; nonguests are charged EC$25 ($9.25) a day. Tennis racquets rent for EC$20 ($7.40) per hour.

If you're in the southern part of the island, a good, new program is offered by the **Jalousie Hilton,** at Soufrière (☎ 758/459-7666). Vernon Lewis, the top-ranked player in St. Lucia and an 11-time Davis Cup singles winner, is the pro. You'll find four brand-new Laykold tennis courts (three lit for night play). Hotel guests play for free (though they pay for lessons). Nonguests can play for EC$25 ($9.25) per hour.

OTHER WATER SPORTS   Unless you're interested in scuba (in which case you should head for the facilities at the Anse Chastenet Hotel), the best all-around water-sports center is **St. Lucian Watersports,** at the Rex St. Lucian Hotel (☎ 758/452-8351). Waterskiing costs $12 for a 10- to 15-minute ride. Windsurfers can be rented for $15 for half an hour or $22 an hour. Snorkeling is free for guests of the hotel; nonguests pay $8 per hour, including equipment.

6 Exploring the Island

Lovely little towns, beautiful beaches and bays, mineral baths, banana plantations—St. Lucia has all this and more. You can even visit a volcano.

ORGANIZED TOURS   Most hotel front desks will make arrangements for tours that take in all the major sights of St. Lucia. For example, **Sunlink Tours,** Reduit Beach Avenue (☎ 758/452-8232), offers many island tours, including full-day boat trips along the west coast of Soufrière, the Pitons, and the volcano; the cost is $80 per person. Plantation tours go for $56, and jeep safaris can be arranged for $80. One of the most popular jaunts is a rain-forest ramble for $55, and there's also a daily shopping tour for $20. The company has tour desks and/or representatives at most of the major hotels.

CASTRIES   The capital city has grown up around its **harbor,** which occupies the crater of an extinct volcano. Charter captains and the yachting set drift in here, and large cruise-ship wharves welcome vessels from around the world. Because it has been hit by several devastating fires (most recently in 1948) that destroyed almost all the old buildings, the town today has a look of newness, with glass-and-concrete (or steel) buildings replacing the French colonial or Victorian look typical of many West Indian capitals.

Castries may be architecturally dull, but its **public market** is one of the most fascinating in the West Indies, and our favorite people-watching site on the island. It goes full blast every day of the week except Sunday, and is most active on Friday and Saturday mornings. The market stalls are a block from Columbus Square along Peynier Street, running down toward the water. The country women dress up in traditional garb and cotton headdresses; the number of knotted points on top reveals their marital status (ask one of the locals to explain it to you). The luscious fruits and vegetables of St. Lucia may be new to you; the array of color alone is astonishing. Sample one of the numerous varieties of bananas—they're allowed to ripen on the tree, and taste completely different from those picked green and sold at supermarkets in the United States. Nearby, weather-beaten men sit playing warrie, a fast game using pebbles on a carved board. You can also pick up St. Lucian handcrafts such as baskets and unglazed pottery here.

To the south of Castries looms **Morne Fortune,** the inappropriately named "Hill of Good Luck" (though no one ever had much luck here). In the 18th century, some of the most savage battles between the French and the British took place here. You can visit the military cemetery, a small museum, the old powder magazine, and the "Four

Apostles Battery" (a quartet of grim muzzle-loading cannons). Government House, now the official residence of the governor-general of St. Lucia, is one of the few examples of Victorian architecture that escaped destruction by fire. The private gardens are beautifully planted, aflame with scarlet and purple bougainvillea. Morne Fortune also offers what many consider the most scenic lookout perch in the Caribbean. The view of the harbor of Castries is panoramic: You can see north to Pigeon Island or south to the Pitons; on a clear day, you may even spot Martinique. To reach Morne Fortune, head east on Bridge Street.

○ **PIGEON ISLAND NATIONAL LANDMARK**   St. Lucia's first national park was originally an island flanked by the Caribbean on one side and the Atlantic on the other. It's now joined to the mainland island by a causeway. On its west coast are two white-sand beaches (see "Beaches," above). There's also a restaurant, Jambe de Bois, named after a wooden-legged pirate who once used the island as a hideout.

Pigeon Island offers an **Interpretation Centre,** equipped with artifacts and a multimedia display on local history, ranging from the Amerindian occupation of A.D. 1000 to the Battle of the Saints, when Admiral Rodney's fleet set out from Pigeon Island and defeated Admiral De Grasse in 1782. The Captain's Cellar Olde English Pub lies under the center and is evocative of an 18th-century English bar.

Pigeon Island, only 44 acres in size, got its name from the red-neck pigeon, or ramier, that once made this island home. It's ideal for picnics, weddings, and nature walks. The park is open daily from 9am to 5pm, charging an entrance fee of EC$10 ($3.70). For more information, call the **St. Lucia National Trust** (☎ 758/ 452-5005).

RODNEY BAY   This scenic bay is a 15-minute drive north of Castries. Set on a man-made lagoon, it has become a chic center for nightlife, hotels, and restaurants— in fact, it's the most active place on the island at night. Its marina is one of the top water-sports centers in the Caribbean, and a destination every December for the Atlantic Rally for Cruisers, when yachties cross the Atlantic to meet and compare stories.

MARIGOT BAY   Movie crews, including those for Rex Harrison's *Dr. Doolittle* and Sophia Loren's *Fire Power,* have used this bay, one of the most beautiful in the Caribbean, for background shots. Eight miles south of Castries, it's narrow yet navigable by yachts of any size. Here Admiral Rodney camouflaged his ships with palm leaves while lying in wait for French frigates. The shore, lined with palm trees, remains relatively unspoiled, but some building sites have been sold. It's a delightful spot for a picnic. A 24-hour ferry connects the bay's two sides.

SOUFRIÈRE   This little fishing port, St. Lucia's second-largest settlement, is dominated by two pointed hills called ○ **Petit Piton and Gros Piton.** The Pitons, two volcanic cones rising to 2,460 and 2,619 feet, have become the very symbol of St. Lucia. Formed of lava and rock, and once actively volcanic, they are now covered in green vegetation. Their sheer rise from the sea makes them a landmark visible for miles around, and waves crash at their bases. It's recommended that you only attempt to climb Gros Piton, but doing so requires the permission of the **Forest and Lands Department** (☎ 758/ 450-2231) and the company of a knowledgeable guide.

Near Soufrière lies the famous "drive-in" volcano, ○ **Mount Soufrière,** a rocky lunar landscape of bubbling mud and craters seething with sulfur. You literally drive your car into an old (millions of years) crater and walk between the sulfur springs and pools of hissing steam. Entrance costs EC$3 ($1.10) per person and includes the services of your guide, who will point out the blackened waters, among the few of their kind in the Caribbean. Hours are daily from 9am to 5pm; for more information, call ☎ 758/459-5500.

Discovering "Forgotten" Grande Anse

The northeast coast is the least visited and least accessible part of the island, but contains the most dramatic rockbound shores interspersed with secret sandy coves. The government has set Grand Anse aside as a nature reserve, so it will never be developed. The terrain is arid and can be unwelcoming, but is fascinating nonetheless. Grande Anse is home to some rare bird species, notably the white-breasted thrasher, as well as the fer-de-lance, the only poisonous snake on the island (but visitors report rarely seeing one). Its series of beaches—Grande Anse, Petite Anse, and Anse Louvet—is a nesting ground for sea turtles, including the hawksbill, the green turtle, the leatherback, and loggerhead. Nesting season lasts from February to October. Many locals tackle the poor road in a four-wheel-drive vehicle, especially the bumpiest part from Desbarra to Grande Anse.

Nearby are the ✪ **Diamond Mineral Baths** (☎ 758/452-4759) in the **Diamond Botanical Gardens.** Deep in the lush tropical gardens is the Diamond Waterfall, one of the geological attractions of the island. Created from water bubbling up from sulfur springs, the waterfall changes colors (from yellow to black to green to gray) several times a day. Nearby, the baths were constructed in 1784 on the orders of Louis XVI, whose doctors told him these waters were similar in mineral content to the waters at Aix-les-Bains, they were intended to provide recuperative effects for French soldiers fighting in the West Indies. The baths have an average temperature of 106°F. For EC$7 ($2.60), you can bathe and try out the recuperative effects for yourself.

From Soufrière in the southwest, the road winds toward Fond St-Jacques, where you'll have a good view of mountains and villages as you cut through St. Lucia's Cape Moule-à-Chique tropical rain forest. You'll also see the Barre de l'Isle divide.

7 Nature Reserves

The fertile volcanic soil of St. Lucia sustains a rich diversity of bird and animal life. Some of the richest troves for ornithologists are in protected precincts off the St. Lucian coast, in either of two national parks, Frigate Islands Nature Reserve and the Maria Islands Nature Reserve.

The **Fregate Islands** are a cluster of rocks a short distance offshore from Praslin Bay, midway up St. Lucia's eastern coastline. Barren except for tall grasses that seem to thrive in the salt spray, the islands were named after the scissor-tailed frigate birds (*Fregata magnificens*) that breed here. Between May and July, large colonies of the graceful birds fly in well-choreographed formations over islands that you can only visit under the closely supervised permission of government authorities. Many visitors believe that the best way to admire the Fregate Islands (and to respect their fragile ecosystems) is to walk along the nature trail that the St. Lucian government has hacked along the cliff top of the St. Lucian mainland, about 150 feet inland from the shoreline. Even without binoculars, you'll be able to see the frigates wheeling overhead. You'll also enjoy eagle's-eye views of the unusual geology of the St. Lucian coast, which includes sea caves, dry ravines, a waterfall (which flows only during rainy season), and a strip of mangrove swamp.

The **Maria Islands** are larger and more arid and are almost constantly exposed to salt-laden winds blowing up from the equator. Set to the east of the island's southernmost tip, off the town of Vieux Fort, they contain a strictly protected biodiversity. The approximately 30 acres of cactus-dotted land comprising the two largest islands (Maria

Major and Maria Minor) are home to more than 120 species of plants, lizards, butterflies, and snakes that are believed to be extinct in other parts of the world. These include the large ground lizard (*Zandolite*) and the nocturnal, nonvenomous kouwes snake (*Dromicus ornatus*).

The Marias are also a bird refuge, populated by such species as the sooty tern, the bridled tern, the Caribbean martin, the red-billed tropicbird, and the brown noddy, which usually builds its nest under the protective thorns of prickly pear cactus.

If permission is granted, visitors will set foot in either park as part of a group that arrives by boat under the supervision of a qualified guide. Guided full-day tours cost $30 for the Frigates and $114 for the Marias (the Marias jaunt includes lunch). These must be arranged through the staff of the **St. Lucia National Trust** (☎ 758/ 452-5005), who will supply further details.

8 Shopping

Most of the shopping is in Castries, where the principal streets are William Peter Boulevard and Bridge Street. Many stores will sell you goods at duty-free prices (providing you don't take the merchandise with you but have it delivered to the airport or cruise dock). There are some good (but not remarkable) buys in bone china, jewelry, perfume, watches, liquor, and crystal.

POINTE SERAPHINE

Built for the cruise-ship passenger, Pointe Seraphine, in Castries, has the best collection of shops on the island, together with offices for car rentals, organized taxi service (for sightseeing), a bureau de change, a Philatelic Bureau, an information center, and international phones. Cruise ships berth right at the shopping center. Under red roofs in a Spanish-style setting, the complex requires that you present a cruise pass or an airline ticket to the shopkeeper when purchasing goods. Visitors can take away their purchases, except liquor and tobacco, which will be delivered to the airport. The center is open in winter, Monday to Friday from 8am to 5pm and Saturday from 8am to 2pm; off-season, Monday to Saturday from 9am to 4pm. It's also open when cruise ships are in port.

Little Switzerland (☎ 758/452-7587) sells a broad-based but predictable array of luxury goods. Prices of the porcelain, crystal, perfume, and jewelry are usually around 25% lower than on the North American mainland; wise shoppers should be alert to special promotions. Although it can't compete with the inventory at Little Switzerland, **Colombian Emeralds** (☎ 758/453-7233) has a more diverse selection of watches, gemstones, and gold chains. Of special value are the watches, which sometimes sell for up to 40% less than equivalent retail prices in North America.

Studio Images (☎ 758/452-6883) offers designer fragrances, including some exotic locally made concoctions, often 20% to 40% lower than Stateside prices. The store also carries the latest Sony electronics, leather accessories from Ted Lapidus, Samsonite luggage, and a wide collection of souvenirs.

The **Land Shop** (☎ 758/452-7488) specializes in elegant handbags, garment bags, and briefcases. Prices are at least 25% less than equivalent items sold in North America, and your purchases are, like everything else in the complex, tax-free. Also available is a selection of shoes, although the inventory for women is more varied and interesting than the choices for men.

Oasis (☎ 758/452-1185) sells well-known, brand-name resort clothing. Look for Revo sunglasses, Reef and Naot footwear, Kipling bags, Gottex swimwear, and casual clothing by Gear. There's also a wide range of quality T-shirts for adults and children.

Peer (☎ **758/453-0815**) stocks high-quality, creative, colorful prints and embroidery designs on T-shirts, shorts, and more. There's a large range for children, plus bags, caps, and women's wear. It's a good place to visit for a wearable souvenir or gift. **Benetton** (☎ **758/452-7685**) carries T-shirts, tennis shirts, shorts, suits, and children's wear. Prices are about 20% lower than Stateside.

ELSEWHERE ON THE ISLAND

GABLEWOODS MALL   On Gros Islet Highway, 2 miles north of Castries, this mall contains three restaurants and one of the densest concentrations of shops on the island. The best clothing and sundry shop is **Top Banana** (☎ **758/451-6389**), which carries beachwear, scuba and snorkeling equipment, gifts, inflatable rafts, and casual resort wear. Other branches of this store can be found at both the Rex St. Lucian Hotel and the Windjammer Resort.

Made in St. Lucia (☎ **758/453-2788**) sells only gifts and souvenirs made by local St. Lucia craftspeople. The merchandise includes wood carvings, clay cooking pots, sandals, spices and cooking sauces, T-shirts, paintings, and such jewelry items as necklaces and "love beads" made from seeds and dried berries.

Another worthwhile outlet here is **Sea Island Cotton Shop** (☎ **758/451-6946**), offering an array of quality T-shirts, hand-painted souvenirs, Caribbean spices, beach and swimwear, and elegantly casual clothing.

ALSO IN OR NEAR CASTRIES   At **Noah's Arkade,** Jeremie Street (☎ **758/ 452-2523**), many of the Caribbean handcrafts and gifts are routine tourist items, yet you'll often find something interesting if you browse around: local straw place mats, baskets, rugs, wall hangings, maracas, shell necklaces, locally made bowls, dolls dressed in banana leaves, and warri boards. Additional branches are at Hewanorra International Airport and the Pointe Seraphine duty-free shopping mall.

Bagshaws, La Toc, just outside Castries (☎ **758/451-9249**), is the leading island hand-printer of silk-screen designs. The birds (look for the St. Lucia parrot), butterflies, and flowers of St. Lucia are incorporated into their original designs. The highlights are an extensive line of vibrant prints on linen, clothing and beachwear for both men and women, and the best T-shirt collection on St. Lucia. At La Toc Studios, the printing process can be viewed Monday through Friday. There are three other retail outlets: in the Pointe Seraphine duty-free shopping mall (☎ **758/452-7570**), in Rodney Bay (☎ **758/452-9435**), and at the "Best of St. Lucia" at Hewanorra International Airport, Vieux Fort (☎ **758/454-7784**).

Caribelle Batik, Howelton House, 37 Old Victoria Road, the Morne (☎ **758/ 452-3785**), a 5-minute drive from Castries, is where you can watch St. Lucian artists creating intricate patterns and colors through the ancient art of batik. You can also purchase batik in cotton, rayon, and silk, made up in casual and beach clothing, plus wall hangings and other gift items. Drinks are served in the Dyehouse Bar and Terrace in the renovated Victorian-era building.

Vincent Joseph Eudovic is a master artist and wood carver whose sculptures have gained increasing fame. You can view and purchase his work at **Eudovic Art Studio,** Goodlands, Morne Fortune (☎ **758/452-2747;** fax 758/459-0124). He usually carves his imaginative, free-form sculptures from local tree roots, such as teak, mahogany, and red cedar. Ask to be taken to his private studio, where you'll see his remarkable creations. Eudovic has recently added 10 simply furnished guest rooms, some with kitchenette. These are among the bargains of the island, renting for $40 double without kitchenette, $50 double with kitchenette. Each room has a private bathroom, cable TV, and ceiling fans.

CHOISEUL The coastal village of Choiseul, southwest of Castries, was named during St. Lucia's French-speaking regime, and has ever since been the home of the descendants of Carib Indians whose bloodlines mingled long ago with African slaves. The village's artistic centerpiece is the **Choiseul Art & Craft Center,** La Fargue (☎ 758/459-3226), a government-funded retail outlet and training school that perpetuates the tradition of handmade Amerindian pottery and basketware. Look for place mats, handbags, and even artfully contrived bassinets, priced from EC$250 ($92.50) each, that might make a worthwhile present for expectant parents-to-be.

9 St. Lucia After Dark

There isn't much except the entertainment offered by hotels. In the winter, at least one hotel offers a steel band or calypso music every night of the week. Otherwise, check to see what's happening at **Capone's** (☎ 758/452-0284) and the **Green Parrot** (☎ 758/452-3167), both in Castries.

Indies, at Rodney Bay (☎ 758/452-0727), is a split-floor, soundproof dance club with a large wooden dancing area and stage. There's also a trio of bars, with smoking and no-smoking sections. The DJs keep the joint jumping, with both West Indian and international sounds, often American. The action gets going Wednesday, Friday, and Saturday from 11pm to 4am. There's a cover ranging from EC$15 to EC$25 ($5.55 to $9.25). Indies has opened a bar around the side of the building called the **Back Door,** featuring alternative music and reggae. A sort of rock and sports bar, it serves snacks until 3am.

The Lime at Rodney Bay is a restaurant that operates the **Late Lime Night Club,** Reduit Beach (☎ 758/452-0761), offering entertainment Wednesday to Saturday from 10pm until the crowd folds. Wednesday, Friday, and Saturday are disco nights. The cover is EC$15 ($5.55).

If you'd like to go barhopping, begin at **Waves,** Choc Bay, Castries (☎ 758/451-3000), which is popular with both locals and visitors. Some nights, there's live music or karaoke. **Banana Split,** on St. George's Street in Castries (☎ 758/450-8125), is another popular hangout that often offers live entertainment, as does **Shamrocks Pub,** Rodney Bay (☎ 758/452-8725). This Irish-style pub is especially popular among boaters and gets really lively on weekends.

24 St. Maarten/St. Martin

For an island with a big reputation for its restaurants, hotels, and energetic nightlife, St. Maarten is small—only 37 square miles, about half the area of Washington, D.C. An island divided between the Netherlands and France, St. Maarten (Sint Maarten) is the Dutch half, while St. Martin is French. Legend has it that a gin-drinking Dutchman and a wine-guzzling Frenchman walked around the island to see how much territory each could earmark for his country in a day; the Frenchman outwalked the Dutchman, but the canny Dutchman got the more valuable piece of property.

The divided island is the smallest territory in the world shared by two sovereign states. The only way you'll know you're crossing an international border is when you see the sign BIENVENUE PARTIE FRANÇAISE, attesting to the peaceful coexistence between the two nations. The island was officially split in 1648, and many visitors still ascend Mount Concordia, near the border, where the agreement was reached. Even so, St. Maarten changed hands 16 times before it became permanently Dutch.

Returning visitors who have been "off island" for a while are often surprised and shocked upon arrival in the St. Maarten of today. No longer a sleepy Caribbean backwater, it has expanded like a boomtown in recent years. Many hotels and restaurants sustained serious structural damage from Hurricane Luis in September 1995, but have since reopened with freshly renovated facilities, new and often better menus, and energized staffs. A sense of freshness and rejuvenation now permeates the island.

In fact, you can live far more luxuriously on St. Maarten than you ever could before. Duty-free shopping has turned the island into a virtual mall, and the capital, Philipsburg, is often bustling with cruise-ship hordes. The nightlife is among the best in the Caribbean, with lively happy hours and casinos galore. Sunshine is pretty much guaranteed year-round on St. Maarten, so you can swim, snorkel, and sail almost any day. The island's 36 white-sand beaches remain unspoiled, and the clear turquoise waters are even more enticing.

Despite its natural beauty, much has been lost to the bulldozer on St. Maarten, too. This is obviously not an island for people who don't like crowds, so if "getting away from it all" is your prerogative, we suggest heading over to the nearby Dutch islands of St. Eustatius (Statia) and Saba. Nevertheless, in spite of its problems, including crime, occasional weather woes, traffic congestion, and corruption, St. Maarten continues to attract massive numbers of visitors who want a Caribbean island vacation with a splash of Las Vegas.

The Dutch capital, **Philipsburg,** curves like a toy village along Great Bay. The town lies on a narrow sand isthmus separating Great Bay and the Great Salt Pond. The capital was founded in 1763 by Commander John Philips, a Scot in Dutch employ. To protect Great Bay, Fort Amsterdam was built in 1737.

The main thoroughfare is busy **Front Street,** which stretches for about a mile and is lined with stores selling international merchandise, such as French fashions and Swedish crystal. More shops are along the little lanes, known as *steegijes,* that connect Front Street with Back Street, another shoppers' haven.

The French side of the island has a slightly different character. There are no dazzling sights, no spectacular nightlife. Even the sports scene on St. Martin isn't as well organized as on many Caribbean islands (though the Dutch side has golf and other diversions). Most people come to St. Martin just to relax on its many white-sand beaches. Mostly they come to sample "France in the tropics."

French St. Martin does, however, boast some of the best cuisine in the Caribbean, as well as an extraordinary number of bistros and restaurants. It has a distinctly French air. Policemen, for example, wear *képis.* The towns have names like Colombier and Orléans, the streets are *rues,* and the French flag flies over the *gendarmerie* in Marigot, the capital. Its advocates cite it as distinctly more sophisticated, prosperous, stylish, and cosmopolitan than its neighboring *départements d'outre-mer,* Guadeloupe and Martinique.

French St. Martin is governed from Guadeloupe and has direct representation in the government in Paris. The principal town on the French side is **Marigot,** the seat of the subprefect and municipal council. Visitors come here not only for shopping, as the island is a free port, but also to enjoy the excellent cookery in the Creole bistros.

Marigot is not quite the same size as its counterpart, Philipsburg, in the Dutch sector. It has none of the frenzied pace of Philipsburg, which is often overrun with cruise-ship passengers. In fact, Marigot looks like a French village transplanted to the Caribbean. If you climb the hill over this tiny port, you'll be rewarded with a view from the old fort.

About 20 minutes by car beyond Marigot is **Grand-Case,** a small fishing village that's an outpost of French civilization, with many good restaurants and a few places to stay.

1 Essentials

VISITOR INFORMATION

If you're going to **Dutch St. Maarten,** contact the St. Maarten Tourist Office, 675 Third Ave., Suite 1806, New York, NY 10017 (☎ 800/786-2278 or 212/953-2084). In Canada, the office is at 243 Ellerslie Ave., Willowdale, Toronto, Ontario M2N 1Y5 (☎ 416/223-3501). Once on the island, go to the **Tourist Information Bureau,** in the Imperial Building at 23 Walter Nisbeth Rd. (☎ 599/5-22337), open Monday to Friday from 8am to noon and 1 to 5pm.

For **French St. Martin,** you can get information from one of the French government tourist offices at 444 Madison Ave., New York, NY 10022 (☎ 212/529-9069); 9454 Wilshire Blvd., Suite 715, Beverly Hills, CA 90212 (☎ 310/271-6665), and 676 N. Michigan Ave., Suite 3360, Chicago, IL 60611 (☎ 312/751-7800). You can also call **France-on-Call** at ☎ 900/990-0040 at the rate of 50¢ per minute. The tourist board on French St. Martin, called the **Office du Tourisme,** is at the port de

St. Maarten/St. Martin

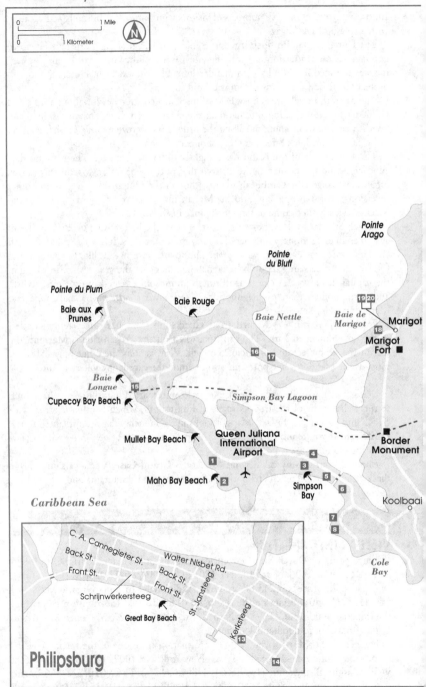

0   1 Mile

0   1 Kilometer

Pointe Arago

Pointe du Bluff

Pointe du Plum

Baie Rouge

Baie aux Prunes

Baie Nettle

Baie de Marigot

19 20

Marigot

18

Marigot Fort ■

16

17

Baie Longue

15

Simpson Bay Lagoon

Cupecoy Bay Beach

Mullet Bay Beach

Queen Juliana International Airport

Border Monument

1

4

Maho Bay Beach

2

3

5

Simpson Bay

6

Koolbaai

Caribbean Sea

7

8

Cole Bay

C. A. Cannegieter St.

Back St.

Walter Nisbet Rd.

Front St.

Back St.

Front St.

Schrijnwerkersteeg

St. Jansteeg

Ketksteeg

Great Bay Beach

13

14

Philipsburg

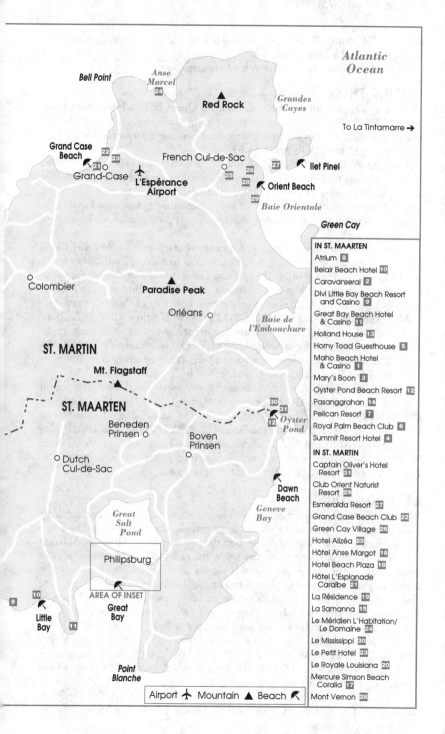

Atlantic Ocean

Bell Point

Anse Marcel **24**

Red Rock

Grandes Cayes

To La Tintamarre →

Grand Case Beach **22** **23**

21 Grand-Case

French Cul-de-Sac

L'Espérance Airport

27 Ilet Pinel

25 **26**

28 Orient Beach

29

Baie Orientale

Green Cay

Colombier

Paradise Peak

Orléans

Baie de l'Embouchure

ST. MARTIN

Mt. Flagstaff

ST. MAARTEN

Beneden Prinsen

Boven Prinsen

30

31 Oyster Pond

12

Dutch Cul-de-Sac

Dawn Beach

Geneve Bay

Great Salt Pond

Philipsburg

AREA OF INSET

Great Bay

9

10

11

Little Bay

Point Blanche

IN ST. MAARTEN

Atrium **8**

Belair Beach Hotel **10**

Caravanserai **2**

Divi Little Bay Beach Resort and Casino **9**

Great Bay Beach Hotel & Casino **11**

Holland House **13**

Horny Toad Guesthouse **5**

Maho Beach Hotel & Casino **1**

Mary's Boon **3**

Oyster Pond Beach Resort **12**

Pasanggrahan **14**

Pelican Resort **7**

Royal Palm Beach Club **6**

Summit Resort Hotel **4**

IN ST. MARTIN

Captain Oliver's Hotel Resort **31**

Club Orient Naturist Resort **29**

Esmeralda Resort **27**

Grand Case Beach Club **22**

Green Cay Village **26**

Hotel Alizéa **25**

Hôtel Anse Margot **16**

Hotel Beach Plaza **18**

Hôtel L'Esplanade Caraïbe **21**

La Résidence **19**

La Samanna **15**

Le Méridien L'Habitation/ Le Domaine **24**

Le Mississippi **30**

Le Petit Hotel **23**

Le Royale Louisiana **20**

Mercure Simson Beach Coralia **17**

Mont Vernon **28**

Airport ✈ Mountain ▲ Beach 🏖

601

Marigot (☎ **0590/87-57-21**), open Monday to Friday from 8:30am to 1pm and 2:30 to 5:30pm, Saturday from 8am to noon.

On the Web, point your browser to **www.st-martin.org**.

GETTING THERE

There are two airports on the island. St. Maarten's **Queen Juliana International Airport** (☎ **599/5-54211**) is the second busiest in the Caribbean, topped only by San Juan, Puerto Rico. You can also fly to the smaller **L'Espérance Airport,** in Grand-Case on French St. Martin (☎ **0590/87-53-03**).

American Airlines (☎ **800/433-7300** in the U.S.; www.aa.com) offers more options and more frequent service into St. Maarten than any other airline—one daily nonstop flight from both New York's JFK and Miami. Additional nonstop daily flights into St. Maarten are offered by American and its local affiliate, **American Eagle** (same toll-free number), from San Juan. Ask about American's package tours, which can save you a bundle.

Other air service is provided by **Continental Airlines** (☎ **800/231-0856;** www.flycontinental.com), offering daily flights out of its hub in Newark, New Jersey, and **LIAT** (☎ **800/468-0482** in the U.S. and Canada), with three flights out of San Juan. These latter flights stop first at Tortola (capital of the British Virgin Islands) before going on to St. Maarten. Even so, the trip usually takes only 90 minutes.

ALM Antillean Airlines (☎ **800/327-7230** in the U.S.; www.alm-airlines.com) offers nonstop daily service in winter from the airline's home base on Curaçao. In the off-season, there are two flights Sunday through Tuesday and again on Friday. **US Airways** (☎ **800/428-4322;** www.usairways.com) offers nonstop service from Baltimore on Saturday and Sunday and from Charlotte, North Carolina, on Sunday.

If you're coming from St. Barts, there are at least three airlines that can haul you on the short route directly to French-speaking St. Martin. They include **Air Guadeloupe** (☎ **0590/87-10-36** on St. Martin) and its two subsidiaries, **Air St-Martin** (☎ 0590/87-25-38) and **Air St-Barthélemy** (☎ **0590/87-76-59**). Collectively, they maintain between 15 and 20 daily flights, each about 10 minutes in duration, from St. Barts, about a third of which land at L'Espérance. A one-way flight between St. Barts and French St. Martin is 259 F ($44.05) per person.

GETTING AROUND

BY TAXI For visitors, the most common means of transport is a taxi. Since taxis are unmetered on both sides of the island, always agree on the rate before getting into a cab. Rate schedules are slightly different on the two sides of the island. **St. Maarten taxis** have minimum fares for two passengers, and each additional passenger pays $2 extra. One piece of luggage per person is allowed free; each additional piece is 50¢ extra. Fares are 25% higher between 10pm and midnight, and 50% higher between midnight and 6am. On the Dutch side, a typical fare from Queen Juliana Airport to the Maho Beach Hotel is $5; from Philipsburg to Queen Juliana Airport, $10.

St. Martin fares are also for two passengers, but allow a supplement of about $1 for each suitcase or valise. These fares are in effect from 7am to 10pm; after that, they go up by 25% until midnight, rising by 50% after midnight. On the French side, the fare from Marigot to Grand-Case is $10, from Juliana Airport to Marigot and from Juliana Airport to La Samanna $14.

For late-night cab service on St. Maarten, call ☎ **599/5-54317.** A **Taxi Service & Information Center** operates at the port of Marigot (☎ **0590/87-56-54**) on the French side of the island.

BY RENTAL CAR   Because of the island's size and diversity, car rentals are practical, particularly if you want to experience both the Dutch and the French sides. The taxi drivers' union strictly enforces a law that forbids anyone from picking up a car at the airport. As a result, every rental agency delivers cars directly to your hotel (only if you've booked in advance), where an employee will complete the paperwork. If you prefer to rent your car upon arrival, you can head for one of the tiny rental kiosks that lie across the road from the airport, but beware of long lines. In recent years, policies against renting a car on the Dutch side to someone staying on the French have been less strict. But know in advance that the policy of car-rental outfits toward their counterparts on the opposite side of the St. Maarten/St. Martin border seems about as changeable as the dishes at a local buffet table. You may or may not be able to return your car at the island's counterpart; check carefully before you go.

Bear in mind that **Budget** (☎ **800/527-0700** in the U.S., 599/5-54030 on the Dutch side, or 0590/87-38-22 on the French side), **Hertz** (☎ **800/654-3001** in the U.S., 599/5-54314 on the Dutch side, or 0590/87-40-68 on the French side), and **Avis** (☎ **800/331-1212** in the U.S., 599/5-52847 on the Dutch side, or 0590/87-50-60 on the French side) each maintain an office on both sides of the island. Another national chain represented is **National Car Rental** (☎ **800/328-4567** in the U.S., 599/5-42168 in Cole Bay, or 599/5-96856 at Queen Juliana Airport). All these companies charge roughly equivalent rates.

All three major car-rental agencies require that renters be at least 25 years old. Your credit-card issuer may provide insurance coverage, so check before your trip; otherwise, it may be wise to buy the fairly cheap collision-damage waiver (CDW) when you rent.

Drive on the right-hand side (on both the French and Dutch sides of the island), and don't drink and drive. Traffic jams are common near the island's major settlements, so be prepared to be patient. International road signs are observed, and there are no Customs formalities at the border between the island's political divisions.

BY MINIBUS   This is a reasonable means of transport on St. Maarten/St. Martin if you don't mind inconveniences, and at times overcrowding. Buses run daily from 7am to midnight and serve most of the major locations on both sides of the island. The most popular run is from Philipsburg on the Dutch side to Marigot on the French side. Privately owned and operated, minibuses tend to follow specific routes, with fares ranging from $1.15 to $2.

BY BICYCLE   Of course, it's far cheaper to get around the island by scooter or bike than by rented car. The best deal is at **Rent 2 Wheels,** Low Lands Road, Nettle Bay (☎ **0590/87-20-59**), just across the border on the French side. It rents scooters for 138 F ($23.45) per day, with motorbikes beginning at 250 F ($42.50).

Fast Facts: St. Maarten & St. Martin

Banking Hours   On the Dutch side, most banks are open Monday to Thursday from 8:30am to 1pm, Friday from 8:30am to 1pm and 4 to 5pm. On the French side, they are also usually open every weekday afternoon from 2 to 4 or 5pm.

Currency   The legal tender on the Dutch side is the **Netherlands Antilles guilder (NAf);** the official exchange rate is NAf 1.77 for each U.S.$1. However, U.S. dollars are easily, willingly, and often eagerly accepted on St. Maarten. On the French side, the currency, officially at least, is the **French franc (F);** the current exchange rate is 5.90 F to U.S.$1 (1 F = 17¢ U.S.), but check the most up-to-date quotation at the time of your visit. Nevertheless, U.S. dollars seem to be preferred wherever you go. Since that seems to be true regardless of which side of the island you're on, *prices in this chapter are given in U.S. currency unless otherwise designated.*

Documents   U.S., British, and Canadian citizens should have a passport, plus an ongoing or a return ticket and a confirmed hotel reservation.

Electricity   Dutch St. Maarten uses the same voltage (110 volts AC, 60 cycles) with the same electrical configurations as the United States, so adapters and transformers are not necessary. However, on French St. Martin, you'll need transformers and adapters. To simplify things, many hotels on both sides of the island have installed built-in sockets suitable for both European and North American appliances.

Emergencies   On the Dutch side, call the **police** at ☎ **599/5-22222** or an **ambulance** at ☎ **599/5-22111.** On the French side, you can reach the **police** by dialing ☎ **17** or 0590/87-50-06. In case of **fire,** dial ☎ **18.**

Hospitals   On the Dutch side, go to the **Medical Center,** Welegen Road, Cay Hill (☎ **599/5-31111**). On the French side, the local hospital is **Hospital de Marigot,** in Marigot (☎ **0590/29-57-57** or 0590/29-57-48).

Language   The language on the St. Maarten side is officially Dutch, but most people speak English. The same is true for St. Martin, although this is a French possession. A patois is spoken only by a small segment of the local populace.

Safety   Crime is on the rise on St. Maarten and, in fact, has become quite serious. If possible, avoid night driving—it's particularly unwise to drive on remote, unlit, back roads at night. Also, let that deserted, isolated beach remain so. You're safer in a crowd, although under no circumstances should you ever leave anything unguarded on the beach. The crime wave hitting Dutch St. Maarten also plagues French St. Martin.

Taxes & Service Charges   There is no departure tax imposed for departures from Espérance Airport on the French side. However, for departures from Juliana Airport on the Dutch side, there's a departure tax of $20 ($6 if you're leaving the island for St. Eustatius or Saba).

On the Dutch side, an 8% government tax is added to hotel bills, and, in general, hotels also add a 10% or 15% service charge. If service has not been added (unlikely), it's customary to tip around 15% in restaurants.

On the French side, your hotel is likely to add a 10% to 15% service charge to your bill to cover tipping. Likewise, most restaurant bills include the service charge.

Telephone   To call Dutch St. Maarten from the United States, dial **011** (the international access code), then **599** (the country code for the Netherlands Antilles), and finally **5** (the area code for Dutch St. Maarten) followed by the five-digit local number.

To make a call within Dutch St. Maarten, you need only the five-digit local number. But if you're calling "long distance" from the Dutch side of the island to the French side of the island, dial **00,** followed by **590** (the international access code for French St. Martin) and the six-digit local number.

If you're on the French side of the island and want to call anyone on the Dutch side, you'll have to treat the call the same way: Dial **00,** followed by **599,** then **5** and the five-digit local number. Know in advance that calls between the French and Dutch sides are considered long-distance calls and are much, much more expensive than you might have imagined, considering the relatively short distances involved.

French St. Martin is linked to the Guadeloupe telephone system. To call French St. Martin from the United States, dial **011** (the international access code), then **590** (the country code for Guadeloupe) and the six-digit local number.

To make a call from French St. Martin to any point within French St. Martin, no codes are necessary—just dial the local six-digit French number.

Time   St. Maarten and St. Martin operate on Atlantic standard time year-round. Thus in winter, if it's 6pm in Philipsburg, it's 5pm in New York. During daylight saving time in the United States, the island and the U.S. East Coast are on the same time.

Water   The water of St. Martin is safe to drink. In fact, most hotels serve desalinated water.

Weather   The island has a year-round temperature of about 80°F.

2 Where to Stay

IN ST. MAARTEN

A government tax of 8% and a service charge of 10% to 15% are added to your hotel bill. Ask about this when you book a room to save yourself a shock when you check out.

EXPENSIVE

Atrium. 6 Bill Foley Rd., Pelican Keys, Simpson Bay, St. Maarten, N.A. ☎ **599/5-42126.** Fax 599/5-42128. 87 units. A/C TV TEL. Winter $180 studio; $260 one-bedroom apt; $390 two-bedroom apt; $520 penthouse. Off-season $150 studio; $215 one-bedroom apt; $330 two-bedroom apt; $440 penthouse. AE, MC, V.

Atrium is one of the newest hotels in St. Maarten and one of the few that emerged almost unscathed from the twin hurricanes of 1995. Its secret, according to island engineers, is its structure of reinforced concrete and tempered sliding-glass doors that bend before they break. The hotel rises nine floors above a beachfront within a 5-minute walk of its much larger and less upscale sibling, the Pelican Resort, where guests must go for amenities like casinos, tennis, water sports, and fine dining. The Atrium does, however, maintain its own pool, snack bar, and bar. The guest rooms boast views over the hills, the lagoon, and/or the sea; private balconies; and a summery decor with lots of tile and wicker. Most of the spacious units have king beds; all contain kitchenettes, safes, and tiled bathrooms with hair dryers and combination shower/tubs.

Belair Beach Hotel. Little Bay (P.O. Box 940), Philipsburg, St. Maarten, N.A. ☎ **800/622-7836** in the U.S., or 599/5-23362. Fax 599/5-25295. E-mail: bbhotel@sintmaarten.net. 72 units. A/C TV TEL. Winter $255–$355 one-bedroom suite for 2; $299–$454 two-bedroom suite for 3. Off-season $209 one-bedroom suite for 2; $284 two-bedroom suite for 3. Children 17 and under stay free in parents' suite (subject to availability). AE, DC, DISC, MC, V.

One of the most surprising things about this breezy, oceanfront condo right on Little Bay Beach, a 10-minute taxi ride east of the airport, is the size of the accommodations: They're all suites. Each contains a large bedroom, two full bathrooms with hair dryers and combination shower/tubs, a fully equipped kitchen, and a 21-foot terrace with a sweeping view of the sea. The suites are privately owned, but rented to visitors when their owners are not on the island. The Sugar Bird Café serves breakfast, lunch, and dinner in a casual atmosphere. Extras include an on-site grocery, a beach with a seafront freshwater pool, two tennis courts, water sports, laundry, baby-sitting, a car-rental desk, and an activities desk. Many visitors find this place a good value, considering the amenities—especially the kitchen—and the family package rate.

The Caravanserai. 2 Beacon Hill Road, St. Maarten, NA. ☎ **800/616-1154** in the U.S., or 599/5-54000. Fax 599/5-54001. 52 units. TV TEL. Winter $250 double; $290–$350 one-bedroom suite. Off-season $175 double; $215–$290 one-bedroom suite. AE, DC, MC, V.

In 1996, a team of new St. Maarten–based entrepreneurs acquired a long-standing resort, and immediately began a program of upgrading the existing infrastructure. Set within a grove of palm trees on a private coral promontory, it enjoys a location that's usually calm, quiet, and restful except for the occasional noise of a low-flying jet taking off or landing at the nearby airport. Lying adjacent to Burgeaux Bay, the architecture incorporates natural woods and stone, Moorish arches, and tropical furnishings including lots of rattan and bamboo. Accommodations are spread out in at least 10 low-rise, cement-sided buildings, none of which rises more than two stories above the sandy terrain. Bedrooms are medium-sized to spacious, fitted with king or double beds, plus small but well-equipped bathrooms with hair dryers. The property contains a large terrace where drinks are served and live music is sometimes performed. Facilities include two tennis courts, three pools, two restaurants, and a fitness center.

Divi Little Bay Beach Resort and Casino. Little Bay (P.O. Box 961), Philipsburg, St. Maarten, N.A. ☎ **800/367-3484** in the U.S., or 599/5-22333. Fax 599/5-23911. www. diviresorts.com. E-mail: reserve@diviresorts.com. 210 units. A/C TV TEL. Winter $209–$320 double; $280–$325 one-bedroom apt; $425 two-bedroom apt; $525 three-bedroom apt. Off-season $150–$235 double, $215–$275 one-bedroom apt; $375 two-bedroom apt; $475 three-bedroom apt. AE, DC, MC, V.

Built on a desirable peninsula whose 22 acres slope from a point within a 10-minute drive east of the airport, this hotel originated as a simple guest house in 1955, and soon became famous as the vacation home of the Netherlands' Queen Juliana, Prince Bernhard, and Queen Beatrix. After dozens of enlargements and modifications, it was severely damaged during the hurricanes of the early 1990s, then rebuilt in 1997 as the flagship and premier emissary of the well-respected Divi chain. Its new design incorporates beige stucco walls, terra-cotta roofs, two pools, and postmodern references to Dutch colonial architecture. Gardens are carefully landscaped, and at this writing, Divi had promised to improve the nearby beach after its erosion during the decade's tropical storms. This hotel development is larger than its 210 units imply, since much of the site is devoted to time-share units. The result is a solidly entrenched residential apartment complex that's enhanced with hotel-style amenities and services. Accommodations are airy, accented with ceramic tiles and pastel colors; most units have kitchens. Bathrooms tend to be small and compact, but have adequate shelf space and a combination shower/tub.

Dining/Diversions: There's a poolside indoor/outdoor eatery, a more formal dining room, and two bars, one of which features live music on some evenings.

Amenities: Three pools, two tennis courts. In the upper altitudes of the property are the ruins of Fort Amsterdam, once Dutch St. Maarten's most prized military stronghold and today a decorative and much-respected historical site. A concierge helps arrange water sports.

Great Bay Beach Hotel & Casino. Little Bay Rd. (P.O. Box 310), Philipsburg, St. Maarten, N.A. ☎ **800/223-0757** or 599/5-22446. Fax 599/5-23859. 285 units. A/C TV TEL.

All-inclusive rates: Winter $330–$380 double; $350–$410 suite. Off-season $260–$290 double; $270–$330 suite. Accommodations only: Winter $190–$235 double; $210–$260 suite. Off-season $130–$160 double; $150–$185 suite. AE, DC, MC, V.

This deluxe resort is at the southwestern corner of Great Bay, and is unusual in that it offers both an all-inclusive rate and an EP rate (room only). Within walking distance of Philipsburg, it's ideal for shopping excursions. The hotel received a $10-million renovation, followed by a second renovation after Hurricane Luis dropped in. However, it still lacks any real charm and is short on atmosphere. All guest rooms, average in size, have been refurbished and contain bland furniture, a terrace or patio, and a king or two full beds. The corner ocean rooms are the most expensive and the most preferred. The bathrooms have Valentino-designed tiles, black marble bidets, and combination shower/tubs.

The hotel has a casino and nightclub, plus two dining areas, serving a standard international cuisine. There's also one all-weather tennis court and two freshwater pools, which are infinitely preferable to the polluted water at the beach. Laundry and baby-sitting are available.

Horny Toad Guesthouse. Simpson Bay, St. Maarten, N.A. ☎ **800/417-9361**, ext. 3013, or 599/5-54323. Fax 599/5-53316. E-mail: hornytod@sintmaarten.net. 8 units. Winter $198 double. Off-season $107 double. Extra person $40 in winter, $25 in off-season. DC, MC, V.

Many guests consider this the most homey and welcoming guest house on St. Maarten. It's the well-maintained domain of a pair of expatriates from the snows of Maine, Earle and Betty Vaughn. Seven units are in an amply proportioned beachside house originally built in the 1950s as a private home by the island's former governor. The eighth room is in half of an octagonal "round house" known for its large windows and views of the sea. Guest rooms range from medium-size to spacious, and each has a kitchenette, a recently renewed mattress, and a small but well-kept private bathroom. The Vaughns' tenure here began in 1979 when they checked in as overnight guests. So charmed were they that they bought the place 2 years later. There's no pool, no restaurant, and no organized activities of any kind, although the beach is a few steps away, and a pair of gas-fired barbecues act as excuses for impromptu get-togethers by resident guests and owners. The only drawback is that the hotel is near the airport, but the roar of jumbo jets is heard only a few times a day for a few moments. Children 7 and under are not encouraged, but families with children over 7 often retreat here to avoid the megaresorts, and second-timers quickly become "part of the family."

Maho Beach Hotel & Casino. Maho Bay, Philipsburg, St. Maarten, N.A. ☎ **599/5-52115.** Fax 599/5-53410. 616 units. A/C TV TEL. Winter $205–$410 double; $350–$440 suite; $590 two-bedroom unit. Off-season $110–$325 double; $200–$360 suite; $460 two-bedroom unit. AE, DC, MC, V.

Separated into three distinct sections, each built over an 8-year period beginning in the mid-1980s, this megaresort is the largest hotel on the island. It was massively renovated following hurricane damage in 1995. Set along the busy coastal road adjacent to a crescent-shaped beach, the hotel is unified by its trademark color scheme of pink and white. About a third of the rooms contain microwaves and fridges, and each has wicker furniture, Italian tiles, and plush upholstery. All units are fairly roomy and conservatively but comfortably furnished. Walk-in closets are an added plus. Bathrooms are spacious with bidets and combination shower/tubs. The hotel's only drawbacks are its very large size and the thundering noise of planes landing at the airport (2 minutes away) several times a day.

Dining/Diversions: Because of its size, the hotel contains 10 independently operated restaurants, more than any other hotel on the island. The Casino Royale, across the street, is the largest on the island. La Luna, an open-air disco, is an island hot spot.

Amenities: Four tennis courts, two outdoor pools with a view of Maho Bay, health-club spa, duty-free shopping (70 boutiques), water sports at the beach at the bottom of the hill. Laundry, baby-sitting.

Oyster Pond Beach Resort. Oyster Pond (P.O. Box 239), Philipsburg, St. Maarten, N.A. ☎ 599/5-36040. Fax 599/5-36695. www.where2stay.com. E-mail: oyster@sintmaarten.net. 40 units. A/C TV TEL. Winter $200–$275 double; $290–$600 suite. Off-season $120–$175 double; $190–$400 suite. AE, DISC, MC, V.

At the end of a twisting, scenic road, this elegant retreat is designed for vacationers who don't like overly commercialized megaresorts, like Maho Beach. However, by 2000 it will lose a great deal of intimacy itself, with the construction of new accommodations which will bring the room count up to 89. On a circular harbor on the eastern shore, near the French border, the fortresslike structure stands guard over a 35-acre protected marina and has a private, sandy half-moon beach. There's a central courtyard and an alfresco lobby, with white wicker and fine paintings. More than half the units are suites or duplexes, and most have a West Indian decor. The bedrooms offer balconies overlooking the pond or sea; the most elegant and expensive accommodations are the tower suites. Rooms are airy and fairly spacious, each with coffeemakers, robes, and hair dryers.

Dining: Off the courtyard, and opening onto the sea, is a bar/lounge that's as warm and comfortable as a private home. The dining room is exceptional, and the chef turns out a well-prepared continental cuisine with some Creole dishes.

Amenities: Freshwater pool (22 by 44 feet). Laundry.

Royal Palm Beach Club. P.O. Box 3035, Airport Blvd., Simpson Bay. ☎ **599/5-43732.** Fax 599/5-43727. E-mail: elawrence@sunterra.com. 140 units. A/C TV TEL. Winter $364 for up to 6. Off-season $264 for up to 6. AE, MC, V.

The beauty of renting here is the direct access to Simpson's Bay Beach. Accommodations occupy five floors of a white-and-peach building. Each unit is more or less the same, with two bedrooms, two bathrooms, cool ceramic tile floors, ceiling fans and air-conditioning, and simple, summery furniture (including a sofa bed) that was for the most part refurbished or replaced in 1996. The bathrooms are compact, with shower stalls. There's a pool on the premises, but that's about it—you won't find any bars, restaurants, or communal spaces at this apartment complex. Most people rent here for the privacy and anonymity.

MODERATE/INEXPENSIVE

Holland House. Front St. (P.O. Box 393), Philipsburg, St. Maarten, N.A. ☎ **800/223-9815** in the U.S., or 599/5-22572. Fax 599/5-24673. 60 units. A/C TV TEL. Winter $140–$175 for up to 3; $185–$200 suite. Off-season $84–$109 for up to 3; $124–$139 suite. AE, DC, DISC, MC, V.

Located in the heart of town, this hotel rents cozy medium-sized apartments decorated with furnishings from the Netherlands and the United States, with an emphasis on rattan. Units have exposure to the street or to the (polluted) beach, and most contain a tiny kitchenette, ideal for light cooking. The suites are very spacious. Bathrooms are small but efficiently arranged. You're right on the beach, where you can order drinks at the bar. An open-air dining terrace fronts Great Bay, and the hotel is near all the major restaurants and shops of Philipsburg. Even if you're not staying here, you might want to call and reserve a table for dinner; this is one of the few hotels that serves authentic Dutch specialties at its Governor's Restaurant. International and Indonesian specialties are also featured.

✪ **Mary's Boon.** Simpson Bay (P.O. Box 2078, Philipsburg), St. Maarten, N.A. ☎ **599/ 5-54235.** Fax 599/5-53403. 14 units. A/C TV TEL. Winter $125–$195 apt for two. Off-season $90–$125 apt for two. MC, V. Take the first right turn from the airport toward Philipsburg.

Built in 1968 near the beach, this small-scale inn is like something out of a West Indies Hemingway story. The name is an amalgam of its founder (Mary Pomeroy) and her companion, Mr. Boon, although their legacy is dimly remembered since new owners, Karla and Mark Cleveland, took over in 1996. Everything about the place exudes an informal and relaxed hospitality. Each unit contains a kitchen of its own, there's an honor bar in the communal living room, and a garden blooms lushly whenever it isn't being massacred by a hurricane. Damage from the storms of 1995 instigated a renovation that was sorely needed. There's an on-site restaurant serving West Indian and international food, open every night for dinner except during October (the inn, however, stays open during that period). Don't expect luxury or opulence of any kind: The rooms are comfortable and outfitted with ceiling fans, rattan and wicker furniture, and louvered windows open to seafront breezes. All but four units are air-conditioned. Each unit has twin beds, often pushed together, and small, well-maintained bathrooms. Noise is sometimes bothersome from planes taking off from the nearby airport, but big planes are a factor only two or three times a day, and only land during daylight hours.

Pasanggrahan. 15 Front St. (P.O. Box 151), Philipsburg, St. Maarten, N.A. ☎ **599/ 5-23588.** Fax 599/5-22885. 28 units. Winter $128–$168 double. Off-season $78–$110 double. AE, MC, V. Closed Sept.

Pasanggrahan is the Indonesian word for guest house, and this one is West Indian in style. A small, informal place, it's right on the busy, narrow main street of Philipsburg, toward the end of the mountain side of Front Street. It's set back under tall trees, with a white wooden veranda. The interior has peacock bamboo chairs, Indian spool tables, and a gilt-framed oil portrait of Queen Wilhelmina. So many guests asked to see the bedroom where the queen and her daughter, Juliana, stayed during World War II that the management turned it into the Sydney Greenstreet Bar. The small- to medium-size renovated bedrooms have queen, double, or king beds with good mattresses and in some cases Saban bedspreads; some are in the main building and others are in an adjoining annex. All accommodations have ceiling fans, and all but six are air-conditioned. Bathrooms are small but tidy. Set among the wild jungle of palms and shrubbery is the Pasanggrahan Restaurant, open from 7am to 11pm. The private beach is only 50 feet away.

Pelican Resort. Simpson Bay (P.O. Box 431), Philipsburg, St. Maarten, N.A. ☎ **800/ 550-7088** in the U.S., or 599/5-42503. Fax 954/484-1182. www.pelicanresort.com. 342 units. A/C TV TEL. Winter $80–$160 studio for 2; $120–$140 one-bedroom suite for 4; $200–$350 two-bedroom suite for 6; $250–$400 three-bedroom suite for 8. Off-season $60–$80 studio for 2; $90–$120 one-bedroom suite for 4; $150–$200 two-bedroom suite for 6, $200–$250 three-bedroom suite for 8. 7-night minimum stay usually required in winter. AE, DISC, MC, V.

The Pelican, built in 1979 on 12 acres of land near the airport, is the largest time-share facility on St. Maarten, and the staff appears at times more interested in hawking these properties than in running a hotel. Nevertheless, it's worthy of consideration if other major resorts are fully booked. Although many of the suites are leased for predesignated periods throughout the year, others are rented as they become available by the on-site managers. Accommodations, which contain ceiling fans and full kitchens, are arranged into village-style clusters separated from other units by lattices, hibiscus hedges, and bougainvillea. Each unit is fairly spacious, equipped with blandly international furnishings and comfortable king or double beds; most units have patios or verandas, and some have hair dryers. Scattered around the property are a lily pond, many small waterways, and an orchid garden.

The Pelican Reef Restaurant is one of the island's best steak-and-seafood places, with a waterfront ambience and an extensive wine list. The casual Crocodile Express Café offers good and reasonable fare, and the Italian Connection delivers pizza and pasta. There's also a cozy bistro with a European-style menu. Amenities include five tennis courts, six pools, a playground, 1,400 feet of ocean-front marina, and the unique L'Aqualine health and beauty center (see "A Spa" under section 5, below). Water sports, laundry, and baby-sitting can be arranged.

Summit Resort Hotel. P.O. Box 456, Simpson Bay Lagoon, St. Maarten, N.A. ☎ **599/ 5-52150**, or 718/518-7470 in New York City. Fax 599/5-52615, or 718/518-0534 in New York City. E-mail: resort@idt.net. 53 units. A/C MINIBAR TV TEL. Winter $140–$155 double without kitchen; $180–$195 double with kitchen. Off-season $110 double without kitchen; $150 double with kitchen. AE, DISC, MC, V.

This place is pleasant and uncomplicated. The cluster of one- and two-story bunga- lows is adjacent to a lagoon, within a 10-minute walk of Cupecoy Beach, although there is an on-site pool overlooked by a restaurant. The verandas of some rooms look over the lagoon; others face gardens or other verandas. A shuttle bus will take you free to the beach (some visitors prefer to walk); it charges $5 for an excursion to Philips- burg and its shops and casinos. The accommodations have undergone a major reno- vation, and colors have been brightened with a tropical motif. Rooms come in standard size with two double beds, plus a sitting area and a fridge. The more spacious deluxe rooms have both a king-size bed and a queen-size sofa bed, full kitchen facili- ties, tile floors, an in-room safe, and a sitting and dining area. Most of the units have combination shower/tubs. Guests can use the tennis court for free.

IN ST. MARTIN

Hotels on French St. Martin add a 10% service charge and a *taxe de séjour*. This visi- tors' tax on rooms differs from hotel to hotel, depending on its classification, but is often $4 a day.

VERY EXPENSIVE

Esmeralda Resort. Parc de la Baie Orientale (B.P. 5141), 97150 St. Martin, F.W.I. ☎ **800/622-7836** in the U.S., or 0590/87-36-36. Fax 0590/87-35-18. 54 units. A/C TV TEL. Winter $300–$450 double; from $450 suite. Off-season $180–$250 double; from $300 suite. Rates include continental breakfast. AE, MC, V.

Originally conceived as a site for a single private villa, and then for a semiprivate club, this hillside housing development, like something in Arizona, is a 25-minute taxi ride northeast of Queen Juliana Airport. Opening onto Orient Beach, the Esmeralda blos- somed into a full-scale resort in the early 1990s, offering views over Orient Bay and a decidedly French focus. Each of the 18 Spanish mission–style, tile-roofed villas can be configured into four separate units by locking or unlocking the doors between rooms. Each individual unit contains a king or two doubles, a kitchenette, a bathroom, a pri- vate terrace, a personal safe, and a private entrance. Each villa has a communal pool, which creates the feeling of a private club.

Dining/Diversions: The resort's bar and grill (Le Coco Beach) lies close to the nearby beach. There's also an impressive, relatively upscale restaurant, L'Astrolabe, for more formal dining. The hotel maintains cooperative relationships with several local beach bars, any of which allows guests of Esmeralda to sign for food and drinks throughout the day and evening.

Amenities: 17 pools, two tennis courts, day and night scuba diving, snorkeling, horseback riding, waterskiing. Room service (for breakfast and dinner), laundry, baby-sitting, massage.

Green Cay Village. Parc Baie Orientale, B.P. 3006, 97064 St. Martin, F.W.I. ☎ **0590/ 87-38-63.** Fax 0590/87-39-27. 48 units. A/C TV TEL. Winter $342 one-bedroom villa for two; $414 two-bedroom villa for four; $557 three-bedroom villa for six. Off-season $257 one-bedroom villa for two persons; $329 two-bedroom villa for four; $414 three-bedroom villa for six. 3-night minimum stay required in winter. AE, DC, MC, V.

Set on the barren, scrub-covered heights overlooking Orient Bay, a 15-minute walk to its beach, this compound consists of 16 cream-colored villas, built during the early 1990s. Each villa contains three spacious bedrooms, three bathrooms, a shared living room, a kitchenette, a pool, and airy, summery furniture and upholsteries that are well suited to surviving in the salty air. Bathrooms are small but have adequate shelf space. Guests here tend to be urban escapees looking for peace and solitude—thus tend to appreciate this establishment's utter lack of group activities. Management is insouciant and very, very French; unless you happen to visit during a busy period, such as Christmastime, it does everything possible not to house strangers within the respective bedrooms of the same villa. Consequently, for the price of a one-bedroom villa, you and your partner are likely to have lots of privacy and even unrestricted solitary use of the villa's small but refreshing pool, its living room, and its outdoor dining terrace. There's no restaurant on the premises. In fact, there are very few additional amenities at all here, although someone at the reception desk (open only from 7am to 10pm daily) will direct you to any of several nearby choices.

✪ **La Samanna.** Baie Longue (B.P. 4077), 97064 St. Martin CEDEX, F.W.I. ☎ **800/ 854-2252** or 0590/87-64-00. Fax 0590/87-87-86. 83 units. A/C MINIBAR TV TEL. Winter $600 double; $750–$3,150 suites and villas. Off-season $325–$450 double; $450–$2,750 suites and villas. AE, MC, V.

Luxurious and sybaritic, this world-class resort was once a semi-private club on the isolated, scrub-covered flatlands near a 1½-mile stretch of one of St. Martin's finest beaches. Since then, the resort has earned a reputation as a sleek, sexy, and stylish complex where off-the-record celebrity visits are relatively commonplace. After serious damage during the 1995 hurricane, the resort was acquired by Orient Express Hotels and made especially competitive with a massive infusion of cash and a major overhaul. Although the place is pricey, the new management is taking well-publicized pains to expose a well-heeled but more general audience to its pleasures.

In 1997, rows of mature royal palms were added to enhance the 55-acre property's front entrance, lavish art objects were imported from Morocco's sub-Sahara and the jungles of northern Thailand, and the banal-looking terra-cotta floors of the resort's reception area were replaced with Mediterranean blue- and-white tiles. Ironically, although many of La Samanna's buildings were damaged during the hurricanes, the storms enlarged its adjoining beach with tons of fresh sand. An all-new fourth floor was added as the site for one of the grandest suites in the Caribbean. Additionally, TVs and VCRs were added to each room, and everything was brightened up. Today, the resort is more evocative of France's Côte d'Azur or Morocco than the Caribbean, and it remains what the French call *intime, tranquille,* and artfully *informel.* Regardless of their size, most units have private terraces. Suites and villas come with spacious bedrooms with luxurious beds, fully equipped kitchens, living and dining rooms, and large patios. The baths are simpler than might be expected, but well designed nonetheless, with bidets, hand-painted Mexican tiles, hair dryers, and robes.

Dining: Guests enjoy French cuisine alfresco, on a candlelit terrace overlooking Baie Longue. After dinner, the bar becomes a disco. At the poolside grill, waiters serve food, St-Tropez style, on the beach.

Amenities: Fitness and activity center with daily aerobics classes, outdoor pool, waterskiing, three tennis courts, library, sailboat rentals, boutique. 24-hour room service, laundry, baby-sitting, massages; a hotel driver meets all guests at the airport.

Le Méridien L'Habitation/Le Domaine. Anse Marcel (B.P. 581, 97150 Marigot), St. Martin, F.W.I. ☎ **800/543-4300** in the U.S., or 0590/87-67-00. Fax 0590/87-30-38. E-mail: meridiensxmresa@caraibes.com. 396 units. A/C MINIBAR TV TEL. Winter $320–$570 double; $460–$950 suite. Off-season $190–$220 double; $290–$350 suite. AE, DC, MC, V. Closed Sept.

Since its expansion in 1992, this has become the largest resort complex on the French side of the island, and one of its most heavily promoted, often attracting French-speaking tour groups. It's tucked under Pigeon Pea Hill, opening onto one of the tiny island's most scenic white-sand beaches, some 1,600 feet of it. Its older section (L'Habitation), with less panoramic bedroom views, was erected in the mid-1980s on a 150-acre tract of rugged scrubland nestled between the sea and a mountain ridge. In the early 1990s, after the project had been purchased by Air France, work began on Le Domaine, a few steps to the west of the original complex. Today, both resorts are fully integrated, sharing all entertainment, dining, drinking, and recreational facilities.

Accommodations at both resorts are in a string of neo-Victorian two- and three-story buildings ringed with lattices, gingerbread, and verandas. Most of the rooms in Le Domaine overlook the ocean, and are thus more expensive. The rooms in L'Habitation mostly open onto a 120-slip marina and a garden. All rooms and suites are comfortably and stylishly furnished, each with quality mattresses, soundproofing, a balcony or terrace, a two-sink bathroom, and an airy, tropical decor, which, along with special children's programs such as the Pirates' Club, make this an ideal place for families.

Dining: The pool bar (Le Carbet) resembles a tile-sheathed gazebo on stilts at the edge of the water. Breakfast buffets are served in Le Balaou, while Le President BBQ offers grilled meats and seafood at lunch or dinner. Pastas, grills, and Italian food are served in La Veranda, while La Belle France features an haute Caribbean cuisine.

Amenities: Three pools, nightclub complex, 100-slip marina. When enough children are in attendance to justify its expense, a Pirates' Club offers a wide range of activities for ages 2 to 14. Guests have complimentary access to Le Privilege Resort and Spa, a complex on the hill linked by frequent minibus service from the hotel. Both fitness training and European spa–style treatments are featured, including aerobics classes, tennis, body building, squash, and racquetball. Room service (from 7am to 11pm), laundry, baby-sitting (from 7am to 11pm).

Le Mississippi. Oyster Pond, 9150 St. Martin, F.W.I. ☎ **0590/87-33-81.** Fax 0590/87-31-52. 19 units. A/C MINIBAR TV TEL. Winter $470–$600 double; $600–$710 triple; $655–$820 suite quad; $655–$745 cottage quad. Off-season $390–$510 double; $545–$565 triple; $620–$655 suite quad; $590–$655 cottage quad. AE, DC, MC, V. Closed Sept.

Set on a hillside in a sprawling garden, on the heights looking down over Oyster Pond, this resort was initially developed by France-based investors in 1993, and then closed for almost all of 1997 in the wake of a series of disastrous hurricanes. In 1998, much rebuilt and refurbished, it reopened as a new and untested entity struggling for market recognition in a highly competitive marketplace. It offers attractive lodgings and a small-scale, somewhat sleepy format that will appeal to anyone looking for calm non-involvement and recuperation from stress-filled urban life. The nearest beach (Dawn

Beach) is a 12- to 15-minute walk from the hotel, down a winding pathway. The resort consists of a series of dark-stained wooden buildings arranged around a square-shaped pool. Six of the units are independent cottages, each with its own Jacuzzi, and each with a noticeable lack of the whimsical gingerbread that adorns many of its Creole-inspired competitors. Suites are spacious, with posh features including marble and tile floors, luxury beds, VCRs and stereos, and full American-style kitchens with microwaves and dishwashers. Baths are adorned with pink Portuguese marble and come with whirlpool tubs. Cottages are equally luxurious with king-sized beds and antique-style tubs. From the windows of some of the accommodations, and from the terrace of the appealing restaurant, Mahogany (see "Where to Dine," below), you'll have sweeping water views as far away as St. Barts and Saba.

EXPENSIVE

Captain Oliver's Resort. Oyster Pond, 97150 St. Martin, F.W.I. ☎ **0590/87-40-26.** Fax 0590/87-40-84. www.captainolivers.com. E-mail: captoli@wanadoo.fr. 50 units. A/C MINIBAR TV TEL. Winter $175–$270 junior suite for 2. Off-season $120–$205 junior suite for 2. Rates include American breakfast. AE, DC, MC, V.

Smaller and a bit sleepier than Meridien's L'Habitation/La Domaine, and with a greater sense of intimacy and calm, this is one of the more appealing, upper-middle bracket hotels of French St. Martin, comparable in some ways to the Esmeralda Resort, to which it's sometimes compared. At the French–Dutch border 10 miles east of Queen Juliana Airport, this hotel is near the prestigious Oyster Pond Hotel on the Dutch side. After the 1995 hurricanes, much time and money was spent on upgrading the compound. The pink bungalows, with a bit of gingerbread, are set in a labyrinth and connected by boardwalks. High on a hill, they command panoramic views, and from the large terraces you can gaze over to St. Barts. The accommodations, which are clustered three to a bungalow, are furnished in white rattan and decorated with local prints, and come with kitchenettes, marble-trimmed bathrooms with double sinks, large double closets, and many amenities. Each junior suite has two beds and a sofa bed, which makes them perfect for families.

Dining: Captain Oliver's Restaurant serves French and Creole cuisine. The Iguana pool bar is open daily from noon to midnight. The Dinghy Dock, a breakfast room and snack bar, is open daily from 7am to midnight.

Amenities: Scuba-diving facilities, outdoor pool, private taxi boat to nearby beach, boutiques. Room service (from 7am to 10:30pm), laundry, baby-sitting.

Club Orient Naturist Resort. Baie Orientale, 97150 St. Martin, F.W.I. ☎ **800/828-9356** or 0590/87-33-85. Fax 0590/87-33-76. E-mail: clubo@virtualaccess.net. 110 units. A/C. Rates per couple: Winter $205 studio; $240–$260 minisuite; $305–$340 chalet. Off-season $135 studio; $150–$165 minisuite; $180–$195 chalet. AE, DC, DISC, MC, V.

Isolated from the rest of St. Martin, this is the only resort in the French West Indies that's committed to the creation of a safe and socially acceptable environment for nudists. Established in the late 1970s by a Dutch-born family, and completely rebuilt after its devastation by hurricanes in 1995, it welcomes a European and North American clientele. There's a great beach here and a restaurant, the Papagayo, where you can dine alfresco, literally. However, most guests opt to cook their own meals, as each unit has its own kitchenette (there's an on-site minimarket). Accommodations, set in red-pine chalets imported from Finland, are utterly plain and simple; all have outside showers and most have porches. Beds are rather basic, but still comfortable enough. There's no pool on the premises, but the chalets are right on the beach.

Grand Case Beach Club. Rue du Petit-Plage Grand-Case, 97150 St. Martin, F.W.I. ☎ **800/447-7462** in the U.S., or 0590/87-51-87. Fax 0590/87-59-93. 100 units. A/C TV

TEL. Winter $230–$285 double; $285–$350 one-bedroom suite; $440–$465 two-bedroom suite. Off-season $135–$180 double; $180–$195 one-bedroom suite; $310–$335 two-bedroom suite. Rates include continental breakfast. AE, DISC, MC, V.

This restored condo complex, a quintet of motel-like buildings with white trim, sits directly on the sands of Grand Case Beach. Because of its position in a garden that's awfully close to the level of the waves, the hotel's buildings tend to suffer heavy damage during storms. As such, after its original construction in 1977, the entire place received an almost complete overhaul after the hurricanes of 1995. The medium-sized accommodations contain private patios or balconies, kitchenettes, mostly white and rather simple decor, and views of either the garden or the sea. Guest rooms come with king or double beds, foldout couches, wall safes, and simple white-tiled bathrooms. Everything here is extremely informal: This is the kind of place where you don't need much more than a bathing suit.

Dining: Although there's a bar and a simple, summery restaurant on the premises, many guests prepare their meals in their kitchenettes.

Amenities: Pool; beach boutique; water-sports facilities, including waterskiing, snorkeling, and sailing; free use of St. Martin's first artificial-grass tennis courts; car-rental facilities. Laundry, baby-sitting.

Hotel Alizéa. Mont Vernon 25, 97150 St-Martin, F.W.I. ☎ **0590/87-33-42.** Fax 0590/ 87-41-15. www.west-indies-online.com/alizea. E-mail: alizea@wanadoo.fr. 26 units. A/C TV TEL. Winter $185 double; $265 bungalow. Off-season $126 double; $186 bungalow. Discounts offered for stays of 1 week or more. Rates include continental breakfast. AE, MC, V. After passing through Grand-Case, turn left and follow the signs along the cul-de-sac.

On the northeastern end of the island, this is the smallest hotel in a district with some of the biggest resorts. The inn opens onto a panoramic vista of Orient Bay. A pool is on the premises, but the beach is just a 5-minute hike through fields and across a road. All accommodations were renovated after the damages of the 1995 hurricane, and each contains a kitchenette (with fridge) set on an open-air veranda, a light and airy collection of wooden furniture, a color scheme of Caribbean pastels, and a private safe. We like the Creole Rooms in the main building, which open onto the water and feature mosquito netting draped over king-sized beds. The bungalows are equally comfortable, designed in a West Indian style with ceramic tile floors. These contain king or twin beds, plus sofa beds that are ideal for families. Bathrooms are plain but have double vanities, bidets, and showers.

There are no on-site facilities for lunch, since a half-dozen or so beachfront restaurants are nearby. A set-price dinner, however, can be ordered at Le Mango, the hotel restaurant, for between 120 F to 155 F ($20.40 to $26.35). Philippe Thevenet, your English-speaking manager, works hard to provide what guests need within the context of a very laissez-faire environment.

Hôtel Anse Margot. Baie Nettlé (B.P. 4071, 97060 Marigot), St. Martin, F.W.I. ☎ **0590/ 87-92-01.** Fax 0590/87-92-13. 92 units. A/C TV TEL. Winter $187–$244 double; $316–$377 suite. Off-season $150–$176 double; $286 suite. AE, DC, MC, V.

This French-owned resort, just west of Marigot, consists of eight pastel-colored buildings. Built in 1988, and renovated in 1996, they sit on a narrow strip of scrub-covered sand that separates the ocean from the largest of the island's saltwater lagoons. Nettlé Beach, across from the hotel, is best for swimming, while sunbathers (though not swimmers) can visit the beach along Simpson Bay. Each of the resort's multistory buildings is embellished with ornate balconies and gingerbread in a stylized version of colonial Creole architecture. Guest rooms, ranging from small to spacious, are done in a French Antillean decor of pastel florals; the many amenities include small fridges.

Many units also have their own private balconies. Especially inviting is suite no. 916, a two-story unit with rattan furnishings and French doors opening onto a large tiled balcony. Bathrooms are tiled and well equipped, with sufficient shelf space and bidets.

Dining/Diversions: Entre Deux Mers serves French cuisine. The resort's social center rises like a well-designed miniature temple, with a pair of pools flanking it on either side. After dark, a pianist performs live music, which might include Piaf or jazz.

Amenities: Scuba diving, two outdoor pools, two Jacuzzis, waterskiing, sailboat rentals, boutiques. Room service (available during normal meal hours), laundry, babysitting.

Hotel Beach Plaza. Baie de Marigot, 97150 St. Martin. ☎ **0590/87-87-00.** Fax 0590/ 87-18-87. 144 units. A/C MINIBAR TV TEL. Winter $203–$275 double; from $405 suite. Off-season $160–$190 double; from $291 suite. Rates include buffet breakfast. AE, MC, V.

Set closer to Marigot than many of its middle-bracket competitors in Baie Nettlé, this three-story hotel lies within a cluster of buildings mostly composed of condominiums. Built in 1996, and painted in shades of blue and white, it's set midway between the open sea and the lagoon, giving all rooms water views. Inside, the decor is pure white accented with varnished, dark-tinted woods and an inviting tropical motif. Each room contains a balcony, tile floors, native art, a private safe, and simple hardwood furniture, including a writing desk and comfortable beds. Bathrooms have hair dryers and generous shelf space. There's a water-sports kiosk for sailing, windsurfing, snorkeling, and scuba, plus a pool that's visible from the windows of Le Corsaire, the restaurant. There's also two bars, one beside the pool, another with a resident pianist. The congenial staff is rightfully proud of the hotel's position as a worthy competitor among the more deeply entrenched properties nearby.

✪ **Hôtel L'Esplanade Caraïbe.** (B.P. 5007), Grand-Case, 97150 St. Martin, F.W.I. ☎ **800/ 633-7411** or 0590/87-06-55. Fax 0590/87-29-15. www.esplanade-caraibes.com. E-mail: esplanade@wanadoo.fr. 24 units. A/C TV TEL. Winter $240–$280 double studio; $320 suite. Off-season $170–$200 double studio; $230 suite. AE, MC, V.

Although the hamlet of Grand-Case has always been known for its potpourri of many different restaurants, its hotel choices were rather limited. In 1992, this changed with the construction of an elegant collection of suites on a steeply sloping hillside above the town's approach road from Marigot. Covered with cascades of bougainvillea, and accented with a vaguely Hispanic overlay of white walls, hand-painted tiles, and cream-colored roofs, the resort's various elements are connected by a network of concrete steps that add to the layout's drama. There's a pool, a series of terraced gardens, and access to a beach that you reach after a 6-minute walk on a winding, stair-dotted pathway. All views from the guest rooms and their terraces are angled out toward the sea. Each unit contains a kitchen with a large fridge, up-to-date cookware, and a coffeemaker; a blue, green, and white color scheme with lots of exposed mahogany and wicker furniture; and especially comfortable queen beds with firm French mattresses. Bathrooms are beautifully equipped right down to mosquito milk in the toiletries baskets, bidets, and thick towels. The loft suites on the upper floors are worth the cost, as they include a sofa bed that can sleep extra guests, an upstairs master bedroom with a king bed, and a partial bath downstairs. The only on-site dining option is a cocktail bar open in midwinter only.

Le Petit Hotel. Grand Case (B.P. 5007), 97150 St. Martin, F.W.I. ☎ **0590/29-09-65.** Fax 0590/87-09-19. www.lepetithotel.com. 10 units. A/C TV TEL. Winter $250 studio for two; $340 one-bedroom apt for up to four. Off-season $160 studio for two; $220 one-bedroom apt for up to four. AE, DISC, MC, V.

Set on a small parcel of property that's squeezed between other buildings, with direct access to the sands of Grand Case Beach, this is a well-managed, thoughtfully designed hotel that opened late in 1996 in the wake of Hurricane Luis. Much of its appeal derives from its hard-working and articulate manager, Kristin Petrelluzi, who offers advice on any of two dozen restaurants in nearby Grand Case, and who wisely—in light of the competition—does not maintain an on-site restaurant of her own. Nine of the spacious units are studios, while the 10th is a one-bedroom apartment. Each has a kitchenette with everything from a can opener to champagne glasses, as well as a microwave, a fridge, a coffeemaker, and a two-burner stove. (There's no oven, but no one ever seems inspired to actually bake during their stay here.) All units have balconies or outdoor terraces, plus furnishings that are both durable and comfortable. The small bathrooms come with shower stalls and hair dryers.

Mont Vernon. Baie Orientale Chevrise (B.P. 1174, 97062 Marigot), St. Martin, F.W.I. ☎ **0590/87-62-00.** Fax 0590/87-37-27. www.hotelmontvernon.com. E-mail: stm@ bluebayresorts.com. 394 units. A/C TV TEL. Rates per couple: Winter $354–$404 junior suite; $454 suite. Off-season $254–$304 junior suite; $354 suite. Rates include buffet breakfast. Children under 12 stay free in parents' suite. AE, MC, V.

Opened in 1989, this resort complex with a lacy gingerbread architecture offers junior suites and two-room suites, with private balconies opening onto the water. Accommodations are housed in 10 party-colored buildings, painted in vivid shades of pink, blue, green, or yellow, in the Creole style. The guest rooms are among the island's most spacious, with many amenities such as fridges, hair dryers, and gigantic showers. Despite the hotel's large size, the staff works hard to provide what guests need. It's a favorite among package-tour groups, especially those originating in France. The hotel suffered severe damage from the 1995 hurricanes, but was completely rebuilt and reconfigured in 1996.

Dining: There's a 200-seat main restaurant, La Creole; a 50-seat main bar and patio; an 80-seat beach bar; and a 100-seat pool snack bar with a barbecue, called Le Sloop. French, Italian, and Creole cuisine are offered.

Amenities: Duty-free shopping arcade, large pool with sundeck, tennis courts, archery, water-sports center where deep-sea fishing can be arranged. Laundry, baby-sitting, massage.

MODERATE/INEXPENSIVE

La Résidence. Rue du Général-de-Gaulle (B.P. 679), Marigot, 97150 St. Martin, F.W.I. ☎ **800/423-4433** in the U.S., or 0590/87-70-37. Fax 0590/87-90-44. 21 units. A/C MINIBAR TV TEL. Year-round $94 double. Rates include continental breakfast. AE, MC, V.

In the commercial center of town (and favored by business travelers for its location), La Résidence has a concrete facade enlivened with neo-Victorian gingerbread fretwork. A bar with a soaring tent serves drinks to guests relaxing on wicker and bentwood furniture. The small bedrooms are arranged around a landscaped central courtyard with a fish-shaped fountain. Each rooms contains minimalist decor, and all but a few have sleeping lofts and a duplex design of mahogany-trimmed stairs and balustrades. Mattresses are a bit thin, but acceptable. Bathrooms are also small, with shower stalls. The hotel is known for its French and Creole restaurant. Room service is available as well.

Le Royale Louisiana. Rue du Général-de-Gaulle, Marigot, 97150 St. Martin, F.W.I. ☎ **0590/87-86-51.** Fax 0590/87-96-49. 58 units. A/C TV TEL. Winter 440 F–490 F ($74.80–$83.30) double; 610 F–690 F ($103.70–$117.30) duplex. Off-season 410 F ($69.70) double; 640 F ($108.80) duplex. Rates include continental breakfast. AE, MC, V.

Occupying a prominent position in the center of Marigot, 10 miles north of Queen Juliana Airport, this hotel is designed in a hip-roofed French-colonial Louisiana style; its rambling balconies are graced with ornate balustrades. Each small- to medium-size guest room contains big sunny windows and modern furniture. Standard rooms have either king- or queen-size beds. Duplexes, ideal for families, have a sitting room with a sofa bed on the lower floor, with a bedroom and bathroom on the upper level. Note that duplex rates are not based on the number of occupants. Bathrooms are well maintained but a bit cramped, with shower stalls. The hotel restaurant serves a simple breakfast, plus salads and sandwiches at lunch. A bar on the premises is open in the evening, but no meals are served.

Mercure Simson Beach Coralia. Baie Nettlé (B.P. 172, 97150 Marigot), St. Martin, F.W.I. ☎ **800/221-4542** or 0590/87-54-54. Fax 0590/87-92-11. 175 units. A/C TV TEL. Winter $159–$179 studio for 2; $224–$244 duplex. Off-season $124–$144 studio for 2; $171–$191 duplex. Rates include buffet breakfast. AE, DC, MC, V.

One of the most stylish hotels in its price bracket on the French side of the island is operated by the French hotel conglomerate Accor. It's good value for the money, especially since each unit contains a kitchenette. The complex occupies a flat, sandy stretch of land between a saltwater lagoon and the beach, 5 miles west of Queen Juliana Airport. Decorated throughout in ocean-inspired pastels, its five three-story buildings are each evocative of a large, many-balconied Antillean house. In its center, two pools serve as the focal point for a bar built out over the lagoon, an indoor/outdoor restaurant, and a flagstone terrace that hosts steel bands and evening cocktail parties. Each unit, in addition to the kitchenette, offers ceiling fans and simple, durable wicker furniture. The most desirable accommodations, on the third (top) floor, contain sloping ceilings sheltering sleeping lofts and two bathrooms. Laundry and baby-sitting are available.

3 Where to Dine

IN ST. MAARTEN
EXPENSIVE

Antoine's. 103 Front St., Philipsburg. ☎ **599/5-22964.** Reservations recommended, especially in winter. Main courses $17.75–$36. AE, MC, V. Daily 11:30am–10pm. FRENCH/CREOLE/ITALIAN.

This restaurant offers *la belle cuisine* in an atmospheric setting by the sea. Antoine's has a certain sophistication and style, backed up by first-class service and an impressive wine list. Start off with an aperitif in the bar while you peruse the menu. The cuisine is mainly old continental favorites. The Gallic specialties with Creole overtones are among the best on the island, ranking favorably with any of the better restaurants in the French zone. The Italian dishes, however, are better at Da Livio (see below). Gazpacho and vichyssoise appear on the menu, but we prefer to begin with the chef's savory kettle of fish soup. A quite good homemade pâté would also make a suitable opening. The menu is almost equally divided between meat and fish dishes. If featured, opt for the baked red snapper fillet, which is delicately flavored with white wine, lemon, shallots, and a butter sauce. Although the veal and beef dishes are shipped in frozen, they're thawed out and fashioned into rather delectable choices, especially the veal scaloppine with a mustard-and-cream sauce that's smooth and perfectly balanced.

✪ Da Livio Ristorante. 189 Front St., Philipsburg. ☎ **599/5-22690.** Reservations recommended for dinner. Main courses $16–$25 lunch, $19–$34 dinner. AE, MC, V. Mon–Fri noon–2pm; Mon–Sat 6:30–10pm. ITALIAN.

This is the finest Italian dining in St. Maarten. The food is consistently excellent, and the staff is graciousness itself (something rarely found on the island). The place is as Italian as they come, even if all the staff isn't. Bergamasco Livio himself hails from near Venice, and he purchases most of his ingredients from the finest suppliers in his home country. At the bottom of Front Street, with a panoramic view of the Great Bay, the restaurant sets a romantic mood in the evening with background music. Since 1979, and in spite of hurricanes, Da Livio has been turning out the classics, offering daily specials with an emphasis on fresh pastas, fresh local fish, and such favorites as lobster and prime meats. We love the homemade manicotti della casa, filled with ricotta, spinach, and a zesty tomato sauce. For a main course, we suggest you tear into Fra Diavolo with linguine or the tender and juicy veal chop with sage-flavored butter. Tony Bennett and even Eddie Murphy have sung the praises of these dishes. This is obviously a kitchen staff who cares, even going so far as to grow tomatoes in their own garden.

✪ **Le Perroquet.** 72 Airport Rd., a short walk from the airport. ☎ 599/5-54339. Reservations recommended. Main courses $18–$28. AE, DISC, MC, V. Tues–Sun 6–10pm. Closed Sept. FRENCH.

St. Maarten's version of the famed Chicago restaurant is in a typical West Indian house with shutters open to the trade winds blowing around Simpson Bay Lagoon. Monsieur Pierre Castagne, a French chef of exceptional ability, offers such dishes as fillet of boar and ostrich breast (yes, that's right), but you can also order more familiar fare, beginning with a savory fish soup or a fresh mâche salad, moving on to a delectable mussels marinara, savory duck with Grand Marnier orange sauce, or perfectly cooked red snapper in garlic sauce. Some of the specialties are wheeled in on a table so you can make a visual selection—a nice touch.

✪ **Saratoga.** Simpson Bay Yacht Club, Airport Rd. ☎ 599/5-42421. Reservations recommended. Main courses $18–$26. AE, MC, V. Mon–Sat 6:30–10:30pm. AMERICAN.

This is the most creative and cutting-edge restaurant in St. Maarten—it's more closely aligned with trends you'd expect in Los Angeles or New York than in the Caribbean. The result is a burgeoning business that's both laid-back and intensely choreographed at the same time. Thanks to the impressive quantities of varnished mahogany that line much of the interior, this place, which resembles a Spanish colonial structure from the outside, is also one of the most beautiful on the island. You might like a pre-dinner drink ("ultra-premium margaritas" and vodka martinis are the house specialties) in the bar. Seating is either indoors or on a marina-side veranda. The menu changes daily, but there's always an artfully contrived low-fat selection like onion-crusted salmon served on a compote of lentils and sweet corn. Yellowfin tuna might be grilled with basmati rice or wasabi-flavored butter and daikon leaves. Long Island duckling is served with a sauce that varies from night to night, depending on the inspiration of the chef. Examples include confit of duck with green peppercorn sauce, with roasted garlic sauce, or with blackberry-flavored port sauce. Another dish is crispy-fried black sea bass with an Asian-style sauce of fermented black beans and scallions. Grilled salmon is sometimes served either wasabi-flavored or ginger-flavored with flying-fish caviar, and rack of venison is often featured with port or some other sauce concocted by owner/chef John Jackson, who hails, incidentally, from Saratoga Springs, New York.

Spartaco. Almond Grove Plantation Estate, Cole Bay. ☎ 599/5-45379. Reservations recommended. Main courses $12–$24. AE, MC, V. Tues–Sun 6–11pm. Closed Sept–Oct. ITALIAN.

Spartaco is in a residential suburb midway between Philipsburg and the airport. Guests sit in the main dining room, whose decor features strong doses of 1930s art deco and some high-tech touches, or on a breeze-filled, wraparound veranda. Season after season, Spartaco has continued to be the leader in Italian cuisine—and not the pizza and spaghetti selections too often passed off as Italian. Here you get the real thing, which includes fresh black tagliolini (angel-hair pasta flavored with squid ink) served with shrimp, parsley, and garlic sauce. One of the most worthy dishes is the swordfish Mediterranean, composed of parsley, garlic, capers, and an olive oil that owner Spartaco Sargentoni imports from his relatives, who produce it on a farm outside Florence. The antipasti, from squid and mussels to eggplant and carpaccio, make a fine beginning.

MODERATE/INEXPENSIVE

✪ **Cheri's Café.** 45 Cinnamon Grove Shopping Centre, Maho Beach. ☎ **599/5-53361.** Reservations not accepted. Main courses $5.75–$19.75. MC, V. Daily 11am–midnight. AMERICAN.

American expat Cheri Baston's island hot spot was winner of the *Caribbean Travel and Life* readers' pick for best bar in the West Indies. Known for its inexpensive food and live bands, it is by now an island institution. This open-air cafe, serving some 400 meals a night, is really only a roof without walls, and it's not even on a beach. But people flock to it anyway, devouring 18-ounce steaks, simple burgers, and grilled fresh-fish platters. The clientele covers everybody from rock bands to movie stars, high rollers at the casino to beach bums. Some come for the inexpensive food, others for the potent drinks, many to dance to the music. The bartender's special is a frozen "Straw Hat" made with vodka, coconut, tequila, pineapple and orange juices, and strawberry liqueur. Maybe even one more ingredient, we suspect—although nobody's talking.

Chesterfields. Great Bay Marina, Philipsburg. ☎ **599/5-23484.** Reservations recommended. Main courses $3.50–$6 breakfast, $6.95–$13.95 lunch, $14.95–$18.95 dinner. MC, V. Daily 7:30am–10:30pm. AMERICAN/CARIBBEAN.

Just a few steps from Great Bay Marina, east of Philipsburg, this restaurant occupies a breezy veranda that's popular among yachties. Breakfasts are hearty and wholesome, and eye-opening main courses like the seafood omelets are especially tasty. Besides dispensing bottled beer and mixed drinks from midmorning until long after sundown, the bar does a brisk lunch business as well, serving platters of fish, grilled steaks and other meats, sandwiches, and salads. Dinners are more elaborate, and include yellowfin tuna or mahimahi, which can be either grilled and served with garlic butter, or pan-fried with a Creole sauce. Roasted duck, accompanied by banana-pineapple sauce, has been a longtime favorite here. The Wednesday-night special is prime rib, served with heaping portions of sautéed mushrooms.

Don Carlos Restaurant. Airport Rd., Simpson Bay. ☎ **599/5-53112.** Main courses $10.50–$28.50. AE, DC, DISC, MC, V. Daily 7:30am–10pm. MEXICAN/CARIBBEAN/INTERNATIONAL.

This down-home restaurant is just 5 minutes east of the airport, with a view of arriving and departing planes from the floor-to-ceiling windows surrounded by international flags. The place provides consistently decent fare at reasonable prices. Owners Shenny and Carl Wagner invite you for a drink in their Pancho Villa Bar before your meal in the hacienda-style dining room, with a multilingual staff. Quantity, instead of quality, is the rule here, but diners seem to view this as a fun choice.

The Greenhouse. Bobby's Marina (off Front St.), Philipsburg. ☎ **599/5-22941.** Main courses $8.95–$15.95. AE, MC, V. Daily 11am–1am. AMERICAN.

Open to a view of the harbor, the Greenhouse is filled with plants, as befits its name. As you dine, breezes filter through the open-air eatery. The menu features the ever-popular catch of the day as well as burgers, pizza, and salads. Dinner specials might include fresh lobster Thermidor, Jamaican jerk pork, or salmon in a light dill sauce. Some of the island's best steaks are served here, each cut certified Angus beef, including a New York strip, a T-bone, a porterhouse, or a filet mignon. The chef specializes in chicken, ranging from mango chicken to chicken parmigiana. Happy hour, daily from 4:30 to 7pm, features half-price appetizers and two-for-one drinks. The DJ not only plays music but also gives prizes to Bingo champs and trivia experts. Pool tables and video games will keep you entertained.

✪ **Lynette's.** Simpson Bay Blvd. ☎ **599/5-52865.** Reservations recommended. Main courses $13.75–$32. AE, MC, V. Winter daily 11:30am–10:30pm. Off-season daily 6–10:30pm. WEST INDIAN.

This is the most noteworthy West Indian restaurant on St. Maarten. It's completely unpretentious, and rich in local flavors and understated charm. The creative forces here are St. Maarten–born Lynette Felix, along with Clayton Felix, who serve up flavorful ethnic food from a location near the airport. The setting is a concrete-sided, wood-trimmed building beside the highway, with a color scheme of pink, maroon, cream, and brown. The menu reads like a lexicon of tried-and-true Caribbean staples, including colombos (ragoûts) of goat and chicken, stuffed crab backs, curried seafood, and fillet of snapper with green plantains. An ideal lunch might be a brimming bowlful of pumpkin (squash) soup followed by one of the main-course salads. The herbed lobster version, when available, is particularly succulent. The dishes here have true island flavor.

Wajang Doll. 167 Front St., Philipsburg. ☎ **599/5-22687.** Reservations required. 14-dish dinner $18.90, 19-dish dinner $24.90. AE, MC, V. Mon–Sat noon–2pm and 6:30–10pm. Closed Sept. INDONESIAN.

Housed in a wooden West Indian building on the main street of town, Wajang Doll is the best Indonesian restaurant in the Caribbean. A low-slung front porch lets you watch the pedestrian traffic outside, and the big windows in back overlook the sea. The restaurant is known for its 19-dish dinner, known as a *rijstaffel* (rice table). The cuisine varies from West Java to East Java, and the chef crushes his spices every day for maximum pungency, according to an ancient craft. The specialties include a spicy seafood tofu and tempura made from soy bean, plus zestily flavored Javanese chicken dishes.

IN ST. MARTIN
IN & AROUND MARIGOT

La Brasserie de Marigot. 11 rue du Général-de-Gaulle. ☎ **0590/87-94-43.** Main courses 45 F–88 F ($7.65–$14.95). AE, MC, V. Mon–Sat 7am–9pm, Sun 9am–4pm. FRENCH.

This is where the local French eat. Set in a former bank, it has a marble-and-brass decor, a sort of retro 1950s style with green leather banquettes. Entrees include pot-au-feu, stuffed snapper with conch, fillet of beef with mushroom sauce, veal with goat cheese, even chicken on a spit and steak tartare, all those good dishes that the French enjoyed at blue-collar bistros "between the wars." Naturally, you can order interesting terrines here, and wine is sold by the glass, carafe, or bottle. The kitchen also prepares a handful of Caribbean dishes, such as swordfish in garlic sauce. The brasserie, located in the center of town, is air-conditioned, with sidewalk tables overlooking the pedestrian traffic outside. It also features the most glamorous take-out service on St. Martin. For good food at good prices, this is an excellent choice.

La Maison sur le Port. Blvd. de France. ☎ **0590/87-56-38.** Reservations recommended. Main courses $14–$19 lunch, $17.50–$38 dinner; fixed-price dinner $23.75. AE, DISC, MC, V. Mon–Sat noon–2:30pm and daily 6–10:30pm. FRENCH.

Overall, this is a rather grand, rather Parisian, and rather upscale choice. French cuisine is served in an elegant, refined atmosphere, with a view of three waterfalls in the garden. The tables are dressed with snowy tablecloths and Limoges china. At lunch, served on the covered terrace, you can choose from a number of salads as well as fish and meat courses. Dinner choices include fresh fish, such as snapper, salmon, or fresh-caught swordfish with coconut sauce; and fillet of lamb, veal, or steak. Duck with mango has always been a specialty, as has bouillabaisse or giant shrimp in garlic butter. The cookery is grounded firmly in France, but there are Caribbean twists and flavors, which come as delightful surprises. The wine list has an extensive selection of imported French options at moderate prices. Many guests come here at sundown to enjoy the harbor view.

✪ **La Vie en Rose.** Blvd. de France at rue de la République. ☎ **0590/87-54-42.** Reservations recommended, especially in winter and as far in advance as possible. Main courses $14–$23 lunch, $26.85–$40.30 dinner. AE, MC, V. Daily 11:30am–2:30pm and 6:30–9:45pm. FRENCH.

The dining room in this balconied second-floor restaurant evokes the 1920s with its ceiling fans and candlelight. If you don't like the parlor, you can sit on a little veranda overlooking the harbor (request this when you make your reservation). Even though the menu is classic French, it nevertheless has Caribbean flavor. Lunches are relatively simple affairs, with an emphasis on fresh, meal-sized salads, simple grills that include steaks and fresh fish, and sandwiches. Dinners are more elaborate, and might begin with a seafood tartare with medaillons of lobster, or fried foie gras with pears marinated in red wine. Main courses include grilled fillet of red snapper with fresh basil sauce, fresh medaillons of lobster floating on a bed of Caribbean lime sauce, boneless breast of duck with raspberry sauce and fried bananas, and an unusual version of roasted rack of lamb with a gratin of goat cheese and sliced potatoes.

Le Mini Club. Rue de la Liberté. ☎ **0590/87-50-69.** Reservations required. Fixed-price menu $23; Wed and Sat dinner buffet $40. AE, MC, V. Daily noon–3pm and 6–11pm. FRENCH/CREOLE.

After you climb a flight of wooden stairs, you'll find yourself in an environment like a treehouse built among coconut palms. Suspended on a wooden deck above the sands of the beach, this establishment is filled with Haitian murals and grass carpeting. It's not the best and certainly not the most innovative restaurant on the island, but it has many fans, as it uses quality ingredients and prepares every dish exceedingly well. The specialties include lobster soufflé (made for two or four people), an array of fish and vegetable terrines, red snapper with Creole sauce, sweetbreads in puff pastry, and many kinds of salad. Dessert might be bananas flambéed with cognac. Lavish buffets are held every Wednesday and Saturday night, with unlimited wine included. The restaurant is along the seafront at Marigot.

Mahogany. In Le Mississippi Hotel, Oyster Pond. ☎ **0590/87-33-81.** Reservations recommended. Main courses 110 F–165 F ($18.70–$28.05); set-price menus 220 F–380 F ($37.40–$64.60). AE, DC, MC, V. Daily noon–2pm and 7–9:30pm. FRENCH/INTERNATIONAL.

This relative newcomer to St. Martin's restaurant scene has appealed to many with its rather formal French menu and its position on a covered, woodsy-looking veranda whose views extend out over neighboring St. Barts and Saba. You might begin with a drink at the circular bar before migrating to your table. The menu has been decidedly influenced by the grand culinary traditions of Paris. Examples include homemade foie gras or smoked salmon, a "crème brûlée" of crayfish in an herbal infusion of verveine flavored with bacon, suprême of red snapper with a crystalline of fresh vegetables, and rosettes of Peking duck with lavender-flavored honey and sherry-flavored vinaigrette. The cuisine remains always inventive, always consistently good.

IN & AROUND GRAND-CASE

This isolated beach town, a scant mile-long brush stroke of Antillean houses, has the greatest concentration of restaurants in the Caribbean. They line the seafront, a virtual movie set of the colonial Caribbean.

Hévéa. 163 Blvd. de Grand-Case. ☎ **0590/87-56-85.** Reservations required. Main courses 100 F–130 F ($17–$22.10); menu Creole (featuring West Indian items) 145 F ($24.65). AE, MC, V. Daily 6:30–11pm. Closed Sept–Oct. FRENCH.

Normandy-born restaurateurs own this place, the most obviously French of any restaurant in Grand-Case. After storm damage in 1995, it reopened with Louis XV chairs, Norman artifacts, candlelight, and a sense of formality. There are fewer than a dozen tables, so advance reservations are usually crucial. Start with the Caesar salad, which remains the best on the island. In honor of their Norman roots, the owners prepare such classic dishes as *darne* of kingfish; scallops *Dieppoise* (with a cream-flavored mussel sauce); and one of the great dishes of the conservative French repertoire, escalopes of veal *Pays d'Auge,* made with apple brandy (Calvados) and cream. You might also try the terrine of duck or foie gras maison. To remind you that you're in the West Indies, there's a set-price all-Creole menu, a platter of West Indian smoked fish, and American-style lobster with tomato sauce and herbs.

La Marine. 158 Blvd. de Grand-Case. ☎ **0590/87-02-31.** Reservations recommended. Main courses $19–$30. AE, MC, V. Mon–Sat noon–2:30pm and 6–10:30pm. Closed Sept 1 to mid-Oct; no lunch during the off-season. FRENCH.

Set on the seaward side of the main road running through Grand-Case, this is one of the most appealing restaurants in town, set in an antique, much-enlarged Creole house with a blue-and-white color scheme. The capable chef here is Gilles Briand, who crafts sophisticated variations on classical French cuisine. Everything is made fresh from ingredients imported at frequent intervals from the French or U.S. mainland. Worthy beginnings include lobster-stuffed ravioli with Antillean herbs, a galette of crabmeat with a confit of red peppers, and a *croustillant* of snails with vinaigrette made from equal portions of cider vinegar and balsamic vinegar. There's also a roulade of halibut with Japanese algae, stuffed with a mixture of crabmeat and smoked salmon, then drizzled with a curry sauce. To represent old-fashioned, 19th-century provincial fare is a confit of rabbit cooked in goose fat, served with cabbage stuffed with smoked lard, and accompanied by a chive-flavored cream sauce.

✪ L'Auberge Gourmande. 89 Blvd. de Grand-Case. ☎ **0590/87-73-37.** Reservations required. Main courses $18–$32. MC, V. Winter Thurs–Tues, with seatings at 7 or 9pm. Off-season Thurs–Tues 6–10pm (seatings any time). Closed June. FRENCH.

If you appreciate decent French food, a family ambience, and professional service, this is the place for you. The restaurant, in a century-old French Antillean house with a nautical atmosphere, is run by chef Philippe Cassan and his wife, Christine. No one pretends that the cuisine is the finest on the island, but it's both honest and straight-forward. Begin with vichyssoise, onion soup, or perhaps the mussel soup flavored with orange. Among their classic dishes are pork tenderloin with an old-fashioned mustard sauce, and a fillet of beef with either a blue-cheese or black-pepper sauce. Also excellent is the duck breast with a honey-and-lemon sauce. More recent and more innovative items on the menu include foie gras sautéed with a sherry-flavored vinaigrette, scallops in a creamy saffron sauce, and medaillons of lobster in a white butter sauce. For dessert, try the profiteroles. Ask about le service au vin, which allows you to taste several wines throughout the course of your meal.

✪ **Le Cottage.** 97 Blvd. de Grand Case. ☎ **0590/29-03-30.** Reservations recommended. Main courses 105 F–145 F ($17.85–$24.65). AE, DC, MC, V. Daily 6:30–11pm. FRENCH/ CREOLE.

One of our favorite restaurants in a town that's loaded with worthy contenders is set in what looks like a private house, on the landward side of the main road running through Grand Case. Owned by Bruno Lemoine, its atmosphere is at least partly influenced by the Burgundy-born wine steward, Stephane Émorine, who shows a canny intuition at recommending a sophisticated medley of wines that are sold by the glass, and that are specifically selected to complement each course of the French and Caribbean cuisine. Menu items include both rustic *cuisine du terroir* (such as roasted rack of lamb with a cream-based *pistou* sauce) and dishes more closely linked to Creole traditions, including a fillet of local dorado served with a reduction of crayfish, or a blaff (stew) of red snapper flavored with Creole herbs. Other dishes seem to go beyond Creole classics, onto a creative level all their own. One example is scallops in puff pastry, with a unique form of tea that's brewed from flap mushrooms and mint leaves. Meals tend to begin dramatically with such dishes as a *charlotte* of crayfish and avocados with a citrus sauce, a tartare of tuna and salmon with mustard-flavored vinaigrette, and a salad of crispy vegetables with balsamic-oil dressing.

✪ **Villa Plantation (Michel Royer).** Orient Bay. ☎ **0590/29-57-68.** Reservations recommended. Main courses 82 F–220 F ($13.95–$37.40); menu dégustation 400 F ($68). AE, MC, V. Wed–Mon 7–10:30pm. Closed Sept–Oct. FRENCH/CARIBBEAN.

St. Martin's most celebrated new restaurant has managed to attract dozens of clients from the international world of show biz and media since it was founded in 1996. Set on an eastward-facing slope above the waters of Orient Bay, in a villa with two dining rooms and a terrace, it's the personal statement of Michel Royer, who won many awards in his native Lyon and Bordeaux, including the coveted maître cuisinier de France. The decor includes pineapple friezes and painted furniture, whose depictions of vines and flowers were executed during slow periods by Mr. Royer himself. The menu dégustation is a personalized ritual of five courses and three desserts, each selected by the owner/chef according to the season and the availability of the ingredients. Choices from the à la carte menu include an escalope of warm foie gras with raspberry vinegar, asparagus tips in puff pastry served with asparagus-stuffed morels, guinea fowl steeped in its own juices and served with Provençal herbs and white truffle oil, and a fillet of beef with a mustard-flavored and nettle-based cream sauce. Everyone's favorite dessert is a crisp version of caramelized banana flambé, with a sauce made from aged rum.

4 Beaches

The island has 36 beautiful white-sand beaches, and it's fairly easy to find a part of the beach for yourself. Most beaches have recovered from the erosion caused by the 1995 hurricane. *Warning:* If it's too secluded, be careful. It's unwise to carry valuables to the beach; there have been reports of robberies on some remote strips.

Regardless of where you stay, you're never far from the water. If you're a beach sampler, you can often use the changing facilities at some of the bigger resorts for a small fee. Nudists should head for the French side of the island, although the Dutch side is getting more liberal about such things. Here's a rundown of the best, starting on the Dutch side of the island.

On the west side of the island, west of the airport, **Mullet Bay Beach** is filled with white sand and shaded by palm trees. Once it was the most crowded beach on the island, but St. Maarten's largest resort, Mullet Bay, remains closed at press time, enabling you to find your place in the sun today. Weekdays are best, as many locals flock here on weekends. Water-sports equipment can be rented at a kiosk here.

West of the airport, **Maho Bay Beach,** at the Maho Beach Hotel and Casino, is shaded by palms and is ideal in many ways, if you don't mind the planes taking off and landing. This is one of the island's busiest beaches, buzzing with windsurfers. Food and drink can be purchased at the hotel.

Stretching the length of Simpson Bay Village are the mile-long white sands of crescent-shaped **Simpson Bay Beach,** west of Philipsburg before you reach the airport. This beach is popular with windsurfers, and it's an ideal place for a stroll or a swim. Water-sports equipment rentals are available here, but there are no changing rooms or other facilities.

Great Bay Beach is preferred if you're staying along Front Street in Philipsburg. This mile-long beach is sandy, but since it borders the busy capital, it may not be as clean as some of the more remote choices. On a clear day, you'll have a view of Saba. Immediately to the west, at the foot of Fort Amsterdam, is picturesque **Little Bay Beach**—but it, too, can be overrun with tourists. When you tire of the sands here, you can climb up to the site of Fort Amsterdam itself. Built in 1631, it was the first Dutch military outpost in the Caribbean. The Spanish captured it two years later, making it their most important bastion east of Puerto Rico. Only a few of the fort's walls remain, but the view is panoramic.

Dawn Beach is noted for its underwater tropical beauty, with some of the island's most beautiful reefs immediately offshore. Visitors talk ecstatically of its incredible sunrises. Dawn is suitable for swimming and offers year-round activities such as sand-castle-building contests and crab races. There's plenty of wave action for both surfers and windsurfers. The road to this beach is bumpy, but worth the effort. Nearby are the pearly white sands of **Oyster Pond Beach,** near the Oyster Pond Hotel northeast of Philipsburg. Bodysurfers like the rolling waves here.

Beyond the sprawling Mullet Beach Resort on the Dutch side, the popular **Cupecoy Bay Beach** is just north of the Dutch-French border, on the western side of the island. It's a string of three white-sand beaches set against a backdrop of caves, beautiful rock formations, and cliffs that provide morning shade. There are no restaurants, bars, or other facilities here, but locals come around with coolers of cold beer and soda. The beach has two parking lots, one near Cupecoy and Sapphire beach clubs, the other a short distance to the west. Parking costs $2. You must descend stone-carved steps to reach the sands. Cupecoy is also the island's major gay beach.

Top rating on St. Martin goes to **Baie Longue** on the French side, a beautiful beach that's rarely overcrowded. Chic and very expensive La Samanna opens onto this beachfront. Its reef-protected waters are ideal for snorkeling, but there is a strong undertow. Baie Longue is to the north of Cupecoy Beach, reached via the Lowlands Road. Don't leave any valuables in your car, as many break-ins have been reported along this occasionally dangerous stretch of highway.

If you continue north along the highway, you'll reach another long and popular stretch of sand and jagged coral, **Baie Rouge.** Swimming is excellent here, and snorkelers are drawn to the rock formations at both ends of the beach. This intimate little spot is especially lovely in the morning. There are no changing facilities, but a local kiosk sells cold drinks.

Orient Beach is the island's only official nudist beach, so anything—or nothing—goes in terms of attire. There's steady shoreside action here: bouncy Caribbean bands, refreshments of all kinds, water sports, and clothing, crafts, and jewelry vendors. Our favorite spot is the open-air bar/restaurant **Kontiki** (☎ **0590/87-43-27**), offering fresh lobster and reasonably good sushi for lunch. Club Orient, the nude resort, is at the end of the beach; voyeurs from cruise ships can always be spotted here. This is also a haven for windsurfers.

White-sand **Grand Case Beach** is right in the middle of the town of Grand Case and is likely to be crowded, especially on weekends. The waters are very calm here, making swimming excellent. A small but select beach, it has its own charm, with none of the carnival-like atmosphere of Orient Beach.

Finally, for the most isolated and secluded beach of all, you have to leave St. Martin. **Ilet Pinel,** off the coast at Cul de Sac, is reached by a $5 boat ride off the northeast coast. Once on this islet, you'll find no residents (except wild goats), phones, or electricity. You will find fine white-sand beaches, reefs idyllic for snorkeling, and waters great for bodysurfing. There are even two beach bars: Pitou's and Karibuni. Both rent lounge chairs and serve dishes such as lobster, ribs, and grilled chicken.

5 Sports & Outdoor Pursuits

DEEP-SEA FISHING   Pelican Watersports, on the Dutch side, at the Pelican Resort and Casino, Simpson Bay (☎ **599/5-42640**), is part of one of the island's most comprehensive resorts. Their 31-foot Blackfin is available for deep-sea-fishing expeditions priced at $450 for a half-day (from 8am to noon) or $850 for a full-day (from 8am to 4pm) excursion.

GOLF   The **Mullet Bay Resort** (☎ **599/5-52801**, ext. 1850), on the Dutch side, has an 18-hole Joseph Lee–designed course, one of the most challenging in the Caribbean. Mullet Pond and Simpson Bay Lagoon provide both beauty and hazards. Greens fees are $62 for 9 holes or $108 for 18 holes. Clubs cost $21 for 9 holes or $26 for 18 holes.

HORSEBACK RIDING   Crazy Acres, Dr. J. H. Dela Fuente Street, Cole Bay (☎ **599/5-42793**), on the Dutch side, is your best bet for riding expeditions. Two experienced escorts accompany a maximum of six people on the 2½-hour outings, which are offered Monday to Saturday at 9:30am and 2:30pm. The cost is $55 per person. Riders of all levels of experience are welcome. Reserve at least a day in advance; riding lessons are available as well.

SCUBA DIVING   Scuba diving is excellent around **French St. Martin,** with reef, wreck, night, cave, and drift diving; the depth of dives is 20 to 70 feet. Off the northeastern coast on the French side, dive sites include Ilet Pinel, for shallow diving; Green Key, a barrier reef; and Tintamarre, for sheltered coves and geologic faults. To the north, Anse Marcel and neighboring Anguilla are good choices. Most hotels will arrange scuba excursions on request.

The island's premier dive operation is **Marine Time,** whose offices are based in the same building as L'Aventure, Chemin du Port, Marigot (☎ **0590/87-20-28**). Operated by England-born Philip Baumann and his Mauritius-born colleague, Corine Mazurier, it offers morning and afternoon dives in deep and shallow water, wreck dives, and reef dives, at a cost of $45 per dive. A resort course for first-time divers with reasonable swimming skills costs $80 and includes 60 to 90 minutes of instruction in a swimming pool, then a one-tank dive above a coral reef. Full PADI certification costs $400, an experience that requires 5 days and includes classroom training, sessions with

---

Butterflies in Bucolic St. Martin

Far from the crowds, you may want to seek out the little village of **Orléans** (also called the French Quarter), the island's oldest French settlement. Its houses (*cases*) are set in meadows that blossom with hibiscus, bougainvillea, and wisteria. On the road to Bayside and Galion is the charming **Butterfly Farm,** route de Baie L'Embouchure (☎ 0590/87-31-21), an Eden-like setting created and run by two Englishmen. Visitors are offered a rare insight into the amazing transformations from egg to butterfly. You'll learn all about these delicate creatures and meet such beauties as the Brazilian Blue Morpho and the Cambodian Wood Nymph. Mornings are an ideal time to visit.

---

a SCUBA tank within the safety of a swimming pool, and three open-water dives. Snorkeling trips cost $25 for a half day or $75 for a full day, plus $10 for equipment rental.

You can also try **Blue Ocean Watersport & Dive Center,** BP 4079, Baie Nettlé, St. Martin (☎ 0590/87-89-73). A certified one-tank dive costs $45, including equipment. A PADI certification course is available for $350, and takes 4 to 5 days. Three one-tank dives are offered for $120, five dives for $175. Snorkeling trips, more modestly priced at $30, are conducted daily from 1:30 to 4:30pm.

Dutch St. Maarten's crystal-clear bays and countless coves make for good scuba diving as well as snorkeling. Underwater visibility runs from 75 to 125 feet. The biggest attraction for divers is the 1801 British man-of-war, HMS *Proselyte,* which came to a watery grave on a reef a mile off the coast. Most of the big resorts have facilities for scuba diving and can provide information about underwater tours, for photography as well as for night diving.

We recommend **Pelican Watersports,** Pelican Resort and Casino, Simpson Bay (☎ 599/5-42640). Its PADI-instructed program features the most knowledgeable guides on the island, each familiar with St. Maarten dive sites. Divers are taken out in custom-built 28- and 35-foot boats. A single-tank dive costs $45; a double-tank dive, $90. Snorkeling trips can also be arranged, as can trips to nearby islands, including Saba, Anguilla, and St. Barts.

SNORKELING The calm waters ringing the shallow reefs and tiny coves found throughout the island make it a snorkeler's heaven. The waters off the northeastern shores of French St. Martin have been classified as a regional underwater nature reserve, **Réserve Sous-Marine Régionale.** The area, comprising Flat Island (also known as Tintamarre), Pinel Islet, Green Key, Proselyte, and Petite Clef, is thus protected by official government decree. The use of harpoons is strictly forbidden. Equipment can be rented at almost any hotel.

One of St. Martin's best sources for snorkeling and other beach diversions is **Carib Watersports** (☎ 0590/87-51-87), a clothing store, art gallery, and water-sports kiosk on the beachfront of the Grand-Case Beach Club. Its French and American staff, supervised by Michigan-born Marla Welch, provides information on island activities and rents paddleboats for $15 an hour, low-velocity motorized boats for $20 an hour, and chaise longues with beach umbrellas. The main allure, however, is the guided, hour-long snorkeling trips to St. Martin's teeming offshore reefs. The most visible of these are the waters surrounding Creole Rock, an offshore clump of reef-ringed boulders rich in underwater fauna. The 2-hour trips depart daily at 2:30pm and cost $25, with all equipment included. Reservations are recommended.

A SPA **L'Aqualine,** at the Pelican Resort and Casino, Simpson Bay (☎ 599/ 5-42426), on the Dutch side, is a world-class European health, fitness, and beauty spa that offers services ranging from water aerobics to massage, cellulite therapy to body sculpting. Spa services include waxing, medical pedicures, manicures, body peels, facials, and beauty treatments. Facilities include eight separate treatment rooms, saunas, a steam room, and an ice-plunge and therapy pool. Hours are Monday to Saturday from 9am to 6pm.

TENNIS You can try the courts at most of the large resorts, but you must call first for a reservation. Preference, of course, is given to hotel guests. On the Dutch side, there are three lit courts at **Pelican Resort Club** at Simpson Bay (☎ 0599/ 54-25-03); another three lit courts at **Divi Little Bay Beach Resort,** Little Bay Road (☎ 0599/52-54-10); and yet another three at **Maho Beach Hotel,** Maho Bay (☎ 0599/55-21-15). On the French side, **Privilège Resort & Spa,** Anse Marcel (☎ 0590/87-38-38), offers six lit courts; **Hotel Mont Vernon,** Baie Orientale (☎ 0590/87-62-00), has two lit courts; and **Nettlé Beach Club,** Sandy Ground Road (☎ 0590/87-6-68), has three lit Laykold courts.

WATERSKIING & PARASAILING Most of French St. Martin's large beachfront hotels maintain facilities for waterskiing and parasailing, often from kiosks that operate on the beach. Waterskiing averages $40 per 20-minute ride. Two independent operators on Orient Bay, close to the cluster of hotels near the Esmeralda Hotel, include **Kon Tiki Watersports** (☎ 0590/87-46-89) and **Bikini Beach Watersports** (☎ 0590/87-43-25). High-velocity, highly maneuverable jet skis rent for around $45 per half-hour session; parasailing, which involves hanging from a parachute above waterskis while being towed behind a motorboat, costs $50 for 10 minutes.

Jet-skiing and waterskiing are also especially popular in Dutch St. Maarten. The unruffled waters of Simpson Bay Lagoon, the largest in the West Indies, are ideal for these sports.

WINDSURFING Because of prevailing winds and waters that are protected from violent waves by offshore reefs, most windsurfers gravitate to the strip of sand on the island's easternmost edge, most notably Coconut Grove Beach, Orient Beach, and to a lesser extent, Dawn Beach, all in French St. Martin. The best of the several outfitters here is **Tropical Wave,** Coconut Grove, Le Galion Beach, Baie de l'Embouchure (☎ 0590/87-37-25). Set midway between Orient Beach and Oyster Pond, amid a sunblasted, scrub-covered landscape isolated from any of the island's big hotels, its combination of wind and calm waters is considered almost ideal by windsurfing aficionados. Operated by American-born Patrick Turner, Tropical Wave is the island's leading sales agent for Mistral Windsurfers. They rent for $20 an hour, with instruction offered at $30 an hour.

In Dutch St. Maarten, visitors usually head to Simpson Bay Lagoon.

6 Cruises & Tours

CRUISES A popular pastime is a day of picnicking, sailing, snorkeling, and sightseeing aboard one of several boats providing the service. The sleek sailboats usually pack large wicker hampers full of provisions and stretch tarpaulins over sections of the deck to protect sun-shy sailors.

In Dutch St. Maarten, the traditional clipper *Random Wind* makes day trips that circumnavigate the island, carrying 15 passengers at a cost of $70 each, including a lunch bar and snorkeling. Reservations can be made at Simpson Bay Marina

(☎ **0599/57-57-42**). A Wednesday breakfast cruise, from 9am to 1pm, costs $50 per person and includes a real French breakfast, complete with mimosas. A Wednesday sunset cruise, from 5 to 6:30pm, costs $30.

Experienced skippers also make 1-day voyages to St. Barts in the French West Indies and to Saba, another of the Dutch Windwards in the Leewards; they stop long enough for passengers to visit the island ports, shop, and have lunch. To arrange a trip, ask at your hotel or at the **St. Maarten Tourist Bureau,** 23 Walter Nisbeth Rd., Philipsburg (☎ **599/5-22337**).

If you'd like to see some of the other islands nearby, the best deal is offered by *Voyager I* and *Voyager II.* Daily sails to St. Barts cost $50 round-trip; to Saba, $60 round-trip. Children under 12 pay half. These are good-value trips well worth the time and money. For details, call **Dockside Management,** in Philipsburg (☎ **599/5-24096**).

SIGHTSEEING TOURS   The only companies offering bus tours of the island are **Dutch Tours,** Cougar Road, 8 Unit One (☎ **599/5-23316**), and **St. Maarten Sightseeing Tours** (☎ **599/5-53921**), whose buses can accommodate between 22 and 52 people. They are only configured for large groups, and are very difficult to prearrange.

In Dutch St. Maarten, you can also hire a taxi driver as your guide; a 2½-hour tour of the entire island costs $30 to $35 for up to two passengers, and $7.50 to $10 for each additional passenger.

In French St. Martin, you can book 2-hour sightseeing trips around the island either through **St. Martin's Taxi Service & Information Center,** in Marigot (☎ **0590/87-56-54**), or at any hotel desk. The cost is $50 for one or two passengers, plus $10 for each additional person.

7 Shopping

IN ST. MAARTEN

St. Maarten is not only a free port—there's also no local sales taxes. Prices are sometimes lower here than anywhere else in the Caribbean except possibly St. Thomas. On some items (fine liqueurs, cigarettes, Irish linen, German cameras, French perfumes), we've found prices 30% to 50% lower than in the United States or Canada. Many well-known shops on Curaçao have branches here, in case you're not going on to the ABC islands (Aruba, Bonaire, and Curaçao).

Except for the boutiques at resort hotels, the main shopping area is in the center of **Philipsburg**. Most of the shops are on **Front Street** (called Voorstraat in Dutch), which is closer to the bay, and **Back Street** (Achterstraat), which runs parallel.

In general, prices marked on the merchandise are fixed. At small, very personally run shops, where the owner is on site, some bargaining might be in order.

New Amsterdam Store, 66 Front St. (☎ **559/5-22787**), has been a tradition in the islands since 1925. This general store sells a little bit of everything—from fine linen to fashion, footwear to swimwear, even porcelain. If your time is limited, you might want to visit this place first. Prices are competitive with other stores in town touting similar merchandise.

Old Street Shopping Center, with entrances on Front Street and Back Street (☎ **599/5-24712**), is east of the courthouse. Its lion's-head fountain is the most photographed spot on St. Maarten. Built in a West Indian–Dutch style, it features more than two dozen shops and boutiques. The stores are open Monday to Saturday from 9:30am to 6pm, but the Philipsburg Grill and Ribs Company is open on Sunday if a cruise ship docks.

Colombian Emeralds International, Old Street Shopping Center (☎ **599/5-23933**), sells unmounted emeralds from Colombia, as well as emerald, gold,

People Watching in Philipsburg

The picturesque Dutch capital of St. Maarten is filled with West Indian cottages, decorated with gingerbread trim. At Wathey Square (pronounced *watty*), the heartbeat of the thriving, bustling little town, you can sit and watch the world go by: tourists and cruise-ship passengers, trinket peddlers and shopkeepers. It's like a bustling souk all day. Directly off the square is the town's densest concentration of restaurants, cafes, and shops. Follow any narrow alleyway leading to an arcade, where you'll find flower-filled courtyards, more shops, and plenty of eateries.

---

diamond, ruby, and sapphire jewelry. Prices are approximately the same as in other outlets of this famous Caribbean chain, and if you're seriously shopping for emeralds, this is the place. There are some huckster vendors around the island pawning fakes off on unsuspecting tourists; Colombian Emeralds offers the genuine item.

Caribbean Camera Centre, 79 Front St. (☎ 599/5-25259), has a wide range of merchandise, but it's always wise to know the prices charged back home. Cameras here may be among the cheapest on St. Maarten; however, if you're going to St. Thomas, we've discovered better deals there.

Little Europe, 80 Front St. (☎ 599/5-24371), is an upscale purveyor of all the "finer things" in life. It's favored by cruise-ship passengers because its prices are inexpensive compared to North American boutiques. Inventory includes porcelain figurines by Hummel, jewelry, and watches by Concorde, Piaget, Corum, and Movado.

Little Switzerland, 52 Front St. (☎ 599/5-23530), is part of a chain of stores spread throughout the Caribbean. These fine-quality European imports are made even more attractive by the prices, often 25% or more lower than Stateside. Elegant famous-name watches, china, crystal, and jewelry are for sale, plus perfume and accessories. Little Switzerland has the best overall selection of these items of any shop on the Dutch side.

At **Shipwreck Shop,** Front Street (☎ 599/5-22962), you'll find West Indian hammocks, beach towels, salad bowls, baskets, jewelry, T-shirts, postcards, books, and much more. It's also the home of wood carvings, native art, sea salt, cane sugar, and spices—in all, a treasure trove of Caribbean handcrafts. If you're looking for affordable gifts or handcrafts in general, this might be your best bet.

Guavaberry Company, 8–10 Front St. (☎ 599/5-22965), sells the rare "island folk liqueur" of St. Maarten, which for centuries was made only in private homes. Sold in square bottles, the product is made from rum that's given a unique flavor with rare berries usually grown in the hills in the center of the island. Don't confuse guavaberries with guavas—they're very different. The liqueur has a fruity, woody, almost bittersweet flavor. You can blend it with coconut for a unique guavaberry colada or pour a splash into a glass of icy champagne.

Antillean Liquors, Queen Juliana Airport (☎ 599/5-54267), has a complete assortment of liquor and liqueurs, cigarettes and cigars. Prices are generally lower here than in other stores on the island, and the selection is larger. The only local product sold is the Guavaberry island liqueur.

IN ST. MARTIN

Many day-trippers come over to Marigot from the Dutch side just to visit the French-inspired boutiques and shopping arcades. Because it's also a duty-free port, you'll find some of the best shopping in the Caribbean. There's a wide selection of European merchandise, much of it luxury items such as crystal, fashions, fine liqueurs, and cigars, sometimes at 25% to 50% less than in the United States and Canada. Whether you're seeking jewelry, perfume, or St. Tropez bikinis, you'll find it in one of the boutiques along **rue de la République** and **rue de la Liberté** in Marigot. Look especially for French luxury items, such as Lalique crystal, Vuitton bags, and Chanel perfume.

Prices are often quoted in U.S. dollars, and salespeople frequently speak English. Credit cards and traveler's checks are generally accepted. When cruise ships are in port on Sunday and holidays, some of the larger shops stay open.

At harborside in Marigot, there's a lively **morning market** with vendors selling spices, fruit, shells, and handcrafts. Shops here tend to be rather upscale, catering to passengers of the small but choice cruise ships that dock offshore.

At **Port La Royale,** the bustling center of everything, mornings are even more active: Schooners unload produce from the neighboring islands, boats board guests for picnics on deserted beaches, a brigantine sets out on a sightseeing sail, and a dozen different little restaurants are readying for the lunch crowd. The largest shopping arcade on St. Martin, it has many boutiques, some of which come and go with great rapidity.

Another complex, the **Galerie Périgourdine,** facing the post office, also has a cluster of boutiques. Here you might pick up designer wear for both men and women, including items from the collection of Ted Lapidus.

Act III, 3 rue du Général-de-Gaulle (☎ 0590/29-28-43), is almost always cited as the most glamorous women's boutique in St. Martin. It prides itself on its evening gowns and chic cocktail dresses, and limits its roster of bathing suits to a simple collection that appears only in spring. If you've been invited to a reception aboard a private yacht, this is the place to find the right outfit. Designers include Alaïa, Thierry Mugler, Gianni Versace, Christian Lacroix, Cerruti, and Gaultier. The bilingual staff is accommodating, tactful, and charming.

La Romana, 12 rue de la République (☎ 0590/87-88-16), specializes in chic women's clothing that's a bit less pretentious and more fun and lighthearted than the selection at Act III. Italian rather than French designers are emphasized, including lines such as Anna Club and Ritmo de la Perloa, plus La Perla swimwear, Moschino handbags, and perfumes. A small collection of menswear is also available.

The popular chain **Little Switzerland** has a branch here on rue de la République (☎ 0590/87-50-03). This outlet is different from the one on the Dutch side, with a concentration on French products. The widest array of duty-free luxury items in French St. Martin is available here, including French perfume and leather goods.

Maneks, 24 rue de la République (☎ 0590/87-54-91), has a little bit of everything: video cameras, electronics, household appliances, liquors, gifts, souvenirs, beach accessories, film, watches, T-shirts, sunglasses, and Majorca pearls. The staff even sells Cuban cigars, but these can't be brought back into the United States.

Lipstick, Port La Royale, rue Kennedy (☎ 0590/87-73-24), is the leading purveyor of cosmetics and skin-care products on French St. Martin, with a beauty parlor one floor above street level. It carries virtually every conceivable cosmetic or beauty aid made by Chanel, Lancôme, Guerlain, Yves St. Laurent, Dior, and Shiseido. Hair removal, massage, manicures, pedicures, facials, and hair styling are available. Another outlet a few storefronts away, on rue de la République (☎ 0590/87-53-92), sells cosmetics but does not offer beauty treatments.

Gingerbread & Mahogany Gallery, 4–14 Marina Royale (☎ 0590/87-73-21), is among the finest galleries. Owner Simone Seitre is one of the most knowledgeable purveyors of Haitian art in the Caribbean. Even if you're not in the market for an expensive piece, you'll find dozens of charming and inexpensive handcrafts. The little gallery is a bit hard to find (on a narrow alleyway at the marina), but it's worth the search.

✪ **Roland Richardson,** boulevard de France (☎ **0590/87-32-24**), has a beautiful gallery on the waterfront in Marigot. A native of St. Martin, Mr. Richardson is one of the Caribbean's premier artists, working in oil, watercolors, pastels, and charcoal. Called a "modern-day Gauguin," he is known for his landscapes, portraits, and colorful still lifes. His work has been exhibited in more than 70 one-man and group exhibitions in museums and galleries around the world. Gallery hours are Monday through Friday from 10am to 6pm and Saturday from 9am to 2pm; special appointments are available.

8 St. Maarten/St. Martin After Dark

IN ST. MAARTEN

On the Dutch side, there are few real nightclubs. After-dark activities begin early here, as guests select their favorite nook for a sundowner, perhaps the garden patio of **Pasanggrahan** (see "Where to Stay," above). The most popular bar on the island is **Cheri's Café** (see "Where to Dine," above).

Each evening, visitors watch for the legendary **"green flash,"** an atmospheric phenomenon described by Hemingway—it sometimes occurs in these latitudes just as the sun drops below the horizon. Guests have been known to break into a round of applause at a particularly spectacular sunset.

Many hotels sponsor **beachside barbecues** (particularly in season) with steel bands, native music, and folk dancing. Outsiders are welcomed at most of these events, but call ahead to see if it's a private affair.

One of the new clubs to open is **Axum,** 7 Front St., above the St. Maarten Historical Museum, in Philipsburg. This music hall, exhibition center, and popular bar is open Tuesday to Sunday beginning at 9pm; the cover is $5 but could vary depending on the entertainment. Often featured are blues, reggae, and jazz, even poetry readings. It has no phone, but information is available from the **Mosera Fine Arts Gallery** next door (☎ **0599/52-05-54**).

Casino Royale, at the Maho Beach Hotel on Maho Bay (☎ **599/5-52115**), opened in 1975. It has 16 blackjack tables, six roulette wheels, and three craps and three Caribbean stud-poker tables. The casino offers baccarat, mini-baccarat, and more than 250 slot machines. It's open daily from 1pm to 4am. The **Casino Royale Piano Bar** is open nightly from 9:30pm, featuring the best of jazz, pop, and Caribbean music. There's no cover, and a snack buffet is complimentary.

The **Pelican Resort Club,** Simpson Bay (☎ **599/5-42503**), has a popular Las Vegas–style casino with a panoramic view of the bay. It offers two craps tables, three roulette tables, nine blackjack tables, two stud-poker tables, and 120 slot machines. Pelican also features horse racing, bingo, and sports nights with events broadcast via satellite, plus nightly dancing on the Pelican Reef Terrace and island shows featuring Caribbean bands. It's open daily from 1pm to 3am.

The Roman-themed **Coliseum Casino,** on Front Street in Philipsburg (☎ **599/5-32102**), which opened in 1990, has taken several steps to attract gaming enthusiasts, especially "high rollers," and has the highest table limits ($1,000 maximum) on St. Maarten. Upon the management's approval, the Coliseum also offers credit lines for clients with a good credit rating at any U.S. casino. The Coliseum features more than 200 slot machines, four blackjack tables, three poker tables, and two roulette wheels. The Coliseum is open daily from 11am to 3am.

Sports fans gravitate to **Lightning Casino,** Cole Bay (☎ **0599/54-32-90**), where wide-screen TVs show baseball, soccer, boxing, hockey, basketball, and football, along with horse racing. This casino is near the airport and will send a shuttle to pick you up, regardless of where you are on island.

Golden Casino, at the Great Bay Beach Hotel, in Philipsburg (☎ **0599/52-24-46**), appeals particularly to its guests but also attracts visitors from around the island. Payback on its slots goes as high as $2,500.

Also worth a visit 24 hours a day is **Atlantis Casino,** at beautiful Cupecoy Beach (☎ **0599/54-60-0**), only a short distance from both Maho Bay and Mullet Bay. There's a private gaming room for higher stakes baccarat, French roulette, chemin de fer, and seven-card poker.

Right in the heart of Philipsburg's shopping-crazed Front Street, **Rouge et Noir** (☎ **0599/52-29-52**), has a futuristic design. It offers slot machines, a Sigma Derby horse machine, video Keno, and video poker. It opens Monday to Saturday at 9am and Sunday at 11am to snag cruise-ship passengers.

Gaining in popularity is **Paradise Plaza Casino** (☎ **0599/53-27-21**), also located on Front Street. It opens at 10am daily, making it a hit with cruise-ship passengers as well.

IN ST. MARTIN

Some St. Martin hotels have dinner dancing, piano-lounge music, and even discos. But the most popular after-dark pastime is leisurely dining.

Le Prive, rue de la République, in Marigot (☎ **0590/87-01-97**), is the most talked-about, most stylish, and most popular nightclub on the island's French side. Designed in a modern style that evokes an upscale yacht club, it's a high-energy, multicultural disco, where even 40-year-olds feel comfortable mingling with the island's young and energetic. The club has a state-of-the-art sound system and top DJs. The view of Marigot from its balcony is panoramic. The club is open daily from 11pm to 4:30am, charging a cover of $10.

Le Club One, auberge de la Mer, La Marina, Marigot (☎ **0590/87-98-41**), is one floor above street level in a modern building facing the boats and yachts bobbing at anchor near the center of Marigot. Its fans, who descend on it every night from both sides of the island, view it as a Gallic/Caribbean version of a British pub, where recorded funk, reggae, and rap encourage some folks to dance. The cover is $8. Hours are nightly from 10pm to 1am.

The island attracts a lot of gay visitors, especially to its nude beaches, but there is little gay nightlife other than the **Pink Mango,** Residence Laguna Beach at Nettle Bay (☎ **0590/87-59-99**). This charming, rather small club lies behind the residence itself. To reach it, go to the far right section of this former hotel's parking lot, walk along the building, and keep to your left. When you see a rainbow flag, press a buzzer. Gay men of all ages (and a few women) flock here. The club opens nightly at 10pm but doesn't really get crowded until midnight. It keeps going until 3am or later.

St. Vincent & the Grenadines

One of the major British Windward Islands, sleepy St. Vincent is only now awakening to tourism, which hasn't yet reached massive proportions the way it has on nearby St. Lucia. Sailors and the yachting set have long known of St. Vincent and its satellite bays and beaches in the Grenadines, and until recently it was a well-kept vacation secret.

Visit St. Vincent for its botanical beauty, and the Grenadines for the best sailing waters in the Caribbean. Don't come for nightlife, grand cuisine, or fabled beaches. There are some white-sand beaches near Kingstown on St. Vincent, but most of the other beaches ringing the island are of black sand. The yachting crowd seems to view St. Vincent merely as a launching pad for the 40-plus-mile string of the Grenadines, but the island still has a few attractions that make it worth exploring on its own.

Unspoiled by the fallout that mass tourism sometimes brings, the people actually treat visitors like human beings: Met with courtesy, they respond with courtesy. British customs predominate, along with traces of Gallic cultural influences, but all with a distinct West Indian flair.

South of St. Vincent, the small chain of islands called the Grenadines extends for more than 40 miles and offers the finest yachting in the eastern Caribbean. The islands are strung like a necklace of precious stones and have such romantic-sounding names as Bequia, Mustique, Canouan, and Petit St. Vincent. We'll explore Union and Palm Islands, and Mayreau as well. A few of the islands have accommodations, but many are so small and so completely undeveloped that they attract only beachcombers and stray boaters.

Populated by the descendants of African slaves and administered by St. Vincent, the Grenadines collectively add up to a land mass of 30 square miles. These bits of land, often dots on nautical charts, may lack natural resources, but they're blessed with white-sand beaches, coral reefs, and their own kind of sleepy beauty. If you don't spend the night in the Grenadines, you should at least go over to one of them for the day, and enjoy a picnic lunch (which your hotel will pack for you) on one of the long stretches of beach.

1 Essentials

VISITOR INFORMATION

In the United States, you can get information at the **St. Vincent and Grenadines Tourist Office,** 801 Second Ave., 21st Floor, New York,

NY 10017 (☎ **800/729-1726** or 212/687-4981), or 6505 Cove Creek Place, Dallas, TX 75240 (☎ **800/235-3029** or 214/239-6451).

Canadians can go to 32 Park Rd., Toronto, Ontario N4W 2N4 (☎ **416/924-5796**).

The Web site for St. Vincent and the Grenadines is **www.vincy.com**.

On St. Vincent, the local **Department of Tourism** is on Upper Bay Street, Government Administrative Centre, Kingstown (☎ **784/457-1502**).

GETTING THERE

In the eastern Caribbean, St. Vincent—the "gateway to the Grenadines" (the individual islands are discussed later in this chapter)—lies 100 miles west of Barbados, where most visitors from North America fly first and then make connections to St. Vincent's **E. T. Joshua Airport** and on to the Grenadines. For details on getting to Barbados from North America, see chapter 6. However, the transfer through Barbados is no longer necessary, as **American Eagle** (☎ **800/433-7300** or 784/456-5000) has one flight daily from San Juan, making it more convenient than ever to get here.

Air Martinique (☎ **784/458-4528**) runs once-daily service between Martinique, St. Lucia, St. Vincent, and Union Island.

Increasing numbers of visitors prefer the dependable service of one of the best charter airlines in the Caribbean, **Mustique Airways** (☎ **784/458-4380**), which makes frequent runs from St. Vincent to the major airports of the Grenadines. With advance warning, Mustique Airways will arrange specially chartered (and reasonably priced) transport for you and your party to and from many of the surrounding islands (including Grenada, Aruba, St. Lucia, Antigua, Barbados, Trinidad, and any others in the southern Caribbean). The price of these chartered flights is less than you might expect and often matches the fares on conventional Caribbean airlines. The airline currently owns seven small aircraft, none of which carries more than nine passengers.

GETTING AROUND ST. VINCENT

BY TAXI The government sets the rates for fares, but taxis are unmetered; the wise passenger will always ask the fare before getting in. Figure on spending EC$15 to EC$20 ($5.55 to $7.40) or more to go from the E. T. Joshua Airport to your hotel. You should tip about 12% of the fare.

You can also hire taxis to take you to the island's major attractions. Most drivers seem to be well-informed guides (it won't take you long to learn everything you need to know about St. Vincent). You'll spend EC$40 to EC$50 ($14.80 to $18.50) per hour for a car holding two to four passengers.

BY RENTAL CAR Driving on St. Vincent is a bit of an adventure because of the narrow, twisting roads. *Drive on the left.* To drive like a Vincentian, you'll soon learn to sound your horn a lot as you make the sharp curves and turns. If you present your valid U.S. or Canadian driver's license at the police department, on Bay Street in Kingstown, and pay an EC$40 ($14.80) fee, you'll get a temporary permit to drive.

The major car-rental companies do not have branches on St. Vincent. Rental cars cost EC$140 to EC$200 ($51.80 to $74) a day, but that must be determined on the

---

Special Events

Early July brings the weeklong **Carnival,** one of the largest in the eastern Caribbean. The festivities include steel-band and calypso competitions, along with the crowning of the king and queen of the carnival.

spot. Contact **Kim's Rentals,** on Grenville Street in Kingstown (☎ 784/456-1884), or **Star Garage,** also on Grenville Street in Kingstown (☎ 784/456-1743).

BY BUS Flamboyantly painted "alfresco" buses travel the principal roads of St. Vincent, linking the major towns and villages. The price is low, depending on where you're going, and the experience will connect you with the locals. The central departure point is the bus terminal at the New Kingstown Fish Market. Fares range from EC$1 to EC$6 (40¢ to $2.20).

Fast Facts: St. Vincent & the Grenadines

Banking Hours Most banks are open Monday to Thursday from 8am to either 1 or 3pm, and Friday from either 8am to 5pm or from 8am to 1pm and 3 to 5pm, depending on the bank.

Currency The official currency of St. Vincent is the **Eastern Caribbean dollar (EC$),** worth about 37¢ in U.S. money. *Most of the quotations in this chapter appear in U.S. dollars,* unless marked EC$. Most restaurants, shops, and hotels will accept payment in U.S. dollars or traveler's checks.

Documents British, Canadian, and U.S. citizens should have proof of identity and a return or ongoing airplane ticket. Passports or birth certificates with a photo ID are sufficient.

Electricity Electricity is 220 volts AC (50 cycles), so you'll need an adapter and a transformer. Some hotels have transformers, but it's best to bring your own.

Emergencies In case of emergency, dial ☎ 999.

Hospitals There are two hospitals on St. Vincent, both in Kingstown: **Kingstown General Hospital** (☎ 784/456-1185) and **Medical Associates Clinic** (☎ 784/457-2598).

Language English is the official language.

Pharmacies On St. Vincent, try **Deane's Pharmacy,** Halifax Street, Kingstown (☎ 784/457-2056), open Monday through Friday from 8:30am to 4:30pm and Saturday from 8:30am to 12:30pm.

Post Office The **General Post Office,** on Halifax Street in Kingstown (☎ 784/456-1111), is open Monday to Friday from 8:30am to 3pm and Saturday from 8:30 to 11:30am. There are sub–post offices in 56 districts throughout the country, including offices on the Grenadine islands of Bequia, Mustique, Canouan, Mayreau, and Union Island.

Safety St. Vincent and its neighboring islands of the Grenadines are still safe to visit. In Kingstown, the capital of St. Vincent, chances are you'll encounter little serious crime. However, take the usual precautions and never leave valuables unguarded.

Taxes & Service Charges The government imposes an airport departure tax of EC$30 ($11.10) per person. A 7% government occupancy tax is charged for all hotel accommodations. Hotels and restaurants add a 10% to 15% service charge.

Telephone To call St. Vincent from the United States, dial **1,** then **784** (the area code for St. Vincent) and the local seven-digit number.

Time Both St. Vincent and the Grenadines operate on Atlantic standard time year-round: When it's 6am on St. Vincent, it's 5am in New York. During daylight saving time in the United States, St. Vincent keeps the same time as the U.S. East Coast.

Water   In St. Vincent and the Grenadines, stick to bottled water.

Weather   The climate of St. Vincent is pleasantly cooled by the trade winds year-round. The tropical temperature is in the 78° to 82°F range. The rainy season is May to November.

2 Where to Stay on St. Vincent

Don't expect high-rise resorts here; everything is kept small. The places are comfortable, not fancy, and you usually get a lot of personal attention from the staff. Most hotels and restaurants add a 7% government tax and a 10% to 15% service charge to your bill; ask about this when you register.

VERY EXPENSIVE

Young Island. P.O. Box 211, Young Island, St. Vincent, W.I. ☎ **800/223-1108** in the U.S. and Canada, or 784/458-4826. Fax 784/457-4567. www.travelsource.com/exotic/ youngisland.html. E-mail: y-island@caribsurf.com. 30 units. Winter $450–$610 cottage for two. Off-season $325–$480 cottage for two. Extra person $90. Rates include MAP (breakfast and dinner). Ask about "lovers' packages" (bargain deals offered in the off-season). AE, MC, V.

This 32-acre resort, which might have attracted Gauguin, is supposedly where a Carib tribal chieftain kept his harem. It lies just 200 yards off the south shore of St. Vincent, to which it's linked by a ferry from the pier right on Villa Beach, a 5-minute ride. Hammocks are hung under thatched roofs, and the beach is of brilliant white sand. Set in a tropical garden are wood-and-stone Tahitian cottages (all for couples), with bamboo decor and outdoor showers in little rock grottoes—very romantic. Floors are of tile and terrazzo, covered with rush rugs. The spacious accommodations come with queen or king beds (rarely a twin), fridges, private safes, and generous storage space. Some units open onto the beach; others are on a hillside. Some guests have complained of hearing "domestic noises" in the rooms adjoining them.

Dining/Diversions: Food and service are not always of a high standard, in spite of the longtime fame of this hotel. Dining is by candlelight, and dress is informal. Sometimes a steel band plays for after-dinner dancing, and strolling singers serenade diners. On some nights, the hotel transports guests over to its other island, Fort Duvemette, for a cocktail party.

Amenities: Pool (modeled on a tropical lagoon and set in landscaped grounds) and a saltwater lagoon fish pond (at the far end of the beach, where you can hear parrots and macaws chattering), tennis court (lit at night), Carib canoes and Sailfish. All water sports (such as scuba diving and waterskiing) are available. Room service (for breakfast), baby-sitting.

EXPENSIVE

✪ **Camelot Inn.** Kingstown Park St., P.O. Box 787, Kingstown, St. Vincent, W.I. ☎ **809/ 456-2100.** Fax 809/456-2233. http://vincy.com/camelot. E-mail: caminn.caribsurf. com. 22 units. A/C TV TEL. Winter $275–$300 double; $400–$450 suite. Off-season $225–$250 double; $300–$350 suite. Rates include MAP (breakfast and dinner) and afternoon tea. AE, MC, V.

Set in an upscale residential neighborhood on the sloping heights above Kingstown, with a view sweeping out over the capital and the sea, this guest house opened in 1996. Originally built in 1781 as a private villa by the island's first French governor, and radically renovated in the mid-1990s, it retains most of its original stonework, an exterior sheathing of glistening white clapboards, plus modern bathrooms whose terra-cotta basins were hand-painted by friends of the owners. Each pastel bedroom has a

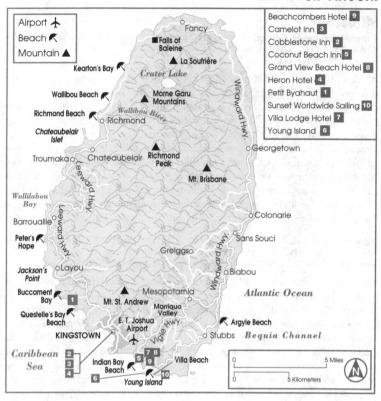

St. Vincent

Airport ✈
Beach ⚓
Mountain ▲

Beachcombers Hotel **9**
Camelot Inn **3**
Cobblestone Inn **2**
Coconut Beach Inn **5**
Grand View Beach Hotel **8**
Heron Hotel **4**
Petit Byahaut **1**
Sunset Worldwide Sailing **10**
Villa Lodge Hotel **7**
Young Island **6**

Fancy
Falls of Baleine
La Soufrière
Crater Lake
Kearton's Bay
Morne Garu Mountains
Wallibou Beach
Wallibou River
Richmond Beach
Richmond
Chateaubelair Islet
Georgetown
Troumaka
Chateaubelair
Richmond Peak
Mt. Brisbane
Wallilabou Bay
Leeward Hwy.
Barrouallie
Colonarie
Peter's Hope
Sans Souci
Jackson's Point
Layou
Greiggso
Biabou
Windward Hwy.
Buccament Bay **1**
Mesopotamia
Atlantic Ocean
Mt. St. Andrew
Questelle's Bay Beach
Marriqua Valley
E. T. Joshua Airport
Argyle Beach
KINGSTOWN
Stubbs
Bequia Channel
Caribbean Sea
2 **3** **4**
Indian Bay Beach
5 **7 8** **9**
Villa Beach
6
10
Young Island
Vigie Hwy.

0   5 Miles
0   5 Kilometers

N

---

private patio that opens directly onto a garden where afternoon tea is served amid flowering shrubbery. St. Vincent's most elegant accommodations are handsomely decorated with ceiling fans, Spanish rattan, frames of Mexican silver, private safes, and in some cases antique phones and love seats. Each unit has a combination tub/shower, a scale, deluxe toiletries, and a hair dryer. There's a pool, a small gym, a bar, and a restaurant, King Arthur's (see "Where to Dine," below).

Grand View Beach Hotel. P.O. Box 173, Villa Point, St. Vincent, W.I. ☎ **800/223-6510** in the U.S., or 784/458-4811. Fax 784/457-4174. www.grandviewhotel.com. E-mail: grandview@caribsurf.com. 19 units. MINIBAR TV TEL. Winter $210 double; from $270 suite. Off-season $130 double; from $190 suite. MAP (breakfast and dinner) $38 per person extra. AE, DC, MC, V. Villa Point is 5 minutes from the airport and 10 minutes from Kingstown.

Owner/manager F. A. (Tony) Sardine named this place well: The "grand view" promised is of islets, bays, yachts, Young Island, headlands, lagoons, and sailing craft. On well-manicured grounds, this resort is set on 8 acres of gardens. The converted plantation house is a large, white, two-story mansion. The most luxurious guest rooms are in a Mediterranean-style modern wing. The other units are on the upper level of a former great house, somewhat evoking the qualities of a B&B. Twin beds come with crisp white sheets and fine mattresses. Twelve units are air-conditioned. Most of the bathrooms are shower only, but come with hair dryers.

The West Indian fare served here is average. Amenities include room service, laundry, baby-sitting, a pool, tennis and squash courts, and a fitness club with a range of exercise options, plus a sauna and massage.

MODERATE

Sunset Worldwide Sailing. P.O. Box 133, Blue Lagoon, St. Vincent, W.I. ☎ and fax **784/ 458-4308.** E-mail: sunsailsva@caribsurf.com. 19 units. A/C TV. Winter $100–$120 double. Off-season $76–$86 double. AE, MC, V.

A two-story group of rambling modern buildings crafted from local wood and stone, this hotel lies 4 miles from the airport on the main island road, opening onto a narrow, curved, black-sand beach. There's a pleasantly breezy bar with open walls and lots of exposed planking, often filled with seafaring folk. As you relax, you'll overlook a moored armada of boats tied up at a nearby marina. A two-tiered pool, terraced into a nearby hillside, offers two lagoon-shaped places to swim. Snorkeling, windsurfing, and daily departures on sailboats to Mustique and Bequia can be arranged through the hotel. Each of the medium-size, high-ceilinged guest rooms has a balcony, and about half the rooms are air-conditioned. The bedrooms are well maintained and cared for, with ceramic-tile floors and good furnishings. Bathrooms are in the standard motel style, with shower stalls. Room service and laundry are available.

Villa Lodge Hotel. P.O. Box 1191, Villa Point, St. Vincent, W.I. ☎ **784/458-4641.** Fax 784/457-4468. E-mail: villodge@caribsurf.com. 10 units. A/C TV TEL. Winter $120 double; $140 triple; $150 quad. Off-season $105 double; $115 triple; $125 quad. AE, MC, V.

Set on a residential hillside a few minutes southeast of the center of Kingstown and the E. T. Joshua Airport, this place is a favorite of visiting businesspeople. Because of its access to a beach and its well-mannered staff, it evokes the feeling of a modern villa. It's ringed with tropical, flowering trees and shrubs growing in the gardens. The air-conditioned rooms have ceiling fans, king-size beds, minifridges, hair dryers, comfortable rattan and local mahogany furniture, and small bathrooms. The hotel also rents eight apartments in its Breezeville Apartments complex, charging year-round prices of $130 for a double, $135 for a triple, and $145 for a quad.

There's a wood-sheathed bar on the second floor with a view of Young Island and the Grenadines, and a dining room where good food is served, usually from a fixed-price menu. There's also a bar and restaurant down by the pool. Services offered include room service, laundry, and baby-sitting.

INEXPENSIVE

✪ **Beachcombers Hotel.** Villa Beach (P.O. Box 126, Kingstown), St. Vincent, W.I. ☎ **784/ 458-4283.** Fax 784/458-4385. 13 units. TEL. Year-round $83 double. AE, MC, V.

This relative newcomer, established by Richard and Flora Gunn, immediately became a far more inviting choice than the traditional budget favorites, the Heron and Cobblestone. It's in a tropical garden right on the beach, adjacent to Sunset Shores. A pair of chaletlike buildings house the small- to medium-size accommodations, all with private bathrooms and tasteful decor. They're cooled by ceiling fans, although a few rooms have air-conditioning as well. The standard of cleanliness and maintenance is the finest on the island. Try for room nos. 1, 2 or 3, as they are not only the best but also open onto the water. Two units have small kitchenettes. Bathrooms are a bit cramped, with shower only. The hotel has a health spa (Mrs. Gunn is a massage and beauty therapist). And, astonishingly for a B&B, the Beachcombers offers a steam room, sauna, and even facials and aromatherapy. The Beachbar & Restaurant, a favorite gathering place for locals, fronts an open terrace, and serves an excellent cuisine. Daughter Cheryl, who mastered her cooking skills in England, is the chef.

Cobblestone Inn. Bax St. (P.O. Box 867, Kingstown), St. Vincent, W.I. ☎ **784/456-1937.** Fax 784/456-1938. 20 units. A/C TEL. Year-round $60 double; $70 triple. AE, DC, DISC, MC, V.

Originally built as a warehouse for sugar and arrowroot in 1814, the core of this historic hotel is made of stone and brick. Today, it's one of the most famous hotels on St. Vincent, known for its labyrinth of passages, arches, and upper hallways. To reach the high-ceilinged reception area, you pass from the waterfront through a stone tunnel into a chiseled courtyard. At the top of a massive sloping stone staircase, you're shown to one of the simple, old-fashioned bedrooms. Most of the small units contain TVs, and some have windows opening over the rooftops of town. The most spacious is no. 5, but it opens onto a noisy street. Mattresses are well worn but still comfortable, and the bathrooms are very tiny, with showers only. Meals are served on a third-floor eagle's aerie high above the hotel's central courtyard. Rows of windows and rattan furnishings in its adjacent bar create one of the most frequented hideaways in town. The hotel is convenient to town, but it's a 3-mile drive to the nearest beach.

Coconut Beach Inn. Indian Bay (P.O. Box 355, Kingstown), St. Vincent, W.I. ☎ or fax **784/457-4900.** 11 units. Year-round $65–$75 double. Rates include breakfast. AE, MC, V.

This owner-occupied inn, restaurant, and bar is 5 minutes (2 miles) south of the airport and 5 minutes from Kingstown. The hotel, which grew out of a villa constructed in the 1930s by one of the region's noted eccentrics, lies across the channel from the much more expensive Young Island. Its seaside setting makes it a choice for swimming and sunbathing. Island tours, such as sailing the Grenadines, can be arranged, as can diving, snorkeling, and mountain climbing. There's minimum comfort here: Each small guest room is furnished in a straightforward modern style, with a tiny bathroom with a shower only. A beach bar at water's edge serves tropical drinks, and an open-air restaurant opens onto a view of Indian Bay and features West Indian and Vincentian cooking prepared from local ingredients. Steaks, Cornish game hens, and hamburgers round out the fare.

Heron Hotel. Upper Bay St. (P.O. Box 226), Kingstown, St. Vincent, W.I. ☎ **784/457-1631.** Fax 784/457-1189. 13 units. A/C TEL. Year-round $58.50 double; $62.50 suite. Rates include full breakfast. AE, MC, V.

This respectable but slightly run-down hotel is among the most historic buildings on St. Vincent. Built of local stone and tropical hardwoods, it served as a warehouse in the late–18th century, then later provided lodgings for colonial planters doing business along the wharves of Kingstown. Operating in its present format since 1960, it occupies the second story of a building whose ground floor is devoted to shops. Some of the simple and rather small rooms overlook an inner courtyard; others face the street. Room no. 15 is the largest of the lot. Accommodations have simple and time-worn furnishings, including mattresses ready for retirement, rather garish floral draperies, single beds, and extremely cramped bathrooms with shower stalls. Although you don't get grand comfort here, the price is hard to beat, and the staff most hospitable. The hotel attracts a clientele of moderately eccentric guests, some of whom conduct business in the heart of the island's capital, while others want to be near the docks in time for early-morning departures. The on-site restaurant is busiest at lunch (it may close after dusk, so dinner reservations are important). Overall, this place exudes a sense of old-fashioned timelessness and dignified severity you'll almost never find in modern resorts.

Petit Byahaut. Petit Byahaut Bay, St. Vincent, W.I. ☎ and fax **784/457-7008.** www. outahere.com/petitbyahaut. E-mail: petitbyahaut@carisurf.com. 6 tents. Year-round $350 double per day, or $1,700 for 5 days/5 nights. Rates are all-inclusive. Scuba packages available. AE, MC, V.

This adventurous place attracts snorkelers, scuba divers, hikers, and nature lovers. Lying 4½ miles north of Kingstown on the leeward coast and accessible only by boat, it accepts no more than 14 guests at a time, who are housed in roomy tents with fresh-water showers and large roofed decks. Opening onto a horseshoe-shaped bay, the complex stands in a 50-acre private valley. Foliage between the tents provides privacy. A seaside bar and restaurant offers wholesome meals, picnics are prepared during the day, and dinner is served by candlelight. The snorkeling and scuba diving right off the beach are excellent, and water-sports equipment is provided. A house-party atmosphere prevails.

3 Where to Dine on St. Vincent

Most guests eat at their hotels on the Modified American Plan (breakfast and dinner), and many Vincentian hostelries serve authentic West Indian cuisine. There are also a few independent restaurants, but not many.

Basil's Bar & Restaurant. Bay St., Kingstown. ☎ **784/457-2713.** Reservations recommended. Main courses EC$37–EC$57 ($13.70–$21.10); lunch buffet EC$32 ($11.85). AE, MC, V. Mon–Sat 8am–10pm. SEAFOOD/INTERNATIONAL.

This enclave is a less famous annex of the legendary Basil's Beach Bar on Mustique. It's set within the early-19th-century walls of an old sugar warehouse, beneath the previously recommended Cobblestone Inn. The air-conditioned interior is accented with exposed stone and brick, soaring arches, and a rambling mahogany bar, which remains open throughout the day. The food is quite acceptable, but nowhere near as good as that enjoyed by Princess Margaret or Mick Jagger at Basil's other bar on Mustique. The menu might include lobster salad, shrimp in garlic butter, sandwiches, hamburgers, and barbecued chicken. Dinners feature grilled lobster, escargots, shrimp cocktail, grilled red snapper, and grilled filet mignon, all fairly standard dishes of the international repertoire. You can order meals here throughout the day and late into the evening—until the last satisfied customer leaves.

Bounty. Egmont St., Kingstown. ☎ **784/456-1776.** Snacks and sandwiches EC$.75–EC$8 (30¢–$2.95); main courses EC$6–EC$15 ($2.20–$5.55). No credit cards. Mon–Fri 8am–5pm, Sat 8am–1:30pm. AMERICAN/WEST INDIAN.

In the red-brick Troutman Building in the center of Kingstown, you'll find the extremely affordable Bounty serving the local workers (the true power-lunch venue is Basil's, recommended above). A friendly local staff greets you, and people who work nearby frequent the place, making it their second home. Fill up on pastries of all kinds, rotis (Caribbean burritos), hot dogs, hamburgers, and sandwiches, along with home-made soups, fish-and-chips, quiche, and pizza. The cookery is just as simple as the surroundings. The interesting collection of drinks includes passion fruit and golden apple. An on-site gallery sells works by local artists.

✪ **French Restaurant.** Villa Beach. ☎ **784/458-4972.** Reservations recommended. Lunch EC$10–EC$90 ($3.70–$33.30); dinner main courses EC$46–EC$90 ($17–$33.30). AE, MC, V. Daily noon–2pm and 7–9:30pm. Closed Sept–Oct. FRENCH/SEAFOOD.

In a clapboard house 2 miles from the airport, near the pier where the ferry from Young Island docks, this is one of the most consistently good restaurants on the island. It offers a long, semishadowed bar, which you pass on your way to the rear veranda. Here, overlooking the moored yachts off the coast of Young Island, you can enjoy well-seasoned, Gallic-inspired food. Surrounded by vine-laced lattices, you can order seafood casserole or curried conch, shrimp in garlic sauce, fresh fish in a ginger and peppercorn sauce, or lobster fresh from the tank. Lunch is simpler and cheaper, with fresh fish, seafood kebabs, grilled cheese steak, and spicy pineapple conch. The staff is inexperienced, but the food makes up for it.

Juliette's Restaurant. Egmont St., Kingstown. ☎ **784/457-1645.** Rotis and sandwiches EC$5–EC$6 ($1.85–$2.20); fixed-price menu EC$11–EC$12 ($4.05–$4.45). No credit cards. Mon–Fri 8:30am–5pm, Sat 8:30am–2pm. WEST INDIAN.

Set amid the capital's cluster of administrative buildings, across from the National Commercial Bank, this restaurant serves up more lunches to office workers than any other establishment in town. Meals are served in a clean and respectable dining area headed by a veteran of the restaurant trade, Juliette Campbell. (Ms. Campbell's husband is the island's well-known attorney general.) Menu items include soups, curried mutton, an array of fish, stewed chicken, stewed beef, and sandwiches. Many of the platters are garnished with fried plantains and rice. Although Juliette's opens early, it doesn't serve breakfast, offering only snacks or lunch-type items in the morning. This is the type of cuisine you are likely to be served in a decent family-style boarding house in St. Vincent.

King Arthur's Restaurant. In the Camelot Inn, Kingstown Park St. (a 10-minute drive from the center of town), Kingstown. ☎ **809/456-2100.** Reservations recommended. Set-price lunch $20; set-price dinner $40. Daily noon–2:30pm and 7–9:30pm. INTERNATIONAL.

Set on a terrace whose views sweep over a garden, the faraway sea, and the commercial core of downtown Kingstown, this restaurant is in a prosperous-looking house that was built in the 1790s by St. Vincent's first governor under the French regime. More stylish and a bit more formal than many of its competitors, it focuses on international cuisine and set-price menus whose composition changes according to the seasons and the inspiration of the chef. Choices may include pumpkin soup, Chinese spring rolls, several kinds of salads, fillet of fresh salmon with chef's potatoes, and baked Vienna-style chicken served with glazed vegetables.

Lime N' Pub Restaurant. Opposite Young Island at Villa. ☎ **784/458-4227.** Main courses EC$45–EC$140 ($16.65–$51.80). AE, DC, MC, V. Daily noon–midnight. WEST INDIAN/ INDIAN.

This is one of the island's most popular restaurants, opposite the superexpensive Young Island Hotel, right on Young Island Channel. It's the most congenial pub on St. Vincent, with a wide selection of pub grub, including pizzas. There's even a live lobster pond. A local band enlivens the atmosphere a few times a week in winter. In the more formal section of this indoor and alfresco restaurant, you can partake of some good West Indian food, along with dishes from India or the international kitchen. The rotis win high praise, but we gravitate to the fresh fish and lobster dishes instead. Coconut shrimp is generally excellent. Service is among the most hospitable on the island.

Rooftop Restaurant & Bar. Bay St., Kingstown. ☎ **784/457-2845.** Reservations recommended for dinner. Lunch platters EC$20 ($7.40); dinner main courses EC$20–EC$50 ($7.40–$18.50). AE, DISC, MC, V. Mon–Sat 8:30am–10pm. WEST INDIAN/INTERNATIONAL.

This restaurant does a thriving business thanks to its well-prepared food and its location three stories above the center of Kingstown. After you climb some flights of stairs, you'll see a bar near the entrance, an indoor area decorated in earth tones, and a patio open to the prevailing breezes. Lunches stress traditional Creole recipes using fresh fish, chicken, mutton, beef, and goat. Dinners are more international, and may include lobster, an excellent snapper with lemon-butter and garlic sauce, steaks with onions and mushrooms, and several savory preparations of pork. Every Wednesday and Friday, there's a karaoke sing-along; Saturday is family night, with a barbecue and a steel band after 6pm. In addition, 60 different drinks are featured at the bar.

4 St. Vincent Beaches

All beaches on St. Vincent are public, and many of the best ones border hotel properties, which you can patronize for drinks or lunch. Most of the resorts are in the south, where the beaches have golden-yellow sand. The only real white-sand beach on St. Vincent is Young Island, which is private (see "Where to Stay on St. Vincent," above, for a review of this expensive resort property). Many of the beaches in the north have sands of a lava-ash color. The safest swimming is on the leeward beaches; the surf on the windward or eastern beaches is often rough and can be quite dangerous.

The island's most frequented strip is narrow **Villa Beach,** only a 10-minute drive from Kingstown. Its tranquil Caribbean waters make swimming safe here, and numerous simple cafes and water-sports stands are ready to serve you. The drawback to this beach: Its sands can barely accommodate the crowds who flock here; weekends can be particularly bad.

Nearby **Indian Bay Beach** is similar to Villa Beach and also attracts lots of Vincentians on weekends. Monday through Thursday, however, you'll probably have plenty of room on the narrow strip. The sand here is slightly golden in color, but tends to be rocky. The reef-protected tranquil waters are ideal for both swimming and snorkeling. You'll find both bars and restaurants here.

Heading north from Kingstown, you'll reach **Buccament Bay,** where the waters are clean, clear, and tranquil enough for swimming. This beach is very tiny, however, and its sand is of the black volcanic variety. In the same area, **Questelle's Bay Beach** (pronounced keet-*ells*) is also on the leeward, tranquil Caribbean side of the island. The black-sand beach, next to Camden Park, is very similar to Buccament Bay.

Only the most die-hard frequent the beaches on the east coast, or windward side. This is where the big breakers roll in from the Atlantic. Don't plan to go swimming in these rough waters—a beach picnic might be more appropriate. The best beaches, all with black volcanic sand, are found at **Kearton's Bay** and at **Peter's Hope,** and **Richmond,** all reached along the leeward highway running up the west coast of St. Vincent.

5 St. Vincent Sports & Outdoor Pursuits

FISHING   It's best to go to a local fisher for advice if you're interested in this sport, which your hotel can also arrange for you. The government of St. Vincent doesn't require visitors to have a license. It's sometimes possible to accompany a fisher on a trip, perhaps 4 or 5 miles from shore. A modest fee should suffice. The fishing fleet leaves from the leeward coast at Barrouallie. They've been known to return to shore with everything from a 6-inch redfish to a 20-foot pilot whale.

HIKING   Exploring St. Vincent's hot volcano, **La Soufrière,** is an intriguing adventure. As you travel the island, you can't miss its cloud-capped splendor. This volcano has occasionally captured the attention of the world. The most recent eruption was in 1979, when it spewed ashes, lava, and hot mud that covered the vegetation on its slopes. Belching rocks and black curling smoke filled the blue Caribbean sky. About 17,000 people were evacuated from a 10-mile ring around the volcano.

Fortunately, the eruption was in the sparsely settled northern part of the island. The volcano lies away from most of the tourism and commercial centers of St. Vincent, and even if it should erupt again, volcanologists don't consider it a danger to visitors lodged at beachside hotels along the leeward coast.

At the rim of the crater, you'll be rewarded with one of the most panoramic views in the Caribbean. That is, if the wind doesn't blow too hard and make you topple over into the crater itself! *Take extreme caution.* Looking inside, you can see the steam rising from the crater.

Even if you're an experienced hiker, don't attempt to explore the volcano without a guide. Also, wear suitable hiking clothes and be sure that you're in the best of health before making the arduous journey. The easiest route is the 3-mile-long eastern approach from Rabacca. The more arduous trail, longer by half a mile, is the western trail from Chateaubelair, which definitely requires a guide. The round-trip to the crater takes about 5 hours.

The **St. Vincent Forestry Headquarters,** in the village of Campden Park, about 3 miles from Kingstown along the west coast (☎ 784/457-8594), offers a pamphlet on hiking to La Soufrière. It's open Monday to Friday from 8am to noon and 1 to 4pm. **HazEco Tours** (☎ 784/457-8634) offers guided hikes up to La Soufrière, costing $100 per couple, including lunch.

If you don't want to face Soufrière, the best hikes are the **Vermont Nature Trails.** These marked trails (get a map at the tourist office) take you through a rain forest and pass long-ago plantations reclaimed by nature. If it's your lucky day, you might even see the rare St. Vincent parrot with its flamboyant plumage. Wear good hiking shoes and your antimosquito cologne. Call **Sailor's Wilderness Tours** in Kingstown (☎ 784/457-1274) to get directions.

SAILING & YACHTING   St. Vincent and the Grenadines are one of the great sailing centers of the Caribbean. If you want to go bareboating, you can obtain a fully provisioned yacht. If you're a well-heeled novice, you can hire a captain and a crew. Any hotel can recommend charter yachts. We suggest **Nicholson Yacht Charters** (☎ 800/662-6066 in the U.S.) and the **Lagoon Marina and Hotel,** in the Blue Lagoon area (☎ 800/327-2276 or 784/458-4308). The latter offers 44-foot crewed sloops, costing from $400 a day.

SNORKELING & SCUBA DIVING   The best area for snorkeling and scuba diving is the Villa/Young Island section on the southern end of the island.

Dive St. Vincent, on the Young Island Cut (☎ 784/457-4928), has been owned and operated by a transplanted Texan, Bill Tewes, for more than a decade. The oldest and best dive company, it now has two additional dive shops: **Dive Canouan,** at the Tamarind Beach Hotel on Canouan Island (☎ 784/458-8044), and **Grenadines Dive,** at the Sunny Grenadines Hotel on Union Island (☎ 784/458-8138). The shops have a total of six instructors and three dive masters, as well as seven dive boats. All shops offer dive/snorkel trips as well as sightseeing day trips and dive instruction. Single-tank dives cost $50 and two-tank dives go for $90, including all equipment and instructors and/or dive master guides. Dive packages are also available.

TENNIS   **Young Island Resort,** on Young Island (☎ 784/458-4826), and the **Grand View Beach Hotel,** at Villa Point (☎ 784/458-4811), have tennis courts.

6 Exploring St. Vincent

KINGSTOWN   Lush and tropical, the capital isn't as architecturally fascinating as St. George's on Grenada. Some English-style houses do exist, many of them looking as if they belonged in Penzance, Cornwall, instead of the Caribbean. However, you can still meet old-timers if you stroll on Upper Bay Street. White-haired and bearded, they can be seen loading their boats with produce grown on the mountain, before heading to some secluded beach in the Grenadines. This is a chief port and gateway to the Grenadines, and you can see the small boats and yachts that have dropped anchor here. The place is a magnet for charter sailors. On Saturday morning, the **market** at the south end of town is at its most active.

At the top of a winding road on the north side of Kingstown, **Fort Charlotte** (☎ 784/456-1165) was built on Johnson Point around the time of the American Revolution. The ruins aren't much to inspect; the reason to come here is the view. The fort sits atop a steep promontory some 640 feet above the sea. From its citadel, you'll have a commanding sweep of the leeward shores to the north, Kingstown to the south, and the Grenadines beyond. On a clear day, you can even see Grenada. Three cannons used to fight off French troops are still in place. You'll see a series of oil murals depicting the history of black Caribs. Admission is free, and it's open 24 hours.

The second major sight is the ✪ **Botanic Gardens,** on the north side of Kingstown at Montrose (☎ 784/457-1003). Founded in 1765 by Governor George Melville, they're the oldest botanic gardens in the West Indies. In this Windward Eden, you'll see 20 acres of such tropical exotics as teak, almond, cinnamon, nutmeg, cannonball, and mahogany; some of the trees are more than 200 years old. One of the breadfruit trees was reputedly among those original seedlings brought to this island by Captain Bligh in 1793. There's also a large *Spachea perforata* (the Soufrière tree), a species believed to be unique to St. Vincent and not found in the wild since 1812. The gardens are open daily from 6am to 6pm; admission is free.

✪ **THE LEEWARD HIGHWAY**   The leeward or west side of the island has the most dramatic scenery. North of Kingstown, you rise into lofty terrain before descending to the water again. There are views in all directions. Here you can see one of the finest petroglyphs in the Caribbean: the massive **Carib Rock,** with a human face carving dating back to A.D. 600.

Continuing north you reach **Barrouallie,** where there's a Carib stone altar. Even if you're not into fishing, you might want to spend some time in this village, where some whalers still occasionally set out in brightly painted boats armed with harpoons, Moby Dick–style, to seek the elusive whale. While Barrouallie may be one of the few outposts in the world where whaling is still carried on, Vincentians point out that it doesn't endanger an already endangered species, since so few are caught each year. If one is caught, it's an occasion for festivities.

The highway continues to **Chateaubelair,** the end of the line. Here you can swim at the attractive **Richmond Beach** before heading back to Kingstown. In the distance, the volcano, La Soufrière, looms menacingly in the mountains.

The adventurous set out from here to see the **Falls of Baleine,** 7½ miles north of Richmond Beach on the northern tip of the island, accessible only by boat. Baleine is a freshwater falls that comes from a stream in the volcanic hills. If you're interested in making the trip, check with the tourist office in Kingstown for tour information.

THE WINDWARD HIGHWAY   This road runs along the eastern Atlantic coast from Kingstown. Waves pound the surf, and panoramic seascapes are all along the rocky shores. If you want to go swimming on this often-dangerous coast, stick to the sandy spots, as they offer safer shores. This road will take you past coconut and banana plantations and fields of arrowroot.

North of Georgetown is the **Rabacca Dry River,** which shows the flow of lava from the volcano when it erupted at the beginning of the 20th century. The journey from Kingstown to here is only 24 miles, but it will seem like much longer. For those who want to go the final 11 miles along a rugged road to **Fancy,** the northern tip of the island, you'll need a Land Rover, Jeep, or Moke.

MARRIQUA VALLEY   Sometimes known as the Mesopotamia Valley, this area is one of the lushest cultivated valleys in the eastern Caribbean. Surrounded by mountain ridges, the drive takes you through a landscape planted with nutmeg, cocoa, coconut, breadfruit, and bananas. The road begins at the Vigie Highway, east of the airport; surrounded by mountain ridges, it opens onto a panoramic view of Grand Bonhomme Mountain, rising 3,180 feet. At Montréal, you'll come upon natural mineral springs where you can have lunch and take a dip. Only rugged vehicles should make this trip.

Around Kingstown, you can also enjoy the **Queen's Drive,** a scenic loop into the high hills to the east of the capital. From here, the view is panoramic over Kingstown and its yacht-clogged harbor to the Grenadines in the distance.

7 St. Vincent Shopping

You don't come to St. Vincent to shop, but once here, you might pick up some of the Sea Island cotton fabrics and clothing that are local specialties. In addition, Vincentian artisans make pottery, jewelry, and baskets.

Since Kingstown consists of about 12 small blocks, you can walk, browse, and see about everything in a single morning's shopping jaunt. Try to be in town for the colorful, noisy **Friday-morning market.** You might not purchase anything, but you'll surely enjoy the riot of color.

Noah's Arkade, Bay Street, Kingstown (☎ 784/457-1513), sells gifts from the West Indies, including wood carvings, T-shirts, and a wide range of books and souvenirs. Noah's has a shop at the Frangipani Hotel in Bequia.

At **Sprott Brothers,** Homeworks, Bay Street (☎ 784/457-1121), you can buy clothing designed by Vincentians, along with an array of fabrics, linens, and silk-screened T-shirts, and even Caribbean-made furniture. In fact, there's a little bit of everything here.

Juliette's Fashions, Back Street (☎ 784/456-1143), owned and operated by the same entrepreneur who runs Juliette's Restaurant, is the best-stocked and most glamorous women's clothing store on St. Vincent—but that's not saying a lot. Beneficiary of its owner's frequent buying trips to Miami and New York, it's one of the few outlets on the island to sell semiformal evening wear.

St. Vincent Philatelic Services, Bonadie's Building, Bay Street (☎ 784/457-1911), is the largest operating bureau in the Caribbean, and its issues are highly acclaimed by stamp collectors around the world.

Y. de Lima, Bay and Egmont streets (☎ 784/457-1681), is well stocked with cameras, stereo equipment, toys, clocks, binoculars, and the best selection of jewelry on the island.

To add to your music collection, you can visit **Music World,** Egmont Street (☎ 784/547-1884), where you can listen to and purchase the latest soca, reggae, and calypso.

The typical Caribbean duty-free goods are found at **Voyager,** Halifax Street (☎ 784/456-1686), including quality jewelry, French perfumes, leather goods, and Swiss watches.

At the airport, you can drop into **Carsyl Duty-Free Liquors** (☎ 784/457-2706), where you'll find liquor at prices often 40% off Stateside.

8 St. Vincent After Dark

The nightlife focus is mainly on the hotels, where activities are likely to include barbecues and dancing to steel bands. In season, at least one hotel seems to have something planned every night during the week. Beer is extremely cheap at all the places noted below.

The **Aquatic Club,** adjacent to the departure point of the ferryboat from St. Vincent to Young Island (☎ 784/458-4205), is the loudest and most raucous nightspot on St. Vincent. It's a source of giddy fun to its fans and a sore bone of contention to nearby hotel guests, who claim they can't sleep because of the noise. On Friday, Saturday, and Sunday nights, things heat up by 11pm and continue until as late as 3am. During the other nights of the week, the place functions as a bar. Centered around an open-sided veranda and an outdoor deck, it's open every night from 9pm to 2 or 3am. Saturday night, there's a cover of EC$15 ($5.55).

The **Attic,** in the Kentucky Building, Melville and Back streets, Kingstown (☎ 784/457-2558), features jazz and easy-listening music. Music is live only on Friday and Saturday; Tuesday and Thursday it's recorded, and Wednesday is karaoke night. Fish and burgers are available. There's usually a cover of EC$10 ($3.70).

Emerald Valley Casino, Penniston Valley (☎ 784/456-7140), is not one of the Caribbean's glamorous casinos. This "down-home" spot offers a trio of roulette tables, three blackjack tables, and one Caribbean stud-poker table. You can also play craps here. There's also a bar, and you can order food. If you've got nothing else to do, you might consider a visit any time Wednesday through Monday from 9pm to 3am.

Touch Entertainment Centre (TEC), Grenville Street, Kingstown (☎ 784/457-1825), opposite KFC on the top floor of the Cambridge Building, is the best-known nightspot in the region. With advanced lighting, it's a soundproof (from the outside), air-conditioned environment, popular with tourists. Every Wednesday night in summer is disco night, especially for the young and restless. Friday and Sunday nights, the club has a house party with a DJ. Surprisingly, it's not open on Saturday night.

9 The Grenadines

GETTING THERE

BY PLANE Four of the Grenadines—Bequia, Mustique, Union Island, and Canouan—have small airports, the landing spots for flights on **Mustique Airways** (☎ 784/458-4380 on St. Vincent). Its planes are technically charters, although flights depart St. Vincent for Bequia daily at 8am. The cost is $43 round-trip.

BY BOAT The ideal way to go, of course, is to hire your own yacht, as many wealthy visitors do. A far less expensive option is to take a mail, cargo, or passenger boat, as the locals do, but you'll need time and patience. However, boats do run on schedules. The **government mail boat,** MV *Baracuda* (☎ 784/456-5180), leaves St. Vincent on Monday and Thursday at 10:30am, stops at Bequia, Canouan, and Mayreau, and arrives at Union Island at about 3:45pm. On Tuesday and Friday, the boat leaves Union Island at about 6:30am, stops at Mayreau and Canouan, reaches Bequia at about 10:45am, and makes port at St. Vincent at noon. One-way fares from St. Vincent to Bequia are EC$10 ($3.70) Monday to Friday, and EC$12 ($4.45) on weekends. To Canouan, it's EC$13 ($4.80); Mayreau, EC$15 ($5.55); and Union Island, EC$20 ($7.40).

Monday through Saturday, you can also reach Bequia on the *Admiral I* and *II.* For information on these sea trips, inquire at the **Tourist Board,** Upper Bay Street, in Kingstown (☎ 784/457-1502).

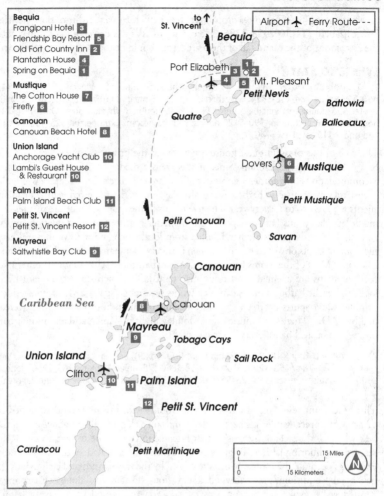

Bequia
Frangipani Hotel **3**
Friendship Bay Resort **5**
Old Fort Country Inn **2**
Plantation House **4**
Spring on Bequia **1**

Mustique
The Cotton House **7**
Firefly **6**

Canouan
Canouan Beach Hotel **8**

Union Island
Anchorage Yacht Club **10**
Lambi's Guest House
 & Restaurant **10**

Palm Island
Palm Island Beach Club **11**

Petit St. Vincent
Petit St. Vincent Resort **12**

Mayreau
Saltwhistle Bay Club **9**

Airport ✈ Ferry Route - - -

to ↑
St. Vincent

Bequia

Port Elizabeth **3** ○ **1**
 2
✈ **4** **5** Mt. Pleasant
 Petit Nevis

Battowia

Quatre *Baliceaux*

Dovers ○ **6** *Mustique*
 7

Petit Mustique

Petit Canouan

Savan

Canouan

Caribbean Sea

 8 ✈○ Canouan

Mayreau
 9 *Tobago Cays*

Union Island △ *Sail Rock*

Clifton ○ **10**
 11 *Palm Island*

 12 *Petit St. Vincent*

Carriacou *Petit Martinique*

0 —————————— 15 Miles
0 —————————— 15 Kilometers

N

BEQUIA

Only 7 square miles of land, Bequia (pronounced *BECK-wee*) is the largest of the Grenadines. It's the northernmost island in the chain (only 9 miles south of St. Vincent), offering quiet lagoons, reefs, and long stretches of nearly deserted beaches. Its population of some 6,000, descended from seafarers and other early adventurers, will give you a friendly greeting. Of the inhabitants, 10% are of Scottish ancestry, who live mostly in the Mount Pleasant region. A feeling of relaxation and informality prevails on Bequia.

GETTING AROUND

Rental cars, owned by locals, are available at the port, or you can hire a **taxi** at the dock to take you around the island or to your hotel. Taxis are reasonably priced, but an even better bet are the so-called **dollar cabs,** which take you anywhere on the island for a small fee. They don't seem to have a regular schedule—you just flag one down.

Before going to your hotel, drop in at the circular **Tourist Information Centre,** Port Elizabeth (☎ **809/458-3286**). Here you can ask for a driver who's familiar with the attractions of the island (all of them are). You should negotiate the fare in advance.

WHERE TO STAY

✪ **Frangipani Hotel.** P.O. Box 1, Bequia, The Grenadines, St. Vincent, W.I. ☎ **784/ 458-3255.** Fax 784/458-3824. www.heraldsvg.com. E-mail: frangi@caribsurf.com. 15 units. Winter $55 double without bathroom, $130–$150 double with bathroom. Off-season $40 double without bathroom, $90–$120 double with bathroom. Extra person $25. Children 12 and under $15. AE, DISC, MC, V.

The core of this pleasant guest house originated as the private, shingle-covered home of a 19th-century sea captain. Since it was transformed into a hotel, it has added accommodations that border a sloping tropical garden in back. The complex overlooks the island's most historic harbor, Admiralty Bay, and is the preferred venue for many clients who return to it every year. The five rooms in the original house are smaller and much less glamorous (and cheaper) than the better-outfitted accommodations in the garden. The garden units are handcrafted from local stone and hardwoods, and have tile floors, carpets of woven hemp, wooden furniture (some made on St. Vincent), and balconies. Most of the rooms have a small private bathroom with a shower; otherwise, corridor baths are adequate and tidily maintained. The open-sided restaurant overlooks the yacht harbor. Guests can play tennis or arrange scuba dives, sailboat rides, or other water sports nearby. (The nearest scuba outfitter, Sunsports, is fully accredited by PADI.) There's live music every Monday night in winter, and an outdoor barbecue, with a steel band, every Thursday night.

✪ **Friendship Bay Resort.** Friendship Cove (P.O. Box 9), Bequia, The Grenadines, St. Vincent, W.I. ☎ **784/458-3222.** Fax 784/458-3840. 28 units. Winter $165–$250 double; $300–$350 suite. Off-season $125–$175 double; $225 suite. Rates include continental breakfast. MC, V.

This beachfront resort offers well-decorated rooms with private verandas, nestled in 12 acres of tropical gardens. The complex stands on a sloping hillside above one of the best white-sand beaches on the island, at Friendship Cove. Guests have a view of the sea and neighboring islands. Brightly colored curtains, handmade wall hangings, and grass rugs decorate the rooms, which are cooled by the trade winds and ceiling fans (in lieu of air-conditioning). Driftwood and various flotsam art, along with sponge-painted walls, evoke a beachcomber's retreat. The accommodations have generous storage space, beds draped in mosquito netting, and small, shower-only bathrooms. The most requested units are those set directly on the ocean. The owners have added a beach bar and offer a local string band on Wednesday and Saturday. The food is good, with many island specialties on the menu. You can enjoy water sports, tennis, or boat excursions here.

Old Fort Country Inn. Mount Pleasant, Bequia, The Grenadines, St. Vincent, W.I. ☎ **784/ 458-3440.** Fax 784/457-3340. www.vincy.com/oldfort. E-mail: the view@caribsurf. com. 6 units. Winter $240 double. Off-season $210 double. Rates include MAP (breakfast and dinner). MC, V.

A special hideaway has been created from the ruins of a French-built plantation house commanding the best views on Bequia. Set on 30 tropical acres at a point 450 feet above the sea, the climate is excellent, with no mosquitoes. The property dates from at least 1756 (it may be older), and the 3-foot-thick walls are made from cobblestones. In the reconstruction, the owner matched the original style by using the old stones with exposed ceiling beams and rafters, creating a medieval feel. The views from the spacious bedrooms are the best of any hotel on the island. Each unit has modern

Scandinavian-style furnishings, a private balcony or terrace, and a shower-only bathroom. An unstocked fridge can be supplied upon request. The rooms aren't airconditioned, but trade winds seem to suffice. The atmospheric restaurant holds eight tables, serving fine four- or five-course dinners of Creole and Mediterranean specialties, including a whole barbecued fish. On the property are nature trails, a beach that's a 10-minute hike from the hotel, and a 15-by-30-foot freshwater pool, with views of the ocean on three sides.

✪ **Plantation House.** Admiralty Bay (P.O. Box 16), Bequia, The Grenadines, St. Vincent, W.I. ☎ **784/458-3425.** Fax 784/458-3612. E-mail: planthouse@caribsurf.com. 27 units. A/C MINIBAR TV TEL. Winter $449–$496 double. Off-season $302–$359 double. Rates include MAP (breakfast and dinner). AE, MC, V.

Completely renovated in 1989, the Plantation House is on Admiralty Bay, just a 5-minute walk from the center of town. The informal hotel is the most luxurious place to stay on the island. The accommodations consist of 17 peach-and-white West Indian cottages (each with its own private porch), luxury beachfront units with fans, and five deluxe air-conditioned rooms in the main house. Spacious guest rooms have a kind of colonial elegance and fresh-looking Caribbean style, with such touches as bamboo and flower prints. Two of the rooms share a private terrace overlooking Admiralty Bay. The tiled, shower-only bathrooms come with hair dryers and deluxe toiletries. On-site facilities include a dining room that serves excellent cuisine (see "Where to Dine," below), a bar, a beach-bar grill, and a kidney-shaped beachside pool, all set on 10 acres of tropical gardens. Barbecues, tennis, and scuba diving are offered.

Spring on Bequia. Spring Bay, Bequia, The Grenadines, St. Vincent, W.I. ☎ **784/458-3414,** or 612/823-1202 in Minneapolis. Fax 784/457-3305. 10 units. Winter $130–$210 double. Off-season $70–$140 double. MAP (breakfast and dinner) $40 per person extra. AE, DC, DISC, MC, V. Closed end of June to Oct.

In the late 1960s, the Frank Lloyd Wright design of this hotel won an award from the American Institute of Architects. Fashioned from beautifully textured honey-colored stone, it has a flattened hip roof inspired by the old plantation houses of Martinique. Constructed on the 18th-century foundations of a West Indian homestead, it sits in the middle of 28 acres of hillside orchards, producing oranges, grapefruit, bananas, breadfruit, plums, and mangos. Thanks to the almost constant blossoming of one crop or another, it always feels like spring here (hence the name of the establishment). From the main building's stone bar and open-air dining room, you might hear the bellowing of a herd of cows. All guest rooms have terraces; the three units in the main building are less spacious and darker than the others. Each room is ringed with stone and contains Japanese-style screens to filter the sun. The high pyramidal ceilings and the constant trade winds keep things cool in the rooms (which lack fans and air-conditioning). The twin or double platform beds are draped in mosquito netting, and the bathrooms have stone-grotto-like showers that utilize solar-heated water. All remains very quiet and tranquil here, as the place has long since been bypassed by other more glitzy and happening resorts in the Grenadines. The sandy beach is a 3-minute walk away through a coconut grove, but it's too shallow for good swimming. There's a pool and a tennis court on site.

WHERE TO DINE

The food is good and healthy here—lobster, chicken, and steaks from such fish as dolphin (mahimahi), kingfish, and grouper, plus tropical fruits, fried plantains, and coconut and guava puddings made fresh daily. Even the beach bars are kept spotless.

Frangipani. In the Hotel Frangipani, Port Elizabeth. ☎ **809/458-3255.** Reservations required for dinner. Breakfast EC$18 ($6.65); lunch EC$6–EC$40 ($2.20–$14.80); dinner main courses EC$30–EC$70 ($11.10–$25.90); fixed-price dinner EC$45–EC$80 ($16.65–$29.60). AE, MC, V. Daily 7:30am–5pm and 7–9pm. Closed Sept. CARIBBEAN.

This waterside dining room is one of the best restaurants on the island. The yachting crowd often comes ashore to dine here. With the exception of the juicy steaks imported for barbecues, only local food is used in the succulent specialties. Lunches, served throughout the day, include sandwiches, salads, and seafood platters. Dinner specialties include conch chowder, baked chicken with rice-and-coconut stuffing, lobster, and an array of fresh fish. A Thursday-night barbecue with live entertainment is an island event.

Friendship Bay Resort. Port Elizabeth. ☎ **784/458-3222.** Reservations required for dinner. Main courses EC$20–EC$45 ($7.40–$16.65) lunch, EC$35–EC$80 ($12.95–$29.60) dinner. AE, MC, V. Daily noon–3pm and 7:30–10pm. Closed Sept–Oct 15. INTERNATIONAL/WEST INDIAN.

Guests dine in a candlelit room high above a sweeping expanse of seafront on a hillside rich with the scent of frangipani and hibiscus. Lunch is served at the Spicy 'n Herby beach bar, but dinner is more elaborate. Meals, based on fresh ingredients, might include grilled lobster in season, curried beef, grilled or broiled fish (served Creole style with a spicy sauce), shrimp curry, and charcoal-grilled steak flambé. Dishes are flavorsome and well prepared. An island highlight is the Friday- and Saturday-night "jump-up" (like a Caribbean hoedown) and barbecue.

✪ **Le Petit Jardin.** Backstreet, Port Elizabeth. ☎ **784/458-3318.** Reservations recommended. Main courses EC$40–EC$80 ($14.80–$29.60). AE, DC, MC, V. Daily 11:30am–2pm and 6:30–9:30pm. INTERNATIONAL.

Set in a varnished wooden house behind the post office, this restaurant is the slow-moving but likable creation of the Belmar family, who focus on as many fresh ingredients as the vagaries of the local fishing fleet will allow. You'll dine within view of a garden, in a likable ambience inspired by both the British and French West Indies. Menu items include grilled swordfish with lemon sauce; grilled lobster, shrimp and vegetable kebabs; chipped steak in cream sauce; and conventional grilled sirloin.

✪ **Plantation House.** Admiralty Bay. ☎ **784/458-3425.** Reservations Required. Main courses EC$50–EC$120 ($18.50–$44.40). AE, MC, V. Daily 7–10pm. CREOLE/INTERNATIONAL/CARIBBEAN.

This is the premier dining spot on the island. Although informal, evenings here are the most elegant on Bequia. The chef emphasizes fresh ingredients, a blend of some of the finest of European cookery along with West Indian spice and flair. Try the chicken Cordon Bleu with mousseline potatoes, christophene in cheese sauce, and buttered pumpkin, or the roast breast of duck with orange sauce. Curried conch is a local specialty.

Whaleboner Inn. Admiralty Bay, Port Elizabeth. ☎ **784/458-3233.** Reservations required for dinner. Main courses $20–$32. AE, MC, V. Daily 8am–10:30pm. Next to the Hotel Frangipani, directly south of Port Elizabeth. CARIBBEAN/SEAFOOD.

An enduring favorite, the Whaleboner is still going strong, serving dishes with the most authentic island flavor on Bequia. Inside, the bar is carved from the jawbone of a giant whale, and the bar stools are made from the vertebrae. The owners offer the best pizza on the island, along with a selection of fish-and-chips and well-made sandwiches for lunch. At night, you may want one of the wholesome dinners, including a choice of lobster, fish, chicken, or steak. We prefer the curried-conch dinner beginning with the callaloo soup. The bar often stays open later than 10:30pm, depending on the crowd.

EXPLORING BEQUIA

Obviously, the secluded beaches are tops on everyone's list of Bequia's attractions. As you walk along the beaches, especially near Port Elizabeth, you'll see craftspeople building boats by hand, a method passed on by their ancestors. Whalers sometimes still set out from here in wooden boats with hand harpoons, just as they do from a port village on St. Vincent.

Dive Bequia, Gingerbread House, Admiralty Bay (P.O. Box 16), Bequia (☎ 784/458-3504), specializes in diving and snorkeling. Scuba dives cost $50 for one, $85 for two in the same day, and $400 for a 10-dive package. Introductory lessons go for $15 per person; a four-dive open-water certification course is $400. Snorkeling trips are $15 per person. These prices include all the necessary equipment.

The main harbor village, **Port Elizabeth** is known for its safe anchorage, Admiralty Bay. The bay was a haven in the 17th century for the British, French, and Spanish navies, as well as for pirates. Descendants of Captain Kydd (a.k.a. Kidd) still live on the island. Today, the yachting set anchors here.

There aren't many sights after you leave Port Elizabeth, so you'll probably have your driver, booked for the day, drop you off for a long, leisurely lunch and some time on a beach. You will pass a fort with a harbor view as well as Industry Estates, which has a Beach House restaurant serving a fair lunch. At **Paget Farm,** you can wander into an old whaling village and maybe inspect a few jawbones left over from the catches of yesterday.

At **Moonhole,** there's a vacation and retirement community built into the cliffs like a free-form sculpture. These are private homes, of course, and you're not to enter without permission. For a final look at Bequia, head up an 800-foot hill that the local people call **"The Mountain."** From that perch, you'll have a 360-degree view of St. Vincent and the Grenadines to the south.

SHOPPING

This is not a particularly good reason to come to Bequia, but there are some interesting stores.

The **Crab Hole,** next door to the Plantation House, Admiralty Bay (☎ 784/458-3290), is the best of the shops scattered along the water. Guests can visit the silk-screen factory in back, then make purchases at the shop in front, including sterling-silver and 14-karat-gold jewelry.

At **Noah's Arkade,** in the Frangipani Hotel, Port Elizabeth (☎ 784/458-3424), island entrepreneur Lavinia Gunn sells Vincentian and Bequian batiks, scarves, hats, T-shirts, pottery, dolls, baskets, and homemade jellies concocted from grapefruit, mango, and guava, plus West Indian cookbooks and books on tropical flowers and reef fish.

Anyone on the island can show you the way to the workshops of **Sargeant's Model Boatshop Bequia,** Front Street, Port Elizabeth (☎ 784/458-3344), west of the pier past the oil-storage facility. Sought out by yacht owners looking for a scale-model reproduction of their favorite vessel, Lawson Sargeant is the self-taught wood carver who established this business. The models are carved from a soft local wood called gumwood, then painted in brilliant colors. When a scale model of the royal family's yacht, *Britannia,* was commissioned in 1985, it required 5 weeks of work and cost $10,000. You can pick up a model of a Bequia whaling boat for much less. The Sargeant family usually keeps 100 model boats in many shapes and sizes in inventory.

MUSTIQUE

This island of luxury villas, which someone once called "Georgian West Indian," is so remote and small it almost deserves to be unknown, and it would be if it weren't for Princess Margaret and other world-class celebrities (including Truman Capote, Paul Newman, Mick Jagger, Raquel Welch, Richard Avedon, and Prince Andrew) who have cottages here.

The island, privately owned by a consortium of businesspeople, is only 3 miles long and 1 mile wide, and it has only one major hotel. It's located 15 miles south of St. Vincent. After settling in, you'll find many good white-sand beaches against a backdrop of luxuriant foliage. Our favorite is **Macaroni Beach,** where the water is turquoise.

On the northern reef of Mustique lies the wreck of the French liner *Antilles,* which ran aground on the Pillories in 1971. Its massive hulk, now gutted, can be seen cracked and rusting a few yards offshore—an eerie sight.

If you wish to tour the small island, you can rent a **Mini-Moke** to see some of the most elegant homes in the Caribbean. To stay on Mustique, you can even rent Princess Margaret's place, **Les Jolies Eaux** (Pretty Waters)—that is, if you can afford it. A five-bedroom/five-bathroom house with a large pool, it accommodates 10 guests and is available only when Her Royal Highness is not in residence. If you rent it, the princess will require references.

GETTING THERE & GETTING AROUND

Mustique Airways (☎ 784/458-4380 in St. Vincent) maintains two daily commuter flights between St. Vincent and Mustique. Flights depart St. Vincent daily at 7:30am and 4:30pm, landing on Mustique about 10 minutes later, then heading immediately back to St. Vincent. The airport closes at dusk.

Once here, you can call **Michael's Taxi** (☎ 784/458-4621, ext. 448), but chances are someone at the Cotton House will already have seen you land.

WHERE TO STAY

✪ **The Cotton House.** Mustique, The Grenadines, St. Vincent, W.I. ☎ **800/826-2809** in the U.S., or 784/456-4777. Fax 784/456-5887. E-mail: cottonhouse@caribsurf.com. 20 units. MINIBAR TEL. Winter $790–$1,500 double. Off-season $590–$1,000 double. Rates include MAP (breakfast and dinner). AE, MC, V.

The Caribbean's most exclusive hotel, once operated as a private club, is as casually elegant and palpably British as its clientele. The 18th-century main house is built of coral and stone and was painstakingly restored, reconstructed, and redecorated by Oliver Messel, uncle by marriage to Princess Margaret. The entire property was again renovated in 1996. The style of the hotel is set by the antique loggia, arched louvered doors, and cedar shutters. The decor includes everything from Lady Bateman's steamer trunks to a scallop-shell fountain on a quartz base, where guests sit and enjoy their sundowns, perhaps after an afternoon on the tennis court or in the pool. Guest rooms are in two fully restored Georgian houses, a trio of cottages, a newer block of four rooms, and a five-room beach house, all of which open onto windswept balconies or patios. Extras include private safes, ceiling fans, and king-size beds dressed in Egyptian cotton and swathed in netted canopies. Bathrooms contain hair dryers, robes, slippers, and toiletries from Floris in London. Some of the more romantic units have wrought-iron four-posters, while some of the bathrooms offer private outdoor showers. The Tower Suite is the most luxurious accommodation, filling the entire second floor. Guests go between two beaches, each only a couple of minutes away on foot—Endeavour Bay, on the leeward side, with calmer waters, and L'Ansecoy, on the other side.

Dining/Diversions: The hotel enjoys an outstanding reputation for its West Indian/continental food and service. Nonguests are welcome to dine here, but must reserve. The hotel also has three bars—you might find Mick Jagger at one of them.

Amenities: Two tennis courts, deep-sea fishing, sailboats, horseback riding. Room service, laundry, baby-sitting.

✪ **Firefly.** Brittania Bay (P.O. Box 349), Mustique, The Grenadines, W.I. ☎ **784/456-3414.** Fax 784/456-3514. www.mustiquefirefly.com. E-mail: fireflymus@caribsurf.com. 4 units. Year-round $350 double; $475–$550 suite. Rates include breakfast. AE, MC, V.

This hotel occupies the stone-sided premises of what was constructed in 1972 as one of the first homes ever built by an expatriate English or North American on Mustique. It functioned as a simple, not particularly glamorous B&B until the late 1990s, when Sussex-born Elizabeth Clayton spent huge sums of money to upgrade and enlarge the hotel and its restaurant. Although it contains only a quartet of bedrooms, it thrives as one of the most consistently popular bars and restaurants on an island where lots of the expatriate residents enjoy partying 'til the wee hours. (The restaurant is recommended in "Where to Dine," below) Each of the guest rooms has a Caribbean decor, ceiling fans, mahogany furniture, an antique four-poster bed, and a bathroom with a sunken Jacuzzi, plus floors and countertops crafted from smooth-worn pebbles set into beds of mortar. The ambience of the place is more that of a private home than a hotel, and an added advantage is the easy accessibility to one of the island's most animated bars and restaurants.

WHERE TO DINE

Basil's Beach Bar. 13 Britannia Bay. ☎ **784/458-4621.** Main courses $25–$40. AE, MC, V. Daily 11am–10:30pm. Bar daily 8am "until very late." SEAFOOD.

Nobody ever visits this island of indigenous farmers and fisherfolk without spending a night drinking at Basil's, a South Seas–type place more authentic than any reproduction in an old Dorothy Lamour flick. It's far beyond its heyday of chicdom—Princess Margaret and Mick Jagger are long gone—but the memories linger on in this gathering place for boaters, built on piers above the sea. Some people come here to drink and see the panoramic view, but Basil's also has a reputation as one of the finest seafood restaurants in the Caribbean. You can dine under the open-air sunscreens or with the sun blazing down on you. On Wednesday night in winter, you can "jump-up" at a barbecue. A boutique is also on the premises.

✪ **The Restaurant at Firefly.** Firefly, Britannia Bay. ☎ **784/456-3414.** Reservations recommended for dinner. Main courses EC$50–EC$85 ($18.50–$31.45). Daily noon–3pm and 7–10pm. Bar daily noon–3am. FRENCH/INTERNATIONAL.

This is one of the island's most consistently popular restaurants, characterized by its bright tropical colors and open-air terraces, a busy bar area where you're likely to see Mustique's glitterati at play, and a menu that's the by-product of a European-trained chef whose earlier venues were very grand and very prestigious. Some of the establishment's tried-and-true dishes include spicy Caribbean crab cakes and pineapple-shrimp curry with rice. Other entrees change with the season and the inspiration of the chef. The drink that's forever associated with this place is the Firefly Special, made with coconut cream, two kinds of rum, fresh papaya, and nutmeg.

CANOUAN

In the shape of a half circle, Canouan is surrounded by coral reefs and blue lagoons. The island is only 3½ miles by 1½ miles, and is visited mainly for its splendid long beaches. Canouan has a population of fewer than 2,000 people, many of whom fish for a living and reside in **Retreat Village,** the island's only hamlet.

The governing island, St. Vincent, is 14 miles to the north, while Grenada is 20 miles to the south. Canouan rises from its sandy beaches to the 800-foot-high peak of Mount Royal in the north, where you'll find unspoiled forests of white cedar.

GETTING THERE

Reaching Canouan by air is slightly different from traveling to the other Grenadines. **Mustique Airways** no longer makes passenger flights from St. Vincent to Canouan; these flights are now flown by **S.V.G.A. Airways** in St. Vincent (☎ 784/456-4942). S.V.G.A. makes two daily flights to Canouan at a cost of EC$160 ($59.20) round-trip. However, **Mustique Airways** (☎ 784/458-4380) does charter flights to Canouan at a cost of $250 one-way, for up to five passengers.

WHERE TO STAY

Canouan Beach Hotel. South Glossy Bay, Canouan, St. Vincent, W.I. (c/o Mr. Joe Nadal, Manager, Canouan Beach Hotel, Canouan Post Office, St. Vincent, W.I.). ☎ **784/458-8888.** Fax 784/458-8875. 32 units. A/C. Winter $183–$210 per person double. Off-season $146–$168 per person double. Rates are all-inclusive, except for alcohol. MC, V. Guests fly to Barbados, where a chartered plane from Mustique Airways takes them on to Canouan (the hotel will arrange this in advance of your arrival); the price is $120 per person one-way from Barbados to Canouan; from the airport, take a 5-minute taxi ride.

Until 1996, this was the only resort on an island with nothing but sandy beaches and a sweltering scrub-covered landscape. Opened in 1984 on 7 acres of glaringly white beachfront on a peninsula jutting out between the Atlantic and the Caribbean, it does a thriving business with escapist Europeans (primarily French, German, and English) in search of few distractions and a life patterned on Gauguin's. Don't expect to find a lot to do other than sleep, swim, sunbathe, snorkel, sail, and reminisce about the life you've left behind. The resort's social center is beneath the sunscreen of a mahogany-trussed parapet whose sides are open, like virtually everything else here, to views of the water. A pair of lush, uninhabited islands lie offshore. Snorkeling, windsurfing, small sailboats, and a catamaran are available without charge to guests. The 36-foot cata-maran departs on seaborne excursions six afternoons a week. All water sports, dining (usually in the form of buffet lunches and barbecue-style suppers), and soft drinks are included in the rates (with extra charges for alcohol). Accommodations are in stone-sided buildings with sliding-glass doors and simple furnishings. The spacious bed-rooms have tile floors, high ceilings, king or twin beds, and basic, shower-only bathrooms. The sunsets here are beautiful, but you'll have to enjoy them with the mos-quitoes.

UNION ISLAND

Midway between Grenada and St. Vincent, Union Island is the southernmost of the Grenadines. It's known for its dramatic 900-foot peak, Mount Parnassus, which yachters can often see from miles away. For those cruising in the area, Union is the port of entry for St. Vincent. Yachters are required to check in with Customs upon entry.

You may sail into Union on a night when the locals are having a "big drum" dance, in which costumed islanders dance and chant to the beat of drums made of goatskin.

GETTING THERE

The island is reached by chartered or scheduled aircraft, cargo boat, private yacht, or mail boat (see "Getting There" at the beginning of this section). **Air Martinique** (☎ 784/458-4528) flies to Union Island from both Martinique and St. Vincent. **Mustique Airways** (☎ 784/458-4380 on St. Vincent) makes one flight per day Monday through Thursday; the fare is $64 round-trip (children under 12 pay half).

WHERE TO STAY & DINE

Anchorage Yacht Club. Clifton, Union Island, The Grenadines, St. Vincent, W.I. ☎ **784/458-8221.** Fax 784/458-8365. 12 units. A/C. Winter $100 double; $150 bungalow or apt. Off-season $70 double; $80 bungalow or apt. Extra person $35. Rates include continental breakfast. MC, V.

This club occupies a prominent position a few steps from the bumpy landing strip that services at least two nearby resorts (Petit St. Vincent and Palm Island) and about a half dozen small islands nearby. As such, something of an airline-hub aura permeates the place, as passengers shuttle between their planes, boats, and the establishment's bar and restaurant. Although at least two other hotels are nearby, this is the most important. It has a three-fold function as a hotel, a restaurant, and a bar, with (under different management) a busy marine-service facility in the same scrubby, concrete-sided compound. Each of the small guest rooms, set between a pair of airy verandas, has white-tile floors and simple, somewhat sunbleached modern furniture. Bathrooms are very small and towels a bit thin, but in this remote part of the world, you're grateful for hot water. The most popular units are the bungalows and cabanas beside the beach.

The yachting club meets in the wood-and-stone bar, which serves breakfast, lunch, and dinner daily. The menu might include fish soup, a wide array of fresh fish, and Creole versions of lamb, pork, and beef. Try the mango daiquiri. The bar is open all day and into the night.

Lambi's Guest House & Restaurant. Clifton Harbour, Union Island, The Grenadines, St. Vincent, W.I. ☎ **784/458-8549.** Fax 784/458-8395. 41 units. Year-round EC$50 ($18.50) single; EC$75 ($27.75) double; EC$90 ($33.30) triple. Main courses EC$30 ($11.10). 50-dish buffet EC$50 ($18.50). Daily 7am–midnight. MC, V. CREOLE/SEAFOOD.

Built partially on stilts on the waterfront in Clifton, this is the best place to sample the local cuisine. *Lambi* means conch in Creole patois, and naturally it's the specialty here—if you've never tried this shellfish before, this is a good place to sample it. You can order various other fresh fish platters as well, depending on the catch of the day, and lobster and crab are frequently available. You can also order the usual chicken, steak, lamb, or pork chops, but all this is shipped in frozen. Fresh vegetables are used whenever possible. In winter, a steel band entertains nightly in the bar, and limbo dancers or even fire dancing will enthrall you.

Upstairs are the dormitory-simple rooms, which each have two double beds, ceiling fans, and a tiny, tiny bathroom.

PALM ISLAND

Is this island a resort or is the resort the island? Casual elegance prevails on these 130 acres in the southern Grenadines. Surrounded by five white-sand beaches, the island is sometimes called "Prune," so we can easily understand the more appealing name change. This little islet offers complete peace and quiet with plenty of sea, sand, sun, and sailing.

GETTING THERE

To get to Palm Island, you must first fly to Union Island. From Union Island, a hotel launch will take you to Palm Island.

WHERE TO STAY & DINE

Palm Island Beach Club. Palm Island, The Grenadines, St. Vincent, W.I. ☎ **888/456-6123** in the U.S., or 784/458-8824. Fax 784/458-8804. www.palmislandresorts.com/rates.htm. E-mail: palm@caribsurf.com. 24 units. Winter $330–$415 double. Off-season $325 double. Rates are all-inclusive. AE, DISC, MC, V.

This place is the fulfillment of John and Mary Caldwell's wish to establish a hotel on an idyllic and isolated island. Their dream-come-true has since attracted such celebs as Ted Kennedy, Barbra Streisand, and Donald Trump. John is nicknamed "Coconut Johnny" because of his hobby of planting palms. He planted hundreds upon hundreds of trees on Prune Island, until its name was changed to Palm Island. This Texan adventurer once set out to sail solo across the Pacific, coming to rest off the coast of Fiji. He made it to Australia, where he constructed his own ketch, *Outward Bound,* loaded his family aboard, and took off again. Eventually he made it to the Grenadines, where he operated a charter business and eventually built this cottage colony on the white-sand beach. Accommodations are in the Beach Club duplex cottages or in the stone-and-wood villas, with louvered walls as well as sliding-glass doors that open onto terraces. All rooms are superior, with ceiling fans, window screens, rattan furniture, beach lounges, small fridges, outdoor walled patios on the oceanfront, and tiny bathrooms with showers.

Dining/Diversions: Good, plentiful food is served in a South Seas–style pavilion. The nautically oriented guests like to have tall drinks at the Sunset Beach Bar or at the nearby Yacht Club Bar and Restaurant. There are barbecues twice a week, calypso on Wednesday, and a Saturday-evening "jump-up."

Amenities: Sailboats and scuba equipment are available for rental, and snorkeling gear, table tennis, and Sunfish sailing are offered free. Guests can also make day sails to Tobago Cays and Mayreau on a 37-foot *CSY* yacht.

PETIT ST. VINCENT

A private island 4 miles from Union in the southern Grenadines, this speck of land is rimmed with white-sand beaches. On 113 acres, it's an out-of-this-world corner of the Caribbean that's only for self-sufficient types who want to escape from just about everything.

GETTING THERE

The easiest way to get to Petit St. Vincent is to fly to Union Island via St. Vincent. Make arrangements with the hotel to have its "PSV boat" pick you up on Union Island.

WHERE TO STAY & DINE

✪ **Petit St. Vincent Resort.** Petit St. Vincent, The Grenadines, St. Vincent, W.I. (For reservations, P.O. Box 12506, Cincinnati, OH 45212.) ☎ **800/654-9326** or 513/242-1333 in the U.S., or 784/458-8801. Fax 784/458-8428. www.psvresort.com. E-mail: psv@fuse.net. 22 units. MINIBAR. Winter $490–$770 cottage for 2. Off-season $490–$625 cottage for two. Rates are all-inclusive. AE, V (personal checks accepted and preferred). Closed Sept–Oct.

Petit St. Vincent Resort has a nautical chic. It was conceived by Hazen K. Richardson, who had to do everything from planting trees to laying cables on the 113-acre property. Open to the trade winds, this self-contained cottage colony was designed by a Swedish architect, Arne Hasselquist, who used purpleheart wood and the local stone, called blue bitch (yes, that's right), for the walls. This is the only place to stay on the island, and if you don't like it and want to check out, you'd better have a yacht waiting. But we think you'll be pleased.

The cottages are built on a hillside, with great views, or set conveniently close to the beach. They open onto big outdoor patios and are cooled by trade winds and ceiling fans. Each spacious accommodation has an ample living area, two daybeds, a good-size bedroom with two queen beds, a dressing room, Caribbean-style wicker and rattan furnishings, and a large patio with a hammock for lying back and taking it easy.

When you need something, you simply write out your request, place it in a slot in a bamboo flagpole, and run up the yellow flag. A staff member will arrive on a motorized cart to collect your order.

Amenities include a tennis court, a fitness trail, and a water-sports center with snorkeling gear, the motor launch *Zeus II* for day trips, Sunfish, Hobie Cats, and windsurfing equipment.

MAYREAU

A tiny cay, 1½ square miles of land in the Grenadines, Mayreau is a privately owned island shared by a hotel and a little hilltop village of about 170 inhabitants. It's on the route of the mail boat that plies the seas to and from St. Vincent, visiting Canouan and Union Island as well. It's completely sleepy unless a cruise ship anchors offshore and hustles its passengers over for a lobster barbecue on the beach.

WHERE TO STAY & DINE

Saltwhistle Bay Club. Mayreau, The Grenadines, St. Vincent, W.I. ☎ **784/458-8444.** Fax 784/458-8944. 10 units. Winter $480 double. Off-season $320 double. Children under 18 pay half. Rates include MAP (breakfast and dinner). AE, V. Closed Sept–Oct. Take the private hotel launch from the airport on Union Island ($50 per person round-trip).

This is a last frontier for people seeking a tropical island paradise. Set back from the beach, the accommodations were built by local craftspeople, using local stone and such tropical woods as purpleheart and greenheart. All units are cooled by ceiling fans. Inside, the spacious cottages have an almost medieval feel, with thick stone walls and dark wood furnishings. Air mattresses rest on king or twin beds. Bathrooms are large, with cylindrical stone showers. Slightly less formal and less expensive than the Petit St. Vincent Resort on Petit St. Vincent (see above), to which it's frequently compared, the place caters to escapists with money. By day you can snorkel, fish, windsurf, cruise on a yacht, or just loll in one of the hammocks strung among the trees in the 20-acre tropical garden, perhaps taking a swim off the expanse of white-sand beaches that curve along both the leeward and windward sides of the island. Scuba divers will enjoy exploring the wreck of a 1912 gunboat, in 40 feet of water a few hundred feet offshore. One of the enjoyable excursions available is a "Robinson Crusoe" picnic on a little uninhabited island nearby. The dining room at the hotel is made up of circular stone booths topped by thatch canopies, where you can enjoy seafood fresh from the waters around Mayreau: lobster, curried conch, and grouper. Guests can get acquainted at the bar.

26 Trinidad & Tobago

Trinidad, birthplace of the calypso, steel-drum music, and the limbo, used to be visited only by business travelers in Port-of-Spain. The island was more interested in its oil, natural gas, and steel industries than in tourism. But all that has changed now. Trinidad has become a serious vacation destination, with a spruced-up capital and a renovated airport. The island's sophistication and cultural mélange, which is far greater than that of any other island in the southern Caribbean, is also a factor in increased visitor volume.

Conversely, Tobago, its sibling island, is just as drowsy as ever, and that's its charm. Through the years, the country has been peopled by immigrants from almost every corner of the world: Africa, the Middle East, Europe, India, China, and the Americas. It's against such a background that the island has become the fascinating mixture of cultures, races, and creeds that it is today.

Trinidad, which is about the size of Delaware, and its neighbor island, tiny Tobago, 20 miles to the northeast, together form a nation popularly known as "T&T." South African Bishop Desmond Tutu once dubbed it "The Rainbow Country," for its abundance of floral growth and the diversity of its population. The islands are the southernmost outposts of the West Indies. Trinidad lies only 7 miles from the Paria Peninsula of Venezuela, to which it was once connected in prehistoric times.

The Spanish settled the island, making their first permanent settlement in 1592 and holding onto it longer than they did any of their other real estate in the Caribbean. The English captured Trinidad in 1797, and it remained British until the two-island nation declared its independence in 1962. The British influence is still clearly visible today, from the strong presence of the British dialect to the islanders' fondness for cricket.

1 Essentials

VISITOR INFORMATION

Before you go, information about either Trinidad or Tobago is available by calling the **Tourism Hotline** at ☎ **888/595-4TNT.** You can also contact the **Trinidad & Tobago Tourism Office,** 350 Fifth Ave., Suite 6316, New York, NY 10118 (☎ **800/748-4224**).

Canadians can get information from **Taurus House,** 512 Duplex Ave., Toronto, Ontario M4R 2E3 (☎ **800/267-7600** or 416/485-7827).

There's also an office in England at **International House,** 47 Chase Side, Enfield, Middlesex EN2 6NB2 (☎ **0181/367-3752**).

The islands are on the Web at **www.tidco.co.tt**.

Once you're on Trinidad, you can stop by **TIDCO,** 10–14 Phillips St., Port-of-Spain (☎ **868/623-1932**). There's also an information desk at Piarco Airport (☎ **868/669-5196**).

On Tobago, go to the **Tobago Division of Tourism,** N.I.B. Mall, Level 3, Scarborough (☎ **868/639-2125**), or the information desk at Crown Point Airport (☎ **868/639-0509**).

Fast Facts: Trinidad & Tobago

Banking Hours   Most banks are open Monday to Thursday from 8am to 2pm and Friday from 9am to noon and 3 to 5pm. On Trinidad, the **Bank of Nova Scotia** has an office on Park Street at Richmond Street, Port-of-Spain (☎ **868/ 625-3566** or 868/625-5222). **Citibank** has offices at 12 Queen's Park East, Port-of-Spain (☎ **868/625-1046** or 868/625-1049), and 18–30 High St., San Fernando (☎ **868/652-3691** or 868/652-3293). On Tobago, **First Citizen Bank** has an office on Main Street in Scarborough (☎ **868/639-3111**).

Currency   The **Trinidad and Tobago dollar (TT$)** is loosely pegged to the U.S. dollar at an exchange rate of about $1 US = TT$6 (TT$1 = 16.6¢ US). Ask what currency is being referred to when rates are quoted. We've used a combination of both in this chapter, depending on the establishment. U.S. and Canadian dollars are accepted, particularly in Port-of-Spain. However, you'll usually do better by converting your Canadian or U.S. dollars into local currency. British pounds should be converted into the local currency. *Unless otherwise specified, dollar quotations appearing in this chapter are in U.S. currency.*

Customs   Readers have reported long delays in clearing Customs on Trinidad. Personal effects are duty free, and visitors may bring in 200 cigarettes or 50 cigars plus 1 quart of "spirits."

Documents   Visitors arriving in Trinidad and Tobago should have an ongoing or return ticket from their point of embarkation. A visa is not required for tourist/business stays of less than 6 weeks. You'll be asked to fill out an immigration card upon your arrival, and the carbon copy of this should be saved, as it must be returned to immigration officials when you depart. Citizens of the United States, Britain, and Canada need passports to enter Trinidad and Tobago.

Electricity   The electricity is either 110 or 230 volts AC (60 cycles), so ask when making your hotel reservations if you'll need transformers and/or adapters.

Embassies & High Commissions   In Port-of-Spain on Trinidad, the **U.S. Embassy** is at 7–9 Marli St., 15 Queen's Park West (☎ **868/622-6371**); the **Canadian High Commission** is at Maple House, 3 Sweet Briar Rd., St. Clair (☎ **868/622-6232**); and the **British High Commission** is at 19 St. Clair Ave., St. Clair (☎ **868/622-2748**).

Emergencies   On either Trinidad or Tobago, call the **police** at ☎ **999;** to report a **fire** or summon an **ambulance,** dial ☎ **990.**

Hospital   On Trinidad, the **Port-of-Spain General Hospital** is at 169 Charlotte St. (☎ **868/623-2951**). On Tobago, the **Tobago County Hospital** is on Fort George Street, Scarborough (☎ **868/639-2551**). Medical care is sometimes limited, and physicians and health-care facilities expect immediate cash payment for services. Medical insurance from the United States is not always valid outside the country, but supplemental medical insurance with specific overseas coverage is available. Contact the U.S. Embassy for updates.

Language English is the official language, although you'll hear it spoken with many different accents, including British. Hindi, Chinese, French, and Spanish are also spoken.

Post Office On Trinidad, the main post office (☎ **868/625-2121**) is on Wrightson Road, Port-of-Spain, and is open Monday to Friday from 7am to 5pm.

Safety As a general rule, Tobago is safer than its larger neighbor, Trinidad. Crime does exist, but it's not of raging dimensions. If you can, avoid the downtown streets of Port-of-Spain at night, especially those around Independence Square, where muggings have been reported. Evening jaunts down Wilson Street and the Market of Scarborough are also discouraged. Visitors are open prey for pickpockets during Carnival time, so be alert during large street parties. It would also be wise to safeguard your valuables and never leave them unattended at the beach or even in a locked car.

Taxes & Service Charges The government imposes a 15% value-added tax (VAT) on room rates. It also imposes a departure tax of TT$85 ($13.60) on every passenger more than 5 years old. The big hotels and restaurants add a 10% to 15% service charge to your final tab.

Telephone To call Trinidad and Tobago from the United States, dial **1,** then **868** and the local seven-digit number.

On Trinidad, you can send a cable or fax at **Textel,** 1 Edward St., Port-of-Spain (☎ **868/625-4431**).

Time Trinidad and Tobago time is the same as the U.S. East Coast. When the States go on daylight saving time, when it's 6am in Miami, it's 7am in T&T.

Water On Trinidad and Tobago, stick to bottled water.

Weather Trinidad has a tropical climate all year, with constant trade winds maintaining mean temperatures of 84°F during the day and 74°F at night, with a range of 70° to 90°F. The rainy season runs from May to November, but it shouldn't deter you from visiting; the rain usually lasts no more than 2 hours before the sun comes out again. However, carry along plenty of insect repellent if you visit then.

2 Trinidad

Trinidad is completely different from the other islands of the Caribbean, and that forms part of its charm and appeal. It's not for everyone, though. Because **Port-of-Spain,** the capital, is one of the most bustling commercial centers in the Caribbean, more business travelers than tourists are drawn here. The island, 50 miles long and 40 miles wide, does have beaches, but the best of them are far away from the capital. The city itself, with a population of about 120,000, is hot, humid, and slightly on the dirty side. With the opening of its $2-million cruise-ship complex, Port-of-Spain has become a major port of call for Caribbean cruise lines.

Although Port-of-Spain, with its shopping centers, fast-food joints, modern hotels, and active nightlife, draws mixed reviews from readers, the countryside is calmer. Far

Asa Wright Nature Centre and Lodge 8
Cascadia Hotel 5
Chaconia Inn 6
Kapok Hotel & Restaurant 1
Maracas Bay Hotel 7
Normandie Hotel & Restaurant 2
Trinidad Hilton 3
Trinidad Holiday Inn 4

Airport ✈ Beach 🏖

removed from the traffic jams of the capital, you can explore the fauna and flora of the island. It's estimated that there are some 700 varieties of orchids alone, plus 400 species of birds.

Prices on Trinidad are often lower than on many other islands in the West Indies, such as Barbados. Port-of-Spain abounds in inexpensive inns and guest houses. Since most of the restaurants cater to locals, dining prices reflect the low wages.

The people are part of the attraction on Trinidad, the most cosmopolitan in the Caribbean. The island's polyglot population includes Syrians, Chinese, Americans, Europeans, East Indians, Parsees, Madrasis, Venezuelans, and the last of the original Amerindians, the early settlers of the island. You'll also find Hindustanis, Javanese, Lebanese, African descendants, and Creole mixes. The main religions are Christianity, Hinduism, and Islam. In all, there are about 1.2 million inhabitants, whose language is English, although you may hear speech in a strange argot, Trinibagianese.

One of the most industrialized nations in the Caribbean, and the third-largest exporter of oil in the Western Hemisphere, Trinidad is also blessed with the huge 114-acre Pitch Lake, the source of most of the world's asphalt. It's also the home of Angostura Bitters, the recipe for which is a closely guarded secret.

GETTING THERE

From North America, Trinidad is one of the most distant islands in the Caribbean. Because of the legendary toughness of Trinidadian Customs, it's preferable to arrive during the day (presumably when your stamina is at its peak) if you can schedule it.

Trinidad is the transfer point for many passengers heading on to the beaches of Tobago. For information about getting to Tobago, see section 3 of this chapter.

Most passengers from eastern North America fly **American Airlines** (☎ **800/ 433-7300** or 868/664-4661; www.aa.com), which has connections through New York. American also offers a daily nonstop flight to Trinidad from Miami, which is especially useful for transfers from the Midwest and the West Coast.

Air Canada (☎ **800/268-7240** in Canada, 800/776-3000 in the U.S., or 868/664-4065; www.aircanada.ca) offers two nonstop flights per week from Toronto to Port-of-Spain.

BWIA (☎ **800/538-2942** or 868/625-1010; www.bwee.com) offers service from New York to Port-of-Spain. Some of these flights are nonstop; most of them touch down en route, usually on Barbados or Antigua, before continuing on to Trinidad, the airline's home base. From Miami, BWIA usually offers a daily nonstop flight to Port-of-Spain.

GETTING AROUND

BY TAXI Trinidad taxis are unmetered, and they're identified by their license plates, beginning with the letter *H*. There are also "pirate taxis" as well—private cars that cruise around like a regular taxi and pick up passengers. Maxi Taxis or vans can also be hailed on the street. A fare from Piarco Airport into Port-of-Spain generally costs $20 to $30.

To avoid the anxiety of driving, you can hire a local driver for your sightseeing jaunts. Although it costs more, it alleviates the hassles of badly marked (or unmarked) roads and the sometimes-bizarre local driving patterns. Most drivers will serve as guides. Their rates, however, are based on route distances, so get an overall quotation and agree on the actual fare before setting off.

BY RENTAL CAR Since the island is one of the world's largest exporters of asphalt, Trinidad's some 4,500 miles of roads are well paved. However, outback roads should be avoided during the rainy season, as they're often narrow, twisting, and prone to washouts. Inquire about conditions, particularly if you're headed for the north coast. The fierce traffic jams of Port-of-Spain are legendary, and night driving anywhere on the island is rather hazardous.

If you're brave enough to set out via rental car, arm yourself with a good map and be prepared for a car with a steering wheel mounted on the right side, as *you'll drive on the left*. Visitors with a valid international driver's license or a license from the United States, Canada, France, or the United Kingdom may drive without extra documentation for up to 3 months.

The major U.S.-based car-rental firms currently have no franchises on the island, so you'll have to make arrangements with a local firm (go over the terms and insurance agreements carefully). Count on spending about $40 to $60 per day or more, with unlimited mileage included. Your best bet is one of the firms maintaining offices at Piarco Airport. These include **Southern Sales Car Rentals** (☎ **868/669-2424**), **Econo-Car Rentals** (☎ **868/669-2342**), **Thrifty** (☎ **868/669-0602**), and the simply named **Auto Rentals** (☎ **868/669-2277**).

A word of warning: Although these local car-rental firms technically accept reservations, a car may not be waiting for you even if you reserve.

BY BUS All the cities of Trinidad are linked by regular bus service from Port-of-Spain. Fares are low (about 50¢ for runs within the capital). However, the old buses are likely to be very overcrowded. Try to avoid them at rush hours, and beware of pickpockets.

A Swirl of Color & Sound: The Carnival of Trinidad

Called "the world's most colorful festival," the Carnival of Trinidad is a spectacle of dazzling costumes and gaiety. Hundreds of bands of masqueraders parade through the cities on the Monday and Tuesday preceding Ash Wednesday, bringing traffic to a standstill. The island seems to explode with music, fun, and dancing.

Some of the Carnival costumes cost hundreds of dollars. "Bands" might depict the birds of Trinidad, such as the scarlet ibis and the keskidee, or a bevy of women might come out in the streets dressed as cats. Costumes are also satirical and comical.

Trinidad, of course, is the land of calypso, which grew out of the folk songs of the African–West Indian immigrants. The lyrics command great attention, as they're rich in satire and innuendo. The calypsonian is a poet-musician, and lyrics have often been capable of toppling politicians from office. In banter and bravado, the calypsonian gives voice to the sufferings and aspirations of his people. At Carnival time, the artist sings his compositions to spectators in tents. There's one show a night at each of the calypso tents around town, from 8pm to midnight. Tickets for these are sold in the afternoon at most record shops.

Carnival parties, or fêtes, with three or four orchestras at each one, are public and are advertised in the newspaper. For a really wild time, attend a party on Sunday night before Carnival Monday. To reserve tickets, contact the **National Carnival Committee,** Queen's Park Savannah, Port-of-Spain, Trinidad (☎ **868/627-1358**). Hotels are booked months in advance, and most inns raise their prices—often considerably—at the time.

You can attend rehearsals of steel bands at their headquarters, called panyards, beginning about 7pm. Preliminary band competitions are held at the grandstand of Queen's Park Savannah in Port-of-Spain and at Skinner Park in San Fernando, beginning two weeks before Carnival.

WHERE TO STAY

The number of hotels is limited, and don't expect your Port-of-Spain room to open directly onto a white-sand beach—the nearest beach is a long, costly taxi ride away. Don't forget that a 15% government tax and a 10% service charge will be added to your hotel and restaurant bills. All hotels raise their rates during Carnival (the week before Ash Wednesday).

EXPENSIVE

✪ **Asa Wright Nature Centre and Lodge.** Spring Hill Estate, Arima, Trinidad, W.I. (For information or reservations, call the toll-free number or write Caligo Ventures, 156 Bedford Rd., Armonk, NY 10504.) ☎ **800/426-7781** in the U.S., or 868/667-4655. Fax 868/667-4540. 25 units. Winter $240 double. Off-season $180 double. Rates include all meals, afternoon tea, and a welcoming rum punch. No credit cards.

There really isn't anything else like this in the Caribbean. Known to bird watchers throughout the world, this center sits on 196 remote acres of protected land at an elevation of 1,200 feet in the rain-forested northern mountain range of Trinidad, 10 miles north of Arima, beside Blanchisseuse Road. Hummingbirds, toucans, bellbirds, manakins, several varieties of tanagers, and the rare oilbird are all on the property. Back-to-basics accommodations are available in the lodge, in the 1908 Edwardian main house, or in the cottages built on elevated ground above the main house; none has air-conditioning, TV, or phones. Even though they offer less privacy, we prefer the two rooms in the main house, which offer more atmosphere and are outfitted with dark wood antiques and two king-size beds. Furnishings in the cottages are rather plain but comfortable. Mattresses are a bit thin, but the bird watchers who flock here don't complain. Shower-only baths are a bit cramped, but you generally get hot water—so count yourself lucky.

Guided tours are available on the nature center's grounds, which contain several well-maintained trails and a natural waterfall with a pool in which guests can swim (in lieu of a beach, which involves a 90-minute drive to the coast). Expert instructors conduct summer seminars in natural history, ornithology, and nature photography. The minimum age accepted is 14 if accompanied by an adult, or 17 if unaccompanied.

Trinidad Hilton. Lady Young Rd. (P.O. Box 442), Port-of-Spain, Trinidad, W.I. ☎ **800/HILTONS** in the U.S. and Canada, or 868/624-3211. Fax 868/624-4485. www.hilton.com. E-mail: hiltonpos@wow.net. 394 units. A/C TV TEL. Year-round $205–$270 double; from $450 suite. Rates include breakfast. AE, DC, MC, V.

This is the most dramatic and architecturally sophisticated hotel on Trinidad. Because of its position on some of the steepest terrain in Port-of-Spain, the building's lobby is on its uppermost floor, while the guest rooms are staggered in rocky but verdant terraces that sweep down the hillside. Its location just above Queen's Park Savannah affords most of its rooms a view of the sea and mountains. The hotel offers a wide range of accommodations that get cheaper the higher up they're situated. This is not the greatest Hilton in the world, or even in the Caribbean, but all rooms still meet international first-class standards, with queen or twin beds, balconies, generous closet space, and modern tiled bathrooms with combination shower/tubs. Accommodations in the main wing are the most sought after, as they have good views over Queen's Park Savannah. Only the more expensive units contain hair dryers, scales, private safes, and bars. Executive Floor rooms have upgraded services and amenities.

Dining/Diversions: The main dining room, La Boucan (see "Where to Dine," below), contains museum-quality murals by Geoffrey Holder, one of the island's best-known artists. Less formal are the Pool Terrace and the Gazebo Bar, both of which serve Caribbean and international food and colorful drinks. Saturday from 5pm to 1am, there's live music in the Carnival Bar. *The Taste of Trinidad,* a lively musical show, is offered on Monday night, along with a buffet, for $17.35.

Amenities: Olympic-size pool, pharmacy, bank, two all-weather tennis courts (lit at night), boutiques, business center, fitness center. Room service (from 6am to 11:30pm), concierge, baby-sitting, travel agency, laundry.

MODERATE

Maracas Bay Hotel. Maracas Bay, Trinidad, W.I. ☎ **868/669-1914.** Fax 868/623-1444. 40 units. A/C. Winter $150 double. Off-season $110 double. Rates include MAP (breakfast and dinner) for two occupants. Extra person (up to a total of four) $25. AE, MC, V.

This two-story, white-walled hotel finally opened in 1996 after years in the works. Owned and operated by a local family, it's nestled in a valley, on sloping terrain that lies across the road from Maracas Bay, about 7 miles ("as the crow flies") north of Port-of-Spain. Be warned in advance that dense traffic and a winding road makes this at least a 45-minute drive from the commercial center of the capital. Surprisingly, this is the only beachfront hotel in all of Trinidad, an island not particularly known for its beaches; in this case, you'll have to walk across the coastal road to reach it. There's a bar/lounge, accented with Hindu art, and an unpretentious dining room. Bedrooms contain simple furnishings, spartan white walls, and terra-cotta tile floors. Each unit comes with two queen-size beds and a tiled bathroom with a shower stall.

Trinidad Holiday Inn. Wrightson Rd. at London Rd. (P.O. Box 1017), Port-of-Spain, Trinidad, W.I. ☎ **800/HOLIDAY** in the U.S. and Canada, or 868/625-3366. Fax 868/ 625-4166. www.holidayinn/trinidad.net. E-mail: holidayinn@trinidad.net. 244 units. A/C TV TEL. Year-round $152 double; from $225 suite. AE, MC, V.

Originally built during the 1960s in an international but bland modern style, and proud of its role as the second-largest hotel on Trinidad, the Holiday Inn lies on the northern perimeter of the city's commercial zone, a 5-minute walk from the center. It's a favorite with business travelers, who tolerate the noise and congestion for the convenient location. The recently renovated bedrooms, tastefully decorated in pastels, contain private balconies along with two double beds. The hotel has added two executive floors and such amenities as trouser presses, magnifying mirrors, hair dryers, mahogany furniture, and brass lamps. The bathrooms have combination tub/showers and dual basins in faux marble or granite.

The Olympia Restaurant is adorned with Roman-style pillars, with plants cascading over the top. La Ronde, with a French decor, is the only revolving restaurant in the Caribbean and serves an international cuisine. A bar just above the lobby offers recorded island music. Amenities include gift shops, a full gym, an exotic pool with a "sunken" bar (open 24 hours), a children's pool, a business center, room service, laundry, and baby-sitting.

INEXPENSIVE

Cascadia Hotel. Ariapita Rd., St. Ann's, Trinidad, W.I. ☎ **868/624-0940.** Fax 868/ 627-8046. E-mail: reservations@cascadiahotel.com. 68 units. A/C TV TEL. Year-round $96 double; $121 suite for 2. AE, DC, MC, V. Located about 5 miles northwest of the center of Port-of-Spain.

Originally built in 1986, this modern hotel is a favorite with business travelers. With a vaguely English decor, it has lots of wicker furniture and touches of marble. The hotel is past its prime, but still reasonably comfortable. Each of the pleasant bedrooms contains two phones, a balcony, and unpretentious furniture. Bathrooms are rather standard fare, although they do contain second phones along with shower stalls. On the premises is an oval pool with a "swim-through" bar and a water slide, two squash courts, a gym, and an airy restaurant, the Skyview, serving American-Creole cuisine.

Chaconia Inn. 106 Saddle Rd. (P.O. Box 3340), Maraval, Trinidad, W.I. ☎ **868/628-8603.** Fax 868/628-3214. 31 units. A/C TV TEL. Year-round $75–$85 double; $110–$140 two-bedroom apt. MAP (breakfast and dinner) $30 per person extra. Tax 25% extra. AE, DC, MC, V. Located 3 miles north of Port-of-Spain.

This place offers great value for your money. Named for the country's scarlet national flower, the low-rise Chaconia is a miniature resort in the cool residential valley of Maraval, about 10 miles from Maracas Beach. The buildings are simple, and the furnishings are in a contemporary motel style. You'll be housed in one of three different types of accommodations, including two-bedroom apartments, superior rooms, and standard rooms. All are equipped with TVs, and the superior rooms and apartments also contain fridges. Bathrooms, though small, are tidily maintained. A special feature is the roof garden, where barbecues are staged on Saturday nights.

✪ **Kapok Hotel and Restaurant.** 16–18 Cotton Hill, St. Clair, Trinidad, W.I. ☎ **868/ 622-6441.** Fax 868/622-9677. www.kapok.co.tt/home.html. E-mail: web@kapok.co.tt. 94 units. A/C TV TEL. Year-round $109–$141 double. AE, DC, MC, V.

This modern but unpretentious nine-floor hotel, in the residential suburb of St. Clair, is an efficient, well-maintained operation run by the Chan family. Located a minute's drive and just north from the city's biggest park, the Savannah, the Kapok also lies near the zoo and the Presidential Palace and away from the worst traffic of the city. From its lounge, you'll have panoramic views of the Savannah and the Gulf of Paria. Guests who prefer small- to medium-size hotels will feel at home here. The comfortably appointed, spacious rooms have wicker furnishings and private bathrooms with combination shower/tubs. For a hotel of this price range, it comes as a surprise to find phones with voice mail and dataports, and even room service until 10pm. The rooftop restaurant, Tiki Village, serves Chinese and Polynesian food. In the back is an expanded pool area with a waterfall, garden, menagerie, and sundeck.

Normandie Hotel and Restaurant. 10 Nook Ave., St. Ann's (P.O. Box 851), Port-of-Spain, Trinidad, W.I. ☎ **868/624-1181.** Fax 868/624-0108. 53 units. A/C TV TEL. Year-round $72–$87 double; $97 loft studio for three. Children 11 and under stay free in parents' room. AE, DC, MC, V.

Originally built in the 1930s by two French brothers on the site of an old coconut plantation, this was already a well-established hotel when its owners modernized it in 1986, and again in 1996. It rises around a banyan- and banana-filled courtyard that surrounds an oval-shaped pool. Each guest room has a balcony or patio, plus standard furnishings (mostly twin beds). The more spacious superior units have tiny lofts with queen-size beds. Bathrooms are a bit lackluster with combination tub/showers, low water pressure, and rather thin towels. The cheaper rooms have drawn fire from some readers, especially for the noisy air-conditioning.

Calm and cosmopolitan, the hotel sits 3½ miles northwest of the city center, next to one of the best art galleries on Trinidad; a skylight-covered shopping center; an attractive restaurant, La Fantasie (see "Where to Dine," below); the botanical gardens of Port-of-Spain; and the official residence of the prime minister of Trinidad and Tobago. In addition, brunch, lunch, or tea can be ordered in the hotel's cafe, and the Cascade Club offers entertainment on Friday and Saturday nights.

WHERE TO DINE

The food probably should be better than it is, considering all the different culinary backgrounds that shaped the island, including West Indian, Chinese, French, and Indian.

Stick to local specials such as stuffed crabs or chip-chip (tiny clamlike shellfish), but skip the armadillo or opossum stews. Spicy Indian rotis filled with vegetables or ground meat seem to be everyone's favorite lunch, and the drink of choice is a fresh rum punch flavored with the natively produced Angostura Bitters. Except for a few fancy places, dress tends to be very casual.

EXPENSIVE

✪ **La Boucan.** In the Trinidad Hilton, Lady Young Rd. ☎ **868/624-3211.** Reservations required. Main courses $11–$30; lunch buffet $15. AE, MC, V. Mon–Sat noon–2:30pm and 7–10:30pm. INTERNATIONAL.

The finest hotel restaurant on Trinidad, with some of the most lavish buffets, this establishment satisfies the eye as well as the palate. Taking its name from the smoking process by which pirates and buccaneers used to preserve meat for long voyages, La Boucan incorporates this smoky flavor into many of its West Indian dishes. Against one of its longest walls stretches a graceful mural by Geoffrey Holder, one of the most famous artists and dancers of the Caribbean. Not all dishes reflect the nurturing and refinement they should, but most diners are satisfied with the results. Typical choices include lobster grilled or Thermidor; a daily selection of fish (usually grouper or snapper), which is grilled, poached, or pan-fried according to your wishes and served with herb-butter sauce; pan-fried fillet of shark with a lemon and herb sauce; and U.S. prime rib of beef. The desserts are sumptuous, especially the chocolate crème brûlée and a rich and creamy cheesecake. Live music from a pianist (and on weekends from a dance band) provides entertainment.

La Fantasie. In the Normandie Hotel and Restaurant, 10 Nook Ave., St. Ann's Village. ☎ **868/624-1181,** ext. 3306. Reservations recommended. Lunch main courses TT$50–TT$75 ($8–$12); dinner main courses TT$50–TT$120 ($8–$19.20). AE, DC, MC, V. Daily 7am–11pm. FRENCH/CREOLE.

Off Queen's Park Savannah, and named after the 18th-century plantation that once stood here, La Fantasie is loaded with style and features a tempting modern Creole cuisine. Many of the usually heavy, deep-fried dishes are given a light touch here, creating a sort of *cuisine nouvelle Creole*. Since fresh ingredients are used and deftly handled, no false notes jar the senses. The changing menu might include filet mignon with a tamarind-flavored sauce, chicken curry, locally caught Trinidadian salmon in a wine-based sauce with sultana raisins and bananas, and shrimp with Creole sauce in a pastry shell flavored with cheese. "Fish walk up the hill" is grilled fish with chopped herbs, while "drunken fish" fillet is in a crêpe with a white Creole sauce. End with a Trinidadian fruitcake with a rum-flavored custard, a dish especially popular at Christmas. Our only complaint: You're not exactly pampered here, and service has drawn complaints from readers.

✪ **Solimar.** 6 Nook Ave. (next to the Normandie Hotel and Restaurant, 3½ miles northwest of the city center), St. Ann's. ☎ **868/624-6267.** Reservations recommended. Main courses TT$24–TT$210 ($3.85–$33.60). AE, MC, V. Mon–Sat 6:30–10:30pm. Closed Mon from Mar–Nov; also closed 1 week in mid-May and 2 weeks in mid-Aug (exact dates vary). INTERNATIONAL.

By some estimates, this restaurant offers the most creative cuisine and most original format in Trinidad and Tobago. Established by Joe Brown, an English-born chef who worked for many years in the kitchens of Hilton hotels around the world, it occupies a garden-style building whose open walls are cooled by ceiling fans. As you dine, you'll hear the sound of an artificial waterfall that cascades into a series of fish ponds.

The menu, which changes every 3 months, presents local ingredients inspired by the cuisines of the world. The results are usually very convincing. Dishes might include an English-inspired combination of grilled breast of chicken and jumbo shrimp dressed with a lobster sauce, and a Sri Lankan dish of herb-flavored chicken vindaloo. The restaurant's double-chocolate mousse is the highlight of any meal here.

MODERATE

Restaurant Singho. Long Circular Mall, Level 3, Port-of-Spain. ☎ **868/628-2077.** Main courses TT$85–TT$100 ($13.60–$16); Wed night buffet TT$100 ($16). AE, MC, V. Daily 11am–11pm. CHINESE.

This restaurant, with an almost mystically illuminated bar and aquarium, is on the second floor of one of the capital's largest shopping malls, midway between the commercial center of Port-of-Spain and the Queen's Park Savannah. For Trinidad, this cuisine isn't bad: It's better than your typical chop suey and chow mein joint, and many of its dishes are quite tasty and spicy. À la carte choices include shrimp with oyster sauce, shark-fin soup, stewed or curried beef, almond pork, and spareribs with black-bean sauce. The to-go service is one of the best known in town. The Wednesday-night buffet offers an enormous selection of main dishes, along with heaps of rice and fresh vegetables. Even dessert is included in the set price.

✪ **Veni Mangé.** 67A Ariapata Ave. ☎ **868/624-4597.** Reservations recommended. Main courses $5–$15. AE, MC, V. Daily 11:30am–3pm; Wed 7:30–10pm; Fri open for bar service only 6–11:30pm. CREOLE/INTERNATIONAL.

Originally built in the 1930s and set about a mile west of Port-of-Spain's center, Veni Mangé (whose name means "come and eat") is painted in coral tones and has louvered windows on hinges that ventilate the masses of potted plants. It was established by two of the best-known women in Trinidad, Allyson Hennessy and her sister, Rosemary Hezekiah. Allyson, the Julia Child of Trinidad, hosts a daily TV talk show that's broadcast throughout the island. Best described as a new generation of Creole women, both Allyson and Rosemary (whose parents were English/Venezuelan and African-Caribbean/Chinese) entertain with their humor and charm.

Start with the bartender's special, a coral-colored fruit punch that's a rich, luscious mixture of papaya, guava, orange, and passion-fruit juices. The authentic callaloo soup, according to Trinidadian legend, can make a man propose marriage. The main courses might be curried crab or West Indian hot pot (a variety of meats cooked Creole style), perhaps a vegetable lentil loaf. The helpings are large, but if you still have room, order the pineapple upside-down cake, unless you prefer a homemade version of soursop ice cream or a coconut mousse. Dinner is served only on Wednesday nights and is something of a social event among regulars. On Friday, the bar buzzes, but only snacks and finger foods, "cutters," are served. (Cutters are so named because "they cut the appetite," so you can drink more punch.)

HITTING THE BEACH

Trinidad isn't thought of as beach country, yet it has more beach frontage than any other island in the West Indies. The only problem is that most of its beaches are undeveloped and found in distant, remote places, far removed from Port-of-Spain. The closest of the better beaches, **Maracas Bay,** is a full 18 miles from Port-of-Spain on the North Coast Road. It's a delight to visitors with its protected cove and quaint fishing village. The only drawbacks are the crowds and the strong current. Facilities include rest rooms and snack bars.

Farther up the North Coast Road is **Las Cuevas Bay,** which is far less crowded. The narrow beach is set against a backdrop of palm trees. There are changing rooms and vendors selling luscious tropical fruit juices.

To reach the other beaches, you'll have to range farther afield, perhaps to **Blanchisseuse Bay** on the North Coast Road. This narrow strip of sand set against palms is excellent for a picnic, although there are no facilities here unless you're staying at the resort.

Balandra Bay, on the northeast coast, is frequented by bodysurfers, but the waters generally aren't good for swimming.

Manzanilla Beach, along the east coast of Trinidad, north of Cocos Bay and south of Matura Bay, is not ideal for swimming. Nonetheless, it has some picnic facilities, and the view of the water is dramatic.

SPORTS & OUTDOOR PURSUITS

For serious golf and tennis holidays, we recommend that you try another island.

DEEP-SEA FISHING   Some of the best fishing in the Caribbean is possible in the waters off the northwest coast of Trinidad—or at least Franklin D. Roosevelt used to think so. Try **TNT Charters,** Bayshore, Trinidad & Tobago Yacht Club (☎ **868/637-3644**), where Robert Nunez takes fishers out in his 31-foot boat. Full gear is included in the rates: $275 for 4 hours, $375 for 6 hours, and $425 for 8 hours. The boat is well maintained with air-conditioning and a microwave, and no more than six people are taken out at a time.

GOLF   The oldest golf club on the island, **St. Andrew's Golf Course,** Moka Estate (☎ 868/629-2314), is in Maraval, about 2 miles from Port-of-Spain. This 18-hole course has been internationally acclaimed ever since it hosted the 1976 Hoerman Cup Golf Tournament. There's a full-service clubhouse on the premises. Greens fees are TT$250 ($40) for 18 holes. Clubs cost TT$80 ($12.80). Hours are daily 6am to 6pm.

TENNIS   The **Trinidad Hilton,** Lady Young Road (☎ 868/624-3211), has two chevron courts lit for night play and available only to hotel guests. Reservations are recommended. The cost is $15 per half hour. At the **Trinidad Country Club,** Champs-Elysées, Maraval (☎ 868/622-3470), six courts are lit at night. You must purchase a day pass for TT$30 ($4.80) and pay an additional TT$5 (80¢) per hour of play during the day or TT$10 ($1.60) per hour at night. There are public courts in Port-of-Spain on the grounds of the Prince's Building (ask at your hotel for directions).

EXPLORING TRINIDAD
ORGANIZED TOURS

Sightseeing tours are offered by **The Travel Centre,** Uptown Mall, Edward Street, Port-of-Spain (☎ 868/623-5096), in late-model sedans with a trained driver/guide. Several different tours are offered, including a daily city tour that takes you past (but not inside) the main points of interest of Port-of-Spain. The 2-hour tour costs $22 per person for two, or $16 per person for three or more.

You'll see tropical splendor at its best on a Port-of-Spain/Maracas Bay/Saddle Road jaunt leaving at 1pm daily, lasting 3½ hours. The tour begins with a drive around Port-of-Spain, passing the main points of interest in town and then going on through the mountain scenery over the "Saddle" of the northern range to Maracas Bay, a popular beach. The cost is $35 per person for two, or $25 per person for three or more.

An Island Circle Tour is a 7- to 8-hour journey that includes a lunch stop (though the tour price doesn't include lunch) and a welcome drink. Leaving at 9am daily, your car goes south along the west coast with a view of the Gulf of Paria, across the central plains, through Pointe-à-Pierre and San Fernando, and on eastward into rolling country overlooking sugarcane fields. You then go down into the coconut plantations along the 14-mile-long Mayaro Beach, enjoy a swim and lunch, and return along Manzanilla Beach and back to the city. The cost is $75 per person for two, or $55 per person for three or more.

An especially interesting trip is the 4-hour trek by car and flat-bottomed boat to the Caroni Swamp and Bird Sanctuary, where you'll see rich Trinidad bird life. The guides recommend long pants and long-sleeved, casual attire, along with lots of insect repellent. The cost is $75 per person for two, or $55 per person for three or more.

PORT-OF-SPAIN

One of the busiest harbors in the Caribbean, Trinidad's capital, Port-of-Spain, can be explored on foot. Start out at ✪ **Queen's Park Savannah,** on the northern edge of the city. "The Savannah" consists of 199 acres, complete with soccer, cricket, and rugby fields, and vendors hawking coconut water and rotis. This was once a sugar plantation, until it was swept by a fire in 1808 that destroyed hundreds of homes.

Among the Savannah's outstanding buildings is the pink-and-blue ✪ **Queen's Royal College,** containing a clock tower with Westminster chimes. Today a school for boys, it stands on Maraval Road at the corner of St. Clair Avenue. On the same road, the family home of the Roodal clan is affectionately called **"the gingerbread house"** by Trinidadians. It was built in the baroque style of the French Second Empire.

In contrast, the family residence of the Strollmeyers was built in 1905 and is a copy of a German Rhenish castle. Nearby stands **Whitehall**, which was once a private mansion but today has been turned into the office of the prime minister of Trinidad and Tobago. In the Moorish style, it was erected in 1905 and served as the U.S. Army headquarters in World War II. These houses, including Hayes Court, the residence of the Anglican bishop of Trinidad, and others form what is known as the **"Magnificent Seven"** big mansions standing in a row.

On the south side of Memorial Park, a short distance from the Savannah and within walking distance of the major hotels, stands the **National Museum and Art Gallery,** 117 Frederick St. (☎ **868/623-5941**), open Tuesday to Saturday from 10am to 6pm. The free museum contains a representative exhibition of Trinidad artists, including an entire gallery devoted to Jean Michel Cazabon (1813 to 1888), permanent collections of artifacts giving a general overview of the island's history and culture, Amerindian archaeology, British historical documents, and a small natural-history exhibition including geology, corals, and insect collections. There's also a large display filled with costumes dedicated to the colorful culture of Carnival.

At the southern end of Frederick Street, the main artery of Port-of-Spain's shopping district, stands **Woodford Square.** The gaudy **Red House,** a large neo-Renaissance structure built in 1906, is the seat of the government of Trinidad and Tobago. Nearby stands **Holy Trinity Cathedral,** whose Gothic look may remind you of the churches of England. Inside, search out the marble monument to Sir Ralph Woodford made by the sculptor of Chantry.

Another of the town's important landmarks is **Independence Square,** dating from Spanish days. Now mainly a parking lot, it stretches across the southern part of the capital from the **Cathedral of the Immaculate Conception** to Wrightson Road. The Roman Catholic church was built in 1815 in the neo-Gothic style and consecrated in 1832.

The cathedral has an outlet that leads to the **Central Market,** on Beetham Highway on the outskirts of Port-of-Spain. Here you can see all the spices and fruits for which Trinidad is known. It's one of the island's most colorful sights, made all the more so by the wide diversity of people who sell their wares here.

North of the Savannah, the **Royal Botanical Gardens** (☎ **868/622-4221**) cover 70 acres and are open daily from 9:30am to 6pm; admission is free. The park is filled with flowering plants, shrubs, and rare and beautiful trees, including an orchid house. Seek out also the raw beef tree: An incision made in its bark is said to resemble rare, bleeding roast beef. Guides will take you through and explain the luxuriant foliage. In the gardens is the **President's House,** official residence of the president of Trinidad and Tobago. Victorian in style, it was built in 1875.

Part of the gardens is the **Emperor Valley Zoo** (☎ **868/622-3530**), in St. Clair, which shows a good selection of the fauna of Trinidad as well as some of the usual exotic animals from around the world. The star attractions are a family of mandrills, a reptile house, and open bird parks. You can take shady jungle walks through tropical vegetation. Admission is TT$4 (65¢) for adults, TT$2 (30¢) for children 3 to 12, and free for children under 3. It's open daily from 9:30am to 6pm.

AROUND THE ISLAND

For one of the most popular attractions in the area, the **Asa Wright Nature Centre,** see "Where to Stay," above.

On a peak 1,100 feet above Port-of-Spain, **Fort George** was built by Governor Sir Thomas Hislop in 1804 as a signal station in the days of the sailing ships. Once it could be reached only by hikers, but today it's accessible by an asphalt road. From its citadel, you can see the mountains of Venezuela. Locals refer to the climb up the winding road as "traveling up to heaven." The drive is only 10 miles, but to play it safe, allow about 2 hours.

Pointe-à-Pierre Wild Fowl Trust, 42 Sandown Rd., Point Cumana (☎ 868/ 658-4230, ext. 2512), is a 26-acre bird sanctuary lying a 2-hour drive south of Port-of-Spain. The setting is unlikely, near an industrial area of the state-owned Petrotrin oil refinery, with flames spouting from flare stacks in the sky. However, in this seemingly inhospitable clime, wildfowl flourish amid such luxuriant vegetation as crêpe myrtle, flamboyant soursop and mango trees, even black sage bushes said to be good for high blood pressure. You can spot the yellow-billed jacana, plenty of Muscovies, and, if you're lucky, such endangered species as the toucan or the purple gallinule. Admission is $5, or $2 for kids under 12. Hours are Monday through Friday from 8am to 5pm, Saturday and Sunday by appointment only from 11am to 4pm.

Enhanced by the blue and purple hues of the sky at sunset, clouds of scarlet ibis, the national bird of Trinidad and Tobago, fly in from their feeding grounds to roost at the 40-square-mile ✪ **Caroni Bird Sanctuary** (☎ 868/645-1305), a big mangrove swamp interlaced with waterways. The setting couldn't be more idyllic, with blue, mauve, and white lilies; oysters growing on mangrove roots; and caimans resting on mudbanks. Visitors are taken on a launch through these swamps to see the birds (bring along insect repellent). The most reliable tour operator is **James Meddoo,** Bamboo Grove Settlement, 1 Butler Hwy. (☎ 868/662-7356), who has toured the swamps for some 25 years. His 2½-tour leaves daily at 4pm and costs $10 per person, or $5 for kids. The sanctuary is about a half-hour drive (7 miles) south of Port-of-Spain.

The ✪ **Pitch Lake** is on the west coast of Trinidad, with the village of Le Brea on its north shore. To reach it from Port-of-Spain, take the Solomon Hocoy Highway. It's about a 2-hour drive, depending on traffic. One of the wonders of the world, with a surface like elephant skin, the lake is 300 feet deep at its center. It's possible to walk on its rough side, but we don't recommend that you proceed far. Legend has it that the lake devoured a tribe of Chayma Amerindians, punishing them for eating hummingbirds in which the souls of their ancestors reposed. The lake was formed millions of years ago, and it's believed that at one time it was a huge mud volcano into which muddy asphaltic oil seeped. Churned up and down by underground gases, the oil and mud eventually formed asphalt. According to legend, Sir Walter Raleigh discovered the lake in 1595 and used the asphalt to caulk his ships. Today, the bitumen mined here is used to pave highways throughout the world. A 120-mile tour around the lake takes 5 hours. You'll find some bars and restaurants at Le Brea.

The ✪ **Saddle** is a humped pass on a ridge dividing the Maraval and the Santa Cruz valleys. Along this circular run, you'll see the luxuriant grapefruit, papaya, cassava, and cocoa trees. Leaving Port-of-Spain by Saddle Road, going past the Trinidad Country Club, you pass through Maraval Village and its St. Andrew's Golf Course. The road rises to cross the ridge at the spot from which the Saddle gets its name. After going over the hump, you descend through Santa Cruz Valley, rich with giant bamboo, into San Juan and back to the capital along Eastern Main Road or Beetham Highway. You'll see panoramic views in every direction; this tour takes about 2 hours and covers 18 miles.

Nearly all cruise-ship passengers are hauled along Trinidad's "Skyline Highway," the **North Coast Road.** Starting at the Saddle, it winds for 7 miles across the Northern Range and down to Maracas Bay. At one point, 100 feet above the Caribbean, you'll see on a clear day as far as Venezuela in the west or Tobago in the east, a sweep of some 100 miles.

Most visitors take this route to the beach at **Maracas Bay,** the most splendid on Trinidad. Enclosed by mountains, it has the expected charm of a Caribbean fantasy: white sands, swaying coconut palms, and crystal-clear water.

SHOPPING

One of the large bazaars of the Caribbean, Port-of-Spain has luxury items from all over the globe, including Irish linens, English china, Scandinavian crystal, French perfumes, Swiss watches, and Japanese cameras. Even more interesting are the Asian bazaars, where you can pick up items in brass. Reflecting the island's culture are calypso shirts, sisal goods, woodwork, cascadura bracelets, silver jewelry in local motifs, and saris. For souvenirs, visitors often like to bring back figurines of limbo dancers, carnival masqueraders, or calypso singers.

Stecher's, Excellent City Mall (☎ **868/623-5912**), is the best bet for those luxury items: crystal, watches, jewelry, perfumes, Georg Jensen silver, Lladró, Wedgwood, Royal Doulton, Royal Albert, and other in-bond items that can be delivered to the airport upon your departure. If you don't want to go downtown, you'll find branches at Long Circular Mall and West Mall. You can also pay a last-minute call at their tax-free airport branches or at the cruise-ship complex at the Port-of-Spain docks.

Y. De Lima, 23 Queen St. (☎ **868/623-1364**), is a good store for duty-free cameras and watches, but the main focus is local jewelry. Its third-floor workroom will make whatever you want in jewelry or bronze. You might emerge with anything from steel-drum earrings to a hibiscus-blossom brooch.

Art Creators and Suppliers, Apt. 402, Aldegonda Park, 7 St. Ann's Rd., St. Ann's (☎ **868/624-4369**), is in a banal apartment complex, but the paintings and sculptures here are among the finest in the Caribbean. Among the artistic giants are Glasgow, Robert Mackie, Boscoe Holder, Sundiata, Keith Ward, Jackie Hinkson, and many others.

Gallery 1-2-3-4, in the Normandie Hotel, 10 Nook Ave., St. Ann's Village (☎ **868/625-5502**), is more iconoclastic and less conservative than any other gallery on the island. Since it opened in 1985, it has attracted the attention of the art world for its wide selection of Caribbean artists.

The Market, 10 Nook Ave., St. Ann's (☎ **868/624-1181**), is one of the most fashionable shopping complexes on Trinidad. Some 20 boutiques represent the best jewelers, designers, and art dealers on the island. You'll find a wide assortment of clothing, cosmetics, bags, shoes, china, tableware, handcrafts, and accessories. The complex forms an interconnected bridge among the Normandie Hotel and Restaurant, the restaurant La Fantasie, and Gallery 1-2-3-4.

The Boutique, 43 Syndeham Ave., St. Ann's (☎ **868/624-3274**), is a notable handcrafts outlet and a showcase for batik silks created by Althea Bastien, one of Trinidad's finest artisans. Her fabric art is highly prized but reasonable in price.

If you'd like to go home with some music of Trinidad, head for **Rhyner's Record Shop,** 54 Prince St. (☎ **868/623-5673**), which has the best selection of soca and calypso. There's another branch at the airport.

TRINIDAD AFTER DARK

Mascamp Pub, French Street at Ariapata Avenue, on the western outskirts of Port-of-Spain (☎ **868/623-3745**), is the only venue on Trinidad where calypso music from the island's greatest bands is presented continually throughout the year. (Many similar places offer this music only during Carnival.) Its rootsy, sometimes raucous, and generally high-energy feel is recommended only to adventurous readers who happen to love live music. On Monday, Tuesday, and Thursday, there's only a DJ, but live calypso and its modern variations are the almost exclusive format every Wednesday, Friday, Saturday, and Sunday. There's usually a $2 to $5 cover.

The **Trinidad Hilton,** Lady Young Road, Port-of-Spain (☎ **868/624-3211**), stages a poolside fiesta show every Monday night, with a folkloric performance beginning at 7pm and continuing live until midnight. It features lots of live music, calypso, a steel band, and limbo. It's the most spectacular on Trinidad. The cover (including a buffet dinner with grills) is TT$140 ($22.40).

Other fun joints worth checking out include **Smokey & Bunty,** Western Main Road at Dengue Street, St. James (no phone). Self-billed as a sports bar, it's more a local hangout and gossip center. If you have a rumor to spread in Port-of-Spain, get it going here. As one regular says, "There's no better place in Trinidad for doing nothing."

Moon Over Bourbon Street, Southern Landing, Westmall, Westmoorings (☎ 868/637-3488), offers live music on some nights, Trinidadian comedians on others. It has a long happy hour, and the place is fun, funky, and local, as is the **Blue Iguana,** Main Street, Chaguanas (no phone), which is the best place to go late at night when the clubs close and you're still in a party mood. It's about a half hour west of Port-of-Spain, and opens at 10pm Wednesday to Sunday, seemingly closing when the last customer staggers out.

3 Tobago

Dubbed "the land of the hummingbird," Tobago lies 20 miles northeast of Trinidad, to which it's connected by frequent flights. It has long been known as a honeymooner's paradise. The physical beauty of Tobago is stunning, with its forests of breadfruit, mango, cocoa, and citrus, through which a chartreuse-colored iguana will suddenly dart. Tobago's idyllic natural beauty makes it one of the greatest escapes in the Caribbean. It's for those who like a generous dose of sand, sun, and solitude in a mellow atmosphere.

Unlike bustling Trinidad, Tobago is sleepy, and Trinidadians come here, especially on weekends, to enjoy its wide, sandy beaches. The legendary home of Daniel Defoe's Robinson Crusoe, Tobago is only 27 miles long and 7½ miles wide. The people are hospitable, and their villages are so tiny they seem to blend with the landscape.

The island's villagelike capital and main port, **Scarborough,** lies on the southern coast. Its bay surrounded by a mountainside provides a scenic setting, but the town itself is rather plain. The local market, the Gun Bridge, the Powder Magazine, and Fort King George will provide a good day's worth of entertainment. Most of the shops are clustered in streets around the market.

GETTING THERE

BY PLANE   A recently established Trinidad-based airline, **Air Caribbean** (☎ 868/623-2500), maintains popular shuttle flights between Trinidad and Tobago, departing from Port-of-Spain every 2 hours daily between 6am and 8pm. The final return to Trinidad departs from Tobago daily at 9pm. A round-trip ticket costs $75. Because the beaches of Tobago are a favorite of vacationing Trinidadians, shuttle flights on any airline between the two islands are almost always crowded, and on weekends, sometimes impossibly overbooked. Air Caribbean, however, operates extra flights on Friday, Sunday, and public holidays to meet demands.

LIAT (☎ 800/468-0482 in the U.S. and Canada, or 868/639-0276) has one daily flight from Trinidad to Tobago. If you'd like to skip Trinidad completely, you can book a LIAT flight with direct service to Tobago from either Barbados or Grenada.

American Eagle (☎ 800/433-7300), the regional affiliate of American Airlines, operates daily round-trip flights between San Juan and Tobago. American Airlines also operates a daily nonstop flight between Miami and Trinidad; once on Trinidad, you can make a connecting flight into Tobago.

Tobago's small airport lies at Crown Point, near the island's southwestern tip.

BY BOAT　It's possible to travel between Trinidad and Tobago by ferry service managed and operated by the **Port Authority of Trinidad and Tobago** (☎ 868/623-2901 in Port-of-Spain, 868/639-2417, or 868/639-2416 in Scarborough, Tobago). Call for departure times and more details. Ferries leave once a day; trip time is 5½ to 6 hours. The round-trip fare is TT$50 ($8) in economy or TT$60 ($9.60) in tourist class.

GETTING AROUND

BY TAXI　From the airport to your accommodations, take an unmetered taxi, which will cost $8 to $36, depending on the location of your hotel. You can also arrange (or have your hotel do it for you) a sightseeing tour by taxi. Rates must be negotiated on an individual basis.

BY RENTAL CAR　Contact **Tobago Travel,** Store Bay Road, Milford (☎ 868/639-8778), where the average cost of a vehicle begins at $50 per day, with unlimited mileage, collision-damage coverage, value-added tax, and comprehensive insurance, plus delivery if you're housed in a hotel near the airport. An international driver's license or your valid license from home entitles you to drive on the roads of Tobago. You must be 25 or over to rent a car. *Don't forget to drive on the left.*

BY BUS　Inexpensive public buses travel from one end of the island to the other several times a day. Of course, expect an unscheduled stop at any passenger's doorstep, and never, never be in a hurry.

WHERE TO STAY

The hotels of Tobago attract those who seek hideaways rather than high-rise resorts packed with activities. To save money, it may be best to take the MAP (breakfast and dinner) plan when reserving a room. There's a 15% value-added tax on all hotel bills, and often a service charge of about 10%. Don't forget to ask if the VAT and service charge are included in the prices quoted to you.

VERY EXPENSIVE

✪ **Le Grand Courlan.** Black Rock (P.O. Box 25, Scarborough), Tobago, W.I. ☎ **800/223-6510** in the U.S., 800/424-5500 in Canada , or 868/639-9667. Fax 868/639-9292. E-mail: legrand@trinidad.net. 70 units. A/C MINIBAR TV TEL. Winter $350–$375 double; $605 suite. Off-season $200–$225 double; $375 suite. Extra person $50. Children 4 and under stay and dine free. MAP (breakfast and dinner) $57 per person extra. AE, MC, V. Located 5 miles from Crown International Airport.

Operated by the same owners as the Grafton Beach Resort (see below), this pricey hotel is definitely five-star and definitely deluxe, both rarities on Tobago. It opened in the autumn of 1995 and was named for the bay on which it sits, on the western edge of the island. A soft, sandy beach sits at its door, and everything is set against a backdrop of bougainvillea, white frangipani, and hibiscus. Constructed to fit in with its natural surroundings, the hotel was built of stone and teak harvested from farms on Trinidad, then furnished with handcrafted mahogany pieces and decorated with original artwork. The floors are covered in Italian porcelain tile, while the ceilings are made from Guyana hardwood. The bedrooms are handsomely tropical in decor, with two phones, king-size beds, and large balconies. Bathrooms are small, but nonetheless equipped with robes, hair dryers, scales, mirrored closets, and phones.

Dining/Diversions: The hotel offers a Mediterranean-style bistro and an international à la carte restaurant. The food is among the best on the island—in fact, among the best in the Caribbean. There's also nightly entertainment and a health-food bar.

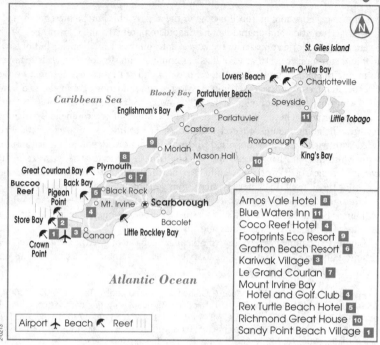

Airport ✈ Beach ⚓ Reef ||||

Arnos Vale Hotel **8**
Blue Waters Inn **11**
Coco Reef Hotel **4**
Footprints Eco Resort **9**
Grafton Beach Resort **6**
Kariwak Village **3**
Le Grand Courlan **7**
Mount Irvine Bay
  Hotel and Golf Club **4**
Rex Turtle Beach Hotel **5**
Richmond Great House **10**
Sandy Point Beach Village **1**

2-0213

Amenities: The spa specializes in cell therapy. It has a koi pond and aerobics and offers consultations in nutrition, fitness coaching, and ozone-and-steam detoxing, even fresh-fruit facials and full-body compression "release" massages. Floodlit tennis court, 80-foot pool, beach cabanas. Water sports can be arranged at the diving center. Laundry, room service.

EXPENSIVE

Arnos Vale Hotel. Arnos Vale Rd., Plymouth, Tobago, W.I. ☎ **868/639-2881.** Fax 868/639-4629. 33 units. A/C TEL. Winter $180 double; $245–$300 suite. Off-season $150 double; $220–$260 suite. AE, MC, V.

Originally built in the 1950s, and set on 150 acres of partially flat, partially sloping land that's very, very private, this was one of the first hotels of Tobago's modern tourist age. Named after a township in England, and renovated in the mid–1990s, it's centered around a two-story, motel-like building of rose-painted concrete that contains all but a handful of the resort's accommodations. Rooms, each with a private patio or veranda, come with a wide spectrum of furniture—including some pieces dating back to the early 1960s, retained because many clients appreciate their slightly battered charm. Only a few units are actually on the beach. Suites are in a handful of fully detached stucco-sided bungalows. Some bathrooms have a combination shower/tub, others shower only. Most of the socializing occurs at the likable bar, where you'll find a TV, strong drinks, and a loyal clientele that returns year after year. Facilities include a pool, tennis courts, and the Arnos Vale Water Wheel Restaurant (see "Where to Dine," below).

✪ **Coco Reef Hotel.** Coconut Beach (P.O. Box 434), Tobago, W.I. ☎ **800/221-1294** or 868/639-8571. Fax 868/639-8574. www.cocoreef.com. E-mail: cocoreef-tobago@ trinidad.net. 135 units. A/C MINIBAR TV TEL. Winter $218–$242 double; from $385 suite or villa. Off-season $170–$218 double; from $350 suite or villa. AE, DC, MC, V.

Set on the eastern shore of Tobago, close to the airport, this hotel represents the radical 1995 renovation and upgrading of a dilapidated property, the Crown Reef. With a certain South Florida pizzazz, it's the largest hotel on the island, boasting lots of facilities and surrounded by 10 acres of grassy, sloping terrain. Its concrete walls (painted to mimic the peachy-pink color of local papaya) and red roofs were inspired by the eclectic architecture of nearby Trinidad. Most accommodations are in the two- and three-story main core, although about a half dozen villas are scattered over the surrounding terrain. The designer incorporated a number of environmentally friendly features, including the use of recycled materials. The bedrooms are spacious and airy, filled with wicker furniture imported from the Dominican Republic, big bathrooms with white tiles and hair dryers, and balcony trim as intricate as Belgian lace. The complex is near a trio of the island's best beaches—Store Bay, Pigeon Point, and Coconut Beach itself, the latter just steps from your room.

Dining: Tamara's, the resort's most formal restaurant, is reviewed below in "Where to Dine." Bachanals is simpler, suitable for sun-flooded lunches and light dinners. Lobster's Cocktail Bar serves drinks and snacks.

Amenities: Sailing, waterskiing, snorkeling, scuba diving, windsurfing, deep-sea fishing, horseback riding, tennis. Spa services include aerobics, massage, weight-loss regimes, and exercise areas.

Grafton Beach Resort. Black Rock (P.O. Box 25, Scarborough), Tobago, W.I. ☎ **800/655-1214** in the U.S., or 868/639-0191. Fax 868/639-0030. www.grandehotels.com. E-mail: grafton@trinidad.net. 116 units. A/C MINIBAR TV TEL. Winter $126–$220 per person. Off-season $105 per person. Suite supplement $70 per person. Rates are all-inclusive. 10% service and 10% tax extra. AE, MC, V. Located 4 miles from the airport.

The most action-oriented resort on the island, this luxurious complex of low-rise, stone-and-stucco buildings lies on 5 acres, 4 miles south of Scarborough between a hill and a white-sand beach. It attracts a mainly European clientele. Rooms are scattered in buildings of three and four floors descending to a good beach. The well-furnished units contain ceiling fans, safes, sliding-glass doors opening onto balconies, and hand-crafted teak furniture. Most bathrooms are small but well appointed, with combination shower/tubs, hair dryers, mirrored closets, and retractable laundry lines.

Dining/Diversions: The resort's pool is ringed with cafe/restaurant tables, and there are several different bars (including a swim-up bar). Both a regional and an international cuisine are served in the Ocean View and Neptunes restaurants. Limbo dancing and calypso, or some other form of entertainment, are featured nightly.

Amenities: Two squash courts, gym, dive shop, outdoor pool; access to a nearby golf course. Room service, laundry, baby-sitting, massages.

Mount Irvine Bay Hotel and Golf Club. Mount Irvine (P.O. Box 222, Scarborough), Tobago, W.I. ☎ **800/74-CHARMS** in the U.S., or 868/639-8871. Fax 868/639-8800. www.spatrick.com/mtirvine. E-mail: mtirvine@tstt.net.tt. 157 units. A/C TV TEL. Winter $266 double; $350 cottage; $720 one-bedroom suite; $1,000 two-bedroom suite. Off-season $199 double; $320 cottage; $720 one-bedroom suite; $1,000 two-bedroom suite. AE, DC, MC, V. About a 5-mile drive northwest of the airport.

Originally established in 1972 on the site of an 18th-century sugar plantation, this 16-acre resort is part of a recreational complex that totals more than 150 acres. Most of the acreage is devoted to the Mount Irvine Golf Course, one of the finest in the Caribbean. The remainder is filled with sprawling lawns and tropical gardens, in the center of which rise a luxurious oval pool and the ruins of a stone sugar mill. The grounds slope down to a good sandy beach. On the hill leading to the beach are the newer and better-maintained cottage suites, covered with heliconia. Most accommodations are in the main building, a two-story, hacienda-inspired wing of rather large but standard guest rooms, each with a view of green lawns and flowering shrubbery. Some of the better units have Queen Anne–style furniture with two-posters. Bathrooms have hair dryers and combination shower/tubs.

Dining/Diversions: The hotel offers three restaurants, including the Sugar Mill. There's also dining at Le Beau Rivage, at the golf course, and at the Jacaranda, which has a high standard of international cuisine. There's dancing almost every evening, and calypso singers are often brought in to entertain guests.

Amenities: Tennis courts, pool with swim-up bar, beauty salon, barbershop, boat rentals; windsurfers and snorkeling equipment available at the beach. Guests become temporary members of the golf club (see "Sports & Outdoor Pursuits," below), and their greens fees are discounted by 30%. Room service (from 7am to 10pm), baby-sitting, laundry, massage.

MODERATE

Blue Waters Inn. Batteaux Bay, Speyside, Tobago, W.I. ☎ **800/742-4276** in the U.S., or 868/660-4341. Fax 868/660-5195. www.bluewatersinn.com. E-mail: bwi@bluewatersinn.com. 45 units. Winter $160 double; $190 efficiency; $330 one-bedroom suite; $490 two-bedroom suite. Off-season $95 double; $125 efficiency; $195 one-bedroom suite; $290 two-bedroom suite. AE, MC, V.

Attracting nature lovers, this property on the northeastern coast of Tobago is nestled along the shore of Batteaux Bay, where a private 1,000-foot-long beach beckons guests. Family-owned and -managed, the inn is about 24 miles from the airport, a 1¼-hour drive along narrow, winding country roads. At this charming and rustic retreat, which extends onto acres of tropical rain forest with myriad exotic birds, butterflies, and other wildlife, the building's entrance almost appears to drop over a cliff, and birds may actually fly through the open windows of the driftwood-adorned dining room. It's a very informal place, so leave your fancy resort wear at home. The inn now offers several newly renovated units with kitchenettes, suitable for families. Two rooms are wheelchair accessible, and all of the basic, no-frills accommodations have ceiling fans and small private showers; several are air-conditioned as well. The second-floor rooms open onto lovely views of the water. The overall level of comfort is that of a standard beachside motel.

The appropriately named Fish Pot offers local seafood and international dishes. Guests can retire to the Shipwreck Bar for Caribbean cocktails. Fishing, tennis, wind-surfing, kayaking, and skin diving can be arranged, as can boat trips (including glass-bottom boats) to Little Tobago. The dive shop is a full-service PADI outfitter.

Footprints Eco Resort. Golden Lane, Colloden Bay Rd., Tobago, W.I. ☎ **800/814-1396** or 868/660-0118. Fax 868/660-0027. www.footprintseco-resort.com. E-mail: footprints@trinidad.net. 9 units. TEL. Winter $140–$275 double; $250 quad. Off-season $95–$224 double; $210 quad. MAP (breakfast and dinner) $30 extra per day. AE, DC, MC, V.

Until 1997, this resort's 61 acres were densely forested with cocoa and fruit trees, with no buildings of any kind. Today, thanks to its development by a local doctor and his daughter, visitors can immerse themselves in a rustic and charming compound of wood-sided, thatch-roofed cottages designed by devoted ecologists. Each was artfully built of recycled lumber, some of it obtained from the local telephone company, with a distinct emphasis on termite-resistant hardwoods such as wallaba and teak. Accommodations are rough-hewn but comfortable, with wooden floors and a lot of idiosyncratic charm. Rooms range from standard doubles to king superior units with fridges. Some rooms have a garden shower, while others contain two full bathrooms with combination shower/tubs. On-site amenities include the Cocoa House restaurant, a network of well-maintained nature trails that fan out across the forested nearby hills, a saltwater pool, a freshwater Jacuzzi, a small-scale library, and a mini-museum that contains Amerindian artifacts uncovered during the excavations on the property. Most guests opt to swim in the resort's pool, although worthwhile beaches, including both Courland Bay and Castara Bay, are a 15-minute drive away. If you want to immerse yourself in local sociology and culture, the staff here will happily arrange diversions such as horseback riding, glass-bottomed boat rides, rain-forest tours, crafts exhibitions, yoga lessons, and massage.

Rex Turtle Beach Hotel. Great Courland Bay (P.O. Box 201, Scarborough), Tobago, W.I. ☎ **868/639-2851,** or 305/471-6170 for reservations. Fax 868/639-1495. 125 units. A/C TV TEL. Winter $195 double. Off-season $155 double. AE, DC, MC, V.

Firmly entrenched as a well-managed middle-bracket choice, and set within a compound of two low-rise buildings adjacent to the tawny-colored sands of Courland Beach, this hotel was built in the early 1970s in an isolated location on the island's southwestern edge, adjacent to the beach. The medium-size rooms have balconies or patios, cream-colored floor tiles, pastel walls, teakwood ceilings, louvered doors, spacious closets, tropical-patterned upholsteries, and simple, summery furnishings. The small bathrooms have individual heaters for hot water, and most contain combination shower/tubs. On the premises are two restaurants, the Kiskadee and the less formal Coffeeshop. The hotel's pool is so small as to be almost ornamental, thus most serious swimmers head for the wide sands of Courland Beach, just a few steps away. You'll also find a kiosk renting snorkeling equipment, a bike-rental shop, a volleyball court, and two separate bars.

✪ Richmond Great House. Belle Garden, Tobago, W.I. ☎ **868/660-4467.** 10 units. Winter $140 double; $160 suite for two; $95 family unit. Off-season $120 double; $140 suite for two; $80 family unit. Room and suite rates include MAP (breakfast and dinner). AE, V. Located a 45-minute drive from the airport.

One of the most charming accommodations on the island is an 18th-century great house set on 6 acres, part of a cocoa- and coconut-growing estate. Near Richmond Beach, on the southern (windward) coast, it's owned by Dr. Hollis R. Lynch, a Tobago-born professor of African history at Columbia University. As befits his profession, he has decorated the mansion with African art along with island antiques. Guests are free to explore the garden and grounds and to enjoy the pool and the barbecue. Most rooms have hardwood floors, country estate–style furnishings, and tasteful but colorful fabrics. Bathrooms are small and strictly functional, with somewhat dated plumbing. Families might want to consider one of the three small, basic family units in the extension to the main house. On the premises are two 19th-century tombs containing the remains of the original English founders of the plantation. Both a regional and an international cuisine are served. Since it's such a small place, the cook asks guests about their culinary preferences.

INEXPENSIVE

Kariwak Village. Local Rd., Store Bay (P.O. Box 27, Scarborough), Tobago, W.I. ☎ **868/639-8545.** Fax 868/639-8441. www.kariwak.co.tt. E-mail: kariwak@tstt.net.tt. 24 units. A/C TEL. Winter $125 double. Off-season $90 double. AE, DC, MC, V.

A self-contained cluster of cottages evoking the South Pacific, this complex is about a 6-minute walk from the beach on the island's western shoreline, a 2-minute drive from the airport. The name is a combination of the two native tribes that originally inhabited Tobago, the Caribs and the Arawaks. During its construction in 1982, the builders made much use of Tobago's palm fronds, raw teak, coral stone, and bamboo. Nine of the accommodations are hexagonal cabanas with two rooms each, opening onto a freshwater pool. Bedrooms are small to medium in size, and often quite dark. Mattresses have been replaced and are quite comfortable, unlike the dull, small bathrooms with shower stalls.

Live entertainment is provided on Friday and Saturday year-round. The food served in the Village Restaurant is among the best on the island, and you may want to come by even if you aren't staying here. A fixed-price meal, either à la carte or one of the weekend buffets, ranges from $20 to $24.

Sandy Point Beach Village. Crown Point, Tobago, W.I. ☎ **868/639-8533.** Fax 868/639-8496. 44 units. A/C TV TEL. Winter $60 double studio; $70 double suite; $90 two-bedroom apartment. Off-season $45 double studio; $50 double suite; $60 two-bedroom apartment. Extra adult $15. Children 11 and under stay in parents' room for $5. MAP (breakfast and dinner) $25 per person extra. MC, V.

Built in two different sections in 1977 and 1991, this miniature vacation village somewhat resembles a Riviera condominium complex. It's just a 3-minute run from the airport, but its shoreside position on the island's southwestern coast makes it seem remote. Airport noise, however, can be a problem. The little village of peaked and gabled roofs is landscaped all the way down to the sandy beach, where there's a rustic Steak Hut, which serves meals throughout the day and evening. The fully equipped accommodations have patios that open toward the sea, living and dining areas with Jamaican wicker furniture, and satellite TV. All but six of the units (those at poolside) contain kitchenettes. Some of the studios have a rustic open stairway leading to a loft with bunk beds, with a twin-bedded room on the lower level as well. On the premises are two pools, a small gym, and a disco in the basement.

WHERE TO DINE
EXPENSIVE

✪ **The Cocoa House.** In Footprints Eco Resort, Golden Lane, Colloden Bay Rd. ☎ **868/860-0118.** Reservations recommended for lunch, required for dinner before 1pm on the day of your intended arrival. Main courses $6–$12 lunch, $16.50–$40 dinner. AE, MC, V. Daily 11:30–1:30pm and 6:30–9pm. WEST INDIAN/TOBAGONIAN.

Proud of its eco-sensitivity (waste water and paper trash are recycled here), this restaurant is a worthy choice because of its allegiance to tried-and-true Tobagan food that's prepared in a style endorsed by many of the island's matriarchs and grandmothers. Its name comes from its unusual roof, made from the fronds of the Timit palm. Old-fashioned drying rooms for cocoa pods were designed with retractable roofs, allowing direct sun to dry the raw product. On balmy evenings, the roof here retracts, allowing views of the setting sun and—a bit later—of the moon and stars. Well-flavored menu items include jerk versions of shrimp, chicken, pork, and beef; duck with either orange or pineapple sauce; and *pelau*, a French-inspired dish that combines rice, chicken, and beef, all of it bound together with rice. For a dish that many Tobagans remember from their childhood, try pork and dumplings.

Le Beau Rivage. In the Mount Irvine Bay Hotel, Tobago Golf Course, Buccoo Bay. ☎ **868/639-8871.** Reservations required. Main courses $16–$28. AE, MC, V. Daily noon–3pm and 7–10pm. Located 5 minutes northwest of the airport. FRENCH/CARIBBEAN.

This restaurant is in a former golf clubhouse with sweeping views of one of Tobago's most historic inlets, Mount Irvine Bay. The food is more competent than exciting, but still quite good. Menu choices vary daily, but might include local ingredients combined with continental inspirations, such as grilled Caribbean lobster, pork tenderloin, and veal cutlet. Dessert may be fresh fruit salad, coconut pie, coconut tart, or fresh mango flan floating on a coulis of tropical fruits.

⭐ **Tamara's.** In the Coco Reef Resort, Coconut Beach. ☎ **868/639-8571.** Reservations recommended. Fixed-price dinner TT$300 ($48). AE, MC, V. Daily 7–10pm. WEST INDIAN/ INTERNATIONAL.

One of the most appealing restaurants on Tobago occupies a two-tiered, stone-and-timber gazebo whose curved edges are open on all sides for maximum exposure to cool breezes. It serves a deliberately upscale cuisine based on West Indian traditions, with lots of international touches thrown in by renowned chef Kenneth Thomas. Amid a color scheme of pink and white, with views over the nearby sea, it serves some of the most sophisticated food in Trinidad and Tobago. Start, perhaps, with homemade veal and bacon terrine or pan-fried scallops with wilted greens and wasabi sauce. Try the lamb loin set on couscous, the char-grilled ocean snapper with a cream mushroom and lemongrass sauce, or most definitely the pork tenderloin garnished with a lima-bean ragoût.

MODERATE/INEXPENSIVE

Arnos Vale Water Wheel Restaurant. Arnos Vale Rd., Plymouth. ☎ **868/639-2881.** Reservations recommended. Main courses TT$40–TT$190 ($6.40–$30.40). AE, MC, V. Daily 11:45am–2:45pm and 6:30–10pm. INTERNATIONAL.

A 5-minute drive from the Arnos Vale Hotel, with which it's associated, this restaurant occupies the weathered premises of what was originally built in the early 1800s as a water-powered mill for the crushing of sugarcane. From a circular room with an antique oven and the wheel's original machinery still in place, you'll look out over the verdant banks of the Franklin River, the seacoast, and the landscapes which once produced some of England's greatest fortunes. Menu items include Cornish hen, shaved pear and Parmesan salad, deviled chicken, caramelized breast of chicken with polenta and callaloo sauce, grilled fish served with a medley of sauces, and at least three different shrimp and lobster dishes. Three times a week, there's a performance of live Trinidad/Tobagan music and dance, whose animated sounds perk up the otherwise calm and quiet landscape of chirping tree frogs and splashing water.

⭐ **The Blue Crab.** Robinson St., Scarborough. ☎ **868/639-2737.** Reservations required for dinner. Lunch TT$25–TT$40 ($4–$6.40); dinner main courses TT$100–TT$130 ($16–$20.80). AE, MC, V. Mon–Fri 11am–3:30pm; daily 7–10pm (but call first to be sure). CARIBBEAN/INTERNATIONAL.

One of our favorite restaurants in the capital, adjacent to the town's only Methodist church, this family-run spot occupies an Edwardian-era house with an oversize veranda. The menu makes the most of local ingredients and regional spices, and is dictated by whatever is available that day in the marketplace. The good, homemade food includes fresh conch, stuffed crab backs, an array of Creole meat dishes grilled over coconut husks, flying fish in a mild curry-flavored batter, shrimp with garlic butter or cream, and a vegetable rice dish of the day. Lobster sometimes appears on the menu.

Dillon's. Milford Rd., near Crown Point. ☎ **868/639-8765.** Reservations recommended. Main courses TT$65–TT$290($10.40–$46.40). AE, MC, V. Daily 6–10pm. Closed 6 weeks May–June. INTERNATIONAL.

Set in a simple house near the Coco Reef Resort and the airport, this restaurant is run by one of Tobago's leading operators of a deep-sea-fishing boat. Consequently, the fish that's featured on the night of your arrival is likely to be the very fresh product of that day's catch. There's both an indoor, air-conditioned room with framed memorabilia of the island's tradition of steel-pan music, and an outdoor terrace with views over the garden. Menu items include fresh barracuda with lemon-butter sauce; T-bone steak with fried onions and tomato; pork tenderloin with a piquant sauce; pan-fried or grilled shrimp served with red wine, garlic, or Creole sauce; and a dessert specialty of ice cream garnished with slices of local fruit.

Jemma's Seaview Kitchen. Speyside. ☎ **868/660-4066.** Reservations recommended. Main courses TT$60–TT$175 ($9.60–$28). MC, V. Sun–Fri 8am–9pm. TOBAGONIAN.

A short walk north of the hamlet of Speyside, on Tobago's northeastern coast, this is one of the very few restaurants in the Caribbean designed as a tree house. Although the simple kitchen is firmly anchored to the shoreline, the dining area is set on a platform nailed to the massive branches of a 200-year-old almond tree that leans out over the water. Some 50 tables are available on a wooden deck that provides a rooflike structure for shelter from the rain. The charming staff serves up main courses that come with soup or salad. Lunch platters include shrimp, fish, and chicken, while dinners feature more elaborate portions of each, as well as steaks, curried lamb, grilled or curried kingfish, lamb chops, and lobster served grilled or Thermidor style. Most dishes are at the lower end of the price scale. No liquor is served.

Old Donkey Cart House. Bacolet St., Scarborough. ☎ **868/639-3551.** Fax 868/639-6124. Reservations required. Main courses TT$50–TT$250 ($8–$40). AE, MC, V. Daily 8am–11pm. INTERNATIONAL.

An unusual and noteworthy restaurant occupies a green-and-white Edwardian house about half a mile south of Scarborough. Its owner, Gloria Jones-Knapp, was once a fashion model in Europe. "Born, bred, and dragged up" on Tobago, she is today the island's leading authority on selected European wines—from Italy, France, Austria, and Germany—that she purchases with her husband. Her restaurant also serves freshly made fruit drinks laced with the local rum. You get the standards here—grilled steaks, stir-fried shrimp, stuffed crab back, homemade pasta, fresh fish, beef Stroganoff, salads, and callaloo soup with crab. Guests dine either in the palm garden or on the verandas of the Hibiscus Bar.

If you're interested, ask about the apartment suites for rent. Doubles go for $80 to $120, including breakfast and taxes.

Papillon. Buccoo Bay Rd., Buccoo Bay. ☎ **868/639-0275.** Reservations recommended. Main courses TT$40–TT$60 ($6.40–$9.60) lunch, TT$80–TT$125 ($12.80–$20) dinner. AE, MC, V. Daily 7:30am–2:30pm and 7–11pm. SEAFOOD/INTERNATIONAL.

Located near the Tobago Golf Club on the corner of Buccoo Bay Road and Mount Irvine, this restaurant offers international specialties with an emphasis on seafood, including kingfish steak, stuffed flying fish, and lobster Buccoo Bay (marinated in sherry wine and broiled with garlic, herbs, and butter sauce). The interior is adorned with pictures that refer to the novel and film *Papillon,* a story about a convict who settles in the Caribbean. For a change of pace, try curried goat, beef Stroganoff, or grilled lamb and beef. There's a patio for alfresco dining.

✪ **Roussell's.** Old Windward Rd., Bacolet. ☎ **868/639-4738.** Reservations recommended. Main courses TT$80–TT$165 ($12.80–$26.40). MC, V. Restaurant Mon–Sat 6:30–11pm; bar Mon–Sat 3–11pm. WEST INDIAN/INTERNATIONAL.

Set in a white-sided building that was originally conceived as a private home, a 2-minute drive north of Scarborough's center, this restaurant is the creative statement of Trinidad-born partners Bobbie Evans and Charlene Goodman. Inside, four dining and drinking rooms open onto an outdoor terrace, where the view sweeps down over the coast and the sea. Look for sculptures by island artists, lots of local business, and extremely good food. Specific dishes change with the availability of ingredients and the whim of the chefs, but are likely to include broiled grouper with fresh Creole sauce, baked chicken with gingered carrots and garlic-coated green beans, and several different preparations of lobster. Dessert might be pineapple pie or a coconut-enriched version of crème brûlée. Just looking for drinks and some friendly chat with a local? The bar stocks wines by the glass, as well as a frothy-looking and deceptively potent pink libation known as Roussell's punch—it's almost guaranteed to change your mind if you thought you never had any particular taste for rum.

HITTING THE BEACH

On Tobago, you can still feel like Robinson Crusoe in a solitary sandy cove—at least for most of the week, before the Trinidadians fly over for a Saturday on the beach.

A good beach, **Back Bay,** is an 8-minute walk from the Mount Irvine Bay Hotel on Mount Irvine Bay. Along the way, you'll pass a coconut plantation and an old cannon emplacement. Snorkeling is generally excellent, even in winter. There are sometimes dangerous currents here, but you can always explore Rocky Point with its brilliantly colored parrot fish. In July and August, the surfing here is the finest in Tobago; it's also likely to be good in January and April. Stop in Scarborough for picnic fixings, which you can enjoy at the picnic tables here; a snack bar sells cold beer and drinks.

Great Courland Bay is known for its calm, gin-clear waters, and is flanked by **Turtle Beach,** named for the sea creatures who nest here. Near Fort Bennett and south of Plymouth, Great Courland Bay is one of the longest sandy beaches on the island and the site of several hotels and a marina.

✪ **Pigeon Point,** on the northwestern coast, is the best-known bathing area with a long coral beach. It's public, but to reach it you must enter a former coconut estate, which charges a fee of TT$10 ($1.60). Set against a backdrop of royal palms, this beach is becoming increasingly commercial. Facilities include food kiosks, crafts shops, a diving concession, paddleboat rentals, changing rooms in thatched shelters, and picnic tables.

Man-O-War Bay is one of the finest natural harbors in the West Indies, at the opposite end of the island, near the little fishing village of Charlotteville. It has a long sandy beach and a government-run rest house. Sometimes local fishermen will hawk the day's catch (and clean it for you as well). Nearby **Lovers' Beach** is accessible only by boat and is famous for its pink sand, formed long ago from crushed sea shells. Negotiate a fee with one of the local boatmen.

Approached from Roxborough on the north side of the island is the half-moon-shaped **Parlatuvier Beach.** However, the setting, with fishing boats and locals, is more bucolic than the swimming. If you can't stand crowds, head for **Englishman's Bay,** on the north coast just west of Parlatuvier. We don't know why this beach is virtually deserted: It's charming, secluded, and good for swimming.

The true beach buff will head for **King's Bay** in the northeast, south of the town of Speyside near Delaford. Against a backdrop of towering green hills, the crescent-shaped grayish-sand beach is one of the best places for swimming.

SPORTS & OUTDOOR PURSUITS

BOATING   The **Rex Turtle Beach Hotel,** Great Courland Bay (☎ 868/639-2851), rents sailboats and is a registered Mistral Sailing Centre. The cost is TT$85 ($13.60) an hour.

GOLF   Tobago is the proud possessor of an 18-hole, 6,800-yard course at Mount Irvine. Called the **Tobago Golf Club** (☎ 868/639-8871), it covers 150 breeze-swept acres and was featured in the *Wonderful World of Golf* TV series. Even beginners agree the course is friendly to golfers. Well-heeled golfers should stay at the Mount Irvine Bay Hotel, where guests are granted temporary membership, use of the clubhouse and facilities, and a 30% discount on greens fees. The course is also open to nonguests, who pay $48 for 18 holes or $30 for 9 holes. Cart rentals are $36 for 18 holes or $20 for 9 holes; clubs cost $15 for 18 holes or $10 for 9 holes.

SCUBA DIVING, SNORKELING & OTHER WATER SPORTS   The unspoiled reefs off Tobago teem with a great variety of marine life. Divers can swim through rocky canyons 60 to 130 feet deep, underwater photographers can shoot pictures they won't find anywhere else, and snorkelers can explore the celebrated Buccoo Reef.

Wreck divers have a new adventure to enjoy with the sinking of the former ferry-boat *Maverick,* in 100 feet of water near Mount Irvine Bay Hotel on Tobago's southwest coast.

The **Rex Turtle Beach Hotel,** Great Courland Bay (☎ 868/639-2851), is the best equipped for water sports. Activities include sailing for TT$85 ($13.60) per hour, windsurfing for TT$100 ($16) per hour, and waterskiing for TT$145 ($23.20) per half hour.

Dive Tobago, Pigeon Point (P.O. Box 53, Scarborough), Tobago (☎ 868/639-0202), is the oldest and most established operation on Tobago, operated by Jay Young, a certified PADI instructor. It offers easy resort courses, single dives, and dive packages, along with equipment rentals. A basic resort course costs $55, although for certification you must pay $300. A one-tank dive goes for $40.

Tobago Dive Experience, at the Turtle Beach Hotel, Black Rock (☎ 868/639-7034), offers scuba dives, snorkeling, and boat trips. All dives are guided, with a boat following. Exciting drift dives are available for experienced divers. A one-tank dive costs $39 without equipment or $46 with equipment; a two-tank dive starts at $70; and a resort course costs $59.

Man Friday Diving, Charlotteville (☎ 868/660-4676), is a Danish-owned dive center with certified PADI instructors and PADI dive masters. It's located right on the beach of Man-O-War Bay at the northernmost tip of Tobago. With more than 40 different dive sites, it's always able to find suitable locations, no matter what the water conditions are. Guided boat trips for certified divers go out Monday through Saturday at 9:30am and 1pm. A resort course costs $75; a PADI open-water certification, $375; a one-tank dive, $35; and a night dive, $50.

TENNIS   The **Rex Turtle Beach Hotel,** Great Courland Bay (☎ 868/639-2851), has two excellent courts open to nonguests, who pay TT$30 ($4.80) per hour (hotel guests play for free). The best courts, however, are at the **Mount Irvine Bay Hotel** (☎ 868/639-8871), where two good courts are available for TT$11.50 ($1.85) per half hour or TT$23 ($3.70) per hour.

EXPLORING TOBAGO

If you'd like a close-up view of Tobago's exotic and often rare tropical birds, as well as a range of other island wildlife and lush tropical flora, naturalist-led field trips are the answer. Each 2- to 3-hour trip leads you to forest trails and coconut plantations, along rivers and past waterfalls; one excursion goes to two nearby islands. Trips cost $45 to $54. For details, contact **Pat Turpin,** Man-O-War Bay Cottages, Charlotteville (☎ 868/660-4327 or 868/660-4328).

Tobago's capital, **Scarborough,** need claim your attention only briefly before you climb up the hill to **Fort King George,** about 430 feet above the town. Built by the English in 1779, it was later captured by the French, then jockeyed back and forth among various conquerors until nature decided to end it all in 1847, blowing off the roofs of its buildings. You can see artifacts displayed in a gallery, plus the ruins of a military hospital.

From Scarborough, you can drive northwest to **Plymouth,** Tobago's other town. Perched on a point at Plymouth is **Fort James,** which dates from 1768. Now it's mainly in ruins.

From Speyside in the north, you can make arrangements with a local fisher to go to **Little Tobago,** a 450-acre offshore island whose bird sanctuary attracts ornithologists. The 20-minute crossing is likely to be rough, but the effort is worth it. Threatened with extinction in New Guinea, many birds, perhaps 50 species in all, were brought over to this little island in the early part of this century. The islet is arid and hilly, with a network of marked trails.

Off Pigeon Point in the south lies ✪ **Buccoo Reef,** where sea gardens of coral and hundreds of fish can be seen in waist-deep water. This is the natural aquarium of Tobago, offering the best snorkeling and scuba diving. Nearly all the major hotels arrange boat trips here. Even nonswimmers can wade knee-deep in the waters. Remember to protect your head and body from the sun and to guard your feet against the sharp coral.

After about half an hour at the reef, passengers reboard their boats and go over to **Nylon Pool,** with its crystal-clear waters. Here in this white-sand bottom, about a mile offshore, you can enjoy a dip in water only 3 or 4 feet deep.

Eco-consciousness on the island was enhanced by the opening of the **Franklyn Water Wheel and Nature Park,** at Arnos Vale, Arnos Vale Estate, Franklyn Road (☎ 868/660-0815). This is the site of Tobago's best preserved water wheel, which once provided power to a sugar estate. The 12-acre estate has walking trails, a restaurant, an outdoor theater, and the old machinery, for the most part still in place. On the trails, you may see butterflies and iguanas, plus mango and citrus orchards where you can pick your own fresh fruit. Admission is TT$10 ($1.60) for adults, TT$5 (80¢) for children. You can visit any time during the day and gain entrance to the site as long as the restaurant is open (before 10pm).

SHOPPING

In Tobago's capital, Scarborough, you can visit the local **market** Monday through Saturday mornings and listen to the sounds of a Creole patois. Scarborough's stores have a limited range of merchandise, more to tempt the browser than the serious shopper.

Farro's, Wilson Road (☎ 868/639-2979), across from the marketplace, offers the tastiest condiments on the island, packed into little straw baskets for you to carry back home. Sample the delectable lime marmalade, any of the hot sauces, the guava jelly, and most definitely the home-canned and homemade chutney from the tamarind fruit.

If you're seeking handcrafts, especially straw baskets, head for the **Souvenir & Gift Shop,** Port Mall (☎ 868/639-5632), also in Scarborough.

Cotton House Fashion Studio, Old Windward Road, in Bacolet (☎ 868/639-2727), is the island's best choice for "hands-on" appreciation of the fine art of batik. In the Indonesian tradition, melted wax is brushed onto fabric, resisting dyes and creating unusual colors and designs. This outlet contains the largest collection of batik clothing and wall hangings on Tobago. Dying techniques are demonstrated to visitors, who can then try their skills at the art form.

TOBAGO AFTER DARK

Your best bet for entertainment is at the **Mount Irvine Bay Hotel** at Mount Irvine Bay (☎ 868/639-8871), where you might find some disco action or a steel band performing by the beach or pool. The **Rex Turtle Beach Hotel,** Great Courtland Bay (☎ 868/639-2851), is the place to be on Wednesday night, when it stages a

Caribbean buffet dinner with cultural entertainment and dancing. You get real West Indian flavor here. Every Saturday night, a steel band is brought in to entertain at a barbecue dinner from 7 to 10pm.

The Grafton Beach Resort at Black Road owns one of the island's most charming bars, **Buccaneer's Beach Bar** (☎ 868/639-0191), across from the resort. Here you'll find a wide wood terrace sheltered by a grove of almond trees. Daily specials written up on a surfboard include burgers, fried fish, and the like (don't expect the elegant beachside Creole cooking of Martinique). The resort itself offers cabaretlike entertainment nightly. Catch if you can a local troupe, Les Couteaux Cultural Group, which performs a version of Tobagonian history set to dance.

The best place for a sundowner is **Pigeon Point Bar** (☎ 868/639-8141). Sit here, sip your drink, and listen to the sounds of steel drums and breakers unfurling on a distant reef. It's quite romantic.

Still want some local action? Drop in at **Bankers,** Store Bay Road at Crown Point (☎ 868/639-7173), an active bar where you'll hear the best soca, reggae, or jazz. If you've been "bad," the DJ might order you to walk the gangplank into the pool. Disco nights are occasionally held at **Starting Gate,** Shirvan Road in Mount Irvine (☎ 868/639-0225), one of the island's friendliest alfresco pubs. Drop in to see what's happening.

27

The U.S. Virgin Islands

The U.S. Virgin Islands are known for their sugar-white beaches, among the finest in the world, and also for duty-free shopping. The most developed island in the chain is **St. Thomas,** whose capital, Charlotte Amalie, holds the largest concentration of shopping in the Caribbean. With a population of some 50,000, tiny St. Thomas isn't exactly a secluded tropical retreat; you'll hardly have its beaches to yourself. The place abounds in bars and restaurants, including fast-food joints, and has a vast selection of hotels in all price ranges.

St. Croix is bigger, but more tranquil. A favorite with cruise-ship passengers (as is St. Thomas), St. Croix touts its shopping and has more stores than most islands in the Caribbean, especially in and around Christiansted, although it's not the shopping mecca Charlotte Amalie is. Its major attraction is Buck Island, a national park that lies offshore. St. Croix is peppered with inns and hotels and is condo heaven.

St. John, the smallest of the three islands, is also the most beautiful and the least developed. It has only two big hotels. Some two-thirds of this island is a national park. Even if you visit only for the day while based on St. Thomas, you'll want to sample the island's dream beach, Trunk Bay.

The U.S. Virgin Islands lie in two bodies of water: St. John is entirely in the Atlantic Ocean, St. Croix is entirely in the Caribbean Sea, and St. Thomas separates the Atlantic and the Caribbean. Directly in the belt of the subtropical, easterly trade winds, these islands enjoy one of the most perfect year-round climates in the world. The U.S. Virgins are at the eastern end of the Greater Antilles and the northern tip of the Lesser Antilles, some 60 miles east of Puerto Rico and 1,100 miles southeast of Miami.

1 Essentials

VISITOR INFORMATION

Before you go, contact the **U.S. Virgin Islands Division of Tourism,** 1270 Ave. of the Americas, New York, NY 10020 (☎ **212/ 332-2222**). Branch offices are at: 225 Peachtree St. NE, Suite 260, **Atlanta, GA** 30303 (☎ **404/688-0906**); 500 N. Michigan Ave., Suite 2030, **Chicago, IL** 60611 (☎ **312/670-8784**); 2655 Le Jeune Rd., Suite 907, **Coral Gables, FL** 33134 (☎ **305/442-7200**); 3460

Wilshire Blvd., Suite 412, **Los Angeles, CA** 90010 (☎ **213/739-0138**); and 900 17th St. NW, Suite 500, **Washington, DC** 20006 (☎ **202/293-3707**).

In **Canada,** go to 3300 Bloor St. West, Suite 3120, Centre Tower, Toronto, ON M8X 2X3, Canada (☎ **416/233-1414**). In **Britain,** contact the office at 2 Cinnamon Row, Plantation Wharf, York Place, London SW11 3TW (☎ **0171/978-5262**).

On the Web, get information at **www.usvi.net**.

GETTING THERE

Before you book your airline ticket on your own, refer to the section on "Package Deals," in chapter 2. You might save a bundle!

It's possible to fly from the mainland of the U.S. directly to St. Thomas and St. Croix, but the only way to get to St. John is by a ferry from St. Thomas or from Jost Van Dyke or Tortola in the British Virgin Islands.

TO ST. THOMAS OR ST. CROIX FROM THE U.S.   Nonstop flights to the U.S. Virgin Islands from either New York or Atlanta usually take 3¾ and 3½ hours, respectively. The flight time between St. Thomas and St. Croix is only 20 minutes. You may save money by flying to San Juan, then changing planes.

American Airlines (☎ **800/433-7300;** www.aa.com) offers frequent service to St. Thomas and St. Croix from the U.S. mainland, with five daily flights from New York to St. Thomas. Summer flights can vary; call for details. Passengers originating in other parts of the world are usually routed to St. Thomas through American's hubs in Miami or San Juan, both of which offer nonstop service (often several times a day) to St. Thomas. Connections from Los Angeles or San Francisco to either St. Thomas or St. Croix are usually made through New York, San Juan, or Miami. One especially convenient nonstop flight from Miami, available only June through August, departs Miami at 5pm and continues to St. Croix, where the plane stays overnight. This late-afternoon departure from Miami allows for connections to the U.S. Virgin Islands from many other destinations within the United States. Flights from Puerto Rico to the U.S. Virgin Islands are on American's partner, **American Eagle** (☎ **800/ 433-7300**), which has 13 nonstop flights daily. American can also arrange great discount packages that include both airfare and hotel.

Delta (☎ **800/221-1212** www.delta-air.com) offers two daily nonstop flights between Atlanta and St. Thomas in winter. **US Airways** (☎ **800/428-4322;** www.usairways.com) has one flight nonstop from Philadelphia to St. Thomas.

TWA (☎ **800/221-2000;** www.twa.com) does not fly nonstop to any of the Virgin Islands, but instead offers connections to other carriers through San Juan. TWA flies into San Juan five times daily from New York's JFK and twice daily from St. Louis with a touchdown in Miami.

Cape Air (☎ **800/352-0714**) has service between St. Thomas and Puerto Rico. This Massachusetts-based airline offers seven flights daily.

TO ST. CROIX FROM ST. THOMAS   It's now easier than ever before to travel between St. Thomas and St. Croix. **American Eagle** (☎ **800/433-7300**) has three flights a day, costing $61 one-way. In addition, **Seaborne Seaplane** (☎ **340/ 773-6442**) offers 10 or 11 round-trip flights daily, going for $55 one-way. Flight time is 30 minutes.

Those who want to make the 40-mile crossing from St. Thomas to St. Croix by **hydrofoil** can call a new service at ☎ **340/776-7417**. The vessel departs twice daily from the harbor at Charlotte Amalie on St. Thomas, arriving at Christiansted on St. Croix in about an hour; it costs $90 round-trip.

A **ferry** service between Charlotte Amalie in St. Thomas and Puerto Rico, with a stop in St. John, is available about once every 2 weeks (sometimes more often in high season). The trip takes about 2 hours, costing $80 one-way or $100 round-trip, including ground transportation to the San Juan airport or Condado. For more information, call ☎ **340/776-6282.**

TO ST. JOHN   The easiest and most common way to get to St. John is by **ferry** (☎ **340/776-6282**), which leaves from the Red Hook landing pier on St. Thomas's eastern tip; the trip takes about 20 minutes each way. Beginning at 6:30am, boats depart more or less every hour. The last ferry back to Red Hook departs from St. John's Cruz Bay at 11pm. The service is frequent and efficient enough that even cruise-ship passengers temporarily anchored in Charlotte Amalie can visit St. John for a quickie island tour. The one-way fare is $3 for adults, $1 for children 10 and under. Schedules can change without notice, so call in advance.

To reach the ferry, take the **Vitran** bus from a point near Market Square (in Charlotte Amalie) directly to Red Hook. The cost is $1 per person each way. In addition, privately owned taxis will negotiate a price to carry you from virtually anywhere to the docks at Red Hook.

It's also possible to board a **boat** for St. John directly at the Charlotte Amalie waterfront for a cost of $7 each way. The ride takes 45 minutes. The boats depart from Charlotte Amalie at 9am and continue at intervals of between 1 and 2 hours, until the last boat departs around 5:30pm. (The last boat to leave St. John's Cruz Bay for Charlotte Amalie departs at 3:45pm.) Call for more information.

Fast Facts: The U.S. Virgin Islands

American Express   The local agent on St. Thomas is Caribbean Travel Agency/Tropic Tours, 14AB The Guardian Building (☎ **340/774-1855**), a 5-minute drive east of Charlotte Amalie's center, opposite Havensight shopping mall; it's open Monday through Friday from 8:30am to 5pm and Saturday from 8:30am to noon. On St. Croix, go to Southerland, Chandler's Wharf, Gallows Bay (☎ **800/260-2603** or 340/773-9500).

Banking Hours   Banks are generally open Monday through Thursday from 9am to 2:30pm, Friday from 9am to 2pm and 3:30 to 5pm.

Currency   The **U.S. dollar** is the unit of currency in the Virgin Islands.

Customs   Every U.S. resident can bring home $1,200 worth of duty-free purchases, including 5 liters of liquor per adult. If you go over the $1,200 limit, you pay a flat 5% duty, up to an additional $1,000. You can also mail home gifts valued at up to $100 per day, which you don't have to declare. (At other spots in the Caribbean, U.S. citizens are limited to $400 or $600 worth of merchandise and a single bottle of liquor.)

Documents   U.S. and Canadian citizens are required to present some proof of citizenship to enter the Virgin Islands, such as a birth certificate with a raised seal along with a government-issued photo ID. A passport is not strictly required, but carrying one is a good idea. The requirements for other citizens are the same as for foreigners entering the U.S. mainland.

Electricity   It's the same as on the mainland: 120 volts AC (60 cycles). No transformer, adapter, or converter is needed for American appliances.

Emergencies   In an emergency, dial ☎ **911.**

Hospitals   On St. Thomas, **Royal Roy Lester Schneider Hospital,** 48 Sugar Estate, Charlotte Amalie (☎ **340/776-8311**), a 5-minute drive east of the town's commercial center, is the largest hospital with the best-equipped emergency room. On St. John, go to **St. John Myrah Keating Smith Community Health Clinic,** 28 Sussanaberg (☎ **340/693-8900**), reached along Route 10, 7 miles east of Cruz Bay. On St. Croix, go to the **St. Croix Hospital,** 6 Diamond Bay, Christiansted (☎ **340/778-6311**).

Safety   The U.S. Virgin Islands have more than their share of crime. Travelers should exercise extreme caution both day and night, especially in the backstreets of Charlotte Amalie on St. Thomas, and in Christiansted and Frederiksted on St. Croix. Muggings are commonplace. Avoid night strolls, especially on the beaches.

Time   The U.S. Virgins are on Atlantic standard time, which is 1 hour ahead of eastern standard time. However, the islands do not observe daylight saving time, so in the summer, the Virgin Islands and the East Coast of the U.S. are on the same time. In winter, when it's 6am in Charlotte Amalie, it's 5am in Miami; during daylight saving time, it's 6am in both places.

Tipping   Tip as you would on the U.S. mainland. Some hotels add a 10% to 15% surcharge to cover service, so check before you wind up paying twice.

Water   Most visitors drink the local tap water with no harmful aftereffects. Those with more delicate stomachs might want to stick to bottled water.

Weather   From November to February, temperatures average about 77°F. Sometimes in August the temperature peaks in the high 80s, but the subtropical breezes keep it comfortably cool in the shade. The temperature in winter may drop into the low 60s, but this rarely happens.

2 St. Thomas

St. Thomas, the busiest cruise-ship harbor in the West Indies, is not the largest of the U.S. Virgins—St. Croix, 40 miles south, holds that title. But bustling Charlotte Amalie is the capital of the U.S. Virgin Islands, and remains the shopping hub of the Caribbean. The beaches on this island are renowned for their white sand and calm, turquoise waters, including the very best of them all, **Magens Bay.** *National Geographic* rated the island as one of the top destinations in the world for sailing, scuba diving, and fishing.

Charlotte Amalie, with its white houses and bright red roofs glistening in the sun, is one of the most beautiful towns in the Caribbean. It's most famous for its shopping, but the town is also filled with historic sights, like Fort Christian, an intriguing 17th-century building constructed by the Danes. The town's architecture reflects the island's culturally diverse past. You'll pass Dutch doors, Danish red-tile roofs, French iron grillwork, and Spanish-style patios.

Because of St. Thomas's thriving commercial activity—as well as its lingering drug and crime problems—the island is often referred to as the most "unvirgin" of the Virgin Islands. Charlotte Amalie's Main Street is virtually a 3- to 4-block-long shopping center. But while this area tends to be overcrowded, for the most part, the island's beaches, major hotels, restaurants, and entertainment facilities are removed from the cruise-ship chaos. And you can always find seclusion at a resort in more remote sections of the island. Hotels on the north side of St. Thomas look out at the Atlantic; those on the south side front the calmer Caribbean Sea.

GETTING AROUND

BY TAXI   Cabs are unmetered, but fares are controlled and widely posted; however, we still recommend that you negotiate a fare with the driver before you get into the car. A typical fare from Charlotte Amalie to Sapphire Beach is $10 per person. Surcharges, from $1.50 to $2, are added after midnight. You'll pay $1 per bag for luggage. For 24-hour radio dispatch taxi service, call ☎ **340/774-7457.** If you want to hire a taxi and a driver (who just may be a great tour guide) for a day, expect to pay about $30 for two passengers for 2 hours of sightseeing; each additional passenger pays $12.

Taxi vans transport 8 to 12 passengers to multiple destinations on the island. It's cheaper to take a van instead of a taxi if you're going between your hotel and the airport. The cost for luggage ranges from 50¢ to $1 per bag.

BY BUS   St. Thomas has the best public transportation of any island in the U.S. chain. Buses, called **Vitrans,** leave from street-side stops in the center of Charlotte Amalie, fanning out east and west along all the most important highways. They run between 5:30am and 10:30pm daily, and you rarely have to wait more than 30 minutes during the day. A ride within Charlotte Amalie is 75¢; anywhere else, $1. The service is safe, efficient, and comfortable. For schedule and bus-stop information, call ☎ **340/774-5678.**

BY RENTAL CAR   St. Thomas has many leading North American car-rental firms at the airport, and competition is stiff. Before you go, compare the rates of the "big three": **Avis** (☎ **800/331-1084**), **Budget** (☎ **800/626-4316**), and **Hertz** (☎ **800/ 654-3001**).

You can often save money by renting from a local agency, although vehicles sometimes aren't as well maintained. Try **Dependable Car Rental,** 3901 B Altona, behind the Bank of Nova Scotia and the Medical Arts Complex (☎ **800/522-3076** or 340/774-2253), which will pick up renters at the airport or their hotel, or the aptly named **Discount Car Rental,** 14 Content, outside the airport on the main highway (☎ **340/776-4858**), which grants drivers a 12% discount on rivals' rates. Its rates are usually among the most reasonable on the island, beginning at $46.95 per day in winter. There is no tax on car rentals in the Virgin Islands.

Warning: Remember to *drive on the left.* This comes as a surprise to many visitors, who expect that U.S. driving practices will hold here. Of course, obey speed limits, which are 20 mph in towns, 35 mph outside. St. Thomas has a high accident rate, as tourists are not used to driving on the left, the hilly terrain hides blind curves and entrance ramps, roads are narrow and poorly lit, and drivers often get behind the wheel after too many drinks. To be on the safe side, consider getting **collision-damage insurance,** which usually costs an extra $14 to $16 per day. Be aware that even with this insurance, you could still get hit with a whopping deductible: The Hertz deductible is the full value of the car; at Avis and Budget, it's $250.

WHERE TO STAY

Nearly every beach on St. Thomas has its own hotel, and the island also has more quaint inns than anyplace else in the Caribbean. If you want to stay here on the cheap, consider one of the guest houses in the Charlotte Amalie area. All the glittering, expensive properties lie in the East End. Remember that hotels in the Virgin Islands slash their prices in summer by 20% to 60%. Unless otherwise noted, the rates listed below do *not* include the 8% government tax.

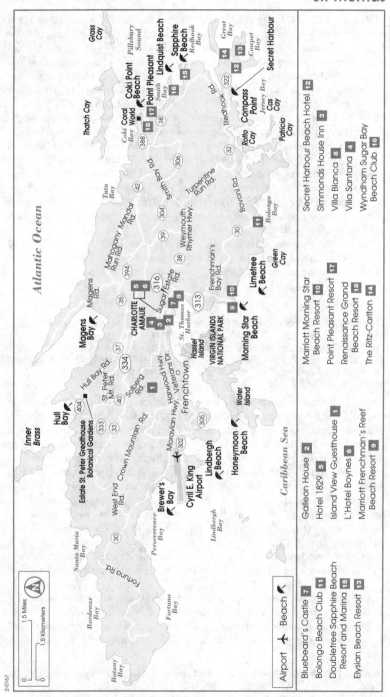

St. Thomas

Atlantic Ocean

Caribbean Sea

Grass Cay
Inner Brass

Thatch Cay

Pillsbury Sound

Great Bay

Congaet Bay

Jersey Bay

Smith Bay

Redhook Bay

Bolongo Bay

Green Cay

Cas Cay

Patricia Cay

Water Island

Hassel Island

St. Thomas Harbor

Frenchtown

CHARLOTTE AMALIE

Lindbergh Bay

Bordeaux Bay

Botany Bay

Santa Maria Bay

Fortuna Bay

Perseverance Bay

West End Rd.

Crown Mountain Rd.

Fortuna Rd.

Moravian Hwy.

Harwood Hwy.

Veterans Dr.

St. Peter Mt. Rd.

Hull Bay Rd.

Solberg Rd.

Magens Rd.

Mahogany Run Rd.

Mandal Run Rd.

Smith Bay Rd.

Sugar Estate Rd.

Weymouth Rhymer Hwy.

Turpentine Run Rd.

Frenchman's Bay Rd.

Bovoni Rd.

Redhook Rd.

Estate St. Peter Greathouse Botanical Gardens

Cyril E. King Airport

VIRGIN ISLANDS NATIONAL PARK

Hull Bay

Magens Bay

Brewer's Bay

Honeymoon Beach

Lindbergh Beach

Morning Star Beach

Limetree Beach

Coki Point Beach

Coki Coral World

Point Pleasant

Lindquist Beach

Sapphire Beach

Secret Harbour

Compass Point

Tutu Bay

0 1.5 Miles
0 1.5 Kilometers

Airport ✈   Beach ⌐

Bluebeard's Castle **7**
Bolongo Beach Club **11**
Doubletree Sapphire Beach Resort and Marina **15**
Elysian Beach Resort **13**

Galleon House **2**
Hotel 1829 **5**
Island View Guesthouse **1**
L'Hotel Boynes **6**
Marriott Frenchman's Reef Beach Resort **9**

Marriott Morning Star Beach Resort **10**
Point Pleasant Resort **17**
Renaissance Grand Beach Resort **18**
The Ritz-Carlton **14**

Secret Harbour Beach Hotel **12**
Simmonds House Inn **3**
Villa Blanca **8**
Villa Santana **4**
Wyndham Sugar Bay Beach Club **16**

691

CONDOS, APARTMENTS & VILLAS   Sometimes you can make a deal on a moderately priced condo, apartment, or villa. We've found that **Calypso Realty,** P.O. Box 12178, St. Thomas, U.S.V.I. (☎ **800/747-4858** or 340/774-1620), has the best offers, especially on rentals from April to mid-December. A studio overlooking Pillsbury Sound often goes for $95 per night off-season or $135 per night in winter.

Another source to check is **McLaughlin Anderson Vacations Ltd.,** 100 Blackbeard's Hill, St. Thomas, U.S.V.I. 00802 (☎ **800/666-6246** or 340/776-0635), which has rentals not only on St. Thomas, but on St. John and St. Croix as well. A one-bedroom villa begins at $1,900 per week in winter, with off-season discounts.

You can also contact **Paradise Properties of St. Thomas,** P.O. Box 9395, St. Thomas, U.S.V.I. 00801 (☎ **800/524-2038** or 340/779-1540; fax 340/779-6109), which currently represents six condo complexes. Rental units range from studio apartments to four-bedroom villas suitable for up to eight people; each has a fully equipped kitchen. A minimum stay of 3 days is required in any season, and 7 nights around Christmas. The prices range from $145 to $490 per day in winter and from $116 to $385 in the off-season.

Linlex Management, P.O. Box 8529, St. Thomas, U.S.V.I. 00801 (☎ **340/775-2600;** fax 340/775-5901) enjoys a repeat business of some 60%. Among other offerings, it rents condo suites featuring private balconies with ocean views, lying a short walk from the beach.

VERY EXPENSIVE

✪ **Doubletree Sapphire Beach Resort and Marina.** Rte. 36, Smith Bay Rd. (P.O. Box 8088), St. Thomas, U.S.V.I. 00801. ☎ **800/524-2090** in the U.S., or 340/775-6100. Fax 340/775-4024. www.usvi.net/hotel/sapphire. 171 units. A/C MINIBAR TV TEL. Winter $315–$385 suite for 2; $550 villa for 2. Off-season $225–$275 suite for 2; $325 villa for 2. Children 12 and under stay free in parents' room and eat for free when accompanied by a parent. AE, DC, MC, V.

This secluded retreat is one of the finest modern luxury resorts in the Caribbean. Guests can arrive by yacht, anchoring in the 67-slip marina, or else secure a suite or villa. Accommodations exude casual elegance and open onto a bay with one of St. Thomas's best and most sensuous beaches. The suites have fully equipped kitchens with microwaves, bedrooms with full bath, living/dining rooms with queen-size sofa beds, and large, fully tiled outdoor galleries complete with lounge furniture. The villas are on two different levels: The main, lower-level villas contain the same amenities as the suites, while the upper-level units feature a second full bathroom, a bedroom and sitting area with a queen-size sofa bed, and a sundeck with outdoor furniture. The suites accommodate one to four guests; the villas, up to six. The resort also boasts a fantastic children's program, which makes this a good choice for families.

Dining/Diversions: The Seagrape is one of the island's finest restaurants. A five-piece band often plays for dancing under the stars. For casual dining, try the Sailfish Café.

Amenities: Beach towels, daily chamber service, guest-services desk, baby-sitting. The Little Gems Kids Klub offers supervised activities for children. A 1-acre freshwater pool, snorkeling equipment, Sunfish sailboats, windsurfing boards, four all-weather tennis courts, waterfront pavilion with snack bar, complete scuba-diving center.

Marriott Frenchman's Reef Beach Resort. Estate Bakkeroe, Flamboyant Point (P.O. Box 7100), St. Thomas, U.S.V.I. 00801. ☎ **800/524-2000** in the U.S., or 340/776-8500. Fax 340/776-3054. www.marriott.vi. E-mail: resorts@marriott.vi. 408 units. A/C MINIBAR TV TEL. Winter $350–$375 double; from $495 suite. Off-season $210–$225 double; from $300 suite. MAP (breakfast and dinner) $61 per person extra. AE, DC, DISC, MC, V.

Frenchman's Reef, 3 miles east of Charlotte Amalie, has an excellent location facing south on a projection of land overlooking both the harbor and the Caribbean. This is a full-service, American-style megaresort; it's not suited to those seeking cozy island ambience. Everywhere you look are facilities devoted to the good life. To reach the private beach, for example, you take a glass-enclosed elevator. The bedrooms vary greatly, but in general are traditionally furnished and quite comfortable, though we find the rooms at the hotel's neighbor, the Morning Star, more luxurious. Nonetheless, the accommodations here have all you'll need for comfort. and the bathrooms are generally spacious.

Dining: Seafood with a continental flair is served at Windows on the Harbour, which resembles the inside of a cruise ship and has a good view. Sunset Grille & Bar offers alfresco dining poolside, with a variety of Caribbean and American fare served all day long. The Captains Café is a favorite port for thirsty visitors; its light menu includes seafood appetizers, sandwiches, salads, and tropical cocktails. All the restaurants of the Marriott Morning Star are also close at hand.

Amenities: Two pools with poolside bar, tennis courts, water sports (snorkeling, scuba diving, sailing, deep-sea fishing). 24-hour room service, laundry, baby-sitting.

Marriott Morning Star Beach Resort. #5 Estate Bakkeroe (P.O. Box 7100), Flamboyant Point, St. Thomas, U.S.V.I. 00801. ☎ **800/524-2000** or 340/776-8500. Fax 340/776-3054. www.marriott.vi. E-mail: resorts@marriott.vi. 96 units. A/C TV TEL. Winter $350–$450 double. Off-season $210–$270 double. MAP (breakfast and dinner) $61 per person extra. AE, DC, DISC, MC, V.

Recently upgraded to the tune of $6 million, this beachside enclave has been enhanced and made more alluring with a striking new Caribbean decor. Both its public areas and its plushly outfitted accommodations are among the best on the island. The resort was built on the landscaped flatlands near the beach of the well-known Marriott Frenchman's Reef Beach Resort, and there's a wide array of water sports. Its five buildings each contain between 16 and 24 units. Guests have the amenities and attractions of the large hotel nearby, yet maintain the privacy of this more exclusive enclave. Each unit has rattan furniture and views of the garden, beach, or the lights of Charlotte Amalie. Bedrooms are roomy and spacious, with fine furnishings and tasteful fabrics. The sound of the surf will lull you into a deep sleep.

Dining/Diversions: Caesar's Ristorante, on Morning Star Beach, serves rather standard Italian fare. More alluring is the oceanside Tavern on the Beach, offering an eclectic menu presented with the flair of fusion and Caribbean cuisine. The Raw Bar is an ideal spot for sunset cocktails, and a variety of restaurants and bars are also available at the adjoining Marriott Frenchman's Reef Beach Resort.

Amenities: Two giant pools; four tennis courts; water-sports program, including parasailing, dive shop, and Jacuzzi. Room service, baby-sitting, valet, plus all the services provided by the Frenchman's Reef next door.

Renaissance Grand Beach Resort. Rte. 38, Smith Bay Rd. (P.O. Box 8267), St. Thomas, U.S.V.I. 00801. ☎ **800/468-3571** in the U.S., or 340/775-1510. Fax 340/775-2185. www.renaissancehotels.com. 316 units. A/C TV TEL. Winter $295–$355 double; $450 one-bedroom suite; $850 two-bedroom suite. Off-season $155–$215 double; $450 one-bedroom suite; $650 two-bedroom suite. MAP (breakfast and dinner) $50 per person extra. AE, DC, DISC, MC, V.

This resort, which occupies 34 acres on the northeast shore of St. Thomas, is perched on a steep hillside above a beautiful, though small, beach. It offers a wide array of sports facilities. The accommodations, all stylishly outfitted, are in seven two-story buildings, designed in the style of beach houses and staggered so that each unit has its own view. The Bougainvillea section is adjacent to the beach, while the units in the

Hibiscus section are literally carved into the hillside. All rooms have quality mattresses, marble foyers, wall-to-wall carpeting, marble bathrooms with hair dryers, private safes, minifridges, robes, irons and ironing boards, and private patios or balconies. The two-story town-house suites and one- or two-bedroom suites have whirlpool spas. This is another good family resort—trained counselors operate a free year-round children's program for ages 3 to 14.

Dining/Diversions: You can enjoy a beachfront meal at Baywinds, which features continental and Caribbean cuisine. Dinner and Sunday brunch are served in Smugglers Bar and Grill. There's a poolside snack bar and live entertainment/dancing in the Baywinds Lounge.

Amenities: Concierge, daily children's program, baby-sitting, laundry, tropical garden tour, 23-hour room service, twice-daily maid service, newspaper and coffee with wake-up call, two pools (and a kiddie pool), water-sports center, on-site full-service dive shop, daily scuba and snorkel lessons, Sunfish sailboats, kayaks, windsurfers, snorkel equipment, six lit tennis courts, exercise facility, newsstand, gift shop, beauty salon. An 18-hole golf course is 10 minutes away.

✪ **The Ritz-Carlton.** Great Bay, St. Thomas, U.S.V.I. 00802. ☎ **800/241-3333** or 340/775-3333. Fax 340/775-4444. 152 units. Winter $450–$575 double; $1,500 suite. Off-season $250–$300 double; $750 suite. AE, DC, DISC, MC, V.

St. Thomas went "ritzy" almost overnight when this chic hotel chain took over the Grand Palazzo, a 15-acre oceanfront estate at the island's eastern tip, 4½ miles southeast of Charlotte Amalie. The Ritz is set amid landscaped gardens and fronted by white-sand beaches. This is St. Thomas's toniest property, edging out Sapphire Beach, Elysian, and the Marriott resorts. More than any other resort in the U.S. Virgin Islands, this deluxe estate blends European elegance with Caribbean style.

Accommodations are in half a dozen three-story villas designed with Italian Renaissance motifs and Mediterranean colors. Guests register in a reception palazzo, whose arches and accents were inspired by a Venetian palace. From the monogrammed bathrobes to the digital in-room safes, the accommodations here have more amenities than those at any other hotel on the island.

Dining/Diversions: The elegant dining room captures the best scenic views of Great Bay and St. John, and serves a refined cuisine that's among the finest of any hotel restaurant on island. The recently upgraded Beach Pavilion Restaurant overlooks tropical gardens and a secluded white-sand beach. The casual Iguana's Restaurant serves a continental breakfast and a lunch with a Caribbean-inspired menu. Guests can participate in the daily supervised feedings of nearby iguanas every morning. There's live entertainment on most nights, at least in season.

Amenities: Private beach with windsurfing, Sunfish and Hobie Cat sailing, and snorkeling; 125-foot free-form pool; complete fitness center; four lit tennis courts; cruises on private catamaran. Diving and deep-sea fishing excursions arranged. Concierge, 24-hour room service, valet, in-room massages, hair salon.

Wyndham Sugar Bay Beach Club. 6500 Estate Smith Bay, St. Thomas, U.S.V.I. 00802. ☎ **800/WYNDHAM** in the U.S., or 340/777-7100. Fax 340/777-7200. www.wyndham. com. 230 units. A/C TV TEL. Winter $396–$580 double; from $650 suite. Off-season $360–$440 double; from $525 suite. Rates are all-inclusive. AE, DC, MC, V.

This hostelry is in the East End of St. Thomas, a 5-minute ride from Red Hook. It's well located for panoramic views, although its secluded beach is really too small for a resort of this size. Many of the rooms are decorated with rattan pieces and pastel color schemes inspired by the tropics, and they contain such extras as dataports and fax, private safes, small fridges, balconies, and ceiling fans, plus roomy marble bathrooms.

Dining/Diversions: The main restaurant, Manor House, offers breakfast and dinner daily, with tables affording views of St. John and the British Virgin Islands. Casual meals are also served poolside. Entertainment is offered nightly. There's an ice-cream parlor in the Main Grove Café.

Amenities: Tennis courts, water sports, three connected freshwater pools with a waterfall, fitness center, nearby golf, Kids Klub, baby-sitting, tour desk.

EXPENSIVE

Bluebeard's Castle. Bluebeard's Hill (P.O. Box 7480), Charlotte Amalie, St. Thomas, U.S.V.I. 00801. ☎ **800/524-6599** in the U.S., or 340/774-1600. Fax 340/774-5134. 170 units. A/C TV TEL. Winter $195–$235 double. Off-season $140–$175 double. Extra person $30. AE, DC, DISC, MC, V.

Bluebeard's is a popular resort set on the side of the bay overlooking Charlotte Amalie. However, its former position as the number-one hotel of the island has long been surpassed by deluxe East End resorts, such as the Ritz-Carlton and Sapphire Beach. The hill surrounding the hotel is now heavily built up with everything from offices to time shares. The guest rooms come in a wide variety of shapes and sizes—all pleasantly but blandly decorated. Many units have a sitting room.

Dining: The Terrace Restaurant commands a panoramic view and serves many delectable American and Caribbean specialties. It offers open-air brunch, lunch, and late-night dining. Other dining choices include Banana Tree Grille (see "Where to Dine" below).

Amenities: Pool, two whirlpools, two championship tennis courts. Free transportation to Magens Bay Beach, a 15-minute drive away.

Bolongo Beach Club. 7150 Bolongo, St. Thomas, U.S.V.I. 00802. ☎ **800/524-4746** or 340/775-1800. Fax 340/775-3208. www.bolongo.com. 83 units. A/C TV TEL. Winter $225 double; $460 all-inclusive double; $325 one-bedroom villa for up to 2; $425 two-bedroom villa for up to 4. Off-season $175 double; $410 all-inclusive double; $210 one-bedroom villa; $275 two-bedroom villa. AE, MC, V.

Here you'll find a half-moon-shaped beach and a cement-sided, pink-walled series of two- and three-story buildings, plus some motel-like units closer to the sands. There's also a social center consisting of a smallish pool and a beachfront bar replete with palm fronds. Many clients check in on the continental plan, which includes breakfast; others opt for all-inclusive plans that include all meals, drinks, a sailboat excursion to St. John, and use of scuba equipment. Rooms are simple, summery, and filled with undistinguished furniture appropriate to the unpretentious, often barefoot style of this resort. Each unit has its own balcony or patio, a private safe, and one king or two double beds. Some of those on the beach come with kitchenettes. Villas (that is, apartment-style condos with full kitchens) are in a three-story building.

Dining: A relatively formal venue, Lord Rumbottom's, serves two-fisted portions of prime rib. The less formal, bistro-style Coconut Henry's offers burgers, sandwiches, salads, and multicolored drinks. Another option for drinking is Iggie's Sing-Along and Sports Bar.

Amenities: Fitness center, three pools, two tennis courts, volleyball, basketball court. St. Thomas Diving Club (an independent outfit) is on the premises. *Heavenly Days*, a 49-passenger catamaran docked right on the hotel's beach, makes frequent cruises to St. John. Baby-sitting can be arranged. The on-site gift shop (Beach Traders) is a registered outlet for Budget Rent-a-Car.

Elysian Beach Resort. 6800 Estate Nazareth, Cowpet Bay, St. Thomas, U.S.V.I. 00802. ☎ **800/753-2554** or 340/775-1000. Fax 340/776-0910. www.kosmasgroup.com. 180 units. Winter $275 double; $295 suite. Off-season $200 double; $225 suite. AE, DC, DISC, MC, V.

This time-share resort on Cowpet Bay in the East End, a 20-minute drive from Charlotte Amalie, has a European kind of glamour. The thoughtfully planned bedrooms contain balconies, and 14 offer sleeping lofts reached by a spiral staircase. The decor is tropical, with rattan and bamboo furnishings, ceiling fans, and natural-wood ceilings. The rooms are in a bevy of four-story buildings connected to landscaped gardens. Of the various units, 43 can be converted into one-bedroom suites, 43 into two-bedroom suites, and 11 into three-bedroom suites. Designer fabrics and white ceramic-tile floors make the tropical living quite grand.

Dining/Diversions: The Palm Court Restaurant offers elegant international dining. The Seabreeze Grill serves light fare right on the beach. Drinks can be ordered at the pool bar or in a first-class lounge. In season, live entertainment is often offered.

Amenities: Fitness center, pool, snorkel gear, canoes, Sunfish sailboats, tennis court, open-air shuttle to town, masseur, baby-sitting.

Point Pleasant Resort. 6600 Estate Smith Bay, St. Thomas, U.S.V.I. 00802. ☎ **800/ 777-1700** or 340/775-7200. Fax 340/776-5694. www.pointpleasantresort.com. E-mail: pointpleasantresort@worldnet.att.net. 95 units. A/C TV TEL. Winter $270–$380 double. Off-season $180–$255 double. AE, DC, DISC, MC, V.

This is a very private, unique resort on Water Bay, on the northeastern tip of St. Thomas, just a 5-minute walk from lovely Stouffer's Beach. These condo units, which are rented when owners are not in residence, are set on a 15-acre bluff with flowering shrubbery, century plants, frangipani trees, secluded nature trails, old rock formations, and lookout points. The villa-style accommodations have light and airy furnishings, mostly rattan and floral fabrics; some units have kitchens. Beds are very comfortable with fine linen and firm mattresses. From your living room, you can look out on a group of islands: Tortola, St. John, and Jost Van Dyke.

Dining/Diversions: The restaurant, Agavé Terrace, is one of the finest on the island. The cuisine, featuring seafood, is a blend of nouvelle American dishes and Caribbean specialties. Local entertainment is provided several nights a week.

Amenities: Complimentary use of a car 4 hours per day, shopping, dinner shuttle, three freshwater pools, lit tennis courts, snorkeling equipment, Sunfish sailboats.

Secret Harbour Beach Hotel. 6280 Estate Nazareth, Nazareth Bay, St. Thomas, U.S.V.I. 00802. ☎ **800/524-2250** or 340/775-6550. Fax 340/775-1501. www. st-thomas.com/shb.vi. 60 units. A/C TV TEL. Winter $275 studio double; $295 one-bedroom suite; $495 two-bedroom suite. Off-season, $169–$189 studio double; $199–$299 one-bedroom suite; $299–$319 two-bedroom suite. Rates include continental breakfast. AE, MC, V.

A favorite with honeymooners, this all-suite resort is on the beach at Nazareth Bay, just outside Red Hook Marina. All four contemporary buildings have southwestern exposure, and each unit has a private deck or patio and a full kitchen. There are three types of accommodations: studio apartments with a bed/sitting-room area, patio, and dressing-room area; one-bedroom suites with a living/dining area, a separate bedroom, and a sundeck; and the most luxurious, a two-bedroom suite with two bathrooms and a private living room.

Dining/Diversions: The Sea Side Restaurant serves both continental and Caribbean cuisine. At the more informal Secret Harbour Beach Cafe, you can eat breakfast or lunch on the outdoor terrace or gazebo. There's also a beachfront bar, where a manager's cocktail party is held weekly.

Amenities: Baby-sitting, daily maid service, five-star PADI dive center and water-sports facility on the beach, catamaran for sailing charters, two all-weather tennis courts, fitness center, freshwater pool, Jacuzzi.

MODERATE/INEXPENSIVE

Galleon House. Government Hill (P.O. Box 6577), Charlotte Amalie, St. Thomas, U.S.V.I. 00804. ☎ **800/524-2052** in the U.S., or 340/774-6952. Fax 340/774-6952. www.st-thomas.com/galleonhouse. 14 units. A/C TV TEL. Winter $79 double without bathroom; $89–$119 double with bathroom. Off-season $59 double without bathroom; $79 double with bathroom. Rates include continental breakfast. AE, DISC, MC, V.

Galleon House is at the east end of Main Street, about a block from the main shopping area of Charlotte Amalie. The good news is that its rates are among the most competitive in town. The bad news is that the hotel lacks state-of-the-art maintenance, is reached only after a difficult climb, and has received some complaints about the attitude of its staff. Nevertheless, it's an acceptable choice if your demands aren't too high. You walk up a long flight of stairs to reach a concrete terrace that doubles as the reception area. The small rooms are scattered in several hillside buildings. Each unit has a ceiling fan, cable TV with HBO, a firm mattress, and so-so air-conditioning, plus a cramped bathroom. There's a small freshwater pool and a sundeck. Breakfast is served on a veranda overlooking the harbor. Magens Beach is 15 minutes away by car or taxi.

✪ **Hotel 1829.** Kongens Gade (P.O. Box 1567), Charlotte Amalie, St. Thomas, U.S.V.I. 00804. ☎ **800/524-2002** in the U.S., or 340/776-1829. Fax 340/776-4313. 15 units. A/C MINIBAR TV TEL. Winter $95–$195 double; from $235 suite. Off-season $75–$145 double; from $170 suite. Rates include continental breakfast. AE, DISC, MC, V.

This is one of the leading small hotels in the Caribbean. Now a national historic site, the inn has serious island charm. It was designed by an Italian architect in a Spanish motif, with French grillwork, Danish bricks, and sturdy Dutch doors. Danish and African labor completed the structure in 1829 (hence the name), and since then it has entertained the likes of Edna St. Vincent Millay and Mikhail Baryshnikov. The place stands right in the heart of town, on a hillside 3 minutes from Government House. Magens Bay is a about a 15-minute ride away. It's a bit of a climb to the top of this multi-tiered structure—note that there are many steps, but no elevator. Amid a cascade of flowering bougainvillea are the upper rooms, which overlook a central courtyard with a miniature pool. The rooms are well designed and attractive, and most face the water. All have old island decor, such as wood beams and stone walls. The smallest units, in the former slave quarters, are the least comfortable.

Island View Guesthouse. 11-C Contant (P.O. Box 1903), Charlotte Amalie, St. Thomas, U.S.V.I. 00803. ☎ **800/524-2023** for reservations only, or 340/774-4270. Fax 340/774-6167. www.st-thomas-com/islandviewguesthouse. E-mail: islandview@worldneet.att.net. 16 units. TV TEL. Winter $65 double without bathroom; $95 double with bathroom; $100 suite. Off-season $50 double without bathroom; $65 double with bathroom; $84 suite. Rates include continental breakfast. AE, MC, V. From the airport, turn right onto Rte. 30; then cut left and continue to the unmarked Scott Free Rd., where you turn left; look for the sign.

Island View is located in a hilly neighborhood of private homes and villas about a 7-minute drive west of Charlotte Amalie and a 20-minute drive from the nearest beach at Magens Bay. Set 545 feet up Crown Mountain, it has sweeping views over Charlotte Amalie and the harbor. It contains main-floor rooms (two without private bathroom) and some poolside rooms, plus six units in a recent addition (three with kitchens and all with balconies). The bedrooms are cooled by breezes and fans, and the newer ones have air-conditioning. Furnishings are very basic. A self-service, open-air bar on the gallery operates on the honor system.

✪ **L'Hotel Boynes.** Blackbeard's Hill, P.O. Box 11611, St. Thomas, U.S.V.I. 00801. ☎ **800/377-2905** or 340/774-5511. Fax 340/774-8509. www.hotelboynes.vi. E-mail: Sboynes@islands.vi. 7 units. A/C TV TEL. Winter $135–$145 double; $195 suite. Off-season $105–$115 double; $165 suite. AE, MC, V.

This cozy, well-run hotel, one of the most historic on St. Thomas, is charming and personalized, with fewer accessories than what you'd find at a megaresort but considerably more charm. The place was originally built 200 years ago from yellow bricks that were carried from Denmark as ballast in the bottoms of sailing ships. Today, it and its half-acre of gardens are often prominently featured in glossy reviews of the island, and photographs over the surrounding harbor and historic zone are among the most widely publicized in the Caribbean. Accommodations have a lot of character, and each one is different, ranging from the Red Room, with Persian carpets and a four-poster bed, to the Whimsy Room, where the bed is actually built into an old Danish oven. All rooms have VCRs and ironing boards. The staff offers a complimentary shuttle to and from the airport and a once-a-day transfer to Magens Bay Beach. On the premises is a sundeck with a plunge pool. Other than breakfast, no meals are served, but there are many restaurants within a 2-minute walk.

✪ **Simmonds House Inn.** 8A Estate Catherineberg, 00804 St. Thomas, U.S.V.I. ☎ **888/ 521-7044** or 340/776-7776. Fax 340/776-7075. 9 units. TEL. Winter $110 double; $130–$150 suite. Off-season $100 double; $100–$130 suite. AE, MC, V.

What's unusual about this hotel is its sense of historic charm, its relatively low rates, and its location. A 10-minute downhill walk leads to the heart of Charlotte Amalie. The steeply sloping 1-acre garden is dotted with venerable mango trees. Bedrooms are cozy and soothing, filled with a combination of genuine antiques and new but traditional-looking furniture. Some of the beds are of the romantic plantation style. Some guests compare staying at this low-tech, non–air-conditioned inn to a visit to Grandma's. There's a six-sided pool in the back garden, and a 150-year-old kitchen that's the site of breakfast every morning. Other than breakfast, no formal meals are served, except by special request (you might ask someone to cook one of the fish you caught on a deep-sea expedition). There's a library and a small TV lounge on the premises.

✪ **Villa Blanca.** 4 Raphune Hill, Rte. 38, Charlotte Amalie, St. Thomas, U.S.V.I. 00801. ☎ **800/231-0034** in the U.S., or 340/776-0749. Fax 340/779-2661. www. st-thomas.com/villablanca. 14 units. TV. Winter $115–$135 double. Off-season $75–$85 double. AE, DC, MC, V.

Small, intimate, and charming, this hotel lies 1½ miles east of Charlotte Amalie on 3 secluded acres of hilltop land, among the most panoramic on the island. The hotel's main building served as the private home of its present owner, Blanca Terrasa Smith, between 1973 and 1985. After the death of her husband, Mrs. Smith added a 12-room annex in the garden and opened her grounds to paying guests. Today, a homelike and caring ambience prevails. Each room contains a ceiling fan and/or air-conditioning, a well-equipped kitchenette, a good bed with a firm mattress, and a private balcony or terrace with sweeping views either eastward to St. John or westward to Puerto Rico and the harbor of Charlotte Amalie. No meals are served. On the premises are a freshwater pool and a large covered patio. The closest beach is Morningstar Bay, about a 4-mile drive away.

Villa Santana. Denmark Hill, St. Thomas, U.S.V.I. 00802. ☎ and fax **340/776-1311.** www.st-thomas.com/villasantana. 7 units. TV TEL. Winter $125–$195 suite for two. Off-season $85–$135 suite for two. AE.

This unique country villa, an all-suite property, was originally built by Gen. Antonio Lopez de Santa Anna of Mexico in the 1850s. It offers a panoramic view of Charlotte Amalie and the St. Thomas harbor. The shopping district in Charlotte Amalie is just a 5-minute walk away; Magens Beach is a 15-minute drive north. Guest rooms are located at La Mansion, the former library of the general; La Terraza, originally the wine cellar; La Cocina de Santa Anna, once the central kitchen for the entire estate; La Casa de Piedra, once the bedroom of the general's most trusted attaché; and La Torre, the old pump house that has been converted into a modern lookout tower. All rooms have fully equipped kitchens, firm mattresses, and ceiling fans. The Mexican decor features clay tiles, rattan furniture, and stonework. The property has a pool, sundeck, and small garden with hibiscus and bougainvillea.

WHERE TO DINE

The St. Thomas dining scene these days is among the best in the West Indies, but it has its drawbacks. Fine dining, and even not-so-fine dining, tends to be expensive, and the best spots (with a few exceptions) are not right in Charlotte Amalie, thus can only be reached by taxi or car.

IN CHARLOTTE AMALIE

The local branch of the **Hard Rock Café** chain is at the International Plaza, the Waterfront (☎ **340/777-5555**). It features live music on Friday and Saturday nights.

Banana Tree Grille. In Bluebeard's Castle Hotel, Bluebeard's Hill. ☎ **340/776-4050.** Reservations recommended. Main courses $12.50–$24.75. AE, MC, V. Tues–Sun 6–9:30pm. INTERNATIONAL.

This place offers candlelit dinners, sweeping views over the busy harbor, and a decor that combines silk and genuine banana plants artfully scattered throughout the restaurant's two dining rooms. The cuisine is creative, the patrons often hip and laid-back. Launch yourself into the repast with one of their accurately named "fabulous firsts," such as tuna wontons with a zippy orange sambal sauce or bacon-wrapped horseradish shrimp grilled and dancing over a mango glaze. Main dishes are filled with flavor, especially the house specialties of sugarcane coco-lacquered tuna, lobster tail tempura with an orange sambal sauce, and the divine mango mustard glazed salmon. Try the aïoli shank, a house specialty, if it's offered: The shank of lamb is slowly braised in Chianti and served with an aïoli sauce over white beans and garlic-mashed potatoes. The desserts are truly decadent, especially accompanied by one of the specialty coffees.

Beni Iguana's Sushi Bar. In the Grand Hotel Court, Veteran's Dr. ☎ **340/777-8744.** Reservations recommended. Sushi $5.50–$15 per portion (two pieces); main courses $8–$15; combo plates for four to five diners $25.50–$35 each. AE, MC, V. Daily 11:30am–10pm. JAPANESE.

It's the only Japanese restaurant on St. Thomas, a change of pace from the Caribbean, steak, and seafood choices nearby. Along with a handful of shops, it occupies the sheltered courtyard and an old cistern across from Emancipation Square Park. You can eat outside, or pass through wide Danish colonial doors into a red- and-black-lacquered interior devoted to a sushi bar and a handful of simple tables. A perennial favorite is the "13" roll, stuffed with spicy crabmeat, salmon, lettuce, cucumbers, and scallions.

✪ **Café Lulu.** Blackbeard's Hill. ☎ **340/714-1641.** Reservations required. Main courses $16.50–$24. AE, DC, MC, V. Mon–Sat 6–10pm. INTERNATIONAL.

Funky and bistro-ish, yet well-grounded in some of the most sophisticated culinary concepts on St. Thomas, this restaurant occupies what was originally a private house set high above Charlotte Amalie's harbor, on Blackbeard's Hill. Patricia Lacorte, one of the premier chefs (and one of the very few female chefs) on the island, prepares a menu that changes frequently. In a dining room that's painted in West Indian style— strong shades of yellow, blue, green, and red—you'll enjoy sweeping panoramas and menu items that include oven-braised lamb shank with garlic mashed potatoes; gaucho steak with Mexican herbs and flavorings; grilled "garlic-stabbed" rib-eye steak with sweet-potato fries and gorgonzola sauce; and barbecued breast of chicken with mashed yams. An especially unusual dish is five-spice Mandarin-style duckling, which is marinated for three days and nights prior to cooking, and served with a vegetable stir-fry.

☼ Hervé Restaurant & Wine Bar. Government Hill (next to the Hotel 1829). **☎ 340/777-9703.** Reservations requested. Main courses $5.50–$16.75 lunch, $17.75–$24.75 dinner. AE, MC, V. Daily 11:30am–3pm and 6–10pm. AMERICAN/CARIBBEAN/FRENCH.

Hervé is the hot restaurant of St. Thomas, surpassing all competition in town, including its next-door neighbor, Hotel 1829. A panoramic view of Charlotte Amalie and a historic setting are minor benefits—it's the cuisine here that matters. Hervé P. Chassin, whose experience has embraced such stellar properties as the Hotel du Cap d'Antibes, is a restaurateur with a vast, classical background. Here in his own unpretentious setting, he offers high-quality food at reasonable prices.

Study the menu in a space decorated with classic black-and-white photographs of St. Thomas at the turn of the century. There are two dining areas: a large open-air terrace and a more intimate wine room. Contemporary American dishes are served with the best of classic France, along with Caribbean touches. Start with the pistachio-encrusted brie, shrimp in a stuffed crab shell, or conch fritters with mango chutney. From here, you can let your taste buds march boldly forward with such temptations as red snapper poached with white wine, or a delectable black-sesame-crusted tuna with a ginger/raspberry sauce. Well-prepared nightly specials of game, fish, and pasta are featured. Desserts here are equally divine—you'll rarely taste a creamier crème caramel or a lighter, fluffier mango or raspberry cheesecake.

Hotel 1829. Kongens Gade (at the east end of Main St.). **☎ 340/776-1829.** Reservations recommended, but not accepted more than 1 day in advance. Main courses $19.50–$32.50; fixed-price dinner $28.50. AE, DISC, MC, V. Daily 6–11pm. CONTINENTAL.

Hotel 1829 is graceful and historic, and its restaurant serves some of the finest food on St. Thomas. Guests head for the attractive bar for a before-dinner drink. Dining is on a 19th-century terrace or in the main room, with walls made from ships' ballast and a floor crafted from 200-year-old Moroccan tiles. The cuisine has a distinctively European twist, with many dishes prepared and served from trolleys beside your table. This is one of the few places in town that serves the finest caviar; other appetizers include goat-cheese bruschetta with roasted-red-pepper hummus. A ragoût of swordfish is made more inviting with pine-nut/basil pesto, and the sautéed snapper in brown butter is always a reliable choice. Mint-flavored roast rack of lamb and Chateaubriand for two are other possibilities.

☼ Virgilio's. 18 Dronningens Gade (entrance on a narrow alley running between Main St. and Back St.). **☎ 340/776-4920.** Reservations recommended. Main courses $8.95–$25 lunch, $12–$35 dinner. AE, MC, V. Mon–Sat 11:30am–10:30pm. NORTHERN ITALIAN.

This is the best northern Italian restaurant in the Virgin Islands. Virgilio's neo-Baroque interior is sheltered under heavy ceiling beams and brick vaulting. A well-trained staff attends to the tables. Owner Virgilio del Mare serves meals against a backdrop of stained-glass windows, crystal chandeliers, and soft Italian music. The *cinco peche* (clams, mussels, scallops, oysters, and crayfish simmered in a saffron broth) is a delectable house special, while the lobster ravioli here is the best there is. Classic dishes are served with a distinctive flair—the rack of lamb, for example, is filled with a porcini mushroom stuffing and glazed with a roasted garlic aïoli. The marinated grilled duck is served chilled. You can even order an individual pesto pizza.

IN FRENCHTOWN

Alexander's. Rue de St. Barthélemy. ☎ **340/776-4211.** Reservations recommended. Main courses $11.75–$19.75 lunch, $15.50–$21.50 dinner. AE, MC, V. Mon–Sat 11:30am–10pm. AUSTRIAN/ITALIAN/SEAFOOD.

Alexander's, west of town, offers 12 tables in air-conditioned comfort, with picture windows overlooking the harbor. There's a heavy emphasis on seafood, plus an increasing Italian slant to the menu. The bacon-wrapped chicken breast stuffed with spinach and Swiss cheese is prepared to perfection, as is the pan-seared herb-crusted lamb tenderloin with a mint port sauce. At lunch, you can enjoy marinated tuna steak or penne in a basil pesto cream sauce, or go for one of the sandwiches, such as a vegetable burger. The top dish, however, is the seafood pasta with an array of mussels, shrimp, clams, crab, and fresh fish. The vegetarian spring rolls are mouthwatering. Alexander's also has a Bar and Grill, open daily from 11am to midnight, and Epernay, a wine bar open Monday through Friday from 4pm to 11pm (until 11:30pm on weekends).

Chart House Restaurant. Villa Olga. ☎ **340/774-4262.** Reservations recommended. Main courses $17.95–$29.95; fixed-price dinner (until 6:30pm) $16.75. AE, DC, DISC, MC, V. Daily 5:30–10pm. STEAKS/SEAFOOD.

The stripped-down 19th-century villa that contains the Chart House was the Russian consulate during the island's Danish administration. It lies a short distance beyond the most densely populated area of Frenchtown village. The dining gallery is a spacious open terrace fronting the sea. Cocktails start daily at 5pm, when the bartender breaks out the ingredients for his special drink known as a Bailey's banana colada. The salad bar here, which comes with dinner, is the best on the island, with a choice of 30 to 40 items. This chain is also known for serving the finest cut of prime rib anywhere. Calamari, pasta dishes, coconut shrimp, Hawaiian chicken, and fresh fish are part of the expanded menu. For dessert, order the famous mud pie.

✪ **Craig & Sally's.** 22 Honduras. ☎ **340/777-9949.** Reservations recommended. Main courses $14.50–$29.50. AE, MC, V. Wed–Fri 11:30am–3pm; Wed–Sun 5:30–10pm. INTERNATIONAL.

This Caribbean cafe is set in an airy, open-sided pavilion in Frenchtown. Its eclectic cuisine is, according to the owner, "not for the faint of heart, but for the adventurous soul." Views of the sky and sea are complemented by a cuisine that ranges from pasta to seafood, with influences from Europe and Asia. Roast pork with clams, filet mignon with macadamia-nut sauce, and grilled swordfish with a sauce of fresh herbs and tomatoes are examples from a menu that changes every day. The lobster-stuffed, twice-baked potatoes are examples of creative cuisine at its most inspired. The wine list is the most extensive and sophisticated on St. Thomas.

ON THE NORTH COAST

✪ **Eunice's Terrace.** 66–67 Smith Bay, Rte. 38 (just east of the Coral World turnoff). ☎ **340/775-3975.** Reservations not accepted. Main courses $10.25–$29.95. AE, MC, V. Mon–Sat 11am–10pm, Sun 5–10pm. CARIBBEAN/AMERICAN.

One of the island's best-known local restaurants is a 30-minute taxi ride east of the airport. Both locals and visitors crowd into its confines for generous platters of savory island food. Dinner specialties include conch fritters, broiled or fried fish (especially mahimahi), sweet-potato pie, and a number of specials usually served with fungi, rice, or plantains. On the lunch menu are fishburgers, sandwiches, and such daily specials as Virgin Islands doved pork or mutton. (Doving, pronounced "*dough*-ving," involves baking sliced meat while basting it with a combination of its own juices, tomato paste,

Kitchen Bouquet, and island herbs.) Key lime pie is a favorite dessert. A popular drink concoction is the "Queen Mary" (tropical fruits laced with dark rum). This little restaurant made news in January 1997, when Bill and Hillary Clinton dined here. They both shared a conch appetizer; he then opted for a local fish ("ole wife"), while the First Lady chose the grilled vegetable plate.

Hartwell's American Brasserie. Mahogany Run. ☎ **340/777-6277.** Reservations recommended. Main courses $16–$22.50. AE, DISC, MC, V. Wed–Sun 6–10pm. INTERNATIONAL.

Set in a wooded valley, close to the 11th hole of the Mahogany Run Golf Course, this restaurant was originally built in the 1750s as a stable for a nearby Danish sugar plantation. Its walls are more than 2 feet thick. Ceiling fans and breezes blowing through the valley keep the place cool. Menu items rotate with the seasons, but are likely to include snails in garlic butter; grilled portobello mushrooms with toasted couscous; and various fresh fish, chicken, and veal dishes. An enduring favorite is shrimp pot pie baked in flaky pastry with a roasted garlic and tomato cream sauce.

Romano's Restaurant. 97 Smith Bay Rd. ☎ **340/775-0045.** Reservations recommended. Main courses $22.95–$29.95; pastas $16.95–$19.95. AE, MC, V. Mon–Sat 6:30–10:30pm. Closed Aug and 1 week in Apr for Carnival. Take the Vitran bus. ITALIAN.

Located on the sandy-bottomed flatlands near Coral World, this hideaway is owned by New Jersey chef Tony Romano, who specializes in a flavorful and herb-laden cuisine that some diners yearn for after too much Caribbean cooking. House favorites include linguine con pesto, four-cheese lasagna, a tender and well-flavored osso buco, scaloppini marsala, and broiled salmon. All desserts are made on the premises. The restaurant, marked by exposed brick and well-stocked wine racks, always seems full of happy, lively diners.

IN & AROUND RED HOOK

Duffy's Love Shack. 650 Red Hook Plaza, Rte. 38. ☎ **340/779-2080.** Main courses $9.25–$14. No credit cards. Daily 11am–2am. AMERICAN/CARIBBEAN.

This is a fun and happening place where you can mingle with the locals. As the evening wears on, the customers become the entertainment, often dancing on tables or forming conga lines. Yes, Duffy's also serves food, a standard American cuisine with Caribbean flair and flavor. The restaurant is open-air, with lots of bamboo and a thatched roof over the bar—in other words, the quintessential island look. Even the menu appears on a bamboo stick, like an old-fashioned fan. Start with a Caribbean egg roll or black-bean cakes, then move on to cowboy steak or voodoo pineapple chicken (in a hot garlic-and-pineapple sauce). Surf-and-turf here means jerk tenderloin and mahimahi. After 10pm, the stove-pot cookery is dropped and a late-night menu appears, mostly sandwiches. The bar business is huge, and the bartender is known for his lethal rum drinks.

East End Sushi & Tempura Bar/Café Wahoo. 6300 Estate Smith Bay (beside the ferry dock to St. John). ☎ **340/775-6350.** Main courses $7–$22 lunch, $16–$35 dinner. AE, MC, V. Mon–Sat 11:30am–3pm and 6–10pm. Take the Red Hook bus. JAPANESE/INTERNATIONAL.

This popular place, built on piers above the sea, has a laid-back atmosphere. The food is good, and much more imaginative than you might think. At lunch, look for fresh sushi and tempura, platters of fish flown in from the U.S. mainland, and to a much lesser extent, local Caribbean fish. Evening choices include soft-shell crab cakes with Caribbean curry sauce, seared yellowfin tuna with wasabi mustard and house-made soy sauce, and Jamaican-style herb-crusted wahoo. The kitchen makes some of its own oils, including orange-pepper oil, basil oil, and various types of vinaigrette. An unusual starter course, at night, is mango-stuffed gnocchi.

AT COMPASS POINT

Raffles. 6300 Frydenhoj, Compass Point, off Rte. 32 (1 mile west of Red Hook). ☎ **809/775-6004.** Reservations recommended. Main courses $15–$24. AE, MC, V. Tues–Sun 6:30–10:30pm. CONTINENTAL/SEAFOOD.

Named after the legendary hotel in Singapore, this establishment is filled with tropical accents more evocative of the South Pacific than of the Caribbean. Peacock chairs and ceiling fans set the mood. We always look for the nightly specials, such as fresh West Indian–style fish (with tomato, garlic, and herbs)—although the regular menu is also enticing. Starters include sautéed conch and the lobster bisque. Everything is accompanied by homemade bread. The chef's excellent seafood pasta is loaded with shrimp, scallops, and mahimahi. The peanut chicken is a delight. In honor of its namesake, the chef prepares steak Raffles in a cream and oyster sauce. One specialty rarely encountered in the Caribbean is beef Wellington in a delectable mushroom duxelle in puff pastry. The pièce de résistance is marinated duck, which is steamed, baked, and served with an orange ginger sauce.

NEAR THE SUB BASE

L'Escargot. 12 Sub Base. ☎ **340/774-6565.** Reservations recommended. Main courses $15–$24. AE, MC, V. Daily 11:45am–2:30pm and 6–10pm. FRENCH/CARIBBEAN.

This place has been in and out of fashion for so long, it's a virtual island legend for its sheer endurance alone. One of the oldest restaurants on St. Thomas, it has been going strong for more than 3 decades. Its focal point is a low-slung semi-outdoor terrace with close-up views of Crown Bay Marina. The first-rate cuisine includes the standard repertoire of French dishes, including rack of lamb with rosemary sauce, scampi in pesto sauce with linguine, grilled swordfish with spicy mango sauce, onion soup, fresh mushroom salad, and chocolate mousse. Many dishes—which change daily—have Caribbean zest and flavor. The sautéed or steamed yellow tail is always perfectly prepared, and many local habitués opt for one of the grilled steaks along with plenty of tropical drinks, of course.

HITTING THE BEACH

Chances are, your hotel will be right on the beach, or very close to one. All the beaches in the Virgin Islands are public, and most lie anywhere from 2 to 5 miles from Charlotte Amalie.

THE NORTH SIDE   ✪ **Magens Bay** lies between two mountains 3 miles north of the capital. *Condé Nast Traveler* named this beach one of the world's 10 most beautiful. Waters here are calm and ideal for swimming, though the snorkeling isn't as good, since the bottom is flat and sandy. The beach is usually terribly overcrowded, though it gets better in the midafternoon. Changing facilities, snorkeling gear, lounge chairs, paddleboats, and kayaks are available. There is no public transportation to get here (though some hotels provide shuttle buses); from Charlotte Amalie, take Route 35 north all the way. The gates to the beach are open daily from 6am to 6pm (after 4pm, you'll need insect repellent). Admission is $1 per person and $1 per car. Don't bring valuables and certainly don't leave anything of value in your parked car.

A marked trail leads to **Little Magens Bay,** a separate clothing-optional beach (especially popular with gay and lesbian visitors). This is also President Clinton's preferred beach on St. Thomas (no, he doesn't go nude).

Two Great Escapes

Water Island, a quarter mile off the coast from the harbor of Charlotte Amalie, is the fourth largest of the U.S. Virgins, with 500 acres of land. At palm-shaded **Honeymoon Beach,** you can swim, snorkel, sail, water ski, or sunbathe, then order lunch or a drink from the beach bar. A ferry, **Launch with Larry** (☎ **340/ 775-8073**), runs between Crown Bay Marina and Water Island several times a day. (Crown Bay Marina is part of the St. Thomas submarine base.)

In the same bay, and even closer to shore, is **Hassel Island.** It's almost completely deserted—its membership in the national parks network prohibits most forms of development. There are no hotels or services of any kind here, and swimming is limited to narrow, rocky beaches. Even so, many visitors hire a boat to drop them off for an hour or 2. A hike along part of the shoreline is a welcome relief from the cruise-ship congestion of Charlotte Amalie. Bringing water and food if you plan to spend more than 3 hours here. **Launch with Larry** (see above) makes the trip here as well. The round-trip fare is only $5, well worth it to escape the hordes for a day.

✪ **Coki Point Beach,** in the northeast near Coral World, is good but often very crowded. It's noted for its warm, crystal-clear water, ideal for swimming, as well as its thousands of rainbow-hued fish swimming among the beautiful corals, which attract snorkelers. Locals even sell small bags of fish food, so you can feed the sea creatures while you're snorkeling. From the beach, there's a panoramic view of offshore Thatch Cay. Concessions can arrange everything from waterskiing to parasailing. An East End bus runs to Smith Bay and lets you off at the gate to Coral World and Coki. Watch out for pickpockets.

Also on the north side is **Renaissance Grand Beach,** one of the island's most beautiful. It opens onto Smith Bay and is near Coral World. Many water sports are available here. The beach is right off Route 38.

THE EAST END   Small and special, **Secret Harbour** is near a collection of condos. With its white sand and coconut palms, it's the epitome of Caribbean charm. The snorkeling near the rocks is some of the best on the island. No public transportation stops here, but it's an easy taxi ride east of Charlotte Amalie heading toward Red Hook.

✪ **Sapphire Beach** is set against the backdrop of the Doubletree Sapphire Beach Resort and Marina, where you can have lunch or order drinks. There are good views of offshore cays and St. John, a large reef is close to the shore, and windsurfers like this beach a lot. Snorkeling gear and lounge chairs can be rented. Take the East End bus from Charlotte Amalie, going via Red Hook. Ask to be let off at the entrance to Sapphire Bay; it's not too far to walk from here to the water.

White-sand **Lindquist Beach** isn't a long strip, but it's one of the island's prettiest. It's between Wyndham Sugar Bay Beach Club and the Sapphire Beach Resort. Many films and TV commercials have used this photogenic beach as a backdrop. It's not likely to be crowded, as it's not very well known.

THE SOUTH SIDE   **Morning Star** (also known as Frenchman's Bay Beach) is near the Marriott Frenchman's Reef Beach Resort, about 2 miles east of Charlotte Amalie. Here, among the often young crowds (many of whom are gay), you can don your most daring swimwear. Sailboats, snorkeling equipment, and lounge chairs are available for rent. The beach is easily reached by a cliff-front elevator at Frenchman's Reef.

Limetree Beach, set against a backdrop of sea-grape trees and shady palms, lures those who want a serene spread of sand where they can bask in the sun and even feed hibiscus blossoms to iguanas. Snorkeling gear, lounge and beach chairs, towels, and drinks are available. There's no public transportation, but the beach can easily be reached by taxi from Charlotte Amalie.

WEST OF CHARLOTTE AMALIE   Near the University of the Virgin Islands in the southwest, **Brewer's Bay** is one of the island's most popular beaches. The strip of white coral sand is almost as long as the beach at Magens Bay. Unfortunately, this isn't the place for snorkeling. Vendors sell light meals and drinks. From Charlotte Amalie, take the Fortuna bus heading west; get off at the edge of Brewers Bay, across from the Reichhold Center.

Lindbergh Beach, with a lifeguard, rest rooms, and a bathhouse, lies at the Island Beachcomber Hotel and is used extensively by locals, who sometimes stage political rallies here as well as Carnival parties. It's not good for snorkeling. Drinks are served on the beach. Take the Fortuna bus route west from Charlotte Amalie.

SPORTS & OUTDOOR PURSUITS

DEEP-SEA FISHING   The U.S. Virgins have excellent deep-sea fishing—some 19 world records (eight for blue marlin) have been set in these waters in recent years. Outfitters abound at the major marinas like Red Hook. We recommend angling off the *Fish Hawk* (☎ 340/775-9058), which Captain Al Petrosky sails out of Fish Hawk Marina Lagoon on the East End. His 43-foot diesel-powered craft is fully equipped with rods and reels. All equipment (but not meals) is included in the price: $450 per half day for up to six passengers. Full-day excursions start at $800.

GOLF   Mahogany Run, on the North Shore at Mahogany Run Road (☎ 800/ 253-7103 or 340/775-6006), is an 18-hole, par-70 course. This beautiful course rises and drops like a roller coaster on its journey to the sea; cliffs and crashing sea waves are the ultimate hazards at the 13th and 14th holes. President Clinton pronounced this course "very challenging." Greens fees are $85 for 18 holes, reduced to $75 in the late afternoon. Carts cost $15.

GYMS   The most reasonably priced club on the island is the **Bayside Fitness Center,** 7140 Bolongo (☎ 340/693-2600), part of the Bolongo Beach complex. It offers weights, cardio, treadmills, and a sauna. A day pass costs $10 for nonguests; it's free to guests of the Bolongo complex. Hours are Monday to Friday from 6am to 9pm and Saturday and Sunday from 8am to 5pm.

HORSE & PONY TOURS   Half Moon Stables (☎ 340/777-6088) offers horse and pony tours of the East End. A secluded trail winds through lush, green hills to a pebble-covered beach. These hour-long guided tours are a great way to explore areas of the island rarely seen from tour buses or rental cars. The cost is $45 per person per hour. Western and English saddles are available.

KAYAK TOURS   Virgin Island Ecotours (☎ 340/779-2155) offers 2½ -hour kayak trips through a mangrove lagoon on the southern coastline. The cost is $50 per person. The tour is led by professional naturalists who allow enough time for 30 minutes of snorkeling.

SCUBA DIVING & SNORKELING   With 30 spectacular reefs just off St. Thomas, the U.S. Virgins have been rated one of the most beautiful areas in the world for scuba diving and snorkeling by *Skin Diver* magazine. For **snorkeling,** we like the waters off **Coki Point,** on the northeast shore of St. Thomas; especially enticing are the coral ledges near Coral World's underwater tower. **Magens Bay** also has great snorkeling year-round. For information on snorkeling cruises, see "Taking to the Seas," below.

Taking to the Seas

On St. Thomas, most of the boat business centers around the Red Hook and Yacht Haven marinas. The 50-foot *Yacht Nightwind,* Sapphire Marina (☎ **340/ 775-4110,** 24 hours a day), offers full-day sails to St. John and the outer islands. The $95 price includes continental breakfast, champagne buffet lunch, and an open bar aboard. You're also given free snorkeling equipment and instruction.

New Horizons, 6501 Red Hook Plaza, Suite 16, Red Hook (☎ **340/ 775-1171**), offers windborne excursions amid the cays and reefs of the Virgin Islands. The two-masted, 63-foot ketch has circumnavigated the globe and has been used as a design prototype for other boats. Owned and operated by Canadian Tim Krygsveld, it contains a hot-water shower, serves a specialty drink called a New Horizons Nooner (with a melon-liqueur base), and carries a complete line of snorkeling equipment for adults and children. A full-day excursion, with an Italian buffet lunch and an open bar, costs $90 per person. Children 2 to 12, when accompanied by an adult, pay $45. Excursions depart daily, weather permitting, from the Doubletree Sapphire Beach Resort & Marina. Call ahead for reservations and information.

New Horizons has recently expanded with another vessel, *New Horizons II,* a 44-foot custom-made speedboat that takes you on a full-day trip to some of the most scenic highlights of the British Virgin Islands, costing $110 for adults or $85 for children 2 to 12. The outfitter also operates **Power Trips** next door, renting out 25-foot Wellcrafts for $245 per day for up to eight people. These boats have fuel-efficient engines and can make it to any of the 10 islands in the vicinity of St. Thomas. The company offers dive and fishing equipment and will supply a captain upon request.

You can avoid the crowds by sailing aboard the *Fantasy,* 6700 Sapphire Village, no. 253 (☎ **340/775-5652;** fax 340/775-6256), which departs from the American Yacht Harbor at Red Hook at 9:30am daily. It takes a maximum of six

As for **scuba diving,** the best dive site off St. Thomas has to be **Cow and Calf Rocks,** off the southeast end (45 minutes from Charlotte Amalie by boat); here you'll discover a network of coral tunnels riddled with caves, reefs, and ancient boulders encrusted with coral. Below is a list of outfitters that can assist you with an underwater adventure.

St. Thomas Diving Club, 7147 Bolongo Bay (☎ **800/538-7348** or 340/ 776-2381), is a full-service, PADI five-star IDC center, the best on the island. An open-water certification course, including four scuba dives, costs $385. An advanced open-water certification course, including five dives that can be accomplished in 2 days, goes for $275. Every Thursday, participants are taken on an all-day scuba excursion that includes a two-tank dive to the wreck of the HMS *Rhone* in the British Virgin Islands; the trip costs $110. A scuba tour of the 350-foot wreck of the *Witshoal* is offered every Saturday for experienced divers only; the cost is $80. You can also enjoy local snorkeling for $30.

DIVE IN!, in the Doubletree Sapphire Beach Resort & Marina, Smith Bay Road, Route 36 (☎ **800/524-2090** or 340/775-6100), is a well-recommended, complete diving center that offers some of the finest services in the U.S. Virgin Islands, including professional instruction (beginner to advanced), daily beach and boat dives, passengers to St. John and nearby islands for swimming, snorkeling, beach-combing, and trolling. Snorkel gear with expert instruction is provided, as is a champagne lunch; an underwater camera is available. The full-day trip costs $95 per person. Also offered is a full-day trip to Jost Van Dyke for $95 per person, including a B.V.I. Customs charge of $15 (no lunch). A half-day sail, morning or afternoon, lasts 3 hours and costs $65. Sunset tours are also popular, with an open bar and hors d'oeuvres, costing $50 per person.

Remember Grace Kelly and Bing Crosby crooning a duet in *High Society?* The *True Love,* 6501 Red Hook Plaza, Suite 54 (☎ 340/779-6547, 24 hours a day), a sleek coast guard–certified 54-foot Malabar schooner, is the very same yacht featured in the classic 1956 film. No longer just for lovers, the craft sails daily from the Doubletree Sapphire Marina for $95 per person. Included in the price is a gourmet lunch, open bar, and snorkeling equipment and lessons.

✪ **American Yacht Harbor,** Red Hook (☎ 800/736-7294 or 340/775-6454), offers both bareboat and fully crewed charters. It leaves from a colorful yacht-filled harbor set against a backdrop of Heritage Gade, a reproduction of a Caribbean village. The harbor is home to numerous boat companies, including day-trippers, fishing boats, and sailing charters. There are also four restaurants on the property, serving everything from continental to Caribbean cuisine. Another reliable outfitter is **Char-teryacht League,** at Flagship (☎ 800/524-2061 or 340/774-3944).

Sailors may want to check out the *Yachtsman's Guide to the Virgin Islands,* available at major marine outlets, at bookstores, through catalog merchandisers, or direct from **Tropic Isle Publishers,** P.O. Box 610938, North Miami, FL 33261-0938 (☎ 305/893-4277). This annual guide, which costs $15.95, is supplemented by sketch charts, photographs, and landfall sketches and charts showing harbors and harbor entrances, anchorages, channels, and landmarks, plus information on preparations necessary for cruising the islands.

custom dive packages, underwater photography and videotapes, snorkeling trips, and a full-service PADI dive center. An introductory course costs $60, with a one-tank dive going for $55, two-tank dives for $70. A six-dive pass costs $195.

TENNIS   The best tennis on the island is at the ✪ **Wyndham Sugar Bay Beach Club,** 6500 Estate Smith Bay (☎ 340/777-7100), which has the Virgin Islands' first stadium tennis court, seating 220, plus six additional Laykold courts lit at night. The cost is $8 an hour. There's also a pro shop.

Another good resort for tennis is the **Bolongo Bay Beach Resort,** Bolongo Bay (☎ 340/775-1800), which has two courts lit until 10pm. They're free to members and hotel guests, but cost $10 for nonguests.

Marriott Frenchman's Reef Tennis Courts, Flamboyant Point (☎ 340/776-8500, ext. 444), has four courts. Again, nonguests are charged $10 per hour per court. Lights stay on until 10pm.

WINDSURFING   This increasingly popular sport is available through the major resorts and at some public beaches, including Brewer's Bay, Morning Star Beach, and Limetree Beach. The **Renaissance Grand Beach Resort,** Smith Bay Road, Route 38 (☎ 340/775-1510), is the major hotel offering windsurfing, with rentals costing $20 per hour.

EXPLORING ST. THOMAS
CHARLOTTE AMALIE

The capital, Charlotte Amalie, where most visitors begin their sightseeing, has all the color and charm of an authentic Caribbean waterfront town. In days of yore, seafarers from all over the globe flocked here, as did pirates and members of the Confederacy, who used the port during the American Civil War. (Sadly, St. Thomas was the biggest slave market in the world.)

The old warehouses once used for storing pirate goods still stand—today, many of them house shops. In fact, the main streets are now a virtual shopping mall and are usually packed. (See "Shopping," below, for our specific recommendations.) Sandwiched among these shops are a few historic buildings, most of which can be covered on foot in about 2 hours. Before setting off, stop off in the **Grand Hotel,** at Tolbod Gade 1, near Emancipation Park. No longer a hotel, it now contains shops and a **visitor center** (☎ 340/774-8784), open Monday to Friday from 8am to 5pm and Saturday from 8am to noon.

Fort Christian. In the town center. ☎ **340/776-4566.** Free admission. Mon–Fri 8:30am–4:30pm.

This imposing structure, which dates from 1672, dominates the center of town. It was named after the Danish king, Christian V, and has been everything from a fort to a governor's residence to a jail. It became a national historic landmark in 1977, but still functioned as a police station, court, and jail until 1983. Now a museum, the fort houses displays on the island's history and culture. Cultural workshops and turn-of-the-century furnishings are just some of the exhibits. A museum shop features local crafts, maps, and prints.

Paradise Point Tramway. ☎ **340/774-9809.** Round-trip $12 adults, $6 children. Daily 9am–5pm.

This contraption affords visitors a dramatic view of Charlotte Amalie harbor, with a ride to a 697-foot peak. The tramway, similar to those used at ski resorts, operates four cars, each with a 10-person capacity, for the 15-minute round-trip ride. It transports customers from the Havensight area to Paradise Point, where they can disembark to visit shops and the popular restaurant and bar.

Seven Arches Museum. Government Hill. ☎ **340/774-9295.** Admission $5. Tues–Sat 10am–3pm or by appointment.

Browsers and gapers love checking out the private home of longtime residents Philibert Fluck and Barbara Demaras. This is an 18th-century Danish house, completely restored to its original condition and furnished with West Indian antiques. You can walk through the yellow ballast arches and visit the great room, with its wonderful view of the busiest harbor in the Caribbean. Night-blooming cacti and iguanas are on the roof of the slave quarters. The admission includes a cold tropical drink served in a walled garden filled with flowers.

Synagogue of Beracha Veshalom Vegmiluth Hasidim. 15 Crystal Gade. ☎ **340/ 774-4312.** Free admission. Mon–Fri 9am–4pm.

This is the oldest synagogue in continuous use under the American flag and the second oldest in the Western Hemisphere. It was erected in 1833 by Sephardic Jews, and still maintains the tradition of having sand on the floor, commemorating the exodus from Egypt. The structure was built of local stone, along with ballast brick from Denmark and mortar made of molasses and sand. Next door, the **Weibel Museum** showcases 300 years of Jewish history. It keeps the same hours.

ELSEWHERE ON THE ISLAND

Route 30 (Veterans Drive) will take you west of Charlotte Amalie to **Frenchtown.** (Turn left at the sign to the Admiral's Inn.) Early French-speaking settlers arrived on St. Thomas from St. Bart's after they were uprooted by the Swedes. Many island residents today are the direct descendants of those long-ago immigrants, who were known for speaking a distinctive French patois.

This colorful village contains a number of restaurants and taverns. Because Charlotte Amalie has become somewhat dangerous at night, Frenchtown has picked up its after-dark business and is the best spot for dancing, drinking, and other local entertainment.

✪ **Coral World Marine Park & Underwater Observatory.** 6450 Coki Point, a 20-minute drive from Charlotte Amalie off Route 38. ☎ **340/775-1555.** Admission $18 adults, $9 children 3–12. Daily 9am–5:30pm.

This marine complex features a three-story underwater observation tower 100 feet offshore. Inside, you'll see sponges, fish, coral, and other aquatic creatures in their natural state. An 80,000-gallon reef tank features exotic marine life of the Caribbean; another tank is devoted to sea predators, with circling sharks and giant moray eels. Activities include daily fish and shark feedings and exotic bird shows. The latest addition to the park is a semisubmarine that lets you enjoy the panoramic view and the "down under" feeling of a submarine without truly submerging.

Coral World's guests can take advantage of adjacent **Coki Beach** for snorkel rentals, scuba lessons, or simply swimming and relaxing. Lockers and showers are available. Also included in the marine park are the Tropical Terrace Restaurant, duty-free shops, and a nature trail.

Estate St. Peter Greathouse Botanical Gardens. At the corner of Rte. 40 (6A St. Peter Mountain Rd.) and Barrett Hill Rd. ☎ **340/774-4999.** Admission $8 adults, $4 children. Daily 9am–4pm.

This estate consists of 11 acres set at the foot of volcanic peaks on the northern rim of the island. The grounds are laced with self-guided nature walks that will acquaint you with some 200 varieties of West Indian plants and trees, including an umbrella plant from Madagascar. From a panoramic deck in the gardens, you can see some 20 of the Virgin Islands, including Hans Lollick, an uninhabited island between Thatched Cay and Madahl Point. The house itself, filled with local art, is worth a visit.

SHOPPING

The discounted, duty-free shopping in the Virgin Islands makes St. Thomas a shopping mecca. It's possible to find well-known brand names here at savings of up to 60% off mainland prices. But be warned—savings are not always so good. Make sure you know the prices back home to determine if you are in fact getting good deals. Having sounded that warning, we'll mention some St. Thomas shops where we have found really good buys.

The best buys include china, crystal, perfume, jewelry (especially emeralds), Haitian art, fashion, watches, and items made of wood. Cameras and electronic items, based on our experience, are not the good buys they're reputed to be. St. Thomas is also the best place in the Caribbean for discounts in porcelain, but remember that U.S. brands may often be purchased for 25% off the retail price on the mainland. Look for the imported patterns for the biggest savings.

Most shops, some of which occupy former pirate warehouses, are open Monday through Saturday from 9am to 5pm. Some stores open Sunday and holidays if a cruise

Going Under: A Submarine Ride

If you really want to get to the bottom of it all, board the air-conditioned *Atlantis* submarine, which takes you on a 1-hour voyage (the whole experience is really 2 hours when you include transportation to and from the sub) to depths of 90 feet, where an amazing world of exotic marine life unfolds. You'll have up-close views of coral reefs and sponge gardens through the sub's 2-foot windows. *Atlantis* divers swim with the fish and bring them close to the windows for photos.

Passengers take a surface boat from the West Indies Dock, right outside Charlotte Amalie, to the submarine, which is near Buck Island (the St. Thomas version, not the more famous Buck Island near St. Croix). The fare is $72 for adults, $36 for ages 4 to 17; children 3 and under are not allowed. The *Atlantis* operates daily November through April, Tuesday through Saturday May through October. Reservations are a must (the sub carries only 30 passengers). For tickets, go to the Havensight shopping mall, building 6, or call ☎ **340/776-5650.**

---

ship is in port. *Note:* Friday is the biggest cruise-ship day at Charlotte Amalie (we once counted eight at once), so try to avoid shopping then.

Nearly all the major shopping is along the harbor of Charlotte Amalie. Cruise-ship passengers mainly shop at the **Havensight Mall** at the eastern edge of town. The principal shopping street is **Main Street,** or Dronningens Gade (its old Danish name). To the north is another merchandise-loaded street called **Back Street,** or Vimmelskaft. Many shops are also spread along the **Waterfront Highway** (Kyst Vejen). Between these major streets is a series of side streets, walkways, and alleys, all filled with shops. You might also browse along Tolbod Gade, Raadets Gade, Royal Dane Mall, Palm Passage, Storetvaer Gade, and Strand Gade.

It's illegal for most street vendors (food vendors are about the only exception) to ply their trades outside of the designated area called **Vendors Plaza,** at the corner of Veterans Drive and Tolbod Gade. Hundreds of vendors converge here at 7:30am; they usually pack up around 5:30pm, Monday through Saturday.

When you completely tire of French perfumes and Swiss watches, head for **Market Square,** also called Rothschild Francis Square. Under a Victorian tin roof, locals with machetes slice open fresh coconuts, while women wearing bandannas sell akee, cassava, and breadfruit.

Other noteworthy shopping districts include **Tillett Gardens,** a virtual oasis of arts and crafts—pottery, silk-screened fabrics, candles, watercolors, jewelry, and more—located on the highway across from Four Winds Shopping Center (take Route 38 east from Charlotte Amalie). A major island attraction in itself is the ✪ **Jim Tillett Art Gallery and Silk Screen Print Studio** (☎ **340/775-1929**), which displays the best work of local artists, including originals in oils, watercolors, and acrylics. The prints are all one of a kind, and prices start as low as $10. The famous Tillett maps on fine canvas are priced from $30.

All the major stores in St. Thomas are located by number on an excellent map in publication *St. Thomas This Week,* distributed free to all arriving plane and boat passengers and at the visitor center. A lot of the stores on the island don't have street numbers, or don't display them, so look for their signs instead.

✪ **Bernard K. Passman,** 38A Main St. (☎ **340/777-4580**), is the world's leading sculptor of black-coral art and jewelry. He's famous for his *Can Can Girl* and his four statues of Charlie Chaplin. After being polished and embellished with gold and diamonds, some of Passman's work has been treasured by royalty. There are also simpler and more affordable pieces for sale.

Gallery Camille Pissarro, Caribbean Cultural Centre, 14 Dronningens Gade (☎ 340/774-4621), is located in the house where Pissarro was born in 1830. In three high-ceilinged and airy rooms, you can see Pissarro paintings relating to the islands. Many prints of local artists are available, and the gallery also sells original batiks, alive in vibrant colors.

Mango Tango Art Gallery, Al Cohen's Plaza, Raphune Hill, Route 38 (☎ 340/777-3060), is one of the largest galleries on island, closely connected with a half-dozen internationally recognized artists who spend at least part of the year in the Virgin Islands. Examples include Don Dahlke, Max Johnson, Anne Miller, David Millard, Dana Wylder, and Shari Erickson. Original works begin at $200; prints and posters are cheaper.

Native Arts and Crafts Cooperative, Tarbor 1 (☎ 340/777-1153), is the largest arts-and-crafts emporium in the U.S. Virgin Islands, offering the output of 90 different artisans. It specializes in items small enough to be packed into a suitcase or trunk, such as spice racks, lamps crafted from conch shells, salad bowls, crocheted goods, and straw goods.

Caribbean Marketplace, Havensight Mall, building 3 (☎ 340/776-5400), carries the best selections of handcrafts, including the Sunny Caribbee line, a vast array of condiments (ranging from spicy peppercorns to nutmeg mustard) and botanical products. Other items range from steel-pan drums from Trinidad to wooden Jamaican jigsaw puzzles, Indonesian batiks, and bikinis from the Cayman Islands. Do not expect very attentive service.

The aromas will lead you to **Down Island Traders,** Veterans Drive (☎ 340/776-4641), which has Charlotte Amalie's most attractive array of spices, teas, candies, jellies, jams, and condiments, most of which are packaged in natural Caribbean products. There's also local cookbooks, silk-screened T-shirts and bags, Haitian metal sculpture, handmade jewelry, Caribbean folk art, and children's gifts.

The clutter and eclecticism of **Carson Company Antiques,** Royal Dane Mall, off Main Street (☎ 340/774-6175), may appeal to you. The shop is loaded with merchandise, tasteless and otherwise, from virtually everywhere. Much of it is meant to appeal to the tastes of cruise-ship passengers. Bakelite jewelry is cheap and cheerful, and the African artifacts are often interesting.

✪ **A. H. Riise Gift & Liquor Stores,** 37 Main St. (☎ 800/524-2037 or 304/776-2303), is St. Thomas's oldest outlet for luxury items such as jewelry, cosmetics, crystal, china, and perfumes. It also offers the widest sampling of liquors on the island. The store boasts a collection of fine jewelry and watches from Europe's leading craftspeople, including Vacheron Constantin, Bulgari, Omega, and Gucci, as well as a wide selection of gold, platinum, and precious gemstone jewelry. Imported cigars are stored in a climate-controlled walk-in humidor. Waterford, Lalique, Baccarat, and Rosenthal are featured in the china and crystal department. Specialty shops in the complex sell Caribbean gifts, books, clothing, food, prints, note cards, and designer sunglasses. Delivery to cruise ships and the airport is free.

One of the island's most famous outlets, **Al Cohen's Discount Liquors,** Long Bay Road (☎ 340/774-3690), occupies a big warehouse at Havensight with a huge selection of liquor and wine. The wine department is especially impressive. You can also purchase fragrances, T-shirts, and souvenirs.

Tropicana Perfume Shoppe, 2 Main St. (☎ 800/233-7948 or 340/774-0010), bills itself as the largest perfumery in the world. It offers all the famous names in perfumes, skin care, and cosmetics, including Lancôme and La Prairie. Men will also find Europe's best colognes and aftershave lotions here.

✪ **Royal Caribbean,** 33 Main St. (☎ 340/776-4110), is the largest camera and electronics store in the Caribbean. It carries Nikon, Minolta, Pentax, Canon, and Panasonic products, plus watches by Seiko, Movado, Corum, Fendi, Philippe Charriol, and Zodiac. There are also leather bags, Mikimoto pearls, 14- and 18-karat jewelry, and Lladró figurines. Another branch is at Havensight Mall (☎ 340/776-8890).

Often called the Tiffany's of the Caribbean, ✪ **Cardow Jewelers,** 39 Main St. (☎ **340/ 776-1140**), boasts the largest selection of fine jewelry in the world. This fabulous shop, where more than 20,000 rings are displayed, offers savings because of its worldwide direct buying, large turnover, and duty-free prices. Unusual and traditional designs are offered in diamonds, emeralds, rubies, sapphires, and pearls. Cardow also has a whole wall of Italian gold chains, and features antique-coin jewelry as well. The Treasure Cove has cases of fine gold jewelry priced under $200.

Cardow's leading competitor is **H. Stern Jewellers,** Havensight Mall (☎ **800/ 524-2024** or 340/776-1223), the international chain with some 175 outlets. Besides this branch, there are two more on Main Street and one at Marriott's Frenchman's Reef. Stern gives worldwide guaranteed service, including a 1-year exchange privilege.

For a decade, the owners of **Blue Carib Gems and Rocks,** 2 Back St., behind Little Switzerland (☎ **340/774-8525**), have scoured the Caribbean for gemstones. The raw stones are cut, polished, and fashioned into jewelry by the lost-wax process. You can see craftspeople at work and view their finished products. A lifetime guarantee is given on all handcrafted jewelry. Since the items are locally made, they are duty free and not included in the $1,200 Customs exemption.

Colombian Emeralds International, Havensight Mall (☎ **340/774-2442**), is renowned throughout the Caribbean for its collection of Colombian emeralds, both set and unset. Here you buy direct from the source, which can mean significant savings. The shop also stocks fine watches. There's another outlet on Main Street.

Connoisseurs of colored gemstones consider **Pierre's,** 24 Palm Passage (☎ **800/ 300-0634** or 340/776-5130), one of the most impressive repositories of collector's items in the Caribbean. It's a branch of a store based in Naples, Florida. You might be new to some of the glittering and mystical-looking gemstones here. Look for alexandrites (garnets in three shades of green); spinels (pink and red); sphenes, yellow-green sparklers from Madagascar (as reflective as high-quality diamonds); and tsavorites, a green stone from Tanzania.

Cosmopolitan, Drakes Passage and the waterfront (☎ **340/776-2040**), draws a lot of repeat business. It carries Bally shoes and handbags; women's and men's swimwear by Gottex, Hom, Lahco, and Fila; ties by Versace and Pancaldi (at least 30% less than the U.S. mainland price); and Nautica sportswear for men (discounted at 10%).

The **Leather Shop,** 1 Main St. (☎ **340/776-0290**), has the best selection of handbags, belts, wallets, and briefcases from Italian designers such as Fendi, Longchamp, Furla, and Il Bisonte. Some of these items are very expensive, of course, but there's also less costly merchandise such as backpacks, carry-ons, and Mola bags from Colombia. The outlet store on Back Street sells close-outs at prices that are sometimes 50% off U.S. mainland tags.

Coki, Compass Point Marina (☎ **340/775-6560**), has a factory 1½ miles from Red Hook amid a little restaurant row, so you might want to combine a dining tour with a shopping expedition. From the expansive cutting boards come some of the most popular varieties of tote bags in the Virgin Islands. These include beach bags, zip-top bags, and drawstring bags crafted from canvas and elegant cotton prints.

The Linen House, A. H. Riise Mall (☎ **340/774-1668**), is considered the best store for linens in the West Indies. You'll find a wide selection of place mats, decorative tablecloths, and many hand-embroidered goods, much of them crafted in China.

The inventory at **Lover's Lane,** Raadets Gade 33, besides Veteran's Drive (☎ **340/ 777-9616**), is as earthy and, in some cases, raunchy, as anything you'll find on St. Thomas. Amid an ever-so-tasteful decor of muted grays and mirrors, the shop sells provocative lingerie; edible panties; inflatable men, women, and sheep; massage aids of every conceivable type; vibrators; and all the lace, leather, or latex you'll need to make your dreams come true.

If you need a beach read, head for the well-stocked **Dockside Bookshop,** Havensight Mall (☎ 340/774-4937), near the cruise-ship dock. It has the best selection of books on island lore as well as a variety of general reading selections.

Modern Music, across from Havensight Mall and the cruise-ship docks (☎ 340/774-3100), features nearly every genre, from rock to jazz to classical, and especially Caribbean. You'll find new releases from island stars such as Jamaica's Byron Lee and the Virgin Islands' The Violators, as well as U.S. groups. There are two other branches, at the Nisky Center (☎ 340/777-7877) and at Four Winds Mall (☎ 340/775-3310).

ST. THOMAS AFTER DARK

St. Thomas has more nightlife than any other island in the Virgins, U.S. and British, but not as much as you might think. Charlotte Amalie is no longer the swinging town it used to be. Many of the streets are dangerous after dark, so visitors have relatively abandoned the town except for a few places, such as the Greenhouse. Much of the action has shifted to **Frenchtown,** which has some great restaurants and bars. However, just as in Charlotte Amalie, some of these little hot spots are along dark, badly lit roads.

Note: Sexual harassment can be a problem in certain bars in Charlotte Amalie, where few single women would want to be alone at night anyway. Any of the major resort hotels is generally safe.

The big hotels, such as Marriott's Frenchman's Reef Beach Resort and Bluebeard's, have the most lively after-dark scene. After a day of sightseeing and shopping in the hot West Indies sun, sometimes your best bet is just to stay at your hotel in the evening, perhaps listening to a local fungi band playing traditional music on homemade instruments. You might also call the **Reichhold Center for the Arts,** University of the Virgin Islands, 2 John Brewer's Bay (☎ 340/693-1550), or check with the tourist office to see what's on at the time of your visit. The lobby displays a frequently changing free exhibit of paintings and sculptures by Caribbean artists. A Japanese-inspired amphitheater is set into a natural valley, with seating space for 1,196. Several different repertory companies of music, dance, and drama perform here. Performances usually begin at 8pm. Tickets range from $12 to $40.

Any savvy insider will tell you to head to the **Bar at Paradise Point** (☎ 340/777-4540) at sunset. It's located 740 feet above sea level (a tram takes you up the hill), across from the cruise-ship dock, and provides excellent photo ops and panoramic views. Get the bartender to serve you his specialty, a "Bushwacker." Sometimes a one-man steel band is on hand to serenade the sunset watchers. You can also order inexpensive food, such as barbecued ribs, hot dogs, and hamburgers. Happy hour, with discounted drinks, begins at 5pm.

Bakkeroe's, at Marriott's Frenchman's Reef, Estate Bakkeroe (☎ 340/776-8500), offers classic pop and rock, with a large stage and the island's finest sound system. Local acts alternate with DJs, and karaoke is inevitably featured. The place gets going nightly at 9pm and generally stays open until the last customers stagger out.

The posh **Baywinds,** at the Renaissance Grand Beach Resort, Smith Bahy Road (☎ 340/775-1510), is a romantic place to be in the evening. Couples dance at the side of the luxurious pool as moonlight glitters off the ocean in the background. Music ranges from jazz to pop. It's open nightly, with live music and dinner from 6pm to midnight.

The scenic **Dungeon Bar,** Bluebeard's Hill (☎ 340/774-1600), overlooking the yacht harbor, offers piano-bar entertainment nightly. It's a popular gathering spot for both locals and visitors. You can dance from 8pm to midnight on Thursday and from 8pm to 1am on Saturday. Entertainment varies from month to month, but a steel band usually comes in on some nights, while other nights are devoted to karaoke or jazz. It's open Tuesday to Friday from 4pm to midnight and Saturday to Monday from 4pm to 1am. There's no cover.

Epernay, rue de St. Barthélemy (next to Alexander's Restaurant), Frenchtown (☎ 340/774-5348), is a stylish watering hole with a view of the ocean. You can order vintage wines and at least six different brands of champagne by the glass. Also available are appetizers, including sushi and caviar, main courses, and tempting desserts, such as chocolate-dipped strawberries. It's open Monday to Wednesday from 11:30am to 11pm, Thursday to Saturday from 11:30am to midnight.

Fat Tuesday, 26A Royal Dane Mall (☎ 340/777-8676), is on the waterfront in downtown Charlotte Amalie. Specialties include the Tropical Itch (a frozen punch made with bourbon and 151 rum) and the Moko Jumbi Juice (vodka, bourbon, 151 rum, and banana and cocoa liqueurs). There's also a variety of beer, highballs, and shooters. The bar has a special event each night. It's open daily from 10am to midnight or 1am (perhaps later on Friday and Saturday, depending on business).

The **Greenhouse,** Veterans Drive (☎ 340/774-7998), a bar/restaurant directly on the waterfront, is one of the few nightspots we recommend in the heart of Charlotte Amalie. Each night features different entertainment, ranging from reggae to disco. There's no cover except on Wednesday and Friday nights, when you pay $5 for the live reggae.

Iggie's Bolongo, Bolongo Beach Resort, 7150 Bolongo (☎ 340/779-2844), functions during the day as an informal, open-air restaurant serving hamburgers, sandwiches, and salads. After dark, it presents karaoke and occasional live entertainment. Call to find out what's happening.

Larry's Hideaway, 10 Hull Bay (☎ 340/777-1898), has a laid-back, casual atmosphere. Many locals like to spend lazy Sunday afternoons here. It's also a cheap place to eat—hot dogs and hamburgers are served until 3:45pm. After 5pm, you can order affordable main courses in the restaurant, including the catch of the day and the chef's pork stew.

Latitude 18, Red Hook Marina (☎ 340/779-2495), is the hot spot on the east coast, where the ferryboats depart for St. John. The ceiling is adorned with boat sails. The place is both a restaurant and bar, opening nightly at 6pm. Live entertainment is featured regularly, especially on Tuesday and Saturday nights. This casual spot is especially popular with locals.

Martini's, in Frenchtown (☎ 340/714-2145), is the newest and hottest club on St. Thomas, with the best martinis on the island. It's open nightly, with live entertainment Thursday through Saturday (for a $5 cover). The club is generally open from 6pm to 12:30am, but hours can vary.

The popular **Turtle Rock Bar,** in the Mangrove Restaurant at the Wyndham Sugar Bay Beach Club, 6500 Estate Smith Bay (☎ 340/777-7100), presents live music, steel bands, and karaoke. There's space to dance, but most patrons just sway and listen to the steel-pan bands that play from 2pm to closing, or the more elaborate bands that play on Tuesday, Sunday, and some other nights. Thursday night is karaoke. Burgers, salads, steaks, and grilled fish are available at the Mangrove Restaurant a few steps away. There's no cover. Happy hour (when most drinks are half price) is 4 to 6pm every night.

The intimate, dimly lit, two-level bar at **Walter's Livingroom,** 3 Trompeter Gade (☎ 340/774-5025), attracts locals, often gay men, in season, drawing more off-island visitors in winter. It's about 100 yards from the island's famous synagogue, in a clapboard town house built around 1935. The music here ranges from the 1950s to the 1970s.

3 St. John

A few miles east of St. Thomas, across a glistening, turquoise channel known as Pillsbury Sound, lies St. John, the smallest and least densely populated of the three main U.S. Virgin Islands.

St. John is a wonder of unspoiled beauty. Along its rocky coastline are beautiful crescent-shaped bays and white-sand beaches, and the interior is no less impressive. The variety of wildlife here is the envy of naturalists around the world. And there are miles of serpentine hiking trails, leading past the ruins of 18th-century Danish plantations to magnificent panoramic views. At scattered intervals along the trails, you can even find mysteriously geometric petroglyphs, of unknown age and origin, incised into boulders and cliffs.

Today, St. John (unlike the other U.S. islands) remains truly pristine, its preservation rigidly enforced by the U.S. Park Service. Thanks to the efforts of Laurance Rockefeller, who purchased acres of land here and donated them to the United States, the island's shoreline waters, as well as more than half of its surface area, comprise the **Virgin Islands National Park.** The hundreds of coral gardens that surround St. John are protected rigorously—any attempt to damage or remove coral from the water is punishable with large and strictly enforced fines.

Despite the unspoiled beauty of much of St. John, the island manages to provide visitors with modern amenities and travel services, including a sampling of restaurants, car-rental kiosks, yacht-supply facilities, hotels, and campgrounds. **Cinnamon Bay,** founded by the National Park Service in 1964, is the most famous campsite in the Caribbean. In addition, the roads are well maintained, and there's even a small commercial center, **Cruz Bay,** on the island's western tip. Don't come here for nightlife, though: St. John is definitely sleepy, and that's why people love it.

To get to St. John, you first pass through St. Thomas, then take the ferry. (There are also ferries from the British Virgin Islands.) See the "Getting There" section at the beginning of this chapter for information on how to get to St. Thomas.

The **tourist office** (☎ **340/776-6450**) is located near the Battery, a 1735 fort that's a short walk from the St. Thomas ferry dock. It's open Monday to Friday from 8am to noon and 1 to 5pm.

GETTING AROUND

BY BUS OR TAXI   The most popular way to get around is by the local **Vitran** service, the same company that runs bus service on St. Thomas. Buses run between Cruz Bay and Coral Bay, costing $1 for adults and 75¢ for children. An open-air **surrey-style taxi** is more fun, however. Typical fares are $4 to Trunk Bay, $5.50 to Cinnamon Bay, or $10 to Mahoe Bay. Between midnight and 6am, fares are increased by 40%. Call ☎ **340/693-7530** for more information.

BY RENTAL CAR OR JEEP   The island's undeveloped roads offers some of the best views anywhere. Because of this, many people opt to rent a vehicle (sometimes with four-wheel drive) to tour the island. Most visitors need a car for only a day or two. Just remember to *drive on the left,* and follow posted speed limits, which are generally very low.

Unless you have luggage, which should probably be locked away in a trunk, you might consider one of the sturdy, open-sided, jeep-like vehicles that offer the best view of the surroundings and the most fun way to tour St. John. Note that most of these vehicles have manual transmission.

The two largest car-rental agencies on St. John are **Hertz** (☎ **800/654-3001** or 340/693-7580) and **Avis** (☎ **800/331-1212** or 340/776-6374). If you want a local

Travel Tip

If you need a pharmacy, or want to purchase film, magazines, books, and other daily necessities, head to **St. John Drugcenter,** in the Boulon Shopping Center, Cruz Bay (☎ **340/776-6353**). It's open Monday to Saturday from 9am to 6pm and Sunday from 10am to 2pm.

firm, try **St. John Car Rental,** across from the post office in Cruz Bay (☎ **340/ 776-6103**). Its stock is limited to Jeep Wranglers, Jeep Cherokees, and Suzuki Side-kicks.

WHERE TO STAY
LUXURY RESORTS

✪ **Caneel Bay.** Virgin Islands National Park, St. John, U.S.V.I. 00831. ☎ **800/928-8889** or 340/776-6111. Fax 340/693-8280. www.roewood-hotels.com. E-mail: caneelbay@worldnet. att.net. 166 units. MINIBAR. Winter $350–$700 double. Off-season $250–$525 double. MAP (breakfast and dinner) $75 per person extra. AE, DC, MC, V.

In 1956, Caneel Bay, the dream and creation of megamillionaire Laurance S. Rocke-feller, became the original ecoresort. Though it's long been one of the premier resorts of the Caribbean, Caneel Bay is definitely not one of the most luxurious. A devoted fan once told us, "It's like living at summer camp." That means no phones or TV in the rooms, and sometimes no air-conditioning. Nevertheless, the movers and shakers of the world continue to descend on this place, though younger people tend to head elsewhere. To attract more families, young children are now allowed here.

The resort lies on a 170-acre portion of the national park, offering a choice of seven beaches. The main buildings are strung along the bays, with a Caribbean lounge and dining room at the core. Other buildings housing guest rooms stand along the beaches. The savvy traveler should request one of the six rooms in cottage no. 7, over-looking two of the most idyllic beaches, Scott and Paradise. Most rooms, however, are set back on low cliffs or headlands. The decor within is understated, with Indonesian wicker furniture, hand-woven fabrics, sisal mats, and plantation fans. Gardens sur-round all buildings. Many of the rooms are being renovated, and air-conditioning—at long last—is being installed in some units.

Dining: The intimate Turtle Bay dining room has made a comeback. You can enjoy drinks at the Caneel Bay Bar, beneath the soaring ceiling of a stone-and-timber pavilion.

Amenities: Full-service dive shop and water-sports activities desk, fitness facility with free weight and cardiovascular training equipment, business center, children's play area, 11 tennis courts, free use of Sunfish sailboats and Windsurfers, pool, snor-keling gear, kayaks, an array of scheduled garden tours, diving excursions to offshore wrecks, deep-sea fishing, free snorkeling lessons, tennis clinics and lessons, baby-sit-ting, valet laundry.

Westin Resort St. John. Great Cruz Bay, St. John U.S.V.I. 00831. ☎ **800/808-5020** or 340/693-8000. Fax 340/693-8888. www.westin.com. 285 units. A/C MINIBAR TV TEL. Winter $425–$575 double; $850–$995 suite. Off-season $254–$420 double; $475–$860 suite. AE, DC, MC, V. Round-trip shuttle bus and private ferryboat transfers from St. Thomas airport $65 per person.

This is the most architecturally dramatic and visually appealing hotel on St. John. The new owners have vastly improved the resort since its less fortunate times in the early 1990s. The complex is set on 34 gently sloping, intricately landscaped acres on the southwest side of the island, and consists of 13 cedar-roofed postmodern buildings,

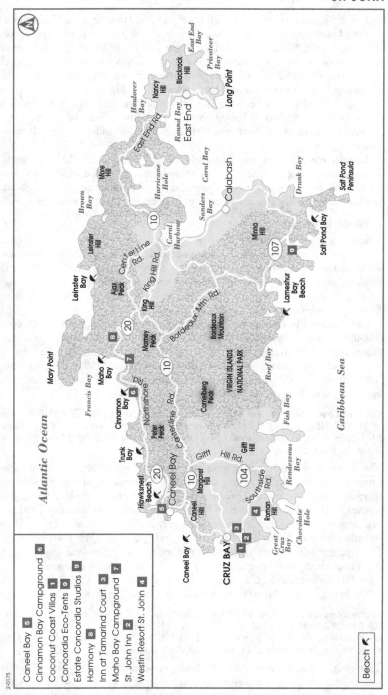

St. John

Atlantic Ocean

Caribbean Sea

Caneel Bay 5
Cinnamon Bay Campground 6
Coconut Coast Villas 1
Concordia Eco-Tents 9
Estate Concordia Studios 9
Harmony 8
Inn at Tamarind Court 3
Maho Bay Campground 7
St. John Inn 2
Westin Resort St. John 4

Beach

2-0175

717

each with ziggurat-shaped angles, soaring ceilings, and large windows. Herringbone-patterned brick walkways connect the gardens (with 400 palms imported from Puerto Rico) with the 1,200-foot beach and the largest pool in the Virgin Islands. Some of the stylish accommodations contain fan-shaped windows and curved ceilings. All units open onto private balconies, and some have their own whirlpools.

Dining: Four separate restaurants keep guests well fed. The most upscale and experimental is Coccoloba. The Beach Café offers both buffet and à la carte meals. Snorkels Bar and Grill is set beside the resort's massive pool. And to ward off hunger pangs between meals, the Mango Deli serves New York–style deli sandwiches and take-away snacks.

Amenities: A pool with more than a half-acre of water surface, six lit tennis courts, fitness center with spa services, 24-hour room service, supervised activities program for children, baby-sitting, laundry, organized diving and fishing excursions, sailboats, windsurfers, snorkeling gear, and a concierge who arranges island tours and car rentals.

CONDOS & VILLAS

Villa vacations are on the rise on St. John for travelers who want a home away from home. There are actually more villa and condo beds available on St. John than there are hotel beds. These units offer spaciousness and comfort, as well as privacy and freedom, and often come with fully equipped kitchens, dining areas, bedrooms, and such amenities as VCRs and patio grills. Rentals range from large multiroom resort homes to simply decorated one-bedroom condos.

Caribbean Villas & Resorts, P.O. Box 458, St. John, U.S.V.I. 00831 (☎ **800/ 338-0987** in the U.S., or 340/776-6152; fax 340/779-4044), the island's biggest real-estate agency, is an excellent choice. Most condos go for less than $210 per night (a Cruz View two-bedroom unit for four costs $220 in winter, $150 in the off-season), though private homes are more expensive. Children 5 and under stay free; no credit cards are accepted.

Coconut Coast Villas. P.O. Box 618, Cruz Bay, St. John, U.S.V.I. 00831. ☎ **800/858-7989** or 340/693-9100. Fax 340/779-4157. www.coconutcoast.com. 9 units. A/C TV TEL. Winter $185–$235 studio; $285–$375 town house. Off-season $110–$145 studio; $175–$235 town house. No credit cards.

This is one of the island's most affordable properties on the water's edge (besides campgrounds), and within walking distance of the center of Cruz Bay. All units are decorated with contemporary Caribbean flair, including artwork by a local Caneel Bay resident. Each of the five studio units has its own kitchen, private bathroom, and private deck overlooking the Caribbean, and can sleep up to three comfortably. More recently built town houses are perfect for groups up to eight. These town houses are fully equipped with everything from coffeemakers to stereos. The small snorkel beach has lounge chairs, where you can sit on a calm day and spot fish swimming close to shore. The home of the helpful managers is right on the property. Car rentals, day trips to Virgin Gorda, and all types of water sports can be arranged, including scuba diving.

Estate Concordia Studios. 20–27 Estate Concordia, Coral Bay, St. John, U.S.V.I. 00830. ☎ **800/392-9004** in the U.S. and Canada, or 212/472-9453 in New York City. Fax 212/ 861-6210 in New York City. 9 units. Winter $135–$190 studio for two. Off-season $95–$150 studio for two. Extra person $25 in winter, $15 in off-season. MC, V.

This environmentally correct, 51-acre development has been widely praised for its integration with the local ecosystem. Its elevated structures were designed to coexist with the stunning southern edge of St. John. The secluded property is nestled on a low cliff above a salt pond, surrounded by hundreds of acres of pristine national park.

It's best for those with a rental vehicle. Each building was designed to protect mature trees, and is connected to its neighbors with boardwalks. The nine studios are contained in six postmodern cottages. Each unit comes with a kitchen, bathroom, balcony, and ceiling fan; some have an extra bedroom. There's also a hillside pool and guest laundry facilities. On-site management assists with activity suggestions. For information on the on-site **Eco-Tents,** refer to "Campgrounds," below.

Harmony. P.O. Box 310, Cruz Bay, St. John, U.S.V.I. 00831. ☎ **800/392-9004** in the U.S. and Canada, 212/472-9453 in New York City, or 340/776-6226. Fax 340/776-6504, or 212/861-6210 in New York City. E-mail: mahony@maho.org. 12 units. Winter $165–$195 studio for 2. Off-season $105–$135 studio for 2. Extra person $25. 7-night minimum stay in winter. DISC, MC, V.

Built on a hillside above the Maho Bay Campground, this is a small-scale cluster of 12 luxury studios in six two-story houses with views sweeping down to the sea. The complex is designed to combine both ecological technology and comfort; it's one of the few resorts in the Caribbean to operate exclusively on sun and wind power. Most of the building materials are derived from recycled materials, including reconstituted plastic and glass containers, newsprint, old tires, and scrap lumber. The managers and staff are committed to offering educational experiences, as well as the services of a small-scale resort. The studios contain tiled bathrooms, kitchenettes, dining areas, and outdoor terraces. Guests can walk a short distance downhill to use the restaurant, grocery store, and water-sports facilities at the Maho Bay campground.

GUEST HOUSES

The following places offer just the basics, but they're fine if you're not too finicky.

The Inn at Tamarind Court. South Shore Rd. (P.O. Box 350), Cruz Bay, St. John, U.S.V.I. 00831. ☎ **800/221-1637** or 340/776-6378. Fax 340/776-6722. www.tamarindcourt.com. E-mail: tamarind@worldnet.att.net. 23 units. Winter $88 double with bathroom; $118 apt; $138 suite. Off-season $68 double with bathroom; $98 apt; $118 suite. Rates include continental breakfast. AE, DISC, MC, V.

Right outside Cruz Bay but still within walking distance of the ferryboat dock, this modest establishment consists of a small hotel and an even simpler West Indian inn. Bedrooms are small, evoking those in a little country motel. Most have twin beds. Bathrooms in the inn are shared; units in the hotel have small private bathrooms. The establishment's social life revolves around its courtyard bar and restaurant, Pa Pa Bulls. From the hotel, you can walk to shuttles taking you to the beaches.

✪ **St. John Inn.** P.O. Box 37, Cruz Bay, St. John, U.S.V.I. 00831. ☎ **800/666-7688** in the U.S., or 340/693-8688. 12 units. A/C TV TEL. Winter $95–$175 double. Off-season $60–$120 double. Extra person $15. Rates include continental breakfast. AE, DC, DISC, MC, V.

The old Cruz Inn, once the budget staple of the island, has been given a new lease on life and reincarnated as the St. John Inn. Although its rates have gone up, it has also been much improved. The inn overlooks Enighed Pond, only a few blocks from the Cruz Bay Dock area. Accommodations have a light, airy, California feel. The small- to medium-size bedrooms have wrought-iron beds and new mattresses, handcrafted pine armoires, and a touch of Ralph Lauren flair to make for an inviting nest. The junior suites contain full sofa beds, kitchenettes, and sitting areas. Bathrooms are small. You can meet fellow guests by the hotel pool or at the bar. The inn offers a 43-foot motor yacht, *Hollywood Waltz,* for daily excursions to private snorkeling spots along the coast and private beaches on uninhabited islands.

CAMPGROUNDS

✪ **Cinnamon Bay Campground.** P.O. Box 720, Cruz Bay, St. John, U.S.V.I. 00831.
☎ **800/539-9998** in the U.S., or 340/776-6330. Fax 340/776-6458. 126 units, none with
bathroom. Winter $95–$105 cottage for two; $75 tent site; $17 bare site. Off-season $63–$68
cottage for two; $48 tent site; $17 bare site (5-day minimum). Extra person $15. AE, MC, V.

This National Park Service campground is the most complete in the Caribbean. The
site is directly on the beach, surrounded by thousands of acres of tropical vegetation.
Life is simple here: You have a choice of a tent, a cottage, or a bare site. At the bare
campsites, nothing is provided except general facilities. The canvas tents are 10 by 14
feet with a floor, and come with a number of extras, including all cooking equipment;
even your linen is changed weekly. The cottages are 15 by 15 feet, consisting of a room
with two concrete walls and two screen walls. They contain cooking facilities and four
twin beds with thin mattresses; two cots can be added. Lavatories and cool-water
showers are in separate buildings nearby. Camping is limited to a 2-week period in any
given year. Near the road is the office, with a grocery and a cafeteria (dinners cost
$15).

Concordia Eco-Tents. 20–27 Estate Concordia, Coral Bay, St. John, U.S.V.I. 00830.
☎ **800/392-9004** or 212/472-9453 for reservations. Fax 212/861-6210. 11 tent-cottages.
Winter $110–$120 tent for two. Off-season $70 tent for two. Extra person $25 in winter, $15
in off-season. DISC, MC, V.

The Eco-Tents are the newest addition to Stanley Selengut's celebrated Concordia
development project on the southern tip of St. John, overlooking Salt Pond Bay and
Ram Head Point. These solar- and wind-powered tent-cottages combine sustainable
technology with some of the most spectacular views on the island. The light framing,
fabric walls, and large screened-in windows lend a tree-house atmosphere to guests'
experience. Set on the windward side of the island, the tent-cottages enjoy natural ventilation from the cooling trade winds. Inside, each has two twin beds with rather thin
mattresses in each bedroom, one or two twin mattresses on a loft platform, and a
queen-size futon in the living-room area (each can sleep up to six people comfortably).
Each kitchen comes equipped with a running-water sink, propane stove, and cooler.
In addition, each Eco-Tent has a small private shower, rather meager towels, and a
composting toilet.

   The secluded hillside location, surrounded by hundreds of acres of pristine national
park land, requires guests to arrange for a rental vehicle. Beaches, hikes, and the shops
and restaurants of Coral Bay are only a 10-minute drive from the property. For a recommendation of regular on-site studios, see the Estate Concordia Studios, above.

✪ **Maho Bay.** P.O. Box 310, Cruz Bay, St. John, U.S.V.I. 00831. ☎ **800/392-9004,**
212/472-9453 in New York City, or 340/776-6226. Fax 340/776-6504, or 212/816-6210 in
New York City. E-mail: mahony@maho.org. 114 tent-cottages, none with bathroom. Winter
$105 tent-cottage for two (minimum stay of 7 nights). Off-season $60 tent-cottage for two.
Extra person $15. MC, V.

Maho Bay, an 8-mile drive northeast from Cruz Bay, is an interesting concept in
ecology vacationing, where you camp close to nature, but with considerable comfort.
It's set on a hillside above the beach surrounded by the Virgin Islands National Park.
To preserve the existing ground cover, all 114 tent-cottages are on platforms above a
thickly wooded slope. Utility lines and pipes are hidden under wooden boardwalks
and stairs. Each tent-cottage, covered with canvas and screens, has two twin beds with
thin mattresses, a couch, electric lamps and outlets, a dining table, chairs, a propane
stove, an ice chest (cooler), linen, thin towels, and cooking and eating utensils. Guests
share communal bathhouses.

Maho Bay's open-air Pavilion Restaurant serves breakfast and dinner. The Pavilion also functions as an amphitheater and community center where various programs are featured. A store sells supplies. The water-sports program here is excellent.

WHERE TO DINE

St. John has some posh dining, particularly at the luxury resorts like Caneel Bay, but it also has West Indian establishments with plenty of local color and flavor. Many of the restaurants here command high prices, but you can lunch almost anywhere at reasonable rates. Dinner is often an event on St. John, since it's about the only form of nightlife the island has.

EXPENSIVE

✪ **Asolare.** Cruz Bay. ☎ **340/779-4747.** Reservations required. Main courses $22–$28. AE, MC, V. Daily 5:30–9:30pm. FRENCH/ASIAN.

This is the most beautiful and elegant restaurant on St. John, with the hippest and best-looking staff. Asolare sits on top of a hill overlooking Cruz Bay and some of the British Virgin Islands. *Asolare* translates as "the leisurely passing of time without purpose," and that's what many diners prefer to do here. The chef roams the world for inspiration, and cooks with flavor and flair, using some of the best and freshest ingredients available on island. To begin, try the prawn and coconut-milk soup or the stone-seared carpaccio. For a main course, you might be tempted by crispy Peking duckling with a chestnut glaze, or perhaps catfish wrapped in banana leaves with a plantain and lime curry sauce. Truly excellent is the lime sauté chicken with a yellow curry sauce and the sashimi tuna on a sizzling plate with a plum-passion fruit sake vinaigrette. For dessert, try the frozen mango guava soufflé or the chocolate pyramid cake.

Ellington's. Gallows Point, Cruz Bay. ☎ **340/693-8490.** Reservations required only for seating upstairs. Main courses $25–$38. AE, MC, V. Daily 4:30–10pm. CONTINENTAL.

Ellington's is set near the neocolonial villas of Gallows Point, to the right after you disembark from the ferry. Its exterior has the kind of double staircase, fan windows, louvers, and low-slung roof found in an 18th-century Danish manor house. Drop in at sunset for a drink on the panoramic upper deck, where an unsurpassed view of St. Thomas and its neighboring cays unfolds. The establishment is named after a local radio announcer, a raconteur and mystery writer whose real-estate developments helped transform St. John into a stylish enclave for the American literati of the 1950s and '60s. The dinner menu changes often to accommodate the freshest offerings of the sea. Conch fritters or toasted ravioli might get you started, or else you could opt for one of the soups—none finer than a Caribbean seafood chowder. For a main course, we always go for the Caribbean mixed grill, with lobster, shrimp, and fresh fish grilled to perfection. Blackened swordfish and wahoo or mahimahi with Cajun spices are also excellent choices, as are the pastas. The chicken martinique comes with pineapples, bananas, and dark rum topped with coconut. Vegetarian specials are also featured nightly.

Le Château de Bordeaux. Junction 10, Centerline Rd., Bordeaux Mountain. ☎ **340/776-6611.** Reservations recommended. Main courses $21–$34. MC, V. Mon–Sat two nightly seatings, 5:30–6:30pm and 7:30–8:45pm. Closed Sun–Mon in summer. CONTINENTAL/CARIBBEAN.

This restaurant is 5 miles east of Cruz Bay, near the geographical center of the island and close to one of its highest points. It's known for having some of the best views on St. John. A lunch grill on the patio serves burgers and drinks Monday through

Saturday from 10am to 4:30pm. In the evening, amid a Victorian decor with lace tablecloths, you can begin with a house-smoked chicken spring roll or a velvety carrot soup. After that, move on to one of the saffron-flavored pastas or a savory West Indian seafood chowder. Smoked salmon and filet mignon are a bow to the international crowd, although the wild-game specials are more unusual. The well-flavored Dijmand pecan-crusted roast rack of lamb with a shallot port reduction is also a good choice. For dessert, there's a changing array of cheesecakes, among other options. The specialty drink is a passion-fruit daiquiri.

✪ **Paradiso.** Mongoose Junction. ☎ **340/693-8899.** Reservations recommended. Main courses $20–$30. AE, MC, V. Daily 11am–3pm and 5:30–9:30pm. Bar daily 5–10pm. Closed Aug–Nov. CONTEMPORARY/AMERICAN.

This is the most talked-about restaurant on St. John, other than Asolare (see above), and the only one that's air-conditioned. The interior has lots of brass, glowing hardwoods, and nautical antiques, not to mention the most beautiful bar on the island, crafted from mahogany, purpleheart, and angelique.

Every dish has real flavor. Try such appetizers as shrimp and lobster dumplings with pineapple salsa and a mango vinaigrette. A roasted garlic Caesar salad with sun-dried tomatoes and a parmesan grizzini is a new twist on this classic dish. But the chefs truly shine in their main dishes, especially pan-roasted sea bass with baby beets and cannellini or grilled veal medallions with pastrami-cured duck breast and arugula. Even chicken breast is given new zest and flair, stuffed with prosciutto, asiago cheese, and basil, and served with garlic mashed potatoes.

MODERATE

Café Roma. Cruz Bay. ☎ **340/776-6524.** Reservations not necessary. Main courses $9–$18. MC, V. Daily 5–10pm. ITALIAN.

This restaurant in the center of Cruz Bay is not a place for great finesse in the kitchen, but it's a long-standing favorite, and has pleased a lot of diners seeking informal meals. To enter, you have to climb a flight of stairs. You might arrive early and have a strawberry colada, then enjoy a standard pasta, veal, seafood, or chicken dish. There are usually 30 to 40 vegetarian items on the menu. The owner claims, with justification, that his pizzas are the best on the island; try the white pizza. Italian wines are sold by the glass or bottle, and you can end the evening with an espresso.

✪ **La Tapa.** Centerline Road, across from Scotia Bank, Cruz Bay. ☎ **340/693-7755.** Reservations recommended. Tapas $4–$5; main courses $15–$25. AE, MC, V. Mon–Sat 6–10pm. INTERNATIONAL.

This is one of our favorite restaurants in Cruz Bay, where you can sample the *tapas*, Spanish-inspired bite-size morsels of fish, meat, or marinated vegetables, accompanied by pitchers of sangria. There's a tiny bar with no more than five stools, a two-tiered dining room, and lots of original paintings (the establishment doubles as an art gallery for emerging local artists). Menu items are thoughtful and well-conceived, and include fast-seared tuna with a Basque-inspired relish of onions, peppers, garlic, and herbs; filet mignon with gorgonzola, caramelized onions, and port; and linguine with shrimp, red peppers, and leeks in a peanut sauce.

Mongoose Deli/Global Village Restaurant. Mongoose Junction. ☎ **340/693-8677.** Reservations not necessary. Sandwiches in deli $5–$9. Main courses in restaurant $6–$10 lunch, $16–$24 dinner. AE, MC, V. Deli daily 7am–8pm; restaurant daily 8:30am–10pm; bar daily 11:30am–midnight or later, depending on business. AMERICAN.

At this popular deli and outdoor restaurant, you'll get hints of the culinary traditions of California, and just a whiff of New Age thinking, in a setting that's soothing, woodsy, and very, very tropical. The to-go service at the deli provides one of the best options on St. John for an overstuffed sandwich. There's a cluster of wooden tables near the deli if you prefer to eat here. Breads are baked fresh every day.

More substantial, and more esoteric, fare is served in the restaurant, where the vegetation of a tropical forest extends up to the deck, and where a high roof and a lack of walls give the impression of eating outdoors. You can always precede or end a meal at the center-stage bar. Perennially popular drinks include rum-and-fruit-based painkillers or a dessert-inspired "chocolate chiquita" (rum, bananas, and chocolate ice cream). Menu items at lunch include quesadillas, burgers, grilled chicken, and blackened tuna sandwiches. At dinner, they include fresh grilled or sautéed fish, often served with a salsa made from local fruits; margarita-marinated shrimp; mahimahi with a cashew crust; and lots of vegetarian options as well.

Morgan's Mango. Cruz Bay (across from the National Park dock). ☎ 340/693-8141. Reservations recommended. Main courses $7.95–$24.95. AE, MC, V. Daily 6–10pm. Bar opens at 5:30pm. CARIBBEAN.

The chefs here roam the Caribbean for tantalizing flavors, which they adapt for their ever-changing menu. The restaurant is easy to spot, with its big canopy, the only protection from the elements. The bar wraps around the main dining room and offers some 30 frozen drinks. Thursday is Margarita Night, when a soft-rock duo plays. Some think the kitchen tries to do too much with the nightly menu, but it does produce some zesty fare—everything from Anegada lobster cakes to a spicy Jamaican pickapepper steak. Try flying fish served as an appetizer, followed by Haitian voodoo snapper pressed in Cajun spices, then grilled and served with fresh fruit salsa. Equally delectable is mahimahi in a Cruzan rum and mango sauce. You can also order more standard steak, chicken, and vegetarian dishes. The knockout dessert is the mango-banana pie.

Pusser's of the West Indies. Wharfside Village, Cruz Bay. ☎ **340/693-8489.** Reservations recommended. Main courses $11.95–$21.95; pizzas $9.95–$11.95. AE, MC, V. Daily 11am–10pm. INTERNATIONAL/CARIBBEAN/PIZZA.

This two-story, air-conditioned store and pub in Cruz Bay overlooks the harbor and is near the ferry dock. You face a choice of three bars here: the Beach Bar, where you can enjoy food while still in your bathing suit; the Oyster Bar, the main dining area; and the Crow's Nest. Each offers the same food, as well as lots of Pusser's Rum, a blend of five West Indian rums that the Royal Navy has served to its men for 3 centuries. You can enjoy traditional English fare, including steak and ale, or try the jerk tuna fillet, the jerk chicken with a tomato-basil sauce over penne, or the spaghetti with lobster cooked in rum, wine, lemon juice, and garlic. Caribbean lobster is another favorite, as is the chicken Tropical, which features coconut-encrusted, pan-seared chicken served up with a rum and banana sauce with macadamia nuts. Finish your meal with Pusser's famous mud pie. The food is satisfying, competent, and not a lot more, but after all that Pusser rum, will you notice?

✪ **Shipwreck Landing.** 34 Freeman's Ground, Rte. 107, Coral Bay. ☎ **340/693-5640.** Reservations requested. Main courses $9.75–$15.25; lunch from $5.75–$10.75. AE, MC, V. Daily 11am–10pm. Bar daily 11am–11pm. SEAFOOD/CONTINENTAL.

Eight miles east of Cruz Bay on the road to Salt Pond Beach, Shipwreck Landing offers palms and tropical plants on a veranda overlooking the sea. The intimate bar specializes in tropical frozen drinks. Lunch isn't ignored here, and there's a lot more than sandwiches, salads, and burgers—try pan-seared blackened snapper in Cajun spices, or conch fritters to get you going. The chef shines brighter at night, though, offering a pasta of the day along with such specialties as a rather tantalizing Caribbean blackened shrimp. A lot of the fare is routine, including New York strip steak and fish-and-chips, but the grilled mahimahi in lime butter is worth the trip. Entertainment, including jazz and reggae, is featured Friday through Sunday nights, with no cover.

INEXPENSIVE

Vie's Snack Shack. East End Rd. (12½ miles east of Cruz Bay). ☎ **340/693-5033.** Main courses $4.95–$6.50. No credit cards. Tues–Sat 10am–5pm (but call first!) WEST INDIAN.

Vie's looks like little more than a plywood-sided hut, but its charming and gregarious owner is known as one of the best local chefs on St. John. Her garlic chicken is famous. She also serves conch fritters, johnnycakes, island-style beef pâtés, and coconut and pineapple tarts. Don't leave without a glass of homemade limeade. The place is open most days, but as Vie says, "Some days, we might not be here at all"—so you'd better call before you head out.

HITTING THE BEACH

The best beach, hands down, is ✪ **Trunk Bay,** the biggest attraction on St. John. To miss its picture-perfect shoreline of white sand would be like touring Europe and skipping Paris. Often cited as one of the loveliest beaches in the Caribbean, it offers ideal conditions for diving, snorkeling, swimming, and sailing. The only drawback is the crowds—watch for pickpockets. Beginning snorkelers in particular are attracted to the underwater trail near the shore (see "Sports & Outdoor Pursuits," below). You can rent snorkel gear here. Lifeguards are on duty. Admission is $4 per person for those over 16. If you're coming from St. Thomas, both taxis and "safari buses" to Trunk Bay meet the ferry from Red Hook when it docks at Cruz Bay.

Caneel Bay, the stomping ground of the rich and famous, has seven beautiful beaches on its 170 acres. However, six of the beaches can only be reached by private boat, and one of those six, beautiful **Hawksnest Beach,** is only available to guests of the resort. The exception is **Caneel Bay Beach,** which is open to everyone and easy to reach from the main entrance of the Caneel resort. A staff member at the gatehouse will provide directions. Safari buses and taxis from Cruz Bay will take you along North Shore Road.

The campgrounds of **Cinnamon Bay** have their own beach, where forest rangers sometimes have to remind visitors to put their swim trunks back on. This is our particular favorite, a beautiful strip of white sand with hiking trails, great windsurfing, ruins, and feral donkeys (don't feed or pet them!). Changing rooms and showers are available, and you can rent water-sports equipment. Snorkeling is especially popular; you'll often see big schools of purple triggerfish. This beach is better in the morning or at midday, as afternoons are likely to be windy. A marked nature trail, with signs identifying the flora, loops through a tropical forest on even turf before leading straight up to Centerline Road.

Maho Bay Beach is immediately to the east of Cinnamon Bay, and also borders campgrounds. As you lie on the sand here, you can take in a whole hillside of pitched tents. This is also a popular beach, often with the campers themselves.

Francis Bay Beach and **Watermelon Cay Beach** are just a few more of the beaches you'll encounter traveling eastward along St. John's gently curving coastline. The beach at **Leinster Bay** is another haven for those seeking the solace of a private sunny retreat. You can swim in the bay's shallow water or snorkel over the spectacular and colorful coral reef, perhaps in the company of an occasional turtle or stingray.

The remote **Salt Pond Bay** is known to locals, but often missed by visitors. It's on the beautiful coast in the southeast, adjacent to Coral Bay. The bay is tranquil, but the beach is somewhat rocky. It's a short walk down the hill from a parking lot (be careful if you park here, as a few cars have recently been broken into). The snorkeling is good, and the bay has some fascinating tidal pools. The Ram Head Trail beginning here and winding for a mile leads to a belvedere overlooking the bay. Facilities are meager but include an outhouse and a scattering of tattered picnic tables.

If you want to escape the crowds, head for **Lameshur Bay Beach,** along the rugged south coast, west of Salt Pond Bay and accessible only via a bumpy dirt road. The sands are beautiful and the snorkeling is excellent. You can also take a 5-minute stroll down the road past the beach to explore the nearby ruins of an old plantation estate that was destroyed in a slave revolt.

Does St. John have a nude beach? Not officially, but lovely **Solomon Bay Beach** is a contender, although park rangers of late have sometimes asked people to put their swimwear back on. Leave Cruz Bay on Route 20 and turn left at the park service sign, about a quarter mile past the visitor center. Park at the end of a cul-de-sac, then walk along the trail for about 15 minutes. Go early, and you'll practically have the beach to yourself.

SPORTS & OUTDOOR PURSUITS

St. John offers some of the best snorkeling, scuba diving, swimming, fishing, hiking, sailing, and underwater photography in the Caribbean. The island is known for Virgin Islands National Park, as well as for its coral-sand beaches, winding mountain roads, hidden coves, and trails that lead past old, bush-covered sugarcane plantations. However, don't visit St. John expecting to play golf.

The most complete line of water-sports equipment available, including rentals for windsurfing, kayaking, and sailing, is offered at the **Cinnamon Bay Watersports Center,** on Cinnamon Bay Beach (☎ 340/776-6330). One- and two-person sit-on-top kayaks rent for $10 to $17 per hour. You can also sail away in a 12- or 14-foot Hobie monohull **sailboat,** for $20 to $30 per hour.

BOAT EXCURSIONS   You can take half- and full-day boat trips, including a full-day excursion to the Baths at Virgin Gorda, for $85. An "Around St. John Snorkel Excursion" costs $50 per person. Call **Vacation Vistas and Motor Yachts** (☎ 340/776-6462) for details. **Cruz Bay Watersports** offers trips to the British Virgin Islands (bring your passport) for $80, including food and beverages.

FISHING   Outfitters located on St. Thomas offer sport-fishing trips here—they'll come over and pick you up. Call the **St. Thomas Sportfishing Center** (☎ 340/775-7990) at Red Hook. **St. John World Class Anglers** (☎ 340/775-4281) offers light-tackle shore and offshore fishing. Count on spending from $350 to $500 per party for a half day of fishing.

HIKING   Because of St. John's semiwild state, many hikers and trekkers consider a visit here among the most rewarding in the Virgin Islands. The terrain ranges from arid and dry (in the east) to moist and semitropical (in the northwest). The island boasts more than 800 species of plants, 160 species of birds, and more than 20 trails maintained in fine form by the island's crew of park rangers. Much of the land on the island is designated as **Virgin Island's National Park.** Visitors are encouraged to stop by the **Cruz Bay Visitor Center,** where you can pick up the park brochure, which includes a map of the park, and the *Virgin Islands National Park News,* which has the latest information on park activities.

St. John is laced with a wide choice of clearly marked walking paths. At least 20 of these originate from North Shore Road (Route 20) or from the island's main east-west artery, Centerline Road (Route 10). Each is marked at its starting point with a pre-planned itinerary; the walks can last anywhere from 10 minutes to 2 hours. Maps are available from the national park headquarters at Cruz Bay.

One of our favorite hikes, the **Annaberg Historic Trail** (identified by the National Park Service as trail no. 10) requires only about a half-mile stroll. It departs from a clearly marked point along the island's north coast, near the junction of routes 10 and 20. This self-guided tour passes the partially restored ruins of a manor house built during the 1700s. Signs along the way give historical and botanical data. Visiting the ruins costs $4 per person for those over 16. If you want to prolong your hiking experience, take the **Leinster Bay Trail** (trail no. 11), which begins near the point where trail no. 10 ends. It leads past mangrove swamps and coral inlets rich with plant and marine life; markers identify some of the plants and animals. For information on the **Cinnamon Bay Trail,** see the Driving Tour in "Exploring St. John."

Another series of hikes traversing the more arid eastern section of St. John originate at clearly marked points along the island's **southeastern tip,** off Route 107. Many of the trails wind through the grounds of 18th-century plantations, past ruined schoolhouses, rum distilleries, molasses factories, and great houses, many of which are covered with lush, encroaching vines and trees.

The **National Park Service** (☎ **340/776-6330** or 340/776-6201) provides a number of ranger-led activities. One of the most popular is the guided 2½-mile **Reef Bay Hike.** Included is a stop at the only known petroglyphs on the island and a tour of the sugar-mill ruins. A park ranger discusses the area's natural and cultural history along the way. The hike starts at 10am on Monday and Thursday, and costs $15 per person. Reservations are required and can be made by phone.

SCUBA DIVING & SNORKELING   **Cruz Bay Watersports,** P.O. Box 252, Palm Plaza, St. John (☎ **800/835-7730** or 340/776-6234), is a PADI and NAUI five-star diving center. Certifications can be arranged through a dive master, for $350. Beginner scuba lessons start at $75. Two-tank reef dives with all dive gear cost $75, and wreck dives, night dives, and dive packages are available. In addition, snorkel tours are offered daily.

Divers can ask about scuba packages at **Low Key Watersports,** Wharfside Village (☎ **800/835-7718** or 340/693-8999). All wreck dives offered are two-tank/two-location dives. One-tank dives cost $55 per person, with night dives going for $65. Snorkel tours are also available at $25 to $35 per person. Parasailing costs $50 per person. The center also rents water-sports gear, including masks, fins, snorkels, and dive skins, and arranges day sailing trips, kayaking tours, and deep-sea fishing.

Snorkeling gear can be rented from the Cinnamon Bay Watersports Center (see above) for $4, plus a $25 deposit. Two of the best **snorkeling spots** around St. John are ✪ **Leinster Bay** and ✪ **Haulover Bay.** Usually uncrowded Leinster Bay offers some of the best snorkeling in the U.S. Virgins. The water is calm, clear, and filled with brilliantly hued tropical fish. Haulover Bay is a favorite among locals. It's often deserted, and the waters often clearer than in other spots around St. John. The ledges, walls, and nooks here are set very close together, making the bay a lot of fun for anyone with a little bit of experience.

At Trunk Bay, you can take the ✪ **National Park Underwater Trail** (☎ **340/776-6201**), stretching for 650 feet, allowing you to identify what you see, everything from false coral to colonial anemones. You'll pass lavender sea fans and schools of silversides. Equipment rental costs $4, with a $25 refundable deposit. Rangers are on hand to provide information.

WINDSURFING   The windsurfing at Cinnamon Bay is some of the best anywhere, for either the beginner or the expert. The **Cinnamon Bay Watersports Center** (see above) rents high-quality equipment for all levels, even for kids. Boards cost $12 an hour; a 2-hour introductory lesson costs $40.

EXPLORING ST. JOHN

The best way to see St. John in a nutshell, especially if you're on a cruise-ship layover, is to take a 2-hour **taxi tour.** The cost is $30 for one or two passengers, or $15 per person for three or more. Almost any taxi at Cruz Bay will take you on these tours, or else you can call **St. John Taxi Association** (☎ 340/693-7530).

Many visitors spend time at **Cruz Bay,** where the ferry docks. This village has interesting bars, restaurants, boutiques, and pastel-painted houses. It's a bit sleepy, but relaxing after the fast pace of St. Thomas. The small **Elaine Ione Sprauve Museum** (☎ 340/776-6359), in the public library at Cruz Bay, exhibits some local artifacts. It's open Monday to Friday from 9am to 5pm; admission is free.

Most cruise-ship passengers dart through Cruz Bay and head for the island's biggest attraction, **Virgin Islands National Park** (☎ 340/776-6201). The park totals 12,624 acres, including submerged lands and water adjacent to St. John, and has more than 20 miles of hiking trails to explore. See "Sports & Outdoor Pursuits," above, for information on trails and organized park activities.

Other major sights on the island include **Trunk Bay** (see "Beaches," above), one of the world most beautiful beaches, and **Fort Berg** (also called Fortsberg), at Coral Bay, which served as the base for the soldiers who brutally crushed the 1733 slave revolt. Finally, try to make time for the **Annaberg Ruins** on Leinster Bay Road, where the Danes maintained a thriving plantation and sugar mill after 1718. It's located off North Shore Road east of Trunk Bay. Admission is $4 for those over 16. On certain days of the week (dates vary), guided walks of the area are given by park rangers. For information on the **Annaberg Historic Trail,** see "Sports & Outdoor Pursuits," above.

SHOPPING

Compared to St. Thomas, St. John's shopping isn't much, but what's here is interesting. The boutiques and shops of Cruz Bay are individualized and quite special. Most of the shops are clustered at **Mongoose Junction,** in a woodsy area beside the roadway, about a 5-minute walk from the ferry dock. We've already recommended restaurants in this complex (see "Where to Dine," above).

Before you leave the island, you'll want to visit the recently expanded **Wharfside Village,** just a few steps from the ferry-departure point. Here in this complex of courtyards, alleys, and shady patios is a mishmash of all sorts of boutiques, along with some restaurants, fast-food joints, and bars.

The most fun shopping on the island takes place on ✪ **St. John Saturday,** a colorful, drum-beating, spice-filled feast for the senses, held on the last Saturday of every month. This daylong event begins early in the morning in the center of town and spills across the park. Vendors hawk handmade items, ranging from jewelry to handcrafts and clothing, and especially food made from local ingredients. One vendor concocts soothing salves from recipes passed on by her ancestors; another designs and makes porcelain earrings; another flavors chicken and burgers with her own wonderful secret hickory barbecue sauce; yet another hollows out and carves gourds from local calabash trees.

Bamboula, Mongoose Junction (☎ 340/693-8699), has an unusual and very appealing collection of gifts from St. John, the Caribbean, India, Indonesia, and Central Africa. Its exoticism is unexpected and very pleasant. The store also has clothing for both men and women under its own label—hand-batiked soft cottons and rayons made for comfort in a hot climate

The Canvas Factory, Mongoose Junction (☎ 340/776-6196), produces its own handmade, rugged, colorful canvas bags, as well as sailing hats, soft-sided luggage, and cotton hats.

The **Clothing Studio,** Mongoose Junction (☎ 340/776-6585), is the Caribbean's oldest hand-painted–clothing studio. Here you can watch talented artists create original designs on fine tropical clothing, including swimwear and daytime and evening clothing, mainly for women and babies, with a few items for men.

Coconut Coast Studios, Frank Bay (☎ 340/776-6944), is the studio of Lucinda Schutt, one of the best watercolorists on the island, and Elaine Estern, who's especially known for her Caribbean landscapes. Elaine is the official artist for Westin Resorts; Lucinda is the artist for Caneel Bay. It's located 5 minutes from Cruz Bay; walk along the waterfront, bypassing Gallows Point.

At **Donald Schnell Studio,** Mongoose Junction (☎ 340/776-6420), Mr. Schnell and his assistants have created one of the finest collections of handmade pottery, sculpture, and blown glass in the Caribbean. The staff can be seen working daily. They're known for their rough-textured coral work. Water fountains are a specialty item, as are house signs and coral-pottery dinnerware.

Fabric Mill, Mongoose Junction (☎ 340/776-6194), features silk-screened and batik fabrics from around the world. Vibrant rugs and bed, bath, and table linens can add a Caribbean flair to your home. Whimsical soft sculpture, sarongs, scarves, and handbags are also made here.

Pusser's of the West Indies, Wharfside Village, Cruz Bay (☎ 340/693-8489), is a unique store/restaurant with a large collection of classically designed old-world travel and adventure clothing, along with unusual accessories.

R and I Patton Goldsmithing, Mongoose Junction (☎ 340/776-6548), is one of the oldest businesses on the island. Three-quarters of the merchandise here is made on St. John. There's a large selection of jewelry in sterling silver, gold, and precious stones. Also featured are the works of goldsmiths from outstanding American studios, as well as Spanish coins.

ST. JOHN AFTER DARK

Bring a good book. When it comes to nightlife, St. John is no St. Thomas, and everybody here seems to want to keep it that way. Most people are content to have a leisurely dinner and then head for bed.

Among the popular bars of Cruz Bay, **Pusser's,** at Wharfside Village, has the most convivial atmosphere. The **Caneel Bay Bar,** at the Caneel Bay Resort (☎ 340/776-6111), presents live music nightly from 8:30 to 11pm. The most popular drinks here include the Cool Caneel (local rum with sugar, lime, and anisette) and the trademark of the house, the Plantation Freeze (lime and orange juice with three different kinds of rum, bitters, and nutmeg).

The two places above are very touristy. If you'd like to drink and gossip with the locals, try **JJ's Texas Coast Café,** Cruz Bay (☎ 340/776-6908), a real dive, across the park from the ferry dock. The margaritas here are deservedly called lethal.

Also at Cruz Bay, check out the action at **Fred's** (☎ 340/776-6363), across from the Lime Inn. Fred's brings in bands and has dancing on Wednesday, Friday, and Sunday nights. It's just a little hole-in-the-wall and can get crowded fast.

The best sports bar on the island is **Skinny Legs,** Emmaus, Coral Bay, beyond the fire station (☎ 340/779-4982). This shack made of tin and wood happens to have the best hamburgers in St. John. (The chili dogs aren't bad, either.) The yachting crowd likes to hang out here, though you wouldn't know it at first glance—it often seems that the richer they are, the poorer they dress. The bar has a satellite dish, dartboard, and horseshoe pits. Live music is presented at least once a week.

Morgan's Mango (☎ 340/693-8141), a restaurant, is also one of the hottest watering holes on the island. It's in Cruz Bay, across from the national park dock.

Count yourself lucky if you get in on a crowded night in winter. The place became famous locally when it turned away Harrison Ford, who was vacationing at Caneel Bay. Thursday is Margarita Night.

As a final option, check out **Sea Breeze,** 4F Little Plantation, Coral Bay on Salt Pond Road (☎ **340/693-5824**), a laid-back, popular local hangout, where you can not only drink and enjoy live entertainment, but also order three meals a day. Each night a different chef demonstrates his or her specialties. The Sunday brunch from 9am to 2pm is an island highlight. Try the barbecued beef sandwich.

4 St. Croix

At 84 square miles, St. Croix is the largest of the U.S. Virgin Islands. At the east end—which actually is the easternmost point of the United States—the terrain is rocky and arid. The west end is lusher, and even includes a small "rain forest" of mango, mahogany, tree ferns, and dangling lianas. Between the two extremes are beautiful beaches, rolling hills, pastures, and, increasingly, miles of condos.

Columbus named the island *Santa Cruz* (Holy Cross) when he landed here on November 14, 1493. He anchored his ship off the north shore, but was quickly driven away by the spears, arrows, and axes of the Carib Indians. The French laid claim to the island in 1650, and the Danes purchased it from them in 1773. Under Danish rule, slave labor and sugarcane fields proliferated during a golden era for both planters and pirates, which came to an end in the latter half of the 19th century. Danish influence still permeates the island today.

See "Getting There" at the beginning of the chapter for details on flights to St. Croix.

GETTING AROUND

BY TAXI At Alexander Hamilton Airport, you'll find official taxi rates posted. From the airport, expect to pay about $12 for a ride to Christiansted and about $10 to Frederiksted. As the cabs are unmetered, agree on the rate before you get in. The **St. Croix Taxicab Association** (☎ 340/778-1088) offers door-to-door service.

BY BUS Air-conditioned buses run between Christiansted and Frederiksted about every 30 minutes daily between 5:30am and 9pm. They start at Tide Village, to the east of Christiansted, and go along Route 75 to the Golden Rock Shopping Center. They then make their way to Route 70, with stopovers at the Sunny Isle Shopping Center, La Reine Shopping Center, St. George Village Botanical Garden, and Whim Plantation Museum, before reaching Frederiksted. Bus service is also available from the airport to both Christiansted and Frederiksted. The fare is $1, or 50¢ for seniors. For more information, call ☎ **340/778-0898.**

BY RENTAL CAR Not to beat a dead horse, but do remember: *Driving is on the left.* In most rural areas, the speed limit is 35 mph; certain parts of the major artery, Route 66, are 55 mph. In towns and urban areas, the speed limit is 20 mph. Keep in mind that if you're going into the "bush country," you'll find the roads very difficult. Sometimes the government smoothes the roads out before the rainy season begins (often in October or November), but they deteriorate rapidly.

St. Croix offers moderately priced car rentals, even on cars with automatic transmission and air-conditioning. However, because of the island's higher-than-normal accident rate (which is partly the result of visitors who forget about driving on the left-hand side of the road), insurance costs are a bit higher than usual. **Avis** (☎ 800/331-2112), **Budget** (☎ 888/227-3359 or 340/778-9636), and **Hertz** (☎ 800/654-3001 or 340/778-1402) all maintain headquarters at the airport; look for their kiosks near the baggage-claim areas. Each of these three companies offers Suzuki Swifts, Suzuki Esteems, and Ford Escorts.

Collision-damage insurance costs $13.95 per day, depending on the company, and we feel it's a wise investment. Some credit-card companies grant collision-damage protection if you pay for the rental with their card. Verify coverage before you go.

BY BICYCLE **St. Croix Bike and Tours,** 5035 Cotton Valley, Christiansted (☎ 340/773-5004), offers bike rentals. Its 21-speed mountain bikes are best suited for the rugged terrain of St. Croix. The company also features a moderate 12-mile historical ecotour, which runs along the rolling western coast, and a 14-mile ridgeline tropical mountain-bike tour for the more experienced biker. Guides are knowledgeable about the social, political, and natural history of the island. Call for more information.

WHERE TO STAY

All rooms are subject to an 8% hotel room tax, which is not included in the rates given below.

VERY EXPENSIVE

✪ **Buccaneer.** 2 miles east of Christiansted on Rte. 82 (P.O. Box 25200), Gallows Bay, St. Croix, U.S.V.I. 00824. ☎ **800/255-3881** in the U.S., or 340/773-2100. Fax 340/773-8215. 150 units. A/C TEL. Winter $210–$575 double. Off-season $210–$390 double. Rates include continental breakfast. AE, DC, DISC, MC, V.

This large, luxurious, family-owned resort covers 240 acres and contains three of the island's best beaches. It also offers the best sports program on St. Croix. The property was once a cattle ranch and a sugar plantation; its first estate house, which dates from the mid–17th century, stands near a freshwater pool. Accommodations are either in the main building or in one of the beachside properties. The baronially arched main building has a lobby opening on drinking or viewing terraces, with a sea vista on two sides and Christiansted to the west. The rooms are fresh and comfortable, though some of the standard units are a bit small. All have wicker furnishings, fridges, and private safes. The best bathrooms are in the "Beachside Doubloons," and come complete with whirlpool tubs.

Dining/Diversions: Breakfast and dinner are served at the Terrace Restaurant and at the Little Mermaid Restaurant. Lunch is offered at the Mermaid and the Grotto. Dino's, long a popular St. Croix institution, has also opened here. (See "Where to Dine," below, for separate reviews on the Terrace Restaurant and Dino's.) There's nightly entertainment at the Terrace Lounge, with music ranging from jazz to steel drums.

Amenities: Pool, eight championship tennis courts, fitness center and health spa, 18-hole golf course, Kids Camp program (ages 2 to 12), 2-mile jogging trail. Trips to Buck Island can be arranged.

Sunterra Resorts Carambola Beach. P.O. Box 3031, Kingshill, St. Croix, U.S.V.I. 00851. ☎ **340/778-3800.** Fax 340/778-1682. www.sunterra.com. 151 units. A/C MINIBAR TV TEL. Winter $275–$370 double; $600 suite. Off-season $185–$270 double; $410 suite. AE, CB, DC, DISC, MC, V.

This hotel is set on 28 acres above Davis Bay, about a 30-minute drive from Christiansted. It's one of the largest hostelries on St. Croix, and lies adjacent to an outstanding golf course designed by Robert Trent Jones, Sr. Guests are housed in red-roofed, two-story buildings, each of which contains six units. The accommodations are furnished in rattan and wicker, with pastel colors; each has a balcony partially concealed from outside view, overlooking either the garden or sea. Rooms have an upmarket flair, with louvered doors, tile floors, and sometimes such extras as

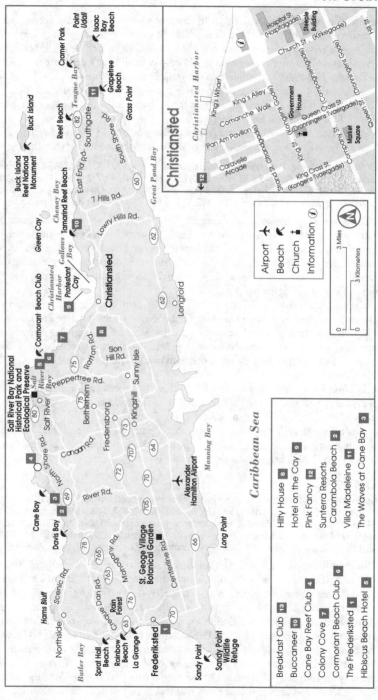

St. Croix

Christiansted

Hospital St. (Hospitalsgade)
Steeple Building
Church St. (Kirkegade)
King's Wharf
King's Alley
Comanche Walk
Government House
Pan Am Pavilion
Queen Cross St. (Dronningens Tvaergade)
Stand St. (Strandgade)
King St. (Kongens Gade)
Company St. (Compagniensgade)
Queen St. (Dronningens Gade)
Hill St.
Caravelle Arcade
Market Square
King Cross St. (Kongens Tvaergade)

Christiansted Harbor

Point Udall
Isaac Bay Beach
Cramer Park
Grapetree Beach
Reef Beach
Teague Bay
Buck Island
Grass Point
Southgate
East End Rd.
South Shore Rd.
Buck Island Reef National Monument
Chenay Bay
Tamarind Reef Beach
Green Cay
Gallows Bay
Great Pond Bay
1 Hills Rd.
Lowry Hills Rd.
Christiansted Harbor
Protestant Cay
Cormorant Beach Club
Christiansted
Longford
Salt River Bay National Historical Park and Ecological Preserve
Salt River Bay
Salt River
North Shore Rd.
Peppertree Rd.
Rattan Rd.
Sion Hill Rd.
Sunny Isle
Manning Bay
Bethlehem
Fredensborg
Kingshill
Cane Bay
Davis Bay
River Rd.
Canaan Rd.
Alexander Hamilton Airport
Long Point
Harms Bluff
Northside
Butler Bay
Scenic Rd.
Creque Dan Rd.
Mahogany Rd.
St. George Village Botanical Garden
Centerline Rd.
Sprat Hall Beach
Rainbow Beach
La Grange
Rain Forest
Frederiksted
Sandy Point
Sandy Point Wildlife Refuge

Caribbean Sea

Airport
Beach
Church
Information

3 Miles
3 Kilometers

Hilty House 8
Hotel on the Cay 9
Pink Fancy 12
Sunterra Resorts Carambola Beach 2
Villa Madeleine 11
The Waves at Cane Bay 3

Breakfast Club 13
Buccaneer 10
Cane Bay Reef Club 4
Colony Cove 7
Cormorant Beach Club 6
The Frederiksted 1
Hibiscus Beach Hotel 5

731

screened-in porches with rocking chairs. Bathrooms are luxurious and roomy, with oversized showers (with seats) and tiled vanities. If you want the very finest room here, ask for the Davis Bay Suite, which was a former Rockefeller private beach home. Its veranda alone is capable of entertaining 100 people, should that many drop in on you.

Dining: The most elegant dining choice is the Mahogany Room. The food's almost as good at the Cruzian Grill. Nonguests might also want to stop by for a meal. The Sunday brunch here is an island tradition, and a buffet is usually staged one night a week (call the hotel desk for confirmation).

Amenities: Large pool, four hard-surface tennis courts, 18-hole golf course, 24-hour room service, baby-sitting, concierge who can arrange tours, car rentals.

✪ **Villa Madeleine.** 8 miles east of Christiansted at Teague Bay (P.O. Box 26160), St. Croix, U.S.V.I. 00824. ☎ **800/496-7379** or 340/778-8782. Fax 340/773-2150. 43 units. A/C TV TEL. Winter $325 one-bedroom villa; $425 two-bedroom villa. Off-season $200 one-bedroom villa, $275 two-bedroom villa. AE, MC, V. Children 11 and under discouraged.

This 6½-acre property has some of the island's poshest rooms. It's very independent of everything else on St. Croix—guests arrive here and aren't heard from again until they leave. Many of the well-heeled occupants are retirees who live here full-time. The focal point is the great house, whose Chippendale balconies and proportions emulate the Danish colonial era. Inside, a splendidly conceived decor incorporates masses of English chintz and mahogany paneling.

Each stylish one- or two-bedroom villa has its own kitchen, privacy wall, and plunge pool. The marble bathrooms have double dressing areas and oversized showers. The villas comprising the resort are handled by different management companies; therefore, service and standards can vary greatly depending on which one you're assigned. Beach-lovers willingly travel the third of a mile to the nearest beaches, Reef and Grapetree.

Dining: On the premises is the Café Madeleine, a continental restaurant with a piano bar. The Turf Club is a New York–style steakhouse decorated with horse-racing memorabilia. The Turf allows smoking, including cigars.

Amenities: Small library with writing tables, games room for cards and billiards, laundry room, tennis courts, golf course below the property, concierge, laundry, maid service every 3 days, baby-sitting (with advance notice).

EXPENSIVE

Cormorant Beach Club. 4126 La Grande Princesse (about 3 miles northwest of Christiansted, beside route 75), St. Croix, U.S.V.I. 00820. ☎ **800/548-4460** in the U.S., or 340/778-8920. Fax 340/778-9218. www.cormorant-stcroix.com. 38 units. A/C TV TEL. Winter $180–$210 double; $265 suite. Off-season $130–$160 double; $225 suite. Extra bed $10. AE, DC, DISC, MC, V. Dive, golf, scuba, and "commitment ceremony" packages available.

This is the poshest gay resort in the Caribbean Basin, dwarfing all competition. About 70% of its clientele are gay males, mostly from the eastern United States or California. The 12-acre property is designed in a boxy, modern-looking series of rectangles, with strong horizontal lines and outcroppings of exposed natural stone. It strikes a well-coordinated balance between seclusion and accessibility. Long Reef, one of the better-known zoological phenomena of the Caribbean, lies a few hundred feet offshore from the resort's sandy beachfront. The social life here revolves around a wood-sheathed, high-ceilinged clubhouse, whose walls were removed to give guests a firsthand taste of the salty air and views of the sea. Off the central core is a bar (see "St. Croix After Dark," below) and an airy dining room that had to be rebuilt in the wake of Hurricane Marilyn.

Bedrooms contain a restrained decor of cane and wicker furniture, coffeemakers, spacious bathrooms with hair dryers, and sliding-glass doors that flood the interior with sunlight. During the lifetime of this edition, expect further improvements that will probably include the addition of a gym and a renewed emphasis on landscaping.

The restaurant, with its adjacent bar area, is St. Croix's leading gay eatery (see "Where to Dine," below). Facilities include a freshwater pool, two tennis courts, snorkeling facilities, and croquet. The staff can arrange golf, scuba, horseback riding, sailing, and island tours.

Hibiscus Beach Hotel. 4131 La Grande Princesse (next to the Cormorant, 10 minutes from Christiansted), St. Croix, U.S.V.I. 00820. ☎ **800/442-0121** or 340/773-4042. Fax 340/773-7668. www.lhibiscus.com. E-mail: hibiscus@worldnet.att.net. 37 units. A/C MINIBAR TV TEL. Winter $180–$190 double; $290 efficiency. Off-season $130–$140 double; $220 efficiency. Honeymoon, dive, and golf packages available. AE, DISC, MC, V.

This hotel, located on one of the island's best beaches, attracts a lively clientele. Each guest room is a retreat unto itself, with a private patio or balcony and a view of the Caribbean, plus tasteful Caribbean furnishings and floral prints. Other amenities include in-room safes and fresh flowers every day. Bathrooms are small but well maintained. The hotel also offers a seaside pool and a beachfront restaurant and bar, which offers good-value theme buffets. Complimentary snorkeling equipment is provided.

MODERATE

✪ **Hilty House.** Questa Verde Rd. (P.O. Box 26077), Gallows Bay, St. Croix, U.S.V.I. 00824. ☎ and fax **809/773-2594.** E-mail: hiltyhouse@worldnet.att.net. 6 units. Winter $110 double; $115–$135 cottage. Off-season $95 double; $100–$110 cottage. 3-night minimum stay in cottages. Maximum of three people per room. Room rates include continental breakfast. No credit cards. Children under 12 not accepted.

This bed-and-breakfast is located on the east side of St. Croix, on a hilltop surrounded by mountains. It's a 15-minute ride from the airport, and the nearest beach is a 10-minute ride away. The place is housed in a 200-year-old building that was once a rum distillery. Upon arriving, guests pass through a shaded courtyard to a set of iron gates that lead to the inn's gardens. There's a large pool, decorated with hand-painted tile. The beautifully appointed plantation-style house has a high-ceilinged living room and an enormous fireplace. The master bedroom is the most lavish room, with a four-poster bed and sunken shower over which hangs a chandelier. There are also two self-catering cottages that can be rented. Accommodations are generous in size, containing fine beds and small but beautifully kept bathrooms. The Danish Kitchen, one of the cottages, has a covered porch, TV, and phone. A three-course dinner, for a set price of $25, is usually served on Monday night. The overall atmosphere here is very homey and warm.

Hotel on the Cay. Protestant Cay, Christiansted, St. Croix, U.S.V.I. 00820. ☎ **800/524-2035** or 340/773-2035. Fax 809/773-7046. 55 units. A/C TV TEL. Winter $162 double; $192 suite. Off-season $107 double; $137 suite. Extra person $25. AE, DISC, MC, V.

With its buff-colored stucco, terra-cotta tiles, and archways, this rather sterile-looking hotel evokes Puerto Rico or the Dominican Republic, but it's the most prominent building on a 3-acre island set in the middle of Christiansted's harbor. Reaching it requires a 4-minute boat ride from a well-marked quay in the town center (hotel guests ride free; nonguests pay $3 round-trip). Its position in the clear waters of the harbor is both its main allure and its main drawback: Its wide sandy beaches provide the only pollution-free swimming in the town center, but it's the first hotel to be wiped off the map when a hurricane strikes.

In theory, this place should be a lavishly landscaped, upscale retreat; unfortunately, it's not. Nonetheless, it does provide adequate, unfrilly, and clean accommodations near the beach. Units are fairly roomy; most have two double beds, glass tables, wicker armchairs, desks and bureaus, adequate closet space, and laminate baths. Rooms open onto small metal-railed balconies with a view of the garden or the Christiansted harbor.

Breakfast, lunch, and tropical drinks are served daily from 7am to 5pm in a shed-style restaurant, the Harbormaster. Dinner is only served on Tuesday night; it's a beach barbecue, complete with steel band and a "Moko Jumbi" (traditional stilt walkers) floor show.

INEXPENSIVE

❂ **Breakfast Club.** 18 Queen Cross St., Christiansted, U.S.V.I. 00820. ☎ **340/773-7383.** Fax 340/773-8642. E-mail: reservations@the-breakfast-club.christiansted.vi.us. 9 units. Year-round $55 double. Rates include breakfast. AE, V. Free parking.

Here you'll get the best value of any bed-and-breakfast on St. Croix. This comfortable place combines a 1950s compound of efficiency apartments with a traditional-looking stone house that was rebuilt from a ruin in the 1930s. Each of the units has a kitchenette, a cypress-sheathed ceiling, white walls, a beige tile floor, and simple, summery furniture. Bathrooms are small and adequately maintained. The centerpiece of the place is the hot tub on a raised deck, where impromptu parties are likely to develop at random hours of the day or night, and where views stretch as far off as St. John. Toby Chapin, the Ohio-born owner, cooks one of the most generous and appealing breakfasts on the island; try the banana pancakes or the chili rellenos.

The Frederiksted. 20 Strand St., Frederiksted, St. Croix, U.S.V.I. 00840. ☎ **800/595-9519** in the U.S., or 340/772-0500. 40 units. A/C TV TEL. Winter $95–$105 double. Off-season $85–$95 double. Extra person $10. AE, DC, MC, V.

This contemporary four-story inn is a good choice for the heart of historic Frederiksted. It's located in the center of town, about a 10-minute ride from the airport. Much of the activity takes place in the outdoor tiled courtyard, where guests enjoy drinks and listen to live music on Friday and Saturday nights. There's also a small pool here. The somewhat tattered bedrooms are like those of a motel on the mainland, with good ventilation but bad lighting. They're done in a tropical motif of pastels and are equipped with small fridges. The best (and most expensive) rooms are those with an ocean view; they're subject to street noise, but have the best light. A full breakfast is served at the poolside patio. The nearest beach is Dorch Beach, a 1-mile walk or a 5-minute drive from the hotel, along the water.

❂ **Pink Fancy.** 27 Prince St., Christiansted, St. Croix, U.S.V.I. 00820. ☎ **800/524-2045** in the U.S., or 340/773-8460. Fax 340/773-6448. www.pinkfancy.com. 13 units. A/C TV TEL. Winter $75–$120 double. Off-season $65–$90 double. Extra person $15. Children 11 and under stay free in parents' room. Rates include continental breakfast. AE, MC, V.

This small, unique hotel is a block from the Annapolis Sailing School. You get more atmosphere here than anywhere else in town; guests quickly get to know each other around the bar, turning the place into a bit of a social gathering. The oldest part of the four-building complex is a historic 1780 Danish town house. In the 1950s, the hotel became a mecca for writers and artists, including, among others, Noël Coward. Guest rooms have a bright, tropical feel, with ceiling fans, floral prints, and rattan furnishings. The medium-size bathrooms have combination shower/tubs. There's also a pool and a bar, which offers free drinks from 4 to 6pm. A complimentary breakfast is offered as well.

Condo Complexes

If you're interested in a villa or condo rental, contact the properties listed below or **Island Villas,** Property Management Rentals, 6 Company St., Christiansted, St. Croix, U.S.V.I. 00820 (☎ **800/626-4512** or 340/773-8821; fax 340/773-8823), which offers some of the best accommodations on the island. Some are very private residences with pools; many are on the beach. They range from one-bedroom units to five-bedroom villas, with prices from $975 to $10,000 per week year-round.

Cane Bay Reef Club. P.O. Box 1407, Kingshill, St. Croix, U.S.V.I. 00851. ☎ **800/253-8534** in the U.S., or 340/778-2966. Fax 340/778-2966. www.canebay.com. 8 units. Winter $145–$230 suite for two. Off-season $90–$115 suite for two. Extra person $15. AE, DISC, MC, V.

This is one of the little gems of the island, offering large suites, each with a living room, a full kitchen, and a balcony overlooking the water. It's located on the north shore of St. Croix, about a 20-minute taxi ride from Christiansted, fronting the rocky Cane Bay Beach near the Waves at Cane Bay. The decor is breezily tropical, with cathedral ceilings, overhead fans, and Chilean tiles. Bedrooms are spacious, cool, and airy, with comfortable beds and fine mattresses; living rooms also contain futons. Bathrooms are medium in size and excellently maintained. Guests enjoy the pool, and local rum drinks are served at the patio bar.

Colony Cove. 3221 Estate Golden Rock (about a mile west of Christiansted), St. Croix, U.S.V.I. 00820. ☎ **800/828-0746** in the U.S., or 340/773-1965. Fax 340/773-5397. www.usvi.net/hotel/colony. E-mail: colcove@islands.vi. 60 units. A/C TV TEL. Winter $195 apt for 2; $235 apt for 4. Off-season $135 apt for 2; $155 apt for 4. Extra person $20 in winter, $10 in summer. Children under 6 stay free. AE, MC, V. Go east on Rte. 75 heading toward Christiansted as far as Five Corners; turn left and pass Mill Harbor; Colony Cove is the next driveway to the left.

Of all the condo complexes on St. Croix, Colony Cove is the most like a full-fledged hotel, with a relatively large staff on hand. Its four three-story buildings ring a swimming pool next to a palm-dotted beach. Apartments contain a washer and dryer (rare for St. Croix), a kitchen with microwave, an enclosed veranda or gallery, two air-conditioned bedrooms, and a pair of bathrooms. All have a light, airy, tropical feel. The kitchens are especially modern. Facilities include a snack bar, an on-site water-sports center, and two tennis courts.

The Waves at Cane Bay. Cane Bay (P.O. Box 1749, Kingshill), St. Croix, U.S.V.I. 00851. ☎ **800/545-0603** in the U.S., or 340/778-4945. Fax 340/778-4945. www.thewavesatcanebay.com. 12 units. A/C TV. Winter $140–$195 double. Off-season $85–$140 double. Extra person $20. AE, DC, DISC, MC, V. From the airport, go left on Rte. 64; after 1 mile, turn right on Rte. 70; after another mile, go left at the junction with Rte. 75; after 2 miles, turn left at the junction with Rte. 80; follow for 5 miles.

This intimate and tasteful property is about 8 miles from the airport, midway between the island's two biggest towns. It's set on a well-landscaped plot of oceanfront property on Cane Bay, the heart of the best scuba and snorkeling at Cane Bay Beach, though the beach here is rocky and tends to disappear at high tide. There's a PADI dive shop on the property. Accommodations are in two-story units with screened-in verandas, all directly on the ocean. The high-ceilinged rooms come with fresh flowers, well-stocked kitchens, private libraries, tile floors, and shower-only bathrooms. A two-room villa next to the main building has a large oceanside deck. The beachside bar serves as the social center, and a restaurant on the premises is open Monday through Saturday in the evenings.

WHERE TO DINE
IN CHRISTIANSTED

Comanche Club. 1 Strand St. ☎ **340/773-2665.** Reservations recommended. Main courses $9.95–$18; lunch from $12. AE, MC, V. Mon–Sat 11:30am–2:30pm and 5:30–9:30pm. CARIBBEAN/CONTINENTAL.

Relaxed yet elegant, Comanche is one of the island's most popular restaurants. The specialties are eclectic—everything from fish and conch chowder to shark cakes. Each night, a different special and a different local dish is featured. Other choices include salads, a cold buffet, curries, fish sautéed with lemon butter and capers, and typical West Indian dishes such as conch Creole with fungi. There's also standard international dishes such as filet mignon in a béarnaise sauce.

✪ **Indies.** 55–56 Company St. ☎ **340/692-9440.** Reservations recommended. Main courses $13.50–$21.50. AE, DISC, MC, V. Mon–Fri 11:30am–2:30pm; daily 5:30–9:30pm. CARIBBEAN/INTERNATIONAL.

Catherine Plav-Drigger is one of the best chefs in the Caribbean, and at her restaurant you're likely to get your finest meal on St. Croix. Indies is a welcoming retreat, set in a 19th-century courtyard lined with antique cobblestone. You dine adjacent to a carriage and cookhouse from the 1850s in a sheltered courtyard protected from the noise of the street outside. The menu changes depending on what's fresh. The fresh fish and lobster are caught in Caribbean waters, and local seasonal fruits and vegetables are featured. Try the swordfish with fresh artichokes, shiitake mushrooms, and thyme, or perhaps the baked wahoo with lobster curry and fresh chutney and coconut. Soup choices may include an excellent island lobster and shrimp bisque or a spicy black-bean soup. A different pasta dish is offered nightly. All the desserts are freshly made.

✪ **Kendricks.** 2132 Company St. ☎ **340/773-9199.** Reservations required for dinner upstairs. Main courses $19–$24. AE, MC, V. Mon–Sat 6–9:30pm. FRENCH/CONTINENTAL.

This restaurant, the island's toniest, has moved out to Gallows Bay, overlooking Christiansted Harbor, but its local fans have followed. It has both upstairs and downstairs dining rooms, the downstairs being more informal. Some of its recipes have been featured in *Bon Appétit,* and deservedly so. You'll immediately warm to such specialties as homemade eggplant ravioli with a tomato-basil butter or grilled filet mignon with black truffle in a bordelaise sauce. The signature appetizer is seared scallops and artichoke hearts in a lemon-cream sauce. Another great choice is the pecan-crusted roast pork loin with a ginger mayonnaise.

Luncheria Mexican Food. In the historic Apothecary Hall Courtyard, 2111 Company St. ☎ **340/773-4247.** Main courses $5–$10.50. No credit cards. Mon–Fri 11am–9pm, Sat noon–9pm. MEXICAN/CUBAN/PUERTO RICAN.

This Mexican restaurant offers some of the best dining values on the island. You get the usual tacos, tostadas, burritos, nachos, and enchiladas, as well as chicken fajitas, enchiladas verde, and arroz con pollo (spiced chicken with brown rice). Daily specials feature both low-calorie and vegetarian choices (the chef's refried beans are lard-free), and whole-wheat tortillas are offered. The complimentary salsa bar has mild to hot sauces, plus jalapeños. More recently, some Cuban and Puerto Rican dishes have appeared on the menu, including a zesty chicken curry, black-bean soup, and roast pork. The bartender makes the island's best margaritas.

Nolan's Tavern. 5A Estate St. Peter (2 miles east of Christiansted's harbor), Christiansted East. ☎ **340/773-6660.** Reservations recommended only for groups of six or more. Burgers $7–$8.50; main courses $12.75–$16.25. AE, DISC, MC, V. Kitchen daily 5–9pm, bar from 3pm. INTERNATIONAL/WEST INDIAN.

This is the best place to go for a warm, cozy tavern with no pretensions. It's across from the capital's most visible elementary school, the Pearl B. Larsen School. Your host is Nolan Joseph, a Trinidad-born chef who makes a special point of welcoming guests and offering "tasty food and good service." No one will mind if you stop in just for a drink. Mr. Joseph, referred to by some diners as "King Conch," prepares that mollusk in at least half a dozen ways, including versions with curry, Creole sauce, and garlic-pineapple sauce. He reportedly experimented for 3 months to perfect a means of tenderizing the conch without artificial chemicals. His ribs are also excellent.

Paradise Café. 53B Company St. (at Queen Cross St., across from Government House). ☎ **340/773-2985.** Breakfast $3.50–$7.50; lunch $4–$9; dinner $13–$22. MC, V. Mon–Sat 7:30am–3pm and 5–10pm. DELI/AMERICAN.

This place is a neighborhood enclave of savvy locals seeking good food and great value. Its brick walls and beamed ceiling were originally part of an 18th-century great house. New York–style deli fare is served during the day. Enjoy the savory homemade soups or freshly made salads, to which you can add grilled chicken or fish. At breakfast, you can select from an assortment of omelets, or try the steak and eggs. Dinners are more elaborate. The 12-ounce New York strip steak and the freshly made pasta specialties are good choices. Appetizers include stuffed mushrooms and crab cakes.

St. Croix Brewery & Fish House. King's Alley Walk. ☎ **340/713-9820.** Reservations recommended for upstairs dining room. Platters in Brew Pub $8–$11.50; main courses in upstairs restaurant $12–$21. AE, MC, V. Mon–Sat 4–11pm. AMERICAN.

This fish house and brewery boasts one of the best harbor views in Christiansted. It's the only licensed microbrewery in the U.S. Virgin Islands. Beer choices include a pale ale ("Frigate"), a red beer ("Blackbeard's"), and a dark stout ("Jump-Up"), all of which have already earned a formidable reputation on the island. Many patrons come just to drink, staying until the pub's closing, at around 1am. But if you're hungry, a roster of burgers and sandwiches is served on street level at lunch and dinner. In the evening, the upstairs dining room offers a two-fisted menu that includes garlic-stuffed fillet steak, New York–style pepper steak, brown ale chicken, and fish prepared in four or five different ways, including fried in a beer batter, blackened, broiled, and pan-seared.

Tutto Bene. 2 Company St. ☎ **340/773-5229.** Reservations accepted only for parties of five or more. Lunch $5.95–$10.95; dinner main courses $12.95–$24.95. AE, V. Mon–Fri 11:30am–2:30pm, daily 6–10pm. ITALIAN.

Tutto Bene, located in the heart of town, has more the allure of a bistro-cantina than of a full-fledged restaurant. The Connecticut-born owner, Tony Cerruto, believes in simple, hearty, and uncomplicated *paysano* dishes, the kind mammas fed their sons in the old country. You'll dine on wooden tables covered with painted tablecloths, amid warm colors and often lots of hubbub. Menu items are written on a pair of oversize mirrors against one wall. At lunch, you can enjoy bistro-style veggie frittatas, a chicken pesto sandwich, or spinach lasagna. A full range of delectable pastas and well-prepared seafood is offered nightly. Fish might be served parmigiana, or you can order seafood Genovese with mussels, clams, and shrimp in a white wine/pesto sauce over linguine. If you don't feel like eating, there's a large mahogany bar in back that does a brisk business of its own.

IN FREDERIKSTED

Blue Moon. 17 Strand St. ☎ **340/772-2222.** Main courses $14–$18.50. AE, DISC, MC, V. Tues–Fri 11:30am–2pm, Tues–Sat 6–9:30pm, Sun 11am–2pm and 6–9pm. Closed Aug. INTERNATIONAL/CAJUN.

The best little bistro in Frederiksted becomes a hot, hip spot during Sunday brunch and on Friday nights when it offers entertainment. The 200-year-old stone house on the waterfront is a favorite of visiting jazz musicians, and tourists have now discovered—but not ruined—it. It's decorated with funky, homemade art from the States, including a trash-can–lid restaurant sign. The atmosphere is casual and cafelike. Begin with the "lunar pie," with feta cheese, cream cheese, onions, mushrooms, and celery in phyllo pastry, or else the artichoke-and-spinach dip. Main courses include the catch of the day and, on occasion, Maine lobster. The clams served in garlic sauce are also from Maine. Vegetarians opt for the spinach fettuccine. There's also the usual array of steak and chicken dishes. Save room for the yummy guava pie.

Le St. Tropez. Limetree Court, 67 King St. ☎ **340/772-3000.** Reservations recommended. Main courses $14.50–$24.50. AE, DISC, MC, V. Mon–Fri 11:30am–2:30pm and 6–10pm, Sat 6–10:30pm. FRENCH/MEDITERRANEAN.

This is the most popular bistro in Frederiksted. Since it's small, it's always better to call ahead for a table. If you're visiting for the day, make this bright little cafe your lunch stop, and enjoy crêpes, quiches, soups, or salads in the sunlit courtyard. At night, the atmosphere glows with candlelight, and assumes more *joie de vivre*. Try the Mediterranean cuisine, beginning with mushrooms aïoli and escargots Provençale, or one of the freshly made soups. Main dishes are likely to include medaillons of beef with two mushrooms, the fish of the day, or a magret of duck. Ingredients are always fresh and well prepared.

Villa Morales. Plot 82C, off Route 70 (about 2 miles from Frederiksted), Estate Whim. ☎ **340/772-0556.** Reservations recommended. Main courses $6–$28. AE, MC, V. Tues–Wed 11am–6pm; Thurs–Sat 11am–10pm. PUERTO RICAN.

This inland spot hosts one of the premier Puerto Rican restaurants on St. Croix. You can choose between indoor and outdoor seating areas. No one will mind if you come here just to drink. A cozy bar is lined with the memorabilia collected by several generations of the family who maintain the place. Look for a broad cross-section of Hispanic tastes here, including many that Puerto Ricans remember from their childhoods. Savory examples include fried snapper with white rice and beans, stewed conch, roasted or stewed goat, and stewed beef. Meal platters are garnished with beans and rice. Most of the dishes are at the lower end of the price scale. About once a month, the owners transform the place into a dance hall, bringing in live salsa and merengue bands (the cover ranges from $5 to $12).

AROUND THE ISLAND

Cormorant Beach Club Restaurant. 4126 La Grande Princesse. ☎ **340/778-8920.** Reservations recommended. Main courses $5–$9.50 lunch, $14.50–$19.50 dinner. AE, DC, DISC, MC, V. Daily 11:30am–3pm and 6–9:30pm. INTERNATIONAL.

This is the premier gay restaurant on St. Croix. Both it and its bar are a mecca for gay and gay-friendly people who appreciate its relaxed atmosphere, well-prepared food, and gracefully arched premises overlooking the sea. The menu isn't particularly ambitious, but food items are flavorful and generous. Lunch specialties include at least three meal-size salads, club sandwiches, burgers, and fresh fish of the day. Dinner might begin with carrot-ginger soup or Caribbean spring rolls with chutney; main courses include steak au poivre, chicken breast stuffed with spinach and feta, grilled New Zealand lamb chops, and grilled fillets of salmon with roasted poblano orange sauce. Desserts feature tropical fruits baked into tempting pastries such as warm apple crunch cake, Key lime pie, or kahlua-flavored cheesecake.

✪ **Dino's Bistro.** In the Buccaneer, Gallows Bay. ☎ **340/773-2100.** Reservations recommended. Main courses $25–$30. AE, CB, DC, DISC, MC, V. Thurs–Mon 6–9:30pm. ITALIAN/MEDITERRANEAN.

This successful Italian restaurant is located within one of St. Croix's best resorts. It offers views of the sea as well as of the lights of Christiansted. Chef Dino DiNatale is back, zestier and better than ever. He serves the finest, most up-to-date Italian cuisine on the island. You might begin with an array of antipasti delectably prepared from fresh ingredients. That old favorite of every Sicilian paysano, black linguine with squid, is given an original touch here. Mushroom fettuccine is another noteworthy choice, as is the local fish du jour prepared in several different ways—one of our favorites is with cilantro, tomato, and ginger. An innovative pasta dish is fettuccine Caribbean, with chicken, rum, black beans, ginger, cilantro, and both sweet and hot peppers.

Duggan's Reef. East End Rd., Teague Bay. ☎ **340/773-9800.** Reservations required for dinner in winter. Main courses $17–$37; pastas $13–$17. AE, MC, V. Daily noon–3pm and 6–9:30pm. Bar daily 11am–11:30pm. Closed for lunch in summer. CONTINENTAL/CARIBBEAN.

Duggan's Reef is one of the most popular restaurants on St. Croix. It's set only 10 feet from the still waters of Reef Beach and makes an ideal perch for watching the windsurfers and Hobie Cats careening through the nearby waters. At lunch, a simple array of salads, crêpes, and sandwiches is offered. The more elaborate night menu features the popular house specialties: Duggan's Caribbean lobster pasta and Irish whiskey lobster. Begin with fried calamari or a conch chowder. Main dishes include New York strip steak, veal piccata, and pastas. The local catch of the day can be baked, grilled, blackened Cajun style, or served island style (with tomato, pepper, and onion sauce).

The Galleon. East End Rd., Green Cay Marina, 5000 Estate Southgate. ☎ **340/773-9949.** Reservations recommended. Main courses $18.50–$38. AE, MC, V. Daily 6–10pm. Go east on Rte. 82 from Christiansted for 5 minutes; after going a mile past the Buccaneer, turn left into Green Cay Marina. FRENCH/NORTHERN ITALIAN.

The Galleon, which overlooks the ocean, is a local favorite, and deservedly so. It offers the cuisine of northern Italy and France, including osso buco, just as good as that served in Milan. Freshly baked bread, two fresh vegetables, and rice or potatoes accompany main dishes. The menu always includes at least one local fish, such as wahoo, tuna, swordfish, mahimahi, or even fresh Caribbean lobster. Or you might order a perfectly done rack of lamb, which will be carved right at your table. There's an extensive wine list, including many sold by the glass. Music from a baby grand accompanies your dinner.

Sprat Hall Beach Restaurant. A mile north of Frederiksted on Rte. 63. ☎ **340/772-5855.** Lunch $7–$15. No credit cards. Daily 10am–4pm (hot food 11:30am–2:30pm). CARIBBEAN.

This informal spot is on the western coast, near Sprat Hall Plantation. It's the best place on the island to combine lunch and a swim. The restaurant has been in business since 1948, feeding both locals and visitors. Try such local dishes as conch chowder, pumpkin fritters, tannia soup, and the fried fish of the day. These dishes have authentic island flavor, perhaps more so than any other place on St. Croix. You can also get salads and burgers. The bread is baked fresh daily. The owners charge $2 for use of the showers and changing rooms.

HITTING THE BEACH

Beaches are St. Croix's big attraction. The problem is that getting to them from Christiansted, home to most of the hotels, isn't always easy. It can also be expensive, especially if you want to go back and forth every day of your stay. Of course, you can always rent a condo right on the water.

The most celebrated beach is offshore ✪ **Buck Island,** part of the U.S. National Park network. Buck Island is actually a volcanic islet surrounded by some of the most stunning underwater coral gardens in the Caribbean. The white-sand beaches on the southwest and west coasts are beautiful, but the snorkeling is even better. The islet's interior is filled with such plants as cactus, wild frangipani, and pigeonwood. There are picnic areas for those who want to make a day of it. Boat departures are from Kings Wharf in Christiansted; the ride takes half an hour. For more information, see the box "A Day on Buck Island," below.

Your best choice for a beach in Christiansted is the one at the **Hotel on the Cay.** This white-sand strip is on a palm-shaded island. To get here, take the ferry from the fort at Christiansted; it runs daily from 7am to midnight. The 4-minute trip costs $3, free for guests of the Hotel on the Cay.

Five miles west of Christiansted is the **Cormorant Beach Club,** where some 1,200 feet of white sand shaded by palm trees attract a gay crowd. Since a reef lies just off the shore, snorkeling conditions are ideal.

We highly recommend both **Davis Bay** and ✪ **Cane Bay**—they're the type of beaches you'd expect to find on a Caribbean island, with palms, white sand, and good swimming and snorkeling. Because they're on the north shore, these beaches are often windy, and their waters are not always tranquil. The snorkeling at Cane Bay is truly spectacular; you'll see elkhorn and brain corals, all lying some 250 yards off the "Cane Bay Wall." Cane Bay adjoins Route 80 on the north shore. Davis Beach doesn't have a reef; it's more popular among bodysurfers than snorkelers. There are no changing facilities. It's near Carambola Beach Resort.

On Route 63, a short ride north of Frederiksted, lies **Rainbow Beach,** which offers white sand and ideal snorkeling conditions. Nearby, also on Route 63, about 5 minutes north of Frederiksted, is another good beach, called **La Grange.** Lounge chairs can be rented here, and there's a bar nearby.

Sandy Point, directly south of Frederiksted, is the largest beach in all the U.S. Virgin Islands. Its waters are shallow and calm, perfect for swimming. Try to concentrate on the sands and not the unattractive zigzagging fences that line the beach. Take the Melvin Evans Highway (Route 66) west from the Alexander Hamilton Airport.

There's an array of beaches at the **East End** of the island; they're somewhat difficult to get to, but much less crowded. The best choice here is **Isaac Bay Beach,** ideal for snorkeling, swimming, or sunbathing. Windsurfers like **Reef Beach,** which opens onto Teague Bay along Route 82, East End Road, a half-hour ride from Christiansted. You can get food at Duggan's Reef. **Cramer Park** is a special public park operated by the Department of Agriculture. It's lined with sea-grape trees and has a picnic area, a restaurant, and a bar. **Grapetree Beach** is off Route 60 (the South Shore Road). Water sports are popular here.

SPORTS & OUTDOOR PURSUITS

Some of the best snorkeling, diving, and hiking is found on Buck Island. See "A Day on Buck Island," below.

FISHING The fishing grounds at **Lang Bank** are about 10 miles from St. Croix. Here you'll find kingfish, dolphin fish, and wahoo. Using light-tackle boats to glide along the reef, you'll probably turn up jack or bonefish. At **Clover Crest,** in Frederiksted, local anglers fish right from the rocks.

Serious sportfishers can board the *Fantasy,* a 38-foot Bertram special available for 4-, 6-, or 8-hour charters, with bait and tackle included. It's anchored at St. Croix Marina, Gallows Bay. Reservations can be made by calling ☎ **340/773-7165** during the day, or 340/773-0917 at night. The cost for 6 passengers is $375 for 4 hours, $500 for 6 hours, and $600 for 8 hours.

GOLF   St. Croix has the best golfing in the U.S. Virgins. Guests staying on St. John and St. Thomas often fly over for a day's round on one of the island's three courses.

The ✪ **Carambola Golf Course,** on the northeast side of St. Croix (☎ 340/778-5638), was created by Robert Trent Jones, Sr., who called it "the loveliest course I ever designed." It's been likened to a botanical garden. The par-3 holes here are known to golfing authorities as the best in the tropics. The greens fee of $70 in winter, or $48 in summer, allows you to play as many holes as you like. Cart rentals are mandatory and cost $13 for 18 holes.

The **Buccaneer,** Gallows Bay (☎ 340/773-2100, ext. 738), 2 miles east of Christiansted, has a challenging 5,810-yard, 18-hole course with panoramic vistas. Nonguests of this deluxe resort pay $55 in winter or $45 off-season, including use of a cart.

The **Reef,** on the east end of the island at Teague Bay (☎ 340/773-8844), is a 3,100-yard, 9-hole course, charging greens fees of $10. Carts rent for $5 to $7. The longest hole here is a 579-yard par 5.

HIKING   Scrub-covered hills make up much of St. Croix's landscape. The island's western district, however, includes a dense, 15-acre forest known as the **"Rain Forest"** (though it's not a real one). The network of footpaths here offer some of the best nature walks in the Caribbean. For more details hiking in this area, see "Exploring the 'Rain Forest,' " below. **Buck Island,** just off St. Croix, also offers some wonderful nature trails.

St. Croix Environmental Association, 6 Company St., Christiansted (☎ 340/773-1989), has regularly scheduled hikes from December through March. This is the most visible environmental group on St. Croix. In addition to in-season hikes, the group offers lectures, slide shows, and films on environmental issues. Prices for events vary.

HORSEBACK RIDING   **Paul and Jill's Equestrian Stables,** Sprat Hall Plantation, Route 58 (☎ 340/772-2880), the largest equestrian stable in the Virgin Islands, is known throughout the Caribbean for the quality of its horses. It's set on the sprawling grounds of the island's oldest plantation great house. The operators lead scenic trail rides through the forests, past ruins of abandoned 18th-century plantations and sugar mills, to the tops of the hills of St. Croix's western end. Along the way, the leaders give running commentaries on island fauna, history, and riding techniques. Beginners and experienced riders alike are welcome. A 2-hour trail ride costs $50. Tours usually depart daily in winter at 10am and 4pm, and in the off-season at 5pm, with slight variations according to demand. Reserve at least a day in advance.

SNORKELING & SCUBA DIVING   Sponge life, black coral (the finest in the West Indies), and steep drop-offs into water near the shoreline make St. Croix a snorkeling and diving paradise. The island is home to the largest living reef in the Caribbean, including the fabled north-shore wall that begins in 25 to 30 feet of water and drops to 13,200 feet, sometimes straight down. See "Beaches," above, for information on good snorkeling beaches. **St. Croix Water Sports Center** (see "Windsurfing," below) rents snorkeling equipment for $20 per day.

Buck Island is the major scuba-diving site, with a visibility of some 100 feet. It also has an underwater snorkeling trail. All the minor and major agencies offer scuba and snorkeling tours to Buck Island. See "A Day on Buck Island," below.

Other favorite dive sites include the historic **Salt River Canyon** (northwest of Christiansted at Salt River Bay), the gorgeous coral gardens of **Scotch Banks** (north of Christiansted), and **Eagle Ray** (also north of Christiansted), the latter so named because of the rays that cruise along the wall there. **Cane Bay** is known for its coral canyons.

Davis Bay is the site of the 12,000-foot-deep Puerto Rico Trench. **Northstar Reef,** at the east end of Davis Bay, is a spectacular wall dive, recommended for intermediate or experienced divers only. The wall here is covered with stunning brain corals and staghorn thickets. At some 50 feet down, a sandy shelf leads to a cave where giant green moray eels hang out.

The ultimate night dive is at the **Frederiksted Pier,** whose underwater pilings are carpeted with a mix of rainbow-hued sponges, amber tube worms, and both hard and soft coral. At **Butler Bay,** to the north of the pier on the west shore, three ships were wrecked: the *Suffolk Maid,* the *Northwind,* and the *Rosaomaira,* the latter sitting in 100 feet of water. These wrecks form the major part of an artificial reef system made up mostly of abandoned trucks and cars. This site is recommended for intermediate or experienced divers.

Dive St. Croix, 59 King's Wharf (☎ **800/523-DIVE** in the U.S., or 340/ 773-2628; fax 340/773-7400), operates the 38-foot dive boat *Reliance.* The staff offers complete instruction, from resort courses through full certification, as well as night dives. A resort course is $80, with a two-tank dive going for $75. Scuba trips to Buck Island cost $65, and dive packages begin at $250 for five dives.

V.I. Divers Ltd., in the Pan Am Pavilion on Christiansted's waterfront (☎ **800/544-5911** or 340/773-6045), is the oldest and one of the best dive operations on the island. *Rodales Scuba Diving* magazine rated its staff as among the top 10 worldwide. This full-service PADI five-star facility offers two-tank boat dives, guided snorkeling trips to Green Cay, night dives, and a full range of scuba-training programs. Introductory two-tank dives, which require no experience, cost $75, including all instruction and equipment. A six-dive package goes for $205 and a 10-dive package for $330. A two-tank boat or beach dive is $75. Night dives go for $60. A 2-hour guided snorkel tour costs $75; the boat snorkeling trip to Green Cay, $35.

TENNIS   Some authorities rate the tennis at the ✪ **Buccaneer,** Gallows Bay (☎ **340/773-2100,** ext. 736) as the best in the Caribbean. This resort offers a choice of eight courts, two lit for night play, all open to the public. Nonguests pay $8 per person per hour; you must call to reserve a court. A tennis pro is available for lessons, and there's also a pro shop.

WINDSURFING   The best place for this increasingly popular sport is the **St. Croix Water Sports Center** (☎ **340/773-7060**), located on a small offshore island in Christiansted Harbor and part of the Hotel on the Cay. It's open daily from 10am to 5pm. Windsurfing rentals are $25 per hour. Lessons are available. Sea Doos, which seat two, can be rented for $45 to $55 per half hour. The center also offers parasailing for $65 per person, and rents snorkeling equipment for $20 per day.

EXPLORING ST. CROIX

Taxi tours are the ideal way to explore the island. The cost is around $40 for 2 hours or $60 for 3 hours for one or two passengers. All prices should be agreed upon in advance. For more information, call the **St. Croix Taxi Association** at ☎ **340/ 778-1088.**

CHRISTIANSTED

The picture-book harbor town of the Caribbean, ✪ **Christiansted** is an old, handsomely restored (or at least in the process of being restored) Danish port. On the

Into the Deep without Getting Wet

St. Croix Water Sports Center (☎ **340/773-7060**), located at the Hotel on the Cay, now offers an ideal way for visitors to view the island's aquatic life without getting wet. *Oceanique*, a semi-submersible vessel acting as part submarine and part cruiser, carries visitors on 1-hour excursions through Christiansted harbor and along Protestant Cay. The inch-thick windows lining the vessel's underwater observation room provide views of St. Croix's marine life in a cool and dry environment. This trip is especially popular with children and nonswimmers. Day and night excursions are available for $25 for adults and $15 for children. Call for reservations.

northeastern shore of the island, on a coral-bound bay, the town is filled with Danish buildings erected by prosperous merchants in the booming 18th century. These red-roofed structures are often washed in pink, ocher, or yellow. Arcades over the sidewalks provide shade for shoppers. The whole area around the harbor front has been designated a historic site, including **Government House,** which is looked after by the National Park Service.

You can begin your exploration of the town at the **visitors bureau,** Queen Cross Street (☎ **340/773-0495**), a yellow-sided building with a cedar-capped roof near the harbor. It was originally built as the Old Scalehouse in 1856. In its heyday, all taxable goods leaving and entering the harbor were weighed here.

Steeple Building. On the waterfront off Hospital St. ☎ **340/773-1460.** Admission $2 (also includes admission to Fort Christiansvaern). Daily 8am–5pm.

This building's full name is the Church of Lord God of Sabaoth. It was built in 1753 as St. Croix's first Lutheran church, until it was deconsecrated in 1831; the building subsequently served at various times as a bakery, a hospital, and a school. Today, it houses exhibits relating to island history and culture.

Fort Christiansvaern. ☎ **340/773-1460.** Admission included in the ticket to the Steeple Building. Mon–Thurs 8am–5pm, Fri–Sat 9am–5pm.

This fortress overlooking the harbor is the best-preserved colonial fortification in the Virgin Islands. It's maintained as a historic monument by the National Park Service. Its original four-pronged, star-shaped design was in accordance with the most advanced military planning of its era. The fort is now the site of the St. Croix Police Museum, which has exhibits on police work on the island from the late 1800s to the present.

St. Croix Aquarium. Caravelle Arcade. ☎ **340/773-8995.** Admission $4.50 adults, $2 children. Tues–Sat 11am–4pm.

This aquarium moved here from Frederiksted, and has expanded with many exhibits, including one devoted to "night creatures." In all, it houses some 40 species of marine animals and more than 100 species of invertebrates. A touch pond contains starfish, sea cucumbers, brittle stars, and pencil urchins. The aquarium allows you to become familiar with the marine life you'll see while scuba diving or snorkeling.

FREDERIKSTED

This former Danish settlement at the western end of the island, about 17 miles from Christiansted, is a sleepy port town that comes to life only when a cruise ship docks at its shoreline. Frederiksted was destroyed by a fire in 1879. Its citizens subsequently rebuilt it with wood frames and clapboards on top of the old Danish stone and yellow-brick foundations.

A Day on Buck Island

The crystal-clear water and white coral sand of ✪ **Buck Island**, a satellite of St. Croix, are legendary. Some call this island the single most important attraction of the Caribbean. Only a third of a mile wide and a mile long, Buck Island lies 1½ miles off the northeastern coast of St. Croix. A barrier reef here shelters many reef fish, including queen angelfish and smooth trunkfish. In years past, the island was frequented by the swashbuckling likes of Morgan, Blackbeard, and even Captain Kidd.

Buck Island's greatest attraction is its **underwater snorkeling trails,** which ring part of the island. Equipped with a face mask, fins, and a snorkel, you'll be treated to some of the most beautiful underwater views in the Caribbean. Plan on spending at least two-thirds of a day at this extremely famous ecological site, which is maintained by the National Park Service. There are also many labyrinths and grottoes for **scuba divers.** The sandy **beach** has picnic tables and barbecue pits, as well as rest rooms and a small changing room.

You can follow **hiking trails** through the tropical vegetation that covers the island. Circumnavigating the island on foot takes about 2 hours. Buck Island's trails meander from several points along its coastline to its sun-flooded summit, affording views over nearby St. Croix. *A couple of warnings:* Bring protection from the sun's merciless rays; even more important, don't rush to touch every plant you see. The island's western edge has groves of poisonous machineel trees, whose leaves, bark, and fruit cause extreme irritation if they come into contact with human skin.

Small boats run between St. Croix and Buck Island. Nearly all charters provide snorkeling equipment and allow for 1½ hours of snorkeling and swimming. **Mile Mark Watersports,** in the King Christian Hotel, 59 King's Wharf, Christiansted (☎ **800/523-DIVE** or 340/773-2628), conducts three different types of tours. The first option is a half-day tour aboard a glass-bottom boat departing from the King Christian Hotel, daily from 9:30am to 1pm and 1:30 to 5pm; it costs $35 per person. The second is a more romantic half-day journey aboard one of the company's sailboats, for $45. The third is a full-day tour, offered daily from 10am to 4pm on a 40-foot catamaran, for $70. Included in this excursion is a West Indian barbecue picnic on Buck Island's beach.

Captain Heinz (☎ **340/773-3161** or 340/773-4041) is an Austrian-born skipper with more than 25 years of sailing experience. His trimaran, *Teroro II,* leaves Green Cay Marina "H" Dock at 9am and 2pm, never filled with more than 24 passengers. This snorkeling trip costs $50 in the morning or $45 in the afternoon. The captain is not only a skilled sailor but also a considerate host. He will even take you around the outer reef, which the other guides do not, for an unforgettable underwater experience.

Most visitors begin their tour at russet-colored **Fort Frederik,** at the northern end of Frederiksted next to the cruise-ship pier (☎ **340/772-2021**) This fort, completed in 1760, is said to have been the first to salute the flag of the new United States. When an American brigantine anchored at port in Frederiksted hoisted a homemade Old Glory, the fort returned the salute with cannon fire, violating the rules of neutrality. Also, it was here on July 3, 1848, that Governor-General Peter von Scholten emancipated the slaves in the Danish West Indies, in response to a slave uprising led by a young man named Moses "Buddhoe" Gottlieb. In 1998, a bust of Buddhoe was unveiled here. The fort has been restored to its 1840 appearance, and is today a national historic landmark. You can explore the courtyard and stables. A local history museum has been installed in what was once the Garrison Room. Admission is free. It's open Monday through Saturday from 8:30am to 4:30pm.

The **Customs House**, just east of the fort, is an 18th-century building with a 19th-century two-story gallery. To the south of the fort is the **visitors bureau,** at Strand Street (☎ **340/772-0357**), where you can pick up a free map of the town.

THE "RAIN FOREST"

The island's western district contains a dense, 15-acre forest, called the "Rain Forest" (though it's not a real one). The area is thick with mahogany trees, kapok (silk-cotton) trees, turpentine (red-birch) trees, samaan (rain) trees, and all kinds of ferns and vines. Sweet limes, mangoes, hog plums, and breadfruit trees, all of which have grown in the wild since the days of the plantations, are also interspersed among the larger trees. Crested hummingbirds, pearly eyed thrashers, green-throated caribs, yellow warblers, and perky but drably camouflaged banana quits nest here. The 150-foot-high Creque Dam is the major man-made sight in the area.

The "Rain Forest" is private property, but the owner lets visitors go inside to explore. To experience its charm, some people opt to drive along Route 76 (also known as Mahogany Road), stopping beside the footpaths that meander off on either side of the highway into dry river beds and glens. It's advisable to stick to the best-worn of the footpaths. You can also hike along some of the little-traveled four-wheel-drive roads in the area. Three of the best for hiking are the **Creque Dam Road** (routes 58/78), the **Scenic Road** (route 78), and the **Western Scenic Road** (routes 63/78).

Our favorite trail in this area takes about 2½ hours one-way. From Frederiksted, drive north on route 63 until you reach Creque Dam Road, where you turn right, park the car, and start walking. About a mile past the 150-foot Creque Dam, you'll be deep within the forest's magnificent flora and fauna. Continue along the trail until you come to the Western Scenic Road. Eventually, you reach Mahogany Road (Route 76), near St. Croix Leap Project. Hikers rate this trail moderate in difficulty.

You could also begin near the junction of Creque Dam Road and Scenic Road. From here, your trek will cover a broad triangular swath, heading north and then west along Scenic Road. First, the road will rise, and then descend toward the coastal light-house of the island's extreme northwestern tip, **Hams Bluff.** Most trekkers decide to retrace their steps after about 45 minutes of northwesterly hiking. Real diehards, however, will continue all the way to the coastline, then head south along the coastal road (Butler Bay Road), and finally head east along Creque Dam Road to their starting point at the junction of Creque Dam Road and Scenic Road. Embark on this longer expedition only if you're really prepared for a hike lasting about 5 hours.

SANDY POINT WILDLIFE REFUGE

St. Croix's rarely visited southwestern tip is composed of salt marshes, tidal pools, and low vegetation inhabited by birds, turtles, and other forms of wildlife. More than 3 miles of ecologically protected coastline lie between Sandy Point (the island's most westerly tip) and the shallow waters of the Westend Saltpond. The area is home to colonies of green, leatherback, and hawksbill turtles. It's one of only two such places in U.S. waters. It's also home to thousands of birds, including herons, brown pelicans, Caribbean martins, black-necked stilts, and white-crowned pigeons. As for flora, Sandy Point gave its name to a rare form of orchids, a brown and/or purple variety.

This wildlife refuge is only open on Saturday and Sunday from 6am to 6pm. To get here, drive to the end of Route 66 (Melvin Evans highway) and continue down a gravel road. For guided weekend visits, call the **St. Croix Environmental Association** (☎ **809/773-1989**).

AROUND THE ISLAND

North of Frederiksted, you can drop in at **Sprat Hall,** the island's oldest plantation, or else continue along to the "rain forest" (see above). Most visitors come to the area to see the jagged estuary of the northern coastline's ✪ **Salt River.** The Salt River was where Columbus landed on November 14, 1493. Marking the 500th anniversary of Columbus's arrival, President George Bush signed a bill creating the 912-acre **Salt River Bay National Historical Park and Ecological Preserve.** The park contains the site of the original Carib village explored by Columbus and his men, including the only ceremonial ball court ever discovered in the Lesser Antilles. Also within the park is the largest mangrove forest in the Virgin Islands, sheltering many endangered animals and plants, plus an underwater canyon attracting divers from around the world. Call the **St. Croix Environmental Association,** 3 Arawak Building, Gallows Bay (☎ **340/773-1989**), for information on tours of the area. Tours cost $15 for adults, $10 for children under 10.

St. George Village Botanical Garden of St. Croix. 127 Estate St. (just north of Centerline Road, 4 miles east of Frederiksted), Kingshill. ☎ **340/692-2874.** Admission $5 adults, $1 children 12 and under; donations welcome. Nov–May, daily 9am–5pm; June–Oct, Tues–Sat 9am–4pm.

This is a 16-acre Eden of tropical trees, shrubs, vines, and flowers. The garden is a feast for the eye and the camera, from the entrance drive bordered by royal palms and bougainvillea to the towering kapok and tamarind trees. It was built around the ruins of a 19th-century sugarcane workers' village. Self-guided walking-tour maps are available at the entrance to the garden's great hall. Facilities include rest rooms and a gift shop.

Cruzan Rum Factory. W. Airport Rd., Rte. 64. ☎ **340/692-2280.** Admission $4. Tours given Mon–Fri 9–11:30am and 1–4:15pm.

This factory distills the famous Virgin Islands rum, which some consider the finest in the world. Guided tours depart from the visitors' pavilion; call for reservations and information. There's also a gift shop.

Estate Whim Plantation Museum. Centerline Rd. (2 miles east of Frederiksted). ☎ **340/772-0598.** Admission $6 adults, $1 children. June–Oct, Tues–Sat 10am–3pm; Nov–May, Mon–Sat 10am–4pm.

This restored great house is unique among those of the many sugar plantations whose ruins dot the island. It's composed of only three rooms. With 3-foot-thick walls made of stone, coral, and molasses, the house resembles a luxurious European château. A division of Baker Furniture Company used the Whim Plantation's collection of models for one of its most successful reproductions, the "Whim Museum–West Indies Collection." A showroom here sells the reproductions, plus others from the Caribbean, including pineapple-motif four-poster beds, cane-bottomed planters' chairs with built-in leg rests, and Caribbean adaptations of Empire-era chairs with cane-bottomed seats.

Also on the premises is a woodworking shop that features tools and exhibits on techniques from the 18th century, the estate's original kitchen, a museum store, and a servant's quarters. The ruins of the plantation's sugar-processing plant, complete with a restored windmill, also remain.

SHOPPING

In Christiansted, the emphasis is on hole-in-the-wall boutiques selling one-of-a-kind merchandise; the selection of handmade items is especially strong. Knowing that it can't compete with Charlotte Amalie on St. Thomas, Christiansted has forged its own

Where the Sun First Shines on the U.S.

The rocky promontory of **Point Udall,** jutting into the Caribbean Sea, is the easternmost point of the United States. Diehards go out to see the sun rise, but considering the climb via a rutted dirt road, you may want to wait until there's more light before heading here. Once at the top, you'll be rewarded with one of the best views in the U.S. Virgin Islands. On the way to the lookout point, you'll see "The Castle," a local architectural oddity, owned by the island's most prominent socialite, the Contessa Nadia Farbo Navarro. Point Udall is signposted along Route 82.

identity as the chic spot for merchandise in the Caribbean. All its shops are within about half a mile of each other. The relatively new **King's Alley Complex** (☎ 340/778-8135) is a pink-sided compound filled with the densest concentration of shops on St. Croix.

In recent years, **Frederiksted** has also become a popular shopping destination. Its urban mall appeals to cruise-ship passengers arriving at Frederiksted Pier. The mall is on a 50-foot strip of land between Strand Street and King Street, the town's bustling main thoroughfare.

Below are our favorite shops in Christiansted.

The operators of ✪ **Folk Art Traders,** Strand Street (☎ 340/773-1900), travel throughout the Caribbean ("in the bush") to add to their unique collection of local art and folk-art treasures—Carnival masks, pottery, ceramics, original paintings, hand-wrought jewelry, batiks from Barbados, and high-quality iron sculpture from Haiti. There's nothing else like it in the Virgin Islands.

At the hip and eclectic **From the Gecko,** 1233 Queen Cross St. (☎ 340/778-9433), you can find anything from hand-painted local cottons and silks to that old West Indian staple, batiks. We found the Indonesian collection here among the most imaginative in the U.S. Virgin Islands—everything from ornate candle holders to banana-leaf knapsacks.

Many Hands, in the Pan Am Pavilion, Strand Street (☎ 340/773-1990), sells West Indian spices and teas, locally made shellwork, stained glass, hand-painted china, pottery, and handmade jewelry. The collection of local paintings is intriguing, as is the year-round "Christmas tree."

The **Royal Poinciana,** 1111 Strand St. (☎ 340/773-9892), is the most interesting gift shop on St. Croix, looking like an antique apothecary. You'll find such items as hot sauces, seasoning blends for gumbos, island herbal teas, Antillean coffees, and a scented array of soaps, toiletries, lotions, and shampoos. There's also a selection of museum-reproduction greeting cards and calendars, plus educational but fun gifts for children.

About 60% of the merchandise at **Gone Tropical,** 55 Company St. (☎ 340/773-4696), is made in Indonesia (usually Bali). Prices of new, semiantique, or antique sofas, beds, chests, tables, mirrors, and decorative carvings are the same as (and sometimes less than) those of new furniture in conventional stores. Gone Tropical also sells art objects, jewelry, batiks, candles, and baskets.

The small West Indian cottage of **Crucian Gold,** 59 Kings Wharf (☎ 340/773-5241), holds the gold and silver creations of island-born Brian Bishop. His most popular item is the Crucian bracelet, which contains a "True Lovers' Knot" in its design. The shop also sells hand-tied knots (bound in gold wire), rings, pendants, and earrings.

Elegant Illusions Copy Jewelry, 55 King St. (☎ 340/773-2727), a branch of a hugely successful chain based in California, sells convincing fake jewelry. The look-alikes range in price from $9 to $1,000, and include credible copies of the baroque and antique jewelry your great-grandmother might have worn. If you want the real thing, you can go next door to **King Alley Jewelry** (☎ 340/773-4746), which is owned by the same company and specializes in fine designer jewelry, including Tiffany and Cartier.

Sonya Hough of **Sonya Ltd,** 1 Company St. (☎ 340/778-8605), is the matriarch of a cult of local residents who wouldn't leave home without wearing one of her bracelets. She's most famous for the sterling-silver and gold versions of her C-clasp bracelet. Locals say that if the cup of the "C" is turned toward your heart, it means you're emotionally committed; if the cup is turned outward, it means you're available. Prices range from $20 to $2,500.

Everything sold at **Waterfront Larimar Mines,** the Boardwalk/King's Walk (☎ 340/692-9000), is produced by the largest manufacturer of gold settings for larimar in the world. Discovered in the 1970s, larimar is a pale-blue pectolyte prized for its color. It comes from mines located in only one mountain in the world, on the southwestern edge of the Dominican Republic. Prices range from $25 to $1,000. Although other shops sell the stone as well, this place has the widest selection.

✪ **Little Switzerland,** 1108 King St. (☎ 340/773-1976), is the best source on the island for crystal, figurines, watches, china, perfume, flatware, and fine jewelry. For luxuries like a Rolex watch, Paloma Picasso leather goods, or crystal such as Lalique, Swarovski, and Baccarat, this is the place. It specializes in all the big names. At least a few items are said to sell for up to 30% less than on the U.S. mainland, but don't take anyone's word on that.

The **Coconut Vine,** Pan Am Pavilion (☎ 340/773-1991), is one of the most colorful and popular little boutiques on the island. Hand-painted batiks for both men and women are the specialty.

Urban Threadz/Tribal Threadz, 52C Company St. (☎ 340/773-2883), is the most comprehensive clothing store in Christiansted's historic core, with a two-story, big-city scale and appeal. It's where island residents prefer to shop for hip, urban styles. Men's items are on the street level, women's upstairs. The inventory includes everything from Bermuda shorts to lightweight summer blazers and men's suits. The store carries Calvin Klein, Nautica, and Oakley, among other brands.

The **White House,** King's Alley Walk (☎ 340/773-9222), is about fashion, not politics. Everything is white or off-white—nothing darker than beige is allowed on the premises. The women's clothing here ranges from casual and breezy to dressy.

ST. CROIX AFTER DARK

St. Croix doesn't have the nightlife of St. Thomas. To find the action, you might have consult the publication *St. Croix This Week,* which is distributed free to cruise-ship and air passengers and is also available at the tourist office.

Try to catch a performance of the **Quadrille Dancers,** a real cultural treat. Their dances have changed little since plantation days. The women wear long dresses, white gloves, and turbans, while the men wear flamboyant shirts, sashes, and tight black trousers. After you've learned their steps, you're invited to join the dancers on the floor. Ask at your hotel if and where they're performing.

The 1,100-seat **Island Center** amphitheater, half a mile north of Sunny Isle (☎ 340/778-5272), continues to attract big-name entertainers. Its program is widely varied, ranging from jazz and musical revues to Broadway plays. Consult *St. Croix This Week* or call the center to see what's being presented. The Caribbean Community Theatre and Courtyard Players perform here regularly. Tickets range from $5 to $25.

The big nightlife news on St. Croix is the opening of the casino at the **Divi Carina Bay Resort** (☎ 340/773-3616), which should be up and running sometime in 2000.

If you're looking to hear some live music, try **Blue Moon,** 17 Strand St. (☎ 340/772-2222), a hip little dive and also a good bistro. It's currently the hottest spot in Frederiksted on Fridays, when a five-piece ensemble entertains. There's no cover.

The **Terrace Lounge,** in the Buccaneer, Route 82, Estate Shoys (☎ 340/773-2100), off the main dining room of one of St. Croix's most upscale hotels, welcomes some of the Caribbean's finest entertainers every night, often including a full band.

2 Plus 2 Disco, at the La Grande Princess (☎ 340/773-3710), is a real Caribbean disco. It features the regional sounds of the islands, not only calypso and reggae but also salsa and soca (a hybrid of calypso and reggae). Usually there's a DJ, except on weekends when local bands are brought in. The place isn't fancy or large. Come here for Saturday Night Fever. Hours are Tuesday through Sunday from 8:30pm to 2am and Friday and Saturday from 8pm to either 5 or 6am. The cover is $7 when there's a live band.

For a sunset cocktail, head to the **Marina Bar,** in the King's Alley Hotel, King's Alley/The Waterfront (☎ 340/773-0103).

This bar occupies a great position on the waterfront, on a shaded terrace overlooking the deep-blue sea and Protestant Cay. It's open throughout the day, but the most appealing activities begin right after the last seaplane departs for St. Thomas, around 5:30pm, and continue until 8:30pm. Cocktails made with rum, mango, banana, papaya, and grenadine are the drinks of choice. You can also stave off hunger pangs with burgers, sandwiches, and West Indian–style platters. There's live entertainment most nights, usually street bands. On Monday, you can bet on crab races.

Cormorant Beach Club Bar, 4126 La Grande Princesse (☎ 340/778-8920), is set in a predominantly gay resort about 3 miles northwest of Christiansted. It caters both to resort guests and to gay men and women from other parts of the island. You can sit at tables overlooking the ocean or around an open-centered mahogany bar, adjacent to a gazebo. Excellent tropical drinks are mixed here, including the house specialty, a Cormorant Cooler, made with champagne, pineapple juice, and Triple Sec.

The unique **Mt. Pellier Hut Domino Club,** Montpellier (☎ 340/772-9914), began as a battered snack shack established to serve players of a never-ending domino game. It gradually grew into a drinking and entertainment center, although the game is still going strong. Today, the bar has a beer-drinking pig (Miss Piggy) and a one-man band, Piro, who plays on Sunday. The bartender will serve you a lethal rum-based Mamma Wanna.

Appendix: A Taste of the Caribbean

Below we've compiled an overview of Caribbean cuisine, along with an island-by-island rundown of the best local specialties.

AN OVERVIEW

FRUITS, VEGETABLES & SIDE DISHES The abundance of fruit in the islands is obvious. At breakfast, you'll usually find it freshly sliced, though it's not always ripe enough. Coconut is used in everything from breads to soups. Soursop ice cream appears on some menus, and guava might turn up in anything from juice to cheese. Papaya is called *papaw,* and it will most often be your melon choice at breakfast. Mango is ubiquitous, used not only in chutney but also in drinks and desserts. The avocado, most often called *pears,* is used in fresh seafood salads and often stuffed with fresh crabmeat.

The plantain is similar to a banana. It is not eaten raw, however, but is usually served as a cooked side dish, the way Americans present french fries. Puerto Ricans eat dried plantains, called *tostones,* instead of potato chips.

Two staples of the Caribbean islands have always been rice and pigeon peas. Balls of cornmeal, called fungi, often accompany a salt-pork main dish known as *mauffay.* Sometimes these cornmeal concoctions will appear on the menus of local restaurants as *cou-cou.*

One of the most common vegetables in the islands is christophine (sometimes called *foo foo*), a green, prickly gourd that tastes somewhat like zucchini. Breadfruit, introduced to the islands by Captain Bligh (of Bounty fame), is green and round and used like a potato. Potatoes and yams are also local favorites. The leafy *callaloo* is like spinach and is often served with crab, salt pork, and fresh fish (with floating fungi as a garnish).

In a true local restaurant in the Caribbean, you'll surely find hot peppers on the table—which you should use sparingly. A selection of hot-pepper pastes is called *sambal.*

SEAFOOD Throughout the islands, warm-water lobster is the king of the sea and the most sought after (and most expensive) main course. The catch of the day will most likely be red snapper or grouper, though shark and barracuda are also fairly common.

You should eat barracuda with caution, as it sometimes contains copper deposits. Fish caught north of Antigua, along the Cayman Islands, and in Cuba are said to be at risk. The barracuda in south-lying Barbados are fine and usually very healthy.

"Dolphin," also called *mahimahi,* may appear on the menu as well—but don't worry, this dolphin is a fish and not the playful intelligent mammal you saw in *Flipper.*

DRINKS   Since the late 16th century, rum has been associated with slavery, Yankee traders, pirates, and bootlegging. The names of rum barons became famous around the world: Bacardi, Gonzalez, Myers, and Barcelo, to name only a few. "Kill-devil," as rum was once called, is of course the favorite drink of the islands. Distilled easily from sugarcane, rum played a major role in the history of the West Indies. Today, the rusted machinery and tumble-down ruins of distilleries are tourist stopovers on dozens of Caribbean islands.

Planter's punch is still the most popular drink in the islands, but the average bar in the Caribbean offers a bewildering array of other rum-based drinks as well. Sure, these frosty drinks are pastel-colored and come with cute umbrellas, but they'll get you drunk on very short notice because of their elevated sugar content, the effect of which is exacerbated by the hot climate.

Don't think that the only beer you'll be able to find will be imported from Milwaukee or Holland. Of course, Heineken is ubiquitous, as is Amstel, especially in the Dutch islands, but Red Stripe from Jamaica is the most famous.

Water is generally safe throughout the islands, but many tourists get sick from drinking it simply because it's different from the water they're accustomed to. If it's available, order bottled water.

ISLAND SPECIALTIES

ANGUILLA   Order spiny lobsters if you can get them; they're very good and invariably fresh. Seafood lovers will also enjoy the crayfish, whelk, yellowtail, and red snapper. Some local restaurants serve some of the most elegant continental fare in the West Indies, although they're generally forced to work with frozen ingredients imported from elsewhere, often Miami.

ANTIGUA & BARBUDA   At most restaurants and in most resorts that cater to tourists, you get typical American or continental fare, but a host of French restaurants has opened in the past few years on Antigua. Local food, when it's available on either island, tends to be spicy, with sauces often based on Creole recipes or even on East Indian curry dishes. Expect pepper-pot stew, spareribs, curried goat, and the like. A British heritage lingers in some of the island's blander dishes. If fresh seafood is on the menu, try it.

ARUBA   A few of Aruba's restaurants serve *rijstaffel,* the multidish Indonesian "rice table," or *nasi goreng,* a mini-rijstaffel. In addition, many Chinese restaurants operate in Oranjestad. Though they're a bit heavy for the tropics, Aruban specialties are beginning to appear on menus. *Keshi yena* is Edam cheese filled with a mixture of chicken or beef and flavored with onions, pickles, tomatoes, olives, and raisins. *Sopito de pisca* is a savory fish chowder made with a bouquet of spices. *Funchi,* like a cornmeal pudding of the Deep South, accompanies many regional dishes. Many of the island's top chefs serve French cuisine.

BARBADOS   The famous flying fish appears on every menu. When prepared right, it's a delicacy—moist and succulent, nutlike in flavor, approaching the subtlety of brook trout. Bajans boil it, steam it, bake it, stew it, fry it, and stuff it.

Try the sea urchin, or *oursin,* which you may have already sampled on Martinique and Guadeloupe. Bajans often call these urchins "sea eggs." Crab-in-the-back is another specialty, as is *langouste,* the Barbadian lobster. Dolphin (mahimahi) and salt fish cakes are other popular items. *Cou-cou,* a side dish made from okra and cornmeal, accompanies fish. Yams, sweet potatoes, and *eddoes* (similar to yams) are typical vegetables. Luscious Barbadian fruits include papaya, passion fruit, and mango.

If you hear that any hotel or restaurant is having a *cohobblopot* (or more commonly, a Bajan buffet), call for a reservation. This is a Barbadian term that means "to cook up," and it inevitably will produce an array of local dishes.

BONAIRE   Bonaire's food is generally acceptable, though nearly everything has to be imported. Your best bet is fresh-caught fish and an occasional rijstaffel, the traditional Indonesian "rice table," or local dishes. Popular foods are conch cutlet or stew, pickled conch, red snapper, tuna, wahoo, dolphin (mahimahi), fungi (a thick cornmeal pudding), rice, beans, sate (marinated meat with curried mayonnaise), goat stew, and Dutch cheeses.

THE BRITISH VIRGIN ISLANDS   The food is relatively simple and straightforward, with fresh fish the best choice on the menu. Most other items, including meat and poultry, are shipped in frozen. In most major restaurants and hotels, an American or continental cuisine (with Caribbean influences) prevails. For a taste of authentic island foods, go where the locals go (we'll recommend several good bets in each chapter). Locals give colorful names to the various fish brought home for dinner, everything from "ole wife" to "doctors." "Porgies and grunts," along with yellowtail, kingfish, and bonito, show up on many tables. Fish is usually boiled in a lime-flavored brew seasoned with hot peppers and herbs, and is commonly served with a Creole sauce of peppers, tomatoes, and onions, among other ingredients. Salt fish and rice is another low-cost dish. The fish is flavored with onion, tomatoes, shortening, garlic, and green pepper.

Conch Creole is a tasty stew, flavored with onions, garlic, spices, hot peppers, and salt pork. You might also order a plate of succulent conch fritters if you get the chance. A favorite local dish is chicken and rice, made with Spanish peppers. Curried goat, the longtime "classic" West Indian dinner, is prepared with herbs, including cardamom pods and onions. The famous johnnycakes that accompany many of these fish and meat dishes are deep-fried in fat or baked.

THE CAYMAN ISLANDS   American and continental cooking predominate, although there's also a cuisine known as Caymanian, which features specialties made from turtle. (Environmental groups in the States consider this species to be endangered; however, turtles in the Cayman Islands are not caught in the wild but bred for food.) Fresh fish is the star, and conch is used in many ways. Local lobster is in season from late summer through January. Since most dining places have to rely on imported ingredients, prices tend to be high.

CURAÇAO   The basic cuisine is Dutch, but specialty items are often Latin American and Indonesian. The cuisine strikes many visitors as heavy for the tropics, so you may want to have a light lunch and order the more filling concoctions, such as *rijstaffel,* in the evening. You also may want to finish your meals with Curaçao, the liqueur that made the island famous.

Ertwensoep, the well-known Dutch pea soup, is a popular dish, as is *keshi yena,* which is Edam cheese stuffed with meat and then baked. *Funchi,* a Caribbean cornmeal pudding, accompanies many local dishes. *Sopito,* fish soup often made with coconut water, is an especially good local dish. Conch appears in curries and many other dishes.

DOMINICA   The local delicacy is the fine flesh of the *crapaud* (a frog), called "mountain chicken." Freshwater crayfish is another specialty, as is *tee-tee-ree,* fried cakes made from tiny fish. Stuffed crab back is usually a delight—the backs of red and black land crabs are stuffed with delicate crab-meat and Creole seasonings. The fresh fruit juices of the island are divine, and no one spends a day without at least one rum punch.

THE DOMINICAN REPUBLIC   The national dish is *sancocho,* a thick stew made with meats (maybe seven kinds), vegetables, and herbs, notably marjoram. Another national favorite is *chicharrones de pollo,* pieces of fried chicken and fried green bananas flavored with pungent spices. One of the most typical dishes is *la bandera* (the flag), made with red beans, white rice, and stewed meat. Johnnycakes and *mangu,* a plantain-like dish, are frequently eaten. You can buy johnnycakes on the street corner or at the beach, but you must ask for them as *vaniqueques.*

A good local beer is called Presidente. Wines are imported, so prices tend to run high. Dominican coffee compares favorably with those of Colombia and Brazil.

GRENADA   We have found the food on Grenada to be the best on the British Windward Islands. Many of the chefs are European or European-trained, and local cooks are also on hand to prepare Grenadian specialties, such as conch (called *lambi* here), lobster, callaloo soup (with greens and crab), and soursop or avocado ice cream. Turtle steaks appear on many menus, although this is an endangered species. The national dish, called "oil down," consists of breadfruit and salt pork covered with dasheen leaves and steamed in coconut milk (it's not the favorite of every visitor). Some 22 kinds of fish, including fresh tuna, dolphin (mahimahi), and barracuda, are caught off the island's shores, and most are good eating. Naturally, the spices of the island, such as nutmeg, are used plentifully. Meals are often served family style in an open-air setting with a view of the sea.

GUADELOUPE   The Creole cuisine of Guadeloupe is similar to Martinique's, and we think it's the best in the Caribbean. The island's chefs have been called "seasoned sorcerers." Creole cooking has African roots and is based on seafood. Out in the country, every cook has his or her own herb garden, since the cuisine makes great use of herbs and spices. Except in the major hotels, most restaurants are family-run, offering real homemade cooking. Best of all, you usually get to dine alfresco.

Stuffed, stewed, skewered, or broiled spiny lobsters, as well as clams, conch, oysters, and octopus, are presented with French taste and subtlety. Every good chef knows how to make *colombo,* a spicy rich stew of poultry, pork, or beef served with rice, herbs, sauces, and a variety of seeds. Another Creole favorite is *calalou* (callaloo in English), a soup of spinachlike callaloo greens flavored with savory herbs. Yet another traditional French Caribbean dish is *blaff,* fresh seafood poached in clear stock and usually seasoned with hot peppers.

JAMAICA   There is great emphasis on seafood. Rock lobster appears on every menu—grilled, Thermidor, cold, hot. Ackee and saltfish, the national dish, is a concoction of salt cod and a brightly colored vegetable that looks and tastes something like scrambled eggs. *Escovitch* (marinated fish) is usually fried and then simmered in vinegar with onions and peppers. Curried mutton and goat are popular, as is pepper pot, all highly seasoned.

Jerk pork is found everywhere, but is best in country areas, where it's bar-becued slowly over wood fires until crisp and brown. Rice and peas (really red beans) are usually served with onions, spices, and salt pork. Vegetables are exotic: breadfruit, imported by Captain Bligh in 1723; *callaloo,* rather like spinach, used in pepper pot; *cho-cho,* served boiled or stuffed; and green bananas and plantains, fried or boiled and served with almost everything. Then there's pumpkin, which goes into soup or is served on the side, boiled and mashed with butter. Sweet potatoes appear with main courses, but there's also a sweet-potato pudding made with sugar and coconut milk, flavored with cinnamon, nutmeg, and vanilla.

You'll come across dishes with really odd names: *stamp and go* are saltfish cakes eaten as appetizers; *dip and fall back* is a salty stew with bananas and dumplings; and *rundown* is mackerel cooked in coconut milk, often eaten for breakfast. Patties (meat pies) are another staple snack; the best on the island are in Montego Bay. Boiled corn, roast yams, roast saltfish, fried fish, soups, and fruits are all sold at roadside stands.

In some parts of Jamaica, "tea" is used to describe any nonalcoholic drink, a tradition that dates from plantation days. Fish tea is actually a bowl of hot soup made from freshly caught fish. Skyjuice, a favorite with Jamaicans on hot afternoons, is sold by street vendors from not-always-sanitary carts. It consists of shaved ice with sugar-laden fruit syrup and is sold in small plastic bags with a straw. Coconut water is a refreshing drink, especially when you stop by the road to have a local vendor chop open a fresh coconut.

Rum punches are everywhere, and the local beer is Red Stripe. The island produces many liqueurs, the most famous being Tía Maria, made from coffee beans. Rumona is another good one to take home with you. Bellywash, the local name for limeade, will supply the extra liquid you may need to counteract the heat. Blue Mountain coffee is the best, but tea, cocoa, and milk are usually available to round off a meal.

MARTINIQUE   See Guadeloupe, above.

NEVIS   On Nevis, the local food is good. Suckling pig is roasted with many spices, and eggplant is used in a number of tasty ways, as is avocado. (You may see turtle on some menus, but remember that this is an endangered species.)

PUERTO RICO   Although Puerto Rican cooking has similarities to Cuban, Spanish, and Mexican cuisine, it uses indigenous seasonings and ingredients such as cilantro, papaya, *cacao, nispero, apio,* plantains, and *yampee.*

Cocina Criola (Creole cooking) was initiated by the Arawaks and Taínos, the original inhabitants of the island. Long before Columbus arrived, these peaceful people thrived on a diet of corn, tropical fruits, and seafood. When Ponce de León arrived with Columbus in 1508, the Spanish added beef, pork, rice, wheat, and olive oil to the island's foodstuffs. Soon after, the Spanish began planting sugarcane and importing slaves from Africa, who brought with them okra and taro, known in Puerto Rico as *yauita.* The mingling of flavors and ingredients from different ethnic groups created Puerto Rican cuisine.

Lunch and dinner generally begin with sizzling hot appetizers such as *bacalaitos* (crunchy cod fritters), *surullitos* (sweet, plump cornmeal fingers), and *empanadillas* (crescent-shaped turnovers filled with lobster, crab, conch, or beef). Next, a bowl of steaming *asopao* (a hearty gumbo soup with rice and chicken or shellfish) may be followed by *lechón asado* (roast suckling pig), *pollo en vino dulce* (succulent chicken in wine), or *bacalao* (dried salted cod mixed with various roots and tubers and fried). No matter the selection, main dishes are served with salted tostones (deep-fried plantains or green bananas) and plentiful portions of rice and beans.

The aroma that wafts from kitchens throughout Puerto Rico comes from *adobo* and *sofrito*—blends of herbs and spices that give many of the native foods their distinctive taste and color. *Adobo,* made from peppercorns, oregano, garlic, salt, olive oil, and lime juice or vinegar, is rubbed into meats before they are roasted. *Sofrito,* a potpourri of onions, garlic, and peppers browned in olive oil or lard and colored with *achiote* (annatto seeds), imparts a bright-yellow color to the island's rice, soups, and stews.

Dessert is usually flan (custard) or perhaps *nisperos de batata* (sweet-potato balls made with coconut, cloves, and cinnamon). Finish your meal with Puerto Rican coffee—strong, black, and aromatic.

Rum is the national drink, and you can buy it in almost any shade. On Puerto Rico, it's quite proper to order a cold beer before even looking at the menu; one local choice is India, famous for its pure water. However, most Puerto Ricans drink a golden brew known as Medalla.

SABA   No one visits for the food. Caribbean and continental dishes prevail, but there is no really outstanding restaurant. Most of the food is imported.

ST. BARTHÉLEMY   St. Barts is one of the few islands in the Caribbean where haute cuisine prevails. Perhaps it's somewhat incongruous in a tropical setting, but some excellent continental cuisine is served. There are almost no local dishes, except fresh fish and lobster, though some dishes are given Caribbean flavor. Chicken breast, for instance, is served with mango sauce, and prawns are pan-fried Creole style. Antillean stuffed crab is a regular feature, as is a colombo of lamb (stew flavored with curry and roasted bananas). Chances are, however, that the chef will serve you sole with champagne sauce or fillet of beef in pepper sauce, as in France.

ST. EUSTATIUS   Often called Statia, this Dutch island isn't going to produce any gourmet cookbooks. Most of the food is imported, and restaurants are adequate, not exciting. Some restaurants attempt French cuisine with generally frozen ingredients. Local bistros serve some regional cooking such as stewed conch, salt fish with johnnycakes, or curried goat.

ST. KITTS   On St. Kitts, most guests eat at their hotels, but the island has a number of good restaurants where you can find spiny lobster, crab back, pepper-pot stew, breadfruit, and curried conch. The drink of the island is Cane Spirit Rothschild (CSR), a pure sugarcane liqueur developed by Baron Edmond de Rothschild. Islanders mix it with Ting, a bubbly grapefruit soda.

ST. LUCIA   Try to break free of your hotel and dine in one of St. Lucia's little character-loaded restaurants (we make suggestions in chapter 23). The local food is excellent and reflects the years of French and British occupation. St. Lucia's marketplace offers the ingredients for local dishes, including callaloo soup (fresh greens, dumplings, and salted beef), *pouile dudon* (a sweet, zesty chicken dish), and breadfruit cooked on open hot coals. Pumpkin soup, flying fish, lobster, and *tablette* (a coconut sugar candy that resembles white coral) round out the menu choices.

ST. MAARTEN/ST. MARTIN   This island, part Dutch, part French, has a truly excellent cuisine, in spite of its heavy reliance on imported ingredients. Here you'll find classic French, American, and continental dishes, with a touch of West Indian spice and flavors. The French classics served here include frogs' legs and escargots. Caribbean offerings, inspired by Martinique, include *crabes farcis* (stuffed crab), *blaff* (seafood poached and seasoned with peppers), and curried colombo (a stew with chicken, mutton, or goat).

Nearby Anguilla supplies a never-ending basket of spiny lobsters, the most delectable dish on the island. Dutch specialties are rare, although there's plenty of tasty Dutch beer. A lot of good French wine, served by either the bottle or the carafe, is also shipped into the island.

ST. VINCENT & THE GRENADINES Most dining takes place in the hotels, although a few local bistros serve West Indian food like Creole-style fish and callaloo soup. Mostly locals try to serve what they've heard foreigners like, including frozen steak flown in from Chicago, frozen shrimp from Latin America, and frozen french fries from who-knows-where. Local bartenders take pride in the variety of their rum punches as well as their lethal effects.

TRINIDAD & TOBAGO The food on these islands is as varied and cosmopolitan as the islanders themselves. Although this was a British colony for years, English cuisine never made much of an impression here. Red-hot curries testify to Trinidad's strong East Indian influence, and some Chinese dishes are about as good here as any you'd find in Hong Kong. You'll also find Creole, Spanish, and French fare. A typical savory offering is a *rôti,* a king-size crêpe, highly spiced and filled with chicken, shellfish, or meat. Of course, you may prefer to skip such local delicacies as opossum stew and fried armadillo and be aware that in Trinidad there's a tendency to deep-fry everything. Naturally, your fresh rum punch will have a dash of Angostura Bitters.

Tobago has fewer dining choices than Trinidad. Your best bet is local fish dishes, such as stuffed kingfish in Creole sauce. Local crayfish is also good, and lobster appears on some menus, perhaps stuffed into a crêpe. One island favorite that appears frequently is seafood casserole with ginger wine. Some typical Tobago dishes include baby shark marinated in lime and rum and conch stewed with coconut and rum.

THE U.S. VIRGIN ISLANDS Although a lot of the food is imported (often from Miami or Puerto Rico) and frozen, St. Thomas, and to a lesser extent St. Croix and St. John, serve some of the finest American and continental cuisine in the Caribbean. Very experienced chefs, especially from Europe, are often brought in during the winter season to tempt your taste buds. A whole range of ethnic restaurants exists as well, including Chinese, Mexican, and Italian.

The most famous soup of the islands is *kallaloo,* or *callaloo,* made in an infinite number of ways from a leafy green vegetable similar to spinach. This soup is flavored with salt beef, pig mouth, pig tail, ham bone, fresh fish, crabs, or perhaps conch, along with okra, onions, and spices. Many soups are sweetened with sugar and contain fruits. The classic red-bean soup made with pork or ham, various spices, and tomatoes, is sugared to taste. Tannia soup is made from the root of the so-called Purple Elephant Ear. Salt-fat meat and ham, along with tomatoes, onions, and spices, are added to the tannias.

Souse is an old-time favorite made with the feet, head, and tongue of the pig, and flavored with a lime-based sauce and various spices. Salt-fish salad is traditionally served on Holy Thursday or Good Friday, as well as at other times. It's made with boneless salt fish, potatoes, onions, boiled eggs, and an oil-and-vinegar dressing.

Herring gundy is an old-time island favorite made with salt herring, potatoes, onions, sweet and hot green peppers, olives, diced beets, raw carrots, herbs, and boiled eggs. Seasoned rice is popular with Virgin Islanders, who often serve several starches at one meal. Most often rice is flavored with ham or salt pork, tomatoes, garlic, onion, and shortening. Fungi is a simple cornmeal dumpling that can be made more interesting with the addition of various ingredients, such as okra. Sweet fungi becomes a dessert, with sugar, milk, cinnamon, and raisins.

Okra (often spelled *ochroe* in the islands) is a mainstay vegetable, often accompanying beef, fish, or chicken. It's fried in an iron skillet after it's flavored with hot pepper, tomatoes, onions, garlic, and bacon fat or butter. *Accra,* another popular dish, is made with okra, black-eyed peas, salt, and pepper. It's dropped into boiling fat and fried until golden brown.

The classic vegetable dish—some families serve it every night—is peas and rice, made with pigeon peas flavored with ham or salt meat, onion, tomatoes, herbs, and sometimes slices of pumpkin.

Sweet-potato pone is a classic dessert, made with sugar, eggs, butter, milk, salt, cinnamon, raisins, and chopped almonds. The exotic fruits of the islands lend themselves to various homemade ice creams, including mango. Orange-rose sherbet is made by pounding rose petals into a paste and flavoring it with sugar and orange juice. Guava ice cream is a delectable flavor, as are soursop, banana, and papaya. Sometimes dumplings are served for dessert, made with guava, peach, plum, gooseberry, cherry, or apple.

Frommer's Online Directory

by Michael Shapiro

Frommer's Online Directory is researched and written by Michael Shapiro, author of "Internet Travel Planning" published by The Globe Peque Press.

Frommer's Online Directory is a new feature designed to help you take advantage of the Internet to better plan your trip. Part I lists some general Internet resources that can make any trip easier, such as sites for booking airline tickets. It's not meant to be a comprehensive list—rather, it's a discriminating selection of useful sites to get you started. In Part II, you'll find some top online guides specifically for the Caribbean, organized by island.

1 The Top Travel-Planning Web Sites

Among the most popular sites are online travel agencies. The top agencies, including Expedia, Preview Travel, and Travelocity, offer an array of tools that are valuable even if you don't book online. You can check flight schedules, hotel availability, car-rental prices, or even get paged if your flight is delayed.

While online agencies have come a long way over the past few years, they don't always yield the best price. Unlike a travel agent, for example, they're unlikely to tell you that you can save money by flying a day earlier or a day later. On the other hand, if you're looking for a bargain fare, you might find something online that an agent wouldn't take the time to dig up. Because airline commissions have been cut, a travel agent may not find it worthwhile spending half an hour trying to find you the best deal. On the Net, you can be your own agent and take all the time you want.

Online booking sites aren't the only places to book airline tickets—all major airlines have their own Web sites and often offer incentives, such as bonus frequent-flyer miles or Net-only discounts, for buying online. These incentives have helped airlines capture the majority of the online booking market. According to Jupiter Communications, online agencies such as Travelocity booked about 80 percent of tickets purchased online in 1996, but by 1999 airline sites (such as **www.ual.com**) were projected to own about 60 percent of the online market, with online agencies' share of the pie dwindling each year.

Below are the Web sites for some of the airlines serving Caribbean airports. These sites offer schedules and flight booking, and some have pages where you can sign up for e-mail alerts on weekend deals and other late-breaking bargains.

Far more people look online than book online, partly due to fear of putting their credit cards through on the Net. Though secure encryption has made this fear less justified, there's no reason why you can't find a flight online and then book it by calling a toll-free number or contacting your travel agent. To be sure you're in secure mode when you book online, look for a little icon of a key (in Netscape) or a padlock (Internet Explorer) at the bottom of your Web browser.

Aeromexico **www.aeromexico.com**
Air Aruba **www.interknowledge.com/air-aruba**
Air Canada **www.aircanada.ca**
Air France **www.airfrance.com**
Air Jamaica **www.airjamaica.com**
ALM **www.alm-airlines.com**
American Airlines **www.aa.com**
British Airways **www.british-airways.com**
BWIA **www.bwee.com**
Canadian Airlines International **www.cdnair.ca**
Cayman Airways **www.caymanairways.com**
Continental Airlines **www.continental.com**
Delta Air Lines **www.delta-air.com**
Iberia **www.iberia.com**
Mexicana Airlines **www.mexicana.com**
Northwest Airlines **www.nwa.com**
Trans World Airlines (TWA) **www.twa.com**
United Airlines **www.ual.com**
US Airways **www.usairways.com**

WHEN SHOULD YOU BOOK ONLINE?

Online booking is not for everyone. If you prefer to let others handle your travel arrangements, one call to an experienced travel agent should suffice. But if you want to know as much as possible about your options, the Net is a good place to start, especially for bargain hunters.

The most compelling reason to use online booking is to take advantage of special offers and Internet-only fares that must be purchased online. Another advantage is that you can cash in on incentives for booking online, such as rebates or bonus frequent-flyer miles.

Online booking works best for trips within North America—for international tickets, it's usually cheaper and easier to use a travel agent or consolidator.

Online booking is certainly not for those with a complex international itinerary. If you require follow-up services, such as itinerary changes, use a travel agent. Though Expedia and some other online agencies employ travel agents available by phone, these sites are geared primarily for self-service.

LEADING BOOKING SITES

Below are listings for the top travel booking sites. The starred selections are the most useful and best designed sites.

Cheap Tickets. www.cheaptickets.com
Essentials: Discounted rates on domestic and international airline tickets and hotel rooms.

Take a Look at Frommer's Site

We highly recommend Arthur Frommer's Budget Travel online (**www.frommers.com**) as an excellent travel planning resource. Of course, we're a little biased, but you will find indispensable travel tips, reviews, monthly vacation giveaways, and online booking.

Subscribe to Arthur Frommer's Daily Newsletter (**www.frommers.com/newsletters**) to receive the latest travel bargains and insider tips. You'll read daily headlines and articles from the dean of travel himself, highlighting last-minute deals on airfares, accommodations, cruises, and package vacations. You'll also find great travel advice by checking our Tip of the Day or Hot Spot of the month.

Search our Destinations archive (**www.frommers.com/destinations**) of more than 200 domestic and international destinations for great places to stay, tips for getting there, and what to do while you're there. Once you've researched your trip, you might try our online reservation system (**www.frommers.com/booktravelnow**) to book your dream vacation at affordable prices.

Sometimes discounters such as Cheap Tickets have exclusive deals that aren't available through more mainstream channels. Registration at Cheap Tickets requires inputting a credit-card number before getting started, so many people elect to call the company's toll-free number rather than booking online. Cheap Tickets actually regards this policy as a selling point, arguing that "lookers" who don't intend to buy will be scared off by its "credit card first" approach and won't bog down the site with their queries. Despite its misguided credit-card policy, Cheap Tickets is worth the effort, as its fares can be substantially lower than those offered by its competitors.

✪ **Expedia. expedia.com**
Essentials: Domestic and international flight, hotel, and rental-car booking; late-breaking travel news; destination features and commentary from travel experts; deals on cruises and vacation packages. Free (one-time) registration is required for booking.

Expedia makes it easy to handle flight, hotel, and car booking on one itinerary, so it's a good place for one-stop shopping. The hotel search offers crisp, zoomable maps to pinpoint most properties; click on the camera icon to see images of the rooms. But like many online databases, Expedia focuses on the major chains, such as Hilton and Hyatt, so don't expect too many one-of-a-kind resorts or B&Bs here.

Once you're registered, you can start booking with the Roundtrip Fare Finder on the home page, which expedites the process. After selecting a flight, you can hold it until midnight the following day or purchase online. If you think you might do better through a travel agent, you'll have time to try to get a lower price. (You may do better with a travel agent, since Expedia's computer reservation system does not include all airlines.)

Expedia's World Guide, offering destination information, is a glaring weakness—it takes a lot of page views to get very little information. However, Expedia compensates by linking to other Microsoft Network services, which offer entertainment and dining advice for many of the cities it covers.

Preview Travel. www.previewtravel.com
Essentials: Domestic and international flight, hotel, and rental-car booking; Travel Newswire fare sales; deals on cruises and vacation packages. Free (one-time)

registration is required for booking. Preview offers express booking for members, but at press time, this feature was buried below the fold on Preview's reservation page.

Preview features the most inviting interface for booking trips, though the wealth of graphics involved can make the site somewhat slow to load. Use Farefinder to quickly find the lowest current fares on flights to dozens of major cities. Carfinder offers a similar service for rental cars, but you can only search airport locations, not city pick-up sites.

Preview has a great feature called the Best Fare Finder; after it searches for the best deal on your itinerary, it will check flights that are a bit later or earlier to see if it might be cheaper to fly at a different time. While these searches have become quite sophisticated, they still occasionally overlook deals that might be uncovered by a top-notch travel agent. If you have the time, explore the options online and then call an agent to see if you can get a better price.

With Preview's Fare Alert feature, you can select up to three routes and receive e-mail notices when the fare drops below your target amount. For example, you can tell Preview to alert you when the round-trip fare from New York to Maui drops below $500. If it does, you'll get an e-mail telling you the current fare.

Minor quibbles: When you search for a fare, hotel, or car (at least at press time), Preview launches an annoying little "Please Wait" window that gets in the way of the main browser window, even when your results begin to appear. The hotel search feature is intuitive, but the images and maps aren't as crisp as those at Expedia. Also, all sorts of extraneous information that's irrelevant to most travelers is listed on maps.

Note to AOL Users: You can book flights, hotels, rental cars, and cruises on AOL at keyword: Travel. The booking software is provided by Preview Travel and is similar to Preview on the Web. Use the AOL "Travelers Advantage" program to earn a 5% rebate on flights, hotel rooms, and car rentals.

Priceline.com. www.priceline.com

Priceline lets you "name your price" for domestic and international airline tickets. In other words, you select a route and dates, guarantee with a credit card, and make a bid for what you're willing to pay. If one of the airlines in Priceline's database has a fare that's lower than your bid, your credit card will automatically be charged for a ticket.

But you can't say when you want to fly—you have to accept any flight leaving between 6am and 10pm, and you may have to make a stopover. No frequent-flyer miles are awarded, and tickets are non-refundable and can't be exchanged for another flight. So if your plans change, you're out of luck. Priceline can be good for travelers who have to take off on short notice (and who are thus unable to qualify for advance-purchase discounts). But be sure to shop around first—if you overbid, you'll be required to purchase the ticket and Priceline will pocket the difference.

Travelocity. www.travelocity.com

Essentials: Domestic and international flight, hotel, and rental-car booking; deals on cruises and vacation packages. Travel Headlines spotlights latest bargain airfares. Free (one-time) registration is required for booking.

Travelocity almost got it right. Its Express Booking feature enables travelers to complete the booking process more quickly than they could at Expedia or Preview, but Travelocity gums up the works with a page called "Featured Airlines." Big placards of several featured airlines compete for your attention—if you want to see the fares for all available airlines, click the much smaller box at the bottom of the page labeled "Book a Flight."

Some have worried that Travelocity, which is owned by American Airlines' parent company AMR, directs bookings to American. This doesn't seem to be the case; we've booked there dozens of times and have always been directed to the cheapest listed flight. But this "Featured Airlines" page seems to be Travelocity's way of trying to cash in with ads and incentives for booking certain airlines. (*Note:* It's hard to blame these booking services for trying to generate some revenue; many airlines have slashed commissions to $10 per domestic booking for online transactions, so these virtual agencies are groping for revenue streams.) There are rewards for choosing one of the featured airlines. You'll get 1,500 bonus frequent-flyer miles if you book through United's site, for example, but the site doesn't tell you about other airlines that might be cheaper. If the United flight costs $150 more than the best deal on another airline, it's not worth spending the extra money.

On the plus side, Travelocity has some leading-edge tools. Fare Watcher e-mail is an "intelligent agent" that keeps you informed of the best fares offered for the round-trips of your choice. Whenever the fare changes by $25 or more, Fare Watcher will alert you by e-mail. If you own an alphanumeric pager with national access that can receive e-mail, Travelocity's Flight Paging system can alert you if your flight is delayed. Finally, though Travelocity doesn't include every budget airline, it does include Southwest, the leading U.S. budget carrier.

FINDING LODGINGS ONLINE

While the services above offer hotel booking, it can be best to use a site devoted primarily to lodging in order to find properties that aren't listed on more general online travel agencies. Some specialize in a particular type of accommodation, such as B&Bs, which you won't find on the more mainstream booking services. Other services, such as TravelWeb, offer weekend deals on major chain properties, which cater to business travelers and have more empty rooms on weekends.

All Hotels on the Web. www.all-hotels.com
This site doesn't include *all* the hotels on the Web, but it does have tens of thousands of listings throughout the world. Bear in mind that each hotel listed has paid a small fee (of $25 and up) for placement, so it's not an objective list; it's more like a book of online brochures.

InnSite. www.innsite.com
This site has B&B listings for all 50 U.S. states and dozens of countries around the globe. Find an inn at your destination, have a look at images of the rooms, check prices and availability, and then send e-mail to the innkeeper if you have further questions. This is an extensive directory of B&Bs, but only includes listings if the proprietor submitted one (*note:* it's free to get an inn listed). The descriptions are written by the innkeepers and many listings link to the inn's own Web sites, where you can find more information and images.

Places to Stay. www.placestostay.com
Mostly one-of-a-kind places in the U.S. and abroad that you might not find in other directories, with a focus on resort accommodations. Again, this isn't a comprehensive directory, but can give you a sense of what's available at different destinations.

✪ TravelWeb. www.travelweb.com
TravelWeb lists more than 16,000 hotels worldwide, focusing on chains such as Hyatt and Hilton, and you can book almost 90 percent of these online. TravelWeb's Click-It Weekends, updated each Monday, offers weekend deals at many leading hotel chains. TravelWeb is the online home for Pegasus Systems, which provides transaction processing systems for the hotel industry.

LAST-MINUTE DEALS & OTHER ONLINE BARGAINS

There's nothing airlines hate more than flying with lots of empty seats. The Net has enabled airlines to offer last-minute bargains to entice travelers to fill those seats. Most of these are announced on Tuesday or Wednesday and are valid for travel the following weekend, but some can be booked weeks or months in advance. You can sign up for weekly e-mail alerts at airlines' sites, or check sites such as WebFlyer (see below) that compile lists of these bargains. To make it easier, visit a site that will round up all the deals and send them in one convenient weekly e-mail. But last-minute deals aren't the only online bargains—other sites can help you find value even if you can't wait until the eleventh hour.

✪ 1travel.com. www.1travel.com
Here you'll find deals on domestic and international flights, cruises, hotels, and all-inclusive resorts such as Club Med. 1travel.com's Saving Alert compiles last-minute air deals so you don't have to scroll through multiple e-mail notices. A feature called "Drive a little using low-fare airlines" helps map out strategies for using alternate airports to find lower fares. And Farebeater searches a database that includes published fares, consolidator bargains, and special deals exclusive to 1travel.com. *Note:* The travel agencies listed by 1travel.com have paid for placement.

BestFares. www.bestfares.com
Bargain-seeker Tom Parsons lists some great bargains on airfares, hotels, rental cars, and cruises, but the site is poorly organized. News Desk is a long list of hundreds of bargains, but they're not broken down into cities or even countries, so it's not easy trying to find what you're looking for. If you have time to wade through it, you might find a good deal. Some material is available only to paid subscribers.

Go4less.com. www.go4less.com
Specializing in last-minute cruise and package deals, Go4less has some eye-popping offers, such as off-peak Caribbean cruises for under $100 per day. The site has a clean design, but the bargains aren't organized by destination. However, you can avoid sifting through all this material by using the Search box and entering vacation type, destination, month, and price.

Moment's Notice. www.moments-notice.com
As the name suggests, Moment's Notice specializes in last-minute vacation and cruise deals. You can browse for free, but if you want to purchase a trip you have to join Moment's Notice, which costs $25.

Smarter Living. www.smarterliving.com
Best known for its e-mail dispatch of weekend deals on 20 airlines, Smarter Living also keeps you posted about last-minute bargains on everything from Windjammer Cruises to flights to Iceland.

A Handy Tip

While most people learn about last-minute weekend deals from e-mail dispatches, it can be best to find out precisely *when* these deals become available and check airlines' Web sites at this time. To find out when these special offers become available, check the pages devoted to the deals on airlines' Web pages. Because these deals are limited, they can vanish within hours, sometimes even minutes, so it pays to log on as soon as they're available.

○ WebFlyer. **www.webflyer.com**
WebFlyer is the ultimate online resource for frequent flyers and also has an excellent
listing of last-minute air deals. Click on "Deal Watch" for a round-up of weekend deals
on flights, hotels, and rental cars from domestic and international suppliers.

TRAVELER'S TOOLKIT

Seasoned travelers always carry some essential items to make their trips easier. The following is a selection of online tools to smooth your journey.

ATM LOCATORS

Visa (**www.visa.com/pd/atm**)
MasterCard (**www.mastercard.com/atm**)
Find ATMs in hundreds of cities in the U.S. and around the world. Both include maps
for some locations and both list airport ATM locations, some with maps.

○ Foreign Languages for Travelers. **www.travlang.com**
Learn basic terms in more than 70 languages and click on any underlined phrase to
hear what it sounds like. (*Note:* Free audio software and speakers are required.)

Intellicast. **www.intellicast.com**
Weather forecasts for all 50 states and cities around the world. Note that temperatures
are in Celsius for many international destinations, so don't think you'll need that
winter coat for your next trip to Athens.

MapQuest. **www.mapquest.com**
Specializing in U.S. maps but capable of generating maps for dozens of international
cities, MapQuest enables you to zoom in on a destination and locate restaurants,
hotels, and other attractions on maps.

○ Net Cafe Guide. **www.netcafeguide.com**
Locate Internet cafes at hundreds of locations around the globe. Catch up on your
e-mail, log onto the Web, and stay in touch with the home front, usually for just a few
dollars per hour.

Universal Currency Converter. **www.xe.net/currency**
See what your dollar or pound is worth in more than a hundred other countries.

U.S. Customs Service Traveler Information. **www.customs.ustreas.gov/travel/**
index.htm
Wondering what you're allowed to bring in to the U.S.? Check at this thorough site,
which includes maximum allowance and duty fees.

2 The Top Web Sites for the Caribbean

GENERAL CARIBBEAN GUIDES

This section has some general Web sites covering the Caribbean, while successive sections list useful sites for each island. Keep in mind that many of the best Web sites for
the Caribbean contain pages dedicated to individual destinations.

Calabash Skyviews. **www.skyviews.com**
Skyviews provides free print maps to visitors in the Caribbean; its online guide covers
about 20 islands, with solid information on sightseeing, getting around (including driving tours), beaches, and shopping. Also included: the requisite dining and lodging
advice, plus links to tour operators and outfitters.

Check Your E-mail at Internet Cafes While Traveling

Until a few years ago, most travelers who checked their e-mail while traveling carried a laptop, but this posed some problems. Not only are laptops expensive, but they also can be difficult to configure, incur expensive connection charges, and are attractive to thieves. Thankfully, Web-based free e-mail programs have made it much easier to stay in touch.

Just open an account at a freemail provider, such as Hotmail (hotmail.com) or Excite Mail (mail.excite.com), and all you'll need to check your mail is a Web connection, easily available at Net cafes and copy shops around the world. After logging on, just point the browser to www.hotmail.com, enter you username and password, you'll have access to your mail.

Internet cafes have become ubiquitous, so for a few dollars an hour you'll be able to check your mail and send messages back to colleagues, friends, and family. If you already have a primary e-mail account, you can set it to forward mail to your freemail account while you're away. Freemail programs have become enormously popular because they enable everyone, even those who don't own a computer, to have an e-mail address they can check wherever they log onto the Web.

Caribbean-On-Line. www.caribbean-on-line.com
This general guide to the Caribbean can help you find tour operators, golf courses, sailing trips, and more. You'll also find advice on getting there, accommodations, restaurants, and shopping.

The Civilized Explorer: Caribbean. www.cieux.com/trinfo3.html
A healthy collection of links to more than two dozen Caribbean destinations. Consider this site a port of embarkation rather than a destination in itself.

✪ **InterKnowledge: The Caribbean. www.interknowledge.com/indx02.htm**
About a dozen destinations are covered here, mostly with official tourism bureau information. But don't let that discourage you—there's also advice on golf, fishing, beaches, and points of interest, as well as a calendar of events.

Island Connoisseur: The Caribbean Super Site. caribbeansupersite.com
Use the pull-down menu on the home page to choose one of more than two dozen Caribbean destinations. Some of the general information is pretty thin, but you'll find a nice collection of links to Web sites featuring everything from dining to travelogues.

TravelFacts. www.travelfacts.com
Select your destination using the pull-down menu and you'll find extensive listings for sightseeing, tours, dining, lodging, shopping and more. Some of the navigation can be clunky; for example, at press time, instead of finding all the essential information for a restaurant on one page, you have to click on separate links for details, contact info, etc.

Turqoise Net. www.turq.com
A bare-bones guide to some of the islands with information on lodging and dining; it does have links to some properties' own Web sites, which can be useful. You'll also find links to tourism offices, news from the Caribbean, maps, weather, and a photo album.

Your Caribbean Travel Planner. caribbeantravel.com
A general introduction from the Caribbean Hotel Association, including maps, hotel listings, activities, and more.

ANGUILLA

The Anguilla Guide. net.ai
A basic yet informative guide including information on restaurants, beaches, activities, and lodging, with links to company's own Web sites, where you can see images of hotels, for example. The activities section is especially useful with links for hiking, horseback riding, nightlife, galleries, and more.

Anguilla Home Page. anguillahomepage.ai
Another extensive guide to dining, accommodations, and events, with lots of links to companies' own Web sites. You'll also find information on and images of beaches as well as advice for getting there.

Official Tourist Guide of Anguilla. www.candw.com.ai/~atbtour
Get the basics from Anguilla's tourism board—you'll find answers to frequently asked questions, e-mail addresses for tourist-board reps, and advice on activities, dining, and accommodations.

ANTIGUA & BARBUDA

✪ Antigua and Barbuda. www.antigua-barbuda.org
An extensive, well-designed, and informative guide from the Antigua & Barbuda Department of Tourism. The site covers approximately 20 subjects, from Carnival to transportation. You'll also find information on events such as Sailing Week. If you check only one Web site before you go, this should be the one.

Antigua Today. antiguatoday.com
This collection of Antigua Web pages includes more than 400 referrals to hotels, restaurants, and other sites in Antigua. There's also a short tour of the island, but at press time, it loaded extremely slowly.

ARUBA

Arikok National Park. www.arubanationalparks.com
A guide to the wildlife and activities in this Aruban national park.

Aruba Experience. www.aruba-experience.com
Tips on dining, shopping, and nightlife from the pages of this free tourist magazine.

Aruba Gourmet Restaurant Guide. www.arubadining.com
Information on the island's restaurants and a dine-around program sponsored by the Aruba Gastronomic Association.

Aruba Tourism Authority. www.aruba.com
An updated events calendar plus listings for shopping, dining, accommodations, and activities. Use the links and e-mail addresses here to get in touch with tour operators and outfitters.

✪ Visit Aruba. www.visitaruba.com
This Web site really gets it. Rather than trying to imitate a guide book, Visit Aruba offers features that complement this print guide. You'll find a news desk listing the latest happenings, trip reports from other travelers, a map of dive sites, even local recipes and Top 40 hits that you can listen to online. Of course you'll also find information on dining and shopping, as well as bulletin boards where you can read others' postings or pose a question of your own.

BARBADOS

Barbados Tourism Encyclopedia. barbados.org
Information on events, special vacation-package discounts, and advice on dining and lodging from the Barbados Tourism Authority. You'll also find maps, sightseeing tours, and shopping tips.

✪ Fun Barbados. funbarbados.com
This site lives up to its name—after you spend a few minutes here, you'll be itching to get to the islands. There's extensive information, from the basics (shopping, lodging, dining) to the more esoteric (biking, gardens, caves). You'll also find tips on island tours, a beach guide, and a nightlife calendar.

BONAIRE

✪ Bonaire: Dutch Caribbean. www.bonaire.org
Windsurfing at Lac Bay is just one of Bonaire's many attractions, but the picture here, with the caption "This color has *not* been retouched—Lac Bay really is this blue," may be enough to send you on your way. This well-designed site from Bonaire's tourism office covers lodging and dining but offers much more. You'll find advice for getting off the beaten path, a primer on the local language, a calendar of events, and tips on enjoying a myriad of outdoor activities.

Bonaire Restaurant Association. www.bonairerestaurants.com
A nice roundup of local eateries with menus (including prices) and specials for some of those listed.

InfoBonaire. www.infobonaire.com
The extensive events calendar is the most useful part of this site. You'll also find the basics for dining, lodging, shopping, and getting around.

THE BRITISH VIRGIN ISLANDS

British Virgin Islands Welcome. www.bviwelcome.com
There's nothing spectacular about this site, but it does have solid information on dining, lodging, and—best of all—activities. Click on "At Sea" and use the pull-down menu to choose from scuba, kayaking, and other water sports.

J ScubaMom's BVI Resort Reviews. www.scubamom.com/bvi
Lynn McKamey (a.k.a. ScubaMom) offers extensive personal reviews of resorts and dive spots around the British Virgin Islands. You'll also find lots of pictures and maps, which can make pages slow to load, but they're worth the wait. This is a personal effort that shows how helpful an individual's Web page can be.

Ultimate BVI. www.ultimatebvi.com
While you'll find advice on dining, accommodations, and shopping here, most useful are the sections on diving and boating, with information on charters and e-mail links that let you contact the proprietors. One really annoying aspect of this site is that it opens a new browser window (which slows down surfing) when you click on some links.

Welcome to the British Virgin Islands. www.britishvirginislands.com
A well-designed but not very extensive guide to some of the BVI's hotels, restaurants, and shops. Most useful are the sections on boating and water sports, where you can explore your options and use e-mail to connect with outfitters before you go.

THE CAYMAN ISLANDS

Cayman Islands. www.caymans.com

At press time, this site greeted visitors with an ugly "For Sale" sign on the home page (the Web site was up for sale), but don't let that turn you away. There's some great stuff here, such as a long list of recipes from the islands (iced coconut soup or banana mudslide, anyone?). But don't expect much from the calendar of events—at this writing, it hadn't been updated in 2 years.

The Cayman Islands Department of Tourism. www.caymanislands.ky
Find out about the Batabano Carnival or get up to speed on the Cayman Islands International Fishing Tournament. This site smartly features upcoming happenings on its home page, while also offering advice on dining, lodging, and shopping.

✪ **Cayman Web World. cayman.com.ky**
Diving in Stingray City, where it appears you can pet the rays, is just one of the many attractions featured here. Cayman Web World does a fine job highlighting the islands' attractions (including those on Little Cayman and Cayman Brac), and also includes advice on dining, lodging, and shopping.

CURACAO

✪ **Curacao.com. www.curacao.com**
With a seemingly endless number of links, this site can help you find a beach, a restaurant, or a club for some late-night festivities. Curacao.com is well organized and has extensive sections on culture, tours, and events.

Official Curacao Tourism Site. www.curacao.org
If you can get past the hideous design, you might find some serviceable information on dining, lodging, diving, and other activities.

DOMINICA

Dominica: The Nature Island of the Caribbean. www.dominica.dm
From the rain forest to the boiling lakes, this official site gives the low-down on the best ways to spend your time on Dominica. You'll also find a photo gallery, maps, and a calendar of events that includes festivals.

A Virtual Dominica. www.delphis.dm/home.htm
Wondering where the best dive spots are, or where you can find the best places to see whales? This is your site. You'll find advice on where to dive as well as dive operators who can outfit you, basic lodging information with links to some of the properties' own sites, 360-degree views of the island, and forums where you can exchange messages with others interested in the island.

THE DOMINICAN REPUBLIC

Debbie's Dominican Republic Travel Page. www.computan.on.ca/ ~pdowney/travel.html
This is a personal page from a Canadian sun-worshipper who offers advice on what to expect, what to pack, and what to do. She offers space for others to submit their reviews as well, so you can read a wide range of personal opinions here.

Dominican Republic Vacation Planner. www.domrep-hotels.com.do/ welcome-eng.htm
A fairly useful roundup of hotels (mostly upscale) with detailed information and images. Another section helps you figure out how to spend your days with tips on beaches, diving, golf, and more.

Hispaniola.com. www.hispaniola.com
While this site has reams of valuable information on what to do, where to go, and how to get there, the design (at least at press time) is challenging, to say the least—it's like trying to read through prison bars, but still worth the effort.

GRENADA

Grenada: The Spice of the Caribbean. www.grenada.org
This site, from the Grenada Board of Tourism, includes basic visitor information and the latest on the Grenada Spice Jazz Festival, the Grenada Dive Festival, and many other happenings around the island.

Grenada Travellers' Guide. www.travelgrenada.com
From attractions and tours to spices and recipes, this site captures the flavor of Grenada and can help you get the most from your trip. You'll find sections on shopping, water sports, cruises, accommodations, and weddings.

GUADELOUPE

Antilles Info Tourisme: Guadeloupe. www.antilles-info-tourisme.com/ guadeloupe
Enjoy a virtual sightseeing tour or stock up on ideas for how to spend your time while on Guadeloupe. You'll also find basics on dining, accommodations, nightlife, and even some local recipes. This colorful site is illuminated with nice photography and captures the essence of the "butterfly island."

Guadeloupe: The Civilized Island. www.cieux.com/gdlp.html
While this is not the best organized site, it can help you learn more about Guadeloupe, letting you see restaurants' specialties, lots of nice photos, ideas for activities such as climbing the volcano, and insider advice—such as where to find a clothing-optional beach on this civilized island.

JAMAICA

Discover Jamaica. www.discoverjamaica.com
Though this is a pretty generic site, you can find solid descriptions of Jamaica's regions, including dining, lodging, and activities. For example, click on Ocho Rios, then on Attractions, and find an online brochure from Blue Mountain Bicycle Tours, complete with vivid images and contact information.

Jamaica Tourist Board. www.jamaicatravel.com
This official site does a nice job of providing detailed information on activities (such as a listing of golf courses), accommodations (searchable by region and amenities), and events (with an updated calendar).

J Real Jamaican Tourist. www.jamaicans.com/tourist/index.htm
An insider's guide to the island written from a Jamaican's perspective. This site offers advice on avoiding tourist traps and dealing with local hustlers, as well as an "A-to-Z" guide with information on flying to Jamaica, events, golf, and weather.

MARTINIQUE

See Caribbean: Martinique. www.see-caribbean.com/martinique
A pretty thin site, but it does have some nice images.

Tourist Martinique. **www.touristmartinique.com**
A decent general introduction to Martinique: Learn about local festivals, find out where to charter a boat, and peruse general visitor information including advice on dining, lodging, nightlife, and getting around.

NEVIS

The "Non-Tourist-Trap" Guide to Nevis, West Indies. **nevis1.com**
While some sections of this site are a bit thin, it's a solid, all-around guide with a refreshingly personal perspective.

PUERTO RICO

Escape to Puerto Rico. **escape.topuertorico.com**
This is an all-in-one site for those looking for more information on hotels. You'll find links to some properties that include both images and lengthy lists of amenities. There's also tips on restaurants, activities, and much more.

J Let's Dine Puerto Rico. **letsdine.com**
A well-organized site where you can search for restaurants by cuisine type or neighborhood. You can also find specialty places, such as vegetarian restaurants.

Vieques Island. **vieques-island.com**
A homespun site for this little island off the coast of Puerto Rico. The site's creator says this island, with a population of less than 10,000 and not too many visitors, has beaches to die for.

Welcome to Puerto Rico. **welcome.topuertorico.org**
Much of the information here is quite similar to what you'll find in this book—some of the descriptions, in fact, were lifted verbatim from an earlier edition of this Frommer's guide. But beyond that are some useful links to help you get oriented, as well as ideas for how to spend your time on Puerto Rico.

SABA

Dive Saba. **www.divesaba.com**
While this site focuses on diving (with listings for all three of the island's dive shops!), you'll also find information on lodging, dining, and more.

Saba Online. **saba-online.com**
This hub site links out to dozens of useful Web pages, including sites on Saba's natural wonders, local artists, and dive shops. You'll also find basic information on lodging, dining, and shopping.

ST. BARTHÉLEMY

A Visitor's Guide to St. Barthélemy. **www.st-barths.com/guide.html**
While many people come to St. Barts simply to lie around, there's lots to do, if you're up for it. Among the categories on this site: the Place, the People, Beaches, and Cultural Events. There's also tips on getting around, lodging, dining, and shopping.

ST. EUSTATIUS

Dive Statia. **www.iland.net/divestatia**
This diving guide combines insider advice with underwater photography for a well-rounded introduction to the island's reefs.

St. Eustatius Tourist Office. **www.turq.com/statia**
You won't find much here that isn't already in this guidebook, but there are some pictures and links to hotels and dive outfitters.

ST. KITTS

J Accenting St. Kitts & Nevis. **www.stkitts-nevis.com**
Whether your interest is golfing, fishing, boating, or just about anything else, you'll likely find some information here to help you plan your stay. You'll also find tips on dining, lodging, and nightlife.

St. Kitts & Nevis Explorer. **www.chrisevelyn.com/St.Kitts-Nevis/home.htm**
This is a personal guide with virtual tours and advice on attractions and lodging, but beware: It can be very slow to load.

ST. LUCIA

St. Lucia Hotel and Tourism Association. **www.stluciatravel.com.lc**
This is a boosterish guide but may give you some ideas for places to stay or things to do. There's even information on planning a honeymoon.

St. Lucia Tourist Board. **www.stlucia.org**
Looking for the line-up for this year's jazz fest? If you won't be around in May for the festival, there's a calendar of other happenings, plus extensive listings of dining and lodging choices.

ST. MAARTEN/ST. MARTIN

Mr. St. Martin. **www.mrstm.com**
The self-proclaimed authority on St. Maarten/St. Martin, this site is a place to find a hotel or a restaurant, chat online with others about the island, or check the weather.

Sint Maarten Saint Martin. **www.St-Maarten-St-Martin.com**
From the scenic images of beaches and virtual reality panoramas to solid nuts-and-bolts advice on getting there and getting around, this site will whet your appetite for a visit to this island, whatever you choose to call it.

ST. VINCENT & THE GRENADINES

St. Vincent & the Grenadines. **vincy.com/svg**
Images and guides for St. Vincent and each of the Grenadines. Select "Island Tour" for a clickable map, then choose the islands you want to learn about. Turn the pages of the virtual Photo Album or browse through the Attractions section.

✪ ScubaMom's St. Vincent & the Grenadines. **www.scubamom.com/grenadines**
An up-close-and-personal guide complete with many stunning photographs. ScubaMom reviews several island resorts and gives you the inside scoop on what to see and where to go. Though the name suggests this is a scuba site, it's really more of a travelogue.

TRINIDAD & TOBAGO

Discover Trinidad & Tobago. **www.carib-link.net/discover**
You can almost hear the steel drums and feel the pulse of Carnival at this site. The photos are vibrant and the descriptions enticing. This isn't the place for detailed visitor information, but the site can still help you sample the flavors of T&T.

✪ Welcome to Trinidad and Tobago. **www.visitTNT.com**
This site goes beyond solid coverage of basic visitor information. There's an entire section on Carnival, complete with pictures from recent celebrations and Carnival dates all the way to 2009 for you plan-ahead types. To learn more about lodging, you can take a look at some hotels through links to their own Web sites—and in some cases, book online.

THE U.S. VIRGIN ISLANDS

Caribbean Villas and Resorts. **caribbeanvilla.com**
Sneak a peak at the dozens of villas and condos listed here—some are offered at a 10 to 20 percent discount for "last-minute" reservations (about a month or less in advance). You'll also find useful links to other local services, from Jeep rentals to dive shops.

United States Virgin Islands Tourist Guide. **www.usvi.net**
This site includes a photographic tour of the three main islands, as well as updates on nightlife and festivals. The accommodations information is generic, although you can link to full hotel brochures with descriptions, photos, lists of amenities, and seasonal discounts.

United States Virgin Islands Travel Guide. **www.virginisles.com**
This extensive guide is a bit boosterish but valuable for its extensive coverage of what to see and do. While the site isn't deep (you won't find coverage of individual restaurants, for example), it is broad, encompassing beaches, weddings, family vacations (hmmm, maybe this is a natural progression), and all the basics on sightseeing.

Index

General Index

General Index

General Index

ACCOMMODATIONS

FROMMER'S® COMPLETE TRAVEL GUIDES

FROMMER'S® DOLLAR-A-DAY GUIDES

Australia from $50 a Day
California from $60 a Day
Caribbean from $70 a Day
England from $70 a Day
Europe from $60 a Day
Florida from $60 a Day

Hawaii from $70 a Day
Ireland from $50 a Day
Israel from $45 a Day
Italy from $70 a Day
London from $85 a Day
New York from $80 a Day

New Zealand from $50 a Day
Paris from $85 a Day
San Francisco from $60 a Day
Washington, D.C.,
  from $60 a Day

FROMMER'S® PORTABLE GUIDES

Acapulco, Ixtapa &
  Zihuatanejo
Alaska Cruises & Ports of Call
Bahamas
Baja & Los Cabos
Berlin
California Wine Country
Charleston & Savannah
Chicago

Dublin
Hawaii: The Big Island
Las Vegas
London
Maine Coast
Maui
New Orleans
New York City
Paris

Puerto Vallarta, Manzanillo
  & Guadalajara
San Diego
San Francisco
Sydney
Tampa & St. Petersburg
Venice
Washington, D.C.

FROMMER'S® NATIONAL PARK GUIDES

Family Vacations in the
  National Parks
Grand Canyon

National Parks of the
  American West
Rocky Mountain

Yellowstone & Grand Teton
Yosemite & Sequoia/
  Kings Canyon
Zion & Bryce Canyon

FROMMER'S® GREAT OUTDOOR GUIDES

New England
Northern California

Southern California & Baja
Washington & Oregon

FROMMER'S® MEMORABLE WALKS

Chicago
London

New York
Paris

San Francisco
Washington D.C.

FROMMER'S® IRREVERENT GUIDES

Amsterdam
Boston
Chicago
Las Vegas

London
Los Angeles
Manhattan

New Orleans
Paris
San Francisco

Seattle & Portland
Vancouver
Walt Disney World
Washington, D.C.

FROMMER'S® BEST-LOVED DRIVING TOURS

America
Britain
California

Florida
France
Germany

Ireland
Italy
New England

Scotland
Spain
Western Europe

THE COMPLETE IDIOT'S TRAVEL GUIDES

Boston
Chicago
Cruise Vacations
Planning Your Trip to Europe
Florida
Hawaii

Ireland
Las Vegas
London
Mexico's Beach Resorts
New Orleans
New York City

Paris
San Francisco
Spain
Walt Disney World
Washington, D.C.

WHEREVER YOU TRAVEL, *H*ELP IS NEVER FAR AWAY.

From planning your trip to providing travel assistance along the way, American Express® Travel Service Offices are always there to help you do more.

Caribbean

BAHAMAS
Playtours (R)
303 Shirley St.
Nassau
(242) 322-2931

BARBADOS
Barbados International Travel Service
Horizon House
McGregor St.
(246) 431-2423

BRITISH VIRGIN ISLANDS
Travel Plan Ltd. (R)
Romasco Place
Road Town
Tortola
(284) 494-6239

U.S. VIRGIN ISLANDS
Southerland Tours (R)
Chandlers Wharf
Gallows Bay
St. Croix
(340) 773-9500

CAYMAN ISLANDS
Cayman Travel Services, Ltd. (R)
Shedden Rd., Elizabethan Sq.
George Town
Grand Cayman
(345) 949-8755/5400

JAMAICA
Grace Kennedy Travel Ltd. (R)
19-21 Knutsford Blvd.
Kingston 5
(876) 929-6290

MARTINIQUE
Roger Albert Voyages (R)
7 Rue Victor Hugo
Fort de France
(596) 71-71-71/71-42-20

PUERTO RICO
Travel Network (R)
1035 Ashford Ave.
Condado Area
San Juan
(787) 725-0960

ST. KITTS
Kantours (R)
Liverpool Row
Basseterre
(869) 465-2098

ST. MAARTEN
S.E.L. Maduro & Sons, (W.I.) Inc. (R)
Emmaplein Bldg. One
Philipsburg
(599)(5) 22678

do more AMERICAN EXPRESS

Travel

www.americanexpress.com/travel

American Express Travel Service Offices are found in central locations throughout the Caribbean.